Microsoft® Office 2016

IN PRACTICE

excel

COMPLETE

Microsoft® Office
2016 IN PRACTICE
excel COMPLETE

Kathleen Stewart

MORAINE VALLEY COMMUNITY COLLEGE

Randy Nordell

AMERICAN RIVER COLLEGE

McGraw Hill Education

MICROSOFT OFFICE 2016: IN PRACTICE EXCEL COMPLETE

5 6 7 8 9 SCI 20 19 18

ISBN 978-1-259-76267-3
MHID 1-259-76267-X

Chief Product Officer, SVP Products & Markets: *G. Scott Virkler*
Managing Director: *Scott Davidson*
Executive Brand Manager: *Wyatt Morris*
Executive Director of Development: *Ann Torbert*
Senior Product Developer: *Alan Palmer*
Executive Marketing Managers: *Tiffany Russell & Debbie Clare*
Director, Content Design & Delivery: *Terri Schiesl*
Program Manager: *Mary Conzachi*
Content Project Manager: *Rick Hecker*
Buyer: *Jennifer Pickel*
Designer: *Matt Backhaus*
Cover Image: © *Chris Ryan/Getty Images*
Senior Digital Product Analyst: *Thuan Vinh*
Compositor: *SPi Global*
Printer: *RR Donnelley*

Library of Congress Cataloging-in-Publication Data

Names: Stewart, Kathleen, author. | Nordell, Randy, author.
Title: Microsoft Office 2016: in practice Excel complete / Kathleen Stewart,
    Moraine Valley Community College, Randy Nordell, American River College.
Description: New York, NY: McGraw-Hill/Irwin, [2016]
Identifiers: LCCN 2016024353 | ISBN 9781259762673 (alk. paper)
Subjects: LCSH: Microsoft Excel (Computer file) | Business—Computer
    programs. | Electronic spreadsheets.
Classification: LCC HF5548.4.M523 S7367 2016 | DDC 005.54—dc23
LC record available at https://lccn.loc.gov/2016024353

www.mhhe.com

dedication

Robert, thank you for your gift of quiet support as I worked on this book. Many thanks also to understanding family and friends who listened and offered encouragement, ideas, and suggestions.

—Kathleen Stewart

Bob and Lanita, thank you for generously allowing me to use the cabin where I completed much of the work on this book. Don and Jennie, thank you for teaching me the value of hard work and encouraging me throughout the years. Kelsey and Taylor, thank you for keeping me young at heart. Kelly, thank you for your daily love, support, and encouragement. I could not have done this without you. I'm looking forward to spending more time together on our tandem!

—Randy Nordell

brief contents

contents

CHAPTER 7: WORKING WITH TEMPLATES AND SHARING WORK | E7-434

CHAPTER 8: EXPLORING DATA ANALYSIS AND BUSINESS INTELLIGENCE | E8-495

APPENDICES

GLOSSARY

INDEX

about the authors

KATHLEEN STEWART, M.S. Ed., M.B.A.

Kathleen Stewart is retired from her role as professor and department chairperson for the Information Management Systems Department at Moraine Valley Community College in Palos Hills, Illinois. She has a master's degree in occupational education from Southern Illinois University in Carbondale and an MBA from Loyola University in Chicago. She has authored Microsoft Office texts for many years for McGraw-Hill and has been involved in corporate training in the Chicago area. When not occupied by a writing project, she enjoys traveling, working on her golf game, literacy tutoring, and exploring cultural activities in the city.

RANDY NORDELL, Ed.D.

Randy Nordell is a professor of business technology at American River College in Sacramento, California. He has been an educator for over 25 years and has taught at the high school, community college, and university levels. He holds a bachelor's degree in business administration from California State University, Stanislaus, a single-subject teaching credential from Fresno State University, a master's degree in education from Fresno Pacific University, and a doctorate in education from Argosy University. Randy is the lead author of the *Microsoft Office 2013: In Practice* and *Microsoft Office 2016: In Practice* series of texts. He is also the author of *101 Tips for Online Course Success* and *Microsoft Outlook 2010*. Randy speaks regularly at conferences on the integration of technology into the curriculum. When not teaching and writing, he enjoys spending time with his family, cycling, skiing, swimming, backpacking, and enjoying the California weather and terrain.

What We're About

We wrote *Microsoft Office 2016: In Practice* to meet the diverse needs of both students and instructors. Our approach focuses on presenting Office topics in a logical and structured manner, teaching concepts in a way that reinforces learning with practice projects that are transferrable, relevant, and engaging. Our pedagogy and content are based on the following beliefs.

Students Need to Learn and Practice Transferable Skills

Students must be able to transfer the concepts and skills learned in the text to a variety of projects, not simply follow steps in a textbook. Our material goes beyond the instruction of many texts. In our content, students practice the concepts in a variety of current and relevant projects *and* are able to transfer skills and concepts learned to different projects in the real world. To further increase the transferability of skills learned, this text is integrated with SIMnet so students also practice skills and complete projects in an online environment.

Your Curriculum Drives the Content

The curriculum in the classroom should drive the content of the text, not the other way around. This book is designed to allow instructors and students to cover all the material they need to in order to meet the curriculum requirements of their courses no matter how the courses are structured. *Microsoft Office 2016: In Practice* teaches the marketable skills that are key to student success. McGraw-Hill's Custom Publishing site, **Create,** can further tailor the content material to meet the unique educational needs of any school.

Integrated with Technology

Our text provides a fresh and new approach to an Office applications course. Topics integrate seamlessly with SIMnet with 1:1 content to help students practice and master concepts and skills using SIMnet's interactive learning philosophy. Projects in SIMnet allow students to practice their skills and receive immediate feedback. This integration with SIMnet meets the diverse needs of students and accommodates individual learning styles. Additional textbook resources found in SIMnet (Resources and Library sections) integrate with the learning management systems that are widely used in many online and onsite courses.

Reference Text

In addition to providing students with an abundance of real-life examples and practice projects, we designed this text to be used as a Microsoft Office 2016 reference source. The core material, uncluttered with exercises, focuses on real-world use and application. Our text provides clear step-by-step instructions on how readers can apply the various features available in Microsoft Office in a variety of contexts. At the same time, users have access to a variety of both online (SIMnet) and textbook practice projects to reinforce skills and concepts.

instructor walkthrough

Textbook Learning Approach

Microsoft Office 2016: In Practice uses the *T.I.P. approach:*

- **T**opic
- **I**nstruction
- **P**ractice

Topic

- Each Office application section begins with foundational skills and builds to more complex topics as the text progresses.
- Topics are logically sequenced and grouped by topics.
- Student Learning Outcomes (SLOs) are thoroughly integrated with and mapped to chapter content, projects, end-of-chapter review, and test banks.
- Reports are available within SIMnet for displaying how students have met these Student Learning Outcomes.

Instruction (How To)

- *How To* guided instructions about chapter topics provide transferable and adaptable instructions.
- Because *How To* instructions are not locked into single projects, this textbook functions as a reference text, not just a point-and-click textbook.
- Chapter content is aligned 1:1 with SIMnet.

Practice (Pause & Practice and End-of-Chapter Projects)

- Within each chapter, integrated Pause & Practice projects (three to five per chapter) reinforce learning and provide hands-on guided practice.
- In addition to Pause & Practice projects, each chapter has 10 comprehensive and practical practice projects: Guided Projects (three per chapter), Independent Projects (three per chapter), Improve It Project (one per chapter), and Challenge Projects (three per chapter). Additional projects can also be found in the Library or Resources section of SIMnet.
- Pause & Practice and end-of-chapter projects are complete content-rich projects, not small examples lacking context.
- Select auto-graded projects are available in SIMnet.

Chapter Features

All chapters follow a consistent theme and instructional methodology. Below is an example of chapter structure.

Main headings are organized according to the *Student Learning Outcomes (SLOs)*.

SLO 1.1	**Creating, Saving, and Opening a Workbook**

In Microsoft Excel, the file that you open, edit, and save is a *wor...*
contains *worksheets*, which are comparable to individual pages in a W...
sheet is also referred to as a *spreadsheet* or a *sheet*, and you can use t...
ably. This text also uses the terms "workbook" and "file" interchange...

and build charts. With Excel, you can create simple to com...
books. This chapter presents basic procedures for creating an...

STUDENT LEARNING OUTCOMES (SLOs)

After completing this chapter, you will be able to:

SLO 1.1 Create, save, and open an Excel workbook (p. E...

SLO 1.2 Enter and edit labels and values in a worksheet...

SLO 1.3 Use the *SUM* function to build a simple formula (...

SLO 1.4 Format a worksheet with font attributes, borders... (p. E1-21).

SLO 1.5 Modify columns and rows in a worksheet (p. E1-3...

SLO 1.6 Insert, delete, and move worksheets in a workbo...

SLO 1.7 Modify the appearance of a workbook by adjust... views, and freezing panes (p. E1-42).

SLO 1.8 Review and prepare a workbook for final distrib... setting properties, and adjusting page setup o...

A list of Student Learning Outcomes begins each chapter. All chapter content, examples, and practice projects are organized according to the chapter SLOs.

CASE STUDY

Throughout this book you have the opportunity to put into practice the application features that you are learning. Each chapter begins with a case study that introduces you to the Pause & Practice projects in the chapter. These Pause & Practice projects give you a chance to apply and practice key skills in a realistic and practical context. Each chapter contains three to five Pause & Practice projects.

Paradise Lakes Resort (PLR) is a vacation company with properties located throughout northern Minnesota. PLR staff use Excel to track revenue, to monitor expenses, to

maintain employee records, and similar tasks. In the Pause & Practice projects for Chapter 1, you create, edit, and format a workbook that displays categories of revenue for one week.

Pause & Practice 1-1: Open, edit, and save a workbook.

Pause & Practice 1-2: Use *SUM* and format data in a worksheet.

Pause & Practice 1-3: Edit columns, rows, and sheets in a workbook.

Pause & Practice 1-4: Finalize a workbook for distribution.

The *Case Study* for each chapter is a scenario that establishes the theme for the entire chapter. Chapter content, examples, figures, Pause & Practice projects, SIMnet skills, and projects throughout the chapter are closely related to this case study content. The three to five Pause & Practice projects in each chapter build upon each other and address key case study themes.

How To instructions enhance transferability of skills with concise steps and screen shots.

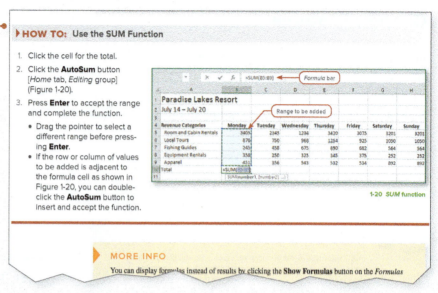

How To instructions are easy-to-follow concise steps. Screen shots and other figures fully illustrate How To topics.

Students can complete hands-on exercises in either the Office application or in SIMnet.

Pause & Practice projects give you a chance to apply and practice key skills in a realistic and practical context. Each chapter contains three to five Pause & Practice projects.

Paradise Lakes Resort (PLR) is a vacation company with properties located throughout northern Minnesota. PLR staff use Excel to track revenue, to monitor expenses, to

Pause & Practice 1-1: Open, edit, and save a workbook.

Pause & Practice 1-2: Use *SUM* and format data in a worksheet.

Pause & Practice 1-3: Edit columns, rows, and sheets in a workbook.

Pause & Practice 1-4: Finalize a workbook for distribution.

Pause & Practice projects, which each covers two to three of the student learning outcomes in the chapter, provide students with the opportunity to review and practice skills and concepts. Every chapter contains three to five Pause & Practice projects.

More Info provides readers with additional information about chapter content.

Another Way notations teach alternative methods of accomplishing the same task or feature such as keyboard shortcuts.

> **▶ ANOTHER WAY**
>
> Press **Esc** to leave the Excel *Start* page and open a blank workbook.

Marginal notations present additional information and alternative methods.

End-of-Chapter Projects

Ten learning projects at the end of each chapter provide additional reinforcement and practice for students. Many of these projects are available in SIMnet for completion and automatic grading.

- ***Guided Projects (three per chapter):*** Guided Projects provide guided step-by-step instructions to apply Office features, skills, and concepts from the chapter. Screen shots guide students through the more challenging tasks. End-of-project screen shots provide a visual of the completed project.
- ***Independent Projects (three per chapter):*** Independent Projects provide students further opportunities to practice and apply skills, instructing students what to do, but not how to do it. These projects allow students to apply previously learned content in a different context.
- ***Improve It Project (one per chapter):*** In these projects, students apply their knowledge and skills to enhance and improve an existing document. These are independent-type projects that instruct students what to do, but not how to do it.
- ***Challenge Projects (three per chapter):*** Challenge Projects are open-ended projects that encourage creativity and critical thinking by integrating Office concepts and features into relevant and engaging projects.

Appendix

- ***Office 2016 Shortcuts:*** Appendix A covers the shortcuts available in Microsoft Office and within each of the specific Office applications. Information is in table format for easy access and reference.

Additional Resources in SIMnet

Students and instructors can find the following resources in the Library or Resources sections in SIMnet.

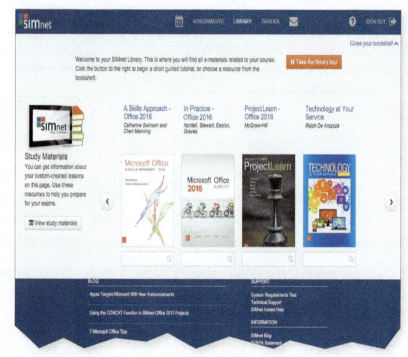

Student Resources

- **Data Files:** Files contain start files for all Pause & Practice, Capstone, and end-of-chapter projects.
- **SIMnet Resources:** Resources provide getting started and informational handouts for instructors and students.
- **Check for Understanding:** A combination of multiple choice, matching, and short answer questions are available at the end of each SIMbook chapter in SIMnet to assist students in their review of the skills and concepts covered in the chapter.

Capstone Projects

- **Integrating Applications:** Projects provide students with the opportunity to learn, practice, and transfer skills using multiple Office applications.
- **Integrating Skills:** Projects provide students with a comprehensive and integrated review of all of the topics covered in each application (Word, Excel, Access, and PowerPoint). Available in individual application texts.

Instructor Resources

- **Instructor's Manual:** An Instructor's Manual provides teaching tips and lecture notes aligned with the PowerPoint presentations for each chapter.
- **Test Bank:** The extensive test bank integrates with learning management systems (LMSs) such as Blackboard, WebCT, Desire2Learn, and Moodle.
- **PowerPoint Presentations:** PowerPoint presentations for each chapter can be used in onsite course formats for lectures or can be uploaded to LMSs.
- **SIMnet Resources:** These resources provide getting started and informational handouts for instructors.
- **Solution Files:** Files contain solutions for all Pause & Practice, Capstone, and end-of-chapter projects.

acknowledgments

REVIEWERS

We would like to thank the following instructors, whose invaluable insights shaped the development of this series.

Scott Straub
College of Western Idaho

Jeremy Eason
West Georgia Technical College

Linda Johnsonius
Murray State University

Barbara West
Central Georgia Technical College

Yvonne Galusha
University of Iowa

Jean Finley
Asheville Buncombe Technical Community College

Candace S. Garrod
Red Rocks Community College

Marianne Dougherty
Middlesex County College

Adam Rosen
LIM College

Peter F. Meggison
Massasoit Community College

Robert Doyle
Dona Ana Community College

Pamela Silvers
Asheville-Buncombe Technical Community College

Lisa Cady
University of Arkansas - Fort Smith

Richard Johnsen
County College of Morris

Joan Butler
Manchester Community College

Robert Nichols
College of DuPage

Anna Tsipenyuk
LIM College

Brian Fox
Santa Fe College

Leilani Benoit
Dona Ana Community College

Uma Sridharan
Presbyterian College

Marianne Daugharthy
College of Western Idaho

Tom Moore
Kapiolani Community College

Diane Morris
Tyler Junior College

Brenda McFarland
Asheville-Buncombe Technical Community College

Mitch Pendleton
LDS Business College

Tony Hunnicutt
College of the Ouachitas

Jeanine Taylor
Bryan University

Darin Bell
Treasure Valley Community College

Martha Guzman
Taller San Jose

Mary Jean Blink
Mount St. Joseph University

Ralph Dickerson
The Atlanta Workforce Development Agency

Robert LaRocca
Keiser University

Jenna Dulak
Hilbert College

Carole Eustice
Clark College

Brad West
Sinclair Community College

Gwyn Ebie
Colorado Mountain College

Susan Paulsen
Community College of Vermont

Karen A. Myers
Fisher College

Gary Judd
Trinity Baptist College

Letty Barnes
Lake Washington Institute of Technology

Tiffinee Morgan
West Kentucky Community and Technical College

Carol Lee
Central Georgia Technical College

Ronald Creel
Troy University

John Sehloff
Bethany Lutheran College

Samuel Gabay
Chicago ORT Technical Institute

Bonnie Armendariz
Bakersfield College, Bakersfield California

Sherry E. Jacob
Jefferson Community and Technical College

Tuncay Bayrak
Western New England University

Mandy Burrell
Holmes community college

Denver Riffe
American National University

Dan Lowrance
LDS Business College

Velma Latson
Bowie State University

Marilyn Mendoza
Franklin Career Institute

Lisa McCool
Alfred State College

Pamela Sorensen
Santa Rosa Junior College

Peggy Batchelor
Furman University

Larry Fudella
Erie Community College

Chet Cunningham
Madisonville Community College

Lauri Smedley
Sacramento City College

Gary Ewen
Colorado Christian University

Amanda Hardin
Mississippi Delta Community College

Rob Durrance
Keiser University

Alli Vainshtein
Riverland Community College

George C. Holder
Cloud County Community College

Colin Onita
University of Akron

Melissa Nemeth
Indiana University Kelley School of Business

Keith Conn
Cleveland Institute of Electronics

Phil Young
Baylor University

Laura Earner
Saint Xavier University

Josanne Ford
Metropolitan Career Center Computer Technology Institute

Darla Hunt
Maysville Community and Technical College

Christopher VanOosterhout
Muskegon Community College

Mark Webb
Illinois Central College

David Raney
Cuyamaca College

Christine Wolfe
Ohio University Lancaster

Dan Guerra
Community Business College

Samuel Abraham
Siena Heights University

Sandra Carriker
North Shore Community College

Shelly Smith
Valley College- Beckley

Tahir Aziz
Long Beach City College

Kin Lam
Medgar Evers College/CUNY

Sherry Grosso
University of South Carolina

Regena Aye
Allen Community College

Paul Weaver
Bossier Parish Community College

Brian McDaniel
Palo Alto College

Stephen Arney
Washburn Institute of Technology

Lynn Wermers
North Shore Community College

Lois McWhorter
Somerset Community College

J. Kirk Atkinson
Western Kentucky University

Salina Chahal
UEI College

Dana Fellows
Whiteside Area Career Center

John Golofski
Everest Institute

Eileen Dewey
Rose State College

Nasser Tadayon
Southern Utah University

Tina Denmark
Montgomery College

Delores Vance
Hazard Community and Technical College

Brad Thomas
Olivet Nazareth University

Steven Mark Sachs
Los Angeles Valley College

Andrew Smith
Marian University

Nelly Delessy
Miami Dade COllege

Richard Patterson
Peirce College

Michael Goeken
Northwest Vista College

Janice Flegle
Thomas Edison State College

Sara Rutledge
Mount Aloysius College

Seyed Roosta
Albany State University

Jim Flannery
Central Carolina Community College

Lynn Krausse
Bakersfield College

Kay Hammond
Lindenwood University

Penny Pereira
Indiana University-Purdue University Fort Wayne

Kevin Lambert
Southeast Kentucky Community and Technical College

Adam Rosen
LIM College

Cheri Whalen
Odessa College

Karr Dyal
LIM College

Shirley Birenz
New York University College of Dentistry

Jose Valdes
IBMC College

Gary DeLorenzo
California University of Pennsylvania

Kristin Roberts
Grand Rapids Community College

Michael Gray
Lane Community College

Ed Jaramillo
Peninsula College

Debasish Banerjee
Western Carolina University

Jenny Elshtain
Indiana University East

Sarah Rencher
Coconino Community College

Debbi Dybevik
Washtenaw Community College

Ann Kiefer
Chippewa Valley Technical College

Keff Lagoditz
American International College

Barbara Lave
Clark College

Morris Pondfield
Towson University

Peter Meggison
Massasoit Community College

Anne Acker
Jacksonville University

Gary Mosley
Southern Wesleyan University

Patrick J. Nedry
Monroe County Community College

Wasim A. Alhamdani
Kentucky State University

Bruce Baginski
Craven Community College

Diane Kosharek
Madison Area Technical College (Madison College)

Christina Shaner
Evergreen Valley College

Thomas Magliolo
Alvin Community College

Dmitriy Kupis
St. Joseph's College

Craig Brigman
Liberty University

Janak Shah
Berkeley college

Gary McFall
Purdue University
Phil Feinberg
Palomar College
Sheila Sicilia
Onondaga Community College
Randy Hollifield
McDowell Technical Community College
Bala R. Subramanian
Kean University
Marie Schmitz
Erie Community College
Tamar Mosley
Meridian Community College
David Bell
Pacific Union College
Jack Tan
University of Wisconsin - Eau Claire
Richard Brown
Loyola University Maryland
Narcissus Shambare
College of Saint Mary
S. E. Rouse
University of Southern Mississippi
Robert Doyle
Dona Ana Community College
David Welch
Nashville State Community College
Chen Ye
Purdue University Calumet
Bahadir Akcam
Western New England University
Frank Lucente
Westmoreland County Community College
Ted Janicki
University of Mount Olive
Kenneth R. Mayer, Jr.
Lipscomb University
Tamar Mosley
Meridian Community College
Pat McMahon
South Suburban College
Maureen Greenbaum
Union County College
Paulinus Ozor-Ilo
Gadsden State Community College
Michael Haugrud
Minnesota State University Moorhead
John Finley
Columbus State University
Philip Reaves
University of West Georgia
Cerro Coso Community College
Michael Leih
Trevecca Nazarene University
Shahla Durany
Tarrant County College - South Campus
Gary Sibbitts
St. Louis Community College at Meramec
Sandro Marchegiani
University of Pittsburgh at Johnstown
Sambit Bhattacharya
Fayetteville State University
Christine Peterson
Saint Paul College
C. Steven Hunt
Morehead State University
Shirley Nagg
Everest College
Ruth Parker
Rowan-Cabarrus Community College
Cecil Lawson
Evergreen Valley College
Adnan Turkey
DeVry College of New York
Janet Nicolaus
Mitchell Technical Institute
Mohammad Morovati
College of Dupage
Anthony Kapolka
Wilkes University

Steven Singer
Kapi'olani Community College
Bill Mills
East Texas Baptist University
Michele Schutte
Delaware Technical Community College - Terry Campus
Mark Evans
American National University
Syed Raza
Talladega College
Pam Gilmore
Reedley College
Philip Kim
Walsh University
Jeanann Boyce
Montgomery College
MaryJo Slater
Community College of Beaver County
JoAnn Brannen
Abraham Baldwin Agricultural College
Robert Patrick Sheridan
Northeast Iowa Community College
Sherry Muse
American Institute
Marcus Lacher
Minnesota State Community and Technical College
John Hupp
Columbus State University
Bernard Ku
Austin Community College
Theresa Meza
James Sprunt Community College
Jeremy A. Pittman
Coahoma Community College
LeAnne Lovering
Augusta Technical College
Lois Ann ONeal
Rogers State University
Lucy DeCaro
College of the Sequoias
Fredrick Bsharah
Cape Cod Community College
Timothy Holston
Mississippi Valley State University
Robert Balicki
Wayne County Community College District
Anita Beecroft
Kwantlen Polytechnic University
Margaret Cooksey
Tallahassee Community College
Susan Jackson
University of New Mexico-Valencia Campus
Beverly Forney
Clackamas Community College
Yves Durand
Keiser University
Cindi Nadelman
New England College
Susan Mahon
Collin College
Anthony Cameron
Fayetteville Tech Comm College
W. Randy Somsen
Brigham Young University-Idaho
Leanne Ruff
Blue Ridge Community College
Jan Wilms
Union University
Diane Bigger
LDS Business College
Michael Kurhan
Burlington County College
Vincent Yip
Umpqua Community College
Cheryl Jordan
San Juan College
Md Manzoor Murshed
Upper Iowa University
Pengtao Li
California State University, Stanislaus

George Sweiss
Governors State University Ill
Sharon M. Hope
Maria College
Ann Konarski
Baker College - Port Huron
Saiid Ganjalizadeh
Metropolitan School of Professional Studies
Brittany Bright
University of Arkansas
Iftikhar Sikder
Cleveland State University
Robin Fuller
Mississippi Gulf Coast Community College
Trude Pang
Kapiolani Community College
Tanya Patrick
Clackamas Community College
Tom Sill
Northwest University
Diane Franklin
Uintah Basin Applied Technology College
Cameron Spears
Hillsborough Community College
Kristi Smith
Allegany College of Maryland
Philip H. Nielson
Salt Lake Community College
Angela Nino
Richland College
Rajkumar Kempaiah
College of Mount Saint Vincent
Jeff Hansen
Treasure Valley Community College
J. F. Pauer
Bowling Green State University Firelands Campus
Ryan Carter
Mayland Community College
Kungwen (Dave) Chu
Purdue University Calumet
Bruce Haft
Glendale College
Tahir Aziz
J. Sargeant Reynolds Community College
Mercedes N. Alafriz
University of Phoenix/WIU
Dusty Anderson
Bluefield College
Keith Grubb
Rowan-Cabarrus Community College
Denise Reimer
Iowa Lakes Community College
Michael Sisk
Cleveland Community College
Anna Beavers
Laney College
Ted Tedmon
North Idaho College
Paulette Bell
Santa Rosa Junior College
Kevin Wyzkiewicz
Delta College
Uma Sridharan
Presbyterian College
Frank Tatum
Patrick Henry Community College
Jean Welsh
Lansing Community College
Karen Poland
Bryant and Stratton College
Aaron Tenenbaum
Brooklyn College
Susan Burden
Moberly Area Community College
Jim Patterson
Paradise Valley Community College
Richard Johnsen
County College of Morris
Ann Henry
Opportunity Center, Inc.,
ServiceSource - Delaware

Cathy Urbanski
Chandler-Gilbert College
Panda Jones
Gwinnett Technical College
Roni Ettleman
Atchison High School
Georgia Vanderark
Stark State College
Kevin Bradford
Somerset Community College - KCTCS
Shan Bhagoji
Monroe College
Anita Laird
Schoolcraft College
Carmen M. Aponte
Ana G. Mendez University System
Roberto Ordonez
Southern Adventist University
Marni Ferner
University of North Carolina Wilmington
Alisa Kadenic-Newman
NHTI
Andrea Langford
Ohio Valley Goodwill Industries
Barbara Schwartz
Pine Manor College
Carolyn Hill
Tallahassee Community College
Tracy Richardson
Eastern Maine Community College
Steve Nichols
Metropolitan Community College
Adell Brooks
Hinds Community College
Don Gaber
University of Wisconsin - Eau Claire
Laurie Zouharis
Suffolk University
Jill Fisher
Indian Capital Technology Center—Bill Willis Campus
Daniel Lowrance
Salt Lake Community College
Dee Hobson
Richland College
Matthew Macarty
University of New Hampshire
Jackie Porter
El Centro College
Alton Tripp
Northern Virginia Community College
Jan Repnow
Minot State University
Muhammad Obeidat
Southern Poly State University
Kirk McLean
LIM College
Saiid Ganjalizadeh
Northern Virginia Community College
Masoud Naghedolfeizi
Fort Valley State University
Kevin Fishbeck
University of Mary
Judy Smith
University District of Columbia
Mary Williams
University of Akron
Lisa Cady
University of Arkansas - Fort Smith (UAFS)
Phyllis Hutson
Southern Arkansas University Tech
Madison Ngafeeson
Northern Michigan University
Mandy Reininger
Chemeketa Community College
Lennie Alice Cooper
Miami Dade College - North Campus
Robert Pavkovich
Fortis College
Augustine Brennan
Erie Community College South

Judy Paternite
Kent State University Geauga

Brian Bradley
College of DuPage

Wilma Andrews
Virginia Commonwealth University

Anna Fitzpatrick
Rowan College at Gloucester County

Abdul Sattar
Bridgewater State University

Annette Kerwin
College of DuPage

Carolyn Barren
Macomb Community College

Matthew Marie
Aquinas College

Michael C. Theiss
University of Wisconsin Colleges

Kimberly Campbell
Eastern Maine Community College

Kamiyar Maleky
American River College

Chris Cheske
Lakeshore Technical College

Teresa Ferguson
Seattle Vocational Institute

Candace S. Garrod
Red Rocks Community College

Amiya K. Samantray
Marygrove College

Alex Morgan
DeAnza College

Howard Divins
DuBois Business College

Reshma R. Tolani
Charter College

Melinda White
Seminole State College

Michelle Thompson
Hillsborough Community College

Roy Stewart
Harris-Stowe State University

Joan Butler
Manchester Community College

Gary Moore
Caldwell Community College and Technical Institute

Brian Downs
Century College

Mitch Pendleton
LDS Business College

Meg Stoner
Santa Rosa Junior College

Orletta E. Caldwell
Grand Rapids Community College

Julia Basham
Southern State Community College

Mary Ann Culbertson
Tarrant County College Northwest Campus

Michael Carrington
Northern Virginia Community College

Freddy Barton
Tampa Vocational Institute

Sandy Keeter
Seminole State College

Harold Gress, Jr.
Wilson College

Sujing Wang
Lamar University

Brent Nabors
Clovis Community College Center

Dennis Walpole
University of South Florida

LaToya Smith
Piedmont Community College

Kyu Lee
Saint Martin's University

Lacey Lormand
University of Louisiana at Lafayette

Rebecca Bullough
College of the Sequoias

Mark Vancleve
Terronez

Raj Parikh
Westwood College

Carolyn Carvalho
Kent State University

Gerry Young
Vance Granville Community College

Marie Hartlein
Montgomery County Community College

Doug Read
Ball State University

Marie Guest
North Florida Community College

Gloria Sabatelli
Butler County Community College

Rose Steimel
Kansas Wesleyan University

Ronald Johnson
Central Alabama Community College

Eddie Bannister
Keiser University-Pembroke Pines, FL

Gustavo Diaz
Broward College

Pamela Lewis
Wilson Community College

James Schaap
Grand Rapids Community College

Gregory Latterell
Alexandria Technical and Community College

David Lewis
Bryant and Stratton College

Pamela Van Nutt
American National University - Martinsville, VA

Cheryl Miller
Bay College

James Anderson
Bay College

Darryl Habeck
Milwaukee Area Technical College

Dorvin Froseth
United Tribes Technical College

Wade Graves
Grayson College

Brenda McFarland
Asheville-Buncombe Technical Community College

Cherie M. Stevens
South Florida State College

Sandra Tavegia
The Community College of Baltimore County

Robyn Barrett
St Louis Community College - Meramec

Sharon Breeding
Bluegrass Community and Technical College

Theodore Tielens
Mt. San Jacinto

Lynda Hodge
Guilford Technical Community College

James Graves
College of Southern Maryland

Mike Michaelson
Palomar College

Kristi Parker
Baptist Bible College

Cheri Broadway
Jacksonville University

Anna Tsipenyuk
LIM College

Pamela Silvers
Asheville-Buncombe Technical Community College

Clarence Stokes
American River College

Cheryl D. Green
Delgado Community College

Kenneth N. Bryant
Kentucky State University

James Cammack
Lamar State College Port Arthur

Bryan Moss
San Jacinto College

Becky McAfee
Hillsborough Community College

David Gomillion
Northern Michigan University

Steven Bale
Truckee Meadows Community College

Julie Craig
Scottsdale Community College

Ashley Harrier
Hillsborough Community College

Brian Fox
Santa Fe College

Alicen Flosi
Lamar University

Karl Smart
Central Michigan University

David Little
High Point University

Paula Gregory
Yavapai College

Gary Sorenson
Northwest Technical College, Bemidji

Linda Lau
Longwood University

Frank Clements
State College of Florida

Keith Hood
Indiana Purdue Fort Wayne

Timothy Ely
Harcum College

Deborah Sahrbeck
North Shore Community College, Danvers, MA

Barbara West
Central Georgia Technical College

Shondra Greene
Albany State University

Amy Giddens
Central Alabama Community College

Dishi Shrivastava
University of North Florida

Patricia Frederick
Del Mar College

Bill Hammerschlag
Brookhaven College

Vinzanna Leysath
Allen University

Robert Nichols
College of DuPage

Corrine Sweet
Darton State College

Michael Magro
Shenandoah University

Vijay K Agrawal
University of Nebraska at Kearney

Timothy Ely
Harcum College

Rosie L. Inwang
Olive-Harvey College

Milledge Mosby
Prince George's Community College

Michael Torguson
Rogue Community College

Linda Phelps
Northwest Arkansas Community College

Corey DeLaplain
Keiser University Online

Lisa Lopez
Southern Wesleyan University

John Marek
Houston Community College

Lori Krei
Iowa Lakes Community College

Sharon Sneed
Eastfield Community College

Michael C. Johnson
ACD Computer College

Ben Martz
Northern Kentucky University

Russ Dulaney
Rasmussen College

Linda Johnsonius
Murray State University

Ionie Pierce
LIM College

Jo Ann Koenig
Indiana University-Purdue University Indianapolis

James Reneau
Shawnee State University

Wanda Gibson
Consolidated School of Business

David Milazzo
Niagara County Community College

John S. Galliano
University of Maryland University College

Lee Janczak
Lackawanna College

Philip Raphan
Broward College North Campus

Larry Schulze
San Antonio College

David Easton
Waubonsee Community College

Doug Baker
Kent State University

Alanna Duley
College of Western Idaho

Helen Slack
Mahoning County Career and Technical Center

Carolyn Golden
Huston-Tillotson University

Terri Tiedeman
Southeast Community College

Edwin Harris
University of North Florida

Jeff Lehman
Huntington University

Aimee Durham
Rowan-Cabarrus Community College

Denise Askew
Rowan-Cabarrus Community College

Curby Simerson
Randolph Community College

Cindi Albrightson
Southwestern Oklahoma State University

Amanda Kaari
Central Georgia Tech

Ruben Ruiz
Morton College

Riza Marjadi
Murray State University

Annette Yauney
Herkimer Couny Community College

Donna Maxson
Lake Michigan College

Benjamin White
Bainbridge State College

Joy Flanders
Central Methodist University

Jill McCollum
Southern Arkansas University Tech

Sonya Sample
Greenville Technical College

Michelle Chappell
Henderson Community College

Shawn Brown
Ashland Community and Technical College

Sherry Cox
Broward College

Bonnie J. Tuggle-Ziglar
Brookstone College of Business

Fernando Wilches
Ana G. Mendez University System

Doreen Palucci
Wilmington University

Thomas Seeley
Urbana University

Victor Wotzkow
New Professions Technical Institute

Ahmed Kamel
Concordia College, Moorhead
Marie Campbell
Idaho State University-College of Technology
Sue McCrory
Missouri State University
Somone Washington
Broward College Online
Johnnie Nixon
King's College
Gloria Hensel
Matanuska-Susitna College University of Alaska Anchorage
Gary Cotton
American River College,
Kingsley Meyer
University of Rio Grande / Rio Grande Community College
Martha Merrill
Pellissippi State Community College
Olusade Ajayi
Germanna Community College
Pat Pettit
Millikin University
Mary Evens
Clark College
Michelle Masingill
North Idaho College
Mark Douglas
Our Lady of the Lake University
Rhonda Lucas
Spring Hill College
Anita Sutton
Germanna Community College

S. E. Beladi
Broward College
Ronda Thompson .
Keene State College
Lyn Snyder
Owens Community College
Mark Connell
SUNY at Cortland
Guarionex Salivia
Minnesota State University
David Arevigian
Monroe County Community College
Verlan Erickson
Western Dakota Technical Institute
John Robinson
Cumberland County College
Allan Greenberg
New York University
Debra Adams
Mott Community College
Bobbie Hawkins
Southwest TN Community College
Nancy Stephens
Chemeketa Community College
Jeremy Harris
Evangel University
Kim Mangan
Manor College
Judith Scheeren
Westmoreland County Community College
Darrelyn Relyea
Grays Harbor College
Jay F. Miller
Union College, Barbourville

Deborah Franklin
Bryant and Stratton College
Nina Fontenot
South Louisiana Community College
Jim Speers
Southeastern Oklahoma State University
Jennifer Klenke
East Central College
Young Baek
Los Angeles City College
Carl Rebman
University of San Diego
Shelly Knittle
Alaska Career College
Natunya Johnson
Holmes Community College
Linda Lemley
Pensacola State College
Ranida Harris
Indiana University Southeast
Kelly Young
Lander University
Karin Stulz
Northern Michigan University
Cathie Phillips
Lamar State College-Orange
James Brown
Central Washington University
H. Roger Fulk
Rhodes State College
Dan Britton
Chemeketa Community College
Olivia Kerr
El Centro College

Michelle Dawson
Missouri Southern State University
Dianne Hargrove
College of Health Care Professions
Shannon Shoemaker
SUNY Delhi
Bruce Caraway
Lone Star College - University Park
Richard DiRose
Hillsborough Community College - South Shore

TECHNICAL EDITORS

Karen May
Blinn College
Andrea Nevill
College of Western Idaho
Richard Finn
Moraine Valley Community College
Chris Anderson
North Central Michigan College
Gena Casas
Florida State College
Leon Blue
Pensacola State College
Mary Carole Hollingsworth
Georgia Perimeter College
Amie Mayhall
Olney Central College
Julie Haar
Alexandria Technical and Community College
Diane Santurri
Johnson & Wales University
Ramona Santa Maria
Buffalo State College

Thank you to the wonderful team at McGraw-Hill for your confidence in us and support throughout this project. Alan, Wyatt, Tiffany, Debbie, Rick, and Julianna, we thoroughly enjoy working with you all! A special thanks to Debbie Hinkle for her thorough and insightful review of the series. Thank you also to Laurie Zouharis, Amie Mayhall, Sarah Clifford, Rebecca Leveille, Jane Holcombe, and all of the reviewers and technical editors for your expertise and invaluable insight, which helped shape this book.

—Kathleen and Randy

Intro Chapter

Windows 10, Office 2016, and File Management

CHAPTER OVERVIEW

Microsoft Office 2016 and Windows 10 introduce many new features, including cloud storage for your files, Office file sharing, and enhanced online content. The integration of Office 2016 and Windows 10 means that files are more portable and accessible than ever when you use *OneDrive*, Microsoft's free online cloud storage. The new user interface for Office 2016 and Windows 10 allows you to work on tablet computers and smartphones in a consistent working environment that resembles that of your desktop or laptop computer.

STUDENT LEARNING OUTCOMES (SLOs)

After completing this chapter, you will be able to:

SLO Intro.1 Explore the features of Windows 10 (p. OI-2).

SLO Intro.2 Use the basic features of Office 2016 and navigate the Office 2016 working environment (p. OI-10).

SLO Intro.3 Create, save, close, and open Office files (p. OI-17).

SLO Intro.4 Customize the view and display size in Office applications and work with multiple Office files (p. OI-25).

SLO Intro.5 Print, share, and customize Office files (p. OI-28).

SLO Intro.6 Use the *Ribbon*, tabs, groups, dialog boxes, task panes, galleries, and the *Quick Access* toolbar (p. OI-33).

SLO Intro.7 Use context menus, mini toolbars, keyboard shortcuts, and function keys in Office applications (p. OI-37).

SLO Intro.8 Organize and customize Windows folders and Office files (p. OI-42).

CASE STUDY

Throughout this book you have the opportunity to put into practice the application features that you are learning. Each chapter begins with a case study that introduces you to the Pause & Practice projects in the chapter. These Pause & Practice projects give you a chance to apply and practice key skills in a realistic and practical context. Each chapter contains three to five Pause & Practice projects.

American River Cycling Club (ARCC) is a community cycling club that promotes fitness. ARCC members include recreational cyclists who enjoy the exercise and camaraderie as well as competitive cyclists who compete in road, mountain, and cyclocross races throughout the cycling season. In the Pause & Practice projects, you incorporate many of the topics covered in the chapter to create, save, customize, manage, and share Office 2016 files.

OFFICE

OI-1

Pause & Practice Intro-1: Customize the Windows *Start* menu and *Taskbar*, create and save a PowerPoint presentation, create a folder, open and rename an Excel workbook, and use Windows 10 features.

Pause & Practice Intro-2: Modify the existing document, add document properties, customize the Quick Access toolbar, export the document as a PDF file, and share the document.

Pause & Practice Intro-3: Copy and rename files, create a folder, move files, create a zipped folder, and rename a zipped folder.

SLO INTRO. 1

Using Windows 10

Windows 10 is the *operating system* that controls computer functions and the working environment. Windows 10 uses the familiar **Windows desktop**, **Taskbar**, and **Start menu**, and you can customize the working environment. You can install traditional applications (**apps**), such as Microsoft Office, to your computer. Also, you can add modern apps from the Microsoft Store similar to how you add an app to your smartphone. Your **Microsoft account** is used to store your Microsoft settings, download apps from the Microsoft Store, and connect you to Microsoft Office, *OneDrive*, and *Office Online*.

Windows 10

The Windows 10 operating system controls interaction with computer hardware and software applications. **Windows 10** has a revised user interface that utilizes an updated **Start menu**, where you can select and open a program. Alternatively, you can use the *Taskbar* on the Windows desktop, which has the familiar look of previous versions of Windows. When you log in to Windows 10 using your Microsoft account, it synchronizes your Windows, Office, and **OneDrive** cloud storage among computers.

Microsoft Account

In Windows 10 and Office 2016, your files and account settings are portable. In other words, your Office settings and files can travel with you and be accessed from different computers. You are not restricted to a single computer. When you sign in to Windows 10 using your Microsoft account (user name and password), Microsoft uses this information to transfer your Windows and Office 2016 settings to the computer you are

Intro-1 Create a Microsoft account

using. Your Microsoft account not only signs you in to Windows and Office but also to other free Microsoft online services, such as *OneDrive* and **Office Online**. If you don't have a Microsoft account, you can create a free account at https://signup.live.com (Figure Intro-1).

Windows Desktop and Taskbar

The Windows desktop is the working area of Windows. When you log in to Windows, the desktop displays (Figure Intro-2). The *Taskbar* displays at the bottom of the desktop. You can open programs and folders from the *Taskbar* by clicking on an icon on the *Taskbar* (see Figure Intro-2). You can pin apps and other Windows items, such as the *Control Panel* or *File Explorer*, to the *Taskbar* (see "Customize the Taskbar" later in this section).

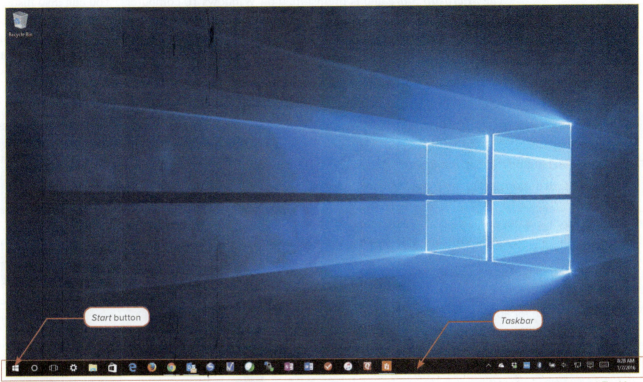

Intro-2 Windows desktop and *Taskbar*

Intro-3 Windows *Start* menu

Start Menu

Windows 10 utilizes a redesigned *Start* menu (Figure Intro-3), that you open by clicking the **Start button** located in the bottom left of the *Taskbar*. From the *Start* menu, you can open programs, files, folders, or other Windows resources. The *Start* menu is divided into two main sections. The left side of the *Start* menu displays **Most Used** items, buttons to open the **File Explorer** and **Settings** windows, the **Power** button, and **All apps**, which displays an alphabetical listing of all applications installed on your computer. The right side of the *Start* menu displays apps as tiles (large and small buttons) you can click to open an application or window.

You can customize which apps and items appear on either side of the *Start* menu, arrange and group apps on the *Start* menu, resize the *Start* menu, and display the *Start* menu as a **Start page** when you log in to Windows (similar to the *Start* page in Windows 8 and 8.1). See "Customize the Start Menu" later in this section for information about customizing the *Start* menu.

Add Apps

Windows 10 uses the term *apps* generically to refer to applications and programs. Apps include the Windows 10 Weather app, Microsoft Excel program, Control Panel, Google Chrome, or *File Explorer*. Many apps are preinstalled on a Windows 10 computer, and you can add apps to your computer. You can install an app such as Office 2016 or Quicken by downloading it from a web site or from a program DVD. These are referred to as ***traditional apps***.

The ***Microsoft Store*** app is preinstalled on Windows 10 computers. You can also install apps such as Netflix, Trip Advisor, and The Weather Channel from the Microsoft Store. These apps are referred to as ***modern apps*** and look and function similar to apps you install on your smartphone. Many apps in the Microsoft Store are free and others are available for purchase.

▶**HOW TO:** Add an App from the Microsoft Store

1. Click the **Start** button to open the *Start* menu.
2. Click the **Store** button (tile) to open the Microsoft Store app (Figure Intro-4).
   - If the *Store* tile is not available on the *Start* menu, click **All apps** on the *Start* menu, scroll down, and click **Store** in the alphabetic listing of all apps.
3. Select an app in the Microsoft Store (Figure Intro-5).
   - The Microsoft Store has different categories of apps.
   - You can search for apps by typing key words in the *Search* box in the upper right.
   - When you select an app, a description and screen shots of the app displays.
4. Click the **Free**, **Free trial**, or price button to install the app.
   - You must have a payment method stored in your Microsoft account to purchase apps from the Microsoft Store.
5. Click **Open** to open the installed app.
   - When you install an app, the app is listed in the *Recently added* area on the *Start* menu and *All apps* list of applications.

Intro-4 Store button on the Start menu

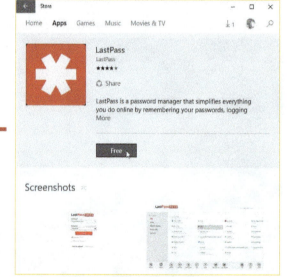

Customize the Start Menu

When you start using Windows 10 or after you have installed either traditional or modern apps, you can customize what appears on your *Start* menu and resize the *Start*

Intro-5 Install an app from the Microsoft Store

menu. When you *pin* an app to the *Start* menu, the app tile remains on the right side of the *Start* menu. Pin the apps you most regularly use, unpin the apps you don't want to display on the *Start* menu, and rearrange and resize apps tiles to your preference.

▶**HOW TO:** Customize the Start Menu

1. Move an app tile by clicking and dragging the app tile to a new location on the *Start* menu. The other app tiles shuffle to accommodate the placement of the app tile.

2. Remove an app tile from the *Start* menu by right-clicking the app tile you want to remove and selecting **Unpin from Start** from the context menu (Figure Intro-6).

   • The app tile is removed from the *Start* menu, but the program or task is not removed from your computer.

Intro-6 Unpin an app from the *Start* menu

3. Pin an app tile to the *Start* menu by clicking **All apps** at the bottom of the *Start* menu, right-clicking the app to pin, and selecting **Pin to Start** (Figure Intro-7).

   • Drag the newly added app tile to the desired location on the Start menu.

Intro-7 Pin an app to the *Start* menu

4. Resize an app tile by right-clicking the app tile, selecting **Resize**, and selecting **Small**, **Medium**, **Wide**, or **Large**.

   • Some apps only have *Small*, *Medium*, and *Wide* size options.

5. Turn on or off the live tile option by right-clicking the app tile and selecting **Turn live tile on** or **Turn live tile off**.

   • Live tile displays rotating graphics and options on the app tile. When this option is turned off, the name of the app displays on the tile.

6. Uninstall an app by right-clicking the app you want to uninstall and selecting **Uninstall**.

   • Unlike the unpin option, this option uninstalls the program from your computer, not just your *Start* menu.

7. Resize the *Start* menu by clicking and dragging the top or right edge of the *Start* menu.

8. Use a full screen *Start* menu by clicking the **Start** button to open the *Start* menu, selecting **Settings** to open the *Settings* window, clicking the **Personalization** button, clicking the **Start** option at the left, selecting **Use Start full screen**, and clicking the **X** in the upper right to close the *Settings* window (Figure Intro-8).

   • The *Start* menu expands to the full screen when opened.

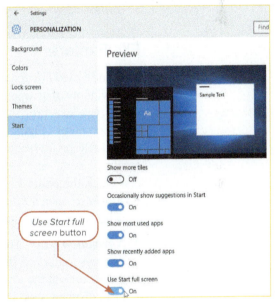

Intro-8 Use full screen *Start* menu

Customize the Taskbar

The *Taskbar* is located at the bottom of the Windows desktop, and you can quickly open an app by clicking a button on the *Taskbar* rather than opening it from the *Start* menu. You can customize the *Taskbar* by pinning, unpinning, and rearranging apps on the *Taskbar*.

▶HOW TO: Customize the Taskbar

1. Pin an app to the *Taskbar* by clicking the *Start* menu, right-clicking an app, clicking **More**, and selecting **Pin to taskbar** (Figure Intro-9).
   - You can also pin an app to the *Taskbar* from the *All apps* list in the *Start* menu.
2. Unpin an app from the *Taskbar* by right-clicking an app on the *Taskbar*, and selecting **Unpin from taskbar** (Figure Intro-10).
   - You can also unpin apps from the *Taskbar* by right-clicking the app in the *Start* menu, clicking **More**, and selecting **Unpin from taskbar**.
3. Rearrange apps on the *Taskbar* by clicking and dragging the app to the desired location on the *Taskbar* and release.

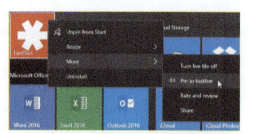

Intro-9 Pin an app to the *Taskbar*

Intro-10 Unpin an app from the *Taskbar*

> ▶ **MORE INFO**
>
> If using a touch screen, you can press and hold an app on the *Start* menu or *Taskbar* to display the app options.

File Explorer

The redesigned *File Explorer* in Windows 10 is a window that opens on your desktop where you can browse for files stored on your computer (Figure Intro-11). You can open a file or folder, move or copy items, create folders, and delete files or folders. Click the **Start** button and select **File Explorer** to open a *File Explorer* window.

The *File Explorer* has different areas:

- **Navigation pane**: The *Navigation* pane displays folders on the left. The **Quick access** area at the top of the *Navigation* pane displays shortcuts to favorite folders. You can pin or unpin folders in the *Quick access* area of the *Navigation* pane.

Intro-11 *File Explorer* window

- **Navigation buttons**: The navigation buttons (*Back*, *Forward*, *Recent location*, and *Up*) are located directly above the *Navigation* pane and below the *Ribbon*. Use these buttons to navigate a File Explorer window.
- **Folder pane**: When you select a folder in the *Navigation* pane, the contents of the folder displays in the *Folder* pane to the right of the *Navigation* pane. Double-click a folder or file in the *Folder* pane to open it.
- **Ribbon**: The *Ribbon* at the top of the *File Explorer* is collapsed by default. When you click a tab on the *Ribbon*, it expands to display the options on the tab. The main tabs of

the *Ribbon* are *File*, *Home*, *Share*, and *View*. Other context-sensitive tabs open when you select certain types of files. For example, the *Picture Tool Manage* tab opens when you select a picture file.

- **Quick Access toolbar**: The *Quick Access* toolbar is above the *Ribbon*. From the *Quick Access* toolbar, you can click the **New Folder** button to create a new folder or **Properties** to display the properties of a selected file or folder. You can add buttons, such as *Rename*, to the *Quick Access* toolbar.
- **Search**: The *Search* text box is located on the right of the *File Explorer* window below the *Ribbon*. Type key words in the *Search* text box to find files or folders.

OneDrive

OneDrive is a cloud storage area where you can store files in a private and secure online location that you can access from any computer. When you store your files in *OneDrive*, the files are actually saved on both your computer and on the cloud. *OneDrive* synchronizes your files so when you change a file it is automatically updated on the *OneDrive* cloud.

With Windows 10, the ***OneDrive folder*** is one of your storage location folder options, similar to your *Documents* or *Pictures* folders (Figure Intro-12). You can save, open, and edit your *OneDrive* files from a *File Explorer* folder. Your *OneDrive* folder looks and functions similar to other Windows folders.

In addition to the *OneDrive* folder on your computer, you can also access your *OneDrive* files online using an Internet browser such as Microsoft Edge, Google Chrome, or Mozilla Firefox. When you access *OneDrive* online using a web browser, you can upload files, create folders, move and copy files and folders, and create Office files using *Office Online* (*Office Online* is discussed in *SLO Intro.2: Using Office 2016*).

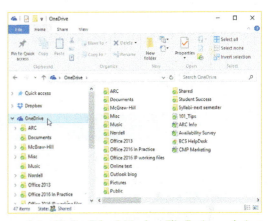

Intro-12 *OneDrive* folder in a *File Explorer* window

▶**HOW TO: Use OneDrive Online**

1. Open an Internet browser window and navigate to the *OneDrive* web site (www.onedrive.live.com), which takes you to the *OneDrive* sign in page.
   - You can use any Internet browser to access *OneDrive* (Microsoft Edge, Google Chrome, Mozilla Firefox).
2. Click the **Sign in** button, type your Microsoft account email address, and click **Next**.
3. Type your Microsoft account password and click **Sign in** (Figure Intro-13). You are taken to your *OneDrive* page.
   - If you are on your own computer, check the **Keep me signed in** box to stay signed in to *OneDrive* when you return to the page.

☁️ **OneDrive**

Microsoft account What's this?

| Email or phone |

| Password |

☐ Keep me signed in

Sign in

Can't access your account?

Sign in with a single-use code

Don't have a Microsoft account? **Sign up now**

Intro-13 Log in to *OneDrive* online

- The different areas of *OneDrive* are listed under the *OneDrive* heading on the left (Figure Intro-14).
- Click **Files** to display your folders and files in the folder area.
- At the top of the page, buttons and drop-down menus list the different actions you can perform on selected files and folders.

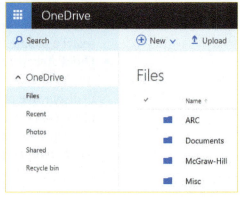

Cortana

In addition to using the search tools in the *File Explorer*, you can also use **Cortana**, which is new in Windows 10. While the search feature in the *File Explorer* searches only for content on your computer, *Cortana* searches for content on your computer, on the Internet, and in the Microsoft Store. You can either type key words for a search or use voice commands to search for content.

When you open *Cortana*, other content, such as weather, upcoming appointments, and popular news stories, displays in the *Cortana* pane.

▶**HOW TO:** Search Using Cortana

1. Click the **Cortana** button on the *Taskbar* to open the *Cortana* pane (Figure Intro-15).

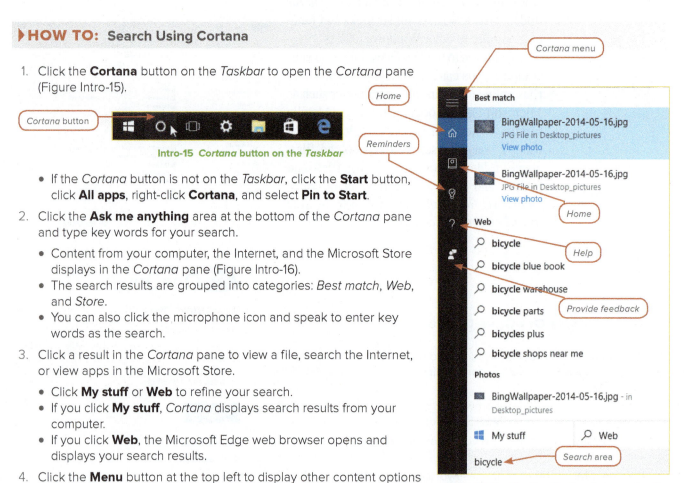

Intro-15 *Cortana* button on the *Taskbar*

- If the *Cortana* button is not on the *Taskbar*, click the **Start** button, click **All apps**, right-click **Cortana**, and select **Pin to Start**.

2. Click the **Ask me anything** area at the bottom of the *Cortana* pane and type key words for your search.
   - Content from your computer, the Internet, and the Microsoft Store displays in the *Cortana* pane (Figure Intro-16).
   - The search results are grouped into categories: *Best match*, *Web*, and *Store*.
   - You can also click the microphone icon and speak to enter key words as the search.

3. Click a result in the *Cortana* pane to view a file, search the Internet, or view apps in the Microsoft Store.
   - Click **My stuff** or **Web** to refine your search.
   - If you click **My stuff**, *Cortana* displays search results from your computer.
   - If you click **Web**, the Microsoft Edge web browser opens and displays your search results.

4. Click the **Menu** button at the top left to display other content options in the *Cortana* pane (see Figure Intro-16).
   - The other content options are *Home*, *Notebook*, *Reminders*, *Help*, and *Feedback*.

Intro-16 Use *Cortana* to search your computer, the Internet, and the Microsoft Store

Task View

A new feature to Windows 10 is **Task View**. *Task View* displays all open apps and windows as tiles on your desktop, and you can choose which item to display or close. This feature is very helpful when you have multiple items open and want to select or close one.

Task View button

▶**HOW TO: Use Task View**

1. Click the **Task View** button on the *Taskbar* (Figure Intro-17).
   - All open apps and windows display on the desktop (Figure Intro-18).

Intro-17 *Task View* **button on the** *Taskbar*

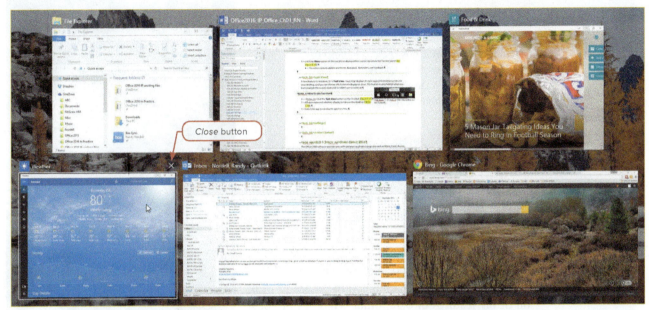

Close button

Intro-18 *Task View* **with open apps and windows displayed on the desktop**

2. Select the app or window to open or close.
   - Click a tile to open an app. The app opens and *Task View* closes.
   - Click the **X** in the upper right corner of an app to close an app. *Task View* remains open when you close an app.

Settings

In Windows 10, the **Settings** window is the redesigned *Control Panel* (although the *Control Panel* is still available). The *Settings* window is where you change global Windows settings, customize the Windows environment, add devices, and manage your Microsoft account. Click the **Settings** button on the *Taskbar* or *Start* menu to open the *Settings* window (Figure Intro-19). The following categories are available in the *Settings* window:

Search area

Intro-19 *Settings* **window**

- *System*: Display, notifications, apps, and power
- *Devices*: Bluetooth, printers, and mouse
- *Network & Internet*: Wi-Fi, airplane mode, and VPN
- *Personalization*: Background, lock screen, and colors
- *Accounts*: Your account, sync settings, work, and family
- *Time & Language*: Speech, region, and date
- *Ease of Access*: Narrator, magnifier, and high contrast
- *Privacy*: Location and camera
- *Update & Security*: Windows Update, recovery, and backup

> ### MORE INFO
>
> If you can't find an item in *Settings*, use the *Search* dialog box (*Find a setting*) in the upper right corner and type key words. If *Settings* is not available on the *Taskbar*, you can find it in the *All apps* list on the *Start* menu.

Action Center

The **Action Center** in Windows 10 provides a quick glance of notifications and buttons to open other commonly used settings and features in Windows. The *Action Center* displays notifications such as emails and Windows update notifications. Or you can click an action button to turn on or off features or open other windows or apps such as the *Settings* menu (*All Settings* button) or OneNote (*Note* button). Click the **Action Center** button on the right side of the *Taskbar* to open the *Action Center* pane on the right side of your screen (Figure Intro-20).

Intro-20 *Action Center*

SLO INTRO. 2

Using Office 2016

Office 2016 includes common software applications such as Word, Excel, Access, and PowerPoint. These applications give you the ability to work with word processing documents, spreadsheets, presentations, and databases in your personal and business projects.

Office 2016 and Office 365

Microsoft Office is a suite of personal and business software applications (Figure Intro-21). **Microsoft Office 2016** and **Microsoft Office 365** are the same software products; the difference is how you purchase the software. Office 2016 is

Intro-21 **Microsoft Office** application tiles on the *Start* menu

the traditional model of purchasing the software, and you own that software for as long as you want to use it. Office 365 is a subscription that you pay monthly or yearly, similar to how you purchase Netflix or Spotify. If you subscribe to Office 365, you automatically receive new versions of the software when they are released.

The common applications typically included in Microsoft Office 2016 and 365 are described in the following list:

- **Microsoft Word**: Word processing software used to create, format, and edit documents such as reports, letters, brochures, and resumes.
- **Microsoft Excel**: Spreadsheet software used to perform calculations on numerical data such as financial statements, budgets, and expense reports.
- **Microsoft Access**: Database software used to store, organize, compile, and report information such as product information, sales data, client information, and employee records.
- **Microsoft PowerPoint**: Presentation software used to graphically present information in slides such as a presentation on a new product or sales trends.
- **Microsoft Outlook**: Email and personal management software used to create and send email and create and store calendar items, contacts, and tasks.
- **Microsoft OneNote**: Note-taking software used to take and organize notes, which can be shared with other Office applications.
- **Microsoft Publisher**: Desktop publishing software used to create professional-looking documents containing text, pictures, and graphics such as catalogs, brochures, and flyers.

Office Desktop Apps, Office Universal Apps, and Office Online

Office desktop apps are the full-function Office 2016 or 365 programs installed on your computer (PC or Mac). Both Office 2016 and Office 365 are considered Office desktop apps. Because of the increased popularity and capabilities of tablets and mobile devices, Office software is also available for both tablets and smartphones. *Office universal apps* are the Office 365 programs that can be installed on tablets or other mobile devices. Office universal apps do not have the full range of advanced features available in Office desktop applications, but Office universal apps provide users the ability to create, edit, save, and share Office files using many of the most common features in the Office suite of programs.

> **MORE INFO**
>
> Office universal apps are also referred to as *Office mobile apps*.

Intro-22 *Office Online*

Office Online is free online software from Microsoft that works in conjunction with your Microsoft account and *OneDrive* (Figure Intro-22). With *Office Online*, you can work with Office files online through a web browser, even on computers that do not have Office 2016 or 365 installed. This is a useful option when you use a computer at a computer lab or use a friend's computer that does not have Office installed.

You can access *Office Online* from your *OneDrive* web page to create and edit Word documents, Excel workbooks, PowerPoint presentations, and OneNote notebooks. *Office Online* is a scaled-down version of Office 2016/365 and not as robust in terms of features, but you can use it to create, edit, print, share, and collaborate on files. If you need more advanced features, you can open *Office Online* files in Office 2016.

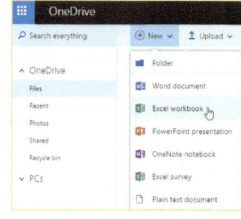

▶HOW TO: Create an Office Online File

1. Open an Internet browser Window, navigate to the *OneDrive* web site (www.onedrive.live.com), and log in to *OneDrive*. If you are not already logged in to *OneDrive*, use the following steps.

   - Click the **Sign in** button, type your Microsoft account email address, and click **Next**.
   - Type your Microsoft account password and click **Sign in** to open your *OneDrive* page.

Intro-23 Create an Office Online file from your online *OneDrive* page

2. Click the **New** button and select the type of *Office Online* file to create (Figure Intro-23).

   - A new file is created and opens in the *Office Online* program.
   - The new file is saved in your *OneDrive* folder (both online and on your computer).

3. Rename the file by clicking on the file name at the top of the file, typing a new file name, and pressing **Enter** (Figure Intro-24).

   - You can also click the **File** tab to open the *Backstage* view, select *Save As*, and choose **Save As** or **Rename**.
   - Click the **OPEN IN [OFFICE APPLICATION]** button (for example **OPEN IN EXCEL**) to open the file in the Office desktop application (see Figure Intro-24).

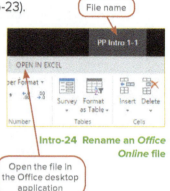

Intro-24 Rename an *Office Online* file

Open the file in the Office desktop application

4. Close the browser tab or window to close the file.

   - *Office Online* automatically saves the file as you make changes.

Open an Office Desktop Application

When using Windows 10, you open an Office desktop application by clicking the application tile on the *Start* menu or the application icon on the *Taskbar*. If your *Start* menu and *Taskbar* do not have the Office applications displayed, click the **Start** button, select **All apps**, and select **Word 2016**, **Excel 2016**, **Access 2016**, or **PowerPoint 2016** to launch the application (Figure Intro-25).

You can also use *Cortana* to quickly locate an Office desktop app (Figure Intro-26).

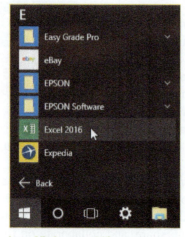

Intro-25 Open an Office desktop app from the *All apps* area on the *Start* menu

Intro-26 Use *Cortana* to find and open an app

Office Start Page

Most of the Office applications (except Outlook and OneNote) display a ***Start page*** when you launch the application (Figure Intro-27). From this *Start* page, you can create a new blank file (for example a Word document, an Excel workbook, an Access database, or a PowerPoint presentation), create a file from an online template, search for an online template, open a recently used file, or open another file. These options vary depending on the Office application.

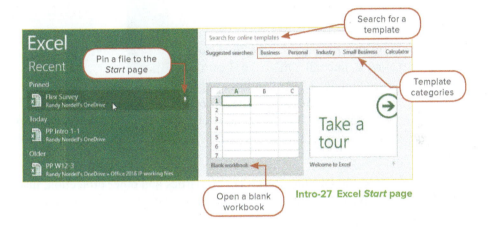

Intro-27 Excel *Start* page

▶**HOW TO:** Use the Office Start Page

1. Open a file listed in the *Recent* area on the left side of the *Start* menu by clicking the file to open. The file opens in the working area of the Office application.

   • The *Recent* area on the left side of the *Start* page lists files you have recently used and files that are pinned to the *Start* page.

2. Open a new blank file by clicking the **Blank *[file type]*** tile (*Blank workbook*, *Blank document*, etc.) to the right of the *Recent* area.

   • You can also press the **Esc** key to exit the *Start* page and open a new blank file.

3. Open an existing file that is not listed in the *Recent* area by clicking the **Open Other Workbooks** link (Figure Intro-28). The *Open* area on the *Backstage* view displays.

   • Click the **Browse** button to open the *Open* dialog box where you can locate and open a file.
   • You can also select a different location, *OneDrive* or *This PC*, and select a file to open.

4. Open a template by clicking a template file on the right or searching for templates.

   • Search for a template by typing key words in the *Search* area on the *Start* page.
   • Click a link to one of the categories below the *Search* area to display templates in that category.

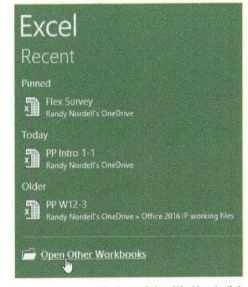

Intro-28 *Open Other Workbooks* link on the *Start* page

5. Pin a frequently used file to the *Start* page by clicking the **Pin** button.
    - The *Pin* button is on the right side of items listed in the *Recent* area and at the bottom right of templates displayed in the *Templates* area (to the right of the *Recent* area).
    - Pinned files display at the top of the *Recent* area.

Intro-29 *Backstage* view in Excel

> **MORE INFO**
>
> In Access, you have to open an existing database or create a new one to enter the program.

Backstage View

Office incorporates the ***Backstage view*** into all Office applications (including *Office Online* apps). Click the **File** tab on the *Ribbon* to open the *Backstage* view (Figure Intro-29). *Backstage* options vary on the different Office applications. The following list describes common tasks you can perform from the *Backstage* view:

- ***Info***: Displays document properties and other protection, inspection, and version options.
- ***New***: Creates a new blank file or a new file from a template or theme.
- ***Open***: Opens an existing file from a designated location or a recently opened file.
- ***Save***: Saves a file. If the file has not been named, the *Save As* dialog box opens when you select this option.
- ***Save As***: Opens the *Save As* dialog box.
- ***Print***: Prints a file, displays a preview of the file, or displays print options.
- ***Share***: Invites people to share a file or email a file.
- ***Export***: Creates a PDF file from a file or saves as a different file type.
- ***Close***: Closes an open file.
- ***Account***: Displays your Microsoft account information.
- ***Options***: Opens the *[Application] Options* dialog box (for example *Excel Options*).

Office Help—Tell Me

In all the Office 2016/365 applications, ***Tell Me*** is the new help feature (Figure Intro-30). This new help feature displays the commands in the Office application related to your search. The *Help* feature in older versions of Office displayed articles describing the feature and how to use it. The new *Tell Me* feature provides command options that take you directly to a command or dialog box. For example if you type *PivotTable* in the *Tell Me* search box in Excel, the results include the option to open the *Create PivotTable* dialog box, as well as other options such as *Recommended PivotTables* and *Summarize with PivotTable*.

Intro-30 *Tell Me* search box

▶HOW TO: Use Tell Me

1. Place your insertion point in the **Tell Me** search box at the top of the *Ribbon* (see Figure Intro-30).

2. Type key words for the command or feature for which you are searching.

3. Select an option from the list of displayed search results (Figure Intro-31).

   - When you select a search result, it may apply a command, open a dialog box, or display a gallery of command choices.

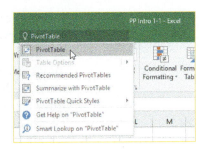

Intro-31 *Tell Me* **search results**

▶ **ANOTHER WAY**

Alt+Q places the insertion point in the *Tell Me* dialog box.
The previous *Help* feature is still available in Office 2016/365. Press **F1** to open the *Help* dialog box.

Mouse and Pointers

If you are using Office on a desktop or laptop computer, use your mouse (or touch pad) to navigate around files, click tabs and buttons, select text and objects, move text and objects, and resize objects. The following table lists mouse and pointer terminology used in Office:

Mouse and Pointer Terminology

Term	Description
Pointer	When you move your mouse, the pointer moves on your screen. A variety of pointers are used in different contexts in Office applications. The following pointers are available in most of the Office applications (the appearance of these pointers varies depending on the application and the context used): • *Selection pointer:* Select text or an object. • *Move pointer:* Move text or an object. • *Copy pointer:* Copy text or an object. • *Resize pointer:* Resize objects or table columns or rows. • *Crosshair:* Draw a shape.
Insertion point	The vertical flashing line indicating where you type text in a file or text box. Click the left mouse button to position the insertion point.
Click	Click the left mouse button. Used to select an object or button or to place the insertion point in the selected location.
Double-click	Click the left mouse button twice. Used to select text.
Right-click	Click the right mouse button. Used to display the context menu and the mini toolbar.
Scroll	Use the scroll wheel on the mouse to scroll up and down through your file. You can also use the horizontal or vertical scroll bars at the bottom and right of an Office file window to move around in a file.

Touch Mode and Touch Screen Gestures

The new user interface in Windows 10 and Office 2016 has improved touch features to facilitate the use of Windows and the Office applications on a tablet computer or smartphone. On tablets and smartphones, you use a touch screen rather than using a mouse, so the process of selecting text and objects and navigating around a file is different from a computer without a touch screen.

In Office 2016/365, *Touch mode* optimizes the Office working environment when using a computer with a touch screen to provide more space between buttons and commands. Click the **Touch/Mouse Mode** button on the *Quick Access* toolbar (upper left of the Office app window) and select **Touch** from the drop-down list to enable *Touch* mode (Figure Intro-32). To turn off *Touch* mode, select **Mouse** from the *Touch/Mouse Mode* drop-down list.

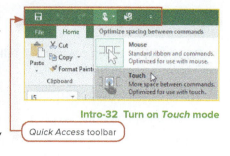

Intro-32 Turn on *Touch* mode

Quick Access toolbar

> **MORE INFO**
>
> The *Touch/Mouse Mode* button displays on the *Quick Access* toolbar when using a touch-screen computer.

The following table lists common gestures used when working on a tablet or smartphone (these gestures vary depending on the application used and the context):

Touch Screen Gestures

Gesture	Used To	How To
Tap	Select text or an object or position the insertion point. Double tap to edit text in an object or cell.	
Pinch	Zoom in or resize an object.	
Stretch	Zoom out or resize an object.	
Slide	Move an object or selected text.	
Swipe	Select text or multiple objects.	

> **MORE INFO**
>
> Window 10 has a *Tablet mode* that optimizes all of Windows and apps for touch screens. When you turn on the *Tablet mode* feature in Windows, the *Touch mode* in Office apps turns on automatically. Click the **Action Center** button on the Windows *Taskbar* and click the **Tablet mode** button to turn on this feature in Windows.

SLO INTRO. 3

Creating, Saving, Closing, and Opening Files

Creating, saving, opening, and closing files is primarily done from the *Start* page or *Backstage* view of the Office application you are using. These areas provide you with many options and a central location to perform these tasks. You can also use shortcut commands to create, save, and open files.

Create a New File

When you create a new file in an Office application, you can create a new blank file or a new file based on a template (in PowerPoint, you can also create a presentation based on a theme). On the *Start* page, click **Blank [file type]** to create a new blank file in the application you are using (in Word, you begin with a blank document; in Excel, a blank workbook; in Access, a blank desktop database; and in PowerPoint, a blank presentation).

▶ **HOW TO:** Create a New File from the Start Page

1. Open the Office application you want to use. The *Start* page displays when the application opens (Figure Intro-33).

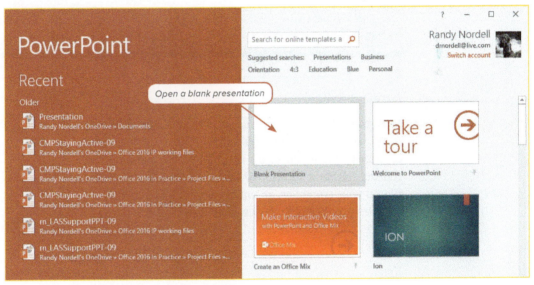

Intro-33 *Start* page in PowerPoint

2. Click **Blank [file type]** or select a template or theme to use for your new blank file. A new file opens in the application you are using.
   - The new file is given a generic file name (for example *Document1, Book1,* or *Presentation1*). You can name and save this file later.
   - When creating a new Access database, you are prompted to name the new file when you create it.
   - A variety of templates (and themes in PowerPoint only) display on the *Start* page, but you can search for additional online templates and themes using the *Search* text box at the top of the *Start* page.

> ▶ **MORE INFO**
>
> **Esc** closes the *Start* page and takes you into the Office application (except in Access).

If you have been using an application already and want to create a new file, you create it from the *Backstage* view. From the *Backstage* view, the new file options are available in the *New* area.

▶HOW TO: Create a New File from the Backstage View

1. Click the **File** tab to display the *Backstage* view.
2. Select **New** on the left to display the *New* area (Figure Intro-34).
3. Click **Blank [file type]** or select a template or theme to use in your new blank file. A new file opens in the application.
   - The new file is given a generic file name (*Document1*, *Book1*, or *Presentation1*). You can name and save this file later.
   - When you are creating a new Access database, you are prompted to name the new file when you create it.

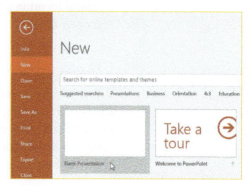

Intro-34　*New* area on the *Backstage* view in PowerPoint

▶ ANOTHER WAY

Ctrl+N opens a new file from within an Office application. In Access, **Ctrl+N** opens the *New* area in the *Backstage* view.

Save a File

In Access, you name a file as you create it, but in Word, Excel, and PowerPoint, you name a file after you have created it. When you save a file, you type a name for the file and select the location to save the file. You can save a file on your computer, an online storage location such as *OneDrive*, or portable device, such as a USB drive.

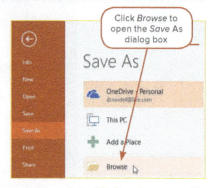

Click *Browse* to open the *Save* As dialog box

Intro-35　*Save As* area on the *Backstage* view in PowerPoint

▶HOW TO: Save a File

1. Click the **File** tab to display the *Backstage* view.
2. Select **Save** or **Save As** on the left to display the *Save As* area (Figure Intro-35).
   - If the file has not already been saved, clicking *Save* or *Save As* takes you to the *Save As* area on the *Backstage* view.
3. Click the **Browse** button to open the *Save As* dialog box (Figure Intro-36).
   - You can also select a different location (*OneDrive* or *This PC*) and select a folder from the list of folders at the right to open the *Save As* dialog box.
4. Select a location to save the file in the *Folder* list on the left.

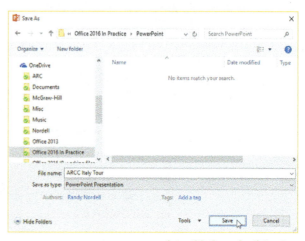

Intro-36　*Save As* dialog box

5. Type a name for the file in the *File name* area.
   - By default, Office selects the file type, but you can change the file type from the *Save as type* drop-down list.
6. Click **Save** to close the dialog box and save the file.

Create a New Folder When Saving a File

When saving files, it is a good idea to create folders to organize your files. Organizing your files in folders makes it easier to find your files and saves you time when you are searching for a specific file (see *SLO Intro.8: Organizing and Customizing Folders and Files* for more information on this topic). When you save an Office file, you can also create a folder in which to store that file.

▶ **HOW TO:** Create a New Folder When Saving a File

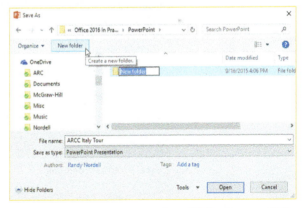

1. Click the **File** tab to display the *Backstage* view.
2. Select **Save As** on the left to display the *Save As* area.
3. Click **Browse** to open the *Save As* dialog box.
4. Select a location to save the file in the *Folder* list on the left.
5. Click the **New Folder** button to create a new folder (Figure Intro-37).
6. Type a name for the new folder and press **Enter**.

Intro-37 Create a new folder

Save As a Different File Name

After you have saved a file, you can save it again with a different file name. If you do this, you have preserved the original file, and you can continue to revise the second file for a different purpose.

> **▶HOW TO:** Save as a Different File Name

1. Click the **File** tab to display the *Backstage* view.
2. Select **Save As** on the left to display the *Save As* area.
3. Click the **Browse** button to open the *Save As* dialog box.
4. Select a location to save the file in the *Folder* list on the left.
5. Type a new name for the file in the *File name* area.
6. Click **Save** to close the dialog box and save the file.

Office 2016 File Types

When you save an Office file, by default Office saves the file in the most recent file format for that application. You also have the option of saving files in older versions of the Office application you are using. For example, you can save a Word document as an older version to share with or send to someone who uses an older version of Word. Each file has an extension at the end of the file name that determines the file type. The ***file name extension*** is automatically added to a file when you save it. The following table lists common file types used in the different Office applications:

Office File Types

File Type	Extension	File Type	Extension
Word Document	*.docx*	Access Database	*.accdb*
Word Template	*.dotx*	Access Template	*.accdt*
Word 97-2003 Document	*.doc*	Access Database (2000-2003 format)	*.mdb*
Rich Text Format	*.rtf*	PowerPoint Presentation	*.pptx*
Excel Workbook	*.xlsx*	PowerPoint Template	*.potx*
Excel Template	*.xltx*	PowerPoint 97-2003 Presentation	*.ppt*
Excel 97-2003 Workbook	*.xls*	Portable Document Format (PDF)	*.pdf*
Comma Separated Values (CSV)	*.csv*		

Close a File

You can close a file using the following different methods:

- Click the **File** tab and select **Close** on the left.
- Press **Ctrl+W**.
- Click the **X** in the upper right corner of the file window. This method closes the file and the program if only one file is open in the application.

When you close a file, you are prompted to save the file if it has not been named or if changes were made after the file was last saved (Figure Intro-38). Click **Save** to save and close the file or click **Don't Save** to close the file without saving. Click **Cancel** to return to the file.

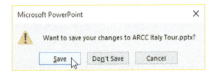

Intro-38 Prompt to save a document before closing

Open an Existing File

You can open an existing file from the *Start* page when you open an Office application or while you are working on another Office file.

▶ **HOW TO:** Open a File from the Start Page

1. Open an Office application to display the *Start* page.
2. Select a file to open in the *Recent* area on the left (Figure Intro-39). The file opens in the Office application.
   - If you select a file in the *Recent* area that has been renamed, moved, or on a storage device not connected to the computer, you receive an error message.
3. Alternatively, click the **Open Other [file type]** (for example *Open Other Presentations*) (see Figure Intro-39) link to open the *Open* area of the *Backstage* view (Figure Intro-40).

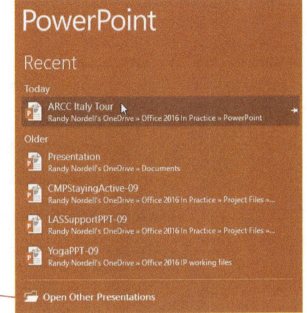

Intro-39 Open a file from the *Start* page

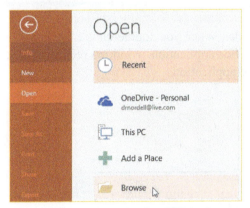

Intro-40 *Open* area on the *Backstage* view

4. Click the **Browse** button to open the *Open* dialog box (Figure Intro-41).
5. Select a location from the *Folder* list on the left.
6. Select the file to open and click the **Open** button.
   - If the file opens in *Protected View*, click the **Enable Editing** button to allow you to edit the file.

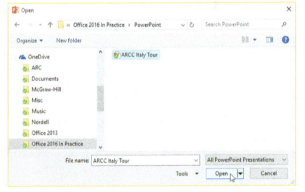

Intro-41 *Open* dialog box

When working on a file in an Office application, you might want to open another file. You can open an existing file from within an Office application from the *Open* area on the *Backstage* view.

> **HOW TO:** Open a File from the Backstage View

1. Click the **File** tab from within an open Office application to open the *Backstage* view.
2. Click **Open** on the left to display the *Open* area on the *Backstage* view (see Figure Intro-40).
3. Click the **Browse** button to open the *Open* dialog box (see Figure Intro-41).
   - You can also select a file to open from the list of *Recent* files on the right of the *Open* area on the *Backstage* view.
4. Select a location from the *Folder* list on the left.
5. Select the file to open and click the **Open** button.
   - If the file opens in *Protected View*, click the **Enable Editing** button to allow you to edit the file.

> **ANOTHER WAY**
>
> Press **Ctrl+F12** to open the *Open* dialog box when you are in the working area of an Office application (except in Access). On some laptops, you might have to press **Fn+Ctrl+F12**.

You can also open a file from a *File Explorer* folder. When you double-click a file in a *File Explorer* folder, the file opens in the appropriate Office application. Windows recognizes the file name extension and launches the correct Office application.

PAUSE & PRACTICE: INTRO-1

For this project, you log in to Windows using your Microsoft account, customize the Windows *Start* menu and *Taskbar*, create and save a PowerPoint presentation, create a folder, open and rename an Excel workbook, and use Windows 10 features.

File Needed: ***ARCC2018Budget-Intro.xlsx*** *(Student data files are available in the* Library *of your SIMnet account)*
Completed Project File Names: ***[your initials] PP Intro-1a.pptx*** and ***[your initials] PP Intro-1b.xlsx***

1. Log in to Windows using your Microsoft account if you are not already logged in.
   a. If you don't have a Microsoft account, you can create a free account at https://signup.live.com.
   b. If you are using a computer on your college campus, you may be required to log in to the computer using your college user name and password.
2. Customize the *Start* menu to include Office 2016 apps. If these apps tiles are already on the *Start* menu, skip steps 2a–e. You can pin other apps of your choice to the *Start* menu.
   a. Click the **Start** button at the bottom left of your screen to open the *Start* menu.

b. Click **All apps** at the bottom left of the *Start* menu (Figure Intro-42). The list of apps installed on the computer displays on the left side of the *Start* menu.

c. Locate and right-click **Access 2016** and select **Pin to Start** (Figure Intro-43). The app displays as a tile on the right side of the *Start* menu.

d. Repeat step 2c to pin **Excel 2016**, **PowerPoint 2016**, and **Word 2016** apps to the *Start* menu.

e. Display the *Start* menu and drag these Office app tiles so they are close to each other.

f. Click the **Start** button (or press the **Esc** key) to close the *Start* menu.

Intro-42 *All apps* button on the *Start* menu

3. Use *Cortana* and the *Start* menu to pin Office 2016 apps to the *Taskbar*.

a. Click the **Cortana** button (to the right of the *Start* button) on the *Taskbar* and type *Access*. *Cortana* displays content matching your search.

b. Right-click the **Access 2016** option near the top of the *Cortana* pane and select **Pin to taskbar** (Figure Intro-44). The app pins to the *Taskbar*.

c. Click the **Start** button to open the *Start* menu.

d. Right-click the **Excel 2016** tile on the right side of the *Start* menu, click **More**, and select **Pin to taskbar**. The app pins to the *Taskbar*.

e. Use either of the methods described above to pin the **PowerPoint 2016** and **Word 2016** apps to the *Taskbar*.

f. Drag the Office apps on the *Taskbar* to rearrange them to your preference.

Intro-43 Pin Access 2016 app to *Start* menu

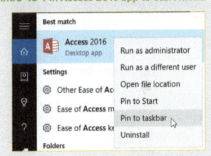

Intro-44 Use *Cortana* to find an Office app and pin it to the *Taskbar*

4. Create a PowerPoint presentation and save the presentation in a new folder.

a. Click the **PowerPoint 2016** app tile on your *Start* menu to open the application.

b. Click **Blank Presentation** on the PowerPoint *Start* page to create a new blank presentation.

c. Click the **Click to add title** placeholder and type American River Cycling Club to replace the placeholder text.

d. Click the **File** tab to open the *Backstage* view and click **Save As** on the left to display the *Save As* area.

e. Click **Browse** to open the *Save As* dialog box (Figure Intro-45).

f. Select a location to save the file from the *Folder* list on the left. If the *OneDrive* folder is an option, select **OneDrive**. If it is not, select the **Documents** folder in the *This PC* folder. You can also save to a portable storage device if you have one.

g. Click the **New Folder** button to create a new folder.

h. Type American River Cycling Club as the name of the new folder and press **Enter** (Figure Intro-46).

i. Double-click the **American River Cycling Club** folder to open it.

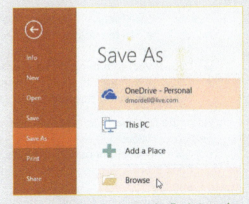

Intro-45 *Save As* area on the *Backstage* view in PowerPoint

j. Type [your initials] PP Intro-1a in the *File name* area.

k. Click **Save** to close the dialog box and save the presentation. Leave the file and PowerPoint open.

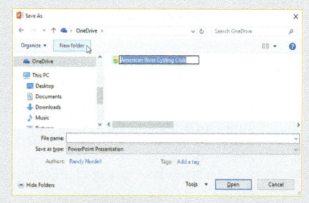

5. Open an Excel file and save as a different file name.

a. Return to the Windows *Start* menu.

b. Click the **Excel 2016** app button on the *Taskbar* to open it.

c. Click the **Open Other Workbooks** link on the bottom left of the Excel *Start* page to display the *Open* area of the *Backstage* view.

d. Click **Browse** to open the *Open* dialog box (Figure Intro-47).

e. Browse to your student data files and select the *ARCC2018Budget-Intro* file.

f. Click **Open** to open the workbook. If the file opens in *Protected View*, click the **Enable Editing** button.

g. Click the **File** tab to open the *Backstage* view.

h. Click **Save As** on the left to display the *Save As* area and click **Browse** to open the *Save As* dialog box.

i. Locate the **American River Cycling Club** folder (created in step 4h) in the *Folder* list on the left and double-click the folder to open it.

j. Type [your initials] PP Intro-1b in the *File name* area.

k. Click **Save** to close the dialog box and save the workbook. Leave the file and Excel open.

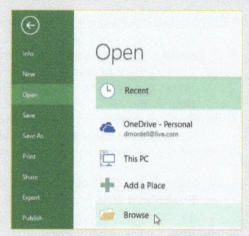

Intro-47 *Open* area on the *Backstage* view

6. Use the *Tell Me* feature in Excel to find a command.

a. Click the **Tell Me** search box on the *Ribbon* of the Excel window and type PivotTable (Figure Intro-48).

b. Click **PivotTable** to open the *Create PivotTable* dialog box.

c. Click the **X** in the upper right corner of the *Create PivotTable* dialog box to close it.

Intro-48 Use the *Tell Me* feature to find a command

7. Open the *Microsoft Store* app, the *Action Center*, and the *Settings* window.

a. Click the **Cortana** button and type Microsoft Store.

b. Click **Store** at the top of the *Cortana* pane to open the *Store* app.

c. Click **Apps** in the top left and browse the available apps in the Microsoft Store.

d. Click the **Minimize** button in the upper right corner of the *Store* window to minimize this app (Figure Intro-49). The app is still open, but it is minimized on the *Taskbar*.

Intro-49 *Minimize* button on an app window

e. Click the **Action Center** button on the right side of the *Taskbar* to display the *Action Center* pane at the right (Figure Intro-50).

Intro-50 Windows 10 *Action Center*

Intro-51 *Task View* button on the *Taskbar*

SLO INTRO. 4

Working with Files

When you work with Office files, a variety of display views are available. You can change how a file displays, adjust the display size, work with multiple files, and arrange the windows to view multiple files. Because most people work with multiple files at the same time, Office makes it easy and intuitive to move from one file to another or to display multiple document windows at the same time.

File Views

Each of the different Office applications provides you with a variety of ways to view your document. In Word, Excel, and PowerPoint, the different views are available on the *View tab* (Figure Intro-52). You can also change views using the buttons on the right side of the *Status bar* at the bottom of the file window (Figure Intro-53). In Access, the differ-

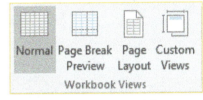

Intro-52 *Workbook Views* group on the *View* tab in Excel

Intro-53 PowerPoint views on the *Status* bar

ent views for each object are available in the *Views* group on the *Home* tab.

The following table lists the views that are available in each of the different Office applications:

File Views

Office Application	Views	Office Application	Views
Word	*Read Mode* *Print Layout* *Web Layout* *Outline* *Draft*	**Access** *(Access views vary depending on active object)*	*Layout View* *Design View* *Datasheet View* *Form View* *SQL View* *Report View* *Print Preview*
Excel	*Normal* *Page Break Preview* *Page Layout* *Custom Views*	**PowerPoint**	*Normal* *Outline View* *Slide Sorter* *Notes Page* *Reading View* *Presenter View*

Change Display Size

You can use the *Zoom* feature to increase or decrease the display size of your file. Using *Zoom* to change the display size does not change the actual size of text or objects in your file; it only changes the size of your display. For example, if you change the *Zoom* level to 120%, you increase the display of your file to 120% of its normal size (100%), but changing the display size does not affect the actual size of text and objects in your file. You could also decrease the *Zoom* level to 80% to display more of your file on the screen.

You can increase or decrease the *Zoom* level several different ways. Your *Zoom* options vary depending on the Office application you are using.

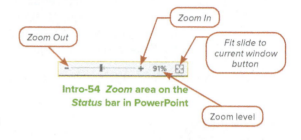

Intro-54 *Zoom* area on the *Status* bar in PowerPoint

- **Zoom level** *on the Status* bar (Figure Intro-54): Click the **+** or **−** button to increase or decrease *Zoom* level in 10% increments.
- **Zoom group** *on the View tab* (Figure Intro-55): The *Zoom* group includes a variety of *Zoom* options. The options vary depending on the Office application.
- **Zoom dialog box** (Figure Intro-56): Click the **Zoom** button in the *Zoom* group on the *View* tab or click the **Zoom level** on the *Status* bar to open the *Zoom* dialog box.

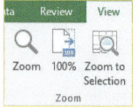

Intro-55 *Zoom* group in Excel

> ▶ **MORE INFO**
>
> The *Zoom* feature is only available in Access in *Print Preview* view when you are working with reports.

Manage Multiple Open Files and Windows

When you are working on multiple files in an Office application, each file is opened in a new window. You can **minimize** an open window to place the file on the Windows *Taskbar* (the bar at the bottom of the Windows desktop), **restore down** an open window so it does not fill the entire computer screen, or **maximize** a window so it fills the entire computer screen. The *Minimize, Restore Down/Maximize,* and *Close* buttons are in the upper right of a file window (Figure Intro-57).

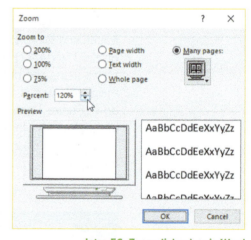

Intro-56 *Zoom* dialog box in Word

> ▶ **MORE INFO**
>
> You can open only one Access file at a time. If you open another Access file, the first one closes.

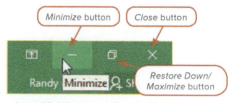

Intro-57 Window options buttons

- *Minimize*: Click the **Minimize** button (see Figure Intro-57) to hide the active window. When a document is minimized, it is not closed. It is minimized to the *Taskbar* so the window is not displayed on your screen. Place your pointer on the application icon on the Windows *Taskbar* to display thumbnails of open files. You can click an open file thumbnail to display the file (Figure Intro-58).

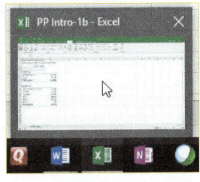

Intro-58 Display minimized file on the *Taskbar*

- *Restore Down/Maximize*: Click the **Restore Down/ Maximize** (see Figure Intro-57) button to decrease the size of an open window or maximize the window to fill the entire screen. This button toggles between *Restore Down* and *Maximize*. When a window is restored down, you can change the size of a window by clicking and dragging a border of the window. You can also move the window by clicking and dragging the title bar at the top of the window.
- *Close*: Click the **Close** button (see Figure Intro-57) to close the window. If there is only one open file, the Office application also closes when you click the *Close* button on the file.

You can switch between open files or arrange the open files to display more than one window at the same time. The following are several methods to do this:

- *Switch Windows button*: Click the **Switch Windows** button [*View* tab, *Window* group] (not available in Access) to display a drop-down list of open files. Click a file from the drop-down list to display the file.

> ► **ANOTHER WAY**
>
> Click the Windows **Task View** button on the *Taskbar* to tile all open windows and apps on the desktop.

- *Windows Taskbar*: Place your pointer on an Office application icon on the Windows *Taskbar* to display the open files in that application. Click a file thumbnail to display it (see Figure Intro-58).
- *Arrange All button*: Click the **Arrange All** button [*View* tab, *Window* group] to display all windows in an application. You can resize or move the open file windows.

Snap Assist

The *Snap Assist* feature in Windows provides the ability to position an open window to the left or right side of your computer screen and fill half the screen. When you snap an open window to the left or right side of the screen, the other open windows tile on the opposite side where you can select another window to fill the opposite side of the computer screen (Figure Intro-59).

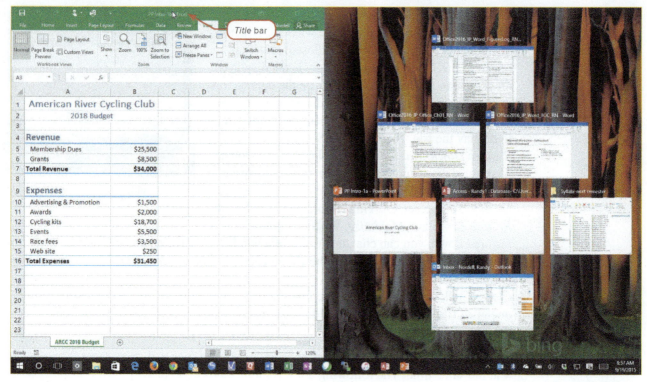

Intro-59 Windows *Snap Assist* feature

▶ **HOW TO:** Use Snap Assist

1. Click the **title bar** of an open window.
2. Drag it to the left or right edge of the computer screen and release the pointer.
   - The window snaps to the side of the screen and fills half of the computer screen (see Figure Intro-59).
   - The other open windows and apps display as tiles on the opposite side.
   - If you're using a touch screen computer, you can use *Snap Assist* by pressing and holding the title bar of an open window and dragging to either side of the computer screen.
3. Select a tile of an open window or app to fill the other half of the screen.

> **MORE INFO**
>
> *Snap Assist* also allows you to snap a window to a quadrant (quarter rather than half) of your screen. Drag the **title bar** of an open window to one of the four corners of your computer screen.

SLO INTRO. 5

Printing, Sharing, and Customizing Files

On the *Backstage* view of any of the Office applications, you can print a file and customize how a file is printed. You can also export an Office file as a PDF file in most of the Office applications. In addition, you can add and customize document properties for an Office file and share a file in a variety of formats.

Print a File

You can print an Office file if you need a hard copy. The *Print* area on the *Backstage* view displays a preview of the open file and many print options. For example, you can choose which page or pages to print and change the margins of the file in the *Print* area. Print settings vary depending on the Office application you are using and what you are printing.

▶**HOW TO:** Print a File

1. Open the file you want to print from a Windows folder or within an Office program.
2. Click the **File** tab to open the *Backstage* view.
3. Click **Print** on the left to display the *Print* area (Figure Intro-60).
   - A preview of the file displays on the right. Click the **Show Margins** button to adjust margins or **Zoom to Page** button to change the view in the *Preview* area. The *Show Margins* button is only available in Excel.
4. Change the number of copies to print in the *Copies* area.
5. Click the **Printer** drop-down list to choose from available printers.
6. Customize what is printed and how it is printed in the *Settings* area.
   - The *Settings* options vary depending on the Office application you are using and what you are printing.
   - In the *Pages* area (*Slides* area in PowerPoint), you can select a page or range of pages (slides) to print.
   - By default all pages (slides) are printed when you print a file.
7. Click the **Print** button to print your file.

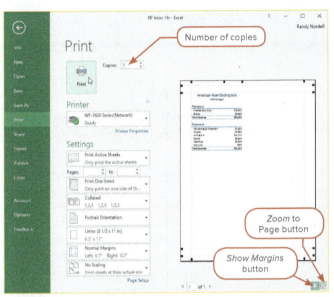

Intro-60 *Print* area on the *Backstage* view

▶ **ANOTHER WAY**

Press **Ctrl+P** to open the *Print* area on the *Backstage* view.

Export as a PDF File

Portable document format, or **PDF**, is a specific file format that is often used to share files that are not to be changed or to post files on a web site. When you create a PDF file from an Office application file, you are actually exporting a static image of the original file, similar to taking a picture of the file.

The advantage of working with a PDF file is that the format of the file is retained no matter who opens the file. PDF files open in the Windows Reader app or Adobe Reader, which is free software that is installed on most computers. Because a PDF file is a static image of a file, it is not easy for other people to edit your files. When you want people to be able to view a file but not change it, PDF files are a good choice.

▶HOW TO: Export a File as a PDF File

1. Open the file you want to export as a PDF file.

2. Click the **File** tab and click **Export** to display the *Export* area on the Backstage view (Figure Intro-61).

3. Select **Create PDF/XPS Document** and click the **Create PDF/XPS**. The *Publish as PDF or XPS* dialog box opens.

   - XPS (XML Paper Specification) format is an alternative to a PDF file. XPS is a Microsoft format and is not widely used.

4. Select a location to save the file.

5. Type a name for the file in the *File name* area.

6. Click **Publish** to close the dialog box and save the PDF file.

   - A PDF version of your file may open. You can view the file and then close it.

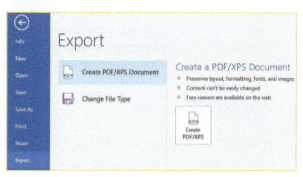

Intro-61 *Export* a file as a PDF file

▶ **MORE INFO**

Microsoft Word can open PDF files, and you can edit and save the file as a Word document.

Document Properties

Document properties are hidden codes in a file that store identifying information about that file. Each piece of document property information is called a ***field***. You can view and modify document properties in the *Info* area of the *Backstage* view.

Some document properties fields are automatically generated when you work on a file, such as *Size*, *Total Editing Time*, *Created*, and *Last Modified*. Other document properties fields, such as *Title*, *Comments*, *Subject*, *Company*, and *Author*, can be modified. You can use document property fields in different ways such as inserting the *Company* field in a document footer.

▶HOW TO: View and Modify Document Properties

1. Click the **File** tab and click **Info**. The document properties display on the right (Figure Intro-62).

2. Click the text box area of a field that can be edited and type your custom document property information.

3. Click the **Show All Properties** link at the bottom to display additional document properties.

   - Click **Show Fewer Properties** to collapse the list and display fewer properties.
   - This link toggles between *Show All Properties* and *Show Fewer Properties*.

4. Click the **Back** arrow to return to the file.

Intro-62 Document properties

Share a File

Windows 10 and Office 2016 have been enhanced to help you share files and collaborate with others. The *Share* area on the *Backstage* view lists different options for sharing files from within an Office application. When you save a file to your *OneDrive*, Office provides a variety of options to share your file (Figure Intro-63). The two main sharing options are **Share with People** and **Email**. Within these two categories, you have a variety of ways to share a file with others. Your sharing options vary depending on the Office application you are using. The following list describes the sharing options available in the Office applications:

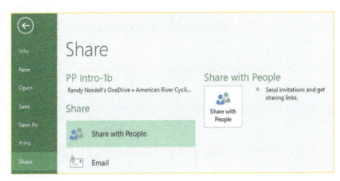

Intro-63 Share options on the Backstage view

- **Word**: *Share with People*, *Email*, *Present Online*, and *Post to Blog*
- **Excel**: *Share with People* and *Email*
- **Access**: No *Sharing* option on the *Backstage* view
- **PowerPoint**: *Share with People*, *Email*, *Present Online*, and *Publish Slides*

▶HOW TO: Share a File

1. Click the **File** tab to open the *Backstage* view and select **Share** on the left.
   - If your file is not saved in *OneDrive*, you are directed to first save the file to the cloud (*OneDrive*). Click the **Save to Cloud** button and save your file in *OneDrive*.
   - If your file is not saved to *OneDrive*, you will not have all available sharing options.

2. Share a *OneDrive* file with others by clicking **Share with People** on the left and then clicking the **Share with People** button on the right (see Figure Intro-63).
   - The *Backstage* view closes and the *Share* pane opens on the right side of the file (Figure Intro-64).
   - Alternatively, click the **Share** button in the upper right corner of the Office application window to open the *Share* pane (Figure Intro-65).
   - Type an email address in the *Invite people* text box. If you want to share the file with more than one person, separate email addresses with a semicolon.
   - Select **Can edit** or **Can view** from the permission drop-down list, which controls what others can do with your file.
   - You can include a message the recipients will receive.
   - Click the **Share** button below the message to send a sharing email to recipients.
   - Alternatively, click the **Get a sharing link** option at the bottom of the *Share* pane to create an *edit link* or *view-only link* (Figure Intro-66). You can then copy the sharing link and email it to others or post it in an online location.

Intro-64 Share pane

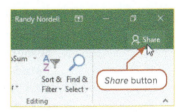

Intro-65 The Share button opens the Share pane

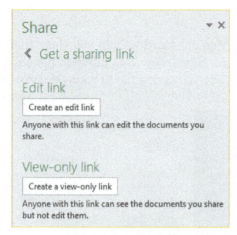

Intro-66 *Get a sharing link* options in the *Share* pane

Intro-67 *Email* share options in the *Share* area on the *Backstage* view

3. Share a file through email by clicking the **Email** button on the left side of the *Share* area on the *Backstage* view and selecting an option (Figure Intro-67).

- These *Email* share options use Microsoft Outlook (email and personal management Office application) to share the selected file through email.
- The *Email* share options include *Send as Attachment*, *Send a Link*, *Send as PDF*, *Send as XPS*, and *Send as Internet Fax*.
- A description of each of these *Email* share options are provided to the right of each option.

> **MORE INFO**
>
> Sharing options are also available if you save files to other online storage locations such as Dropbox and Box.

Program Options

Using the program options, you can apply global changes to the Office program. For example, you can change the default save location to your *OneDrive* folder or you can turn off the *Start* page that opens when you open an Office application.

Click the **File** tab and select **Options** on the left to open the **[Program] Options** dialog box (Word Options, Excel Options, etc.) (Figure Intro-68). Click one of the categories on the left to display the category options on the right. The categories and options vary depending on the Office application you are using.

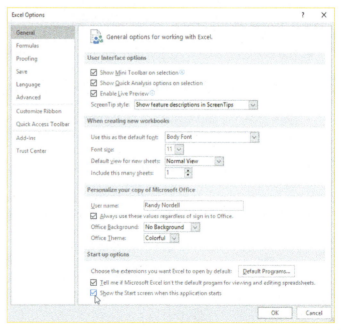

Intro-68 *Excel Options* dialog box

Using the Ribbon, Tabs, and Quick Access Toolbar

You can use the *Ribbon*, tabs, groups, buttons, drop-down lists, dialog boxes, task panes, galleries, and the *Quick Access* toolbar to modify your Office files. This section describes different tools you can use to customize your files.

The Ribbon, Tabs, and Groups

The **Ribbon**, which appears at the top of an Office file window, displays the many features available to use on your files. The *Ribbon* is a collection of **tabs**. On each tab are **groups** of features. The tabs and groups that are available on each Office application vary. Click a tab to display the groups and features available on that tab.

Some tabs always display on the *Ribbon* (for example the *File* tab and *Home* tabs). Other tabs are **context-sensitive**, which means that they only appear on the *Ribbon* when you select a specific object. Figure Intro-69 displays the context-sensitive *Table Tools Field* tab that displays in Access when you open a table.

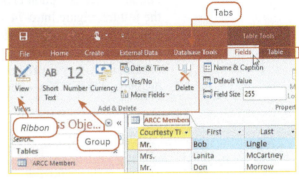

Intro-69 Context-sensitive *Table Tools Fields* tab displayed

Ribbon Display Options

The *Ribbon* displays by default in Office applications, but you can customize how the *Ribbon* displays. The **Ribbon Display Options** button is in the upper right corner of an Office application window (Figure Intro-70). Click the **Ribbon Display Options** button to select one of the three options:

Intro-70 *Ribbon Display Options*

- **Auto-Hide Ribbon**: Hides the *Ribbon*. Click at the top of the application to display the *Ribbon*.
- **Show Tabs**: *Ribbon* tabs display. Click a tab to open the *Ribbon* and display the tab.
- **Show Tabs and Commands**: Displays the *Ribbon* and tabs, which is the default setting in Office applications.

> **MORE INFO**
>
> **Ctrl+F1** collapses or expands the *Ribbon*.

Buttons, Drop-Down Lists, and Galleries

Groups on each of the tabs contain a variety of **buttons**, **drop-down lists**, and **galleries**. The following list describes each of these features and how they are used:

- **Button**: Applies a feature to selected text or object. Click a button to apply the feature (Figure Intro-71).

- **Drop-down list**: Displays the various options available for a feature. Some buttons are drop-down lists only, so when you click one of these buttons the drop-down list of options appears (Figure Intro-72). Other buttons are **split buttons**, which have both a button you click to apply a feature and an arrow you click to display a drop-down list of options (Figure Intro-73).
- **Gallery**: Displays a collection of option buttons. Click an option in a gallery to apply the feature. Figure Intro-74 is the *Styles* gallery. You can click the **More** button to display the entire gallery of options or click the **Up** or **Down** arrow to display a different row of options.

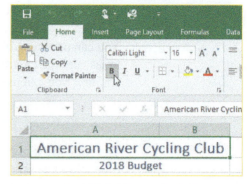

Intro-71 *Bold* button in the *Font* group on the *Home* tab

Up and Down buttons

More button

Intro-74 *Styles* gallery in Word

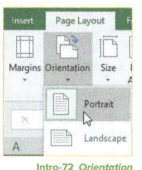

Intro-72 *Orientation* drop-down list

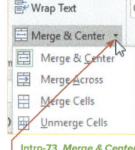

Intro-73 *Merge & Center* split button—button and drop-down list

Click the arrow on a split button to display the drop-down list

Dialog Boxes, Task Panes, and Launchers

Not all of the features that are available in an Office application are displayed in the groups on the tabs. Additional options for some groups display in a **dialog box** or **task pane**. A **launcher**, which is a small square in the bottom right of some groups, opens a dialog box or displays a task pane when you click it (see Figure Intro-76).

- **Dialog box**: A new window that opens to display additional features. You can move a dialog box by clicking and dragging the title bar, which is the top of the dialog box where the title is displayed. Figure Intro-75 shows the *Format Cells* dialog box that opens when you click the *Alignment* launcher in Excel.

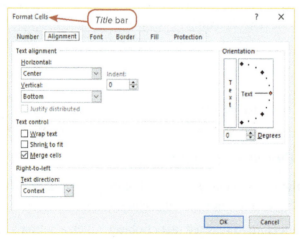

Title bar

Intro-75 *Format Cells* dialog box

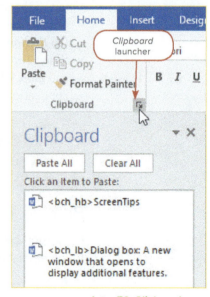

Clipboard launcher

Intro-76 *Clipboard* pane

- **Task pane**: Opens on the left or right of the Office application window. Figure Intro-76 shows the *Clipboard* pane, which is available in all Office applications. Task panes are named according to their feature (for example *Clipboard* pane or *Navigation* pane). You can resize a task pane by clicking and dragging its left or right border. Click the **X** in the upper right corner to close a task pane.

ScreenTips

ScreenTips display descriptive information about a button, drop-down list, launcher, or gallery selection. When you place your pointer on an item on the *Ribbon*, a *ScreenTip* displays information about the selection (Figure Intro-77). The *ScreenTip* appears temporarily and displays the command name, keyboard shortcut (if available), and a description of the command.

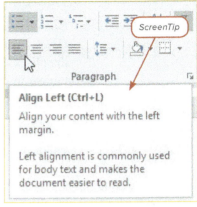

Intro-77 *Align Left ScreenTip*

Radio Buttons, Check Boxes, and Text Boxes

Dialog boxes and task panes contain a variety of features you can apply using ***radio buttons***, ***check boxes***, ***text boxes***, ***drop-down lists***, and other buttons (Figure Intro-78).

- ***Radio button***: A round button you click to select one option from a list of options. A selected radio button has a solid dot inside the round button.
- ***Check box***: A square button you click to select one or more options. A check appears in a check box you have selected.
- ***Text box***: An area where you can type text.

A task pane or dialog box may also include drop-down lists or other buttons that open additional dialog boxes. Figure Intro-78 shows the *Page Setup* dialog box in Excel, which includes a variety of radio buttons, check boxes, text boxes, drop-down lists, and other buttons that open additional dialog boxes (for example the *Print* and *Options* buttons).

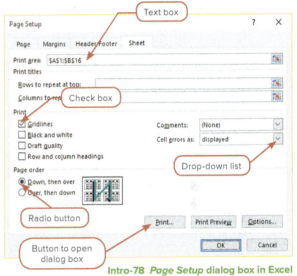

Intro-78 *Page Setup* dialog box in Excel

Quick Access Toolbar

The ***Quick Access toolbar*** is located above the *Ribbon* on the upper left of each Office application window. It contains buttons to apply commonly used commands such as *Save*, *Undo*, *Redo*, and *Open* (Figure Intro-79). The *Undo* button is a split button. You can click the

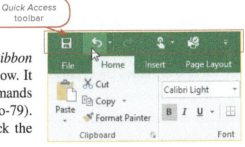

Intro-79 *Quick Access* toolbar

button to undo the last action performed or you can click the drop-down arrow to display and undo multiple previous actions.

Customize the Quick Access Toolbar

You can customize the *Quick Access* toolbar to include features you regularly use, such as *Quick Print*, *New*, and *Spelling & Grammar*. The following steps show how to customize the *Quick Access* toolbar in Word. The customization process is similar for the *Quick Access* toolbar in the other Office applications.

▶HOW TO: Customize the Quick Access Toolbar

1. Click the **Customize Quick Access Toolbar** drop-down list on the right edge of the *Quick Access* toolbar (Figure Intro-80).

2. Select a command to add to the *Quick Access* toolbar. The command displays on the *Quick Access* toolbar.
   - Items on the *Customize Quick Access Toolbar* drop-down list with a check mark are commands that are displayed on the *Quick Access* toolbar.
   - Deselect a checked item to remove it from the *Quick Access* toolbar.

3. Add a command that is not listed on the *Customize Quick Access Toolbar* by clicking the **Customize Quick Access Toolbar** drop-down list and selecting **More Commands**. The *Word Options* dialog box opens with the *Quick Access Toolbar* area displayed (Figure Intro-81).

4. Click the **Customize Quick Access Toolbar** drop-down list on the right and select **For all documents** or the current document.
   - If you select *For all documents*, the change is made to the *Quick Access* toolbar for all documents you open in Word.
   - If you select the current document, the change is made to the *Quick Access* toolbar in that document only.

5. Select the command to add from the alphabetic list of commands on the left and click the **Add** button.
   - If you can't find the command you're looking for, click the **Choose commands from** drop-down list and select **All Commands**.
   - The list on the right contains the commands that display on the *Quick Access* toolbar.

6. Rearrange commands on the *Quick Access* toolbar by selecting a command in the list on the right and clicking the **Move Up** or **Move Down** button.

7. Click **OK** to close the *Word Options* dialog box.

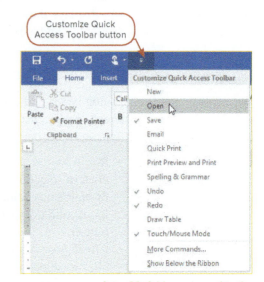

Customize Quick Access Toolbar button

Intro-80 Add a command to the *Quick Access* toolbar

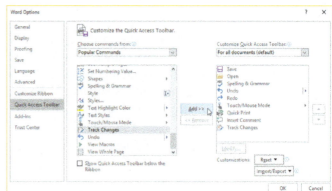

Intro-81 Customize the *Quick Access* toolbar in the *Word Options* dialog box

SLO INTRO. 7

Using Context Menus, the Mini Toolbars, and Keyboard Shortcuts

Most of the commands you use for formatting and editing your files display in groups on the tabs. But many of these features are also available using content menus, mini toolbars, and keyboard shortcuts. You can use these tools to quickly apply formatting or other options to text or objects.

Context Menu

A *context menu* displays when you right-click text, a cell, or an object such as a picture, drawing object, chart, or *SmartArt* (Figure Intro-82). The context menu is a vertical list of options, and the options are context-sensitive, which means they vary depending on what you right-click.

Context menus include options that perform an action (*Cut* or *Copy*), open a dialog box or task pane (*Format Cells* or *Hyperlink*), or display a drop-down list of selections (*Filter* or *Sort*).

Mini Toolbar

The *mini toolbar* is another context menu that displays when you right-click or select text, a cell, or an object in your file (see Figure Intro-82). The mini toolbar is a horizontal rectangular menu that lists a variety of formatting options. These options vary depending on what you select or right-click. The mini toolbar contains a variety of buttons and drop-down lists. The mini toolbar typically displays above the context menu. The mini toolbar automatically displays when you select text or an object, such as when you select a row of a table in Word or PowerPoint.

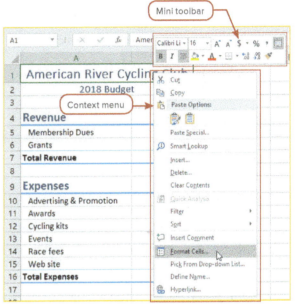

Intro-82 Context menu and mini toolbar

Keyboard Shortcuts

You can also use a *keyboard shortcut* to quickly apply formatting or perform commands. A keyboard shortcut is a combination of keyboard keys that you press at the same time. These can include the **Ctrl**, **Shift**, **Alt**, letter, number, and function keys (for example **F1** or **F7**). The following table lists common Office keyboard shortcuts.

Common Office Keyboard Shortcuts

Keyboard Shortcut	Action or Displays	Keyboard Shortcut	Action or Displays
Ctrl+S	Save	Ctrl+Z	Undo
F12	*Save As* dialog *box*	Ctrl+Y	Redo or Repeat
Ctrl+O	*Open* area on the *Backstage* view	Ctrl+1	Single space
Shift+F12	*Open* dialog box	Ctrl+2	Double space
Ctrl+N	New blank file	Ctrl+L	Align left
Ctrl+P	*Print* area on the *Backstage* view	Ctrl+E	Align center
Ctrl+C	Copy	Ctrl+R	Align right
Ctrl+X	Cut	F1	*Help* dialog box
Ctrl+V	Paste	F7	*Spelling* pane
Ctrl+B	Bold	Ctrl+A	Select All
Ctrl+I	Italic	Ctrl+Home	Move to the beginning
Ctrl+U	Underline	Ctrl+End	Move to the end

> **MORE INFO**
> See Appendix A for additional Office 2016 keyboard shortcuts.

Function Keys on a Laptop

Intro-83 Function key

When using a laptop computer, function keys perform specific Windows actions on your laptop, such as increase or decrease speaker volume, open Windows *Settings*, or adjust the screen brightness. So when using a numbered function key, such as **F12** as a shortcut to open the *Save As* dialog box in an Office application, you may need to press the ***function key*** (**Fn** or **fn**) on your keyboard in conjunction with a numbered function key to activate the command (Figure Intro-83). The *function key* is typically located near the bottom left of your laptop keyboard next to the *Ctrl* key.

PAUSE & PRACTICE: INTRO-2

For this project, you work with a document for the American River Cycling Club. You modify the existing document, add document properties, customize the *Quick Access* toolbar, export the document as a PDF file, and share the document.

File Needed: ***ARCCTraining-Intro.docx*** *(Student data files are available in the* Library *of your SIMnet account)*
Completed Project File Names: ***[your initials] PP Intro-2a.docx*** and ***[your initials] PP Intro-2b.pdf***

1. Open Word 2016 and open the **ARCCTraining-Intro** file from your student data files. If the file opens in *Protected View*, click the **Enable Editing** button.

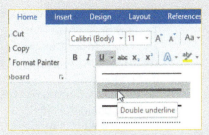

2. Save this document as [your initials] PP Intro-2a in the *American River Cycling Club* folder in your *OneDrive* folder.
   a. In *Pause & Practice Intro-1*, you created the *American River Cycling Club* folder in *OneDrive* or other storage area. Save this file in the same location.
   b. If you don't save this file in *OneDrive*, you will not be able to complete steps 7 and 9 in this project.

Intro-84 Apply *Double underline* to selected text.

3. Use a button, drop-down list, and dialog box to modify the document.
   a. Select the first heading, "**What is Maximum Heart Rate?**"
   b. Click the **Bold** button [*Home* tab, *Font* group].
   c. Click the **Underline** drop-down arrow and select **Double underline** (Figure Intro-84).
   d. Click the **launcher** in the *Font* group [*Home* tab] to open the *Font* dialog box (Figure Intro-85).
   e. In the *Size* area, select **12** from the list or type 12 in the text box.
   f. In the *Effects* area, click the **Small caps** check box to select it.
   g. Click **OK** to close the dialog box and apply the formatting changes.
   h. Select the next heading, "**What is Target Heart Rate?**"
   i. Repeat steps 3b–g to apply formatting to selected text.

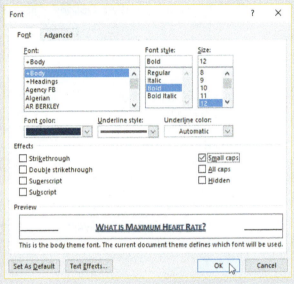

Intro-85 *Font* dialog box

4. Add document properties.
   a. Click the **File** tab to display the *Backstage* view.
   b. Select **Info** on the left. The document properties display on the right.
   c. Click the **Add a title** text box and type ARCC Training.
   d. Click the **Show All Properties** link near the bottom to display additional document properties.
   e. Click the **Specify the subject** text box and type Heart rate training.
   f. Click the **Specify the company** text box and type American River Cycling Club.
   g. Click the **Back** arrow on the upper left to close the *Backstage* view and return to the document.

5. Customize the *Quick Access* toolbar.
   a. Click the **Customize Quick Access Toolbar** drop-down arrow and select **Open** (Figure Intro-86).
   b. Click the **Customize Quick Access Toolbar** drop-down arrow again and select **Spelling & Grammar**.

Intro-86 *Customize Quick Access Toolbar* drop-down list

c. Click the **Customize Quick Access Toolbar** drop-down arrow again and select **More Commands**. The *Word Options* dialog box opens (Figure Intro-87).

d. Select **Insert Comment** in the list of commands on the left.

e. Click the **Add** button to add it to your *Quick Access* toolbar list on the right.

f. Click **OK** to close the *Word Options* dialog box.

g. Click the **Save** button on the *Quick Access* toolbar to save the document.

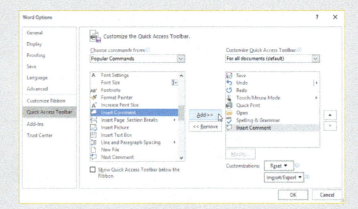

Intro-87 Customize the *Quick Access* toolbar in the *Word Options* dialog box

6. Export the file as a PDF file.

a. Click the **File** tab to go to the *Backstage* view.

b. Select **Export** on the left.

c. Select **Create PDF/XPS Document** and click the **Create PDF/XPS** button. The *Publish as PDF or XPS* dialog box opens (Figure Intro-88).

d. Select the **American River Cycling Club** folder in your *OneDrive* folder as the location to save the file.

e. Type [your initials] PP Intro-2b in the *File name* area.

f. Deselect the **Open file after publishing** check box if it is checked.

g. Select the **Standard (publishing online and printing)** radio button in the *Optimize for* area.

h. Click **Publish** to close the dialog box and create a PDF version of your file.

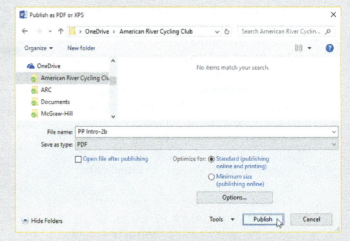

Intro-88 *Publish as PDF or XPS* dialog box

7. Get a link to share a document with your instructor. If your file is not saved in *OneDrive*, skip steps 7 and 9.

a. Click the **Share** button in the upper right of the Word window. The *Share* pane opens on the right side of your document.

b. Click **Get a sharing link** at the bottom of the *Share* pane.

c. Click the **Create an edit link** button.

d. Click **Copy** to copy the edit link (Figure Intro-89).

Intro-89 Copy a sharing link

8. Save and close the document (Figure Intro-90).

American River Cycling Club

www.arcc.org   Cycling...a way of life   info@arcc.org

WHAT IS MAXIMUM HEART RATE?

The maximum heart rate is the highest your pulse rate can get. To calculate your **predicted maximum heart rate**, use this formula:

(Example: a 40-year-old's predicted maximum heart rate is 180.)

Your actual maximum heart rate can be determined by a graded exercise test. Please note that some medicines and medical conditions might affect your maximum heart rate. If you are taking medicines or have a medical condition (such as heart disease, high blood pressure, or diabetes), always ask your doctor if your maximum heart rate/target heart rate will be affected.

WHAT IS TARGET HEART RATE?

You gain the most benefits and decrease the risk of injury when you exercise in your target heart rate zone. Usually this is when your exercise heart rate (pulse) is 60 percent to 85 percent of your maximum heart rate. Do not exercise above 85 percent of your maximum heart rate. This increases both cardiovascular and orthopedic risk and does not add any extra benefit.

When beginning an exercise program, you might need to gradually build up to a level that is within your target heart rate zone, especially if you have not exercised regularly before. If the exercise feels too hard, slow down. You will reduce your risk of injury and enjoy the exercise more if you don't try to over-do it.

To find out if you are exercising in your target zone (between 60 percent and 85 percent of your maximum heart rate), use your heart rate monitor to track your heart rate. If your pulse is below your target zone (see the chart below), increase your rate of exercise. If your pulse is above your target zone, decrease your rate of exercise.

MAX AND TARGET HEART RATES

AGE	PREDICTED MAX HEART RATE	TARGET HEART RATE (60-85% OF MAX)
20	✓ 200	120-170
25	✓ 195	117-166
30	✓ 190	114-162
35	✓ 185	111-157
40	✓ 180	108-153
45	✓ 175	105-149
50	✓ 170	102-145
55	✓ 165	99-140
60	✓ 160	96-136
65	✓ 155	93-132
70	✓ 150	90-128

Intro-90 PP Intro-2a completed

9. Email the sharing link to your instructor.
   a. Using your email account, create a new email to send to your instructor.
   b. Include an appropriate subject line and a brief message in the body.
   c. Press **Ctrl+V** to paste the link to your document in the body of the email.
   d. Send the email message.

Organizing and Customizing Folders and Files

The more you use your computer to create and use files, the more important it is to stay organized. You can use **folders** to store related files, which makes it easier for you to find, edit, and share your files. For example, you can create a folder for the college you attend. Inside the college folder, you can create a folder for each of your courses. Inside each of the course folders you might create a folder for student data files, solution files, and group projects. Folders can store any type of files; you are not limited to Office files.

Create a Folder

In *SLO Intro.3: Creating, Saving, Closing, and Opening Files*, you learned how to create a new folder when saving an Office file in the *Save As* dialog box. You can also create a Windows folder using *File Explorer*. You can create folders inside other folders.

▶HOW TO: Create a Windows Folder

1. Click the **Start** button and select **File Explorer** to open a *File Explorer* window.
   - Your folders and computer locations are listed on the left.
2. Select the location in the *Navigation* pane on the left where you want to create a new folder.
3. Click **Home** tab, and click the **New folder** button [*New* group]. A new folder is created (Figure Intro-91).
   - The *New Folder* button is also on the *Quick Access* toolbar in the *File Explorer* window.
4. Type the name of the new folder and press **Enter**.

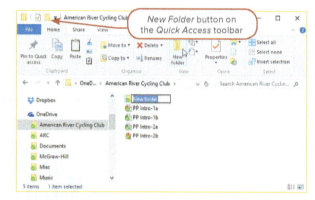

Intro-91 Create a new Windows folder

> ### ▶ ANOTHER WAY
> **Ctrl+Shift+N** creates a new folder in a Windows folder.

Move and Copy Files and Folders

Moving a file or folder is cutting it from one location and pasting it in another location. Copying a file or folder creates a copy of it, and you can paste in another location so the file or folder is in two or more locations. If you move or copy a folder, the files in the folder are moved or copied with the folder. Move or copy files and folders using the *Move to* or *Copy to* buttons on the *Home* tab of *File Explorer*, keyboard shortcuts (**Ctrl+X, Ctrl+C, Ctrl+V**), or the drag-and-drop method.

To move or copy multiple folders or files at the same time, press the **Ctrl** key and select multiple items to move or copy. Use the **Ctrl** key to select or deselect multiple non-adjacent files or folders. Use the **Shift** key to select a range of files or folders. Click the first file or folder in a range, press the **Shift** key, and select the last file or folder in the range to select all of the items in the range.

1. Click the **Start** button and select **File Explorer** to open a *File Explorer* window.
2. Select a file or folder to move or copy.
   - Press the **Ctrl** key to select multiple files or folders.
3. Click the **Home** tab in the *File Explorer* window.
4. Click the **Move to** or **Copy to** button [*Organize* group] and select the location where you want to move or copy the file or folder (Figure Intro-92).

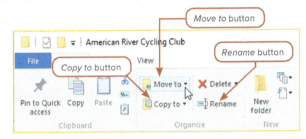

Intro-92 Move or copy a selected file or folder

   - If the folder you want is not available, select **Choose location** to open the *Move Items* or *Copy Items* dialog box.
   - To use the keyboard shortcuts, press **Ctrl+X** to cut the file or folder or **Ctrl+C** to copy the file or folder from its original location, go to the desired new location, and press **Ctrl+V** to paste it.
   - To use the drag-and-drop method to move a file or folder, select the file or folder and drag and drop to the new location.
   - To use the drag-and-drop method to copy a file or folder, press the **Ctrl** key, select the file or folder, and drag and drop to the new location.

> ▶ **ANOTHER WAY**
>
> Right-click a file or folder to display the context menu where you can select **Cut, Copy,** or **Paste.**

Rename Files and Folders

You can rename a file or folder in a *File Explorer* window. When you rename a file or folder, only the file or folder name changes, and the contents of the file or folder do not change.

1. Click the **Start** button and select **File Explorer** to open a *File Explorer* window.
2. Select the file or folder you want to rename.
3. Click the **Rename** button [*Home* tab, *Organize* group] (see Figure Intro-92).
4. Type the new name of the file or folder and press **Enter**.

> ▶ **ANOTHER WAY**
>
> Select a file or folder to rename, press **F2**, type the new name, and press **Enter**. You can also right-click a file or folder and select **Rename** from the context menu.

Delete Files and Folders

You can also easily delete files and folders. When you delete a file or folder, it is moved from its current location to the ***Recycle Bin*** on your computer where deleted items are stored. If a file or folder is in the *Recycle Bin*, you can restore this item to its original location or move it to a different location. You also have the option to permanently delete a file or folder; the item is deleted and not moved to the *Recycle Bin*. If an item is permanently deleted, you do not have the restore option.

▶HOW TO: Delete Files and Folders

1. Open a *File Explorer* window and select the file or folder you want to delete.
   - You can select multiple files and folders to delete at the same time.
2. Click the **Delete** drop-down arrow [*Home* tab, *Organize* group] to display the list of delete options (Figure Intro-93).
   - The default action when you click the *Delete* button (not the drop-down arrow) is *Recycle*.
3. Delete a file by selecting **Recycle**, which moves it to the *Recycle Bin*.
   - *Recycle* deletes the item(s) and moves it to the *Recycle Bin*.
   - When you *Recycle* an item, you are not by default prompted to confirm the deletion. Select **Show recycle confirmation** from the *Delete* drop-down list to receive a confirmation dialog box each time you delete or recycle an item.
4. Permanently delete a file by selecting **Permanently delete**. A confirmation dialog box opens. Click **Yes** to confirm the deletion.
   - *Permanently delete* deletes the item(s) from your computer.

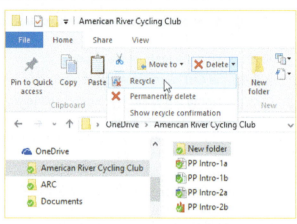

Intro-93 Delete selected folder

> **ANOTHER WAY**
>
> Press **Ctrl+D** or the **Delete** key on your keyboard to recycle selected item(s).
> Press **Shift+Delete** to permanently delete selected item(s).

Create a Zipped (Compressed) Folder

If you want to share multiple files or a folder of files with classmates, coworkers, friends, or family, you can *zip* the files into a *zipped folder* (also called a *compressed folder*). For example, you can't attach an entire folder to an email message, but you can attach a zipped folder to an email message. Compressing files and folders decreases their size. You can zip a group of selected files, a folder, or a combination of files and folders, and then share the zipped folder with others through email or in a cloud storage location such as *OneDrive*.

▶HOW TO: Create a Zipped (Compressed) Folder

1. Open a *File Explorer* window.
2. Select the file(s) and/or folder(s) you want to zip (compress).
3. Click the **Zip** button [*Share* tab, *Send* group] (Figure Intro-94). A zipped folder is created.
   - The name of the zipped folder is the name of the first item you selected to zip. You can rename this folder.
   - The icon for a zipped folder looks similar to the icon for a folder except it has a vertical zipper down the middle of the folder.

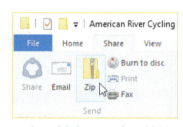

Intro-94 Create a zipped folder

Extract a Zipped (Compressed) Folder

If you receive a zipped folder via email or download a zipped folder, save the zipped folder to your computer and then you can *extract* its contents. Extracting a zipped folder creates a regular Windows folder from the zipped folder.

▶ **HOW TO:** Extract a Zipped (Compressed) Folder

1. Select the zipped folder to extract.
2. Click the **Compressed Folder Tools** tab.
3. Click the **Extract all** button (Figure Intro-95). The *Extract Compressed (Zipped) Folders* dialog box opens (Figure Intro-96).
4. Click **Extract** to extract the folder.
   - Both the extracted folder and the zipped folder display in the folder where they are located.
   - If you check the **Show extracted files when complete** check box, the extracted folder will open after extracting.

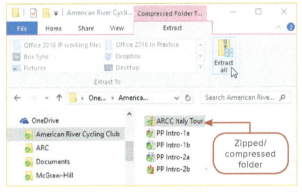

Intro-95 **Extract files from a zipped folder**

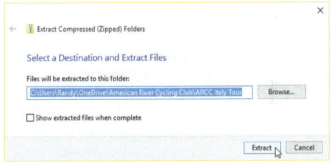

Intro-96 *Extract Compressed (Zipped) Folders* **dialog box**

For this project, you copy and rename files in your *OneDrive* folder on your computer, create a folder, move files, create a zipped folder, and rename a zipped folder.

Files Needed: *[your initials] PP Intro-1a.pptx, [your initials] PP Intro-1b.xlsx, [your initials] PP Intro-2a.docx, [your initials] PP Intro-2b.docx,* and *ARCC_Membership-Intro.accdb (Student data files are available in the* Library *of your SIMnet account)*
Completed Project File Names: *[your initials] PP Intro-1a.pptx, [your initials] PP Intro-1b.xlsx, [your initials] PP Intro-2a.docx, [your initials] PP Intro-2b.docx, [your initials]PP Intro-3.accdb,* and *ARCC Italy Tour-2018* (zipped folder)

1. Copy and rename a file.
   a. Click the Windows **Start** button and click **File Explorer** to open a *File Explorer* window. If *File Explorer* is not available on the *Start* menu, use *Cortana* to find and open a *File Explorer* window.
   b. Browse the *File Explorer* window to locate your student data files.
   c. Select the **ARCC_Membership-Intro** file.
   d. Click the **Copy to** button [*Home* tab, *Organize* group] and select **Choose location** from the drop-down list to open the *Copy Items* dialog box.
   e. Browse to locate the *American River Cycling Club* folder you created in *Pause & Practice: Intro-1*.
   f. Select the **American River Cycling Club** folder and click the **Copy** button to copy the **ARCC_Membership-Intro** file to the *American River Cycling Club* folder (Figure Intro-97). The *Copy Items* dialog box closes and the file is copied.

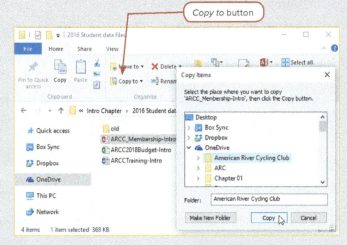

Intro-97 *Copy Items* dialog box

   g. In the open *File Explorer* window, browse to locate the *American River Cycling Club* folder and double-click the folder to open it.
   h. Click the **ARCC_Membership-Intro** file in the *American River Cycling Club* folder to select it.
   i. Click the **Rename** button [*Home* tab, *Organize* group], type [your initials] PP Intro-3 as the new file name, and press **Enter** (Figure Intro-98).

2. Create a new folder and move files.
   a. With the *American River Cycling Club* folder still open, click the **New folder** button [*Home* tab, *New* group] (see Figure Intro-98).
   b. Type ARCC Italy Tour as the name of the new folder and press **Enter**.

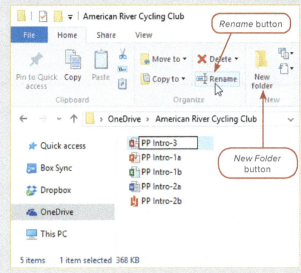

Intro-98 Rename a file

c. Select the *[your initials] PP Intro-1a* file.

d. Press the **Ctrl** key, select the *[your initials] PP Intro-1b*, *[your initials] PP Intro-2a*, *[your initials] PP Intro-2b*, and *[your initials] PP Intro-3* files, and release the **Ctrl** key. All five files should be selected.

e. Click the **Move to** button [*Home* tab, *Organize* group] and select **Choose location** to open the *Move Items* dialog box (Figure Intro-99).

f. Browse to locate the *ARCC Italy Tour* folder in the *Move Items* dialog box.

g. Select the **ARCC Italy Tour** folder and click the **Move** button to move the selected files to the *ARCC Italy Tour* folder.

h. Double-click the **ARCC Italy Tour** folder to open it and confirm the five files are moved.

i. Click the **Up** or **Back** arrow above the *Navigation* pane to return to the *American River Cycling Club* folder (see Figure Intro-99).

3. Create a zipped folder.

a. Select the **ARCC Italy Tour** folder.

b. Click the **Zip** button [*Share* tab, *Send* group]. A zipped (compressed) folder is created.

c. Place the insertion point at the end of the zipped folder name, type –2018, and press **Enter** (Figure Intro-100).

4. Email the zipped folder to your instructor.

a. Use your email account to create a new email to send to your instructor.

b. Include an appropriate subject line and a brief message in the body.

c. Attach the **ARCC Italy Tour-2018** zipped folder to the email message and send the email message.

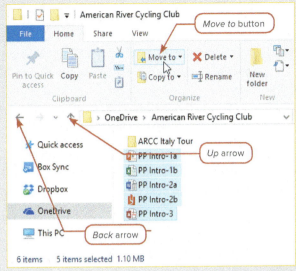

Intro-99 Move selected files to a different folder

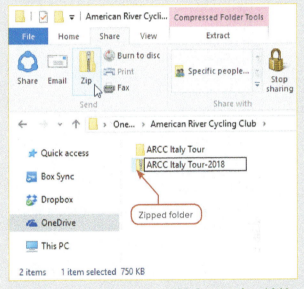

Intro-100 Create a zipped folder

Chapter Summary

Intro.1 Explore the features of Windows 10 (p. OI-2).

- *Windows 10* is a computer operating system.
- A *Microsoft account* is a free account you create. When you create a Microsoft account, you are given an email address, a *OneDrive* account, and access to *Office Online*.
- The *Windows desktop* is the working area of Windows 10 and the *Taskbar* displays at the bottom of the desktop. You can rearrange icons on and pin applications to the *Taskbar*.
- Use *Start menu* in Windows 10 to select a task. You can pin applications to the *Start* menu and customize the arrangement of apps.
- *Most Used* items, *File Explorer*, *Settings*, the *Power* button, and *All apps* options display to the left of the *Start* menu.
- *Apps* are the applications or programs installed on your computer. App buttons are arranged in tiles on the Windows 10 *Start* menu.
- The *Microsoft Store* is a Windows 10 app you use to search for and install apps on your computer.
- You can install both *traditional apps* and *modern apps* in Windows 10.
- You can customize the *Start* menu and *Taskbar* to add, remove, or arrange apps.
- The *File Explorer* is a window that displays files and folders on your computer.
- *OneDrive* is the cloud storage area where you can store files in a private and secure online location.
- In Windows 10, the *OneDrive folder* is one of your file storage location options.
- You can access your *OneDrive* folders and files using an Internet browser window.
- *Cortana* is a search tool in Windows 10 used to locate information on your computer and the Internet.
- *Task View* displays all open apps and windows as tiles on your desktop where you can select an app or window to display or close.
- *Settings* is the redesigned *Control Panel* where you change many Windows settings.

- The *Action Center* displays notifications and buttons to open many common Windows settings and features.

Intro.2 Use the basic features of Office 2016 and navigate the Office 2016 working environment (p. OI-10).

- *Office 2016* is application software that includes *Word*, *Excel*, *Access*, *PowerPoint*, *Outlook*, *OneNote*, and *Publisher*.
- *Office 2016* and *Office 365* include the same application products, but they differ in how you purchase them.
- *Office desktop apps* are the full-function Office 2016 or 365 products you install on your laptop or desktop computer.
- *Office universal apps* are a scaled-down version of Office applications you install on a tablet or mobile device.
- *Office Online* is free online software that works in conjunction with your online *Microsoft* account.
- When you open each of the Office applications, a *Start page* displays where you can open an existing file or create a new file.
- In the *Backstage view* in each of the Office applications, you can perform many common tasks such as saving, opening an existing file, creating a new file, printing, and sharing.
- *Tell Me* is the Office help feature that displays Office commands related to specific topics.
- Use the mouse (or touch pad) on your computer to navigate the pointer on your computer screen. Use the pointer or click buttons to select text or objects.
- When using Office 2016 on a touch-screen computer, use the touch screen to perform actions. You can choose between *Touch Mode* and *Mouse Mode* in Office applications.

Intro.3 Create, save, close, and open Office files (p. OI-17).

- You can create a new Office file from the *Start* page or *Backstage* view of the Office application you are using.
- When you save a file for the first time, assign the file a file name.

- You can create folders to organize saved files, and you can save a file as a different file name.
- A variety of different file types are used in each of the Office applications.
- You can close an Office file when you are finished working on it. If the file has not been saved or changes have been made to the file, you are prompted to save the file before closing.
- In each of the Office applications, you can open an existing file from the *Start* page or from the *Open* area on *Backstage* view.

Intro.4 Customize the view and display size in Office applications and work with multiple Office files (p. OI-25).

- Each Office application has a variety of display views.
- You can select an application view from the options on the *View tab* or the view buttons on the *Status bar*.
- The *Zoom* feature changes the display size of your file.
- You can *minimize*, *restore down*, or *maximize* an open Office application window.
- You can work with multiple Office files at the same time and switch between open files.
- *Snap Assist* enables you to arrange an open window on one side of your computer screen and select another window to fill the other side of the screen.

Intro.5 Print, share, and customize Office files (p. OI-28).

- You can print a file in a variety of formats. The *Print* area on the *Backstage* view lists your print options and displays a preview of your file.
- You can export a file as a *PDF (portable document format)* file and save the PDF file to post to a web site or share with others.
- *Document properties* store information about a file.
- You can share Office files in a variety of ways and allow others to view or edit shared files. To share a file with others, save the file in *OneDrive*.

- Program options are available on the *Backstage* view. You can use the program options to apply global changes to an Office application.

Intro.6 Use the *Ribbon,* tabs, groups, dialog boxes, task panes, galleries, and the *Quick Access* toolbar (p. OI-33).

- The *Ribbon* appears at the top of an Office window. It contains *tabs* and *groups* with commands to format and edit files.
- The *Ribbon Display Options* provides different ways the *Ribbon* displays in Office applications.
- Within groups on each tab are a variety of *buttons*, *drop-down lists*, and *galleries*.
- *Dialog boxes* contain additional features not always displayed on the *Ribbon*.
- Click the *launcher* in the bottom right corner of some groups to open a dialog box for that group.
- A *ScreenTip* displays information about commands on the *Ribbon*.
- Dialog boxes contain *radio buttons*, *check boxes*, *drop-down lists*, and *text boxes* you can use to apply features.
- The *Quick Access toolbar*, which contains buttons that allow you to perform commands, displays in all Office applications in the upper left.
- You can add or remove commands on the *Quick Access* toolbar.

Intro.7 Use context menus, mini toolbars, keyboard shortcuts, and function keys in Office applications (p. OI-37).

- A *context menu* displays when you right-click text or an object. The context menu contains different features depending on what you right-click.
- The *mini toolbar* is another context menu that displays formatting options.
- You can use *keyboard shortcuts* to apply features or commands.
- Some of the numbered *function keys* perform commands in Office applications. On laptops, you may have to press the function key (**Fn** or **fn**) to activate the numbered function keys.

Intro.8 Organize and customize Windows folders and Office files (p. OI-42).

- **Folders** store and organize your files.
- You can create, move, or copy files and folders. Files stored in a folder are moved or copied with that folder.
- You can rename a file to change the file name.
- When you delete a file or folder, it is moved to the **Recycle Bin** on your computer by default. Alternatively, you can permanently delete files and folders.
- You can **zip** files and/or folders into a **zipped (compressed) folder** to email or share multiple files as a single file.
- When you receive a zipped folder, you can **extract** the zipped folder to create a regular Windows folder and access its contents.

Check for Understanding

The SIMbook for this text (within your SIMnet account) provides the following resources for concept review:

- Multiple choice questions
- Short answer questions
- Matching exercises

For these projects, you use your *OneDrive* to store files. If you don't already have a Microsoft account, see *SLO Intro.1: Using Windows 10* for information about creating a free personal Microsoft account.

Guided Project Intro-1

For this project, you organize and edit files for Emma Cavalli at Placer Hills Real Estate. You extract a zipped folder, rename files, manage multiple documents, apply formatting, and export as a PDF file. [Student Learning Outcomes Intro.1, Intro.2, Intro.3, Intro.4, Intro.5, Intro.6, Intro.7, Intro.8]

Files Needed: **CavalliFiles-Intro** (zipped folder) *(Student data files are available in the* Library *of your SIMnet account)*

Completed Project File Names: **PHRE** folder containing the following files: **BuyerEscrowChecklist-Intro**, **CavalliProspectingLetter-Intro**, *[your initials]* **Intro-1a.accdb**, *[your initials]* **Intro-1b.xlsx**, *[your initials]* **Intro-1c.docx**, and *[your initials]* **Intro-1d.docx**

Skills Covered in This Project

- Copy and paste a zipped folder.
- Create a new folder in your *OneDrive* folder.
- Extract a zipped folder.
- Move a file.
- Rename a file.
- Open a Word document.

- Use *Task View* to switch between two open Word documents.
- Save a Word document with a different file name.
- Change display size.
- Use a mini toolbar, keyboard shortcut, context menu, and dialog box to apply formatting to selected text.
- Export a document as a PDF file.

1. Copy a zipped folder and create a new *OneDrive* folder.
   a. Click the Windows **Start** button and click **File Explorer** to open the *File Explorer* window. If *File Explorer* is not available on the *Start* menu, use *Cortana* to find and open the *File Explorer* window.
   b. Browse in the *File Explorer* window to locate your student data files.
   c. Select the **CavalliFiles-Intro** zipped folder from your student data files and press **Ctrl+C** or click the **Copy** button [*Home* tab, *Clipboard* group] to copy the folder.
   d. Select your **OneDrive** folder on the left of the *File Explorer* window, and click the **New folder** button [*Home* tab, *New* group] to create a new folder. If you don't have *OneDrive* available, create the new folder in a location where you store your files.
   e. Type PHRE and press **Enter**.
   f. Press **Enter** again to open the *PHRE* folder or double-click the folder to open it.
   g. Press **Ctrl+V** or click the **Paste** button [*Home* tab, *Clipboard* group] to paste the copied **CavalliFiles-Intro** zipped folder in the *PHRE* folder.

2. Extract a zipped folder.
   a. Select the **CavalliFiles-Intro** zipped folder.
   b. Click the **Compressed Folder Tools Extract** tab and click the **Extract all** button. The *Extract Compressed (Zipped) Folders* dialog box opens.
   c. Uncheck the **Show extracted files when complete** box if it is checked.
   d. Click the **Extract** button (Figure Intro-101). The zipped folder is extracted, and the *PHRE* folder now contains two *CavalliFiles-Intro* folders. One folder is zipped and the other is a regular folder.

e. Select the zipped ***CavalliFiles-Intro*** folder and click the **Delete** button [*Home* tab, *Organize* group] to delete the zipped folder.

3. Move and rename files.
   a. With the *PHRE* folder still open, double-click the **CavalliFiles-Intro** folder to open it.
   b. Click the first file, press and hold the **Shift** key, and click the last file to select all four files.
   c. Press **Ctrl+X** or click the **Cut** button [*Home* tab, *Clipboard* group] to cut the files from the current location (Figure Intro-102).
   d. Click the **Up** arrow to move up to the *PHRE* folder.
   e. Press **Ctrl+V** or click the **Paste** button [*Home* tab, *Clipboard* group] to paste and move the files.
   f. Select the ***Cavalli files-Intro*** folder and press **Delete** to delete the folder.
   g. Select the ***CavalliPHRE-Intro*** file and click the **Rename** button [*Home* tab, *Organize* group].
   h. Type [your initials] Intro-1a and press **Enter**.
   i. Right-click the ***FixedMortgageRates-Intro*** file and select **Rename** from the context menu.
   j. Type [your initials] Intro-1b and press **Enter**.

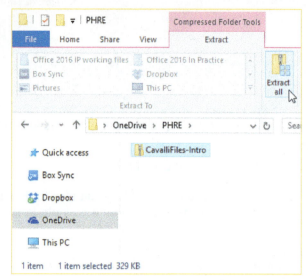

Intro-101 Extract a zipped folder

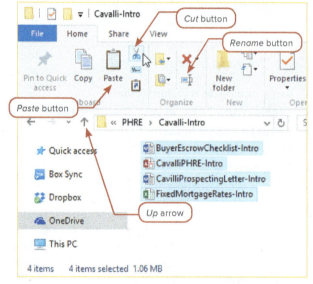

Intro-102 *Cut* files to move from a folder

4. Open two Word documents and rename a Word document.
   a. Press the **Ctrl** key and click the ***BuyerEscrowChecklist-Intro*** and ***CavalliProspectingLetter-Intro*** files to select both files.
   b. Press the **Enter** key to open both files in Word. If the files open in *Protected View*, click the **Enable Editing** button.
   c. Press the **Task View** button on your *Taskbar* (Figure Intro-103). All open windows display as tiles on your desktop.
   d. Select the ***BuyerEscrowChecklist-Intro*** document.
   e. Click the **File** tab to open the *Backstage* view and select **Save As** on the left.
   f. Click the **Browse** button to open the *Save As* dialog box.
   g. Type [your initials] Intro-1c in the *File name* text box and click **Save**. The file is saved in the *PHRE* folder.
   h. Click the **X** in the upper right corner of the Word window to close the document. The *CavalliProspectingLetter-Intro* document remains open.

5. Change display size and edit and rename a Word document.
   a. Press the **Task View** button on your *Taskbar* and select the ***CavalliProspectingLetter-Intro*** document.

Intro-103 *Task View* button on the *Taskbar*

b. Click the **Zoom In** or **Zoom Out** button in the bottom right of the document window to change the display size to **120%** (Figure Intro-104).

Intro-104 Use *Zoom* to change the display size to 120%

c. Select "**Placer Hills Real Estate**" in the first body paragraph of the letter and the mini toolbar displays (Figure Intro-105).

d. Click the **Bold** button on the mini toolbar to apply bold formatting to the selected text.

e. Select "**Whitney Hills resident**" in the first sentence in the second body paragraph and press **Ctrl+I** to apply italic formatting to the selected text.

f. Select the text that reads "**Emma Cavalli**," below "Best regards,".

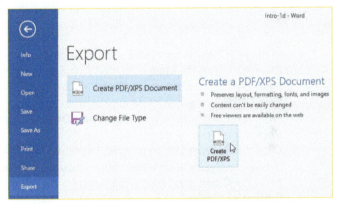

Intro-105 Use the mini toolbar to apply formatting

g. Right-click the selected text and select **Font** from the context menu to open the *Font* dialog box.

h. Check the **Small Caps** box in the *Effects* area and click **OK** to close the *Font* dialog box.

i. With "**Emma Cavalli**" still selected, click the **Bold** button [*Home* tab, *Font* group].

j. Click the **File** tab, select **Save As** on the left, and click the **Browse** button to open the *Save As* dialog box.

k. Type [your initials] Intro-1d in the *File name* text box and click **Save**.

6. Export a Word document as a PDF file.

a. With the *[your initials] Intro-1d* still open, click the **File** tab to open the *Backstage* view.

b. Select **Export** on the left, select **Create PDF/XPS Document** in the *Export* area, and click the **Create PDF/XPS** button (Figure Intro-106). The *Publish as PDF or XPS* dialog box opens.

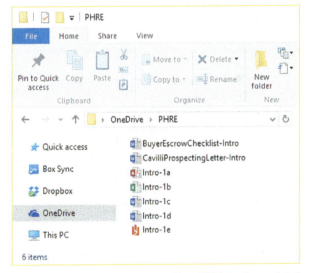

Intro-106 Export as a PDF file

c. Deselect the **Open file after publishing** check box if it is checked.

d. Select the **Standard (publishing online and printing)** radio button in the *Optimize for* area.

e. Type [your initials] Intro-1e in the *File name* text box and click **Publish**.

f. Click the **File** tab to open the *Backstage* view and select **Save** on the left.

g. Click the **X** in the upper right corner of the Word window to close the document and Word.

7. Your *PHRE* folder should contain the files shown in Figure Intro-107.

Intro-107 Intro-1 completed

Guided Project Intro-2

For this project, you modify an Excel file for Hamilton Civic Center. You create a folder, rename a file, add document properties, use *Tell Me* to search for a topic, share the file, and export a file as a PDF file.
[Student Learning Outcomes Intro.1, Intro.2, Intro.3, Intro.5, Intro.6, Intro.7, Intro.8]

File Needed: ***HCCYoga-Intro.xlsx*** *(Student data files are available in the* Library *of your SIMnet account)*
Completed Project File Names: ***[your initials] Intro-2a.xlsx*** and ***[your initials] Intro-2b.pdf***

Skills Covered in This Project

- Open Excel and an Excel workbook.
- Create a new folder.
- Save an Excel workbook with a different file name.

- Add document properties to a file.
- Use *Tell Me* to search for a topic.
- Open a Word document.
- Share a file.
- Export a file as a PDF file.

1. Open Excel 2016 and open an Excel workbook.
   a. Click the Windows **Start** button and click **Excel 2016** to open this application. If Excel 2016 is not available on the *Start* menu, click the **Cortana** button on the *Taskbar*, type Excel, and then click **Excel 2016** in the search results to open it.
   b. From the Excel *Start* page, click **Open Other Workbooks** to display the *Open* area of the *Backstage* view.
   c. Click the **Browse** button to open the *Open* dialog box.
   d. Browse to the location where your student data files are stored, select the ***HCCYoga-Intro*** file, and click **Open** to open the Excel workbook. If the file opens in *Protected View*, click the **Enable Editing** button.

2. Save a file as a different file name in your *OneDrive* folder.
   a. Click the **File** tab to open the *Backstage* view and select **Save As** on the left.
   b. Click the **Browse** button to open the *Save As* dialog box.
   c. Select the **OneDrive** folder on the left and click the **New folder** button to create a new folder (Figure Intro-108). If *OneDrive* is not a storage option, select another location to create the new folder.
   d. Type HCC and press **Enter**.
   e. Double-click the **HCC** folder to open it.
   f. Type [your initials] Intro-2a in the *File name* area and click **Save** to close the dialog box and save the file.

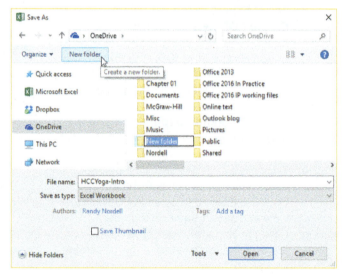

Intro-108 Create a new folder from the *Save As* dialog box

3. Add document properties to the Excel workbook.
   a. Click the **File** button to open the *Backstage* view and select **Info** on the left if it is not already selected. The document properties displays on the right.
   b. Place your insertion point in the *Title* text box ("Add a title") and type Yoga Classes as the worksheet title.

c. Click the **Show All Properties** link at the bottom of the list of properties to display more properties (Figure Intro-109).

d. Place your insertion point in the *Company* text box and type Hamilton Civic Center as the company name.

e. Click the **Back** arrow in the upper left of the *Backstage* window to return to the Excel workbook.

4. Use *Tell Me* to search for a topic.

a. Click the **Tell Me** search box at the top of the *Ribbon* and type Cell formatting (Figure Intro-110).

b. Select **Get Help on "Cell formatting"** to open the *Excel 2016 Help* dialog box.

c. Click the first result link to display information about the topic.

d. Click the **Back** arrow to return to the search list.

e. Click the **X** in the upper right corner to close the *Excel 2016 Help* dialog box.

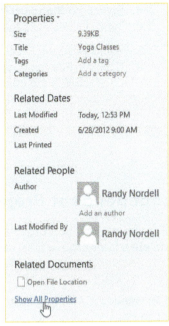

Intro-109 Add document properties

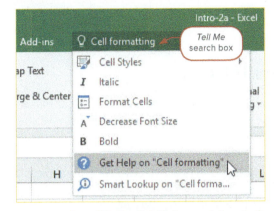

Intro-110 Use *Tell Me* to search for a topic

5. Share an Excel workbook with your instructor. If your file is not saved in *OneDrive*, skip step 5.

a. Click the **Share** button in the upper right of the Excel worksheet. The *Share* pane opens on the right side of the worksheet (Figure Intro-111).

b. Type your instructor's email address in the *Invite people* area.

c. Select **Can edit** from the drop-down list below the email address if it is not already selected.

d. Type a brief message in the body text box.

e. Click the **Share** button.

f. Click the **X** in the upper right corner of the *Share* pane to close the pane.

g. Press **Ctrl+S** to save the worksheet.

6. Export an Excel file as a PDF file.

a. Click the **File** tab to open the *Backstage* view.

b. Select **Export** on the left, select **Create PDF/XPS Document** in the *Export* area, and click the **Create PDF/XPS** button (Figure Intro-112). The *Publish as PDF or XPS* dialog box opens.

c. Deselect the **Open file after publishing** check box if it is checked.

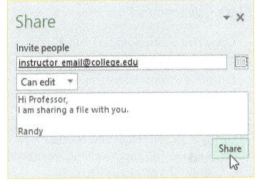

Intro-111 *Share* pane

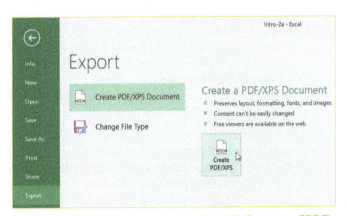

Intro-112 Export as a PDF file

d. Select the **Standard (publishing online and printing)** radio button in the *Optimize for* area.

e. Type [your initials] Intro-2b in the *File name* text box and click **Publish**.

7. Save and close the Excel file.

a. Click the **File** tab to open the *Backstage* view and select **Save** on the left.

b. Click the **X** in the upper right corner of the Excel window to close the file and Excel.

Independent Project Intro-3

For this project, you organize and edit files for Courtyard Medical Plaza. You extract a zipped folder, delete a folder, move files, rename files, export a file as a PDF file, and share a file.
[Student Learning Outcomes Intro.1, Intro.2, Intro.3, Intro.5, Intro.8]

File Needed: ***CMPFiles-Intro*** (zipped folder) *(Student data files are available in the* Library *of your SIMnet account)*

Completed Project File Names: ***[your initials] Intro-3a.pptx***, ***[your initials] Intro-3a-pdf.pdf***, ***[your initials] Intro-3b.accdb***, ***[your initials] Intro-3c.xlsx***, and ***[your initials] Intro-3d.docx***

Skills Covered in This Project

- Copy and paste a zipped folder.
- Create a new folder in your *OneDrive* folder.
- Extract a zipped folder.
- Delete a folder.

- Move a file.
- Rename a file.
- Open a PowerPoint presentation.
- Export a file as a PDF file.
- Open a Word document.
- Share a file.

1. Copy a zipped folder and create a new *OneDrive* folder.

   a. Open a *File Explorer* window, browse to locate the ***CMPFiles-Intro*** zipped folder in your student data files and copy the zipped folder.

   b. Go to your *OneDrive* folder and create a new folder named Courtyard Medical Plaza within the *OneDrive* folder. If *OneDrive* is not a storage option, select another location to create the new folder.

2. Paste a copied folder, extract the zipped folder, and move files.

   a. Paste the zipped folder in the *Courtyard Medical Plaza* folder.

   b. Extract the zipped folder and then delete the zipped folder.

   c. Open the ***CMPFiles-Intro*** folder and move all of the files to the *Courtyard Medical Plaza* folder.

   d. Return to the *Courtyard Medical Plaza* folder to confirm the four files were moved.

   e. Delete the ***CMPFiles-Intro*** folder.

3. Rename files in the *Courtyard Medical Plaza* folder.

   a. Rename the ***CMPStayingActive-Intro*** PowerPoint file to [your initials] Intro-3a.

   b. Rename the ***CourtyardMedicalPlaza-Intro*** Access file to [your initials] Intro-3b.

   c. Rename the ***EstimatedCalories-Intro*** Excel file to [your initials] Intro-3c.

   d. Rename the ***StayingActive-Intro*** Word file to [your initials] Intro-3d.

4. Export a PowerPoint file as a PDF file.

   a. From the *Courtyard Medical Plaza* folder, open the ***[your initials] Intro-3a*** file. The file opens in PowerPoint. If the file opens in *Protected View*, click the **Enable Editing** button.

   b. Export this file as a PDF file. Don't have the PDF file open after publishing and optimize for **Standard** format.

   c. Save the file as [your initials] Intro-3a-pdf and save in the *Courtyard Medical Plaza* folder.

   d. Close the PowerPoint file and exit PowerPoint.

5. Share a file with your instructor. If your files are not saved in *OneDrive*, skip step 5.

   a. Return to your *Courtyard Medical Plaza* folder and open the **Intro-3d** file. The file opens in Word. If the file opens in *Protected View*, click the **Enable Editing** button.

   b. Open the *Share* pane.

   c. Type your instructor's email address and select **Can edit** from the permission drop-down list.

   d. Type a brief message and **Share** the file.

   e. Close the *Share* pane.

   f. Save and close the document and exit Word.

6. Close the *File Explorer* window containing the files for this project (Figure Intro-113).

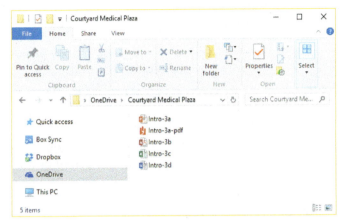

Intro-113 Intro-3 completed

Independent Project Intro-4

For this project, you modify a Word file for Life's Animal Shelter. You create a folder, rename a document, add document properties, modify a document, create a sharing link, export a document as a PDF file, and create a zipped folder.
[Student Learning Outcomes Intro.1, Intro.2, Intro.3, Intro.5, Intro.6, Intro.7, Intro.8]

File Needed: **LASSupportLetter-Intro.docx** (*Student data files are available in the* Library *of your SIMnet account*)
Completed Project File Names: **[your initials] Intro-4a.docx**, **[your initials] Intro-4b.pdf**, *and* **LAS files** (zipped folder)

Skills Covered in This Project

- Open a Word document.
- Create a new folder.
- Save a file with a different file name.
- Apply formatting to selected text.
- Add document properties to the file.
- Create a sharing link.
- Export a file as a PDF file.
- Create a zipped folder.

1. Open a Word document, create a new folder, and save the document with a different file name.

   a. Open Word 2016.

   b. From the Word *Start* page, open the **LASSupportLetter-Intro** document from your student data files. If the file opens in *Protected View*, click the **Enable Editing** button.

    c. Open the **Save As** dialog box and create a new folder named LAS in your *OneDrive* folder. If *OneDrive* is not a storage option, select another location to create the new folder.

    d. Save this document in the *LAS* folder and use [your initials] Intro-4a as the file name.

2. Apply formatting changes to the document using a dialog box, keyboard shortcut, and mini toolbar.

    a. Select "**To**:" in the memo heading and use the launcher to open the *Font* dialog box.

    b. Apply **Bold** and **All caps** to the selected text.

    c. Repeat the formatting on the other three memo guide words "**From**:," "**Date**:," and "**Subject**:".

    d. Select "**Life's Animal Shelter**" in the first sentence of the first body paragraph and press **Ctrl+B** to apply bold formatting.

    e. Select the first sentence in the second body paragraph ("**Would you again consider** . . .") and use the mini toolbar to apply **italic** formatting.

3. Add the following document properties to the document:
Title: Support Letter
Company: Life's Animal Shelter

4. Get a link to share this document with your instructor and email your instructor the sharing link.

    a. Open the *Share* pane and click **Get a sharing link** at the bottom of the *Share* pane.

    b. Create an edit link to send to your instructor.

    c. Copy the edit link.

    d. Open the email you use for this course and create a new email message to send to your instructor.

    e. Type your instructor's email address, include an appropriate subject line, and type a brief message in the body of the email message.

    f. Paste (**Ctrl+V**) the sharing link in the body of the email message and send the message.

    g. Click the **Task View** button on the Windows *Taskbar* and select the ***Intro-4a*** document to display this document.

    h. Close the *Share* pane.

    i. Use the **Save** command on the *Quick Access* toolbar to save the file before continuing.

7. Export this document as a PDF file.

    a. Export this file as a PDF file. Don't have the PDF file open after publishing and optimize for **Standard** format.

    b. Save the file as [your initials] Intro-4b and save in the *LAS* folder.

    c. Save and close the document and exit Word.

8. Create a zipped folder.

    a. Using *File Explorer*, open the **LAS** folder in your *OneDrive* folder.

    b. Select the two files and create a zipped folder.

    c. Rename the zipped folder LAS files.

9. Close the open *File Explorer* window (Figure Intro-114).

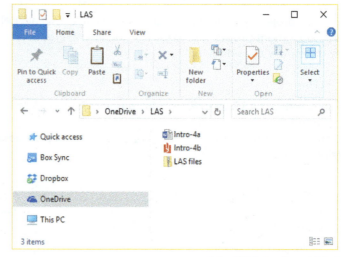

Intro-114 Intro-4 completed

Challenge Project Intro-5

For this project, you create folders to organize your files for this class and share a file with your instructor.
[Student Learning Outcomes Intro.1, Intro.5, Intro.8]

Files Needed: Student data files for this course
Completed Project File Name: Share a file with your instructor

Using *File Explorer*, create *OneDrive* folders to contain all of the student data files for this class. Organize your files and folders according to the following guidelines:

- Create a *OneDrive* folder for this class.
- Create a *Student data files* folder inside the class folder.
- Copy and paste the student data files in the *Student data files* folder.
- Extract student data files and delete the zipped folder.
- Create a *Solution files* folder inside the class folder.
- Inside the *Solution files* folder, create a folder for each chapter.
- Create a folder to store miscellaneous class files such as the syllabus and other course handouts.
- Open one of the student data files and share the file with your instructor.

Challenge Project Intro-6

For this project, you save a file as a different file name, customize the *Quick Access* toolbar, share a file with your instructor, export a file as a PDF file, and create a zipped folder.
[Student Learning Outcomes Intro.1, Intro.2, Intro.3, Intro.5, Intro.6, Intro.8]

File Needed: Use an existing Office file
Completed Project File Names: *[your initials] Intro-6a* and *[your initials] Intro-6b*

Open an existing Word, Excel, or PowerPoint file. Save this file in a *OneDrive* folder and name it [your initials] Intro-6a. If you don't have any of these files, use one from your Pause & Practice projects or select a file from your student data files.

With your file open, perform the following actions:

- Create a new folder on OneDrive and save the file to this folder using a different file name.
- Customize the *Quick Access* toolbar to add command buttons. Add commands such as *New*, *Open*, *Quick Print*, and *Spelling* that you use regularly in the Office application.
- Share your file with your instructor. Allow your instructor to edit the file.
- Export the document as a PDF file. Save the file as [your initials] Intro-6b and save it in the same *OneDrive* folder as your open file.
- Zip the files in the folder.

Microsoft® Office

excel

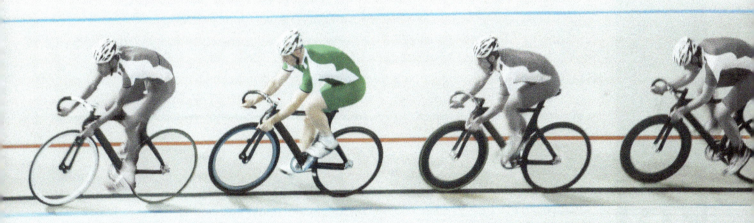

Creating and Editing Workbooks

CHAPTER OVERVIEW

Microsoft Excel (Excel) is spreadsheet software for creating an electronic workbook. A workbook consists of rows and columns used to organize data, perform calculations, print reports, and build charts. With Excel, you can create simple to complex personal or business workbooks. This chapter presents basic procedures for creating and editing an Excel workbook.

STUDENT LEARNING OUTCOMES (SLOs)

After completing this chapter, you will be able to:

SLO 1.1 Create, save, and open an Excel workbook (p. E1-3).

SLO 1.2 Enter and edit labels and values in a worksheet (p. E1-6).

SLO 1.3 Use the *SUM* function to build a simple formula (p. E1-19).

SLO 1.4 Format a worksheet with font attributes, borders, fill, cell styles, and themes (p. E1-21).

SLO 1.5 Modify columns and rows in a worksheet (p. E1-31).

SLO 1.6 Insert, delete, and move worksheets in a workbook (p. E1-37).

SLO 1.7 Modify the appearance of a workbook by adjusting zoom size, changing views, and freezing panes (p. E1-42).

SLO 1.8 Review and prepare a workbook for final distribution by spell checking, setting properties, and adjusting page setup options (p. E1-47).

CASE STUDY

Throughout this book you have the opportunity to put into practice the application features that you are learning. Each chapter begins with a case study that introduces you to the Pause & Practice projects in the chapter. These Pause & Practice projects give you a chance to apply and practice key skills in a realistic and practical context. Each chapter contains three to five Pause & Practice projects.

Paradise Lakes Resort (PLR) is a vacation company with properties located throughout northern Minnesota. PLR staff use Excel to track revenue, to monitor expenses, to maintain employee records, and similar tasks. In the Pause & Practice projects for Chapter 1, you create, edit, and format a workbook that displays categories of revenue for one week.

Pause & Practice 1-1: Open, edit, and save a workbook.

Pause & Practice 1-2: Use *SUM* and format data in a worksheet.

Pause & Practice 1-3: Edit columns, rows, and sheets in a workbook.

Pause & Practice 1-4: Finalize a workbook for distribution.

Creating, Saving, and Opening a Workbook

In Microsoft Excel, the file that you open, edit, and save is a ***workbook***. Each workbook contains ***worksheets***, which are comparable to individual pages in a Word document. A worksheet is also referred to as a ***spreadsheet*** or a ***sheet***, and you can use these terms interchangeably. This text also uses the terms "workbook" and "file" interchangeably.

Create a New Workbook

By default, a new workbook includes one worksheet, but a workbook can include multiple sheets. The worksheet ***tab*** is located near the bottom left of the workbook window and is labeled *Sheet1*.

When you first open Excel, the ***Excel Start page*** displays. From the *Start* page, you can create a new blank workbook, open a recently saved workbook, or create a workbook from an Excel template (a model workbook). Click **Blank workbook** to start a new blank workbook. You can also select *Blank workbook* from the *New* area in the *Backstage* view.

> **ANOTHER WAY**
>
> Press **Esc** to leave the Excel *Start* page and open a blank workbook.

▶ **HOW TO:** Create a New Workbook

1. Click the **File** tab to display the *Backstage* view.
2. Select **New** on the left to display the *New* area in the *Backstage* view (Figure 1-1).

1-1 *Backstage* view for creating new workbooks

3. Click **Blank workbook** to create a new blank workbook.

> **ANOTHER WAY**
>
> Press **Ctrl+N** to open a new workbook.

Save and Close a Workbook

When you open a blank workbook, Excel automatically assigns a file name, such as *Book1*. The first time you save a workbook, you should type a descriptive file name for the workbook in the *Save As* dialog box. You can save a workbook on your computer, in a *OneDrive* folder, or on external media.

▶ HOW TO: Save a New Workbook

1. Click the **File** tab to display the *Backstage* view.
2. Select **Save As** on the left to display the *Save As* area.
   - You can press **Ctrl+S** to open the *Save As* area in the *Backstage* view for a workbook that has not yet been saved.
3. Select the location to save your workbook.
   - Click **This PC** to see recently used folders.
   - Click **Browse** to open the *Save As* dialog box for further navigation.
   - Click **OneDrive** to see your cloud folder names.
4. Click the folder name to open the *Save As* dialog box (Figure 1-2).
5. Type the file name in the *File name* area.
6. Click **Save** to close the *Save As* dialog box.

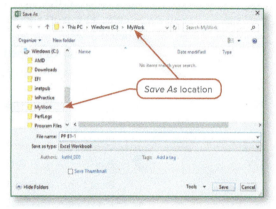

1-2 *Save As* dialog box

▶ ANOTHER WAY

Press **F12** (**FN+F12**) to open the *Save As* dialog box.

Once a workbook has been saved, you can re-save it with the same file name by pressing **Ctrl+S** or by clicking the **Save** button in the *Quick Access toolbar*.

To close a workbook, click the **File** tab and choose **Close**. You can press **Ctrl+W** or **Ctrl+F4** to close a workbook, too. These commands leave Excel running with a blank screen so that you can open another file or start a new workbook.

You can also click the **X** (**Close** button) in the upper right corner of the window. If the workbook is the only one open, this command closes the file and exits Excel. If multiple workbooks are open, clicking the *Close* button closes only the active workbook.

Open a Workbook

A workbook can be opened from the *Start* page, the *Open* area in the *Backstage* view, or the *Open* dialog box. When a workbook is opened from an Internet or unrecognized source, it opens in **Protected View**. Click **Enable Editing** when you know that it is safe to work with the file.

▶ HOW TO: Open a Workbook

1. Click the **File** tab to open the *Backstage* view.
2. Click **Open** to display the *Open* area.

3. Select the location where the workbook is stored.

- The *Recent* list displays workbook file names on the right.
- The *This PC* option lists recently used folder names.
- Click **Browse** to locate a folder.

4. Click the folder name that stores the file.

5. Select the workbook name and click **Open** (Figure 1-3).

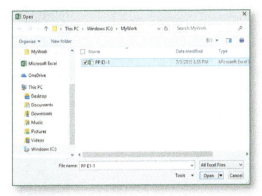

1-3 *Open* dialog box

> **ANOTHER WAY**

Ctrl+O displays the *Open* area in the *Backstage* view. **Ctrl+F12** displays the *Open* dialog box.

> **MORE INFO**

From an Explorer window, you can double-click a workbook file name to launch Excel and open the workbook.

Save a Workbook with a Different File Name

To preserve an existing workbook, you can open and save it with a different file name, creating a copy of the original file with a new name. Follow the same steps that you would when saving a new workbook.

> **HOW TO:** Save a Workbook with a Different File Name

1. Click the **File** tab to open the *Backstage* view.
2. Click **Save As** to display the *Save As* area.
3. Navigate to and select the folder name to open the *Save As* dialog box.
   - You can press **F12** (**FN+F12**) to open the *Save As* dialog box.
4. Type the name in the *File name* area.
5. Click **Save** to close the *Save As* dialog box and save the file.

Workbook File Formats

Excel workbooks are saved as *.xlsx* files, indicated as *Excel Workbook* in the *Save As* dialog box. You can save a workbook in other formats for ease in sharing data. For example, you can save a workbook in *Excel 97-2003* format so that a coworker with an earlier version of Excel can use the data. Or you can create a PDF file of a workbook to provide data to users who do not have Excel.

The *Save as type* area of the *Save As* dialog box lists available formats (Figure 1-4). The following table lists common formats for saving an Excel workbook.

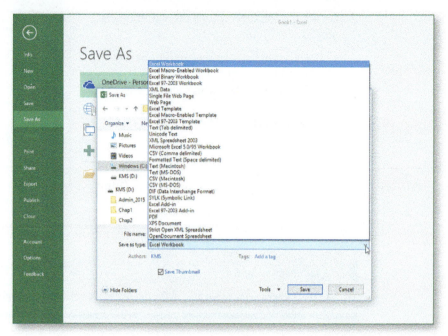

1-4 Workbook file formats

Save Formats

Type of Document	File Name Extension	Uses of This Format
Excel Workbook	.xlsx	Excel workbook compatible with versions 2010 and later
Excel Macro-Enabled Workbook	.xlsm	Excel workbook with embedded macros
Excel 97-2003 Workbook	.xls	Excel workbook compatible with older versions of Microsoft Excel
Excel Template	.xltx	Model or sample Excel workbook stored in the Custom Office Templates folder
Excel Macro-Enabled Template	.xltm	Model or sample Excel workbook with embedded macros stored in the Custom Office Templates folder
Portable Document Format (PDF)	.pdf	An uneditable image of the workbook for viewing that can be opened with free software
Text (tab-delimited)	.txt	Data only with columns separated by a tab character. File can be opened by many applications.
Comma Separated Values (CSV)	.csv	Data only with columns separated by a comma. File can be opened by many applications.
OpenDocument Spreadsheet	.ods	Workbook for the Open Office suite as well as Google Docs
Web Page	.htm, .html	Excel workbook formatted for posting on a web site that includes data, graphics, and linked objects

SLO 1.2

Entering and Editing Data

A worksheet consists of columns and rows. Columns are labeled with letters and rows are labeled with numbers. You enter data in a *cell*, which is the intersection of a column and a row. Each cell is identified with a *cell reference* (or *cell address*), the column letter and row number that represents the location of the cell. Cell A1 is the intersection of column A and row 1. A rectangular group of cells is a **range**. The range address **A1:B3** identifies six cells in two columns and three rows.

You see column and row headings as well as gridlines on the worksheet to help you identify the location of data. You can change these options from the *View* tab if you prefer to see a cleaner background for your work. The *Gridlines* and *Headings* settings in the *Show* group are toggles that display or hide these features.

> **MORE INFO**
>
> From the *View* tab, you can also display or hide the formula bar and the ruler.

Enter Labels and Values

Data in a worksheet cell is text, a number, or a formula. A **label** is text that displays a name, a main title, row or column titles, and similar descriptive information. Labels are not included in calculations. A **value** is a number that can be used in a calculation or is the result of a calculation. A **formula** is a calculation or expression that displays a result.

When you type data that includes alphabetic characters and numbers, Excel treats that data as a label. Examples include a street address or an ID such as ABC123. When you type data with numbers that are not used in calculations, enter the data as a label by typing an apostrophe (') before the data. Examples of this type of data include a telephone or Social Security number without hyphens.

> **MORE INFO**
>
> If you type a Social Security number *with* hyphens, Excel will identify it as a label.

When a label in a cell is longer or wider than the cell, the label spills into an empty adjacent cell. If adjacent cells are not empty, the label is truncated or cut off in the cell, but the entire entry is visible in the **Formula bar**. The *Formula* bar appears below the *Ribbon* and displays the contents of the selected cell. When a value is too large for the width of the cell, the cell displays a series of # symbols or shows the value in exponential notation (part of the number with E+n as in 1235E+4). You can simply widen the column to see all cell contents.

To enter data, click the cell with the pointer to select and activate the cell. The pointer appears as a solid, white cross (a thick plus sign) when selecting data in the worksheet. The **active cell** displays a solid border, and its address appears in the **Name box** (Figure 1-5).

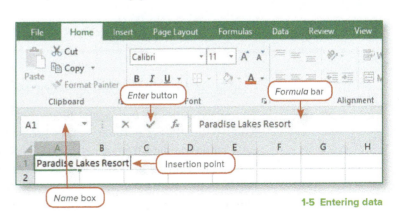

1-5 Entering data

1. Select the cell and type the data.
   - The label or value appears in the cell with an insertion point and in the *Formula* bar.
2. Press **Enter** to complete the entry and activate the cell below.
   - Press **Tab** to complete the entry and activate the cell to the right.
   - Press any keyboard directional arrow key to complete the entry and activate the cell in the direction of the arrow.
   - Press **Ctrl+Enter** to complete the entry and keep the current cell active.
   - Click the **Enter** button in the *Formula* bar to complete the entry and keep the cell active.

Edit Cell Contents

You can edit cell data as you type or after the entry is complete. To edit as you type, press the **Backspace** key to delete characters to the left of the insertion point. Or use arrow keys to move the insertion point and press the **Delete** key to erase characters to the right of the insertion point. To edit a completed entry, start *Edit* mode by double-clicking the cell or by pressing **F2 (FN+F2)**. The word "Edit" appears in the *Status* bar to alert you that data entry is in progress. Position the insertion point either in the cell or in the *Formula* bar, make the change, and press any completion key.

When using some keyboard function keys, you may need to press the **FN** key with the function key to access the command. This depends on the type of computer as well as the keyboard. This text will show a shortcut like this **F2 (FN+F2)** as a reminder to note your keyboard layout.

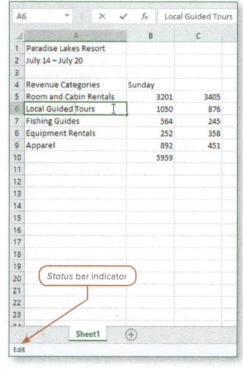

1-6 *Edit* mode

1. Double-click the cell to be edited.
   - You can also click the cell and press **F2 (FN+F2)** to start *Edit* mode.
2. Position the insertion point in the cell or the *Formula* bar (Figure 1-6).
3. Edit the data.
4. Press **Enter**.

Replace or Clear Cell Contents

To replace data in a cell, select the cell and type the new data. Then press **Enter**, click the **Enter** button in the *Formula* bar, or press any completion key. The new data displays in the cell. To delete data from a cell, select the cell and press **Delete** or click the **Clear** button [*Home* tab, *Editing* group]. From the **Clear** button options, you can choose *Clear All, Clear Formats,* or *Clear Contents* (Figure 1-7). Pressing the **Delete** key removes the contents and preserves formatting.

► **HOW TO:** Clear Cell Contents

1. Select the cell or cells.
2. Press **Delete** on the keyboard.

   • Click the **Clear** button [*Home* tab, *Editing* group] and choose an option.
   • *Clear All* removes formatting and content.
   • *Clear Formats* only clears formatting and keeps data.
   • *Clear Contents* deletes content but keeps formatting.

1-7 *Clear* button options

Align and Indent Cell Contents

Excel recognizes a combination of letters, numbers, spaces, and other characters as a label. Labels are aligned on the left and bottom of the cell. When you type only numbers into a cell, Excel identifies the entry as a value. Values are aligned on the right and bottom of the cell.

You can change the vertical and horizontal ***alignment*** of data in a cell from the *Alignment* group on the *Home* tab (Figure 1-8). Horizontal alignment choices are *Align Left*, *Center*, and *Align Right*. Vertical alignment options are *Top Align*, *Middle Align*, and *Bottom Align*.

An ***indent*** moves cell contents away from the left edge of the cell. In Figure 1-8, labels in rows 5:9 are offset from the label in row 4. The **Increase Indent** button [*Home* tab, *Alignment* group] moves cell contents one space to the right if the data is left-aligned. You can remove an indent by clicking the **Decrease Indent** button [*Home* tab, *Alignment* group].

1-8 Alignment and indent options

► **HOW TO:** Align and Indent Text

1. Select the cell.
2. Click a horizontal text alignment button [*Home* tab, *Alignment* group].

   • *Center* positions a label midway between the left and right boundaries of the cell.
   • *Align Left* starts a label at the left boundary of the cell.
   • *Right Align* sets a label to end at the right cell boundary.

3. Click a vertical text alignment button [*Home* tab, *Alignment* group].

   • *Middle Align* positions data midway between the top and bottom cell boundaries.
   • *Top Align* places data at the top cell boundary.
   • *Bottom Align* aligns data at the bottom boundary of the cell.

4. Click an indent button [*Home* tab, *Alignment* group].

   • The *Increase Indent* button moves data toward the right cell boundary.
   • The *Decrease Indent* button moves data toward the left cell boundary.

In addition to horizontal and vertical settings, the *Alignment* group on the *Home* tab includes the *Orientation* button to display data vertically or at an angle. These settings are also available in the *Format Cells* dialog box on the *Alignment* tab (Figure 1-9).

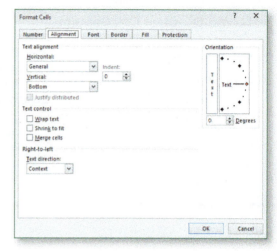

> **MORE INFO**
>
> Click the **Alignment** launcher [*Home* tab, *Alignment* group] or press **Ctrl+1** to open the *Format Cells* dialog box.

1-9 *Alignment* tab, *Format Cells* dialog box

Select Cells

As you format or edit a worksheet, the first step is to select the cell or cells to be edited. Select a single cell by clicking it. Select a range by clicking the first cell and dragging the pointer in any direction to select adjacent cells. The following table outlines basic selection methods.

Selection Methods

Selection	Instructions
Entire Column or Row	Point to and click the column heading. Point to and click the row heading.
All Worksheet Cells	Press **Ctrl+A** or click the **Select All** button (above the row 1 heading and to the left of the column A heading). 
Adjacent Cells by Dragging the Pointer	Click the first cell and drag the selection pointer over the cells to be included. Release the pointer button.
Adjacent Cells Using the Shift Key and the Pointer	Click the first cell, press **Shift**, and click the last cell in the range.
Adjacent Cells Using the Shift and Arrow Keys	Click the first cell, press **Shift**, and press any **Arrow** key.
Nonadjacent Cells	Click a cell or select the first range, press **Ctrl**, and select the next cell or range. Release the pointer button first; then release the **Ctrl** key.
Single Cell or Range Using the *Name Box*	Type a cell or range address in the *Name* box and press **Enter**.

You can see selected cell ranges in Figure 1-10.

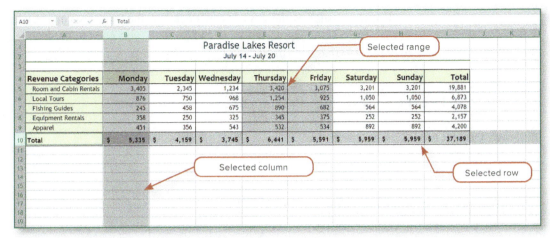

1-10 Selected cells in a worksheet

The pointer changes shape depending on the current task or mode. The following table describes the shapes and indicates when they appear.

Pointer Shapes

Pointer Icon	Pointer Use
⊕	**Selection pointer** (thick, white cross or plus sign) selects a cell or range; the selection pointer appears when you move the pointer over a cell.
+	**Fill pointer** (crosshair or thin, black plus sign) copies cell contents or completes a series; it appears when you place the pointer on the *Fill Handle*, the tiny, black square in the bottom right corner of a selected cell or range.
✛	**Move pointer** (solid, white arrow with a black four-pointed arrow) moves data; it appears when you place the pointer on the border of a selected cell or range.
22	**Resize pointer** (two-pointed arrow) adjusts a formula cell range or an object; it appears when you place the pointer on a selection handle in a formula range or on a sizing handle for a selected object.

The Fill Handle

A *series* is a list of labels or values that follows a pattern. An example of a label series is the days of the week or the months of the year. A series of values is 1, 3, 5, 7, 9. Excel recognizes patterns and can complete most series with the *Fill Handle*. If there is no recognizable series, the *Fill Handle* copies the data.

The *Fill Handle* is a small, black square in the lower right corner of the cell or selected range. You drag this handle across the cell range for the series or to copy data. When you release the pointer button, the data is completed, and the *Auto Fill Options* button displays near the end of the series. This button provides choices for how to complete the series, but you usually need not make any changes.

For series such as the days of the week and the months, you only need enter the first item in the series. For other series, such as 2, 4, 6, 8, you need to enter at least two items for Excel to recognize the pattern.

▶ **HOW TO:** Use the Fill Handle to Create a Series

1. Type the first item in the series and press **Enter**.
   - Press **Ctrl+Enter** to keep the cell active.
   - Type two or three entries to identify a custom series.
2. Select the cell with the entry.
   - Select all cells with data that identify the series.
3. Point to the *Fill Handle* to display the *Fill* pointer (thin, black plus sign) (Figure 1-11).

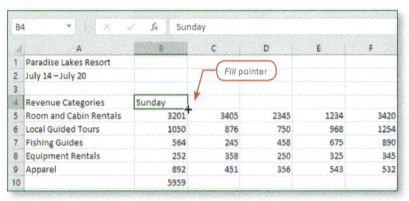

1-11 Use the *Fill Handle* to complete a series

4. Click and drag the *Fill* pointer through the last cell for the series.
   - A series can be horizontal or vertical.
   - You can double-click the *Fill* pointer to complete data down a column if other columns are already completed to the last row.
5. Release the pointer button.
   - The series is complete and the *Auto Fill Options* button appears.
6. Click the **Auto Fill Options** button.
   - Choose an option as desired (Figure 1-12).
7. Press **Esc** to remove the *Auto Fill Options* button or continue to the next task.

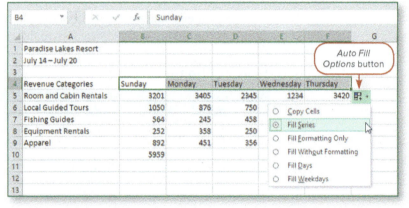

1-12 Completed series with *Auto Fill Options* button

AutoComplete

AutoComplete is an Excel feature that displays a suggested label in a column when the first character or two that you type matches a label already in the column. *AutoComplete* enables you to quickly and accurately complete repetitive data. It works only for data that is alphanumeric, not for a column of values.

In a column that lists city names, for example, a particular city name might be repeated many times. The first time it appears, you type it as usual. On the second and succeeding occurrences of the name, as soon as you type the first character, Excel completes the label but waits for you to accept it. If the *AutoComplete* suggestion is correct, press **Enter**. If the suggestion is not correct, continue typing the label as needed.

Excel usually makes a suggestion after you type a single character in a cell in the column. If the column has more than one entry that begins with that character, type a second character and *AutoComplete* makes another or a better suggestion.

▶ HOW TO: Use AutoComplete

1. Type the first character in a label.

   - A suggested label appears in the cell.
   - Type a second and third character when there are many labels that begin with the same letter.
   - You can type uppercase or lowercase characters to display an *AutoComplete* suggestion.

2. Press **Enter** to accept the *AutoComplete* suggestion (Figure 1-13).

   - Continue typing to ignore an *AutoComplete* suggestion.
   - Press **Enter** to complete a new label.

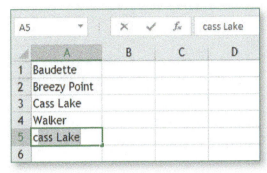

1-13 *AutoComplete* **suggestion**

Cut, Copy, and Paste Cell Contents

Excel has the same *Cut*, *Copy*, and *Paste* commands as other Windows applications. Use the **Cut** command to move data from one location to another. The **Copy** command duplicates cell contents to a different location. The **Paste** command places cut or copied data in the selected location. Data is cut or copied from a **source cell** or range and is pasted in a **destination cell** or range. When you cut or copy data, it is usually stored on the Windows *Clipboard* as well as the *Office Clipboard*.

Move or Cut Cell Contents

You can move data using drag and drop, keyboard shortcuts, or *Cut* and *Paste* in the *Clipboard* group on the *Home* tab. Drag and drop is quick when you want to move or copy cells within a visible range on the worksheet. When you use the drag-and-drop method, the source data is not stored on either clipboard.

▶ HOW TO: Move Data Using Drag and Drop

1. Select the cell(s) to be moved.

2. Point to a border of the selection to display a move pointer (white arrow with four-pointed arrow).

3. Click and drag the selection to the new location (Figure 1-14).

   - A preview selection shows the destination address.

4. Release the pointer button.

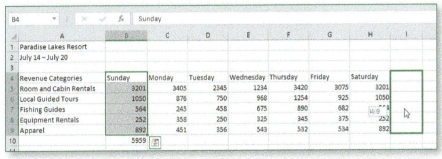

1-14 **Drag and drop to move data**

When you use the *Cut* command from the *Ribbon* or the keyboard, the selected data is placed on both clipboards. You can paste once from the Windows *Clipboard*. You can paste multiple times from the *Office Clipboard*. There are three methods to cut data:

- *Ribbon* buttons: **Cut** and **Paste** buttons [*Home* tab, *Clipboard* group]
- Shortcut commands: **Ctrl+X** to cut and **Ctrl+V** to paste
- Context menu: Right-click and select **Cut**; right-click and select **Paste**

▶ HOW TO: Move Data Using Cut and Paste

1. Select the cell or range to be moved.
2. Click the **Cut** button [*Home* tab, *Clipboard* group].
   - A moving border surrounds the source cell(s) (Figure 1-15).
3. Select the destination cell.
   - Select the top-left cell in a destination range.
4. Click the **Paste** button [*Home* tab, *Clipboard* group].
   - If the destination cell(s) are not empty, pasted data overwrites existing data.

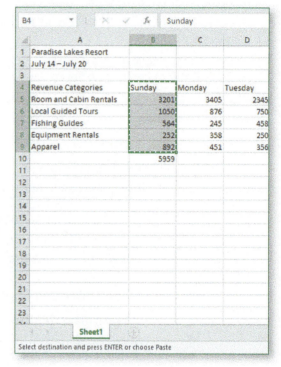

1-15 Cut data has moving border

The Office Clipboard

The **Office Clipboard** stores cut or copied data from Office applications and makes the data available for pasting in any application. The *Office Clipboard* can hold up to 24 items with each cut or copied item appearing, in turn, at the top of the pane. Click the **Clipboard** launcher to open the *Clipboard* task pane.

▶ HOW TO: Use the Office Clipboard

1. Click the **Home** tab.
2. Click the **Clipboard** launcher to open the *Clipboard* pane (Figure 1-16).
3. Click **Clear All** to empty the *Clipboard*.
   - The button is grayed out if there is no data on the clipboard.

4. Select data to be cut or copied.

5. Click the **Copy** button [*Home* tab, *Clipboard* group].

   - Use any *Cut* or *Copy* command from the *Ribbon* or keyboard.
   - Each item rotates into the first position in the *Clipboard* pane.

6. Select a destination cell.

7. Click the item icon in the *Clipboard* to paste it.

   - You can paste an item multiple times in different locations.

8. Click the **Close** button (X) to hide the *Clipboard*.

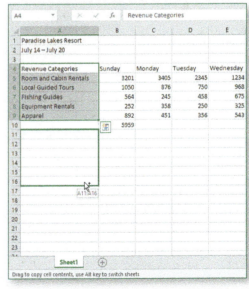

1-16 *Clipboard* pane

> **MORE INFO**
>
> To remove an item from the *Clipboard* task pane, click its drop-down arrow and choose **Delete**.

Copy Cell Contents

Copying data places a duplicate on the *Clipboard* so that it can be pasted in another location. When you use a *Ribbon*, keyboard, or context menu command, you can paste the data multiple times. You can copy data using the drag-and-drop method and paste it multiple times, even though the copied data is not placed on the *Clipboard*.

The *Copy* command stores data on the *Clipboard*, and the *Paste* command duplicates *Clipboard* contents in the worksheet.

- *Ribbon* buttons: **Copy** and **Paste** buttons [*Home* tab, *Clipboard* group]
- Shortcut commands: **Ctrl+C** to copy and **Ctrl+V** to paste
- Context menu: Right-click and choose **Copy**; right-click and choose **Paste**

> **HOW TO:** Copy Data Using Drag and Drop

1. Select the cell(s) to be copied.

2. Point to a border of the selection to display the move pointer.

3. Press **Ctrl** to display the copy pointer.

   - The copy pointer is a white arrow with a tiny plus sign.

4. Drag the selection to the desired location (Figure 1-17).

   - A preview selection shows where the copy will be pasted.

5. Continue to press **Ctrl** and drag to the next location for another copy.

6. Release the pointer button first and then release **Ctrl**.

1-17 Copy data using drag and drop

Paste Options

When you paste data, you can choose how it is copied in the new location. You can paste data and formatting, only the data, only the formatting, and so on. To see the options, click the lower half of the **Paste** button [*Home* tab, *Clipboard* group] to open the ***Paste Options*** gallery. The gallery also displays when you right-click a destination cell.

The table describes the icons in the *Paste Options* gallery:

Paste Options

Group	Paste Icon	Paste Option	Description
Paste		Paste	Copies all data and formatting; this is the default option.
		Formulas	Copies all data and formulas, but no formatting
		Formulas & Number Formatting	Copies all data and formulas with formatting
		Keep Source Formatting	Copies all data and formatting; same as *Paste*
		Match Destination Formatting	Copies data and applies formatting used in the destination
		No Borders	Copies all data, formulas, and formatting except for borders
		Keep Source Column Widths	Copies all data, formulas, and formatting and sets destination column widths to the same width as the source columns
		Transpose	Copies data and formatting and reverses data orientation so that rows are pasted as columns and columns are pasted as rows
		Merge Conditional Formatting	Copies data and *Conditional Formatting* rules. This option is available only if the copied data has conditional formatting.
Paste Values		Values	Copies only formula results (not the formulas) without formatting
		Values & Number Formatting	Copies only formula results (not the formulas) with formatting
		Values & Source Formatting	Copies only formula results (not the formulas) with all source formatting
Other Paste Options		Formatting	Copies only formatting, no data
		Paste Link	Pastes a 3-D reference to data or a formula
		Picture	Pastes a selectable picture object of the data. Data is static, but the object can be formatted like any object.
		Linked Picture	Pastes a selectable picture object of the data. The copied data is dynamic and reflects edits made in the source data. The picture can be formatted like any object.

PAUSE & PRACTICE: EXCEL 1-1

In this project, you open an Excel workbook that tracks revenue for one week at Paradise Lakes Resort. You add labels and values to complete the report; align labels; and edit, cut, and paste data. Your worksheet will have deliberate spelling errors for checking in a later Pause & Practice exercise.

File Needed: ***ParadiseLakes-01**.xlsx*
Completed Project File Name: ***[your initials] PP E1-1**.xlsx*

1. Open a workbook.
   a. Click the **File** tab and click **Open**.
   b. Navigate to the folder where your data files are stored.
   c. Double-click the name of the folder to open it.
   d. Locate the file name ***ParadiseLakes-01*** and click to select it.
   e. Click **Open**.
   f. Click **Enable Editing** if the workbook has opened in *Protected View* (Figure 1-18).

1-18 Worksheet opened in *Protected View*

2. Save the workbook with a different name.
   a. Press **F12** (**FN+F12**) to open the *Save As* dialog box.
   b. Select a location to save the workbook.
   c. Change the file name to [your initials] PP E1-1 in the *File name* area.
   d. Click **Save** to save the file and close the *Save As* dialog box.

3. Enter data.
   a. Click cell **A1** and type Paradise Lakes Resort.
   b. Press **Enter**.
   c. Click cell **A10**, type Total, and press **Enter**.
   d. Type the values shown below in cells **G5:H9**.

	G	H
5	3075	3201
6	925	1050
7	682	564
8	375	252
9	534	892

4. Use the *Fill Handle* to complete a series.
   a. Click **B4**.
   b. Point to the *Fill Handle* (small, black square in the lower right corner) until the *Fill* pointer (thin, black plus sign) appears.
   c. Click and drag the *Fill* pointer to reach cell **H4**.
   d. Release the pointer button.

5. Edit worksheet data.
   a. Click cell **B10**.
   b. Press **Delete** to remove the contents.
   c. Double-click cell **A4** to start *Edit* mode.
   d. Click to position the insertion point and delete the "i" in "Categories" to create a deliberate spelling error.
   e. Press **Enter** to accept the edit.
   f. Click cell **A9** and type Aparel with the error. You will correct errors in Pause & Practice 1-4.
   g. Press **Enter** to replace the entry.

6. Indent and align text.
   a. Select cells **A5:A9**.
   b. Click the **Increase Indent** button twice [*Home* tab, *Alignment* group].
   c. Select cells **B4:H4**.
   d. Click the **Center** button [*Home* tab, *Alignment* group].

7. Cut and paste data.
   a. Select cells **B4:B9**.
   b. Click the **Cut** button [*Home* tab, *Clipboard* group].
   c. Click cell **I4**.
   d. Click the **Paste** button [*Home* tab, *Clipboard* group].
   e. Select cells **C4:I9**.
   f. Point to any border of the selected range to display a four-pointed arrow with a white arrow.
   g. Drag the range to start in cell **B4** and release the pointer button.
   h. Click cell **A1**.

8. Save and close the workbook (Figure 1-19).
   a. Press **Ctrl+S** to save the workbook with the same file name.
   b. Click the **Close** button in the upper right corner to exit Excel.

	A	B	C	D	E	F	G	H
1	Paradise Lakes Resort							
2	July 14 – July 20							
3								
4	Revenue Categores	Monday	Tuesday	Wednesday	Thursday	Friday	Saturday	Sunday
5	Room and Cabin Rentals	3405	2345	1234	3420	3075	3201	3201
6	Local Tours	876	750	968	1254	925	1050	1050
7	Fishing Guides	245	458	675	890	682	564	564
8	Equipment Rentals	358	250	325	345	375	252	252
9	Aparel	451	356	543	532	534	892	892
10	Total							
11								

1-19 PP E1-1 completed

Using the SUM Function

A *formula* calculates a result for numeric data in a cell. A *function* is a built-in formula. *SUM* is a function that adds the values in a cell range. The terms "formula" and "function" are used interchangeably.

To use the *SUM* function, click the cell where you want to show a total. Then click the **AutoSum** button [*Home* tab, *Editing* group]. Excel inserts the function =SUM() with a suggested range of cells to be added between the parentheses. If that range is correct, press **Enter**, **Ctrl+Enter**, or click the **Enter** button in the *Formula* bar to complete the function. If the suggested range is not correct, you can select a different range or choose cells individually and then press a completion key. The sum is shown in the cell, and the function is visible in the *Formula* bar.

ANOTHER WAY

The *Function Library* group on the *Formulas* tab has an *AutoSum* button. You can also enter = SUM() in a cell by pressing **Alt** and the **+/=** key on the top keyboard row.

 HOW TO: Use the SUM Function

1. Click the cell for the total.

2. Click the **AutoSum** button [*Home* tab, *Editing* group] (Figure 1-20).

3. Press **Enter** to accept the range and complete the function.

   - Drag the pointer to select a different range before pressing **Enter**.
   - If the row or column of values to be added is adjacent to the formula cell as shown in Figure 1-20, you can double-click the **AutoSum** button to insert and accept the function.

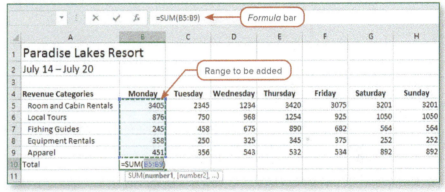

1-20 *SUM* function

MORE INFO

You can display formulas instead of results by clicking the **Show Formulas** button on the *Formulas* tab or by pressing **Ctrl+~**.

Function Syntax

An Excel function has *syntax*, the required elements and the order of those elements for the function to work. Every function starts with the equals sign [=] followed by the name of the function and a set of parentheses. Within the parentheses, you enter the argument(s). An *argument* is the cell reference or value required to complete the function. A function can have a single or multiple arguments. In = SUM(B5:B9), the argument is the range B5:B9. Multiple arguments in a function are separated by commas. There are three arguments in this function: =SUM(B5, B10, B15).

> SUM(B5:B9)
>
> SUM(B5, B10, B15)

Copy the SUM Function

The *SUM* function can be copied using regular copy and paste commands as well as the *Fill Handle*. When *SUM* is used to total data in rows or columns, you can enter the formula in the first column or row and copy it to the other locations. In Figure 1-21, for example, the same function is used in cells B10 through H10, each with its own argument. The formula in cell B10 is =SUM(B5:B9), the formula for cell C10 is =SUM(C5:C9) and so on. When a function is copied into adjacent cells, use the *Fill Handle*. Excel copies the formula and adjusts each argument based on the location in the worksheet.

▶ HOW TO: Use the Fill Handle to Copy a Function

1. Click the cell with the function to be copied.
2. Point to the *Fill Handle* in the lower right corner.

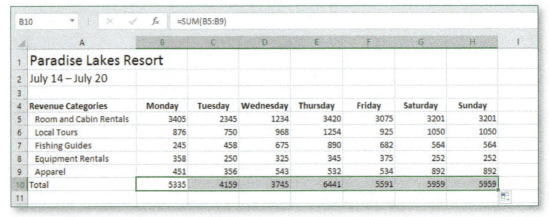

B10				f_x	=SUM(B5:B9)			
	A	B	C	D	E	F	G	H
1	Paradise Lakes Resort							
2	July 14 – July 20							
3								
4	Revenue Categories	Monday	Tuesday	Wednesday	Thursday	Friday	Saturday	Sunday
5	Room and Cabin Rentals	3405	2345	1234	3420	3075	3201	3201
6	Local Tours	876	750	968	1254	925	1050	1050
7	Fishing Guides	245	458	675	890	682	564	564
8	Equipment Rentals	358	250	325	345	375	252	252
9	Apparel	451	356	543	532	534	892	892
10	Total	5335	4159	3745	6441	5591	5959	5959
11								

1-21 Use the *Fill Handle* to copy a function

3. Click and drag the *Fill* pointer across the cells where the function should be pasted (Figure 1-21).

> ▶ **ANOTHER WAY**
>
> You can use regular copy and paste commands to copy a function or formula to any location on the worksheet.

Edit the Function Argument

If you edit a value in a cell that is referenced in a formula or function, the results are automatically recalculated. If you must change a cell or range argument in a function, however, you use *Edit* mode to enter new references. In *Edit* mode, you can make a change in the *Formula* bar or in the cell. You can often use the **Range Finder** to drag or select a new range, too. The *Range Finder* is an Excel feature that highlights and color-codes formula cells as you enter or edit a formula or function.

▶ **HOW TO:** Edit an Argument Range in the Formula Bar

1. Select the cell with the function.

2. Click the argument cell range in the *Formula* bar.

   - The *Range Finder* highlights the argument range in the worksheet.
   - The range is color-coded in the *Formula* bar to match the highlighted range (Figure 1-22)

3. Type the new cell references in the *Formula* bar.

4. Press **Enter**.

   - You can click the **Enter** button in the *Formula* bar to complete the edit.

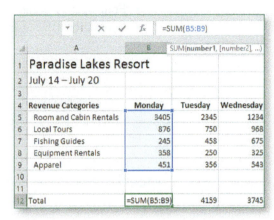

1-22 Argument range is color-coded

You can drag a *Range Finder* handle to select a different argument range, expanding or shrinking the number of included cells. This is easy to do when the formula cell is not adjacent to the range.

▶ **ANOTHER WAY**

Double-click the cell with the function and edit the argument in the cell.

▶ **HOW TO:** Edit an Argument Range by Dragging

1. Double-click the cell with the function.

   - *Edit* mode starts (Figure 1-23).

2. Drag the selection handle down to expand the argument range.

   - Drag the selection handle up to shrink the argument range.

3. Press **Enter** to complete the change.

   - Click the **Enter** button in the *Formula* bar.

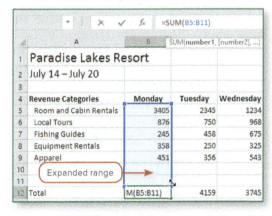

1-23 Edit a cell reference range by dragging

SLO 1.4

Formatting a Worksheet

A new workbook uses a default **theme** named *Office* which is a collection of fonts, colors, and special effects. The default theme applies the 11 point Calibri font and the *General* number format to all cells. You can change the theme as well as individual font attributes, or you can add fill and borders to highlight or emphasize data.

Font Face, Size, Style, and Color

A *font* is a type design for alphanumeric characters, punctuation, and keyboard symbols. *Font size* specifies the size of the character, measured in *points* (pt.). A point is equal to 1/72 of an inch. The *font style* refers to the thickness or angle of the characters and includes settings such as **bold**, <u>underline</u> or *italic*. *Font color* is the hue of the characters in the cell. You can apply any of these font attributes to a single cell or a range of cells.

Default font attributes for Excel 2016 workbooks are:

- Font: Calibri
- Font size: 11 point
- Font color: Black, Text 1

> **MORE INFO**
>
> The font list displayed on your computer depends on your Windows installation and other applications that are installed.

▶ **HOW TO:** Customize Font, Style, Font Size, and Font Color

1. Select the cell or range to be formatted.
   - You can format cells before any data is entered if you prefer.
2. Click the **Font** drop-down list [*Home* tab, *Font* group].
   - A list of available fonts is displayed.
3. Point to a font name.
   - *Live Preview* shows the selected data with the new font applied (Figure 1-24).
4. Click the **Font Size** drop-down list [*Home* tab, *Font* group] and select a size.
   - *Live Preview* shows the selected data in the new size.
   - You can type a custom size in the *Font Size* area.
   - You can also click the **Increase Font Size** or **Decrease Font Size** button [*Home* tab, *Font* group] to adjust the font size in 1-point increments.
5. Click the **Bold**, **Italic**, or **Underline** button [*Home* tab, *Font* group] to apply a style.
   - You can apply multiple styles.
6. Click the **Font Color** drop-down list [*Home* tab, *Font* group] and select a color.
   - Click the **Font Color** button (not the arrow) to apply the most recent font color shown on the button.

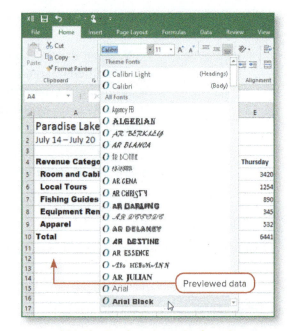

1-24 *Live Preview* when selecting a font name

The *mini toolbar* includes common commands from the *Font*, *Alignment*, and *Number* groups. It appears when you right-click a cell or selected range (Figure 1-25).

1-25 Mini toolbar

The *Format Cells* dialog box includes basic format settings and more. It has six tabs: *Number, Alignment, Font, Border, Fill,* and *Protection*.

- Mini toolbar: Right-click a cell or selected range.
- *Format Cells* dialog box: Click the **Font** launcher in the *Font* group, press **Ctrl+1** or right-click a selected cell and choose **Format Cells** (Figure 1-26).

The Format Painter

The *Format Painter* copies formatting attributes and styles from one cell to another cell or range. You can apply your custom formats without having to redefine each attribute, saving time and ensuring an exact duplicate.

1-26 *Format Cells* **dialog box**

▶ **HOW TO:** Use the Format Painter

1. Select a cell that contains the formatting you want to copy.
2. Click the **Format Painter** button [*Home* tab, *Clipboard* group].
   - The pointer changes to a thick, white cross with a tiny paint brush.
   - Double-click the **Format Painter** button to lock it for painting formats to multiple areas in the worksheet.
3. Click the cell or drag across the range to be formatted (Figure 1-27).
4. Release the pointer button.
   - The *Format Painter* is canceled.
   - If the *Format Painter* command is locked, click the **Format Painter** button or press **Esc** to turn it off.

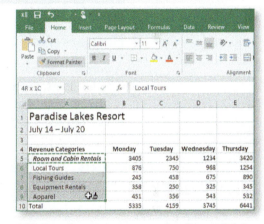

1-27 Copy formats to a range using *Format Painter*

Number Formats

You can format values with currency symbols, decimal points, commas, percent signs, and more so that data is quickly recognized and understood. The *Number* group on the *Home* tab includes command buttons for *Accounting, Percent,* and *Comma* styles as well as command buttons to *Increase Decimal* or *Decrease Decimal*. Dates and times are values, and *Date* and *Time* formats are included in the *Number* group. From the *Format Cells* dialog box, you can apply and customize these number formats or create your own format.

▶ **HOW TO:** Format Numbers

1. Select the cell or range of values.
2. Click a command button [*Home* tab, *Number* group] (Figure 1-28).

- Click the **Number Format** drop-down list to choose a format.
- Press **Ctrl+1** to open the *Format Cells* dialog box and click the **Number** tab to select a format.

3. Click the **Increase Decimal** or **Decrease Decimal** button to control the number of decimal places.

- When a cell displays a series of pound or number symbols (#####), you can widen the column to see the value.

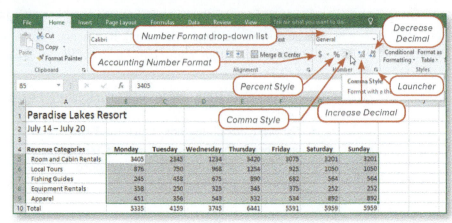

1-28 *Number* group on the *Home* tab

> **ANOTHER WAY**
>
> Click the **Number** launcher [*Home* tab] to open the *Format Cells* dialog box.

Borders and Fill

A **border** is an outline for a cell or a range. You can design a border to separate main or column headings, to emphasize totals, or to group data. **Fill** is a background color or pattern and is used to highlight or draw attention to data. You can use the *Ribbon* or the *Format Cells* dialog box to apply borders and fill color.

▶ **HOW TO: Add Borders and Fill Using the Ribbon**

1. Select the cell or range.
2. Click the arrow next to the **Borders** button [*Home* tab, *Font* group].
   - The **Borders** button shows the most recently used border style.
3. Select a border option from the list (Figure 1-29).
   - To remove a border, choose **No Border**.
4. Click the arrow for the **Fill Color** button [*Home* tab, *Font* group].
   - Click the **Fill Color** button to apply the most recently selected color.
   - To remove a fill, choose **No Fill**.

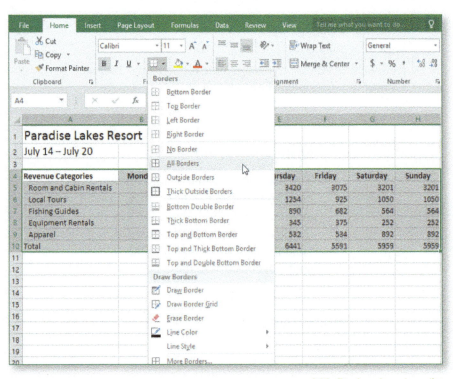

1-29 *Borders* drop-down list

5. Select a color tile in the palette (Figure 1-30).

   - *Live Preview* displays the cell or range with the color applied.
   - Click **More Colors** to build a custom color.

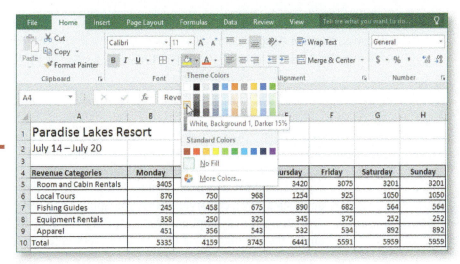

1-30 *Fill Color* palette

The *Format Cells* dialog box has a *Border* tab and a *Fill* tab. From the *Border* tab, you can choose a different line style, a different color, or different positions for the border. From the *Fill* tab, you can design patterned or gradient fills. A **pattern** fill uses crosshatches, dots, or stripes. A **gradient** is a blend of two or more colors. Use fill choices carefully, because they affect the readability of your data.

▶ **HOW TO:** Add Borders and Fill Using the Format Cells Dialog Box

1. Select the cell or range.

2. Click the **Font** launcher [*Home* tab, *Font* group] to open the *Format Cells* dialog box.

   - Press **Ctrl+1** to open the *Format Cells* dialog box.
   - Right-click a cell in the range and select **Format Cells**.

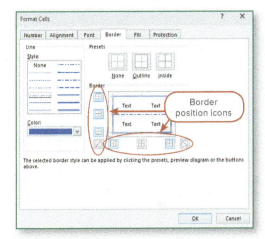

1-31 Build a custom border in the *Format Cells* dialog box

3. Click the **Border** tab (Figure 1-31).

   - Click **None** to remove all borders.

4. Choose a color from the *Color* drop-down list.

   - Select the color before choosing a line style or location.

5. Select a line style in the *Style* area.

6. Click **Outline** in the *Presets* area to apply an outside border.

   - The *Preview* area shows the border.
   - Build a custom border by clicking the desired icons in the *Border* area or by clicking the desired position in the *Preview* area.

7. Click the **Fill** tab (Figure 1-32).

1-32 *Fill* tab in the *Format Cells* dialog box and *Fill Effects* dialog box

8. Select a color tile in the *Background Color* area.
   - Select a color from the *Pattern Color* list and select a pattern from the *Pattern Style* list.
   - Click **Fill Effects** to apply a gradient. Choose two colors, a shading style, and a variant.
9. Click **OK** to close the *Format Cells* dialog box.

Cell Styles

A *cell style* is a set of formatting elements that includes font style, size, color, alignment, borders, and fill as well as number formats. Like other formatting, you select the cell or range and then apply a cell style. When you apply a cell style, the style format overwrites individual formatting already applied. After a cell style is applied, however, you can individually change any of the attributes. The *Cell Styles* gallery is located in the *Styles* group on the *Home* tab.

> **MORE INFO**
>
> Your screen size and settings determine if you see part of the *Cell Styles* gallery in the *Ribbon* or only the *Cell Styles* button.

▶ **HOW TO:** Apply Cell Styles

1. Select the cell or range.
2. Click the **More** button in the *Cell Styles* gallery.
   - Click the **Cell Styles** button [*Home* tab, *Styles* group] to open the gallery (Figure 1-33).

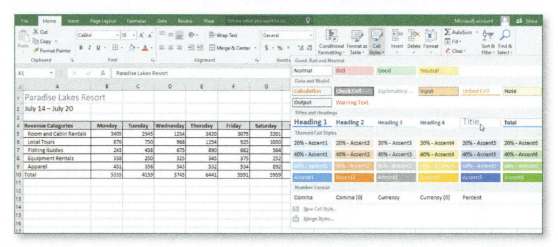

1-33 *Cell Styles* gallery and *Live Preview* for selected cell

3. Point to a style name to see a *Live Preview* in the worksheet.
4. Click a style name to apply it.

Workbook Themes

A workbook *theme* is a professionally designed set of fonts, colors, and effects. When you change the workbook theme, data formatted with theme settings are reformatted with the new theme fonts, colors, and effects. You can change the theme to quickly restyle a worksheet without having to individually edit cell formats throughout the sheet.

A theme includes a font name for headings and one for body text, and some themes use the same font for both. You can see the names of *Theme Fonts* at the top of the *Font* list. *Theme Colors* are identified in the color palettes for the **Fill** and **Font Color** buttons [*Home* tab, *Font* group]. Cell styles use font and color settings from the theme.

The *Themes* gallery lists built-in themes, and there are additional themes available online. You can also create and save your own theme.

▶ **HOW TO:** Change the Workbook Theme

1. Click the **Theme** button [*Page Layout* tab, *Themes* group]
   - The *Themes* gallery opens.
2. Point to a theme name.
   - *Live Preview* displays the worksheet with new format settings (Figure 1-34).

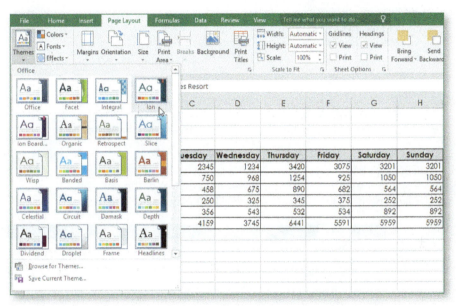

1-34 *Themes* gallery and a *Live Preview* in the worksheet

3. Click a theme icon to apply a different theme.
   - Display the **Font** button list [*Home* tab, *Font* group] to see the new theme font names at the top of the list.
   - Display the **Font Color** and **Fill Color** button galleries [*Home* tab, *Font* group] to see new theme colors.

▶ **MORE INFO**

Rest the pointer on the **Themes** button [*Page Layout* tab, *Themes* group] to see the name of the current theme.

In this project, you open the workbook you created in *Pause & Practice Excel 1-1*. You add totals using *SUM* and copy the function using *AutoFill*. Your format changes result in truncated or cutoff data; you learn how to adjust column widths in the next learning objective and will fix this problem in the next Pause & Practice project.

File Needed: *[your initials] PP E1-1.xlsx*
Completed Project File Name: *[your initials] PP E1-2.xlsx*

---

1. Open a workbook and save it as a different name.
   a. Click the **File** tab and choose **Open**. If you have just started Excel and the file name appears in the *Recent* list in the Excel *Start* page, click the name to open it. Otherwise, click **Open Other Workbooks** at the bottom of the *Start* page.
   b. Locate the folder where your file is stored.
   c. Open *[your initials] PP E1-1*. (Click **Enable Editing** if the workbook has opened in *Protected View*).
   c. Press **F12** (**FN+F12**) to open the *Save As* dialog box.
   d. Locate the folder where your files are saved.
   e. Edit the file name to [your initials] PP E1-2 and click **Save**.

2. Calculate daily totals using *SUM*.
   a. Click cell **B10**.
   b. Click the **AutoSum** button [*Home* tab, *Editing* group].
   c. Press **Enter** to accept the suggested range and to complete the formula.

3. Copy a function using the *Fill Handle*.
   a. Click cell **B10**.
   b. Point to the *Fill Handle* in the lower right corner of the cell.
   c. Click and drag the *Fill* pointer to cell **H10** (Figure 1-35). Release the pointer button.

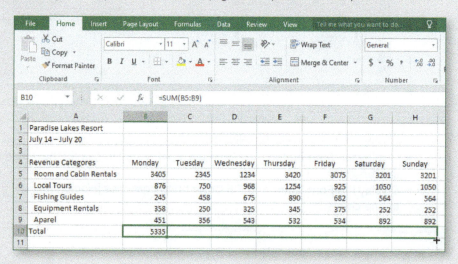

1-35 Copy a function with the *Fill* pointer

4. Calculate sales category totals.
   a. Click cell **J5**.
   b. Double-click the **AutoSum** button [*Home* tab, *Editing* group] to accept and complete the formula.

5. Edit the argument cell range.
   a. Click cell **J5**.
   b. Click the *Formula* bar within the range **B5:I5**.
   c. Position the insertion point and edit the range to **B5:h5**. When you type the "h," you will see a *Formula AutoComplete* list which you can ignore (Figure 1-36).
   d. Press **Enter** to accept the new range.

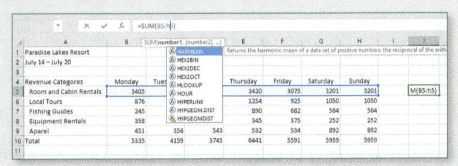

1-36   Edit the cell reference in the *Formula* bar

6. Copy a function using the *Fill Handle*.
   a. Select cell **J5** and point to the *Fill Handle*.
   b. Click and drag the *Fill* pointer to cell **J10**. Release the pointer button.

7. Drag and drop to move a cell range.
   a. Select cells **J5:J10**.
   b. Point to any border of the selected range to display the move pointer.
   c. Drag the range to cells **I5:I10**.
   d. In cell **I4**, type Total.

8. Apply cell styles.
   a. Select cell **A1** and click the **Cell Styles** button or the **More** button [*Home* tab, *Styles* group] to open the *Cell Styles* gallery.
   b. Click **Title** in the *Titles and Headings* group.
   c. Select cell **A2** and click the **Cell Styles** button or the **More** button [*Home* tab, *Styles* group].
   d. Select **Heading 2** in the *Titles and Headings* group.
   e. Select cells **A10:I10** and open the *Cell Styles* gallery [*Home* tab, *Styles* group].
   f. Select **Total** in the *Titles and Headings* group.
   g. Select cells **A4:A10**, press **Ctrl**, and select cells **B4:I4** to add them to the selection.
   h. Open the *Cells Style* gallery and select **20%, Accent1** in the *Themed Cell Styles* category.
   i. Click cell **F1** to deselect cells and view the styles.

9. Change the theme and apply font attributes.
   a. Click the **Themes** button [*Page Layout* tab, *Themes* group] and choose **Facet** from the gallery.
   b. Select cell **A4** and click the **Home** tab.
   c. Click the **Font** drop-down list [*Font* group] and select **Candara** in the *All Fonts* section.
   d. Click the **Font Size** drop-down list and select **16 pt**.
   e. Click the **Bold** button [*Font* group].
   f. Select cells **A5:I10**.
   g. Click the **Font Size** drop-down list and choose **12 pt**.

10. Use the *Format Painter*.
    a. Click cell **A4**.
    b. Click the **Format Painter** button [*Home* tab, *Clipboard* group].
    c. Drag to paint cells **B4:I4** and release the pointer button (Figure 1-37).

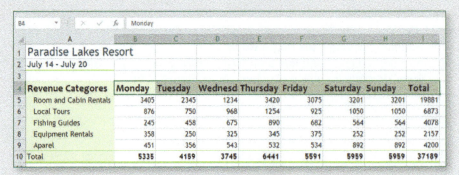

Revenue Categores	Monday	Tuesday	Wednesd	Thursday	Friday	Saturday	Sunday	Total
Room and Cabin Rentals	3405	2345	1234	3420	3075	3201	3201	19881
Local Tours	876	750	968	1254	925	1050	1050	6873
Fishing Guides	245	458	675	890	682	564	564	4078
Equipment Rentals	358	250	325	345	375	252	252	2157
Aparel	451	356	543	532	534	892	892	4200
Total	5335	4159	3745	6441	5591	5959	5959	37189

1-37 Paint the format from cell A4

11. Apply number formats and align text.
    a. Select cells **B5:I9**.
    b. Click the **Comma Style** button [*Home* tab, *Number* group] and leave cells B5:I9 selected.
    c. Click the **Decrease Decimal** button [*Home* tab, *Number* group] two times while cells B5:I9 are selected.
    d. Select cells **B10:I10**.
    e. Click the **Accounting Number Format** button [*Home* tab, *Number* group]. You may see a series of # symbols in the cells.
    f. Click the **Decrease Decimal** button [*Home* tab, *Number* group] two times.
    g. Select cells **B4:I4**.
    h. Click the **Align Right** button [*Home* tab, *Alignment* group]. Not all labels are visible with this alignment setting.
    i. Apply **Bold** to cell **A10**.

12. Add borders.
    a. Select cells **A4:I10** and click the **Border** button arrow [*Home* tab, *Font* group].
    b. Select **All Borders**. The border format from the *Total* cell style in row 10 is overwritten with the *All Borders* format.
    c. Select cells **A10:I10** and press **Ctrl+1** to open the *Format Cells* dialog box.
    d. Click the **Border** tab.
    e. Click the bottom border icon In the *Border* preview area to remove the border (Figure 1-38).
    f. Click the double solid line style (second column, seventh style).
    g. In the preview area, click the bottom border position to reset the border (Figure 1-39).
    h. Click **OK** to close the *Format Cells* dialog box and to apply the new border.
    i. Select cells **A2:I2** and open the *Format Cells* dialog box.
    j. Click the **Border** tab and click the bottom border position two times to remove the bottom border.
    k. Click the **Color** drop-down list, and select **Dark Green, Accent 2, Darker 25%**.

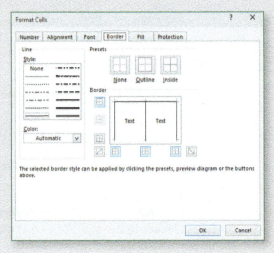

1-38 Remove the bottom border

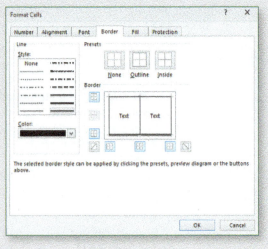

1-39 Reset the bottom border

l. Select the thick, solid line style (second column, fifth style).

m. In the preview area, click the bottom border location to reset the border.

n. Click **OK** and then click cell **A1**.

13. Click the **Save** button in the *Quick Access* toolbar.

14. Click the **File** tab and click **Close**, or press **Ctrl+W** to close the workbook (Figure 1-40).

	A	B	C	D	E	F	G	H	I
1	Paradise Lakes Resort								
2	July 14 - July 20								
3									
4	**Revenue Categores**	**Monday**	**Tuesday**	**ednesday**	**Thursday**	**Friday**	**Saturday**	**Sunday**	**Total**
5	Room and Cabin Rentals	3,405	2,345	1,234	3,420	3,075	3,201	3,201	19,881
6	Local Tours	876	750	968	1,254	925	1,050	1,050	6,873
7	Fishing Guides	245	458	675	890	682	564	564	4,078
8	Equipment Rentals	358	250	325	345	375	252	252	2,157
9	Aparel	451	356	543	532	534	892	892	4,200
10	**Total**	$ 5,335	$ 4,159	$ 3,745	$ 6,441	$ 5,591	$ 5,959	$ 5,959	$ 37,189
11									

1-40 PP E1-2 completed

SLO 1.5

Modifying Columns and Rows

A worksheet has a default number of rows and columns, each in the default width and height for the workbook theme. There are over 1 million rows and more than 16,000 columns available for use. You can modify the width of a column, insert columns, change the height of a row, delete a column, and more.

> **MORE INFO**
>
> Unused rows and columns are ignored when you print a worksheet with default print settings.

Adjust Column Width and Row Height

The default width for a column in a worksheet using the Office theme is 8.43 characters (64 pixels) in the default font. Column width can be set to any value between 0 and 255 characters. The default height of each row is 15 points (20 pixels). A *pixel* measures one screen dot. You can change *column width* or *row height* by dragging the border between column or row headings, by using the context menu, or by selecting a command from the **Format** button list [*Home* tab, *Cells* group]. You can adjust one or more columns or rows at the same time.

▶ **HOW TO:** Change Column Width or Row Height

1. Select one or more cells in the same column.
    - The cells need not be in adjacent rows.
2. Click the **Format** button [*Home* tab, *Cells* group].
3. Select **Row Height**.
    - The *Row Height* dialog box opens.

4. Enter a height in points and click **OK**.

  • The row height is adjusted for the rows in which you selected cells.

5. Select one or more cells in the same row.

  • The cells need not be in adjacent columns.

6. Click the **Format** button [*Home* tab, *Cells* group].

7. Select **Column Width**.

  • The *Column Width* dialog box opens.

8. Enter a new width in characters and click **OK** (Figure 1-41).

1-41 Change the column width for several columns

> **MORE INFO**
>
> Click the **Format** button [*Home* tab, *Cells* group] and select **Default Width** to change the default column width for the entire worksheet.

You can quickly change column widths and row heights using the worksheet headings. Point to the border between two column or row headings and click and drag to set a new width or height. When you point to a border, the pointer changes to a resize arrow, and you will see a *ScreenTip* with the setting as you drag. You can use this method with multiple columns or rows, too. Drag across the headings to select the number of columns or rows to be adjusted, and then click and drag any border in the selected group.

AutoFit Columns and Rows

The **AutoFit** feature resizes column width or row height to fit the width or height of the longest or tallest entry. The quickest way to *AutoFit* a column is to double-click the right border of the column heading (Figure 1-42). To *AutoFit* a row, double-click the bottom border of the row heading. You can *AutoFit* multiple columns or rows by first selecting them and double-clicking any border within the selection. You can also use the *AutoFit Column Width* or the *AutoFit Row Height* commands on the **Format** button in the *Cells* group on the *Home* tab.

▶ **HOW TO: AutoFit Column Width or Row Height**

1. Point to the border to the right of the column heading or below the row heading.

  • Drag to select more than one column or row.

2. Double-click the resize arrow.

  • All selected columns and rows are set to fit the longest or tallest entry.

1-42   Double-click a column border to *AutoFit* its width to the longest item

Wrap Text, Merge Cells, and Center Across Selection

When a label is too long for the column width, it spills into an empty adjacent cell. If that adjacent cell is not empty, a long label may be cut off within the cell. You can widen the column, or you can wrap text. Wrapped text is often used to show lengthy column titles on more than one line (Figure 1-43).

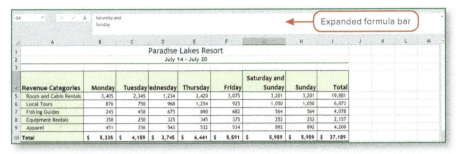

1-43 Label in cell G4 is wrapped to two lines; *Formula* bar is expanded

The ***Wrap Text*** command displays a label on multiple lines within the cell, splitting the label between words to fit the width of the column. You can control where the label splits by inserting a manual ***line break***. Press **Alt+Enter** after the word where you want a new line to start. When using multi-line labels, you can expand the *Formula* bar by clicking the **Formula Bar** expand or collapse button at the right edge of the *Formula* bar.

> **MORE INFO**
>
> After using the *Wrap Text* command, you may need to adjust the column width or row height to better display the label.

> ▶**HOW TO:** Wrap Text in a Cell

1. Select the cell with the label.
2. Click the **Home** tab.
3. Click the **Wrap Text** button in the *Alignment* group.
   - To control the split, edit the cell and click at the desired location. Press **Alt+Enter** to insert a manual line break and then press **Enter** to finish.
4. Adjust the column width and row height as desired.

> **ANOTHER WAY**
>
> As you type a label, press **Alt+Enter** at the point where a new line should start, finish the label, and press **Enter**. The *Wrap Text* command is automatically enabled.

The ***Merge & Center*** command combines two or more cells into one cell and centers the data within the combined cell. This command is a quick way to center a main label over multiple columns. Because the result is one large cell, you can format the area with special fill effects. When you use *Merge & Center*, the data must be in the upper left cell of the selection.

The *Merge & Center* button [*Home* tab, *Alignment* group] includes options to merge cells without centering and to unmerge cells.

▶ **HOW TO:** Merge and Center

1. Select the cells to be merged and centered.

   - You can merge and center the cells first and then enter the data.

2. Click the **Home** tab.

3. Click the **Merge & Center** button [*Alignment* group] (Figure 1-44).

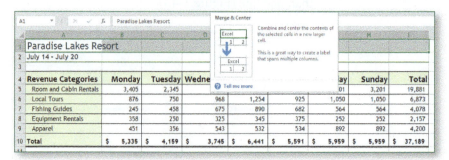

1-44 **Select cells to merge and center**

The ***Center Across Selection*** command horizontally centers multiple rows across multiple columns. When you have two or three rows of labels to center, you can select the entire range and center them with one command. This command does not merge cells, and you can still insert and delete rows and columns in the centered area.

The *Center Across Selection* command is on the *Alignment* tab in the *Format Cells* dialog box.

▶ **HOW TO:** Center Across a Selection

1. Select the cell range that includes the data to be centered.

   - Select all rows with data to be centered.
   - Select columns to identify the range over which the labels should be centered.

2. Click the **Alignment** launcher [*Home* tab, *Alignment* group].

3. Click the **Horizontal** drop-down arrow and choose **Center Across Selection** (Figure 1-45).

4. Click **OK**.

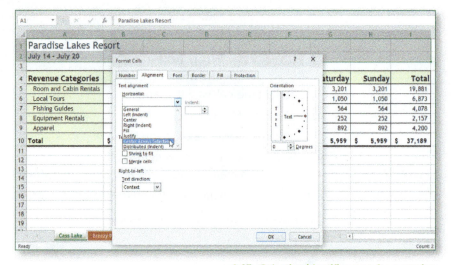

1-45 **Selection identifies area for centering**

Insert and Delete Columns and Rows

You can insert or delete rows or columns in a worksheet. When you do, Excel moves existing data to make room for new data or to fill the gap left by deleted data. Functions or formulas are automatically updated to include an inserted row or column, and they reflect deleted rows or columns in the argument or range.

You can insert rows and columns from options on the **Insert** button [*Home* tab, *Cells* group]. You can also right-click a column or row heading and choose **Insert** from the context menu. To insert multiple columns or rows, first select the number of columns or rows that you want to insert. For example, if you want to insert two columns to the left of column A, select columns A:B. Then use any **Insert** command to insert two new columns.

HOW TO: Insert a Column or a Row

1. Select a cell in the column to the right of where a new column is to be inserted.
2. Click the arrow on the **Insert** button [*Home* tab, *Cells* group].
3. Select **Insert Sheet Columns**.
   - A column is inserted to the left of the current column.
4. Right-click the row heading below the row where a new row should appear.
5. Choose **Insert** from the context menu (Figure 1-46).
   - A row is inserted above the selected row.

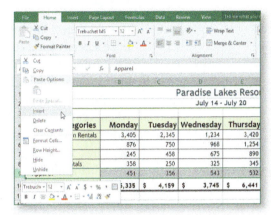

1-46 Insert a row above row 9

When you delete a column or row, data is deleted and remaining columns and rows shift to the left or up. Most functions or formulas are updated if you delete a row or column that is within the argument range.

You can delete rows and columns from the **Delete** button [*Home* tab, *Cells* group] or from the context menu. To delete multiple columns or rows, select them and use the **Delete** command.

> **ANOTHER WAY**
>
> Select a cell and press **Ctrl+plus sign (+)** in the numeric keypad. Choose **Entire Column** or **Entire Row** and press **Enter**. Press **Ctrl+minus sign (−)** in the numeric keypad to delete a column or row.

HOW TO: Delete Columns or Rows

1. Select a cell in the column to be deleted.
2. Click the arrow on the **Delete** button [*Home* tab, *Cells* group].
3. Select **Delete Sheet Columns**.
   - The entire column is deleted.
   - Remaining columns shift to the left.
4. Right-click the row heading for the row to be deleted.
   - The context menu opens.
5. Choose **Delete**.
   - The entire row is deleted.
   - Remaining rows shift up.

Hide and Unhide Columns and Rows

If a worksheet has more data than necessary for your current task, you can hide data to optimize screen space. In a checkbook register with data for several years, you might want to hide rows from two years ago so that you only see the current year's data. You should not delete the old data because it is necessary for record-keeping.

Hidden rows and columns are available and included in calculations and can be shown whenever necessary. The *Hide* and *Unhide* commands apply to columns or rows; you cannot hide cells. When a column or row is hidden, there is a tiny gap between the column or row headings. In addition, column or row headings are not consecutive, so you can quickly identify what is hidden.

► **HOW TO:** Hide and Unhide Columns or Rows

1. Click the row or column heading of the row or column to be hidden.
   - Select multiple row or column headings as desired.
   - Rows or columns need not be adjacent.
2. Right-click one of the selected row or column headings.
   - The context menu opens.
3. Select **Hide** (Figure 1-47).
   - The entire row or column is hidden.
   - Formula references to hidden cells are maintained.
4. Drag across the column or row headings where there are hidden columns or rows.
   - Drag from the column to the left of a hidden column to one column to the right of a hidden column.
   - Drag from the row above hidden rows to one row below hidden rows.
5. Right-click one of the selected row or column headings.
   - The context menu opens.
6. Select **Unhide**.

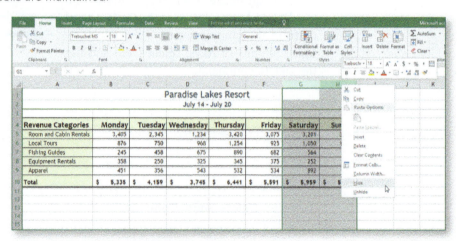

1-47 Hide two columns

SLO 1.6

Modifying Worksheets

Each worksheet in an Excel workbook has a worksheet tab near the bottom left of the Excel window that displays the name of the sheet. A new workbook starts with one sheet, but the number of worksheets is limited only by the size of memory on the computer. You can insert and delete sheets, rename them, and change the tab color. You can also hide, copy, or move sheets.

Insert and Delete Worksheets

You can keep related worksheets in a single workbook for ease in managing your files and tasks. For example, a monthly workbook could include revenue and expense, payroll, and customer data sheets. When there are multiple worksheets in a workbook, activate a sheet by clicking its tab name.

You can insert worksheets from the **Insert** button [*Home* tab, *Cells* group] or by simply clicking the **New Sheet** button to the right of the tab names. You can also right-click an existing sheet tab and choose **Insert** to open an *Insert* dialog box. Inserted worksheets are named *SheetN*, where *N* is the next available number.

To delete the active worksheet, right-click the sheet tab and select **Delete**. You can also click the arrow on the **Delete** button [*Home* tab, *Cells* group] and select **Delete Sheet**.

> **MORE INFO**
>
> Press **Ctrl+Page Down** to move to the next worksheet in the tab order. Press **Ctrl+Page Up** to move to the previous sheet.

▶ **HOW TO:** Insert and Delete Worksheets

1. Click the **New Sheet** button (plus sign) to the right of the worksheet tabs (Figure 1-48).
   - A new sheet is inserted to the right of the active sheet.
2. Click the arrow on the **Insert** button [*Home* tab, *Cells* group].
3. Select **Insert Sheet**.
   - A new sheet is inserted to the left of the active sheet.
4. Right-click a tab and select **Insert**.
   - The *Insert* dialog box opens.
5. Select **Worksheet** and click **OK**.
   - The new sheet is inserted to the left of the active sheet.
6. Right-click a sheet tab and choose **Delete**.
   - The sheet is deleted.
7. Click the arrow on the **Delete** button [*Home* tab, *Cells* group] and select **Delete Sheet**.
   - The sheet is deleted.

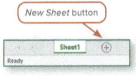

New Sheet button

1-48 *New Sheet* **button**

> **ANOTHER WAY**
>
> Press **Shift+F11** to insert a worksheet to the left of the active sheet.

Rename Worksheets and Change Tab Color

New worksheets are named *Sheet1*, *Sheet2*, and so on, but you can rename a worksheet to identify its contents and purpose. The tab width adjusts to display the name, so if you use lengthy names, you limit the number of tabs visible at the same time. When you cannot see all the tabs, use the *tab scrolling buttons* located to the left of the leftmost tab name. Move forward and backward through the tabs, or you can right-click a tab scrolling button to display the *Activate* dialog box with a list of existing worksheet names (Figure 1-49). The tab scrolling buttons are enabled when needed.

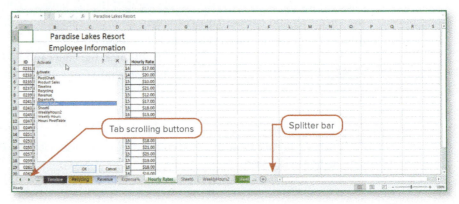

1-49   Activate dialog box and tab scrolling buttons

You can apply a *tab color* to further distinguish a particular sheet. The color palette includes tiles for theme and standard colors as well as an option to build a custom color.

▶ **HOW TO:** Rename a Worksheet and Apply a Tab Color

1. Double-click the worksheet tab.
   - You can right-click the tab and select **Rename**.
2. Type the new name on the tab and press **Enter**.
   - You can click the **Format** button [*Home* tab, *Cells* group] and select **Rename Sheet**.
3. Right-click the worksheet tab.
4. Choose **Tab Color** from the context menu to open the palette (Figure 1-50).
   - You can click the **Format** button [*Home* tab, *Cells* group] and select **Tab Color**.

1-50   Change the tab color

5. Select a color.

6. Click another tab to better see the tab color.

Move and Copy Worksheets

You can rearrange (move) tabs to display the worksheets in your preferred left-to-right order. You can also move worksheets to another workbook.

You can copy a worksheet to make an exact duplicate of the data and formatting. When you copy a worksheet, the copy is named with the same name as the original followed by a number in parentheses (i.e., *January (2)*).

When moving sheets within a workbook, you simply drag the tab to the desired location. When moving or copying to another workbook, however, use the ***Move or Copy*** dialog box.

You can move or copy multiple sheets, too. Select sheet names using **Ctrl** or **Shift**. The word *[Group]* displays in the title bar. After you complete the move or copy command, right-click any tab in the group and choose **Ungroup**.

▶ **HOW TO:** Move and Copy Worksheets

1. Point to the worksheet tab to be moved.

2. Drag the pointer to the desired location in the tab names.
   - A triangle and a worksheet icon preview where the worksheet will be moved (Figure 1-51).

3. Release the pointer button.

4. Right-click the worksheet tab to be copied.

5. Select **Move or Copy**.
   - The *Move or Copy* dialog box opens.
   - You can also click the **Format** button [*Home* tab, *Cells* group] to select **Move or Copy Sheet**.

6. Click the **To book** drop-down arrow and choose a workbook name.
   - To copy the sheet in the same workbook, choose its name.
   - To copy the worksheet into a different workbook, choose its name; the workbook must be open.

7. In the *Before sheet* list, choose a sheet name as desired.
   - Choose **(move to end)** to place the copied sheet as the last tab.

8. Select the **Create a copy** box (Figure 1-52).

9. Click **OK** to close the dialog box.
   - The copied worksheet has the same name as the original followed by *(2)*.

10. Rename the copied sheet as desired.

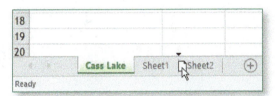

1-51 Drag a sheet tab to a position

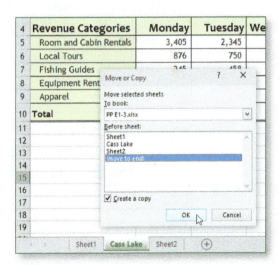

1-52 *Move or Copy* dialog box

▶ **ANOTHER WAY**

To copy a worksheet by dragging, press **Ctrl** and drag the tab to the desired location for the copy.

In this project, you open *[your initials] PP E1-2* and adjust column heights and row widths, insert a row, merge and center cells, and add borders. You also copy and rename sheets, apply tab colors, and delete worksheets.

File Needed: *[your initials] PP E1-2.xlsx*
Completed Project File Name: *[your initials] PP E1-3.xlsx*

---

1. Open the *[your initials] PP E1-2* workbook completed in *Pause & Practice 1-2*.

2. Save the file as [your initials] PP E1-3.

3. Change the width of columns B through I.
   a. Point to the column **B** heading to display a down-pointing arrow.
   b. Click and drag to reach column **I**.
   c. Click the **Format** button [*Home* tab, *Cells* group].
   d. Select **Column Width** from the menu.
   e. Enter 14 in the *Column Width* dialog box.
   f. Click **OK** to set the new width for the selected columns.

4. Change the row height for rows 4 and 10.
   a. Click the row **4** heading.
   b. Press **Ctrl** and click the row **10** heading. Two rows are selected.
   c. Right-click the row **4** heading.
   d. Choose **Row Height** from the menu.
   e. Enter 24 as the new height.
   f. Click **OK** to set the row height for both rows.

5. Insert a row.
   a. Right-click row heading **9**.
   b. Choose **Insert**. The inserted row is row 9, and the remaining rows have shifted down.
   c. In cell **A9**, type Food & Beverage. The new row uses the same format as the other rows (Figure 1-53).
   d. Press **Enter**.

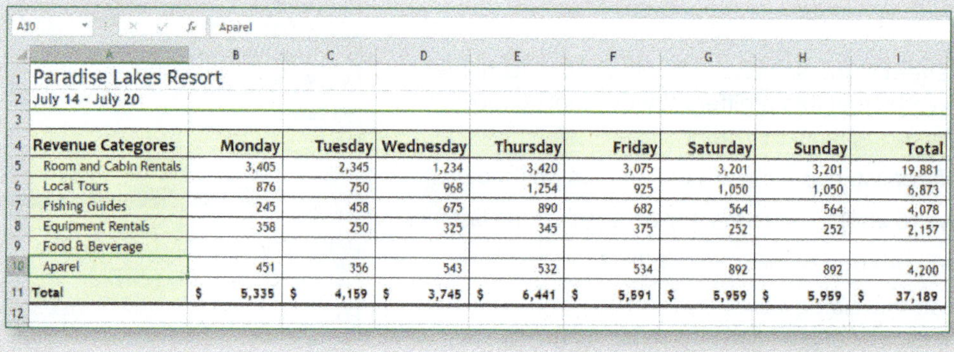

	A	B	C	D	E	F	G	H	I
	A10			*fx*	Aparel				
1	Paradise Lakes Resort								
2	July 14 - July 20								
3									
4	**Revenue Categores**	Monday	Tuesday	Wednesday	Thursday	Friday	Saturday	Sunday	Total
5	Room and Cabin Rentals	3,405	2,345	1,234	3,420	3,075	3,201	3,201	19,881
6	Local Tours	876	750	968	1,254	925	1,050	1,050	6,873
7	Fishing Guides	245	458	675	890	682	564	564	4,078
8	Equipment Rentals	358	250	325	345	375	252	252	2,157
9	Food & Beverage								
10	Aparel	451	356	543	532	534	892	892	4,200
11	**Total**	$ 5,335	$ 4,159	$ 3,745	$ 6,441	$ 5,591	$ 5,959	$ 5,959	$ 37,189
12									

1-53 New row and label inserted

6. Hide a row.
   a. Select cell **A9**.
   b. Click the **Format** button [*Home* tab, *Cells* group].
   c. Select **Hide & Unhide** in the *Visibility* category.
   d. Select **Hide Rows**. The selected row is hidden.

7. Center titles across a selection.
   a. Select cells **A1:I2**.
   b. Click the **Alignment** launcher [*Home* tab, *Alignment* group].

c. Click the **Horizontal** drop-down arrow and choose **Center Across Selection**.
d. Click **OK**.

8. Rename a worksheet and change the tab color.
   a. Double-click the **Sheet1** tab name.
   b. Type Cass Lake.
   c. Press **Enter**.
   d. Right-click the **Cass Lake** tab name and select **Tab Color**.
   e. Select **Green Accent 1, Darker 50%** (fifth column).

9. Copy and rename a worksheet.
   a. Right-click the **Cass Lake** tab.
   b. Choose **Move or Copy**. The *Move or Copy* dialog box opens.
   c. Choose **(move to end)** in the *Before Sheet* list.
   d. Select the **Create a copy** box.
   e. Click **OK**. The copied sheet is named *Cass Lake (2)*.
   f. Double-click the **Cass Lake (2)** tab, type Breezy Point, and press **Enter**.
   g. Right-click the **Breezy Point** tab and choose **Tab Color**.
   h. Format the tab color to **Orange, Accent 4, Darker 25%**.
   i. Select cells **B5:H10** and press **Delete** (Figure 1-54).
   j. Press **Ctrl+Home**.

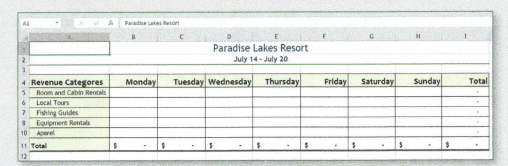

1-54   Data deleted on copied sheet

10. Click the **Cass Lake** tab and press **Ctrl+Home**.

11. Press **Ctrl+S** to save the workbook.

12. Click the **File** tab and click **Close** to close the workbook (Figure 1-55).

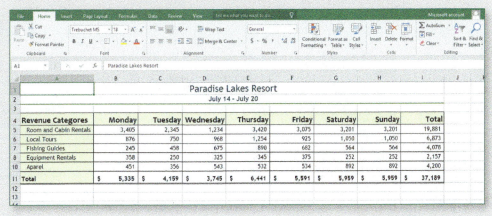

1-55   PP E1-3 completed worksheet

Modifying the Appearance of the Workbook

You can adjust how you see data in a worksheet to make your work as easy as possible. You can select a view, zoom in or out on the data, freeze parts of the screen, split the worksheet into two panes, and switch between multiple open windows.

Workbook Views

The *View* tab has a *Workbook Views* group with three main views or layouts for working in an Excel worksheet. The views are **Normal**, **Page Layout**, and **Page Break Preview**.

- *Normal* view is the default and is used to create and modify a worksheet.
- *Page Layout* view opens the header and footer areas, indicates margin areas, and shows rulers.
- *Page Break Preview* displays printed pages with dashed or dotted lines to mark where new pages start.

There are buttons for *Normal* view, *Page Layout* view, and *Page Break Preview* on the right side of the *Status* bar.

> **MORE INFO**
>
> The **Ribbon Display Options** button (on the right of the workbook title bar) can be used to hide the *Ribbon* for maximum screen space in any workbook view.

HOW TO: Switch Workbook Views Using the Status Bar

1. Click the **View** tab.
   - The *Normal* button is activated in the *Workbook Views* group.
2. Click the **Page Layout** button in the *Status* bar.
   - This view displays the header, the footer, and margin areas (Figure 1-56).

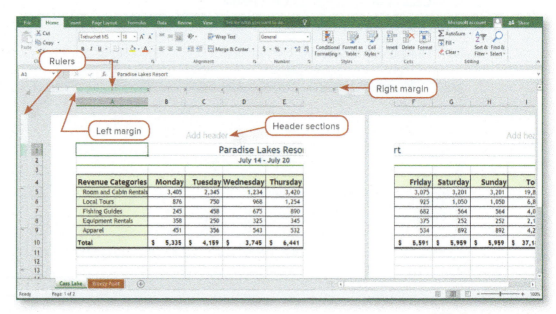

1-56 *Page Layout* view

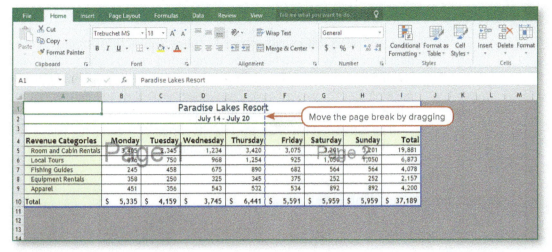

1-57 *Page Break Preview*

3. Click the **Page Break Preview** button in the *Status* bar.

   • If the data does not fit on a single page, a dashed line indicates where the second page will start (Figure 1-57).

4. Click the **Normal** button in the *Status* bar.

Zoom Options

You can change a sheet's magnification to see more of the data at once (zoom out) or to scrutinize content more carefully (zoom in). There is a *Zoom* group on the *View* tab as well as *Zoom* controls in the *Status* bar.

The *Status* bar controls include a **Zoom In** button, a **Zoom Out** button, and the **Zoom** slider. The slider is the vertical bar in the middle of the horizontal line which you can drag to change the magnification level.

▶ **HOW TO:** Change Zoom Levels

1. Click the **Zoom In** button in the *Status* bar.

   • The magnification is increased in 10% increments with each click.

2. Click the **Zoom Out** button in the *Status* bar.

   • The magnification is decreased in 10% increments with each click.

3. Drag the **Zoom** slider in the middle of the horizontal line to the left or right to set a value (Figure 1-58).

   • The magnification percentage is displayed to the right of the line.

4. Click the **Zoom** button [*View* tab, *Zoom* group].

   • The *Zoom* dialog box includes preset values.

5. Click a radio button to choose a *Magnification* level.

   • Select **Fit selection** for a selected range to fill the screen.
   • Choose **Custom** to enter any magnification value.

6. Click **OK**.

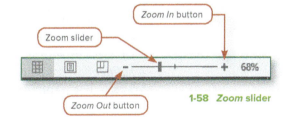

1-58 *Zoom* slider

> **ANOTHER WAY**
>
> The *Zoom* group [*View* tab] has *100%* and *Zoom to Selection* buttons.

Freeze Panes

In a worksheet with many rows and columns of information, it is not possible to see all the data at once. As you scroll to see information on the right, related labels or values on the left scroll out of view. The *Freeze Panes* command locks rows or columns in view so that you can position data for easy review. The worksheet is divided into two or four panes (sections) with a thin, black border to indicate the divisions.

The active cell becomes the top left corner of the moving pane. For example, if you select cell B5 and select the *Freeze Panes* command, column A and rows 1:4 are stationary.

▶ HOW TO: Freeze and Unfreeze Panes

1. Select a cell in the worksheet.
   - Click a cell one row below the last row to be frozen.
   - Click a cell one column to the right of the last column to be locked.
2. Click the **Freeze Panes** button [*View* tab, *Window* group].
   - Select **Freeze Top Row** to lock row 1 in view, regardless of the active cell.
   - Choose **Freeze First Column** to keep the first column in view, regardless of the active cell.
3. Select **Freeze Panes**.
   - All rows above and all columns to the left of the active cell are locked in position.
   - A thin, black border identifies frozen rows and columns.
4. Scroll the data in any direction (Figure 1-59).
5. Click the **Freeze Panes** button [*View* tab, *Window* group].
6. Select **Unfreeze Panes**.
   - The black border is removed.

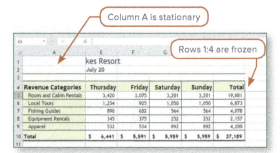

1-59 *Freeze Panes* **results when cell B5 is selected and columns B:D are scrolled left**

Split a Worksheet into Panes

The *Split* command divides a worksheet into two or four display panes. Each pane shows the same sheet, but you can arrange each pane to show different or the same rows and columns. There is only one active cell, and you may not see it in all the panes. Because it is one worksheet, an edit can be made in any pane.

The panes are split based on the position of the active cell when you give the command. A *splitter bar* is a light gray bar that spans the window, either horizontally, vertically, or both. You can drag a splitter bar to resize the panes.

▶ HOW TO: Split a Worksheet

1. Select the cell for the location of a split.
   - Click a cell in column A (except cell A1) to split the worksheet into two horizontal panes.
   - Click a cell in row 1 (but not cell A1) to split the worksheet into two vertical panes.
   - Click a cell to split the worksheet into four panes.
2. Click the **Split** button [*View* tab, *Window* group].

3. Drag a splitter bar to resize a pane (Figure 1-60).

4. Click the **Split** button [*View* tab, *Window* group] to remove the split.

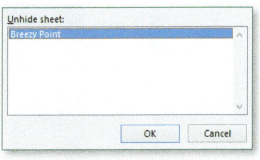

1-60 Split worksheet

> ### ANOTHER WAY
> You can remove a window split by double-clicking the splitter bar.

Hide or Unhide Worksheets

A *hidden worksheet* is a worksheet whose tab is not displayed. It is part of the workbook and can be referenced in calculations. A worksheet might be hidden to prevent accidental changes to it, or it might hold data that should not be easily visible. You can hide a worksheet using the **Format** button [*Home* tab] or by right-clicking the sheet tab. You cannot hide a worksheet if it is the only sheet in the workbook.

> ### MORE INFO
> The command to print an *Entire Workbook* does not print a hidden worksheet.

▶ HOW TO: Hide and Unhide Worksheets

1. Right-click the sheet tab to hide.
   - Press **Ctrl** to select multiple sheets, then right-click any one of the selected tabs.
2. Select **Hide**.
   - The worksheet tab is hidden.
3. Right-click any worksheet tab.
4. Select **Unhide**.
   - The *Unhide sheet* dialog box opens.
5. Select the tab name to unhide (Figure 1-61).
6. Click **OK**.

Unhide sheet:

Breezy Point

OK   Cancel

1-61 *Unhide sheet* **dialog box**

> ### MORE INFO
> The *Hide* command on the *View* tab hides a workbook. A hidden workbook can be used to store programming routines such as macros or external reference data that should be protected from viewing or accidental editing.

Switch Windows Command

When more than one workbook is open, the *Switch Windows* command changes or cycles through open workbooks. You can switch windows from the *Ribbon*, from the Windows taskbar, or with the keyboard shortcut **Ctrl+F6**. When you click the **Switch Windows** button [*View* tab, *Window* group], a menu lists the names of open workbooks so that you can select one. To use the Windows taskbar, point to the Excel icon to see a thumbnail with the file name of each open workbook and click the one to be edited. The keyboard shortcut toggles between the last two viewed workbooks.

When only two workbooks are open, you can view them side by side. The *View Side by Side* button is grayed out when only one workbook is open. For side-by-side viewing, you can scroll the windows together or separately. *Synchronous Scrolling* moves both workbooks in the same direction at the same time. This is especially helpful when worksheets have the same types of data in the same locations. Synchronous scrolling is automatically enabled when you choose the *View Side by Side* command.

> ▶ **HOW TO:** Switch Windows Using the Ribbon
>
> 1. Open two or more workbooks.
> 2. Click the **Switch Windows** button [*View* tab, *Window* group].
>   - The names of open workbooks are listed.
> 3. Click the name of the workbook to view.

> ▶ **MORE INFO**
>
> If three or more workbooks are open when you select the *View Side by Side* command, the *Compare Side by Side* dialog box opens with the names of open workbooks. The one you select is displayed side by side with the active workbook.

View Multiple Worksheets

The *New Window* command opens a new separate window with the same workbook. The new window displays the workbook name in the title bar followed by a colon and number. Combined with the *Arrange All* command, you can position different parts of the workbook to make comparisons or monitor changes as you work. Figure 1-62 shows different sheets in the same workbook.

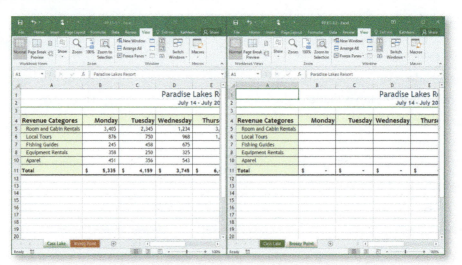

1-62   Two windows for a workbook

> ▶ **MORE INFO**
>
> You can open as many windows as needed and arrange them all.

1. Click the **View** tab and click the **New Window** button [*Window* group].
   - A second window opens for the same workbook and is active.
   - Both windows are maximized.
2. Click the **Arrange All** button [*View* tab, *Window* group].
   - The *Arrange Windows* dialog box opens.
3. Choose an option for arranging the windows.
   - The active window is arranged on the left (vertically tiled) or at the top (horizontally tiled).
   - If several workbooks are open but only the active workbook has multiple windows, choose **Windows of active workbook** so that only those windows are arranged.
4. Click **OK**.
   - The active window is arranged on the left or at the top.
5. Click the **Maximize** button in either title bar.
   - The window is full size.
6. Click the **Close** button (**X**) in the title bar to close the window.
   - The other window is displayed at its tiled size.
7. Click the **Maximize** button.

SLO 1.8

Finalizing a Workbook

Before you distribute your work to others, make sure that it is ready for sharing. A quick spell check can help locate and correct misspelled labels. You can enter document properties or insert headers and footers to help identify your work. You can control how your worksheet prints by setting margins, changing the orientation, or adjusting page breaks.

Check Spelling

The *Spelling* command scans a worksheet and locates words that do not match entries in the main Office dictionary; it also finds duplicate words. The dictionary is shared among all Office applications, and you can add labels to it, such as unusual or technical words. You can spell check the entire worksheet or a selected range.

The *Spelling* dialog box includes options for handling an error as shown in the following table:

Spelling Dialog Box Options

Option	Action
Ignore Once	Skips the occurrence of the label
Ignore All	Skips all occurrences of the same spelling of the label
Add to Dictionary	Adds the label to the default dictionary
Change	Changes the label to the highlighted entry in the *Suggestions* box
Change All	Same as *Change*, but changes the same label throughout the worksheet
Delete	Appears for *Repeated Word*. Click to delete one occurrence of the label.
AutoCorrect	Adds the label to the *AutoCorrect* list
Options	Opens the *Excel Options* dialog box to the *Proofing* tab for changing default settings
Undo Last	Reverses the most recent correction
Cancel	Discontinues spell checking

1. Press **Ctrl+Home** to move to cell **A1**.
   - Start at the beginning of the worksheet.
   - Select a range to limit spell checking to that group of cells.

2. Click the **Review** tab and click the **Spelling** button [*Proofing* group].
   - The first error is located.
   - A list of suggested corrections is displayed.

3. Select the correct spelling in the list.
   - If there is no acceptable suggestion, click the **Not in Dictionary** box and type the correct spelling of the label.

4. Click **Change** to replace the misspelled label (Figure 1-63).

5. Click **Close** when spelling is complete.

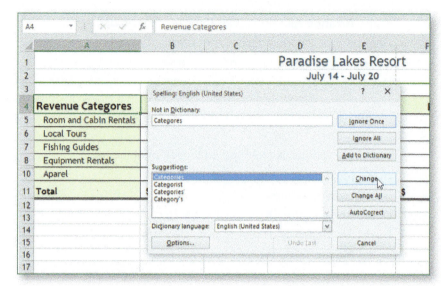

1-63 *Spelling* dialog box

Document Properties

A **document property** or **metadata** is a field of information. Metadata are settings and content including the author name, the date the file was created, the type and size of file, and more. Some properties are uneditable such as dates and file size; these settings are automatically updated. You can edit other document properties, including *Title*, *Author*, and *Subject*. A partial list of properties is available in the *Backstage* view on the right in the *Info* pane.

▶ **HOW TO:** Add Document Properties in Backstage View

1. Click the **File** tab to display the *Backstage* view.

2. Select **Info** if it is not already selected.
   - Property field names are listed.
   - An editable property has an entry box.

3. Click an entry box to enter or edit an item (Figure 1-64).

4. Return to the workbook and save the file.

1-64 Workbook properties

The Properties Dialog Box

You can review all properties in the *Properties* dialog box. The *General*, *Statistics*, and *Contents* tabs list uneditable metadata. The *Summary* tab has properties such as the title, subject, and keywords. Keywords are used in file search commands. On the *Custom* tab, you can choose an additional property and type a default value.

> **HOW TO:** Open the Properties Dialog Box
>
> 1. Display the *Backstage* view and click **Info**.
> 2. Click the **Properties** button.
> 3. Select **Advanced Properties**.
>   - The *Properties* dialog box opens (Figure 1-65).
> 4. Click a tab to view or edit a property.
> 5. Click **OK** to close the dialog box.

1-65 *Properties* dialog box

The Page Setup Dialog Box

The *Page Setup* dialog box offers several command groups for controlling how a worksheet prints. The commands are from the *Sheet Options*, *Scale to Fit*, and *Page Setup* groups on the *Page Layout* tab as well as commands for setting headers and footers. The **Page Setup** launcher [*Page Layout* tab, *Page Setup* group] opens the dialog box.

> **ANOTHER WAY**
>
> Open the *Page Setup* dialog box by clicking the launcher in the *Scale to Fit* or the *Sheet Options* group on the *Page Layout* tab.

Each tab in the *Page Setup* dialog box has a *Print*, a *Print Preview*, and an *Options* button (Figure 1-66). The *Options* button opens the *Printer Properties* dialog box. The following table summarizes commands on each tab in the *Page Setup* dialog box:

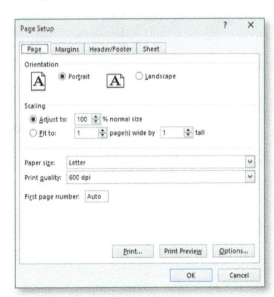

1-66 *Page* tab in the *Page Setup* dialog box

Page Setup Dialog Box Options

Tab	Available Settings
Page	Set the *Orientation* to *Portrait* or *Landscape*. Use *Scaling* to shrink or enlarge the printed worksheet to the paper size. Choose a *Paper size* or set *Print quality*. Define the *First page number*.
Margins	Adjust *Top*, *Bottom*, *Left*, and *Right* worksheet margins. Set *Header* and *Footer* top and bottom margins. *Center on page* horizontally and/or vertically.
Header/Footer	Choose a preset header or footer layout. Create a custom header or footer. Specify first and other page headers. Set header and footers to scale with worksheet and to align with margins.
Sheet	Identify a *Print area* other than the entire worksheet. Identify *Print titles* to repeat on each page. Print *Gridlines*, *Row and column headings*, *Comments*, and *Error messages*.

> **MORE INFO**
>
> You can make changes to multiple worksheets at the same time from the *Page Setup* dialog box. Select the tabs first to group the worksheets.

> **ANOTHER WAY**
>
> Open the *Page Setup* dialog box by clicking the *Page Setup* link in the *Print* area on the *Backstage* view.

Margins, Page Orientation, and Paper Size

A new Excel workbook uses the following default settings:

- Top and bottom margins: 0.75"
- Left and right margins: 0.7"
- Header and footer margins: 0.3"
- Portrait orientation
- Letter size paper

The *Margins* button [*Page Layout* tab, *Page Setup* group] lists *Normal*, *Wide*, and *Narrow* for margin settings as well as *Custom Margins*. When you select **Custom Margins**, the *Page Setup* dialog box opens to the *Margins* tab. Here you can set any value for any margin area, including the header and the footer. You can also center the page horizontally or vertically from this tab.

The *Orientation* button [*Page Setup* group, *Page Layout* tab] has two choices, *Portrait* or *Landscape*. A portrait page is taller than it is wide. A landscape page is wider than it is tall. The *Size* button lists paper sizes, but your printer must be able to accommodate the size.

You can modify settings for one worksheet or for several worksheets at a time. To format multiple worksheets, you need to group the worksheet tabs. Do this by clicking the first tab name, holding down **Shift**, and clicking the last tab name to select all sheets between those two names. You can also click the first tab name, press **Ctrl**, and click nonadjacent sheet names to create a group.

HOW TO: Set Margins, Page Orientation, and Paper Size

1. Click the **Margins** button [*Page Layout* tab, *Page Setup* group].
2. Select **Custom Margins** to open the *Page Setup* dialog box (Figure 1-67).
   - The dialog box opens to the *Margins* tab.
3. Type each margin setting as desired.
   - You can use the spinner buttons to change the margin value.
4. Select the **Horizontally** box in the *Center on page* area.
   - This command centers the data between the left and right margins.
   - You can also vertically center the data on the page.
5. Click the **Page** tab in the *Page Layout* dialog box.
6. Select the radio button for **Portrait** or **Landscape**.
7. Click the **Paper size** arrow and select a paper size.
   - The default paper size is 8½ × 11", which is called *Letter*.
8. Click **OK** to close the dialog box.

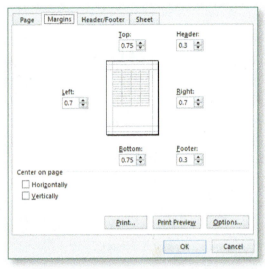

1-67 *Margins* tab in the *Page Setup* dialog box

Headers and Footers

A **header** is information that prints at the top of each page. A **footer** is data that prints at the bottom of each page. You can use a header or a footer to display identifying information such as a company name or logo, page numbers, the date, or the file name.

Each header or footer has left, middle, and right sections. Information in the left section is left aligned, data in the middle section is centered, and material in the right section is right aligned. You can select a predefined header and footer, or you can create your own.

Headers and footers are not visible in *Normal* view, but you can see them in *Page Layout* view or *Print Preview*. Headers and footers are inserted and edited in *Page Layout* view at the top or bottom of the worksheet.

> **HOW TO:** Insert a Header and Footer Using the Ribbon

1. Select the worksheet.
   - You can select more than one worksheet to apply the same header or footer.
2. Click the **Insert** tab.
3. Click the **Header & Footer** button [*Text* group].
   - The view changes to *Page Layout* view.
   - Three header sections are visible at the top of the worksheet.
   - The *Header & Footer Tools Design* tab is active.
4. Click a header section.
5. Click an element name in the *Header & Footer Elements* group [*Header & Footer Tools Design* tab].
   - A code is inserted with an ampersand (&) and the element name enclosed in square brackets (Figure 1-68).
   - You can type your own label in a section.
   - You can select and delete codes and text in a section.
6. Click the **Go To Footer** button [*Header & Footer Tools Design* tab, *Navigation* group].
7. Click a footer section.
8. Click an element name in the *Header & Footer Elements* group [*Header & Footer Tools Design* tab].
   - The related code is inserted.
   - You can type your own label in a footer section.
   - You can select and delete codes and text in a section.
9. Click any worksheet cell.
   - The header and footer appear as they will print.
   - The *Header & Footer Tools Design* tab is hidden.
10. Click the **Normal** button in the *Status* bar.
    - The header and footer are not visible in *Normal* view.

1-68 Header section in *Page Layout* view

> **ANOTHER WAY**
>
> To insert a built-in header or footer, click the **Header or Footer** button [*Header & Footer Tools Design* tab, *Header & Footer* group] and make a selection.

> **MORE INFO**
>
> In a typed header or footer label such as "Research & Development," type two ampersands in the section like this: *Research && Development*. This distinguishes the required ampersand from the one used in an element code such as &[Date].

You can also use the *Page Setup* dialog box to insert a header or a footer. There is a *Header & Footer* tab which includes the preset headers and footers as well as a *Custom Header* or *Custom Footer* option.

▶ HOW TO: Insert Headers or Footers on Multiple Sheets

1. Select a single or multiple worksheet tabs.
   - Click the first worksheet tab for the group, press **Shift**, and click the last tab.
   - Click a worksheet tab, press **Ctrl**, and click a nonadjacent tab.
   - Right-click any tab and click **Select All Sheets**.
2. Click the **Page Setup** launcher [*Page Layout* tab, *Page Setup* group].
   - The *Page Setup* dialog box opens.
3. Click the **Header/Footer** tab.
4. Click the arrow for the *Header* or the *Footer* text box (Figure 1-69).
   - A list of built-in header or footer layouts opens.
   - Choose **(none)** to remove a header or footer.
5. Choose a predefined header or footer.
   - The header or footer is displayed in the preview area.
6. Click **Custom Header** or **Custom Footer** to open the *Header* or *Footer* dialog box (Figure 1-70).
7. Click a section.
8. Click a button to insert an element.
   - Point to a button to see its *ScreenTip*.
   - The text or code appears in the section.
9. Click **OK** to close the *Header* or *Footer* dialog box.
   - The custom header or footer is displayed in the preview area.
10. Click **OK** to close the *Page Setup* dialog box.
11. Right-click a sheet tab and choose **Ungroup Sheets**.

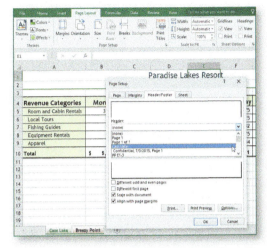

1-69 Select a built-in header or footer in the *Page Setup* dialog box

1-70 *Footer* dialog box

You can remove a header or footer in *Page Layout* view or from the *Page Setup* dialog box. To remove headers and footers from multiple worksheets, select the sheet tabs so that they are grouped. In *Page Layout* view, click the header or footer section and delete labels and codes. From the *Page Setup* dialog box, you can simply select **(none)** from the *Header* or *Footer* drop-down list.

▶ HOW TO: Remove Headers and Footers

1. Select the worksheet(s).
2. Click the **Page Setup** launcher [*Page Layout* tab, *Page Setup* group].
3. Click the **Header/Footer** tab.
4. Click the **Header** or **Footer** drop-down list and select **(none)**.
5. Click **OK** to close the *Page Setup* dialog box.
6. Ungroup sheets if needed.

Page Breaks

A *page break* is a printer code that starts a new page. When worksheet data spans more than one printed page, automatic page breaks are inserted based on the paper size, the margins, and scaling. Automatic page breaks readjust as you add or delete data. You can insert manual page breaks, too. Manual page breaks do not adjust as you make edits.

In *Page Break Preview*, an automatic page break displays as a dotted or dashed blue line. A manual page break appears as a solid, blue line.

▶ HOW TO: Insert a Page Break

1. Select the cell for the location of a page break.
   - Select a cell in column A below the row where you want to start a new page.
   - Select a cell in row 1 to the right of the column where you want to start a new page.
   - Select a cell below and to the right of where new pages should start.
2. Click the **Page Layout** tab.
3. Click the **Breaks** button.
4. Select **Insert Page Break** (Figure 1-71).
   - A manual page break is shown as a thin, solid line in the worksheet in *Normal* view.

1-71 Page break inserted after column D

Preview and Move a Page Break

In *Page Break Preview*, you can move an automatic or a manual page break by dragging its blue line. You can see how the data is affected and evaluate the new printed pages. Depending on the amount of data, as you move one page break, another automatic break may be inserted. When you move an automatic page break, it becomes a manual page break.

> ▶ **MORE INFO**
>
> To move a page break in *Normal* view, you must delete the existing break and insert a new one; you cannot drag the line.

▶ HOW TO: Preview and Move a Page Break

1. Click the **Page Break Preview** button in the *Status* bar.
   - You can adjust the zoom size in *Page Break Preview*.
2. Point to the page break (dashed or solid, blue line) to display a two-pointed arrow.
3. Drag the pointer to a new location (Figure 1-72).
   - You cannot drag an automatic page break to the right of its current location.

4. Release the pointer button.

- A manual page break appears as a solid, blue line.
- Another automatic page break may be inserted if the data requires it.

5. Click the **Normal** button in the *Status* bar.

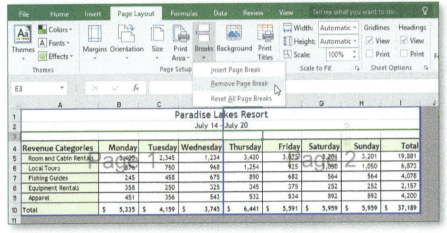

1-72 Drag a page break line to a new position

Remove a Manual Page Break

You can remove a manual page break in *Normal* view or *Page Break Preview*. Click a cell immediately to the right of or below the break and then click the **Remove Page Break** button [*Page Layout* tab, *Page Setup* group]. When you delete a manual page break, Excel may insert a new automatic page break.

> **MORE INFO**
>
> An automatic page break can be "deleted" by inserting a manual page break before it.

▶ **HOW TO:** Remove a Manual Page Break

1. Click the **Page Break Preview** button in the *Status* bar.

2. Click a cell immediately to the right of or below the page break to be removed.

3. Click the **Breaks** button [*Page Layout* tab, *Page Setup* group].

- You can select **Reset All Page Breaks** to remove all manual page breaks.

4. Click **Remove Page Break** (Figure 1-73).

- An automatic page break is inserted if required.

1-73 Remove a manual page break

> **ANOTHER WAY**
>
> In *Page Break Preview*, you can drag a manual page break off the page to the right. Excel will insert an automatic page break if required by the margins and other settings.

Customize Print Settings

You can print the entire workbook, the current worksheet, or a selected cell range by making a choice in the *Settings* area in the *Backstage view* for the *Print* command. The *Sheet Options* and *Page Setup* groups on the *Page Layout* command tab include additional options for repeating titles, displaying a background image, and printing gridlines, column letters, and row numbers.

Gridlines, the vertical and horizontal lines that form the columns and rows, are a visual guide to your working on the sheet. Row and column headings serve a similar purpose—to help you navigate in a worksheet. By default, the gridlines and headings do not print but you can print them from an option on the *Page Layout* tab.

A **print title** is a row or column of data that is repeated on each printed page. For example, you can print main labels from rows 1:3 and from column A on each printed page of a 20-page worksheet.

 HOW TO: Print Gridlines, Print Titles, and Column and Row Headings

1. Click the **Page Layout** tab.

2. Select the **Print** box under *Gridlines* in the *Sheet Options* group.

3. Select the **Print** box under *Headings* in the *Sheet Options* group.

4. Click the **Print Titles** button [*Page Layout* tab, *Page Setup* group].
   - The *Page Setup* dialog box opens to the *Sheet* tab.

5. Select the **Rows to repeat at top** box.

6. Drag to select the heading(s) for the row(s) to print on each page.
   - The dialog box collapses as you select row headings.
   - The dialog box expands when you release the pointer button.
   - You can type a reference such as $1:$3 to repeat data in the first three rows.

7. Select the **Columns to repeat at left** box (Figure 1-74).

8. Drag to select the heading(s) for the column(s) to print on each page.
   - The dialog box collapses as you select column headings.
   - You can type a reference such as $A:$A to repeat data in column A.

9. Click **OK**.

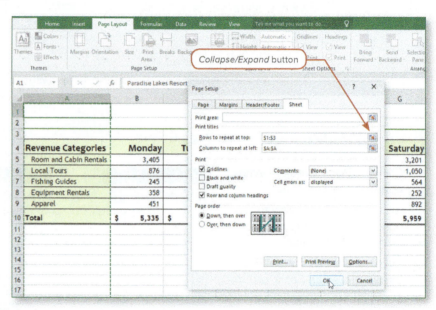

1-74 *Sheet* tab in the *Page Setup* dialog box

ANOTHER WAY

You can print *Gridlines* and *Row and column headings* from an option in the *Page Setup* dialog box.

Scale to Fit

The **Scale to Fit** command enlarges or shrinks printed data to fit a specific number of pages or a particular paper size. You can scale printed data as a percentage of normal size or by setting the number of pages. Normal size is how the data would print in the current font size and is shown as *Automatic* in the *Scale to Fit* group [*Page Layout* tab].

 HOW TO: Scale to Fit

1. Click the **Page Layout** tab.

2. Click the **Width** drop-down list [*Scale to Fit* group] and select an option.

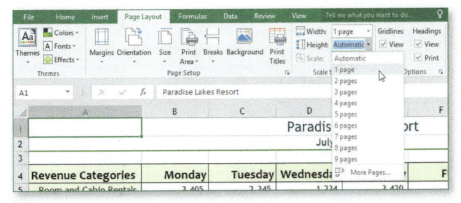

1-75 *Scale to Fit* options

3. Click the **Height** drop-down list [*Scale to Fit* group] and select an option (Figure 1-75).

   • You can click the **Scale** button spinner arrows to set a percentage of the normal size.

▶ **ANOTHER WAY**

Click the **Scale to Fit** launcher [*Page Layout* tab, *Scale to Fit* group] to open the *Page Setup* dialog box and set options in the *Scaling* area.

Print Area

A **print area** is the data that prints when you give a *Print* command. The default is the entire worksheet, but you can identify any range of cells as a print area. You can add adjacent data to a print area, and you can clear a print area to return to the default.

▶ **HOW TO: Set and Clear a Print Area**

1. Select the cells to print.

   • You can select nonadjacent ranges but they print on separate pages.

2. Click the **Page Layout** tab.

3. Click the **Print Area** button [*Page Setup* group] (Figure 1-76).

4. Select **Set Print Area**.

   • You can see the print area in the *Backstage view* for the *Print* command and in *Page Break Preview*.
   • A print area is saved with the workbook.

5. Click the **Print Area** button [*Page Layout* tab, *Page Setup* group].

6. Select **Clear Print Area**.

   • All print areas are cleared.
   • The default print area of the entire sheet is reset.

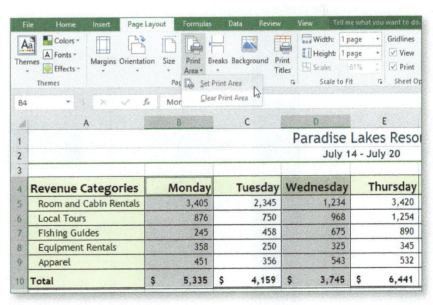

1-76 **Nonadjacent print areas**

Print a Worksheet or Workbook

The *Print* command in the *Backstage view* provides a preview so that you can make changes before actual printing. The *Show Margins* button toggles the display of margin and column markers which can be dragged to new settings. The *Zoom to Page* button toggles between two zoom settings for the preview.

▶ **HOW TO:** Preview and Print a Worksheet

1. Click the **File** tab and select **Print**.
   - You can also click **Print Preview** in the *Page Setup* dialog box to open the *Print* command in the *Backstage* view.
2. Click **Show Margins** to display margin and column markers (Figure 1-77).
3. Click **Zoom to Page** to toggle between zoom sizes.
4. Set the number of *Copies*.
   - Type a number or use the spinner arrows.
5. Click the **Printer** arrow.
   - Choose the printer name.
   - Make sure the printer is ready.

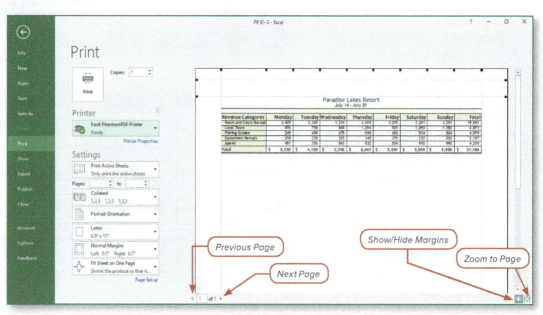

1-77 *Backstage* view for *Print*

6. Click the **Settings** arrow.
   - The active sheets are the default.
   - Cell ranges must be selected in order to print a selection.
   - The workbook setting prints all worksheets.
7. Specify which pages to print.
   - The default is all pages of the worksheet.
   - Click the **Next Page** or **Previous Page** arrow to navigate through multiple pages.
8. Verify orientation, paper size, margin settings, and scaling.
   - You can make changes from the *Page Setup* dialog box by clicking the **Page Setup** link at the bottom of the *Settings* area.
9. Click **Print**.
   - The data is sent to the printer.
   - The *Backstage view* closes.

> **ANOTHER WAY**
> Press **Ctrl+P** to open the *Print* command in the *Backstage view*.

PAUSE & PRACTICE: EXCEL 1-4

In this project, you open *[your initials] PP E1-3.xlsx* to unhide a row, add data, and hide a sheet. You also spell check a worksheet, set document properties, and finalize the workbook for distribution.

File Needed: *[your initials] PP E1-3.xlsx*
Completed Project File Name: *[your initials] PP E1-4.xlsx*

1. Open *[your initials] PP E1-3* completed in *Pause & Practice 1-3*.

2. Save the workbook as [your initials] PP E1-4.

3. Select the **Cass Lake** worksheet.

4. Unhide row 9.
   a. Click and drag to select row headings **8:10**.
   b. Right-click either of the selected row headings.
   c. Choose **Unhide** from the context menu.

5. Enter the following data in cells **B9:H9**. The data is formatted the same as row 8.

	B	C	D	E	F	G	H
Food & Beverage	254	209	198	402	519	677	399

6. Hide a worksheet.
   a. Right-click the **Breezy Point** tab.
   b. Choose **Hide**.

7. Check spelling.
   a. Press **Ctrl+Home**.
   b. Click the **Spelling** button [*Review* tab, *Proofing* group].
   c. Click **Change** to accept the suggested correction for "Categores."
   d. Click **Change** to accept the suggested correction for "Aparel."
   e. Click **OK** when spell checking is finished.
   f. Press **Ctrl+Home**.

8. Enter document properties.
   a. Click the **File** tab to display the *Backstage* view.
   b. Click the **Show All Properties** link at the bottom of the properties list.
   c. Click the *Title* text box and type PP Excel 1-4.
   d. Click the *Subject* text box and type Weekly Revenue.
   e. In the *Status* text box, type Draft (Figure 1-78).

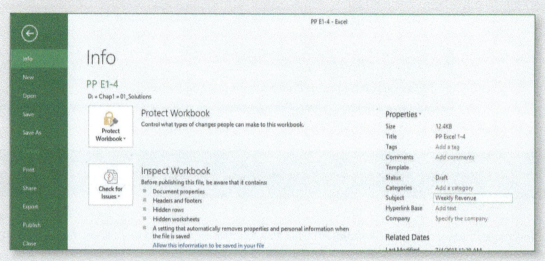

1-78 Properties in *Backstage* view

   f. Click the **Show Fewer Properties** link at the bottom of the properties list.
   g. Return to the worksheet.

9. Change page setup options.
   a. Click the **Page Layout** tab.
   b. Click the **Orientation** button and select **Landscape**.
   c. Click the **Page Setup** launcher to open the *Page Setup* dialog box.
   d. On the **Page** tab, click the **Fit to** button.
   e. Set **1** page wide and **1** page tall.
   f. Click the **Margins** tab.
   g. Select the **Horizontally** box in the *Center on page* area.
   h. Do not close the dialog box.

10. Add a header and footer.
   a. Click the **Header/Footer** tab.
   b. Click the **Header** drop-down list and select *[your initials] PP E1-4*. The file name displays in the preview center section.
   c. Click the **Footer** drop-down list and select **Cass Lake** to insert the sheet name in the center section of the footer.
   d. Click **OK** to close the *Page Setup* dialog box.

11. Preview and print the worksheet.
    a. Click the **File** tab and select **Print**. *Print Preview* displays how the worksheet will print.
    b. Select the printer.
    c. Click **Print** to print the worksheet.

12. Save and close the workbook (Figure 1-79).

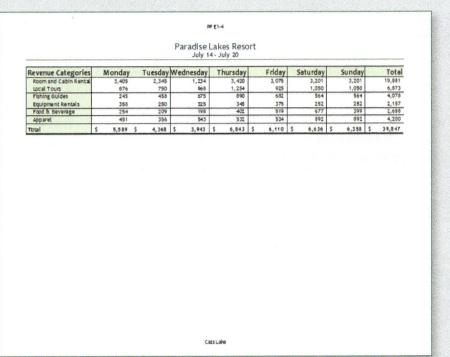

PP E1-4

Paradise Lakes Resort
July 14 - July 20

Revenue Categories	Monday	Tuesday	Wednesday	Thursday	Friday	Saturday	Sunday	Total
Room and Cabin Rental	3,405	2,345	1,234	3,420	3,075	3,201	3,201	19,881
Local Tours	676	750	968	1,254	925	1,050	1,050	6,673
Fishing Guides	245	458	675	890	682	564	564	4,078
Equipment Rentals	358	250	325	346	375	252	252	2,157
Food & Beverage	254	209	198	402	519	677	399	2,658
Apparel	451	356	543	532	534	892	892	4,200
Total	$ 5,589	$ 4,368	$ 3,943	$ 6,843	$ 6,110	$ 6,636	$ 6,358	$ 39,847

Cass Lake

1-79 PP E1-4 completed

Chapter Summary

1.1 Create, save, and open an Excel workbook (p. E1-3).

- A new Excel workbook has one worksheet and is named *BookN*, with numbers assigned in order throughout a work session.
- Save a workbook with a descriptive name that identifies the contents and purpose.
- Create a new workbook from the *Excel Start* page or from the *New* command on the *File* tab.
- A workbook that is opened or copied from an online source will open in **Protected View**.
- An Excel workbook is an *.xlsx* file, but it can be saved in other formats for easy sharing of data.

1.2 Enter and edit labels and values in a worksheet (p. E1-6).

- Data is entered in a cell which is the intersection of a column and a row. Each cell has an address or reference.
- Data is recognized as a label or a value. Labels are not used in calculations. A label is left-aligned in the cell; a value is right-aligned.
- A **formula** is a calculation that displays a value as its result in the worksheet.
- Press **F2 (FN+F2)** or double-click a cell to start *Edit* mode. After making the change, press **Enter** to complete the edit.
- Horizontal alignment options for cell data include *Align Left*, *Center*, and *Align Right*. Data can also be indented from the cell border. Vertical alignment choices are *Top Align*, *Middle Align*, and *Bottom Align*.
- A group or selection of cells is a **range**. You can use the pointer and keyboard shortcuts to select a range.
- Use the **Fill Handle** to create a series that follows a pattern. The *Fill Handle* copies data when there is no pattern.
- **AutoComplete** supplies a suggestion for a column entry that begins with the same character as a label already in the column.
- Cut, copy, and paste commands include drag and drop as well as regular Windows **Cut**, **Copy**, and **Paste** buttons on the *Home* tab, context menus, and keyboard shortcuts.

1.3 Use the *SUM* function to build a simple formula (p. E1-19).

- A **function** is a built-in formula. Results appear in the worksheet cell, but the function is displayed in the *Formula* bar.
- The *AutoSum* button [*Home* tab, *Editing* group] inserts the *SUM* function in a cell to add the values in a selected range.
- Each function has **syntax** which is its required parts in the required order. A function begins with an equals sign (=), followed by the name of the function. After the name, the function **argument** is shown in parentheses.
- You can change a function argument by entering new cell references in the *Formula* bar or by dragging the range border in the worksheet.
- When you copy a function, Excel adjusts cell references to match their locations in the worksheet.

1.4 Format a worksheet with font attributes, borders, fill, cell styles, and themes (p. E1-21).

- Apply font attributes from the *Font* group on the *Ribbon* or from the *Format Cells* dialog box.
- Font attributes include the **font** name or face, the **font size**, font styles such as bold, italic, and underline, and the **font color**.
- Number formats include decimals, commas, currency symbols, and percent signs. They also determine how negative values appear in the worksheet.
- Number formats are applied from the *Ribbon* or the *Format Cells* dialog box.
- The **Format Painter** copies formatting from one cell to another.
- Add borders or fill color to cells for easy identification, clarification, and emphasis.
- A **cell style** is a preset collection of font, font size, alignment, color, borders, and fill color and is based on the theme.
- A **theme** is a collection of fonts, colors, and special effects for a workbook.
- You can use themes and cell styles to quickly format a worksheet with consistent, professionally designed elements.

1.5 Modify columns and rows in a worksheet (p. E1-31).

- The default column width and row height depend on the font size defined by the workbook theme.
- You can change the width of a column or the height of a row by dragging the border between the headings.
- *AutoFit* a column or row by double-clicking the border between the headings.
- The **Format** button [*Home* tab, *Cells* group] includes commands to change **row height** and **column width**.
- Insert or delete a column or a row by right-clicking the column or row heading and choosing *Insert* or *Delete*.
- The *Insert* and *Delete* buttons include commands for inserting and deleting rows and columns.
- Display a label on multiple lines in a cell using the **Wrap Text** command to split the label.
- The **Merge & Center** command combines two or more cells into one and centers the data within that new cell.
- The **Center Across Selection** command can be used to center multiple rows of data across the same range.
- One or multiple rows or columns can be hidden, but they are still available for use in a formula.

1.6 Insert, delete, and move worksheets in a workbook (p. E1-37).

- The number of worksheets in a workbook is limited only by the amount of computer memory.
- You can click the *New Sheet* button next to the worksheet tabs to insert a new sheet in a workbook.
- The *Insert* and *Delete* buttons include options to insert and delete worksheets.
- You can double-click a worksheet tab, type a name, and press **Enter** to rename a sheet.
- You can apply a **tab color** to distinguish a particular sheet by changing the background color.

- Move a worksheet tab to another location in the list of tabs by dragging it to that location.
- You can create an exact duplicate of a worksheet in the same or another workbook with the **Move or Copy** command or the context menu.

1.7 Modify the appearance of a workbook by adjusting zoom size, changing views, and freezing panes (p. E1-42).

- A workbook can be viewed in three ways: **Normal**, **Page Layout**, and **Page Break Preview**.
- Switch views from the *Status* bar buttons or from the *Workbook Views* group on the *View* tab.
- Adjust the zoom size to display more or less data on screen. Zoom controls are available in the *Status* bar and from the *View* tab.
- Use the **Freeze Panes** command to lock selected rows or columns on screen so that you can scroll data while keeping important data in view.
- The **Split** command divides the screen into multiple sections so that you can see different areas of a large worksheet at once.
- You can hide a worksheet from view and unintended editing.
- When multiple workbooks are open, the **Switch Windows** command lists the open workbook names.
- You can switch among open workbooks from the Windows taskbar.
- The **New Window** command displays the same workbook in a second window. Use this command with the **Arrange All** command to view different areas or sheets of a workbook at the same time.

1.8 Review and prepare a workbook for final distribution by spell checking, setting properties, and adjusting page setup options (p. E1-47).

- Spell checking a workbook follows the same steps as other Office applications.
- A **document property** is **metadata** stored with the file.

- Some properties are supplied by Excel and cannot be edited. Other document properties are added or edited by the user.
- Several properties are visible and can be edited in the *Info* area in the *Backstage* view.
- You can open the *Properties* dialog box to build or edit properties.
- The *Page Layout* tab includes commands to set page margins and orientation.
- **Headers** and **footers** can be added to print at the top and bottom of each page.
- When a worksheet fills more than one printed page, Excel inserts automatic page breaks.
- You can insert manual **page breaks** to change where a new page starts.
- From commands on the *Page Layout* tab or in the *Page Setup* dialog box, you can print **gridlines** as well as row and column headings.

- You can make additional changes to the printed worksheet from the **Print** area in the *Backstage* view. These include choosing to print only a selection or the entire workbook.

Check for Understanding

The SIMbook for this text (within your SIMnet account) provides the following resources for concept review:

- Multiple choice questions
- Matching exercises
- Short answer questions

Guided Project 1-1

Life's Animal Shelter (LAS) maintains data in an Excel workbook that tracks daily expenses for categories that include supplies, animal food, and wages. You will create a new workbook for the current week, enter and format the data, and prepare the workbook for distribution.
[Student Learning Outcomes 1.1, 1.2, 1.3, 1.4, 1.5, 1.6, 1.7, 1.8]

File Needed: None
Completed Project File Name: **[your initials] Excel 1-1.xlsx**

Skills Covered in This Project

- Create and save a workbook.
- Enter labels and values.
- Use the *Fill Handle*.
- Set column widths and row heights.
- Merge and center labels.
- Apply a workbook theme and cell styles.

- Apply font attributes and insert borders.
- Use *SUM* and set number formatting.
- Copy and rename worksheets.
- Set worksheet tab color.
- Change page setup options.
- Use spell check.
- Adjust zoom size and freeze panes.

1. Create and save a workbook.
   a. Click the **File** tab to open the *Backstage* view.
   b. Select **New** and then click **Blank workbook**.
   c. Click the **Save** button on the *Quick Access* toolbar to open the *Save As* dialog box.
   d. Select the folder to save the workbook, or **Browse** to a location on *OneDrive*, your computer, or external media.
   e. Name the workbook [your initials] Excel 1-1 in the *File name* area.
   f. Click **Save**.

2. Enter data with deliberate errors.
   a. In cell **A1**, type Life's Aminal Shelter with the spelling error and press **Enter**.
   b. In cell **A2**, type Setember 1 through 7 with the spelling error and press **Enter**.
   c. In cell **A4**, type Expens Categories and press **Enter**.

3. Adjust column width.
   a. Point to the border between the column **A** and column **B** headings to display a two-pointed arrow.
   b. Double-click to *AutoFit* column **A**.

4. Enter labels and values as shown in Figure 1-80.

	A	B	C	D	E	F	G	H
1	Life's Aminal Shelter							
2	Setember 1 through 7							
3								
4	Expens Categories	Monday						
5	Pet nutrition	55.25	47.5	38.55	27.45	42.5	35.25	51.75
6	Veterinary supplies	27.85	32.35	35	25	28.5	38.75	44.85
7	Shelter supplies	78	56.45	65.35	55	70	60.25	45.35
8	Salaries and wages	475						
9	Utilities (prorated)	45						
10								

1-80 Labels and values to be entered with errors in cells A1:A2 and A4

5. Use the *Fill Handle* to fill a series and copy data.
   a. Select cell **B4**.
   b. Click and drag the *Fill* pointer to cell **H4**.
   c. Select cells **B8:B9**. There is one *Fill Handle* shown in cell B9.
   d. Click and drag the *Fill* pointer to cell **H9**. When there is no discernible pattern, the *Fill Handle* copies data.
   e. Point to the border between the column **D** and column **E** headings to display a two-pointed arrow.
   f. Double-click to *AutoFit* column **D**.

6. Merge and center labels.
   a. Select cells **A1:H1** and click the **Merge & Center** button [*Home* tab, *Alignment* group].
   b. Select cells **A2:H2** and click the **Merge & Center** button [*Home* tab, *Alignment* group].
   c. Select cells **B4:H4**.
   d. Click the **Center** button [*Home* tab, *Alignment* group].

7. Choose a workbook theme.
   a. Click the **Themes** button [*Page Layout* tab, *Themes* group].
   b. Choose **Integral** from the gallery.
   c. Click the **Home** tab. All labels and values are set in the **Tw Cen MT** font.

8. Apply cell styles.
   a. Select cell **A1** and click the **Cells Styles** button or the **More** button [*Home* tab, *Styles* group].
   b. Select **Title** in the *Titles and Headings* category. For the *Integral* theme, a title is format in the *Tw Cen MT Condensed* font, 18 points.
   c. Select cell **A2** and click the **Cells Styles** or the **More** button [*Home* tab, *Styles* group].
   d. Select **Heading 2** in the *Titles and Headings* category. The second level heading uses *Tw Cen MT* bold, 13 points. Both styles use a dark blue color.
   e. Select cells **A4:A9**.
   f. Press **Ctrl** and select cells **B4:H4**. Two ranges are selected.
   g. Click the **Cells Styles** or the **More** button [*Home* tab, *Styles* group].
   h. Select **40%, Accent 1** in the *Themed Cell Styles* category.
   i. Click the **Bold** button [*Home* tab, *Font* group].
   j. Select cell **A10**.
   k. Type Total and press **Enter**. The format from the column is automatically applied.

9. Apply font attributes.
   a. Select cells **A4:H10**.
   b. Click the **Font size** drop-down list [*Home* tab, *Font* group] and select **12**.
   c. Change the font size for cell **A2** to **14**.
   d. Select cells **A5:A9**.
   e. Click the **Increase Indent** button [*Home* tab, *Alignment* group] two times.
   f. Select cell **A10** and click the **Align Right** button [*Home* tab, *Alignment* group].

10. Use the *SUM* function and copy a formula.
    a. Select cell **B10**.
    b. Click the **AutoSum** button [*Home* tab, *Editing* group] and press **Enter** to accept the suggested range.
    c. Select cell **B10** and drag the *Fill* pointer to cell **H10**.

11. Apply number formatting.
    a. Select cells **B5:H10**.
    b. Click the **Accounting Number Format** button [*Home* tab, *Number* group]. Column widths are adjusted to accommodate the values.
    c. Click the **Decrease Decimal** button [*Home* tab, *Number* group] two times. Column widths do not adjust.

12. Change row heights.
    a. Click the heading for row **4**.
    b. Press **Ctrl** and click the row **10** heading. Two rows are selected.
    c. Right-click the row **4** heading.
    d. Choose **Row Height** and type 25 as the new height.
    e. Click **OK**.
    f. Click the heading for row **5** and drag down to select rows **5:9**.
    g. Point to the bottom border of the row **9** heading to display the resize arrow.
    h. Drag the pointer down to reach a height of **21.00 (28 pixels)** and release the pointer button (Figure 1-81).

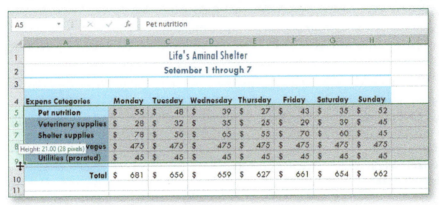

1-81 Change row heights for rows 5:9

13. Insert a row and change column width.
    a. Select cell **A9** and then right-click row heading **9**.
    b. Choose **Insert** from the context menu. The new row is located above the selected row; other rows shift down.
    c. In cell **A9**, type Cages and equipment.
    d. Point to the border between columns **A** and **B** to display the resize arrow.
    e. Drag the pointer to a width of **22.50 (185 pixels)** and release the pointer button.

14. Enter the following data in row **9**. A zero (0) is displayed as a small dash.

	B	C	D	E	F	G	H
Cages and equipment	35	35	25	0	0	35	40

15. Insert borders and change the font size.
    a. Select cells **A4:H11**.
    b. Click the **Borders** button drop-down list and choose **All Borders**.
    c. Select cell **A2** and press **Ctrl+1** to open the *Format Cells* dialog box.
    d. Click the **Border** tab.
    e. Click the blue bottom border in the preview area to remove it.
    f. Click the **Color** drop-down arrow and select **Black, Text 1**.
    g. Click to select the solid, thick line (second column, sixth style) in the *Style* group,
    h. Click the bottom border In the preview area (Figure 1-82).
    i. Click **OK**.
    j. Select cell **A1** and change the font size to **24**.

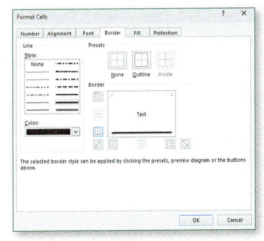

1-82 Create a custom border

16. Rename the sheet and set the tab color.
    a. Double-click the **Sheet1** tab name.
    b. Type Week 1 and press **Enter**.
    c. Click the **Format** button [*Home* tab, *Cells* group].
    d. Select **Tab Color** in the *Organize Sheets* category.
    e. Select **Blue Accent 2, Darker 50%**.

17. Spell check a worksheet.
    a. Press **Ctrl+Home** to go to cell **A1**.
    b. Click the **Spelling** button [*Review* tab, *Proofing* group].
    c. Type Animal in the *Not in Dictionary* box and click **Change**.
    d. Choose "September" in the *Suggestions* list and click **Change**.
    e. Correct "Expens" when the error is located.
    f. Click **OK**.
    g. Press **Ctrl+Home**.

18. Change page setup options.
    a. Click the **Page Layout** tab and click the **Page Setup** launcher.
    b. On the **Page** tab, select the **Landscape** radio button.
    c. Click the **Margins** tab.
    d. Select the **Horizontally** box under *Center on page*.
    e. Click the **Header/Footer** tab.
    f. Click the **Header** drop-down list and choose *[your initials] Excel 1-1* to insert the file name in the center section.
    g. Click **OK**.
    h. Press **Ctrl+F2** to preview the worksheet.
    i. Press **Esc** to close the *Backstage* view.

19. Copy and edit a worksheet.
    a. Right-click the **Week 1** tab name.
    b. Select **Move or Copy** from the menu.
    c. Select **(move to end)** in the *Before sheet* list.
    d. Select the **Create a copy** box and click **OK**.
    e. On the copied worksheet, select cells **B5:H10** and delete the data.
    f. Double-click cell **A2** to start *Edit* mode.
    g. Change "September 1 through 7" to September 8 through 14.
    h. Double-click the **Week 1 (2)** tab name.
    i. Type Week 2 and press **Enter**.
    j. Right-click the **Week 2** tab name and choose **Tab Color**.
    k. Select **Green Accent 4, Darker 50%**.

20. Click the **Week 1** sheet tab.

21. Click the **File** tab and select **Print** to preview the **Week 1** worksheet.

22. Change the zoom size and freeze panes.
    a. Select cell **B5**.
    b. Click the **Zoom In** button in the *Status* bar five times.
    c. Click the **Freeze Panes** button [*View* tab, *Window* group].
    d. Choose **Freeze Panes**.
    e. Scroll the window on the right so that column **F** is immediately to the right of column **A** (Figure 1-83).
    f. Select cell **A1**.

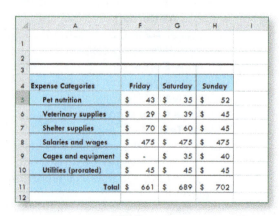

1-83 Panes frozen and positioned

23. Save and close the workbook (Figure 1-84).

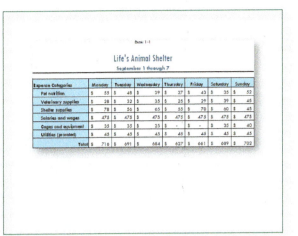

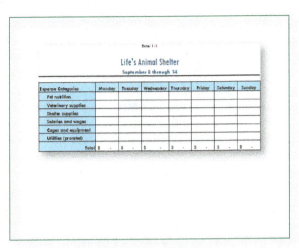

Guided Project 1-2

In this project, you edit a worksheet for Eller Software Services representative Adam White. He maintains client data with sales revenue and specific products or services. You plan to format the data, complete the calculation, and prepare the worksheet for sharing with management.
[Student Learning Outcomes 1.1, 1.2, 1.3, 1.4, 1.5, 1.6, 1.8]

File Needed: ***EllerSoftwareServices-01.xlsx*** [*Student data files are available in the Library of your SIMnet account.*]
Completed Project File Name: ***[your initials] Excel 1-2*.xlsx**

Skills Covered in This Project

- Open and save a workbook.
- Choose a workbook theme.
- Enter and copy labels using the *Fill Handle*.
- Set font attributes and number formats.
- Use *SUM*.

- Center labels across a selection.
- Change page orientation and scale a worksheet for printing.
- Design borders.
- Insert a row and hide a column.
- Rename and apply color to sheet tabs.
- Adjust page setup options.

1. Open the workbook **EllerSoftwareServices-01.xlsx** from your student data files. If the workbook has opened in *Protected View*, click **Enable Editing** in the security bar.

2. Save the workbook with a new file name.
   a. Press **F12** (**FN+F12**) to open the *Save As* dialog box.
   b. Navigate to the folder where your files are stored.
   c. Rename the file [your initials] Excel 1-2.
   d. Click **Save**.

3. Choose a workbook theme.
   a. Click the **Themes** button [*Page Layout* tab, *Themes* group].
   b. Choose **Ion** from the gallery. A different font, *Century Gothic*, is used for all data in the worksheet.
   c. Double-click the border between the column **C** and column **D** headings to *AutoFit* column **C**.

4. Enter and copy data.
   a. Select cell **F5**, type **MN**, and press **Enter**.
   b. Select cell **F5** and point to the *Fill Handle*.
   c. Click and drag the *Fill* pointer to cell **E13**.

5. Format data.
   a. Select cells **D5:D13**.
   b. Press **Ctrl+1** to open the *Format Cells* dialog box.
   c. Click the **Number** tab.
   d. In the *Category* list, click **Special**.
   e. Select **Phone Number** in the *Type* list and click **OK** (Figure 1-85).
   f. Select cells **I6:I13**.
   g. Click the **Comma Style** button [*Home* tab, *Number* group].
   h. Select cell **I5**.
   i. Click the **Accounting Number Format** button [*Home* tab, *Number* group]. A series of # symbols means the column is not wide enough to display the data (Figure 1-86).

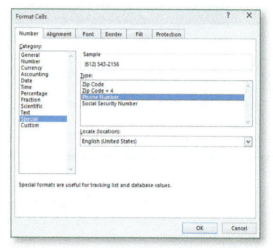

1-85   Special number format

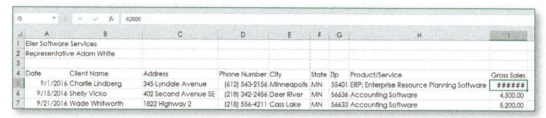

1-86   Column I is not wide enough

   j. Double-click the border between the column **I** and column **J** headings to *AutoFit* column **I**.

6. Enter and edit the reference range for the *SUM* function.
   a. Click cell **A15**, type Total, and press **Enter**.
   b. Select cell **I15**.
   c. Click the **AutoSum** button [*Home* tab, *Editing* group]. The suggested range includes an empty row.
   d. Click cell **I5** and drag to select cells **I5:I13**. Your selected range is highlighted and shown in the *Formula* bar and in the cell (Figure 1-87).
   e. Press **Enter** to accept the range. The *Accounting Number* format is applied.

7. Center labels across a selection.
   a. Select cells **A1:I2** and click the **Alignment** launcher [*Home* tab, *Alignment* group].
   b. Click the **Horizontal** arrow and select **Center Across Selection**.
   c. Click **OK**.

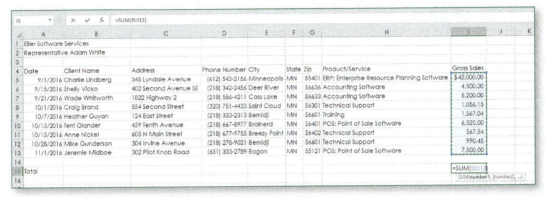

1-87 New range selected for SUM

8. Apply font attributes and cell styles.
   a. Select cell **A1**, click the **Font Size** drop-down list [*Home* tab, *Font* group], and select **24**.
   b. Select cell **A2** and change the font size to **18**.
   c. Select cells **A4:A15**, press **Ctrl**, and then select cells **B4:I4**.
   d. Click the **Cell Styles** button or the **More** button and select **40% - Accent3** in the *Themed Cell Styles* category.
   e. While the cells are selected, click the **Bold** button [*Home* tab, *Font* group].
   f. Select cell **I15** and apply the **Total** cell style.
   g. Select cells **A4:I4**.
   h. Click the **Font Size** drop-down list [*Home* tab, *Font* group] and select **12**.
   i. Click the **Center** button [*Home* tab, *Alignment* group].
   j. *AutoFit* column **D**.
   k. Select cell **A15** and click the **Align Right** button [*Home* tab, *Alignment* group].

9. Edit a label.
   a. Double-click cell **H9** to start *Edit* mode.
   b. Press **Home** to position the insertion point before the word "Training".
   c. Type ERP and press **Spacebar**.
   d. Press **Enter**.

10. Insert a row.
    a. Right-click row heading **10**.
    b. Choose **Insert** from the context menu.
    c. In cell **A10**, type 10/10/16 and press **Tab**.
    d. Complete the data as shown here. For the phone number, do not type any spaces; it is automatically formatted when you press **Tab** to move to the next cell.

    B10   Hillary Marschke
    C10   245 West Third Avenue
    D10   3203555443 (press **Tab**)
    E10   sa (press **Tab**)
    F10   m (press **Tab**)
    G10   56301
    H10   t (press **Tab**)
    I10   750

11. Apply borders.
    a. Select cells **A4:I14**.
    b. Click the **Border** drop-down arrow [*Home* tab, *Font* group] and choose **All Borders**.

c. Select cells **A16:I16**.

d. Press **Ctrl+1** to open the *Format Cells* dialog box and click the **Border** tab.

e. Select the solid, single line (first column, sixth option) in the *Style* list.

f. Click the top border In the *Border* preview area.

g. Select the solid, double line (second column, seventh option) in the *Style* list.

h. Click the bottom border In the *Border* preview area (Figure 1-88).

i. Click **OK**.

j. Select cells **A15:I16**.

k. Click the **Border** arrow [*Home* tab, *Font* group] and choose **Left Border**.

l. Click the **Border** arrow [*Home* tab, *Font* group] and choose **Right Border**.

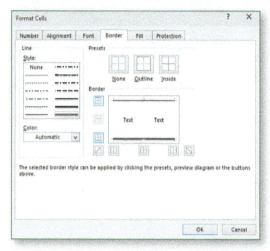

1-88 **Design a double border**

12. Hide a column.

a. Right-click the column **F** heading.

b. Select **Hide**.

c. Press **Ctrl+Home**.

13. Rename and color a sheet tab.

a. Double-click the **Sheet1** tab.

b. Type MN Clients and press **Enter**.

c. Right-click the **MN Clients** tab.

d. Select **Tab Color** and choose **Gold, Accent 3**.

14. Change page setup options.

a. Click the **Page Layout** tab.

b. Click the **Orientation** button [*Page Setup* group] and choose **Landscape**.

c. In the *Scale to Fit* group, click the **Width** arrow and choose **1 page**.

d. Click the **Insert** tab.

e. Click the **Header & Footer** button In the *Text* group. The view switches to *Page Layout* with the insertion point in the center header section. The *Header & Footer Tools Design* toolbar displays.

f. Click the **Go to Footer** button in the *Navigation* group.

g. Click the **Footer** button in the *Header & Footer* group (Figure 1-89).

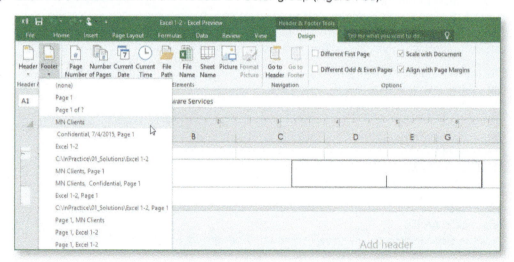

1-89 **Select a built-in footer**

h. Choose **MN Clients** to insert the sheet name in the footer. The *Header & Footer Tools Design* toolbar closes.

i. Click the **Normal** button in the *Status* bar. The footer is not visible in this view.

15. Preview and print the worksheet.
    a. Select **Print** from the *File* tab.
    b. Review the worksheet layout.
    c. Click **Print** or press **Esc** to return to the workbook.

16. Save and close the workbook (Figure 1-90).

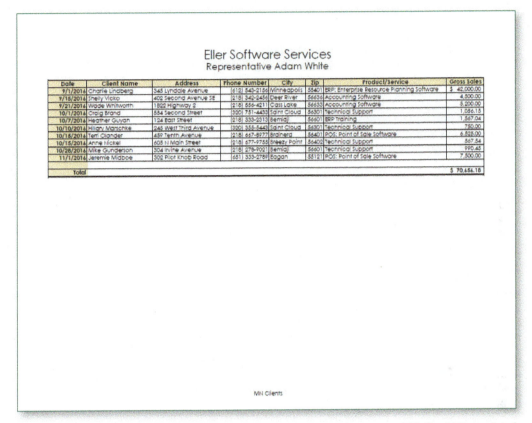

Eller Software Services
Representative Adam White

Date	Client Name	Address	Phone Number	City	Zip	Product/Service	Gross Sales
9/1/2016	Charlie Lindberg	345 Lyndale Avenue	(612) 543-2156	Minneapolis	55401	ERP: Enterprise Resource Planning Software	$ 42,000.00
9/15/2016	Shelly Vicko	402 Second Avenue SE	(218) 342-2456	Deer River	56636	Accounting Software	4,500.00
9/21/2016	Wade Whitworth	1822 Highway 2	(218) 556-4211	Cass Lake	56633	Accounting Software	5,200.00
10/1/2016	Craig Brand	554 Second Street	(320) 751-4433	Saint Cloud	56301	Technical Support	1,056.15
10/7/2016	Heather Guyan	124 East Street	(218) 333-2313	Bemidji	56601	ERP Training	1,567.04
10/10/2016	Hilary Marschke	245 West Third Avenue	(320) 355-5443	Saint Cloud	56301	Technical Support	750.00
10/15/2016	Terri Olander	459 Tenth Avenue	(218) 667-8977	Brainerd	56401	POS: Point of Sale Software	6,525.00
10/15/2016	Anne Nickel	605 N Main Street	(218) 677-9755	Breezy Point	56402	Technical Support	567.54
10/28/2016	Mike Gunderson	304 Irvine Avenue	(218) 278-9021	Bemidji	56601	Technical Support	990.45
11/1/2016	Jeremie Midboe	302 Pilot Knob Road	(651) 333-2789	Eagan	55121	POS: Point of Sale Software	7,500.00
Total							$ 70,656.18

MN Clients

1-90 Excel 1-2 completed

Guided Project 1-3

In this project, you edit a worksheet for Wear-Ever Shoes that tracks their product inventory. You change the zoom size, reset the panes, and format data. You copy an existing formula to calculate the value of the current stock and insert a column for new data. After adjusting print options, you set a print area for a specific product line.

[Student Learning Outcomes 1.1, 1.2, 1.4, 1.5, 1.6, 1.7, 1.8]

File Needed: ***WearEverShoes-01.xlsx*** [*Student data files are available in the Library of your SIMnet account.*]
Completed Project File Name: *[your initials] Excel 1-3.xlsx*

Skills Covered in This Project

- Open and save a workbook.
- Change zoom size and remove a split.
- Freeze panes.
- Format labels and values.
- Use the *Fill Handle* to copy a formula and fill a series.
- Check spelling.
- Apply a workbook theme, cell styles, and font attributes.
- Merge and center labels.
- Insert a column and adjust column widths and row heights.
- Adjust alignment, indents, and borders.
- Rename the sheet tab.
- Use *Page Layout* view to insert a footer.

1. Open and rename a workbook.
   a. Open the workbook **WearEverShoes-01.xlsx** from your student data files. If the workbook has opened in *Protected View*, click **Enable Editing** in the security bar.
   b. Press **F12** (**FN+F12**) and locate the folder where your files are saved.
   c. Save the workbook as [your initials] Excel 1-3.

2. Remove a split and freeze panes.
   a. Click the **Split** button [*View* tab, *Window* group]. The split is removed.
   b. Click cell **A4** to freeze the column titles at this position.
   c. Click the **Freeze Panes** button [*View* tab, *Window* group].
   d. Choose **Freeze Panes**. There is a solid border between rows 3 and 4 to mark the pane.
   e. Scroll to row **31** and click cell **E31**. The column titles are frozen.
   f. Type 3 and press **Enter** (Figure 1-91).
   g. Press **Ctrl+Home**. The insertion point returns to cell **A4**.

E31	▼	✕ ✓ fx	3				
◢	A	B	C	D	E	F	G	H
1	Wear-Ever Shoes							
2	Current Stock							
3	Product ID	Product	Color	Size	Quantity	Men's or V	Cost	Value
16	WE013	Comfy Walking Shoes	Taupe	7.5	2	W	47.5	
17	WE014	Comfy Walking Shoes	Brown	8	3	W	47.5	
18	WE015	Lazy Flip-Flops	Pink	6	4	W	7.5	
19	WE016	Lazy Flip-Flops	Pink	7	0	W	7.5	
20	WE017	Lazy Flip-Flops	Pink	8	2	W	7.5	
21	WE018	Lazy Flip-Flops	White	6	3	W	7.5	
22	WE019	Lazy Flip-Flops	White	7	1	W	7.5	
23	WE020	Lazy Flip-Flops	White	8	2	W	7.5	
24	WE021	Lazy Flip-Flops	Brown	8	2	M	7.5	
25	WE022	Lazy Flip-Flops	Brown	9	4	M	7.5	
26	WE023	Lazy Flip-Flops	Brown	10	2	M	7.5	
27	WE024	Lazy Flip-Flops	Brown	11	2	M	7.5	
28	WE025	Seriously Tall Boots	Black	6	0	W	42.5	
29	WE026	Seriously Tall Boots	Black	6.5	0	W	42.5	
30	WE027	Seriously Tall Boots	Black	7	1	W	42.5	
31	WE028	Seriously Tall Boots	Black	7.5	3	W	42.5	

1-91 Panes frozen at cell A4

3. Change zoom size and unfreeze the pane.
   a. Click the **100%** button [*View* tab, *Window* group].
   b. Click the **Freeze Panes** button [*View* tab, *Window* group].
   c. Choose **Unfreeze Panes**.
   d. Click cell **A1**.

4. Check spelling in the worksheet.
   a. Click the **Spelling** button [*Review* tab, *Proofing* group]. The first occurrence of "Hikin" is found as misspelled.
   b. Select **Hiking** in the *Suggestions* list.
   c. Click **Change All** to correct all occurrences of the misspelled word (Figure 1-92).
   d. Click **OK**.

5. Use the *Fill Handle* to copy a formula.
   a. Click **H4**. The formula is visible in the *Formula* bar. The formula multiplies the quantity by the cost to calculate the value of the current stock (Figure 1-93).
   b. Point to the *Fill Handle* for cell **H4**.
   c. Double-click the *Fill* pointer. The formula is copied down the entire column.
   d. Press **Ctrl+Home**.

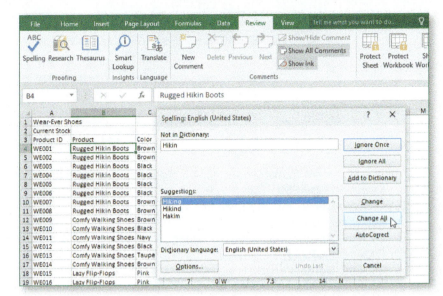

1-92 Change all occurrences of a misspelled word

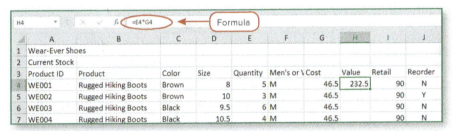

1-93 Formula to be copied

6. Click the **Themes** button [*Page Layout* tab, *Themes* group] and choose **Ion** from the gallery.

7. Merge and center the titles.
   a. Select cells **A1:J1** and click the **Merge & Center** button [*Home* tab, *Alignment* group].
   b. Merge and center cells **A2:J2**.

8. Apply cell styles and adjust row height.
   a. Select cell **A1**, click the **Cell Styles** button or the **More** button [*Home* tab, *Styles* group], and select **Title** in the *Titles and Headings* category.
   b. Select cell **A2** and apply the **Heading 4** style.
   c. Click the **Font Size** arrow [*Home* tab, *Font* group] and select **14 pt**. Your font size change overwrites the font size of the cell style.
   d. Point to the row **1** heading and drag to select row headings **1:2**.
   e. Click the **Format** button [*Home* tab, *Cells* group] and choose **Row Height**.
   f. Type **22** as the new row height and press **Enter**.
   g. Select cells **A3:J3**.
   h. From the *Cell Styles* gallery [*Home* tab], select **40% - Accent3**.
   i. Apply **bold** to the selected cells.
   j. Click the row **3** heading.
   k. Point to the bottom border of the row heading to display the resize arrow.
   l. Drag the resize arrow to **21.00 (28 pixels)** as the new row height and release the pointer button (Figure 1-94).
   m. Click the **Zoom Out** button in the *Status* bar if necessary so that you can see all rows (1:39).

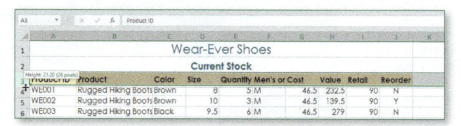

1-94 Adjust row height from the row heading

9. Change alignment, format values, apply borders, and increase the indent.
   a. Select cells **D4:F39**.
   b. Click the **Center** button [*Home* tab, *Alignment* group].
   c. Select cells **G4:H39**.
   d. Click the **Accounting Number Format** button [*Home* tab, *Alignment* group].
   e. Click cells **A3:J39**.
   f. Click the **Borders** drop-down arrow [*Home* tab, *Font* group] and select **All Borders**.
   g. While the cells are selected, click the **Font size** drop-down arrow [*Home* tab, *Font* group] and choose **12**.
   h. Select cells **B4:C39** and click the **Increase Indent** button [*Home* tab, *Alignment* group] one time. This moves the label away from the border for easier reading.
   i. Click and drag to select columns **A:J**.
   j. Double-click the border between columns J and K to *AutoFit* the selected columns (Figure 1-95).
   k. Select and **center** align the labels in row **3**.

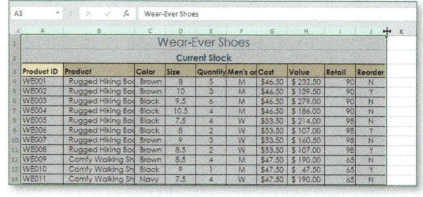

1-95 Select column headings to AutoFit

10. Insert a column and fill data.
    a. Right-click column heading **B**.
    b. Choose **Insert** from the context menu.
    c. In cell **B3**, type Disc? and press **Enter**.
    d. In cell **B4**, type No and press **Enter**.
    e. In cell **B5**, type No and press **Enter**.
    f. In cell **B6**, type Yes and press **Enter**.
    g. Select cells **B4:B6** and increase the indent twice.
    h. Select cells **B4:B6** and double-click the *Fill* pointer (Figure 1-96).
    i. Select cells **A4:A39** and increase the indent one time.
    j. Press **Ctrl+Home**.

11. Rename the sheet tab.
    a. Double-click the **Sheet1** tab.
    b. Type Inventory and press **Enter**.

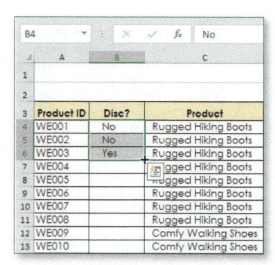

1-96 Double-click the Fill pointer to complete a series

12. Use *Page Layout* view to insert a footer.
   a. Click the **Page Layout** button in the *Status* bar.
   b. Click the center header section. The *Header & Footer Tools Design* tab is active.
   c. Click the **Header & Footer Tools Design** tab.
   d. Click the **Go to Footer** button [*Header & Footer Tools Design* tab, *Navigation* group].
   e. Click the middle section if necessary.
   f. Click the **File Name** button in the *Header & Footer Elements* group. The code is *&[File]*.
   g. Click a worksheet cell to see the file name.
   h. Switch to *Normal* view and press **Ctrl+Home**.

13. Change page setup options.
   a. Click the **Page Layout** tab and click the **Page Setup** launcher.
   b. Display the *Page* tab and select the **Landscape** radio button under *Orientation*.
   c. Select the **Fit to** radio button and enter 1 page wide by 1 tall.
   d. Click **OK**.

14. Set a print area.
   a. Select cells **A1:K11**.
   b. Click the **Page Layout** tab.
   c. Click the **Print Area** button [*Page Setup* group] and select **Set Print Area**.
   d. Press **Ctrl+Home**.
   e. Click the **File** tab and select **Print** to preview the worksheet print area.
   f. Print the area and return to *Normal* view.

15. Click the **Save** button in the *Quick Access* toolbar to save the workbook changes. The print area is saved.

16. Close the workbook (Figure 1-97).

Wear-Ever Shoes
Current Stock

Product ID	Disc?	Product	Color	Size	Quantity	Men's or Women's	Cost	Value	Retail	Reorder
WE001	No	Rugged Hiking Boots	Brown	8	5	M	$ 46.50	$ 232.50	90	N
WE002	No	Rugged Hiking Boots	Brown	10	3	M	$ 46.50	$ 139.50	90	Y
WE003	Yes	Rugged Hiking Boots	Black	9.5	6	M	$ 46.50	$ 279.00	90	N
WE004	No	Rugged Hiking Boots	Black	10.5	4	M	$ 46.50	$ 186.00	90	N
WE005	No	Rugged Hiking Boots	Black	7.5	4	W	$ 53.50	$ 214.00	98	N
WE006	Yes	Rugged Hiking Boots	Black	8	2	W	$ 53.50	$ 107.00	98	Y
WE007	No	Rugged Hiking Boots	Brown	9	3	W	$ 53.50	$ 160.50	98	N
WE008	No	Rugged Hiking Boots	Brown	8.5	2	W	$ 53.50	$ 107.00	98	Y
WE009	Yes	Comfy Walking Shoes	Brown	8.5	4	M	$ 47.50	$ 190.00	65	N
WE010	No	Comfy Walking Shoes	Black	9	1	M	$ 47.50	$ 47.50	65	Y
WE011	No	Comfy Walking Shoes	Navy	7.5	4	W	$ 47.50	$ 190.00	65	N
WE012	Yes	Comfy Walking Shoes	Black	8	1	W	$ 47.50	$ 47.50	65	Y
WE013	No	Comfy Walking Shoes	Taupe	7.5	2	W	$ 47.50	$ 95.00	65	N
WE014	No	Comfy Walking Shoes	Brown	8	3	W	$ 47.50	$ 142.50	65	Y
WE015	Yes	Lazy Flip-Flops	Pink	6	4	W	$ 7.50	$ 30.00	14	N
WE016	No	Lazy Flip-Flops	Pink	7	0	W	$ 7.50	$ -	14	N
WE017	No	Lazy Flip-Flops	Pink	8	2	W	$ 7.50	$ 15.00	14	Y
WE018	Yes	Lazy Flip-Flops	White	6	3	W	$ 7.50	$ 22.50	14	N
WE019	No	Lazy Flip-Flops	White	7	1	W	$ 7.50	$ 7.50	14	N
WE020	No	Lazy Flip-Flops	White	8	2	W	$ 7.50	$ 15.00	14	Y
WE021	Yes	Lazy Flip-Flops	Brown	8	2	M	$ 7.50	$ 15.00	14	Y
WE022	No	Lazy Flip-Flops	Brown	9	4	M	$ 7.50	$ 30.00	14	N
WE023	No	Lazy Flip-Flops	Brown	10	2	M	$ 7.50	$ 15.00	14	Y
WE024	Yes	Lazy Flip-Flops	Brown	11	2	M	$ 7.50	$ 15.00	14	Y
WE025	No	Seriously Tall Boots	Black	6	0	W	$ 42.50	$ -	80	Y
WE026	No	Seriously Tall Boots	Black	6.5	0	W	$ 42.50	$ -	80	Y
WE027	Yes	Seriously Tall Boots	Black	7	1	W	$ 42.50	$ 42.50	80	Y
WE028	No	Seriously Tall Boots	Black	7.5	3	W	$ 42.50	$ 127.50	80	N
WE029	No	Seriously Tall Boots	Black	8	2	W	$ 42.50	$ 85.00	80	Y
WE030	Yes	Seriously Tall Boots	Black	8.5	1	W	$ 42.50	$ 42.50	80	Y
WE031	No	Glide Running Shoes	White	8	6	M	$ 48.00	$ 288.00	75	N
WE032	No	Glide Running Shoes	White	9	6	M	$ 48.00	$ 288.00	75	N
WE033	Yes	Glide Running Shoes	White	10	6	M	$ 48.00	$ 288.00	75	N
WE034	No	Glide Running Shoes	Black	8	2	M	$ 48.00	$ 96.00	75	N
WE035	No	Glide Running Shoes	Black	9	3	M	$ 48.00	$ 144.00	75	N
WE036	Yes	Glide Running Shoes	Black	10	1	M	$ 48.00	$ 48.00	75	Y

Excel 1-3

1-97 Excel 1-3 completed

Independent Project 1-4

As staff at Blue Lake Sports Company, you are expected to prepare the monthly sales worksheet. You edit and format data, complete calculations, and prepare the workbook for distribution. You also copy the sheet for next month's data.
[Student Learning Outcomes 1.1, 1.2, 1.3, 1.4, 1.5, 1.6, 1.8]

File Needed: **BlueLakeSports-01.xlsx** [Student data files are available in the Library of your SIMnet account.]
Completed Project File Name: **[your initials] Excel 1-4.xlsx**

Skills Covered in This Project

- Open and save a workbook.
- Choose a workbook theme.
- Edit and format data.
- Center labels across a selection.

- Use *SUM* and the *Fill Handle*.
- Adjust column width and row height.
- Insert a header and a footer.
- Adjust page layout options.
- Copy and rename a worksheet.

---

1. Open **BlueLakeSports-01.xlsx** from your student data files. If the workbook has opened in *Protected View*, click **Enable Editing** in the security bar.

2. Save the workbook as [your initials] Excel 1-4 in your usual location.

3. Apply the **Slice** theme to the worksheet.

4. Edit worksheet data.
   a. Edit the title in cell **A2** to display Monthly Sales by Department.
   b. Edit cell **D6** to 1950.

5. Select cells **A1:F2** and apply the *Center Across Selection* command.

6. Select and delete row **8**.

7. Use the *Fill Handle* to complete a series.
   a. Select cell **B3**.
   b. Use the *Fill Handle* to complete the series to **Week 4** in column **E**.
   c. *AutoFit* the columns to display the complete label.

8. Use *SUM* and the *Fill Handle* to calculate totals.
   a. Use the **AutoSum** button to build a *SUM* function in cell **F4**.
   b. Use the *Fill Handle* to copy the formula in cell **F4** to cells **F5:F16**.
   c. Delete the contents of cell **F17** if you copied the formula to that cell.
   d. Select cells **B17:F17** and click the **AutoSum** button. The *SUM* formula is inserted, and a **Quick Analysis** options button appears (Figure 1-98).
   e. Press **Esc** to ignore the *Quick Analysis* options.

1-98 *AutoSum* complete with *Quick Analysis* button

9. Format labels and values.
   a. Select cells **A1:A2** and increase the font size to **18**.
   b. Increase the row height of rows **1:2** to **24 (32 pixels)**.
   c. Format cells **A3:F3** as **Bold** and increase the row height to **18 (24 pixels)**.
   d. Center the data in cells **B3:F3**.
   e. Format all values with **Comma Style** and decrease the decimal two times.
   f. Apply the **All Borders** format to cells **A3:F17**.
   g. Select cells **B17:F17** and apply the **Accounting Number Format** with no decimal places.
   h. *AutoFit* each column that does not display all data.

10. Finalize the worksheet.
   a. Click the **Insert** tab and click the **Header & Footer** button.
   b. In the right header section, insert the **Sheet Name** field.
   c. Go to the footer and click the right section.
   d. Type [your first and last name] (Figure 1-99).

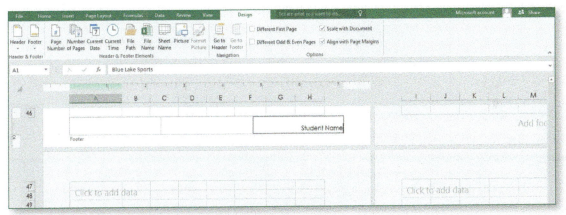

1-99 Add a footer in *Page Layout* view

   e. Click a cell in the worksheet and return to *Normal* view.
   f. Center the worksheet horizontally on the page.

11. Copy and rename a worksheet.
   a. Right-click the *January* sheet tab and choose **Move or Copy**.
   b. Make a copy of the sheet at the end.
   c. Rename the copied sheet February.
   d. Format the *February* sheet tab color to **Dark Blue, Accent 1**.
   e. Delete the values in cells **B4:E16** and press **Ctrl+Home**.
   f. Return to the *January* sheet.

12. Preview the *January* sheet.

13. Save and close the workbook (Figure 1-100).

Blue Lake Sports
Monthly Sales by Department

January

Department	Week 1	Week 2	Week 3	Week 4	Total
Apparel	2,600	3,200	3,800	3,700	13,300
Baseball	3,500	1,200	1,350	2,100	8,150
Basketball	1,800	1,800	1,950	1,400	6,950
Bike & Skate	1,500	1,325	1,225	2,450	6,500
Fitness	2,650	2,875	3,250	3,775	12,550
Footwear	1,875	2,675	3,575	3,250	11,375
Game Room	1,300	1,500	1,900	1,050	5,750
Golf	4,750	875	925	5,400	11,950
Hockey	850	1,875	1,950	750	5,425
Hunting	2,000	1,000	650	725	4,375
Lacrosse	1,750	1,800	1,750	1,375	6,675
Running	1,925	2,400	2,800	2,650	9,775
Winter Sports	1,250	34,350	2,750	550	38,900
Total	$27,750	$56,875	$27,875	$29,175	$141,675

Student Name

Blue Lake Sports
Monthly Sales by Department

February

Department	Week 1	Week 2	Week 3	Week 4	Total
Apparel					-
Baseball					-
Basketball					-
Bike & Skate					-
Fitness					-
Footwear					-
Game Room					-
Golf					-
Hockey					-
Hunting					-
Lacrosse					-
Running					-
Winter Sports					-
Total	$ -	$ -	$ -	$ -	$ -

Student Name

1-100 Excel 1-4 completed

Independent Project 1-5

Clemenson Imaging employs certified staff to perform mobile medical imaging at several hospitals state-wide. Your worksheet maintains a log of which hospitals were visited and what images were made. You need to format the data and finalize the worksheet.
[**Student Learning Outcomes 1.1, 1.2, 1.3, 1.4, 1.5, 1.6, 1.7, 1.8**]

File Needed: ***ClemensonImaging-01.xlsx*** [*Student data files are available in the Library of your SIMnet account.*]
Completed Project File Name: ***[your initials] Excel 1-5.xlsx***

Skills Covered in This Project

- Open and save a workbook.
- Use *SUM*.
- Unfreeze panes and change the zoom size.
- Format data.
- Merge and center labels.
- Adjust column width and row height.
- Design borders.
- Copy a sheet and rename a tab.
- Add document properties.
- Change page layout options.

1. Open ***ClemensonImaging-01.xlsx*** from your student data files and save it as [your initials] Excel 1-5. If the workbook has opened in *Protected View*, click **Enable Editing** in the security bar.

2. Edit the label in cell **A1** to insert LLC after "Clemenson Imaging." Edit the label in cell **A2** to show "Second Quarter . . ." instead of "First Quarter."

3. Merge and center the label in cell **A1** across the worksheet data and then do the same for the label in cell **A2**.

4. Scroll to and select cell **A41**. Type Total. Right-align this label and apply bold format.

5. Use *SUM* in cell **F41** to add the values in cells **F5:F40**.

6. Unfreeze the panes and set a zoom size to display rows 1:30.

7. *AutoFit* columns **D** and **G**.

8. Format data.
   a. Click cell **A1** and set the font size to **18**.
   b. Change the label in cell **A2** to a font size of **14**.
   c. Select cells **A4:H4** and apply bold and center.
   d. Format cells **A4:H4** to use the **White, Background 1, Darker 15%** fill color.
   e. Format the row height for row **4** to **21.00 (28 pixels)**.
   f. Select cells **A4:H41** and apply **All Borders**.
   g. Select cells **A41:H41** and apply the fill color **White, Background 1, Darker 15%**.
   h. Make the value in cell **F41** bold.

9. Set page layout options.
   a. Change the page orientation to **Landscape**.
   b. Center the worksheet horizontally.
   c. Scale the sheet to fit on a single page.
   d. Add a footer that displays the current date in the left section and your first and last name in the right section.
   e. *Autofit* columns that do not display all the data.

10. Add document properties.
    a. Click the **File** tab and select **Info**.
    b. Click the **Properties** drop-down arrow and select **Advanced Properties**.
    c. Click the **Title** box and type Procedures.
    d. Click the **Author** box and type your first and last name (Figure 1-101).
    e. Return to the worksheet.

1-101 *Properties* **dialog box**

11. Rename *Sheet1* as Qtr 2.

12. Copy the *Qtr 2* sheet and place it at the end. Name the copy Qtr 3. Set this tab color to **Blue, Accent 1, Darker 50%**.

13. On the *Qtr 3* sheet, edit the label in cell **A2** to show "Third Quarter . . .".

14. Delete the contents of cells **A5:H40** on the *Qtr 3* sheet.

15. Select cell **A5** and return to the *Qtr 2* sheet.

16. Press **Ctrl+Home** and preview the entire workbook (Figure 1-102).

17. Save and close the workbook (Figure 1-103).

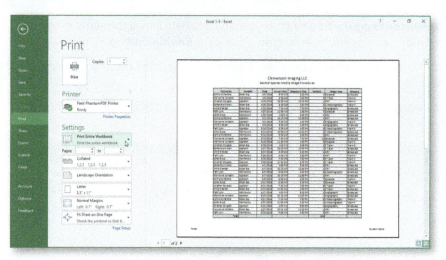

1-102 Entire workbook selected for preview and print

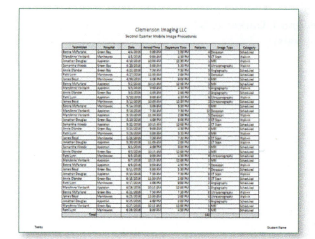

1-103 Excel 1-5 completed

Independent Project 1-6

As accounts receivable clerk for Livingood Income Tax & Accounting, you track daily payments from clients in an Excel worksheet. After entering the data, you format the worksheet and prepare it for distribution to coworkers.

[Student Learning Outcomes 1.1, 1.2, 1.3, 1.4, 1.5, 1.6, 1.8]

File Needed: None
Completed Project File Name: *[your initials] Excel 1-6.xlsx*

Skills Covered in This Project

- Create and save a workbook.
- Enter labels, dates, and values.
- Use the *Fill Handle* to build series.
- Use *SUM*.
- Change font size and attributes.
- Adjust column width and row height.
- Choose a theme and cell styles.
- Choose page layout options.
- Rename and apply color to sheet tabs.

1. Create a new workbook and save it as [your initials] Excel 1-6. If the workbook has opened in *Protected View*, click **Enable Editing** in the security bar.

2. Apply the **Organic** theme for the workbook.

3. In cell **A1**, type Livingood Income Tax and Accounting and press **Enter**

4. In cell **A2**, type Accounts Receivable and press **Enter**.

5. In row **4**, type the labels as shown here in Figure 1-104:

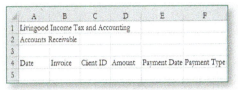

1-104 Data to be entered

6. *AutoFit* or widen the columns to display each label in row 4 in its cell.

7. In cell **A5**, type 8/18/17 to enter the date. In cell **A6**, type 8/20/17 to set a pattern for the dates.

8. Select cells **A5:A6** and use the *Fill Handle* to fill in dates to cell A15.

9. In cell **B5**, type 1001 for the first invoice number. In cell **B6**, type 1002 to set a pattern for the invoice numbers.

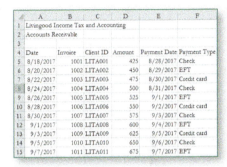

1-105 All columns filled

10. Select cells **B5:B6** and use the *Fill Handle* to fill in invoice numbers to reach cell B15.

11. In cell **C5**, type LITA001 as the first client ID. In cell **C6**, type LITA002 to set a pattern.

12. Use the *Fill Handle* to complete the client ID numbers.

13. Type 425 in cell **D5**. In cell **D6**, type 450 to set the pattern and fill in the amounts.

14. Type the first two payment dates in column **E** and fill the cells (Figure 1-105).

15. Type the first three payment types in cells **F5:F7** and then use the *Fill Handle* to complete the cells in column F.

16. Format data.
    a. Select cells **C5:C15**, increase the indent one time, and *AutoFit* the column. Do the same for the payment type data.
    b. Format the values in column **D** as **Accounting Number Format**.
    c. Select cells **A1:A2** and change the font size to **18**. Center the labels across cells **A1:F2**.
    d. Select the labels in row **4** and apply bold format center alignment.
    e. *AutoFit* columns that do not show all the data.
    f. Apply **All Borders** to cells **A4:F15**. Apply an **Outside Border** for cells **A1:F2**.
    g. Apply the **Green, Accent 1, Lighter 60%** fill color to cells **A1:F2** and **A4:F4**.
    h. Apply the **Green, Accent 1, Lighter 60%** fill color to cells **A6:F6**.
    i. Use the **Ctrl** key to select the data in rows **8**, **10**, **12**, and **14** and apply the same fill color.

17. Rename *Sheet1* as AR and set the tab color to **Green, Accent 1**.

18. Define page layout and add document properties.
    a. Center the worksheet horizontally on the page.
    b. Create a header with the sheet name in the left section and your name in the right section.
    c. Delete an existing author name and key your first and last name as *Author* in the *Properties* dialog box.
    d. Type Receivables in the *Title* box (Figure 1-106).
    e. Preview your worksheet.

1-106 Properties entered in dialog box

E1-83

19. Save and close the workbook (Figure 1-107).

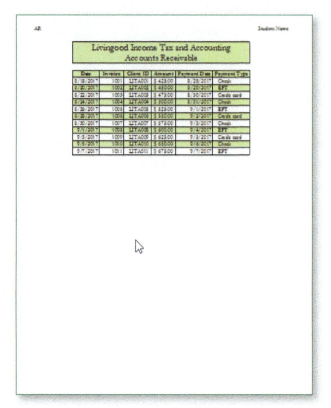

1-107 Excel 1-6 completed

Improve It Project 1-7

In this project, you complete a worksheet that maintains flight statistics for Boyd Air. The data has been imported from the reservation system, and you now need to add finishing touches.
[**Student Learning Outcomes 1.1, 1.2, 1.3, 1.4, 1.5, 1.6, 1.7, 1.8**]

File Needed: **BoydAir-01.xlsx** [*Student data files are available in the Library of your SIMnet account.*]
Completed Project File Name: **[your initials] Excel 1-7.xlsx**

Skills Covered in This Project

- Open and save a workbook.
- Change the zoom level and remove a split.
- Enter and merge and center labels.
- Insert a row and set column width.
- Format data.
- Use *SUM*.
- Apply cell styles.
- Rename and color the sheet tab.
- Adjust page layout options.
- Add document properties.

1. Open the workbook **BoydAir-01.xlsx** from your student data files. If the workbook has opened in *Protected View*, click **Enable Editing** in the security bar.

2. Save the workbook as [your initials] Excel 1-7.

3. Remove the split from the window.

4. Type Boyd Air in cell **A1** and Flight Statistics in cell **A2**.

5. Merge and center the labels in cells **A1** and **A2**. Change the font size for both labels to **16**.

6. Insert a row at row **3**.

7. Select the labels in row **4** and make them bold and centered. *AutoFit* columns to show each label in row 4.

8. Change the zoom size to **100%**.

9. Select cells **B5:D18**, press **Ctrl**, and select cells **G5:G18**. Increase the indent one time.

10. Apply **All Borders** for cells **A4:H19**.

11. Calculate the total number of passengers in cell **H19**.

12. Apply the **Accent2** cell style to cells **A3:H3** and cells **A20:H20**.

13. Select cells **A3:H3** and **A20:H20** and apply an **Outside Border**.

14. Modify page layout options.
    a. Change the orientation to **Landscape**.
    b. Center the worksheet horizontally on the page.
    c. Show the file name in the left header section.
    d. Type your first and last name in the right header section.

15. Name the sheet tab Feb-Mar and format the tab color as **Orange, Accent 2**.

16. Set the document properties to show your first and last name as the *Author*. In the *Title* field, type Flight Stats.

17. Preview your worksheet.

18. Save and close the workbook (Figure 1-108).

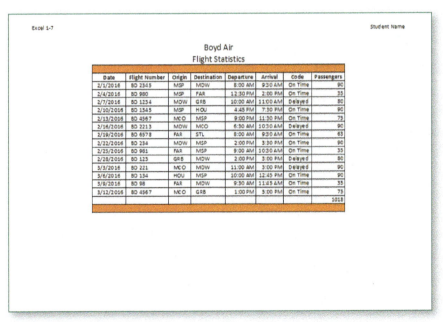

1-108 Excel 1-7 completed

Challenge Project 1-8

In this project, you create a workbook that lists and tracks candy and beverage sales at a gourmet chocolate store for selected holidays or special events. You enter and format the data and then finalize the workbook for distribution.
[Student Learning Outcomes 1.1, 1.2, 1.3, 1.4, 1.5, 1.6, 1.8]

File Needed: None
Completed Project File Name: *[your initials] Excel 1-8.xlsx*

Create a new workbook and save it as [your initials] Excel 1-8. Modify your workbook according to the following guidelines:

- Choose a workbook theme.
- Determine and type a name for the store in cell **A1**. In cell **A2**, type Sales by Holiday.
- Starting in cell **B3**, type names of four chocolate candies and one chocolate beverage (cells B3:F3).
- Type the names of five holidays, celebrations, or special events in cells **A4:A8**.
- Fill in values to reflect dollar or unit sales, and format these values appropriately.
- Calculate a total for each holiday and a total for each candy or beverage. Add labels for these values.
- Use cell styles, borders, fill color, or other formatting to design your worksheet.
- *AutoFit* columns and adjust row heights as needed.
- Insert a footer that includes your name in one section and the date in another section.
- Use portrait orientation and fit the worksheet to a single page. Center it horizontally.
- Name the sheet tab and set a tab color.
- Enter the company name in the *Title* field in the document properties.

Challenge Project 1-9

In this project, you create a worksheet for a photography club that rents retail space for selling used equipment. The equipment includes camera bodies, lenses, tripods, cases, accessories, books, and more. You are building the worksheet so that expected selling prices can be entered each month for each item.
[Student Learning Outcomes 1.1, 1.2, 1.4, 1.5, 1.6, 1.7, 1.8]

File Needed: None
Completed Project File Name: *[your initials] Excel 1-9.xlsx*

Create a new workbook and save it as [your initials] Excel 1-9. Modify your workbook according to the following guidelines:

- Create and type a name for the photography club as a main label. As a second label, type a label that specifies the purpose of the worksheet.
- In cell **B3**, type Jan. Fill the months to **Dec** in column **M**.
- Starting in cell **A4**, type the names of ten items related to any type of photography equipment in column **A**. Research a web site that sells similar items.

- As the January price for the first item, type a value that makes sense as a resale price. For the February price, type a value that is a few dollars more than the January price. Select these two cells and fill prices for the remaining months.
- Repeat the tasks in the previous step for each of the ten items to fill in values for all the items.
- Use cell styles, borders, fill color, or other formatting to design the worksheet.
- Adjust column widths and row heights.
- Insert a header that includes your name in the right section.
- Use landscape orientation and fit the worksheet to a single page.
- In the document properties, enter the club's name in the *Author* field.
- Name the worksheet tab and choose a tab color.
- Split the sheet at cell **G1**. Arrange the data so that you see cell **A1** in each window.

Challenge Project 1-10

In this project, you create a spreadsheet that details your expected monthly income and expenses. [Student Learning Outcomes 1.1, 1.2, 1.3, 1.4, 1.5, 1.6, 1.8]

File Needed: None
Completed Project File Name: *[your initials] Excel 1-10.xlsx*

Create a new workbook and save it as [your initials] Excel 1-10. Modify your workbook according to the following guidelines:

- Type the main label Expected Monthly Income and Estimated Expenses. Type your name as a second label.
- Type Income in cell **A3**. In cells **A4:A7**, enter labels for four categories of income. For example, you may have regular wages from one or more jobs, interest from a certificate of deposit, rent from property that you own, income from Internet sales, etc. Include descriptive labels, enter values in column **B**, and include a total income calculation using *SUM*.
- In cell **D3**, type Expenses. In cells **D4:D9**, enter labels for six categories of expenses. These include rent, a mortgage payment, insurance, loan payments, food, clothing, entertainment, transportation, and so on. Complete labels, enter values in column **E**, and use *SUM* to calculate total expenses.
- Format the data with borders, fill color, font styles, and number formats. Adjust page layout options so that the sheet fits on a single portrait page.
- Spell check the sheet.
- Name the sheet Jan and choose a tab color.
- Copy the sheet and name the copy Feb. Choose a different tab color.
- Delete the expense amounts on the *Feb* sheet.
- Make a copy of the *Feb* sheet to create a worksheet for March.
- Add document properties to identify the workbook.

Working with Formulas and Functions

CHAPTER OVERVIEW

With its capabilities in mathematical, scientific, engineering, and other calculations, Excel is a valuable tool for business, government, education, and you. You can use Excel to create a simple addition formula or a sophisticated calculation with layers of arithmetic. In this chapter, you learn how to build a basic formula and how to use mathematical rules. You also explore Excel function categories.

STUDENT LEARNING OUTCOMES (SLOs)

After completing this chapter, you will be able to:

SLO2.1 Build and edit basic formulas (p. E2-89).

SLO2.2 Set mathematical order of operations in a formula (p. E2-91).

SLO2.3 Use absolute, mixed, relative, and 3D references in a formula (p. E2-93).

SLO2.4 Use formula auditing tools in a worksheet (p. E2-99).

SLO2.5 Work with *Statistical* and *Date & Time* functions (p. E2-106).

SLO2.6 Work with functions from the *Financial*, *Logical*, and *Lookup & Reference* categories (p. E2-114).

SLO2.7 Build functions from the *Math & Trig* category (p. E2-122).

CASE STUDY

In the Pause & Practice projects in this chapter, you work with a multi-sheet workbook for Paradise Lakes Resort (PLR), the northern Minnesota chain of resorts. You build formulas to complete a simple income statement, to calculate data for the boutique division, and to track information about the youth camp.

Pause & Practice 2-1: Build and audit formulas in a worksheet.

Pause & Practice 2-2: Insert *Statistical* and *Date & Time* functions in a workbook.

Pause & Practice 2-3: Use *Financial*, *Logical*, *Lookup*, and *Math & Trig* functions in a workbook.

EXCEL

Building and Editing a Formula

An Excel *formula* is an expression or statement that uses common arithmetic operations to carry out a calculation. Basic arithmetic operations are addition, subtraction, multiplication, and division. The formula is entered in a cell and refers to other cells or ranges in the worksheet or workbook. The formula appears in the *Formula* bar, but the results appear in the cell.

You learned in Chapter 1 that a function is a built-in formula. Like a function, a formula begins with an equals sign (=). After the equals sign, you enter the address of the first cell, followed by the arithmetic operator, followed by the next cell in the calculation. An example of a simple addition formula is **=B5+B6** which adds the values in cells B5 and B6.

Basic arithmetic operators are listed in the table. Enter arithmetic operators using the numeric keypad or the symbols on the number keys at the top of the keyboard.

In the multiplication formula **=C5*C6**, the value in cell C5 is multiplied by the value in cell C6. You can use cell references in a formula or a value known as a *constant*. In the formula **=D5*85%**, the constant is 85%.

Character	Arithmetic Operator
+	Addition
−	Subtraction
*	Multiplication
/	Division

Type a Formula

For a simple formula, you can easily type it. Click the cell, type the equals sign, type the first cell address, type the operator, type the next cell address, and so on. Press any completion key when the formula is finished. Formulas are not case sensitive, so you can type cell addresses in lowercase letters. Excel automatically converts cell references to uppercase when the formula is completed. If you press **Esc** before completing a formula, it is canceled and nothing is entered in the cell.

As you type a cell address after the equals sign, *Formula AutoComplete* displays a list of functions and range names that match the character that you typed. You can ignore the list and continue typing. In addition, the *Range Finder* highlights and color codes each cell as you type its address.

▶ **HOW TO:** Type a Formula

1. Click the cell for the formula.
2. Type an equals sign (=) to begin the formula.
3. Type the column letter for the first cell reference (Figure 2-1).
   - *Formula AutoComplete* displays a list of functions and range names.
   - You can type a lowercase or uppercase character.
4. Type the row number for the cell reference.
   - The *Range Finder* color codes the cell and its reference.
5. Type the arithmetic operator.
6. Type the cell address for the next reference.

2-1 *Formula AutoComplete* while typing a formula

7. Press **Enter**.
   - The result displays in the cell where the formula is located (Figure 2-2).
   - The *Formula* bar displays the formula.
   - You can click the **Enter** button (the check mark) on the *Formula* bar to complete a formula.
   - You can press **Ctrl+Enter** to complete a formula.

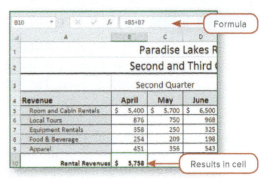

2-2 Formula and result

Point and Click to Build a Formula

Instead of typing a cell address, you point to and click the cell to enter its address in a formula. This method guards against your typing the wrong address. You will not see a *Formula AutoComplete* list, but the *Range Finder* will highlight and color code the cells.

▶**HOW TO:** Point and Click to Build a Formula

1. Click the cell for the formula.
2. Type an equals sign (=) to start the formula.
3. Point to and click the first cell for the formula.
   - The reference is entered in the cell and in the *Formula* bar.
   - The *Range Finder* highlights and color codes the reference.
   - If you click the wrong cell, click the correct cell to replace the address.
4. Type the arithmetic operator.
5. Point to and click the next cell for the formula (Figure 2-3).
   - The reference is entered in the cell and in the *Formula* bar.
   - The *Range Finder* highlights and color codes the reference.
6. Press **Enter**.
   - The result displays in the cell.
   - The *Formula* bar displays the formula.
   - Click the **Enter** button on the *Formula* bar or press **Ctrl+Enter** to complete a formula.

2-3 Point and click to build a formula

Edit a Formula

You edit a formula in *Edit* mode by double-clicking its cell or by clicking the *Formula* bar while the cell is active. The *Range Finder* highlights and color codes the formula cell as well as the cells used in the formula. You can add or remove cells and operators to build a new formula in the cell or in the *Formula* bar.

> **ANOTHER WAY**
>
> Click the cell and press **F2 (FN+F2)** to start *Edit* mode.

▶ HOW TO: Edit a Formula

1. Double-click the formula cell.

    - The *Range Finder* highlights and color codes the cells.

2. Edit the formula in the cell (Figure 2-4).

    - Edit the cell address or type a different operator.
    - Select a cell address and click a different cell to replace the reference.
    - You can make the same edits in the *Formula* bar.

3. Press **Enter**.

    - Click the **Enter** button on the *Formula* bar or press **Ctrl+Enter** to complete a formula.

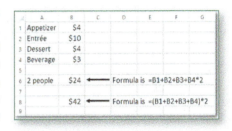

2-4 Edit a formula in the cell

SLO 2.2

Setting Mathematical Order of Operations

A formula can have more than one operator, such as a combination of addition and multiplication. Figure 2-5 illustrates two formulas a restaurant might use to calculate a bill for a couple who ordered the same items. The formula in cell B6 lists the additions first and multiplies by 2; the total of $24 is incorrect. The formula in cell B8 is the same except for the parentheses; the correct amount is $42.

	A	B	C	D	E	F	G
1	Appetizer	$4					
2	Entrée	$10					
3	Dessert	$4					
4	Beverage	$3					
5							
6	2 people	$24	← Formula is =B1+B2+B3+B4*2				
7							
8		$42	← Formula is =(B1+B2+B3+B4)*2				
9							

2-5 Formulas with multiple operators

Excel follows *mathematical order of operations*, which is the sequence of arithmetic calculations. The order in which the mathematics in a formula is carried out depends on the operator as well as left-to-right order. The basic sequence is left to right, but multiplication and division are done before addition and subtraction. This concept is also known as *order of precedence* or *math hierarchy*.

You control the order of operations with parentheses. The formula in cell B8 (Figure 2-5) uses parentheses to reorder the calculation. The parentheses group the addition ($4+$10+$4+$3 = 21) and then multiplies by 2 ($21*2 = 42).

In a formula with multiple operators, references enclosed in parentheses are calculated first. If a value with an exponent exists, it is calculated next. Multiplication and division follow and finally addition and subtraction. When two operators have the same precedence, Excel calculates them from left to right.

Mathematical Order of Precedence

Operator	Operation	Order or Precedence
()	**Parentheses**	First
^	**Exponent**	Second
*	**Multiplication**	Third
/	**Division**	Third
+	**Addition**	Fourth
−	**Subtraction**	Fourth

Exponents raise a number to a power. The formula **3^3** multiplies 3 * 3 * 3, 27. Use the caret symbol (**^**) to build a formula with an exponent.

Multiple Operators in a Formula

When different operators are used in a formula, you must determine how the calculation should be completed and if parentheses are necessary to set the proper order. Here are formulas with two operators. Since addition and subtraction are equal in priority, Excel calculates from left to right.

$$2 + 5 - 3 = 4 \qquad 5 + 1 - 3 = 3$$

Below are formulas with two operators with different priority. Excel calculates the multiplication first and then follows left to right order.

$$2 + 5 * 3 = 17 \qquad 2 * 5 + 3 = 13$$

Consider this formula with three different operators. Since multiplication and division are equal priority but higher than addition, the multiplication is first, followed by the division (left to right). The result of those calculations is added to 5.

$$= 2 * 5/2 + 5 = 10$$

▶ HOW TO: Use Multiple Operators in a formula

1. Type = to start the formula.

2. Type ((left parenthesis) to start the calculation that should have priority.

   - The calculation in parentheses can occur anywhere in the formula.

3. Click the first cell for the calculation to be enclosed in parentheses.

4. Type the arithmetic operator.

5. Click the next cell for the calculation to be enclosed in parentheses.

6. Type) (right parenthesis) to end the calculation with priority (Figure 2-6).

   - You must have matching parentheses.

7. Complete the formula.

8. Press **Enter**.

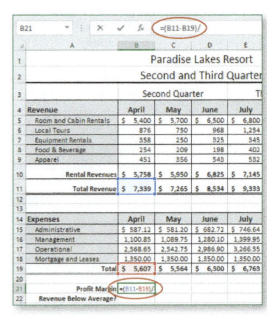

2-6 Set the order of operation with parentheses

Using Absolute, Mixed, Relative, and 3D References

Cell references in a formula are identified in different ways. How a cell reference is identified affects how the formula is adjusted when it is copied.

- A *relative cell reference* is the location of a cell, such as cell **B2**. In column B, the formula is **=B5+B7**, but when copied to column C, it is **=C5+C7**. When you copy a formula with relative references, copied references are updated to the new locations.
- An *absolute cell reference* is indicated with dollar signs as in cell **$B$2**. When an absolute reference is copied, it does not change. In the formula **=$B$6−C7**, $B$6 would not change when copied anywhere in the workbook. C7, on the other hand, would reflect where the copy is located. You can type the dollar signs in an absolute reference, but it is easier to use the **F4 (FN+F4)** function key. When building a formula, enter the cell address and then press **F4 (FN+F4)**.
- A *mixed cell reference* has one relative and one absolute reference. Cell **$B2** is a mixed reference. When it is copied, it always refers to column B, but the row number updates relative to where the copy is located. The formula **=$B5+C$6** has two mixed references. When copied, this formula will always show column B for the first address and row 6 for the second address.
- A *3D cell reference* is a cell located in another worksheet in the same workbook. It can be absolute, mixed, or relative. A 3D reference includes the name of the sheet as in **Sheet2!B2** or **Inventory!$B2**. The sheet name is followed by an exclamation point. When you point and click to build a 3D reference, the sheet name and exclamation point are automatically entered. When the sheet name includes special characters (@, #, &, etc.), the name is enclosed in single quotes as in **'Inventory#'!$B2**. When you type a 3D reference, you must spell the sheet name correctly and include the exclamation point and single quotes.

The following table illustrates each cell reference type:

Cell Reference Types

Cell Reference	Reference Type	Behavior When Copied
B2	Relative	Cell address updates to new location(s).
$B$2	Absolute	Cell address does not change.
$B2	Mixed	Column does not change; row updates to new location(s).
B$2	Mixed	Row does not change; column updates to new location(s).
Sheet2!B2	3D Relative	Cell address updates to new location(s).

> **MORE INFO**
>
> When used in a reference, the dollar sign ($) and the exclamation point (!) are identifiers. The dollar sign is not treated as a currency symbol, and the exclamation point is not considered punctuation.

Copy a Formula with a Relative Reference

When a formula with relative references is copied, the copied formulas use cell addresses that reflect their locations in the worksheet. In the Paradise Lakes worksheet shown in Figure 2-7, the formula to calculate rental revenue in cell B10 is **=B5+B7**. The formula for cell C10 is **=C5+C7**. The formula in cell B10 can be copied to cells C10:G10 and will automatically adjust for each column.

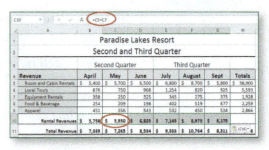

2-7 Copy a formula with a relative reference

▶ **HOW TO:** Copy a Formula with a Relative Reference

1. Select the cell with the formula.
   - You can select multiple adjacent cells.
2. Press **Ctrl+C** to copy the formula(s).
   - Click and drag the *Fill* pointer if the copies are adjacent to the original formula(s).
   - Use the **Copy** button on the *Home* tab if you prefer.
3. Select the destination cell or range.
   - Click the first cell in a destination range when pasting multiple cells.
4. Press **Ctrl+V** to paste the formula (see Figure 2-7).
   - The pasted formula reflects its location on the worksheet.
   - Ignore the **Paste Options** button.
   - Use the **Paste** button on the *Home* tab if you prefer.

Build and Copy a Formula with an Absolute Reference

An absolute reference in a formula maintains that address when copied. An example is a worksheet in which expenses are calculated as a percentage of revenue. You type the percentage once in a worksheet cell, use an absolute reference to that cell in the first formula, and copy the formula.

To change a cell address to an absolute reference, press the **F4 (FN+F4)** function key while keying or editing the formula. The first press of the key inserts dollar signs for the row and column reference. Another press of the **F4 (FN+F4)** key makes it a mixed reference, and each press of the key cycles through the next option.

▶ **HOW TO:** Build and Copy a Formula with an Absolute Reference

1. Click the cell for the formula.
2. Type an equals sign (=) to begin the formula.
3. Click the cell to be referenced in the formula.
4. Press **F4 (FN+F4)**.
   - The reference becomes absolute (Figure 2-8).
5. Complete the formula and press **Enter**.

2-8 Make a reference absolute

6. Select the cell with the formula.

7. Press **Ctrl+C** to copy the formula(s).

   - Click and drag the *Fill* pointer if the copies are adjacent to the original formula.
   - Use the **Copy** button on the *Home* tab if you prefer.

8. Select the destination cell or range.

9. Press **Ctrl+V** to paste the formula.

   - The pasted formula uses the same cell reference as the original.
   - Use the **Paste** button on the *Home* tab if you prefer.
   - Ignore the **Paste Options** button.

> **MORE INFO**
>
> When you type a constant in a formula, such as **=B7*12**, the constant (12) is treated as an absolute value.

Build and Copy a Formula with a Mixed Reference

A mixed cell reference has one relative and one absolute reference in the cell address. Part of the copied formula is unchanged and part is updated. A mixed reference has one dollar sign. You still use the **F4 (FN+F4)** function key, because each press of the key cycles through displaying the dollar signs in different combinations.

> **HOW TO:** Build and Copy a Formula with a Mixed Reference

1. Click the cell for the formula.

2. Type an equals sign (=) to begin the formula.

3. Click the cell to be referenced in the formula.

4. Press **F4 (FN+F4)**.

   - The reference is absolute.

5. Press **F4 (FN+F4)** again.

   - The column reference is relative and the row reference is absolute.

6. Press **F4 (FN+F4)** again (Figure 2-9).

   - The row reference is relative and the column reference is absolute.

7. Complete the formula and press **Enter**.

8. Select the formula cell.

9. Press **Ctrl+C** to copy the formula(s).

   - Drag the *Fill* pointer if copies are adjacent to the original formula.
   - You can use the **Copy** button on the *Home* tab.

10. Click the destination cell or range.

11. Press **Ctrl+V** to paste the formula.

    - The pasted formula keeps the absolute part of the reference but updates the relative part.
    - Use the **Paste** button on the *Home* tab if you prefer.

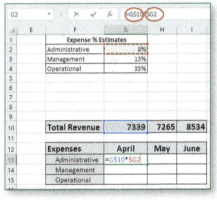

2-9 Formula with a mixed reference

Create a Formula with a 3D Reference

An important feature of an Excel workbook is that you can refer to data on any sheet in a formula. This type of formula is called a **3D reference**, because it uses more than one sheet or surface to calculate a result.

A 3D reference includes the name of the worksheet and can be absolute, mixed, or relative.

Sample 3D References

Cell on Sheet1	Formula on Sheet1	Results
B4	=B3+Sheet2!B3+Sheet3!B3	Adds the values in cell B3 on Sheet1, Sheet2, and Sheet3
B7	=SUM(B4:B6)+Sheet2!A12	Adds the values in cells B4:B6 on Sheet1 to the value in cell A12 on Sheet2
C8	=C7*Sheet2!$D$4	Multiplies the value in cell C7 by the value in cell D4 on Sheet2
D10	=Sheet2!$B$2/Sheet3!B2	Divides the value in cell B2 on Sheet2 by the value in cell B2 on Sheet3

> **MORE INFO**
>
> An external reference formula refers to a cell in another workbook. It can be absolute, mixed, or relative. An external reference includes the name of the workbook in square brackets as in **[PLRSales]Sheet!B$2**.

▶ HOW TO: Create a Formula with a 3D Reference

1. Click the cell for the formula.
2. Type **=**.
3. Select the sheet tab with the cell to be used in the formula.
4. Click the required cell.
   - Press **F4 (FN+F4)** to make the reference absolute or mixed as needed.
5. Type the operator (Figure 2-10).
6. Click the next cell for the formula.
   - The next cell can be on the same or another sheet.
7. Type the next operator and complete the formula as needed.
8. Press **Enter** or any completion key.

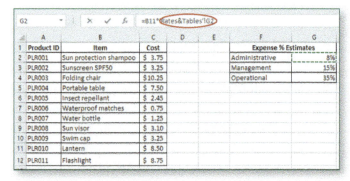

2-10 3D cell reference

Range Names and Formula AutoComplete

A **range name** is a label assigned to a single cell or a group of cells. You can use range names instead of cell references in a formula. Instead of **=B11*10%**, you can name cell B11 as "Revenue" to build the formula **=Revenue*10%**. Descriptive range names help you interpret a formula. In addition, named cell ranges appear in the *Formula AutoComplete* list for ease in building formulas. A named cell range is an absolute reference in a formula.

You create a range name from the *Name* box or from the *Defined Names* group on the *Formulas* tab. The *Name Manager* command in this group enables you to create, edit, and delete range names. If you alter a range name, Excel automatically updates formulas that use that range name. There is also a command that enables you to name a range and apply it to existing formulas that refer to those cells.

Follow these basic rules for naming a cell range:

- Begin a range name with a letter.
- Use a short, descriptive name.
- Do not use spaces or special characters in a range name.
- Separate words in a range name with an underscore as in "First_Qtr," or use initial caps for each word such as "FirstQtr."
- Do not name a range with a single character such as "N."
- Do not name a range with a cell reference such as "B2."

To use the name in a formula, type the first character of the name when it is required to display the *Formula AutoComplete* list. You may need to type a second character to see the name in a workbook that has many range names. Select the range name in the list and press **Tab**, or double-click the name to enter it in the formula. Range names are automatically substituted in formulas when you select the named cell range in the worksheet while building a formula.

▶ **HOW TO:** Name a Range and Use Formula AutoComplete

1. Select the cell or range to be named.
2. Click the **Name** box at the left of the *Formula* bar.
3. Type the name and press **Enter** (Figure 2-11).
4. Click the cell for the formula.
5. Type = to start the formula
6. Type the first one or two letters of the range name.

   - The *Formula AutoComplete* list shows range and function names.
   - The list is alphabetical, and function names are uppercase.

7. Find the range name and double-click it (Figure 2-12).

   - The name is inserted in the formula.
   - You can also click the name in the list to highlight it and press **Tab**.

8. Complete the formula.
9. Press **Enter** when the formula is complete.

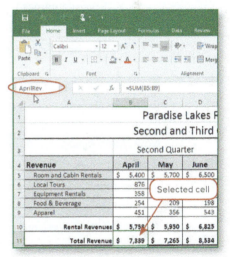

2-11 Name a range in the *Name* box

2-12 Use *Formula AutoComplete* with a range name

In addition to selecting cell ranges to name them, you can use row and column labels to create range names. The *Create from Selection* button on the *Formulas* tab automatically assigns range names based on labels in the top row, the left column, or both.

▶ HOW TO: Create Names from a Selection

1. Select the range including row or column labels (or both) (Figure 2-13).
   - Values and related labels must be adjacent.
2. Click the **Create from Selection** button [*Formulas* tab, *Defined Names* group].
   - The *Create Names from Selection* dialog box opens.
3. Select the **Top row** or **Left column** box.
   - You can choose both options if appropriate for the data.
   - There are options for the bottom row and right column.
4. Click **OK**.
5. Click the **Name box** arrow on the *Formula* bar.
   - All range names are listed.

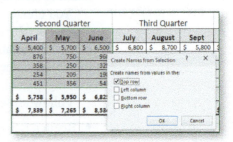

2-13 *Create Names from Selection* **dialog box**

The **Define Name** button [*Formulas* tab, *Defined Names* group] opens the *New Name* dialog box. Here you can type the name, enter a comment, select the cells, and specify a *scope*. The scope determines if the range applies to a particular sheet or to the entire workbook. By default, a range name applies to the workbook. If you use the name "JanSales" on Sheet1, you cannot use it again on Sheet2, unless you scope each name to a particular sheet. When you scope names to a worksheet, you can use the name multiple times in the workbook.

▶ HOW TO: Define and Scope a Range Name

1. Select the cell range to be named.
2. Click the **Define Name** button [*Formulas* tab, *Defined Names* group].
   - The *New Name* dialog box opens.
3. Type the range name in the *Name* box.
4. Click the **Scope** drop-down list (Figure 2-14).
   - Choose the name of a worksheet as desired.
5. Select or edit the *Refers to* entry.
   - The selected cell range address displays.
   - If no cells are selected, you can type or select the range address.
6. Click **OK**.

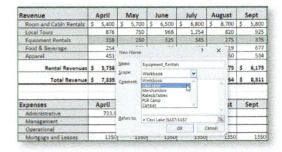

2-14 *New Name* **dialog box**

The *Use in Formula* button [*Formulas* tab, *Defined Names* group] displays a list of range names for insertion in a formula. You can do the same from the *Paste Name* dialog box, opened when you press the **F3 (FN+F3)** function key.

▶ HOW TO: Paste a Range Name in a Formula and Paste a List

1. Click the formula cell and type **=**.
2. Press **F3 (FN+F3)** to open the *Paste Name* dialog box.
   - Range names are listed in alphabetical order.

3. Find the range name and double-click it (Figure 2-15).
   - You can also highlight the range name and press **Enter** or click **OK**.
   - The range name displays in the formula.
   - The worksheet displays the highlighted range.
4. Complete the formula and press **Enter**.
5. Click a blank cell in an unused area of the worksheet.
   - You can select a cell on another worksheet.
6. Click the **Use in Formula** button [*Formulas* tab, *Defined Names* group].
7. Select **Paste Names**.
   - The *Paste Name* dialog box opens.
8. Click **Paste List**.
   - A list of range names and cell references is pasted.
   - You can edit and format these cells.

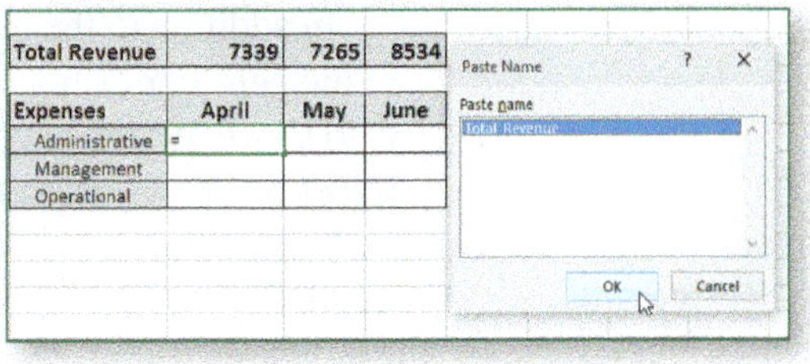

2-15 Choose a range name for the formula

SLO 2.4

Using Formula Auditing Tools

Formula auditing is the process of reviewing formulas for accuracy. Excel automatically audits formulas as you enter them and when you open a workbook based on its error checking rules [*File* tab, *Options*, *Formulas* pane]. Excel recognizes many errors, but not all of them. For example, if you type a formula that multiplies the values in two cells when it should add the values, you must find that error on your own. There are also circumstances when Excel identifies an error, but the formula is correct.

MORE INFO

You can set whether automatic error checking is enabled and you can select which rules are used in the *Excel Options* dialog box.

When Excel finds an error in a formula, it displays a small green error triangle in the top left corner of the cell. Click the cell to see the *Trace Error* button and point to the button to see a *ScreenTip* about the error. The *Trace Error* button has a drop-down list with options for dealing with the error.

HOW TO: Trace an Error

1. Click the cell with the triangle error.
   - The *Trace Error* button appears.
2. Point to the **Trace Error** button to display a *ScreenTip*.
3. Click the **Trace Error** drop-down list (Figure 2-16).
   - Options for handling the error are listed.
4. Choose an option for the error.
   - The options depend on the type of error.
   - Select **Ignore Error** if the formula is correct.

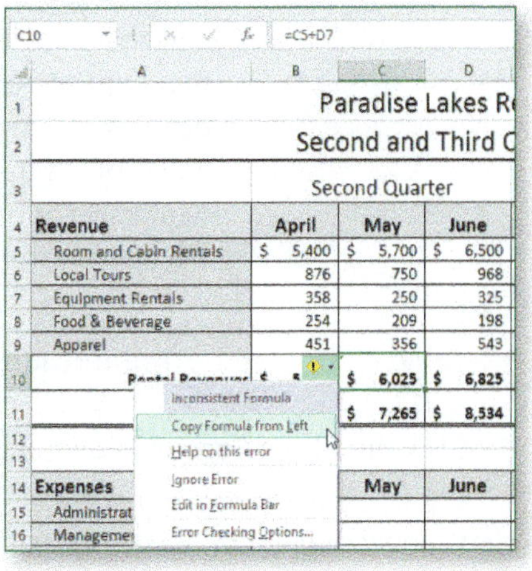

2-16 *Trace Error* button and its drop-down list

In addition to the green triangle error, Excel functions can result in a standard error message in the cell. For example, if you create a division formula that divides by a blank cell, the result is *#DIV/0!* When you click the **Trace Error** button, it is identified as a division by zero error. Excel error messages occur for a syntax error, such as spelling a function name incorrectly, using an incorrect operator or symbol, having the wrong number of arguments, and so on. A standard error message starts with the number sign (#) and ends with an exclamation point (!).

> ### MORE INFO
>
> From the *Go to Special* dialog box [**Find & Select** button, *Home* tab, *Editing* group], you can highlight cells with formula errors, blank cells, and cells with precedents and dependents. This command helps identify potential problems in a workbook.

The Formula Auditing Group

The *Formula Auditing* group on the *Formulas* tab has tools to check formulas for logic, consistency, and accuracy. These commands enable you to examine what contributes to a formula and analyze if the formula is correct. The tools are helpful but they do require that you correct the problem.

Button	Description
Trace Precedents	Displays lines with arrows to identify all cells referenced in the formula in the active cell
Trace Dependents	Displays lines with arrows to all cells that use the active cell directly or indirectly in a formula
Remove Arrows	Removes all lines and arrows from the *Trace Precedents* or *Trace Dependents* buttons
Show Formulas	Displays formulas in the cells
Error Checking	Checks data against the error rules in Excel Options
Evaluate Formula	Steps through each part of a formula and displays an outcome for each part so that an error can be isolated
Watch Window	Opens a floating window that displays selected cells and values for monitoring

Trace Precedents and Dependents

A ***precedent*** is a cell that contributes to the formula results. Excel displays lines from the formula cell to each precedent cell for an easy way to audit your formula. A ***dependent*** is a cell that is affected by the active cell. Excel displays lines from the active cell to each cell that depends on the value in that cell. When the lines and arrows are blue, the precedents or dependents do not have an error. If the lines and arrows are red, the precedents or dependents have some type of recognized error. If a precedent or dependent cell is located on a different worksheet, a black line and arrow point to a small worksheet icon, but this does not identify the actual error cell address.

▶ HOW TO: Use Formula Auditing Tools

1. Click the **Show Formulas** button [*Formulas* tab, *Formula Auditing* group].
   - Each formula displays in its cell.
   - Show or hide formulas by pressing **Ctrl+~**.
2. Select the formula cell.

3. Click the **Trace Precedents** button [*Formulas* tab, *Formula Auditing* group].

   - Lines and arrows identify cells that contribute to the formula results (Figure 2-17).
   - You can trace precedents and dependents with formulas shown or hidden.

4. Click the **Remove Arrows** button [*Formulas* tab, *Formula Auditing* group].

   - Clicking the button removes all arrows.
   - Click the **Remove Arrows** drop-down list to specify the type of arrow to remove.

5. Click a cell that is referenced in a formula.

   - The cell need not have a formula.

6. Click the **Trace Dependents** button [*Formulas* tab, *Formula Auditing* group].

   - Lines and arrows trace to cells that are affected by the active cell.

7. Click the **Remove Arrows** button [*Formulas* tab, *Formula Auditing* group].

8. Click the **Show Formulas** button [*Formulas* tab, *Formula Auditing* group].

   - Formulas are hidden.
   - Show or hide formulas by pressing **Ctrl+~**.

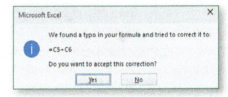

2-17 *Trace Precedents* **arrows with formulas shown**

> **MORE INFO**
>
> In a complex worksheet with sophisticated formulas, click the **Trace Precedents** button [*Formulas* tab, *Formula Auditing* group] once to trace the first layer of precedents. Then click the button again to trace the precedents of the precedents.

The Formula Correction Message Window

As you complete a formula with a minor error (e.g. typing "5c" as a cell address), Excel displays a message box with information about the error (Figure 2-18). For many of these types of errors, review the suggested correction and select **Yes**. For an error that Excel finds but cannot offer a solution, a message box opens with suggestions but you need to solve the problem on your own.

2-18 Formula correction message window

Circular Reference

A *circular reference* is an error that occurs when a formula includes the cell address of the formula. For example, if the formula in cell **B10** is **=B5+B10**, the reference is circular. When you try to complete such a formula, a message box opens as shown in Figure 2-19. The *Status* bar displays the location of circular references, but Excel does not correct this type of error. You can keep a circular reference in a worksheet, but the formula results are inaccurate.

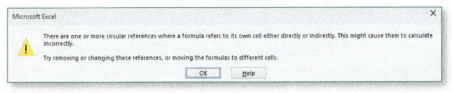

2-19 Circular reference and its message window

PAUSE & PRACTICE: EXCEL 2-1

For this project, you build formulas in a Paradise Lakes Resort worksheet. You use mixed and absolute references, a 3D reference, and set order of precedence. You also name cell ranges and use auditing tools.

File Needed: **ParadiseLakes-02.xlsx** *[Student data files are available in the* Library *of your SIMnet account.]*
Completed Project File Name: **[your initials] PP E2-1.xlsx**

1. Open the **ParadiseLakes-02.xlsx** workbook from your student data files.

2. Save the workbook as [your initials] PP E2-1. (If the workbook opens in *Protected View*, click **Enable Editing**.)

3. Enter and copy an addition formula.
   a. Click cell **B10** on the **Cass Lake** sheet.
   b. Type = to start a formula.
   c. Click cell **B5** to insert the first rental item in the formula.
   d. Type + as the mathematical operator.
   e. Click cell **B7** to add the second rental item. The formula is **=B5+B7** (Figure 2-20).
   f. Press **Enter** or click the **Enter** button on the *Formula* bar. The result is $5,758.
   g. Select cell **B10** and point to the *Fill* handle.
   h. Drag the *Fill* pointer to copy the formula to cells **C10:H10**. Ignore the *Auto Fill Options* button.

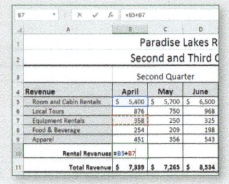

2-20 Point and click to build a formula

4. Create and copy a 3D formula with absolute cell references.
   a. Select cell **B15**. Administrative expense is calculated by multiplying the total revenue for the month by a set percentage.
   b. Type = to start the formula.
   c. Click cell **B11**, the total revenue for April.
   d. Type * to indicate multiplication.
   e. Click the **Rates&Tables** sheet tab. The sheet name is inserted in the *Formula* bar with single quotes and an exclamation point.
   f. Click cell **G2**, the percentage for administrative expenses. The cell address is added to the formula.
   g. Press **F4 (FN+F4)** to make the reference absolute (Figure 2-21).
   h. Press **Enter**. The formula is complete and the *Cass Lake* sheet is active.
   i. Select cell **B15** and drag the *Fill* pointer to copy the formula to cells **C15:G15**. The reference to cell G2 does not change, but the reference to cell B11 does (Figure 2-22).

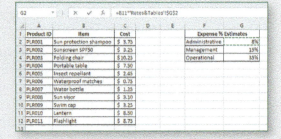

2-21 Absolute 3D reference in the formula

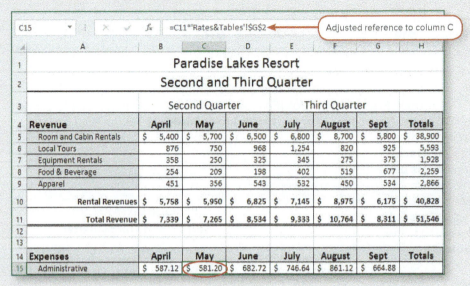

2-22 Copied formula with absolute reference

5. Create and copy a 3D formula with mixed references.
   a. Select cell **B16**. Management expense is calculated by multiplying the total revenue for the month by the set percentage.
   b. Type **=** to start the formula.
   c. Click cell **B11**, the total revenue for April.
   d. Press **F4 (FN+F4)** to make the reference absolute ($B$11).
   e. Press **F4 (FN+F4)** to make the reference mixed with the row reference absolute (B$11). When the formula is copied, the row will not change but the column reference will (Figure 2-23).
   f. Type ***** for multiplication.
   g. Click the **Rates&Tables** sheet tab. The sheet name is inserted in the *Formula* bar.
   h. Click cell **G3**, the percentage for management expenses.
   i. Press **F4 (FN+F4)** to make the reference absolute ($G$3).
   j. Press **F4 (FN+F4)** to make the reference mixed with the row reference absolute (G$3).
   k. Press **F4 (FN+F4)** to make the reference mixed with the column reference absolute ($G3) (Figure 2-24). When the formula is copied, the column will not change but the row will.

2-23 Mixed cell reference

G3		✕ ✓	f_x	=B$11*'Rates&Tables'!$G3		
	A	B	C	D	E	F	G
1	Product ID	Item	Cost			Expense % Estimates	
2	PLR001	Sun protection shampoo	$ 3.75			Administrative	8%
3	PLR002	Sunscreen SPF50	$ 3.25			Management	15%
4	PLR003	Folding chair	$10.25			Operational	35%
5	PLR004	Portable table	$ 7.50				

2-24 Absolute reference to column G

l.   Press **Enter**. The formula is complete and the *Cass Lake* sheet is active.
   m.   Select cell **B16** and drag its *Fill* pointer to cell **B17**.
   n.   Keep cells **B16:B17** selected and drag the *Fill* pointer for cell B17 to copy the formulas to cells **C16:G17**.

6.   Use *Formula Auditing* tools.
   a.   Click cell **D17** to view how the mixed reference formula has been copied.
   b.   Click the **Trace Precedents** button [*Formulas* tab, *Formula Auditing* group]. The formula refers to cell D11 on the **Cass Lake** sheet and to the **Tables&Rates** sheet.
   c.   Click cell **E16** and click the **Trace Precedents** button. The formula refers to cell E11 on the **Cass Lake** sheet and to the **Tables&Rates** sheet (Figure 2-25).
   d.   Click the **Remove Arrows** button [*Formulas* tab, *Formula Auditing* group].
   e.   Click the **Show Formulas** [*Formulas* tab, *Formula Auditing* group] to see all formulas. This view does not display number formatting (Figure 2-26).

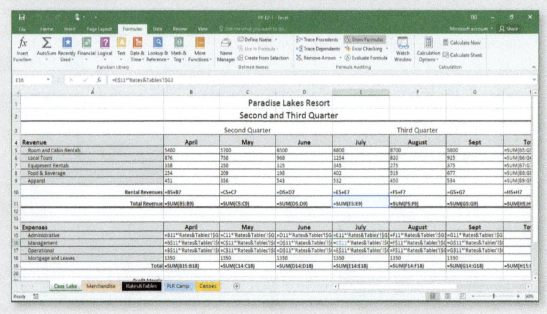

2-25 Formula precedents

2-26 Formulas displayed in worksheet

   f.   Click the **Show Formulas** [*Formulas* tab, *Formula Auditing* group] to hide the formulas.

7. Edit a formula and correct an error.
   a. Select cells **H15:H18** and click the **AutoSum** button [*Home* tab, *Editing* group]. The *SUM* function displays in each cell.
   b. Widen column **H** to display all data.
   c. Double-click cell **H16** to start *Edit* mode.
   d. Edit the cell range to **B15:G16** and press **Enter** to create a deliberate error. The green error triangle appears in the upper right corner of the cell.
   e. Click cell **H16** to display the **Trace Error** button and then click the button. This formula is now inconsistent with others in the column (Figure 2-27).

H16	▼ : × ✓ *fx*	=SUM(B15:G16)					

	A	B	C	D	E	F	G	H
1	Paradise Lakes Resort							
2	Second and Third Quarter							
3			Second Quarter			Third Quarter		
4	Revenue	April	May	June	July	August	Sept	Totals
5	Room and Cabin Rentals	$ 5,400	$ 5,700	$ 6,500	$ 6,800	$ 8,700	$ 5,800	$ 38,900
6	Local Tours	876	750	968	1,254	820	925	5,593
7	Equipment Rentals	358	250	325	345	275	375	1,928
8	Food & Beverage	254	209	198	402	519	677	2,259
9	Apparel	451	356	543				2,866
10	Rental Revenues	$ 5,758	$ 5,950	$ 6,825	$	Inconsistent Formula		$ 40,828
11	Total Revenue	$ 7,339	$ 7,265	$ 8,534	$	Copy Formula from Above		$ 51,546
12						Help on this error		
13						Ignore Error		
14	Expenses	April	May	June		Edit in Formula Bar		Totals
15	Administrative	$ 587.12	$ 581.20	$ 682.72	$	Error Checking Options...		$ 4,123.68
16	Management	$ 1,100.85	$ 1,089.75	$ 1,280.10	$ 1,399.95	$ 1,614.60	$ 1,24⚠️ ▾	$ 11,855.58
17	Operational	$ 2,568.65	$ 2,542.75	$ 2,986.90	$ 3,266.55	$ 3,767.40	$ 2,908.85	$ 18,041.10

2-27 *Trace Error* button and options

   f. Select **Copy Formula from Above** to correct the error.
   g. Click cell **H16** and click the **Trace Precedents** button [*Formulas* tab, *Formula Auditing* group]. The formula refers to the correct cells in row 16.
   h. Click the **Remove Arrows** button [*Formulas* tab, *Formula Auditing* group].

8. Set mathematical order of operations.
   a. Select cell **B21**. Profit margin, as a percentage, is revenue minus expenses divided by revenue. The formula is **=(B11−B19)/B11**; the parentheses are necessary so that the subtraction is done before the division.
   b. Type **=(** to start the formula and insert the opening parenthesis.
   c. Click cell **B11**, the total revenue for April.
   d. Type **−** for subtraction.
   e. Click cell **B19**, total expenses for April.
   f. Type **)** to set the precedence with the closing parenthesis.
   g. Type **/** for division and click cell **B11** (Figure 2-28).
   h. Press **Enter**. The result is formatted as *Accounting Number* format to match the source cells and displays a zero due to rounding.

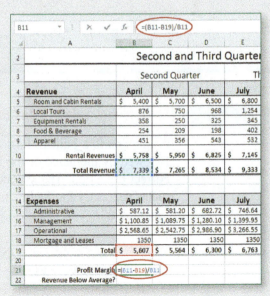

2-28 Set arithmetic order

i. Click cell **B21** and click the **Percent Style** button [*Home* tab, *Number* group].

j. Copy the formula in cell **B21** to cells **C21:G21**.

9. Name a cell range.

a. Select cell **H11** and click the **Name** box.

b. Type TotalRevenue in the *Name* box and press **Enter**.

c. Select cells **B11:G11**.

d. Click the **Define Name** button [*Formulas* tab, *Defined Names* group].

e. Type Monthly_Rev in the *Name* box and click **OK** (Figure 2-29).

f. Click cell **A1**.

g. Click the **Name box** arrow and choose **TotalRevenue**. Cell H11 is selected.

h. Click the **Name box** arrow and choose **Monthly_Rev**. Cells B11:G11 are selected.

New Name	? ☓
Name:	Monthly_Rev
Scope:	Workbook
Comment:	
Refers to:	='Cass Lake'!$B$11:$G$11

OK   Cancel

2-29 Use the *New Name* dialog box to name a range

10. Format cells **B16:H18** as **Comma Style**. Decrease the decimal two times.

11. Select cells **B15:H15** and decrease the decimal two times.

12. Press **Ctrl+Home**. Save and close the workbook (Figure 2-30).

Paradise Lakes Resort							
Second and Third Quarter							
	Second Quarter			Third Quarter			
Revenue	April	May	June	July	August	Sept	Totals
Room and Cabin Rentals	$ 5,400	$ 5,700	$ 6,500	$ 6,800	$ 8,700	$ 5,800	$ 38,900
Local Tours	876	750	968	1,254	820	925	5,593
Equipment Rentals	358	250	325	345	275	375	1,928
Food & Beverage	254	209	198	402	519	677	2,259
Apparel	451	356	543	532	450	534	2,866
Rental Revenues	$ 5,758	$ 5,950	$ 6,825	$ 7,145	$ 8,975	$ 6,175	$ 40,828
Total Revenue	$ 7,339	$ 7,265	$ 8,534	$ 9,333	$ 10,764	$ 8,311	$ 51,546
Expenses	April	May	June	July	August	Sept	Totals
Administrative	$ 587	$ 581	$ 683	$ 747	$ 861	$ 665	$ 4,124
Management	1,101	1,090	1,280	1,400	1,615	1,247	$ 7,782
Operational	2,569	2,543	2,987	3,267	3,767	2,909	$ 18,041
Mortgage and Leases	1350	1350	1350	1350	1350	1350	$ 8,100
Total	$ 5,607	$ 5,564	$ 6,300	$ 6,763	$ 7,593	$ 6,170	$ 37,997
Profit Margin	24%	23%	26%	28%	29%	26%	
Revenue Below Average?							

2-30 PP E2-1 completed

SLO 2.5

Working with Statistical and Date & Time Functions

A function is a built-in formula. Like a formula, a function starts with an equals sign (=) followed by the name of the function. Each function has its own syntax, its set of rules for correct execution. The syntax includes arguments, which are cell references and other elements necessary for the function to work properly.

> **MORE INFO**
>
> A formula such as **=B2+B3−B6** is usually not called a function since it has no function name.

Excel functions are grouped into categories on the *Formulas* command tab in the *Function Library* group. This group also has an *Insert Function* button which opens the *Insert Function* dialog box. From this dialog box, you can display an alphabetical list of all functions, a list by category, or a recently used list. You can also search for a function by name in this dialog box.

The *Statistical* function category includes calculations that determine an average, a maximum, a minimum, and a count. These common functions are options on the *AutoSum* button on the *Home* tab. The *Formulas* tab also has an *AutoSum* button with the same options.

AVERAGE Function

The *AVERAGE* function calculates the arithmetic **mean** of a range of cells. The mean is determined by adding all the values and dividing the result by the number of values. The *AVERAGE* function ignores empty cells or cells that include labels. When calculating an average, do not include total values in the range to be averaged.

The *AVERAGE* function has one argument, *numberN*. A number argument can be a range such as B11:G11. You can average up to 255 numbers (or ranges). The proper syntax for an *AVERAGE* function is:

> **=AVERAGE(number1, [number2], [number3], . . .)**

The *Number1* argument is required and others are optional.

When you choose a function from the *AutoSum* button, you will see the function name, an assumed range within parentheses, and an **Argument ScreenTip** below the cell that displays the syntax. When you choose to type a function, the *ScreenTip* shows the next argument in bold type as a guideline.

▶ **HOW TO:** Use the AVERAGE Function

1. Click the cell for the function.
2. Click the **AutoSum** button arrow [*Formulas* tab, *Function Library* group].
3. Select **Average**.
   - The function and an assumed argument range display in the *Formula* bar and in the cell.
4. Select the correct cell range (Figure 2-31).
   - You can type cell addresses rather than selecting cells.
   - When the selected cells have been named, the range name is substituted in the formula.

2-31 *AVERAGE* function

5. Press **Enter**.
   - You can use any completion key.

COUNT Functions

There are five functions in the *Statistical* category that are *COUNT* functions which tally the number of items in a range. The basic *COUNT* function is an option on the *AutoSum* button, but it appears in the list as *Count Numbers*. The *COUNT* function includes only cells with values in its result.

From the *Statistical* group, you can choose *COUNTA* which includes cells with values and labels. There is a *COUNTBLANK* function that counts cells that are empty. The following table describes the *Statistical COUNT* functions.

Statistical COUNT Functions

Count Functions	Description	Example Syntax
COUNT (Count Numbers)	Counts the cells in a range that contain values	=COUNT(A1:A15)
COUNTA	Counts the cells in a range that contain any data type	=COUNTA(A1:A15)
COUNTBLANK	Counts empty cells in a range	=COUNTBLANK(A1:A15)
COUNTIF	Counts the cells in a range that meet the criteria argument	=COUNTIF(A1:A15, "Services")
COUNTIFS	Counts the cells in one or more criteria ranges that meet respective criteria arguments	=COUNTIFS(B2:B5, "=A", C2:C5, "=21")

The *COUNT* function has one argument, *valueN*. You can count up to 255 cells or ranges. The proper syntax for a *COUNT* function is:

=COUNT(value1, [value2], [value3], . . .)

The *Value1* argument is required.

▶**HOW TO:** Use the COUNT Function

1. Click the cell for the function.
2. Click the **AutoSum** button arrow [*Formulas* tab, *Function Library* group].
3. Select **Count Numbers**.
   - The *COUNT* function is inserted with an assumed range.
   - The function appears in the cell and in the *Formula* bar (Figure 2-32).

B5 =COUNT(B5:G5)

Paradise Lakes Resort

Second and Third Quarter

	Second Quarter			Third Quarter			
Revenue	**April**	**May**	**June**	**July**	**August**	**Sept**	**Totals**
Room and Cabin Rentals	$ 5,400	$ 5,700	$ 6,500	$ 6,800	$ 8,700	$ 5,800	$ 38,900
Local Tours	876	750	968	1,254	820	925	5,593
Equipment Rentals	358	250	325	345	275	375	1,928
Food & Beverage	254	209	198	402	519	677	2,259
Apparel	451	356	543	532	450	534	2,866
Rental Revenues	**$ 5,758**	**$ 5,950**	**$ 6,825**	**$ 7,145**	**$ 8,975**	**$ 6,175**	**$ 40,828**
Total Revenue	**$ 7,339**	**$ 7,265**	**$ 8,534**	**$ 9,333**	**$ 10,764**	**$ 8,311**	**$ 51,546**

Expenses	**April**	**May**	**June**	**July**	**August**	**Sept**	**Totals**
Administrative	$ 587	$ 581	$ 683	$ 747	$ 861	$ 665	$ 4,124
Management	1,101	1,090	1,280	1,400	1,615	1,247	$ 7,732
Operational	2,569	2,543	2,987	3,267	3,767	2,909	$ 18,041
Mortgage and Leases	1350	1350	1350	1350	1350	1350	$ 8,100
Total	**$ 5,607**	**$ 5,564**	**$ 6,300**	**$ 6,763**	**$ 7,593**	**$ 6,170**	**$ 37,997**

Total Revenue	
Average Monthly Revenue	
Maximum Cabin Revenue	$ 6,483.33
Minimum Tour Revenue	
Number of Months	=COUNT(B5:G5)

COUNT(value1, [value2], ...)

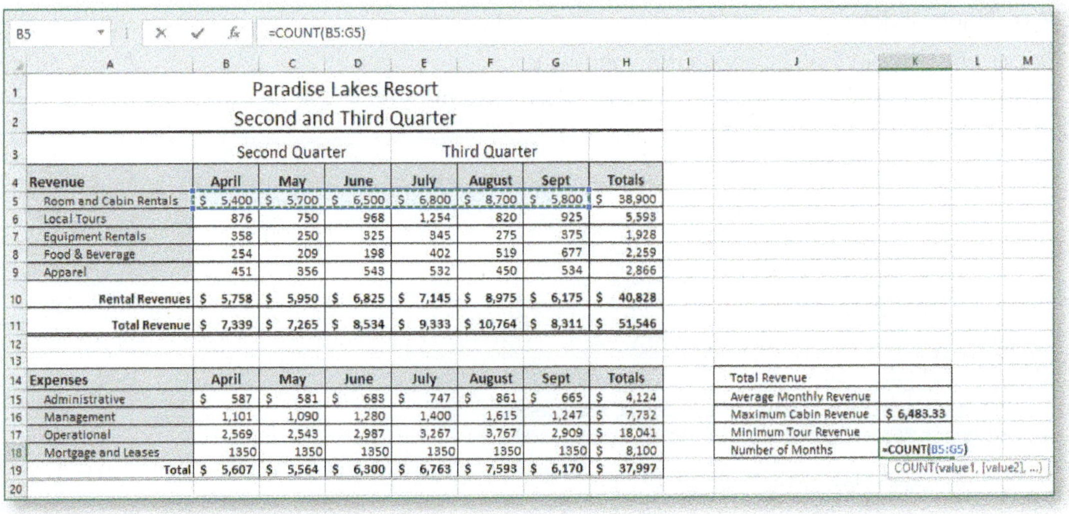

2-32 ***COUNT* function**

4. Select the correct cell range.
   - You can type cell addresses rather than selecting cells.
5. Press **Enter** or any completion key.

MORE INFO

If you use *COUNT* with a range of labels, the result is zero (0).

MAX and MIN Functions

The *MAX* function finds the largest value in a range, and the *MIN* function finds the smallest value. Both functions are options on the *AutoSum* button. Each has one argument, the cells to be evaluated.

The proper syntax for *MAX* and *MIN* functions is:

=MAX(number1, [number2], [number3], . . .)
=MIN(number1, [number2], [number3], . . .)

In many worksheets, an argument range is a group of adjacent cells such as B11:G11, but the cells need not be next to each other. You can select individual cells anywhere in the worksheet for an argument, and they are separated by commas as in =MAX(B11, B15, B18).

HOW TO: Use the MAX Function with Nonadjacent Cells

1. Click the cell for the function.
2. Click the **AutoSum** button arrow [*Formulas* tab, *Function Library* group].

3. Select **Max** (Figure 2-33).

- The function displays in the cell and in the *Formula* bar.
- The *Argument ScreenTip* shows the next argument in bold **number1**.

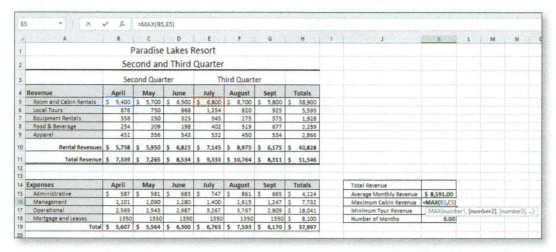

2-33 Use nonadjacent cells for MAX

4. Click the first cell to be evaluated.

5. Type **,** (a comma) to separate the arguments.

- The *Argument ScreenTip* shows the next argument in bold **number2**.

6. Click the next cell to be evaluated.

7. Type a comma **,** to add additional cells to the argument.

8. Press **Enter** when all the cells are listed.

AutoCalculate

The ***AutoCalculate*** feature is located on the right side of the *Status* bar where statistical and mathematical results are displayed for selected cells. The calculations are *Average*, *Count*, *Numerical Count*, *Maximum*, *Minimum*, and *Sum*. The *Count* calculation is the equivalent of *COUNTA*, and *Numerical Count* is the same as *COUNT*. *AutoCalculate* allows you to see results without inserting a function in the worksheet. You can see and change which calculations are visible by right-clicking that area of the *Status* bar to open the *Customize Status Bar* menu.

▶ **HOW TO: Use AutoCalculate**

1. Select the cell range or individual cells in the worksheet.

2. View the results on the *Status* bar (Figure 2-34).

- Selected options appear on the *Status* bar when appropriate; there is no *SUM* when you select labels.

3. Right-click the right side of the *Status* bar.

- The *Customize Status Bar* menu opens.
- If a function has a check mark to the left, it is active.

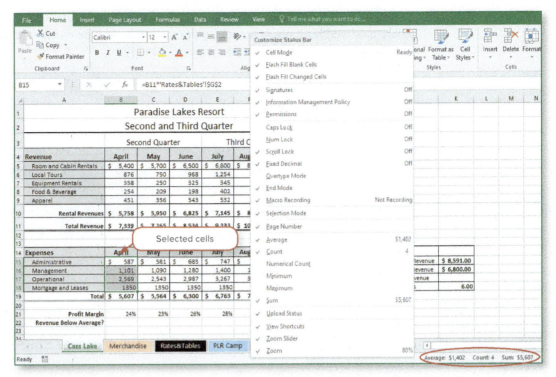

2-34 *AutoCalculate* results and other *Status* bar options

4. Select a calculation name to activate it and show it on the *Status* bar.

5. Select a calculation name with a check mark to hide it from the *Status* bar.

TODAY and NOW Functions

The *Date & Time* category has many functions for date and time arithmetic, for converting dates and times to values, and for controlling how dates and times are displayed.

The *TODAY* function inserts the current date in the cell and updates each time the workbook is opened. It uses the computer's clock, and the syntax is =TODAY(). The parentheses are necessary, but there are no arguments. The *NOW* function uses the syntax =NOW() and has no arguments. These two functions are *volatile* which means that the result depends on the current date, time, and computer.

After either function is inserted, you can format results to show both the date and the time. The *Format Cells* dialog box has a *Date* category and a *Time* category with many preset styles. There are also two date formats available from the *Number Format* list [*Home* tab, *Number* group], *Short Date* and *Long Date*.

In its handling of dates, Excel treats each date as a *serial number*, a unique value assigned to each date. Excel starts by setting January 1, 1900, as number 1; January 2, 1900 is number 2, and so on. January 1, 2018, is number 43101. You can see the serial number for any date by applying the *General* format to the cell.

> **MORE INFO**
>
> On the *Advanced* pane in the *Excel Options* dialog box [*File* tab], you can set a 1904 date system which matches the date system in the Macintosh operating system.

You can select **TODAY** or **NOW** from the *Date & Time* function category. Since they are widely used and have no arguments, you may prefer to type either with the help of *Formula AutoComplete*.

> **HOW TO:** Insert TODAY with Formula AutoComplete

1. Click the cell.

2. Type =to to display a filtered *Formula AutoComplete* list (Figure 2-35).

   - The list appears as soon as you type a character.
   - Each additional character further limits the list of names.

3. Point to the function name and double-click.

   2-35 *Formula AutoComplete* list

   - Instead of double-clicking the name, point and click once to select it and press **Tab**.
   - The name and parentheses are inserted.
   - If you accidentally press **Enter** to select a name and see an error in the cell, delete the cell contents and try again.

4. Press **Enter** to complete the function (Figure 2-36).

   - Excel supplies the closing parenthesis.
   - The current date is shown in the cell.
   - The *TODAY* function has no arguments.

   2-36 **TODAY inserted in cell**

PAUSE & PRACTICE: EXCEL 2-2

For this project, you open your Pause & Practice file and insert Excel functions to complete more of the worksheet. You insert functions from the *AutoSum* button and by typing. You also use *AutoCalculate* to check results.

File Needed: ***[your initials] PP E2-1.xlsx***
Completed Project File Name: ***[your initials] PP E2-2.xlsx***

---

1. Open the ***[your initials] PP E2-1.xlsx*** workbook completed in *Pause & Practice 2-1* and save it as [your initials] PP E2-2.

2. Enter functions using the *AutoSum* button.
   a. Click the **Cass Lake** worksheet tab and select cell **K14**.
   b. Click the **AutoSum** arrow button [*Formulas* tab, *Function Library* group].
   c. Choose **Sum**. The function name and parentheses are inserted, and a *Function ScreenTip* is visible.
   d. Select cells **B11:G11**. The range is highlighted on screen, and Excel has substituted the defined name that you set in *Pause & Practice 2-1* (Figure 2-37).
   e. Press **Enter**.
   f. Select cell **K15** and click the **AutoSum** arrow button [*Formulas* tab, *Function Library* group].
   g. Choose **Average**. The name and parentheses are inserted.
   h. Select cells **B11:G11**. The range is highlighted, but the range name is substituted.
   i. Press **Enter**. Average sales are $8,591.

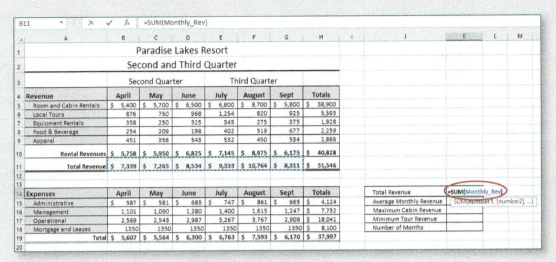

| B11 | | ▼ | : | × | ✓ | f_x | =SUM(Monthly_Rev) | | | | | | |

Paradise Lakes Resort
Second and Third Quarter

	April	May	June	July	August	Sept	Totals
		Second Quarter			Third Quarter		
Revenue	**April**	**May**	**June**	**July**	**August**	**Sept**	**Totals**
Room and Cabin Rentals	$ 5,400	$ 5,700	$ 6,500	$ 6,800	$ 8,700	$ 5,800	$ 38,900
Local Tours	876	750	968	1,254	820	925	5,593
Equipment Rentals	358	250	325	345	275	375	1,928
Food & Beverage	254	209	198	402	519	677	2,259
Apparel	451	356	543	532	450	534	2,866
Rental Revenues	$ 5,758	$ 5,950	$ 6,825	$ 7,145	$ 8,975	$ 6,175	$ 40,828
Total Revenue	$ 7,339	$ 7,265	$ 8,534	$ 9,333	$ 10,764	$ 8,311	$ 51,546

Expenses	**April**	**May**	**June**	**July**	**August**	**Sept**	**Totals**			
Administrative	$ 587	$ 581	$ 683	$ 747	$ 861	$ 665	$ 4,124	Total Revenue	=SUM(Monthly_Rev)
Management	1,101	1,090	1,280	1,400	1,615	1,247	$ 7,782	Average Monthly Revenue	SUM(number1, [number2], …)
Operational	2,569	2,543	2,987	3,267	3,767	2,909	18,041	Maximum Cabin Revenue	
Mortgage and Leases	1350	1350	1350	1350	1350	1350	8,100	Minimum Tour Revenue	
Total	$ 5,607	$ 5,564	$ 6,300	$ 6,763	$ 7,593	$ 6,170	$ 37,997	Number of Months	

2-37 Range name substituted in formula

3. Enter the *MAX* function by typing.
   a. Select cell **K16**.
   b. Type =ma to display the *Formula AutoComplete* list. You only need type as many characters as necessary to see the function name.
   c. Point to **MAX** in the list, click to select it, and press **Tab** (Figure 2-38).
   d. Select cells **B5:G5** for the *number1* argument. This range is not named.
   e. Press **Enter**. Excel supplies the closing parenthesis.

2-38 Choose *MAX* from *Formula AutoComplete* list

4. Copy and edit a function.
   a. Select cell **K16** and use the *Fill* pointer to copy the formula to cell **K17**.
   b. Double-click cell **K17**. Note that the argument cell range was updated because it was a relative reference.
   c. Replace the function name *MAX* in the cell with **min** (Figure 2-39).
   d. Press **Enter**. The minimum value is $750.

2-39 Edit a function name

5. Type the *COUNT* function.
   a. Select cell **K18**.
   b. Type =cou to display the *Formula AutoComplete* list.
   c. Double-click **COUNTA** in the list. This function counts cells with labels and values. The *ScreenTip* shows the first argument as *value1*.
   d. Select cells **B4:G4** to count the months. The formula is =COUNTA(B4:G4).
   e. Press **Enter**. The final parenthesis is supplied, and the result is 6.00.
   f. Select cells **K14:K18** and decrease the decimal two times.
   g. Apply the **General** format to cell **K18** [*Home* tab, *Number* group, *Number Format* drop-down list].

6. Check results with *AutoCalculate*.
   a. Select cells **B11:G11**.
   b. Right-click near the middle of the *Status* bar to display the options.
   c. Verify that **Average, Count,** and **Sum** are checked.
   d. Left-click anywhere in the *Status* bar to close the menu.
   e. Compare the values shown in the *Status* bar with the results in column K.

7. Insert the *TODAY* function.
   a. Select cell **A25**.
   b. Click the **Formulas** tab.
   c. Click the **Date & Time** button [*Function Library* group].
   d. Find and select **TODAY**. A *Function Arguments* dialog box notes that this function does not have any arguments and that it is volatile (Figure 2-40).
   e. Click **OK**. The current date is inserted.
   f. Press **Ctrl+Home**.

9. Save and close the workbook (Figure 2-41).

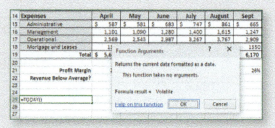

2-40 *Function Arguments* dialog box for *TODAY*

Paradise Lakes Resort								
Second and Third Quarter								
	Second Quarter			Third Quarter				
Revenue	April	May	June	July	August	Sept	Totals	
Room and Cabin Rentals	$ 5,400	$ 5,700	$ 6,500	$ 6,800	$ 8,700	$ 5,800	$ 38,900	
Local Tours	876	750	968	1,254	820	925	5,593	
Equipment Rentals	358	250	325	345	275	375	1,928	
Food & Beverage	254	209	198	402	519	677	2,259	
Apparel	451	356	543	532	450	534	2,866	
Rental Revenues	$ 5,758	$ 5,950	$ 6,825	$ 7,145	$ 8,975	$ 6,175	$ 40,828	
Total Revenue	$ 7,339	$ 7,265	$ 8,534	$ 9,333	$ 10,764	$ 8,311	$ 51,546	
Expenses	April	May	June	July	August	Sept	Totals	
Administrative	$ 587	$ 581	$ 683	$ 747	$ 861	$ 665	$ 4,124	Total Revenue	$ 51,546
Management	1,101	1,090	1,280	1,400	1,615	1,247	7,732	Average Monthly Revenue	$ 8,591
Operational	2,569	2,543	2,987	3,267	3,767	2,909	18,041	Maximum Cabin Revenue	$ 8,700
Mortgage and Leases	1350	1350	1350	1350	1350	1350	8,100	Minimum Tour Revenue	$ 750
Total	$ 5,607	$ 5,564	$ 6,300	$ 6,763	$ 7,593	$ 6,170	$ 37,997	Number of Months	6
Profit Margin	24%	23%	26%	28%	29%	26%		
Revenue Below Average?								
(Current Date)								

2-41 PP E2-2 completed

SLO 2.6

Working with Financial, Logical, and Lookup Functions

The *Financial* category includes functions that determine loan payments, the amount of interest earned, the rate of return on an investment, and more. Most of the functions in the *Logical* category display TRUE or FALSE as the result, but the *IF* function is in this group. An *IF* function can test if monthly revenue is above or below average and display "Yes" or "No" in the cell. The *Lookup & Reference* category is used to find and display information from a list in the workbook. For example, you might use a *Lookup* function to insert a price from a price list.

The Function Arguments Dialog Box

Functions require arguments in a particular order. They are easy to learn and build when you use the *Function Arguments* dialog box. This dialog box opens when you choose a function name from a category on the *Formulas* tab or when you use the *Insert Function* dialog box.

The *Function Arguments* dialog box shows each argument with an entry box and an explanation (Figure 2-42). You can select cells to enter an address, or you can type directly in the entry box. In addition to doing the work for you, the *Function Arguments* dialog box helps you learn the proper syntax for a function.

Function arguments may be required or optional. Optional arguments generally add some level of refinement to the calculation. In the *Function Arguments* dialog box and the

ScreenTip, a required argument name is shown in bold. When you use *Formula AutoComplete* to build a function, the *ScreenTip* shows optional arguments in square brackets (e.g., [type]).

When you are not sure about a function's name or category, you can search for it in the *Insert Function* dialog box. Open this dialog box by clicking the **Insert Function** button on the *Formulas* tab [*Function Library* group] or the same button to the left of the *Formula* bar. In the search area, type the name of the function or a brief description of what you want the function to do. For example, you can type "rate of return" to list *Financial* functions that calculate a rate of return for an investment.

2-42 *Function Arguments* dialog box for *AVERAGE*

▶ **ANOTHER WAY**

Shift+F3 opens the *Insert Function* dialog box.

PMT Function

The *PMT* function is in the *Financial* category. It calculates a constant loan payment amount for a period of time at a stated interest rate. When you borrow money for tuition or to buy a car, you can use the *PMT* function to determine your monthly payment for a selected payback time.

The *PMT* function has five arguments. Three of them are required: *rate*, *nper*, and *pv*. The other arguments are optional, *fv* and *type*. The proper syntax for a *PMT* formula is:

=PMT(rate, nper, pv, [fv], [type])

- **Rate** is the interest rate, a percentage of the amount borrowed. Most rates are set at a yearly rate. To determine monthly payments, you must divide the rate by 12.
- **Nper** is the total number of periods for repayment. If you make monthly payments for five years, the *nper* argument is 60.
- **Pv** is the present value, the amount borrowed.
- **Fv** is any future value after the last payment, an amount still owed at the end of the loan. When the *fv* argument is omitted, it means zero or that you have paid back the entire amount.
- **Type** indicates if payments are made at the beginning or the end of the period. Most loan payments are at the beginning of the period, because the interest amount is less. The number *1* is used to set payment at the beginning of the period.

Figure 2-43 shows a PMT function in cell B7 **=PMT(B6/12,B5*12,B4,,1)**. In the *Formula* bar, arguments are separated by commas. Where there are two commas with nothing between them, an argument has been omitted. In this case, it is the *fv* argument.

B6/12 is the interest *rate* divided by 12 to determine a monthly payment.
B5*12 is the *nper* argument, the number of years times 12, to determine the total number of payments.
B4 is the *pv* argument, the amount of money borrowed.
1 is the *type* argument and indicates that payment occurs at the beginning of the period.

The *PMT* result is a negative number, because the function is calculated from the borrower's point of view. It is money paid out.

2-43 *PMT* function is in cell B7

▶ HOW TO: Use the PMT Function

1. Click the cell where the function results should display.

2. Click the **Insert Function** button to the left of the *Formula* bar.

   • The *Insert Function* dialog box opens.

3. Type payment in the *Search for a function* box.

4. Click **Go** (Figure 2-44).

   • A list of functions that include some type of payment displays.

5. Select **PMT** and click **OK**.

   • The *Function Arguments* dialog box opens.
   • The dialog box includes a description of the function.

6. Click the **Rate** box and click the cell with the interest rate.

   • You can type the rate in the entry box with the percent sign.
   • An explanation of the argument is displayed.

7. Type */12* immediately after the address in the *Rate* box.

   • Divide by 12 for monthly payments.
   • If payments are quarterly, divide by 4.

8. Click the **Nper** box and click the cell that contains the loan term.

9. Type **12* immediately after the address in the *Nper* box.

   • If the loan term is years and payments are quarterly, multiply by 4.
   • If the cell already displays the total number of payments, just click to enter the address.

10. Click the **Pv** box and click the cell that contains the amount of the loan.

11. Click the **Type** box.

    • The *Fv* argument is usually omitted, because loans require a zero balance at the end.

12. Type *1* in the *Type* box to set a payment at the beginning of the period (Figure 2-45).

    • Most loan payments are at the beginning, because the payment is less than if it were at the end of the period.

13. Click **OK**.

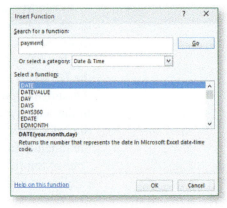

2-44 *Insert Function* dialog box

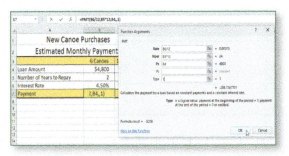

2-45 *Function Arguments* dialog box for *PMT*

> ▶ **MORE INFO**
>
> To show the payment as a positive value, type a minus sign (−) before the loan amount in the worksheet or before its cell address in the *Function Arguments* dialog box.

> ▶ **ANOTHER WAY**
>
> Choose the *PMT* function from the **Financial** button [*Formulas* tab, *Function Library* group].

IF Function

The *IF* function tests a condition or statement; if it is true, there is a specified result; if it is false, there is an alternative result. In the Paradise Lakes revenue worksheet, you can use an

IF formula to determine if each month's revenue is above average. If it is, you can display "Yes," in the cell, and if it is not, you can display "No."

> **MORE INFO**
>
> An *IF* function is similar to an *IF* statement in many programming languages.

An *IF* function has three arguments, and its syntax is:

=IF(logical_test, value_if_true, value_if_false)

- The **logical_test** is the value or statement to be evaluated.
- The **value_if_true** is the result displayed in the cell when the *logical_test* is true. You can select a cell, enter text, or use a formula for this argument.
- The **value_if_false** is the result displayed in the cell when the *logical_test* is false. You can select a cell, enter text, or use a formula for this argument.

An *IF* function can use comparison or logical operators in its arguments. The following table describes the comparison operators:

Comparison Operators

Operator	Description
=	Equal to
<>	Not equal to
>	Greater than
>=	Greater than or equal to
<	Less than
<=	Less than or equal to

Figure 2-46 has an *IF* function in cell D5 **=IF(B5>=4,18,20)**. When you use the *Function Arguments* dialog box to build a function, the commas to separate arguments are entered automatically.

B5>=4 is the *logical_test*. It determines if the value in cell B5 is equal to or greater than 4. Cell B5 is a relative reference so when the formula is copied, it will update to show the new row. The *value_if_true* argument is **18**. If the age is 4 or higher, the fee is $18. This value is a constant. It does not change when the formula is copied. The *value_if_false* argument is **20**, another constant. If the age is not 4 or higher, it must be lower and the fee is $20. The constant does not change when the formula is copied.

2-46 *IF* function in cell D5

You can insert the *IF* function from the *Logical* category on the *Formulas* tab, from the *Insert Function* button, or by typing it. When you type an *IF* function, you must type the commas to separate arguments, and you must enclose text arguments within quotation marks.

▶ HOW TO: Build an IF Function

1. Click the cell for the function.
2. Click the **Logical** button [*Formulas* tab, *Function Library* group].
   - The list of *Logical* functions opens.
3. Select **IF** in the list.
   - The *Function Arguments* dialog box for *IF* opens.
4. Click the **Logical_test** box.
5. Click the cell that will be evaluated.
   - Make the reference absolute if you know that the formula will be copied and that the reference should not change.
6. Type a comparison operator immediately after the cell address.
7. Type a value or click a cell to complete the expression to be tested.
   - You can build a statement such as B11=K15 or B11<10000.
   - Make a cell reference absolute or mixed if necessary.
8. Click the **Value_if_true** box.
9. Type the label or click a cell that contains data that should be displayed if the *logical_test* is true.
   - You can type a value in the text box.
10. Click the **Value_if_false** box.
11. Type the label or click a cell that contains data that should be displayed if the *logical_test* is false (Figure 2-47).
    - Results for the current cell are displayed in the *Function Arguments* dialog box.

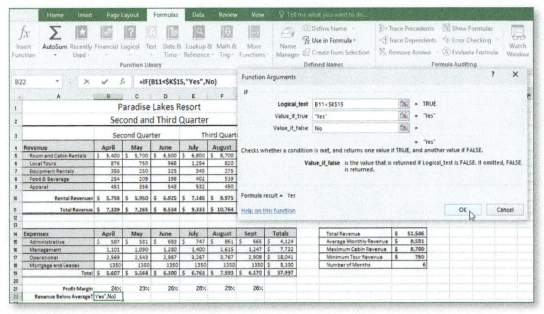

2-47 *Function Arguments* dialog box for *IF*

12. Click **OK**.

MORE INFO

The *value_if_false* argument for the *logical_test* can be another *IF* function which allows you to test for more than one possibility.

Lookup Functions

A *Lookup* function displays a piece of data from a range of cells in another part of the workbook. There are two *Lookup* functions: *VLOOKUP* (vertical) and *HLOOKUP* (horizontal). These two functions have the same syntax and similar arguments. *VLOOKUP* uses a lookup table that is organized in columns, and *HLOOKUP* uses a lookup range that is laid out in rows.

A *VLOOKUP* function has four arguments, and the syntax is:

=VLOOKUP (lookup_value, table_array, col_index_num, [range_lookup])

- The **lookup_value** is the data to be found or looked up. It is usually a cell address, but you can type a value or a text string. The function locates this *lookup_value* in the first column of the table array. It then displays data from the designated column in the same row as the *lookup_value*.
- The **table_array** is a range of cells, sorted in ascending order by the first column. The range can be located on a different worksheet or in a different workbook. It is good practice to name the range so that its reference is absolute.
- The **col_index_num** sets which column in the *table_array* contains the data to be displayed in the result. The columns are counted from left to right.
- The **[range lookup]** is optional and is often omitted. This argument is either TRUE or FALSE. TRUE means that Excel finds the closest match to the *lookup_value*, not always a good choice. If the data in the table array is sorted, TRUE will generally return the correct match. When you set this argument to FALSE, the data can be in any order.

Figure 2-48 shows a *VLOOKUP* function in cell D3 in the worksheet on the left. The result (250) is from the third column in row 6 in the table array in the worksheet on the right. These are two sheets in the same workbook.

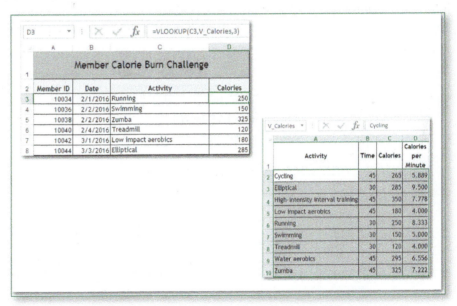

2-48 VLOOKUP function in cell D3 on the left

=VLOOKUP(C3,V_Calories,3)

The *lookup_value* argument is cell C3 ("Running").
The *table_array* argument is a named cell range, *V_Calories*. The "V" is a reminder that this range is a vertical lookup table. The *V_Calories* range is cells A2:D10 in the sheet on the right. The *col_index_num* argument is *3* so that the result is from the third column, the "Calories" column, in the *V_Calories* range.
The *range_lookup* argument is omitted or TRUE. The data in the table array (on the right) is sorted so TRUE is acceptable for this argument.

You can insert the *VLOOKUP* function from the *Lookup & Reference* category on the *Formulas* tab or by searching for it in the *Insert Function* dialog box. When you are experienced using the function, you can type it in the cell and use *Formula AutoComplete*.

▶ HOW TO: Enter the VLOOKUP Function

1. Click the cell for the function.
2. Click the **Lookup & Reference** button [*Formulas* tab].
3. Select **VLOOKUP**.
   - The *Function Arguments* dialog box opens.
   - Move the dialog box if it covers data that you need to see or select.
4. Click the **Lookup_value** box.
5. Click the cell to be matched.
   - The *lookup_value* is typically a cell in the same row as the function.
   - This reference is usually relative.
6. Click the **Table_array** box.
7. Select the cell range with the lookup data.
   - When the lookup table is named, the range name is substituted.
   - The *Function Arguments* dialog box collapses while you select cells.
8. Press **F4 (FN+F4)** to make the reference absolute if cell addresses are used.
   - When a range name has been substituted, you need not do this.
9. Click the **Col_index_num** box.
10. Type the column number, counting from the left, that contains the data to be displayed (Figure 2-49).
    - The result for the current cell is displayed in the dialog box.

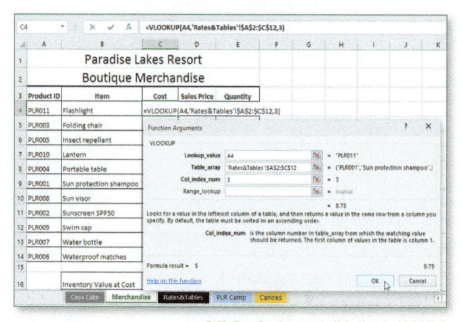

2-49 *Function Arguments* dialog box for *VLOOKUP*

11. Leave the *Range_lookup* argument box empty if the data in the table array is sorted.
12. Click **OK**.

The *HLOOKUP* function has a *row_index_num* argument instead of the *col_index_num* argument. *The table_array* is set up horizontally as seen in Figure 2-50, and the first row is arranged in alphabetical order from left to right. The *HLOOKUP* function is in cell C6 in the sheet on the left. The lookup table is named *H_Fees*, shown in the sheet on the right.

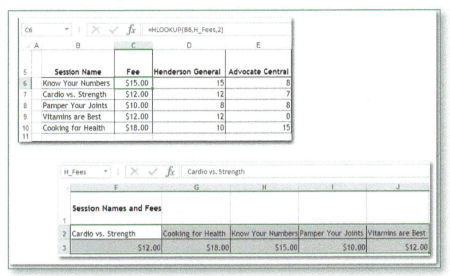

2-50 *HLOOKUP* in cell C6

=HLOOKUP(B6,H_Fees,2)

The *lookup_value* argument is cell B6 ("Know Your Numbers").
The *table_array* argument is a named cell range, *H_Fees*. The "H" is a visual cue for a horizontal lookup table. The *H_Fees* range is cells F2:J3 on the right.
The *row_index_num* argument is *2* so that the data shown in cell C6 is from the second row of the *H_Fees* range.
The *range_lookup* argument is omitted, because the data range is sorted alphabetically from left to right.

>
> **MORE INFO**
>
> The *range_lookup* argument TRUE (or omitted) finds the largest value that is less than or equal to the *lookup_value*.

▶ **HOW TO:** Use The HLOOKUP Function

1. Click the cell for the function.
2. Click the **Lookup & Reference** button [*Formulas* tab].
3. Select **HLOOKUP**.
   - The *Function Arguments* dialog box opens.
4. Click the **Lookup_value** box.
5. Click the cell to be matched.
   - The *lookup_value* is typically a cell in the same row as the function.
   - This reference is usually relative.
6. Click the **Table_array** box.

7. Select the cell range with the lookup data.
   - When the lookup table is named, the range name is substituted.
   - The *Function Arguments* dialog box collapses while you select cells.
8. Press **F4 (FN+F4)** to make the reference absolute when cell addresses are used.
9. Click the **Row_index_num** box.
10. Type the row number, counting the first row of the *table_array* as 1 (Figure 2-51).
    - The result for the current cell is displayed in the dialog box.

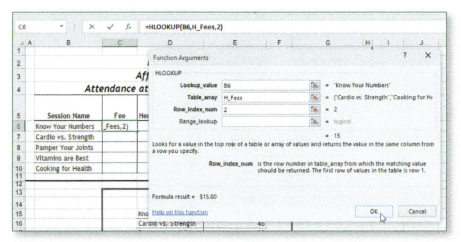

2-51 *HLOOKUP Function Arguments* **dialog box**

11. Leave the *Range_lookup* argument box empty if the data in the table array is sorted.
12. Click **OK**.

SLO 2.7

Using Math & Trig Functions

You have already used *SUM* from the *Math & Trig* function category. There are functions in this category to display the absolute value of data, one to calculate the cosine of an angle, or one that returns the power of a number. You might recognize the function *PI* or π from a math class. Three *Math & Trig* functions that are often used in business or personal calculations are *ROUND*, *SUMIF*, and *SUMPRODUCT*.

ROUND Function

Rounding means that a value is adjusted to display a specified number of decimal places or a whole number. You can round the numbers on your tax return in the United States which means that you need not show any cents, just dollars.

The *ROUND* function has two arguments, *number* and *num_digits*.

=ROUND(number, num_digits)

- The **number** is the cell or the value to be adjusted.
- The **num_digits** sets the number of decimal places for rounding. When this argument is zero (0), the value is displayed as the nearest whole number. When the *num_digits* argument is greater than zero, the value is rounded to that number of decimal places. You can use a negative number for the *num_digits* argument which rounds the value to the left of the decimal point. Make sure you understand the results when you round to the left of the decimal point.

When a value used in rounding is 5 or greater, results round up to the next digit. If you round 5.523 to show zero (0) decimal places, it rounds up to display as 6 because the value after the decimal point is 5. If you round 5.423 to two places, it rounds to 5.42 because the value used for rounding is 3. The *Increase Decimal* and *Decrease Decimal* buttons follow these rounding principles for displaying values in the cell as do the *Accounting Number* and *Currency* formats. These formats, however, keep the full unrounded value in the cell and use that value in calculations.

MORE INFO

When a value is rounded, the rounded value is used in calculations, not the full unrounded number.

▶ **HOW TO:** Use the ROUND Function

1. Click the cell for the function.
2. Type **=rou** and press **Tab**.
   - *Formula AutoComplete* inserts the function in the cell.
   - The *number* argument is bold in the *ScreenTip*.
3. Select the cell to be rounded.
   - The cell address appears in the cell and in the *Formula* bar.
   - You can type a value if there is no cell reference.
4. Type **,** (a comma) to separate the arguments.
   - The *num_digits* argument is bold in the *ScreenTip*.
5. Type a number to set the number of decimal places (Figure 2-52).
6. Press **Enter**.

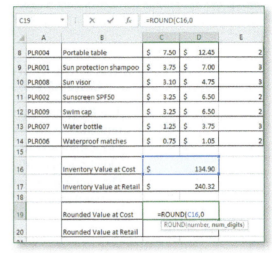
2-52 Type the *ROUND* function

MORE INFO

Excel has a *ROUNDDOWN* function that always rounds a number down. The *ROUNDUP* function rounds a value up.

SUMIF Function

The *SUMIF* function controls which data in a range is included in the total. It allows you to eliminate cells from the calculation by criteria that you set. *Criteria* are restrictions, conditions, or rules that must be met. In a *SUMIF* function, cell values are included in the sum only if they match the criteria.

The *SUMIF* function has three arguments.

=SUMIF (range, criteria, [sum_range])

- The **range** is the range of cells to be evaluated or searched, the values that are compared to the criteria.
- The **criteria** argument defines which cells from the range should be included in the sum. You can use comparison operators, cell references, a value, or text. When you use text or a comparison operator, the criteria must be enclosed in quotation marks.

- The *[sum_range]* is the cell range to be summed. This argument is optional, because it is omitted when the range to be summed is the same as the *range* argument.

Figure 2-53 illustrates a *SUMIF* function in cell I5 that totals sales for products that have a price greater than $10.

2-53 *SUMIF* function in cell I5

=SUMIF($D$4:$D$14,">=10",$F$4:$F$14)

The *range* argument is the sales price column, cells $D$4:$D$14. It is an absolute reference so that the formula can be copied.

The *criteria* argument is >=10, shown in quotation marks. The quotation marks are added automatically when you use the *Function Arguments* dialog box.

The *sum_range* argument is cells $F$4:$F$14, the cells to be added if the price is greater than 10.

> **MORE INFO**
>
> You can use wildcards (* or ?) in a criteria argument. For example, to sum sales for all items that begin with the letter S, use **s*** as the criteria. Criteria are not case-sensitive.

HOW TO: Build a SUMIF Function

1. Click the cell for the function.
2. Click the **Math & Trig** button [*Formulas* tab, *Function Library* group].
3. Select **SUMIF**.
4. Click the **Range** box.
5. Select the cell range to be compared against the criteria.
   - Make the reference absolute if the formula might be copied.
   - Press **F3 (FN+F3)** to paste a range name rather than selecting the range.
6. Click the **Criteria** box.
   - Type text to be compared or a value to be matched.
   - Type an expression with operators to be evaluated.
   - Quotation marks are automatically supplied.

7. Click the **Sum_range** box (Figure 2-54).
   - Select the cells to be added.
   - If the cells to be added are the same as those in the *range* argument, leave the entry blank.

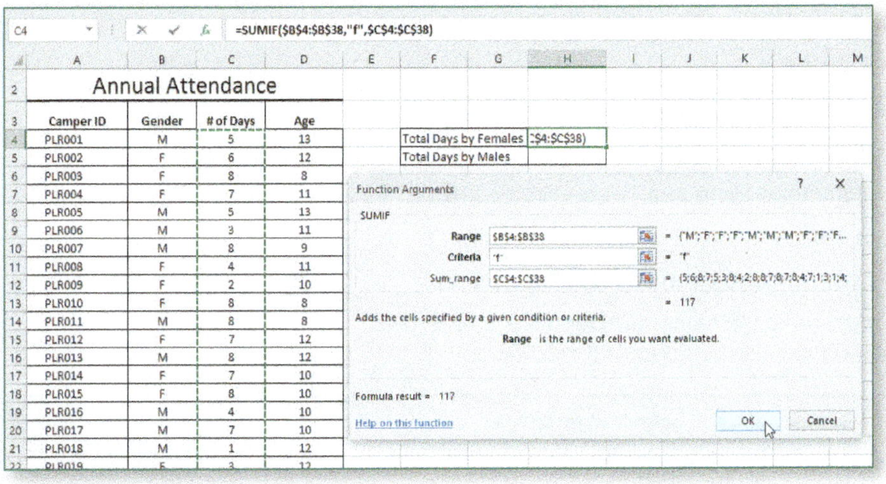

2-54 *Function Arguments dialog box for Sumif*

8. Click **OK**.

SUMPRODUCT Function

The *SUMPRODUCT* function calculates the sum of the product of several ranges. It multiplies the cells identified in its *array* arguments and then it totals those individual products. A ***product*** is the result of a multiplication problem; 4 is the product of 2 times 2. An ***array*** is a range of cells in a row or a column. An array has a ***dimension***, which is the number of columns or rows. The arrays A1:A5 and C1:C5 have the same dimension, five rows and one column.

The *SUMPRODUCT* function has the following syntax.

=SUMPRODUCT(array1, array2, [arrayN])

- The ***array1*** argument is the first range of cells for the multiplication.
- The ***array2*** argument is the range that is multiplied by the corresponding cells in the *array1* range. These two ranges must have the same number of cells, the same dimension.

It is possible to use more than two arrays so that you could have an *array3* argument or even more.

In Figure 2-55, the *SUMPRODUCT* function in cell C22 multiplies the first array C6:C20 by the corresponding values in cells F6:F20 and totals those products.

=SUMPRODUCT(C6:C20,F6:F20)

The value in cell C6 is multiplied by cell F6, cell C7 is multiplied by cell F7, and so on. Those individual products are summed, and the result is $249.15.

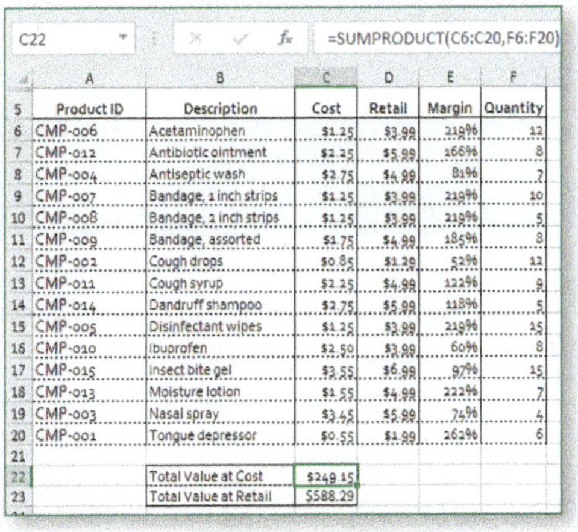

2-55 *SUMPRODUCT* in cell C22

1. Click the cell for the function.
2. Click the **Math & Trig** button [*Formulas* tab, *Function Library* group].
3. Select **SUMPRODUCT**.
   - The *Function Arguments* dialog box opens.
4. Click the **Array1** box.
5. Select the first cell range to be multiplied.
6. Click the **Array2** box.
7. Select the next cell range to be multiplied (Figure 2-56).
   - Both arrays must have the same number of cells and rows.
   - Use as many arrays as required for the calculation.

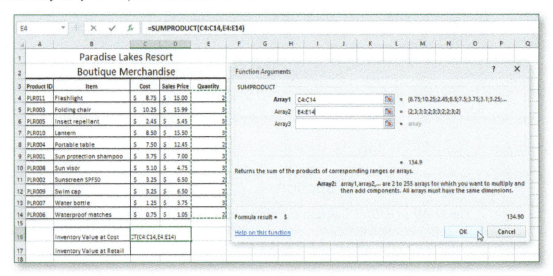

2-56 *Function Arguments* dialog box for *SUMPRODUCT*

8. Click **OK**.

> **MORE INFO**
>
> If an array in a *SUMPRODUCT* formula includes an empty cell, Excel treats that value as 0, but the multiplication by zero does not affect the sum.

PAUSE & PRACTICE: EXCEL 2-3

For this project, you continue working on the workbook for Paradise Lakes. You calculate totals related to camp attendance and merchandise inventory using functions from the *Math & Trig*, *Financial*, *Logical*, *Lookup & Reference*, and *Date & Time* categories.

File Needed: *[your initials] PP E2-2.xlsx*
Completed Project File Name: *[your initials] PP E2-3.xlsx*

1. Open the *[your initials] PP E2-2.xlsx* workbook completed in *Pause & Practice 2-2* and save it as [your initials] PP E2-3.

2. Click the **Cass Lake** worksheet tab.

3. Enter an *IF* function to determine if a month's revenue was below average.
   a. Click cell **B22** and click the **Formulas** tab.
   b. Click the **Logical** button In the *Function Library* group and select **IF**. The *Function Arguments* dialog box opens.
   c. Click the **Logical_test** text box and click cell **B11**.
   d. After "B11" in the *Logical_test* box, type < for a less than operator.
   e. Click cell **K15** and press **F4 (FN+F4)** to make this an absolute reference.
   f. Click the **Value_if_true** box and type Yes. You need not type quotation marks when you use the *Function Arguments* dialog box.
   g. Press **Tab** to move to the *Value_if_false* box. Excel supplies the quotation marks for "Yes."
   h. Type No (Figure 2-57).
   i. Click **OK**. For April, the result is *Yes*.
   j. Click cell **B22** and click the **Center** button [*Home* tab, *Font* group].
   k. Use the *Fill* pointer to copy the formula in cell **B22** to cells **C22:G22**.
   l. Press **Ctrl+Home**.

2-57 Build an *IF* function

4. Use *SUMIF* to calculate results.
   a. Click the **PLR Camp** worksheet tab. The number of attendees is tracked with the camper's ID, gender, and age.
   b. Select cell **H4**, and click the **Formulas** tab.
   c. Click the **Math & Trig** button in the *Function Library* group and select **SUMIF**.
   d. Click the **Range** text box and select cells **B4:B38**.
   e. Press **F4 (FN+F4)** to make the reference absolute.
   f. Press **Tab** and type f in the *Criteria* box. Criteria are not case-sensitive. The cells in column B will be checked to determine if they show "F."
   g. Click the **Sum_range** box, select cells **C4:C38**, and press **F4 (FN+F4)**. The values in this range will be summed for those rows in which the gender is F (Figure 2-58).
   h. Click **OK**. Female camp days are 117.
   i. Click cell **H4** and use the *Fill* pointer to copy the formula to cell **H5**.
   j. Edit the formula in cell **H5** to show m instead of "f."

2-58 Build a *SUMIF* function

5. Use *VLOOKUP* to display costs.
   a. Click the **Merchandise** sheet tab and select cell **C4**. Individual costs are missing, but they are listed on the **Rates&Tables** sheet.
   b. Click the **Lookup & Reference** button [*Formulas* tab, *Function Library* group].
   c. Select **VLOOKUP**.
   d. Click the **Lookup_value** box and select cell **A4**.
   e. Click the **Table_array** box. The table with the costs is on the **Rates&Tables** sheet.
   f. Click the **Rates&Tables** worksheet tab and select cells **A2:C12**. This array or range includes the ID, the name, and the cost. The costs are in column C, the third column from the left.

g. Press **F4 (FN+F4)** to make the array an absolute reference.

h. Click the **Col_index_num** box and type 3. The ID in cell A4 will be located in cells A2:C12 on the **Rates&Tables** sheet, and the cost in the third column will be displayed.

i. Click the **Range_lookup** box and type false (Figure 2-59).

j. Click **OK**. The cost for the first item is $8.75.

k. Copy the formula in cell **C4** to cells **C5:C14**.

2-59 Build a *VLOOKUP* function

6. Use *SUMPRODUCT* to calculate inventory values.
   a. Click cell **C16**. This is a merged and centered cell.
   b. Click the **Formulas** tab.
   c. Click the **Math & Trig** button in the *Function Library* group and select **SUMPRODUCT**.
   d. Click the **Array1** box and select cells **C4:C14**. There are 11 values in this range.
   e. Click the **Array2** box and select cells **E4:E14**. There are 11 values in this range, and each one will be multiplied by the corresponding value in the same row in column C.
   f. Click **OK**. The value of the inventory at cost is 134.9.
   g. Click cell **C17**, type =sump, and press **Tab**. The function is inserted and the *ScreenTip* shows the next argument, *array1*.
   h. Select cells **D4:D14** and type , (a comma) to separate the first argument from the second.
   i. Select cells **E4:E14** (Figure 2-60). You need not type the closing parenthesis.
   j. Press **Enter**. The value is 240.32.
   k. Select cells **C16:C17** and apply the **Accounting Number** format.

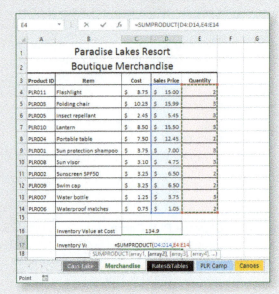

2-60 Type a *SUMPRODUCT* function

7. Use the *ROUND* function.
   a. Select cell **C19**.
   b. Click the **Math & Trig** button [*Formulas* tab, *Function Library* group].
   c. Select **ROUND**.
   d. In the *Number* text box, click cell **C16**.
   e. Type 0 in the *Num_digits* text box.
   f. Press **Enter**. The value is rounded up to $135.00.
   g. Copy the formula in cell **C19** to cell **C20**. The value from cell C17 is rounded down to $240.00.

8. Use the PMT function to determine payments for new canoe purchases.
   a. Click the **Canoes** sheet tab and click cell **B7**.
   b. Click the **Formulas** tab and the **Financial** button [*Function Library* group].
   c. Select **PMT**.
   d. Click the **Rate** box and click cell **B6**.
   e. Immediately after "B6," type /12 to divide the rate by 12 for monthly payments.

f. Click the **Nper** box and click cell **B5**. Type *12 to multiply by 12 for 12 months per year.

g. Click the **Pv** box and click cell **B4**. This is the amount of the loan.

h. Click the **Fv** box. Leave this blank to indicate no balance due at the end of the loan term.

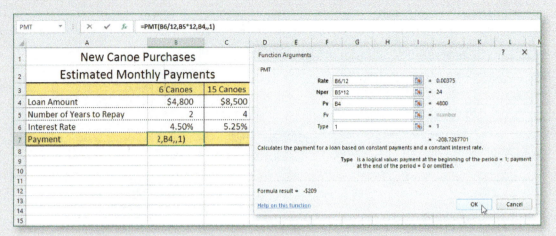

2-61 **PMT function for payment at the beginning of the period**

i. Click the **Type** box and type 1. The payment will made at the beginning of the month (Figure 2-61).

j. Click **OK**. The payment is −$209, a negative value because it is money paid out. This cell was formatted to show no decimal places.

9. Type the PMT function.

a. Click cell **C7**.

b. Type =pm, and press **Tab**. The *ScreenTip* shows the first argument, *rate*.

c. Click cell **C6** and type /12,. This divides the rate by 12 and enters a comma to separate the arguments (Figure 2-62).

d. Click cell **C5** for the *nper* argument, type *12, to multiply by 12 and enter a comma to separate the arguments.

e. Click cell **C4** for the *pv* argument, the amount of the loan.

f. Type , (a comma) to move to the *fv* argument.

g. Type , (another comma) to move to the *type* argument. *Formula AutoComplete* lists two options for the argument (Figure 2-63).

h. Double-click **1-beginning of the period** in the *ScreenTip*.

i. Press **Enter**. The payment is −$196.

j. Press **Ctrl+Home**.

2-62 **Type a PMT function**

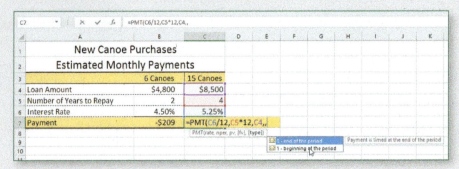

2-63 *Formula AutoComplete* **for argument choices**

10. Save and close the workbook (Figure 2-64).

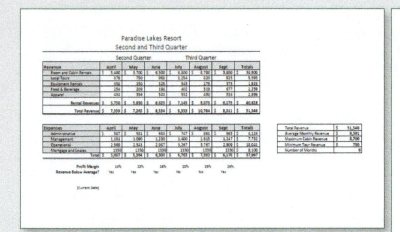

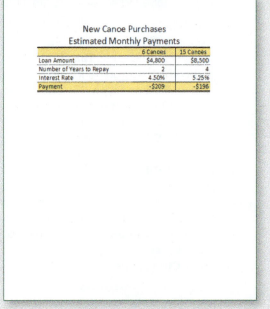

2-64 PP 2-3 completed

Chapter Summary

2.1 Build and edit basic formulas (p. E2-89).

- A *formula* is a calculation that uses arithmetic operators, worksheet cells, and constant values. Basic arithmetic operations are addition, subtraction, multiplication, and division.
- You can type a formula in the cell or you can point and click to select cells.
- When you type a formula, **Formula AutoComplete** displays suggestions for completing the formula.
- Formulas are edited in the *Formula* bar or in the cell to change cell addresses, use a different operator, or add cells to the calculation.

2.2 Set mathematical order of operations (p. E2-91).

- Excel follows mathematics rules for the order in which operations are carried out when a formula has more than one operator.
- You can control the sequence of calculations by placing operations that should be done first within parentheses.
- Use the following acronym to help remember the order of arithmetic operations: **P**lease **E**xcuse **M**y **D**ear **A**unt **S**ally (**P**arentheses, **E**xponentiation, **M**ultiplication, **D**ivision, **A**ddition, **S**ubtraction).

2.3 Use absolute, mixed, relative, and 3D references in a formula (p. E2-93).

- A *relative cell reference* in a formula is the cell address which, when copied, updates to the address of the copy.
- An **absolute cell reference** is the cell address with dollar signs as in $A$5. This reference does not change when the formula is copied.
- A **mixed cell reference** contains one relative and one absolute address as in $B5 or B$5. When copied, the absolute part of the reference does not change.
- A **3D cell reference** is a cell in another worksheet in the same workbook. It includes the name of the worksheet followed by an exclamation point as in *Inventory!B2*.
- You can name a single cell or a group of cells with a defined **range name**.
- You can use range names in formulas instead of cell addresses.

- *Formula AutoComplete* displays range names so that you can paste them in a formula.
- A named range is an absolute reference.

2.4 Use formula auditing tools in a worksheet (p. E2-99).

- Excel highlights several types of formula errors as you work, but you still need to review errors and make corrections.
- Excel automatically error-checks formulas based on its internal rules. A potential error is marked in the upper left corner of the cell with a small triangle.
- **Formula auditing** tools include several commands to aid your review of workbook formulas and functions.
- The *Formula Auditing* group on the *Formulas* tab includes the *Trace Precedents* and *Trace Dependents* buttons.
- A **circular reference** is an error that occurs when a formula includes the address of the formula.
- Some errors are noted as you press a completion key and can be quickly corrected by accepting the suggested correction in the message window.

2.5 Use *Statistical* and *Date & Time* functions (p. E2-106).

- The *AVERAGE* function calculates the arithmetic mean by adding values and dividing by the number of values.
- The *COUNT* function tallies the number of cells in a range. There are different *COUNT* functions based on whether cell contents are labels, values, or blank.
- *MAX* and *MIN* functions find the largest and the smallest values, respectively, in a range.
- Commonly used statistical functions are options on the *AutoSum* button.
- The **AutoCalculate** feature displays numerical results such as *Sum*, *Average*, and *Count* on the *Status* bar for selected cells.
- The *Date & Time* category includes a *TODAY* function and a *NOW* function that display the current date and time.

2.6 Work with functions from the *Financial*, *Logical*, and *Lookup & Reference* categories. (p. E2-114).

- Use the *Function Arguments* dialog box for help in completing an Excel function.

E2-131

- The *Function Arguments* dialog box includes a description of the function and an explanation of each argument.
- The *PMT* function from the *Financial* category calculates a constant payment amount for a loan.
- The *Logical* function *IF* evaluates a statement or condition and displays a particular result when the statement is true and another result when the condition is false.
- A *Lookup* function displays data from a cell located in another part of the workbook.
- Two widely used *Lookup* functions are *VLOOKUP* (vertical) and *HLOOKUP* (horizontal).

2.7 Build functions from the *Math & Trig* category (p. E2-122).
- The *ROUND* function adjusts a value up or down based on the number of decimal places.

- The *SUMIF* function includes cells in a total only if they meet a set criteria or condition.
- The *SUMPRODUCT* function multiplies corresponding cells from an **array** and then totals the results of each multiplication.

Check for Understanding

The SIMbook for this text (within your SIMnet account) provides the following resources for concept review:

- Multiple choice questions
- Matching exercises
- Short answer questions

Guided Project 2-1

Courtyard Medical Plaza (CMP) has doctor offices, a pharmacy, x-ray and lab services, insurance and billing support, optometry and dental facilities, and onsite dining. You will complete an inventory worksheet for the pharmacy as well as insurance and payment data for the optometry group.
[Student Learning Outcomes 2.1, 2.2, 2.3, 2.4, 2.5, 2.6, 2.7]

File Needed: **CourtyardMedical-02.xlsx** *[Student data files are available in the Library of your SIMnet account.]*
Completed Project File Name: **[your initials] Excel 2-1.xlsx**

Skills Covered in This Project

- Build and copy formulas.
- Name cell ranges.
- Use *AVERAGE*, *MAX*, and *MIN*.
- Use relative, mixed, absolute, and 3D cell references in formulas.
- Use *SUMIF*.
- Check results with *AutoCalculate*.
- Use the *VLOOKUP* function.
- Set mathematical order of operations.
- Use formula auditing tools.
- Use the *PMT* and *SUMPRODUCT* functions.
- Insert the *TODAY* function.

1. Open the **CourtyardMedical-02.xlsx** workbook from your student data files and save it as [your initials] Excel 2-1.

2. Enter and copy subtraction formulas.
    a. Click cell **E2** on the **Lookup_Data** worksheet. To calculate the dollar amount of the margin, subtract the cost from the retail price.
    b. Type an equals sign (=) to start the formula.
    c. Click cell **D2**, the retail price.
    d. Type a minus sign, or hyphen (−) to subtract, and click cell **C2**, the cost.
    e. Click the **Enter** button (check mark) on the *Formula* bar. The pointer stays in the formula cell. The margin for acetaminophen is $1.49.
    f. Drag the *Fill* pointer to copy the formula in cell **E2** to cells **E3:E16**. The *Auto Fill Options* button appears near cell E16.
    g. Click the **Auto Fill Options** button and choose **Fill Without Formatting** (Figure 2-65). This option copies the formula without the top border from cell E2.
    h. Format cells **E3:E16** as **Currency**.
    i. Click the **Optometry** sheet tab and select cell **G5**.
    j. Type = to start the formula to subtract the deductible amount from the billed amount.
    k. Click cell **E5**, the billed amount.
    l. Type −, click cell **F5**, the deductible amount, and press **Enter**.
    m. Copy the formula in cell **G5** to cells **G6:G24** without formatting to maintain the fill color.

E2	▾	✕ ✓	*fx*	=D2-C2

⊿	A	B	C	D	E	F
1	Product ID	Description	Cost	Retail	Margin	
2	CMP-006	Acetaminophen	$2.50	$3.99	$1.49	
3	CMP-001	Tongue depressor	$0.55	$1.99	$1.44	
4	CMP-002	Cough drops	$0.85	$1.29	$0.44	
5	CMP-003	Nasal spray	$3.45	$5.99	$2.54	
6	CMP-004	Antiseptic wash	$2.75	$4.99	$2.24	
7	CMP-005	Disinfectant wipes	$1.25	$3.99	$2.74	
8	CMP-007	Bandage, 1 inch strips	$1.25	$3.99	$2.74	
9	CMP-008	Bandage, 2 inch strips	$1.25	$3.99	$2.74	
10	CMP-009	Bandage, assorted	$1.75	$4.99	$3.24	
11	CMP-010	Ibuprofen	$2.50	$3.99	$1.49	
12	CMP-011	Cough syrup	$2.25	$4.99	$2.74	
13	CMP-012	Antibiotic ointment	$2.25	$5.99	$3.74	
14	CMP-013	Moisture lotion	$1.55	$4.99	$3.44	
15	CMP-014	Dandruff shampoo	$2.75	$5.99	$3.24	
16	CMP-015	Insect bite gel	$3.55	$6.99	$3.44	
17						
18				⊙	Copy Cells	
19				○	Fill Formatting Only	
20				○	Fill Without Formatting	
21				○	Flash Fill	
22						

2-65 Copy without formatting to preserve borders

3. Name cell ranges.
   a. Select cells **E5:E24**. This named range will refer to the billable amounts.
   b. Click the **Name** box.
   c. Type Billables in the *Name* box and press **Enter**.
   d. Click the **Lookup_Data** worksheet tab.
   e. Select cells **A2:D16**. This named range will not include the calculated margin.
   f. Click the **Name** box.
   g. Type Costs in the *Name* box and press **Enter**.
   h. Select cells **H2:I5** and click the **Formulas** tab.
   i. Click the **Create from Selection** button [*Defined Names* group]. Excel will create range names based on the labels in the column on the left.
   j. Select the **Left column** box and click **OK**.
   k. Click cell **A1** and click the **Name** box arrow to see the range names in the worksheet (Figure 2-66).

2-66 Range names in the worksheet

4. Use range names with *AVERAGE*, *MIN*, and *MAX*.
   a. Click the **Optometry** sheet tab and select cell **D27**.
   b. Type =aver and press **Tab**.
   c. Select cells **E5:E24** and press **Enter**. The range name is substituted in the formula when you select the cells in the worksheet.
   d. Select cell **D28**, click the **AutoSum** button arrow [*Home* tab, *Editing* group], and select **Max**.
   e. Select cells **E5:E24** and press **Enter**.
   f. Use *MIN* in cell **D29** with the same cell range.

5. Set the order of operations in a 3D formula.
   a. Click the **Insurance** sheet tab and select cell **D5**. The total with service charge is calculated by multiplying 1 plus the percentage times the billed amount. The percentages are on the **Lookup_Data** sheet in named ranges.
   b. Type = and click cell **C5**.
   c. Type *(immediately after **C5**. The next part of the formula will be calculated first.
   d. Type 1+ immediately after the left parenthesis. The calculation is (1+ the percentage).
   e. Click the **Lookup_Data** sheet tab. The sheet name is displayed in the *Formula* bar.
   f. Click cell **I2**. The range name is substituted. Because it is an absolute reference, the sheet name is removed (Figure 2-67).
   g. Press **Enter**. Because the formula refers to another sheet and a range name, the missing parenthesis is not automatically supplied (Figure 2-68).
   h. Click **Yes** to accept the suggested correction.
   i. Copy the formula to cells **D5:D9** for the Green Cross patients.

2-67 3D formula with a range name

6. Edit and copy a formula.
   a. Click cell **D9** and copy the formula to cell **D10**.
   b. Double-click cell **D10** to start *Edit* mode.
   c. Select the range name **Green_Cross** in the cell or *Formula* bar (Figure 2-69).
   d. Click the **Lookup_Data** sheet tab and select cell **I3**. The *IrisMed* range name replaces *Green_Cross*, and the parenthesis is maintained.

2-68 Formula correction message window

e. Press **Enter**. Four decimal places are shown for some results.
f. Copy the formula in cell **D10** to cells **D11:D16**.
g. Double-click cell **D16** and select **IrisMed** in the cell or in the *Formula* bar.
h. Press **F3 (FN+F3)** to open the *Paste Name* dialog box.
i. Select **Medeye** in the list and click **OK**.
j. Press **Enter**.
k. Copy the formula in cell **D16** to cells **D17:D20**.
l. Complete the formulas for Westville insurance.

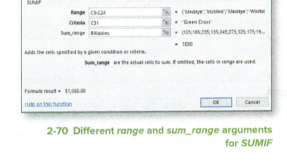

2-69 Edit the range name in a formula

7. Format cells **D5:D24** as **Currency** from the *Number Format* drop-down list. The values are rounded to two decimals places.

8. Use the *SUMIF* function to calculate billable amounts by insurance company.
a. Click the **Optometry** worksheet tab and select cell **D31**.
b. Click the **Math & Trig** button [*Formulas* tab, *Function Library* group].
c. Select **SUMIF**.
d. Click the **Range** box and select cells **C5:C24**.
e. Click the **Criteria** box and select cell **C31** to use a relative reference to the company name.
f. Click the **Sum_range** text box and select cells **E5:E24**. The range name is substituted (Figure 2-70).
g. Click **OK**. The result is 1030, the total amount billed to Green Cross.

2-70 Different *range* and *sum_range* arguments for *SUMIF*

9. Verify results with *AutoCalculate*.
a. Select cells **E13:E15**.
b. Press **Ctrl** and select cells **E20:E21**. These are the billable amounts for the Green Cross insurance company.
c. Compare the *SUM* in the *Status* bar with the result in cell **D31** (Figure 2-71).

10. Copy the *SUMIF* function with a relative reference.
a. Select cell **D31**.
b. Drag the *Fill* pointer to copy the formula in cell **D31** to cells **D32:D34**. The *Auto Fill Options* button appears near cell D34.
c. Select cell **D32**. The reference to cell C31 in the original formula is updated to cell C32 in the copied formula (Figure 2-72).

2-71 *AutoCalculate* results in Status bar

11. Format cells **D31:D34** as **Currency** from the *Number Format* drop-down list. Press **Ctrl+Home**.

12. Use *VLOOKUP* with a range name to display costs.

    a. Click the **Pharmacy** worksheet tab and select cell **C6**. Cost and retail prices are missing.

    b. Click the **Lookup & Reference** button [*Formulas* tab, *Function Library* group] and select **VLOOKUP**.

    c. Click the **Lookup_value** box and click cell **A6**. The ID in column A will be located in the table array.

    d. Click the **Table_array** box. All prices are in the *Lookup_Data* sheet.

    e. Click the **Lookup_Data** sheet tab and select cells **A2:D16**. This range *Costs* is substituted when you select the cells; the range name is not substituted if you type the range address. Notice that the cost is in the third column.

    f. Click the **Col_index_num** box and type 3 (Figure 2-73).

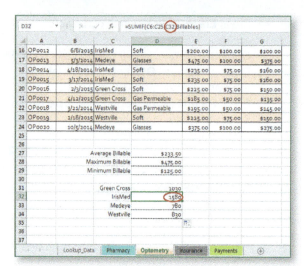

2-72 *Relative reference is adjusted after copying*

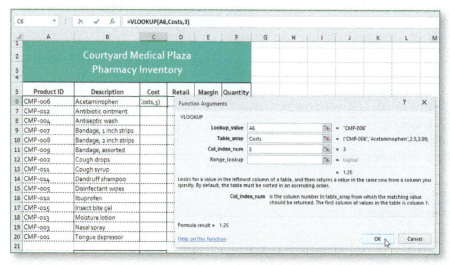

2-73 *VLOOKUP and its arguments*

    g. Click **OK**. The acetaminophen cost is 1.25.

    h. Copy the formula in cell **C6** to cells **C7:C20** without formatting. Format cells **C6:C20** as **Currency**.

13. Type the *VLOOKUP* function.

    a. Click cell **D6**.

    b. Type **=vl** and press **Tab**. The first argument is *lookup_value*.

    c. Select cell **A6** and type a comma (,) to separate the arguments. The next argument is *table_array*.

    d. Type costs,. You can type the name or select it in the *Formula AutoComplete* list (Figure 2-74).

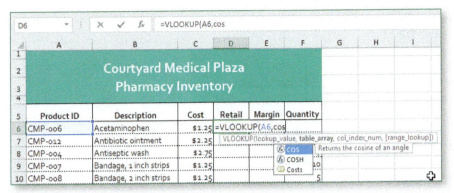

2-74 Formula AutoComplete shows range names

e. Type **4** for the *Col_index_num* argument, because the retail price is in the fourth column of the *Costs* range.

f. Press **Enter**. The closing parenthesis is supplied, and the retail price for acetaminophen is 3.99.

g. Copy the formula in cell **D6** to cells **D7:D20** without formatting and then format the cells as **Currency**.

14. Set order of precedence in a formula.
   a. Click cell **E6**. The formula to calculate the margin subtracts the cost from the retail price and then divides by the cost. The margin is shown as a markup percentage.
   b. Type **=(** to start the formula and enter the opening parenthesis.
   c. Click cell **D6** for the retail price.
   d. Type **–** and click cell **C6** to subtract the cost from the retail price.
   e. Type **)** for the closing parenthesis. This forces the subtraction to be carried out first.
   f. Type **/** for division and click cell **C6** to divide the results by the cost (Figure 2-75).
   g. Press **Enter**. The results are formatted as currency.
   h. Apply **Percent Style** to cell **E6**. A margin of 219% means that the retail price is more than two times the cost.
   i. Copy the formula in cell **E6** to cells **E7:E20** without formatting; then apply **Percent Style** to cells **E7:E20**.

2-75 Formula with multiple operators

15. Trace precedents and dependents for formulas.
   a. Select cell **C6**.
   b. Click the **Trace Precedents** button [*Formulas* tab, *Formula Auditing* group]. The formula uses data from another worksheet and from cell **A6**.
   c. Select cell **E6** and click the **Trace Precedents** button.
   d. Select cell **D7** and click the **Trace Dependents** button. The arrow points to cell **E7**.
   e. Click the **Remove Arrows** button [*Formulas* tab, *Formula Auditing* group].

16. Enter a *SUMPRODUCT* function to calculate inventory values.
   a. Click cell **C22**.
   b. Click the **Math & Trig** button [*Formulas* tab, *Function Library* group] and select **SUMPRODUCT**.
   c. Click the *Array1* box and select cells **C6:C20**.
   d. Click the *Array2* box and select cells **F6:F20**. Both arrays have the same dimension (Figure 2-76).
   e. Click **OK**. The result in E22 is 249.15. Each value in column C is multiplied by its corresponding value in column E, and those results are summed.

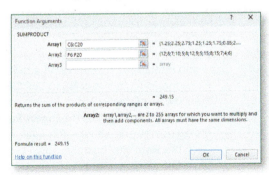

2-76 Two arrays for SUMPRODUCT

17. Type the *SUMPRODUCT* function.
    a. Click cell **D23**.
    b. Type =sump and press **Tab**. The first argument is *array1*.
    c. Select cells **D6:D20** and type a comma (,) to separate the arguments. The next argument is *array2*.
    d. Select cells **F6:F20** and press **Enter** (Figure 2-77). The result is 588.29.
    e. Format cells **D22:D23** as **Currency**. Press **Ctrl+Home**.

18. Use *PMT* to calculate patient payments.
    a. Click the **Payments** sheet tab and select cell **B6**.
    b. Click the **Financial** button [*Formulas* tab, *Function Library* group] and select **PMT**.
    c. Click the **Rate** box and type 2.75%/12. You can type the rate when it is not shown in a cell. Yearly rates are divided by 12 for monthly payments.
    d. Click the **Nper** box and type 24. The length of the loan is indicated in the label in cell A4. Two-year financing means 24 monthly payments.
    e. Click the **Pv** box and click cell **A6**, the amount of a loan.
    f. Press **F4 (FN+F4)** to make the reference absolute ($A$6). Press **F4 (FN+F4)** again to make a mixed reference A$6.
    g. Press **F4 (FN+F4)** once more to make the reference mixed $A6.
    h. Click the **Type** box and type 1 for payment at the beginning of the month. The *Fv* argument is blank (Figure 2-78).
    i. Click **OK**. The payment for financing $500 is ($21.39).
    j. Copy the formula to cells **B7:B11**. The reference to cell $A6 is mixed, and the *rate* and *nper* values that you typed are absolute.

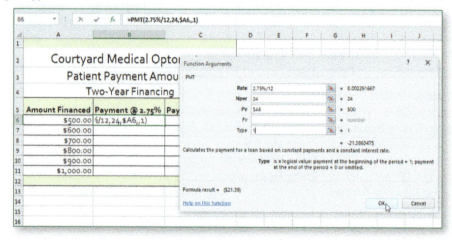

2-77 Both arrays have the same dimension

2-78 PMT arguments

19. Copy and edit a *PMT* function with a mixed reference.
    a. Copy the formula in cell **B6** to cell **C6**. The reference to cell $A6 is correct, but you need to edit the *Rate* argument.
    b. Select cell **C6** and click the **Insert Function** button in the *Formula* bar. The *Function Arguments* dialog box opens with the formula.
    c. Click the **Rate** text box and edit the calculation to 3.25%/12.
    d. Click **OK**. The payment for financing $500 at 3.25% is ($21.49).
    e. Copy the formula to cells **C7:C11**.

20. Enter the TODAY function.
    a. Select cell **A14**.
    b. Type =to, press **Tab**, and press **Enter**.
    c. Press **Ctrl+Home**.

21. Save and close the workbook (Figure 2-79).

Courtyard Medical Optometry

Bill Date	Insurance	Amount	Total with Service Charge
9/7/2013	Green Cross	$195.00	$198.90
8/15/2015	Green Cross	$200.00	$204.00
11/14/2014	Green Cross	$225.00	$229.50
2/3/2015	Green Cross	$225.00	$229.50
4/12/2015	Green Cross	$185.00	$188.70
5/6/2013	IrisMed	$185.00	$188.98
2/1/2015	IrisMed	$275.00	$280.91
3/7/2015	IrisMed	$325.00	$331.99
6/8/2015	IrisMed	$200.00	$204.30
4/18/2014	IrisMed	$235.00	$240.05
3/17/2014	IrisMed	$235.00	$239.11
3/3/2014	Medeye	$125.00	$127.19
8/12/2014	Medeye	$235.00	$239.11
7/8/2014	Medeye	$245.00	$249.29
5/3/2014	Medeye	$475.00	$483.31
10/5/2014	Medeye	$375.00	$381.56
4/4/2014	Westville	$135.00	$137.70
12/3/2014	Westville	$175.00	$178.50
3/21/2014	Westville	$195.00	$198.90
2/18/2015	Westville	$225.00	$229.50

2-79 Completed Excel 2-1

Guided Project 2-2

Hamilton Civic Center (HCC) is a nonprofit community fitness center with an indoor pool, sauna, indoor track, project room, racquetball courts, meeting rooms, and a boutique. In this workbook, you complete tasks related to health seminars, a member challenge, and the daycare program.
[**Student Learning Outcomes 2.1, 2.2, 2.3, 2.4, 2.5, 2.6, 2.7**]

File Needed: ***HamiltonCivic-02.xlsx*** *[Student data files are available in the* Library *of your SIMnet account.]*
Completed Project File Name: ***[your initials] Excel 2-2.xlsx***

Skills Covered in This Project

- Create and copy formulas.
- Name cell ranges.
- Use relative and absolute references.
- Set mathematical order of operations.

- Use *AutoCalculate* and formula auditing tools.
- Use *VLOOKUP* and *HLOOKUP*.
- Create an *IF* function.
- Create a *SUMIF* function.
- Use the *TODAY* function.

1. Open the ***HamiltonCivic-02.xlsx*** workbook from your student data files and save it as [your initials] Excel 2-2.

2. Name cell ranges.
   a. On the *Seminars* sheet, select cells **B6:B10**, and click the **Name** box.
   b. Type Seminars in the *Name* box and press **Enter**.
   c. Click the **Data** sheet tab. You will name the cell ranges used in the *Lookup* functions.
   d. Select cells **A2:D10** and click the **Name** box.
   e. Type V_Calories in the *Name* box and press **Enter**. This will remind you that this range is a vertical table array.
   f. Select cells **F2:J3** and click the **Name** box.
   g. Type H_Fees and press **Enter**. This range is a horizontal table array.

3. Enter and copy a division formula.
   a. Select cell **D2** on the **Data** worksheet. To calculate calories per minute, divide the total calories by the number of minutes.
   b. Type an equals sign (**=**) to start the formula.
   c. Click cell **C2**, the total number of calories. This formula uses relative references.
   d. Type **/** for division.
   e. Click cell **B2**, the number of minutes, and press **Enter**. As many decimal places as fit in the cell are displayed (Figure 2-80).
   f. Drag the *Fill* pointer to copy the formula in cell **D2** to cells **D3:D10**. Ignore the *Auto Fill Options* button.
   g. While cells **D2:D10** are selected, click the **Decrease Decimal** button [*Home* tab, *Number* group] two times. The sets the same number of decimal positions for all results.

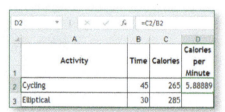

2-80 Decimal positions fill the cell

4. Use *HLOOKUP* with a range name to display fees.
   a. Click the **Seminars** worksheet tab and select cell **C6**. Fees are in the *H_Fees* range.
   b. Click the **Lookup & Reference** button [*Formulas* tab, *Function Library* group] and select **HLOOKUP**.
   c. Click the **Lookup_value** box and click cell **B6**.
   d. Click the **Table_array** box.

e. Type h_fees the name of the range. It is not case sensitive, and quotation marks are not necessary.

f. Click the **Row_index_num** box and type 2 because the fees are in the second row of the *H_Fees* range (Figure 2-81).

g. Click **OK**. The fee is $15.00.

h. Copy the formula in cell **C6** to cells **C7:C10**.

5. Enter and copy an addition formula.

a. Click cell **E15** and type an equals sign (=) to start the formula.

b. Click cell **D6**, the number of attendees for the seminar in Hendersonville.

c. Type + for addition.

d. Click cell **E6** to add the number of attendees for Advocate Central.

e. Type +, click cell **F6**, type +, and click cell **G6** (Figure 2-82).

f. Press **Enter**.

g. Drag the *Fill* pointer to copy the formula in cell **E15** to cells **E16:E19**. Ignore the *Auto Fill Options* button.

h. Click cell **E20**, click the **AutoSum** button [*Home* tab, *Editing* group], and press **Enter**. The total is 209 attendees.

6. Set order of operations in a formula.

a. Select cell **E24**. The fee is multiplied by the sum of the attendees at each hospital. Cells D6:G6 must be added first and that result is multiplied by cell C6.

b. Type = to start the formula and click cell **C6**.

c. Type * to multiply.

d. Type (for the opening parenthesis. This forces the addition to be carried out first.

e. Click cell **D6**, type +, click cell **E6**, type +, click cell **F6**, type +, and click cell **G6**.

f. Type) for the closing parenthesis (Figure 2-83).

g. Press **Enter**. The result is 705.

h. Format cell **E24** as **Currency** and copy the formula to cells **E25:E28**.

i. Click cell **E29**, click the **AutoSum** button [*Home* tab, *Editing* group], and press **Enter**.

7. Use *AutoCalculate* and formula auditing tools.

a. Select cells **E24:E28**.

b. Compare the *SUM* in the *Status* bar with the result in cell E29.

c. Select cell **E15**.

2-81 Arguments for *HLOOKUP*

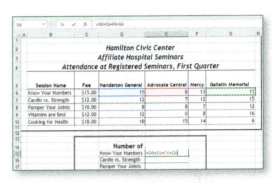

2-82 Simple addition formula

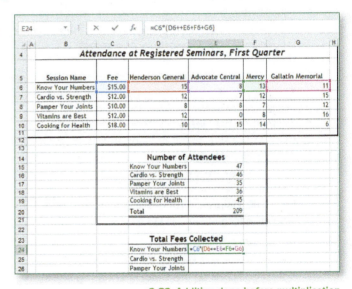

2-83 Addition done before multiplication

d. Click the **Trace Precedents** button [*Formulas* tab, *Formula Auditing* group].
e. Click the **Trace Dependents** button. The formula in cell E15 has both precedent and dependent cells (Figure 2-84).
f. Click the **Remove Arrows** button [*Formulas* tab, *Formula Auditing* group].

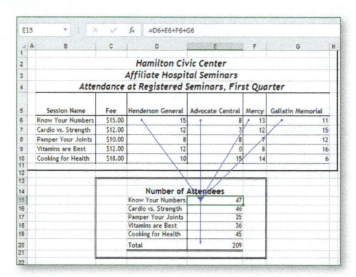

2-84 Precedent and dependent cells

8. Use *VLOOKUP* with a range name to display calories expended.
   a. Click the **Data** sheet tab.
   b. Click the **Name** box arrow and select **V_Calories**. Notice that total calories are in the third column.
   c. Click the **Calorie Tracking** sheet tab and select cell **D3**. Calories by activity are within the range *V_Calories*.
   d. Click the **Lookup & Reference** button [*Formulas* tab, *Formula Auditing* group] and select **VLOOKUP**.
   e. Click the **Lookup_value** box and click cell **C3**. The activity name in column C will be located in the table array.
   f. Click the **Table_array** box and press **F3 (FN+F3)** to open the *Paste Name* dialog box.
   g. Double-click **V_Calories** to insert it.
   h. Click the **Col_index_num** box and type 3 (Figure 2-85).
   i. Click **OK**. Calories for the first activity are 250.
   j. Copy the formula in cell **D3** to cells **D4:D23**.

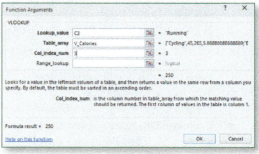

2-85 Arguments for the *VLOOKUP* function

9. Build a *SUMIF* formula with absolute and relative references.
   a. Select cell **D28** on the **Calorie Tracking** sheet.
   b. Click the **Recently Used** button [*Formulas* tab, *Function Library* group].
   c. Look for and choose **SUMIF**. (If you do not see *SUMIF* in the list, click the **Math & Trig** button to find and select **SUMIF**.)
   d. Click the **Range** box and select cells **C3:C23**, the range that will be evaluated.
   e. Press **F4 (FN+F4)** to make the cell references absolute.
   f. Click the **Criteria** box and select cell **C28** to find rows with "cycling" as the activity.
   g. Click the **Sum_range** box and select cells **D3:D23**, the values to be summed if the activity is cycling.

h. Press **F4 (FN+F4)** to make the references absolute (Figure 2-86).
i. Click **OK**. The result is 795 calories.

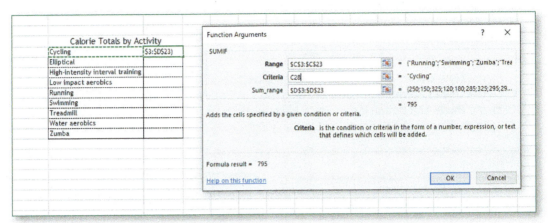

2-86 *SUMIF* function for cycling

10. Copy the formula in cell **D28** to cells **D29:D36** without formatting (Figure 2-87).

11. Create an *IF* function to calculate a fee based on age.
    a. Click the **Day Care** sheet tab and select cell **D5**.
    b. Click the **Logical** button [*Formulas* tab, *Function Library* group] and select **IF**.
    c. Click the **Logical_test** box and click cell **B5**.
    d. Type **>=4** to test if the child is 4 years old or greater.
    e. Click the **Value_if_true** box and click cell **I9**. The fee for a child 4 years old or greater is $18.
    f. Press **F4 (FN+F4)** to make the reference absolute.
    g. Click the **Value_if_false** box and click cell **I8**. If the child is not 4 years old or greater, the child is between 1 and 3 years old.
    h. Press **F4 (FN+F4)** to make the reference absolute (Figure 2-88).
    i. Click **OK**. The fee for Mary is $18.
    j. Format the result as **Currency**.
    k. Copy the formula in cell **D5** to cells **D6:D14**.

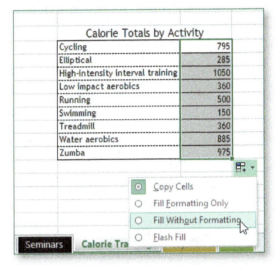

2-87 Copy the formula without formatting

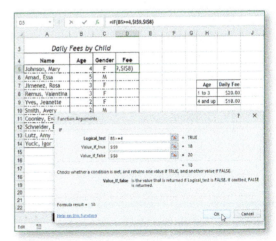

2-88 *IF* function to determine the fee

12. Insert the current date as a function.
    a. Click the **Data** sheet tab and click cell **A12**.
    b. Type **=to** and press **Tab** to select the function.
    c. Press **Enter**.
    d. Press **Ctrl+Home**.

13. Paste range names.
    a. Click the **New sheet** button in the sheet tab area.
    b. Click the **Use in Formula** button [*Formulas* tab, *Defined Names* group] and select **Paste Names**.
    c. Click the **Paste List** button in the *Paste Name* dialog box.
    d. *AutoFit* each column and name the tab Range Names.

14. Save and close the workbook (Figure 2-89).

Hamilton Civic Center
Affiliate Hospital Seminars
Attendance at Registered Seminars, First Quarter

Session Name	Fee	Henderson General	Advocate Central	Mercy	Gallatin Memorial
Know Your Numbers	$18.00	18	8	13	11
Cardio vs. Strength	$12.00	12	7	12	15
Pamper Your Joints	$10.00	8	8	7	12
Vitamins are Best	$12.00	12	0	8	16
Cooking for Health	$18.00	10	15	14	6

Number of Attendees
Know Your Numbers	47
Cardio vs. Strength	46
Pamper Your Joints	35
Vitamins are Best	36
Cooking for Health	45
Total	209

Total Fees Collected
Know Your Numbers	$705.00
Cardio vs. Strength	$552.00
Pamper Your Joints	$350.00
Vitamins are Best	$432.00
Cooking for Health	$810.00
Total	$2,949.00

Member Calorie Burn Challenge

Member ID	Date	Activity	Calories
10034	2/1/2016	Running	250
10036	2/2/2016	Swimming	150
10038	2/3/2016	Zumba	325
10040	2/4/2016	Treadmill	120
10042	3/1/2016	Low impact aerobics	180
10044	3/3/2016	Elliptical	285
10046	3/5/2016	Zumba	325
10048	3/7/2016	Water aerobics	295
10050	3/9/2016	Water aerobics	295
10034	3/11/2016	Low impact aerobics	180
10036	3/13/2016	Cycling	265
10038	3/15/2016	Cycling	265
10040	3/17/2016	Water aerobics	295
10042	3/19/2016	High-intensity interval training	350
10044	3/21/2016	High-intensity interval training	350
10046	3/23/2016	Cycling	265
10048	3/25/2016	Treadmill	120
10050	3/27/2016	Zumba	325
10036	3/29/2016	High-intensity interval training	350
10034	3/31/2016	Treadmill	120
10042	4/2/2016	Running	250

Hamilton Civic Center

Summer Day Care

Daily Fees by Child

Name	Age	Gender	Fee
Johnson, Mary	4	F	$18.00
Amad, Essa	5	M	$18.00
Jimenez, Rosa	3	F	$20.00
Remus, Valentina	3	F	$20.00
Yves, Jeanette	2	F	$20.00
Smith, Avery	3	M	$20.00
Cooney, Evan	5	M	$18.00
Schneider, Ellery	1	F	$20.00
Lutz, Amy	4	F	$18.00
Yuole, Igor	3	M	$20.00

Age	Daily Fee
1 to 3	$20.00
4 and up	$18.00

Calorie Totals by Activity
Cycling	795
Elliptical	285
High-intensity interval training	1050
Low impact aerobics	360
Running	500
Swimming	150
Treadmill	360
Water aerobics	885
Zumba	975

H_Fees	=Data!$F$2:$J$3	
Seminars	=Seminars!$B$6:$B$10	
V_Calories	=Data!$A$2:$D$10	

Activity	Time	Calories	Calories per Minute
Cycling	40	265	6.640
Elliptical	30	285	9.500
High-intensity interval training	45	350	7.770
Low impact aerobics	45	180	4.000
Running	30	250	8.331
Swimming	30	150	5.000
Treadmill	20	120	6.000
Water aerobics	45	295	6.556
Zumba	45	325	7.244

Session Names and Fees
Cardio vs. Strength	Cooking for Health	Know Your Numbers	Pamper Your Joints	Vitamins are Best
$12.00	$18.00	$18.00	$10.00	$12.00

2-89 Excel 2-2 completed

Guided Project 2-3

Sierra Pacific Community College District (SPCCD) consists of four individual community colleges. The workbook for this project includes an amortization schedule for student loans and a fee and credit hour summary for several departments.
[Student Learning Outcomes 2.1, 2.2, 2.3, 2.4, 2.5, 2.6, 2.7]

File Needed: **SierraPacific-02.xlsx** *[Student data files are available in the Library of your SIMnet account.]*
Completed Project File Name: *[your initials] Excel 2-3.xlsx*

Skills Covered in This Project

- Name cell ranges.
- Create and copy formulas.
- Set mathematical order of operations.
- Use absolute references in formulas.

- Insert the current date as a function.
- Use the *PMT* function.
- Audit formulas.
- Use *SUMIF* and *SUMPRODUCT*.

1. Open the **SierraPacific-02.xlsx** workbook from your student data files and save it as [your initials] Excel 2-3.

2. Set range names for the workbook.
   a. On the **Student Loan** sheet, select cells **B5:C8**.
   b. Click the **Create from Selection** button [*Formulas* tab, *Defined Names* group].
   c. Verify that the **Left column** box in the *Create Names from Selection* dialog box is selected.
   d. Deselect the **Top row** box if it is checked and click **OK**.
   e. Select cells **E5:F7**. Repeat steps a–d to create range names.
   f. Click the **Name Manager** button [*Formulas* tab, *Defined Names* group] to view the names in the *Name Manager* dialog box (Figure 2-90).
   g. Click **Close**.

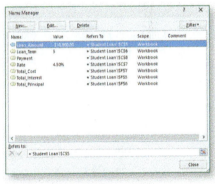

2-90 *Name Manager dialog box*

3. Enter a *PMT* function.
   a. Select **C8**.
   b. Click the **Financial** button [*Formulas* tab, *Function Library* group] and select **PMT**.
   c. Click the **Rate** box and click cell **C7**. The range name *Rate* is substituted.
   d. Type **/12** immediately after **Rate** to divide by 12 for monthly payments.
   e. Click the **Nper** box and click cell **C6**. The substituted range name is *Loan_Term*.
   f. Type ***12** after **Loan_Term** to multiply by 12.
   g. Click the **Pv** box and type a minus sign (−) to set the argument as a negative amount.
   h. Click cell **C5** (*Loan_Amount*) for the *pv* argument. A negative loan amount reflects the lender's perspective, since the money is paid out now (Figure 2-91).

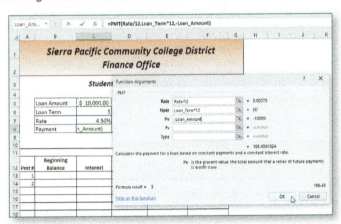

2-91 *Pv argument is negative in the PMT function*

    i. Leave the *Fv* and *Type* boxes empty.

    j. Click **OK**. The payment for a loan at this rate is $186.43, shown as a positive value.

4. Create a total interest formula.

    a. Click cell **F5** (*Total_Interest*). This value is calculated by multiplying the monthly payment by the total number of payments to determine total outlay. From this amount, you subtract the loan amount.

    b. Type **=** and click cell **C8** (the *Payment*).

    c. Type ***** to multiply and click cell **C6** (*Loan_Term*).

    d. Type ***12** to multiply by 12 for monthly payments.

    e. Type **−** immediately after ***12** to subtract.

    f. Click cell **C5** (the *Loan_Amount*). The formula is *Payment*Loan_Term*12−Loan_Amount*. Parentheses are not required, because the multiplications are done from left to right, followed by the subtraction (Figure 2-92).

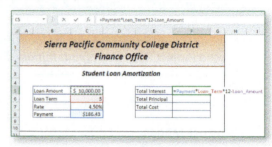

2-92 Left-to-right operations

    g. Press **Enter**. The result is $1,185.81.

5. Create the total principal formula and the total loan cost.

    a. Select cell **F6** (*Total_Principal*). This value is calculated by multiplying the monthly payment by the total number of payments. From this amount, subtract the total interest.

    b. Type **=** and click cell **C8** (the *Payment*).

    c. Type ***** to multiply and click cell **C6** (*Loan_Term*).

    d. Type ***12** to multiply by 12 for monthly payments.

    e. Type **−** immediately after ***12** to subtract.

    f. Click cell **F5** (the *Total_Interest*). The formula is *Payment*Loan_Term*12−Total_Interest*.

    g. Press **Enter**. Total principal is the amount of the loan.

    h. Click cell **F7**, the *Total_Cost* of the loan. This is the total principal plus the total interest.

    i. Type **=**, click cell **F5**, type **+**, click cell **F6**, and then press **Enter**.

6. Build an amortization schedule.

    a. Click cell **B13**. The beginning balance is the total cost of the loan.

    b. Type **=**, click cell **F7**, and press **Enter**.

    c. Format the value as **Accounting Number Format**.

    d. Select cell **C13**. The interest for each payment is calculated by multiplying the balance in column B by the rate divided by 12.

    e. Type **=** and click cell **B13**.

    f. Type ***(** and click cell **C7**.

    g. Type **/12)**. Parentheses are necessary so that the division is done first (Figure 2-93).

    h. Press **Enter** and format the results as **Accounting Number Format**.

    i. Select cell **D13**. The portion of the payment that is applied to the principal is calculated by subtracting the interest portion from the payment.

    j. Type **=**, click cell **C8** (the *Payment*).

    k. Type **−**, click cell **C13**, and press **Enter**.

    l. Click cell **E13**. The total payment is the interest portion plus the principal portion.

    m. Type **=**, click cell **C13**, type **+**, click cell **D13**, and then press **Enter**. The value matches the amount in cell **C8**.

    n. Select cell **F13**. The ending balance is the beginning balance minus the payment.

    o. Type **=**, click cell **B13**, type **−**, click cell **E13**, and then press **Enter**. The ending balance is $10,999.38.

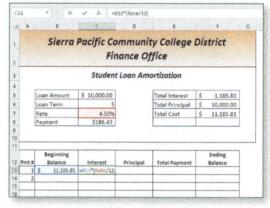

2-93 The interest formula

B13	=Total_Cost
C13	=B13*(Rate/12)
D13	=Payment−C13
E13	=C13+D13
F13	=B13−E13

7. Fill data and copy formulas.
   a. Select cells **A13:A14**. This is a series with an increment of 1.
   b. Drag the *Fill* pointer to reach cell **A72**. This sets 60 payments for a five-year loan term.
   c. Select cell **B14**. The beginning balance for the second payment is the ending balance for the first payment.
   d. Type **=**, click cell **F13**, and press **Enter**.
   e. Double-click the *Fill* pointer for cell **B14** to fill the formula down to row **72**. The results are zero until the rest of the schedule is complete.
   f. Select cells **C13:F13**.
   g. Double-click the *Fill* pointer at cell **F13**. All of the formulas are filled (copied) to row **72** (Figure 2-94).
   h. Scroll to see the values in row **72**. The loan balance reaches 0.
   i. Press **Ctrl+Home**.

8. Build a multiplication formula and set order of mathematical operations.
   a. Click the **Fees & Credit** sheet tab and select cell **F7**. Credit hours times number of sections times the fee calculates the total fees from a course.
   b. Type **=**, click cell **C7**, type *****, click cell **D7**, type *****, click cell **E7**, and then press **Enter**. No parentheses are necessary because multiplication is done in left to right order.
   c. Select cell **G7**. Fee collected per credit hour is determined by dividing the value in cell F7 by the number of sections times credit hours times average enrollment.
   d. Type **=**, click cell **F7**, and type **/ (**. Parentheses are necessary so that left to right order is overridden.
   e. Click cell **C7**, type *****, and click cell **D7**.
   f. Type *****, click cell **C20**, and press **F4 (FN+F4)** to make the reference absolute (Figure 2-95).
   g. Press **Enter**. A message box notes that the closing parenthesis is missing.
   h. Click **Yes** in the message box.
   i. Select cells **F7:G7** and double-click the *Fill* pointer to copy the formulas.
   j. Format cells **G7:G18** as **Currency** and set a bottom border for cells **F18:G18**.

9. Use *SUMIF*.
   a. Select cell **D26**. Fees by department can be calculated.
   b. Click the **Math & Trig** button [*Formulas* tab, *Function Library* group] and select **SUMIF**.
   c. Click the **Range** box and select cells **A7:A18**. This range will be matched against the criteria.
   d. Press **F4 (FN+F4)** to make the reference absolute.
   e. Click the **Criteria** box and type bio.
   f. Click the **Sum_range** box, select cells **F7:F18**, and press **F4 (FN+F4)**.

	A	B	C	D	E	F
12	Pmt #	Beginning Balance	Interest	Principal	Total Payment	Ending Balance
13	1	$ 11,185.81	$ 41.95	$ 144.48	$ 186.43	$ 10,999.38
14	2	$ 10,999.38	$ 41.25	$ 145.18	$ 186.43	$ 10,812.95
15	3	$ 10,812.95	$ 40.55	$ 145.88	$ 186.43	$ 10,626.52
16	4	$ 10,626.52	$ 39.85	$ 146.58	$ 186.43	$ 10,440.09
17	5	$ 10,440.09	$ 39.15	$ 147.28	$ 186.43	$ 10,253.66
18	6	$ 10,253.66	$ 38.45	$ 147.98	$ 186.43	$ 10,067.23
19	7	$ 10,067.23	$ 37.75	$ 148.68	$ 186.43	$ 9,880.80
20	8	$ 9,880.80	$ 37.05	$ 149.38	$ 186.43	$ 9,694.37
21	9	$ 9,694.37	$ 36.35	$ 150.08	$ 186.43	$ 9,507.94
22	10	$ 9,507.94	$ 35.65	$ 150.78	$ 186.43	$ 9,321.51
23	11	$ 9,321.51	$ 34.96	$ 151.47	$ 186.43	$ 9,135.08
24	12	$ 9,135.08	$ 34.26	$ 152.17	$ 186.43	$ 8,948.65
25	13	$ 8,948.65	$ 33.56	$ 152.87	$ 186.43	$ 8,762.22
26	14	$ 8,762.22	$ 32.86	$ 153.57	$ 186.43	$ 8,575.79
27	15	$ 8,575.79	$ 32.16	$ 154.27	$ 186.43	$ 8,389.36
28	16	$ 8,389.36	$ 31.46	$ 154.97	$ 186.43	$ 8,202.93
60	48	$ 2,423.59	$ 9.09	$ 177.34	$ 186.43	$ 2,237.16
61	49	$ 2,237.16	$ 8.39	$ 178.04	$ 186.43	$ 2,050.73
62	50	$ 2,050.73	$ 7.69	$ 178.74	$ 186.43	$ 1,864.30
63	51	$ 1,864.30	$ 6.99	$ 179.44	$ 186.43	$ 1,677.87
64	52	$ 1,677.87	$ 6.29	$ 180.14	$ 186.43	$ 1,491.44
65	53	$ 1,491.44	$ 5.59	$ 180.84	$ 186.43	$ 1,305.01
66	54	$ 1,305.01	$ 4.89	$ 181.54	$ 186.43	$ 1,118.58
67	55	$ 1,118.58	$ 4.19	$ 182.24	$ 186.43	$ 932.15
68	56	$ 932.15	$ 3.50	$ 182.93	$ 186.43	$ 745.72
69	57	$ 745.72	$ 2.80	$ 183.63	$ 186.43	$ 559.29
70	58	$ 559.29	$ 2.10	$ 184.33	$ 186.43	$ 372.86
71	59	$ 372.86	$ 1.40	$ 185.03	$ 186.43	$ 186.43
72	60	$ 186.43	$ 0.70	$ 185.73	$ 186.43	$ 0.00

2-94 Formulas copied down columns

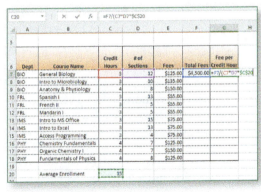

2-95 Formula to calculate fee per credit hour

g. Click **OK**. Total fees for the Biology department are 13350.

h. Format the results as **Currency**.

10. Copy a *SUMIF* function and check formula errors.

a. Click cell **D26** and drag its *Fill* pointer to copy the formula to cells **D27:D29** without formatting.

b. Double-click cell **D27**. You need to change the criteria.

c. Edit the criteria argument in the *Formula* bar or in the cell to display frl. Do not change the quotation marks or any other punctuation (Figure 2-96).

d. Press **Enter** or click the **Enter** button in the *Formula* bar. An error triangle appears in the top left corner of cell **D27**.

e. Click cell **D27** and point to its **Trace Error** button to see the *ScreenTip* (Figure 2-97). The formula has different criteria than the immediately preceding formula, but this is correct.

f. Click the **Trace Error** button and choose **Ignore Error**.

g. Double-click cell **D28** and edit the criteria argument to display ims.

h. Edit the argument in cell **D29** to show the department initials.

i. Format cells **D27:D29** as **Currency**.

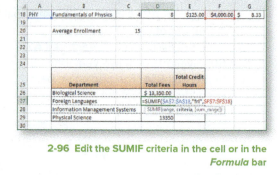

2-96 Edit the SUMIF criteria in the cell or in the *Formula* bar

11. Use *SUMPRODUCT* and trace an error.

a. Select cell **E26** and click the **Formulas** tab.

b. Click the **Math & Trig** button in the *Function Library* group and select **SUMPRODUCT**.

c. Click the **Array1** box and select cells **C7:C9**, credit hours for courses in the Biology Department.

d. Click the **Array2** box and select cells **D7:D9**, the number of sections for the Biology Department.

e. Click **OK**. The Biology Department has 98 total credit hour offerings.

f. Click cell **E26** and point to its **Trace Error** button. The formula omits adjacent cells in columns C and D, which is correct.

g. Click the **Trace Error** button and select **Ignore Error**.

2-97 *Trace Error* button and its *ScreenTip*

12. Copy and edit *SUMPRODUCT*.

a. Click cell **E26** and drag its *Fill* pointer to copy the formula to cells **E27:E29** without formatting.

b. Click cell **E27** and click the **Insert Function** button in the *Formula* bar.

c. Select and highlight the range in the *Array1* box and select cells **C10:C12**. The range you select replaces the range in the dialog box (Figure 2-98).

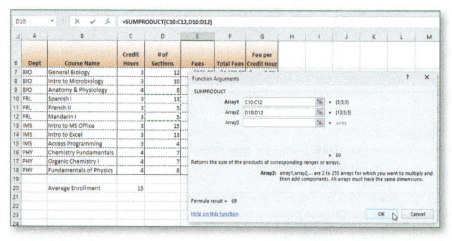

2-98 Replace the *ArrayN* arguments

d. Select the range in the *Array2* box and select cells **D10:D12**.

e. Click **OK**.

f. Edit and complete the formulas in cells **E28:E29** and ignore errors.

13. Insert the current date as a function.

a. Select cell **G30**.

b. Type **=to** and press **Tab** to select the function.

c. Press **Enter**.

d. Press **Ctrl+Home**.

14. Paste range names.

a. Click the **New sheet** button in the sheet tab area.

b. Name the new sheet **Range Names**.

c. Press **F3 (FN+F3)** to open the *Paste Name* dialog box.

d. Click the **Paste List** button.

e. *AutoFit* each column.

15. Save and close the workbook (Figure 2-99).

Sierra Pacific Community College District
Finance Office

Student Loan Amortization

Loan Amount	$ 10,000.00		Total Interest	$	1,185.81
Loan Term	5		Total Principal	$	10,000.00
Rate	4.50%		Total Cost	$	11,185.81
Payment	$186.43				

Pmt #	Beginning Balance		Interest		Principal		Total Payment		Ending Balance	
1	$	11,185.81	$	41.95	$	144.48	$	186.43	$	10,999.38
2	$	10,999.38	$	41.25	$	145.18	$	186.43	$	10,812.95
3	$	10,812.95	$	40.55	$	145.88	$	186.43	$	10,626.52
4	$	10,626.52	$	39.85	$	146.58	$	186.43	$	10,440.09
5	$	10,440.09	$	39.15	$	147.28	$	186.43	$	10,253.66
6	$	10,253.66	$	38.45	$	147.98	$	186.43	$	10,067.23
7	$	10,067.23	$	37.75	$	148.68	$	186.43	$	9,880.80
8	$	9,880.80	$	37.05	$	149.38	$	186.43	$	9,694.37
9	$	9,694.37	$	36.35	$	150.08	$	186.43	$	9,507.94
10	$	9,507.94	$	35.65	$	150.78	$	186.43	$	9,321.51
11	$	9,321.51	$	34.96	$	151.47	$	186.43	$	9,135.08
12	$	9,135.08	$	34.26	$	152.17	$	186.43	$	8,948.65
13	$	8,948.65	$	33.56	$	152.87	$	186.43	$	8,762.22
14	$	8,762.22	$	32.86	$	153.57	$	186.43	$	8,575.79
15	$	8,575.79	$	32.16	$	154.27	$	186.43	$	8,389.36
16	$	8,389.36	$	31.46	$	154.97	$	186.43	$	8,202.93
17	$	8,202.93	$	30.76	$	155.67	$	186.43	$	8,016.50
18	$	8,016.50	$	30.06	$	156.37	$	186.43	$	7,830.07
19	$	7,830.07	$	29.36	$	157.07	$	186.43	$	7,643.64
20	$	7,643.64	$	28.66	$	157.77	$	186.43	$	7,457.21
21	$	7,457.21	$	27.96	$	158.47	$	186.43	$	7,270.78
22	$	7,270.78	$	27.27	$	159.16	$	186.43	$	7,084.35
23	$	7,084.35	$	26.57	$	159.86	$	186.43	$	6,897.92
24	$	6,897.92	$	25.87	$	160.56	$	186.43	$	6,711.49
25	$	6,711.49	$	25.17	$	161.26	$	186.43	$	6,525.06
26	$	6,525.06	$	24.47	$	161.96	$	186.43	$	6,338.63
27	$	6,338.63	$	23.77	$	162.66	$	186.43	$	6,152.20
28	$	6,152.20	$	23.07	$	163.36	$	186.43	$	5,965.77
29	$	5,965.77	$	22.37	$	164.06	$	186.43	$	5,779.34
30	$	5,779.34	$	21.67	$	164.76	$	186.43	$	5,592.91

Sierra Pacific Community College District
Credit Hours and Fees by Department

Dept	Course Name	Credit Hours	# of Sections	Fees	Total Fees	Fee per Credit Hour
BIO	General Biology	3	12	$125.00	$4,500.00	$ 8.33
BIO	Intro to Microbiology	3	10	$135.00	$4,050.00	$ 9.00
BIO	Anatomy & Physiology	4	8	$150.00	$4,800.00	$ 10.00
FRL	Spanish I	3	13	$55.00	$2,145.00	$ 3.67
FRL	French II	3	5	$55.00	$825.00	$ 3.67
FRL	Mandarin I	3	5	$55.00	$825.00	$ 3.67
IMS	Intro to MS Office	3	15	$75.00	$3,375.00	$ 5.00
IMS	Intro to Excel	3	13	$75.00	$2,925.00	$ 5.00
IMS	Access Programming	3	4	$75.00	$900.00	$ 5.00
PHY	Chemistry Fundamentals	4	7	$125.00	$3,500.00	$ 8.33
PHY	Organic Chemistry I	4	7	$150.00	$4,200.00	$ 10.00
PHY	Fundamentals of Physics	4	8	$125.00	$4,000.00	$ 8.33

Average Enrollment — 15

Department	Total Fees	Total Credit Hours
Biological Science	$ 13,350.00	98
Foreign Languages	$ 3,795.00	69
Information Management Systems	$ 7,200.00	96
Physical Science	$ 11,700.00	88

Loan_Amount	='Student Loan'!$C$5
Loan_Term	='Student Loan'!$C$6
Payment	='Student Loan'!$C$8
Rate	='Student Loan'!$C$7
Total_Cost	='Student Loan'!$F$7
Total_Interest	='Student Loan'!$F$5
Total_Principal	='Student Loan'!$F$6

2-99 Completed Excel 2-3

31	$	5,592.91	$	20.97	$	165.46	$	186.43	$	5,406.48
32	$	5,406.48	$	20.27	$	166.16	$	186.43	$	5,220.05
33	$	5,220.05	$	19.58	$	166.86	$	186.43	$	5,033.62
34	$	5,033.62	$	18.88	$	167.55	$	186.43	$	4,847.19
35	$	4,847.19	$	18.18	$	168.25	$	186.43	$	4,660.75
36	$	4,660.75	$	17.48	$	168.95	$	186.43	$	4,474.32
37	$	4,474.32	$	16.78	$	169.65	$	186.43	$	4,287.89
38	$	4,287.89	$	16.08	$	170.35	$	186.43	$	4,101.46
39	$	4,101.46	$	15.38	$	171.05	$	186.43	$	3,915.03
40	$	3,915.03	$	14.68	$	171.75	$	186.43	$	3,728.60
41	$	3,728.60	$	13.98	$	172.45	$	186.43	$	3,542.17
42	$	3,542.17	$	13.28	$	173.15	$	186.43	$	3,355.74
43	$	3,355.74	$	12.58	$	173.85	$	186.43	$	3,169.31
44	$	3,169.31	$	11.88	$	174.55	$	186.43	$	2,982.88
45	$	2,982.88	$	11.19	$	175.24	$	186.43	$	2,796.45
46	$	2,796.45	$	10.49	$	175.94	$	186.43	$	2,610.02
47	$	2,610.02	$	9.79	$	176.64	$	186.43	$	2,423.59
48	$	2,423.59	$	9.09	$	177.34	$	186.43	$	2,237.16
49	$	2,237.16	$	8.39	$	178.04	$	186.43	$	2,050.73
50	$	2,050.73	$	7.69	$	178.74	$	186.43	$	1,864.30
51	$	1,864.30	$	6.99	$	179.44	$	186.43	$	1,677.87
52	$	1,677.87	$	6.29	$	180.14	$	186.43	$	1,491.44
53	$	1,491.44	$	5.59	$	180.84	$	186.43	$	1,305.01
54	$	1,305.01	$	4.89	$	181.54	$	186.43	$	1,118.58
55	$	1,118.58	$	4.19	$	182.24	$	186.43	$	932.15
56	$	932.15	$	3.50	$	182.93	$	186.43	$	745.72
57	$	745.72	$	2.80	$	183.63	$	186.43	$	559.29
58	$	559.29	$	2.10	$	184.33	$	186.43	$	372.86
59	$	372.86	$	1.40	$	185.03	$	186.43	$	186.43
60	$	186.43	$	0.70	$	185.73	$	186.43	$	0.00

Independent Project 2-4

Central Sierra Insurance (CSI) sets bonus percentages based on commissions earned by each agent and calculates totals by branch office. This workbook also tracks fundraising efforts of employees for a community event.

[**Student Learning Outcomes 2.1, 2.2, 2.3, 2.5, 2.6, 2.7**]

File Needed: **CentralSierra-02.xlsx** *[Student data files are available in the* Library *of your SIMnet account.]*
Completed Project File Name: ***[your initials] Excel 2-4.xlsx***

Skills Covered in This Project

- Create, copy, and edit formulas.
- Name cell ranges.
- Set mathematical order of operations.
- Set cell references to be absolute.
- Use the *NOW* function.
- Use *HLOOKUP* and *VLOOKUP* functions.
- Use the *SUMIF* function.
- Build an *IF* function.

1. Open the **CentralSierra-02.xlsx** workbook from your student data files and save it as [your initials] Excel 2-4. Review the data on each sheet.

2. On the **Tables** sheet, select cells **A6:B10** and create range names from this selection.

3. Select cells **B1:F2** and click the **Name** box. Name this as H_Rates.

4. Create an *HLOOKUP* function to display the bonus rate.
   a. Click the **Commissions** sheet tab and select cell **F5**.
   b. Start the *HLOOKUP* function and use cell **E5** as the *lookup_value*.
   c. For the *table_array* argument, use the **H_Rates** range.
   d. Use the second row for the *row_index_num* argument (Figure 2-100).

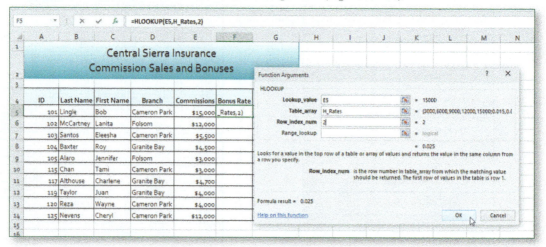

2-100 *HLOOKUP* function to display bonus rate

5. Format the results as **Percent Style** with two decimal places.

6. Copy the formula in cell **F5** to cells **F6:F14**.

7. Set order of operations to calculate total earnings.
   a. Select cell **G5**.
   b. Build a formula to add the commissions amount (E5) to the commissions amount times the rate (F5*E5). Use parentheses to set the multiplication as the first calculation.
   c. Copy the formula in cell **G5** to cells **G6:G14**.

8. Create and copy a *SUMIF* function to calculate total earnings by branch office.
   a. Select cell **E18**.
   b. Start the *SUMIF* function with cells **$D$5:$D$14** as the *Range* argument.
   c. The *Criteria* argument is a relative reference to cell **C18**.
   d. Select cells **G5:G14** for the *Sum_range* argument and make the references absolute.
   e. Copy the formula in cell **E18** to cells **E19:E20** without formatting.
   f. Format cells **E18:E20** as **Currency**.

9. Total the earnings in cell **E21**.

10. Create and format the current date.
    a. Select cell **G23** and insert the *NOW* function.
    b. Select cell **G23** and click the **Number** group launcher [*Home* tab]. On the *Number* tab, select the **Date** category.
    c. Scroll the *Type* list to find the date that displays the month spelled out, the date, a comma, and a four-digit year (Figure 2-101).
    d. Click **OK**. Press **Ctrl+Home**.

11. Create and copy a *VLOOKUP* function to display goals for each funding source.
    a. Click the **Family Day** sheet tab and select cell **F6**.
    b. Start the *VLOOKUP* function and use cell **E6** as the *lookup_value*.
    c. Click the **Tables** sheet tab for the *table_array* argument and use cells **$A$6:$B$10**.
    d. Use the second column as the *col_index_num* argument.
    e. Copy the formula in cell **F6** to cells **F7:F20** without formatting to preserve the fill color.
    f. Format cells **F7:F20** as **Currency** with no decimal places.

12. Create and copy an *IF* function.
    a. Select cell **H6** and start an *IF* function.
    b. Type a *logical_argument* to determine if cell **G6** is greater than or equal to (>=) cell **F6**.
    c. Type **Yes** as the *Value_if_true* argument and **No** as the *Value_if_false* argument.
    d. Copy the formula in cell **H6** to cells **H7:H20** without formatting to maintain the fill color.
    e. Center align cells **H6:H20**.
    f. Press **Ctrl+Home**.

13. Insert a new sheet at the end of the tab names and paste the range names starting in cell A1. Name the worksheet as Range Names.

14. Save and close the workbook (Figure 2-102).

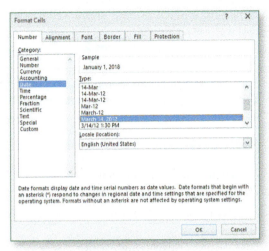

2-101 Date format selected

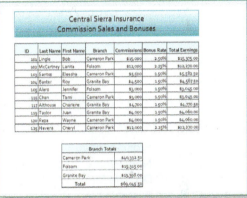

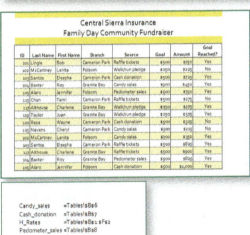

2-102 Excel 2-4 completed

Independent Project 2-5

San Diego Sailing keeps data about its fleet of rental and charter boats in a workbook. One of the sheets is missing a piece of data and another sheet has circular reference errors. You will complete work on these sheets, calculate projected rates for each boat, and build basic statistics about past rentals.
[**Student Learning Outcomes 2.1, 2.2, 2.3, 2.4, 2.5, 2.6, 2.7**]

File Needed: ***SanDiegoSailing-02.xlsx*** *[Student data files are available in the* Library *of your SIMnet account.]*
Completed Project File Name: ***[your initials] Excel 2-5.xlsx***

Skills Covered in This Project

- Create and copy formulas.
- Use formula auditing tools.
- Set mathematical order of operations.
- Use relative, mixed, and 3D cell references.
- Use *COUNTIF* and *SUMIF* functions.
- Build an *IF* formula.
- Insert the *TODAY* function.

1. Open the ***SanDiegoSailing-02.xlsx*** workbook from your student data files. When a workbook has a circular reference, a message box appears immediately as you open it (Figure 2-103).

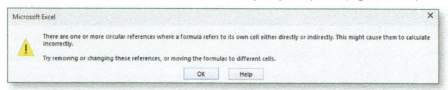

2-103 Circular reference message

2. Click **OK** in the message box. There is a message in the *Status* bar that there are *Circular References*.

3. Save the workbook as [your initials] Excel 2-5. Review the data on each sheet.

4. Use formula auditing tools.
   a. Click the **New Prices** sheet tab and review the *Status* bar.
   b. Click cell **D5**. The formula should be 1 plus the value in cell D4.
   c. Click the **Formulas** tab and click the **Trace Precedents** button in the *Formula Auditing* group. The worksheet icon means that the formula has a 3D reference to another sheet.
   d. Click the **Evaluate Formula** button [*Formula Auditing* group]. The circular reference is identified (Figure 2-104).
   e. Click **Close** and click the **Remove Arrows** button [*Formula Auditing* group].

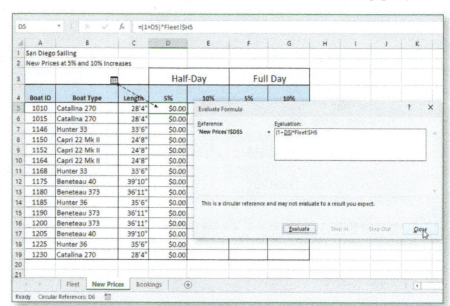

2-104 *Evaluate Formula* dialog box

5. Edit and copy a formula with mixed references.
   a. Edit the formula in cell D5 to show **D$4** instead of "D5." The formula multiplies one plus the percentage value in cell D4 by the current rate on the **Fleet** sheet ($H5). With an absolute reference to row 4 and column H on the **Fleet** sheet, you can copy the formula down the column (Figure 2-105).

2-105 Mixed reference in the edited formula

   b. Copy the formula in cell **D5** to cells **D6:D19** without formatting to preserve the border. When the circular reference message box opens, click **OK**.
   c. Select cells **D5:D19** and drag the *Fill* pointer to copy the formulas to cells **E5:E19**.
   d. Click cell **E6**. The formula is adjusted to use the percentage value in cell E4. Note also that the reference on the **Fleet** sheet ($H6) is adjusted to show the correct row.

6. Build a formula with mixed references.
   a. Click cell **F5** and type **=(1+** to start the formula.
   b. Select cell **F4** and make it an absolute reference to the row but not the column.
   c. Type **)*** for the closing parenthesis and multiplication.
   d. Click cell **I5** on the **Fleet** sheet, and make the reference absolute for the column but not the row (Figure 2-106).

2-106 Mixed references in the new formula

   e. Copy the formula down column F without formatting to preserve the border.
   f. Format cells **F5:F19** as **Currency** and then copy cells **F5:F19** to cells **G5:G19**.

7. Build an *IF* function formula.
   a. Click the **Fleet** sheet tab and select cell **G5**. Rental boats must be able to seat 8 or more people to have a stove in the galley.
   b. Create an *IF* function in which the *logical_test* argument determines if there are 8 or more seats.
   c. Use **Yes** for the *value_if_true* argument. Use **No** for the *value_if_false* argument.
   d. Copy the formula to cells **G6:G19** without formatting and then center the data in column G.

8. Insert the *TODAY* function in cell **B21**. Format the date to show the month spelled out, the date, and four digits for the year.

9. Create a division formula.
   a. Click the **Bookings** sheet tab and select cell **F5**. Average revenue per passenger can be determined by dividing the fee by the number of passengers.
   b. Build the division formula.
   c. Copy the formula in cell **F5** to cells **F6:F19**.

10. Create and copy a *COUNTIF* function to count bookings by boat type.
    a. Select cell **D27**.
    b. Start the *COUNTIF* function from the *Statistical* category by clicking the **More Functions** button in the *Function Library* group.
    c. Use cells **$C$5:$C$19** as the *Range* argument.
    d. To set a *Criteria* argument that will select all boats in the "Beneteau" group, the criteria is **ben***. If you type the formula, include quotation marks.
    e. Copy the formula in cell **D27** to cells **D28:D30**.
    f. Edit the criteria in each copied formula in cells **D28:D30** to reflect the boat type.

11. Create and copy a *SUMIF* function to calculate total revenue by boat type.
    a. Select cell **E27**.
    b. Start the *SUMIF* function with cells **$C$5:$C$19** as the *Range*.

c. The *Criteria* is ben*.
d. The *Sum_range* is cells **$E$5:$E$19**.
e. Copy the formula in cell **E27** to cells **E28:E30**.
f. Edit the criteria in each copied formula in cells **E28:E30** as needed.

12. Complete formatting.
    a. Apply the **Currency** format to all values that represent money.
    b. Format the labels in cells **A1:A2** as **18** point.
    c. Select cells **A1:F2** and center them across the selection.
    d. Merge and center the label in cell **C25** over cells C25:E25 and format it at **16** points.
    e. Bold and center the labels in rows **4** and **26**.
    f. Select cells **A4:F19** and apply **All Borders**. Do the same for cells **C25:E30**.
    g. Center the page horizontally.

13. Save and close the workbook (Figure 2-107).

San Diego Sailing Bookings
Revenue per Passenger

Date	Boat ID	Boat Type	# of Passengers	Total Fees	Revenue per Passenger
4/5/2016	1010	Catalina 270	4	$525.00	$191.25
4/8/2016	1015	Catalina 270	6	$850.00	$141.67
4/11/2016	1146	Hunter 33	6	$500.00	$83.33
4/14/2016	1150	Capri 22 Mk II	6	$525.00	$87.50
4/17/2016	1152	Capri 22 Mk II	4	$325.00	$81.25
4/20/2016	1164	Capri 22 Mk II	3	$475.00	$158.33
4/23/2016	1168	Hunter 33	6	$725.00	$120.83
4/26/2016	1175	Beneteau 40	10	$850.00	$85.00
4/29/2016	1180	Beneteau 373	8	$350.00	$43.75
5/2/2016	1185	Hunter 36	8	$650.00	$81.25
5/5/2016	1190	Beneteau 373	10	$625.00	$62.50
5/8/2016	1200	Beneteau 373	8	$725.00	$90.63
5/11/2016	1205	Beneteau 40	12	$850.00	$70.83
5/14/2016	1225	Hunter 36	8	$725.00	$90.63
5/17/2016	1230	Catalina 270	6	$675.00	$112.50

Bookings by Type

	Count	Total Revenue
Beneteau	5	$3,400.00
Capri 22 Mk II	3	$1,325.00
Catalina 270	3	$2,050.00
Hunter	4	$2,600.00

San Diego Sailing
Rental and Charter Fleet

Boat ID	Boat Type	Length	Model Year	Seats	Sleeps	Galley with Stove	Half-Day Rate	Full Day Rate
1010	Catalina 270	28'4"	2000	8	6	Yes	$375.00	$650.00
1015	Catalina 270	28'4"	2001	8	6	Yes	$425.00	$725.00
1146	Hunter 33	33'6"	2004	10	6	Yes	$350.00	$500.00
1150	Capri 22 Mk II	24'8"	2005	6	4	No	$325.00	$500.00
1152	Capri 22 Mk II	24'8"	2005	6	4	No	$325.00	$500.00
1164	Capri 22 Mk II	24'8"	2006	6	4	No	$325.00	$500.00
1168	Hunter 33	33'6"	2007	10	6	Yes	$425.00	$725.00
1175	Beneteau 40	39'10"	2008	12	6	Yes	$489.00	$750.00
1180	Beneteau 373	36'11"	2009	10	6	Yes	$369.00	$725.00
1185	Hunter 36	35'6"	2009	10	6	Yes	$349.00	$550.00
1190	Beneteau 373	36'11"	2010	10	6	Yes	$369.00	$625.00
1200	Beneteau 373	36'11"	2010	10	6	Yes	$369.00	$625.00
1205	Beneteau 40	39'10"	2012	12	6	Yes	$489.00	$750.00
1225	Hunter 36	35'6"	2012	10	6	Yes	$349.00	$725.00
1230	Catalina 270	28'4"	2012	8	6	Yes	$439.00	$675.00

San Diego Sailing
New Prices at 5% and 10% Increases

Boat ID	Boat Type	Length	Half-Day 5%	Half-Day 10%	Full Day 5%	Full Day 10%
1010	Catalina 270	28'4"	$393.75	$412.50	$682.50	$715.00
1015	Catalina 270	28'4"	$446.25	$467.50	$761.25	$797.50
1146	Hunter 33	33'6"	$367.50	$385.00	$525.00	$550.00
1150	Capri 22 Mk II	24'8"	$341.25	$357.50	$525.00	$550.00
1152	Capri 22 Mk II	24'8"	$341.25	$357.50	$525.00	$550.00
1164	Capri 22 Mk II	24'8"	$341.25	$357.50	$525.00	$550.00
1168	Hunter 33	33'6"	$446.25	$467.50	$761.25	$797.50
1175	Beneteau 40	39'10"	$513.45	$537.90	$787.50	$825.00
1180	Beneteau 373	36'11"	$387.45	$405.90	$761.25	$797.50
1185	Hunter 36	35'6"	$366.45	$383.90	$577.50	$605.00
1190	Beneteau 373	36'11"	$387.45	$405.90	$656.25	$687.50
1200	Beneteau 373	36'11"	$387.45	$405.90	$656.25	$687.50
1205	Beneteau 40	39'10"	$513.45	$537.90	$787.50	$825.00
1225	Hunter 36	35'6"	$366.45	$383.90	$761.25	$797.50
1230	Catalina 270	28'4"	$460.95	$482.90	$708.75	$742.50

2-107 Excel 2-5 completed

Independent Project 2-6

Placer Hills Real Estate has regional offices throughout central California, and each office tracks its listings and sales data. In the workbook, you need to insert agent names, calculate market days, and determine sale price as a percentage of list price. You also calculate summary statistics.
[Student Learning Outcomes 2.1, 2.3, 2.5, 2.6, 2.7]

File Needed: **PlacerHills-02.xlsx** [Student data files are available in the Library of your SIMnet account.]
Completed Project File Name: **[your initials] Excel 2-6.xlsx**

Skills Covered in This Project

- Create and copy formulas.
- Use dates in a subtraction formula.
- Name cell ranges.
- Use relative and 3D cell references in formulas.
- Use the VLOOKUP function.
- Use AVERAGE, MAX, MIN, and COUNT.
- Use COUNTIF.

1. Open the **PlacerHills-02.xlsx** workbook from your student data files and save it as [your initials] Excel 2-6. Review the data on each sheet.

2. Build a subtraction formula with dates.
   a. Select cell **N4** on the **Listings** sheet. You can subtract the older date from the later date to determine the number of days on the market.
   b. Type = and click cell **M4**, the sold date.
   c. Type − for subtraction and click cell **B4**, the listing date.
   d. Press **Enter**. The result is formatted as a date (Figure 2-108).

2-108 Result is formatted as a date

   e. Copy the formula in cell **N4** to cells **N5:N12** without formatting to preserve the fill color.
   f. Format cells **N4:N12** as **General**.

3. Calculate the sold price as a percentage of the list price.
   a. Select cell **P4** and type =.
   b. Build a formula to divide the selling price by the list price.
   c. Copy the formula without formatting and format the column as **Percent Style** with **two** decimal places.

4. Use the VLOOKUP function to insert the agent's last name in a new column.
   a. Insert a column at column **D**.
   b. Type Name in cell **D3** and click cell **D4**.
   c. Start a VLOOKUP function and set the agent ID (C4) as the lookup_value argument.
   d. Use an absolute reference to cells **A2:B7** on the **Agents** sheet for the table_array argument. Do not include column titles in a table array.
   e. Enter the appropriate number for the col_index_num argument to display the agent's last name.
   f. Copy the formula without formatting to display each agent's name and AutoFit the column width.

5. Name cell ranges.
   a. Select cells **E3:E12**.
   b. Press **Ctrl** and select cells **G3:G12**, **L3:L12**, and **P3:P12**.
   c. Click the **Create from Selection** button [Formulas tab, Defined Names group] and use the **Top row** to create range names.

d. Press **Ctrl+Home**.

e. Set this sheet to fit one page, landscape orientation.

f. Insert a footer that displays your name in the right section.

	A	B
1	Placer Hills Real Estate	
2	Roseville Office Statistics	
3		
4	Average List Price	$297,400
5	Highest List Price	$385,000
6	Lowest List Price	$227,000
7	Number of Listings	9
8		
9	Number of Brick Homes	on,br*)
10	Number of Frame Homes	
11	Number of Stone Homes	
12		
13	Number of Homes in Auburn	
14	Number of Homes in Lincoln	
15	Number of Homes in Rocklin	
16	Number of Homes in Roseville	
17		

2-109 Arguments for COUNTIF

6. Calculate statistics for the agency.

   a. Click the **Statistics** sheet tab and select cell **B4**.

   b. Click the **AutoSum** button arrow and choose *Average*. There is no assumed range.

   c. Press **F3 (FN+F3)** to open the *Paste Name* dialog box.

   d. Choose **List_Price** and click **OK**. Press **Enter**.

   e. Continue on this sheet to calculate the highest and lowest list prices as well as the number of listings. Be careful to select the correct range name.

7. Use *COUNTIF* to calculate statistics.

   a. Select cell **B9**.

   b. Click the **More Functions** button in the *Function Library* group, choose **Statistical**, and select **COUNTIF**.

   c. For the *Range* argument, use the range name **Construction** (Figure 2-109).

   d. Type br* for the *Criteria* and click **OK**.

   e. Copy the formula and edit the criteria for cells **B10:B11**.

   f. Start a new *COUNTIF* function in cell **B13** with the appropriate range name. Then copy and edit the formula for cells **B14:B16**. Be sure to use criteria that will distinguish between the two city names that begin with "ro."

8. Center the sheet horizontally. Add a footer with your name in the center section.

9. Save and close the workbook (Figure 2-110).

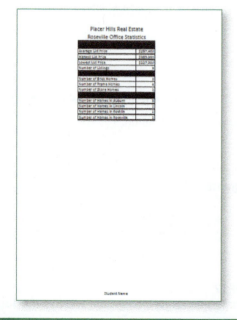

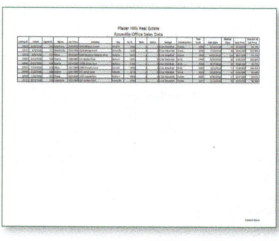

2-110 Excel 2-6 completed

Improve It Project 2-7

Mary's Rentals serves light-to-heavy equipment rental needs of contractors as well as the general public. Data has been imported from an Access database and needs to be handled for better management in Excel. Once that is done, you can calculate several statistics for the company.
[Student Learning Outcomes 2.1, 2.3, 2.4, 2.5, 2.7]

File Needed: ***MarysRentals-02.xlsx*** *[Student data files are available in the* Library *of your SIMnet account.]*
Completed Project File Name: *[your initials] Excel 2-7.xlsx*

Skills Covered in This Project

- Use formula auditing tools.
- Name cell ranges.
- Create, copy, and edit formulas.

- Use relative references and range names in formulas.
- Use *Statistical* functions.
- Use functions from the *Math & Trig* category.

1. Open the ***MarysRentals-02.xlsx*** workbook from your student data files and save it as [your initials] Excel 2-7. The *Equipment* sheet is an inventory of equipment available for rental.

2. Correct errors on the *Rentals* sheet.
   a. Click the **Rentals** tab. This data was imported from an Access database, and there are error triangles in many cells.
   b. Select cells **A2:A47** and click the **Trace Error** button near cell A2 (Figure 2-111). This data was imported as text (labels) but should be set as values.
   c. Select **Convert to Number**. The data is formatted as a value and is right-aligned.
   d. Repeat for cells **B2:C47**.
   e. Center align cells **E2:E47**. This column specifies whether the rental was daily, weekly, or monthly.
   f. Press **Ctrl+Home**.

3. Name cell ranges.
   a. Select cells **B1:B47**, press **Ctrl**, and select cells **E1:E47** and cells **I1:I47**.
   b. Create names from the selection.
   c. Press **Ctrl+Home**.

4. Create and copy a *SUMIF* function with a relative reference.
   a. Click the **Generators** sheet tab and select cell **C5**.
   b. Start the *SUMIF* function with *Equipment_ID* as the *Range* argument.
   c. The *Criteria* argument is cell **A5**.
   d. The *Sum_range* argument is the *Total_Cost* range.
   e. Copy the formula in cell **C5** to cells **C6:C7**. The relative cell reference to cell A5 is adjusted.
   f. Format cells **C5:C7** as **Currency** with no decimal places.

5. Build a custom border.
   a. Select cells **A4:C7**.
   b. Press **Ctrl+1** to open the *Format Cells* dialog box and click the **Border** tab.
   c. In the *Presets* section, click the **Outline** button.
   d. In the *Style* section, click the dotted line style (second option, first column, just below *None*).

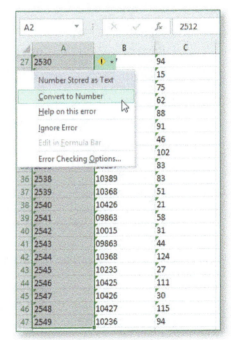

2-111 *Trace Error* button for a selected range

e. Click the middle horizontal position in the *Border* preview area.

f. In the *Style* section, click the single solid line style (last option, first column).

g. Click the middle vertical position in the *Border* preview area (Figure 2-112).

h. Click **OK**.

6. Complete formatting.
   a. Apply bold and centering to cells **A4:C4**.
   b. Format cells **A1:A2** to **16** points.
   c. Select cells **A1:C2** and use **Center Across Selection**.
   d. Center the sheet horizontally.
   e. Insert a header with your name in the right section.

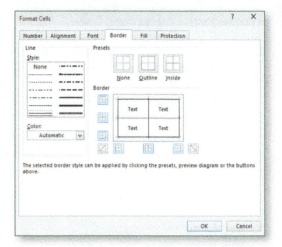

2-112 Build a custom border in the *Format Cells* dialog box

7. Use *SUMIF* to calculate daily, weekly, and monthly income rentals.
   a. Click the **Income Data** sheet tab and select cell **B4**.
   b. Start the *SUMIF* function with **Type** as the *Range* argument.
   c. Type d for daily income as the *Criteria* argument.
   d. The *Total_Cost* range is the *Sum_range* argument.
   e. In cells **B5:B6**, enter *SUMIF* formulas or copy and edit the formula in cell B4.
   f. Use *SUM* in cell **B7**.
   g. Format cells **B4:B7** as **Currency** with no decimal places.

8. Use *COUNTIF* to count rentals by type.
   a. Select cell **B9** and start the *COUNTIF* function from the *Statistical* category.
   b. Use the range name **Type** as the *Range* argument. The *Criteria* is d.
   c. Create a separate formula in cells **B10:B11**, or copy and edit the formula in cell B9.

9. Add a border and fill.
   a. Select cells **A3:B12**.
   b. Click the **Font** group launcher [*Home* tab] and click the **Border** tab.
   c. Click the **Outline** button in the *Presets* section.
   d. In the *Style* section, click the single solid line style (last option, first column).
   e. Click the middle vertical position in the *Border* preview area.
   f. In the *Style* section, click the dotted line style (second option, first column).
   g. Click the middle horizontal position in the *Border* preview area.
   h. Click **OK**.
   i. Select cells **A3:B3, A8:B8,** and **A12:B12**.
   j. Click the arrow with the **Fill Color** button and choose **Black, Text 1, Lighter 50%**.
   k. Select cells **A1:B2** and use **Center Across Selection**.
   l. Increase the font size for cells **A1:B2** to **16**.
   m. Center the sheet horizontally.
   n. Insert a footer with your name in the right section.

10. Save and close the workbook (Figure 2-113).

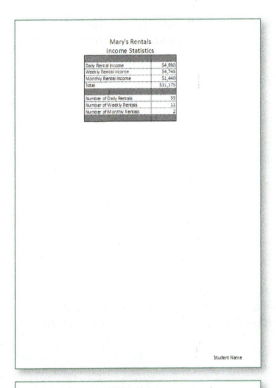

Mary's Rentals
Income Statistics

Daily Rental Income	$4,990
Weekly Rental Income	$4,745
Monthly Rental Income	$1,440
Total	$11,175
Number of Daily Rentals	59
Number of Weekly Rentals	11
Number of Monthly Rentals	2

Student Name

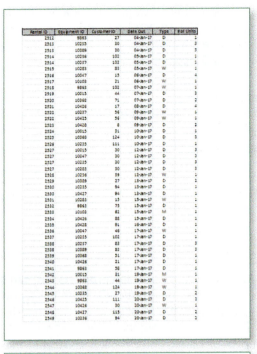

Rental ID	Equipment ID	Customer ID	Date Out	Type	# of Units
2512	9863	27	04-Jan-17	D	1
2513	10235	30	04-Jan-17	D	3
2513	10389	30	04-Jan-17	D	3
2514	10236	102	05-Jan-17	D	1
2514	10237	102	05-Jan-17	D	1
2515	10283	83	05-Jan-17	W	1
2516	10047	15	06-Jan-17	D	4
2517	10103	21	06-Jan-17	W	1
2518	9863	102	07-Jan-17	W	1
2519	10015	44	07-Jan-17	D	3
2520	10398	71	07-Jan-17	D	2
2521	10426	17	08-Jan-17	D	4
2522	10237	56	09-Jan-17	W	1
2522	10425	56	09-Jan-17	W	1
2523	10428	8	09-Jan-17	D	2
2524	10015	31	10-Jan-17	D	1
2525	10360	124	10-Jan-17	D	3
2526	10235	111	10-Jan-17	D	1
2527	10015	30	12-Jan-17	D	3
2527	10047	30	12-Jan-17	D	3
2527	10235	30	12-Jan-17	D	3
2527	10283	30	12-Jan-17	D	3
2528	10236	29	13-Jan-17	W	1
2529	10389	27	13-Jan-17	D	2
2530	10235	94	13-Jan-17	D	1
2530	10427	94	13-Jan-17	D	1
2531	10283	15	15-Jan-17	W	1
2532	9863	73	15-Jan-17	D	1
2533	10103	82	15-Jan-17	M	1
2534	10426	88	15-Jan-17	D	1
2535	10428	81	16-Jan-17	D	1
2536	10047	46	17-Jan-17	W	1
2537	10235	102	17-Jan-17	D	1
2538	10237	83	17-Jan-17	D	3
2538	10389	83	17-Jan-17	D	3
2539	10368	51	17-Jan-17	D	1
2540	10426	21	17-Jan-17	D	1
2541	9863	56	17-Jan-17	D	1
2542	10015	31	19-Jan-17	M	1
2543	9863	44	19-Jan-17	W	1
2544	10368	124	19-Jan-17	D	1
2545	10235	27	19-Jan-17	D	2
2546	10425	111	20-Jan-17	D	1
2547	10426	30	20-Jan-17	W	1
2548	10427	115	20-Jan-17	D	2
2549	10236	94	20-Jan-17	D	2

Student Name

Mary's Rentals
Generator Rental Data

ID	Name	Total
10015	Generator Portable Makita 1000W	$570
10103	Generator Towable PowerPro 25KW	$1,440
10425	Generator Portable Makita 1000W	$210

Date Due	Rate	Total Cost
05-Jan-17	$160.00	$160.00
07-Jan-17	$10.00	$30.00
07-Jan-17	$60.00	$180.00
06-Jan-17	$35.00	$35.00
06-Jan-17	$200.00	$200.00
12-Jan-17	$480.00	$480.00
10-Jan-17	$225.00	$900.00
13-Jan-17	$360.00	$360.00
14-Jan-17	$640.00	$640.00
10-Jan-17	$30.00	$90.00
09-Jan-17	$15.00	$30.00
12-Jan-17	$35.00	$140.00
16-Jan-17	$800.00	$800.00
16-Jan-17	$120.00	$120.00
11-Jan-17	$40.00	$80.00
12-Jan-17	$30.00	$30.00
13-Jan-17	$15.00	$45.00
11-Jan-17	$10.00	$10.00
15-Jan-17	$30.00	$90.00
15-Jan-17	$225.00	$675.00
15-Jan-17	$10.00	$30.00
15-Jan-17	$120.00	$360.00
19-Jan-17	$140.00	$140.00
15-Jan-17	$60.00	$120.00
14-Jan-17	$10.00	$10.00
14-Jan-17	$120.00	$120.00
22-Jan-17	$480.00	$480.00
16-Jan-17	$160.00	$160.00
15-Feb-17	$1,080.00	$1,080.00
16-Jan-17	$35.00	$35.00
17-Jan-17	$40.00	$40.00
24-Jan-17	$900.00	$900.00
18-Jan-17	$10.00	$10.00
20-Jan-17	$200.00	$600.00
20-Jan-17	$60.00	$180.00
18-Jan-17	$15.00	$15.00
18-Jan-17	$35.00	$35.00
18-Jan-17	$160.00	$160.00
19-Feb-17	$360.00	$360.00
26-Jan-17	$640.00	$640.00
26-Jan-17	$45.00	$45.00
21-Jan-17	$10.00	$20.00
23-Jan-17	$30.00	$90.00
27-Jan-17	$140.00	$140.00
22-Jan-17	$120.00	$240.00
22-Jan-17	$35.00	$70.00

2-113 Excel 2-7 completed

Challenge Project 2-8

For this project, you create a workbook for a hair products company that includes an inventory list and an invoice form. You use *VLOOKUP* to enter the cost of the product on the invoice and then calculate a total with taxes for each product.
[Student Learning Outcomes 2.1, 2.2, 2.3, 2.5, 2.6]

File Needed: None
Completed Project File Name: *[your initials] Excel 2-8.xlsx*

Create and save a workbook as [your initials] Excel 2-8. Modify your workbook according to the following guidelines:

- In cell **A1**, type a name for the hair products company. In cell **A2**, type Customer Invoice. In cells **A4:D4**, enter these labels: Product ID, Cost, Quantity, and Total with Tax. Do not include a comma or a period. Name this sheet tab Invoice.
- Insert a new sheet and name it Stock. In cells **A1:C1**, enter labels for Product ID, Name, and Cost with no punctuation.
- In cells **A2:C11**, enter data for ten products that can be purchased from your company. Use *AutoFill* to create a series for the *Product ID*. Since this range will be used as the table array in a *VLOOKUP* function, the product IDs must be in ascending order, either A to Z or low value to high value. Name the cell range Stock (without the labels in row 1).
- Below the *Stock* range, enter Tax Rate as a label. In a cell either to the right or below the label, enter 3.75% as the rate.
- On the *Invoice* sheet, type any three of the product IDs in cells **A5:A7**. Use *VLOOKUP* in column B to display the cost. In the *Quantity* column, type three values to indicate the number ordered.
- In the *Total with Tax* column, build a formula to multiply the cost by the quantity ordered. This result should be multiplied by one plus the tax rate on the *Stock* sheet. Show a grand total in row 8.
- Use the *TODAY* function in cell **A10** on the *Invoice* sheet and format the date to show the date, the month with a three-letter abbreviation, and the year as two-digits.
- Complete formatting on the *Invoice* sheet. Select a workbook theme if desired, use cell styles, or build your own designs.
- Add a header that shows your name in the right section.
- Set document properties to show your name as the author and the company name as the title. Spell check the workbook if necessary.

Challenge Project 2-9

For this project, you create a workbook for a mobile services provider to calculate revenue from purchased mobile apps. You enter and format data and use *SUMPRODUCT* to determine revenue by category.
[Student Learning Outcomes 2.1, 2.3, 2.5, 2.7]

File Needed: None
Completed Project File Name: *[your initials] Excel 2-9.xlsx*

Create and save a workbook as [your initials] Excel 2-9. Modify your workbook according to the following guidelines:

- In cell **A1**, enter a name for your mobile services company.
- In cell **A2**, type Last Month's Activity.
- In cells **B3:D3**, enter the labels App Name, Times Downloaded, and Cost.
- In cell **A4**, type Books as the first category. In cells **A7, A10,** and **A13,** type the names of three other categories of mobile applications. Examples might be Travel, Entertainment, Games, Health, Sports, and so on.
- In cells **B5:D6**, complete data for two apps in the *Books* category. Then do the same for the other categories.
- Starting in row **18**, create a section that calculates revenue from each app category using the *SUMPRODUCT* function.
- In a cell below the data, use the *TODAY* function and format the date to show a short date.
- Select a workbook theme if desired, use cell styles, or set your own formatting.
- Add a footer that shows the current date in the left section and your name in the right section.
- Set document properties to show your name as the author and a title of your choice. Spell check the workbook if necessary.

Challenge Project 2-10

In this project, you create a workbook that calculates monthly payments for a major purchase at four possible interest rates and different payback times.
[**Student Learning Outcomes 2.1, 2.3, 2.4, 2.5, 2.6**]

File Needed: None
Completed Project File Name: *[your initials] Excel 2-10.xlsx*

Create and save a workbook as [your initials] Excel 2-10. Modify your workbook according to the following guidelines:

- Enter main labels that identify the worksheet and your proposed purchase.
- Build the first section for a *PMT* formula with the labels Loan, Rate, Term, and Payment. Since you plan to copy the section to show other possibilities, do not use range names.
- Fill in values for the loan amount, an interest rate, and the term. Include the percent sign when you type the interest rate. For the term, you can use the number of years or the number of months.
- Use *PMT* to calculate the payment made at the beginning of the month (*Type* argument). If you set months for the term, do not multiply the *Nper* argument by 12.
- Copy the entire section once below the current location with a blank row or two between. Then copy these two groupings one or two columns to the right. You should have four possible payment scenarios on the sheet.
- Edit the interest rate and term for each of the copied sections. Be consistent in how you indicate the term of the loan (years or months). Assume that the loan amount is the same.
- In a row below the data, use the *TODAY* function and format the date to show a short date.
- Make formatting choices to building an easy-to-read report for your possibilities.
- Add a footer with your name in the right section.
- Set document properties to show your name as the author, and spell check the workbook if necessary.

CHAPTER 3

Creating and Editing Charts

CHAPTER OVERVIEW

In addition to building formulas and functions in a worksheet, you can use Excel to graph or chart data. After selecting values and labels, you can quickly create a professional looking chart with a few clicks of the mouse. This chapter introduces you to the basics of creating, editing, and formatting Excel charts.

STUDENT LEARNING OUTCOMES (SLOs)

After completing this chapter, you will be able to:

SLO 3.1 Create Excel chart objects and chart sheets (p. E3-163).

SLO 3.2 Use quick layouts and chart styles to design a chart (p. E3-167).

SLO 3.3 Edit chart elements including titles, data labels, and source data (p. E3-172).

SLO 3.4 Format chart elements with shape styles, fill, outlines, and special effects (p. E3-179).

SLO 3.5 Use pictures, shapes, and *WordArt* in a chart (p. E3-183).

SLO 3.6 Build pie charts and combination charts (p. E3-188).

SLO 3.7 Create sunburst and waterfall charts (p. E3-191).

SLO 3.8 Insert and format sparklines in a worksheet (p. E3-194).

CASE STUDY

In the Pause & Practice projects in this chapter, you use data in a Paradise Lakes Resort workbook to build charts that compare revenue categories for two quarters. You build column and pie charts as objects and separate sheets. You also add trendlines and sparklines to further illustrate aspects of the data.

Pause & Practice 3-1: Create and edit column and bar charts.

Pause & Practice 3-2: Edit and format charts and chart elements.

Pause & Practice 3-3: Create and format pie, combo, and sunburst charts and insert sparklines.

Creating a Chart Object and a Chart Sheet

An Excel *chart* is a visual representation of numeric data in a worksheet. A chart helps you identify trends, make comparisons, and recognize patterns in the numbers. Charts are dynamic and linked to the data, so when values in the worksheet change, the chart is automatically redrawn. You can display a chart in the worksheet with its data, or you can place a chart on its own sheet.

There are different kinds of charts, and Excel can recommend the best chart type based on your selected data. It is essential, however, that you select appropriate data for a chart, because it is possible to build charts that illustrate nothing of any consequence. With experience and practice, you will learn how to create charts that have meaning to your work.

Create a Chart Object

A *chart object* is a selectable item surrounded by a square border that is separate from worksheet data. A chart object contains chart elements such as titles, axes, and gridlines, and each element is selectable, too. You can size and position a chart object in a worksheet, and you can size and position each chart element on the chart.

Source data are the cells that contain values and labels to be graphed in a chart. When you select data for a chart, you usually do not include sums, averages, or similar calculations. In Figure 3-1, the source data includes the series names in column A, the category names in row 4,

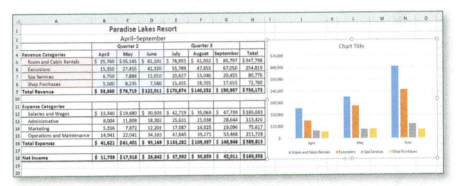

3-1 Chart object and its source data

and four values for each of three months. Each of the values is a *data point*, a cell containing a value. Each group of data points or values is a *data series*. In this example, there are four data series, one for each revenue category. Each data series has a name or label.

The text label that describes a data series is a *category label*. In Figure 3.1, the category labels are the month names.

> ### ANOTHER WAY
> You can create a default chart object by selecting the data and pressing **Alt+F1**.

Data for a chart is best arranged with labels and values in adjacent cells and no empty rows. If you do not include labels for the source data, there are no labels in the chart to describe the data. An empty row within the source data is graphed as a data point with a value of zero (0) and will distort the chart's ability to illustrate a comparison or trend.

When you select contiguous source data (all cells are next to each other), the **Quick Analysis** button appears in the lower right corner of the selection. The *Quick Analysis* tool lists command groups you would be likely to use for the selected data, such as *Formatting, Charts,* or *Totals.* When you select the *Charts* command, Excel shows recommended chart types. As you point to each type, you see a preview of the chart. Click the preferred type to create the chart object in the worksheet.

▶ **HOW TO:** Create a Chart Object from the Quick Analysis Tool

1. Select the source data range with labels and values.
   - The *Quick Analysis* button appears at the lower right corner of the range.
2. Click the **Quick Analysis** button.
   - A dialog box with command categories opens.
3. Select **Charts**.
   - Possible chart types are listed (Figure 3-2).
4. Point to a chart type.
   - A preview of the chart object is displayed.
5. Click to select the chart type.
   - The chart object displays in the worksheet.

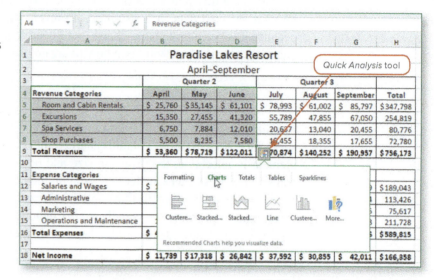

3-2 Chart options for selected data

Excel Chart Types

Excel has many chart types and most types have subtypes or variations. The most common chart types are column or bar, line, and pie, but Excel can build powerful scientific and statistical charts. The following table describes Excel chart types:

Excel Chart Types

Chart Type	Purpose	Data Example	Categories (Labels)	Values (Numbers)
Column	Illustrates data changes over a period of time or shows comparisons among items	Monthly sales data for three automobile models	Horizontal axis	Vertical axis
Bar	Displays comparisons among individual items or values at a specific period of time	Number of pairs sold for eight shoe styles	Vertical axis	Horizontal axis
Pie	Uses one data series to display each value as a percentage of the whole	Expenses or revenue by department for one quarter		One data series shown by slice size
Line	Displays trends in data over time, emphasizing the rate of change	Number of weekly web site views over a ten-week period	Horizontal axis	Vertical axis
Area	Displays the magnitude of change over time and shows the rate of change	Yearly consumption of apples, bananas, and pears over a ten-year period	Horizontal axis	Vertical axis

Continued

Chart Type	Purpose	Data Example	Categories (Labels)	Values (Numbers)
XY (Scatter) or Bubble	Displays relationships among numeric values in two or more data series; these charts do not have a category.	Number of times a patient visits a doctor, amount billed to insurance, and cost billed to patient	Horizontal axis (value 1-x)	Vertical axis (value 2-y)
Stock	Displays three series of data to show fluctuations in stock prices from high to low to close	Opening, closing, and high price for Microsoft stock each day for 30 days	Horizontal axis	Vertical axis
Surface	Displays optimum combinations of two sets of data on a surface	Perceived outside temperature at ten temperature and ten humidity levels	Horizontal axis (value 1-x)	Horizontal axis (value 1-x)
Radar	Displays the frequency of multiple data series relative to a center point. There is an axis for each category.	Style, comfort, and value ratings for three snow boot styles	NA	NA
TreeMap	Displays a hierarchical view of data with different sized and colored rectangles and sub-rectangles to compare the sizes of groups	Soda sales by product name, continent, country, and city	NA	NA
Sunburst	Displays a hierarchical view of data with concentric rings. The top hierarchy is the inner ring and each outer ring is related to its adjacent inner ring.	Tablet sales by screen size, continent, country, and city	NA	NA
Histogram	Column-style chart that shows frequencies within a distribution	Number of students in each of five grade categories for an exam	Horizontal axis	Vertical axis
Box & Whisker	Displays the distribution of data with minimum, mean, maximum, and outlier values	Sales prices of home in five suburbs during a three-week period	Horizontal axis	Vertical axis
Waterfall	Plots each element in a running total and displays negative and positive effects of each on the total	Banking or savings account register	Horizontal axis	Vertical axis
Funnel	Plots values that progressively decrease from one stage or process to the next	Job applications received, applications selected, initial interviews, team interviews, HR interview, job offer	Vertical axis	Horizontal axis
Combo Chart	Uses two types of charts to graph values that are widely different	Line chart for number of monthly web site visits and a column chart for monthly sales of online golf gloves	Either	Either

Size and Position a Chart Object

When you select a chart object, it is active and surrounded by eight selection handles. A *selection handle* is a small circle shape on each corner and in the middle of each side. To select the chart object, point to its border and click. When the chart object is selected, the *Range Finder* highlights the source data in the worksheet. When you point to a selection handle, you will see a two-pointed resize arrow. Drag a corner handle to size the height and width proportionally.

To move a chart object, point to the chart border to display a four-pointed move pointer. Then drag the chart object to the desired location.

When a chart is active or selected, the *Chart Tools Design* and *Format* tabs are available in the *Ribbon* and three *Quick Chart Tools* are available in the top right corner of the object: *Chart Elements, Chart Styles,* and *Chart Filters.*

> **MORE INFO**
>
> You can select individual elements or parts of the chart, and each element has its own selection handles.

▶ **HOW TO:** Move and Size a Chart Object

1. Select the chart object.
   - Point to the border of the chart and click.
2. Point to the outside border of the chart to display a move pointer.
   - Point anywhere along the border.
3. Drag the chart object to a new location and release the pointer button (Figure 3-3).
4. Point to a corner selection handle to display a resize arrow.
5. Drag the pointer to resize the chart proportionally.

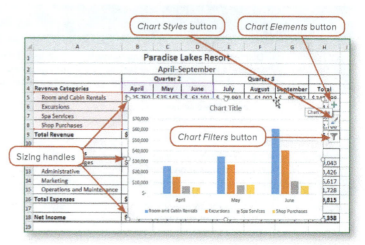

3-3 Selected chart object and move pointer

Create a Chart Sheet

A ***chart sheet*** is an Excel chart that is displayed on its own sheet in the workbook. A chart sheet does not have rows, columns, and cells, but the chart is linked to its data on the source worksheet.

From the *Quick Analysis* tool or the *Insert* tab, Excel creates a chart object. You must move the chart object to its own sheet with the *Move Chart* button on the *Chart Tools Design* tab. Excel uses default sheet names *Chart1, Chart2,* and so on, but you can type a descriptive name in the *Move Chart* dialog box, or you can rename the sheet at any time.

You can create an automatic column chart sheet by selecting the data and pressing the **F11** (**FN+F11**) function key.

> ▶ **MORE INFO**
>
> When the *Recommended Charts* button does not recommend a chart type, select the source data again in a left-to-right order. If there are still no suggestions, click the **All Charts** tab and choose a type.

Source data for a chart need not be contiguous. The *Quick Analysis* tool does not appear for noncontiguous data, but you can click the **Recommended Charts** button in the *Charts* group on the *Insert* tab. The *Insert Chart* dialog box opens and recommends chart types.

▶ **HOW TO:** Create a Chart Sheet for Noncontiguous Cells

1. Select the values and labels for the chart.
   - Select the first range, press the **Ctrl** key, and select each range (Figure 3-4).
2. Click the **Recommended Charts** button [*Insert* tab, *Charts* group].
   - The *Insert Chart* dialog box opens.
   - You can click the **All Charts** tab to select any chart type.
3. Click the thumbnail for a chart type to preview the results.

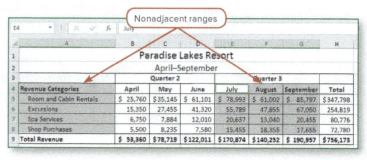

3-4 Source data ranges that are not next to each other

4. Click the preferred chart type and click **OK**.
   - The chart object is active.
   - The *Chart Tools* tabs are available.
5. Click the **Move Chart** button [*Chart Tools Design* tab, *Location* group].
6. Click the **New sheet** radio button (Figure 3-5).
7. Type a descriptive name for the chart sheet.
8. Click **OK**.

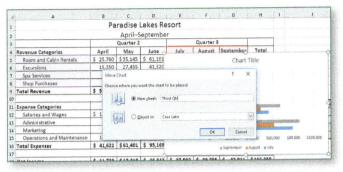

3-5 *Move Chart* dialog box

SLO 3.2

Using Quick Layouts and Chart Styles

A newly created chart has a default layout, color, and style. Excel has various tools to help you enhance the appearance of your chart for originality, readability, and appeal. The *Chart Tools Design* tab includes commands for selecting a chart layout, choosing a chart style, or changing the color scheme.

Apply a Quick Layout

A **chart layout** is a set of elements and the location of those elements. Elements are individual parts of a chart such as a main title, a legend, and axis titles. The *Quick Layout* button [*Chart Tools Design* tab, *Chart Layouts* group] opens a gallery of predefined layouts (Figure 3-6). As you point to an option in the gallery, *Live Preview* redraws the chart. When a chart layout adds an element such as a title, the element displays a generic label like "Chart Title." You can add or remove individual elements, as well as edit placeholder text.

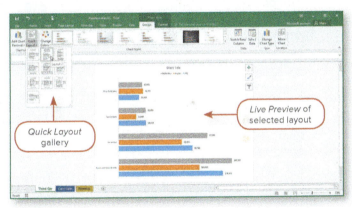

3-6 *Quick Layout* gallery

▶ **HOW TO:** Apply a Quick Layout to a Chart

1. Select the chart object or the chart sheet tab.
2. Click the **Quick Layout** button [*Chart Tools Design* tab, *Chart Layouts* group].
   - The gallery displays thumbnail images of each layout.
   - Quick layouts are named *Layout 1* through the last number.
3. Point to a layout to preview it in the chart.
4. Click a thumbnail to select it.
   - The chart is reformatted with the *Quick Layout* elements.

Apply a Chart Style

A **chart style** is a preset combination of colors and effects for a chart, its background, and its elements. The chart styles that are available for a chart are based on the current workbook theme. If you change the theme, the chart style colors are updated, and your chart reflects the new color palette. You can find chart styles in the *Chart Styles* group on the *Chart Tools Design* tab. Like a chart layout, you can preview the effects of a chart style as you point to each style in the gallery.

> **HOW TO: Apply a Chart Style**

1. Select the chart object or the chart sheet tab.

2. Click the *Chart Styles* **More** button to open the gallery or point to a *Style* thumbnail [*Chart Tools Design* tab, *Chart Styles* group].

   - The number of styles depends on the chart type (Figure 3-7).
   - Chart styles are named *Style 1* through the last number.

3. Point to a style thumbnail to see a *Live Preview* in the chart.

4. Click to select a style.

   - The chart is redrawn with the selected style.

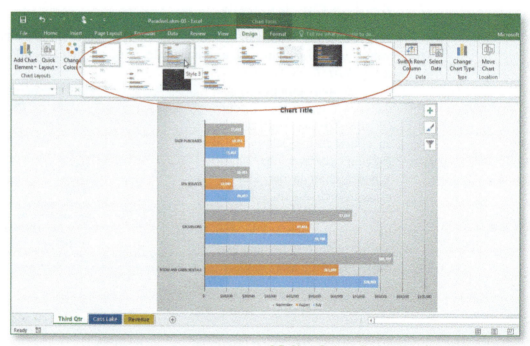

3-7 *Chart Styles* gallery and preview of selected style

Change Chart Colors

The workbook theme and the chart style form the basis for a chart's color scheme. The *Chart Styles* group [*Chart Tools Design* tab] includes a *Change Colors* button with optional color palettes. These palettes are divided into *Colorful* and *Monochromatic* groups.

▶ HOW TO: Change Chart Colors

1. Select the chart object or the chart sheet tab.

2. Click the **Change Colors** button [*Chart Tools Design* tab, *Chart Styles* group].
   - A gallery of color palettes opens (Figure 3-8).
   - Color schemes are named *Color 1* through the last number.

3. Point to a palette to see a *Live Preview* in the chart.

4. Click to select a palette.
   - The chart is formatted with new colors.

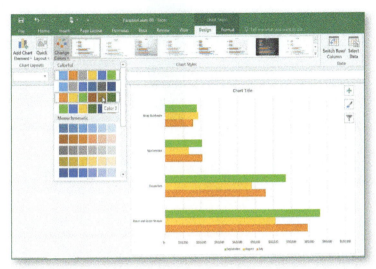

3-8 *Change Colors* **gallery**

Print a Chart

A chart object can be printed on the page with worksheet data, or it can be printed separately. To print a chart with the data, deselect the chart object by clicking a worksheet cell. Size and position the chart and scale the sheet to fit a printed page. Then use regular *Page Setup* commands to complete the print task, such as choosing the orientation or inserting headers or footers.

> ▶ **MORE INFO**
>
> When you insert a header or footer in a selected chart object, that header or footer is not inserted on the worksheet.

To print only the chart object on its own sheet, select it and use regular *Print* and *Page Setup* options. A selected chart object, by default, prints scaled to fit a landscape page. A chart sheet also prints in landscape orientation fit to the page.

▶ HOW TO: Print a Chart with Its Source Data

1. Click any cell in the worksheet.
   - Size and position the chart object as needed.

2. Click the **File** tab to open the *Backstage* view (Figure 3-9).

3. Select **Print**.

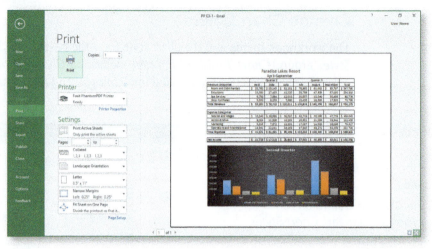

3-9 Print a chart with the data

4. Choose print settings as needed.
   - Set margins and scale the sheet to fit.
5. Click **Print**.

PAUSE & PRACTICE: EXCEL 3-1

In this project, you insert a clustered column chart object in a worksheet that tracks revenue and expenses for Paradise Lakes Resort. You also insert a clustered bar chart sheet to highlight second quarter results.

File Needed: *ParadiseLakes-03.xlsx* [Student data files are available in the Library of your SIMnet account.]
Completed Project File Name: *[your initials] PP E3-1.xlsx*

1. Open the *ParadiseLakes-03* workbook from your student data files and save it as [your initials] PP E3-1.

2. Create a chart object.
   a. Select cells **A4:D8** on the **Cass Lake** sheet. These are labels and values for the chart.
   b. Click the **Quick Analysis** button and select **Charts**.
   c. Click **Clustered Column**.

3. Position and size the chart object.
   a. Click the chart object if it is not selected.
   b. Point to the chart border to display a move pointer.
   c. Drag the chart object so that its top left corner is at cell **A20**.
   d. Point to the lower right selection handle to display a resize arrow.
   e. Drag the pointer to reach cell **H35**.

4. Choose a quick layout.
   a. Select the chart object if necessary.
   b. Click the **Quick Layout** button [*Chart Tools Design* tab, *Chart Layouts* group].
   c. Click **Layout 3** (Figure 3-10).

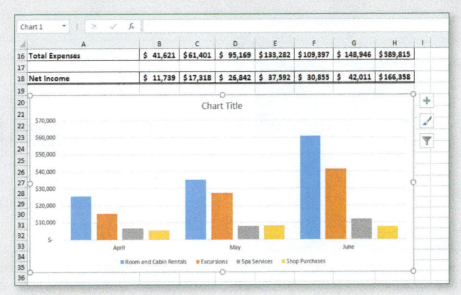

16	Total Expenses	$ 41,621	$61,401	$ 95,169	$133,282	$109,397	$ 148,946	$589,815
17								
18	Net Income	$ 11,739	$17,318	$ 26,842	$ 37,592	$ 30,855	$ 42,011	$166,358

3-10 Chart object sized and positioned

5. Create a chart sheet.
   a. Select cells **A4:A8**.
   b. Press **Ctrl** and select cells **E4:G8**.
   c. Click the **Recommended Charts** button [*Insert* tab, *Charts* group].
   d. Select **Clustered Bar**.
   e. Click **OK**. The chart object is inserted and selected.
   f. Click the **Move Chart** button [*Chart Tools Design* tab, *Location* group].
   g. Click the **New sheet** radio button.
   h. Type Qtr 3 as the sheet name.
   i. Click **OK**. The chart sheet tab is active.

6. Choose a chart style.
   a. Click the **More** button to open the *Chart Styles* gallery [*Chart Tools Design* tab, *Chart Styles* group].
   b. Select **Style 7**.

7. Preview the charts.
   a. Select the **Qtr 3** sheet if necessary.
   b. Click the **File** tab to open the *Backstage* view.
   c. Choose **Print** to preview the chart sheet (Figure 3-11).
   d. Click the **Back** button to return to the worksheet.
   e. Click the **Cass Lake** worksheet tab and select cell **A1**.
   f. Click the **File** tab and select **Print**. The worksheet and chart are previewed on a single page.
   g. Click the **Back** button to return to the worksheet.

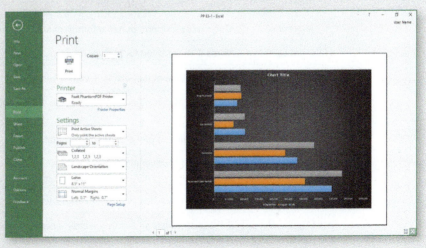

3-11 Print preview for chart sheet

8. Save and close the workbook (Figure 3-12).

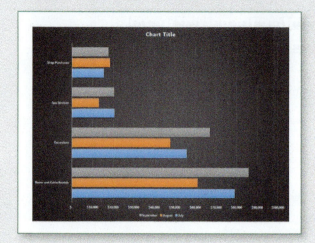 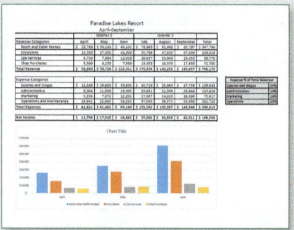

3-12 PP E3-1 completed chart object and chart sheet

Editing Chart Elements and Data

A ***chart element*** is a separate, clickable, editable object. The chart layout and style affects which elements are initially displayed, but you can add, remove, format, size, and position elements as you design a chart. The following table describes common chart elements:

Excel Chart Elements

Element	Description
Axis	Horizontal or vertical boundary that identifies what is plotted
Axis title	Optional description for the categories or values
Chart area	Background for the chart; can be filled with a color, gradient, or pattern
Chart floor	Base or bottom for a 3D chart
Chart title	Optional description or name for the chart
Chart wall	Vertical background for a 3D chart
Data label	Optional element that displays values with the marker for each data series
Data marker	Element that represents individual values. The marker is a bar, a column, a slice, or a point on a line.
Data point	A single value or piece of data from a data series
Data series	Group of related values that are in the same column or row and translate into the columns, lines, pie slices, and other markers
Gridline	Horizontal or vertical line that extends across the plot area to help in identifying values
Horizontal (category) axis	Describes what is shown in the chart and is created from row or column headings. In a bar chart, the category axis is the vertical axis; the category axis is the horizontal axis in a column chart.

Continued

Element	Description
Legend	Element that explains symbols, textures, or colors used to differentiate data series
Plot area	Rectangular area bounded by the horizontal and vertical axes
Tick mark	Small line or marker on an axis to guide in reading values
Trendline	Line or curve that displays averages in the data and can be used to forecast future averages
Vertical (value) axis	Shows the numbers on the chart. In a bar chart, the vertical axis is along the bottom; in a column chart, the vertical axis is along the side.

MORE INFO

Not all charts have all elements. For example, a pie chart does not have any axes or axes titles.

Add and Remove Chart Elements

When you point to a chart element, a *ScreenTip* describes it. When you click the element, it is active and surrounded by selection handles, as shown for the legend in Figure 3-13. In addition to clicking, you can select an element from the *Chart Elements* drop-down list on the *Chart Tools Format* tab. The name of the selected element appears in the *Chart Elements* box.

You show or hide chart elements from the *Chart Elements* button in the top right corner of a chart. When you click the button, the *Chart Elements* pane opens with a list of available elements for the chart type. In this pane, select or deselect the box to show or remove an element. To hide the pane, click the **Chart Elements** button again.

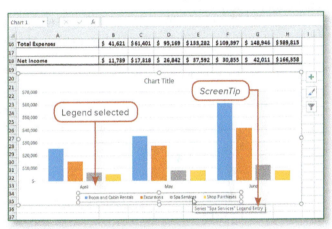

3-13 Selected legend and ScreenTip for a data series

ANOTHER WAY

Click the **Add Chart Element** button [*Chart Tools Design* tab, *Chart Layouts* group] to show a chart element.

Chart and Axes Titles

Chart layouts may include placeholders, which are text box objects, for a main chart title and for axes titles. If the quick layout does not include titles, you can add them. In either case, you must edit the placeholder text.

A main chart title is usually positioned above the chart, but within the chart area. Once you insert the text box, you can select it and move it anywhere on the chart. You might use an axis title to clarify what is represented by the categories or the values. If the chart represents the data well, axes titles are often not necessary.

▶HOW TO: Insert a Chart Title

1. Click the chart object or the chart sheet tab.
2. Click the **Chart Elements** button in the top right corner of the chart.
3. Select the **Chart Title** box.
   - The *Chart Title* placeholder displays above the chart.
4. Click the **Chart Title** arrow in the *Chart Elements* pane to select a position for the title.
5. Triple-click the *Chart Title* placeholder text to select it (Figure 3-14).
   - The mini toolbar opens.
6. Type a title to replace the placeholder text.
7. Click the chart border.
   - The title object is deselected.
   - If you press **Enter** while typing in the text box, you insert a new line in the title. Press **Backspace** to remove it and then click the chart border.

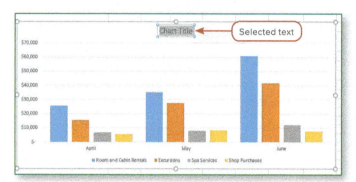

3-14 Placeholder text to be edited

To edit placeholder text, you can also select the object and type text in the *Formula* bar. Then press **Enter**, or click the **Enter** button in the *Formula* bar to complete it. The label appears in the *Formula* bar as you type, and you will not see it on the chart until you press **Enter**.

All text within an object can be formatted with font attributes from the *Font* and *Alignment* groups [*Home* tab] when the element is selected. When you want to apply a format to a portion of the text, click to place an insertion point inside the element and select the characters to be changed.

> ▶ **MORE INFO**
>
> When you double-click a chart element, its *Format* pane opens with format and design choices for that element.

Removing a chart element makes more room for the actual chart. In Figure 3-15, for example, the vertical axis title "Dollars" is probably not necessary. By removing it, the chart resizes to fit the chart area. You can always show the element again if you change your mind.

To delete a chart element,

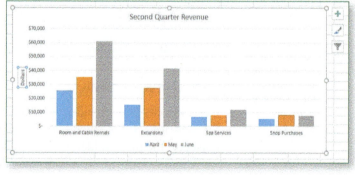

3-15 Delete an axis title to make more room for the chart

select it and press **Delete**. You can confirm which element is selected in the *Chart Elements* box on the *Chart Tools Format* tab [*Current Selection* group].

1. Click the chart element.
   - The element displays selection handles.
   - Confirm which element is selected in the *Chart Elements* list box [*Chart Tools Format* tab, *Current Selection* group].
2. Press **Delete**.
   - The chart resizes to fit the area.
   - You can also right-click the chart element and choose **Delete**.

> **ANOTHER WAY**
>
> To remove an element, click the **Chart Elements** button in the top right corner of the chart and deselect the box for that element.

Data Labels

Data labels display the number represented by a column, bar, pie slice, or other marker on the chart. Because the value axis uses a scale, it cannot show a precise value, but a data label can display that number. Data labels should be used when there are not too many data series because they can clutter a chart. Or you can select just one or two of the data points (the individual bars or columns) and show labels for only that data.

Data labels are displayed from the *Chart Elements* button on the chart or from the same button on the *Chart Tools Design* tab [*Chart Layouts* group].

▶ **HOW TO:** Add Data Labels

1. Select the chart object or the chart sheet tab.
2. Click the **Chart Elements** button in the top right corner of the chart.
3. Select the **Data Labels** box.
   - *Live Preview* shows data labels for each data point in the data series
4. Point to **Data Labels** in the pane and point to its arrow (Figure 3-16).
   - Position choices for the labels are listed.
   - *Live Preview* updates as you point to each option.
5. Choose a location for the data labels.

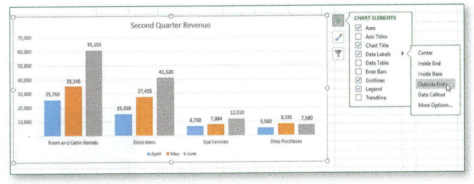

3-16 Data labels shown outside bar markers

Data Table

A chart ***data table*** is a columnar display of the values for each data series in a chart, located just below the chart. When your readers do not have access to the source data for a chart, a data table can supply valuable information.

To include a data table below your chart, you can use the *Add Chart Element* button on the *Chart Tools Design* tab in the *Chart Layouts* group or the *Chart Elements* button on the chart. You can show a data table with or without legend markers, a mini legend to the left of the table (Figure 3-17).

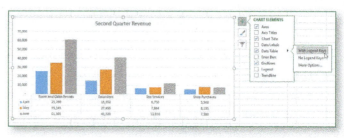

3-17 Data table element for a chart

Trendlines

A **trendline** is a chart element that plots patterns using a moving average of the current data. It uses a straight or curved line and can extend past the data to predict future averages. Some charts cannot display a trendline, such as a stacked chart, a pie chart, or a 3D chart. A basic linear trendline is appropriate for values that tend to increase or decrease as time passes. A trendline traces data for one data series as seen in

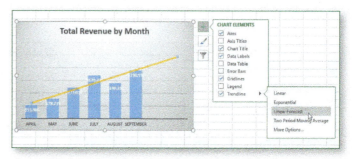

3-18 Column chart with "Total Revenue" linear trendline

Figure 3-18. If you have multiple data series, as in a typical column chart, you can add a trendline for each series.

> ▶ **ANOTHER WAY**
>
> Right-click a data series marker (its column) and choose **Add Trendline** to open the *Format Trendline* task pane and build a trendline.

▶ HOW TO: Add a Trendline to a Chart

1. Click the chart object or the chart sheet tab.
2. Click the **Chart Elements** button in the top right corner of the chart.
3. Select the **Trendline** box in the *Chart Elements* pane.
   - The *Add Trendline* dialog box lists the names of the data series.
   - When there is only one data series, the trendline is added to the chart.
4. Choose a data series for the trendline and click **OK** (Figure 3-19).
5. Point to the **Trendline** arrow in the *Chart Elements* pane.
   - Choose **Linear** to show a line for existing data.
   - Choose **Linear Forecast** to build a line for current and future data.

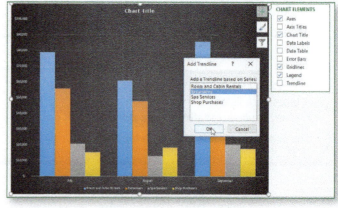

3-19 *Add Trendline* dialog box for chart with multiple data series

Switch Row and Column Data

Excel plots the data series based on the number of rows and columns selected in the worksheet and the chart type. Based on your choices, Excel determines if the labels are along the bottom or the side of the chart. When necessary, you can change which data series is plotted on the x-axis and which is plotted on the y-axis. In a column chart, the x-axis is along the bottom of the chart; the y-axis is along the left.

▶ **HOW TO: Switch Row and Column Data**

1. Click the chart object or the chart sheet tab.
2. Click the **Switch Row/Column** button [*Chart Tools Design* tab, *Data* group] (Figure 3-20).
   - The data series become the categories.
   - You can toggle between how columns and rows are plotted.

3-20 Column and row data switched

Change the Chart Type

When a chart does not depict what you intended, you need a variety of chart types for a project, or you simply prefer a different chart, you can easily change the chart type. Changing the type assumes that the source data is the same and that it can be graphed in the new chart. You should not, for example, change a column chart with three data series into a pie chart, because a pie chart has only one series. The resulting chart would not represent the data as expected.

The *Change Chart Type* button is on the *Chart Tools Design* tab in the *Type* group. For a selected chart object or sheet, you can also right-click and choose **Change Chart Type** from the context menu. The *Change Chart Type* dialog box has *Recommended Charts* and *All Charts* tabs like the *Insert Chart* dialog box.

▶ **HOW TO: Change the Chart Type**

1. Click the chart object or chart sheet.
2. Click the **Change Chart Type** button [*Chart Tools Design* tab, *Type* group].
   - The *Change Chart Type* dialog box opens.

3. Click the **Recommended Charts** tab.

  • Click **All Charts** tab if the recommended charts are not adequate.

4. Click a thumbnail image to preview the chart in the dialog box.

5. Select a chart type and click **OK**.

Filter Source Data

A chart displays all the categories and all the data series. You can, however, filter or refine which data is displayed by hiding categories or series. A *filter* is a requirement or condition that identifies which data is shown and which is hidden. Chart filters do not change the underlying cell range for a chart, but they enable you to focus on particular data.

You filter chart data from the *Chart Filters* button in the top right corner of the chart or in the *Select Data Source* dialog box.

▶**HOW TO:** Filter Source Data

1. Select the chart object or chart sheet tab.

2. Click the **Chart Filters** button in the top right corner.

  • The *Chart Filters* pane shows a check mark for series and categories that are shown.

3. Deselect the box for a series or category to be hidden.

4. Click **Apply** (Figure 3-21).

  • The chart is redrawn.

5. Click the **Chart Filters** button to close the pane.

  • You can show the hidden data when desired.

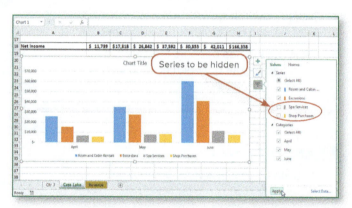

3-21 *Chart Filters* pane

Edit Source Data

The cells used to build a chart are its source data. This data can be edited to change, add, or remove cells. In a column chart, for example, you can add a data series, or another column. To add or delete a data series in a chart object, select the chart and drag the sizing arrow in the lower right corner of the highlighted cell range to expand or shrink the data range, as shown in Figure 3-22. Removing cells from the data range deletes that data series from the chart.

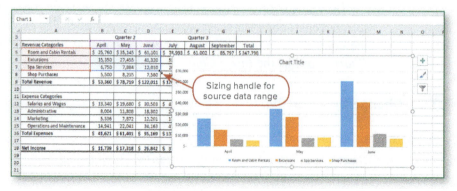

3-22 The "Shop Purchases" column will be removed from chart

To edit the source data for a chart sheet, click the **Select Data** button on the *Chart Tools Design* tab [*Data* group] to open the *Select Data Source* dialog box.

> **HOW TO: Add a Data Series in a Chart Sheet**

1. Click the chart sheet tab.

2. Click the **Select Data** button [*Chart Tools Design* tab, *Data* group].

   - The *Select Data Source* dialog box opens.
   - The worksheet is active, and the source cells are highlighted.

3. Select the new cell range in the worksheet (Figure 3-23).

   - If the cell ranges are not adjacent, select the first one, type a comma, and select the next range.
   - You can type cell addresses in the *Chart data range* box rather than selecting cells.

4. Click **OK**.

   - The chart sheet is active and redrawn with the edited source data range.

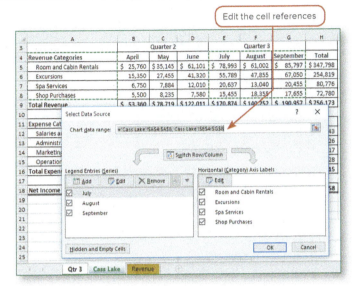

3-23 *Select Data Source* dialog box for a chart sheet

> **ANOTHER WAY**
>
> You can open the *Select Data Source* dialog box by clicking **Select Data** at the bottom of the *Chart Filters* pane. You can define filters from this dialog box by selecting or deselecting a series or category name box.

SLO 3.4

Formatting Chart Elements

Quick Layout and *Chart Styles* apply formatting, but you can change most attributes to personalize your work. Making your own format choices enables you to distinguish your charts from those of other Excel users. You can also use company, association, or school colors and images to further differentiate your charts.

Some chart elements consist of a group of related elements. A data series, for example, is the group of values for a particular item. Within each data series, there are data points. You can format the entire data series or an individual data point.

When you select a chart element, certain options on the *Chart Tools Design* tab apply to only that element. When the chart area (background) is selected, for example, you can change only its fill or border color.

Apply a Shape Style

A *shape style* is a predesigned set of borders, fill colors, and effects for a chart element. *Shape fill* is the background color, and *shape outline* is the border around the element. *Shape effects* include shadows, glows, bevels, or soft edges. All of these commands are available in the *Shape Styles* group on the *Chart Tools Format* tab.

Shape styles are shown in a gallery and are grouped as *Theme Styles* or *Presets*. Point to an icon to see a *ScreenTip* with a descriptive name and click an icon to apply it to the selected element. *Live Preview* is available for a chart object but not for a chart sheet.

▶ HOW TO: Apply a Shape Style

1. Select the chart element.
   - Confirm or select a chart element by clicking the **Chart Elements** drop-down arrow [*Chart Tools Format* tab, *Current Selection* group] and choosing the name.
   - If you accidentally open the *Format* task pane for a chart element, close it.
2. Click the **More** button [*Chart Tools Format* tab, *Shape Styles* group].
   - Each icon in the *Shape Styles* gallery displays fill, outline, and effects (Figure 3-24).
   - Point to an icon to see its name and *Live Preview* in a chart object.
3. Click a shape style icon.
   - The chart element is reformatted.

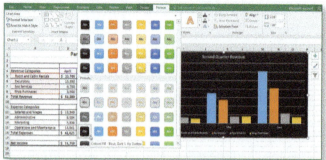

3-24 *Shape Style* gallery for the chart area

Apply Shape Fill, Outline, and Effects

Fill color, outline width and color, and special effects are available separately, and your choices override shape style settings already applied.

For fill color, you choose from the gallery, standard colors, or a custom color. After you choose a color, you can refine it to use a gradient, a variegated blend of the color.

▶ HOW TO: Apply Gradient Fill to a Chart Element

1. Select the chart element.
   - Confirm or select a chart element from the **Chart Elements** list [*Chart Tools Format* tab, *Current Selection* group].
2. Click the **Shape Fill** button [*Chart Tools Format* tab, *Shape Styles* group].
   - The gallery and menu options are listed.
3. Point to a color tile to see its name in a *ScreenTip*.
   - *Live Preview* applies the color to an element in a chart object.
4. Select a color tile to apply the color.
5. Click the **Shape Fill** [*Chart Tools Format* tab, *Shape Styles* group].
6. Choose **Gradient** to open the gallery (Figure 3-25).
7. Point to a tile to see its description.
8. Click the preferred gradient.

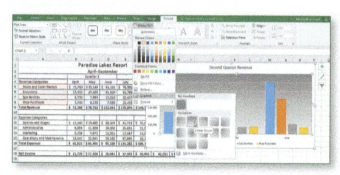

3-25 *Shape Fill* and *Gradient* galleries

The outline for a shape is a border that surrounds or encircles the element. Not all chart elements are suited to an outline, but elements such as the chart or plot area often benefit from the use of an outline. When you add an outline to a chart element, you can select a weight or thickness for the line as well as a color. The thickness of an outline is measured in points, like fonts. Excel provides a gallery of weights to help you visualize the width. After you apply an outline, it is easier to see the effect if you deselect the chart object.

▶ HOW TO: Apply an Outline to a Chart Element

1. Select the chart element.
2. Click the **Shape Outline** button [*Chart Tools Format* tab, *Shape Styles* group].
   - The gallery and menu options are listed.
3. Choose a color.
4. Click the **Shape Outline** button [*Chart Tools Format* tab, *Shape Styles* group].
5. Click **Weight** to open its gallery.
6. Choose a width for the outline (Figure 3-26).
7. Click a worksheet cell or another chart element to see the outline.

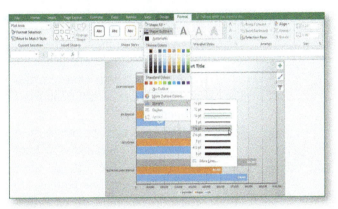

3-26 *Outline color* and *Weight* galleries

Special effects that are commonly used are bevels and shadows, because they give an element a realistic, three-dimensional look. These effects are best used on larger elements, such as the chart area, because they can overwhelm smaller elements.

To remove an effect, select the element and click the **Shape Effects** button. Choose the effect group to select the first option such as **No Shadow** or **No Bevel**.

▶ HOW TO: Apply an Effect to a Chart Element

1. Select the chart element.
2. Click the **Shape Effects** button [*Chart Tools Format* tab, *Shape Styles* group].
   - The gallery lists effect groups and then variations for each group.
3. Select a group for the effect (Figure 3-27).
   - If a group name is grayed out, it is not available for the selected element.
4. Point to an icon to see its name.
5. Click to choose an effect.
6. Click a worksheet cell or another chart element to see the outline.

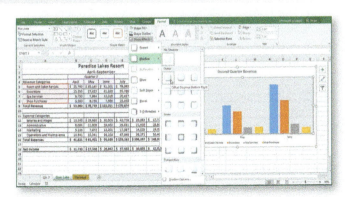

3-27 *Shape Effects* gallery for the plot area

The Format Task Pane

Every chart element has a *Format* task pane that consolidates shape, fill, and color options and provides custom commands for the element. To open the *Format* pane for a chart element, double-click the element or right-click it and choose **Format** [*Element Name*] from the menu. The *Format* pane opens to the right of the workbook window and automatically updates to reflect the selected element.

> **ANOTHER WAY**
>
> Open a *Format* task pane for a selected object by clicking the **Format Selection** button [*Chart Tools Format* tab, *Selection* group].

A task pane lists command options at the top of the pane. In Figure 3-28, *Title Options* and *Text Options* are available because the selected element is a chart title. The small triangle next to the first *Options* name enables you to choose a different chart element.

For each options group, most *Format* task panes have at least two buttons. The *Fill & Line, Effects,* and *Options* buttons are common, but there are other buttons for selected elements. Point to a button to see its *ScreenTip.* When you click a button, the pane displays relevant commands.

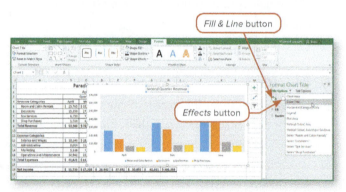

3-28 *Format Chart Title* pane

> **MORE INFO**
>
> Expand or collapse a command group in the *Format* task pane by clicking the command name.

► **HOW TO:** Use the Format Task Pane to Change Shape Fill

1. Double-click the chart element.
   - The *Format* task pane for the element opens on the right.
   - Select another element in the chart to see its task pane.
   - You can also select an element and click the **Format Selection** button [*Chart Tools Format* tab, *Current Selection* group] to open the task pane.
2. Click the name of the *Options* group at the top of task pane.
   - For some chart elements, there is only one group.
3. Click the **Fill & Line** button in the *Format* task pane.
4. Click **Fill** to expand the group.
5. Click the **Fill Color** button to open the gallery (Figure 3-29).
6. Choose the desired color.

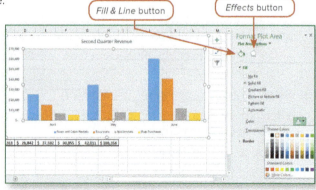

3-29 *Fill & Line* command in the *Format Plot Area* task pane

While the *Fill & Line* and *Effects* buttons offer similar commands for all elements, the *Options* button in a *Format* task pane is specific to the element. For a data series in a column chart, for example, these commands determine whether numbers are shown to the right or left of the chart (secondary or primary axis), or whether the columns overlap. A pie chart, on the other hand, has options that allow you to rotate the pie or explode slices.

▶ **HOW TO:** Use the Format Task Pane to Format Data Labels

1. Double-click a data label element in the chart.
   - Right-click an element and choose **Format Data Labels**.
   - All data labels for one series are selected.

2. Choose **Label Options** at the top of the task pane.
   - Point to a button to see a *ScreenTip*.
   - *Text Options* are also available.

3. Click the **Label Options** button.

4. Click **Label Options** or **Number** to expand the command group.

5. Select format options for the labels (Figure 3-30).
   - Formats are applied as you select them.

6. Close the task pane.

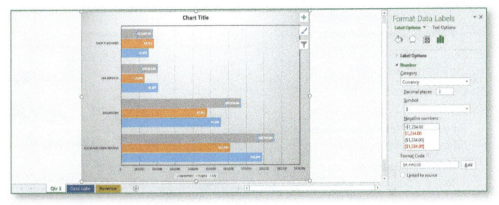

3-30 *Format Data Labels* pane

SLO 3.5

Using Pictures, Shapes, and WordArt in a Chart

A chart can be enhanced with pictures, shapes, or *WordArt*. Pictures can be inserted as separate design objects on the chart, or they can be used as fill for a chart element. You can draw a shape such as an arrow or a lightning bolt to highlight a particular data point on a chart. *WordArt* is often applied to a chart title for a distinctive look.

Use a Picture as Shape Fill

An image can be used to fill the chart area, the plot area, or a marker, especially bars, columns, or pie slices. You have probably seen bar charts with stick figures to illustrate population numbers or column charts with tiny automobile images to show auto sales. You can use an image file from your computer, from external media, or from an online source. And always verify that you have permission to use an image in your work.

The size and design of the picture is important, and you should guard against making the chart appear busy. You can edit some attributes of a picture in Excel, but this depends on the picture format.

A picture is inserted from the **Fill** command on the *Format* task pane for the element. After you have inserted a picture, the task pane displays *Stretch* and *Stack* options. *Stretch* enlarges and elongates a single copy of a picture to fill the element. The *Stack* choice sizes and repeats the image to fill the area. There is also a *Stack and Scale* setting for precise matching of the number of images used per unit of value.

HOW TO: Use a Picture as Fill

1. Double-click the chart element for the fill.
   - The *Format* task pane opens.
   - You can also right-click the element and choose **Format [*Element Name*]**.
2. Click the **Fill & Line** button in the *Format* task pane.
3. Click **Fill** to expand the group.
4. Select the **Picture or texture fill** radio button.
   - If the last-used picture or texture displays in the chart element, ignore it. It will be replaced.
5. Click **Online** to search for an image or click **File** to choose a stored image.
6. Find and insert the image.
   - The picture is placed in the chart element.
7. Click the **Stack** button in the task pane (Figure 3-31).
   - Copies of the picture fill the element.

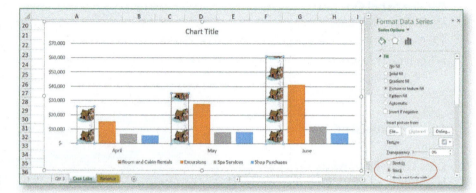

3-31 Image used as fill for data series

Insert Shapes

The *Shapes* gallery is located in the *Insert Shapes* group on the *Chart Tools Format* tab. These predefined shapes include arrows, lines, circles, and other basic figures. Shapes can be used to highlight or emphasize a point in the chart. They can be drawn anywhere on the chart, but are usually placed on the background or the plot area so they do not obscure any data. A shape, once drawn, is a clickable, selectable object. When it is selected, the *Picture Tools Format* tab is available with commands for altering the appearance of the shape and there is also the *Format Shape* task pane.

HOW TO: Insert a Shape in a Chart

1. Select the chart object or the chart sheet tab.
2. Click the **More** button [*Chart Tools Format* tab, *Insert Shapes* group].

3. Select the shape.

4. Click and drag to draw the shape on the chart (Figure 3-32).

   - The shape is selected.

5. Type text for the shape.

   - Text is optional.
   - Some shapes cannot display text.

6. Click the **Drawing Tools Format** tab to format the shape.

   - You can also apply formatting from the *Format Shape* task pane.

7. Click a worksheet cell or another chart element to deselect the shape.

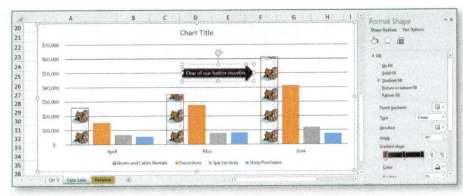

3-32 **Shape inserted in chart**

▶ **ANOTHER WAY**

Insert a shape from the *Shapes* button on the *Insert* tab [*Illustrations* group].

Use WordArt in a Chart

WordArt is a text box with preset font style, fill, and effects. *WordArt* is best used for main titles, because it can make smaller elements unreadable. You apply a *WordArt* style from the *Chart Tools Format* tab, *WordArt Styles* group. You can further design a *WordArt* style by individually changing its fill, outline, and effects.

▶ **MORE INFO**

You can insert a *WordArt* text box from the *Insert* tab [*Text* group] and position it on the chart.

▶ **HOW TO:** Use WordArt in a Chart

1. Select the chart title object.

   - You can also apply *WordArt* to an axis title, a data label, or the legend.

2. Click the **More** button to open the *WordArt Styles* gallery [*Chart Tools Format* tab, *WordArt Styles* group].

3. Point to a style icon to see a *ScreenTip* with a description.

   - The styles use colors and effects from the workbook theme.
   - *Live Preview* works in a chart object but not on a chart sheet.

4. Click the preferred style (Figure 3-33).

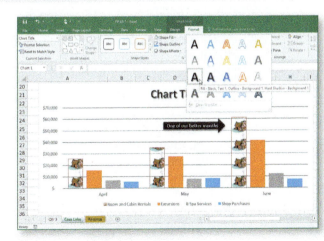

3-33 *WordArt Style* **gallery for selected chart title**

For this project, you open your Pause & Practice file to edit and format the Paradise Lakes Resort charts. You switch row and column data, remove chart elements, and change the chart type. Finally, you format the charts for increased visual appeal.

File Needed: *[your initials] PP E3-1.xlsx*
Completed Project File Name: *[your initials] PP E3-2.xlsx*

1. Open the *[your initials] PP E3-1* workbook completed in *Pause & Practice 3-1* and save it as [your initials] PP E3-2.

2. Switch the row and column data in the chart object.
   a. Click the **Cass Lake** worksheet tab.
   b. Point to the border or edge of the chart object and click to select it.
   c. Click the **Switch/Row Column** button [*Chart Tools Design* tab, *Data* group].

3. Edit, add, and remove chart elements.
   a. Click to select the chart title box.
   b. Point to the placeholder text and triple-click to select all of it.
   c. Type Second Quarter Activity.
   d. Click the chart border to deselect the title.
   e. Click the **Chart Elements** button in the top right corner of the chart.
   f. Select the **Axis Titles** box.
   g. Select the horizontal *Axis Title* placeholder below the columns and press **Delete**.
   h. Select the vertical *Axis Title* placeholder.
   i. Click the *Formula* bar, type Revenue, and press **Enter** (Figure 3-34).
   j. Click a worksheet cell to deselect the chart object.

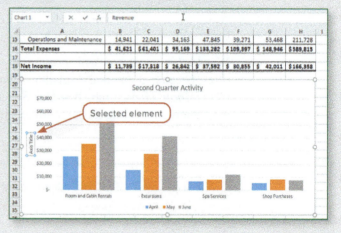

3-34 Edit the text in the *Formula* bar

4. Change the chart type.
   a. Click the **Qtr 3** sheet tab.
   b. Click the **Change Chart Type** button [*Chart Tools Design* tab, *Type* group].
   c. Click the **Recommended Charts** tab.
   d. Find and select the first **Clustered Column** in the pane on the left.
   e. Click **OK**.

5. Filter the source data.
   a. Click the **Chart Filters** button at the top right corner of the chart.
   b. Deselect the **Excursions** box in the *Series* area.
   c. Click **Apply**.
   d. Click the **Chart Filters** button to close the pane (Figure 3-35).

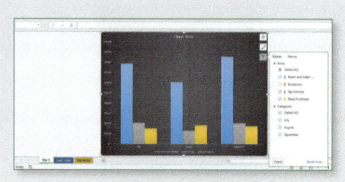

3-35 Filtered data in chart

6. Apply shape styles and outlines to chart elements.
   a. Click the **Cass Lake** tab and select the chart object.
   b. Click the **Chart Elements** drop-down arrow [*Chart Tools Format* tab, *Current Selection* group].
   c. Choose **Plot Area** to select the plot area of the chart.
   d. Click the **More** button [*Chart Tools Format* tab, *Shape Styles* group].
   e. Click **Subtle Effect – Gold**, **Accent 4** in the fourth row in the *Theme Styles* group.
   f. Click the drop-down arrow for the **Shape Outline** button [*Chart Tools Format* tab, *Shape Styles* group].
   g. Choose **Black**, **Text 1** in the top row of the *Theme Colors*.
   h. Click the **Chart Elements** drop-down arrow [*Chart Tools Format* tab, *Current Selection* group].
   i. Choose **Vertical (Value) Axis Major Gridlines** to select the major gridlines in the plot area.
   j. Click the icon with the **Shape Outline** button [*Chart Tools Format* tab, *Shape Styles* group] to apply the last-used color (**Black**, **Text 1**).
   k. Click the **Chart Elements** drop-down arrow [*Chart Tools Format* tab, *Current Selection* group] and choose **Chart Area**.
   l. Apply **Black**, **Text 1** for the outline (Figure 3-36).
   m. Click a worksheet cell.

3-36 Plot area formatted

7. Use a picture as fill.
   a. Click the **Qtr 3** tab.
   b. Double-click one of the "Room and Cabin Rentals" columns to open the *Format Data Series* task pane.
   c. Click the **Fill & Line** button.
   d. Click **Fill** to expand the command group.
   e. Select the **Picture or texture fill** button.
   f. Click **Online**, type log cabin in the *Bing Image Search* box, and press **Enter**.
   g. Choose an image and insert it (Figure 3-37). If you choose an image that cannot be used as fill, a message appears in the columns; just select a different picture.
   h. Select the **Stack** radio button in the *Format Data Series* task pane.
   i. Click **Fill** to collapse the command group and click **Border** to expand its group.
   j. Select the **Solid line** button.
   k. Click the **Color** button and choose **Black**, **Text 1**.
   l. Close the task pane.

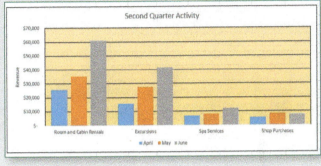

3-37 Online search for a picture as fill

8. Use *WordArt* in a chart.
   a. Triple-click the **Chart Title** placeholder text to select the text.
   b. Type Third Quarter Activity.
   c. Triple-click the new label and change the font size to **32 pt**.
   d. Click the border area of the chart title to display the selection handles.
   e. Click the **More** button [*Chart Tools Format* tab, *WordArt Styles* group].
   f. Choose **Fill – Gray-25%**, **Background 2**, **Inner Shadow** (third row).

9. Format the legend.
   a. Click to select the legend.
   b. Click the **Home** tab and change the font size to **12 pt**.
   c. Click the chart border to deselect the legend.
   d. Click a worksheet cell and press **Ctrl+Home**.

10. Save and close the workbook (Figure 3-38).

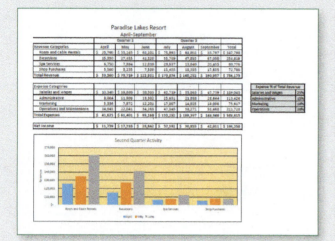

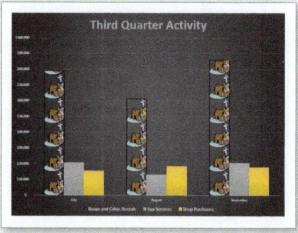

3-38 PP E3-2 completed worksheet and chart sheet

SLO 3.6

Building Pie and Combination Charts

A pie chart represents one set of related values and shows the proportion of each value to the total. A combination chart uses at least two sets of values and plots each data series with a different chart type. A combination chart can also have two value axes, one on the left and one on the right.

Create a 3-D Pie Chart

A pie chart graphs one data series and illustrates how each number relates to the whole. Be cautious about the number of categories, because a pie chart with hundreds of slices is difficult to interpret and does not depict the relationship among the values.

As you develop chart-building skills, you can choose a type from the *Charts* group on the *Insert* tab. When you select a chart type button, you see a gallery with available subtypes. As you point to each subtype, *Live Preview* previews the chart.

From the *Insert Pie or Doughnut Chart* button on the *Insert* tab, you can select from a gallery of 2-D or 3-D pie types as well as a doughnut shape (Figure 3-39). A doughnut chart is a pie chart with a hollow center. There are also options for a pie chart with a bar or another pie chart.

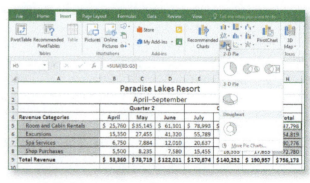

3-39 Selected data series and categories for a pie chart

1. Select the cells that include the values and the category labels.
   - The labels and values need not be adjacent.
2. Click the **Insert Pie or Doughnut Chart** button [*Insert* tab, *Charts* group].
3. Choose **3-D Pie**.
   - A pie chart object is placed in the worksheet.
4. Click the **Move Chart** button [*Chart Tools Design* tab, *Location* group].
5. Click the **New sheet** button.
6. Type a name for the chart sheet.
7. Click **OK**.

Pie Chart Elements and Options

In a pie chart, the data series is represented by the whole pie. A data point is a slice of the pie. You can format the data series as a whole, or you can format individual slices.

A pie chart can display a legend and a title. It does not, however, have axes and does not use axes titles. Data labels can be used in place of a legend, because they show the same information.

Custom commands for a pie chart are the angle of the first slice and the percent of explosion. These commands are available on the *Format* task pane for the data series (the whole pie) or for a selected data point (one slice). The angle of the first slice allows you to rotate the pie. The first slice starts at the top of the chart at 0° (zero degrees). As you increase that value, the slice arcs to the right. *Live Preview* displays the results, too.

Exploding a pie slice emphasizes that slice, because it moves the slice away from the rest of the pie. This uses more white space in the chart, and the pie gets smaller. You set explosion as a percentage.

1. Double-click the pie shape.
   - The *Format Data Series* task pane opens.
   - You can also right-click the pie shape and choose **Format Data Series**.
2. Click the **Series Options** button.
3. Drag the vertical slider to set the *Angle of first slice*.
   - The percentage is shown in the entry box.
   - You can also type a percentage or use the spinner arrows to set a value.
4. Click the data point (slice) to explode.
   - The *Format Data Point* task pane opens.
5. Drag the vertical slider to set the *Pie Explosion* (Figure 3-40).
   - The percentage is shown in the entry box.
   - The larger the percentage, the farther the slice is from the rest of the pie.
   - You can type a percentage or use the spinner arrows to set a value.

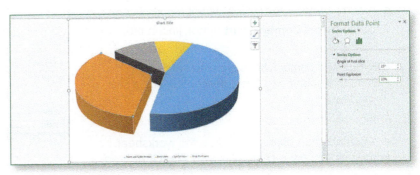

3-40 Exploded pie slice with angle of first slice changed

Create a Combination Chart

A combination chart includes at least two chart types such as a line chart and a column chart. Paradise Lakes Resort can use a combination chart to compare revenue from cabin and room rentals to total revenue. These two values reflect a different scale of numbers, so showing one series as a line and the other as a column focuses the comparison (Figure 3-41).

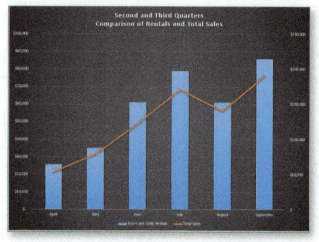

3-41 Line-Column combination chart

The most common combination of chart types is line and column, but you can also use a line and area combination. Excel offers an option to create a custom combination, but it is best to use this only after you have experience charting your data.

Create a combination chart from the *Insert Combo Chart* button in the *Charts* group on the *Insert* tab as well as from the *All Charts* tab in the *Insert Chart* dialog box.

▶ HOW TO: Create a Combination Chart

1. Select the cell ranges for the chart.
   - The cell ranges need not be contiguous.
2. Click the **Insert Combo Chart** button [*Insert* tab, *Charts* group].
   - Suggested combinations are displayed.
   - Point to a subtype to see a description and a *Live Preview* (Figure 3-42).
3. Select the chart subtype.
   - A combo chart object displays in the worksheet.
   - You can move the chart to its own sheet if desired.

3-42 Insert Combo Chart button options

Combination Chart Elements and Options

A combination chart has at least two data series, each graphed in its own chart type. Keep this type of chart relatively simple, because its purpose is to compare unlike items and too many data series complicate what viewers see.

In a combination chart, you can display values on two vertical axes. The axis on the left is the primary axis; the one on the right is secondary (Figure 3-43). This option is best when the values are very different or use a different scale.

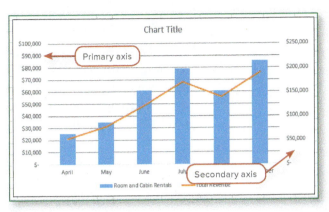

3-43 Secondary axis for a combo chart

For the secondary axis, Excel builds the number scale based on the data. Select the data series to be plotted on the secondary axis and choose the option from the *Series Options* command group in the *Format* task pane. You can also define a secondary axis in the *Insert Chart* or the *Change Chart Type* dialog boxes.

A combination chart has the same elements and commands as a regular column or line chart. You can apply chart styles and layouts, as well as shape fill, outline, effects, pictures, shapes, and *WordArt*.

▶ **HOW TO: Display a Secondary Axis on a Combination Chart**

1. Select the chart object or the chart sheet tab.
2. Select the data series to be shown on the secondary axis.
   - Select the line or any column in a line-column combo chart.
   - You can also choose the data series from the *Chart Elements* box [*Chart Tools Format* tab, *Current Selection* group].
3. Click the **Format Selection** button [*Chart Tools Format* tab, *Current Selection* group].
4. Click the **Series Options** button in the task pane (Figure 3-44).
5. Click the **Secondary Axis** radio button.
   - Additional options for the axis depend on the chart type.
6. Close the *Format Data Series* task pane.

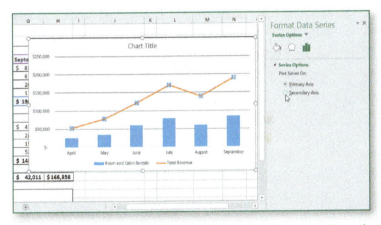

3-44 *Format Data Series* task pane to define a secondary axis

---

SLO 3.7

Creating Sunburst and Waterfall Charts

New chart types in Excel 2016 visualize data in ways that previously required engineering or similar specialized software. With a sunburst chart, you can show relationships between multiple categories of data. A waterfall chart depicts a running total for financial data so that you can assess the impact of negative and positive cash flows. These charts have many characteristics of standard Excel charts, but they have a few limitations related to requirements for the data they plot.

Create a Sunburst Chart

A *sunburst chart* is a hierarchy chart that illustrates the relationship among categories and subcategories of data. It resembles a doughnut chart with concentric rings for each layer of data as shown in Figure 3-45. A *hierarchy* is a division of data that identifies a top group followed by lesser groups. The student population at your college can be illustrated in a hierarchy with gender at the top, followed by age group, then home city, followed by area of study, and so on.

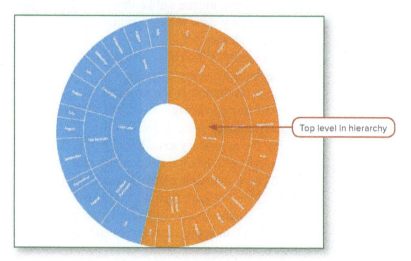

Top level in hierarchy

3-45 Sunburst chart for third quarter revenue for two locations

Paradise Lakes Resort keeps a record of revenue by location, category, and month. The inner ring in Figure 3-45 is the top level of the hierarchy, the location. The second level is the revenue category (Rentals, Excursions, etc.), and the outside ring is the month's revenue. From the chart, you can see that Baudette contributed slightly more than half of the total revenue and that the boutique purchases at Cass Lake were high.

A sunburst chart has one data series and no axes. It can display a title, data labels, and a legend. The *Chart Tools Design* and *Format* tabs provide basic options for fine-tuning the appearance of the chart.

The *Insert Hierarchy Chart* button [*Insert* tab, *Charts* group] has two subtypes, *Sunburst* and *TreeMap*. These subtypes can handle large amounts of data, but be careful not to build charts that are difficult to interpret due to their size.

> ### ▶ MORE INFO
>
> A *TreeMap* chart illustrates hierarchical data using rectangles of various sizes and colors to represent the divisions and subdivisions.

▶ HOW TO: Create a Sunburst Chart

1. Select the source data with labels and values.
   - The **Quick Analysis** button appears, but the *Charts* group does not include the *Sunburst* chart type.
2. Click the **Insert Hierarchy Chart** button [*Insert* tab, *Charts* group].
   - A menu lists the subtypes.
3. Point to **Sunburst** to see a *Live Preview*.

4. Click **Sunburst** to select it.
    - A chart object is placed in the worksheet.
5. Click the **Move Chart** button [*Chart Tools Design* tab, *Location* group].
6. Select **New sheet**.
7. Type a name for the chart sheet and click **OK**.
    - The *Chart Tools Design* and *Format* tabs are available.
8. Click the sunburst shape to select the circle.
9. Point to a category name in the inner ring and click to select the data point.
    - The category and its related items are selected (Figure 3-46).

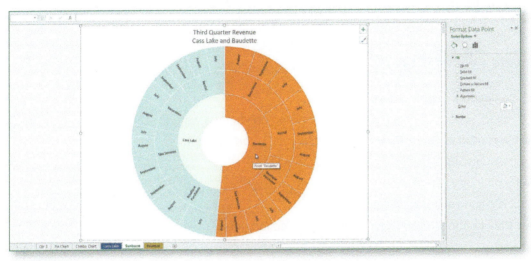

3-46 Sunburst chart sheet with selected data point

10. Format the data point as desired.
    - If the *Format Data Point* task pane is not open, click the **Format Selection** button [*Chart Tools Format* tab, *Current Selection* group].
11. Click outside the chart background to deselect the chart.

> **MORE INFO**
>
> The *Hierarchy* charts do not appear in any *Recommended Charts* list, but they are listed on the *All Charts* tab.

Create a Waterfall Chart

A **waterfall chart** is a financial chart that displays a moving total for positive and negative values. A waterfall chart graphs how each expense or outlay affects the account. You might, for example, build a waterfall chart to visualize your monthly income sources (inflows) and expenditures (outlays) to watch how you spend your resources.

In Figure 3-47, it is obvious that payroll consumes most of the cash account for Paradise Lakes Resort. In a waterfall chart, the depth or height of the marker indicates the value. In the figure, the beginning balance and ending total markers rest on the bottom axis. The other amounts are described as floating.

A waterfall chart plots one data series and has a legend that clarifies the increase, decrease, and total colors. A waterfall chart can also include axes, titles, gridlines, and data labels.

The *Insert Waterfall or Stock Chart* button is in the *Charts* group on the *Insert* tab. These charts do not appear in the *Recommended Charts* list, but they are available on the *All Charts* tab.

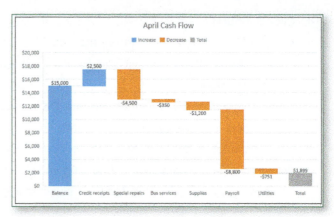

3-47 Waterfall chart for cash flow

▶ **HOW TO:** Create a Waterfall Chart Sheet

1. Select the source data with labels and values.
   - The *Quick Analysis* button appears but does not have an option for a waterfall chart.
2. Click the **Insert Waterfall or Stock Chart** button [*Insert* tab, *Charts* group].
   - A menu lists the subtypes.
3. Click **Waterfall**.
   - A chart object is placed in the worksheet.
4. Click the **Move Chart** button [*Chart Tools Design* tab, *Location* group].
5. Select **New sheet**.
6. Type a name for the chart sheet and click **OK**.
   - The *Chart Tools Design* and *Format* tabs are available.
7. Click a column marker to select the data series.
8. Click the ending marker to select only it.
9. Click the **Format Selection** button [*Chart Tools Format* tab, *Current Selection* group].
10. Click the **Series Options** button in the task pane.
11. Expand the *Series Options* group.
12. Select the **Set as total** box (Figure 3-48).
    - The marker rests on the bottom axis and is no longer floating.
13. Close the task pane and click outside the chart to deselect it.

3-48 Set a marker as a total

SLO 3.8

Inserting and Formatting Sparklines

Sparklines are miniature charts in a cell or cell range. They can be used to illustrate trends and patterns without adding a separate chart object or sheet. They do not have the same characteristics as an Excel chart.

Sparklines are created from a selected data range and placed in a location range, usually next to the data (Figure 3-49). They are embedded in the cell, almost like a background. If you enter a label or value in a cell with a sparkline, that data appears on top of the sparkline.

3-49 Column sparklines in a worksheet

Insert Sparklines

There are three sparkline types: *Line*, *Column*, and *Win/Loss*. The *Sparklines* commands are located on the *Insert* tab of the worksheet. The *Data Range* is the range of cells to be graphed, and the *Location Range* is the cell or range for the sparklines. The **Sparkline Tools Design** tab opens when you select the sparkline group.

▶ **HOW TO:** Insert Column Sparklines in a Worksheet

1. Select the cell range of data to be graphed.
2. Click the **Column Sparkline** button [*Insert* tab, *Sparklines* group].
   - The selected range address is shown in the *Data Range* entry box.
   - You can select or edit the data range here.
3. Click the *Location Range* box.
4. Select the cell or range for the sparklines (Figure 3-50).
5. Click **OK**.

3-50 *Create Sparklines* dialog box

Sparkline Design Tools

When sparklines are selected, the *Sparkline Tools Design* tab opens. This context-sensitive tab includes several options for changing the appearance of the sparklines. There is a *Sparkline Style* option that changes the color scheme for the sparkline group, but you can also change colors with the *Sparkline Color* command. The *Marker Color* command enables you to choose a different color for identified values. A **marker** for a sparkline is the data point value. You can use different colors to highlight the high, low, first, or last value as well as negative values.

When you define a location range for sparklines, they are embedded as a group. If you select any cell in the sparkline range, the entire group is selected. Subsequent commands affect all sparklines in the group. From the *Group* section on the *Sparkline Tools Design* tab, you can ungroup the sparklines so that you can format them individually.

From the *Sparkline Tools Design* tab, you can also change the type of sparkline, such as making a column sparkline into a line sparkline. The *Show* group lists the marker values that can be highlighted. When you select one of these options, that marker in the sparkline is formatted with a different color.

► HOW TO: Format Sparklines

1. Click a cell with a sparkline.
   - The sparkline group is selected.
2. Click the *Sparkline Line Tools Design* tab.
3. Click the **More** button [*Sparkline Tools Design* tab, *Style* group].
4. Choose a sparkline style.
   - The sparkline group is recolored.
5. Select the **High Point** box in the *Show* group (Figure 3-51).
   - A default color based on the sparkline style is applied to the highest value in the sparkline for each row.
6. Click the **Sparkline Color** button [*Sparkline Tools Design* tab, *Style* group].
7. Choose a color for the sparkline group.
   - The sparkline group is recolored, and the color from the *Sparkline Style* is overridden.
8. Click the **Marker Color** button [*Sparkline Tools Design* tab, *Style* group].
9. Choose **High Point** and select a color.
   - The color for the highest value is reset.

3-51 *High Point* marker selected for sparklines

Clear Sparklines

You can remove sparklines from a worksheet with the *Clear* command in the *Group* group on the *Sparkline Tools Design* tab. After sparklines are cleared, you may also need to delete the column where they were located or reset row heights and column widths.

► HOW TO: Clear Sparklines

1. Select any cell in the sparklines range.
2. Click the arrow with **Clear Selected Sparklines** button [*Sparkline Tools Design* tab, *Group* group].
3. Choose **Clear Selected Sparklines Groups**.

> **MORE INFO**
>
> When you ungroup sparklines, you can select a single sparkline cell and clear it.

PAUSE & PRACTICE: EXCEL 3-3

For this project, you complete Paradise Lakes' revenue report by inserting a pie chart that shows the proportion of each revenue category. You also insert a combination chart sheet to compare rentals with total revenue and a sunburst chart to analyze third quarter revenue. Finally, you insert sparklines in the worksheet.

File Needed: *[your initials] PP E3-2.xlsx*
Completed Project File Name: *[your initials] PP E3-3.xlsx*

1. Open the *[your initials] PP E3-2* workbook completed in *Pause & Practice 3-2* and save it as [your initials] PP E3-3.

2. Create a pie chart for total sales revenue.
   a. Select the **Cass Lake** tab.
   b. Select cells **A5:A8** as the category.
   c. Press **Ctrl** and select cells **H5:H8** as the data series.
   d. Click the **Insert Pie or Doughnut Chart** button [*Insert* tab, *Charts* group].
   e. Choose **3-D Pie**.
   f. Click the **Move Chart** button [*Chart Tools Design* tab, *Location* group].
   g. Click the **New sheet** button and type Pie Chart as the sheet name.
   h. Click **OK**.

3. Format a pie chart.
   a. Select the **Pie Chart** tab.
   b. Click the **Chart Title** placeholder to select it and then triple-click the **Chart Title** placeholder text.
   c. Type Second and Third Quarters and press **Enter**.
   d. Type Sources of Revenue on the second line.
   e. Drag to select the first line of the title.
   f. Use the mini toolbar to change the font size to **24 pt**.
   g. Drag to select the second line of the title.
   h. Use the mini toolbar to change the font size to **18 pt**. (Figure 3-52).

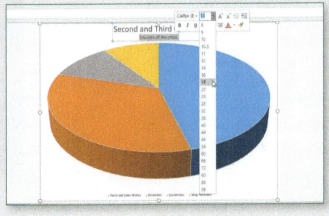

3-52 Chart titles typed and font size changed

   i. Click the chart border to deselect the title.
   j. Double-click the pie to open the *Format Data Series* task pane.
   k. Click the **Series Options** button in the *Format Data Series* task pane.
   l. Click the **Room and Cabin Rentals** slice to change to the *Format Data Point* task pane.
   m. Set the pie explosion percentage at **10%**.
   n. Close the task pane.
   o. Select the legend at the bottom of the chart to display selection handles.
   p. Click the **Home** tab and change the font size to **14 pt** (Figure 3-53).

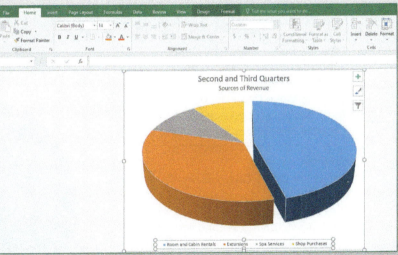

3-53 Selected legend with new font size

4. Create a combination chart for total sales revenue and room and cabin rentals.
   a. Select the **Cass Lake** tab.
   b. Select cells **A4:G5** as one data series and category.

c. Press **Ctrl** and select cells **A9:G9** as another data series and category.

d. Click the **Insert Combo Chart** button [*Insert* tab, *Charts* group].

e. Choose **Clustered Column – Line on Secondary Axis**.

f. Click the **Move Chart** button [*Chart Tools Design* tab, *Location* group].

g. Click the **New sheet** button and type Combo Chart as the sheet name.

h. Click **OK**.

5. Format a combination chart.

a. Select the **Combo Chart** tab, select the **Chart Title** placeholder, and then triple-click the placeholder text.

b. Type Second and Third Quarters and press **Enter**.

c. Type Comparison of Rentals and Total Revenue on the second line.

d. Click the chart border to deselect the chart title.

e. Choose **Style 6** [*Chart Tools Design* tab, *Chart Styles* group] (Figure 3-54).

f. Click the background to deselect the chart.

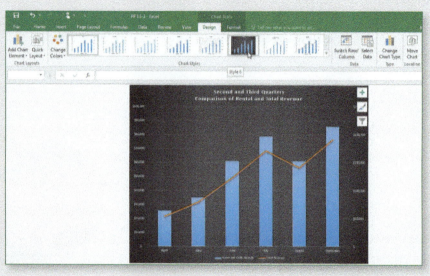

3-54 Combo chart with Style 6

6. Create a sunburst chart for third quarter revenue analysis.

a. Select the **Revenue** tab.

b. Select cells **A5:D28** as the data series and categories. This chart will illustrate revenue for Cass Lake and Baudette.

c. Click the **Insert Hierarchy Chart** button [*Insert* tab, *Charts* group].

d. Choose **Sunburst**.

e. Click the **Move Chart** button [*Chart Tools Design* tab, *Location* group].

f. Click the **New sheet** button and type Sunburst as the sheet name.

g. Click **OK**.

h. Select the **Chart Title** placeholder and type Third Quarter Revenue.

i. Press **Enter** and type Cass Lake and Baudette on the second line (Figure 3-55).

j. Click the chart border to deselect the title object.

k. Click to select the title object and change its font size to **16 pt**.

l. Click the background to deselect the chart.

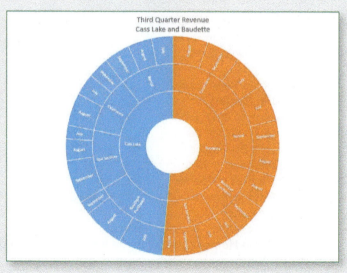

3-55 Sunburst chart with edited title

7. Insert sparklines in a worksheet.
   a. Select the **Cass Lake** tab.
   b. Right-click the column **H** heading and choose **Insert** to insert a new column.
   c. Select the cell range **B5:G8** as the data to be charted with sparklines.
   d. Click the **Column Sparkline** button [*Insert* tab, *Sparklines* group].
   e. Click the **Location Range** box, and select cells **H5:H8**.
   f. Click **OK**.

8. Format sparklines.
   a. Click the **Sparkline Color** button [*Sparkline Tools Design* tab, *Style* group] and select **Green**, **Accent 6**, **Darker 25%**.
   b. Select the sparkline group if necessary, click the **Format** button [*Home* tab, *Cells* group], and change the **Row Height** to **30 (40 pixels)**.
   c. Format column **H** to a width of **16.00 (117 pixels)**.
   d. Press **Ctrl+Home**.

9. Save and close the workbook (Figure 3-56).

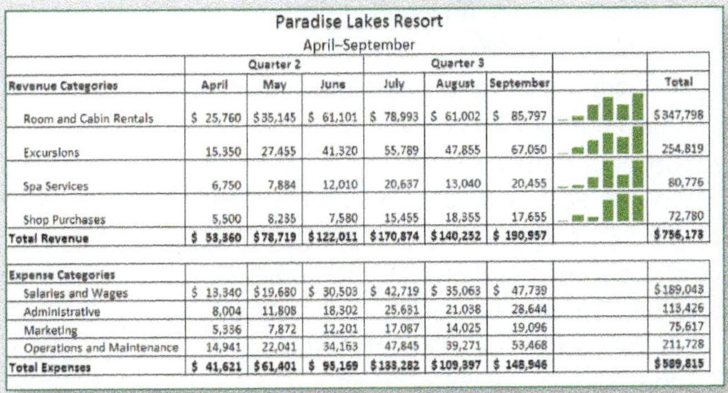

Paradise Lakes Resort									
April–September									
		Quarter 2			Quarter 3				
Revenue Categories	April	May	June	July	August	September			Total
Room and Cabin Rentals	$ 25,760	$35,145	$ 61,101	$ 78,993	$ 61,002	$ 85,797			$347,798
Excursions	15,350	27,455	41,320	55,789	47,855	67,050			254,819
Spa Services	6,750	7,884	12,010	20,637	13,040	20,455			80,776
Shop Purchases	5,500	8,235	7,580	15,455	18,355	17,655			72,780
Total Revenue	$ 53,360	$78,719	$122,011	$170,874	$140,252	$ 190,957			$756,173
Expense Categories									
Salaries and Wages	$ 13,340	$19,680	$ 30,503	$ 42,719	$ 35,063	$ 47,739			$189,043
Administrative	8,004	11,808	18,302	25,681	21,038	28,644			113,426
Marketing	5,336	7,872	12,201	17,087	14,025	19,096			75,617
Operations and Maintenance	14,941	22,041	34,163	47,845	39,271	53,468			211,728
Total Expenses	$ 41,621	$61,401	$ 95,169	$133,282	$109,397	$ 148,946			$589,815

3-56 PP E3-3 completed worksheet

Chapter Summary

3.1 Create Excel chart objects and chart sheets (p. E3-163).

- A **chart** is a visual representation of worksheet data.
- A **chart object** is a selectable item or element in a worksheet.
- A **chart sheet** is an Excel chart on its own tab in the workbook.
- The cells with values and labels used to build a chart are its **source data**.
- Chart objects and sheets are linked to their source data and contain editable chart elements such as data labels or a chart title.
- Commonly used chart types are *Column, Line, Pie,* and *Bar,* and Excel can build sophisticated statistical, financial, and scientific charts.
- You can size and position a chart object in a worksheet, or move it to its own sheet using the *Move Chart* button in the *Location* group on the *Chart Tools Design* tab.
- The *Quick Analysis* tool includes a command group for charts, and it appears when the selected source data is contiguous.

3.2 Use Quick layouts and chart styles to design a chart (p. E3-167).

- A **chart layout** is a set of elements and their locations in a chart.
- The *Quick Layout* button [*Chart Tools Design* tab, *Chart Layouts* group] includes predefined layouts for the current chart type.
- A **chart style** is a predefined combination of colors and effects for chart elements.
- Chart styles are based on the current workbook theme.
- The *Change Colors* command [*Chart Tools Design* tab, *Chart Styles* group] provides quick color palettes for customizing a chart.
- A chart object can be printed with its worksheet data or on its own sheet.
- A chart sheet prints on its own page in landscape orientation.

3.3 Edit chart elements including titles, data labels, and source data (p. E3-172).

- A **chart element** is a selectable and editable part or item in the chart.

- Chart elements include chart and axes titles, data labels, legends, gridlines, and more, depending on the type of chart.
- Excel plots data based on the number of rows and columns selected and the chart type, but you can switch the row and column data.
- You can change some chart types into another type using the *Change Chart Type* button on the *Chart Tools Design* tab.
- Chart data can be filtered to hide and display values or categories without changing the source data.
- Source data for a chart can be edited to use a different cell range or to add or remove a data series.

3.4 Format chart elements with shape styles, fill, outlines, and special effects (p. E3-179).

- A **shape style** is a predesigned set of fill colors, borders, and effects.
- **Shape fill**, **outline**, and **effects** can also be applied to a chart element from the *Chart Tools Format* tab.
- A chart element has a *Format* task pane that includes fill, outline, and effects commands as well as specific options for the element.
- Most formats can also be applied to a selected chart element from the *Home* tab.

3.5 Use pictures, shapes, and *WordArt* in a chart (p. E3-183).

- For chart shapes that have a fill color, you can use a picture as fill.
- Images used as fill can be from your own or online sources, but not all pictures work well as fill.
- Shapes are predefined outline drawings available from the *Insert Shapes* group on the *Chart Tools Format* tab or from the *Illustrations* group on the *Insert* tab.
- Shapes can be placed on a chart to highlight or draw attention to a particular element.
- **WordArt** is a text box with a preset design, often used to format a chart title.

3.6 Build pie charts and combination charts (p. E3-188).

- A pie chart has one data series and shows each data point as a slice of the pie.

- A pie chart does not have axes, but it does have options to rotate or explode slices.
- A combination chart uses at least two chart types to highlight, compare, or contrast differences in data or values.
- You can format a combination chart to show a secondary axis when values are widely different or use different scales.

3.7 Create sunburst and waterfall charts (p. E3-191).

- A *sunburst chart* has one data series that is grouped in a *hierarchy*.
- A sunburst chart illustrates the relationship among the hierarchies in a pie-like chart with concentric rings.
- A *waterfall chart* depicts a running total for positive and negative values.
- A waterfall chart is used for financial or other data that shows inflows and outlays of resources.

- A waterfall chart resembles a column chart and has category and value axes.
- You can place a sunburst chart or a waterfall chart as an object or on a separate sheet.

3.8 Insert and format sparklines in a worksheet (p. E3-194).

- A *sparkline* is a miniature chart in a cell or range of cells in the worksheet.
- Three sparkline types are available: *Line*, *Column*, and *Win/Loss*.
- When inserted in a range of cells, sparklines are grouped and can be ungrouped.
- The *Sparkline Tools Design* tab is visible when a sparkline is selected and includes formatting options such as setting the color or identifying high and low values.

Check for Understanding

The SIMbook for this text (within your SIMnet account) provides the following resources for concept review:

- Multiple choice questions
- Matching exercises
- Short answer questions

Guided Project 3-1

Life's Animal Shelter (LAS) is an animal care and adoption agency that accepts unwanted and abandoned domestic animals. For this project, you create expense charts and insert sparklines to help the agency track expenses for the first six months of the year. You also build a waterfall chart to graph cash flow for a month.
[Student Learning Outcomes 3.1, 3.2, 3.3, 3.4, 3.5, 3.6, 3.7, 3.8]

File Needed: **LAS-03.xlsx** [Student data files are available in the Library of your SIMnet account.]
Completed Project File Name: **[your initials] Excel 3-1.xlsx**

Skills Covered in This Project

- Create a chart object.
- Create a chart sheet.
- Apply *Quick Layout* and chart styles.
- Add and format chart elements.
- Change the chart type.
- Filter the data series.
- Insert a shape in a chart.
- Create and format a combination chart.
- Insert and format sparklines in a worksheet.
- Create and format a waterfall chart.

1. Open the **LAS-03** workbook from your student data files and save it as [your initials] Excel 3-1.

2. Create a pie chart object.
   a. Select the **Jan-June** sheet and select cells **A5:A10**. Press **Ctrl** and select cells **I5:I10**.
   b. Click the **Insert Pie or Doughnut Chart** button [*Insert* tab, *Charts* group].
   c. Select the **2D-Pie** chart subtype.

3. Create a chart sheet.
   a. Select the pie chart object.
   b. Click the **Move Chart** button [*Chart Tools Design* tab, *Location* group].
   c. Click the **New sheet** button.
   d. Type Pie Chart in the text box.
   e. Click **OK**.

4. Apply a chart style.
   a. Click the **More** button [*Chart Tools Design* tab, *Chart Styles* group].
   b. Select **Style 12**.

5. Edit and format chart elements.
   a. Click the chart title element.
   b. Click the *Formula* bar, type January through June Expenses, and press **Enter**.
   c. Triple-click the new label in the chart and change the font size to **28 pt**.
   d. Click the legend element to select it and to deselect the title element.
   e. Click the **Font Size** arrow [*Home* tab, *Font* group] and change the legend size to **12 pt**.
   f. Select the *Chart Area* element, the chart background.
   g. Click the **Shape Outline** button [*Chart Tools Format* tab, *Shape Styles* group].
   h. Choose **Black, Text 1** as the color.
   i. Click the **Shape Outline** button again.

j. Choose **Weight** and select **1 pt**.

k. Click outside the chart background to see the outline (Figure 3-57).

6. Create a bar chart object.

   a. Click the **Jan-June** sheet tab.

   b. Select cells **A4:G9** as source data, omitting the *Rent* expense.

   c. Click the **Quick Analysis** button and select **Charts**.

   d. Select **Clustered Bar**.

   e. Point to the chart border to display a move pointer.

   f. Drag the chart object so that its top left corner is at cell **A13**.

   g. Point to the bottom right selection handle to display a resize arrow.

   h. Drag the pointer to reach cell **I30** (Figure 3-58).

7. Change the chart type.

   a. Click the bar chart object.

   b. Click the **Change Chart Type** button [*Chart Tools Design* tab, *Type* group].

   c. Click the **Recommended Charts** tab.

   d. Choose **Clustered Column** in the left pane.

   e. Click **OK**.

8. Filter the source data.

   a. Click the column chart object.

   b. Click the **Chart Filters** button in the top right corner of the chart.

   c. Deselect the **January**, **February**, and **March** boxes.

   d. Click **Apply** in the *Chart Filters* pane (Figure 3-59).

   e. Click the **Chart Filters** button to close the pane.

9. Edit, format, and add chart elements.

   a. Click the chart title object.

   b. Click the *Formula* bar.

   c. Type Second Quarter Variable Expenses and press **Enter**.

   d. Click the **Chart Elements** arrow [*Chart Tools Format* tab, *Current Selection* group] and choose **Chart Area**.

   e. Click the **Shape Outline** button [*Chart Tools Format* tab, *Shape Styles* group].

   f. Choose **Black**, **Text 1** as the color.

   g. Click the **Shape Outline** button again and choose **Weight** and **1 pt**.

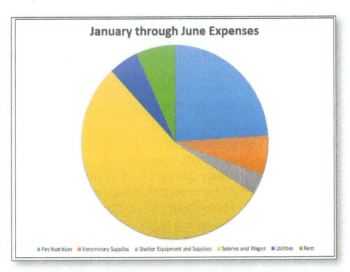

3-57 Pie Chart sheet with format changes

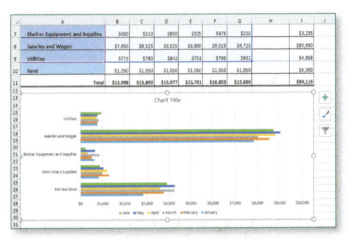

3-58 Bar chart object sized and positioned

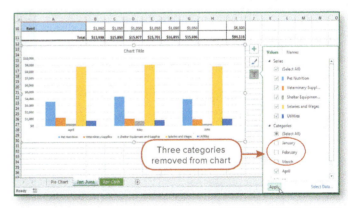

Three categories removed from chart

3-59 Chart filters applied

E3-203

h. Click the **Change Colors** button [*Chart Tools Design* tab, *Chart Styles* group].

i. Choose **Color 3** in the *Colorful* group.

j. Click the **Chart Elements** arrow [*Chart Tools Format* tab, *Current Selection* group] and choose **Plot Area**.

k. Click the **Shape Fill** button [*Chart Tools Format* tab, *Shape Styles* group].

l. Choose **Gold**, **Accent 4**, **Lighter 80%** as the color.

m. Click a worksheet cell.

10. Create a combination chart sheet.

a. Select cells **A9:G9**. Press **Ctrl** and select cells **A11:G11**.

b. Click the **Insert Combo Chart** button [*Insert* tab, *Charts* group].

c. Select the **Clustered Column-Line** chart subtype.

d. Click the **Move Chart** button [*Chart Tools Design* tab, *Location* group].

e. Click the **New sheet** button, type Combo Chart as the name, and click **OK**.

f. Double-click the line marker in the chart.

g. Click the **Series Options** button in the *Format Data Series* task pane.

h. Select the **Secondary Axis** box in the task pane (Figure 3-60).

i. Close the task pane.

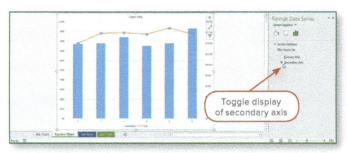

Toggle display of secondary axis

3-60 Combo chart and a secondary axis

11. Edit and format chart elements.

a. Edit the chart title placeholder to Utilities Expense and Total Expenses.

b. Select the chart area.

c. Apply a **1 pt**. **Black, Text 1** outline to the chart area.

d. Click one of the column markers to select the data series.

e. Click the **More** button [*Chart Tools Format* tab, *Shape Styles* group].

f. Select **Moderate Effect – Black**, **Dark 1** in the *Theme Styles* group.

g. Click the line marker.

h. Click the **Shape Outline** button [*Chart Tools Format* tab, *Shape Styles* group].

i. Choose **Gold, Accent 4** as the color.

j. Click the **Shape Outline** button again and choose **Weight** and **3 pt** (Figure 3-61).

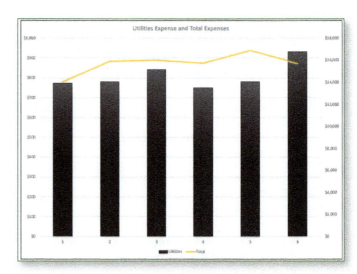

3-61 Line and column formatted in combo chart

12. Insert sparklines in the worksheet.

a. Click the **Jan-June** sheet tab.

b. Select cells **B5:G9** as the data range.

c. Click the **Column Sparkline** button [*Insert* tab, *Sparklines* group].

d. Select cells **H5:H9** for the *Location Range* and click **OK**.

e. Click the **Sparkline Color** button [*Sparkline Tools Design* tab, *Style* group].

f. Choose **White, Background 1, Darker 50%**.

13. Insert a shape in a chart.
    a. Select the column chart object.
    b. Click the **More** button [*Chart Tools Format* tab, *Insert Shapes* group].
    c. Select the **Text Box** shape [*Basic Shapes* group].
    d. Draw a text box like the one shown in Figure 3-62.
    e. Type Utilities are to be removed from an updated chart per management request.
    f. Drag a selection handle to size the text box shape if necessary.
    g. Point to a border of the *Text Box* shape to display a four-pointed arrow and position it if needed.

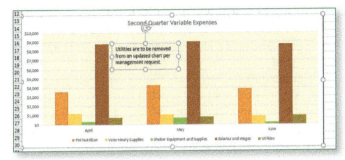

3-62 Text box shape inserted in chart

14. Click a worksheet cell and press **Ctrl+Home**.

15. Create a waterfall chart object.
    a. Select the **Apr Cash** sheet tab.
    b. Select cells **A5:B14**. This data represents cash coming in and going out for April.
    c. Click the **Insert Waterfall or Stock Chart** button [*Insert* tab, *Charts* group].
    d. Select **Waterfall**.

16. Size and position a chart object.
    a. Point to the chart border to display the move pointer.
    b. Drag the chart object so that its top left corner is at cell **C1**.
    c. Point to the bottom right selection handle to display the resize arrow.
    d. Drag the pointer to cell **L20**.

17. Format chart elements.
    a. Double-click the Net Cash column marker and then click the marker again to open the *Format Data Point* pane.
    b. Click the **Series Options** button in the task pane and expand the *Series Options* group.
    c. Select the **Set as total** box.
    d. Triple-click the chart title placeholder text and type April Cash Flow.
    e. Select the chart area and apply a **1 pt. black** outline.
    f. Click a worksheet cell and press **Ctrl+Home**.

18. Save and close the workbook (Figure 3-63).

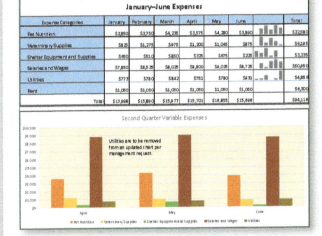

3-63 Excel 3-1 completed worksheets and charts

Guided Project 3-2

Wear-Ever Shoes is a shoe outlet with several locations. In a worksheet that tracks sales of popular items for the past six months, you create a bar chart to compare the number of pairs sold by style. You also create a combination chart to compare number of pairs sold and unit cost for each style. For another set of data, you create a sunburst chart to illustrate sales by shoe style, gender, and color.
[Student Learning Outcomes 3.1, 3.2, 3.3, 3.4, 3.5, 3.6, 3.7]

File Needed: *WearEverShoes-03.xlsx* [Student data files are available in the Library of your SIMnet account.]
Completed Project File Name: *[your initials] Excel 3-2.xlsx*

Skills Covered in This Project

- Create a chart sheet.
- Change the chart type.
- Apply a chart style.

- Add and format chart elements.
- Use a picture as fill.
- Create and format a combination chart.
- Use *WordArt* in a chart.
- Create and format a sunburst chart.

1. Open the *WearEverShoes-03* workbook from your student data files and save it as [your initials] Excel 3-2.

2. Create a column chart sheet.
   a. Select cells **A5:B16** on the **Unit Sales** sheet.
   b. Click the **Quick Analysis** button and choose **Charts**.
   c. Select **Clustered Column**.
   d. Click the **Move Chart** button [*Chart Tools Design* tab, *Location* group].
   e. Click the **New sheet** button.
   f. Type Sales Chart and click **OK**.

3. Change the chart type.
   a. Click the **Sales Chart** sheet tab if necessary.
   b. Click the **Change Chart Type** button [*Chart Tools Design* tab, *Type* group].
   c. Click the **Recommended Charts** tab.
   d. Choose **Clustered Bar** in the left pane and click **OK**.

4. Apply a chart style.
   a. Click the **Chart Styles** button in the top right corner of the chart.
   b. Select **Style 7**.
   c. Click the **Chart Styles** button to close the pane.

5. Add fill color to a data series.
   a. Double-click one of the bars to open the *Format Data Series* task pane.
   b. Click the **Fill & Line** button in the task pane.
   c. Click **Fill** to expand the command group.
   d. Select the **Vary colors by point** box.

6. Use a picture as fill for a data point.
   a. Click the "Classy Pumps" bar to display its *Format Data Point* task pane.
   b. Click the **Fill & Line** button in the task pane.
   c. Click **Fill** to expand the command group.
   d. Click the **Picture or texture fill** button.
   e. Click **Online** to open the *Insert Pictures* dialog box.
   f. Type heels in the *Bing Image Search* box and press **Enter** (Figure 3-64).

g. Select an image and click **Insert**.

h. Click the **Stack** radio button in the task pane.

i. Close the task pane and click the chart border.

3-64 Online image search for fill in a data point

7. Create a combination chart sheet.

   a. Click the **Unit Sales** sheet tab.

   b. Select cells **A5:A16**. Press **Ctrl** and select cells **E5:F16**.

   c. Click the **Insert Combo Chart** button [*Insert* tab, *Charts* group].

   d. Select the **Clustered Column-Line on Secondary Axis** chart subtype.

   e. Click the **Move Chart** button [*Chart Tools Design* tab, *Location* group].

   f. Click the **New sheet** button.

   g. Type Cost&Retail and click **OK**.

8. Edit chart elements.

   a. Click the chart title placeholder.

   b. Type Cost and Selling Price Comparison in the *Formula* bar and press **Enter**.

   c. Select the chart title box.

   d. Click the **Home** tab and change the font size to **20 pt**.

   e. Select the chart area and apply a **¾ pt. black** outline.

   f. Select one of the column shapes.

   g. Click the **More** button [*Chart Tools Format* tab, *Shapes Styles* group].

   h. Choose **Intense Effect - Blue, Accent 1** in the bottom row of the *Theme Styles* gallery.

   i. Select the line marker.

   j. Click the **Shape Outline** button [*Chart Tools Format* tab, *Shape Styles* group] and choose **Black, Text 1** as the color.

   k. Change the weight of the line to **3 pt**.

9. Use *WordArt* in a chart.

   a. Click the chart title.

   b. Click the **More** button [*Chart Tools Format* tab, *WordArt Styles* group].

   c. Choose **Fill - Black, Text 1, Shadow** in the first row of the gallery.

   d. Click the chart border to deselect the title.

10. Create a sunburst chart.

    a. Click the **Grouped Sales** sheet tab.

    b. Select cells **A5:D24**.

    c. Click the **Insert Hierarchy Chart** button [*Insert* tab, *Charts* group].

    d. Click **Sunburst** to select it.

    e. Click the **Move Chart** button [*Chart Tools Design* tab, *Location* group].

    f. Select **New sheet**, type Sunburst, and click **OK**.

11. Format a sunburst chart.

    a. Click the chart title element.

    b. Triple-click the placeholder text to select it.

    c. Type Sales by Style, Color, and Gender.

    d. Click the sunburst shape to select the circle.

e. Point to the **Comfy Walking Shoes** arc in the inner ring and click twice to select the data point. The data point is the wedge that represents two colors of the style. You can confirm your selection on the *Chart Tools Format* tab in the *Current Selection* group. It should display "Branch Comfy Walking."

f. Click the **Format Selection** button [*Chart Tools Format* tab, *Current Selection* group].

g. Click the **Fill & Line** button.

h. Click **Fill** to expand the command group.

i. Choose **Solid fill** and click the **Color** button.

j. Choose **Orange**, **Accent 6**, **Lighter 40%**.

k. Close the task pane.

l. Click outside the chart background to deselect the chart.

12. Save and close the workbook (Figure 3-65).

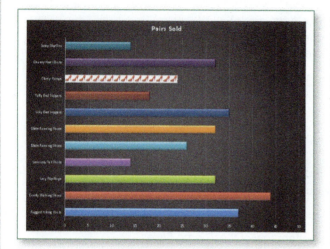

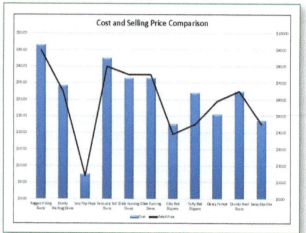

3-65 Excel 3-2 completed chart sheets

Guided Project 3-3

Blue Lake Sports has locations in several major cities and tracks sales by department in each store. For this project, you create a pie chart that shows each store's share of golf-related sales for the first quarter. You also create a line chart to illustrate week-to-week sales for specific departments in one of the stores and insert sparklines in the data.
[Student Learning Outcomes 3.1, 3.2, 3.3, 3.4, 3.6, 3.8]

File Needed: **BlueLakeSports-03.xlsx** [Student data files are available in the Library of your SIMnet account.]
Completed Project File Name: **[your initials] Excel 3-3.xlsx**

Skills Covered in This Project

- Create, size, and position a pie chart object.
- Apply a chart style.
- Change the chart type.

- Add and format chart elements.
- Create a line chart sheet.
- Apply a chart layout.
- Insert and format sparklines in a worksheet.

1. Open the **BlueLakeSports-03** workbook from your student data files and save it as [your initials] Excel 3-3.

2. Create a pie chart object.
   a. Select the **Revenue by Department** sheet, select cells **A4:F4**, press **Ctrl**, and select cells **A13:F13**.
   b. Click the **Recommended Charts** button [Insert tab, Charts group].
   c. Choose **Pie** and click **OK**.

3. Apply a chart style.
   a. Select the chart object.
   b. Click the **More** button [Chart Tools Design tab, Chart Styles group].
   c. Select **Style 12**.

4. Size and position a chart object.
   a. Point to the chart object border to display the move pointer.
   b. Drag the chart object so its top left corner is at cell **A21**.
   c. Point to the bottom right selection handle to display the resize arrow.
   d. Drag the pointer to cell **G36**.

5. Change the chart type.
   a. Select the pie chart object and click the **Change Chart Type** button [Chart Tools Design tab, Type group].
   b. Select the **All Charts** tab and choose **Pie** in the left pane.
   c. Choose **3-D Pie** and click **OK**.

6. Format pie chart elements.
   a. Double-click the pie to open its Format Data Series task pane.
   b. Click the **Atlanta** slice to update the pane to the Format Data Point task pane. (Rest the pointer on a slice to see its identifying ScreenTip.)
   c. Click the **Series Options** button in the Format Data Series task pane.
   d. Set the pie explosion percentage at **10%**.
   e. Close the task pane.
   f. Click the chart object border to deselect the **Atlanta** slice.

7. Add and format chart elements in a pie chart.
   a. Click the **Chart Elements** button in the top right corner of the chart.
   b. Select the **Data Labels** box.

   c. Click the **Data Labels** arrow to open its submenu and choose **More Options**.

   d. Click the **Label Options** button In the *Format Data Labels* pane.

   e. Click **Label Options** to expand the group.

   f. Select the **Percentage** box.

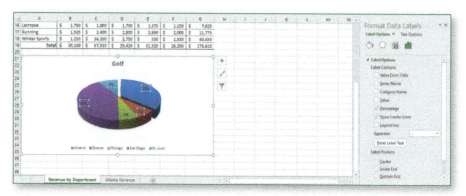

3-66 *Format Data Point* task pane for data labels

   g. Deselect the **Value** box (Figure 3-66).

   h. Press **Ctrl+B** to apply bold.

   i. Change the font size to **12 pt** [*Home* tab, *Font* group].

   j. Click the chart object border to select it.

   k. Click the **Shape Outline** button [*Chart Tools Format* tab, *Shape Styles* group] and choose **Purple, Accent 4, Darker 50%**.

   l. Click the **Shape Outline** button and choose **Weight** and **1 pt**.

   m. Click a worksheet cell.

8. Create a line chart sheet.

   a. Select the **Atlanta Revenue** sheet tab.

   b. Select cells **A4:E7**.

   c. Click the **Quick Analysis** button and choose **Charts**.

   d. Select **Line**.

   e. Click the **Move Chart** button [*Chart Tools Design* tab, *Location* group].

   f. Click the **New sheet** button.

   g. Type Promo Depts and click **OK**.

9. Apply a chart layout.

   a. Click the **Quick Layout** button [*Chart Tools Design* tab, *Chart Layouts* group].

   b. Select **Layout 5** to add a data table to the chart sheet (Figure 3-67).

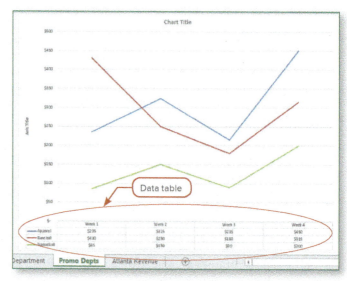

3-67 **Data table added by** *Quick Layout*

10. Change the chart type.

   a. Click the **Change Chart Type** button [*Chart Tools Design* tab, *Type* group].

   b. Select the **All Charts** tab and choose **Line with Markers** in the *Line* category.

   c. Click **OK**.

11. Edit chart elements in a line chart.
    a. Click the chart title placeholder.
    b. Type Special Promotion Departments in the formula bar and press **Enter**.
    c. Click the vertical axis title placeholder.
    d. Type Dollar Sales in the formula bar and press **Enter**.
    e. Click the **Chart Elements** drop-down arrow [*Chart Tools Format* tab, *Current Selection* group].

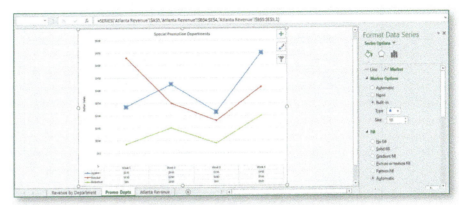

    f. Choose **Series "Apparel"** to select the line in the chart.

3-68 Marker options for the data series

    g. Click the **Format Selection** button [*Chart Tools Format* tab, *Current Selection* group].
    h. Click the **Fill & Line** button in the *Format Data Series* task pane.
    i. Click **Marker** and then click **Marker Options** to expand the group (Figure 3-68).
    j. Choose **Built-in** and select **10 pt**.
    k. Click the *Series Options* triangle at the top of the task pane and choose **Series "Baseball"** (Figure 3-69).
    l. Apply the same marker changes for the baseball series.
    m. Select the basketball series and make the same marker changes.
    n. Close the task pane and click outside the chart.

12. Insert sparklines in the worksheet.
    a. Click the **Atlanta Revenue** tab.
    b. Right-click the column **F** heading and choose **Insert**.
    c. Select cells **B5:E18** as the data range.
    d. Click the **Line Sparkline** button [*Insert* tab, *Sparklines* group].
    e. Select cells **F5:F18** in the *Location Range* box.
    f. Click **OK**.

13. Format sparklines in worksheet.
    a. Click the **Format** button [*Home* tab, *Cells* group] and change the **Row Height** to **24**.
    b. Click the **Format** button [*Home* tab, *Cells* group] and set the **Column Width** to **35**.
    c. Select the **Markers** box in the *Show* group in the *Sparkline Tools Design* tab.
    d. Click the **Sparkline Color** button [*Sparkline Tools Design* tab, *Style* group].
    e. Choose **Black**, **Text 1** for the line color.
    f. Click cell **A1**.

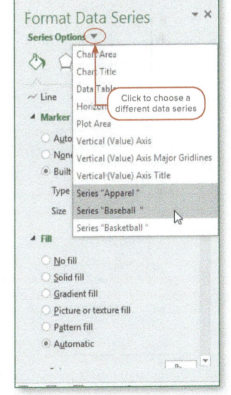

3-69 New data series selected

14. Change the page orientation to landscape.

15. Save and close the workbook (Figure 3-70).

Blue Lake Sports
First Quarter Sales by City

Department	Atlanta	Boston	Chicago	San Diego	St. Louis	Total
Apparel	$ 2,600	$ 3,200	$ 3,800	$ 3,700	$ 3,200	$ 16,500
Baseball	$ 3,500	$ 1,200	$ 1,350	$ 2,100	$ 2,475	$ 10,625
Basketball	$ 1,800	$ 1,800	$ 2,250	$ 1,400	$ 1,750	$ 9,000
Bike & Skate	$ 1,500	$ 1,325	$ 1,225	$ 2,450	$ 1,650	$ 8,150
Exercise	$ 2,650	$ 2,875	$ 3,250	$ 3,775	$ 2,950	$ 15,500
Fishing	$ 2,350	$ 1,035	$ 1,250	$ 2,750	$ 1,450	$ 8,835
Footwear	$ 1,875	$ 2,675	$ 3,575	$ 3,250	$ 2,950	$ 14,325
Game Room	$ 1,300	$ 1,500	$ 1,900	$ 1,050	$ 1,275	$ 7,025
Golf	$ 4,750	$ 875	$ 925	$ 5,400	$ 1,250	$ 13,200
Hockey	$ 850	$ 1,875	$ 1,950	$ 750	$ 1,650	$ 7,075
Hunting	$ 2,000	$ 1,000	$ 650	$ 725	$ 950	$ 5,325
Lacrosse	$ 1,750	$ 1,800	$ 1,750	$ 1,375	$ 1,150	$ 7,825
Running	$ 1,925	$ 2,400	$ 2,800	$ 2,650	$ 2,000	$ 11,775
Winter Sports	$ 1,250	$ 34,350	$ 2,750	$ 550	$ 1,550	$ 40,450
Total	$ 30,100	$ 57,910	$ 29,425	$ 31,925	$ 26,250	$ 175,610

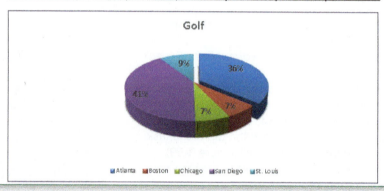

3-70 Excel 3-3 completed worksheet and charts

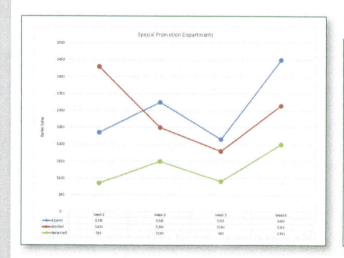

Independent Project 3-4

For this project, you create a column chart to illustrate April–September revenue for Classic Gardens and Landscapes. You also build a pie chart sheet to graph the proportion that each category contributes to total revenue.
[Student Learning Outcomes 3.1, 3.2, 3.3, 3.4, 3.5, 3.6]

File Needed: **ClassicGardens-03.xlsx** [Student data files are available in the Library of your SIMnet account.]
Completed Project File Name: **[your initials] Excel 3-4.xlsx**

Skills Covered in This Project

- Create a chart object.
- Size and position a chart object.
- Edit and format chart elements.
- Edit the source data for a chart.
- Build a pie chart sheet.
- Use texture as fill.
- Add and format data labels in a chart.

1. Open the **ClassicGardens-03** workbook from your student data files and save it as [your initials] Excel 3-4.

2. Create a **Clustered Column** chart object for cells **A4:G9**.

3. Move the chart object so that its top left corner is at cell **A12**. Size the bottom of the chart to reach cell **H30**.

4. Edit the chart title to display CGL Major Sales Revenue on one line and Second and Third Quarters on the second line.

5. Apply chart **Style 14** to the chart.

6. Format the first line of the chart title to a font size of **20 pt**. Format the second title line as **16 pt**.

7. Apply a **½ point Black**, **Text 1** outline to the chart area.

8. Verify that the chart is still selected. In the highlighted range in the worksheet, drag the resize pointer to remove the Design Consulting data series from the chart (Figure 3-71).

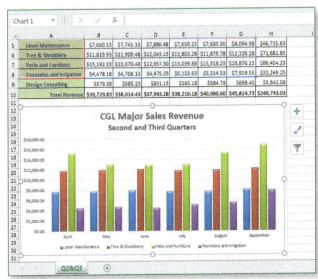

3-71 Resize the chart by dragging the resize pointer

9. Create a 3-D Pie chart for cells **A4:A9** and cells **H4:H9**. Move the chart to its own sheet named Revenue Breakdown.

10. Edit the chart title to display Revenue by Category. Change the font size to **32**.

11. Select the legend and change the font size to **12**.

12. Apply the **Woven mat** texture fill to the Patio and Furniture slice.

13. Add data labels to display in the center of each slice.
    a. Display the Format Data Labels task pane, choose the **Accounting** format, and set **0** decimal places.
    b. While the data labels are selected, change the font size to **14 pt** and apply **bold** [Home tab, Font group].

14. Deselect the chart.

15. Save and close the workbook (Figure 3-72).

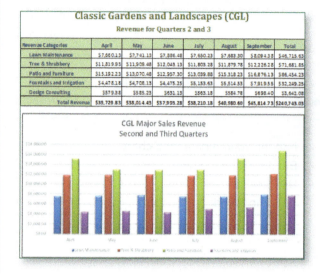

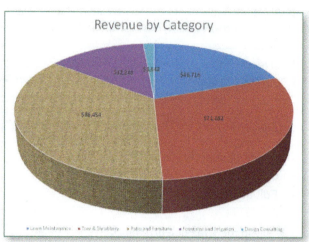

3-72 Excel 3-4 completed chart sheets

Independent Project 3-5

For this project, you create a stacked bar chart to illustrate projected tuition and fee amounts for Sierra Pacific Community College District (SPCCD). You also create a pie chart to show total projected revenue for the time period and add sparklines to the worksheet.
[Student Learning Outcomes 3.1, 3.2, 3.3, 3.4, 3.6, 3.8]

File Needed: **SierraPacific-03.xlsx** [Student data files are available in the Library of your SIMnet account.]
Completed Project File Name: **[your initials] Excel 3-5.xlsx**

Skills Covered in This Project

- Create a chart object.
- Size and position a chart object.
- Apply a chart style.
- Switch row and column data.

- Edit chart source data.
- Create a pie chart sheet.
- Edit and format chart elements.
- Insert and format sparklines in a sheet.

1. Open the **SierraPacific-03** workbook from your student data files and save it as [your initials] Excel 3-5.

2. Select cells **A3:E7** and use the *Quick Analysis* tool to create a stacked bar chart object.

3. Size and position the chart below the worksheet data in cells **A10:G28**.

4. Apply **Chart Style 6**.

5. Edit the chart title to display Tuition Revenue Projection.

6. Apply a ½ pt **Dark Blue**, **Text 2** outline to the chart object.

7. Edit the source data to remove the utilization and facilities fees from the chart.

8. Switch the row and column data for the chart so that semester names are shown on the vertical axis.

9. Create a 3-D pie chart sheet for cells **A4:A7** and cells **F4:F7**. Move the chart to a new sheet named Total Revenue.

10. Apply **Chart Style 3** and a **black ½ pt** outline.

11. Edit the chart title to Projected Revenue Sources.

12. Format the legend font size to **12 pt**.

13. Create a column sparkline with cell **G8** as the location range for cells **B8:E8**. Format cell **G8** with an **Outside Border** [*Home* tab, *Font* group].

14. Save and close the workbook (Figure 3-73).

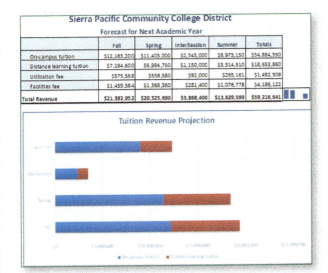
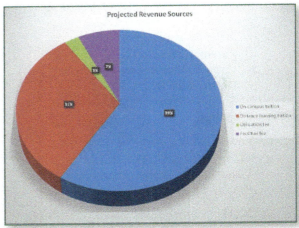

3-73 Excel 3-5 completed worksheet and chart

Independent Project 3-6

Courtyard Medical Plaza (CMP) is a full-service medical office complex providing customers with a variety of medical services in one location. For this project, you create charts to illustrate data about the number of procedures performed at CMP as well as how patients came to the facility. Your final task is to prepare a waterfall chart for the operations account.
[Student Learning Outcomes 3.1, 3.2, 3.3, 3.4, 3.5, 3.7]

File Needed: **CourtyardMedical-03.xlsx** [*Student data files are available in the Library of your SIMnet account.*]
Completed Project File Name: **[your initials] Excel 3-6.xlsx**

Skills Covered in This Project

- Create a column chart sheet.
- Add and edit chart elements.
- Add and format a trendline in a chart.
- Insert a text box shape in a chart.
- Display gridlines in a chart.
- Use gradient fill for a chart object.
- Create a waterfall chart.

1. Open the **CourtyardMedical-03** workbook from your student data files and save it as [your initials] Excel 3-6.

2. Select the **Patient Arrivals** worksheet. Create a clustered column chart sheet for cells **A5:M5** and cells **A7:M7**. Move the chart to its own sheet named Immed Care.

3. Edit the chart title to display Immediate Care Patient Count.

4. Click the **Chart Elements** button and select **Trendline**.

5. Click the options arrow next to **Trendline** and select **More Options** to open the *Format Trendline* task pane.
   a. In the *Forecast* group, set the **Forward** value to **12**.
   b. Choose **Olive Green, Accent 3, Darker 50%** for the line color.
   c. Set the **Width** of the trendline to **4 pt**.

6. Draw a *Text Box* shape between the 300 and 400 gridlines and type The number of patients who come in for Immediate Care services will continue to grow. (Figure 3-74).

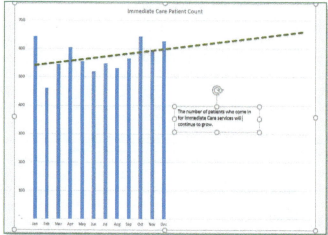

3-74 Text box shape in a chart

7. Select the **Procedures Count** worksheet and use the *Quick Analysis* tool to create a clustered column chart for cells **A5:D16** on its own sheet named Procedures Chart.

8. Edit the chart title to Number of Procedures on the first line and Three-Month Period on the second line.

9. Change the chart type to a clustered bar chart.

10. Click the **Chart Elements** button. Show **Primary Major Vertical**, **Primary Major Horizontal** and **Primary Minor Vertical** gridlines. Format each gridline element to use **Black, Text 1, Lighter 50%**.

11. Use the **Shape Fill** button to format the plot area to **Tan, Background 2**.

12. Select the **Operations** sheet tab and create a waterfall chart object for cells **A3:B9**.

13. Position the waterfall chart object so that its top left corner is at cell **A11**. Size the object to reach cell **I28**.

14. Select the ending balance marker and set it as a total.

15. Edit the chart title placeholder to CMP Operations Account.

16. Select the chart area and apply a **1 pt black** outline.

17. Click a worksheet cell and press **Ctrl+Home**.

18. Save and close the workbook (Figure 3-75).

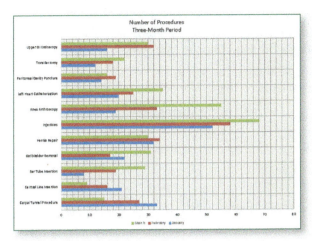

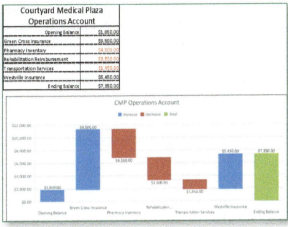

Improve It Project 3-7

Central Sierra Insurance is a multi-office insurance company that handles commercial and personal insurance products. In this project, you add missing data and verify that the charts are updated.
[Student Learning Outcomes 3.2, 3.3, 3.4]

File Needed: **CentralSierra-03.xlsx** [Student data files are available in the Library of your SIMnet account.]
Completed Project File Name: **[your initials] Excel 3-7.xlsx**

Skills Covered in This Project

- Edit source data.
- Switch row and column data.
- Change chart colors.
- Apply a chart style.
- Add and format elements in a chart.
- Change the chart type.

1. Open the **CentralSierra-03** workbook from your student data files and save it as [your initials] Excel 3-7. There are two chart objects on the worksheet.

2. Insert a new row at row 8.

3. Type Motorcycle in cell **A8**. In cells **B8:D8**, type these values: 15, 82, and 24.

4. Change the pie chart object to a **3-D Pie** and apply **Chart Style 3**. Notice that a data series for "Motorcycle" has been added.

5. Switch the row and column data for the column chart. The data series for "Motorcycle" is not included.

6. Click the **Select Data** button [Chart Tools Design tab, Data group] and reset the source data to show cells **A5:D10**.

7. Change the column chart color scheme to **Color 11** in the Monochromatic list.

8. Format chart elements.
   a. Use the **Shape Fill** button [Chart Tools Format tab, Shape Styles group] to apply **Olive Green, Accent 3** fill for the **Side Wall** of the column chart.
   b. Use the **Shape Fill** button to apply the **Linear Down** gradient in the Light Variations group to the side wall.

   c. Apply the same fill and gradient to the **Walls** element.

   d. Apply the **Olive Green**, **Accent 3**, **Lighter 60%** with no gradient to the **Floor** element.

   e. Select the horizontal gridlines and use the **Shape Outline** button to format them with **Black**, **Text 1**, **Lighter 50%**.

9. Select the pie chart object and change the colors to **Color 11** in the *Monochromatic* group.

10. Use **Olive Green**, **Accent 3** as shape fill for the pie chart area with a **Linear Down** gradient from the light variations.

11. Apply a **½ pt Olive Green**, **Accent 3**, **Darker 25%** outline to both chart objects.

12. Save and close the workbook (Figure 3-76).

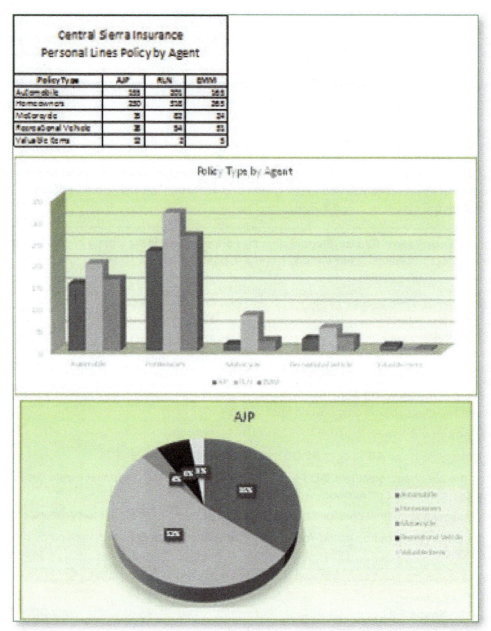

3-76 Excel 3-7 Completed worksheet with charts

Challenge Project 3-8

For this project, you build a worksheet by copying a worksheet from one of the student data files, editing data, and creating a TreeMap chart.
[Student Learning Outcomes 3.1, 3.2, 3.3, 3.7]

File Needed: **WearEverShoes-03.xlsx** [Student data files are available in the Library of your SIMnet account.]
Completed Project File Name: **[your initials] Excel 3-8.xlsx**

Create a new workbook and save it as [your initials] Excel 3-8. Modify your workbook according to the following guidelines:

- Open the **WearEverShoes-03** workbook from your student data files.
- Copy the **Grouped Sales** sheet to **[your initials] Excel 3-8**. Close **WearEverShoes-03**.
- Rename the *Grouped Sales* sheet as My Groups.
- Delete column **C** to create two levels in the hierarchy, the style name and the color. Each item has a value.
- Select a topic of interest or relevance to you that can be placed in a two-level hierarchy like the worksheet. Examples are college department and course name; company name and functional area; state and city; music type and song title. Assign different values if appropriate to your data.
- Edit the data in the worksheet to reflect your groups and subgroups. Edit the title labels also.
- Type a main and secondary title for your data. Format your worksheet.
- Select the appropriate data and create a *TreeMap* hierarchy chart on its own sheet.
- Edit the chart title and apply a chart style.
- Edit the source data to increase or decrease values and see how the *TreeMap* is adjusted.

Challenge Project 3-9

For this project, you create a worksheet and accompanying charts to track daily usage of your smartphone, tablet, or smart watch.
[Student Learning Outcomes 3.1, 3.2, 3.3, 3.4, 3.5, 3.6]

File Needed: None
Completed Project File Name: **[your initials] Excel 3-9.xlsx**

Create a new workbook and save it as [your initials] Excel 3-9. Modify your workbook according to the following guidelines:

- Enter the days of the week as column headings, starting in cell B2.
- As row headings starting in cell A3, type the names of five daily tasks or activities for your device. Examples are "Send text," "Receive phone call," "Use GPS," "View video," or similar tasks.
- Enter a value for the number of times you perform each task on each day.
- Type a main title for your data in row 1. Format your data.
- Create a column chart object that compares the number of times for each task on Monday.

- Size and position the chart object below the worksheet data.
- Change the layout or apply a chart style.
- Edit the chart title placeholder to display an appropriate title.
- Format chart elements to create an attractive, easy-to-understand chart of your data.
- For the task with the greatest Monday value, create another column chart that displays daily numbers for that one task.
- Size and position this chart object below the first chart.
- Format the second chart to complement the first chart.

Challenge Project 3-10

For this project, you create a worksheet with a column/line combo chart that compares air temperature and humidity level in your city or town for 10 days. You also insert a single sparkline in the data.
[Student Learning Outcomes 3.1, 3.2, 3.3, 3.4, 3.6, 3.8]

File Needed: None
Completed Project File Name: *[your initials] Excel 3-10.xlsx*

Create a new workbook and save it as [your initials] Excel 3-10. Modify your workbook according to the following guidelines:

- In a worksheet, enter dates in cells **A4:A13** for each of the last 10 days or each of the next 10 days.
- In column B, enter a recorded or predicted temperature in degrees for each date at 12 noon. Use an online weather reference or a weather app.
- In column C, enter corresponding humidity levels as percentages. Use the same weather reference or make an estimate.
- Type a main title for the data as well as column labels.
- Create a clustered column/line combo chart with a secondary axis for the percentages. Move the chart to its own sheet.
- Change the layout or apply a chart style.
- Edit and format the chart elements as needed.
- In the worksheet, select the range of temperature values as the data range for a line sparkline. As the location range, select cell **D14**. Format column D as **32.00 (229 pixels)** wide.
- Format the sparkline and adjust row heights to better display the data and the sparkline.

EXCEL

CHAPTER 4

Formatting, Organizing, and Getting Data

CHAPTER OVERVIEW

Excel can use data from many sources as well as provide data to other programs. When data is shared among applications, the data is usually in a list or table layout like a database. This chapter covers how to format data as an Excel table, how to sort and filter data, how to get data from other sources, and how to build a *PivotTable*.

STUDENT LEARNING OUTCOMES (SLOs)

After completing this chapter, you will be able to:

SLO 4.1   Create and format a list as an Excel table (p. E4-222).

SLO 4.2   Apply *Conditional Formatting* rules as well as *Color Scales, Icon Sets,* and *Data Bars* (p. E4-228).

SLO 4.3   Sort data by one or more columns or by attribute (p. E4-234).

SLO 4.4   Filter data by using *AutoFilters* and by creating an *Advanced Filter* (p. E4-238).

SLO 4.5   Use subtotals, groups, and outlines for tabular data in a worksheet (p. E4-242).

SLO 4.6   Import data into an Excel worksheet from a text file, a database file, and other sources (p. E4-248).

SLO 4.7   Export Excel data as a text file and into a Word document (p. E4-254).

SLO 4.8   Build and format a *PivotTable* (p. E4-258).

CASE STUDY

For the Pause & Practice projects in this chapter, you create worksheets for Paradise Lakes Resort. To complete the work, you format a list as an Excel table, sort and filter data, import and clean data, and create a *PivotTable*.

Pause & Practice 4-1: Format data as an Excel table and set conditional formatting.

Pause & Practice 4-2: Sort, filter, and subtotal data.

Pause & Practice 4-3: Import and *Flash Fill* data in a workbook.

Pause & Practice 4-4: Create and format a *PivotTable* and a *PivotChart*.

Creating and Formatting an Excel Table

An Excel *table* is a list of related pieces of information that is formatted with a title row followed by rows of data (Figure 4-1). When data is in table format, you can organize, sort, filter, and calculate data easily and quickly, much like a database.

The **header row** is the first row of a table with descriptive titles or labels. Each row of data is a **record** and each column is a **field.** The label in the header row is sometimes referred to as the **field name.** When you format Excel data as a table, follow these guidelines to optimize your tables for use of Excel commands:

4-1 Excel table

- Type descriptive labels in the first row and begin each label with a letter, not a number.
- Assign each header a unique label; do not repeat any of the descriptive labels.
- Keep the same type of data within each column (e.g., text or values).
- Do not leave blank rows within the data.
- Keep the table separate from other data on the worksheet.

Create an Excel Table

When data is arranged as a list and conforms to the guidelines just described, a simple format command creates an Excel table. Select the data and click the **Format as Table** button in the *Styles* group on the *Home* tab to open the *Table Styles* gallery. Choose a style and click **OK** in the *Format as Table* dialog box. When the data is selected, you can also click the **Table** button in the *Tables* group on the *Insert* tab to open the *Format as Table* dialog box and create the table with a default style.

After your data is formatted as a table, each label in the header row displays an **AutoFilter** arrow, and the *Table Tools Design* tab opens with command groups for modifying the table. Recall from Chapter 3 that a filter is criteria that determines which data is shown and which is hidden. From *AutoFilter* arrows, you can show records for employees in a particular location or for revenue from certain months.

> **MORE INFO**
>
> *AutoFilter* arrows replace the worksheet column headings when you scroll down in a table with many records. *AutoFilter* arrows do not print.

▶ **HOW TO:** Create an Excel Table

1. Select the cells to be formatted as a table.
   - Include the header row with column titles.
2. Click the **Format as Table** button [*Home* tab, *Styles* group] to open the table gallery.
3. Choose a table style from the *Table Styles* gallery (Figure 4-2).

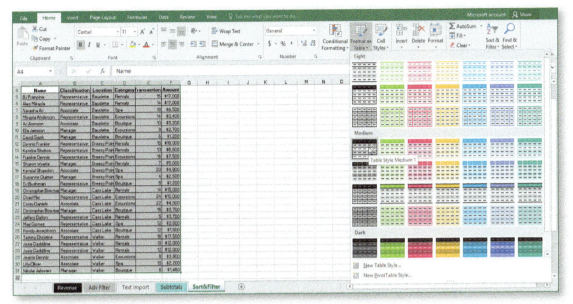

4-2 *Table Styles* gallery and selected data

- Table styles are organized in light, medium, and dark categories.

4. Confirm the cell range in the *Format As Table* dialog box.

   - You can drag to select a different range, if necessary.

5. Select the **My table has headers** box in the *Format As Table* dialog box.

   - When the selected range does not have column titles, Excel inserts a row above the data with the labels *Column1, Column2,* and so on. You can edit these names.

6. Click **OK**.

   - When the selected range includes data from an outside source, you will see a message box asking to remove the data connection. Click **Yes** to create the table (Figure 4-3).

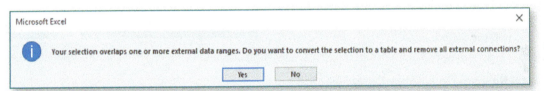

4-3 Message box for data from an outside source

▶ **ANOTHER WAY**

Select the header and data rows, click the **Quick Analysis** tool, and choose **Tables**. Then click the **Table** button to format the data in a default table style. This method is not available for data from an outside source.

Table Styles and Options

A *table style* is a predesigned set of format settings with a color scheme, alternating fill for rows and columns, vertical and horizontal borders, and more. You select a style when you create a table from the **Format as Table** button, but you can apply a different style at any time. Predefined table styles are classified as *Light, Medium,* and *Dark* and use colors based on the workbook theme. You can remove a style by selecting *None* in the *Light* group.

▶ HOW TO: Apply a Table Style

1. Click any cell within the table.
   - The *Table Tools Design* tab opens.
2. Click the **More** button [*Table Tools Design* tab, *Table Styles* group].
   - The *Table Styles* gallery opens.
   - Styles are named *Table Style Light 1, Table Style Medium 4, Table Style Dark 8,* and so on.
   - The *None* style is the first icon in the *Light* group.
3. Point to a style icon to see a *Live Preview* in the table.
4. Click to select and apply a style.

> ▶ **MORE INFO**
>
> You can create and save a custom table style by clicking the **More** button in the *Table Styles* group [*Table Tools Design* tab] and choosing **New Table Style**.

The *Table Style Options* group on the *Table Tools Design* tab includes commands for showing or hiding various parts of the table such as the header row or a total row. When you show a total row, a blank row inserts as the last row, and you can choose which calculation displays in each column. Other options are banded columns or rows, which alternate fill or borders. There is also a command to apply bold to data in the first or last column, or both. You can also hide the *AutoFilter* arrows.

▶ HOW TO: Display a Total Row in a Table

1. Click any cell within the table.
   - The *Table Tools Design* tab opens.
2. Select the **Total Row** box [*Table Tools Design* tab, *Table Style Options* group].
   - The total row displays as the last row in the table.
3. Click a cell in the total row and click its arrow to open the calculation list.
   - The default calculation is *Sum* for numeric data.
4. Choose the calculation for the column (Figure 4-4).
   - You can use *Count* for alphanumeric columns.

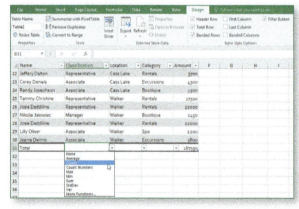

4-4 Table with total row

The Table Tools and Properties Groups

The *Tools* group on the *Table Tools Design* tab includes commands to remove duplicate records and to convert the table to a regular cell range. The *Insert Slicer* command opens a filter window for hiding or showing records in the table. The *Properties* group includes the table name and a command to resize the table.

A **duplicate row** is a record in a table that has exactly the same information in one or more columns. The *Remove Duplicates* command scans a table to locate and delete rows with repeated data in the specified columns. In the *Remove Duplicates* dialog box, you set which columns might have duplicate data. If you check all the columns, a row must have the same data in every column as another row.

▶ HOW TO: Remove Duplicates

1. Click any cell within the table.
2. Click the **Remove Duplicates** button [*Table Tools Design* tab, *Tools* group] (Figure 4-5).
3. Select the box for each column that might have duplicate data.

   - Click **Unselect All** to remove all check marks and select a single label.
   - Excel recognizes headers and does not scan them for duplicate content.

4. Click **OK**.

   - A message box indicates how many duplicate values were removed and how many unique values remain.

5. Click **OK**.

   - The rows are removed from the table.
   - The command does not preview which rows are deleted.
   - You can **Undo** this command if needed.

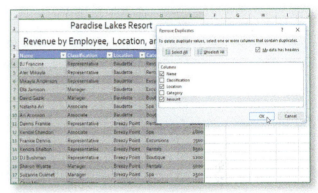

4-5 Remove Duplicates dialog box

The *Insert Slicer* command opens a floating window that is used as a visual filter, allowing you to work with smaller pieces of large datasets. If a table has 10,000 records but you are concerned with one location or category, you can insert a slicer to control which records display in the table. A *Slicer* window is an object that can be sized and positioned, and it displays selection handles like other objects. The *Slicer Tools Options* tab is available when a slicer object is active with settings to customize the floating window.

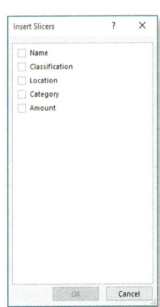

▶ HOW TO: Insert a Slicer

1. Click any cell within the table.
2. Click the **Insert Slicer** button [*Table Tools Design* tab, *Tools* group] (Figure 4-6).

   - The *Insert Slicers* dialog box lists all field names in the table.

3. Select the box for the field to be used for filtering.

   - You can select more than one field to open multiple slicers.

4. Click **OK**.

   - The *Slicer* window is a selectable object.
   - All records display in the table.

5. Click an item name to filter the data.

   - The records are filtered.
   - You can press **Ctrl** and click another item to use more than one filter.
   - You can also toggle the **Multi-Select** button in the *Slicer* title bar so that you can click or tap to select multiple items for filtering.

4-6 Insert Slicers dialog box

6. Click the **Clear Filter** button in the *Slicer* title bar.

   • All the records display.

7. Click the **More** button [*Slicer Tools Options* tab, *Slicer Styles* group].

8. Select a style for the *Slicer*.

9. Click the **Columns** spinner button [*Slicer Tools Options* tab, *Buttons* group] to set the number of columns in the *Slicer* (Figure 4-7).

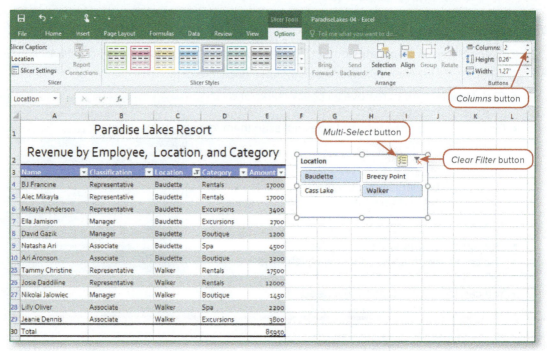

4-7 *Slicer* window for a table

10. Click and drag a corner selection handle to resize the *Slicer*.

    • You can set a specific size in the *Size* group [*Slicer Tools Options* tab].

11. Press **Delete** to remove the *Slicer* window.

    • The *Slicer* window must be selected to be deleted.

The *Convert to Range* command removes table formatting and options, but it does keep font style and fill colors. You may need to convert a table to a range when combining data from different sources or when sharing data with applications that require unformatted data.

▶ **HOW TO:** Convert a Table to a Range

1. Click any cell within the table.

2. Click the **Convert to Range** button [*Table Tools Design* tab, *Tools* group] (Figure 4-8).

3. Click **Yes** in the message box.

   • The data is shown as a regular range of cells.
   • Font size, font style, and colors remain.
   • You can format the data as needed.

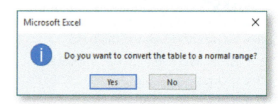

4-8 *Convert to Normal Range* message box

Tables are named automatically as *TableN* where *N* is a number. To change the name to a more descriptive label, click the **Table Name** box in the *Properties* group on the *Table Tools Design* tab and type the name. You cannot use spaces in a table name, and table names in a workbook must be unique. From the *Properties* group, you can also open the *Resize Table* dialog box to select an expanded or reduced cell range for the table. A table also has a resize arrow in its bottom right cell that you can drag to grow or shrink the table. Tables grow automatically when you press **Tab** after the last item in the last row to start a new record.

Structured References and Table Formulas

In addition to the table name, each column is assigned a name using the label in its header row. The column name with its table name is known as a ***structured reference.*** An example is *Table1[Category]* as the reference for the category column in *Table1*. Column names are enclosed in square brackets. In addition to column names, there are specific item names. They are *#All, #Data, #Headers, #This Row,* and *#Totals,* each preceded by the # symbol as an identifier.

Structured references are supplied automatically in formulas making it easy to identify what is being calculated. When you point to build a formula, you will see [@*ColumnName*] as the reference with @ inserted as an identifier (Figure 4-9). The table name and structured reference names appear in *Formula AutoComplete* lists, and you can refer to those ranges in formulas outside the table. As you work with structured references, you can expand the *Formula* bar to better see a lengthy formula. The **Expand/Collapse Formula Bar** button is on the right edge of the *Formula* bar.

Tables are automatically expanded to include a new column when you type a label adjacent to the last row heading. As part of its *Table AutoExpansion* feature, Excel copies a formula to complete a column with a calculation.

▶ **HOW TO: Add a Calculation Column in a Table**

1. Select the cell to the right of the last column heading in the table.
2. Type the new column label and press **Enter**.
   - A column is added to the table.
3. Select the cell below the new label.
4. Type = to start a formula.
5. Click the table cell with the value to be used in the formula.
   - The column name in square brackets preceded an @ symbol is inserted.
6. Complete the formula (Figure 4-9).

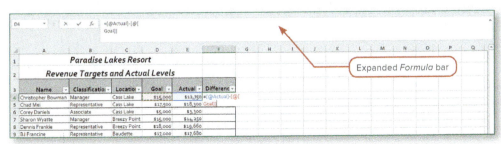

4-9 **Structured references in a table**

- You can refer to other cells in the table or the worksheet or type a constant.

7. Press **Enter**.

- The formula is copied down the entire column.
- You can enter the formula in any row in the column for it to be copied.

SLO 4.2 Applying Conditional Formatting

Conditional formatting commands apply formats to cells only when the cells meet the criteria. For example, you can use conditional formatting to display revenue amounts below a certain level in a bold red font. Conditional formatting is dynamic; the formatting adapts if the data changes.

Basic conditional formatting commands are *Highlight Cells Rules* and *Top/Bottom Rules*. For these commands, you set the rule or criteria in a dialog box and choose the format. Another type of conditional formatting is *data visualization*, in which the cell displays a fill color, a horizontal bar, or an icon.

Highlight Cells Rules

Highlight Cells Rules use relational or comparison operators to determine if the value or label should be formatted. *Highlight Cells Rules* include common operators such as *Equal To* and *Greater Than*. You can also create your own rule using other operators or a formula.

You can access all of the conditional formatting options from the *Conditional Formatting* button in the *Styles* group on the *Home* tab (Figure 4-10). You can also choose a default conditional formatting rule from the *Quick Analysis* tool options.

4-10 *Highlight Cells Rules* menu

▶ **HOW TO:** Create a "Less Than" Highlight Cells Rule

1. Select the cell range.
2. Click the **Conditional Formatting** button [*Home* tab, *Styles* group].
3. Select **Highlight Cells Rules** and select **Less Than**.
   - The *Less Than* dialog box opens.
4. Type a value in the *Format cells that are LESS THAN* box.
   - *Live Preview* applies the default format to cells that meet the criteria.

5. Click the arrow for the *with* box.

   - A list of preset formats is available.

6. Choose a format (Figure 4-11).

   - You can choose *Custom Format* to open the *Format Cells* dialog box and build a format.

7. Click **OK**.

   - Formatting is applied to cells that meet the criteria.
   - Click a cell away from the range to better see the formatting.

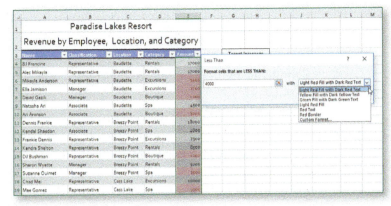

4-11 *Less Than* dialog box

Top/Bottom Rules

Top/Bottom Rules use ranking to format the highest (top) or lowest (bottom) items, either by number or percentage. You set the number or percentage in the dialog box as well as the format. You can also set a rule to format values that are above or below average (Figure 4-12).

For a selected range, the *Formatting* group in the *Quick Analysis* tool provides the most likely conditional formatting choices.

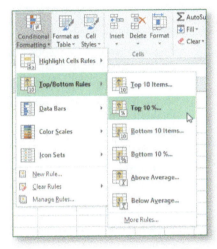

4-12 *Top/Bottom Rules*

▶ **HOW TO:** Create a Top 10% Rule

1. Select the cell range.

   - The *Quick Analysis* button appears in the bottom right cell of the range.

2. Click the **Quick Analysis** button.

3. Choose **Formatting**.

   - Commonly used conditional format choices are listed.

4. Choose **Top 10%** (Figure 4-13).

   - The number of cells equal to the *Top 10%* of the number of cells in the column are formatted with a default format.
   - You can edit the format to use different attributes.

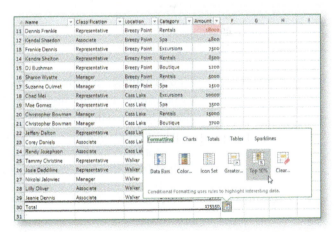

4-13 *Quick Analysis* options for conditional formatting

Use a Formula for a Rule

In addition to the *Highlight Cells* or *Top/Bottom* rules, you can create a conditional formatting formula using operators, criteria, and settings in the *New Formatting Rule* dialog box. You can, for example, build a rule to format cells in the amount column if the location is Baudette. A formula must result in either TRUE or FALSE (a Yes or No question) to be used as criteria.

▶ HOW TO: Use a Formula in a Conditional Formatting Rule

1. Select the cell range.
2. Click the **Conditional Formatting** button [*Home* tab, *Styles* group].
3. Select **New Rule**.
   - The *New Formatting Rule* dialog box opens.
   - The choices in the dialog box update based on the rule type.
4. Choose **Use a formula to determine which cells to format** in the *Select a Rule Type* list.
5. In the *Edit the Rule Description* area, type = in the *Format values where this formula is true* box.
   - You must start the formula with an equals sign (=).
   - The formula must be built so that the result is either TRUE or FALSE.
6. Type the formula.
   - Use relative cell references to the first row of data (Figure 4-14).
   - When you click to enter the cell reference, it is absolute; press **F4 (FN+F4)** to make it relative.
   - Text in the formula must be enclosed in quotation marks.
7. Click **Format** to open the *Format Cells* dialog box.
8. Build the format and click **OK**.
9. Click **OK** to close the *New Formatting Rule* dialog box.
   - Cells that meet the formula condition are formatted.

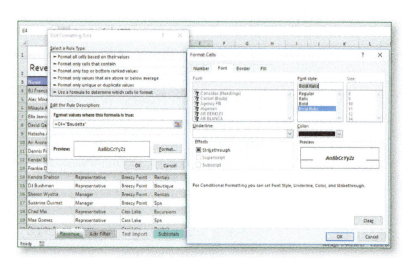

4-14 *New Formatting Rule* and *Format Cells* dialog boxes

Data Bars, Color Scales, and Icon Sets

Data visualization formats cells with icons, fill color, or shaded bars to distinguish values. Visualization formats highlight low, middle, or top values or compare the values to each other. Data visualization commands are *Data Bars, Color Scales,* and *Icon Sets.*

These three commands are part of the conditional formatting group, because they apply a rule for determining what is shown in the cell. You can choose which colors or icons are applied from the *Conditional Formatting* button [*Home* tab, *Styles* group]. When you select an option from the *Quick Analysis* button, however, a default choice is applied.

▶ HOW TO: Format Data with Data Bars

1. Select the cell range.
2. Click the **Quick Analysis** button.
3. Choose **Formatting**.
   - *Data Bars* compare the value in each cell to the other values in the range by the length of the bar.
   - *Color Scales* use a variation of two or three colors to indicate low, middle, and high values.

- *Icon Sets* inserts icons that represent the upper, middle, or lower values of the cell range.

4. Choose **Data Bars** (Figure 4-15).
   - A default data bar style and color is applied.

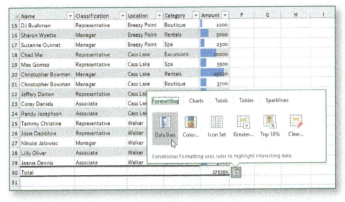

4-15 Setting *Data Bars* from the *Quick Analysis* button

Manage Conditional Formatting Rules

You can edit any conditional formatting rule, including data visualization commands, from the *Conditional Formatting Rules Manager* dialog box. From this dialog box, you can reset the range to be formatted, change the actual format, change the rule, or delete the rule.

If you select the formatted range before you start the *Manage Rules* command, the rule for that selection is shown in the *Conditional Formatting Rules Manager* dialog box. You can also show all the rules in the current or another sheet (Figure 4-16).

When you click **Edit Rule**, the *Edit Formatting Rule* dialog box opens. This dialog box is similar to the *New Formatting Rule* dialog box, and you set options the same way.

4-16 *Conditional Formatting Rules Manager* dialog box

▶**HOW TO:** Manage Conditional Formatting Rules

1. Select the formatted cell range.
2. Click the **Conditional Formatting** button [*Home* tab, *Styles* group].
3. Choose **Manage Rules**.
   - *Current Selection* is listed in the *Show formatting rules for* box.
   - Choose **This Worksheet** to list all rules in the worksheet.
4. Select the rule name to be modified.
5. Select **Edit Rule**.
   - The *Edit Formatting Rule* dialog box opens.
   - The current *Rule Description* displays.
   - You can select another rule type in the top half of the dialog box.
6. Make choices to change the rule in the *Edit the Rule Description* area.
   - The options depend on the rule type (Figure 4-17).
   - Click **Format** when available to open the *Format Cells* dialog box.

4-17 *Edit Formatting Rule* dialog box for data bars

7. Click **OK** to close the *Edit Formatting Rule* dialog box.

8. Click **OK** to close the *Conditional Formatting Rules Manger* dialog box.

You can clear conditional formatting from a selected range or from the entire sheet. For a selected range, click the **Quick Analysis** button and choose **Clear...** You can also choose **Clear Rules** from the *Conditional Formatting* button menu.

PAUSE & PRACTICE: EXCEL 4-1

For this project, you format data as a table, add a total row, and remove duplicate records. As you complete formulas on the sheet, you see structured references. You also set conditional formatting with data bars.

File Needed: *ParadiseLakes-04.xlsx* *[Student data files are available in the* Library *of your SIMnet account.]*
Completed Project File Name: *[your initials] PP E4-1.xlsx*

1. Open the ***ParadiseLakes-04*** workbook from your student data files and save it as [your initials] PP E4-1.

2. Click the **Revenue** sheet tab.

3. Format data as an Excel table.
   a. Select cells **A3:E30**.
   b. Click the **Format as Table** button [*Home* tab, *Styles* group].
   c. Select **Table Style Medium 20** from the gallery.
   d. Verify that the **My table has headers** box is selected in the *Format As Table* dialog box.
   e. Click **OK**.

4. Add a total row to a table.
   a. Click a cell within the table.
   b. Select the **Total Row** box [*Table Tools Design* tab, *Table Style Options* group].
   c. Click cell **D31** and choose **Count** from the drop-down list.
   d. Select cells **E4:E31** and format them as **Currency**. Decrease the decimal two times to show zero decimal places (Figure 4-18).

5. Remove duplicate rows in a table.
   a. Click a cell within table.
   b. Click the **Remove Duplicates** button [*Table Tools Design* tab, *Tools* group].
   c. Click **Unselect All** to deselect all the boxes.
   d. Select the **Name** box and the **Amount** box. When you can look for duplicate data in specific columns, you can speed up search activities.
   e. Click **OK** in the *Remove Duplicates* dialog box. There is one record that will be removed, the one for Josie Daddiline. The records for Christopher Bowman are not duplicated in the selected columns.
   f. Click **OK** in the message box.

Paradise Lakes Resort				
Revenue by Employee, Location, and Category				
Name	Classification	Location	Category	Amount
BJ Francine	Representative	Baudette	Rentals	$17,000
Alec Mikayla	Representative	Baudette	Rentals	$17,000
Mikayla Anderson	Representative	Baudette	Excursions	$3,400
Ella Jamison	Manager	Baudette	Excursions	$2,700
David Gazik	Manager	Baudette	Boutique	$1,200
Natasha Ari	Associate	Baudette	Spa	$4,500
Ari Aronson	Associate	Baudette	Boutique	$3,200
Dennis Frankie	Representative	Breezy Point	Rentals	$18,000
Kendal Shaedon	Associate	Breezy Point	Spa	$4,800
Frankie Dennis	Representative	Breezy Point	Excursions	$7,500
Kendra Shelton	Representative	Breezy Point	Rentals	$8,500
DJ Bushman	Representative	Breezy Point	Boutique	$1,200
Sharon Wyatte	Manager	Breezy Point	Rentals	$5,000
Suzanne Ouimet	Manager	Breezy Point	Spa	$2,500
Chad Mei	Representative	Cass Lake	Excursions	$10,000
Mae Gomez	Representative	Cass Lake	Spa	$3,500
Christopher Bowman	Manager	Cass Lake	Rentals	$15,000
Christopher Bowman	Manager	Cass Lake	Boutique	$3,700
Jeffery Dalton	Representative	Cass Lake	Rentals	$3,700
Corey Daniels	Associate	Cass Lake	Excursions	$4,500
Randy Josephson	Associate	Cass Lake	Boutique	$1,500
Tammy Christine	Representative	Walker	Rentals	$17,500
Josie Daddiline	Representative	Walker	Rentals	$12,000
Nikolai Jalowiec	Manager	Walker	Boutique	$2,450
Josie Daddiline	Representative	Walker	Rentals	$12,000
Lilly Oliver	Associate	Walker	Spa	$2,200
Jeanie Dennis	Associate	Walker	Excursions	$3,800
Total			27	$187,350

4-18 Data formatted as a table

6. Apply conditional formatting using data bars.
   a. Select cells **E4:E29**.
   b. Click the **Conditional Formatting** button [*Home* tab, *Styles* group].
   c. Point to **Data Bars** to see its menu.
   d. Select **Blue Data Bar** in the *Gradient Fill* group (Figure 4-19).

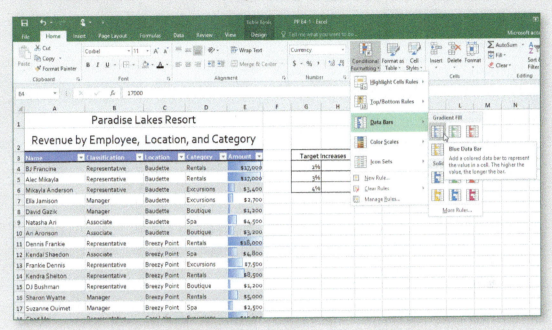

4-19 Choose a gradient fill for data bars

7. Manage conditional formatting rules.
   a. Select cells **E3:E29**.
   b. Click the **Conditional Formatting** button [*Home* tab, *Styles* group].
   c. Choose **Manage Rules**.
   d. Click **Edit Rule**.
   e. Click the **Color** arrow for **Fill** in the *Bar Appearance* area.
   f. Choose **Gold, Accent 3**.
   g. Click the arrow for **Border** in the *Bar Appearance* area.
   h. Choose **No Border** (Figure 4-20).
   i. Click **OK** to close the *Edit Formatting Rule* dialog box.
   j. Click **OK** to close the *Conditional Formatting Rules Manager* dialog box.

8. Refer to a structured reference in a formula.
   a. Select cell **H4** and type = to start a formula.
   b. Click cell **E30** to insert a structured reference to the total in the Amount column.
   c. Type * (1+, click cell **G4**, and type) to calculate a new total that reflects a 2% increase (Figure 4-21).

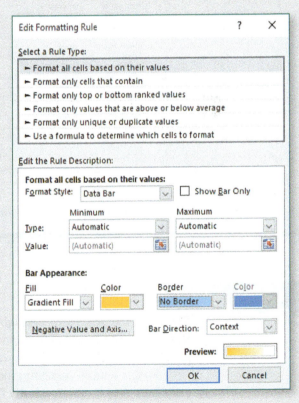

4-20 Edit the rule for data bars

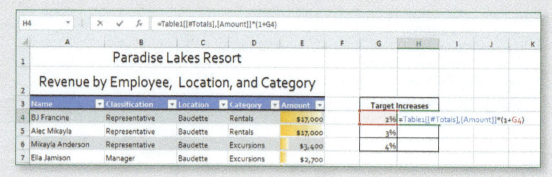

Cell reference bar: H4 | =Table1[[#Totals],[Amount]]*(1+G4)

4-21 Structured reference in a formula

d. Press **Enter**. The target total is $178,857.
e. Copy the formula to cells **H5:H6**.

9. Save and close the workbook (Figure 4-22).

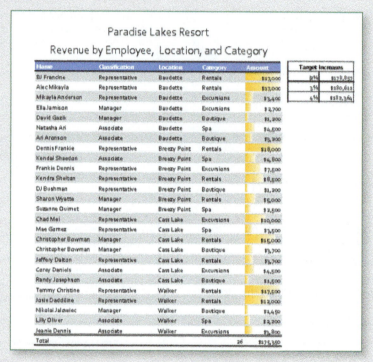

4-22 Completed PP E 4-1

SLO 4.3

Sorting Data

Sorting is the process of arranging rows of data in an identified order. For Paradise Lakes Resort, you can arrange the revenue table by employee classification to compare results for a particular job title. Or you may want to order the rows from highest amount to lowest.

You sort data in ascending or descending order. *Ascending* order sorts data alphabetically from A to Z or numerically from smallest to largest value. In a *descending* sort, data are arranged alphabetically Z to A or numerically from largest to smallest value.

Sort Options

To be sorted, data must be organized in rows and columns like an Excel table, but it need not be formatted as a table. In addition to text or number sorting, you can sort data by fill color, font color, or cell icon from *Conditional Formatting*.

The *Sort & Filter* button on the *Home* tab in the *Editing* group lists *A to Z* sort, *Z to A* sort, and *Custom Sort* (multiple columns) commands. The same commands are available in the *Sort & Filter* group on the *Data* tab as separate buttons.

Sort Data by One Column

When data has a header row followed by rows of data with at least one empty row above and below the data, you can click any cell in the column you want to sort and choose a sort command. Excel recognizes and sorts the entire dataset.

Data to be sorted can be text, numbers, or dates. Dates are treated as values. An ascending sort (smallest to largest) arranges dates so that the earliest date is first. A descending date sort organizes the data so that the most current date is first.

You can undo a sort task by clicking the **Undo** button [*Quick Access* toolbar]. You can also sort data many times to arrange it in your preferred order.

▶ **HOW TO:** Sort Data by a Single Column

1. Select a cell in the column to be used for sorting.
   - Click a cell with data, not the column header.
2. Click the **Sort A to Z** button [*Data* tab, *Sort & Filter* group] (Figure 4-23).
   - The records are arranged in alphabetical or smallest-to-largest order based on the first character in each cell in the column.
   - If the first character in an alphanumeric column is a value or special character, that record is sorted at the top.
3. Click the **Sort Z to A** button [*Data* tab, *Sort & Filter* group].
   - The records are arranged in reverse alphabetical or largest-to-smallest order based on the first character.
   - If the first character in an alphanumeric column is a value or special character, that record is sorted at the bottom.

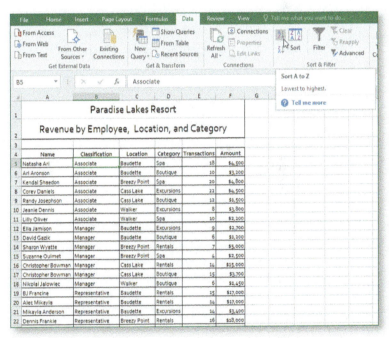

4-23 "Classification" column sorted A to Z

▶ **ANOTHER WAY**

To sort by a single column, right-click a cell in the column, choose **Sort**, and then choose the type of sort.

Sort Data by Multiple Columns

You can sort data by more than one column. An example of data that is often sorted by two columns is a list with cities in one column and states or provinces in another. Such data is sorted by state so that Alabama is before Arizona, and within a particular state, the cities are also sorted alphabetically. When you use the *Sort & Filter* button [*Home* tab, *Editing* group] or a sort button on the *Data* tab, you sort first by the least important field. You can also use the *Sort* dialog box which opens when you click the **Sort** button [*Data* tab, *Sort & Filter* group] or when you choose **Custom Sort** from the *Sort & Filter* button options.

The data in Figure 4-24 are sorted by two columns, classification and amount. When you use the *Sort* dialog box, you set the *Classification* field first and then the *Amount*. When you use the *Sort & Filter* button, you sort first by the *Amount* and then by the *Classification*.

	A	B	C	D	E	F
2	Revenue by Employee, Location, and Category					
4	Name	Classification	Location	Category	Transactions	Amount
5	Randy Josephson	Associate	Cass Lake	Boutique	12	$1,500
6	Lilly Oliver	Associate	Walker	Spa	10	$2,200
7	Ari Aronson	Associate	Baudette	Boutique	10	$3,200
8	Jeanie Dennis	Associate	Walker	Excursions	8	$3,800
9	Natasha Ari	Associate	Baudette	Spa	18	$4,500
10	Corey Daniels	Associate	Cass Lake	Excursions	22	$4,500
11	Kendal Shaedon	Associate	Breezy Point	Spa	20	$4,800
12	David Gazik	Manager	Baudette	Boutique	6	$1,200
13	Nikolai Jalowiec	Manager	Walker	Boutique	6	$1,450
14	Suzanne Ouimet	Manager	Breezy Point	Spa	4	$2,500
15	Ella Jamison	Manager	Baudette	Excursions	9	$2,700
16	Christopher Bowman	Manager	Cass Lake	Boutique	15	$3,700
17	Sharon Wyatte	Manager	Breezy Point	Rentals	7	$5,000
18	Christopher Bowman	Manager	Cass Lake	Rentals	14	$15,000
19	DJ Bushman	Representative	Breezy Point	Boutique	5	$1,200
20	Mikayla Anderson	Representative	Baudette	Excursions	14	$3,400
21	Mae Gomez	Representative	Cass Lake	Spa	12	$3,500
22	Jeffery Dalton	Representative	Cass Lake	Rentals	5	$3,700
23	Frankie Dennis	Representative	Breezy Point	Excursions	16	$7,500
24	Kendra Shelton	Representative	Breezy Point	Rentals	10	$8,500

4-24 Data sorted by "Classification" and "Amount"

▶HOW TO: Sort Data by Multiple Columns

1. Select a cell in the range to be sorted.
   - Click a cell with data, not the column header.
2. Click the **Sort** button [*Data* tab, *Sort & Filter* group].
   - The *Sort* dialog box opens.
   - The range is highlighted in the worksheet.
   - You can click the **Sort & Filter** button [*Home* tab, *Editing* group] and select **Custom Sort**.
3. Select the **My data has headers** box if your data has a header row.
4. Click the **Sort by** arrow and select the column heading for the first sort level.
5. Click the **Sort On** arrow.
   - Use *Values* for text or numbers.
   - If the data has a cell attribute such as a font color, select the name of the attribute.
6. Click the **Order** arrow and choose a sort option.
   - For columns with numbers or dates, the options are *Smallest to Largest* and *Largest to Smallest*.
   - The *Custom List* option provides special sorting orders for days of the week and months of the year so that data is sorted chronologically.
7. Click **Add Level** to add a second sort column.
8. Click the **Then by** arrow and select the second column heading.
9. Click the **Sort On** arrow and choose **Values** or an attribute.
10. Click the **Order** arrow and choose a sort order (Figure 4-25).
    - Click the **Options** button in the *Sort* dialog box to specify case-sensitive sorting or to change the orientation of ascending and descending sorts.
11. Click **OK**.

4-25 Sort dialog box

Sort Data by Cell Attribute

An *attribute* is a setting or property. Cell attributes that can be used for sorting are font color, fill color, and cell icon. These choices are options for the *Sort On* choice in the *Sort* dialog box, and they are listed when you choose **Sort** from a cell's context menu.

When you sort by font or cell color, the *Order* choices are the colors used in the column. You choose a color and set its position in the sorted column.

A cell icon is the symbol placed in a cell by conditional formatting. Column E in Figure 4-26 has an icon set sorted with hollow icons on the top.

	A	B	C	D	E
2	Revenue by Employee, Location, and Category				
3					
4	Name	Classification	Location	Category	Amount
5	Mikayla Anderson	Representative	Baudette	Excursions	☆ $3,400
6	Ella Jamison	Manager	Baudette	Excursions	☆ $2,700
7	Nikolai Jalowiec	Manager	Walker	Boutique	☆ $1,450
8	Lilly Oliver	Associate	Walker	Spa	☆ $2,200
9	Jeanie Dennis	Associate	Walker	Excursions	☆ $3,800
10	Natasha Ari	Associate	Baudette	Spa	☆ $4,500
11	Kendal Shaedon	Associate	Breezy Point	Spa	☆ $4,800
12	Frankie Dennis	Representative	Breezy Point	Excursions	☆ $7,500
13	Sharon Wyatte	Manager	Breezy Point	Rentals	☆ $5,000
14	Corey Daniels	Associate	Cass Lake	Excursions	☆ $4,500
15	BJ Francine	Representative	Baudette	Rentals	★ $17,000
16	Alec Mikayla	Representative	Baudette	Rentals	★ $17,000
17	Dennis Frankie	Representative	Breezy Point	Rentals	★ $18,000
18	Kendra Shelton	Representative	Breezy Point	Rentals	★ $8,500
19	Chad Mei	Representative	Cass Lake	Excursions	★ $10,000
20	Christopher Bowman	Manager	Cass Lake	Rentals	★ $15,000
21	Tammy Christine	Representative	Walker	Rentals	★ $17,500

4-26 Data sorted by the cell icon in "Amount" column

▶ HOW TO: Sort Data by Cell Attribute

1. Select a cell in the column to sort.
2. Click the **Sort** button [*Data* tab, *Sort & Filter* group].
   - The *Sort* dialog box opens.
   - You can also click the **Sort & Filter** button [*Home* tab, *Editing* group] and select **Custom Sort**.
3. Select the for **My data has headers** box if the data has a header row.
4. Click the **Sort by** arrow and select the column heading.
5. Click the **Sort On** arrow and choose the attribute.
   - The column must have data with different font colors, cells with different fill colors, or cell icons.
6. Click the leftmost **Order** arrow and choose a color or icon.
7. Click the rightmost **Order** arrow and choose **On Top** or **On Bottom**.
8. Click **Add Level**.
9. Click the **Then by** arrow and select the same column heading.
10. Click the **Sort On** arrow and choose the attribute.
11. Click the leftmost **Order** arrow and choose a color or icon.
12. Click the rightmost **Order** arrow and choose **On Top** or **On Bottom** (Figure 4-27).
    - Add and define as many sort levels as there are colors or icons to be sorted.
13. Click **OK**.

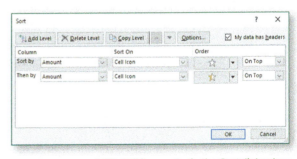

4-27 Cell icon order in the *Sort* dialog box

Sort Data in an Excel Table

When data is formatted as a table, you can sort from the *AutoFilter* arrows with each label in the header row. Sort choices are listed at the top of the pane that opens when you click an *AutoFilter* arrow.

▶ **HOW TO:** Sort Data in an Excel Table

1. Click the **AutoFilter** arrow for the column heading that represents the lowest sort level.
   - The *AutoFilter* pane lists sort choices at the top.
2. Choose **Sort A to Z** or **Sort Smallest to Largest** (Figure 4-28).
   - *Sort Smallest to Largest* appears for numeric data.
   - The table is sorted by the column.
3. Click the **AutoFilter** arrow for the column heading that represents the top sort level.
4. Choose **Sort A to Z** or **Sort Smallest to Largest**.
   - The table maintains the sort order from the first selected column within the sorted data for the top-level column.

4-28 *AutoFilter* arrow sort choices

Filtering Data

You can usually work more efficiently when you filter large amounts of data to show rows of importance to your task. You can, for example, filter data to show records for the year, the month, the individual, the product, or similar grouping. When you filter data, information that does not meet the requirements is temporarily hidden. A filter specifies which data are shown and which are hidden.

AutoFilters

In list-type data or an Excel table, the *Filter* button [*Data* tab, *Sort & Filter* group] displays or hides the *AutoFilter* arrow for each label in the header row. When you click an *AutoFilter* arrow, a pane displays sort options, filter types based on the data type, and check boxes for every piece of data. You can select boxes to mark which records display, or you can build a filter.

▶ **HOW TO:** Display and Use AutoFilters

1. Select a cell in the list.
2. Click the **Filter** button [*Data* tab, *Sort & Filter* group].
   - *AutoFilter* arrows appear in the header row with each label.
   - *AutoFilter* arrows display by default in an Excel table.
3. Click the **AutoFilter** arrow for the column used for filtering.
   - All items are selected and displayed in the data.
   - Filter options depend on the type of data in the column.
4. Click the **(Select All)** box to remove all check marks.
5. Select the box for each item to be shown (Figure 4-29).
6. Click **OK**.
   - Records that meet the criteria display with row headings in blue.
   - Records that do not meet the criteria and their row numbers are hidden.
   - A filter symbol appears with the column *AutoFilter* arrow.

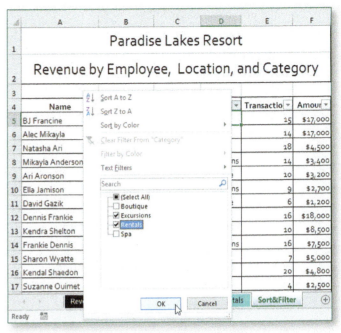

4-29 *AutoFilter* for "Category" column

To remove a filter and display the complete list, click the **AutoFilter** arrow for the column and choose **Clear Filter From (ColumnName)**. You can also click the **Clear** button in the *Sort & Filter* group on the *Data* tab.

Custom AutoFilter

A ***custom AutoFilter*** is criteria that you build in a dialog box. A custom *AutoFilter* gives you more options for how rows display, because you can use multiple criteria with *AND* and *OR*. For a column with alphanumeric data, *Text Filters* are available, and there are *Number Filters* and *Date Filters* for columns with those types of data. Operators use common words such as *Equals, Begins With,* or *Contains* (Figure 4-30).

▶ **ANOTHER WAY**

An *AutoFilter* arrow and a *Slicer* window display the same results.

4-30 Text filters for a custom *AutoFilter*

1. Select a cell in the data to filter.
2. Click the **Filter** button [*Data* tab, *Sort & Filter* group] to display *AutoFilter* arrows for the header row.
3. Click the **AutoFilter** arrow for the column used for filtering.
4. Select **Text Filters** and choose an operator.
   - The *Custom AutoFilter* dialog box opens.
5. Type criteria for the first operator in the box on the right.
   - You can also select a value from the drop-down list.
   - You can use wildcard characters.
6. Click the **And** or **Or** radio button.
   - *Or* conditions include rows that match either criteria.
   - *And* conditions are more restrictive and require that both criteria be met.
7. Click the arrow to choose a second operator.
   - A second operator is optional.
8. Type or select criteria for the second operator (Figure 4-31).
9. Click **OK**.
   - Rows in the data are filtered.

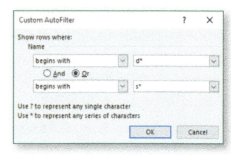

4-31 *Custom AutoFilter* dialog box

Advanced Filter

For an *Advanced Filter,* you build a criteria range separate from the data and type the conditions within that range. You can show the results in the data range, or you can display filtered data in another location on the sheet. Using another location for results allows you to create separate reports with filtered rows while the main list displays all data. An *Advanced Filter* requires more set-up work but allows you to apply more complex filters. You can even use a formula in the criteria.

A *criteria range* is at least two rows in which the first row must use the same column names as the data; the second row is where criteria is entered. You need not use all column names, and you can use more than one row for criteria. You can create a criteria range in empty rows anywhere on the worksheet or on another sheet. In Figure 4-32, the criteria range is cells G5:K6.

	A	B	C	D	E	F	G	H	I	J	K
1		Paradise Lakes Resort									
2		Revenue by Employee, Location, and Category									
3											
4	Name	Classification	Location	Category	Amount				Criteria Area		
5	BJ Francine	Representative	Baudette	Rentals	★ $17,000		Name	Classification	Location	Category	Amount
6	Alec Mikayla	Representative	Baudette	Rentals	★ $17,000			assoc*			>2500
7	Mikayla Anderson	Representative	Baudette	Excursions	☆ $3,400						
8	Ella Jamison	Manager	Baudette	Excursions	☆ $2,700						
9	David Gazik	Manager	Baudette	Boutique	☆ $1,200						
10	Natasha Ari	Associate	Baudette	Spa	★ $4,500						
11	Ari Aronson	Associate	Baudette	Boutique	☆ $3,200						
12	Dennis Frankie	Representative	Breezy Point	Rentals	★ $18,000						
13	Kendal Shaedon	Associate	Breezy Point	Spa	☆ $4,800				Results or Extract Area		
14	Frankie Dennis	Representative	Breezy Point	Excursions	☆ $7,500		Name	Classification	Location	Category	Amount
15	Kendra Shelton	Representative	Breezy Point	Rentals	★ $8,500						
16	DJ Bushman	Representative	Breezy Point	Boutique	☆ $1,200						
17	Sharon Wyatte	Manager	Breezy Point	Rentals	☆ $5,000						
18	Suzanne Ouimet	Manager	Breezy Point	Spa	☆ $2,500						
19	Chad Mei	Representative	Cass Lake	Excursions	★ $10,000						

4-32 *Advanced Filter* set up

Multiple rows below the header row in the criteria range set *AND* or *OR* conditions. If you enter criteria on the same row, they are treated as *AND* conditions. In Figure 4-32, "assoc*" in cell H6 and ">2500" in cell K6 are criteria. Both criteria must be met for a record to be displayed. For an *OR* condition, use a second (or third) row in the criteria range. An *OR* filter displays a record if any one of the requirements is met.

To show filtered results in another location, you also create an ***output*** or ***extract range***. You specify one row for this range, and it should include the same column headings as the data. In Figure 4-32, the extract range is cells G14:K14. Filtered rows are copied below these headings and take up as many rows as necessary. The output range must be on the same worksheet as the data, but you can copy the results to another sheet or another workbook.

▶ **HOW TO:** Create an Advanced Filter

1. Select labels in the header row for fields that will be used for filtering.
   - You can copy all the labels in the header row if preferred.
2. Copy the labels to a *Criteria* area.
   - The criteria area can be on the same or another sheet in the workbook.
   - If the criteria range is above the data, leave at least one blank row between it and the data.
3. Copy the labels again to an *Extract* area.
   - The output or extract area must be on the same sheet as the data.
   - Leave blank rows below the labels for the filtered results.
4. Type criteria in the criteria range.
   - Criteria is not case sensitive.
   - You can use wildcard characters in the criteria.
5. Click a cell in the data range.
6. Click the **Advanced** button [*Data* tab, *Sort & Filter* group].
   - The *Advanced Filter* dialog box opens.
7. Select **Copy to another location** In the *Action* group.
8. Verify or select the range (including the header row) in the *List range* box.
   - If the data range is named, press **F3 (FN+F3)** and select the name.
9. Select the criteria cell range with its header row in the *Criteria range* box.
   - If the criteria range is named, press **F3 (FN+F3)** and select the name.
   - You can type cell references to identify the criteria range.
10. Select the extract range in the *Copy to* box.
    - This range is the row of labels.
11. Click **OK** (Figure 4-33).

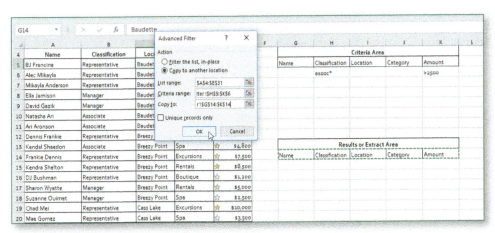

4-33 *Advanced Filter* dialog box

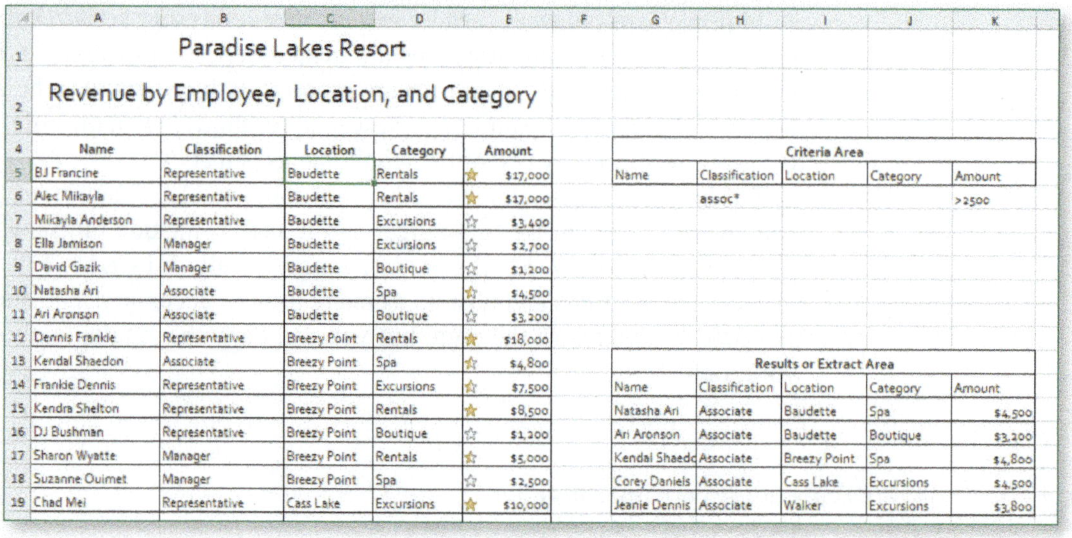

4-34 *Advanced Filter* results copied to another location

- Filtered rows are copied to the output range below the copied labels (Figure 4-34).

> **MORE INFO**
>
> Enter < > as criteria to display records that have any entry in the column. Enter = as criteria to show rows that have no entry in the column.

SLO 4.5

Using Subtotals, Groups, and Outlines

A *subtotal* is a summary row for data that is grouped. A *group* is a set of data that has the same entry in one or more columns. You can see groups by "Location" with a subtotal in the "Amount" column in Figure 4-35. An *outline* is a summary that groups records so that individual groups can be displayed or hidden from view. These three features are Excel commands that make it easy to organize and calculate results for worksheets with large sets of data.

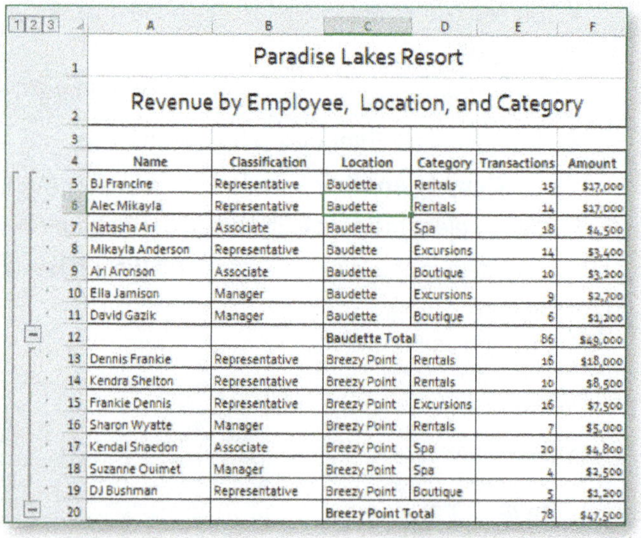

4-35 Grouped rows with a subtotal in "Amount" column

The Subtotal Command

The **Subtotal** command in the *Outline* group on the *Data* tab inserts summary rows for a sorted list and formats the data as an *outline*. The *Subtotal* command is available for a normal range of cells, not an Excel table. The *Subtotal* command includes *SUM, AVERAGE, MAX,* or *MIN* as well as other *Statistical* functions.

To use the *Subtotal* command, the data should have a header row with data rows following, and you must sort the rows by the main field (column) to be summarized or totaled. To display revenue numbers by location, for example, sort the data by location. The *Subtotal* command groups the rows by this field but can show subtotals for any column.

> ### MORE INFO
>
> If data is formatted as an Excel table, convert it to a normal cell range [*Table Tools Design* tab, *Tools* group] to use the *Subtotal* command.

▶HOW TO: Display Subtotals

1. Sort the data by the column by which subtotals will be calculated.
2. Click a cell in the data range.
3. Click the **Subtotal** button [*Data* tab, *Outline* group].
   - When data has a header row followed by data rows, the range is selected.
4. Click the **At each change in** arrow.
5. Choose the column heading name that was used for sorting.
   - Subtotals need not be shown for this column.
6. Click the **Use function** arrow and select the function.
7. In the **Add subtotal to** list, select each field that should display a subtotal.
   - Make sure the function applies to the column data type; for example, do not use *Sum* for a text column.
8. Choose **Replace current subtotals**.
   - If the range already has subtotals, they are replaced.
9. Choose **Summary below data** (Figure 4-36).
   - The "Summary" row can be placed above the data if you prefer.
   - You can also allow a group to split across pages.
   - You can remove subtotals from this dialog box.
10. Click **OK** (Figure 4-37).
    - A subtotal row appears below each group.
    - A grand total appears after the last row of data.
    - Outline buttons appear to the left of the column and row headings.
    - The outline is expanded, showing all details.

4-36 *Subtotal* dialog box

	A	B	C	D	E	F
4	**Name**	**Classification**	**Location**	**Category**	**Transactions**	**Amount**
5	Ari Aronson	Associate	Baudette	Boutique	10	$3,200
6	David Gazik	Manager	Baudette	Boutique	6	$1,200
7	DJ Bushman	Representative	Breezy Point	Boutique	5	$1,200
8	Christopher Bowm.	Manager	Cass Lake	Boutique	15	$3,700
9	Randy Josephson	Associate	Cass Lake	Boutique	12	$1,500
10	Nikolai Jalowiec	Manager	Walker	Boutique	6	$1,450
11				**Boutique Total**		$12,250
12	Mikayla Anderson	Representative	Baudette	Excursions	14	$3,400
13	Ella Jamison	Manager	Baudette	Excursions	9	$2,700
14	Frankie Dennis	Representative	Breezy Point	Excursions	16	$7,500
15	Chad Mei	Representative	Cass Lake	Excursions	24	$10,000
16	Corey Daniels	Associate	Cass Lake	Excursions	22	$4,500
17	Jeanie Dennis	Associate	Walker	Excursions	8	$3,800
18				**Excursions Total**		$31,900
19	BJ Francine	Representative	Baudette	Rentals	15	$17,000
20	Alec Mikayla	Representative	Baudette	Rentals	14	$17,000
21	Dennis Frankie	Representative	Breezy Point	Rentals	16	$18,000
22	Kendra Shelton	Representative	Breezy Point	Rentals	10	$8,500
23	Sharon Wyatte	Manager	Breezy Point	Rentals	7	$5,000
24	Christopher Bowm.	Manager	Cass Lake	Rentals	14	$15,000
25	Jeffery Dalton	Representative	Cass Lake	Rentals	5	$3,700
26	Tammy Christine	Representative	Walker	Rentals	16	$17,500
27	Josie Daddiline	Representative	Walker	Rentals	10	$12,000
28	Josie Daddiline	Representative	Walker	Rentals	12	$12,000
29				**Rentals Total**		$125,700
30	Natasha Ari	Associate	Baudette	Spa	18	$4,500
31	Kendal Shaedon	Associate	Breezy Point	Spa	20	$4,800
32	Suzanne Ouimet	Manager	Breezy Point	Spa	4	$2,500
33	Mae Gomez	Representative	Cass Lake	Spa	12	$3,500
34	Lilly Oliver	Associate	Walker	Spa	10	$2,200
35				**Spa Total**		$17,500
36				**Grand Total**		$187,350

4-37 "Amount" subtotals for each category

The *Subtotal* command inserts the *SUBTOTAL* function in each cell with a result. Its arguments are *Function_num* and *RefN*. *Function_num* is a number from 1 through 11 that specifies which calculation was selected in the *Subtotal* dialog box. If you chose *Sum*, for example, the function is =SUBTOTAL(9,F5:F11). *Ref1* is the range to be summed.

 MORE INFO

The *Function_num* arguments are in alphabetical order, so that *AVERAGE* is 1, *COUNT* is 2, and so on. You can see the argument list in Excel *Help* for the function.

Outline Buttons

An outline groups and summarizes data. A worksheet can have only one outline; the outline can include all of the worksheet data or a portion of the data. Outlines have levels, indicated by the numbered buttons to the left of the column headings. Each *Outline Level* button shows an increasing level of detail. An outline can have up to eight levels. The worksheet in Figure 4-37 has three levels: a grand total (1), a category total for each group (2), and all the rows (3).

Each group has an *Expand/Collapse* button, shown to the left of the row headings. This button is a toggle and shows a minus sign (−) or a plus sign (+). When an individual group is collapsed, you do not see details for that group, only the subtotal.

▶ **HOW TO:** Use Outline Buttons

1. Click a collapse button (−) to hide details for a group.
   - Only the subtotal row displays.
2. Click an expand button (+) to display details for a group.
3. Click the **Level 1** button (1) to reveal the grand total.
4. Click the **Level 2** button (2) to see the second outline level details (Figure 4-38).
5. Click the **Level 3** button (3) to display all details.

		Revenue by Employee, Location, and Category				
	Name	Classification	Location	Category	Transactions	Amount
12			Baudette Total		86	$49,000
20			Breezy Point Total		78	$47,500
28			Cass Lake Total		104	$42,900
35			Walker Total		62	$48,350
36			Grand Total		330	$187,350

4-38 Level 2 outline results

Create an Auto Outline

An *Auto Outline* inserts groups based on where formulas are located. Consistent data and formulas that follow a pattern are necessary, and the formulas can be in specific rows or columns. The data in Figure 4-39 is grouped by location, and there is a *SUM* formula after each group in column E and F.

When data is not properly formatted, Excel displays a message that an *Auto Outline* cannot be created.

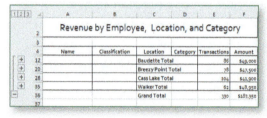

E9   *fx*   =SUM(E5:E8)

	A	B	C	D	E	F
1			Paradise Lakes Resort			
2			Revenue by Employee, Location, and Category			
3						
4	Name	Classification	Location	Category	Transactions	Amount
5	BJ Francine	Representative	Baudette	Rentals	15	$17,000
6	Alec Mikayla	Representative	Baudette	Rentals	14	$17,000
7	Natasha Ari	Associate	Baudette	Spa	18	$4,500
8	Mikayla Anderson	Representative	Baudette	Excursions	14	$3,400
9					61	$41,900
10	Dennis Frankie	Representative	Breezy Point	Rentals	16	$18,000
11	Kendra Shelton	Representative	Breezy Point	Rentals	10	$8,500
12	Frankie Dennis	Representative	Breezy Point	Excursions	16	$7,500
13	Sharon Wyatte	Manager	Breezy Point	Rentals	7	$5,000
14					49	$39,000
15	Christopher Bowman	Manager	Cass Lake	Rentals	14	$15,000
16	Chad Mei	Representative	Cass Lake	Excursions	24	$10,000
17	Corey Daniels	Associate	Cass Lake	Excursions	22	$4,500
18					60	$29,500

4-39 Data sorted by location with formulas for each group

HOW TO: Create an Auto Outline

1. Click a cell within the data range.
2. Click the **Group** button arrow [*Data* tab, *Outline* group].
3. Select **Auto Outline**.
   - Outline level buttons are inserted.
   - The outline is expanded.
4. Click each collapse button to hide details (Figure 4-40).

4-40 *Auto Outline* with two levels

Define Groups

You can create a group, by rows or columns, for data that does not have totals or formulas. This can be a time-consuming task for a large set of records, but you can use groups to hide irrelevant records and concentrate on groups that require editing.

To define groups, data must be sorted or arranged so that you can select a range of cells to indicate the group. In addition, you must insert a blank summary row either above or below the group (or a blank column to the left or right of the group). You can use blank rows to enter subtitles for the data before or after grouping.

The data in Figure 4-41 is sorted by the "Classification" column, so that groups can be created for each job title. Note that a blank row has been inserted after each group.

HOW TO: Define a Group

1. Sort the data (or arrange columns) based on the preferred grouping.
2. Insert a blank row at the end of each sort group (or at the start of each group).
   - Insert the blank row above the group if you want to label each group.
   - For column data, the summary column is usually to the right of the group.
3. Select the row or column headings for the first group.
   - Do not include the blank row or column.
   - You can select a range of cells that spans the rows or columns for the group.
4. Click the **Group** button [*Data* tab, *Outline* group].
   - The rows or columns are grouped.
   - Outline level buttons are inserted.
   - The data is expanded.
   - When you select a range of cells, not the row or column headings, the *Group* dialog box opens. Choose **Rows** or **Columns** if the dialog box opens and click **OK**.
5. Repeat steps 1–4 for each group (see Figure 4-41).

4-41 Data sorted by "Classification"; blank rows inserted after each title

PAUSE & PRACTICE: EXCEL 4-2

For this project, you sort and filter data for Paradise Lakes Resort based on location. You use a *Number Filter* to displays records within a range of values, build an advanced filter, and include subtotals in the workbook.

File Needed: *[your initials] PP E4-1.xlsx*
Completed Project File Name: *[your initials] PP E4-2.xlsx*

1. Open the *[your initials] PP E4-1* workbook completed in *Pause & Practice 4-1* and save it as [your initials] PP E4-2.

2. Click the **Sort&Filter** sheet tab.

3. Sort data in a worksheet.
   a. Click cell **A5**.
   b. Click the **Sort** button [*Data* tab, *Sort & Filter* group].
   c. Select the **My data has headers** box, if necessary.
   d. Click the **Sort by** arrow and select **Location**.
   e. Choose **Values** for *Sort On* and **A to Z** for *Order*.
   f. Click **Add Level**.
   g. Click the **Then by** arrow and select **Amount**.
   h. Choose **Values** for *Sort On* and **Largest to Smallest** for *Order* (Figure 4-42).
   i. Click **OK**. The data in is sorted alphabetically by location and then by amount in descending order.

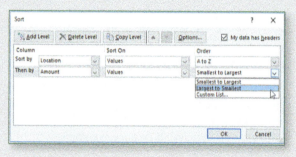

4-42 **Multiple column sort with text and numeric data**

4. Use a *Number AutoFilter*.
   a. Click cell **A5**.
   b. Click the **Filter** button [*Data* tab, *Sort & Filter* group] to display *AutoFilter* arrows.
   c. Click the *AutoFilter* arrow for "Amount."
   d. Point to **Number Filters** and select **Between**.
   e. Type 5000 in the **is greater than or equal to** box.
   f. Type 10000 in the **is less than or equal to** box (Figure 4-43).
   g. Click **OK**.

5. Click the **Adv Filter** sheet tab.

6. Set a criteria range.
   a. In cell **H6**, type assoc*.
   b. Type >1500 in cell **K6**.

7. Run an *Advanced Filter*.
   a. Click cell **A5**.
   b. Click the **Advanced** button [*Data* tab, *Sort & Filter* group].
   c. Select the **Copy to another location** radio button.
   d. Verify that cells **A4:E31** are identified in the **List range** box.

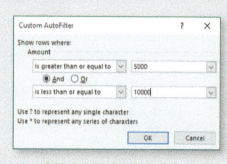

4-43 *Custom AutoFilter* dialog box for "Amount" between $5,000 and $10,000

e. Click the **Criteria range** box and select cells **G5:K6**.

f. Click the **Copy to** box and select cells **G14:K14** (Figure 4-44).

g. Click **OK**. Six records are extracted and displayed.

	A	B	C	D	E	F	G	H	I	J	K
4	Name	Classification	Location	Category	Amount				Criteria Area		
5	BJ Francine	Representative	Baudette	Rentals	☆ $17,000		Name	Classification	Location	Category	Amount
6	Alec Mikayla	Representative	Baudette					assoc*			>1500
7	Mikayla Anderson	Representative	Baudette								
8	Ella Jamison	Manager	Baudette								
9	David Gazik	Manager	Baudette								
10	Natasha Ari	Associate	Baudette								
11	Ari Aronson	Associate	Baudette								
12	Dennis Frankie	Representative	Breezy Poin						Results or Extract Area		
13	Kendal Shaedon	Associate	Breezy Poin				Name	Classification	Location	Category	Amount
14	Frankie Dennis	Representative	Breezy Poin								
15	Kendra Shelton	Representative	Breezy Poin								
16	DJ Bushman	Representative	Breezy Point	Boutique	☆ $1,200						
17	Sharon Wyatte	Manager	Breezy Point	Rentals							

Advanced Filter dialog box:
Action
○ Filter the list, in-place
● Copy to another location
List range: `$A$4:$E$31`
Criteria range: `lter'!$G$5:$K$6`
Copy to: `r'!$G$14:$K$14`
☐ Unique records only
[OK] [Cancel]

4-44 Criteria and extract ranges; *Advanced Filter* dialog box

8. Click the **Subtotals** sheet tab.

9. Show subtotals in a list.

a. Click a cell in the **Location** column. The records are sorted by this column.

b. Click the **Subtotal** button [*Data* tab, *Outline* group].

c. Click the **At each change in** arrow and choose **Location**.

d. Click the **Use function** arrow and choose **Sum**.

e. Select **Transactions** and **Amount** in the **Add subtotal to list** box.

f. Click **OK** (Figure 4-45).

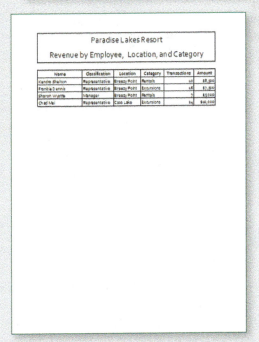

		Criteria Area		
Name	Classification	Location	Category	Amount
	assoc*			>1500

		Results or Extract Area		
Name	Classification	Location	Category	Amount
Natasha Ari	Associate	Baudette	Spa	$4,500
Ari Aronson	Associate	Baudette	Boutique	$3,200
Kendal Shaedon	Associate	Breezy Point	Spa	$4,800
Corey Daniels	Associate	Cass Lake	Excursions	$4,500
Lilly Oliver	Associate	Walker	Spa	$2,200
Jeanie Dennis	Associate	Walker	Excursions	$3,800

Paradise Lakes Resort
Revenue by Employee, Location, and Category

Name	Classification	Location	Category	Transactions	Amount
BJ Francine	Representative	Baudette	Rentals	15	$17,000
Alec Mikayla	Representative	Baudette	Rentals	14	$15,000
Natasha Ari	Associate	Baudette	Spa	18	$4,500
Mikayla Anderson	Representative	Baudette	Excursions	14	$3,400
Ari Aronson	Associate	Baudette	Boutique	10	$3,200
Ella Jamison	Manager	Baudette	Spa	9	$2,700
David Gazik	Manager	Baudette	Boutique	6	$3,200
		Baudette Total		86	$49,000
Dennis Frankie	Representative	Breezy Point	Rentals	16	$18,000
Kendra Shelton	Representative	Breezy Point	Rentals	10	$8,500
Frankie Dennis	Representative	Breezy Point	Excursions	16	$7,000
Sharon Wyatte	Manager	Breezy Point	Rentals	7	$5,000
Kendal Shaedon	Associate	Breezy Point	Spa	20	$4,800
Suzanne Ouimet	Manager	Breezy Point	Spa	4	$3,500
DJ Bushman	Representative	Breezy Point	Boutique	5	$1,200
		Breezy Point Total		78	$47,500
Christopher Bowman	Manager	Cass Lake	Rentals	14	$15,000
Chad Mei	Representative	Cass Lake	Excursions	24	$10,000
Corey Daniels	Associate	Cass Lake	Excursions	22	$4,500
Christopher Bowman	Manager	Cass Lake	Boutique	15	$3,700
Jeffery Delton	Representative	Cass Lake	Spa	6	$3,700
Mae Gomez	Representative	Cass Lake	Spa	12	$3,600
Randy Josephson	Associate	Cass Lake	Boutique	12	$3,500
		Cass Lake Total		104	$44,000
Tammy Christine	Representative	Walker	Rentals	16	$27,500
Josie Daddline	Representative	Walker	Rentals	10	$13,000
Josie Daddline	Representative	Walker	Rentals	11	$13,000
Jeanie Dennis	Associate	Walker	Excursions	8	$3,800
Lilly Oliver	Associate	Walker	Spa	10	$2,200
Nicolai Jalowec	Manager	Walker	Boutique	6	$1,450
		Walker Total		61	$48,950
		Grand Total		330	$187,350

Paradise Lakes Resort
Revenue by Employee, Location, and Category

Name	Classification	Location	Category	Transactions	Amount
Kendra Shelton	Representative	Breezy Point	Rentals	10	$8,500
Frankie Dennis	Representative	Breezy Point	Excursions	16	$7,000
Sharon Wyatte	Manager	Breezy Point	Rentals	7	$5,000
Chad Mei	Representative	Cass Lake	Excursions	24	$10,000

4-45 Completed PP E4-2 worksheets

10. Save and close the workbook.

Importing Data

Importing is the process of getting data from an outside source into an Excel worksheet. For example, you can probably import data from your bank into a worksheet so that you can analyze your transactions. *External data* is data that originated in another program or format. You import or copy external data into Excel from a *source,* which might be a text file, a database, or a web location. Imported data in a worksheet is almost always in list or table format.

The *Get External Data* command group on the *Data* tab establishes a connection to the source so that data can be refreshed. When you copy data into a worksheet using a *Copy and Paste* command, there is no connection to the source. Data connections are discussed later in this section.

Text Files

A *text file* is a document that includes raw data with no formatting. Text files are *.txt* (text) documents such as those created in NotePad or WordPad. Another widely used text format is *.csv* (comma separated values); you might see this type of file when you download a bank statement.

Text files separate data into *fields.* In one method, a character such as a comma or a tab separates the fields, and the file is described as *delimited* (e.g., tab-delimited file). A *delimiter* is the character used to separate the data. Common delimiters are the tab, space, and comma characters.

A second way to separate fields in a text file is by *fixed width*. Each field is a specified number of characters followed by a space. If the first name field is set at 25 characters, the name "Tom," is imported as 3 characters plus 22 spaces. The second field always starts at position 26.

When you click the **From Text** button in the *Get External Data* group on the *Data* tab, the **Text Import Wizard** guides you through the importing steps.(Figure 4-46).

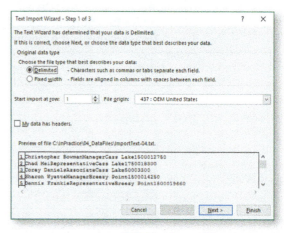

4-46 *Text Import Wizard – Step 1*

> **MORE INFO**
>
> Many legacy or mainframe computer systems use fixed width files for data.

> **HOW TO:** Import a Tab-Delimited Text File into a Worksheet

1. Select the cell in which imported data should begin.

2. Click the **From Text** button [*Data* tab, *Get External Data* group].

3. Navigate to and select the text file name in the *Import Text File* dialog box.

4. Click **Import** (Figure 4-47).

5. Select the **Delimited** radio button in the *Text Import Wizard – Step 1 of 3* window.

   • A preview of the data displays.

4-47 *Import Text File* dialog box

6. Click the spinner arrow for **Start import at row** to set the first row of imported text.

7. Click **Next**.

8. Select the **Tab** box in the *Text Import Wizard – Step 2 of 3* window.
   - The *Data preview* shows how the data will be separated into columns.

9. Click **Next**.
   - The *Step 3 of 3* window allows you to set formats as the data is imported.
   - This is optional; you can format data after it is imported.

10. Click **Finish**.

11. Select the radio button for **Existing worksheet** in the *Import Data* dialog box.
    - You can change or select the beginning cell location.
    - When you choose **New worksheet**, imported data starts at cell A1.

12. Click **OK**.
    - The data is available in the worksheet.

13. Right-click a cell within the imported data and select **Data Range Properties**.
    - The *External Data Range Properties* dialog box opens (Figure 4-48).
    - The *Name* is the name for the data connection.
    - You can specify when and how data is refreshed or updated.

14. Click **OK** to close the *External Data Range Properties* dialog box.

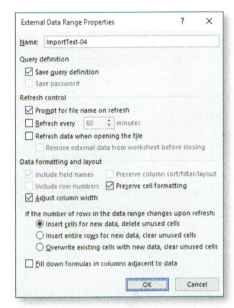

4-48 *External Data Range Properties* **dialog box**

Word Documents

You cannot "import" a Word document into Excel, but you can copy and paste data from Word into a worksheet. You can keep the Word formatting, or you can choose the current worksheet format.

▶ **HOW TO: Copy Data from a Word Document**

1. Select the cell in which imported data should begin.

2. Start Word and open the document.

3. Select the data to be copied.

4. Click the **Copy** button [*Home* tab, *Clipboard* group].

5. Switch to the Excel worksheet.

6. Click the arrow with the **Paste** button [*Home* tab, *Clipboard* group].

7. Choose **Match Destination Formatting** from the *Paste* gallery.
   - The data is pasted in the worksheet.
   - If you click the **Paste** button, data is pasted with the Word format.

> ▶ **ANOTHER WAY**
> Save a Word document as a text file (*.txt*) and import the text file into Excel.

Access Database Files

Most organizations and enterprises maintain large amounts of data in a database. A **database** is a collection of related tables, queries, forms, and reports. **Microsoft Access** is a relational database management system that is part of the Office suite. You can import a table or a query from an Access database into an Excel worksheet. In Access, a table is a data list, and a query is a subset of the list.

When a database includes many tables and queries, the *Select Table* dialog box opens so that you can choose the table or query to import. Access data is imported as an Excel table, a *PivotTable*, or a *PivotChart*.

> **MORE INFO**
>
> If a database has a single table or query, it is automatically imported into Excel; the *Select Table* dialog box does not open.

HOW TO: Import an Access Table into a Worksheet

1. Select the cell in which imported data should begin.
2. Click the **From Access** button [*Data* tab, *Get External Data* group].
3. Navigate to and select the database name in the *Select Data Source* dialog box.
4. Click **Open**.
   - If only one table or query exists in the database, it is imported.
5. Select the name of the table or query in the *Select Table* dialog box (Figure 4-49).
6. Click **OK**.
7. Select **Table** and **Existing worksheet** in the *Import Data* dialog box.
   - You can choose a new worksheet for imported data or select a different cell.
   - You can also import data as a *PivotTable*, a *PivotChart*, or as a connection for later use.
8. Click **OK**.
   - The data is imported in an Excel table.
   - Field names from the Access table or query are column headings in the Excel table.
9. Click the *Table Tools Design* tab.
10. Click the **Properties** button [*External Table Data* group].
    - The *External Data Properties* dialog box opens (Figure 4-50).
    - You can adjust formatting and refresh options.
11. Click the **Connection Properties** button (to the right of the *Name* box).
    - The *Connection Properties* dialog box opens.
    - You can type a description for the data connection.
    - You can set how the data is refreshed or updated.
    - The *Definition* tab identifies the source of the imported data.
12. Click **OK** to close the *Connection Properties* dialog box.
13. Click **OK** to close the *External Data Properties* dialog box.

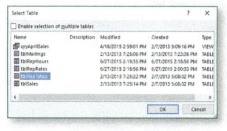

4-49 *Select Table* dialog box

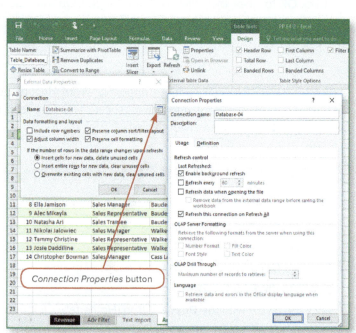

4-50 *External Data Properties* and *Connection Properties* dialog boxes

Web Site Data

Web sites that deal with research, statistics, demographics, and similar public data often have downloadable text or Excel files for importing. Most web sites, however, have protected multimedia content with images, video, and audio, not list-type data for importing into Excel.

When you use the *From Web* command, data are identified by a small red arrow in a yellow-orange box. When you click the arrow, the importable data is selected, and the arrow changes to a blue check mark. Data from a web page establishes a connection to the URL that you can refresh. If the URL changes, you must edit the query to find the new address.

HOW TO: Create a Web Query to Import Data

1. Navigate to the web site and select the URL in the *Address* bar.
2. Press **Ctrl+C** to copy the URL to the Windows *Clipboard*.
3. Select the cell in which imported data should begin.
4. Click the **From Web** button [*Data* tab, *Get External Data* group].
   - The *New Web Query* dialog box opens.
   - Use the resize arrow at the bottom right corner to resize the dialog box.
5. Select the default URL in the *Address* bar in the *New Web Query* dialog box.
6. Press **Ctrl+V** to paste the copied URL in the *Address* bar.
7. Click **Go** or press **Enter**.
   - If an error message box opens about scripts that cannot be run, click **Yes**.
8. Navigate to the data to be imported.
9. Click the **Click to select this table** arrow (yellow-orange arrow) next to data to import (Figure 4-51).
   - The arrow changes to a blue check mark, the **Click to deselect this table** arrow.
10. Click **Import**.
    - The *Import Data* dialog box opens.

4-51 *New Web Query* dialog box

11. Click **OK**.
   • You may see a brief screen message as data is imported.
   • The imported data is unformatted.

Workbook Connections

When you use the *Get External Data* group on the *Data* tab, Excel establishes a connection that you can edit, refresh, name, or remove. A ***connection*** is an identifier and a link for data that originated outside the workbook. All connections are listed in the *Workbook Connections* dialog box. In this dialog box, you can select the connection name and open its *Properties* dialog box to edit various settings.

A data connection to an Internet location is named *Connection*. A data connection to a text or database file is named the same as the original file. You can change the name of a data connection to a descriptive name in the *Properties* dialog box.

When you open a workbook that has data connections, you will usually see a security warning bar at the top of the worksheet. When you are sure that the connection is safe, click **Enable Content** to work with the data.

▶**HOW TO:** Manage Data Connections

1. Click the **Connections** button [*Data* tab, *Connections* group].
   • The *Workbook Connections* dialog box lists current connections.
2. Select the name of the connection.
3. Click the link **Click here to see where the selected connections are used** in the lower pane.
   • This identifies where the data is located in the workbook (Figure 4-52).

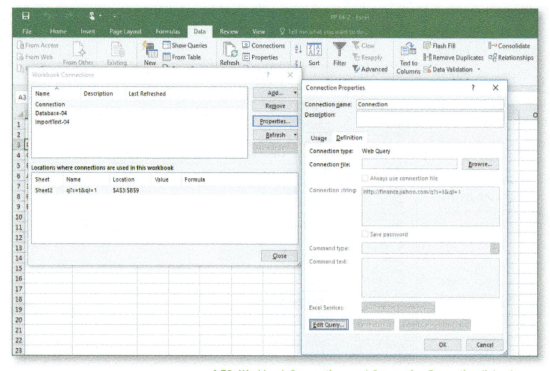

4-52 *Workbook Connections* and *Connection Properties* dialog boxes

4. Click **Refresh** to update the selected connection.

   • The *Import Text File* dialog box opens for a text file so that you can import it again.
   • A database source is automatically refreshed if the file is accessible.
   • An Internet source updates if the URL is accessible.

5. Click **Properties** to open the *Connection Properties* dialog box.

   • You can set how the data are refreshed, change the connection name, or add a description.
   • Click the *Definition* tab to edit a web query to update a URL.

6. Click **OK** to close the *Connection Properties* dialog box.

7. Click **Close** to save changes.

Flash Fill

Imported data often needs to be "cleaned" because it may not be in the correct sort order, it may have missing or incorrect data, and so on. *Flash Fill* is a feature that recognizes a pattern in the first cell and suggests data for the remaining rows in a column. It can be used to quickly complete new, missing, or incorrect data. For example, imagine that imported data lists first and last names in a single column, but you want first and last names in separate columns. Type the first person's name in an empty column next to the original column. As you start to type a second name below the first one, *Flash Fill* previews the completed column. Just press **Enter** to complete the column. Then do the same for the person's last name in the next column to the right. The *Flash Fill Options* button appears after you press **Enter** so that you can undo the fill if necessary or accept all the suggestions.

▶ **HOW TO:** Flash Fill Data in a Worksheet

1. Click the first cell in an empty column next to the original data.

   • The first *Flash Fill* column must be adjacent to the original data.
   • Use an empty column or insert a column.

2. Type the data as you want it to appear.

3. Press **Enter** and type data in the cell below the first cell.

   • The suggested list is previewed.
   • If the suggested list does not appear, try typing a third item in the column (Figure 4-53).
   • The data must be consistent and follow a recognizable pattern.

4. Press **Enter** to complete the *Flash Fill*.

   • If there is no *Flash Fill* suggestion list, click the **Flash Fill** button [*Data* tab, *Data Tools* group] with the insertion point in the column.

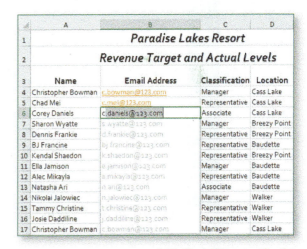

4-53 *Flash Fill* suggestion list

▶ **ANOTHER WAY**

To split data into separate columns, insert blank columns to the right. Select the column to be split and click the **Text to Columns** button [*Data* tab, *Data Tools* group]. Complete the *Convert Text to Columns Wizard*.

Exporting Data

Exporting is the process of saving data in a format that can be used by another program or application. This can be as simple as providing a PDF file for viewing, copying data into Word, or saving worksheet data as a text file.

Export Data as a Text File

Most software applications can read a text file, a common way to transfer or share data. You can save Excel data as a tab-delimited, space-delimited, or comma-delimited file. When you save worksheet data as a text file, Excel renames the sheet with the same file name that you type for the text file. You can save only one worksheet in a text file. If a workbook has multiple sheets, a message box will alert you that only the current sheet will be saved.

▶ **HOW TO:** Save Excel Data as a Tab-Delimited File

1. Click the worksheet tab with data to export.
   - The insertion point can be in any cell.
2. Click the **File** tab and select **Export**.
3. Select **Change File Type**.
4. Select **Text (Tab delimited)** as the file type (Figure 4-54).

4-54 *Export* command in *Backstage* view

5. Click **Save As**.
   - The *Save As* dialog box opens with *Text (tab-delimited)* as the *Save as type.*
6. Navigate to the location for the exported data.
7. Type a file name for the text file in the *File name* box.
8. Click **Save**.
   - If a workbook has more than one sheet, a message box reminds you that only one sheet can be exported. Click **OK** in this message box.
9. Click **Yes** to acknowledge that Excel features may be lost.
   - The worksheet tab has the same name as the exported file.
10. Rename the sheet tab as desired.

11. Click the **File** tab and choose **Save As**.

12. Select **Excel Workbook** as the *Save as type* in the *Save As* dialog box.

13. Navigate to the folder for saved work.

14. Select or type the original workbook file name and click **Save**.

15. Click **Yes** to replace the file.

16. Close the workbook.

- The exported text file is available in the folder selected for saving.
- The original workbook is unchanged and resaved.

> **MORE INFO**
>
> To use Excel data in an Access table, export the data as a text file. You can then import the text file into an Access table.

Export Data via the Clipboard

Excel data can be copied and pasted into a Word document as well as other applications. The *Paste* button gallery in Word has options to paste a table, to paste text separated by tabs or spaces, and to paste a picture object. The *Paste Special* command in the gallery has an option to paste a *Microsoft Excel Worksheet Object*. With this option, you can paste a link to the Excel data in Word to launch Excel, edit the worksheet, and resave the Excel file. You can also paste without a link which opens an Excel window in Word that has most Excel commands but does not affect the original Excel file.

HOW TO: Create a Microsoft Excel Worksheet Object

1. Open the Word document and position the insertion point at the location for the Excel data.

2. Switch to the Excel worksheet.

3. Select the cells to be copied.

4. Click the **Copy** button [*Home* tab, *Clipboard* group].

- The data can be formatted as a table or a normal range.
- You can also press **Ctrl+C** to copy.

5. Switch to the Word document.

6. Click the arrow with the **Paste** button [*Home* tab, *Clipboard* group] and choose **Paste Special**.

7. Select **Microsoft Excel Worksheet Object** in the *Paste Special* dialog box.

8. Select **Paste link** in the *Paste Special* dialog box (Figure 4-55).

9. Click **OK**.

- The data is pasted as a worksheet object.

10. Complete work in the Word document.

- Use horizontal alignment commands to position the object, if necessary.
- You can double-click anywhere in the object to launch Excel and open the source workbook.

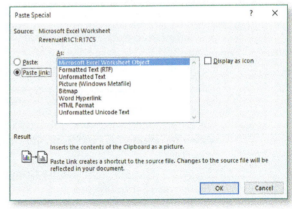

4-55 *Paste Special* dialog box

SharePoint Lists

A **SharePoint server** is a web platform that runs *Microsoft SharePoint,* a family of products that allows for collaboration and simultaneous work by groups of people via the Internet. You can export data in an Excel table to a SharePoint list so that others in your work circle have access to the data. The *Export* button is in the *External Table Data* group on the *Table Tools Design* tab, and it launches the *Export Table to SharePoint List Wizard.* To work with a SharePoint server, you must have an Internet connection and permission from the network administrator.

PAUSE & PRACTICE: EXCEL 4-3

For this project, you import data from a text file into an Excel worksheet, format the data as an Excel table, copy data from a Word document, and use *Flash Fill* to complete the worksheet for Paradise Lakes Resort.

Files Needed: *[your initials] PP E4-2.xlsx, ImportText-04.txt*, and *CopyWord-04.docx* *[Student data files are available in the* Library *of your SIMnet account.]*
Completed Project File Name: ***[your initials] PP E4-3.xlsx***

---

1. Open the ***[your initials] PP E4-2*** workbook completed in *Pause & Practice 4-2* and save it as [your initials] PP E4-3.

2. Import data from a text file.
   a. Select cell **A4** on the **Text Import** tab.
   b. Click the **From Text** button [*Data* tab, *Get External Data* group].
   c. Navigate to and select ***ImportText-04.txt*** from your student data files in the *Import Text File* dialog box.
   d. Click **Import**.
   e. Select **Delimited** in the *Text Import Wizard – Step 1 of 3* dialog box and click **Next**.
   f. Select the **Tab** box in the *Text Import Wizard – Step 2 of 3* dialog box and click **Next**.
   g. Click **Finish** to accept the *General* format.
   h. Click **OK** in the *Import Data* dialog box.

3. Copy data from a Word document.
   a. Select cell **A18**.
   b. Open Microsoft Word and open the ***CopyWord-04*** document from your student data files.
   c. Select all the data and click the **Copy** button [*Home* tab, *Clipboard* group].
   d. Switch to the Excel window.
   e. Click the arrow with the **Paste** button [*Home* tab, *Clipboard* group] and choose **Match Destination Formatting** (Figure 4-56).

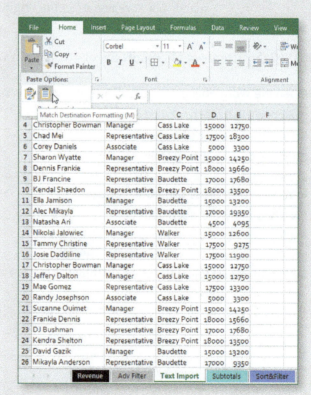

4-56 *Paste Options* **for copied data**

f. Select cells **D4:E27** and apply the **Currency** number format with zero decimals.
   g. Adjust the widths of columns **C:E** to **11.43 (85 pixels)**.

4. Use *Flash Fill* to create an email address column.
   a. Insert a column between columns **A** and **B**.
   b. Type Email Address in cell **B3**.
   c. Increase the width of the "Email Address" column to **31.00 (222 pixels)**.
   d. In cell **B4** type c.bowman@somewhere.com and press **Enter**.
   e. Select cell **B5** and type c.m to start the second address and display the *Flash Fill* suggested list.
   f. Press **Enter**. If the *Flash Fill* suggestion list did not appear, click the **Flash Fill** button [*Data* tab, *Data Tools* group].

5. Format data as an Excel table.
   a. Select cells **A3:F27**. Since the data was imported from different sources, you must select the range.
   b. Click the **Format as Table** button [*Home* tab, *Styles* group].
   c. Choose **Table Style Light 1** and click **OK**. The data connections must be removed to create an Excel table.
   d. Choose **Yes** in the message box (Figure 4-57).

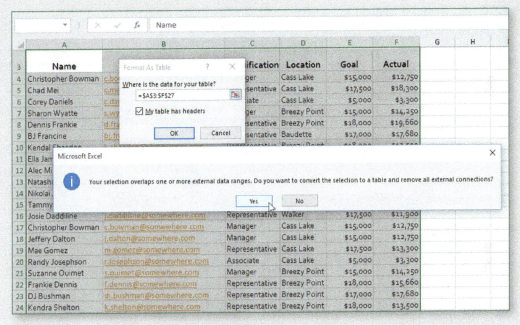

4-57 Message box to remove data connections

6. Add a column with a calculation to a table.
   a. Type Difference in cell **G3** and press **Enter**.
   b. Change the column width to **10.70 (80 pixels)** and use a black bottom border for the cell.
   c. Type **=** in cell **G4** to start the formula and click cell **F4**.
   d. Type **−** for subtraction and click cell **E4** (Figure 4-58).
   e. Press **Enter** to copy the formula in the column.
   f. Select cells **G4:G27** and press **Ctrl+1** to open the *Format Cells* dialog box.
   g. On the *Number* tab, choose **Currency** with zero decimal places and negative numbers in red, and close the dialog box.
   h. Select cells **A1:G1** and click the **Merge & Center** button [*Home* tab, *Alignment* group] to remove the centering. Then click the **Merge & Center** button again to re-center the cells over the new range.
   i. Repeat the steps to re-center cells **A2:G2**.
   j. Change the orientation to **Landscape**.

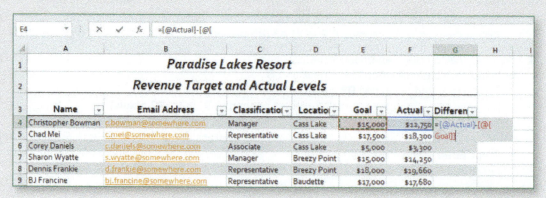

4-58 Structured references in a table formula

7. Save and close the workbook. Close the Word document (Figure 4-59).

Paradise Lakes Resort
Revenue Target and Actual Levels

Name	Email Address	Classification	Location	Goal	Actual	Difference
Christopher Bowman	c.bowman@somewhere.com	Manager	Cass Lake	$15,000	$12,750	$2,250
Chad Mei	c.mei@somewhere.com	Representative	Cass Lake	$17,500	$18,300	$800
Corey Daniels	c.daniels@somewhere.com	Associate	Cass Lake	$5,000	$3,300	$1,700
Sharon Wyatte	s.wyatte@somewhere.com	Manager	Breezy Point	$15,000	$14,250	$750
Dennis Frankie	d.frankie@somewhere.com	Representative	Breezy Point	$18,000	$19,660	$1,660
BJ Francine	bj.francine@somewhere.com	Representative	Baudette	$17,000	$17,680	$680
Kendal Shaedon	k.shaedon@somewhere.com	Representative	Breezy Point	$18,000	$13,500	$4,500
Ella Jamison	e.jamison@somewhere.com	Manager	Baudette	$15,000	$13,200	$1,800
Alec Mikayla	a.mikayla@somewhere.com	Representative	Baudette	$17,000	$19,350	$2,350
Natasha Ari	n.ari@somewhere.com	Associate	Baudette	$4,500	$4,095	$405
Nikolai Jalowiec	n.jalowiec@somewhere.com	Manager	Walker	$15,000	$12,600	$2,400
Tammy Christine	t.christine@somewhere.com	Representative	Walker	$17,500	$5,275	$8,225
Josie Daddiline	j.daddiline@somewhere.com	Representative	Walker	$17,500	$11,900	$5,600
Christopher Bowman	c.bowman@somewhere.com	Manager	Cass Lake	$15,000	$12,750	$2,250
Jeffery Dalton	j.dalton@somewhere.com	Manager	Cass Lake	$15,000	$12,750	$2,250
Mae Gomez	m.gomez@somewhere.com	Representative	Cass Lake	$17,500	$13,300	$4,200
Randy Josephson	r.josephson@somewhere.com	Associate	Cass Lake	$5,000	$3,300	$1,700
Suzanne Ouimet	s.ouimet@somewhere.com	Manager	Breezy Point	$15,000	$14,250	$750
Frankie Dennis	f.dennis@somewhere.com	Representative	Breezy Point	$18,000	$15,660	$2,340
DJ Bushman	dj.bushman@somewhere.com	Representative	Breezy Point	$17,000	$17,680	$680
Kendra Shelton	k.shelton@somewhere.com	Representative	Breezy Point	$18,000	$13,500	$4,500
David Gazik	d.gazik@somewhere.com	Manager	Baudette	$15,000	$13,200	$1,800
Mikayla Anderson	m.anderson@somewhere.com	Representative	Baudette	$17,000	$5,350	$7,650
Ari Aronson	a.aronson@somewhere.com	Associate	Baudette	$4,500	$4,095	$405

4-59 PP E4-3 completed worksheet

Building and Formatting PivotTables

A **PivotTable** is a cross tabulation report based on list-type data. It is a separate worksheet in which you can sort, filter, and calculate large amounts of data. *PivotTables* are analysis tools, an important part of **Business Intelligence (BI)**. Business intelligence is a combination of applications and processes that enable you to "drill-down" into data and assess various types of results or changes. In a table or list with thousands of records, you can build a *PivotTable* to quickly show average revenue by state, by city, or other criteria, and, just as quickly, return to the entire list (Figure 4-60).

PivotTables are interactive, because you rearrange the report for analysis by clicking or dragging. Rearranging data is *pivoting* the data so that you can look at it from a different perspective. It takes time and practice to create and understand all the features of a *PivotTable*, but it is easy to experiment placing fields, sorting data, or filtering results.

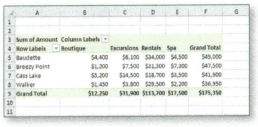

	A	B	C	D	E	F	G
1							
2							
3	Sum of Amount	Column Labels					
4	Row Labels	Boutique	Excursions	Rentals	Spa	Grand Total	
5	Baudette	$4,400	$6,100	$34,000	$4,500	$49,000	
6	Breezy Point	$1,200	$7,500	$31,500	$7,300	$47,500	
7	Cass Lake	$5,200	$14,500	$18,700	$3,500	$41,900	
8	Walker	$1,450	$3,800	$29,500	$2,200	$36,950	
9	Grand Total	$12,250	$31,900	$113,700	$17,500	$175,350	
10							
11							

4-60 An Excel *PivotTable*

Create a PivotTable

Data for a *PivotTable* should follow the same guidelines as those recommended for an Excel table in the beginning of this chapter. Data can be formatted as a table but need not be. A *PivotTable* is placed on its own sheet in the workbook.

The *Tables* group on the *Insert* tab includes the *PivotTable* button as well as the *Recommended PivotTables* button. When you are first learning about *PivotTables*, the *Recommended PivotTables* button may help you gain experience building these reports.

After you create a *PivotTable*, the *PivotTable Tools Analyze* and *Design* tabs are available for additional format choices and data commands.

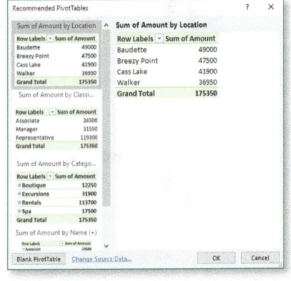

4-61 *Recommended PivotTables* for a data range

▶ **HOW TO: Create a PivotTable**

1. Click a cell in the data range.
   - The data range must have a header row.
2. Click the **Recommended PivotTables** button [*Insert* tab, *Tables* group] (Figure 4-61).
   - A data range is assumed and highlighted in the worksheet.
3. Point to a preview tile on the left to see a *ScreenTip* for the proposed *PivotTable*.
4. Select the preferred *PivotTable* and click **OK**.
   - The *PivotTable* report is created on a separate sheet.

The PivotTable Fields Pane

A *PivotTable* is created on a new sheet in the workbook, and the *PivotTable Fields* pane opens at the right. From this pane, you can add and remove fields from the report and drag field names into different areas in the pane to reset how the data are organized (Figure 4-62).

There are *Filters, Columns, Rows,* and *Values* areas in the pane. Each item from a field in the *Rows* area appears in its own row in the *PivotTable*. Each item in a field in the *Columns* area displays as a column. Columns and rows are usually the categories of data, not the actual values. Fields in the *Values* area are the ones that are summed, averaged, counted, or otherwise used in a calculation. *Filters* are fields placed as separate buttons above the *PivotTable* which act like *AutoFilter* arrows. Row and column labels include a filter arrow in the body of the *PivotTable,* and row data have collapse/expand buttons for certain field layouts. You can filter data from the filter arrows with a field, or you can insert a *Slicer* window.

▶**HOW TO:** Adjust Fields in a PivotTable

1. Click a cell in the body of the *PivotTable.*
2. Drag a field name from the *Choose fields to add to report* area into the *Columns* area in the *PivotTable Fields* pane and release the pointer button.
   - Columns for the field items are added to the report.
   - A grand total column is added.
3. Drag a field name into the *Filters* area and release the pointer button (Figure 4-63).

4-62 *PivotTable Fields* pane

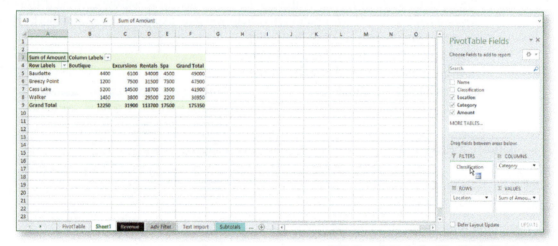

4-63 Drag fields in the *PivotTable Fields* pane

   - The field is added as a filter button in row 1 of the *PivotTable.*
   - No filter is applied.
4. Drag a field name from the *Rows* area to the left and into the worksheet area.
   - The field is removed from the *PivotTable.*
5. Drag a field name from one area in the *PivotTable Fields* pane to another area.
   - The *PivotTable* is updated after each change.

Field Settings

Fields in a *PivotTable* include various settings that depend on the type of data. ***Field Settings*** for a text field include layout and print options as well as subtotal and filter choices. The *Layout* group on the *PivotTable Tools Design* tab includes many of the same commands as the *Field Settings* dialog box.

    The ***Value Field Settings*** for a *PivotTable Values* field determine how data is summarized. The default function is *SUM,* but you can change the function or select a custom percentage, difference, or ranking. From the *Value Field Settings* dialog box, you can edit the label that appears in the *PivotTable,* choose a function, and set how numbers are formatted. To select a field in a *PivotTable,* click the field name in the *Row Labels* row or any cell in the column.

> **ANOTHER WAY**
> You can right-click a field in the *PivotTable* and select **Field Settings** or **Value Field Settings** to open the dialog box.

> **MORE INFO**
> You can show a field more than once in a *PivotTable* and choose different settings for each occurrence.

HOW TO: Change Value Field Settings in a PivotTable

1. Click the arrow for *Sum of [Field Name]* in the *Values* area in the *PivotTable Fields* pane.
2. Select **Value Field Settings** from the menu.
   - The *Value Field Settings* dialog box opens.
   - You can also click one of the field values in the *PivotTable* and click the **Field Settings** button [*PivotTable Tools Analyze* tab, *Active Field* group] to open the dialog box.
3. Click the **Custom Name** box and type a new label as desired.
   - The label cannot be the same as the field name in the *PivotTable Fields* pane.
4. Select the **Summarize Values By** tab, if necessary.
5. Choose the function from the *Summarize value field by* list.
6. Click **Number Format**.
7. Select the preferred number format in the *Format Cells* dialog box (Figure 4-64).

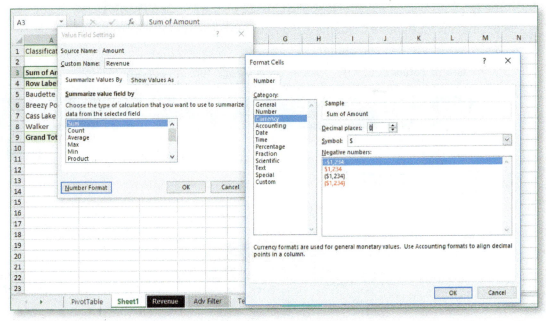

4-64 Value Field Settings dialog box and Number Format options

8. Click **OK** to close the *Format Cells* dialog box.
9. Click **OK** to close the *Value Field Settings* dialog box.
   - The new label displays in the *PivotTable* and in the task pane.
   - The entire field is reformatted.

Format a PivotTable

A *PivotTable* can be formatted from the *PivotTable Tools Design* tab or from the *Home* tab. The *PivotTable Tools Design* tab includes *PivotTable* styles and layout options. *PivotTable* styles are similar to Excel table styles. You can choose from a gallery to apply fill, border, and font color. Changes made from the *PivotTable Tools Design* tab affect the entire table.

The *Layout* group on the *PivotTable Tools Design* tab provides options for displaying subtotals and grand totals. The *Report Layout* command offers choices for the report design and selections for repeated labels. From the *PivotTable Style Options* group, you can choose whether row and column headings are bold and filled and whether columns and rows are banded with fill or borders. These style options are dependent on the *PivotTable* style.

From the *Home* tab, you can change the font size and style, set alignment, and more. When you apply changes from the *Home* tab, the format is applied to the selected cell or cells.

▶ **HOW TO:** Format a PivotTable

1. Click a cell in the *PivotTable.*
2. Click the **More** button for the *PivotTable Styles* group [*PivotTable Tools Design* tab].
   - The style gallery is categorized by light, medium, and dark colors.
3. Point to a style icon to see a *Live Preview.*
   - The styles are named *Pivot Style Light 1, Pivot Style Light 2,* and so on.
   - You can design your own style.
4. Click to select a style.
5. Select the box for **Banded Rows** in the *PivotTable Styles Options* group [*PivotTable Tools Design* tab].
   - The rows are filled or a border is applied, based on the selected *PivotTable* style.
6. Select the box for **Banded Columns** in the *PivotTable Styles Options* group [*PivotTable Tools Design* tab].
   - The columns are filled or a border is applied.
7. Click the **Grand Totals** button [*PivotTable Tools Design* tab, *Layout* group] (Figure 4-65).

4-65 Display or hide total column and row

8. Choose **Off for Rows and Columns**.
   - The total column and row are removed.
   - You can show totals by selecting **On for Columns and Rows**.

Refresh a PivotTable

Although a *PivotTable* is based on worksheet data, the *PivotTable* is not automatically updated if the data are edited. This is a security measure because a *PivotTable* can be associated with data in a different workbook or an external source such as a database. You can use the context-sensitive menu for any cell in the *PivotTable* and choose **Refresh**, or you can click the **Refresh** button in the *Data* group on the *PivotTable Tools Analyze* tab.

MORE INFO

There is a *PivotTable* option to automatically refresh the data each time the workbook is opened. Click the **Options** button [*PivotTable Tools Analyze* tab, *PivotTable* group] and select the **Data** tab.

HOW TO: Refresh Data in a PivotTable

1. Click any cell in the *PivotTable*.
2. Click the **Refresh** button [*PivotTable Tools Analyze* tab, *Data* group].
   - The *PivotTable* data is updated.
   - You can refresh all data connections in the workbook by clicking the arrow for the **Refresh** button and selecting **Refresh All**.

Create a PivotChart

A **PivotChart** contains charted data that updates with the *PivotTable* and has the same field buttons and filter options. The *PivotChart* button is on the *PivotTable Tools Analyze* tab.

A *PivotChart* can be formatted like an Excel chart from its *PivotChart Tools Design* and *Format* tabs. You can select a style, switch row and column data, change the chart type, and so on. When the chart object is selected, you will also see the *PivotChart Tools Analyze* tab with the same commands as the *PivotTable Tools Analyze* tab, and the *PivotChart Fields* pane on the right. A *PivotChart* and its *PivotTable* are linked, and you can make changes from command tabs for the table or the chart.

MORE INFO

You can create a *PivotChart* directly from a list in the worksheet; its underlying *PivotTable* is automatically created.

HOW TO: Create a PivotChart

1. Click a cell in the *PivotTable*.
2. Click the **PivotChart** button [*PivotTable Tools Analyze* tab, *Tools* group].
   - The *Insert Chart* dialog box opens.
3. Select a chart type from the list on the left.
4. Select a subtype for the chart.
5. Click **OK** (Figure 4-66).

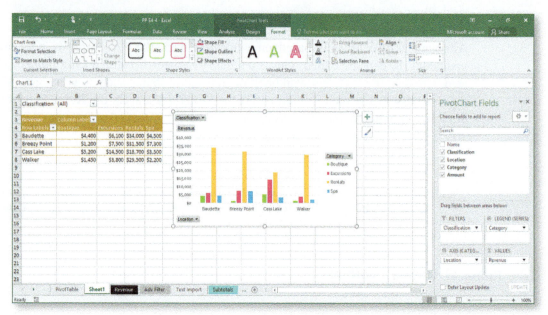

4-66 *PivotChart* inserted as chart object

- The chart displays as a chart object.
- The *PivotChart Tools Analyze, Design,* and *Format* tabs are available.
- The *PivotChart Fields* pane is similar to the *PivotTable Fields* pane.

PAUSE & PRACTICE: EXCEL 4-4

For this project, you create a *PivotTable* for Paradise Lakes Resort using the Excel table as its source. You also create a *PivotChart* and add a slicer to the worksheet. Your workbook now has data connections, so you may see a security warning when you open the file, depending on the settings of your computer.

File Needed: *[your initials] PP E4-3.xlsx*
Completed Project File Name: *[your initials] PP E4-4.xlsx*

1. Open the *[your initials] PP E4-3* workbook completed in *Pause & Practice 4-3*. The security bar informs you that the data connections have been disabled (Figure 4-67).

2. Click **Enable Content**. (If you did not see the security bar, continue to step 3.)

3. Save the workbook as [your initials] PP E4-4.

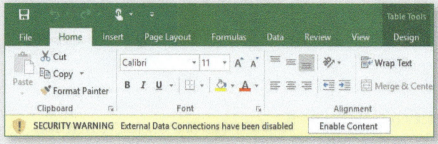

4-67 Security warning for a workbook with data connections

4. Create a *PivotTable*.
   a. Click cell **A4** on the **Revenue** sheet tab.
   b. Click the **Recommended PivotTables** button [*Insert* tab, *Tables* group].

c. Locate and click the **Sum of Amount by Location** preview tile.

d. Click **OK**.

e. Name the worksheet tab PivotTable.

5. Add a field and a *Slicer* window in a *PivotTable*.

   a. Drag the **Category** field from the *Choose fields to add to report* group to the *Columns* area in the *PivotTable Fields* pane.

   b. Click the **Insert Slicer** button [*PivotTable Tools Analyze* tab, *Filter* group].

   c. Select the **Classification** box and click **OK** (Figure 4-68).

   d. Select and drag the *Slicer* window to position it below the *PivotTable*.

6. Format fields in a *PivotTable*.

   a. Right-click cell **B5**.

   b. Choose **Value Field Settings** from the menu.

   c. Click **Number Format** and set **Currency** format with zero decimal places.

   d. Click **OK** to close each dialog box.

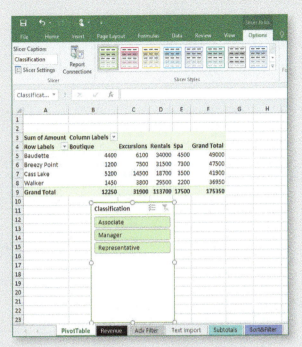

4-68 Field added to *Columns* area and *Slicer* window inserted

7. Create a *PivotChart*.

   a. Click the **PivotChart** button [*PivotTable Tools Analyze* tab, *Tools* group].

   b. Select **Clustered Column** from the *Column* group and click **OK**.

   c. Click the **Quick Layout** button [*PivotChart Tools Design* tab, *Chart Layouts* group].

   d. Select **Layout 3**.

   e. Click to select the **Chart Title** placeholder.

   f. Click the *Formula* bar, type Revenue by Category, and press **Enter**.

   g. Position the chart object so that its top left corner is at cell **H3**.

8. Adjust fields in a *PivotTable* and *PivotChart*.

   a. Click **Representative** in the *Slicer* window. The data is filtered in the *PivotTable* and in the *PivotChart*.

   b. Click the **Category** button in the chart.

   c. Deselect **(Select All)** to remove all the check marks (Figure 4-69).

   d. Select the **Excursions** and **Rentals** boxes and click **OK**.

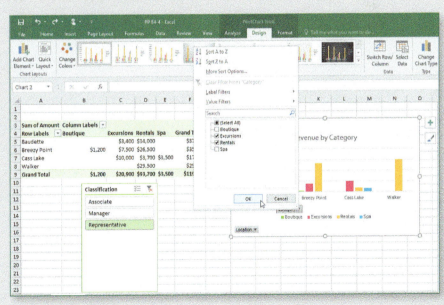

4-69 Data is filtered in the chart and the table

9. Click cell **A1**.

10. Save and close the workbook (Figure 4-70).

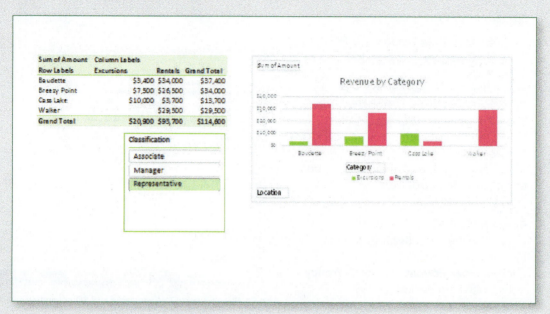

4-70 Completed worksheet for PP E4-4

Chapter Summary

4.1 Create and format a list as an Excel table (p. E4-222).

- An Excel *table* provides enhanced commands for sorting, filtering, and calculating data.
- A table is a list with a *header row, AutoFilter* arrows with the labels in the header row, and the same type of data in each column.
- When any cell in a table is selected, the *Table Tools Design* tab is available with commands for editing and formatting the table.
- A *table style* is a preset combination of colors and borders.
- Table style options enable you to display a total row, to emphasize the first or last column, and to add shading to rows or columns.
- The *Table Tools* group on the *Table Tools Design* tab has commands to remove duplicate rows, to convert a table to a normal cell range, or to insert a *slicer* window for filtering the data.
- The automatic name for a table and several of its parts are *structured references.*
- Structured references appear in *Formula AutoComplete* lists and are substituted automatically in formulas that refer to certain cell ranges in the table.

4.2 Apply *Conditional Formatting* rules as well as *Color Scales, Icon Sets,* and *Data Bars* (p. E4-228).

- *Conditional formatting* formats only cells that meet specified criteria.
- *Highlight Cells Rules* use relational or comparison operators such as *Greater Than* or *Equals* to determine which cells are formatted.
- *Top/Bottom Rules* use ranking or averages to format cells.
- In the *New Rule* dialog box, you can create a rule that uses a formula to determine which cells are formatted.
- *Data visualization* uses rules to format cells with *Icon Sets, Color Scales,* or *Data Bars.*
- You can edit any conditional formatting rule with the *Manage Rules* command.
- Conditional formatting can be removed from a selected cell range or from the entire sheet with the *Clear Rules* command.

4.3 Sort data by one or more columns or by attribute (p. E4-234).

- *Sorting* is a process that arranges data in order, either *ascending* (A to Z) or *descending* (Z to A).
- Data can be sorted by one or by multiple columns.
- For a single column sort, use the *Sort A to Z* or *Sort Z to A* button in the *Sort & Filter* group on the *Data* tab.
- For a multiple column sort, use the *Sort* dialog box by clicking the *Sort* button on the *Data* tab.
- You can perform a multiple column sort within the data by sorting in lowest to highest sort priority.
- From the *Sort* dialog box, data can also be sorted by cell attribute including font color, cell color, or cell icon.
- Data in an Excel table can be sorted from the *AutoFilter* arrows with labels in the header row.

4.4 Filter data by using *AutoFilters* and by creating an *Advanced Filter* (p. E4-238).

- The *Filter* button [*Data* tab, *Sort & Filter* group] displays an *AutoFilter* arrow for each column heading in list-type data.
- From an *AutoFilter* arrow, you can select records to be shown or hidden or build a custom filter.
- A custom *AutoFilter* uses operators such as *Equals* or *Greater Than* as well as AND and OR conditions.
- An *Advanced Filter* provides filter options such as using a formula in the filter definition.
- An *Advanced Filter* requires a criteria range in the same workbook and can display filtered results separate from the data.

4.5 Use subtotals, groups, and outlines for tabular data in a worksheet (p. E4-242).

- The *Subtotal* command inserts summary rows for sorted data using *SUM* or a statistical function.
- The *Subtotal* command formats the data as an *outline,* which groups records so that they can be displayed or hidden.

E4-267

- Outline buttons appear next to row and column headings and determine the level of detail shown in the data.
- An **Auto Outline** creates groups based on formulas that are located in a consistent pattern in a list.
- Groups can be defined by sorting data, inserting blank rows, and using the *Group* button in the *Outline* group on the *Data* tab.

4.6 Import data into an Excel worksheet from a text file, a database file, and other sources (p. E4-248).

- To save time and increase accuracy, you can **import** text files into a worksheet.
- Common text file formats include *.txt* (text) and *.csv* (comma separated values).
- Data in a text file is **delimited** or **fixed width.**
- The **Text Import Wizard** guides you through the steps of importing data.
- You can copy data from a Word document into a worksheet.
- From a **Microsoft Access database,** you can import a table or a query into a worksheet.
- If a web site has table-formatted data, you can use the *From Web* command on the *Data* tab to import data into a worksheet.
- Data that has been imported from a command in the *Get External Data* group establishes a data connection so that the data can be refreshed.
- The **Flash Fill** command recognizes and copies typing actions from one or more cells and suggests data for the remaining rows in the same column.

4.7 Export Excel data as a text file and into a Word document (p. E4-254).

- Data in a worksheet can be exported for use in another program or application.
- Excel data can be exported as a text file.
- Text file formats can be tab-, space-, or comma-delimited.
- The Windows or Office *Clipboard* can be used to copy data from Excel into Word and other programs.

4.8 Build and format a *PivotTable* (p. E4-258).

- A **PivotTable** is a cross-tabulated summary report on its own worksheet.
- When a *PivotTable* is active, the *PivotTable Tools Analyze* and *Design* tabs are available.
- When any cell in a *PivotTable* is selected, the *PivotTable Fields* pane is open on the right side of the window.
- The *PivotTable Fields* pane includes a list of available fields and areas in the report in which the fields can be positioned.
- You can drag field names in the *PivotTable Fields* pane to reposition them and analyze data from a different perspective.
- Fields in a *PivotTable* can be modified and formatted from the *Field Settings* dialog box.
- *PivotTables* can be formatted from the *PivotTable Tools Design* tab, and selected cells can be formatted from the *Home* tab.
- A **PivotChart** is a chart based on a *PivotTable* with the same features as the *PivotTable.*

Check for Understanding

The SIMbook for this text (within your SIMnet account) provides the following resources for concept review:

- Multiple choice questions
- Matching exercises
- Short answer questions

Guided Project 4-1

For this project, you import a text file to complete the inventory worksheet for Wear-Ever Shoes. You use *Flash Fill* to enter product codes and sort the data by supplier and code. You use *AutoFilter* for several tasks, format data as an Excel table, prepare subtotals, build a *PivotTable,* and export data as a text file.
[Student Learning Outcomes 4.1, 4.2, 4.3, 4.4, 4.5, 4.6, 4.7, 4.8]

Files Needed: ***WearEver-04.xlsx*** and ***WearEver-04.txt*** *[Student data files are available in the Library of your SIMnet account.]*
Completed Project File Names: *[your initials] Excel 4-1.xlsx* and *[your initials] Excel 4-1.txt*

Skills Covered in This Project

- Import a text file.
- Use *Flash Fill* to complete data.
- Sort data.
- Use an *AutoFilter*.

- Set conditional formatting.
- Create an Excel table.
- Use the *Subtotal* command.
- Create and format a *PivotTable*.
- Export data as a tab-delimited file.

1. Open the ***WearEver-04*** workbook from your student data files and save it as [your initials] Excel 4-1.

2. Import a text file.
   a. Select cell **I4**.
   b. Click the **From Text** button [*Data* tab, *Get External Data* group].
   c. Find and select the ***WearEver-04.txt*** file from your student data files in the *Import Text File* window.
   d. Click **Import**.
   e. Verify that the **Delimited** button is selected in the first *Wizard* window and click **Next**.
   f. Verify that the **Tab** box is selected and click **Next**.
   g. Do not change any formats and click **Finish**.
   h. Click **OK** in the *Import Data* dialog box. The supplier name and phone number are imported and added to the list.

3. Use the **Format Painter** button to copy formatting from cell **H4** to cells **I4:J4**.

4. *AutoFit* columns **I:J**.

5. Select cells **A1:J2** and click the **Launcher** in the *Alignment* group [*Home* tab]. From the *Horizontal* list, choose **Center Across Selection**.

6. Use *Flash Fill* to insert product codes.
   a. Insert a column between columns **B** and **C**.
   b. Type Code in cell **C4**.
   c. Type RHB in cell **C5**.
   d. Type r and press **Enter** in cell **C6**. Regular *AutoComplete* completes the entries based on what is already in the column.
   e. In cell **C7**, type r and press **Enter**.

f. Click the **Fill** button [*Home* tab, *Editing* group]. The *Flash Fill* suggestion list did not appear because there is no recognizable pattern.

g. Choose **Flash Fill**.

h. *AutoFit* column **C**.

7. Sort data in multiple columns.

a. Click cell **A5**.

b. Click the **Sort** button [*Data* tab, *Sort & Filter* group].

c. Select the **My data has headers** box, if necessary.

d. Click the **Sort by** arrow and choose **Supplier**.

e. Verify that **Values** is selected for *Sort On*.

f. Choose **A to Z** for *Order*.

g. Click **Add Level**.

h. Click the **Then by** arrow and choose **Code**.

i. Verify that **Values** is selected for *Sort On* and that **A to Z** is selected for *Order*.

j. Click **OK** (Figure 4-71).

8. Apply conditional formatting.

a. Select cells **F5:F40**, the quantity in stock.

b. Click the **Conditional Formatting** button [*Home* tab, *Style* group].

c. Click **Highlight Cells Rules** and select **Less Than**.

d. Type 2 in the *Format cells that are LESS THAN* box.

e. Click **OK** to accept the *Light Red Fill with Dark Red Text* format.

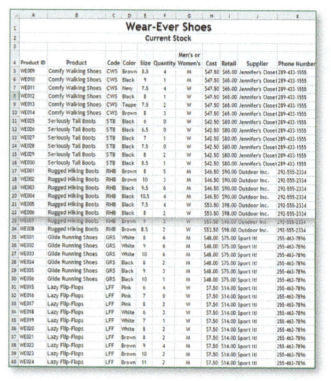

4-71 Data sorted by "Supplier" and "Code"

9. Use an *AutoFilter*.

a. Click cell **A5**.

b. Click the **Filter** button [*Data* tab, *Sort & Filter* group].

c. Click the *AutoFilter* arrow for the **Supplier** column.

d. Deselect the **(Select All)** box to remove all the check marks.

e. Select the **Jennifer's Closet** box.

f. Click **OK**. The data is filtered to show only records from one supplier.

10. Copy the **Inventory** worksheet to the right and name the copy Women's. Set the tab color to **Gold, Accent 4**.

11. Clear a filter and conditional formatting.

a. On the **Women's** sheet, click the *AutoFilter* arrow for the **Supplier** column.

b. Select **Clear Filter from "Supplier."**

c. Click the **Filter** button [*Data* tab, *Sort & Filter* group] to hide the *AutoFilter* arrows.

d. Click the **Conditional Formatting** button [*Home* tab, *Style* group].

e. Select **Clear Rules** and select **Clear Rules From Entire Sheet**.

12. Create an Excel table.

a. Select cells **A4:K40** on the **Women's** sheet.

b. Click the **Format as Table** button [*Home* tab, *Styles* group].

c. Choose **Table Style Medium 5** in the *Table Styles* gallery.

d. Confirm the range in the *Format as Table* dialog box and click **OK**.

e. Select **Yes** in the message box to remove the data connection (Figure 4-72).

13. Add a calculated column to a table.

a. Insert a column at column **J**.

b. Type Markup in cell **J4** and press **Enter**.

c. Type = in cell **J5** to start the formula and click cell **I5**.

d. Type − for subtraction and click cell **H5**.

e. Press **Enter** to copy the formula.

14. Filter data in a table.

a. Click the *AutoFilter* arrow for the **Men's or Women's** column.

b. Deselect the **(Select All)** box to remove all the check marks.

c. Select the **W** box and click **OK**.

d. Press **Ctrl+Home** (Figure 4-73).

15. Copy the **Inventory** worksheet to the end and name the copy Subtotals. Set the tab color to **Orange**, **Accent 6**.

16. Clear a filter and conditional formatting.

a. On the **Subtotals** sheet, clear the filter for the **Supplier**.

b. Click the **Filter** button [*Data* tab, *Sort & Filter* group] to hide the *AutoFilter* arrows.

c. Click the **Conditional Formatting** button [*Home* tab, *Style* group] and clear rules from the sheet.

17. Use the *Subtotal* command.

a. On the **Subtotals** sheet, select cell **J5**. The records are sorted by the "Supplier" column.

b. Click the **Subtotal** button [*Data* tab, *Outline* group].

c. Click the **At each change in** arrow and choose **Supplier**.

d. Click the **Use function** arrow and choose **Count**.

e. Check the **Supplier** box in the *Add subtotal to* area.

f. Deselect any other selected fields in the *Add subtotal to* list (Figure 4-74).

g. Click **OK**. A subtotal row displays at the bottom of each group and shows how many products are available from each supplier.

h. Format the label in cell **I17** as **right-aligned**.

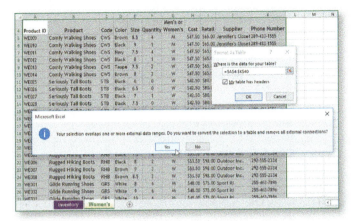

4-72 Data connection will be removed to create the table

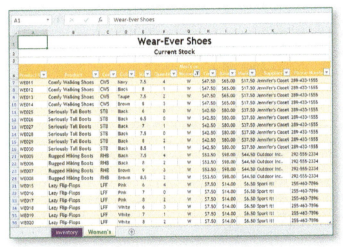

4-73 Table filtered to show women's products

4-74 *Subtotal* dialog box to count number of products by supplier

i. **Right-align** the remaining subtotal labels in column **I** (Figure 4-75).

18. Create a *PivotTable*.
    a. Click the **Inventory** sheet tab and select cell **A5**.
    b. Click the **PivotTable** button [*Insert* tab, *Tables* group].
    c. Verify that the *Table/Range* is **$A$4:$K$40** in the *Create PivotTable* dialog box and that the *New Worksheet* button is selected (Figure 4-76).
    d. Click **OK**. A blank *PivotTable* layout displays on a new sheet.

19. Add fields in a *PivotTable*.
    a. Select the **Product** box in the *PivotTable Fields* pane to place it in the *Rows* area.
    b. Select the **Quantity** box to place it in the *Values* area.
    c. Drag the **Supplier** field name into the *Columns* area.

20. Format a *PivotTable*.
    a. Click the **More** button in the *PivotTable Styles* group [*PivotTable Tools Design* tab].
    b. Select **PivotTable Style Medium 7**.
    c. Select the **Banded Rows** box [*PivotTable Tools Design* tab, *PivotTable Style Options* group].
    d. Select the **Banded Columns** box [*PivotTable Tools Design* tab, *PivotTable Style Options* group] (Figure 4-77).
    e. Name the sheet PivotTable.

21. Copy the **Inventory** worksheet to the end and do not rename it.

22. On the copied sheet, clear the filter from the **Supplier** column and remove the *AutoFilter* arrows.

23. Export data as a tab-delimited file.
    a. Click cell **A1** in the copied sheet.
    b. Click the **File** tab and select **Export**.
    c. Select **Change File Type**.
    d. Select **Text (Tab delimited)** as the file type.
    e. Click **Save As**.
    f. Navigate to the save location for the exported data in the *Save as type* dialog box.
    g. Type Excel 4-1 as the file name.

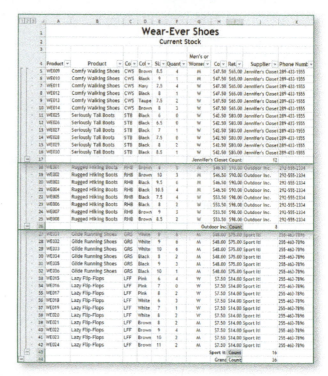

4-75 Subtotals inserted for each group

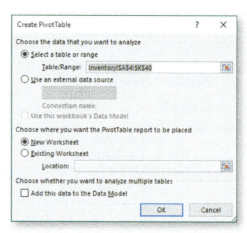

4-76 *Create PivotTable* dialog box

Sum of Quantity	Column Labels			
Row Labels	Jennifer's Closet	Outdoor Inc.	Sport it!	Grand Total
Comfy Walking Shoes	15			15
Glide Running Shoes			24	24
Lazy Flip-Flops			22	22
Rugged Hiking Boots		29		29
Seriously Tall Boots	4			4
Grand Total	19	29	46	94

4-77 Formatted *PivotTable*

h. Click **Save**.

i. Click **OK** in the message box to save only the current sheet (Figure 4-78).

Microsoft Excel   ✕

⚠ The selected file type does not support workbooks that contain multiple sheets.

• To save only the active sheet, click OK.
• To save all sheets, save them individually using a different file name for each, or choose a file type that supports multiple sheets.

[OK]   [Cancel]

4-78 Only the current sheet is saved as a text file

j. Click **Yes** in the message box about features being lost. The sheet is renamed and the data is exported to a *.txt* file.

24. Save the workbook with the same file name.

a. Click the **File** tab and choose **Save As**.

b. Navigate to the folder for saved work.

c. Select **Excel Workbook** as the *Save as type* in the *Save As* dialog box.

d. Select *[your initials] Excel 4-1* from the list.

e. Click **Save** and select **Yes** to replace the *.xlsx* file that you saved at the beginning of this project.

f. Close the workbook (Figure 4-79).

	A	B	C	D	E	F	G	H	I	J	K
1				**Wear-Ever Shoes**							
2				**Current Stock**							
3											
4	Product ▾	Product ▾	Co ▾	Col ▾	Siz ▾	Quant ▾	Men's or Womer ▾	Co ▾	Ret ▾	Supplier ⊤	Phone Numb ▾
5	WE009	Comfy Walking Shoes	CWS	Brown	8.5	4	M	$47.50	$65.00	Jennifer's Closet	289-433-1555
6	WE010	Comfy Walking Shoes	CWS	Black	9	1	M	$47.50	$65.00	Jennifer's Closet	289-433-1555
7	WE011	Comfy Walking Shoes	CWS	Navy	7.5	4	W	$47.50	$65.00	Jennifer's Closet	289-433-1555
8	WE012	Comfy Walking Shoes	CWS	Black	8	1	W	$47.50	$65.00	Jennifer's Closet	289-433-1555
9	WE013	Comfy Walking Shoes	CWS	Taupe	7.5	2	W	$47.50	$65.00	Jennifer's Closet	289-433-1555
10	WE014	Comfy Walking Shoes	CWS	Brown	8	3	W	$47.50	$65.00	Jennifer's Closet	289-433-1555
11	WE025	Seriously Tall Boots	STB	Black	6	0	W	$42.50	$80.00	Jennifer's Closet	289-433-1555
12	WE026	Seriously Tall Boots	STB	Black	6.5	0	W	$42.50	$80.00	Jennifer's Closet	289-433-1555
13	WE027	Seriously Tall Boots	STB	Black	7	1	W	$42.50	$80.00	Jennifer's Closet	289-433-1555
14	WE028	Seriously Tall Boots	STB	Black	7.5	0	W	$42.50	$80.00	Jennifer's Closet	289-433-1555
15	WE029	Seriously Tall Boots	STB	Black	8	2	W	$42.50	$80.00	Jennifer's Closet	289-433-1555
16	WE030	Seriously Tall Boots	STB	Black	8.5	1	W	$42.50	$80.00	Jennifer's Closet	289-433-1555
41											

4-79 Excel 4-1 completed inventory worksheet

Guided Project 4-2

Classic Gardens and Landscapes is building a workbook with data about revenue and promotion campaigns. You copy data from Word and import data from an Access database. You set conditional formatting, format an Excel table, sort and filter data, and build a *PivotTable* and *PivotChart*.
[Student Learning Outcomes 4.1, 4.2, 4.3, 4.4, 4.5, 4.6, 4.7, 4.8]

Files Needed: ***ClassicGardens-04.xlsx***, ***Database-04.accdb***, and ***ClassicGardens-04.docx*** *[Student data files are available in the* Library *of your SIMnet account.]*
Completed Project File Names: *[your initials] Excel 4-2.xlsx* and *[your initials] Excel 4-2.csv*

Skills Covered in This Project

- Copy data from Word.
- Use conditional formatting with an icon set.
- Prepare data for an *Auto Outline*.
- Import a table from a database file.
- Apply a table style and show a total row.
- Sort and filter data in a table.
- Build and format a *PivotTable*.
- Build a *PivotChart*.
- Filter data in a *PivotChart*.
- Export data as a comma-separated text file.

1. Open the **ClassicGardens-04** workbook from your student data files and save it as [your initials] Excel 4-2.

2. Select the **Quarterly** sheet; insert six columns between columns **G** and **H**.

3. Copy data from Word.
    a. Open the Word document **ClassicGardens-04. docx** from your student data files.
    b. Select all the data in Word and copy it.
    c. Select cell **H4** in the Excel workbook.
    d. Click the **Paste** button arrow [*Home* tab, *Clipboard* group] and choose **Match Destination Formatting**.
    e. Select cell **N5** and click the **AutoSum** button [*Home* tab, *Editing* group].
    f. Verify or select the range **B5:M5** and press **Enter**.
    g. Double-click the *Fill* handle for cell **N5** to copy the formula to cells **N6:N10**.
    h. Select cells **H10:M10** and click the **AutoSum** button [*Home* tab, *Editing* group].

4. Apply conditional formatting.
    a. Select cells **N5:N9**.
    b. Click the **Quick Analysis** button.
    c. Verify that **Formatting** is selected.
    d. Choose **Icon Set** (Figure 4-80).The cells display an icon to represent the upper, middle, or lower values of the range.

5. *AutoFit* the columns and make sure all data is visible.

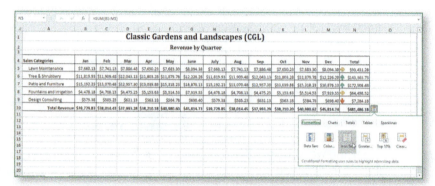

4-80 Icon set conditional formatting

6. Click the **AutoOutline** sheet tab.

7. Use *AutoSum* to calculate subtotals and totals.
    a. Select cells **E5:E18**, press **Ctrl** and select cells **I5:I18**, **M5:M18**, and **Q5:Q18** (Figure 4-81).
    b. Click the **AutoSum** button [*Home* tab, *Editing* group].
    c. Select cells **R5:R18** and click the **AutoSum** button [*Home* tab, *Editing* group]. Excel sums the *Qtr 1, Qtr 2, Qtr 3,* and *Qtr 4* columns.
    d. Select cells **B19:R19** and click the **AutoSum** button [*Home* tab, *Editing* group].
    e. *AutoFit* columns as needed.
    f. Select cells **E21:E25**, press **Ctrl** and select cells **I21:I25**, **M21:M25**, and **Q21:Q25**.
    g. Click the **AutoSum** button [*Home* tab, *Editing* group].

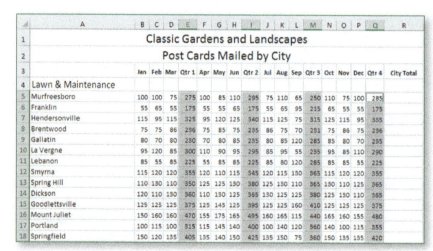

4-81 SUM function used in a consistent pattern

h. Use *AutoSum* in cells **R21:R25**, in cells **E28:E33**, **I28:I33**, **M28:M33**, **Q28:Q33**, and in cells **R28:R33** to complete the worksheet.

i. *AutoFit* the columns.

8. In cell **B35**, type **=** to start a formula.

9. Click cell **B19**, type **+**, click cell **B26**, type **+**, click cell **B34**, and press **Enter**. The formula is **=B19+ B26+B34**.

10. Copy the formula in cell **B35** to cells **C35:R35**. *AutoFit* the columns, if necessary.

11. Create an *Auto Outline*.

a. Click cell **B5**.

b. Click the arrow for the **Group** button [*Data* tab, *Outline* group] and choose **Auto Outline** (Figure 4-82). The *Auto Outline* command uses column and row formulas to group the data.

c. Click the **Level 2** column outline button (above the column headings).Only the quarter totals display (Figure 4-83).

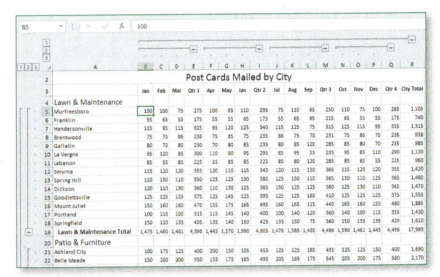

4-82 *AutoOutline* with three row levels and three column levels

12. Import a table from an Access database.

a. Click the **Table** sheet tab.

b. Select cell **A4**.

c. Click the **From Access** button [*Data* tab, *Get External Data* group].

d. Find and select **Database-04.accdb** from your student data files in the *Select Data Source* window.

e. Click **Open**.

f. Click **tblMailings** in the *Select Table* dialog box (Figure 4-84).

g. Click **OK**.

h. Select **Table** and **Existing worksheet** if necessary and click **OK**.

13. Apply a table style and show a total row.

a. Click cell **B5** in the table.

b. Click the **More** button [*Table Tools Design* tab, *Table Styles* group].

c. Choose **Table Style Medium 15**.

d. Select the **Total Row** box [*Table Tools Design* tab, *Table Style Options* group].

e. Click cell **C30** and choose **Sum**. Then copy the formula to cells **D30:M30**.

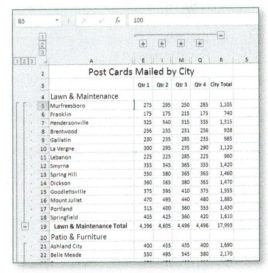

4-83 Outline collapsed at Level 2 column group

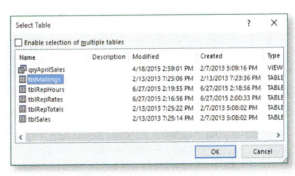

4-84 *Select Table* dialog box for an Access database

14. Sort and filter data in an Excel table.
    a. Click the *AutoFilter* arrow for **City**.
    b. Choose **Sort A to Z**.
    c. Click the *AutoFilter* arrow for **City**.
    d. Select **Text Filters** and **Equals**.
    e. Type c* in the first criteria box to select cities that begin with "C."
    f. Select the **Or** radio button.
    g. Verify that **equals** is selected as the second operator.
    h. Type m* in the second criteria box to select cities that begin with "M" (Figure 4-85).
    i. Click **OK**.

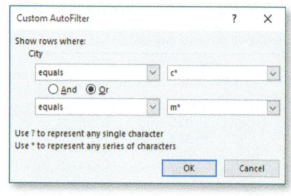

4-85 *Custom AutoFilter* for cities that begin with "C" or "M"

15. Merge and center the labels in rows **1:2** and set them to a font size of **18 pt**. (Figure 4-86).

16. Select the **Pivot Source** sheet tab.

17. Create a *PivotTable*.
    a. Select cell **A5**.
    b. Click the **Recommended PivotTables** button [*Insert* tab, *Tables* group].
    c. Select the **Sum of # of Responses by Department** thumbnail and click **OK**.
    d. Select the **City** and **# Mailed** boxes in the *Choose fields to add to report* area to add them to the report.
    e. Drag the **Department** field from the *Rows* area to the *Filters* area in the *PivotTable Fields* pane (Figure 4-87).

ID	City	Jan	Feb	Mar	Apr	May	Jun	Jul	Aug	Sep	Oct	Nov	Dec
18	Carthage	75	85	95	95	125	100	110	105	105	110	95	125
19	Centerville	150	100	85	100	85	150	85	150	100	85	85	85
20	Charlotte	150	175	205	175	215	135	205	175	255	135	205	205
21	Coopertown	150	225	200	235	200	145	195	250	200	145	200	235
22	Cross Plains	200	200	210	200	215	210	210	200	265	215	210	210
12	Mount Juliet	150	160	160	155	175	165	160	165	115	165	160	155
1	Murfreesboro	100	100	75	100	85	110	75	110	65	110	75	100
Total		975	1045	1030	1060	1100	1015	1040	1155	1105	965	1030	1115

4-86 Imported data sorted and filtered

18. Format a *PivotTable*.
    a. Right-click cell **B4** and select **Value Field Settings** from the context menu.
    b. Click **Number Format**.
    c. Choose **Number** as the *Category*.
    d. Select zero decimal places.
    e. Select the **Use 1000 Separator (,)** box.
    f. Click **OK** to close each dialog box.
    g. Apply the same number format for "Sum of # Mailed" field.
    h. Click the **More** button [*PivotTable Tools Design* tab, *PivotTable Styles* group].
    i. Select **PivotTable Style Medium 9** [*PivotTable Tools Design* tab, *PivotTable Styles* group].
    j. Select the **Banded Rows** box [*PivotTable Tools Design* tab, *PivotTable Styles Options* group].

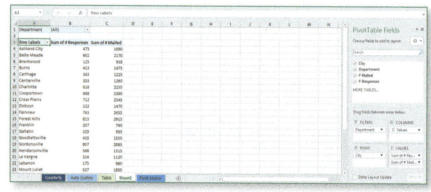

4-87 *PivotTable* layout

k. Select the **Banded Columns** box [*PivotTable Tools Design* tab, *PivotTable Styles Options* group] (Figure 4-88).

19. Create and format a *PivotChart*.
    a. Click the **PivotChart** button [*PivotTable Tools Analyze* tab, *Tools* group].
    b. Select **Bar** as the chart type and **Clustered Bar** as the subtype.
    c. Click **OK**.
    d. Position the chart object so that its top-left corner is at cell **E3**.
    e. Drag the bottom-right selection handle to reach cell **O24**.
    f. Click the **More** button [*PivotChart Tools Design* tab, *Chart Styles* group].
    g. Choose **Style 5**.
    h. Click the **Shape Outline** button [*PivotChart Tools Format* tab, *Shape Styles* group].
    i. Select **Blue, Accent 1**.

20. Filter data in a *PivotChart*.
    a. Click the **Department** filter button in the chart.
    b. Select the **Select Multiple Items** box.
    c. Deselect the **(All)** box.
    d. Select the **Landscape Design** box and click **OK**.
    e. Select cell **A13** to deselect the *PivotTable* and *PivotChart* (Figure 4-89).
    f. Name the sheet PivotTable.

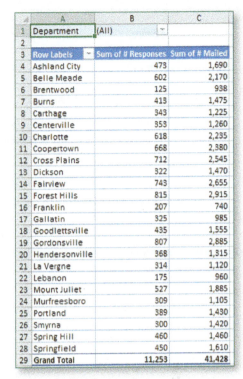

4-88 Formatted *PivotTable*

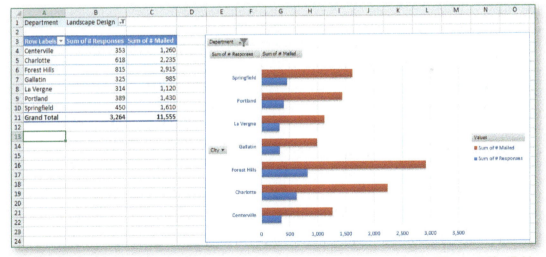

4-89 Filtered data in *PivotChart* and *PivotTable*

21. Export data as a comma-separated file.
    a. Click the **Quarterly** sheet tab.
    b. Click the **File** tab and select **Export**.
    c. Select **Change File Type**.
    d. Select **CSV (Comma delimited)** as the file type.
    e. Click **Save As**.
    f. Navigate to the save location for the exported data in the *Save as type* dialog box.

g. Type Excel 4-2 as the file name.

h. Click **Save**.

i. Click **OK** in the message box to save the current sheet.

j. Click **Yes** in the message box about lost features. The sheet is renamed and the data is exported to a .csv file.

k. Rename the sheet as Quarterly.

22. Save the workbook with the same file name.

a. Click the **File** tab and choose **Save As**.

b. Navigate to the folder for saved work.

c. Select **Excel Workbook** as the *Save as type* in the *Save As* dialog box.

d. Select *[your initials] Excel 4-2* from the list.

e. Click **Save** and click **Yes** to replace the file.

23. Save and close the workbook. Close Word.

Guided Project 4-3

Clemenson Imaging analyzes expense reports from field representatives as well as patient and image data. To complete the worksheets, you format data as a table and build an advanced filter. You import a comma-separated text file (.csv) and use the *Subtotal* command. Finally, you display data in a *PivotTable*.

[**Student Learning Outcomes 4.1, 4.2, 4.3, 4.4, 4.5, 4.6, 4.7, 4.8**]

Files Needed: ***ClemensonImaging-04.xlsx, ClemensonImaging-04.csv,*** and ***ClemensonImaging.docx***
[Student data files are available in the Library *of your SIMnet account.]*
Completed Project File Names: *[your initials] Excel 4-3.xlsx* and *[your initials] Excel 4-3.docx*

Skills Covered in This Project

- Format data as an Excel table.
- Build an *Advanced Filter*.
- Apply conditional formatting to filtered results.
- Sort data by multiple columns.
- Import a comma-separated text file.
- Use the *Subtotal* command.
- Export data via the *Clipboard*.
- Create a *PivotTable*.

1. Open the ***ClemensonImaging-04*** workbook from your student data files and save it as [your initials] Excel 4-3.

2. Copy the **Past&Projected** sheet before the **Criteria** sheet and name the copied sheet Adv Filter.

3. Create and format an Excel table.

a. Select cells **A4:E60** on the **Adv Filter** sheet.

b. Click the **Quick Analysis** tool and choose **Tables**.

c. Click **Table**.

4. Apply a table style.

a. Click cell **A5** in the table.

b. Click the **More** button [*Table Tools Design* tab, *Table Styles* group].

c. Select **Table Style Medium 15**.

5. Create an output range for an *Advanced Filter.*
   a. Select cells **A4:E4** and copy and paste them to cell **G4**.
   b. Type Extract Range in cell **G3** and set the font to **Cambria 16 pt**.
   c. Adjust column widths to show the labels.

6. Create an *Advanced Filter.*
   a. Click the **Criteria** sheet tab.
   b. Type >12/31/16 in cell **A3** to find records after 2016.
   c. Type mri in cell **B3**.
   d. Type >12/31/14 in cell **A4** to find records after 2014.
   e. Type ct scan in cell **B4**. This criteria will find records dated 2017 or later for MRIs *and* records for CT scans after 2014 (Figure 4-90).

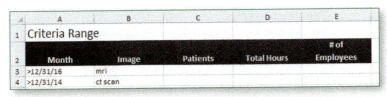

4-90 Criteria for *Advanced Filter*

   f. Click cell **A5** on the **Adv Filter** sheet.
   g. Click the **Advanced** button [*Data* tab, *Sort & Filter* group].
   h. Select the **Copy to another location** radio button.
   i. Verify that the **List range** is cells **A4:E60**. If the range is incorrect, click and drag to select the range including the header row.
   j. Click the **Criteria range** box and select cells **A2:B4** on the **Criteria** sheet.
   k. Click the **Copy to** box and select cells **G4:K4**.
   l. Click **OK** in the *Advanced Filter* dialog box.

7. Sort data in the output range.
   a. Right-click cell **H5**, choose **Sort**, and select **Sort A to Z**.
   b. Right-click cell **G5**, choose **Sort**, and select **Sort Oldest to Newest**. This sorts the results by date, earliest date first.

8. Apply conditional formatting and borders.
   a. Select cells **I5:I14**.
   b. Click the **Conditional Formatting** button [*Home* tab, *Styles* group].
   c. Choose **Highlight Cells Rules** and **Greater Than**.
   d. Type 750 and choose **Green Fill with Dark Green Text**.
   e. Click **OK**.
   f. Select cells **G5:K14** and apply **All Borders** (Figure 4-91).
   g. Press **Ctrl+Home**.

Extract Range				
Month	Image	Patients	Total Hours	# of Employees
Apr 2015	CT Scan	1000	1800	5
Aug 2015	CT Scan	500	2400	3
Dec 2015	CT Scan	500	2400	2
Apr 2016	CT Scan	500	2400	3
Aug 2016	CT Scan	750	2400	3
Dec 2016	CT Scan	500	1800	4
Jan 2017	MRI	1000	1800	3
Apr 2017	CT Scan	750	2400	2
May 2017	MRI	750	3000	4
Aug 2017	CT Scan	500	2400	3

4-91 *Advanced Filter* results

9. Import a comma-separated values text file.
   a. Click the **Expense Info** sheet tab.
   b. Select cell **A5**.
   c. Click the **From Text** button [*Data* tab, *Get External Data* group].
   d. Find and select the **ClemensonImaging-04.csv** file from your student data files in the *Import Text File* window.
   e. Click **Import**.
   f. Select the **Delimited** button in the first *Wizard* window and click **Next**.
   g. Deselect the **Tab** box and select the **Comma** box.
   h. Click **Next**.
   i. Click the date column in the *Data preview* area in the third *Wizard* window.
   j. Click the **Date** radio button in the *Column data format* group (Figure 4-92).

k. Click **Finish**, deselect the **Add this data to the Data Model** box in the *Import Data* dialog box, and click **OK**.

l. Select columns **A:D** and size each column to **12.14 (90 pixels)** wide.

m. Deselect the columns.

10. Use the *Subtotal* command.

a. Click cell **A5**.

b. Click the **Sort A to Z** button [*Data* tab, *Sort & Filter* group] to sort by last name.

c. Click the **Subtotal** button [*Data* tab, *Outline* group].

d. Verify that **Last Name** is selected for **At each change in**.

e. Click the **Use function** arrow and choose **Average**.

f. Check the **Amount** box in the *Add subtotal to* area.

g. Click **OK**.

h. Format the values in column **D** as **Currency** with zero decimal places.

11. Collapse outline groups.

a. Click the collapse symbol (−) for Allen in row **8**.

b. Click the collapse symbol (−) for McAllister (Figure 4-93).

12. Create a *PivotTable*.

a. Click the **Past&Projected** sheet tab.

b. Select cells **A4:E60**.

c. Click the **Quick Analysis** tool and choose **Tables**.

d. Point to each *PivotTable* option to see the *Live Preview*.

e. Choose the option that shows a sum of the employees, the total hours, and the patients (Figure 4-94).

f. Rename the sheet PivotTable.

g. Drag the **Month** field in the *Rows* area in the *PivotTable Fields* pane out of the pane and into the worksheet.

4-92 *Text Import Wizard* to set format

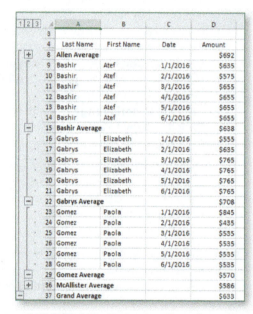

4-93 Subtotals added and outline collapsed for two groups

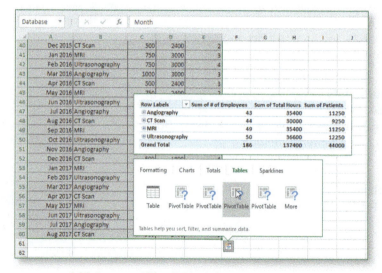

4-94 Suggested *PivotTable* choices from the *Quick Analysis* tool

13. Format a *PivotTable*.
   a. Click cell **C4**.
   b. Click the **Field Settings** button [*PivotTable Tools Analyze* tab, *Active Field* group].
   c. Click **Number Format**.
   d. Choose **Number** as the *Category*.
   e. Select the **Use 1000 Separator (,)** box and set zero decimal places.
   f. Click **OK** to close each dialog box.
   g. Apply the same number format for the "Sum of Patients" field.
   h. Click the **More** button [*PivotTable Tools Design* tab, *PivotTable Styles* group].
   i. Select **PivotTable Style Dark 9** [*PivotTable Tools Design* tab, *PivotTable Styles* group].
   j. Select the **Banded Rows** box [*PivotTable Tools Design* tab, *PivotTable Styles Options* group].
   k. Select the **Banded Columns** box [*PivotTable Tools Design* tab, *PivotTable Styles Options* group] (Figure 4-95).

14. Create and format a *PivotChart*.
   a. Click the **PivotChart** button [*PivotTable Tools Analyze* tab, *Tools* group].
   b. Select **Bar** as the chart type and **Stacked Bar** as the subtype.
   c. Click **OK**.
   d. Position the chart object so that its top-left corner is at cell **A12**.
   e. Drag the bottom-right selection handle to reach cell **J30**.
   f. Click the **More** button [*PivotChart Tools Design* tab, *Chart Styles* group] and choose **Style 8**.
   g. Click the **Change Colors** button [*PivotChart Tools Design* tab, *Chart Styles* group].
   h. Select **Color 5** in the *Monochromatic* group.
   i. Deselect the **# of Employees** box in the *PivotChart Fields* pane (Figure 4-96).
   j. Click cell **A1**.

	A	B	C	D
1				
2				
3	Row Labels	Sum of # of	Sum of Total Hours	Sum of Patients
4	Angiography	43	35,400	11,250
5	CT Scan	44	30,000	9,250
6	MRI	49	35,400	11,250
7	Ultrasonography	50	36,600	12,250
8	Grand Total	186	137,400	44,000

4-95 *PivotTable* with new settings

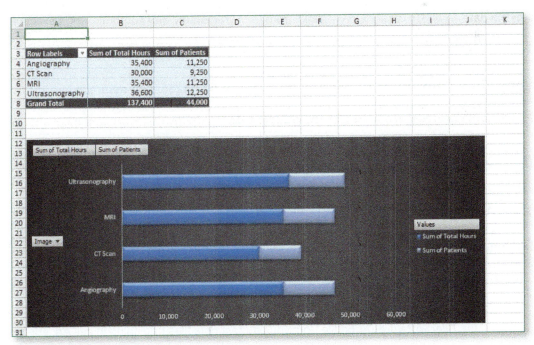

4-96 *PivotChart* object

15. Export data using the *Clipboard*.
    a. Click the **Adv Filter** sheet tab.
    b. Select cells **G4:K14** and click the **Copy** button [*Home* tab, *Clipboard* group].
    c. Open the **ClemensonImaging-04** Word document from your student data files.
    d. Press **Ctrl+End** to position the insertion point.
    e. Click the arrow with the **Paste** button [*Home* tab, *Clipboard* group] and choose **Paste Special**.
    f. Select **Microsoft Excel Worksheet Object** in the *Paste Special* dialog box.
    g. Select the **Paste link** radio button in the *Paste Special* dialog box and click **OK**.
    h. Click the **Center** button [*Home* tab, *Paragraph* group].
    i. Save the Word document as *[your initials] Excel 4-3* in your usual folder (Figure 4-97).
    j. Close Word.

16. Save and close the Excel workbook.

4-97 Word document with pasted Excel object

Independent Project 4-4

Eller Software Services has received contract revenue information in a text file. You import, sort, and filter the data. You also create a *PivotTable,* prepare a worksheet with subtotals, and format related data as an Excel table.
[**Student Learning Outcomes 4.1, 4.3, 4.4, 4.5, 4.6, 4.8**]

Files Needed: ***EllerSoftware-04.xlsx*** and ***EllerSoftware-04.txt*** [*Student data files are available in the Library of your SIMnet account.*]
Completed Project File Name: ***[your initials] Excel 4-4.xlsx***

Skills Covered in This Project

- Import a text file.
- Use *AutoFilters*.
- Sort data by multiple columns.
- Create a *PivotTable*.

- Format fields in a *PivotTable*.
- Use the *Subtotal* command.
- Format data in an Excel table.
- Sort data in an Excel table.

1. Open the ***EllerSoftware-04*** workbook from your student data files and save it as [your initials] Excel 4-4.

2. Import the ***EllerSoftware-04.txt*** file from your student data files beginning in cell **A4**. The text file has a header row and is tab-delimited.

3. Format the values in column **H** as **Currency** with zero decimal places.

4. Click cell **G4** and show *AutoFilter* arrows.

5. Use the *AutoFilter* arrow to sort by date with the earliest date first. Then use the *AutoFilter* arrow to sort by product/service name in ascending order.

6. Filter the *Date* column to show only contracts for **September** using the **All Dates in the Period** option.

7. Select cells **A1:H2** and press **Ctrl+1** to open the *Format Cells* dialog box. On the *Alignment* tab, choose **Center Across Selection**.

8. Change the font size for cells **A1:H2** to **20 pt** (Figure 4-98).

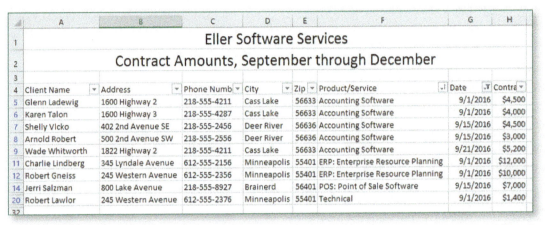

4-98 Imported data sorted and filtered

9. Copy the **Contracts** sheet to the end and name the copy Data.

10. Clear the date filter and hide the *AutoFilter* arrows.

11. Select cell **A5** and click the **PivotTable** button [*Insert* tab] to create a blank *PivotTable* layout on its own sheet named PivotTable.

12. Show the **Product/Service** and **Contract** fields in the *PivotTable*.

13. Drag the **Contract** field from the *Choose fields to add to report* area below the **Sum of Contract** field in the *Values* area so that it appears twice in the report layout and the pane (Figure 4-99).

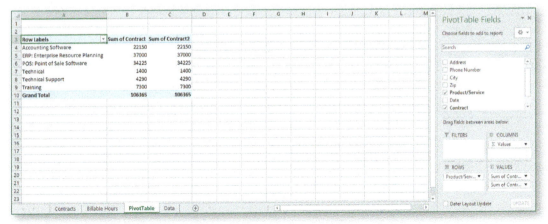

4-99 "Contract" field appears twice in the report

14. Select cell **C4** and click the **Field Settings** button [*PivotTable Tools Analyze* tab, *Active Fields* group]. Type Average Contract as the *Custom Name,* choose **Average** as the calculation, and set the *Number Format* to **Currency** with zero decimal places.

15. Select cell **B4** and set its *Custom Name* to Total Contracts and the number format to **Currency** with zero decimal places.

16. Apply **PivotTable Style Dark 3**.

17. Select the **Data** sheet tab and copy cells **A1:A2**. Paste them in cell **A1** on the **PivotTable** sheet. Set **Align Left** for both cells and **16 pt** as the font size (Figure 4-100).

18. Copy the **Data** sheet to the end and name the copy Subtotals.

19. Select cell **D5** and sort by **City** in **A to Z** order.

20. Use the *Subtotal* command to show a **SUM** for the contract amounts for each city.

21. Click the **Billable Hours** sheet tab and select cell **A4**.

22. Click the **Format as Table** button [*Home* tab, *Styles* group], use **Table Style Medium 10**, and remove the data connections.

23. Type 5% Add On in cell **E4** and press **Enter**.

24. Build a formula in cell **E5** to multiply cell **D5** by **105%**.

25. Select cells **A1:E2** and center them across the selection.

26. Use the *AutoFilter* arrows to sort first by date in oldest to newest order and then by client name in ascending order.

27. Save and close the workbook (Figure 4-101).

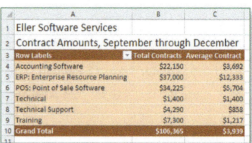

4-100 *Completed PivotTable*

4-101 Completed Excel table and *Subtotals* sheet

Independent Project 4-5

Boyd Air is monitoring flight arrival status as well as capacities. Before formatting the data as an Excel table, you will export it as a text file for use in the reservation software. You will filter the data in the table, build a *PivotTable,* and create a *PivotChart.*
[Student Learning Outcomes 4.1, 4.2, 4.3, 4.4, 4.7, 4.8]

File Needed: ***BoydAir-04.xlsx*** *[Student data files are available in the* Library *of your SIMnet account.]*
Completed Project File Names: ***[your initials] Excel 4-5.xlsx*** and ***[your initials] Excel 4-5.txt***

Skills Covered in This Project

- Export data as a text file.
- Format data as an Excel table.
- Use a number filter in a table.
- Set conditional formatting with an icon set.
- Filter data by cell icon.
- Create and format a *PivotTable.*
- Create and format a *PivotChart.*

1. Open ***BoydAir-04*** workbook from your student data files and save it as [your initials] Excel 4-5.

2. Export the data to a tab-delimited text file named ***[your initials] Excel 4-5*** in your usual location for saving work.

3. Rename the sheet tab Stats after the data is exported.

4. Use the *Save As* command to save and replace ***[your initials] Excel 4-5*** as an **Excel Workbook**.

5. Select cell **A4** and format the data as an Excel table using **Table Style Medium 21**.

6. Copy the **Stats** sheet to the end and name the copy PM Flights.

7. Select the **PM Flights** sheet and use a *Greater Than* filter to display flights with a departure time after 12:00 PM (Figure 4-102).

8. Select the **Stats** worksheet, select cells **I5:I32**, and set conditional formatting to use **3 Stars** from the *Icon Sets.*

9. Build a two-level *Custom Sort* for the *Capacity* column to sort by icon. Show the solid gold star at the top, followed by the half-gold star. The silver star will default to the bottom (Figure 4-103).

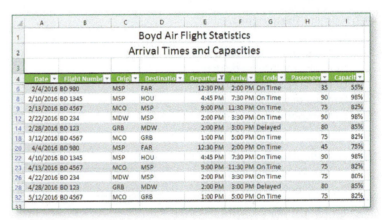

4-102 Filter results for *Departure Time* field

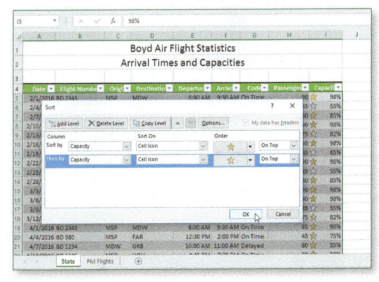

4-103 Custom sort for the *3 Stars* icon set

10. Select the **Stats** worksheet, select cells **A4:I32**, and use the *Quick Analysis* tool to create a *PivotTable* to display average of capacity by origin (Figure 4-104).

11. Select cell **B3** in the *PivotTable* and use **Field Settings** to set a **Number Format** of **Percentage** with two decimal places. Edit the *Custom Name* to display **Average Capacity**.

12. Add the **Passengers** field to the *PivotTable VALUES* area with a sum calculation. Edit the field settings to display **# of Passengers** as the custom name. Set the number format to **Number** with zero decimals and a thousand's separator.

13. Use **PivotTable Style Light 8** for the *PivotTable* and show banded columns and rows.

14. Add a **3-D Pie PivotChart** to the sheet and position the chart object to start in cell **E3**. Size the chart to reach cell **N22**.

15. Select the legend in the chart and set its font size to **11** from the *Home* tab.

16. Show **Data Labels** on the chart positioned at the **Inside End**. Select a data label and format all labels from the *Home* tab as **bold** and **10 pt**.

17. Select cell **A1** and rename the sheet PivotTable&Chart (Figure 4-105).

18. Save and close the workbook.

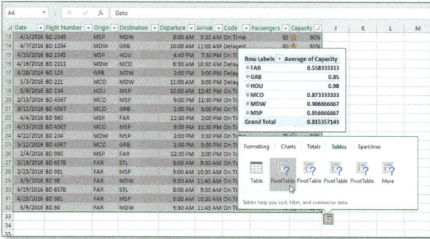

4-104 *PivotTable* suggestions from the *Quick Analysis* tool

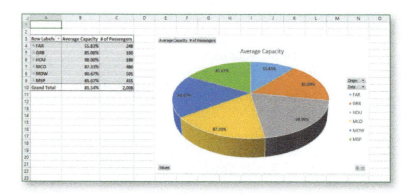

4-105 Excel 4-5 completed sheets

Independent Project 4-6

Life's Animal Shelter has a list of suppliers in a worksheet which must be copied to Word for use by another staff member. You will build an advanced filter to show suppliers for specific product categories and define groups based on supplier name. Your final task is to create an Excel table for sorting and filtering.
[Student Learning Outcomes 4.1, 4.3, 4.4, 4.5, 4.7]

File Needed: **LAShelter-04.xlsx** [Student data files are available in the Library of your SIMnet account.]
Completed Project File Names: **[your initials] Excel 4-6.xlsx** and **[your initials] Excel 4-6.docx**

Skills Covered in This Project

- Copy Excel data to Word.
- Create an advanced filter.
- Use *Flash Fill* to complete a column.
- Format data as a table.
- Filter data.
- Define groups in a worksheet.

1. Open the **LAShelter-04** workbook from your student data files and save it as [your initials] Excel 4-6.

2. Select the **LAS Suppliers** sheet, select cells **A4:D32**, and copy them to the Windows *Clipboard*.

3. Open Word and create a new document.

4. Paste the data into Word with the **Use Destination Styles** option (Figure 4-106).

5. Save the Word document as [your initials] Excel 4-6.docx.

6. Close the Word document and exit Word.

7. Click the **Criteria** sheet tab.

8. Type **cage** in cell **A2** and type **carrier** in cell **A3**. This is *OR* criteria that will find products that include either the word "cage" or the word "carrier."

9. Select the **LAS Suppliers** sheet and format the labels in row **4** as **bold** and **centered** to distinguish the header row from other data.

10. Click cell **A5** on the **LAS Suppliers** sheet.

11. Build an advanced filter that uses the data on the **LAS Suppliers** sheet, the criteria range on the **Criteria** sheet, and cells **F6:G6** as the output range. In the *Advanced Filter* dialog box, select the **Unique records only** box (Figure 4-107).

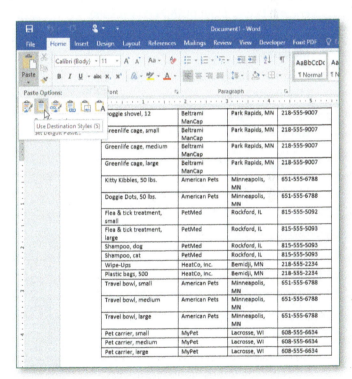

4-106 Word *Paste Options* for Excel data

12. Replace the criteria with *bowl* and *collar* to build a second advanced filter and show the filtered results as indicated on the worksheet.

13. Select cells **A4:D32** and copy them to cell **A4** on the **Table** sheet. Remove all borders.

14. Select cells **A5:A32** and sort the data by product name in ascending order.

15. Type (651) 555-6788 in cell **E5**.

16. Type (2 in cell **E6** and press **Enter** when the *Flash Fill* suggestion appears.

17. Type Phone in cell **E4** and delete column **D**. Set column **D** to a width of **15.71 (115 pixels)**.

18. Format the data as a table using **Table Style Medium 2**.

19. Filter the data to show the suppliers located in Minnesota.

20. Select cells **A1:A2** and remove the **Merge & Center** command. Set both cells to **Align Left**. Then select cells **A1:D2** and use the **Center Across Selection** command (Figure 4-108).

21. Select the **By City** worksheet tab.

22. Sort by **City** in **A to Z** order.

23. Insert a row at row **5** and type Bemidji in cell **A5**. Left-align the label.

24. Insert a row at row **10** and type Houston in cell **A10**. **Bold** the label.

25. Insert blank rows and type labels for the remaining cities.

26. Select the row headings for rows **6:9** and click the **Group** button [*Data* tab, *Outline* group]. Do not include the row with the city name in the group.

27. Repeat the command to group the rows for each city (Figure 4-109).

28. Select and delete column **C**.

29. Collapse the *Houston* and *Minneapolis* groups (Figure 4-110).

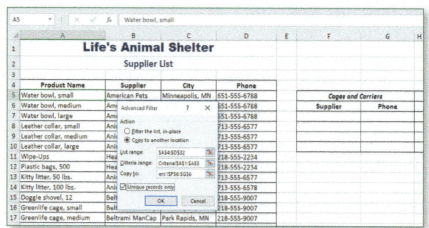

4-107 Advanced filter to select unique records

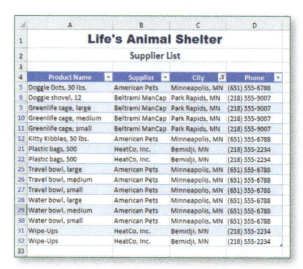

4-108 Completed table

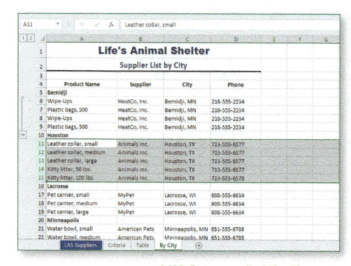

4-109 Data manually defined in groups

Life's Animal Shelter

Supplier List

Product Name	Supplier	City	Phone
Water bowl, small	American Pets	Minneapolis, MN	651-555-6788
Water bowl, medium	American Pets	Minneapolis, MN	651-555-6788
Water bowl, large	American Pets	Minneapolis, MN	651-555-6788
Leather collar, small	Animals Inc.	Houston, TX	713-555-6577
Leather collar, medium	Animals Inc.	Houston, TX	713-555-6577
Leather collar, large	Animals Inc.	Houston, TX	713-555-6577
Wipe-Ups	HeatCo, Inc.	Bemidji, MN	218-555-2234
Plastic bags, 500	HeatCo, Inc.	Bemidji, MN	218-555-2234
Kitty litter, 50 lbs.	Animals Inc.	Houston, TX	713-555-6577
Kitty litter, 100 lbs.	Animals Inc.	Houston, TX	713-555-6578
Doggie shovel, 12	Beltrami ManCap	Park Rapids, MN	218-555-9007
Greenlife cage, small	Beltrami ManCap	Park Rapids, MN	218-555-9007
Greenlife cage, medium	Beltrami ManCap	Park Rapids, MN	218-555-9007
Greenlife cage, large	Beltrami ManCap	Park Rapids, MN	218-555-9007
Kitty Kibbles, 50 lbs.	American Pets	Minneapolis, MN	651-555-6788
Doggie Do's, 30 lbs.	American Pets	Minneapolis, MN	651-555-6788
Flea & tick treatment, small	PetMed	Rockford, IL	815-555-5092
Flea & tick treatment, large	PetMed	Rockford, IL	815-555-5093
Shampoo, dog	PetMed	Rockford, IL	815-555-5093
Shampoo, cat	PetMed	Rockford, IL	815-555-5093
Wipe-Ups	HeatCo, Inc.	Bemidji, MN	218-555-2234
Plastic bags, 500	HeatCo, Inc.	Bemidji, MN	218-555-2234
Travel bowl, small	American Pets	Minneapolis, MN	651-555-6788
Travel bowl, medium	American Pets	Minneapolis, MN	651-555-6788
Travel bowl, large	American Pets	Minneapolis, MN	651-555-6788
Pet carrier, small	MyPet	Lacrosse, WI	608-555-6634
Pet carrier, medium	MyPet	Lacrosse, WI	608-555-6634
Pet carrier, large	MyPet	Lacrosse, WI	608-555-6634

Cages and Carriers		Bowls and Collars	
Supplier	Phone	Supplier	Phone
Beltrami ManCap	218-555-9007	American Pets	651-555-6788
MyPet	608-555-6634	Animals Inc.	713-555-6577

		A	B	C
2			**Supplier List by City**	
3				
4		**Product Name**	**Supplier**	**Phone**
5		**Bemidji**		
6		Wipe-Ups	HeatCo, Inc.	218-555-2234
7		Plastic bags, 500	HeatCo, Inc.	218-555-2234
8		Wipe-Ups	HeatCo, Inc.	218-555-2234
9		Plastic bags, 500	HeatCo, Inc.	218-555-2234
10		**Houston**		
16		**Lacrosse**		
17		Pet carrier, small	MyPet	608-555-6634
18		Pet carrier, medium	MyPet	608-555-6634
19		Pet carrier, large	MyPet	608-555-6634
20		**Minneapolis**		
29		**Park Rapids**		
30		Doggie shovel, 12	Beltrami ManCap	218-555-9007
31		Greenlife cage, small	Beltrami ManCap	218-555-9007
32		Greenlife cage, medium	Beltrami ManCap	218-555-9007
33		Greenlife cage, large	Beltrami ManCap	218-555-9007
34		**Rockford**		
35		Flea & tick treatment, small	PetMed	815-555-5092
36		Flea & tick treatment, large	PetMed	815-555-5093
37		Shampoo, dog	PetMed	815-555-5093
38		Shampoo, cat	PetMed	815-555-5093
39				

4-110 Excel 4-6 completed worksheets

30. Save and close the workbook.

Improve It Project 4-7

Placer Hills Real Estate wants its latest *PivotTable* to show sales by agent listing, but the table needs additional work. In the source data, you also need to highlight certain listings for insurance purposes. In a separate table, you plan to create a calculation column to show the number of market days.
[Student Learning Outcomes 4.1, 4.2, 4.8]

File Needed: **PlacerHills-04.xlsx** *[Student data files are available in the Library of your SIMnet account.]*
Completed Project File Name: *[your initials]* **Excel 4-7.xlsx**

Skills Covered in This Project

- Pivot fields in a *PivotTable*.
- Format fields in a *PivotTable*.
- Add a field to a table.
- Set conditional formatting with a formula.

1. Open the *PlacerHills-04* workbook from your student data files and save it as [your initials] Excel 4-7.

2. Select the **Listings** sheet and use a formula to set conditional formatting for cells **A5:A26**. The formula is =k5="frame" to determine if the construction is frame. Set the format to use light blue fill.

3. Select the **PivotTable** sheet, drag the **City** field out of the *Rows* area, and drag the **Agent ID** field to the *Rows* area.

4. Drag the **Sale Price** field into the *Values* area so that it is shown twice in the *PivotTable*.

5. Format the first occurrence of the **Sales Price** field to show a sum with **Currency** format, zero decimals, and a custom name of Total Sales. Format the second occurrence to show an average with the same **Currency** format and the name Average Sale.

6. Apply **PivotTable Style Light 15**.

7. Select cells **A3:C9** in the *PivotTable*. Click the **Border** button [*Home* tab, *Font* group] and apply **All Borders**. Select cell **A1**.

8. Select the **Table** sheet tab.

9. Type Days in cell **O4**. In cell **O5**, build an *IF* formula to display the number of days on the market. The *logical_test* determines if the sale date is greater than the list date. The *value_if_true* argument is the sale date minus the list date. For the *value_if_false* argument, press **Spacebar** once to leave the cell blank when there is no sale date.

10. Save and close the workbook (Figure 4-111).

4-111 Excel 4-7 completed worksheets

Challenge Project 4-8

For this project, you build a worksheet for a company that sells four varieties of socks in four eastern states. When the data is complete, you will format the data as an Excel table.
[Student Learning Outcomes 4.1, 4.2, 4.3]

File Needed: None
Completed Project File Name: *[your initials] Excel 4-8.xlsx*

Create a new workbook and save it as [your initials] Excel 4-8. Modify your workbook according to the following guidelines:

- Type the labels State, Model, Month, Pairs, and Price in cells **A4:E4**.
- In cells **A5:A8**, type Connecticut, Maine, New Hampshire, and Vermont.
- In cell **B5**, type the style name for one type of sock sold by the company. Copy the name to cells **B6:B8**.
- In cells **C5**, type January and copy the month to cells **C6:C8**.
- In cells **D5:D8**, enter values for how many pairs were sold in each state in January. In column E, enter and copy a price for this sock style.
- Copy cells **A5:E8** and paste the range in cell **A9** to create a February group. Edit the month and the number of pairs sold.
- Copy cells **A5:E12** and paste the range in cell **A13** to create the data for another sock style. In this range, edit the style name, the number of pairs sold, and the price. The price is the same for all rows in this group.
- Copy and paste to complete two more ranges for two sock styles, so that you have January and February data for four sock styles for each state.
- Set conditional formatting to show one of the state names in a format different from the other states.
- Name the sheet Data and make a copy named Table.
- On the **Table** sheet, format the data as an Excel table with a light table style.
- Type Total in cell **F4** and create a formula to calculate the dollar amount of sales in the column.
- Show a total row for the table with results for the number of pairs and sales dollars.
- Add additional formatting to the table as needed.
- Use the *AutoFilter* arrows to sort by style and then by state.
- Enter a name for the company in cell **A1**. Enter a label in cell **A2** that describes the data.

Challenge Project 4-9

For this project, you explore the Bureau of Labor Statistics web site to download data for use in a worksheet. After you have arranged and formatted the data, you copy it to a Word document.
[Student Learning Outcomes 4.1, 4.2, 4.6, 4.7]

File Needed: None
Completed Project File Names: *[your initials] Excel 4-9.xlsx* and *[your initials] Excel 4-9.docx*

Create a new workbook and save it as [your initials] Excel 4-9. Modify your workbook according to the following guidelines:

- Go to www.bls.gov/data.
- Review the subject areas and choose one to explore. Find a topic and subtopic which provides an *.xlsx* file for download.
- Download or copy the data into your worksheet.
- Format the data as an Excel table if it is not already formatted, or apply a different table style.
- Determine and apply conditional formatting for some aspect of the data.
- Determine and set a different sort order.
- Add a main title to your worksheet and set other format attributes to effectively display your information.
- Copy the data to a new Word document and save the Word document as [your initials] Excel 4-9.docx.

Challenge Project 4-10

For this project, you create a worksheet that lists names, birth dates, and hair color for 20 people. You format the list as a table for sorting and filtering. You convert the table to a range and use the *Subtotal* command.
[Student Learning Outcomes 4.1, 4.3, 4.4, 4.5]

File Needed: None
Completed Project File Name: *[your initials] Excel 4-10.xlsx*

Create a new workbook and save it as [your initials] Excel 4-10. Modify your workbook according to the following guidelines:

- Type your first name, your last name, your birthdate, and your hair color in a row using one column for each item.
- Type data for 19 more people, using fictitious or real data. Use birthdates that are the same year as yours as well as four other years, so that your list has only five different years. Use at least three hair colors in your list, such as brown, blond, red.
- Format the data as a table and apply a table style.
- Sort the date by birthdate with the youngest people listed first. Then filter the data to show only those records from the first year listed in the data.
- Make a copy of the sheet and convert the table to a normal range. Use the *Subtotal* command to count the number of persons with each hair color.

CHAPTER 5

Consolidating and Linking Data and Inserting Objects

CHAPTER OVERVIEW

When multiple worksheets have identical layouts and labels, you can summarize data with the *Consolidate* command. You can also link to data in a different workbook to build a formula or display information. In this chapter, you will learn how to consolidate data from multiple sheets in the same workbook and how to link multiple workbooks with an external reference formula. You will also insert *SmartArt* graphics, screenshots, and hyperlinks in a worksheet.

STUDENT LEARNING OUTCOMES (SLOs)

After completing this chapter, you will be able to:

SLO 5.1   Create a static data consolidation (p. E5-294).

SLO 5.2   Create a dynamic data consolidation (p. E5-296).

SLO 5.3   Consolidate data by category (p. E5-298).

SLO 5.4   Group worksheets for editing and formatting (p. E5-299).

SLO 5.5   Link workbooks to consolidate data (p. E5-303).

SLO 5.6   Insert illustrations using *SmartArt*, screenshots, and pictures in a worksheet (p. E5-309).

SLO 5.7   Insert hyperlinks in a worksheet (p. E5-316).

SLO 5.8   Safeguard work by marking it as final or by setting a password (p. E5-318).

CASE STUDY

In the Pause & Practice projects in this chapter, you build consolidated worksheets and link workbooks for Paradise Lakes Resort. You create an illustration to accompany the data and add basic security to the workbook.

Pause & Practice 5-1: Create static and dynamic data consolidations and format grouped sheets.

Pause & Practice 5-2: Link workbooks.

Pause & Practice 5-3: Insert *SmartArt*, hyperlinks, and a screenshot in a workbook; mark a workbook as final.

Creating a Static Data Consolidation

A *consolidated worksheet* summarizes data from multiple sheets with a mathematical or statistical function. The *Consolidate* command on the *Data* tab calculates totals, averages, or other functions for data from multiple worksheets. Worksheets must have common data in the same rows and columns on each sheet for consolidation *by position*.

Each location for Paradise Lakes Resort follows the same layout for its net income worksheet, but the values are different. Figure 5-1 shows the worksheets for two locations. Revenue items and values are in cells A5:D8 on each sheet. When worksheets use the same pattern, the *Consolidate* command gathers data from each sheet to calculate a total, an average, or similar function.

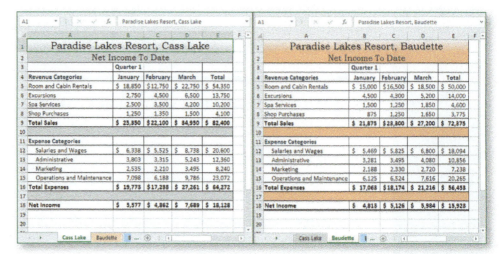

5-1 Two sheets prepared for consolidation by position

A *consolidation worksheet* is a separate summary sheet in the workbook. You create a consolidation sheet by copying one of the *source worksheets*. On the consolidation sheet, delete the contents of cells to be consolidated. You must create the consolidation worksheet before you start the *Consolidate* command.

▶**HOW TO:** Prepare a Consolidation Sheet

1. Copy one of the source worksheets in the workbook.
2. Rename the copied sheet as desired.
3. Delete the contents of cells to be consolidated (Figure 5-2).
   • Do not delete formulas that will be used on the consolidation sheet.

5-2 Copied sheet ready for consolidation

Static Data Consolidation

A *static consolidation* summarizes the data and displays a result on the consolidated sheet. The result does not change when a value on any source worksheet is edited. A static consolidation for the data in Figure 5-1 displays 2,125 in cell B8 on the consolidation sheet. If cell B8 on the Cass Lake sheet is changed after consolidation, cell B8 on the consolidation sheet does not recalculate. When you know that source data is final and will not be edited, you can use a static consolidation.

> **MORE INFO**
>
> If values are edited in source worksheets used in a static consolidation, run the *Consolidate* command again to update results.

▶ **HOW TO:** Create a Static Consolidation

1. Select the cell range to be summarized on the consolidation worksheet.
   - You can also click the first cell in the range.
   - This is the range whose contents were deleted (cells B5:D8 in Figure 5-3).

2. Click the **Consolidate** button [*Data* tab, *Data Tools* group].
   - The *Consolidate* dialog box opens.
   - If recently used cell ranges are listed in the *All references* box, select each reference and click **Delete** in the dialog box.

3. Click the **Function** arrow and choose the function (Figure 5-3).

4. Click the *Reference* box.

5. Click the first worksheet tab name with data to be consolidated.
   - The sheet name displays in the *Reference* box.
   - Move the *Consolidate* dialog box if necessary to select cells.

6. Select the cells to be summarized on the source sheet (Figure 5-4).
   - The *Consolidate* dialog box collapses as you select the range.
   - The reference appears in the *Reference* box.

7. Click **Add** in the *Consolidate* dialog box.
   - The first reference displays in the *All references* list.
   - The first selected sheet tab is active with the range selected.

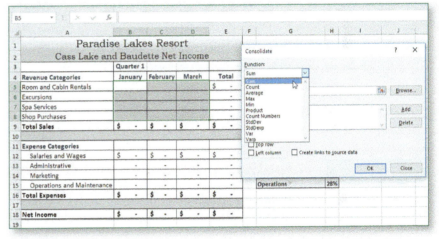

5-3 *Consolidate* dialog box

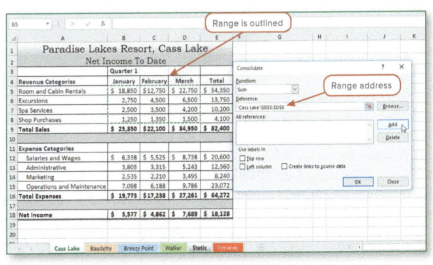

5-4 **Range selected on first sheet**

8. Click the next worksheet tab name with data to be consolidated.
   - The same cell range is selected.
9. Click **Add**.
   - The reference is placed in the *All references* list.
10. Repeat steps 8 and 9 for each worksheet to include in the consolidation (Figure 5-5).
11. Click **OK**.
    - The data is summarized.
    - The consolidated sheet displays a result in each cell (Figure 5-6).

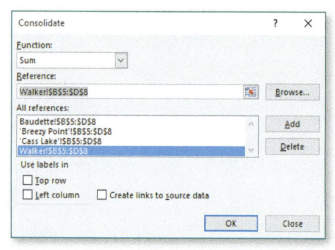

5-5 Data to be consolidated by SUM on four worksheets

	A	B	C	D	E
1	Paradise Lakes Resort				
2	Consolidate Results				
3		Quarter 1			
4	Revenue Categories	January	February	March	Total
5	Room and Cabin Rentals	$ 51,050	$51,100	$ 76,750	$178,900
6	Excursions	15,980	12,555	21,050	49,585
7	Spa Services	8,200	10,000	11,695	29,895
8	Shop Purchases	4,875	8,000	9,700	22,575
9	Total Sales	$ 80,105	$81,655	$119,195	$280,955
10					
11	Expense Categories				
12	Salaries and Wages	$ 20,026	$20,414	$ 29,799	$ 70,239
13	Administrative	12,016	12,248	17,879	42,143
14	Marketing	8,011	8,166	11,920	28,096
15	Operations and Maintenance	22,429	22,863	33,375	78,667
16	Total Expenses	$ 62,482	$63,691	$ 92,972	$219,145
17					
18	Net Income	$ 17,623	$17,964	$ 26,223	$ 61,810

5-6 Consolidated results

SLO 5.2

Creating a Dynamic Data Consolidation

A *dynamic consolidation* places formulas on the consolidated sheet in an outline. When data on a source worksheet is edited, the formula recalculates. You should use dynamic consolidation when data on source worksheets might be edited after you have created the consolidation worksheet.

> **MORE INFO**
>
> An Excel outline can show or hide details as discussed in *SLO 4.5: Using Subtotals, Outlines, and Groups*.

Dynamic Data Consolidation

You build a dynamic consolidation sheet the same way that you build a static consolidation sheet. In the *Consolidate* dialog box, however, choose the option to create links to the source data. The resulting outline in the consolidation sheet uses 3D reference formulas (Figure 5-7). The formulas identify the sheet name and cell used for consolidation. In a dynamic consolidation, you can expand outline items to display individual values that are summarized.

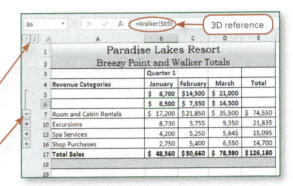

ANOTHER WAY

You can dynamically consolidate data by using 3D references in your own formulas.

5-7 Consolidated results in outline view with 3D references

▶ HOW TO: Create a Dynamic Consolidation

1. Select the cell range to be summarized.
   - The cell contents should be blank.
   - You can also click the first cell in the range.
2. Click the **Consolidate** button [*Data* tab, *Data Tools* group].
   - The *Consolidate* dialog box opens.
   - Select and delete recently used reference ranges in the *All references* box.
3. Click the **Function** arrow and choose the function.
4. Click the *Reference* box.
5. Click the first worksheet tab name with data to be consolidated.
   - The sheet name displays in the *Reference* box.
   - Move the *Consolidate* dialog box if necessary to select cells.
   - You can scroll sheet names as needed.
6. Select the cells to be summarized.
   - The *Consolidate* dialog box collapses as you select the range.
   - The reference appears in the *Reference* box.
7. Click **Add** in the *Consolidate* dialog box.
   - The first reference is listed in the *All references* box.
   - The first selected sheet tab is active with the range selected.
8. Click the next worksheet tab name with data to be consolidated.
   - The same cell range is selected.
9. Click **Add**.
   - The second reference is listed in the *All references* box.
10. Repeat steps 8 and 9 for each worksheet to include in the consolidation.
11. Select the **Create links to source data** box (Figure 5-8).
12. Click **OK** (Figure 5-9).
    - The data is consolidated in outline format.
    - Each item is collapsed.
    - The consolidated sheet displays a 3D reference in each cell above the result cell when the outline is expanded.

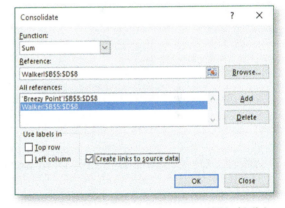

5-8 Data to be consolidated by *SUM* with links

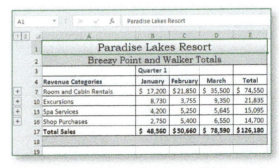

5-9 Dynamic data consolidation results

Consolidating Data by Category

When data in multiple worksheets is arranged differently but has the same row and column labels, you can build a consolidation *by category*. Category refers to the row or column labels. Consolidation by category can be static or dynamic.

Data Consolidation by Category

The worksheets shown in Figure 5-10 have data for January, February, and March. The month names are not arranged in the same way, but they are spelled alike on both sheets.

To consolidate data by category, copy one of the source worksheets. On the consolidation sheet, delete the contents of cells to be consolidated including the labels. For example, in a consolidation for the data in Figure 5-10, delete cells B4:D8 on the consolidation sheet including the month names. When you select the range on each source sheet, select the same range (B4:D8). In the *Consolidate* dialog box, you activate the option to use the top row or left column labels or both.

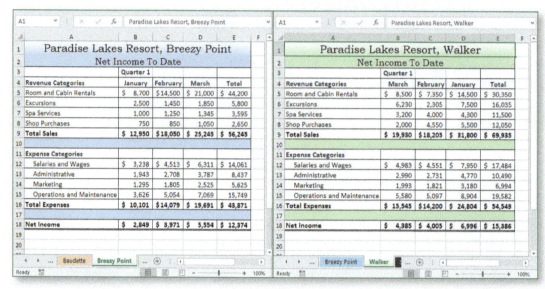

5-10 Data has same labels in different order

▶ HOW TO: Create a Dynamic Data Consolidation by Category

1. Delete the contents of the cells to be summarized including labels on the consolidation sheet.

2. Select the range of cells to be summarized including label cells (Figure 5-11).

3. Click the **Consolidate** button [*Data* tab, *Data Tools* group].
   - The *Consolidate* dialog box opens.
   - Select and delete references in the *All references* box.

4. Click the **Function** arrow and choose the function.

5. Click the first sheet tab name with data to be consolidated.
   - The sheet name displays in the *Reference* box.

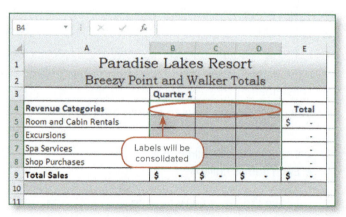

5-11 Consolidation sheet with labels and data deleted

6. Select data and label cells to be summarized.

7. Click **Add** in the *Consolidate* dialog box.
   - The first reference appears in the *All references* list.

8. Click the next worksheet tab name.
   - The same cell range is selected.

9. Click **Add**.
   - The second reference appears in the *All references* list.

10. Repeat steps 8 and 9 for each worksheet to include in the consolidation.

11. Select the **Create links to source data** box.
    - The consolidation can be static if desired.

12. Select the box for **Top row** in the *Use labels in* group (Figure 5-12).
    - Use *Left column* when required.
    - You can select both label positions when needed.

13. Click **OK** (Figure 5-13).
    - Labels display in the consolidated sheet in the same order as the first sheet listed in the *Consolidate* dialog box.
    - The data is consolidated in outline format.
    - Each item is collapsed.
    - The 3D references indicate the cells used for each result on the consolidation sheet.

5-12 *Consolidate* dialog box choices for consolidation by category

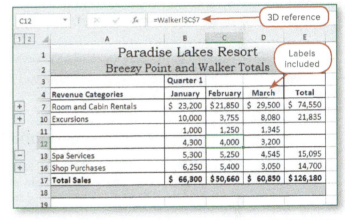

5-13 Consolidation results

Working with Grouped Worksheets

You can group worksheets that have identical layouts for common editing or formatting. Group sheets to change a font, to apply a fill color, to set alignment, to edit data, and more.

Not all commands work for grouped worksheets. For example, you cannot insert a graphic on grouped sheets, nor can you apply conditional formatting. When sheets are grouped and a command is not available, the command button or option is grayed out in the *Ribbon*.

Group Worksheets

When worksheets are grouped, the title bar shows *[Group]* after the file name, and commands or edits affect all sheets in the group. The tabs for grouped worksheets appear white with a hint of the tab color below the sheet name. When grouping sheets, you may find it helpful to set different tab colors so that it is easier to recognize grouped sheets.

To group worksheets, press **Ctrl** or **Shift** to select multiple tab names. Select all sheets in a workbook from the context menu for any tab. To ungroup sheets, click any tab name that is not part of the group. When all sheets are grouped, right-click any tab name and choose **Ungroup Sheets**.

▶ **HOW TO:** Group Worksheets

1. Click the first sheet tab to be included in the group.

2. Press **Shift** and click the last tab name for the group to select adjacent sheets.

   • The first sheet remains visible.

3. Press **Ctrl** and click each tab name to select nonadjacent sheets (Figure 5-14).

4. Right-click any sheet tab and choose **Select All Sheets** to group all sheets in a workbook.

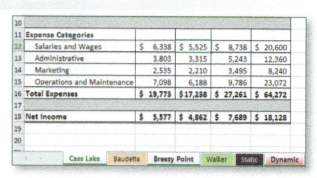

5-14 Nonadjacent grouped worksheets

▶ **MORE INFO**

If you save a workbook while sheets are grouped, the workbook opens with grouped sheets.

Edit and Format Grouped Worksheets

All worksheets in a group are affected by a command, so worksheets should be identical in layout. If they are not, you might make changes that are not appropriate for every sheet in the group.

One command that you *can* apply to grouped sheets that are not identical is a header or footer command. You can also change page orientation for multiple sheets that are not identical.

▶ **HOW TO:** Edit and Format Grouped Sheets

1. Group the worksheets.

2. Click a cell to be edited.

   • Any sheet in the group can be active or visible.

3. Enter data and press **Enter**.

   • The edit is made on all sheets in the group.

4. Select cells to be formatted.

5. Apply the format.

   • The format displays on all sheets in the group.

6. Ungroup the sheets.

For this project, you create a static data consolidation for Paradise Lakes Resort to sum income data. You also create a dynamic consolidation to average income data and group sheets for formatting.

File Needed: **ParadiseLakes-05.xlsx** (Student data files are available in the Library of your SIMnet account)
Completed Project File Name: **[your initials] PP E5-1.xlsx**

---

1. Open the **ParadiseLakes-05** workbook from your student data files and save it as [your initials] PP E5-1.

2. Create a static data consolidation.
   a. Click the **Static** sheet tab.
   b. Select cells **B5:D8** and press **Delete**. The formulas calculate to zero which displays as a hyphen in this worksheet.
   c. Click the **Consolidate** button [*Data* tab, *Data Tools* group].
   d. Verify that the **SUM** function is selected.
   e. If there are references in the *All references* box, select and delete each one.
   f. Click the **Reference** box and click the **Cass Lake** sheet tab.
   g. Select cells **B5:D8**.
   h. Click **Add** in the *Consolidate* dialog box.
   i. Click the **Baudette** sheet tab. Verify that the same cell range (B5:D8) is selected. If it is not selected, select it.
   j. Click **Add** (Figure 5-15).
   k. Click **OK**.

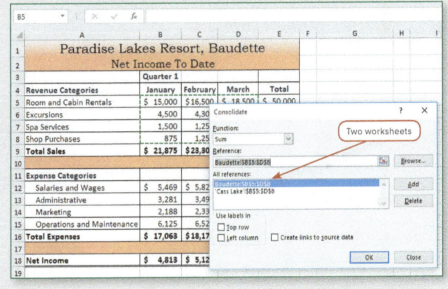

5-15 *Consolidate* dialog box for two worksheets in a static consolidation

3. Create a dynamic data consolidation by category.
   a. Click the **Dynamic** sheet tab.
   b. Select and delete cells **B4:D8**. The labels in row 4 will be consolidated.
   c. Click the **Consolidate** button [*Data* tab, *Data Tools* group].
   d. Click the **Function** drop-down list and choose **AVERAGE**.
   e. If there are references in the *All references* box, select and delete each one.
   f. Click the **Reference** box and click the **Breezy Point** sheet tab.
   g. Select cells **B4:D8** and click **Add** in the *Consolidate* dialog box.
   h. Click the **Walker** sheet tab. Note that the month names are in different order.
   i. Click **Add**.

j. Select the **Top row** box in the *Consolidate* dialog box.

k. Select the **Create links to source data** box (Figure 5-16).

l. Click **OK**. The labels are consolidated in the same order as the **Breezy Point** sheet.

4. Group, format, and edit sheets.

    a. Click the **Cass Lake** sheet tab.

    b. Press **Shift** and click the **Dynamic** sheet tab to group all sheets.

    c. Select cells **A5:A8**.

    d. Click the **Increase Indent** button [*Home* tab, *Alignment* group] two times.

    e. Select cells **B3:D3**.

    f. Click the **Merge & Center** button [*Home* tab, *Alignment* group].

    g. Select cell **A9** and edit the label to show Total Revenue.

    h. Format columns **B:E** to be **10.00 (75 pixels)** wide.

    i. Press **Ctrl+Home**.

    j. Right-click the **Cass Lake** sheet tab and choose **Ungroup Sheets**.

    k. Select the **Dynamic** sheet. The labels on this sheet are not indented because the outline format uses different row numbers.

    l. Select cell **A10**. Press Ctrl and select cell **A13** and then cell **A16**. Increase the indent two times.

    m. Press **Ctrl+Home**.

5. Save and close the workbook (Figure 5-17).

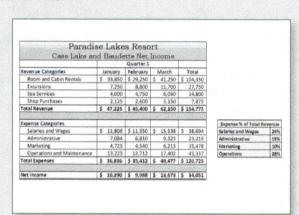

5-16 *Consolidate* dialog box for a dynamic consolidation by category

SLO 5.5

Linking Workbooks

Linking workbooks is the process of referring to data in another workbook. Linking may display data, or it may reference data for a formula. Linked workbooks are referred to as *dependent* and *source workbooks*. A dependent workbook includes or refers to data from another workbook. A source workbook includes data that is referenced in a dependent workbook. For workbooks to be linked, they must be accessible over a network, on the same computer, or in the cloud.

Paradise Lakes Resort maintains a consolidated income workbook (a dependent workbook), but each location builds its own workbook (source workbooks). The consolidated workbook displays up-to-the-minute data because it includes links to each of the individual workbooks.

Link workbooks using the *Consolidate* command, or build formulas that refer to cells in other workbooks. Whether the reference is entered in the *Consolidate* dialog box or in a formula, it is an *external reference* because it refers to cells in another workbook.

Link Workbooks Using the Consolidate Command

An external reference includes the name of the workbook in square brackets, the sheet name, cell address(es), and *identifiers*. An identifier is a character such as an exclamation point that marks or signifies a component of the reference. The complete syntax for an external reference is:

='[WorkbookName]WorksheetName'!CellRange

All workbooks must be open when you use the *Consolidate* command.

▶ **HOW TO: Link Workbooks with a Dynamic Data Consolidation**

1. Open the dependent workbook.
   - This is the workbook that will refer to another workbook.
2. Delete the contents of cells to be consolidated.
3. Open the source workbook.
   - This is workbook with data that is needed to complete the dependent workbook.
   - If there are multiple source workbooks, open each of them.
4. Return to the dependent workbook.
5. Select the range of cells to be consolidated.
6. Click the **Consolidate** button [*Data* tab, *Data Tools* group].
7. Click the **Function** arrow and choose the function.
8. Select and delete references in the *All references* list.
9. Click the *Reference* box.
10. Click the workbook icon on the Windows taskbar for the first source workbook (Figure 5-18).
    - You can also press **Ctrl+F6** to switch to the next open workbook.

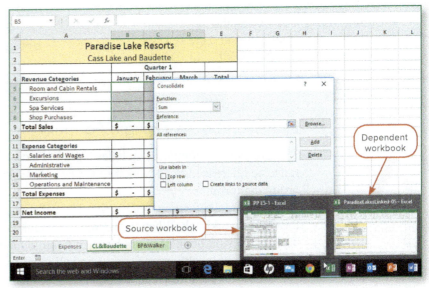

5-18 Open workbook icons on the Windows task bar

11. Select the sheet tab with data to be consolidated.

12. Select the cell range and click **Add**.

   • The reference includes the workbook and sheet names.

13. Click the next tab name and click **Add** (Figure 5-19).

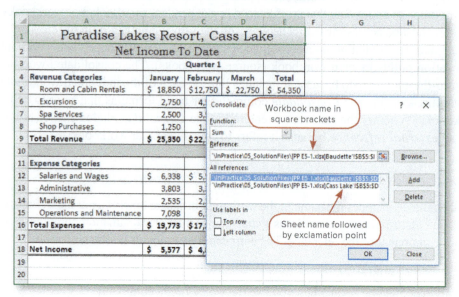

5-19 References with identifiers to another workbook

   • If multiple workbooks are used, click the *Reference* box and click the icon for the next source workbook on the Windows taskbar.

   • Repeat this step for each sheet or workbook to be used as a source in the consolidation.

14. Select the **Create links to source data** box.

15. Click **OK**.

16. Switch to the dependent workbook.

   • The outline is collapsed.

   • External references are placed above the result cell.

   • External references include the name of the workbook, the sheet name, and the cell address or range (Figure 5-20).

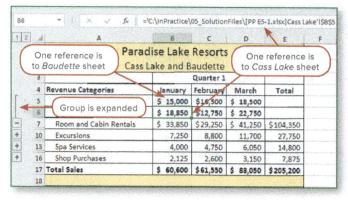

5-20 Dynamic data consolidation with another workbook

Link Workbooks Using a Formula

The *Consolidate* command includes a limited list of functions and requires that the same cell range be referenced in all worksheets. These limitations do not apply in an external reference or linking formula.

An external reference formula refers to cells in another workbook and establishes a link to the source workbook. When the source workbook is open, you can point to build the formula. The source workbook need not be open to build an external reference formula, but you must type the formula with proper syntax and all identifiers.

When you point to create an external reference, it is built with absolute references. You can edit the references to be relative or mixed when you plan to copy the formula.

1. Open the dependent workbook.
   - This is the workbook that will include a formula with references to another workbook.
2. Open all source workbooks.
3. Return to the dependent workbook.
4. Click the cell for the formula.
5. Type = to start the formula.
   - You can enter an Excel function in the dependent workbook.
6. Click the icon on the Windows taskbar for the first source workbook.
7. Click the sheet tab and click the cell for the first argument.
   - The formula displays in the *Formula* bar with identifiers.
8. Type + for addition.
   - You can use any mathematical operator in a formula.
9. Click the next sheet tab.
   - If the next reference is in another workbook, click its icon on the taskbar.
10. Click the cell for the next formula argument (Figure 5-21).
    - The cell address need not be in the same location as the first sheet or workbook.
11. Repeat these steps to build the formula.
12. Press **Enter** (Figure 5-22).
    - The dependent workbook displays the formula result.
    - The reference includes the name of the workbook, the sheet name, and absolute cell references.
    - You can also click the **Enter** button in the *Formula* bar to complete the formula and return to the dependent workbook.

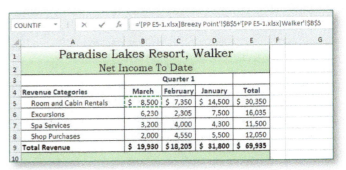

5-21 Formula to link workbooks

5-22 An external reference formula in the dependent workbook

 ANOTHER WAY

Arrange open workbooks side by side or horizontally tiled and switch between them by pointing and clicking.

Examine and Edit Links

An external reference formula creates a ***link*** to the source workbook, a data connection. The link specifies the file name and location at the time the formula was created. You can choose how links are handled when a workbook is opened from the *Trust Center Settings* for *External Content* (Excel *Options*) (Figure 5-23).

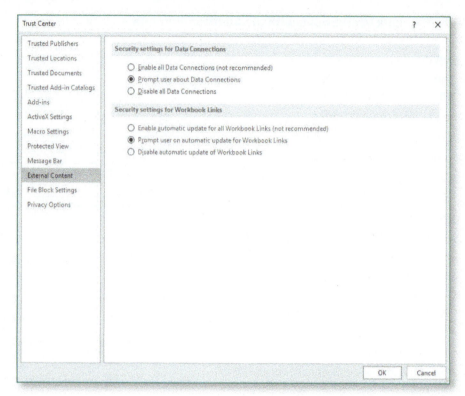

5-23 *Trust Center Settings for External Content*

Links can be updated when the source workbook is accessible. If a source workbook was renamed or moved to another location, the link cannot be updated. When this happens, a dependent workbook shows a result for the formula, but it may not be accurate until you edit the link.

You can break a link to remove the data connection but keep formula results as values in the dependent workbook.

▶ HOW TO: Update Links in a Workbook

1. Open the dependent workbook.
   - This workbook has a formula that refers to another workbook.
   - The source workbook need not be open.

2. Click **Enable Content** in the security message bar.

3. Click **Update** in the message box (Figure 5-24).
   - If the source workbook is accessible, the data is refreshed.
   - If the source workbook is not accessible, a message box displays options to continue or edit the links.

4. Click **Continue** if the links cannot be updated (Figure 5-25).

5-24 **Message box when opening linked workbooks**

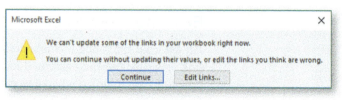

5-25 **Message box when links are not accessible**

5. Click the **Edit Links** button [*Data* tab, *Connections* group].

   - The *Edit Links* dialog box opens.
   - You can open this dialog box at any time to examine links (Figure 5-26).

6. Click **Change Source**.

   - You can find a file that has been moved to change its *Location*.

7. Navigate to find the file and click to select its name.

8. Click **OK** to update the location.

9. Click **Update Values**.

10. Click **Close**.

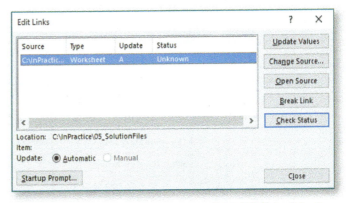

5-26 *Edit Links* dialog box

For this project, you create a dynamic consolidation with links to another workbook. You also create and copy an external reference formula.

Files Needed: ***[your initials] PP E5-1.xlsx*** and ***ParadiseLakesLinked-05.xlsx*** (*Student data files are available in the* Library *of your SIMnet account*)
Completed Project File Name: ***[your initials] PP E5-2.xlsx***

1. Open the ***ParadiseLakesLinked-05*** workbook from your student data files.

2. Save the workbook as [your initials] PP E5-2. This is the dependent workbook.

3. Open the ***[your initials] PP E5-1*** workbook completed in *Pause & Practice 5-1*. This is the source workbook.

4. Use the *Consolidate* command to link workbooks.
   a. Return to the ***[your initials] PP E5-2*** workbook and click the **CL&Baudette** sheet tab.
   b. Select cells **B5:D8**.
   c. Click the **Consolidate** button [*Data* tab, *Data Tools* group].
   d. Select and delete any references in the *All references* list.
   e. Verify that **SUM** is selected as the function.
   f. Click the *Reference* box.
   g. Click the icon on the Windows taskbar for ***[your initials] PP E5-1***.
   h. Click the **Cass Lake** sheet tab and select cells **B5:D8**.
   i. Click **Add**.
   j. Click the **Baudette** sheet tab and click **Add**.
   k. Select the **Create links to source data** box.
   l. Click **OK**.

5. Switch to the ***[your initials] PP E5-2*** workbook and format columns **B:E** to be **10.00 (75 pixels)** wide.

6. Click the *Expand* button for row **7** and click cell **B6** (Figure 5-27).

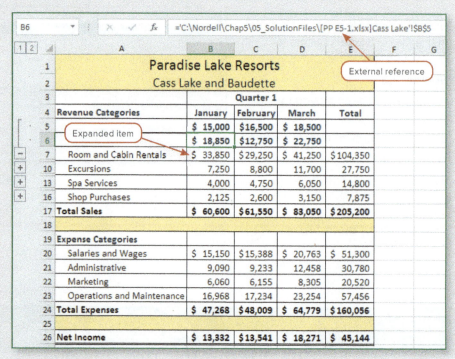

Cell reference: B6 — `='C:\Nordell\Chap5\05_SolutionFiles\[PP E5-1.xlsx]Cass Lake'!$B$5`

External reference

	A	B	C	D	E	F	G
1		Paradise Lake Resorts					
2		Cass Lake and Baudette					
3			Quarter 1				
4	Revenue Categories	January	February	March	Total		
5	Expanded item	$ 15,000	$16,500	$ 18,500			
6		$ 18,850	$12,750	$ 22,750			
7	Room and Cabin Rentals	$ 33,850	$29,250	$ 41,250	$104,350		
10	Excursions	7,250	8,800	11,700	27,750		
13	Spa Services	4,000	4,750	6,050	14,800		
16	Shop Purchases	2,125	2,600	3,150	7,875		
17	Total Sales	$ 60,600	$61,550	$ 83,050	$205,200		
18							
19	Expense Categories						
20	Salaries and Wages	$ 15,150	$15,388	$ 20,763	$ 51,300		
21	Administrative	9,090	9,233	12,458	30,780		
22	Marketing	6,060	6,155	8,305	20,520		
23	Operations and Maintenance	16,968	17,234	23,254	57,456		
24	Total Expenses	$ 47,268	$48,009	$ 64,779	$160,056		
25							
26	Net Income	$ 13,332	$13,541	$ 18,271	$ 45,144		

5-27 Dynamic consolidation

7. Link workbooks using a formula.
   a. Click the **BP&Walker** sheet tab in *[your initials]* **PP E5-2**.
   b. Click cell **B5**.
   c. Type = to start the formula.
   d. Press **Ctrl+F6** or click the icon on the Windows taskbar for *[your initials]* **PP E5-1**.
   e. Click the **Breezy Point** worksheet tab.
   f. Select cell **B5** and type + for addition.
   g. Click the **Walker** sheet tab (Figure 5-28).
   h. Select cell **D5** for the January amount and press **Enter**.

8. Edit and copy the formula.
   a. Select cell **B5** in the **BP&Walker** sheet.
   b. Click the *Formula* bar.
   c. Delete the dollar signs in **$B$5** to display **B5** and in **$D$5** to display **D5**, both relative references (Figure 5-29).
   d. Press **Enter**.
   e. Copy the formula in cell **B5** to cells **B6:B8**.

9. Create, edit, and copy linking formulas.
   a. Select cell **C5** in the **BP&Walker** sheet and type = to start the formula.
   b. Press **Ctrl+F6** or click the icon on the Windows taskbar for *[your initials]* **PP E5-1**.

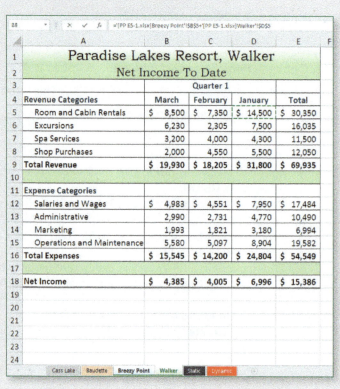

Cell reference: B8 — `='[PP E5-1.xlsx]Breezy Point'!$B$5+'[PP E5-1.xlsx]Walker'!$D$5`

	A	B	C	D	E	F
1		Paradise Lakes Resort, Walker				
2		Net Income To Date				
3		Quarter 1				
4	Revenue Categories	March	February	January	Total	
5	Room and Cabin Rentals	$ 8,500	$ 7,350	$ 14,500	$ 30,350	
6	Excursions	6,230	2,305	7,500	16,035	
7	Spa Services	3,200	4,000	4,300	11,500	
8	Shop Purchases	2,000	4,550	5,500	12,050	
9	Total Revenue	$ 19,930	$ 18,205	$ 31,800	$ 69,935	
10						
11	Expense Categories					
12	Salaries and Wages	$ 4,983	$ 4,551	$ 7,950	$ 17,484	
13	Administrative	2,990	2,731	4,770	10,490	
14	Marketing	1,993	1,821	3,180	6,994	
15	Operations and Maintenance	5,580	5,097	8,904	19,582	
16	Total Expenses	$ 15,545	$ 14,200	$ 24,804	$ 54,549	
17						
18	Net Income	$ 4,385	$ 4,005	$ 6,996	$ 15,386	

Sheet tabs: Cass Lake | Baudette | **Breezy Point** | Walker | Static | Dynamic

5-28 Point to build an external reference formula

c. Click the **Breezy Point** worksheet tab, select cell **C5** and type **+** for addition.

d. Click the **Walker** sheet tab, select cell **C5**, and press **Enter**. The linking formula is calculated in the **BP&Walker** sheet.

e. Select cell **C5** and click the *Formula* bar.

f. Delete the dollar signs in both occurrences of **$C$5** to display **C5**, and press **Enter**.

g. Select cell **D5** and type **=** to start the formula.

h. Press **Ctrl+F6** or click the icon on the Windows taskbar for *[your initials]* **PP E5-1**.

i. Click the **Breezy Point** worksheet tab, select cell **D5**, and type **+** for addition.

j. Click the **Walker** sheet tab, select cell **B5** for March, and press **Enter**.

k. Select cell **D5**, click the *Formula* bar, delete the dollar signs in **$D$5** and **$B$5** to create relative references, and press **Enter**.

l. Select cells **C5:D5** and copy the formulas to cells **C6:D8**.

m. Select and format cells **B6:D8** as **Comma Style** with no decimals.

10. Save and close the workbook (Figure 5-30).

11. Close *[your initials]* **PP E5-1** without saving it.

5-29 Linking formula edited to use relative references

5-30 Completed PP E-2 worksheets

SLO 5.6

Inserting Illustrations in a Worksheet

You can assist readers in understanding and navigating through your work in different ways. For example, include a link to direct users to another worksheet or to other locations in the same sheet. You might include a picture of folder contents to help a coworker learn file location.

SmartArt Graphics

A *SmartArt* graphic is an illustration, usually with text, in an Excel worksheet. Examples of *SmartArt* are organization charts, matrices, pyramids, bulleted lists, and similar diagrams.

SmartArt graphics are text-focused but some may include pictures. Figure 5-31 is a SmartArt graphic with text and pictures.

A SmartArt graphic has a pane for entering text, but you can also type directly inside the component shapes. The text pane appears on the left or right side of the graphic depending where the graphic is positioned. As you type an entry, the text and its shape are sized to fit the content.

A SmartArt graphic is not linked to worksheet data.

5-31 *SmartArt* graphic with four shapes and pictures

▶ HOW TO: Insert a SmartArt Graphic

1. Click the worksheet tab for the *SmartArt*.

2. Click the **Insert a SmartArt Graphic** button [*Insert* tab, *Illustrations* group].
   - The *Choose a SmartArt Graphic* dialog box opens (Figure 5-32).

3. Choose the category from the list on the left.
   - The *All* category displays all available designs.
   - Click a thumbnail image to see a preview and a description on the right.

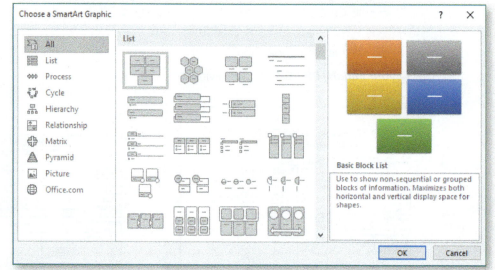

5-32 *Choose a SmartArt Graphic* dialog box

4. Select the *SmartArt* graphic and click **OK** (Figure 5-33).
   - A default object is placed at a default size in the worksheet.
   - The *Name* box displays *Diagram N*, where "N" is a number.
   - Display or hide the text pane by clicking the control at the left or right edge of the graphic frame

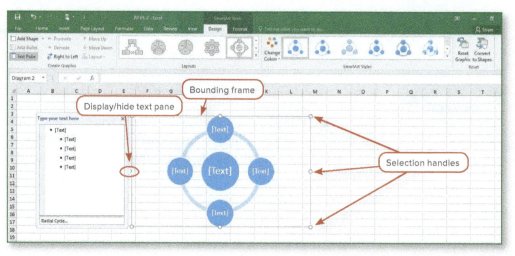

5-33 *SmartArt* graphic with text frame

or by clicking the **Text Pane** button [*SmartArt Tools Design* tab, *Create Graphic* group].

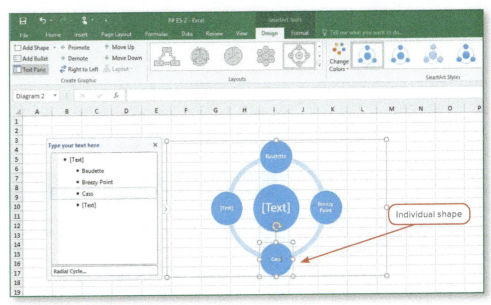

5-34 Text entered in *SmartArt* graphic

5. Click a shape and type the text (Figure 5-34).

- The entry appears in the shape and in the text pane.
- The label is sized to fit the shape as you type.
- You can edit text within the shape or the text pane.
- Each shape has its own selection handles and frame.

6. Click another shape or click the frame of the *SmartArt* object.

SmartArt Tools

A *SmartArt* graphic is an object that you can select, size, and format. It has selection and sizing handles as well as a bounding frame, similar to a chart object. A *SmartArt* graphic is one object that consists of several smaller shapes.

When you insert a *SmartArt* image, it is placed with the default number of shapes. For many *SmartArt* diagrams, you can add or remove shapes. Each individual shape in a *SmartArt* object has its own selection handles, a rotation handle, and a bounding frame.

> **MORE INFO**
>
> A few *SmartArt* shapes are limited in the number of smaller shapes they contain due to the layout and purpose of the diagram.

When a *SmartArt* object is selected, the *SmartArt Tools Design* and *Format* tabs are available. From the tabs, you can change to a different image, choose a style, add a shape, reposition shapes, and add fill, outline, and effects.

A *SmartArt* graphic rests on an invisible, transparent layer in the worksheet, covering cells. You can activate a worksheet cell that appears within the frame of the *SmartArt* by typing the cell address in the *Name* box or by moving the image.

▶ **HOW TO:** Format a SmartArt Graphic

1. Select the *SmartArt* graphic.
   - Click near one of the shapes to select the diagram.
   - The bounding frame is a rectangle that surrounds the graphic.
2. Click the **More** button [*SmartArt Tools Design* tab, *SmartArt Styles* group] to open the gallery.

3. Point to a style thumbnail to see a *Live Preview*.
4. Click a style icon to apply it.
5. Click the **Change Colors** button [*SmartArt Tools Design* tab, *SmartArt Styles* group].
6. Point to a color thumbnail to see a *Live Preview*.
7. Click a color scheme to apply it.
8. Click an individual shape in the graphic.
9. Click the arrow with the **Shape Fill** button [*SmartArt Tools Format* tab, *Shape Styles* group].
10. Choose a color from the gallery (Figure 5-35).
11. Point to a corner sizing handle on the *SmartArt* frame.
    - The pointer displays a resize arrow.
12. Drag the resize arrow to make the graphic larger or smaller.
13. Point to the *SmartArt* frame.
    - The pointer displays a move arrow.
14. Drag the graphic to the desired location.
15. Click a worksheet cell to deselect the *SmartArt* graphic.

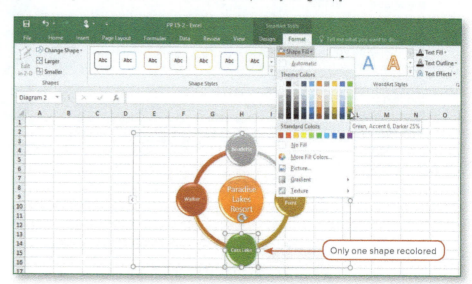

5-35 Shape Fill color gallery for a *SmartArt* shape

Screenshots

A **screenshot** is a picture of a full or partial computer screen inserted as an object in a worksheet. You can capture an image of an open window or select a portion of a document or text from a web site. When capturing screenshots of web pages or another person's work, you should have permission from the author or owner to use the image.

The *Take a Screenshot* button is located on the *Insert* tab in the *Illustrations* group. When you click the button, you see a gallery of open application windows (Figure 5-36). If you select one of the thumbnail windows, a capture of the full screen is placed in your worksheet. To select part of the window, choose **Screen Clipping** from the gallery.

Once you place a screenshot in the worksheet, it is a picture object that you can format, position, and size.

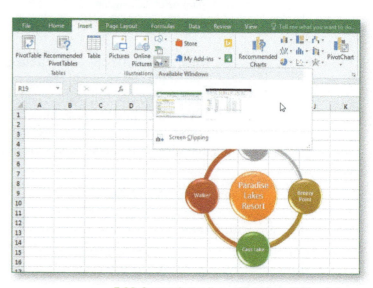

5-36 Screenshot gallery with two available windows

HOW TO: Insert a Screenshot Clipping in a Worksheet

1. Click the sheet tab where the screenshot will be inserted.

2. Open the workbook, document, or web site that contains the content to be captured.
   - Open only two windows or applications.
   - Open another window for the same workbook to capture an image from another worksheet.

3. Click a cell in the worksheet that will hold the captured image.

4. Click the **Take a Screenshot** button [*Insert* tab, *Illustrations* group].

5. From the gallery, choose **Screen Clipping**.
   - The focus switches to the next open window.
   - The entire screen dims in a few seconds.
   - The pointer shape in the dimmed window is a crosshair.

6. Draw a rectangle around the content to be captured with the crosshair pointer. (Figure 5-37).
   - The selected area is no longer dim.

7. Release the mouse button (Figure 5-38).
   - The focus returns to the worksheet.
   - The screenshot displays at a default size and position.

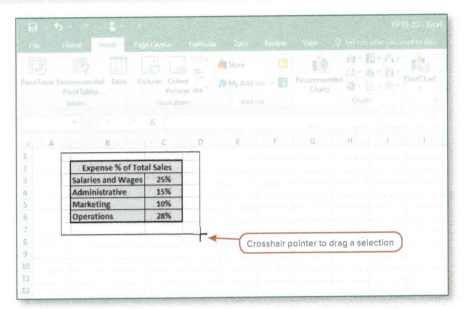

5-37 Dimmed screen for screenshot

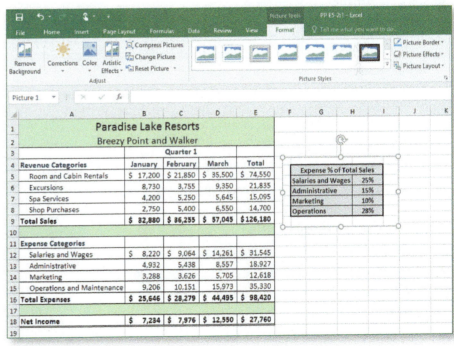

5-38 Screenshot image placed in worksheet

Picture Tools

A screenshot graphic is a picture object with selection and sizing handles, a rotation handle, and a bounding frame. When the object is selected, the *Picture Tools Format* tab is available with command groups for altering the appearance of the image.

Like a *SmartArt* graphic, a screenshot image is placed on the invisible, transparent layer of the worksheet.

> **HOW TO: Work with Picture tools**

1. Select the screenshot or picture object.
   - The bounding frame is rectangular.
   - Selection and sizing handles appear on the bounding frame.

2. Click the **More** button [*Picture Tools Format* tab, *Picture Styles* group].
   - The gallery includes preset combinations of border, fill, and rotation settings.

3. Point to a thumbnail to see a *Live Preview*.

4. Click an icon to apply the style (Figure 5-39).

5. Click the **Artistic Effects** button [*Picture Tools Format* tab, *Adjust* group].

5-39 Style applied to a screenshot

6. Point to a thumbnail to see a *Live Preview*.
   - Many effects may not be appropriate for worksheet images.

7. Click an icon to apply an effect.

8. Click the **Rotate** button [*Picture Tools Format* tab, *Arrange* group].

9. Point to a menu choice to see a *Live Preview*.

10. Click a rotation option to apply the setting.

11. Point to a corner sizing handle on the picture border to display a resize arrow.
    - Use a corner handle to size proportionally.

12. Drag the resize arrow to make the picture larger or smaller.

13. Point to the picture border.
    - The pointer displays a move arrow.

14. Drag the picture to the desired location.

15. Click a worksheet cell to deselect the picture object.

Pictures

You can place pictures in an Excel worksheet for clarification, emphasis, or visual appeal. Insert pictures from a file or online sources. Always investigate copyright issues when you use pictures from outside sources.

The *Pictures* and *Online Pictures* buttons are located on the *Insert* tab in the *Illustrations* group. The *Pictures* command inserts an image from your network, your computer, or your cloud sources. The *Online Pictures* command opens a dialog box in which you search for pictures related to a key term. Excel can use popular image formats such as JPEG, PNG, and TIFF, and you can do simple editing such as changing colors or adding shadows.

> ▶ **MORE INFO**
>
> Do not use too many pictures in a worksheet so that you do not draw attention away from the data.

▶ HOW TO: Insert a Picture from a File

1. Click a blank cell in the worksheet.
2. Click the **Pictures From File** button [*Insert* tab, *Illustrations* group].
   - The *Insert Picture* dialog box opens.
3. Navigate to the location with the image file.
4. Select the image file (Figure 5-40).
   - Adjust the view to show icons if you want to see a thumbnail of the picture.
5. Click **Insert**.
   - The picture appears in the worksheet at a default size and position (Figure 5-41).

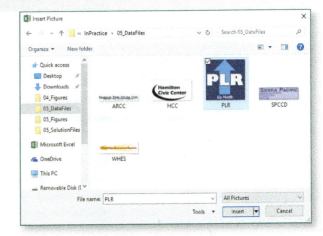

5-40 Select a picture from a file

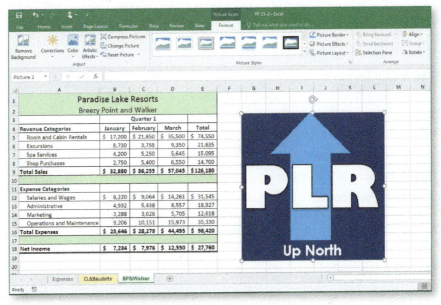

5-41 Picture placed at default size and position

- The picture object is selected.
- The *Picture Tools Format* tab displays.

6. Point to a corner selection handle to display a resize arrow and drag the pointer to shrink or enlarge the image.

7. Point to the image frame to display a move pointer and drag the picture to the desired location in the sheet.

SLO 5.7

Inserting Hyperlinks in a Worksheet

A *hyperlink* is a clickable text string or object that, when clicked, moves the pointer to another location. A hyperlink can also open another workbook or a web page. You might use a hyperlink to open a source workbook, to switch to another worksheet, or to navigate to a *SmartArt* image.

Cell Hyperlinks

A cell hyperlink is a text shortcut or jump term in a cell. It appears as underlined text in the color set in the document theme for hyperlinks. After a hyperlink is created, you can change the font color, font name, and font size from the mini toolbar or from the *Font* group on the *Home* tab.

ANOTHER WAY

The keyboard shortcut to insert a hyperlink is **Ctrl+K**.

The *Hyperlink* button is located on the *Insert* command tab. You can also insert a hyperlink from the shortcut menu for a cell.

MORE INFO

You can choose the hyperlink text color by clicking the *Colors* button on the *Page Layout* tab and selecting *Customize Colors*.

▶ **HOW TO:** Create a Cell Hyperlink

1. Click the cell where the hyperlink text should appear.

2. Click the **Hyperlink** button [*Insert* tab, *Links* group].
   - The *Insert Hyperlink* dialog box opens.

3. Select **Place in This Document** in the *Link to* list on the left.
   - The *Or select a place in this document* box displays locations in the workbook.
   - The names of existing sheets are listed in the *Cell Reference* group.
   - The *Defined Names* group displays range names in the workbook.
   - The *Cell Reference* and *Defined Names* groups have expand and collapse buttons.

4. Select a worksheet name to jump to that sheet.
   - Choose the name of the current sheet if the hyperlink will move to a location on this sheet.

5. Click the *Type the cell reference* box.

6. Type the cell address that should be selected when the hyperlink is clicked.
   - The default is cell **A1**.
7. Click the *Text to display* box and enter text for the hyperlink cell.
   - Select and delete default text.
8. Click the **ScreenTip** button (Figure 5-42).
   - The *Set Hyperlink ScreenTip* dialog box opens.
9. Type an optional *ScreenTip*.
   - The default *ScreenTip* identifies the file and provides basic instructions for a hyperlink.
10. Click **OK** to close the *Set Hyperlink ScreenTip* dialog box.
11. Click **OK** to close the *Insert Hyperlink* dialog box (Figure 5-43).
    - The underlined hyperlink text appears in the cell.
    - When you point to the link, the *ScreenTip* displays.
12. Click the hyperlink to navigate to the location.

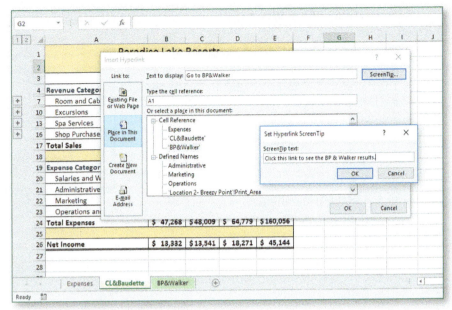

5-42 *Hyperlink* and custom *ScreenTip* dialog boxes

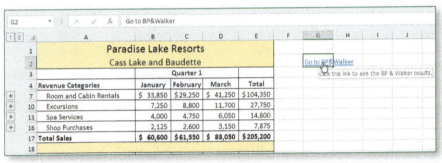

5-43 *Hyperlink* text and its *ScreenTip*

When you choose *Existing File or Web Page* in the *Insert Hyperlink* dialog box, you browse to the location for the file or the web page. The path to the file or the URL for the web address appears in the *Address* box.

Object Hyperlinks

An object hyperlink is a shortcut assigned to an object such as a *SmartArt* graphic, a chart, or a picture. There is no underlined text, but you can use the hyperlink *ScreenTip* to provide information.

▶ **HOW TO:** Create a Hyperlink to Open a File

1. Select the image or object.
   - The selection handles should be visible.
2. Click the **Hyperlink** button [*Insert* tab, *Links* group].
   - The *Insert Hyperlink* dialog box opens.

3. Select **Existing File or Web Page** in the *Link to* list on the left.

    - The *Look in* box displays the name of the current folder.
    - The names of workbooks in the current folder are listed.
    - You can navigate to other folders in this dialog box.

4. Select a workbook name.

    - The file name is entered in the *Address* box (Figure 5-44).

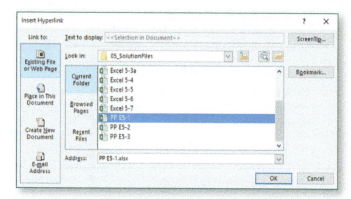

5. Click the **ScreenTip** button.

6. Type text for a *ScreenTip* to describe the action.

7. Click **OK** to close the *Set Hyperlink ScreenTip* dialog box.

8. Click **OK** to close the *Insert Hyperlink* dialog box (Figure 5-45).

5-44 Workbook name selected for hyperlink

9. Click a worksheet cell to deselect the object.

10. Point to the object to see the *ScreenTip*.

11. Click the object to open the file.

    - The file opens with the active sheet and cell based on its last save command.

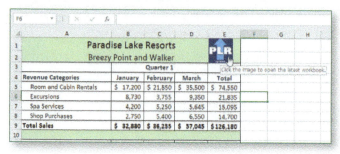

5-45 Object hyperlink in worksheet

To remove a hyperlink from a cell or from an object, right-click the cell or the object and choose **Remove Hyperlink**. You can also edit a hyperlink from the shortcut menu to change the *ScreenTip*, reset the file, or change a URL address.

 SLO 5.8

Safeguarding a Workbook

Excel has two commands that provide a simple level of security to protect your work from unwanted changes. One command is a courtesy message or warning and one command is the assignment of a password.

Mark a Workbook as Final

To let others know that your work is complete and should not be edited, use the *Mark as Final* command which sets a read-only file property. When the workbook opens, you will see a security message bar, an icon in the *Status* bar, and a *[Read-Only]* label in the title bar. You and others can remove the property by clicking the *Edit Anyway* button in the security message bar.

> ### ANOTHER WAY
>
> Remove the *Mark as Final* property by clicking the *Protect Workbook* button [*File* tab, *Info* option] and choosing *Mark as Final*.

▶ HOW TO: Mark a Workbook as Final

1. Save the workbook.
2. Click the **Protect Workbook** button [*File* tab, *Info* option].
   - Protection commands display.
3. Select **Mark as Final**.
   - A message box informs you that the file will be marked and saved (Figure 5-46).
4. Click **OK**.
   - The workbook is resaved with the same file name.
   - If the workbook has not yet been saved, the *Save As* dialog box opens so that you can choose the file location and name.
   - A second message box provides details about the *Mark as Final* command (Figure 5-47). (There is an option to hide this message box, so you may not see it).
5. Click **OK**.
   - The security bar shows the property (Figure 5-48).
   - The icon on the *Status* bar indicates that the workbook is final.

5-46 Message box that workbook will be saved and marked as final

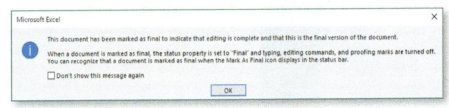

5-47 Details about the *Mark as Final* property

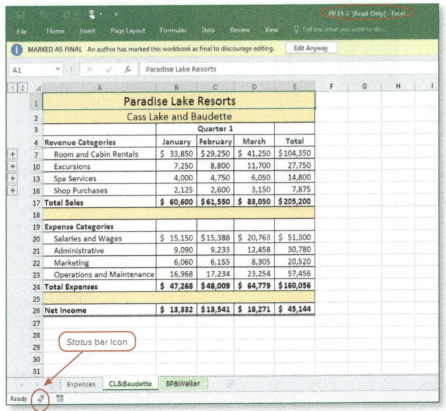

5-48 Workbook that is marked as final

Encrypt a Workbook with a Password

Password protection requires that you type the password as you open the workbook. After you set a password, the *Protect Workbook* button [*File* tab, *Info* pane] indicates that the workbook requires a password as shown in Figure 5-49.

To remove a password, you must open the workbook and enter the password. Then click the **Protect Workbook** button, select **Encrypt with Password**, delete the password, leave the *Password* box empty, and resave the workbook.

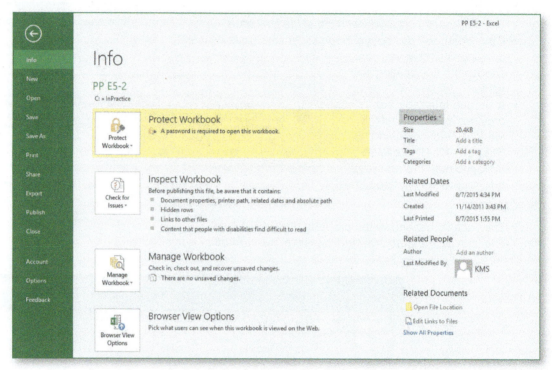

5-49 *Info* pane for a workbook with a password

▶ HOW TO: Password Protect a Workbook

1. Click the **Protect Workbook** button [*File* tab, *Info* pane].
2. Select **Encrypt with Password**.
   - The *Encrypt Document* dialog box opens.
3. Type a password in the *Password* box (Figure 5-50).
   - Passwords are hidden as you type them.
   - Passwords are case sensitive.
4. Click **OK**.
   - The *Confirm Password* dialog box requires that you retype the same password.
5. Retype the password and click **OK**.
6. Click **Close**.
7. Click **Save**.

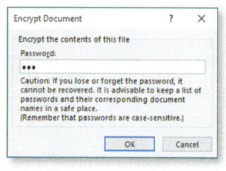

5-50 Passwords are case-sensitive and are hidden as you type them.

For this project, you insert a *SmartArt* graphic to illustrate how revenue results are consolidated for Paradise Lakes Resort. You insert a hyperlink to the *SmartArt*, add the company logo to a sheet, and mark your work as final.

Files Needed: **[your initials] PP E5-2.xlsx** and **PLR.png** (*Student data files are available in the* Library of *your SIMnet account*)
Completed Project File Name: **[your initials] PP E5-3.xlsx**

1. Open the **[your initials] PP E5-2.xlsx** workbook completed in *Pause & Practice 5-2*. Because the workbook includes links, you will see a security warning or a message box (Figure 5-51).

2. Click *Enable Editing* or *Update* to edit the workbook. The message box choice depends on your computer and file management procedures.

3. Save the workbook as
   [your initials] PP E5-3.

5-51 Security message for workbook with links

4. Insert a *SmartArt* graphic.
   a. Click the **New sheet** button.
   b. Name the new sheet SmartArt and position it at the end of the tab names.
   c. Click the **Insert a SmartArt Graphic** button [*Insert* tab, *Illustrations* group].
   d. Select **Cycle** in the list on the left.
   e. Locate and click **Radial Venn** in the gallery of graphics.
   f. Click **OK**. If the text pane for the graphic is open, close it.

5. Add text to a *SmartArt* graphic.
   a. Click the top circle shape.
   b. Type Room and Cabin Rentals. Do not press **Enter**; if you did, press **Backspace**.
   c. Click the leftmost circle shape and type Excursions. If you make an error, click again in the shape and make the correction.
   d. Type Spa Purchases in the bottom circle shape.
   e. Type Shop Purchases in the rightmost shape.
   f. In the center shape, type Total Revenue (Figure 5-52).
   g. Click a cell near the center circle to deselect the shape.

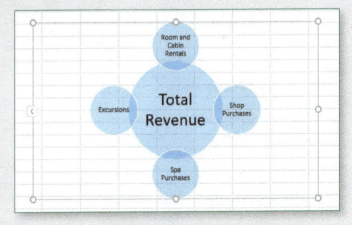

5-52 Text entered in shapes in *SmartArt* graphic

6. Format, position, and size a *SmartArt* graphic.
   a. Click the frame of the *SmartArt* graphic to select it.
   b. Click the **More** button [*SmartArt Tools Design* tab, *SmartArt Styles* group].
   c. Choose **Inset** in the *3-D* group.
   d. Click the **Change Colors** button [*SmartArt Tools Design* tab, *SmartArt Styles* group].
   e. Choose **Colorful – Accent Colors**.
   f. Point to the *SmartArt* frame to display a move pointer.

g. Drag the graphic to position the top left selection handle in cell **A1**. When a *SmartArt* graphic is selected, you can also use a keyboard directional arrow key to nudge the object into position.

h. Point to the bottom right selection handle to display a resize arrow.

i. Drag the frame to reach cell **I22** (Figure 5-53).

j. Click cell **K1** to deselect the *SmartArt*.

7. Insert a hyperlink.

a. Click the **BP&Walker** sheet tab.

b. Select cell **G2**.

c. Click the **Hyperlink** button [*Insert* tab, *Links* group].

d. Select **Place in This Document**.

e. Select the sheet name **SmartArt** in the *Or select a place in this document* list.

f. Select the default text In the *Text to display* box and type View Illustration.

g. Click the **ScreenTip** button and type Click this link to view the graphic. (Figure 5-54).

h. Click **OK** in the *Set Hyperlink ScreenTip* dialog box.

i. Click **OK** in the *Insert Hyperlink* dialog box.

j. Click cell **G3**.

k. Click the link to test it.

8. Insert a picture.

a. Click the **CL&Baudette** sheet tab.

b. Click the **Pictures** button [*Insert* tab, *Illustrations* group].

c. Navigate to the folder with your student data files.

d. Choose **PLR** and click **Insert**.

e. Click the **Height** box [*Picture Tools Format* tab, *Size* group].

f. Replace the default height with .55 and press **Enter**.

g. Click the **Color** button [*Picture Tools Format* tab, *Adjust* group].

h. Select **Gold, Accent color 4 Dark** in the *Recolor* group.

i. Drag and position the image as shown in Figure 5-55.

9. Click cell **A3**.

5-53 Styled and positioned *SmartArt*

5-54 Hyperlink text and *ScreenTip*

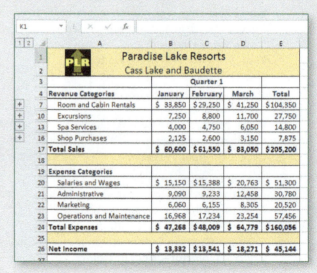

5-55 Image inserted in worksheet

10. Mark a workbook as final.
    a. Click the **File** tab.
    b. Click the **Protect Workbook** button and select **Mark as Final**.
    c. Click **OK** to resave the file.
    d. Click **OK** to close the message box.

11. Close the workbook (Figure 5-56).

Paradise Lake Resorts				
Breezy Point and Walker				
		Quarter 1		
Revenue Categories	January	February	March	Total
Room and Cabin Rentals	$ 17,200	$ 21,850	$ 35,500	$ 74,550
Excursions	8,730	3,755	9,350	21,835
Spa Services	4,200	5,250	5,645	15,095
Shop Purchases	2,750	5,400	6,550	14,700
Total Sales	$ 32,880	$ 36,255	$ 57,045	$ 126,180
Expense Categories				
Salaries and Wages	$ 8,220	$ 9,064	$ 14,261	$ 31,545
Administrative	4,932	5,438	8,557	18,927
Marketing	3,288	3,626	5,705	12,618
Operations and Maintenance	9,206	10,151	15,973	35,330
Total Expenses	$ 25,646	$ 28,279	$ 44,495	$ 98,420
Net Income	$ 7,234	$ 7,976	$ 12,550	$ 27,760

View Illustration

5-56 Completed worksheet for PP E5-3

Chapter Summary

5.1 Create a static data consolidation (p. E5-294).

- A **consolidated worksheet** combines data from multiple worksheets using a mathematical or statistical function.
- When labels and values are in the same position on all worksheets, the consolidation is by position.
- A **static consolidation** places a non-changing result in the consolidation sheet. If the source data is edited, the consolidated sheet is not updated.
- The **Consolidate** button is located on the *Data* tab in the *Data Tools* group.

5.2 Create a dynamic data consolidation (p. E5-296).

- A **dynamic consolidation** places formulas in the consolidation worksheet. If the source data is edited, the consolidated sheet is automatically updated.
- A dynamic data consolidation formats the results as an Excel outline.
- To build a dynamic consolidation, choose the *Create links to source data* option in the *Consolidate* dialog box.

5.3 Consolidate data by category (p. E5-298).

- When labels and values are not in the same position on all worksheets, you may be able to consolidate data by category.
- A category is a row or column label.
- A consolidate by category command includes the label cells on the source worksheets.
- The consolidated sheet displays labels in the same order as the first sheet listed in the *Consolidate* dialog box.
- Consolidation by category can be static or dynamic.

5.4 Group worksheets for editing and formatting (p. E5-299).

- When worksheets are grouped, editing and format commands affect all sheets in the group.
- You can apply formats, enter formulas, or enter data in grouped sheets.
- Not all commands are available in grouped sheets.
- When a command is not available, it is grayed out in the *Ribbon*.
- Press **Shift** or **Ctrl** to group contiguous or non-contiguous sheets.

- Ungroup sheets when finished editing to guard against applying a command in error to the group.

5.5 Link workbooks to consolidate data (p. E5-303).

- **Linking** workbooks is the process of referring to data in another workbook.
- A **dependent workbook** refers to data in another workbook.
- A **source workbook** supplies data to another workbook.
- An **external reference** formula is in a dependent workbook and refers to cells in a source workbook.
- An external reference includes the name of the workbook, the sheet name, cell addresses, and **identifiers**.
- You can **link** workbooks by using the *Consolidate* command on the *Data* tab if all source workbooks are open.
- You can link workbooks by building a formula that refers to another workbook.
- You can point to build an external reference formula if the source workbook is open.
- If the source workbook is not open, build an external reference formula by typing the complete path and file name, the sheet name, cell addresses, and all identifiers.
- The *Excel Trust Center* includes security options for workbooks with links.

5.6 Insert illustrations using *SmartArt*, screenshots, and pictures in a worksheet (p. E5-309).

- A **SmartArt** graphic is an illustration such as a matrix, a cycle diagram, an organization chart, or a process chart.
- A *SmartArt* graphic is a selectable object that you can size, position, and style.
- *SmartArt* graphics are not linked to worksheet data; they contain descriptive text.
- When a *SmartArt* graphic is selected, the *SmartArt Tools Design* and *Format* tabs are available.
- A *SmartArt* graphic consists of several smaller shapes; you can format an individual shape separately.
- A **screenshot** is an image of data on the screen that is inserted as a picture object in a worksheet.

- The **Take a Screenshot** button displays thumbnails of open windows that you can capture as images.
- You can take a *Screen Clipping* by drawing a rectangle around the desired area.
- Pictures can be inserted in a worksheet from a file or from online sources.
- When a picture object is selected, the *Picture Tools Format* tab is available with commands for changing the appearance of the image.

5.7 Insert hyperlinks in a worksheet (p. E5-316).

- A *hyperlink* is a clickable line of text in a cell or a clickable object in a worksheet.
- A hyperlink acts as a jump term or a shortcut to another location in the workbook, on the computer, or in the cloud.
- A cell hyperlink is underlined text in the color specified by the document theme.
- An object hyperlink is a shortcut assigned to an image, a *SmartArt* graphic, or another object.
- The *Hyperlink* button is located in the *Links* group on the *Insert* tab.

5.8 Safeguard work by marking it as final or by setting a password (p. E5-318).

- You can assign a simple level of security to a workbook by marking it as final.
- The *Mark as Final* command is a reminder that the work is complete and should not be edited.
- You can remove the *Mark as Final* setting by clicking **Enable Editing** in the security message bar.
- The *Encrypt with Password* command allows you to assign a password to a workbook.
- You must type the password before the workbook can be opened.
- The *Mark as Final* and *Encrypt with Password* commands are available from the **Protect Workbook** button [*File* tab, *Info* pane].

Check for Understanding

The SIMbook for this text (within your SIMnet account) provides the following resources for concept review:

- Multiple choice questions
- Matching exercises
- Short answer questions

Guided Project 5-1

Blue Lake Sports has maintained sales data about specialty departments. For this project, you reformat worksheets as a group, insert the *SUM* function, build static and dynamic consolidation sheets, insert a *SmartArt* graphic, and create a hyperlink.
[Student Learning Outcomes 5.1, 5.2, 5.4, 5.5, 5.6, 5.7, 5.8]

Files Needed: ***BlueLakeSports-05.xlsx*** and ***BlueLakeSportsLinked-05.xlsx*** *(Student data files are available in the* Library *of your SIMnet account)*
Completed Project File Names: *[your initials] Excel 5-1.xlsx* and *[your initials] Excel 5-1a.xlsx*

Skills Covered in This Project

- Group and format worksheets.
- Edit grouped worksheets.
- Enter a *SUM* function in grouped worksheets.
- Create a static data consolidation.
- Create a dynamic consolidation.
- Link workbooks using the *Consolidate* command.
- Encrypt a workbook with a password.
- Insert and format a *SmartArt* graphic.
- Insert and format a hyperlink.

1. Open the ***BlueLakeSports-05*** workbook from your student data files and save it as [your initials] Excel 5-1.

2. Group and format worksheets.
   a. Right-click the **Quarter 1** tab and choose **Select All Sheets**.
   b. Select cell **A2** and change the font to **Calibri**.
   c. Select cells **A4:E8** and apply **All Borders**.
   d. Select cells **A8:E8** and apply a **Top and Double Bottom Border**.
   e. Click the **Launcher** in the *Page Setup* group on the *Page Layout* tab.
   f. Select the **Horizontally** box on the *Margins* tab to center the data on the page.
   g. Click the **Header/Footer** tab.
   h. Click the *Footer* drop-down arrow and select *[your initials] Excel 5-1*.
   i. Click **OK**.

3. Enter a formula for grouped sheets.
   a. Click cell **E5** and enter a *SUM* function to add cells **B5:D5**.
   b. Select cell **E5** and copy the formula to cells **E6:E7**.
   c. Select cells **B5:E5** and cells **B8:E8**.
   d. Click the **Accounting Number Format** button [*Home* tab, *Number* group].
   e. Click the **Decrease Decimal** button twice [*Home* tab, *Number* group].
   f. Select cells **B6:E7** and click the **Decrease Decimal** button twice [*Home* tab, *Number* group].
   g. Press **Ctrl+Home** (Figure 5-57).
   h. Right-click the **Static** tab and choose **Ungroup Sheets**.

4. Create a static data consolidation.
   a. Select cell **B5** on the **Static** sheet.
   b. Click the **Consolidate** button [*Data* tab, *Data Tools* group].
   c. Choose the **SUM** function.

d. Select each reference, if any, in the *All references* box and click **Delete**.

e. Click the *Reference* box and click the **Quarter 1** worksheet tab.

f. Select cells **B5:D7**.

g. Click **Add** in the *Consolidate* dialog box.

h. Click the **Quarter 2** tab. Verify that cells B5:D7 are selected.

i. Click **Add** in the *Consolidate* dialog box.

j. Add cells **B5:D7** from the **Quarter 3** and **Quarter 4** worksheets to the *All references* list in the *Consolidate* dialog box.

k. Click **OK**. (Figure 5-58).

5. Select cell **A1**.

6. Open the ***BlueLakeSportsLinked-05.xlsx*** workbook from your student data files and save it as [your initials] Excel 5-1a.

7. Tile the windows.
   a. Click the **Arrange All** button [*View* tab, *Window* group].
   b. Choose **Vertical** and click **OK**.

8. Create a dynamic data consolidation by linking workbooks.
   a. Click cell **B5** in *[your initials] Excel 5-1a*.
   b. Click the **Consolidate** button [*Data* tab, *Data Tools* group].
   c. Choose the **SUM** function.
   d. Select each reference in the *All references* box and click **Delete**.
   e. Click the *Reference* box and double-click the **Quarter 1** tab in *[your initials] Excel 5-1*. The first click activates the window; the second click selects the tab.
   f. Select cell **E5** and click **Add** in the *Consolidate* dialog box.
   g. Click the **Quarter 2** tab in *[your initials] Excel 5-1*.
   h. Verify that cell **E5** is selected and click **Add** in the *Consolidate* dialog box.
   i. Add cell **E5** from the **Quarter 3** and **Quarter 4** worksheets to the *All references* list.
   j. Select the **Create links to source data** box (Figure 5-59).
   k. Click **OK**. The result is $2,182,906.

9. Repeat step 8 for the **Golf** and **Winter Sports** categories (cells **E6** and **E7**).

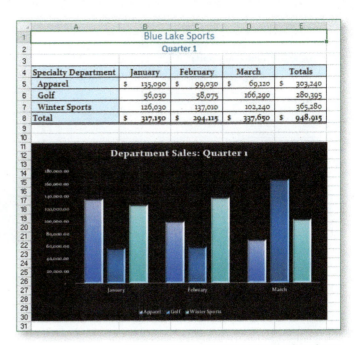

5-57 Completed *Quarter 1* **sheet; other sheets are the same**

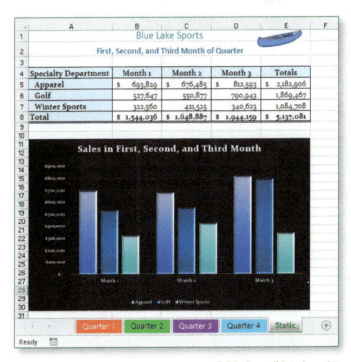

5-58 Consolidated results

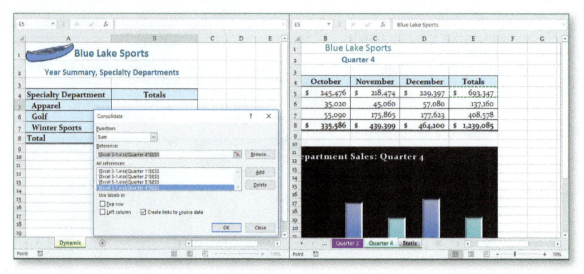

5-59 Dynamic consolidation for Apparel group

10. Click cell **B20** in *[your initials] Excel 5-1a* and click the **AutoSum** button [*Home* tab, *Editing* group].

11. Insert a *SmartArt* graphic.
    a. Click cell **D2** on the **Dynamic** sheet. Maximize the window.
    b. Click the **Insert a SmartArt Graphic** button [*Insert* tab, *Illustrations* group].
    c. Click **Process** in the list at the left.
    d. Find and click **Vertical Equation** in the gallery of graphics.
    e. Click **OK** to insert the *SmartArt* graphic. Close the text pane if necessary.
    f. Click the top left circle shape and type Apparel. Do not press **Enter;** if you did, press **Backspace**.
    g. Click the shape below *Apparel* and type Golf.
    h. Click the **Add Shape** button [*SmartArt Tools Design* tab, *Create Graphic* group] (Figure 5-60).
    i. Click the bottom shape and type Winter Sports.
    j. Click the large circle shape on the right and type Specialty Departments.

12. Format, position, and size a *SmartArt* graphic.
    a. Click the frame of the *SmartArt* graphic to select it.
    b. Click the **More** button [*SmartArt Tools Design* tab, *SmartArt Styles* group].
    c. Choose **Polished** in the 3-D group.
    d. Click the **Change Colors** button [*SmartArt Tools Design* tab, *SmartArt Styles* group].
    e. Choose **Colored Fill – Accent 1** in the *Accent 1* group.
    f. Click the **Shape Fill** button [*SmartArt Tools Format* tab, *Shapes Styles* group].
    g. Choose **White, Background 1, Darker 15%**.

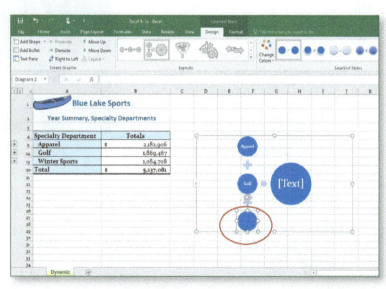

5-60 Shape added to *SmartArt* graphic

h. Click the **Shape Outline** button [*SmartArt Tools Format* tab, *Shapes Styles* group].

i. Choose **Weight** and select **½ pt**.

j. Click the **Shape Outline** button again and choose **Blue, Accent 1**.

k. Point to the *SmartArt* frame to display a move pointer.

l. Drag the graphic to position the top left selection handle in cell **C1**. While the graphic is selected, press the *Up* or *Left* keyboard directional arrow to fine-tune the position of the graphic.

m. Point to the bottom right selection handle to display a resize pointer.

n. Drag the pointer to reach cell **J35**.

13. Click cell **B3** to deselect the *SmartArt*.

14. Save and close the workbook (Figure 5-61).

15. Maximize the window for **[your initials] Excel 5-1**.

16. Insert a hyperlink.
    a. Click the **Quarter 4** sheet tab and select cell **F9**.
    b. Click the **Hyperlink** button [*Insert* tab, *Links* group].
    c. Select **Place in This Document** in the *Insert Hyperlink* dialog box.
    d. In the *Or select a place in this document* list, select **Static** in the *Cell Reference* group.
    e. Select the default text in the *Text to display* box and type See totals.
    f. Click **OK** in the *Insert Hyperlink* dialog box.

17. Format a hyperlink.
    a. Right-click the cell hyperlink.
    b. Format the font size to **16 pt.** from the mini toolbar.
    c. Format the font color to **Blue, Accent 1**.
    d. Click cell **G7** (Figure 5-62).

18. Click the hyperlink to test it.

19. Encrypt a workbook with a password.
    a. Click the **Protect Workbook** button [*File* tab, *Info* pane].

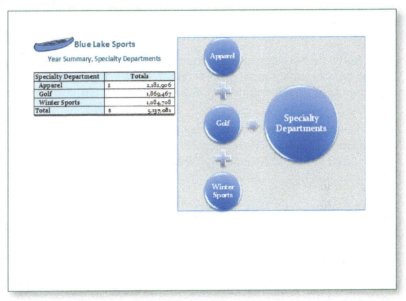

5-61 Completed *SmartArt* graphic and worksheet

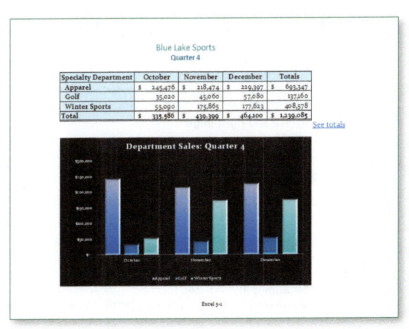

5-62 Completed hyperlink for Excel 5-1

    b. Select **Encrypt with Password**.

    c. Type 123 in the *Password* box.

    d. Click **OK**.

    e. Retype 123 to confirm the password and click **OK**.

    f. Click **Close**.

    g. Click **Save**.

Guided Project 5-2

Eller Software Services has collected monthly data for products and services and can consolidate and link to create management reports. You also format grouped sheets.
[Student Learning Outcomes 5.1, 5.2, 5.3, 5.4, 5.5, 5.6, 5.7, 5.8]

Files Needed: ***EllerSoftware-05.xlsx*** and ***EllerSoftwareLinked-05.xlsx*** (*Student data files are available in the Library of your SIMnet account*)
Completed Project File Names: [***your initials***] ***Excel 5-2.xlsx*** and [***your initials***] ***Excel 5-2a.xlsx***

Skills Covered in This Project

- Group and format worksheets.
- Build a static consolidation by category.
- Build a dynamic data consolidation by position.
- Link workbooks with a formula.
- Insert a screenshot in a worksheet.
- Size and format a screenshot.
- Insert an object hyperlink.
- Mark a workbook as final.

1. Open ***EllerSoftware-05.xlsx*** from your student data files and save it as [your initials] Excel 5-2.

2. Group and format worksheets.
   a. Right-click the **2015** sheet tab and choose **Select All Sheets**.
   b. Select cells **B4:F4** and **B9:F9**.
   c. Click the **Accounting Number Format** button [*Home* tab, *Number* group].
   d. Click the **Decrease Decimal** button [*Home* tab, *Number* group] two times.
   e. Select cells **B5:F8** and apply **Comma Style** with no decimals.
   f. Select cells **B9:F9** and click the **AutoSum** button [*Home* tab, *Editing* group].
   g. Select cell **A9** and **right-align** it.
   h. Select cell **A1**.
   i. Right-click the **2015** tab and choose **Ungroup Sheets**.

3. Click the **2017** sheet tab. Notice that the month names are not in January to April order.

4. Make a copy of the **2017** sheet at the end of the tabs and name the copy as Static.

5. Create a static consolidation by category.
   a. Select cells **B3:E8** on the **Static** sheet and press **Delete**.
   b. Click the **Consolidate** button [*Data* tab, *Data Tools* group].
   c. Select and delete references in the *All references* box, if any.
   d. Verify that **Sum** is the selected function.
   e. Click the *Reference* box and select the **2015** sheet tab.
   f. Select cells **B3:E8** on the **2015** sheet.
   g. Click **Add** in the *Consolidate* dialog box.

h. Click the **2016** tab name and add the same range to the *All references* list.

i. Repeat for the *2017* sheet.

j. Select the **Top row** box in the *Use labels in* group (Figure 5-63).

k. Click **OK**. The months are consolidated in the same order as the months on the first sheet used in the consolidation (2015).

l. Press **Ctrl+Home**.

6. Make a copy of the **2017** sheet at the end and name the copy as Dynamic.

7. Create a dynamic consolidation by category.

a. Select cells **B3:E8** on the **Dynamic** sheet and press **Delete**.

b. Click the **Consolidate** button [*Data* tab, *Data Tools* group].

c. Click the **Function** arrow and choose **Average**.

d. Verify the references in the *All references* box or select the same cells as those used in Step 5 (cells **B3:E8** on the **2015**, **2016**, and **2017** sheets).

e. Verify that the **Top row** box is selected.

f. Select the **Create links to source data** box and click **OK** (Figure 5-64).

8. Edit the label in cell **A2** to insert the word Average before "Billings."

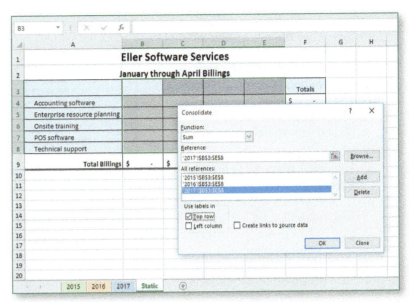

5-63 Consolidating by category

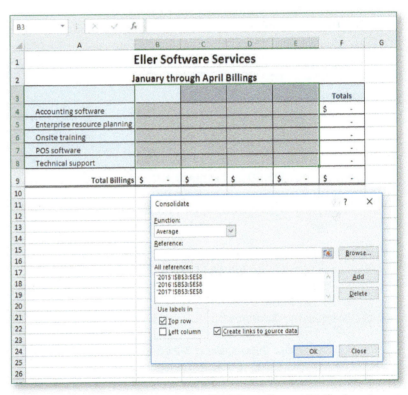

5-64 Dynamic consolidation by category

9. Right-click the column **F** heading and delete the column. Right click the row **24** heading and delete it (Figure 5-65).

10. Open **EllerSoftwareLinked-05.xlsx** from your student data files and save it as [your initials] Excel 5-2a.

11. Click the **Arrange All** button [*View* tab, *Window* group]. Choose **Vertical** and click **OK**. It does not matter which workbook is in the left pane.

12. Link workbooks with a formula.
   a. Select cell **B5** in the *[your initials] Excel 5-2a* workbook and type **=**.
   b. Double-click the **Static** sheet tab in *[your initials] Excel 5-2* to activate it and select cell **E4** (Figure 5-66).
   c. Press **Enter**. The reference is placed with an absolute reference.

13. Copy and edit a linked formula.
   a. Select cell **B5** in *[your initials] Excel 5-2a*.
   b. Click the *Formula* bar and delete both dollar signs. Click after **E4**, type ***125%** to multiply by 125%, and press **Enter** (Figure 5-67).
   c. Copy the formula in cell **B5** to cells **B6:B9** without formatting to preserve the borders.

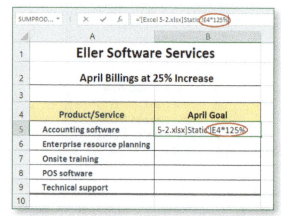

5-65 Completed *Dynamic* sheet

5-66 External reference with absolute reference

   d. Format cells **B5:B9** as **Currency** with zero decimal places.
   e. Maximize the *[your initials] Excel 5-2a* window.

14. Insert and format a screenshot in a workbook.
   a. Switch to the *[your initials] Excel 5-2* workbook and maximize the window.
   b. Select the **Static** sheet tab.
   c. Deselect the **Gridlines** box [*View* tab, *Show* group].
   d. Switch to *[your initials] Excel 5-2a* and select cell **A11**. (It is easier to take screenshots when only the two windows of interest are open, so if you have other programs running, close them and return to *[your initials] Excel 5-2a*.)
   e. Click the **Take a Screenshot** button [*Insert* tab, *Illustrations* group].
   f. Choose **Screen Clipping** from the gallery. The focus switches to *[your initials] Excel 5-2* and the screen dims after a few seconds.
   g. With the crosshair pointer, draw a rectangle to frame cells **A1:F9** for the screenshot and release the mouse button.

5-67 Edit the formula

h. Click the **More** button [*Picture Tools Format* tab, *Picture Styles* group].
i. Find and select **Center Shadow Rectangle** (Figure 5-68).

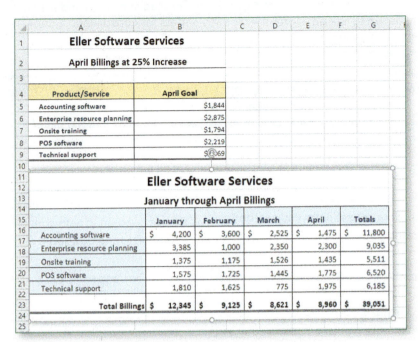

5-68 Screenshot placed in worksheet

15. Insert an object hyperlink.
    a. Select the screenshot if necessary.
    b. Click the **Hyperlink** button [*Insert* tab, *Links* group].
    c. Select **Existing File or Web Page** in the *Insert Hyperlink* dialog box.
    d. Select **Current Folder** in the *Look in* group.
    e. Select *[your initials] Excel 5-2* in the file name list. If your file is not listed, navigate to the correct folder to locate it.
    f. Click **ScreenTip** and type Click to open source file (Figure 5-69).
    g. Click **OK** in the *Set Hyperlink ScreenTip* dialog box.
    h. Click **OK** in the *Insert Hyperlink* dialog box.
    i. Select cell **A1**.

16. Switch to the *[your initials] Excel 5-2* window.

17. Mark a workbook as final.
    a. Click the **File** tab.
    b. Click the **Protect Workbook** button and select **Mark as Final**.
    c. Click **OK** to resave the file.
    d. Click **OK** to close the message box.
    e. Close the workbook.

18. Click the hyperlink in *[your initials] Excel 5-2a* to test it. The *[your initials] Excel 5-2* workbook opens in *Read Only* mode because it is marked as final.

19. Close *[your initials] Excel 5-2*. Save and close *[your initials] Excel 5-2a*.

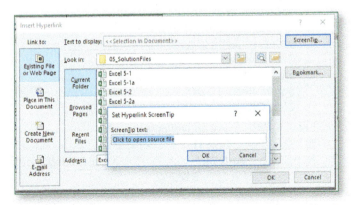

5-69 Hyperlink to open another workbook

Guided Project 5-3

Hamilton Civic Center tracks the number of participants enrolled in classes and seminars. You will create a dynamic consolidation to link data, prepare monthly sheets for consolidation, copy the company logo, and complete work for the summary workbook.
[Student Learning Outcomes 5.1, 5.2, 5.3, 5.4, 5.5, 5.6]

Files Needed: *HamiltonCC-05.xlsx*, *HamiltonCCLinked-05.xlsx*, and *HCC.png* (Student data files are available in the Library of your SIMnet account)
Completed Project File Names: *[your initials] Excel 5-3.xlsx* and *[your initials] Excel 5-3a.xlsx*

Skills Covered in This Project

- Group and format worksheets.
- Create a static data consolidation by category.
- Sort consolidated data.
- Copy a picture.
- Break links in a workbook.
- Link workbooks in the *Consolidate* dialog box.
- Create a dynamic data consolidation.
- Insert, size, and position a picture.

1. Open the *HamiltonCC-05* workbook from your student data files and save it as [your initials] Excel 5-3.

2. Group the worksheets.
   a. Click the **January** worksheet tab.
   b. Press **Shift** and click the **March** tab.

3. Format grouped worksheets.
   a. Select cells **A5:F12**.
   b. Click the arrow with the **Borders** button [*Home* tab, *Font* group] and select **More Borders**.
   c. Click the **Color** arrow and choose **Black, Text 1**.
   d. Click the thin solid line **Style** (bottom choice in the first column of styles).
   e. Click the **vertical middle** of the preview box. If you place a border in the wrong location, click the line in the preview to remove it.
   f. Click the second line **Style** in the first column (two below **None**).
   g. Click the **horizontal middle** of the preview box. This border will appear between rows.
   h. Click the bottom line **Style** in the second column (a double border).
   i. Click the **bottom** of the preview area to place a bottom horizontal border (Figure 5-70).
   j. Click **OK**.

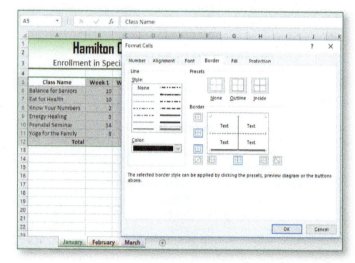

5-70 *Border* tab in *Format Cells* dialog box

4. Enter *SUM* in grouped worksheets.
   a. Select cells **F6:F11**.
   b. Click the **AutoSum** button [*Home* tab, *Editing* group].
   c. Use *SUM* in cells **B12:F12**.
   d. Click cell **A1**.
   e. Right-click the **February** sheet tab and choose **Ungroup Sheets**.

5. Copy a picture.
   a. Click to select the organization logo picture on the **February** sheet.
   b. Press **Ctrl+C** to copy the picture.
   c. Click the **January** sheet tab.
   d. Press **Ctrl+V** to paste the picture.
   e. Point to the picture frame to display a move pointer.
   f. Drag the picture so that it appears in column A to the left of "Hamilton Civic Center." You can nudge the image with any keyboard directional arrow key.
   g. Click cell **B1**.

6. Make a copy of the **March** sheet at the end and name it Quarter 1.

7. Set the tab color to **Black, Text 1**.

8. Edit cell **A3** to read First Quarter Enrollment.

9. Create a static data consolidation by category.
   a. Delete the contents of cells **A6:E11** on the **Quarter 1** sheet. The labels in column A are not in the same order on the quarterly sheets.
   b. Click the **Consolidate** button [*Data* tab, *Data Tools* group].
   c. Choose the **SUM** function.
   d. Select and delete references in the *All references* box.
   e. Click the *Reference* box and click the **January** tab.
   f. Select cells **A6:E11** and click **Add** in the *Consolidate* dialog box.
   g. Click the **February** tab, verify that cells A6:E11 are selected, and click **Add**.
   h. Add the **March** worksheet data to the *All references* list.
   i. Select the **Left column** box in the *Use labels in* group (Figure 5-71).
   j. Click **OK**.

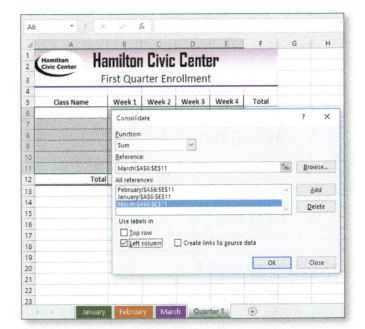

5-71 *Consolidate* dialog box to consolidate by category

10. Sort consolidated data.
    a. Select cells **A6:E11** on the **Quarter 1** sheet.
    b. Click the **Sort & Filter** button [*Home* tab, *Editing* group].
    c. Choose **Sort A to Z**.
    d. Click cell **B1**.

11. Save the *[your initials] Excel 5-3* workbook and leave it open.

12. Open the *HamiltonCCLinked-05* workbook from your student data files. Click **Enable Editing** if updating of links is disabled, or click *Update* or *Continue* without updating. The message box depends on file management procedures on your computer.

13. Save the workbook as [your initials] Excel 5-3a.

14. View and break links in the workbook.
    a. Click cell **D7**. The link is incorrect; it should refer to the **Quarter 1** sheet in *[your initials] Excel 5-3*.
    b. Click the **Edit Links** button [*Data* tab, *Connections* group].

c. Click **Break Link**. When you break a link, formulas are replaced with values and the command cannot be undone (Figure 5-72).

d. Click **Break Links**. Formulas are removed, but the cells display the values.

e. Click **Close**.

5-72 *Edit Links* dialog box and *Break Links* message box

15. Create a dynamic data consolidation to link workbooks.
    a. Select cells **D7:D12** on the **FirstQuarter** sheet.
    b. Click the **Consolidate** button [*Data* tab, *Data Tools* group].
    c. Choose the **SUM** function.
    d. Select and delete references in the *All references* box.
    e. Click the *Reference* box and press **Ctrl+F6** to switch to the *[your initials] Excel 5-3* workbook.
    f. Click the **Quarter 1** sheet tab if necessary.
    g. Select cells **F6:F11**. When there is only one reference, you don't need to click **Add**.
    h. Select the **Create links to source data** box (Figure 5-73).
    i. Click **OK**.
    j. Switch to the *[your initials] Excel 5-3a* workbook if necessary.
    k. Select cell **D19**, click the **AutoSum** button [*Home* tab, *Editing* group], and press **Enter**.

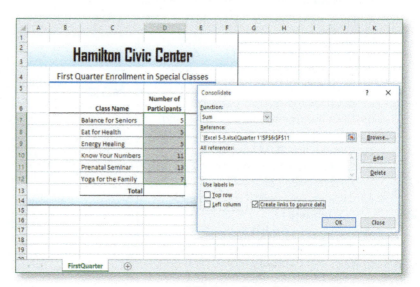

5-73 *Consolidate* dialog box to link workbooks

16. Insert a picture from a file.
    a. Click cell **G2** on the **FirstQuarter** sheet.
    b. Click the **Pictures** button [*Insert* tab, *Illustrations* group].
    c. Find and select **HCC** from your student data files (Figure 5-74).
    d. Click **Insert**. The picture is placed at a default size.

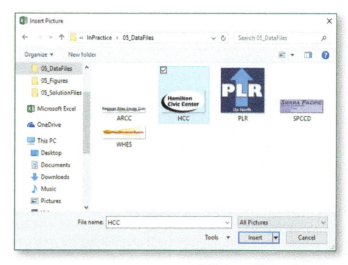

5-74 *Insert Picture* dialog box

e. Click the **Height** box [*Picture Tools Format* tab, *Size* group].

f. Type **.5** to replace the default height and press **Enter**. The image is proportionally resized.

g. Point to the logo frame to display a move pointer.

h. Drag the image to cover cells **A1:B3**.

i. Click cell **C1**.

17. Save and close the *[your initials] Excel 5-3a* workbook. Save and close the *[your initials] Excel 5-3* workbook (Figure 5-75).

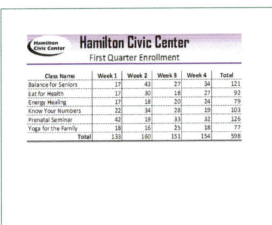

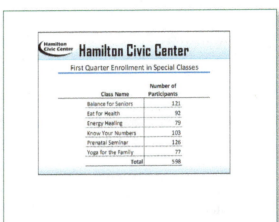

5-75 Completed worksheets for Excel 5-3a

Independent Project 5-4

Wilson Home Entertainment Systems monitors cash flow at their locations separately and consolidates data at the end of the quarter. After the summary is complete, you insert hyperlinks to each of the supporting worksheets.

[Student Learning Outcomes 5.1, 5.2, 5.4, 5.6, 5.7, 5.8]

Files Needed: ***WilsonHome-05.xlsx*** and ***WHES.png*** *(Student data files are available in the* Library *of your SIMnet account)*

Completed Project File Name: *[your initials] Excel 5-4.xlsx*

Skills Covered in This Project

- Group and format worksheets.
- Create a static data consolidation with *SUM*.
- Create a dynamic data consolidation with *AVERAGE*.

- Insert a picture from a file.
- Insert a hyperlink.
- Copy a hyperlink.
- Encrypt a workbook with a password.

1. Open the ***WilsonHome-05*** workbook from your student data files and save it as [your initials] Excel 5-4.

2. Group the **Cash Flow**, **Peoria**, **Champaign**, and **Rockford** sheets.

3. Edit and format grouped sheets.
   a. Select cells **A2:B2** and click the **Launcher** in the *Alignment* group [*Home* tab]. Choose **Center Across Selection** from the *Horizontal* list and click **OK**.
   b. Edit the contents of cell **A10** to read Cash paid for marketing.
   c. Select cell **A1** and ungroup the sheets.

4. Select the **CashFlow** sheet.

5. Build a static consolidation for the *Cash flow from operations* section.
   a. Select cells **B4:B12**.
   b. Use **Sum** to consolidate the data from the three location sheets without links. (Figure 5-76).

6. Build a static consolidation for the *Cash flow from banking and investment* section in cells **B15:B21**. Delete the references in the *Consolidate* dialog box and use **Sum** as the function.

7. Build a static consolidation for the *Cash balance at the beginning of the quarter* amounts in cell **B24** with **Sum** as the function.

8. Insert a picture from a file.
   a. Delete the contents of cell **A1** on the **CashFlow** sheet.
   b. Click cell **D2**.
   c. Click the **Pictures** button [*Insert* tab, *Illustrations* group].
   d. Find and select **WHES** from your student data files.
   e. Click **Insert**. The picture is placed at a default size.
   f. Click the **Height** box [*Picture Tools Format* tab, *Size* group].
   g. Type 1.2 to replace the default height and press **Enter**.
   h. Format the height of row **1** to **86.25 (115 pixels)**.
   i. Point to the logo frame to display a move pointer.
   j. Drag the image to appear in cell **A1** as a main label for the worksheet (Figure 5-77).
   k. Click cell **D2**.

9. Create a dynamic consolidation for *Cash flow from operations* data.
   a. Click the **Averages** sheet tab.
   b. Select cells **B4:B12**.
   c. Use **Average** as the function to consolidate data from the **Peoria**, **Champaign**, and **Rockford** sheets with links to the source data.
   d. Expand the *Cash paid for salaries and wages* group (Figure 5-78).
   e. Select cell **A1**.

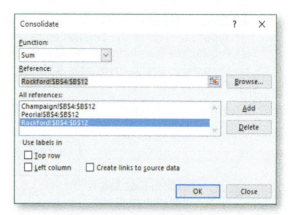

5-76 *Consolidate* dialog box for cash flow

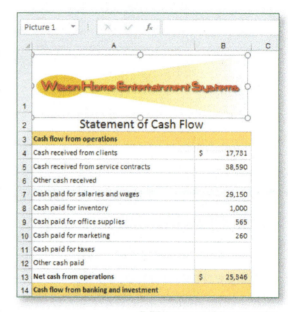

5-77 Image positioned as title

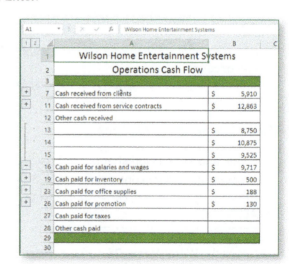

5-78 Completed *Averages* worksheet

10. Insert and copy a hyperlink.
    a. Click cell **D3** on the **Peoria** worksheet.
    b. Create a hyperlink that displays Company Averages and switches to cell **A1** on the **Averages** worksheet.
    c. Right-click cell **D3** and choose **Copy** from the menu.
    d. Select the **Champaign** sheet tab and paste the hyperlink in cell **D3**.
    e. Select the **Rockford** sheet tab and paste the hyperlink in cell **D3**.
    f. Select the **Peoria** sheet, and press **Esc** to remove the copy marquee if it is still visible.
    g. Select cell **D5** and click the hyperlink to test it.

11. Encrypt the workbook with the password abc.

12. Save and close the workbook (Figure 5-79).

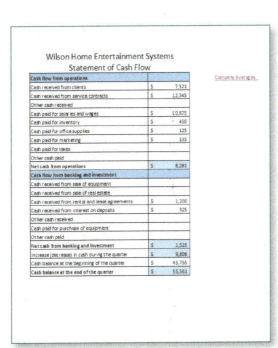

5-79 *Peoria* **worksheet with hyperlink and completed** *CashFlow* **sheet for Excel 5-4**

Independent Project 5-5

At Sierra Pacific Community College, student assignment and exam points are listed on a single sheet but in different name order. You will consolidate by category and copy the results to another sheet. You will also insert the school logo in a footer.
[Student Learning Outcomes 5.1, 5.3, 5.6, 5.8]

Files Needed: *SierraPacific-05.xlsx* and *SPCCD.png* (Student data files are available in the Library of your SIMnet account)
Completed Project File Name: *[your initials] Excel 5-5.xlsx*

Skills Covered in This Project

- Remove the *Mark as Final* property.
- Create a static data consolidation.
- Consolidate data by category.
- Insert a picture from a file in a header.
- Size a picture.
- Change the color of a picture.

1. Open the **SierraPacific-05** workbook and click **Edit Anyway** to remove the *Read-Only* property from the *Mark as Final* command.

2. Save the workbook as [your initials] Excel 5-5. On the **PPT&Access** sheet, student names and points are listed for each segment but not in the same order.

3. Consolidate points by category.
   a. Select cells **I3:K25**. Consolidated data will be placed in this range.
   b. Open the *Consolidate* dialog box.
   c. Select and delete any references in the *All references* list.
   d. Choose **Sum** as the function.
   e. Click the *Reference* box, select cells **A3:C25**, and click **Add**.
   f. Select cells **E3:G25** and click **Add**.
   g. Select the **Top row** and **Left column** boxes (Figure 5-80).
   h. Do not use links.
   i. Click **OK**. The columns are consolidated, and the names are in alphabetical order. The label for the last name column is missing.

4. Copy and format consolidation results.
   a. Select cells **J4:K25** and click the **Copy** button [*Home* tab, *Clipboard* group] (Figure 5-81).
   b. Click the **Total** sheet tab. Student names are already entered in alphabetical order.
   c. Click cell **C4** and click the **Paste** button [*Home* tab, *Clipboard* group].

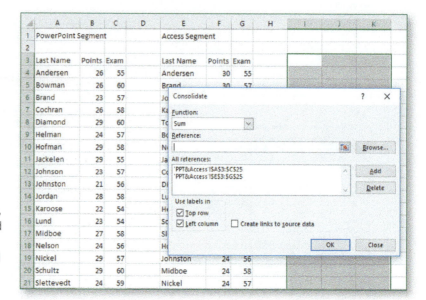

5-80 Consolidating by both label groups

5-81 Copy consolidated values to another sheet

d. Select cell **A4** and click the **Format as Table** button [*Home* tab, *Styles* group].
e. Use **Table Style Medium 16**.
f. Show the **Total Row** with **Average** as the function in the **Points** and **Exams** columns.
g. Format cell **A1** with a **16 pt**. font size.
h. Format row **1** as **22.50 (30 pixels)** high.
i. Type Total in cell **E3**.
j. In cell **E4**, enter a formula to add cells **C4** and **D4**.
k. Show **Average** in the **Total Row** for column **E**.
l. Type Average in cell **A26**, and format it bold and right-aligned.
m. **Center** cells **A3:E3**.

5. Insert a picture from a file in a header.
   a. Click the **Page Layout** view button on the *Status* bar.
   b. Click the right header section.
   c. Click the **Picture** button [*Header & Footer Tools Design* tab, *Header & Footer Elements* group].
   d. In the *Insert Pictures* dialog box, click **Browse** for the *From a file* group.
   e. Find and select **SPCCD** in the folder with your data files.
   f. Click **Insert**. The *&[Picture]* code is placed in the section (Figure 5-82).
   g. Click a worksheet cell. In *Page Layout* view, you can see the picture.

6. Format a picture in a header.
   a. Click the right header section to display the *&[Picture]* code.
   b. Click the **Format Picture** button [*Header & Footer Tools Design* tab, *Header & Footer Elements* group].
   c. Click the **Height** box on the *Size* tab and type .50 to replace the default Height.
   d. Press **Tab**. to move to the *Width* box. When *Lock aspect ratio* is active, the image is automatically proportionally sized.
   e. Click the **Picture** tab in the dialog box.
   f. Click the arrow for **Color** and choose **Grayscale**.
   g. Click **OK** and click a worksheet cell (Figure 5-83).
   h. Click the **Normal** view button on the *Status* bar. You do not see headers in this view.
   i. Press **Ctrl+Home**.

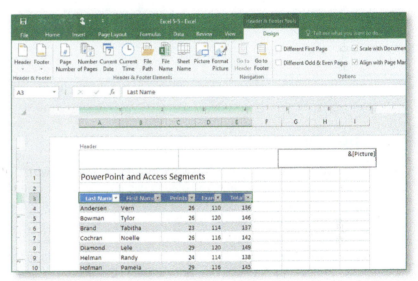

5-82 Picture code in header

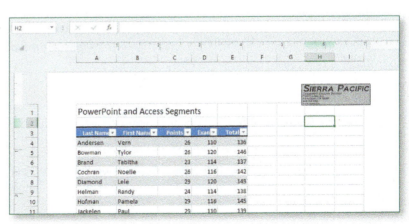

5-83 Reformatted picture

7. Save and close the workbook (Figure 5-84).

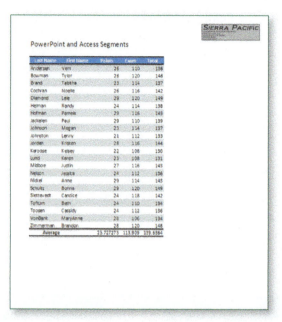

5-84 Completed worksheets for Excel 5-5

Independent Project 5-6

Wear-Ever Shoes plans to link a new workbook to an existing workbook with best-seller data. Your linking formula will use addition, and you plan to use a hyperlink to open the source workbook. You will also illustrate the process to build an external reference formula in a *SmartArt* graphic.
[Student Learning Outcomes 5.5, 5.6, 5.7]

File Needed: ***WearEver-05.xlsx*** (Student data files are available in the Library of your SIMnet account)
Completed Project File Name: ***[your initials] Excel 5-6.xlsx***

Skills Covered in This Project

- Link workbooks with an addition formula.
- Edit and copy an external reference formula.
- Insert a hyperlink.
- Insert a *SmartArt* graphic.

1. Create a new workbook and save it as [your initials] Excel 5-6.

2. Open the ***WearEver-05*** workbook from your student data files.

3. Arrange the two workbooks to be vertically tiled.

4. Copy the **North** worksheet in the ***WearEver-05*** workbook to ***[your initials] Excel 5-6*** by selecting your workbook name from the *To book* list in the *Move or Copy* dialog box. The fill color for the copied sheet is different.

5. In ***[your initials] Excel 5-6***, rename the copied sheet as Totals, and delete **Sheet1**.

6. Prepare the linked workbook.
   a. In *[your initials] Excel 5-6*, delete the contents of cells **B6:B16**.
   b. Select and delete columns **C:D**.
   c. Edit the label in cell **A3** to display Best Sellers All Regions.
   d. Change the sheet tab color to **Orange, Accent 2** and the **Fill Color** for cells **A1:F4** to **Orange, Accent 2, Lighter 60%**.

7. Link workbooks with an addition formula.
   a. Click cell **B6** in *[your initials] Excel 5-6* and type **=** to start the formula.
   b. Add the contents of cell **B6** from each of the sheets in the ***WearEver-05*** workbook in the formula (Figure 5-85). Press **Enter** after the last cell reference.

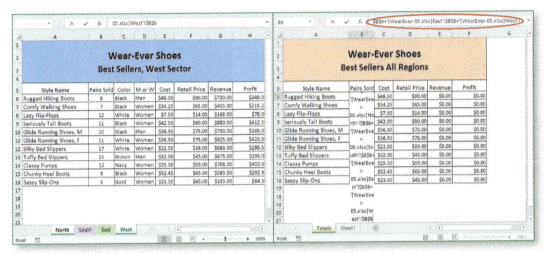

5-85 External reference formula to link workbooks

8. Close the ***WearEver-05*** workbook without saving and maximize your workbook window.

9. Edit and copy an external reference formula.
   a. Click cell **B6** in *[your initials] Excel 5-6*.
   b. Edit the formula to change each absolute reference to a relative reference. Note that the external reference shows the complete path for the source workbook because it is no longer open (Figure 5-86).
   c. Copy the formula to complete the pairs sold column.

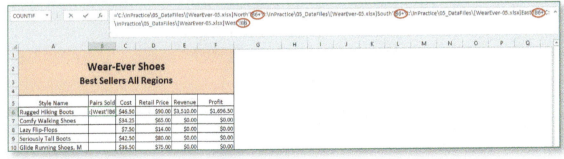

5-86 Formula edited for copying

10. Insert a hyperlink to open the source workbook ***WearEver-05***.
    a. Click cell **G3**.
    b. Create a cell hyperlink and edit the display text to read Open source data.

c. Navigate to the folder with the **WearEver-05** workbook to enter its location in the dialog box.

d. Right-click the hyperlink and format its text color to **Orange, Accent 2**.

e. Test the hyperlink and close the source workbook without saving.

11. Insert a *SmartArt* graphic.

a. Insert a **Basic Process** graphic on the **Totals** sheet.

b. In the leftmost text box, type Create new workbook. Do not press **Enter** after typing the label.

c. Type Open source file in the middle box.

d. Type Copy sheet and delete data in the rightmost box.

e. Click the **Add Shape** button [*SmartArt Tools Design* tab, *Create Graphic* group] (Figure 5-87).

f. Type Build formula in the new shape.

12. Format a *SmartArt* graphic.

a. Click the frame of the *SmartArt* graphic to select it.

b. Click the **More** button [*SmartArt Tools Design* tab, *SmartArt Styles* group].

c. Choose **Brick Scene** in the *3-D* group.

d. Click the **Change Colors** button [*SmartArt Tools Design* tab, *SmartArt Styles* group].

e. Choose **Colorful Range – Accent Colors 2 to 3** in the *Colorful* group.

f. Format the *SmartArt* frame with a **½ pt black** outline.

g. Point to the *SmartArt* frame and drag the graphic to position the top left selection handle in cell **A18**.

h. Point to the bottom right selection handle and resize the frame to reach cell **F35**.

i. Select cell **A1**.

13. Save and close the workbook (Figure 5-88).

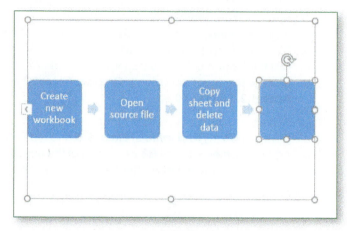

5-87 Fourth shape added to *SmartArt*

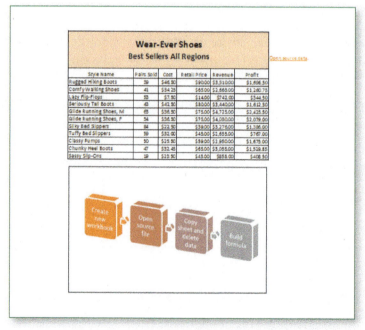

5-88 Completed worksheet for Excel 5-6

Improve It Project 5-7

American River Cycling Club has consolidated data about competitions from April through June. It is a dynamic consolidation but should be static. For this project, you redo the consolidation, improve formatting, and insert the club's logo in a footer.
[Student Learning Outcomes 5.1, 5.2, 5.4, 5.6]

Files Needed: **AmRiverCycling-05.xlsx** and **ARRC.png** *(Student data files are available in the Library of your SIMnet account)*
Completed Project File Name: **[your initials] Excel 5-7.xlsx**

Skills Covered in This Project

- Remove a dynamic consolidation.
- Create a static data consolidation.
- Insert a picture in a footer.
- Group and format worksheets.

1. Open the **AmRiverCycling-05** workbook from your student data files and save it as [your initials] Excel 5-7.

2. On the **Static** sheet, click the Level **2** outline button to expand the outline.

3. Select cells **A4:D7**, turn off the bold font, and use **No Fill**.

4. Select and delete the contents of cells **A4:D48**.

5. Click the arrow with the **Ungroup** button [*Data* tab, *Outline* group] and clear the outline.

6. Select cells **B4:D12** on the **Static** sheet and create a static data consolidation using **Sum** and cells **E4:G12** on each of the supporting worksheets.

7. Format all results as right-aligned. Note that the dates are missing (Figure 5-89).

8. Select the headings for rows **13:48** (to the left of column A) and right-click one of the headings. Choose **Delete** to delete those rows and select cell **A1**.

9. Insert a picture in a footer.
   a. Switch to *Page Layout* view and click the center footer section.
   b. Click the **Picture** button [*Header & Footer Tools Design* tab, *Header & Footer Elements* group].
   c. Click **Browse** in the *From a file* group.
   d. Find and select **ARRC** from your student data files and click **Insert**.
   e. Click a worksheet cell and return to *Normal* view.

10. Group and format worksheets.
    a. Group the four sheets with a state name as the tab name.
    b. Select and delete columns **C:D** in the grouped sheets.
    c. In cell **A1** on the grouped sheets, type American River Cycling Club. Format the font size as **20 pt**.
    d. Type April-June Race Participation in cell **A2** and format the font size as **18 pt**.

5-89 Outline cleared; dates missing

e. Select cells **A1:E2** and use the *Format Cells* dialog box to center across the selection.

f. *AutoFit* columns **A:C**.

g. Format the labels in row **3** bold and centered.

h. Apply **All Borders** to cells **A3:E12**. Apply **Outside Borders** to cells **A1:E2**.

i. Format the **Height** of rows **3:12** to **21.00 (28 pixels)**.

j. Select the dates in column **A** and use the *Format Cells* dialog box to apply a *Date* format that displays the date as *1-Apr*.

k. Open the *Page Setup* dialog box to the *Margins* tab. Center the sheets horizontally on the page.

11. Click cell **A1** and ungroup the sheets.

12. Copy the dates in column **A** on the **Washington** sheet to cell **A4** on the **Static** sheet.

13. Save and close the workbook (Figure 5-90).

American River Cycling Club
April-June Race Participation

Date	City	# of Riders	Male	Female
1-Apr	Algonquin	35	18	17
4-Apr	Blue Island	27	14	13
14-Apr	Cicero	28	12	16
23-Apr	Midlothian	28	12	16
1-May	Peoria	32	16	16
8-May	Rockford	39	20	19
21-May	Salem	35	15	20
1-Jun	Springfield	39	18	21
5-Jun	Urbana	33	18	15

American River Cycling Club
April-June Race Participation

Date	City	# of Riders	Male	Female
1-Apr	Addison	21	11	10
4-Apr	Arlington	21	9	12
14-Apr	Denton	32	20	12
23-Apr	Fort Worth	27	14	13
1-May	Grand Prairie	27	15	12
8-May	Irving	33	18	15
21-May	Plano	27	21	6
1-Jun	River Oaks	29	15	14
5-Jun	San Antonio	22	11	11

American River Cycling Club
April-June Race Participation

Date	City	# of Riders	Male	Female
1-Apr	Arlington	40	24	16
4-Apr	Brookline	37	20	17
14-Apr	Cambridge	28	19	9
23-Apr	Chestnut Hill	38	18	20
1-May	Everett	35	20	15
8-May	Framingham	29	19	10
21-May	Foxboro	29	18	11
1-Jun	Revere	35	21	14
5-Jun	Watertown	39	22	17

American River Cycling Club
Race Participation Totals

Date	# of Riders	Male	Female
1-Apr	117	68	49
4-Apr	115	59	56
14-Apr	114	69	45
23-Apr	121	59	62
1-May	134	72	62
8-May	135	75	60
21-May	121	72	49
1-Jun	132	69	63
5-Jun	121	67	54

AMERICAN RIVER CYCLING CLUB

5-90 Completed worksheets for Excel 5-7

American River Cycling Club
April-June Race Participation

Date	City	# of Riders	Male	Female
1-Apr	Bainbridge Island	21	15	6
4-Apr	Bellevue	30	16	14
14-Apr	Bothell	26	18	8
23-Apr	Kirkland	28	15	13
1-May	Lynnwood	40	21	19
8-May	Parkland	34	18	16
21-May	Poulsbo	30	18	12
1-Jun	Redmond	29	15	14
5-Jun	Tacoma	27	16	11

Challenge Project 5-8

For this project, you work with a classmate (or on your own) to develop source and dependent workbooks. The source workbook includes details about the time spent each weekday on each of five activities for four weeks. The dependent workbook uses external reference formulas to summarize the week's activities.
[Student Learning Outcomes 5.4, 5.5, 5.7]

File needed: None
Completed Project File Names: *[your initials] Excel 5-8.xlsx* and *[your initials] Excel 5-8a.xlsx*

Create a new workbook and save it as [your initials] Excel 5-8. Modify your workbook according to the following guidelines:

- Type the names of the five weekdays as column labels, starting in cell B3.
- Type the names of five tasks or activities as row labels, starting in cell A4. Choose activities such as Prepare meals, Work on class assignments, Exercise or workout, and other daily tasks.
- Name the sheet Week 1 and enter the number of minutes spent each day on each activity.
- Copy the sheet to create separate sheets for weeks 2–4.
- Group the sheets and enter main labels in rows 1:2 to describe the data. Use a formula to total each activity for the week.
- Format the grouped sheets in an attractive, easy-to-view style.
- Ungroup the sheets and edit three values on each of the worksheets for weeks 2–4.
- Create a new workbook named [your initials] Excel 5-8a.
- Copy one of the sheets from *[your initials] Excel 5-8* into this workbook and name the sheet Month.
- Create an external reference formula to add the first task minutes for Monday using *[your initials] Excel 5-8* as the source workbook. Edit and copy the formula.
- Insert a hyperlink in the dependent workbook to open the source workbook.

Challenge Project 5-9

For this project, you build worksheets with data about an activity or concept from your neighborhood or your workplace. You will group sheets for formatting, copy a sheet from one workbook to the other, and insert a *SmartArt* graphic.
[Student Learning Outcome 5.2, 5.4, 5.5, 5.6, 5.7]

File Needed: None
Completed Project File Names: *[your initials] Excel 5-9.xlsx* and *Excel 5-9a.xlsx*

Create a new source workbook and save it as [your initials] Excel 5-9. Modify your workbook according to the following guidelines:

- Key labels and values to illustrate a concept of interest to you. For example, build a worksheet to track the average number of automobiles owned by street in your community, the number of workers by department at your office, travel distances to campus by your classmates, etc.

- Copy the sheet and change one value in each column in the copied sheet.
- Group the sheets and apply formatting that suits both sheets.
- Review the *SmartArt* categories to find a graphic to illustrate a concept related to your data. Place the *SmartArt* on its own sheet. If necessary, add or remove shapes from the graphic.
- Format the *SmartArt* graphic with a style, change the colors, or add fill or a border. Size and position the graphic.
- On each worksheet, insert a hyperlink that switches to the *SmartArt* sheet.
- Save the workbook and leave it open.
- Create a second workbook and save it as [your initials] Excel 5-9a.
- Copy either sheet from *[your initials] Excel 5-9* to *[your initials] Excel 5-9a*.
- Name the copied sheet in *[your initials] Excel 5-9a* to indicate that it is a consolidation worksheet.
- Dynamically consolidate data from the two sheets in *[your initials] Excel 5-9*.
- Save and close both workbooks.

Challenge Project 5-10

For this project, you create a timesheet workbook for five employees. After four weeks, you consolidate data to create a worksheet that displays average number of hours worked on a given day by each employee.
[**Student Learning Outcomes 5.1, 5.4, 5.6, 5.8**]

File Needed: None
Completed Project File Name: *[your initials] Excel 5-10.xlsx*

Create a new workbook and save it as [your initials] Excel 5-10. Modify your workbook according to the following guidelines:

- Insert worksheets so that you have five worksheets in the workbook. Name the sheets Week 1, Week 2, Week 3, Week 4, and Averages.
- Group all the sheets and type the names of five employees in a column as row labels. Use a five- or seven-day workweek, typing the day names as column headings.
- Add a main title to indicate a company name. Enter the number of hours worked by each employee for each day worked (all employees have the same number of hours). Include values that are decimals, such as 5.5 or 6.25, and enter zero (0) in at least five cells.
- Total weekly hours by employee and show the total hours worked by day.
- Apply formatting to the grouped sheets.
- Ungroup the sheets and prepare the *Averages* sheet for consolidation without links. Edit labels as needed and delete the total column and row.
- On the *Averages* sheet, insert a picture from an online source to complement your company name. Size and format the image to enhance the overall appearance of the worksheet.
- Mark the workbook as final.

Exploring the Function Library

CHAPTER OVERVIEW

The Excel *Function Library* includes functions that perform complex and sophisticated calculations for use in business, government, education, and research. In this chapter, you learn about functions in the *Database*, *Logical*, *Date & Time*, *Financial*, and *Text* categories. You also nest functions and build time, date, and statistical calculations.

STUDENT LEARNING OUTCOMES (SLOs)

After completing this chapter, you will be able to:

SLO 6.1   Use *Database* functions such as *DSUM* and *DAVERAGE* (p. E6-350).

SLO 6.2   Build *AND*, *OR*, nested, and *IFS* functions (p. E6-352).

SLO 6.3   Explore the *Lookup & Reference* category with *INDEX*, *MATCH*, and *TRANSPOSE* (p. E6-364).

SLO 6.4   Build date, time, and statistical calculations (p. E6-368).

SLO 6.5   Use *Financial* functions such as *PV*, *FV*, and *NPV* (p. E6-380).

SLO 6.6   Work with *Text* functions including *TEXTJOIN*, *CONCAT*, *EXACT*, and *REPLACE* (p. E6-384).

SLO 6.7   Use multiple criteria in *SUMIFS*, *AVERAGEIFS*, and *COUNTIFS* functions (p. E6-391).

SLO 6.8   Monitor and edit functions with the *Watch Window* and *Find and Replace* (p. E6-394).

CASE STUDY

In the Pause & Practice projects in this chapter, you work on revenue, inventory and forecasting, financial planning, and human resources worksheets for Paradise Lakes Resort (PLR) using Excel functions.

Pause & Practice 6-1: Use *Database* and *Logical* functions.

Pause & Practice 6-2: Work with date and time calculations and *Lookup & Reference* functions.

Pause & Practice 6-3: Build *Financial* and *Text* functions.

Pause & Practice 6-4: Use multiple criteria, the *Watch Window*, and *Find and Replace*.

EXCEL

Working with Database Functions

A *database function* performs a mathematical or statistical calculation only for data that meet the criteria. In a worksheet with revenue numbers for Paradise Lakes Resort, for example, you can use a database function to total results only for Cass Lake.

Database Function Syntax

The term *database* refers to a range of cells that includes a header row and rows of data, like a list or a table. Each row in a database is a *record* and includes the same information for each entity. A column is a *field*.

Database functions use the following syntax:

FunctionName(database, field, criteria)

The first argument, *database*, is the range of cells to be analyzed. You can use a named range or cell addresses. In Figure 6-1, the *database* argument is the named range *List*.

> **MORE INFO**
>
> Press **F3** (**FN+F3**) to paste a range name as an argument.

The *field* argument refers to the column used for the calculation. You can type the column label or the position number of the column in the list. The first column is 1, the second is 2, and so on.

The third argument is *criteria*, a cell range on the same or another sheet where you type specifications. The *criteria* argument includes labels in one row and criteria in the row below. In Figure 6-1, the criteria range is cells B2:B3. Labels in the criteria range must be spelled exactly like those in the database. In Figure 6-1, the *DMAX* function in cell D21 calculates the highest value in the "Goal" column for cells that show "Cass Lake" in the "Location" column.

You can specify *AND* criteria in the same row, build *OR* criteria in separate rows, and use wildcard characters in the criteria.

The following table explains popular *Database* functions.

6-1 *DMAX* function for tabular data

Database Functions

Function Name	Explanation
DAVERAGE	Averages the values of cells in the field (column) that meet the criteria
DCOUNT	Counts cells with values in the field (column) that meet the criteria
DCOUNTA	Counts cells in the field (column) that are not empty that meet the criteria

Function Name	Explanation
DMAX	Displays the largest value in the field (column) that meets the criteria
DMIN	Displays the smallest value in the field (column) that meets the criteria
DSUM	Sums the values of cells in the field (column) that meet the criteria

The *Database* function category is listed in the *Insert Function* dialog box. You can also type = and a few characters of the function name to choose it from the *Formula AutoComplete* list.

▶ **HOW TO:** Build a DSUM Function

1. Copy the labels that are used to specify criteria.
2. Enter criteria below the label in the criteria range.
3. Click the cell for *DSUM* results.
4. Click the **Insert Function** button [*Formulas* tab, *Function Library* group].
5. Choose **Database** in the *Or select a category* list (Figure 6-2).

   - Click a function name in the list to display its description and syntax.

6. Select **DSUM** and click **OK**.

   - The *Function Arguments* dialog box opens.

7. Click the **Database** box.
8. Select the cells in the worksheet.

   - Include the header row and all data rows.
   - Press **F3** (**FN+F3**) to paste a range name instead of selecting cells.

9. Click the **Field** box.
10. Type the field name (column label).

    - The argument is not case sensitive.
    - Quotation marks are automatically supplied when you use the *Function Arguments* dialog box.
    - Type a number to indicate the column's position in the database instead of typing the label.

11. Click the **Criteria** box.
12. Select the criteria range (Figure 6-3).

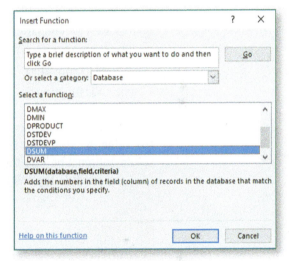

6-2 *Insert Function* dialog box and the *Database* category

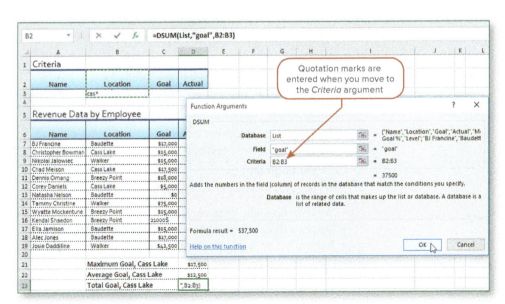

6-3 *Function Arguments* dialog box for *DSUM*

- You can key the range address.
- The criteria range can be located on a different worksheet.

13. Click **OK**.

- Results appear in the cell.
- You can press **Enter** to close the dialog box.

SLO 6.2

Building AND, OR, Nested, and IFS Functions

Functions in the *Logical* group determine if one or all conditions are met and display TRUE or FALSE as the result. The *IFS* function can display text or calculated results as well as TRUE or FALSE.

The AND Function

The *AND* function defines multiple conditions that must be met for a TRUE result. Paradise Lakes Resort can use an *AND* function to determine if an employee met an individual sales goal as well as a department goal.

The syntax for an *AND* function is:

= AND(LogicalN)

An *AND* function has one argument named *LogicalN*. *N* is a number; arguments are named *Logical1*, *Logical2*, *Logical3*, up to *Logical255*. In each *LogicalN* argument, you build a simple statement. An argument such as **D7<C7** means that the value in cell D7 must be less than the value in cell C7 for the result to be TRUE. If you build five *LogicalN* arguments, every statement must be true for the result to display TRUE. If one of those five statements is not true, the result in the cell is FALSE.

> **MORE INFO**
>
> *AND* functions with many arguments are restrictive or limiting.

 HOW TO: Build an AND Function

1. Click the cell for the result.
2. Click the **Logical** button [*Formulas* tab, *Function Library* group].
3. Choose **AND**.
   - Two *LogicalN* argument boxes are listed in the dialog box.
   - Additional arguments become available as you complete the previous argument.
4. Click the **Logical1** box.
5. Build the first statement to be evaluated.
   - You can type the statement.
   - You can select cells in the worksheet or use range names.
   - If the statement includes text, you must enclose the text in quotation marks.
6. Click the **Logical2** box.
   - A third argument box opens.
7. Build the second statement to be evaluated (Figure 6-4).

E6-352

Excel 2016 Chapter 6 Exploring the Function Library

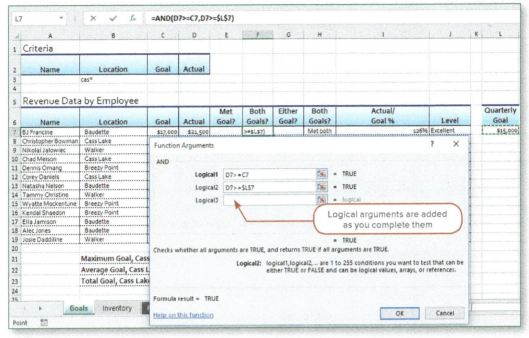

6-4 *AND* function in the *Function Arguments* dialog box

8. Build additional *LogicalN* arguments as needed.

9. Click **OK** or press **Enter**.

- If all statements are true, the word TRUE appears in the cell.
- If one of the statements is false, the word FALSE displays in the cell.

The OR Function

An *OR* function is less restrictive than an *AND* statement. In an *OR* function, if one of the arguments is true, the result is TRUE. All arguments must be false for FALSE to display as the result. You can use up to 255 *LogicalN* arguments.

The syntax for an *OR* function is:

= OR(LogicalN)

> **MORE INFO**
>
> Use absolute or relative cell references in *AND* or *OR* functions as required if the formula will be copied.

▶ **HOW TO: Type an OR Function**

1. Click the cell for the result.

2. Type **=or** and press **Tab**.

- **=OR(** displays in the cell.
- The first argument *logical1* is bold in the *ScreenTip*.

3. Build the first statement to be evaluated.

- You can type the statement.
- Select cells in the worksheet or press **F3 (FN+F3)** to paste a range name.
- If the statement includes text, enclose the text in quotation marks.

4. Type a comma **,** to separate the arguments.
   - The next argument *logical2* appears bold in the *ScreenTip*.
5. Build the second statement to be evaluated (Figure 6-5).

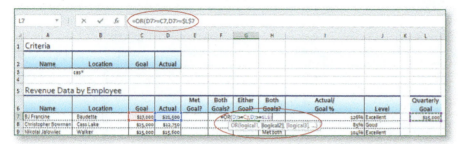

6-5 *OR* **function with two arguments**

6. Type a comma **,** to add another *logicaln* argument.
   - Build additional *logicaln* arguments as needed.
7. Press **Enter** when all arguments are typed.
   - If one statement is true, the word TRUE displays in the cell.
   - If no statement is true, the word FALSE appears in the cell.

The IF Function with AND and OR

A ***nested function*** is a function within a function. Logical functions are commonly nested. For example, use *AND* and *OR* with an *IF* function to build a statement that specifies multiple requirements. You can display a result other than TRUE or FALSE, because the *Value_if_true* and *Value_if_false* arguments in the *IF* function determine the results.

The following table illustrates examples of nesting *AND* or *OR* within an *IF* function in cell D4.

Sample Nested Functions

Function	Arguments	Explanation
=IF(C4>15000, 5000,0)	Logical_test = C4>15000 Value_if_true = 5000 Value_if_false = 0	If the value in cell C4 is greater than 15,000, cell D4 displays 5,000. If the value in cell C4 is less than 15,000, cell D4 displays 0.
=IF(AND(C4>15000,C7>12500), 5000,0)	Logical_test = C4>15000 and C7>12500 Value_if_true = 5000 Value_if_false = 0	If the value is cell C4 is greater than 15,000 **and** if the value in cell C7 is greater than 12,500, cell D4 displays 5,000. If either of these conditions is false, cell D4 displays 0.
=IF(OR(C4>15000,C7>12500), 5000,0)	Logical_test = C4>15000 or C7>12500 Value_if_true = 5000 Value_if_false = 0	If the value is cell C4 is greater than 15,000 **or** if the value in cell C7 is greater than 12,500, cell D4 displays 5,000. Cell D4 displays 0 when the value in cell C4 is equal to or less than 15,000 **and** the value in cell C7 is equal to or less than 12,500.

When you use the *Function Arguments* dialog box to build a nested function, Excel supplies separators and parentheses. Whether you use the dialog box or type a nested function, parentheses are color-coded to help you follow formula syntax. Although Excel automatically enters a closing parenthesis for simple formulas, it may not do so for nested functions. When a parenthesis is missing, Excel may display a message box with a suggested fix.

When using the *Function Arguments* dialog box to build nested functions, you toggle among functions by clicking the function name in the *Formula* bar. The *Function Arguments* dialog box displays arguments for the function that has the focus.

▶ **HOW TO: Nest AND and IF Functions**

1. Click the cell for the result.
2. Type =if (to open the *ScreenTip*.
   - The *logical_test* argument appears bold.
   - The *logical_test* argument is the *AND* function.
3. Type and and press **Tab**.
   - The *ScreenTip* displays arguments for the *AND* function.
4. Type the first *logicalN* statement and type a comma , (Figure 6-6).

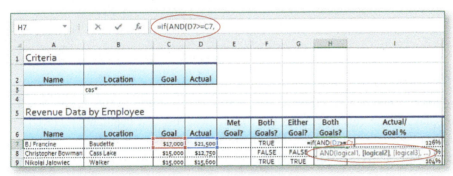

6-6 *AND* function is *logical_test* argument

   - You can select a worksheet cell rather than type the reference.
   - Use absolute or relative references as required.
5. Enter each *logicalN* argument followed by a comma.
6. Type the closing parenthesis and a comma), after the last argument for the *AND* function (Figure 6-7).
   - The focus returns to the *IF* function.

6-7 Closing parenthesis returns focus to *IF* function

7. Enter the *value_if_true* argument.
   - If the argument is text, enclose it in quotation marks.
   - You can select a cell or type its address.
   - Use absolute or relative references as required.
8. Type a comma **,** to move to the *value_if_false* argument.
9. Enter the *value_if_false* argument.
10. Type the closing parenthesis **)** (Figure 6-8).

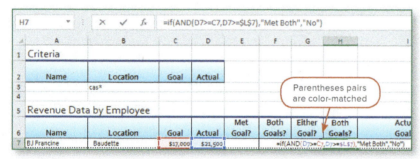

6-8 *AND* function nested within *IF*

11. Press **Enter**.
   - You can click the **Enter** button on the *Formula* bar.

The IFS Function

An *IFS* function has one or more logical tests with corresponding results for each test. The result that displays in the cell represents the first logical test that evaluates to TRUE. Your course grade can be calculated with an *IFS* function as follows:

=IFS(D2>=92,"A",D2>=84,"B",D2>=76,"C",D2<76,"D")

If you receive 92 or more points, the first logical test is TRUE, you receive an A grade, and the *IFS* function ends. When that is not true, the next logical test runs to determine if your score is 84 or higher (but not 92 points or higher). When that is true, the *IFS* function ends, and the result cell displays a B. The third logical test uses 76 points or higher (but not 84 points or higher), and the last test uses fewer than 76 points.

The syntax for an *IFS* function is:

=IFS(logical_test1, value_if_true1, [logical_test2, value_if_true2], ···)

Each *logical_testN* argument must have a *value_if_trueN* argument, and there can be up to 127 logical tests.

IFS functions are usually built from high value to low value.

> **MORE INFO**
>
> In earlier versions of Excel, a nested *IF* formula checked multiple logical tests. In a nested *IF* formula, the number of outcomes minus 1 is the number of logical tests required.

▶ HOW TO: Create an IFS Function

1. Click the cell for the *IFS* function.
2. Click the **Logical** button [*Formulas* tab, *Function Library* group].
3. Choose **IFS** to open the *Function Arguments* dialog box.
4. Enter the *logical_test1* argument.
   - You can click a cell or type its address.
   - You can use an operator to build a statement or expression.
5. Enter the *value_if_true1* result (Figure 6-9).
   - If the *logical_test1* argument is true, this result appears and no more logical tests are run.
   - The *Function Arguments* dialog box enters parentheses and quotation marks as needed.
   - Use uppercase and lowercase as preferred for results.

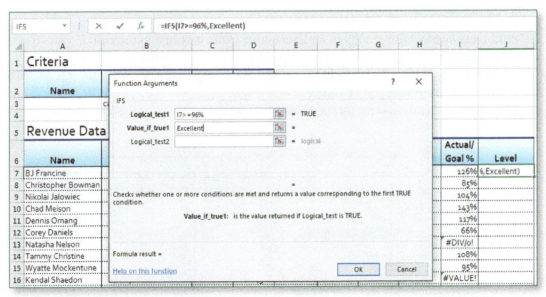

6-9 First logical test in an *IFS* formula

6. Enter the *logical_test2* argument.
   - If the *logical_test1* argument is false, the second test runs.
7. Enter the *value_if_true2* result.
   - If the *logical_test2* argument is true, this result appears and the function ends.
8. Enter *logical_testN* arguments as needed.

9. Enter *value_if_trueN* results for each *logical_testN* argument (Figure 6-10).

- You can use up to 127 *logical_test* arguments.

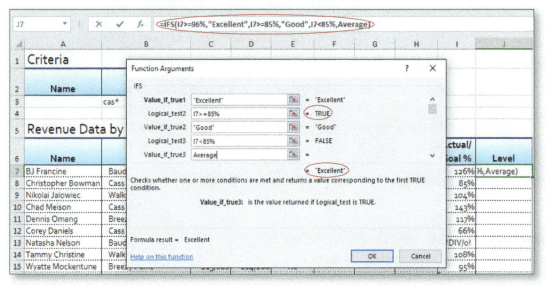

6-10 Three logical tests and results for an *IFS* formula

10. Click **OK**.

- The *value_if_true* argument for the first *logical_test* that is TRUE displays in the cell.

The IFERROR Function

A formula syntax error results in an Excel error value message in the cell. Common syntax errors include typing the letter "o" instead of a zero (0) or typing a letter as part of a value as shown in row 16 in Figure 6-11. Excel displays #VALUE! in the formula cell. When you anticipate an error that you or someone else might make, use the *IFERROR* function to display a specific, custom error message such as "Check that all entries are numbers."

5	Revenue Data by Employee									
6	Name	Location	Goal	Actual	Met Goal?	Both Goals?	Either Goal?	Both Goals?	Actual/ Goal %	Level
7	BJ Francine	Baudette	$17,000	$21,500		TRUE	TRUE	Met Both	126%	Excellent
8	Christopher Bowman	Cass Lake	$15,000	$12,750		FALSE	FALSE		85%	Good
9	Nikolai Jalowiec	Walker	$15,000	$15,600		TRUE	TRUE		104%	Excellent
10	Chad Meison	Cass Lake	$17,500	$25,000		TRUE	TRUE		143%	Excellent
11	Dennis Omang	Breezy Point	$18,000	$21,000		TRUE	TRUE		117%	Excellent
12	Corey Daniels	Cass Lake	$5,000	$3,300		FALSE	FALSE		66%	Average
13	Natasha Nelson	Baudette	$0	$4,050		FALSE	TRUE		#DIV/o!	#DIV/o!
14	Tammy Christine	Walker	$75,000	$81,000		TRUE	TRUE		108%	Excellent
15	Wyatte Mockentune	Breezy Point	$15,000	$14,200		FALSE	FALSE		95%	Good
16	Kendal Shaedon	Breezy Point	21000S	$18,500		FALSE	TRUE		#VALUE!	#VALUE!
17	Ella Jamison	Baudette	$15,000	$13,200		FALSE	FALSE		88%	Good
18	Alec Jones	Baudette	$17,000	$9,350		FALSE	FALSE		55%	Average
19	Josie Daddiline	Walker	$42,500	$56,000		TRUE	TRUE		132%	Excellent

6-11 Standard, default error messages

The *IFERROR* function works only for formulas that can return a standard Excel error value message. When a formula uses incorrect mathematics or the wrong cell address, an error may not be identified or may result in an error triangle, and *IFERROR* is not relevant. The following table lists error values and descriptions.

Excel Error Messages

Error Value	Description
#N/A	A value or an argument is missing.
#VALUE!	An incorrect data type is used (for example a label is used instead of a value).
#REF!	A cell reference is empty, usually because cells were deleted.
#DIV/0!	The formula divides by zero (0) or an empty cell.
#NUM!	The formula uses an invalid numeric entry (for example, it could be a wrong data type or a negative number instead of a required positive value).
#NAME?	The formula uses unrecognized text such as a misspelled function, sheet, or range name.
#NULL!	The formula refers to an intersection of two cell ranges that do not intersect, or uses an incorrect range separator (for example, a semicolon or comma instead of a colon).

An *IFERROR* function has two arguments. The *value* argument is the formula that might display an error message. The *value_if_error* argument is the text that should appear in place of the default Excel error message.

=IFERROR(value, value_if_error)
=IFERROR(A7/A9, "Check the values in column A.")

▶ **HOW TO:** Create an IFERROR Function

1. Click the cell for the result.
   - This is a formula cell that may display a standard error message.
2. Delete the cell contents if the formula is already entered in the cell.
3. Click the **Logical** button [*Formulas* tab, *Function Library* group].
4. Choose **IFERROR**.
5. Enter the *Value* argument.
   - You can key the formula using lowercase letters or select cells in the worksheet.
   - You don't need to key an equals sign when you use the *Function Arguments* dialog box.
6. Enter the *Value_if_error* argument (Figure 6-12).
   - Use uppercase, lowercase, and punctuation as you want it to appear in your message.
   - Quotation marks are supplied when you use the *Function Arguments* dialog box.

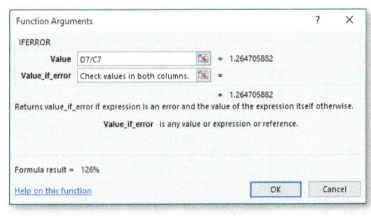

6-12 *IFERROR* with both arguments complete

7. Click **OK**.
   - The error message appears only when there is an error that would have resulted in a standard error message (Figure 6-13).

5	Revenue Data by Employee									
6	**Name**	**Location**	**Goal**	**Actual**	**Met Goal?**	**Both Goals?**	**Either Goal?**	**Both Goals?**	**Actual/ Goal %**	**Level**
7	BJ Francine	Baudette	$17,000	$21,500		TRUE	TRUE	Met Both	126%	Excellent
8	Christopher Bowman	Cass Lake	$15,000	$12,750		FALSE	FALSE	No	85%	Good
9	Nikolai Jalowiec	Walker	$15,000	$15,600		TRUE	TRUE	Met Both	104%	Excellent
10	Chad Meison	Cass Lake	$17,500	$25,000		TRUE	TRUE	Met Both	143%	Excellent
11	Dennis Omang	Breezy Point	$18,000	$21,000		TRUE	TRUE	Met Both	117%	Excellent
12	Corey Daniels	Cass Lake	$5,000	$3,300		FALSE	FALSE	No	66%	Average
13	Natasha Nelson	Baudette	$0	$4,050		FALSE	TRUE	No	Check values in both columns	Excellent
14	Tammy Christine	Walker	$75,000	$81,000		TRUE	TRUE	Met Both	108%	Excellent
15	Wyatte Mockentune	Breezy Point	$15,000	$14,200		FALSE	FALSE	No	95%	Good
16	Kendal Shaedon	Breezy Point	21000S	$18,500		FALSE	TRUE	No	Check values in both columns	Excellent
17	Ella Jamison	Baudette	$15,000	$13,200		FALSE	FALSE	No	88%	Good
18	Alec Jones	Baudette	$17,000	$9,350		FALSE	FALSE	No	55%	Average
19	Josie Daddiline	Walker	$42,500	$56,000		TRUE	TRUE	Met Both	132%	Excellent

6-13 Custom error message appears in place of Excel default message

In this project, you complete calculations for Paradise Lakes Resort using *Database* functions. You also use *Logical* functions to calculate results about employees' revenue accomplishments.

File Needed: ***ParadiseLakes-06.xlsx*** *(Student data files are available in the* Library *of your SIMnet account)*
Completed Project File Name: ***[your initials] PP E6-1.xlsx***

1. Open ***ParadiseLakes-06.xlsx*** from your student data files and save it as [your initials] PP E6-1.

2. Build a *DSUM* function using the *Function Arguments* dialog box.
   a. Click the **Goals** sheet tab and select cell **B3**.
   b. Type cas*. Criteria is not case-sensitive, and wildcard characters are acceptable.
   c. Click cell **C23** and click the **Insert Function** button in the *Formula* bar.
   d. Choose **Database** in the *Or select a category* list.
   e. Select **DSUM** and click **OK**.
   f. Press **F3** (**FN+F3**) in the *Database* box to open the *Paste Names* dialog box.
   g. Choose **List** and click **OK**.
   h. Click the **Field** box and type goal. Entries are not case sensitive.
   i. Click the **Criteria** box and select cells **B2:B3** (Figure 6-14). Quotation marks are entered for the *Field* argument.
   j. Click **OK**. The total for Cass Lake is $37,500.

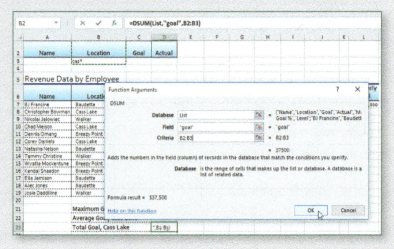

6-14 *DSUM and its arguments*

3. Type a *DAVERAGE* function.

    a. Click cell **C22**.
    b. Type **=dav** to display the *Formula AutoComplete* list and press **Tab**.
    c. Type a lower-case L l for the *database* argument and to open *Formula AutoComplete* again.

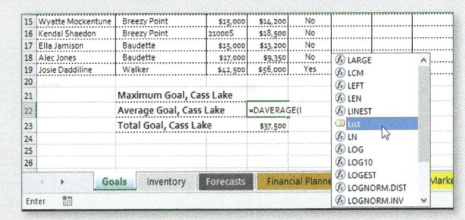

6-15 *DAVERAGE* and *Formula AutoComplete*

    d. Double-click **List** (Figure 6-15).
    e. Type a comma , to move to the *field* argument.
    f. Type **"goal"** including the quotation marks.
    g. Type a comma , to move to the *criteria* argument.
    h. Select cells **B2:B3** and press **Enter**. The closing parenthesis is supplied. The average for Cass Lake is $12,500.

4. Use the *Function Arguments* dialog box or type to create a *DMAX* function in cell **C21** with the same arguments as used in step 3. The maximum value for Cass Lake is $17,500.

5. Use the *Function Arguments* dialog box to build an *AND* function.

    a. Select cell **F7** and click the **Logical** button [*Formulas* tab, *Function Library* group].
    b. Choose **AND**.
    c. Click the **Logical1** argument box.
    d. Select cell **D7**, type **>=**, and select cell **C7**. The first condition is that the value in cell D7 be greater than or equal to the value in cell C7.
    e. Click the **Logical2** box.
    f. Select cell **D7**, type **>=**, select cell **L7**, and press **F4** (**FN+F4**). The reference to cell L7 must be absolute for copying the formula (Figure 6-16).

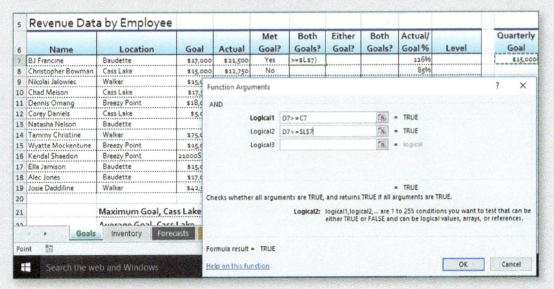

6-16 *AND* function being built

g. Click **OK**. The result for cell F7 is TRUE.

h. Copy the formula in cell **F7** to cells **F8:F19**.

6. Type an *OR* function.

a. Select cell **G7**.

b. Type =or and press **Tab**.

c. Type d7>=c7 for the *logical1* argument.

d. Type a comma , to move to the *logical2* argument.

e. Type d7>=, select cell **L7**, and press **F4** (**FN+F4**) (Figure 6-17).

5	Revenue Data by Employee											Quarterly
6	Name	Location	Goal	Actual	Met Goal?	Both Goals?	Either Goal?	Both Goals?	Actual/ Goal %	Level		Goal
7	BJ Francine	Baudette	$17,000	$21,500	Yes	=OR(d7>=c7,d7>=$L$7			126%			$15,000
8	Christopher Bowman	Cass Lake	$15,000	$12,750	No	FALSE OR(logical1, [logical2], [logical3], ...						
9	Nikolai Jalowiec	Walker	$45,000	$15,600	Yes	TRUE			104%			

6-17 *OR* function typed in the worksheet

f. Press **Enter**. The result for cell G7 is TRUE.

g. Copy the formula in cell **G7** to cells **G8:G19**. *OR* functions are less restrictive than *AND* functions, so more TRUE results display.

7. Nest *AND* and *IF* functions.

a. Select cell **H7**.

b. Type =if(an and press **Tab** (Figure 6-18). The focus is on the *AND* formula as is the *ScreenTip*.

5	Revenue Data by Employee									
6	Name	Location	Goal	Actual	Met Goal?	Both Goals?	Either Goal?	Both Goals?	Actual/ Goal %	Level
7	BJ Francine	Baudette	$17,000	$21,500	Yes	TRUE	TRUE	=if(AND(		
8	Christopher Bowman	Cass Lake	$15,000	$12,750	No	FALSE	FALSE	AND(logical1, [logical2], ...)		
9	Nikolai Jalowiec	Walker	$15,000	$15,600	Yes	TRUE	TRUE	104%		

6-18 *AND* function as logical test for *IF* function

c. Type d7>=c7 for the *logical1* argument.

d. Type a comma , to move to the *logical2* argument.

e. Type d7>=L7 and press **F4** (**FN+F4**) for the *logical2* argument. (You can type a lowercase L).

f. Type a closing parenthesis). The focus and *ScreenTip* return to the *IF* function.

g. Type a comma , to complete the *logical_test* argument for the *IF* function.

h. Type "Met both" including the quotation marks for the *value_if_true* argument.

i. Type a comma , to move to the *value_if_false* argument.

j. Type "No" (Figure 6-19).

5	Revenue Data by Employee											Quarterly
6	Name	Location	Goal	Actual	Met Goal?	Both Goals?	Either Goal?	Both Goals?	Actual/ Goal %	Level		Goal
7	BJ Francine	Baudette	$17,000	$21,500	Yes	=if(AND(d7>=c7,d7>=$L$7),"Met both","No"						$15,000
8	Christopher Bowman	Cass Lake	$15,000	$12,750	No	FALSE IF(logical_test, [value_if_true], [value_if_false])						
9	Nikolai Jalowiec	Walker	$15,000	$15,600	Yes	TRUE	TRUE		104%			

6-19 Arguments for the *IF* function

k. Type a closing parenthesis) and press **Enter**.

l. Copy the formula in cell **H7** to cells **H8:H19**.

8. Create an *IFS* function.

a. Select cell **J7**, click the **Logical** button [*Formulas* tab, *Function Library* group], and choose **IFS**.

b. Select cell **I7** and type >=96% in the *Logical_test1* box.

c. Click the **Value_if_true1** box and type Excellent. If the percentage in cell I7 is 96% or higher, the formula displays *Excellent* and no additional logical tests are run.

d. Click the **Logical_test2** box, select cell I7, and type >= 85%.

e. Click the **Value_if_true2** box and type Good. If the percentage in cell I7 is 85% or higher up to 96%, the formula displays *Good* and no more logical tests are run (Figure 6-20).

f. Click the **Logical_test3** box, select cell I7, and type <85%.

g. Click the **Value_if_true3** box and type Average. If the percentage in cell I7 is less than 85%, the formula displays *Average*.

h. Click **OK**.

i. Increase the indent one time for cell **J7**.

j. Copy the formula in cell **J7** to cells **J8:J19**. Widen the column to show all data if necessary (Figure 6-21).

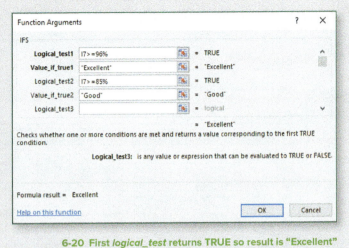

6-20 First *logical_test* returns TRUE so result is "Excellent"

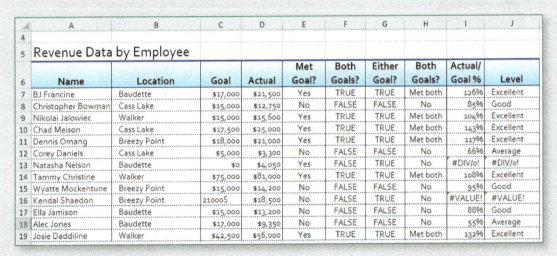

	A	B	C	D	E	F	G	H	I	J
4										
5	Revenue Data by Employee									
6	Name	Location	Goal	Actual	Met Goal?	Both Goals?	Either Goal?	Both Goals?	Actual/ Goal %	Level
7	BJ Francine	Baudette	$17,000	$21,500	Yes	TRUE	TRUE	Met both	126%	Excellent
8	Christopher Bowman	Cass Lake	$15,000	$12,750	No	FALSE	FALSE	No	85%	Good
9	Nikolai Jalowiec	Walker	$15,000	$15,600	Yes	TRUE	TRUE	Met both	104%	Excellent
10	Chad Meison	Cass Lake	$17,500	$25,000	Yes	TRUE	TRUE	Met both	143%	Excellent
11	Dennis Omang	Breezy Point	$18,000	$21,000	Yes	TRUE	TRUE	Met both	117%	Excellent
12	Corey Daniels	Cass Lake	$5,000	$3,300	No	FALSE	FALSE	No	66%	Average
13	Natasha Nelson	Baudette	$0	$4,050	Yes	FALSE	TRUE	No	#DIV/o!	#DIV/o!
14	Tammy Christine	Walker	$75,000	$81,000	Yes	TRUE	TRUE	Met both	108%	Excellent
15	Wyatte Mockentune	Breezy Point	$15,000	$14,200	No	FALSE	FALSE	No	95%	Good
16	Kendal Shaedon	Breezy Point	21000S	$18,500	No	FALSE	TRUE	No	#VALUE!	#VALUE!
17	Ella Jamison	Baudette	$15,000	$13,200	No	FALSE	FALSE	No	88%	Good
18	Alec Jones	Baudette	$17,000	$9,350	No	FALSE	FALSE	No	55%	Average
19	Josie Daddiline	Walker	$42,500	$56,000	Yes	TRUE	TRUE	Met both	132%	Excellent

6-21 *IFS* function results in "Level" column

9. Create an *IFERROR* function.

a. Select cell **I7**. The formula is **=D7/C7**.

b. Delete the contents of cell **I7**.

c. Click the **Logical** button [*Formulas* tab, *Function Library* group] and choose **IFERROR**.

d. In the *Value* argument box, click cell **D7**, type /, and click cell **C7**.

e. Click the *Value_if_error* box.

f. Type Check values in columns C and D. including the period. If the formula results in an error, your message displays instead of a standard error value message.

g. Click **OK**.

h. Copy the formula in cell **I7** to cells **I8:I19**. *AutoFit* column I (Figure 6-22). Column J displays "Excellent" for cells I13 and I16, but the *IFS* formula recalculates when corrections are made in columns C or D.

10. Save and close the workbook.

	A	B	C	D	E	F	G	H	I	J	K	L
1	Criteria											
2	**Name**	**Location**	**Goal**	**Actual**								
3		cas*										
4												
5	Revenue Data by Employee											
6	**Name**	**Location**	**Goal**	**Actual**	**Met Goal?**	**Both Goals?**	**Either Goal?**	**Both Goals?**	**Actual/ Goal %**	**Level**		**Quarterly Goal**
7	BJ Francine	Baudette	$17,000	$21,500	Yes	TRUE	TRUE	Met both	126%	Excellent		$15,000
8	Christopher Bowman	Cass Lake	$15,000	$12,750	No	FALSE	FALSE	No	85%	Good		
9	Nikolai Jalowiec	Walker	$15,000	$15,600	Yes	TRUE	TRUE	Met both	104%	Excellent		
10	Chad Meison	Cass Lake	$17,500	$25,000	Yes	TRUE	TRUE	Met both	143%	Excellent		
11	Dennis Omang	Breezy Point	$18,000	$21,000	Yes	TRUE	TRUE	Met both	117%	Excellent		
12	Corey Daniels	Cass Lake	$5,000	$3,300	No	FALSE	FALSE	No	66%	Average		
13	Natasha Nelson	Baudette	$0	$4,050	Yes	FALSE	TRUE	No	Check values in columns C and D.	Excellent		
14	Tammy Christine	Walker	$75,000	$81,000	Yes	TRUE	TRUE	Met both	108%	Excellent		
15	Wyatte Mockentune	Breezy Point	$15,000	$14,200	No	FALSE	FALSE	No	95%	Good		
16	Kendal Shaedon	Breezy Point	21000S	$18,500	No	FALSE	TRUE	No	Check values in columns C and D.	Excellent		
17	Ella Jamison	Baudette	$15,000	$13,200	No	FALSE	FALSE	No	88%	Good		
18	Alec Jones	Baudette	$17,000	$9,350	No	FALSE	FALSE	No	55%	Average		
19	Josie Daddiline	Walker	$42,500	$56,000	Yes	TRUE	TRUE	Met both	132%	Excellent		
20												
21		Maximum Goal, Cass Lake	$17,500									
22		Average Goal, Cass Lake	$12,500									
23		Total Goal, Cass Lake	$37,500									
24												

6-22 Completed PP E6-1 worksheet

SLO 6.3

Exploring the Lookup & Reference Category

The functions in the *Lookup & Reference* group are used to find, refer to, or manipulate data. These functions do not perform a calculation; they enable you to work with large datasets that might otherwise be unmanageable.

The INDEX Function

The *INDEX* function displays the contents of the cell at the intersection of a specified column and row. In a large inventory sheet that is sorted many times throughout the day, you can use *INDEX* to determine the product name in the third row, fourth column, at any given time. The *INDEX* function is rarely used alone and is generally nested with the *MATCH* function.

The *INDEX* function has two arguments lists. The first list is the array form of the function and includes an array or range of cells, the row number, and the column number as arguments. The syntax for an INDEX function (array form) is:

=INDEX(array, row_num, column_num)

The *array* argument is a cell range to be searched. You can select cells or enter a range name. The *row_num* argument is a row number in the array. The *column_num* argument identifies the column location, counting left to right. When the array consists of one column, a *column_num* argument is not necessary.

The second argument list for *INDEX* is referred to as the reference form, because it has a reference argument to identify multiple cell ranges. The syntax for an INDEX function (reference form) is:

=INDEX(reference, row_num, [column_num], [area_num])

▶ HOW TO: Create an INDEX (Array Form) Function

1. Select the cell for the result.

2. Click the **Lookup & Reference** button [*Formulas* tab, *Function Library* group].

3. Choose **INDEX**.
   - The *Select Arguments* dialog box shows two argument lists (Figure 6-23).

4. Select the first list **array, row_num, column_num** and click **OK**.

5. Select the cell range in the worksheet for the *Array* argument.
   - You can press **F3** (**FN+F3**) and paste a range name.

6. Click the **Row_num** box and type the row number.

7. Click the **Column_num** box and type the column number (Figure 6-24).

8. Click **OK**.
   - The result displays the contents of the cell identified by the *Row_num* and *Column_num* arguments.

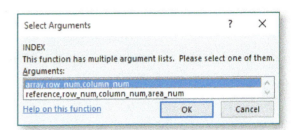

6-23 *Select Arguments* dialog box for *INDEX*

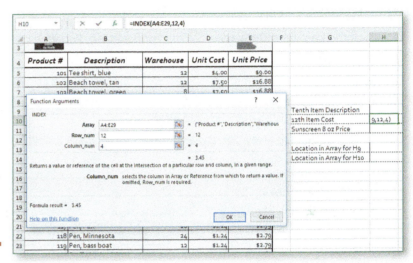

6-24 *Function Arguments* dialog box for *INDEX*

The MATCH Function

The *MATCH* function looks for data that matches your specifications and displays the location of the data within a list. It is similar to *VLOOKUP*, but *MATCH* shows a row or column identifier, not the data. The syntax for a *MATCH* function is:

=MATCH(lookup_value, lookup_array, [match_type])

The *lookup_value* argument is the text or value that you want to locate. You can enter a cell address that contains the data or type a label or value. *Lookup_array* is a range, either a single row or a single column. You can select the range or use a defined name. These two arguments are required.

The *match_type* argument establishes how the *lookup_value* is compared to values in the *lookup_array*. The *match_type* argument is optional, but it is best to use *0* as the *match_type* for an exact match. The following table explains options for the *match_type* argument.

Match_type Argument	Result
1 or omitted	The function finds the largest value that is less than or equal to the lookup_value. The lookup_array must be sorted in ascending order.
0	The function finds the first value that exactly matches the lookup_value. The lookup_array can be in any order.
−1	The function finds the smallest value that is greater than or equal to the lookup_value. The lookup_array must be sorted in descending order.

ANOTHER WAY

Click the **Recently Used** button in the *Function Library* group [*Formulas* tab] to choose a function that you have recently selected.

▶ HOW TO: Build a MATCH Function

1. Select the cell for the result.
2. Click the **Lookup & Reference** button [*Formulas* tab, *Function Library* group].
3. Choose **MATCH**.
4. Select the cell with data to be located and matched for the *Lookup_value* argument.
   - You can type a text entry; quotation marks are entered automatically.
   - This data is located in the lookup array.
5. Click the **Lookup_array** box and select the cell range in the worksheet.
   - The range is a single column or a single row that includes the data you are looking for.
   - If the range has been named, press **F3** (**FN+F3**) to paste the name.
6. Click the **Match_type** box.
7. Type **0** to find an exact match (Figure 6-25).
   - Type **1** or leave the text box empty when the array is sorted in ascending order and you want to find the closest match that is greater than the lookup value.
8. Click **OK**. The relative position of the *lookup_value* in the *lookup_array* displays in the cell.

6-25 *Function Arguments* dialog box for *MATCH*

MATCH Nested in INDEX

The *INDEX* and *MATCH* functions, when used together, work quickly on large sets of data. Although you can often accomplish the same task by sorting, filtering, or using a *LOOKUP* function, these methods can take a long time in a worksheet with millions of records.

Below is an *INDEX* function that nests *MATCH* for the *row_num* and *column_num* arguments. The *INDEX* array argument is the named range "Inventory." The *INDEX* row_num argument is a *MATCH* function that finds and exactly matches the data in cell B15 in cells B5:B29. The *INDEX* column_num argument is a second *MATCH* function that finds and matches the data in cell E4 in cells A4:E4.

> **=INDEX(Inventory,MATCH(B15,B5:B29,0),MATCH(E4,A4:E4,0))**

1. Select the cell for the result.

2. Click the **Lookup & Reference** button [*Formulas* tab, *Function Library* group].

3. Choose **INDEX**.

4. Select the first argument list **array, row_num, column_num** and click **OK**.

5. For the *Array* argument, select the cells in the worksheet.

   - This range is the entire list.
   - Press **F3** (**FN+F3**) to paste a range name.

6. Click the **Row_num** box, click the **Name** box arrow, and choose **MATCH**.

   - Click **More Functions** if necessary to find and select *MATCH*.

7. Select the cell with data to be located and matched as the *Lookup_value* argument for *MATCH*.

   - You can type a text entry.

8. Click the **Lookup_array** box and select the cell range in the worksheet.

   - The range is a single column or a single row that includes the *lookup_value*.
   - If the range has been named, press **F3** (**FN+F3**) to paste the name.

9. Click the **Match_type** box and type **0** (Figure 6-26).

10. Click the name **INDEX** in the *Formula* bar.

    - The *Function Arguments* dialog box presents the *INDEX* function again.
    - Ignore the *Select Arguments* list dialog box if it opens.

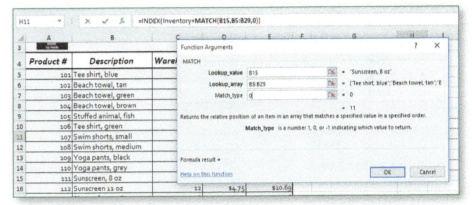

6-26 Complete arguments for the first nested *MATCH*

11. Click the **Column_num** box, click the **Name** box arrow, and choose **MATCH**.

12. Select the cell with data to be located and matched for the *Lookup_value* argument.

    - You can type a text entry.

13. Click the **Lookup_array** box and select the cell range.

    - The range is the single row or column that includes the *lookup_value* argument.

14. Click the **Match_type** box and type **0**.

15. Click the name **INDEX** in the *Formula* bar and click **OK** (Figure 6-27).

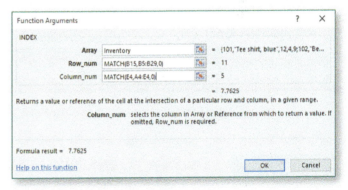

6-27 *MATCH* nested as *column_num* argument

The TRANSPOSE Function

The *TRANSPOSE* function displays columnar data in rows and vice versa, and results are located in multiple cells. An **array formula** is a formula that calculates results across a range of cells. Many Excel functions can be executed as array formulas by pressing **Ctrl+Shift+Enter** as completion keys. These types of formulas are referred to as **CSE** formulas.

An array formula appears in each cell of the results range. The formula includes an equals sign, the name of the function, and the argument in parentheses. The entire function is enclosed in curly braces to indicate that it is an array formula.

{=TRANSPOSE(SheetName!B1:S1)}

The *TRANSPOSE* function has one argument, *array*, which are the cells to be rearranged. To use *TRANSPOSE*, first select the range that will hold the transposed data. If the data occupies 15 columns in a row, select 15 cells in a column to transpose the data.

> ### ANOTHER WAY
> The *Paste Special* dialog box includes an option to transpose copied data.

▶ HOW TO: Create a TRANSPOSE Function

1. Select the cells for transposed results.

2. Click the **Lookup & Reference** button [*Formulas* tab, *Function Library* group].

3. Choose **TRANSPOSE**.

4. Select the cells that are to be transposed for the *Array* argument (Figure 6-28).

   - The cells can be on a different sheet.

5. Press **Ctrl+Shift+Enter**.

   - The formula is inserted in each cell in the selected range.
   - If you press **Enter**, only the first result is calculated.

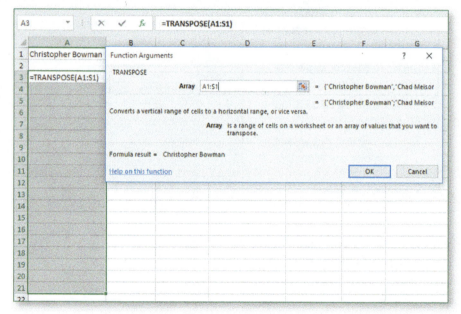

6-28 *TRANSPOSE* arguments

SLO 6.4

Building Date, Time, and Statistical Calculations

Date and time calculations enable you to determine arrival dates, to age accounts receivable, or to figure hours worked. If you depend on market research for your work, concepts such as a mean absolute deviation or a standard deviation are important numbers. These types of tasks can be handled by an Excel formula.

Date and Time Formats

For ease in building date and time calculations, you must understand how dates and times are entered, formatted, and recognized. Excel uses serial numbers for dates which set January 1,

1900, as 1; January 2, 1900, as 2; and so on. For years between 1900 and 1929, you must key "19" to identify the twentieth century; otherwise Excel assumes the twenty-first century.

Dates are often entered in *mm/dd/yy* format in the United States. Excel recognizes a date typed in this style and applies the *Short Date* format. Depending on how you key a date, however, the onscreen format might be different because Excel applies the closest format from its list of preset formats.

> ### MORE INFO
> International and military dates are often entered in *dd/mm/yy* or *yy/mm/dd* format.

Excel uses a 24-hour day in time calculations but can display results using a 12-hour or a 24-hour clock. If you key 14:30 in a cell, Excel displays 2:30 PM in the *Formula* bar. If you key 1:30, the *Formula* bar shows 1:30 AM.

The *Date*, *Time*, and *Custom* categories in the *Format Cells* dialog box provide preset and special display formats for dates and times. From the *Custom* category, scroll a list of formats, choose one that is close to what you prefer, and edit the codes in the *Type* box. When time or date calculations display unexpected results, you should always check and reset the format as needed.

▶ HOW TO: Create Custom Date and Time Formats

1. Type the date and press **Enter**.
   - The date is formatted if it is recognized as a date.
2. Select the cell with the date.
3. Click the **Launcher** for the *Number* group [*Home* tab].
4. Choose **Custom** in the *Category* list.
   - Choose **Date** in the list to select a preset format instead.
5. Scroll the *Type* list and choose a format.
   - The codes for a date are *d*, *y*, and *m* for day, year, and month (Figure 6-29).
   - The *Sample* box previews the formatted date.
6. Click the **Type** box above the list and edit the format codes as desired.
   - You can enter special characters in the *Type* box such as a hyphen or a comma.
7. Press **Enter** or click **OK**.
8. Type the time and press **Enter**.
   - Include **AM** or **PM** to use a 12-hour clock.
   - A colon is required for times not on the hour such as 1:30.
9. Select the cell with the time.
10. Click the **Launcher** for the *Number* group [*Home* tab].
11. Choose **Custom** in the *Category* list.
    - Choose **Time** in the list to select a preset format instead.

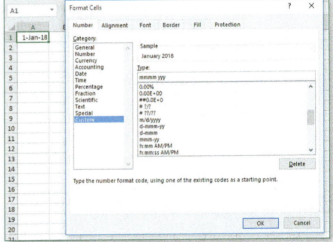

6-29 Build a custom date format

12. Scroll the *Type* list and choose a format.
   - The *Sample* box previews the formatted time.
13. Click the **Type** box and edit the format codes as desired.
   - The codes for a time are *h*, *m*, and *s* for hour, minute, and second (Figure 6-30).
14. Press **Enter** or click **OK**.

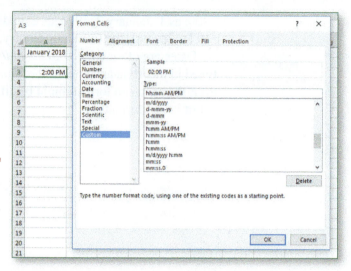

Date Calculations

Date calculations include determining your age, counting the days until your next holiday, or estimating expiration dates. Formula results calculate the number of days, but you can convert days into years (or months). Be careful about mathematical order of preference in date calculations, because formulas typically include multiple operators.

Many date formulas use the *TODAY* function to calculate how much time has passed. To determine your age, for example, subtract your birth date from *TODAY* and divide by 365.25. When you use *TODAY* in a date calculation, you can refer to a cell with the function or enter the function as part of the formula.

> **MORE INFO**
>
> It is common practice to use 365.25 as the number of days in a year which accounts for a leap year every four years.

▶ HOW TO: Calculate Years Passed

1. Enter the *TODAY* function in a cell in the worksheet.
2. Click the cell for the calculated results.
3. Type **=(** to start the formula.
   - The opening parenthesis is necessary so that the subtraction is done first.
4. Click the cell with the *TODAY* function and press **F4 (FN+F4)**.
   - The reference should be absolute if you plan to copy the formula.
5. Type **–** to subtract the next date.
6. Select the cell with the starting date.
   - *TODAY* minus the start date is the subtraction.
   - You can also type the starting date in *mm/dd/yy* format.

7. Type **)/** for the closing parenthesis and division.

8. Type **365.25** to convert the result to years (Figure 6-31).

   - Without the division, the result displays the number of days.

9. Press **Enter**.

   - The result displays as many decimals as will fit in the cell.
   - Format the results with decimal places as desired.

D3			× ✓ fx	=($F$1-C3)/365.25		
◢	A	B	C	D	E	F	G

	A	B	C	D	E	F
1	**PLR Employee Hire Dates**					1/1/2018
2	**First Name**	**Last Name**	**Hire Date**	**Length**		
3	BJ	Francine	03/15/14	=($F$1-C3)/365.25		
4	Alec	Jones	09/18/14			
5	Mikayla	Anderson	07/15/15			
6	Ella	Jamison	05/11/15			
7	David	Gazik	11/14/15			
8	Natasha	Nelson	10/24/15			
9	Ari	Aronson	05/10/16			
10	Dennis	Omang	04/15/16			
11	Kendal	Shaedon	06/14/16			
12	Frankie	Dennis	08/18/16			

6-31 Build a date calculation

Time Calculations

Time calculations include calculating hours worked, upload or delivery times, or processing time. As long as you have a start time and end time, you can determine how many hours have passed. Excel shows time results as a fraction of a 24-hour day, and you can convert to hours by multiplying by 24.

▶ **HOW TO: Calculate Time Passed**

1. Click the cell for the result.

2. Type **=(** to start the formula and enter the opening parenthesis.

   - The parentheses set the subtraction as the first operation.

3. Click the cell with the ending time.

4. Type **–** to subtract.

5. Select the cell with the beginning time (Figure 6-32).

6. Type **)*** for the closing parenthesis and multiplication.

7. Type **24** to convert the result to hours by multiplying by 24.

8. Press **Enter**.

   - The result may be formatted as a time.

9. Select the cell and apply the **General** format [*Home* tab, *Number* group, *Number Format* drop-down list].

   - The time passed is shown with as many decimals as will fit in the cell.
   - Format the results with decimal places as desired.

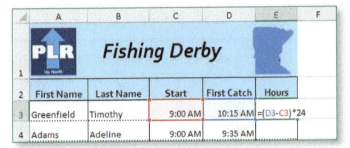

	A	B	C	D	E	F
1	**PLR**	**Fishing Derby**				
2	**First Name**	**Last Name**	**Start**	**First Catch**	**Hours**	
3	Greenfield	Timothy	9:00 AM	10:15 AM	=(D3-C3)*24	
4	Adams	Adeline	9:00 AM	9:35 AM		

6-32 Build a time calculation

> **MORE INFO**
>
> Convert time displayed in hours into minutes by multiplying by 60 or format time with fractions instead of decimals.

The DATEVALUE and TIMEVALUE Functions

Two functions in the *Date & Time* category convert text data into date or time values, *DATEVALUE* and *TIMEVALUE*. This is a common task for date and time data from external sources, because the data often is imported as text. Data to be converted must be in a Microsoft-acceptable arrangement for a date or time.

▶ HOW TO: Use DATEVALUE

1. Click the cell where the converted date should display.
2. Click the **Date & Time** button [*Formulas* tab, *Function Library* group].
3. Choose **DATEVALUE**.
   - The argument is *Date_text*.
4. Select the cell with a date as text (Figure 6-33).
   - You can also type a date in the argument box.
5. Click **OK** or press **Enter**.
   - The date is converted to a serial number.
6. Select the cell and apply a date format.

6-33 *DATEVALUE Function Arguments* dialog box

Forecast Errors and MAD Calculations

A *forecast error* is the difference between actual amounts and predicted values, an important analysis tool for business and research. A forecast error is a *deviation*, a simple subtraction formula. Paradise Lakes Resort can compare the number of products sold with predicted sales to manage inventory. A small forecast error or deviation means good inventory procedures while a large error signifies better control is needed.

A popular measure of how spread out a set of values is from the average (the mean) is the *mean absolute deviation*. Its acronym is **MAD**, and it is a calculation that uses two Excel functions, *ABS* and *AVERAGE*.

When analyzing deviations, it generally is not important whether the value is positive or negative. The *ABS* function displays the numeric value of a number–the value without any sign, the *absolute* value. A MAD formula calculates the absolute difference for each cell and then averages those values.

▶ HOW TO: Build a MAD Calculation

1. Click the cell for the first absolute result.
2. Type =ab and press **Tab**.
   - The *ScreenTip* shows the *number* argument.
3. Click the cell with the forecasted or planned value.

4. Type – and click the cell with the actual value (Figure 6-34).

5. Press **Enter**.

6. Copy the *ABS* formula as needed.

7. Click the cell for the MAD calculation.

8. Type =aver and press **Tab**.

9. Select the cells with absolute values.

10. Press **Enter** (Figure 6-35).

6-34 *ABS* function and argument

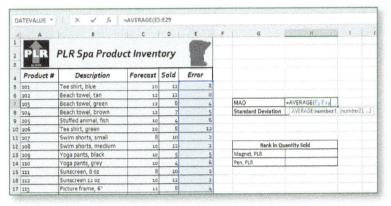

6-35 Calculate the mean absolute deviation

- The result is, on average, how far each deviation or error is from the mean of those errors.

 ANOTHER WAY

The *AVEDEV* function in the *Statistical* category calculates the average deviation of the absolute values in a range.

Standard Deviation

A **standard deviation** measures how broadly values deviate from the mean or average value in a range of numbers, a popular statistical calculation. The *STDEV*.S function applies to sample populations and ignores text and logical values. A **sample** is a subset of a population; a **population** is all the data.

MORE INFO

To calculate the standard deviation for an entire population instead of a sample, use the function **STDEV.P**.

The syntax for a *STDEV*.S function is:

=STDEV.S(number1,[number2],...)

The required argument is *number1*, the first value or range. When the values to be analyzed are not adjacent, you use additional *number* arguments to include each cell in the formula.

▶ **HOW TO:** Use the STDEV.S Function

1. Click the cell for the result.
2. Click the **More Functions** button [*Formulas* tab, *Function Library* group] and choose **Statistical**.
3. Find and choose **STDEV.S**.
4. Select the cells to be analyzed for the *Number1* argument. (Figure 6-36).
5. Click **OK**.

6-36 *STDEV.S Function Arguments* dialog box

▶ **MORE INFO**

The mean square error (MSE) is a measure of variability that uses *SUMSQ* and *COUNT* to sum the squares of the values and divide by the number of values in the range.

The RANK.EQ Function

In a large set of data, use the *RANK.EQ* or the *RANK.AVG* function to calculate where a particular value appears in the dataset. The *RANK* functions identify where the value is relative to all the other values.

The syntax for a *RANK.EQ* function is:

=RANK.EQ(number, ref,[order])

The *Number* is the cell that you want to rank. *Ref* is the range of values in which the *Number* lies. *Order* identifies whether you want the values to be considered in ascending or descending order. Values in descending order place the highest value as rank 1.

When duplicate values exist in the range, *RANK.EQ* shows the lower rank. The *RANK. AVG* function calculates duplicate values with an average rank.

▶ **HOW TO:** Use the RANK.EQ Function

1. Click the cell for the rank result.
2. Click the **More Functions** button [*Formulas* tab, *Function Library* group] and choose **Statistical**.
3. Find and choose **RANK.EQ**.
4. In the *Number* box, select the cell to be ranked.

5. Click the **Ref** box and select the cells with related values (Figure 6-37).

   - This is the range in which the cell to be ranked is located.

6. Leave the **Order** box empty to indicate descending order (top rank is 1).

7. Click **OK**.

   - The value's position in relation to the other values is indicated.

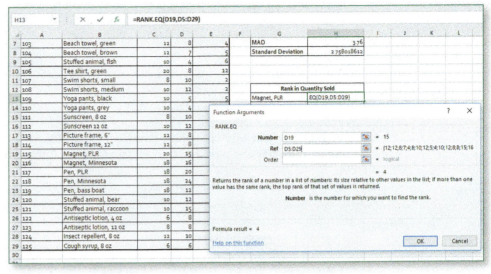

6-37 *RANK.EQ Function Arguments* dialog box

PAUSE & PRACTICE: EXCEL 6-2

In this project, you nest *INDEX* and *MATCH* functions to display information on the inventory worksheet for Paradise Lakes Resort. You transpose data, calculate statistics for inventory data, and prepare time and date calculations.

File Needed: *[your initials] PP E6-1.xlsx*
Completed Project File Name: *[your initials] PP E6-2.xlsx*

1. Open *[your initials] PP E6-1.xlsx* completed in *Pause & Practice 6-1* and save it as [your initials] PP E6-2.

2. Click the **Inventory** worksheet tab.

3. Use the *INDEX* function with one column of data.
   a. Select cell **H9**.
   b. Click the **Lookup & Reference** button [*Formulas* tab, *Function Library* group] and choose **INDEX**.
   c. Select the first argument list **array, row_num, column_num** and click **OK**.
   d. Select cells **B5:B29** for the *Array* argument.
   e. Click the **Row_num** box and type 10 to show data from the tenth row in the range. When using a single column as the array, there is no *Column_num* argument (Figure 6-38).
   f. Click **OK**. *Yoga pants, grey* is the description.

6-38 *INDEX* function to show data from tenth row

4. Use the *INDEX* function with a range name.
   a. Select cell **H10**.
   b. Click the **Recently Used** button [*Formulas* tab, *Function Library* group] and choose **INDEX**.
   c. Select the first argument list and click **OK**.
   d. Press **F3** (**FN+F3**) to open the *Paste List* dialog box in the *Array* argument box.
   e. Choose **Inventory** and click **OK**.
   f. Click the **Row_num** box and type 12 to show data from the twelfth row.
   g. Click the **Column_num** box and type 4 to display data from the Cost column, the fourth column (Figure 6-39).
   h. Click **OK** and format cell **H10** as **Currency**. The cost of the twelfth item, 12 oz. sunscreen, is $4.75.

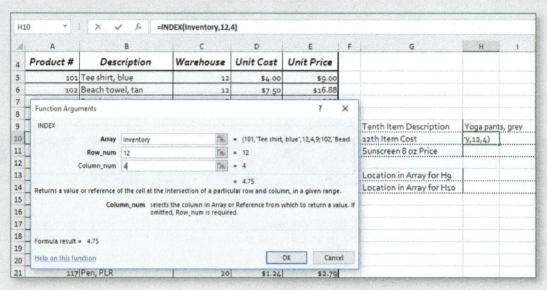

6-39 *INDEX* function to show data from twelfth row, fourth column

5. Use the *MATCH* function.
   a. Select cell **H13**.
   b. Click the **Lookup & Reference** button [*Formulas* tab, *Function Library* group] and choose **MATCH**.
   c. Select cell **H9** for the *Lookup_value* argument.
   d. Click the **Look_up array** box and select cells **B5:B29**. These two arguments will find a match in cells B5:B29 for the data in cell H9.
   e. Click the **Match_type** argument and type 0 to look for an exact match (Figure 6-40).
   f. Click **OK**. The data in cell H9 is located in the tenth row in the array.
   g. Select cell **H14**, type =m and press **Tab**.
   h. Click cell **H10** and type a comma , to move to the array argument.
   i. Select cells **D5:D29** for the *look_up array* and type a comma ,.
   j. Type 0 to look for an exact match.
   k. Press **Enter**. The price in cell H10 is first located in the fifth row.

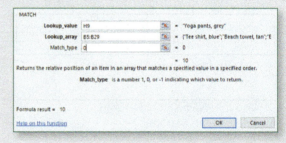

6-40 *MATCH* function for an exact match

6. Nest *INDEX* and *MATCH* functions.
   a. Select cell **H11**.
   b. Click the **Recently Used** button [*Formulas* tab, *Function Library* group] and choose **INDEX**.

c. Select the first argument list and click **OK**.

d. Press **F3** (**FN+F3**) for the *Array* argument, choose **Inventory**, and click **OK**.

e. Click the **Row_num** box, click the **Name** box arrow, and choose **MATCH**.

f. Select cell **B15**, the 8 oz. sunscreen, for the *Lookup_value*.

g. Click the **Lookup_array** box and select cells **B5:B29**.

h. Click the **Match_type** box and type 0. This completes the nested *MATCH* function for the *Row_num* argument (Figure 6-41).

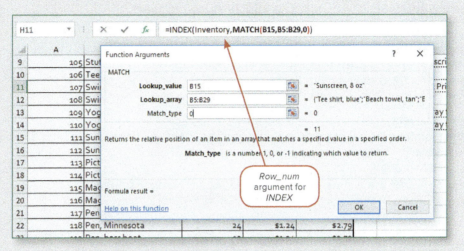

6-41 Nested *MATCH* and *INDEX*

i. Click the word **INDEX** in the *Formula* bar.

j. Click the **Column_num** box for the *INDEX* function.

k. Click the **Name** box arrow and choose **MATCH**.

l. Select cell **E4**, the *Unit Price* label, for the *Lookup_value*.

m. Click the **Lookup_array** box and select cells **A4:E4**, the label row.

n. Click the *Match_type* box and type 0. This is the nested *MATCH* function for the *Column_num* argument.

o. Click the word **INDEX** in the *Formula* bar (Figure 6-42).

6-42 *MATCH* is *Row_num* and *Column_num* arguments

p. Click **OK**. The price for the 8 oz. sunscreen displays unrounded as 7.7625.

q. Format cell **H11** as **Currency**.

7. Calculate the mean absolute deviation (MAD) for forecast errors.
   a. Click the **Forecasts** sheet tab and select cell **E5**.
   b. Type =ab and press **Tab**.
   c. Type c5-d5 and press **Enter**. The closing parenthesis is provided.
   d. Copy the formula in cell **E5** to cells **E6:E29** without formatting. Absolute values do not show any signs.
   e. Select cell **H7**.
   f. Use the *AVERAGE* function with cells **E5:E29** as the argument.

8. Calculate a standard deviation for number sold.
   a. Select cell **H8**.
   b. Type =std, select **STDEV.S** from the list, and press **Tab**.
   c. Select cells **D5:D29** and press **Enter**.

9. Rank products by quantity sold.
   a. Select cell **H13**.
   b. Click the **More Functions** button [*Formulas* tab, *Function Library* group] and choose **Statistical**.
   c. Select **RANK.EQ**.
   d. Select cell **D19**, the number of magnets sold, for the *Number* argument.
   e. Click the **Ref** box and select cells **D5:D29** (Figure 6-43).

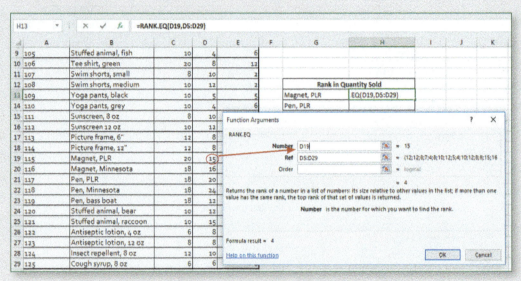

6-43 Rank a value in the list

   f. Click **OK**.
   g. Select cell **H14** and use *RANK.EQ* to rank the quantity sold for the pen.

10. Transpose data using *TRANSPOSE*.
    a. Click the **Transpose** worksheet tab. The data occupies 19 columns in a single row.
    b. Click the **Marketing** worksheet tab.
    c. Select cells **A3:A21**, 19 rows in a single column.
    d. Click the **Lookup & Reference** button [*Formulas* tab, *Function Library* group] and select **TRANSPOSE**.
    e. For the *Array* argument, click the **Transpose** sheet tab and select cells **A1:S1**.
    f. Press **Ctrl+Shift+Enter** to create an array formula (Figure 6-44).

11. Format dates and calculate days employed.
    a. Click the **Hire Dates** sheet tab.
    b. Select cells **C3:C25**. These are serial numbers that represent hire dates.
    c. Click the **Launcher** in the *Number* group [*Home* tab] and select the *Date* category.
    d. Select the format that shows a leading zero **03/14/12** and click **OK**.
    e. Enter the *TODAY* function in cell **A27**.
    f. Select cell **D3**.
    g. Type =(to start a formula.
    h. Click cell **A27** and press **F4 (FN+F4)** to make it absolute.
    i. Type – to subtract and click cell **C3**.
    j. Type)/ for a closing parenthesis and division.
    k. Type 365.25 to convert results to years and press **Enter** (Figure 6-45).
    l. Copy cell **D3** to cells **D4:D25** without formatting.
    m. Format cells **D3:D25** with the **Number** format.

12. Calculate time.
    a. Click the **Derby** sheet tab.
    b. Select cell **E3**. The ending time is the time of the first catch.
    c. Type =(to start a formula.
    d. Click cell **D3**, the end time.
    e. Type – to subtract and click cell **C3**.
    f. Type)* for a closing parenthesis and multiplication.
    g. Type 24 to convert days to hours.
    h. Type *60 to convert hours to minutes (Figure 6-46).
    i. Press **Enter**.
    j. Copy cell **E3** to cells **E4:E8** without formatting.
    k. Format the results as **General** from the *Number Format* list [*Home* tab, *Number* group].

13. Save and close the workbook (Figure 6-47).

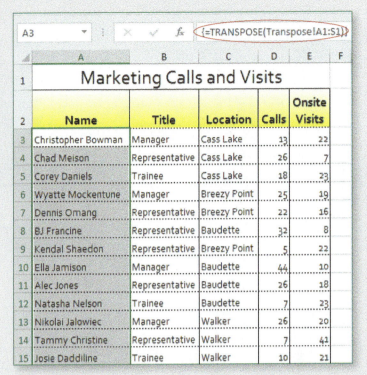

6-44 *TRANSPOSE* in an array formula

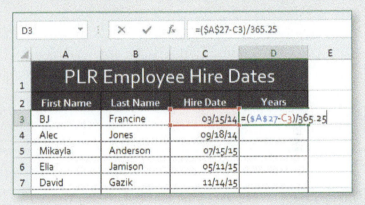

6-45 Calculate years employed

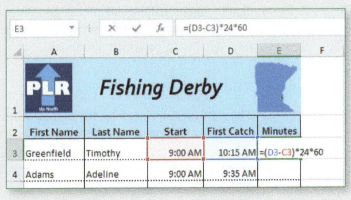

6-46 Calculate time as minutes

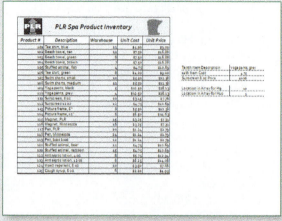

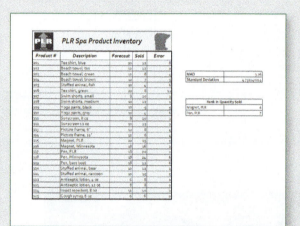

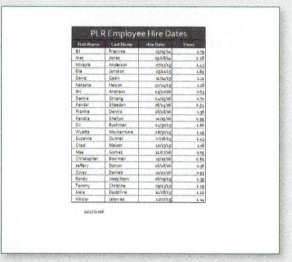

6-47 PP E6-2 completed worksheets

SLO 6.5

Using Financial Functions

Functions in the *Financial* category analyze money transactions such as loans, bond purchases, depreciation, and mortgage amortization. Many *Financial* functions use common arguments including *rate* and *nper*. **Rate** is an interest rate for the time period. **Nper** is the total number of payments or deposits.

The PV Function

The *PV* function calculates the *present value* of a money transaction. If you buy an insurance policy that will pay a specified amount in 20 years, you can use the *PV* function to determine if a lump sum premium paid now is a good value. The *PV* function uses the concept of an **annuity**, a series of equal payments made at the same time of the month or year for a specified period of time.

The syntax for a *PV* function is:

=PV(rate,nper,pmt,[fv],[type])

The *rate*, *nper*, and *pmt* arguments are required. *Rate* and *nper* arguments must use the same time division such as months or years. If you make monthly payments but the interest rate is an annual rate, the rate must be divided by 12. The *pmt* argument is the amount paid each period.

Two optional arguments are *fv* and *type*. The *fv* argument, future value, is a cash balance, if any, at the end of the last period. In the insurance policy example, an *fv* amount is money that you would allow the insurance company to keep. The *type* argument specifies if the payment is made at the beginning or the end of the period. When you receive payments, the beginning of the period is preferable.

▶ HOW TO: Use the PV Function

1. Click the cell for the result.
2. Click the **Financial** button [*Formulas* tab, *Function Library* group] and choose **PV**.
3. Select the cell that contains the interest rate for the *Rate* box.
   - If the interest rate is an annual rate and payments are monthly, type /12 after the cell address.
   - If the interest rate is an annual rate and payments are quarterly, type /4 after the cell address.
   - You can type the interest rate in the entry box as a percent or its decimal equivalent.
4. Click the **Nper** box and select the cell that contains the number of years.
   - If the term is shown in years and payments are monthly, type *12 after the cell address.
   - If the term is shown in years and payments are quarterly, type *4 after the cell address.
   - You can type the total number of payments.
5. Click the **Pmt** box and select the cell that contains the payment amount.
6. Click the **Fv** box and click the cell with the cash balance amount, if any.
   - Type a value in the entry box instead of selecting a cell.
   - Type a zero (0) or leave the entry blank to indicate no cash balance.
7. Click the **Type** box and type 1 if the payment is at the beginning of the period (Figure 6-48).
   - Type 0 or leave the entry blank to indicate payment at the end of the period.

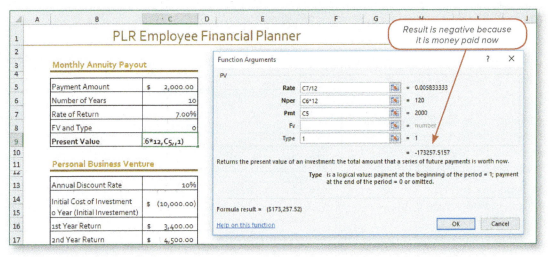

6-48 *Function Arguments dialog box for PV*

8. Click **OK**.

The FV Function

The *FV* function determines the *future value* of a series of payments at the same interest rate for a specified period of time. You can use this function to calculate results for an investment or savings plan in which you plan to deposit a specific amount each period.

The syntax for an *FV* function is:

=FV(rate,nper,pmt,[pv],[type])

Rate, *nper*, and *pmt* are required; *pv* and *type* are optional. The *pv* argument, the present value, might be a required initial investment or an amount already in the account. In a savings or investment plan, the *pv* argument is the amount that you start with.

The *type* argument is either 1 or 0 (or omitted) to indicate if payment is made at the beginning or the end of the period. In a savings plan, payment at the beginning of the period earns interest for the entire period.

▶ HOW TO: Use the FV Function

1. Click the cell for the result.
2. Click the **Financial** button [*Formulas* tab, *Function Library* group] and choose **FV**.
3. Select the cell that contains the interest rate for the *Rate* box.
   - If the interest rate is an annual rate and payments are monthly, type /12 after the cell address.
   - If the interest rate is an annual rate and payments are quarterly, type /4 after the cell address.
   - Type the interest rate in the *Rate* box instead of selecting a cell.
4. Click the **Nper** argument box and select the cell that contains the number of years.
   - If the term is years and payments are monthly, type *12 after the cell address.
   - If the term is years and payments are quarterly, type *4 after the cell address.
   - You can type the total number of payments in the *Nper* box.
5. Click the **Pmt** box and select the cell that contains the payment amount.
   - The payment amount can be formatted as a negative value, because it is money you pay each period.
6. Click the **Pv** box and select the cell with a starting amount, if any.
   - Type a value in the box if the value is not shown in the worksheet.
   - Type a zero (0) or leave the entry blank to indicate no starting amount.
7. Click the **Type** box and type 1 if the payment is at the beginning of the period (Figure 6-49).
   - Type 0 or leave the entry blank to indicate payment at the end of the period.
8. Click **OK**.

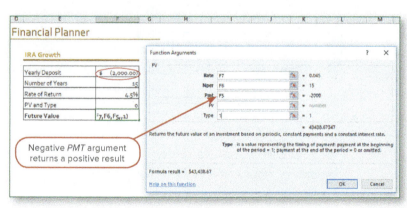

6-49 *Function Arguments* dialog box for *FV*

The NPV Function

The *NPV* function calculates the *net present value* of an investment using a discount rate and a series of future payments and receipts. A **discount rate** represents the cost of financing or the rate of return possible with a competing investment. In the *NPV* function, the series of payments and receipts can vary, unlike the payment amount in *PV* and *FV* functions.

The syntax for a *NPV* function is:

=NPV(rate,value1,value2,...)

Rate is the discount rate, an interest rate. The *valueN* arguments are positive and negative **cash flows**, payments or receipts. *Value* arguments are listed in the order in which they occur. For example, if you earn $3,400 in the first period, that amount is the *value1* argument. The *value2* argument is the next payment or receipt, and so on. A separate initial payment or cost is not a *value* argument but is added to the result of the *NPV* function as a negative amount.

> **MORE INFO**
>
> The *NPV* function assumes that cash flows occur at the end of each period.

▶**HOW TO:** Use the NPV Function

1. Click the cell for the result.
2. Click the **Financial** button [*Formulas* tab, *Function Library* group] and choose **NPV**.
3. Click the cell that contains the discount interest rate for the *Rate* box.
   - Use a percentage (10%) or its decimal equivalent (.1).
   - You can type a value instead of selecting a cell.
4. Click the **Value1** box and select the cell that contains the amount of cash flow at the end of the first period.
   - Cash flow amounts can be negative or positive values.
5. Click the **Value2** argument box and select the cell that contains the amount of cash flow at the end of the second period.
6. Click each additional **Value** box and select the cell (Figure 6-50).
   - For a year with neither a positive or negative cash flow, type a zero (0) as the *ValueN* argument to prevent the sequence of cash flows from moving forward one year.

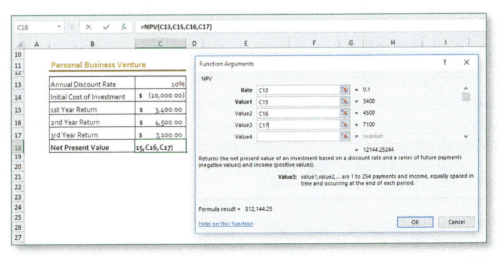

6-50 *Function Arguments* dialog box for *NPV*

7. Click **OK**.

8. To include an initial payment, click the *Formula* bar to edit the formula.

   - The initial payment should be formatted as a negative value.

9. Press **End** to position the insertion point after the closing parentheses and type +.

10. Click the cell with the initial payment and press **Enter** (Figure 6-51).

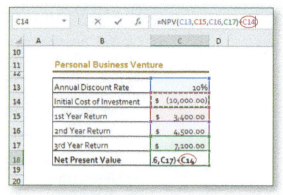

6-51 Edited *NPV* function to include initial cost

SLO 6.6

Working with Text Functions

Text functions split, join, or convert labels and values in a worksheet. With a *Text* function, you can format a value as a label to control alignment or display labels in uppercase or lower case letters.

The TEXTJOIN Function

The *TEXTJOIN* function combines strings of text, values, or characters. A common use of *TEXTJOIN* is to display a person's full name in a single cell by joining two or more cells.

The syntax for a *TEXTJOIN* function is:

=TEXTJOIN(delimiter, ignore_empty, text1, [text2], . . .)

The *delimiter* argument specifies the character used to separate the *TextN* arguments. There can be up to 252 *TextN* arguments but only one delimiter. A *Text* argument can be a cell reference or data that you type.

When you combine text strings, such as first and last names or city, state, and ZIP code, the delimiter is a space character. *TEXTJOIN* results are usually placed in a separate column or row to preserve the original data.

▶ **HOW TO:** Use the TEXTJOIN Function

1. Click the cell for the result.

2. Click the **Text** button [*Formulas* tab, *Function Library* group] and choose **TEXTJOIN**.

3. Press **Spacebar** to insert a space character in the *Delimiter* box.

4. Click the **Ignore_empty** box.

   - Leave this box empty for the default TRUE option.
   - A cell with no data is ignored in the function results.
   - The *Delimiter* space character displays with quotation marks.

5. Click the **Text1** argument box.

6. Select the cell with the first text string to be joined.

   - You can also type a text string, a value, or a punctuation character.

E6-384

7. Click the **Text2** box and select the cell with data to be joined (Figure 6-52).

   - You can use a combination of cell references and typed data among the *TextN* arguments.

8. Complete *TextN* argument boxes as needed.

9. Click **OK**.

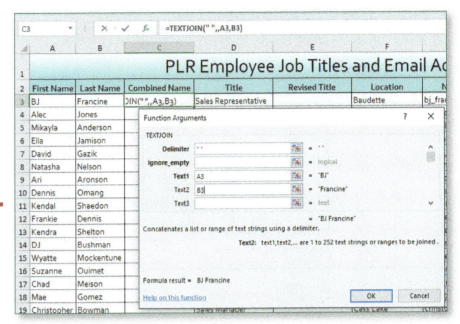

6-52 *Function Arguments* dialog box for *TEXTJOIN*

The CONCAT Function

To *concatenate* means to link or join; the *TEXTJOIN* function concatenates text strings. Excel has another *Text* function *CONCAT* that joins or combines data strings. The *CONCAT* function does not have a *delimiter* argument which enables you to specify a different delimiter between each two *TextN* arguments in the formula.

The syntax for a *CONCAT* function is:

=CONCAT(text1, [text2], . . .)

The *CONCAT* function has one argument *TextN*, where *N* is a number from 1 to 255. The *Text* argument can be a cell reference, data that you type, or a delimiter character.

> ▶ **ANOTHER WAY**
>
> You can join data in a formula using the & operator. The formula **=A1&B1** returns the same result as **=CONCAT(A1,B1)**.

When you concatenate text strings, such as first and last names, you must include space characters to separate words or values. Concatenated results are placed in a separate column or row to preserve original data.

In previous versions of Excel, *CONCAT* was named *CONCATENATE*.

▶ **HOW TO: Use the CONCAT Function**

1. Click the cell for the result.

2. Click the **Text** button [*Formulas* tab, *Function Library* group] and choose **CONCAT**.

3. Select the cell with the first text string for the *Text1* argument.

   - Type a text string rather than selecting a cell.
   - You do not need to include quotation marks when you use the *Function Arguments* dialog box.

4. Click the **Text2** box and enter the next string to be concatenated.
   - You can type a delimiter such as a space, a period, or a comma.
   - You can click a cell with the second text string.
5. Click the **Text3** box and select or type next text string (Figure 6-53).
6. Complete *TextN* argument boxes as needed.

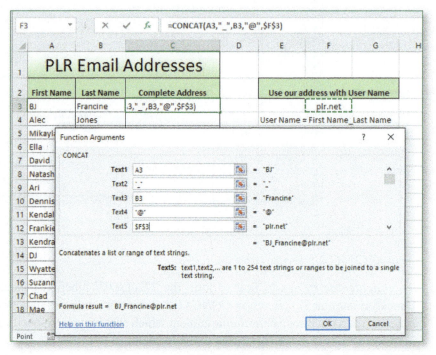

6-53 *Function Arguments* dialog box for *CONCAT*

7. Click **OK**.

> **ANOTHER WAY**
>
> You can include a space or punctuation character immediately after a cell reference in a *TextN* argument box.

> **MORE INFO**
>
> Use *TEXTJOIN* when the same delimiter is necessary for all *TextN* arguments. Use *CONCAT* to build a unique combination of *TextN* arguments and delimiters.

The EXACT Function

The *EXACT* function compares two text strings, values, or characters to determine if they are identical. For example, if you import email names, you can compare imported names to your current list.

The syntax for an *EXACT* function is:

=EXACT(text1, text2)

The *EXACT* function has two required arguments, *Text1* and *Text2*. *Text1* is the first text string, and *Text2* is the second text string. The arguments are case-sensitive, but the function does not check formatting. The result for an *EXACT* function is TRUE or FALSE.

▶ **HOW TO:** Use the EXACT Function

1. Click the cell for the result.
2. Type =ex and press **Tab**.
   - The *text1* argument is bold in the *ScreenTip*.
3. Select the cell or type the text string.
   - If you type the text string, enclose it within quotation marks and use upper- and lowercase as used in the data.
4. Type a comma (,) to move to the *text2* argument.
   - The *text2* argument is bold in the *ScreenTip*.
5. Select the cell or type the second text string (Figure 6-54).
6. Press **Enter**.
   - The closing parenthesis is supplied.
   - The result is TRUE or FALSE.

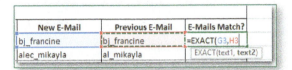

6-54 *EXACT* function has two arguments

The REPLACE Function

The *REPLACE* function allows you to substitute characters for a specified number of characters in existing data. This command is helpful when data in a column follows a pattern. For example, if Paradise Lakes Resort products have an ID that starts with PAR, use the *REPLACE* function to change each ID to PLR.

▶ **ANOTHER WAY**

Use the *SUBSTITUTE* function in the *Text* category to replace specified text within a cell.

The syntax for a *REPLACE* function is:

=REPLACE(old_text, start_num, num_chars, new_text)

The *old_text* argument is the cell with data that you want to change. The *start_num* argument is the position in the cell of the first character to be replaced. If you want to replace the first three characters in a cell, the *start_num* is 1. However, if you want to replace characters in the second word in the cell, you must count each character position, including spaces, to determine the number.

The *num_chars* argument determines how many characters from the *start_num* position are replaced, and the *new_text* argument is the replacement text.

▶ **HOW TO:** Use the REPLACE Function

1. Click the cell for the result.
2. Click the **Text** button [*Formulas* tab, *Function Library* group] and choose **REPLACE**.
3. Select the cell with data to be replaced for the *Old_text* argument.

4. Click the **Start_num** box.
   - Count character positions from the first character on the left.
5. Type a number to indicate the position at which replacement should begin.
6. Click the **Num_chars** box.
   - Count how many characters are to be replaced.
7. Type the number of replacement characters.
8. Click the **New_text** box.
9. Type the replacement text (Figure 6-55).
   - The new text can have more or fewer characters than the *num_chars* argument.
   - Quotation marks are not necessary when you use the *Function Arguments* dialog box.
   - Use upper- and lowercase as required.
10. Press **Enter** or click **OK**.
    - The new text displays in the cell.

6-55 *REPLACE* function has four arguments

PAUSE & PRACTICE: EXCEL 6-3

In this project, you complete a financial planning worksheet for Paradise Lakes Resort staff. You also update the employee data sheet using *Text* functions.

File Needed: *[your initials] PP E6-2.xlsx*
Completed Project File Name: *[your initials] PP E6-3.xlsx*

1. Open *[your initials] PP E6-2.xlsx* completed in *Pause & Practice 6-2* and save it as [your initials] PP E6-3.

2. Click the **Financial Planner** sheet tab.

3. Use the *PV* function.
   a. Select cell **C9**.
   b. Click the **Financial** button [*Formulas* tab, *Function Library* group] and choose **PV**.
   c. Select cell **C7** for the *Rate* argument and type */12* after **C7**, because the payments are monthly.
   d. Click the **Nper** argument box and select cell **C6**.
   e. Type **12* after **C6**, because the term is years but payments are monthly.
   f. Click the **Pmt** box and select cell **C5**.
   g. Press **Tab** two times to skip the *Fv* box and move to the *Type* box.
   h. Type *1* in the *Type* box to indicate payment at the beginning of the period (Figure 6-56).

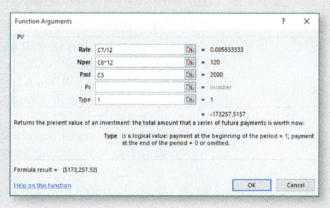

6-56 Payment is made at beginning of period

i. Click **OK**. An annuity or insurance policy costs over $173,000 to pay-out $2,000 monthly for 10 years.

4. Use the *FV* function.
   a. Select cell **F9**.
   b. Click the **Financial** button [*Formulas* tab, *Function Library* group] and choose **FV**.
   c. Click cell **F7** for the *Rate* argument. The payment is once a year and the rate is annual.
   d. Click the **Nper** argument box and select cell **F6**. There is only one payment per year.
   e. Click the **Pmt** box and select cell **F5**. The amount is negative, because you must pay it each year.
   f. Press **Tab** two times to skip the *Pv* box and move to the *Type* box. Leave both boxes empty (Figure 6-57).
   g. Click **OK**. If you invest $2,000 a year in an IRA account that earns 4.5% per year, you will have over $40,000 at the end of 15 years.

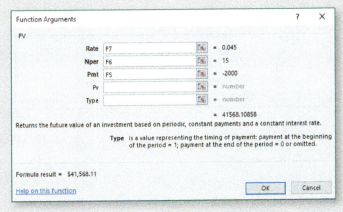

6-57 Rate and payment are yearly

5. Use the *NPV* function.
   a. Select cell **C18**.
   b. Click the **Financial** button [*Formulas* tab, *Function Library* group] and choose **NPV**.
   c. Select cell **C13** for the *Rate* argument.
   d. Click the **Value1** box and select cell **C15**.
   e. Click the **Value2** box and select cell **C16**.
   f. Click the **Value3** box and select cell **C17** (Figure 6-58).

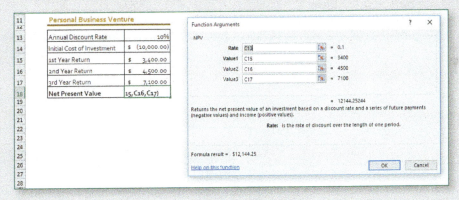

6-58 Initial investment is not a *value* argument

   g. Click **OK**.
   h. Click the *Formula* bar and press **End** to position the insertion point.
   i. Type **+** and select cell **C14** to add the cost of the investment.
   j. Press **Enter**. Based on projected cash flows, the investment has a present value of $2,144.25.

6. Use the *TEXTJOIN* function.
   a. Click the **Title&EMail** sheet tab and select cell **C3**.
   b. Click the **Text** button [*Formulas* tab, *Function Library* group] and choose **TEXTJOIN**.

c. Press **Spacebar** for the *Delimiter* argument.

d. Click the **Text1** box and select cell **A3**. The *Ignore_ empty* argument is blank which means empty cells are ignored.

e. Click the **Text2** box and select cell **B3**.

f. Click **OK**.

g. Copy the *TEXTJOIN* formula in cell **C3** to cells **C4:C25** without formatting.

h. Make column C **19.29 (140 pixels)** wide (Figure 6-59).

7. Use the *REPLACE* function.

a. Select cell **E3**.

b. Click the **Text** button [*Formulas* tab, *Function Library* group] and choose **REPLACE**.

c. Click cell **D3** for the *Old_text* argument.

d. Click the **Start_num** box and type 1.

e. Click the **Num_chars** box and type 5. This preserves the space after the word "Sales."

f. Click the **New_text** box.

g. Type PLR.

h. Press **Enter** or click **OK**.

i. Copy the *REPLACE* formula in cell **E3** to cells **E4:E25** without formatting.

j. Hide column **D** and *AutoFit* column **E**.

8. Use the *EXACT* function.

a. Select cell **I3**.

b. Type =ex and press **Tab**.

c. Select cell **G3** for the *text1* argument and type a comma , to move to the *text2* argument.

d. Select cell **H3** and press **Enter**.

e. Copy the *EXACT* formula in cell **I3** to cells **I4:I25** without formatting.

f. Apply a *Highlight Cells* rule to cells **I4:I25** to show FALSE values in **Light Red Fill with Dark Red Text**.

9. Save and close the workbook (Figure 6-60).

	A	B	C
2	First Name	Last Name	Combined Name
3	BJ	Francine	BJ Francine
4	Alec	Jones	Alec Jones
5	Mikayla	Anderson	Mikayla Anderson
6	Ella	Jamison	Ella Jamison
7	David	Gazik	David Gazik
8	Natasha	Nelson	Natasha Nelson
9	Ari	Aronson	Ari Aronson
10	Dennis	Omang	Dennis Omang
11	Kendal	Shaedon	Kendal Shaedon
12	Frankie	Dennis	Frankie Dennis
13	Kendra	Shelton	Kendra Shelton
14	DJ	Bushman	DJ Bushman
15	Wyatte	Mockentune	Wyatte Mockentune
16	Suzanne	Ouimet	Suzanne Ouimet
17	Chad	Meison	Chad Meison
18	Mae	Gomez	Mae Gomez
19	Christopher	Bowman	Christopher Bowman
20	Jeffery	Dalton	Jeffery Dalton
21	Corey	Daniels	Corey Daniels
22	Randy	Josephson	Randy Josephson
23	Tammy	Christine	Tammy Christine
24	Josie	Daddiline	Josie Daddiline
25	Nikolai	Jalowiec	Nikolai Jalowiec

6-59 *TEXTJOIN* formula shows results in single cell

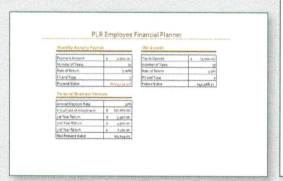

PLR Employee Financial Planner

6-60 Completed worksheets for PP E6-3

Using Multiple Criteria in Functions

You have used multiple arguments in functions and multiple criteria in filters. Three functions combine multiple arguments with multiple criteria: *SUMIFS* in the *Math & Trig* category and *AVERAGEIFS* and *COUNTIFS* in the *Statistical* category.

The SUMIFS Function

The *SUMIFS* function adds or totals cells only if they meet the criteria. In the data shown in Figure 6-61, *SUMIFS* can be used to sum the cells in the "Calls" column if the location is Breezy Point (first criteria) and if the title is Trainee (second criteria).

Marketing Calls and Visits

Name	Title	Location	Calls	Onsite Visits
Christopher Bowman	Manager	Cass Lake	13	22
Chad Meison	Representative	Cass Lake	26	7
Corey Daniels	Trainee	Cass Lake	18	23
Wyatte Mockentune	Manager	Breezy Point	25	19
Dennis Omang	Representative	Breezy Point	22	16
BJ Francine	Representative	Baudette	32	8
Kendal Shaedon	Representative	Breezy Point	5	22
Ella Jamison	Manager	Baudette	44	10
Alec Jones	Representative	Baudette	26	18
Natasha Nelson	Trainee	Baudette	7	23
Nikolai Jalowiec	Manager	Walker	26	20
Tammy Christine	Representative	Walker	7	41
Josie Daddiline	Trainee	Walker	10	21
Tara Miller	Trainee	Breezy Point	32	17
Robert Andrew	Representative	Walker	15	10
Coryn Gomez	Representative	Baudette	35	5
Elizabeth Gabrys	Trainee	Cass Lake	43	9
Rita Larson	Trainee	Walker	6	36
Michael Gentile	Representative	Baudette	38	9

6-61 Criteria from more than one column can be used in *SUMIFS*, *AVERAGEIFS*, or *COUNTIFS*

> **MORE INFO**
>
> The *SUMIFS* function is best used in large lists for which it would be time-consuming to calculate these types of results.

The syntax for a *SUMIFS* function is:

=SUMIFS(sum_range, criteria_range1, criteria1, [criteria_range2, criteria2], . . .)

The three required arguments are *sum_range*, *criteria_range1*, and *criteria1*. The *sum_range* is the cell range to be added. *Criteria_rangeN* is the range of cells that holds the criteria; it must have the same number of rows and columns as the *sum_range*. The *criteriaN* argument is a cell or typed data that must be matched for the cells to be included in the total.

A *SUMIFS* formula includes one *sum_range* and up to 127 *criteria_rangeN* arguments, each with a corresponding *criteriaN* argument.

▶HOW TO: Use SUMIFS

1. Click the cell for the result.
2. Click the **Math & Trig** button [*Formulas* tab, *Function Library* group] and choose **SUMIFS**.
3. Select the cells with data to be totaled for the *Sum_range* argument.
   - You can type cell references instead of selecting them.
4. Click the **Criteria_range1** argument box.
5. Select the range of cells with the first set of data to be matched with criteria.
   - This range must be the same size as the *sum_range*.
6. Click the **Criteria1** argument box.
7. Type the data to be used as a condition.
   - You can use wildcard characters in the criteria.
   - Text criteria are not case-sensitive.
   - If the criteria are located in a cell on the worksheet, you can select the cell.

8. Click the **Criteria_range2** argument box.

9. Select the range with the next set of data to be matched.

   - This range must be the same size as the *sum_range*.

10. Click the **Criteria2** argument box.

11. Type the second requirement or condition (Figure 6-62).

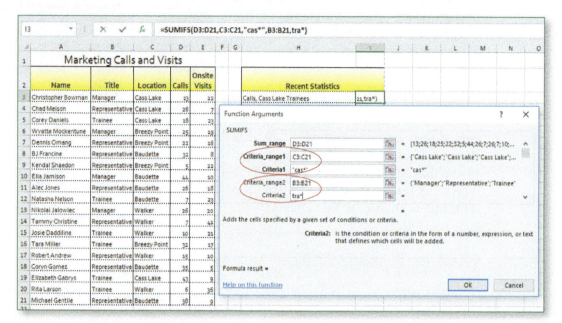

6-62 Data is included in sum only if it meets both criteria

12. Add *Criteria_range* and *Criteria* arguments as needed.

   - The size of each *criteria_range* must match the size of the *sum_range*.
   - Each *criteria_range* argument must have a corresponding *criteria* argument.

13. Click **OK**.

The AVERAGEIFS and COUNTIFS Functions

AVERAGEIFS and *COUNTIFS* perform their computations only when the data meets multiple criteria, like the *SUMIFS* function. For the data in Figure 6-63, use *AVERAGEIFS* to calculate the average number of onsite visits made by Walker representatives.

> **ANOTHER WAY**
>
> Results calculated by *SUMIFS*, *AVERAGEIFS*, or *COUNTIFS* can also be determined by filtering and sorting data in an Excel table.

The syntax for the *AVERAGEIFS* function is:

=AVERAGEIFS(average_range, criteria_range1, criteria1, [criteria_range2, criteria2] . . .)

The three arguments in an *AVERAGEIFS* calculation are *average_range*, *criteria_rangeN*, and *criteriaN*. There is one *average_range*, and the *criteria_range* arguments must be the same size as the *average_range*. You can use up to 127 criteria ranges, and each one must have corresponding criteria.

The syntax for the *COUNTIFS* function is:

=COUNTIFS(criteria_range1, criteria1, [criteria_range2, criteria2] . . .)

The *COUNTIFS* function has multiple *criteria_range* arguments, which are the cell ranges with data to be counted. There is a corresponding *criteria* argument for each *criteria_range* argument, up to 127.

▶**HOW TO:** Use **AVERAGEIFS**

1. Click the cell for the result.
2. Click the **More Functions** button [*Formulas* tab, *Function Library* group] and choose **Statistical**.
3. Choose **AVERAGEIFS**.
4. Select the cells with data to be averaged for the *Average_range* argument.
   • You can type the range address.
5. Click the **Criteria_range1** argument box.
6. Select the range of cells with the first set of data to be matched with criteria.
   • This range must be the same size as the *average_range* argument.
7. Click the **Criteria1** box.
8. Type the data to be used as a condition.
   • Text criteria are not case-sensitive, and you can use wildcard characters.
   • If criteria are located in a worksheet cell, select the cell.
9. Click the **Criteria_range2** argument box.
10. Select the range of cells with the next set of data to be matched.
    • This range must be the same size as the *average_range* argument.
11. Click the **Criteria2** box.
12. Type the second requirement or condition (Figure 6-63).

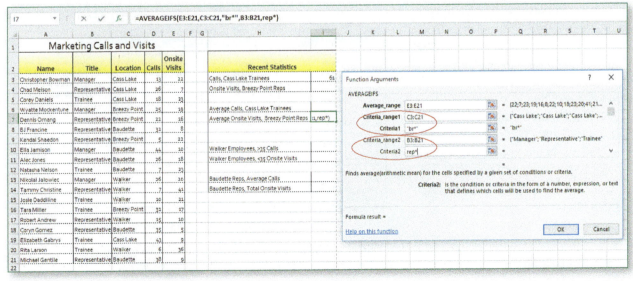

6-63 Data is included in average only if it meets both criteria

13. Add *Criteria_range* and *Criteria* arguments as needed.

- The size of each *criteria_range* must match the size of the *average_range*.
- Each *criteria_range* argument must have a corresponding *criteria* argument.

14. Click **OK**.

SLO 6.8

Monitoring and Editing Functions

With the *Find and Replace* command, you can make batch changes to functions or formulas. You can monitor results in different parts of a large worksheet or in a multi-sheet workbook from the *Watch Window*.

Find and Replace

You can use *Find and Replace* to change a function or an argument throughout a worksheet. In a nested *IF* function used in thousands of rows, use *Find and Replace* to edit a *value_if_true* argument. Or, if you mistakenly used *DAVERAGE* many times when you should have used *DSUM*, find and replace the incorrect function names.

▶ **HOW TO:** Replace a Function Argument

1. Select the cell range with data to be replaced.
2. Click the **Find & Select** button [*Home* tab, *Editing* group] and choose **Replace**.
3. Click **Options>>** to expand the *Find and Replace* options.
4. Click the **Find what** box.
   - Delete existing search strings.
   - If necessary, click the **Format** arrow and clear the find format.
5. Type the data to be replaced.
   - Use uppercase if it will be necessary to match case.
   - Use wildcard characters to shorten a find string.
6. Click the **Replace with** box and type the replacement data.
   - Use uppercase for characters when new text should be capitalized.
7. Select the **Match case** box if appropriate.
8. Select the **Match entire cell contents** box if required.
   - Do not use this choice when looking for a specific part of cell data.
9. Verify or select **Within**, **Search**, and **Look In** options.
10. Click **Find All** (Figure 6-64).
    - Size the *Find and Replace* dialog box to view the results.
11. Click **Replace All**.
    - You can also replace occurrences one at a time if preferred.

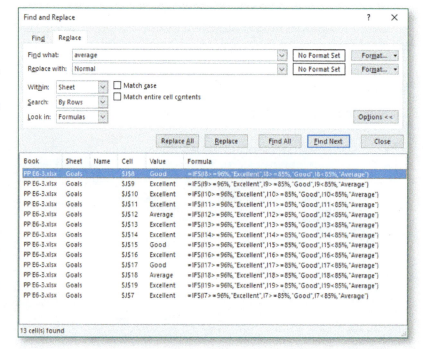

6-64 All occurrences that will be replaced

12. Click **OK** in the message box.

13. Close the *Find and Replace* dialog box.

- You can undo a *Find and Replace* task by pressing **Ctrl+Z** or by clicking the Undo button in the *Quick Access* toolbar.

ANOTHER WAY

Use the *Find and Replace* command to replace formats such as font name, fill color, or border style.

The Watch Window

The *Watch Window* is a floating dialog box with cell addresses and content to monitor while you work in another part of the workbook or worksheet. The *Watch Window* enables you to observe the effects of changes without having to scroll through a large sheet or switch between multiple sheets. You can position and size the *Watch Window* like any dialog box. In addition, when you double-click a cell address in the *Watch Window*, the insertion point moves to that location, like a bookmark.

▶ **HOW TO:** Monitor Changes in the Watch Window

1. Click the **Watch Window** button [*Formulas* tab, *Formula Auditing* group].

- The *Watch Window* opens.

2. Select the first cell or range to monitor and click **Add Watch** in the floating window.

3. Click **Add** in the *Add Watch* dialog box.

4. Repeat steps 2–3 to add cells or ranges to the *Watch Window*.

- Size the *Watch Window* and its columns to see the contents (Figure 6-65).
- Position the window as desired.

5. Edit data in the workbook as needed.

- Switch to another worksheet if necessary.

6. Select a watch in the *Watch Window* and click **Delete Watch** in the floating window.

- Use regular selection methods to select more than one watch.

7. Close the *Watch Window*.

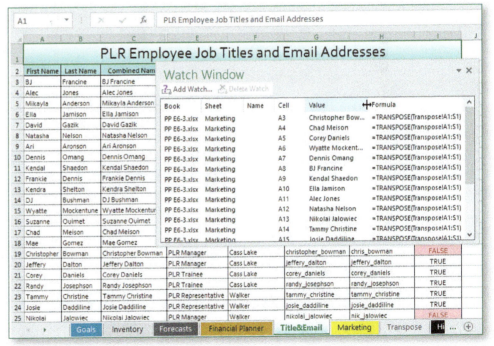

6-65 Resized *Watch Window*

In this project, you use functions from the *Math & Trig* and *Statistical* categories with multiple critieria ranges to analyze Paradise Lakes Resort marketing data. You also update an argument in an *IFS* function and watch changes in transposed data.

File Needed: *[your initials] PP E6-3.xlsx*
Completed Project File Name: *[your initials] PP E6-4.xlsx*

---

1. Open *[your initials] PP E6-3.xlsx* completed in *Pause & Practice 6-3* and save it as [your initials] PP E6-4.

2. Click the **Marketing** sheet tab.

3. Use the *SUMIFS* function.
   a. Select cell **I3**.
   b. Click the **Math & Trig** button [*Formulas* tab, *Function Library* group] and choose **SUMIFS**.
   c. Select cells **D3:D21** for the *Sum_range* argument.
   d. Click the **Criteria_range1** box and select cells **C3:C21**, the location column.
   e. Click the **Criteria1** box and type cas* to include cells with data for Cass Lake.
   f. Click the **Criteria_range2** box and select cells **B3:B21**, the job title column.
   g. Click the **Criteria2** box and type tr* to include trainee data (Figure 6-66).
   h. Click **OK**. The number of calls made by Cass Lake trainees is 61.
   i. Select cell **I4** and use *SUMIFS* to total the number of onsite visits made by Breezy Point representatives.

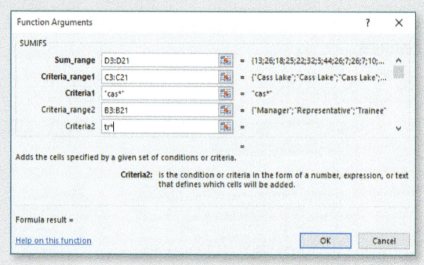

6-66 *SUMIFS* with two criteria ranges

4. Use the *AVERAGEIFS* function.
   a. Select cell **I6**.
   b. Click the **More Functions** button [*Formulas* tab, *Function Library* group] and choose **Statistical**.
   c. Choose **AVERAGEIFS**.
   d. Select cells **D3:D21** for the *Average_range* argument.
   e. Click the **Criteria_range1** box and select cells **C3:C21** for the location.
   f. Click the **Criteria1** box and type cas* for Cass Lake as the location.
   g. Click the **Criteria_range2** box and select cells **B3:B21** for the job title.
   h. Click the **Criteria2** box and type tr* (Figure 6-67).

i. Click **OK**. The average number of calls made by Cass Lake trainees is 30.5.
j. Click cell **I7** and use *AVERAGEIFS* to find the average number of onsite visits made by Breezy Point representatives.

5. Use *COUNTIFS*.
   a. Select cell **I10**.
   b. Click the **More Functions** button [*Formulas* tab, *Function Library* group], **Statistical**, and select **COUNTIFS**.
   c. Select cells **C3:C21** for the *Criteria_range1* argument.
   d. Click the **Criteria1** box and type wa* to include Walker data.
   e. Click the **Criteria_range2** box and select cells **D3:D21**. The function will count the number of cells in which the location is Walker and the number of calls is greater than 35.
   f. Click the **Criteria2** box and type >35 (Figure 6-68).
   g. Click **OK**. No Walker representatives made more than 35 calls.
   h. Click cell **I11** and use *COUNTIFS* to count the number of Walker representatives who made fewer than 35 onsite visits.

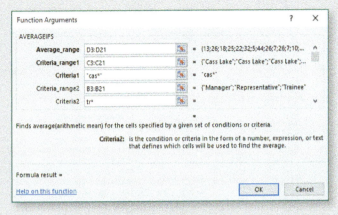

6-67 *AVERAGEIFS* with two criteria ranges

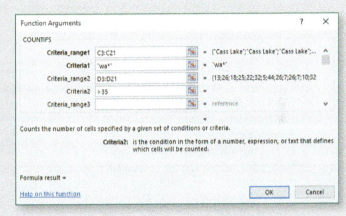

6-68 *COUNTIFS* with two criteria ranges

6. Click cell **I13** and use *AVERAGEIFS* based on the data in cell **H13**.

7. Click cell **I14** and use *SUMIFS*.

8. Watch edits in the *Watch Window*.
   a. Select cells **A3:A21**.
   b. Click the **Watch Window** button [*Formulas* tab, *Formula Auditing* group].
   c. Select and delete any previous watches.
   d. Click **Add Watch**, verify the selection, and click **Add**.
   e. Size the columns in the *Watch Window* to see more data in each column.
   f. Click the **Transpose** sheet tab.
   g. Click cell **B1**, change the name to **Barton Miles**, and press **Enter**. (Figure 6-69). The name is updated on the **Marketing** sheet as shown in the *Watch Window*.
   h. Select the first watch in the *Watch Window*.
   i. Press **Shift** and select the last watch.
   j. Click **Delete Watch** and close the *Watch Window*.

9. Use *Find and Replace*.
   a. Click the **Goals** sheet tab.
   b. Click the **Find & Select** button [*Home* tab, *Editing* group] and choose **Replace**.
   c. Click **Options>>**. When the dialog box is expanded, this command appears as **<<Options**.
   d. If necessary, click the **Format** arrow and clear previous find format settings.

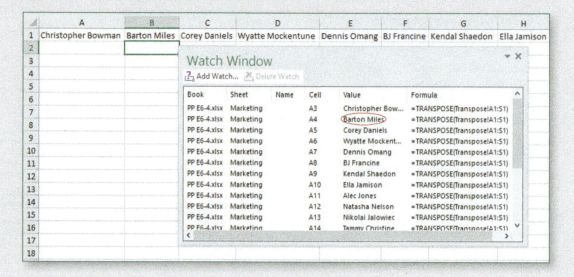

6-69 Name is changed on *Marketing* sheet

e. Click the **Find what** box and delete previous search strings.

f. Type average. The *Find what* string is not case-sensitive.

g. Click the ***Replace with*** box and type Normal.

h. Verify that the **Within** choice is **Sheet**, the **Search** choice is **By Rows**, and the **Look In** choice is **Formulas**.

i. Click **Find All** and size the dialog box to see the listed references.

j. Select the reference for cell **$J$7** in the *Find and Replace* dialog box.

k. Scroll the list, press **Shift**, and select the reference for cell **$J$19**. The selected references exclude cells B22 and D22 (Figure 6-70).

l. Click **Replace All** and then click **OK**.

m. Close the *Find and Replace* dialog box.

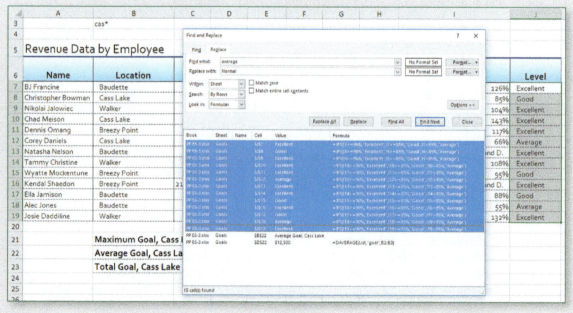

6-70 Select references to be replaced

10. Save and close the workbook (Figure 6-71).

Marketing Calls and Visits

Name	Title	Location	Calls	Onsite Visits
Christopher Bowman	Manager	Cass Lake	13	11
Barton Miles	Representative	Cass Lake	26	7
Corey Daniels	Trainee	Cass Lake	18	23
Wyatte Mockentune	Manager	Breezy Point	15	14
Dennis Omang	Representative	Breezy Point	11	16
BJ Francine	Representative	Baudette	31	8
Kendal Shaedon	Representative	Breezy Point	5	11
Ella Jamison	Manager	Baudette	44	10
Alec Jones	Representative	Baudette	26	18
Natasha Nelson	Trainee	Baudette	7	23
Nikolai Jalowiec	Manager	Walker	26	20
Tammy Christine	Representative	Walker	7	11
Josie Daddiline	Trainee	Walker	10	21
Tara Miller	Trainee	Breezy Point	32	17
Robert Andrew	Representative	Walker	15	10
Coryn Gomez	Representative	Baudette	35	5
Elizabeth Gabrys	Trainee	Cass Lake	43	9
Rita Larson	Trainee	Walker	6	36
Michael Gentile	Representative	Baudette	38	9

Recent Statistics	
Calls, Cass Lake Trainees	61
Onsite Visits, Breezy Point Reps	38
Average Calls, Cass Lake Trainees	30.5
Average Onsite Visits, Breezy Point Reps	19
Walker Employees, >35 Calls	0
Walker Employees, <35 Onsite Visits	3
Baudette Reps, Average Calls	32.75
Baudette Reps, Total Onsite Visits	40

Revenue Data by Employee

Name	Location	Goal	Actual	Met Goal?	Both Goals?	Either Goal?	Both Goals?	Actual/ Goal %	Level
BJ Francine	Baudette	$17,000	$21,500	Yes	TRUE	TRUE	Met both	126%	Excellent
Christopher Bowman	Cass Lake	$15,000	$12,750	No	FALSE	FALSE	No	85%	Good
Nikolai Jalowiec	Walker	$15,000	$15,600	Yes	TRUE	TRUE	Met both	104%	Excellent
Chad Meison	Cass Lake	$17,500	$25,000	Yes	TRUE	TRUE	Met both	143%	Excellent
Dennis Omang	Breezy Point	$18,000	$21,000	Yes	TRUE	TRUE	Met both	117%	Excellent
Corey Daniels	Cass Lake	$5,000	$3,300	No	FALSE	FALSE	No	66%	Normal
Natasha Nelson	Baudette	$0	$4,050	Yes	FALSE	TRUE	No	Check values in columns C and D.	Excellent
Tammy Christine	Walker	$75,000	$81,000	Yes	TRUE	TRUE	Met both	108%	Excellent
Wyatte Mockentune	Breezy Point	$15,000	$14,200	No	FALSE	FALSE	No	95%	Good
Kendal Shaedon	Breezy Point	21000S	$18,500	No	FALSE	TRUE	No	Check values in columns C and D.	Excellent
Ella Jamison	Baudette	$15,000	$13,200	No	FALSE	FALSE	No	88%	Good
Alec Jones	Baudette	$17,000	$9,350	No	FALSE	FALSE	No	55%	Normal
Josie Daddiline	Walker	$42,500	$56,000	Yes	TRUE	TRUE	Met both	132%	Excellent

Quarterly Goal
$15,000

Maximum Goal, Cass Lake	$17,500
Average Goal, Cass Lake	$12,500
Total Goal, Cass Lake	$37,500

6-71 Completed worksheets for PP E6-4

Chapter Summary

6.1 Use *Database* functions such as *DSUM* and *DAVERAGE* (p. E6-350).

- Functions in the *Database* category perform a calculation only when data meet the criteria.
- **Database functions** are used with list or table-type data.
- The syntax for a *Database* function is *FunctionName (database, field, criteria)*.
- The *criteria* argument is a range of cells with labels in one row and criteria below the label row on the same or another sheet.
- The criteria range can use *AND* conditions in the same row or *OR* criteria in separate rows.

6.2 Build *AND*, *OR*, nested, and *IFS* functions (p. E6-352).

- *AND* and *OR* functions return TRUE or FALSE as a result.
- An *AND* function tests multiple conditions and shows TRUE only when all conditions are met.
- An *OR* function tests multiple conditions and shows TRUE if one condition is met and shows FALSE only when all statements are false.
- *AND* and *OR* functions have one argument, *logicalN*, but there can be up to 255 *logicalN* statements.
- A **nested function** is a function within another function.
- *AND* or *OR* are nested within *IF* to check for multiple conditions by using an *AND* or *OR* function as the *logical_test* argument.
- An *IFS* function can use multiple *logical_test* arguments with a corresponding *value_if_true* argument for each test.
- A formula syntax error results in a default error message in the cell such as #N/A or #VALUE!
- For formulas that may result in a default error message, use the *IFERROR* function to display a custom message.

6.3 Explore the *Lookup & Reference* category with *INDEX*, *MATCH*, and *TRANSPOSE* (p. E6-364).

- An *INDEX* function displays the contents of the cell at the intersection of a specified column and row.
- The *MATCH* function returns the relative location of data in a list.

- *MATCH* and *INDEX* are nested to accomplish the same tasks as a *VLOOKUP* formula but at a faster speed.
- Nested *MATCH* and *INDEX* formulas are well-suited to datasets with millions of rows.
- The *TRANSPOSE* function displays columnar data in rows and vice versa.

6.4 Build date, time, and statistical calculations (p. E6-368).

- Date arithmetic is possible because Excel uses a serial numbering system for dates.
- Date and time calculations are straightforward, but an unsuitable format can disguise the results.
- The *Date & Time* function category includes functions that convert text into dates, determine workdays in a range of dates, or display the day of the week for a date.
- Use Excel functions to build common statistical forecasting calculations.
- A **forecast error** is the deviation or difference between actual values and predicted or forecasted values.
- The **mean absolute deviation** (**MAD**) is a statistical measure of how spread out a group of values is from the average.
- A **standard deviation** measures how broadly values vary from the mean (average) value, a common statistical calculation.

6.5 Use *Financial* functions such as *PV*, *FV*, and *NPV* (p. E6-380).

- Financial functions analyze money transactions.
- Many functions in the *Financial* category include **rate** and **nper** arguments and use the concept of an **annuity**, a series of equal payments.
- The *PV* function calculates the current value of regular payments at a set interest rate for a specified period of time.
- The *FV* function calculates the future value of regular payments or deposits invested at a constant interest rate for a specified period of time.
- The *NPV* function calculates the net present value of an investment using a **discount rate** and a series of **cash flows** which can be receipts or payments.

6.6 Work with *Text* functions including *TEXTJOIN, CONCAT, EXACT,* and *REPLACE* (p. E6-384).

- Text functions join, convert, and split labels and values in a worksheet.
- The *TEXTJOIN* function combines up to 252 strings of text, values, or characters in a single cell and uses a delimiter to separate the strings.
- The *CONCAT* function combines up to 255 strings of text, values, or characters in a single cell, and delimiters must be included in the arguments.
- The *EXACT* function compares two text, value, or character strings and displays TRUE if they are identical.
- The *REPLACE* function removes characters in a data string and replaces them with new characters.

6.7 Use multiple criteria in *SUMIFS, AVERAGEIFS,* and *COUNTIFS* functions (p. E6-391).

- The *SUMIFS* function is in the *Math & Trig* category and sums values for cells that meet up to 127 criteria.
- *AVERAGEIFS* and *COUNTIFs* are both in the *Statistical* category.

- *AVERAGIFS* averages values for cells that meet the criteria and *COUNTIFS* counts them.

6.8 Monitor and edit functions with the *Watch Window* and *Find and Replace* (p. E6-394).

- Use the *Find and Replace* command to locate and replace function arguments as well as function names in a workbook.
- The **Watch Window** is a floating dialog box, sized and positioned to show as much data as necessary.
- Add cell references to the *Watch Window* to observe changes in another part of the worksheet or workbook.

Check for Understanding

The SIMbook for this text (within your SIMnet account) provides the following resources for concept review:

- Multiple choice questions
- Matching exercises
- Short answer questions

Guided Project 6-1

In this project, you use *Database* functions to calculate results for the Boyd Air flight schedule. You complete projected versus actual passenger numbers and build a worksheet that tracks flight hours. You also work with *Text* and *Financial* functions.
[Student Learning Outcomes 6.1, 6.2, 6.3, 6.4, 6.5, 6.6, 6.7, 6.8]

File Needed: **BoydAir-06.xlsx** *(Student data files are available in the Library of your SIMnet account)*
Completed Project File Name: **[your initials] Excel 6-1.xlsx**

Skills Covered in this Project

- Use *Database* functions *DAVERAGE*, *DCOUNTA*, and *DMIN*.
- Use *COUNTIFS* and *SUMIFS*.
- Nest *MATCH* and *INDEX* functions.
- Build time and deviation calculations.

- Build *Logical* functions with *IF*, *AND*, and *OR*.
- Create an *IFERROR* formula.
- Build an *IFS* formula.
- Use and nest *Text* functions.
- Create formulas with *Financial* functions.
- Find and replace function arguments.

1. Open the **BoydAir-06** workbook from your student data files and save it as [your initials] Excel 6-1.

2. Use *DCOUNTA* to determine the number of flights originating in Chicago.
   a. Click the **Flight Stats** sheet tab.
   b. Select cells **A4:H18** and name the range Flights. The range includes the labels in row 4.
   c. Click the **Criteria** sheet tab.
   d. Click cell **C2** and type mdw for Midway airport in Chicago.
   e. Click the **Flight Stats** sheet, select cell **E22**, and click the **Insert Function** button on the *Formula* bar.
   f. Choose **Database** in the *Or select a category* list.
   g. Select **DCOUNTA** and click **OK**.
   h. Press **F3** (**FN+F3**) for the *Database* argument to open the *Paste Name* dialog box.
   i. Choose **Flights** and click **OK**.
   j. Click the **Field** argument box and type origin.
   k. Click the **Criteria** argument box and select cells **C1:C2** on the **Criteria** sheet. (Figure 6-72).
   l. Click **OK**. The result is 3.

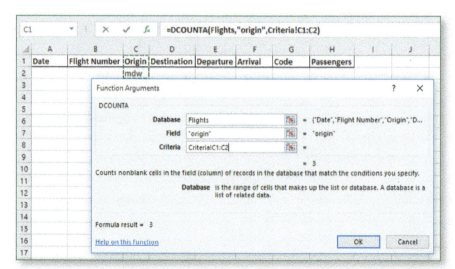

6-72 *DCOUNTA* function to count flights that originated at MDW

3. Use *DCOUNTA* to determine the number of flights terminating in Minneapolis.
   a. Click the **Criteria** sheet tab.
   b. Click cell **D2** and type msp for the Minneapolis-St. Paul airport.
   c. Click the **Flight Stats** sheet tab and select cell **E23**.
   d. Click the **Recently Used** button [*Formulas* tab, *Function Library* group] and select **DCOUNTA**.
   e. Press **F3** (**FN+F3**) for the *Database* argument, choose **Flights**, and click **OK**.
   f. Click the **Field** argument box and type 4 for the fourth column from the left in the range.
   g. Click the **Criteria** box, click the **Criteria** sheet tab, and select cells **D1:D2**.
   h. Click **OK**. The result is 4.

4. Copy cells **A1:H2** on the **Criteria** sheet to cells **A4:H5** and again to cells **A7:H8**. Delete the contents of cells **C5:D5** and **C8:D8**.

5. Select cell **D5** and type grb for the Green Bay airport.

6. Click the **Flight Stats** sheet and select cell **E24**. Start a *DAVERAGE* formula, select the **Flights** range name, and use the "passengers" column. The criteria is located in cells **D4:D5** on the **Criteria** sheet; the result is 77.5

7. Click the **Criteria** sheet tab, select cell **D8**, and type mdw.

8. Click the **Flight Stats** sheet, select cell **E25** and use *DMIN*. The result is 35.

9. Use *COUNTIFS* to count flights delayed into Chicago.
   a. Select cell **E26** on the **Flight Stats** sheet.
   b. Click the **More Functions** button [*Formulas* tab, *Function Library* group] and choose **Statistical**.
   c. Choose **COUNTIFS**.
   d. Select cells **D5:D18** for the *Criteria_range1* argument.
   e. Click the **Criteria1** box and type mdw for Midway airport.
   f. Click the **Criteria_range2** box and select cells **G5:G18**.
   g. Click the **Criteria2** box and type del* for "Delayed" (Figure 6-73).
   h. Click **OK**. The result is 2.

10. Use *SUMIFS* to count total passengers delayed into Chicago.
    a. Select cell **E27**.
    b. Click the **Math & Trig** button [*Formulas* tab, *Function Library* group] and choose **SUMIFS**.
    c. Select cells **H5:H18** for the *Sum_range* argument.
    d. Click the **Criteria_range1** box and select cells **D5:D18**, the destination field.
    e. Click the **Criteria1** box and type mdw.
    f. Click the **Criteria_range2** box and select cells **G5:G18**, the code field.
    g. Click the **Criteria2** box and type del*.
    h. Click **OK**. The count is 170 passengers.

11. Nest *MATCH* with *INDEX* function to display an arrival time.
    a. Select cell **D31**.
    b. Click the **Lookup & Reference** button [*Formulas* tab, *Function Library* group] and choose **INDEX**.
    c. Select the first argument list **array, row_num, column_num** and click **OK**.
    d. Paste the **Flights** range name for the *Array* argument.
    e. Click the **Row_num** box and click the **Name** box arrow.

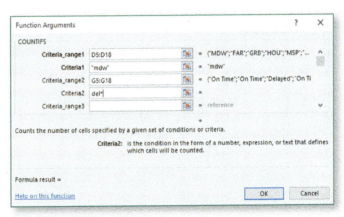

6-73 *COUNTIFS* with two criteria

f. Choose **MATCH** in the list or choose **More Functions** to find and select **MATCH**.

g. Select cell **C31** for the *Lookup_value* box.

h. Click the **Lookup_array** box and select cells **D4:D18**. When the named range includes the header row, the label row is included in the lookup array.

i. Click the **Match_type** box and type 0 to use an exact match.

j. Click the function name **INDEX** in the *Formula* bar. (If an argument lists box opens, click **OK**).

k. Click the **Column_num** box, click the **Name** box arrow, and choose **MATCH**.

l. Select cell **F4** for the *Lookup_value* argument.

m. Click the **Lookup_array** box and select cells **A4:H4**.

n. Click the **Match_type** argument and type 0.

o. Click **INDEX** in the *Formula* bar to see the complete nested formula (Figure 6-74).

p. Click **OK**. The result is formatted as a number.

12. Select cell **D31** and click the **Launcher** in the *Number* group [*Home* tab].

13. Choose the **Time** category and the **1:30 PM** style. Click **OK**.

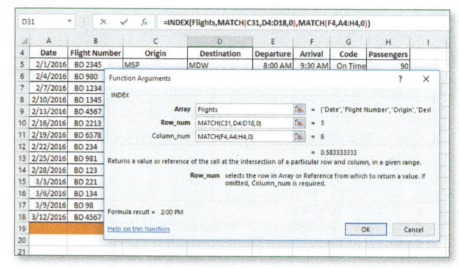

6-74 *MATCH* nested for both *INDEX* arguments

14. Press **Ctrl+Home**.

15. Calculate the difference between scheduled and actual arrival time.

a. Click the **Time Deviations** worksheet tab and select cell **G5**.

b. Type =(and select cell **F5**.

c. Type a minus sign –, select cell **E5**, and type the closing parenthesis).

d. Type *24*60 to convert the result to days and then to minutes (Figure 6-75).

e. Press **Enter**. A negative number of minutes means the flight was early.

f. Copy the formula in cell **G5** to cells **G6:G24**.

16. Calculate the mean absolute deviation (MAD) for arrival times.

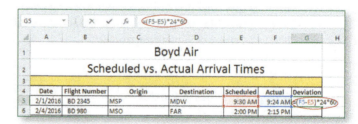

6-75 Time difference is converted to minutes

a. Select cell **I5**.

b. Click the **Math & Trig** button [*Formulas* tab, *Function Library* group] and choose **ABS**.

c. Select cell **G5** for the *Number* argument and click **OK**.

d. Copy the formula in cell **I5** to cells **I6:I24**.

e. Select cell **D27**.

f. Use the *AVERAGE* function to calculate the mean (or average) for cells **I5:I24**. The result is 10.35.

g. Right-click the column **I** heading and choose **Hide**.

17. Calculate the standard deviation for arrival times.
    a. Select cell **D28**.
    b. Click the **More Functions** button [*Formulas* tab, *Function Library* group], choose **Statistical**, and choose **STDEV.S**.
    c. Select cells **G5:G24** and press **Enter**. The result is 13.3111548.
    d. Press **Ctrl+Home**.

18. Build an *IF* function.
    a. Click the **Flight Hours** sheet tab and select cell **F4**.
    b. Click the **Logical** button [*Formulas* tab, *Function Library* group] and choose **IF**.
    c. Click the **Logical_test** argument box, select cell **D4**, and type >20.
    d. Click the **Value_if_true** box and type Yes.
    e. Click the **Value_if_false** box and type No.
    f. Click **OK** or press **Enter**.
    g. Copy the formula to cells **F5:F18** without formatting to preserve the borders.
    h. Center cells **F4:F18**.

19. Use the *Function Arguments* dialog box to enter an *OR* function.
    a. Select cell **G4**, click the **Logical** button [*Formulas* tab, *Function Library* group], and choose **OR**.
    b. Click the **Logical1** argument box, select cell **D4**, and type >20.
    c. Click the **Logical2** box, select cell **E4**, and type >20 (Figure 6-76).

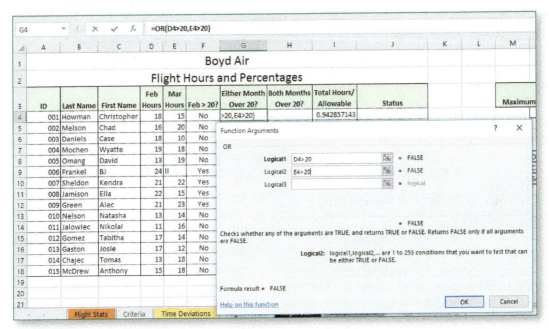

6-76 *OR* formula

    d. Click **OK**. The first result is FALSE.
    e. Copy the formula in cell **G4** to cells **G5:G18** without formatting.

20. Create an *AND* function.
    a. Select cell **H4**, click the **Logical** button [*Formulas* tab, *Function Library* group], and choose **AND**.
    b. Click the **Logical1** box, select cell **D4**, and type >20.
    c. Click the **Logical2** box, select cell **E4**, and type >20.
    d. Click **OK**. The first result is FALSE.
    e. Copy the formula in cell **H4** to cells **H5:H18** without formatting.

21. Use *IFERROR* to display a custom message.
    a. Select cell **I4**. The formula adds the hours for February and March and then divides by the allowable hours in cell N4. There is a standard Excel error message in cell **I9** because the data in cell E9 is text.
    b. Delete the formula in cell **I4**.
    c. Click the **Logical** button [*Formulas* tab, *Function Library* group] and choose **IFERROR**.
    d. Type a left parenthesis (in the *Value* argument box, select cell **D4**, type +, and select cell **E4**.
    e. Type a right parenthesis and a forward slash for division)/, click cell **N4**, and press **F4** (**FN+F4**) to make it absolute.
    f. Click the **Value_if_error** box and type Check values. (Figure 6-77).
    g. Click **OK**.

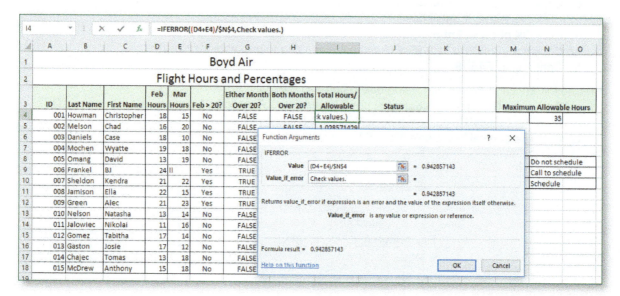

6-77 *IFERROR* formula

    h. Copy the formula in cell **I4** to cells **I5:I18** without formatting. Widen the column to display the complete message.
    i. Format cells **I4:I18** with **Percent Style** and two decimal places.

22. Create an *IFS* function.
    a. Select cell **J4**, click the **Logical** button [*Formulas* tab, *Function Library* group] and choose **IFS**.
    b. Select cell **I4** for the *Logical_test1* box and type >=100%.
    c. Click the **Value_if_true1** box, select cell **N8**, and press **F4** (**FN+F4**).
    d. Click the **Logical_test2** box, select cell **I4**, and type >=91%.
    e. Click the **Value_if_true2** box, select cell **N9**, and press **F4** (**FN+F4**).
    f. Click the **Logical_test3** box, select cell **I4**, and type >=70%.
    g. Press **Tab** to move to the *Value_if_true3* box, select cell **N10**, and press **F4** (**FN+F4**) (Figure 6-78).
    h. Click **OK**.
    i. Copy the formula in cell **I4** to cells **I5:I18** without formatting.
    j. Increase the indent one time for the data in column **J**.
    k. Press **Ctrl+Home**.

23. Create a nested *Text* function with *UPPER* and *CONCAT*.
    a. Click the **Flight Staff** sheet tab and select cell **D4**. Printed labels display first and last names in uppercase characters.
    b. Click the **Text** button [*Formulas* tab, *Function Library* group] and choose **UPPER**. The argument is the *Text* to be shown in uppercase letters.

E6-406

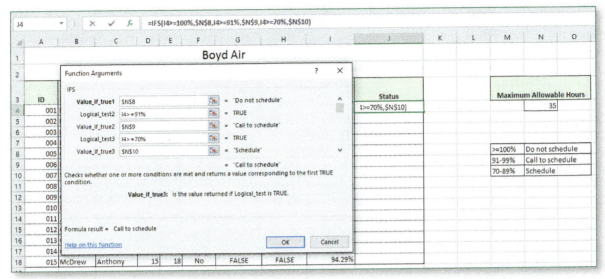

6-78 *IFS* function

c. For the *Text* argument, click the **Name** box arrow, and choose **More Functions**.
d. Choose **Text** as the category, select **CONCAT**, and click **OK**. The *Function Arguments* dialog box shows arguments for the *CONCAT* function.
e. Select cell **C4** for the *Text1* argument.
f. Click the **Text2** argument box and press **Spacebar**.
g. Click the **Text3** argument box and select cell **B4** (Figure 6-79).

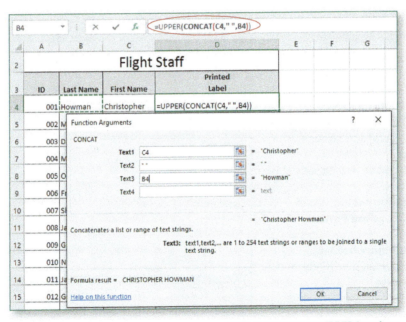

6-79 *CONCAT* and *UPPER* functions

h. Click **OK**.
i. Copy the formula in cell **D4** to cells **D5:D18** without formatting.
j. Press **Ctrl+Home**.

24. Determine the net present value of new equipment purchases.
   a. Click the **Equipment Eval** sheet tab and select cell **C12**.
   b. Click the **Financial** button [*Formulas* tab, *Function Library* group] and choose **NPV**.

c. Select cell **C5** for the *Rate* argument.

d. Click the **Value1** box and select cell **C8**, the expected savings in the first year.

e. Click the **Value2** box and select cell **C9**, expected savings in the second year.

f. For the **Value3** argument, select cell **C10**. (Figure 6-80).

g. Click **OK**.

h. Double-click cell **C12**. Press **End** to position the insertion point at the end of the formula.

i. In the cell or in the *Formula* bar, type **+**, select cell **C6**, and press **Enter** (Figure 6-81). The cost is added to the formula results because it is incurred before savings start.

j. Select cell **C24** and build an *NPV* calculation for an investment at an 8% discount.

25. Use *Find and Replace*.

a. Click the **Flight Hours** sheet tab and select cells **J4:J18**.

b. Click the **Find & Select** button [*Home* tab, *Editing* group] and choose **Replace**.

c. Click **Options> >** to expand the options.

d. Click the **Format** arrow and select **Clear Find Format** if it is available.

e. Click the **Find what** box, select previous data if any, and press **Delete**.

f. Type **91%** to locate "91%" in the *IFS* formula.

g. Click the **Replace with** box and type **90%**.

h. Verify that the **Within** choice is **Sheet**, the **Search** choice is **By Columns**, and the **Look In** choice is **Formulas**.

i. Click **Find All**. Fifteen cells are found (Figure 6-82).

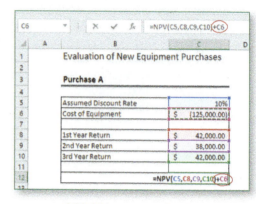

6-80 *NPV* function does not include initial cost

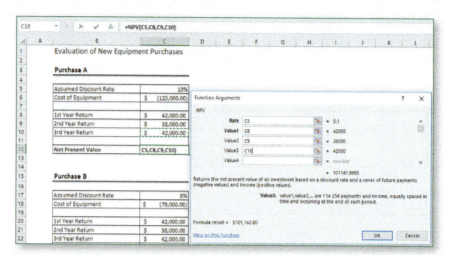

6-81 Add cost to results of *NPV* formula

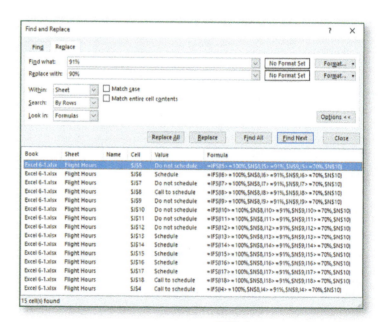

6-82 Arguments to be replaced

j. Click **Replace All** and click **OK**. Close the *Find and Replace* dialog box.

k. Edit cell **M9** to show 90 as the starting percentage.

26. Save and close the workbook (Figure 6-83).

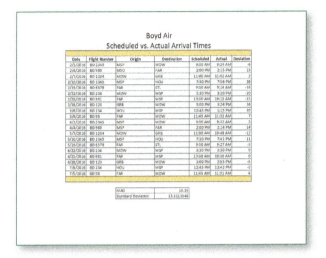

Boyd Air
Scheduled vs. Actual Arrival Times

Date	Flight Number	Origin	Destination	Scheduled	Actual	Deviation
2/1/2016	BD 2345	MSP	MDW	9:30 AM	9:24 AM	-6
2/4/2016	BD 980	MSO	FAR	2:00 PM	2:15 PM	15
2/7/2016	BD 1234	MDW	GRB	11:00 AM	11:02 AM	2
2/10/2016	BD 1345	MSP	HOU	7:30 PM	7:56 PM	26
2/13/2016	BD 6578	FAR	STL	9:30 AM	9:14 AM	-16
2/22/2016	BD 234	MDW	MSP	3:30 PM	3:20 PM	-10
2/25/2016	BD 581	FAR	MSP	10:30 AM	10:15 AM	-15
2/28/2016	BD 123	GRB	MDW	3:00 PM	3:24 PM	24
3/6/2016	BD 134	HOU	MSP	12:45 PM	1:15 PM	10
3/9/2016	BD 98	FAR	MDW	11:45 AM	11:52 AM	7
4/1/2016	BD 2345	MSP	MDW	9:30 AM	9:32 AM	2
4/4/2016	BD 980	MSP	FAR	2:00 PM	2:14 PM	14
5/7/2016	BD 1234	MDW	GRB	11:00 AM	10:48 AM	-12
5/10/2016	BD 1345	MSP	HOU	7:30 PM	7:41 PM	11
5/13/2016	BD 6578	FAR	STL	9:30 AM	9:27 AM	-3
8/22/2016	BD 234	MDW	MSP	3:30 PM	3:30 PM	0
6/25/2016	BD 581	FAR	MSP	10:30 AM	10:30 AM	0
6/28/2016	BD 123	GRB	MDW	3:00 PM	2:55 PM	-5
7/6/2016	BD 134	HOU	MSP	12:45 PM	12:42 PM	-3
7/5/2016	BD 98	FAR	MDW	11:45 AM	11:51 AM	6

MAD	10.35
Standard Deviation	13.3111548

Boyd Air
Flight Hours and Percentages

ID	Last Name	First Name	Feb Hours	Mar Hours	Feb > 20?	Either Month Over 20?	Both Months Over 20?	Total Hours/ Allowable	Status
001	Howman	Christopher	18	15	No	FALSE	FALSE	94.29%	Call to schedule
002	Melson	Chad	16	20	No	FALSE	FALSE	102.86%	Do not schedule
003	Daniels	Case	19	20	No	FALSE	FALSE	86.00%	Schedule
004	Mochen	Wyatte	19	18	No	FALSE	FALSE	105.71%	Do not schedule
005	Omang	David	13	18	No	FALSE	FALSE	91.43%	Call to schedule
006	Frankel	BJ	24	8	Yes	TRUE	FALSE	Check values	Call to schedule
007	Sheldon	Kendra	21	22	Yes	TRUE	TRUE	122.86%	Do not schedule
008	Jamison	Ella	22	15	Yes	TRUE	FALSE	105.71%	Do not schedule
009	Green	Alec	21	20	Yes	TRUE	TRUE	125.71%	Do not schedule
010	Nelson	Natasha	13	14	No	FALSE	FALSE	77.14%	Schedule
011	Jalowiec	Nikolai	11	18	No	FALSE	FALSE	77.14%	Schedule
012	Gomez	Tabitha	17	14	No	FALSE	FALSE	88.57%	Schedule
013	Gaston	Josie	17	12	No	FALSE	FALSE	82.86%	Schedule
014	Chajec	Tomas	11	18	No	FALSE	FALSE	84.37%	Schedule
015	McDrew	Anthony	13	18	No	FALSE	FALSE	94.29%	Call to schedule

Maximum Allowable Hours	35

>=100%	Do not schedule
95-99%	Call to schedule
70-88%	Schedule

Evaluation of New Equipment Purchases

Purchase A

Assumed Discount Rate		10%
Cost of Equipment	$	(125,000.00)
1st Year Return	$	42,000.00
2nd Year Return	$	38,000.00
3rd Year Return	$	42,000.00
Net Present Value		($23,858.00)

Purchase B

Assumed Discount Rate		8%
Cost of Equipment	$	(79,000.00)
1st Year Return	$	42,000.00
2nd Year Return	$	38,000.00
3rd Year Return	$	42,000.00
Net Present Value		$25,808.72

Boyd Air
Flight Staff

ID	Last Name	First Name	Printed Label
001	Howman	Christopher	CHRISTOPHER HOWMAN
002	Melson	Chad	CHAD MELSON
003	Daniels	Case	CASE DANIELS
004	Mochen	Wyatte	WYATTE MOCHEN
005	Omang	David	DAVID OMANG
006	Frankel	BJ	BJ FRANKEL
007	Sheldon	Kendra	KENDRA SHELDON
008	Jamison	Ella	ELLA JAMISON
009	Green	Alec	ALEC GREEN
010	Nelson	Natasha	NATASHA NELSON
011	Jalowiec	Nikolai	NIKOLAI JALOWIEC
012	Gomez	Tabitha	TABITHA GOMEZ
013	Gaston	Josie	JOSIE GASTON
014	Chajec	Tomas	TOMAS CHAJEC
015	McDrew	Anthony	ANTHONY MCDREW

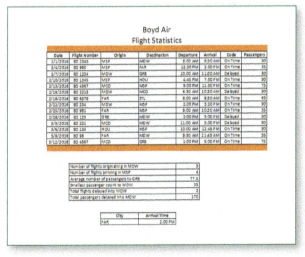

Boyd Air
Flight Statistics

Date	Flight Number	Origin	Destination	Departure	Arrival	Code	Passengers
1/1/2016	BD 2345	MSP	MDW	8:00 AM	9:30 AM	On Time	90
1/4/2016	BD 980	MSP	FAR	12:30 PM	2:00 PM	On Time	35
2/7/2016	BD 1234	MDW	GRB	10:00 AM	11:00 AM	Delayed	30
2/10/2016	BD 1345	MSP	HOU	4:45 PM	7:30 PM	On Time	90
2/13/2016	BD 4567	MCO	MSP	9:00 PM	11:30 PM	On Time	75
2/16/2016	BD 2213	MSP	MCO	6:30 AM	10:30 AM	Delayed	90
2/18/2016	BD 6578	FAR	STL	8:00 AM	9:30 AM	On Time	65
2/22/2016	BD 234	MDW	MSP	2:00 PM	3:30 PM	On Time	90
2/25/2016	BD 981	FAR	MSP	9:00 AM	10:30 AM	On Time	35
2/28/2016	BD 123	GRB	MDW	2:00 PM	3:00 PM	Delayed	30
3/3/2016	BD 221	MCO	MDW	11:00 AM	3:00 PM	Delayed	90
3/6/2016	BD 134	HOU	MSP	10:00 AM	12:45 PM	On Time	90
5/9/2016	BD 98	FAR	MDW	9:30 AM	11:45 AM	On Time	35
3/12/2016	BD 4567	MCO	GRB	1:00 PM	5:00 PM	On Time	75

Number of flights originating in MDW	3
Number of flights arriving in MSP	4
Average number of passengers to GRB	27.5
Smallest passenger count to MDW	35
Total flights delayed into MDW	2
Total passengers delayed into MDW	170

City	Arrival Time
FAR	2:00 PM

6-83 Completed worksheets for Excel 6-1

Guided Project 6-2

In a workbook for Eller Software Services, you calculate deviation statistics for sales by product and city. You verify phone numbers using a *Text* function, develop a worksheet with projected return on investment, and determine representative assignments.
[**Student Learning Outcomes 6.1, 6.2, 6.3, 6.4, 6.5, 6.6, 6.7, 6.8**]

File Needed: ***EllerSoftware-06.xlsx*** *(Student data files are available in the Library of your SIMnet account)*
Completed Project File Name: ***[your initials] Excel 6-2.xlsx***

Skills Covered in this Project

- Calculate the mean absolute deviation (MAD).
- Use the *STDEV.S* function.
- Nest *MATCH* and *INDEX* functions.
- Build *SUMIFS* formulas.
- Use functions from the *Database* category.

- Use *EXACT* to match data.
- Calculate the net present value of an expenditure.
- Create a nested *IF* and *AND* formula.
- Use *Find and Replace* with the *Watch Window*.
- Calculate the number of days between two dates.

1. Open the ***EllerSoftware-06*** workbook from your student data files and save it as [your initials] Excel 6-2.

2. Calculate the mean absolute deviation (MAD) for the difference between estimated and actual sales.
   a. Click the **Revenue** sheet and select cell **I5**.
   b. Type =ab and press **Tab**.
   c. Select cell **H5** for the *number* argument, type – to subtract, select cell **G5**, and press **Enter**.
   d. Copy the formula to cells **I6:I17** without formatting to preserve the fill color.
   e. Select cell **D20** and use the *AVERAGE* function with the cell range **I5:I17**.
   f. Format the results as **Number** from the *Number Format* drop-down list [*Home* tab, *Number* group].

3. Calculate the standard deviation for actual sales.
   a. Select cell **D21**.
   b. Type =std and double-click **STDEV.S** in the list.
   c. Select cells **G5:G17** and press **Enter**. The closing parenthesis is supplied, and the result is 12871.23785.

4. Create a nested function using *INDEX* and *MATCH* to display a phone number.
   a. Select cell **D24** and type Jeremie Midboe.
   b. Select cell **D25**. Click the **Lookup & Reference** button [*Formulas* tab, *Function Library* group] and choose **INDEX**.
   c. Select the first argument list **array, row_num, column_num** and click **OK**.
   d. For the *Array* argument, press **F3** (**FN+F3**) and select **Clients**.
   e. Click the **Row_num** box, click the **Name** box arrow, and choose **More Functions**.
   f. Choose **Lookup & Reference** as the category, select **MATCH**, and press **Enter**. The *Function Arguments* dialog box shows *MATCH* arguments.
   g. Select cell **D24** for the *Lookup_value* argument.
   h. Click the **Lookup_array** box and select cells **A5:A17**. The *MATCH* function finds the value that matches cell D24 in column A.
   i. Click the **Match_type** box and type 0.
   j. Click the name **INDEX** in the *Formula* bar. If the *Select Arguments* dialog box opens, click **OK**.
   k. Click the **Column_num** box, click the **Name** box arrow, and choose **MATCH**.
   l. Type phone number in the *Lookup_value* box.
   m. Click the **Lookup_array** box and select cells **A4:I4**. This *MATCH* function will locate the Phone Number column (Figure 6-84).

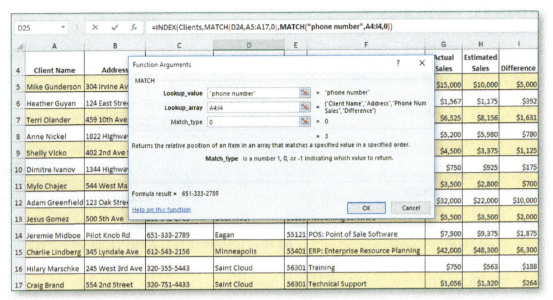

	A	B	C	D	E	F	G	H	I
							Actual Sales	Estimated Sales	Difference
4	Client Name	Address							
5	Mike Gunderson	304 Irvine Av					$15,000	$10,000	$5,000
6	Heather Guyan	124 East Stre					$1,567	$1,175	$392
7	Terri Olander	459 10th Ave					$6,525	$8,156	$1,631
8	Anne Nickel	1822 Highwa					$5,200	$5,980	$780
9	Shelly Vicko	402 2nd Ave					$4,500	$3,375	$1,125
10	Dimitre Ivanov	1344 Highwa					$750	$925	$175
11	Mylo Chajec	544 West Ma					$3,500	$2,800	$700
12	Adam Greenfield	123 Oak Stre					$32,000	$22,000	$10,000
13	Jesus Gomez	500 5th Ave					$5,500	$3,500	$2,000
14	Jeremie Midboe	Pilot Knob Rd	651-333-2789		Eagan	55121	POS: Point of Sale Software	$7,500	$9,375	$1,875
15	Charlie Lindberg	345 Lyndale Ave	612-543-2156		Minneapolis	55401	ERP: Enterprise Resource Planning	$42,000	$48,300	$6,300
16	Hilary Marschke	245 West 3rd Ave	320-355-5443		Saint Cloud	56301	Training	$750	$563	$188
17	Craig Brand	554 2nd Street	320-751-4433		Saint Cloud	56301	Technical Support	$1,056	$1,320	$264

6-84 Nested *MATCH* and *INDEX* functions

n. Click the **Match_type** box and type 0. The formula is
   =INDEX(Clients,MATCH(D24,A5:A17,0), MATCH("phone number",A4:I4,0)).

o. Click **OK**.

p. Select cell **D24**, type Anne Nickel, and press **Enter**. The phone number changes.

5. Use *SUMIFS* to total revenue by category and city.

a. Select cell **G20**.

b. Click the **Math & Trig** button [*Formulas* tab, *Function Library* group] and choose **SUMIFS**.

c. Select cells **G5:G17 f**or the *Sum_range* argument and press **F4** (**FN+F4**) to make it absolute.

d. Click the **Criteria_range1** box, select cells **D5:D17**, the City field, and press **F4** (**FN+F4**).

e. Click the **Criteria1** box and type eag*.

f. Click the **Criteria_range2** box, select cells **F5:F17**, and press **F4** (**FN+F4**).

g. Click the **Criteria2** box, type pos* (Figure 6-85).

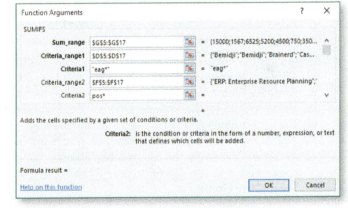

6-85 *SUMIFS* with its arguments

h. Click **OK**.

i. Copy the *SUMIFS* function in cell **G20** to cell **G21**. Edit the formula criteria to show the ERP total for Minneapolis.

j. Format cells **G20:G21** as **Currency** with no decimal places.

6. Use *DAVERAGE* to calculate average sales in Bemidji.

a. Select cells **A4:I17** and name the range SalesData. The range includes column labels.

b. Select cell **G24** and note the label in cell **F24**.

c. Click the **Criteria** sheet tab.

d. Click cell **D2** and type be*.

e. Click the **Revenue** sheet tab.

f. In cell **G24**, click the **Insert Function** button in the *Formula* bar.

g. Choose **Database** in the *Or select a category* list.

h. Select **DAVERAGE** and click **OK**.

i. Press **F3** (**FN+F3**) in the *Database* box, choose **SalesData**, and click **OK**.

j. Click the **Field** box and type actual sales.

k. Click the **Criteria** argument box and select cells **D1:D2** on the **Criteria** sheet (Figure 6-86).

l. Click **OK**.

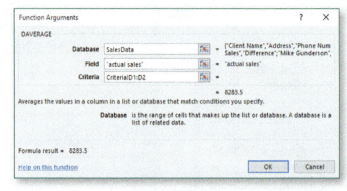

6-86 *DAVERAGE* and its arguments

7. Copy cells **A1:I2** on the **Criteria** sheet to cells **A4:I5** and again to cells **A7:I8**. Delete the contents of cells **D5** and **D7**.

8. Select cell **D5** and type min*. Select cell **D7** and type de*.

9. Click the **Revenue** sheet tab. Select cell **G25** and use *DMAX* to display the top sale in Minneapolis.

10. Select cell **G26** and use *DMIN*.

11. Format cells **G24:G26** as **Currency** with no decimal places and press **Ctrl+Home**.

12. Create a *Text* function with *EXACT*.

a. Click the **Phone Numbers** sheet tab and select cell **D5**. The phone numbers on this sheet will be compared to those on the **Revenue** sheet.

b. Click the **Text** button [*Formulas* tab, *Function Library* group] and choose **EXACT**.

c. Select cell **C5** for the *Text1* argument.

d. Click the **Text2** argument, click the **Revenue** sheet tab, and select cell **C5**.

e. Click **OK**. If the phone number is an exact match, the result is TRUE.

f. Copy the formula in cell **D5** to cells **D6:D17**.

g. Apply a *Highlight Cells* rule to cells **D5:D17** to show FALSE in **Light Red Fill with Dark Red Text**.

h. Press **Ctrl+Home**.

13. Determine the net present value (*NPV*) for client purchases.

a. Click the **Product ROR** sheet tab and select cell **F6**.

b. Click the **Financial** button [*Formulas* tab, *Function Library* group] and choose **NPV**.

c. Select cell **J5** for the *Rate* argument and press **F4** (**FN+F4**).

d. Click the **Value1** box and select cells **B6:E6**, costs and projected savings per year. The cost is paid in increments during the first year and is included as a *Value* argument.

e. Click **OK**. The projected return is $3,729.56.

f. Copy the formula in cell **F6** to cells **F7:F9**.

g. Press **Ctrl+Home**.

14. Create a nested *IF* function with *AND* functions as the logical tests.

a. Click the **Rep Assignments** sheet tab and select cell **F6**.

b. Click the **Logical** button [*Formulas* tab, *Function Library* group] and choose **IF**.

c. In the *Logical_test* box, click the **Name** box arrow, and choose **AND** from the list, or choose **More Functions** to find and select **AND**.

d. Click the **Logical1** argument box, select cell **B6** and type ="yes". Quotations marks are required, but the argument is not case-sensitive.

e. Click the **Logical2** box, select cell **D6**, and type ="yes". The *AND* formula determines if both cells B6 and D6 show "Yes."

f. In the *Formula* bar, click the word **IF** to return to the *IF Function Arguments* dialog box (Figure 6-87).

g. Click the **Value_if_true** box, select cell **I5**, and press **F4** (**FN+F4**). If cells B6 and D6 show "Yes," the rep's name in cell I5 displays.

h. Click the **Value_if_false** box. If the *Logical_test* is false, a second *IF* statement runs.

i. Click **IF** in the *Name* box or choose **More Functions** to find and select **IF**.

j. For the *Logical_test* for the second *IF* statement, click the **Name** box arrow and choose **AND**.

k. Click the **Logical1** box, select cell **C6**, and type ="yes".

l. Click the **Logical2** box, click cell **D6**, and type ="yes". This *AND* formula determines if both cells C6 and D6 show "Yes."

m. In the *Formula* bar, click the second occurrence of **IF** to return to the nested *IF Function Arguments* dialog box (Figure 6-88).

n. Click the **Value_if_true** box, select cell **I6**, and press **F4** (**FN+F4**). If cells C6 and D6 show "Yes," the rep's name in cell I6 displays.

o. Click the **Value_if_false** box, select cell **I7**, and press **F4** (**FN+F4**). If neither *IF* logical test is true, the rep's name in cell I7 displays.

p. Click **OK** and copy the formula in cell **F6** to cells **F7:F18** without formatting.

15. Use *Find and Replace*.

a. Click the **Projects** sheet and select cells **B5:B17**.

b. Click the **Watch Window** button [*Formulas* tab, *Formula Auditing* group].

c. Click **Add Watch** and click **Add**.

d. Click the **Revenue** sheet tab.

e. Click the **Find & Select** button [*Home* tab, *Editing* group] and choose **Replace**.

f. Click **Options >>** to expand the options. If necessary, click the **Format** arrow and clear previous find format settings.

g. Delete previous search strings in the *Find what* box.

h. Click the **Find what** box and type acc*.

i. Click the **Replace with** box and type AR/AP for accounts receivable and accounts payable.

j. Verify that the **Within** choice is **Workbook**.

k. Click **Find All**. Nine occurrences display in the dialog box (Figure 6-89).

l. Click **Replace All**. Close the *Find and Replace* dialog box.

m. Select the first reference in the *Watch Window*, press **Shift**, and click the last reference.

n. Click **Delete Watch** and close the *Watch Window*.

o. Press **Ctrl+Home**.

6-87 First *IF* function and its logical_test argument

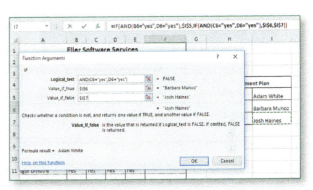

6-88 The second *IF* function in the nested formula

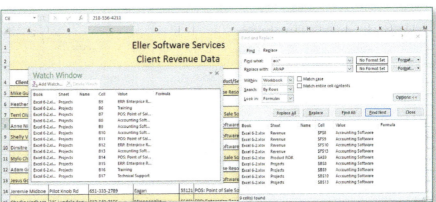

6-89 *Find and Replace* dialog box and *Watch Window*

16. Calculate project duration in days.
    a. Click the **Projects** sheet tab and select cell **E5**.
    b. Type = and click cell **D5**, the ending date.
    c. Type – to subtract and click cell **C5**, the starting date.
    d. Press **Enter**. The result is formatted as a date.
    e. Copy the formula in cell **E5** to cells **E6:E17** without formatting to preserve the fill color.
    f. Format cells **E5:E17** with the **General** format [*Number Format* drop-down list, *Home* tab].
    g. Press **Ctrl+Home**.

17. Save and close the workbook (Figure 6-90).

Eller Software Services
Representative Assignment Based on Client Interest

Client	ERP	HR	POS	AR/AP	Assigned Rep
Elmer Whitestead	Yes	No	Yes	No	Adam White
Gia Mentor	No	No	Yes	No	Josh Haines
Oliver Terry	Yes	Yes	No	Yes	Josh Haines
Nicholas Smith	Yes	Yes	Yes	No	Adam White
Victoria Jones	No	Yes	Yes	No	Barbara Munoz
Igor Dimitre	Yes	Yes	Yes	Yes	Adam White
Mylo Chajec	No	Yes	Yes	No	Barbara Munoz
Lester Simmons	No	Yes	No	Yes	Josh Haines
Kelly MacNeil	Yes	No	Yes	No	Adam White
Jerome Decker	No	Yes	Yes	No	Josh Haines
Charlie Strom	No	Yes	No	No	Josh Haines
Clinton Olmstead	Yes	No	Yes	No	Adam White
Michael Conover	Yes	Ys	Yes	No	Adam White

Assignment Plan

ERP and POS	Adam White
HR and POS	Barbara Munoz
Others	Josh Haines

Eller Software Services
Updated Phone List

Client Name	Address	Phone Number	OK?
Mike Gunderson	304 Irvine Ave	218-278-9021	TRUE
Heather Guyan	124 East Street	218-333-2312	FALSE
Terri Olander	459 10th Avenue	218-667-8977	TRUE
Anne Nickel	1822 Highway 2	218-556-4211	TRUE
Shelly Vicko	402 2nd Ave SE	218-342-2456	TRUE
Dimitre Ivanov	1344 Highway 3	218-556-3009	TRUE
Mylo Chajec	544 West Main	651-345-9000	FALSE
Adam Greenfield	123 Oak Street	612-543-0090	TRUE
Jesus Gomez	500 5th Ave	218-342-8765	TRUE
Jeremie Midboe	Pilot Knob Rd	651-333-2789	TRUE
Charlie Lindberg	345 Lyndale Ave	612-543-3290	FALSE
Hilary Marschke	245 West 3rd Ave	320-355-5443	TRUE
Craig Brand	554 2nd Street	320-751-4433	TRUE

Eller Software Services
Projected Return on Client Investment after 3 Years

Product/Service	Typical Sale	Year 1	Year 2	Year 3	Return
		Savings/Increase in Productivity			
ERP: Enterprise Resource Planning	-$20,000	$8,000	$9,000	$10,000	$3,729.56
Training	-$2,000	$1,500	$2,000	$2,000	$2,711.63
POS: Point of Sale Software	-$4,500	$2,500	$3,500	$3,500	$3,690.70
AR/AP	-$5,000	$2,000	$3,000	$4,500	$3,146.29

Eller Software Services
Project Duration

Project ID	Product/Service	Start	End	Time
ESS014	ERP: Enterprise Resource Planning	5/1/16	6/2/16	32
ESS016	Training	6/3/16	8/5/16	63
ESS018	POS: Point of Sale Software	7/7/16	7/10/16	3
ESS020	AR/AP	9/7/16	11/7/16	61
ESS022	AR/AP	10/2/16	12/21/16	80
ESS024	AR/AP	2/3/17	5/8/17	94
ESS026	POS: Point of Sale Software	4/2/17	4/5/17	3
ESS028	ERP: Enterprise Resource Planning	5/11/17	8/13/17	104
ESS030	AR/AP	5/5/17	8/12/17	99
ESS032	POS: Point of Sale Software	6/6/17	6/10/17	4
ESS034	ERP: Enterprise Resource Planning	7/1/17	8/30/17	60
ESS036	Training	8/5/17	8/15/17	10
ESS038	Technical Support	10/1/17	10/10/17	9

Eller Software Services
Client Revenue Data

Client Name	Address	Phone Number	City	Zip	Product/Service	Actual Sales	Estimated Sales	Difference
Mike Gunderson	304 Irvine Ave	218-278-9021	Bemidji	55601	ERP: Enterprise Resource Planning	$15,000	$11,000	$4,000
Heather Guyan	124 East Street	218-333-2313	Bemidji	56601	Training	$1,567	$1,175	$392
Terri Olander	459 10th Avenue	218-667-8977	Brainerd	56401	POS: Point of Sale Software	$6,525	$4,190	$1,651
Anne Nickel	1822 Highway 2	218-556-4211	Cass Lake	56633	AR/AP	$3,200	$3,980	$780
Shelly Vicko	402 2nd Ave SE	218-342-2456	Deer River	56636	AR/AP	$4,500	$3,175	$1,125
Dimitre Ivanov	1344 Highway 3	218-556-3009	Cass Lake	56633	AR/AP	$750	$925	$175
Mylo Chajec	544 West Main	651-345-9001	Eagan	55121	POS: Point of Sale Software	$3,500	$3,800	$700
Adam Greenfield	123 Oak Street	612-543-0090	Minneapolis	55401	ERP: Enterprise Resource Planning	$11,000	$21,000	$10,000
Jesus Gomez	500 5th Ave	218-342-3765	Deer River	56636	AR/AP	$3,500	$3,500	$3,000
Jeremie Midboe	Pilot Knob Rd	651-333-2789	Eagan	55121	POS: Point of Sale Software	$7,500	$9,375	$1,875
Charlie Lindberg	345 Lyndale Ave	612-543-3156	Minneapolis	55401	ERP: Enterprise Resource Planning	$42,000	$48,500	$6,500
Hilary Marschke	245 West 3rd Ave	320-355-5443	Saint Cloud	56301	Training	$795	$581	$184
Craig Brand	554 2nd Street	320-751-4433	Saint Cloud	56301	Technical Support	$1,056	$1,320	$264

Max	2840.73	POS Sales, Eagan	$11,000
Standard Deviation	12971.21785	ERP, Minneapolis	$14,000

Find Phone for:	Anne Nickel	Average Sale, Bemidji	$4,284
	218-556-4211	Highest Sale, Minneapolis	$42,000
		Lowest Sale, Deer River	$4,500

6-90 Completed worksheets for Excel 6-2

Guided Project 6-3

The Wear-Ever Shoes company maintains inventory data and customer satisfaction survey results in your workbook. You use *Lookup & Reference*, *Database*, and *Logical* functions to complete the data. You also use a *Financial* function to calculate depreciation and a *Text* function to enter email addresses.
[Student Learning Outcomes 6.1, 6.2, 6.3, 6.5, 6.6, 6.7]

File Needed: *WearEverShoes-06.xlsx* *(Student data files are available in the* Library *of your SIMnet account)* **Completed Project File Name: *[your initials] Excel 6-3.xlsx***

Skills Covered in this Project

- Nest the *INDEX* and *MATCH* functions.
- Use *SUMIFS* from the *Math & Trig* category.

- Use *DAVERAGE*.
- Create an *IFS* formula.
- Use a *Text* function to concatenate text strings.
- Calculate depreciation with the *DB* function.

---

1. Open the ***WearEverShoes-06*** workbook from your student data files and save it as [your initials] Excel 6-3.
2. Click the **Inventory** sheet tab.
3. Select cells **A3:I39**, click the **Name** box, type Inventory as the range name, and press **Enter**.
4. Select cell **L5** and type WE006.
5. Create a nested function with *INDEX* and *MATCH* to display inventory for a product.
   a. Select cell **L6**.
   b. Click the **Lookup & Reference** button [*Formulas* tab, *Function Library* group] and choose **INDEX**. Select the first argument list **array, row_num, column_num** and click **OK**.
   c. For the *Array* argument, press **F3 (FN+F3)** and select **Inventory**.
   d. Click the **Row_num** box and click the **Name** box arrow. Choose **MATCH** in the list or choose **More Functions** to find and select **MATCH**. The *INDEX* function uses this *MATCH* statement to find the row.
   e. Click cell **L5** for the *Lookup_value* argument.
   f. Click the **Lookup_array** box and select cells **A3:A39**. This *MATCH* function finds the row that matches cell L5 in column A.
   g. Click the **Match_type** argument and type 0.
   h. Click **INDEX** in the *Formula* bar.
   i. Click the **Column_num** argument, click the **Name** box arrow, and choose **MATCH** (Figure 6-91).

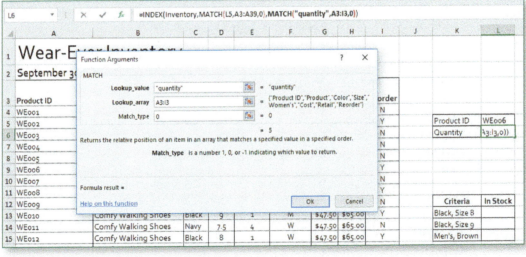

6-91 *MATCH* is nested twice

j. Type quantity in the *Lookup_value* box.

k. Click the **Lookup_array** box and select cells **A3:I3**. This *MATCH* function finds the cell in the "Quantity" column after the row is located by the first *MATCH* function.

l. Click the **Match_type** box and type 0. The formula is
    =**INDEX(Inventory,MATCH(L5,A3:A39,0),MATCH("quantity",A3:I3,0))**.

m. Click **OK**. The result is 2.

n. Click cell **L5**, type WE010, and press **Enter**. The quantity is updated.

6. Use *SUMIFS* to calculate total pairs in stock by specific criteria.

a. Select cell **L13**.

b. Click the **Math & Trig** button [*Formulas* tab, *Function Library* group] and choose **SUMIFS**.

c. Select cells **E4:E39** for the *Sum_range* argument and press **F4** (**FN+F4**).

d. Click the **Criteria_range1** box, select cells **C4:C39**, the Color field, and press **F4** (**FN+F4**).

e. Click the **Criteria1** box and type bla*.

f. Click the **Criteria_range2** box, select cells **D4:D39**, and press **F4** (**FN+F4**).

g. Click the **Criteria2** box and type 8. This criteria specifies the number of black pairs, size 8 (Figure 6-92).

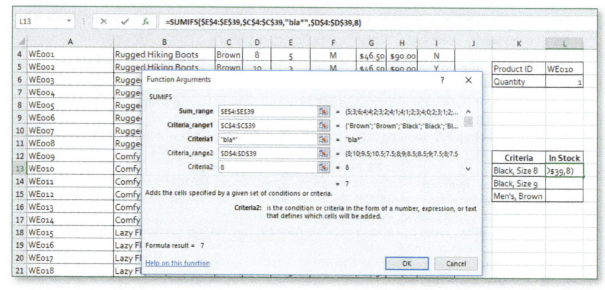

6-92 *SUMIFS* to calculate number by color and size

h. Click **OK**. The result is 7.

i. Select cell **L14** and use *SUMIFS* to sum black, size 9 shoes in stock.

j. Select cell **L15** and use SUMIFS to sum men's brown shoes in stock.

7. Click the **Satisfaction Survey** worksheet tab and review the data.

8. Select cells **A4:H40** and name the range as Survey.

9. Use *DAVERAGE* to summarize customer survey data.

a. Click the **Average Ratings** worksheet tab and select cell **C5** to calculate an average comfort rating for the Rugged Hiking Boots.

b. Click the **Criteria** sheet tab.

c. Select cell **B2** and type rug*.

d. Click the **Average Ratings** sheet tab and verify that cell **C5** is selected.

e. Click the **Insert Function** button [*Formulas* tab, *Function Library* group].

f. Choose **Database** in the *Or select a category* list.

g. Select **DAVERAGE** and click **OK**.

h. Press **F3** (**FN+F3**), choose **Survey** for the *Database* argument, and click **OK**.

i. Click the **Field** box and type comfort.

j. Click the **Criteria** box, select the **Criteria** sheet tab, select cells **B1:B2**, and press **F4** (**FN+F4**) (Figure 6-93).

k. Click **OK**. The result is 7.75.

l. Copy the formula in cell **C5** to cells **D5:F5**.

m. Select cell **D5** and edit the *Field* argument in the formula to show "fit."

n. Repeat step m for cells **E5:F5** to use the correct *Field* argument.

10. Use *DAVERAGE* to summarize survey data.

   a. Select the **Criteria** sheet tab.

   b. Select cell **B5** and type com* to specify the Comfy Walking Shoes.

   c. Click the **Average Ratings** sheet tab and select cell **C6**.

   d. Click the **Recently Used** button [*Formulas* tab, *Function Library* group] and select **DAVERAGE**.

   e. Press **F3** (**FN+F3**) and choose **Survey** for the *Database* argument.

   f. Click the **Field** argument box and type comfort.

   g. Click the **Criteria** box, select cells **B4:B5** on the **Criteria** sheet, and press **F4** (**FN+F4**).

   h. Click **OK**. The result is 7.5.

   i. Copy the formula in cell **C6** to cells **D6:F6**.

   j. Edit the formulas in cells **D6:F6** to use the correct *Field* argument.

11. Build *DAVERAGE* functions for the remaining shoe styles on the **Average Ratings** sheet.

12. Select cells **G5:G9** on the **Average Ratings** sheet, click the **AutoSum** arrow [*Home* tab, *Editing* group], and choose **Average**.

13. Create an *IFS* function.

   a. Select cell **H5**, click the **Logical** button [*Formulas* tab, *Function Library* group], and choose **IFS**.

   b. Click the **Logical_test1** argument, select cell **G5**, and type >=9.

   c. Click the **Value_if_true1** box, click cell **J5**, and press **F4** (**FN+F4**) (Figure 6-94).

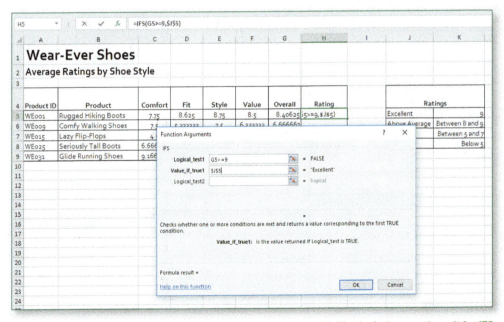

6-93 *DAVERAGE* for comfort rating

6-94 First logical test and result for *IFS*

d. Click the **Logical_test2** box, click cell **G5**, and type $>= 8$.

e. Click the **Value_if_true2** box, click cell **J6**, and press **F4 (FN+F4)**.

f. Click the **Logical_test3** box, click cell **G5**, and type $>= 5$.

g. Click the down scroll arrow to reveal the *Value_if_true3* box, click cell **J7**, and press **F4 (FN+F4)**.

h. Click the down scroll arrow to reveal the *Logical_test4* box, click cell **G5**, and type <5.

i. Click the down scroll arrow to reveal the *Value_if_true4* box, click cell **J8**, and press **F4 (FN+F4)** (Figure 6-95). The complete formula is:

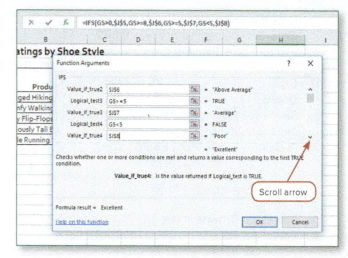

6-95 *IFS function with four logical tests*

$$=IFS(G5>=9,\$J\$5,G5>=8,\$J\$6,G5>=5,\$J\$7,G5<5,\$J\$8)$$

j. Click **OK** and copy the formula to cells **H6:H9**.

k. Make column **H 13.57 (100 pixels)** wide.

14. Calculate depreciation for an asset using a *Financial* function.

a. Click the **Depreciation** sheet tab and select cell **C11**. Depreciation is the decrease in the value of an asset as it ages. The **DB** function calculates the loss in value over a specified period of time at a fixed rate.

b. Click the **Financial** button [*Formulas* tab, *Function Library* group] and choose **DB**.

c. For the *Cost* argument, select cell **C6** and press **F4 (FN+F4)**.

d. Click the **Salvage** box, select cell **C7**, and press **F4 (FN+F4)**. This is the expected value of the equipment at the end of its life.

e. Click the **Life** box, select cell **C8**, and press **F4 (FN+F4)**. This is how long the equipment will be in use.

f. Click the **Period** box and select cell **B11**. The first formula calculates depreciation for the first year (Figure 6-96).

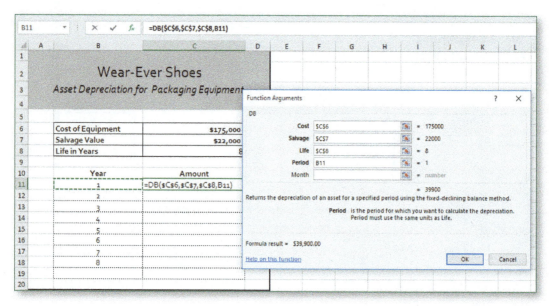

6-96 *DB function to calculate asset depreciation*

g. Click **OK**.

h. Copy the formula in cell **C11** to cells **C12:C18**. Each year's depreciation is less than the previous year's.

i. Select cell **C19** and use **AutoSum**. The total depreciation plus the salvage value is approximately equal to the original cost. It is not exact due to rounding.

15. Use *CONCAT* to build an email address.

a. Right-click any worksheet tab, choose **Unhide**, select **E-Mail**, and click **OK**.

b. Select cell **C5**, type =con, and press **Tab**. The *text1* argument is first.

c. Select cell **A5** and type a comma (,) to move to the *text2* argument.

d. Select cell **B5** and type a comma (,) to move to the *text3* argument.

e. Type "@weshoes.org" including the quotation marks (Figure 6-97).

f. Type the closing parenthesis) and press **Enter**.

g. Copy the formula in cell **C5** to cells **C6:C9**.

16. Save and close the workbook (Figure 6-98).

6-97 *CONCAT* references and typed data

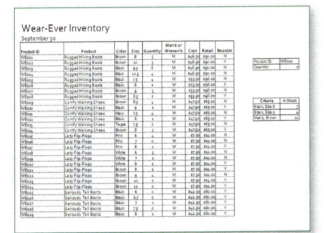

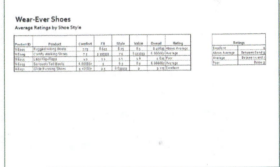

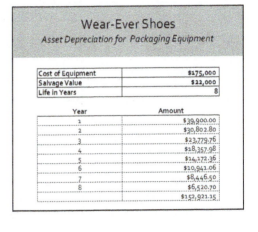

6-98 Completed worksheets for Excel 6-3

Independent Project 6-4

Blue Lake Sports is analyzing the net present value of installing solar panels. They also plan to calculate statistics related to inventory using *Database* and other functions.
[Student Learning Outcomes 6.1, 6.2, 6.4, 6.5, 6.6, 6.8]

File Needed: ***BlueLakeSports-06.xlsx*** *(Student data files are available in the Library of your SIMnet account)*
Completed Project File Name: ***[your initials] Excel 6-4.xlsx***

Skills Covered in this Project

- Calculate the net present value of an investment.
- Use the *REPLACE Text* function.
- Build a MAD calculation.
- Use *RANQ.EQ* to rank sales for a product.
- Use *DAVERAGE* to summarize data.
- Create an *IFS* function.
- Use *Find and Replace* to edit a function argument.

1. Open the ***BlueLakeSports-06*** workbook from your student data files and save it as [your initials] Excel 6-4.

2. Determine the net present value for solar panel installation.
   a. Select cell **C12** on the **Solar Install** sheet and start an *NPV* formula.
   b. Select cell **C10** for the *Rate* argument. This is the interest rate that could be earned if panels are not installed.
   c. Click the **Value1** box and select cell **C5**, the savings during the first year.
   d. For the *Value2* through *Value5* arguments, use cells **C6:C9** (Figure 6-99). (Press **Tab** or click the down scroll arrow to reveal each *Value* box.)

6-99 *Value* arguments for *NPV*

   e. Click **OK**.
   f. Edit the formula to add cell **C4** to the results. The initial cost is added to the results, because the cost is incurred before any savings. (Figure 6-100).

3. Use the *REPLACE* function to update product IDs.
   a. Click the **Inventory** sheet tab and select cell **B5**. New IDs in column B will display "BLS" as the beginning characters instead of "STL" as shown in column A.

b. Use *REPLACE* from the *Text* function category to replace the first three characters in cell **A5** with BLS in uppercase letters (Figure 6-101).

c. Copy the formula and preserve the borders.

4. Calculate the mean absolute deviation (MAD) for differences and the standard deviation for actual sales.

a. Click the **Unit Sales** sheet tab and select cell **G6**.

b. Calculate the absolute value of the difference between the estimated and actual amounts.

c. Click cell **G22** and calculate the mean absolute deviation (MAD).

d. Format the results in cell **G22** to display three decimal positions.

e. Click cell **G23** and use *STDEV.S* to calculate the standard deviation for the actual sales amounts.

5. Click cell **G25** and use *RANK.EQ* to determine the rank in actual sales for the titanium driver.

6. Use *DAVERAGE* to summarize survey data.

a. Click the **Product Evaluation** tab and name cells **A4:E19** as Data. Notice that the "Overall Rating" column is the fifth column in the range.

b. Click the **Criteria** sheet and type ap* in cell **C2** to reference data from the "Apparel" department.

c. Click the **Statistics** tab and select cell **B5**.

d. Use *DAVERAGE* to calculate an overall average for product satisfaction by department. Use the named range **Data** for the *Database* argument. For the *Field* argument, type 5. The *Criteria* argument is cells **C1:C2** on the **Criteria** sheet.

e. Click the **Criteria** sheet. Enter criteria in cells **C5**, **C8**, and **C11** for each of the three remaining departments on the **Statistics** sheet.

f. Click the **Statistics** sheet tab and select cell **B6**. Use *DAVERAGE* and your criteria ranges for cells **B6:B8**.

7. On the **Statistics** sheet, set columns **A:B** each to **16 (133 pixels)** wide.

8. Select cells **A1:B3** and open the *Format Cells* dialog box. Choose **Center Across Selection** on the *Alignment* tab.

9. Center align the labels in row **4** and apply **All Borders** to cells **A4:B8** (Figure 6-102).

6-100 Positive *NPV* is good

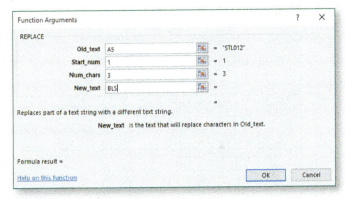

6-101 *REPLACE* function to change three characters

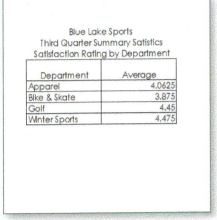

6-102 Completed *Statistics* worksheet

10. Create an *IFS* function.
    a. Click the **Product Evaluation** sheet tab and select cell **F5**. Evaluation criteria and ratings are displayed in rows 21:24.
    b. Start an *IFS* function in cell **F5**, select cell **E5** for the *Logical_test1* box, and type >=4.85.
    c. Click the **Value_if_true1** box, click cell **E21**, and press **F4** (**FN+F4**).
    d. Click the **Logical_test2** box, click cell **E5** and type >=4.35.
    e. Click the **Value_if_true2** box, click cell **E22**, and press **F4** (**FN+F4**).
    f. Click the **Logical_test3** box. Complete the statement and its corresponding *value_if_true* argument.
    g. Complete the fourth logical test and *value_if_true* argument (Figure 6-103) and click **OK**.
    h. Copy the formula in cell **F5** to cells **F6:F19**.

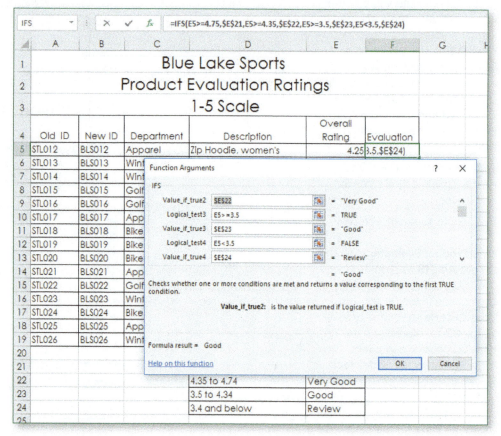

6-103 *IFS* function displays the evaluation

11. Apply **All Borders** to cells **A4:F19** and to cells **D21:E24**.

12. Use **Center Across Selection** for the labels in rows **1:3** and set the font size to **20 pt**.

13. *AutoFit* columns that do not show all the data.

14. Use *Find and Replace* to edit a function argument.
    a. Start a **Replace** command, expand the options, and clear any find format settings.
    b. Replace 4.85 with 4.75 in the worksheet.
    c. Replace 4.84 with 4.74 in the worksheet.
    d. Close the *Find and Replace* dialog box.

15. Save and close the workbook (Figure 6-104).

Blue Lake Sports
Product Evaluation Ratings
1-5 Scale

Old ID	New ID	Department	Description	Overall Rating	Evaluation
STL012	BLS012	Apparel	Zip Hoodie, women's	4.25	Good
STL013	BLS013	Winter Sports	Snowboard, men's	5	Excellent
STL014	BLS014	Winter Sports	Snowboard, women's	4.75	Excellent
STL015	BLS015	Golf	Full Set, Ladies	4.35	Very Good
STL016	BLS016	Golf	Titanium Driver, Men's	4	Good
STL017	BLS017	Apparel	Rain Jacket, girls	5	Excellent
STL018	BLS018	Bike & Skate	Biking helmet, women's	4.75	Excellent
STL019	BLS019	Bike & Skate	Biking helmet, child's	3.25	Review
STL020	BLS020	Bike & Skate	Bicycle Trailer, single	3.5	Good
STL021	BLS021	Apparel	Fleece Sweatshirt, men's	4	Good
STL022	BLS022	Golf	Rangefinder	5	Excellent
STL023	BLS023	Winter Sports	Snow Tube, 44"	4.15	Good
STL024	BLS024	Bike & Skate	Bike Rack, double	4	Good
STL025	BLS025	Apparel	Soft Shell Jacket, boy's	3	Review
STL026	BLS026	Winter Sports	Hockey Facemask, men's	4	Good

4.75 and above	Excellent
4.35 to 4.74	Very Good
3.5 to 4.34	Good
3.4 and below	Review

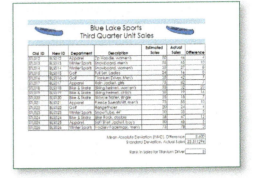

Blue Lake Sports
Third Quarter Unit Sales

Old ID	New ID	Department	Description	Estimated Sales	Actual Sales	Difference
STL012	BLS012	Apparel	Zip Hoodie, women's	50	46	4
STL013	BLS013	Winter Sports	Snowboard, men's	55	65	10
STL014	BLS014	Winter Sports	Snowboard, women's	35	27	8
STL015	BLS015	Golf	Full Set, Ladies	24	16	8
STL016	BLS016	Golf	Titanium Driver, Men's	35	42	7
STL017	BLS017	Apparel	Rain Jacket, girls	75	62	13
STL018	BLS018	Bike & Skate	Biking helmet, women's	55	33	22
STL019	BLS019	Bike & Skate	Biking helmet, child's	30	19	11
STL020	BLS020	Bike & Skate	Bicycle Trailer, single	25	18	7
STL021	BLS021	Apparel	Fleece Sweatshirt, men's	75	85	10
STL022	BLS022	Golf	Rangefinder	20	24	4
STL023	BLS023	Winter Sports	Snow Tube, 44"	55	33	22
STL024	BLS024	Bike & Skate	Bike Rack, double	38	47	12
STL025	BLS025	Apparel	Soft Shell Jacket, boy's	30	46	13
STL026	BLS026	Winter Sports	Hockey Facemask, men's	73	78	5

Mean Absolute Deviation (MAD), Difference [8.600]
Standard Deviation, Actual Sales [23.511294]

Rank in Sales for Titanium Driver [8]

Blue Lake Sports Warehouse Inventory

Old ID	New ID	Department	Description	Qty on Hand
STL012	BLS012	Apparel	Zip Hoodie, women's	24
STL013	BLS013	Winter Sports	Snowboard, men's	34
STL014	BLS014	Winter Sports	Snowboard, women's	22
STL015	BLS015	Golf	Full Set, Ladies	8
STL016	BLS016	Golf	Titanium Driver, Men's	12
STL017	BLS017	Apparel	Rain Jacket, girls	20
STL018	BLS018	Bike & Skate	Biking helmet, women's	25
STL019	BLS019	Bike & Skate	Biking helmet, child's	35
STL020	BLS020	Bike & Skate	Bicycle Trailer, single	15
STL021	BLS021	Apparel	Fleece Sweatshirt, men's	25
STL022	BLS022	Golf	Rangefinder	18
STL023	BLS023	Winter Sports	Snow Tube, 44"	13
STL024	BLS024	Bike & Skate	Bike Rack, double	9
STL025	BLS025	Apparel	Soft Shell Jacket, boy's	14
STL026	BLS026	Winter Sports	Hockey Facemask, men's	16

6-104 Completed worksheets for Excel 6-4

Independent Project 6-5

Classic Gardens and Landscapes counts responses to mail promotions to determine effectiveness. You use *SUMIFS* and a nested *IF* formula to complete the summary. You also calculate insurance statistics and convert birth dates from text to dates.
[Student Learning Outcomes 6.1, 6.2, 6.3, 6.4, 6.7]

File Needed: ***ClassicGardens-06.xlsx*** (Student data files are available in the Library of your SIMnet account)
Completed Project File Name: *[your initials] Excel 6-5.xlsx*

Skills Covered in this Project

- Nest *MATCH* and *INDEX* functions.
- Create *DSUM* formulas.
- Build an *IFS* function.
- Build *SUMIFS* formulas.
- Use *DATEVALUE* to convert text to dates.

1. Open the ***ClassicGardens-06*** workbook from your student data files and save it as [your initials] Excel 6-5.
2. Create a nested *INDEX* and *MATCH* function to display the number of responses from a city.
   a. Click the **Mailings** sheet tab and select and name cells **A3:D28** as Responses.

b. Click the **Mailing Stats** sheet tab.
c. Click cell **B21** and type Carthage.
d. Click cell **C21**, start an **INDEX** function, and select the first argument list option.
e. Choose the **Responses** range for the *Array* argument.
f. Click the **Row_num** box and nest a **MATCH** function. Select cell **B21** for the *Lookup_value* and cells **A3:A28** on the **Mailings** sheet for the *Lookup_array*. Click the **Match_type** argument box and type 0.
g. Click **INDEX** in the *Formula* bar. Click the **Column_num** box and nest a second **MATCH** function to look up cell **D3** on the **Mailings** sheet in the lookup array **A3:D3**.
h. Click the **Match_type** box and type 0 (Figure 6-105).

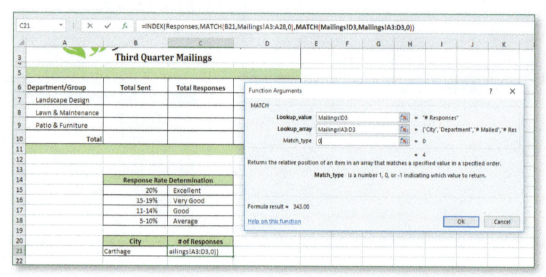

6-105 Nested *MATCH* and *INDEX* functions

i. Format the results to show zero decimal places.
j. Type Smyrna in cell **B21**.

3. Use *DSUM* to summarize mailing data.
   a. On the **Mailings** sheet, note that number sent is located in the third column and response data is in the fourth column.
   b. Click the **Criteria** sheet tab. Select cell **B2** and type lan* to select data for the Landscape Design department.
   c. Click the **Mailing Stats** sheet tab and select cell **B7**.
   d. Use **DSUM** with the range name **Responses** as the *Database* argument. Type 3 for the *Field* argument, and use an absolute reference to cells **B1:B2** on the **Criteria** sheet as the *Criteria* argument.
   e. Copy the formula to cell **C7** and edit the *Field* argument to use the fourth column.
   f. Complete criteria for the two remaining departments on the **Criteria** sheet.
   g. Click the **Mailing Stats** sheet tab and select cell **B8**.
   h. Use *DSUM* in cells **B8:C9** to calculate results for the two departments.

4. Use *SUM* in cells **B10:C10**.

5. Format all values as **Comma Style** with no decimal places.

6. Create an *IFS* function to display a response rating.
   a. Click cell **D7**. The response rate and ratings are shown in rows 14:18.
   b. Start an *IFS* function and select **C7** for the *Logical_test1* argument. Type / for division and select cell **B7**. Type >= 20% to complete the test.

c. Click the **Value_if_true1** box, select **C15**, and press **F4 (FN+F4)** (Figure 6-106).

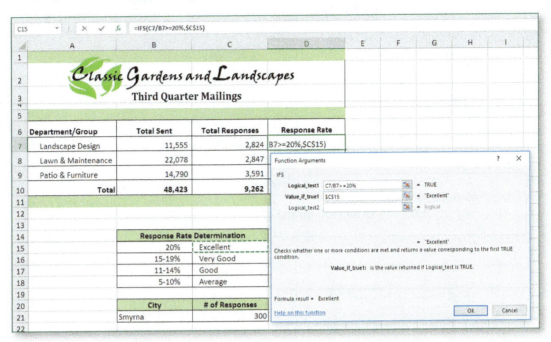

6-106 First logical test and value_if_true arguments

d. Click the **Logical_test2** box, select **C7**, type **/**, select cell **B7**, and type **>=15%**

e. Click the **Value_if_true2** box, click cell **C16**, and press **F4 (FN+F4)**.

f. Complete the third and fourth logical tests and *value_if_true* arguments (Figure 6-107).

g. Copy the formula in cell **D7** to cells **D8:D10**.

7. Use *SUMIFS* to total insurance claims and dependents by city and department.

a. Click the **Employee Insurance** sheet tab and select cell **E25**.

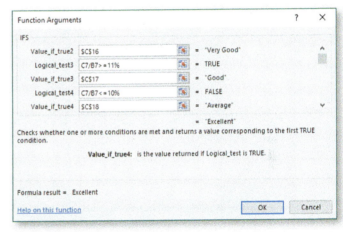

6-107 Completed *IFS* function arguments

b. Use *SUMIFS* with an absolute reference to cells **F4:F23** as the *Sum_range* argument.

c. The *Criteria_range1* argument is an absolute reference to cells **E4:E23** with *Criteria1* that will select the city of Brentwood.

d. The *Criteria_range2* argument is an absolute reference to the department column with criteria that will select the Landscape Design department.

e. Complete *SUMIFS* formulas for cells **E26:E28**.

f. Format borders to remove inconsistencies, if any, and adjust column widths to display data.

8. Use *DATEVALUE* to convert text data to dates.

a. Click the **Birth Dates** sheet tab and select cell **D4**. The dates were imported as text and cannot be used in date arithmetic.

b. Select cells **D4:D23** and cut/paste them to cells **G4:G23**.

c. Select cell **H4** and use *DATEVALUE* to convert the date in cell **G4** to a serial number.

d. Copy the formula to cells **H5:H23**.

e. Select cells **H4:H23** and copy them to the *Clipboard*.

f. Select cell **D4**, click the arrow with the **Paste** button [*Home* tab, *Clipboard* group], and choose **Values** (Figure 6-108).

g. Format the values in column **D** to use the **Short Date** format.

h. Hide columns **G:H**.

i. Apply **All Borders** to the data and make columns **B:D** each **13.57 (100 pixels)** wide.

9. Save and close the workbook (Figure 6-109).

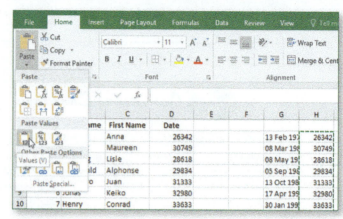

6-108 Only values are pasted

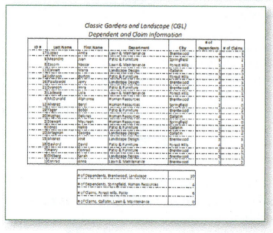

6-109 Completed worksheets for Excel 6-5

Independent Project 6-6

Clemenson Imaging LLC analyzes increased revenue from the purchase and use of CT scan equipment. You determine the number of patients and procedures by technician and location and transpose technician names.
[Student Learning Outcomes 6.3, 6.4, 6.5, 6.6, 6.7]

File Needed: ***ClemensonImaging-06.xlsx*** *(Student data files are available in the* Library *of your SIMnet account)*
Completed Project File Name: *[your initials]* ***Excel 6-6.xlsx***

Skills Covered in this Project

- Calculate the net present value of a purchase.
- Use *TRANSPOSE* to rearrange labels into a column.
- Concatenate cells to display names.
- Use *SUMIFS* to summarize data.
- Calculate procedure times.
- Format times with fractions.

1. Open the ***ClemensonImaging-06*** workbook from your student data files and save it as [your initials] Excel 6-6.

2. Determine the net present value of a new equipment purchase.
   a. Click the **Financials** sheet tab and select cell **H5**.
   b. Use **NPV** with a *Rate* argument of **4.25%**. For the *Value1* argument, select cells **D7:D13**. This is the same as entering each value argument separately.
   c. Edit the formula to add both investment costs (cells **D4** and **D5**) at the end of the formula.

3. Use *TRANSPOSE* to arrange technician names.
   a. Click the **Technicians** sheet tab. The names are in rows.
   b. Select cells **A4:A10**, seven rows in one column.
   c. Select **TRANSPOSE** from the *Lookup & Reference* category and select cells **A1:G1** for the *Array* argument.
   d. Press **Ctrl+Shift+Enter** to complete the array formula.
   e. Repeat the *TRANSPOSE* task for the first names in cells **B4:B10**.
   f. Select cells **A4:B10** and copy them to the *Clipboard*.
   g. Select cell **D4**, click the arrow with the **Paste** button [*Home* tab, *Clipboard* group], and choose **Values** (Figure 6-110).

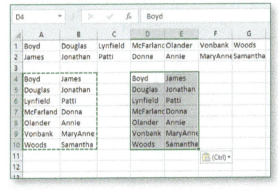

6-110 Transposed and copied data

4. Use *CONCAT* to display technician names.
   a. Click the **Summary** sheet tab.
   b. Select cell **A5** and use *CONCAT* with cell **D4** on the **Technicians** sheet as the *Text1* argument.
   c. The *Text2* argument is a comma and a space.
   d. The *Text3* argument is cell **E4** on the **Technicians** sheet (Figure 6-111).
   e. Copy the formula to display the remaining names and preserve the borders.

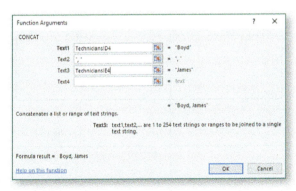

6-111 *CONCAT* with 3D references

5. Use *SUMIFS* to total number of patients by procedure and technician.
   a. Click the **Procedures** tab and name cells **A5:F41** as Data.
   b. Click the **Summary** sheet tab and select cell **C5**.
   c. Use *SUMIFS* with an absolute reference to cells **D5:D41** on the **Procedures** sheet for the *Sum_range*. Since the range name includes the column label, you must include the label in each *CriteriaN* range.
   d. The first criteria range is an absolute reference to the image type column on the **Procedures** sheet. Its corresponding criteria is mri.
   e. The second criteria range is an absolute reference to the technician names column on the **Procedures** sheet.
   f. Type *boyd* for the *Criteria2* argument. This string means that any character(s) can precede or follow "boyd" (Figure 6-112).

6. Copy and edit the *SUMIFS* formula or start a new formula to complete data in cells **C6:C11**.

7. Use *SUMIFS* to total number of patients by category and location in cells **C14:C15**.

8. Look for and correct format inconsistencies.

9. Calculate procedure times.
   a. Click the **Times** sheet tab and select cell **F6**.
   b. Build a formula to subtract the start time from the end time and multiply those results by 24. The result is shown in hours.
   c. Copy the formula to row **41**.
   d. Select cells **F6:F41** and open the *Format Cells* dialog box. On the *Number* tab, choose **Fraction** with a *Type* of **Up to one digit** (Figure 6-113).

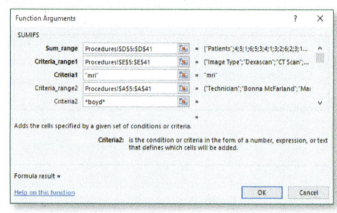

6-112 Wildcard characters in the argument

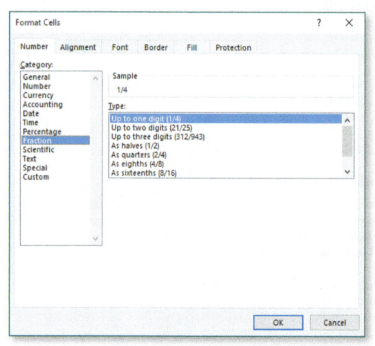

6-113 Time results formatted with fractions

10. Save and close the workbook (Figure 6-114).

Clemenson Imaging
Time Duration for Procedures in Hours

Patient ID	Location	Image Type	Start	End	Duration
CL024	Green Bay	Dexascan	9:15 AM	9:30 AM	1/4
CL027	Manitowoc	CT Scan	1:00 PM	1:45 PM	3/4
CL030	Appleton	MRI	10:15 AM	11:30 AM	1 1/4
CL033	Green Bay	Ultrasonography	9:00 AM	10:00 AM	1
CL036	Green Bay	Angiography	2:30 PM	4:15 PM	1 3/4
CL039	Manitowoc	Dexascan	10:30	11:00 AM	1/2
CL042	Manitowoc	MRI	2:45 PM	4:15 PM	1 1/2
CL045	Appleton	MRI	8:00 AM	10:30 AM	2 1/2
CL048	Appleton	Angiography	1:30 PM	3:45 PM	2 1/4
CL051	Green Bay	Angiography	3:00 PM	4:45 PM	1 3/4
CL054	Appleton	Ultrasonography	1:00 PM	1:45 PM	3/4
CL057	Manitowoc	Ultrasonography	11:30 AM	1:45 PM	2 1/4
CL060	Manitowoc	MRI	10:15 AM	11:30 AM	1 1/4
CL063	Appleton	Dexascan	10:30	11:00 AM	1/2
CL066	Appleton	Dexascan	11:00 AM	11:20 AM	1/3
CL069	Green Bay	CT Scan	2:15 PM	3:30 PM	1 1/4
CL072	Appleton	CT Scan	3:30 PM	5:00 PM	1 1/2
CL075	Green Bay	MRI	8:00 AM	11:00 AM	3
CL078	Manitowoc	MRI	9:00 AM	11:30 AM	2 1/2
CL081	Manitowoc	CT Scan	4:00 PM	5:30 PM	1 1/2
CL084	Appleton	CT Scan	8:00 AM	9:45 AM	1 3/4
CL087	Appleton	MRI	12:00 PM	2:30 PM	2 1/2
CL090	Green Bay	MRI	2:15 PM	4:45 PM	2 1/2
CL093	Manitowoc	Ultrasonography	1:00 PM	1:45 PM	3/4
CL096	Appleton	MRI	10:15 AM	11:30 AM	1 1/4
CL099	Appleton	Dexascan	11:00 AM	11:20 AM	1/3
CL102	Green Bay	Dexascan	8:00 AM	8:20 AM	1/3
CL105	Appleton	CT Scan	2:00 PM	3:30 PM	1 1/2
CL108	Green Bay	CT Scan	3:00 PM	3:45 PM	3/4
CL111	Manitowoc	Angiography	4:00 PM	4:45 PM	3/4
CL114	Appleton	Angiography	3:45 PM	5:00 PM	1 1/4
CL117	Green Bay	Ultrasonography	11:00 AM	11:20 AM	1/3
CL120	Manitowoc	Ultrasonography	12:00 PM	1:30 PM	1 1/2
CL123	Appleton	Angiography	4:00 PM	4:45 PM	3/4
CL126	Green Bay	MRI	10:15 AM	11:30 AM	1 1/4
CL129	Manitowoc	MRI	9:00 AM	11:15 AM	2 1/4

Clemenson Imaging, LLC
Purchase and Training Cost Analysis

Cost of CT Scan Equipment	-$200,000		
Cost of Staff Training	-$25,000	Net Present Value	$22,933.93
Additional Revenue Year 1	$30,000		
Additional Revenue Year 2	$30,000		
Additional Revenue Year 3	$45,000		
Additional Revenue Year 4	$45,000		
Additional Revenue Year 5	$48,000		
Additional Revenue Year 6	$48,000		
Additional Revenue Year 7	$50,000		

Clemenson Imaging
Second Quarter Summary

Technician	Procedure	# of Patients
Boyd, James	MRI	4
Douglas, Jonathan	CT Scan	13
Lynfield, Patti	Angiography	2
McFarland, Donna	Angiography	0
Olander, Annie	MRI	5
Vonbank, MaryAnne	MRI	2
Woods, Samantha	CT Scan	1

Patient Category	Location	# of Patients
Scheduled	Appleton	22
Walk-In	Green Bay	17

6-114 Completed worksheets for Excel 6-6

Improve It Project 6-7

In the Livingood Income Tax and Accounting workbook, you use *IFERROR* to replace a standard error with a custom message. You correct the spelling of a client name throughout the worksheet, incorporate the *TODAY()* function in a concatenated statement, and calculate data about overdue accounts.
[Student Learning Outcomes 6.2, 6.4, 6.6, 6.8]

File Needed: **Livingood-06.xlsx** *(Student data files are available in the* Library *of your SIMnet account)*
Completed Project File Name: *[your initials] Excel 6-7.xlsx*

Skills Covered in this Project

- Use *IFERROR* to display a custom message.
- Add cell references to the *Watch Window*.
- Monitor *Find and Replace* in the *Watch Window*.
- Create a *SUMIF* formula.
- Build a *COUNTIF* formula.
- Concatenate *TODAY()* with text.
- Use date format codes in a function.

---

1. Open the **Livingood-06** workbook from your student data files and save it as [your initials] Excel 6-7.
2. Select cell **E6** on the **Accounts Aging** sheet and review the formula. The formula subtracts the invoice date from today's date in cell G1.
3. Use an *IFERROR* formula in cell **E6** that displays Re-enter date instead of a standard error message.
4. Copy the *IFERROR* formula to cells **E7:E20** and *AutoFit* the column.
5. Select cells **C6:C20** and add them as a watch to the *Watch Window*.
6. Click the **Aging Detail** sheet tab. Build a *Find and Replace* command to replace all occurrences of "accoustaff, inc." with AccounStaff, Inc. throughout the workbook. Close the *Watch Window*.
7. Use *SUMIFS* to calculate totals that are late by 30 days or more.
   a. Click the **Aging Detail** sheet tab.
   b. Name cells **A5:E20** as Detail.
   c. Use *SUMIFS* in cell **H6** to calculate the total due from *AccounStaff* that is 30 or more days late.
   d. Copy or enter a *SUMIFS* formula for *Custom Tax* in cell **H7**.
   e. Format cells **H6:H7** as **Currency**.
8. Use *COUNTIFS* to calculate how many invoices are late by 30 days or more.
   a. Use *COUNTIFS* in cell **I6** to calculate the number of *AccounStaff* invoices that are 30 or more days overdue.
   b. Copy or enter a *COUNTIFS* formula for *Custom Tax* in cell **I7**.
9. Use *CONCAT* to display a sentence about the current date.
   a. Click cell **A22** on the **Aging Detail** sheet and start a *CONCAT* formula.
   b. Type Today is with a space after the word "is" for the *Text1* argument.
   c. Click the **Text2** box and nest the **TEXT** function from the *Text* category.
   d. Type today() for the *Value* argument. The equals sign is not necessary when the function is used as an argument.
   e. Click the **Format_text** box and type mmmm d, yyy. This format spells out the month, uses four digits for the year, and shows the date without leading zeros (Figure 6-115).
   f. Click **OK**.

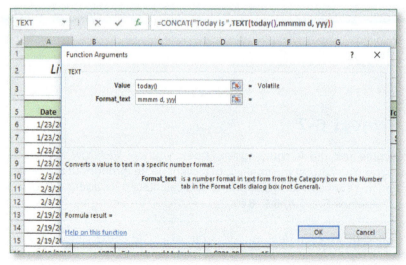

6-115 Nested *TEXT* function with custom date format

10. Save and close the workbook (Figure 6-116).

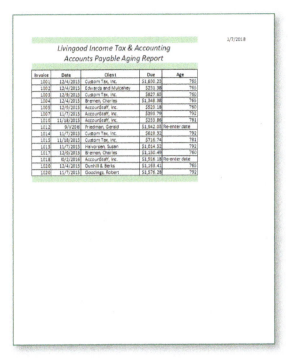

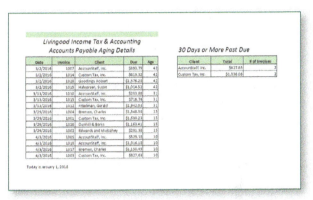

6-116 Completed worksheets for Excel 6-7

Challenge Project 6-8

In this project, you build a list of names and use *Text* functions to create email addresses. You also use the *SUBSTITUTE* function to update the email address list to display a revised name.
[Student Learning Outcome 6.6]

File Needed: None
Completed Project File Name: *[your initials] Excel 6-8.xlsx*

Create and save a workbook as [your initials] Excel 6-8. Modify your workbook according to the following guidelines:

- In cells **A3:B8**, type first and last names for six persons, first names in column A, last names in column B. Names can be friends, relatives, or colleagues.
- In cells **C3:C8**, use *CONCAT* to display an email address for each individual that consists of the first name, an underscore, the last name, and @ with a domain name. Use the same domain name for all, such as "abc.com" or "CompanyA.com."
- In cells **D3:D8**, use *SUBSTITUTE* to change the **Text** in column **C** to a different domain name. For example, change "CompanyA.com" to "CompanyB.com."
- Type labels and apply formatting to complete the worksheet.
- Insert a footer that displays the current date in the left section and your name in the right section.
- Set document properties to show your name as the author and a title of your choice. Spell check the workbook if necessary.

Challenge Project 6-9

In this project, you calculate net present value and internal rate of return for an electric car purchase. You include the increased cost of this type of automobile, a tax credit from your state government, and gasoline cost savings for five years of ownership.
[**Student Learning Outcome 6.5**]

File Needed: None
Completed Project File Name: *[your initials] Excel 6-9.xlsx*

Create and save a workbook as [your initials] Excel 6-9. Modify your workbook according to the following guidelines:

- Enter the following labels in column A: Price Premium, Tax Credit, Year 1 Fuel Savings. Enter labels for fuel savings for years 2–5.
- In column B, enter a value as the price premium for an electric car. This is a negative amount and is how much more an electric car costs than a gasoline-powered car.
- Enter a value for a tax credit that is half the premium value; this is a positive value because it is a savings for you.
- For the fuel savings, estimate a yearly amount based on driving an electric car rather than a gasoline-powered car.
- Enter labels below the data for Net Present Value and Internal Rate of Return.
- Use *NPV* to calculate the net present value of the purchase. For the discount rate, enter a percentage that is close to the percentage you might earn for a moderately safe investment.
- Explore the *IRR* and the *MIRR* functions. Then use either to determine a return rate on the purchase, if any.
- Insert main labels to identify the purpose of the sheet and apply formatting.
- Insert a header that shows the current date in the center section and your name in the right section.
- Edit document properties to show your name as the author.

Challenge Project 6-10

In this project, you create a worksheet that compares year-to-year usage for text messages, tweets, or blog posts. You calculate the percentage change and use *IFERROR* to identify incomplete data.
[**Student Learning Outcome 6.2**]

File Needed: None
Completed Project File Name: *[your initials] Excel 6-10.xlsx*

Create and save a workbook as [your initials] Excel 6-10. Modify your workbook according to the following guidelines:

- Starting in cell **A3**, enter the names of the months from January to December in the column.
- In cells **B2:D2**, enter labels for Year 1, Year 2, and % Change.

- Enter values for January through September for both years. These values can represent the number of tweets, text messages, or other posts of interest to you. Do not enter values for October through December.
- In column D, enter the formula to calculate the percentage change. The formula is year 2's value minus year 1's value divided by year 1's value. Set the order of precedence so that the subtraction is calculated before the division. Format the results as **Percent Style** with two decimal places.
- Copy the formula for all months, including October through December, to display the standard error message *#DIV/0!* in the rows without values.
- Edit or replace the formulas in column D with an *IFERROR* formula to display Missing Data instead of the standard error.
- Insert main labels to identify the purpose of the sheet and complete formatting.
- Insert a header with your name in the right section.
- Edit document properties to show your name as the author.

CHAPTER 7

Working with Templates and Sharing Work

CHAPTER OVERVIEW

Excel templates are model workbooks. When you create a new workbook, you use a template with basic settings, including a document theme, a font name and size, and default margins. You can build an easy-to-use, error-free workbook with a template and commands such as data validation and form controls.

CASE STUDY

In the Pause & Practice projects in this chapter, you work with inventory and guest worksheets for Paradise Lakes Resort (PLR). You save the workbook as a template, add data validation and an option button, and check the workbook for distribution issues.

Pause & Practice 7-1: Create an Excel template and add data validation settings to a worksheet.

Pause & Practice 7-2: Create a workbook from a template, use a data form, add a form control, and set worksheet and workbook protection.

Pause & Practice 7-3: Share and merge workbooks and prepare a workbook for distribution.

Using Excel Templates

A *template* is a prototype or sample workbook. A template can include data, formulas, formatting, charts, images, controls, and more. Templates are best for work that requires the same layout, the same design, and the same data pattern each time you prepare a workbook.

Create a Workbook from a Template

The *Backstage* view for the *New* command displays recently published and popular templates in its *Featured* group. Excel has thousands of templates, and *Backstage* view lists suggested search categories. When you create a workbook from a template, a copy of the template opens as an Excel workbook with the same name as the template followed by a number.

▶ **HOW TO:** Create a Workbook from a Template

1. Click the **New** button [*File* tab].
   - *Backstage* view for *New* displays a thumbnail and name for *Featured* templates.
   - The *Blank workbook* template creates a new workbook.
   - The *Suggested searches* categories locate online templates.
   - Select **PERSONAL** to use a template that you created.

2. Click the thumbnail for the template you want to use.
   - A preview window describes the template (Figure 7-1).

3. Click **Create**.
   - A workbook with the same name as the template followed by a number opens (Figure 7-2).
   - A template can include sample data and multiple sheets.

4. Save the workbook in your usual location with a descriptive name.

7-1 Preview of selected template in *Backstage* view

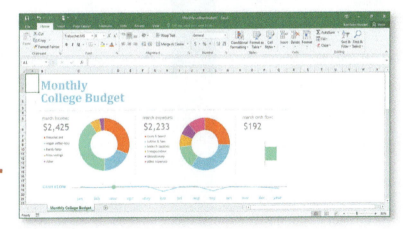

7-2 Workbook created from a template

Save a Workbook as a Template

Published and online templates provide a starting point for a new workbook, but you can create a template from any Excel workbook. When you use the same design, formulas, and objects for a task, you can create a model, save it as a template, and build new workbooks from the template.

When you save a workbook as an Excel template, it is saved in the *Custom Office Templates* folder in the *Documents* folder for the current user at your computer. Your saved templates are available in the *Personal* category in *Backstage* view for the *New* command [*File* tab]. Excel templates are saved with the .xltx file name extension.

> ### MORE INFO
> You can save templates in any folder but their names do not appear in the *Personal* category and they do not open as copies. Change the default folder for personal templates in the *Excel Options* dialog box in the *Save* pane.

Check the *Save Thumbnail* box before you choose the *Save as type* to include a preview for a template. A ***thumbnail*** is a tiny image of the active sheet.

> ### MORE INFO
> A default setting to save thumbnails with all workbooks appears in the *Properties* dialog box on the *Summary* tab. Thumbnails are visible in the *Open* dialog box when you set view options to show icons.

▶ HOW TO: Save a Workbook as a Template

1. Click the **File** tab and choose **Save As**.
2. Choose **This PC**.
3. Click the **More Options** link.
   - The *Save As* dialog box opens.
   - The default name in the *File name* box is highlighted.
4. Type the template name.
5. Click the **Save as type** arrow.
6. Select **Excel Template** (Figure 7-3).
   - Excel selects the default *Custom Office Templates* folder.
   - You can navigate to another folder.
7. Select the **Save Thumbnail** box.
8. Click **Save**.
9. Close the template.

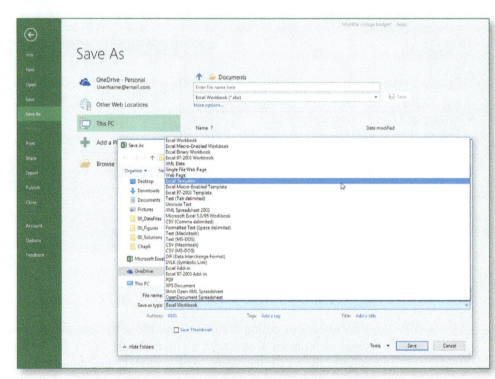

7-3 *Save as type* sets the default templates folder

Setting Data Validation

Data validation is a process in which Excel checks data as it is entered to verify that it matches established requirements. In an inventory worksheet, Paradise Lakes Resort can set a data validation rule that requires the stock quantity to be a positive number. If a user enters a negative number, a pop-up message reminds the person about the error.

Validation Settings

Validation settings are rules applied to data as it is entered. You can build a simple condition using relational operators, such as requiring that the data be a whole number within a range of values or that data be greater than or less than a value. You can allow or prohibit decimal values, specify date or time limits, or limit the length of a text entry. It is also possible to use a list or a formula in a data validation setting.

You usually set data validation for a range of cells before any data is entered. You can set validation after data is entered but already-entered data that does not meet the rule is not automatically identified.

▶ HOW TO: Set Data Validation with an Operator

1. Select the cell or the cell range where data validation settings are required.

2. Click the **Data Validation** button [*Data* tab, *Data Tools* group].

   • The *Data Validation* dialog box has three tabs.

3. Click the **Settings** tab.

4. Click the **Allow** arrow and choose an option.

   • Choose **Whole Number** to set a particular value or range of values.

   • Choose **Any Value** or click **Clear All** to clear validation settings.

5. Click the **Data** arrow and choose an operator.

   • *Data* options are based on the *Allow* choice.
   • Dialog box choices depend on the operator.

6. Enter a value or select a cell to complete the *Data Validation* settings (Figure 7-4).

7. Click **OK**.

   • Cells with data that do not match the criteria are not identified.

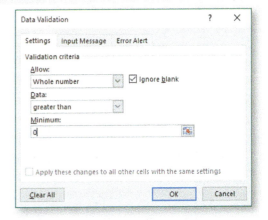

7-4 Data validation settings

Create a Data Validation Input Message

An **input message** is a comment box that appears on screen as soon as a cell with data validation is selected. An input message is a guideline for the person entering data. It might display "Type a value between 1 and 10," or "Choose a name from this list." Figure 7-5 shows an input message before data is entered.

7-5 Input message when the cell is selected

▶HOW TO: Create an Input Message

1. Select the cell or the range with data validation settings.
2. Click the **Data Validation** button [*Data* tab, *Data Tools* group].
3. Click the **Input Message** tab.
4. Verify that the **Show input message when cell is selected** box is selected.
5. Click the **Title** box and type a name or title for the message box.
   - A title is optional.
6. Click the **Input message** box and type the message to appear on screen (Figure 7-6).
   - Use capitalization and punctuation as desired.
   - Be brief to keep the input box small.
7. Click **OK**.

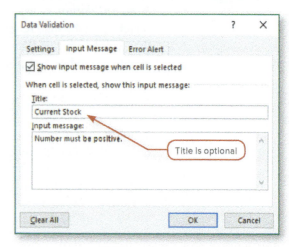

7-6 Input message for data validation

> ### MORE INFO
>
> You can create a custom *ScreenTip* by creating an input message without a data validation setting.

Create a Data Validation Error Alert

An ***error alert*** is a pop-up message that appears after invalid data is entered, as shown in Figure 7-7. You can set an error alert as well as an input message for each data validation setting in a worksheet.

When you create an error alert, you specify the type of warning box. With a *Stop* warning, the user is prohibited from making an entry and can cancel the task or retry. A *Stop* warning displays a white **X** in a red circle.

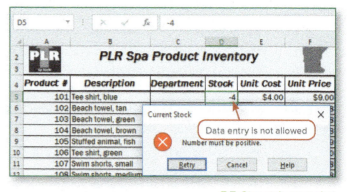

7-7 *Stop* style error alert

When you select a *Warning* box, the message box shows an exclamation point (!) in a yellow triangle. With this type of warning, the entry is allowed or can be edited or canceled. The third warning style is *Information* which allows the entry to be made. This message box includes a lowercase **i** in a blue circle.

> ### MORE INFO
>
> When you allow invalid entries, you can set conditional formatting to highlight invalid entries for review.

After you set the type of warning, you can type an optional title for the message box. The *Error message* is text that appears on screen. The message should clearly and briefly explain what the user should do to create a valid entry.

▶ HOW TO: Create an Error Alert

1. Select the cell or the range with data validation settings.
2. Click the **Data Validation** button [*Data* tab, *Data Tools* group].
3. Click the **Error Alert** tab.
4. Verify that the **Show error alert after invalid data is entered** box is selected.
5. Click the **Style** arrow and choose a warning type.
   - Use a *Stop* style if the entry should not be allowed.
   - Use a *Warning* or *Information* style if the entry is permissible.
6. Click the **Title** box and type a label for the message box.
   - The title is optional.
7. Click the **Error message** box and type the message to appear in the warning box (Figure 7-8).
   - Use capitalization and punctuation as you want it to appear on screen.
   - Check spelling and grammar carefully.
8. Click **OK**.

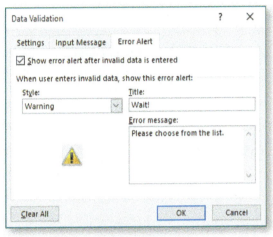

7-8 Warning style error alert

Validation Lists

Data validation includes an option that requires users to select an entry from a list. You can type entries for the list in the dialog box, separating items with commas, or you can select a cell range in the workbook.

With a validation list, the user sees a drop-down arrow when he or she selects the cell as shown in Figure 7-9. It is good practice to enter data in alphabetical or other logical order so that it is easy for the user to find his or her choice.

	A	B	C	D	E
13	Nikolai Jalowiec	Manager	Walker	26	20
14	Tammy Christine	Representative	Walker	10	41
15	Josie Daddiline	Intern	Walker	1	21
16	Tara Miller	Intern	Breezy Point	32	17
17	Robert Andrew	Representative	Walker	15	10
18	Coryn Gomez	Representative	Baudette	35	5
19	Elizabeth Gabrys	Intern	Cass Lake	43	9
20	Rita Larson	Intern	Walker	0	36
21	Michael Gentile	Representative	Baudette	38	9
22	Arthur Greenton	Intern			
23			Baudette		
24			Breezy Point		
25			Cass Lake		
			Walker		

7-9 A data validation list

▶ HOW TO: Set a Data Validation List

1. Select the cell or range for data validation.
2. Click the **Data Validation** button [*Data* tab, *Data Tools* group].
3. Click the **Settings** tab.
4. Click the **Allow** arrow and choose **List**.

5. Click the **Source** entry box and do one of the following:
   - Select the range of cells with the list.
   - Press **F3** (**FN+F3**) to open the *Paste Name* dialog box, choose the name, and click **OK** (Figure 7-10).
   - Type each entry for the list, followed by a comma.
6. Click **OK**.

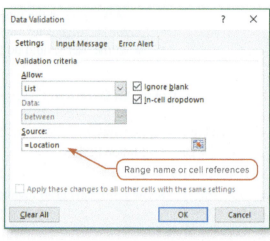

7-10 Validation settings for a list

Circle Invalid Data

Invalid data is a value or label that does not conform to validation criteria. Invalid data can occur because it is possible to copy data into a range with validation settings and because you can set validation after data is already entered.

You can highlight invalid data with the *Circle Invalid Data* command. This command places a red *ellipse* (an elongated circle) around each cell in which the data does not match the validation criteria. The *Circle Invalid Data* command highlights cells. It does not edit or correct the data.

▶ **HOW TO: Circle Invalid Data**

1. Select the cell or range with validation settings.
2. Click the **Data Validation** button [*Data* tab, *Data Tools* group].
3. Select **Circle Invalid Data**.
   - A red ellipse highlights each cell with invalid data (Figure 7-11).
4. Type or select valid data for each invalid entry.
   - The ellipse is removed after valid data is entered.
5. Click the **Data Validation** button [*Data* tab, *Data Tools* group].
6. Select **Clear Validation Circles** to remove ellipses if necessary.

Product #	Description	Department	Stock	Unit Cost	Unit Price
101	Tee shirt, blue		12	$4.00	$9.00
102	Beach towel, tan		12	$7.50	$16.88
103	Beach towel, green	Apparel	-8	$7.50	$16.88
104	Beach towel, brown	Apparel	7	$7.50	$16.88
105	Stuffed animal, fish	Gifts	4	$4.75	$10.69
106	Tee shirt, green	Apparel	8	$4.00	$9.00
107	Swim shorts, small	Apparel	10	$5.50	$12.38
108	Swim shorts, medium	Apparel	12	$5.50	$12.38
109	Yoga pants, black	Apparel	5	$12.50	$28.13
110	Yoga pants, grey	Apparel	4	$12.50	$28.13
111	Sunscreen, 8 oz	Health Aids	10	$3.45	$7.76
112	Sunscreen 12 oz	Health Aids	12	$4.75	$10.69
113	Picture frame, 6"	Gifts	8	$5.50	$12.38
114	Picture frame, 12"	Gifts	8	$6.50	$14.63
115	Magnet, PLR	Gifts	15	$3.25	$7.31
116	Magnet, Minnesota		-16	$3.25	$7.31
117	Pen, PLR		20	$1.24	$2.79
118	Pen, Minnesota	Gifts	24	$1.24	$2.79

PLR Spa Product Inventory

7-11 Invalid data is circled

PAUSE & PRACTICE: EXCEL 7-1

In this project, you save a workbook as a template, set data validation rules, circle invalid data, and remove invalidation circles. You also use input and error alert messages.

File Needed: ***ParadiseLakes-07.xlsx*** *(Student data files are available in the* Library of your SIMnet *account)*
Completed Project File Name: ***[your initials] PP E7-1Template.xltx***

1. Open the *ParadisesLakes-07* workbook from your student data files.

2. Save a workbook as a template.
   a. Click the **File** tab and choose **Save As**.
   b. Select **This PC** and click the **More Options** link to open the *Save As* dialog box.
   c. Type [your initials] PP E7-1Template in the *File name* box.
   d. Select the **Save Thumbnail** box.
   e. Click the **Save as type** arrow and choose **Excel Template**. The default folder for templates is opened.
   f. Click **Save**.

3. Create data validation settings with an operator to require a positive value.
   a. Select cells **D5:D29** on the **Inventory** sheet.
   b. Click the **Data Validation** button [*Data* tab, *Data Tools* group].
   c. Click the **Allow** arrow and choose **Whole Number**.
   d. Click the **Data** arrow and choose **greater than**.
   e. Click the **Minimum** box and type 0.
   f. Do not click **OK**.

4. Create an input message for data validation settings.
   a. Click the **Input Message** tab.
   b. Verify that the **Show input message when cell is selected** box is selected.
   c. Click the **Title** box and type Current Stock.
   d. Click the **Input message** box and type Number must be positive. including the period (Figure 7-12).
   e. Click **OK**. The input message appears because the range is selected.
   f. Select cell **E5** to remove the input message.

5. Circle and delete invalid data.
   a. Click the arrow for the **Data Validation** button [*Data* tab, *Data Tools* group].
   b. Choose **Circle Invalid Data**.
   c. Select each cell with invalid data and press **Delete**. The validation setting requires a value greater than zero, so the circles are not removed (Figure 7-13).
   d. Click the arrow for the **Data Validation** button [*Data* tab, *Data Tools* group] and choose **Clear Validation Circles**.

6. Create data validation settings with a list.
   a. Click the **Validation Lists** sheet tab and select cells **A2:A4**.
   b. Sort the cells in ascending order (A-Z).
   c. Click the **Inventory** sheet tab and select cells **C5:C29**.

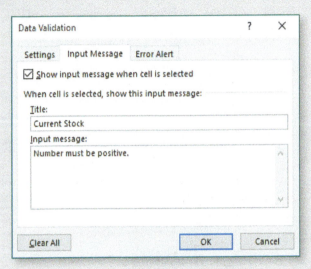

7-12 Input message for the stock number

7-13 Invalid data is circled

d. Click the **Data Validation** button [*Data* tab, *Data Tools* group].

e. Select the **Settings** tab, click the **Allow** arrow, and choose **List**.

f. Click the **Source** box and click the **Validation Lists** worksheet tab.

g. Select cells **A2:A4** and click **OK**.

7. Select cell **C5** and choose **Apparel** from the validation list. Select cell **C6** and choose **Apparel**.

8. Select cell **C20** and choose **Gifts** from the validation list.

9. For cells **C21** and **C23**, choose **Gifts**.

10. For cells **C28:C29**, choose **Health Aids**.

11. Type the list for validation settings and add an error alert.

a. Select the **Responses** sheet tab and select cells **B3:B39**.

b. Click the **Data Validation** button [*Data* tab, *Data Tools* group].

c. Click the **Allow** arrow and choose **List**.

d. Click the **Source** box.

e. Type Intern,Manager,Representative with no space after each comma (Figure 7-14).

f. Click the **Error Alert** tab.

g. Verify that the **Show error alert after invalid data is entered** box is selected.

h. Click the **Style** arrow and choose **Warning**. This style will allow an invalid entry to be made.

i. Click the **Title** box and type Wait!.

j. Click the **Error message** box and type Please choose from the list.

k. Click **OK**.

12. Select cell **B4** and choose **Intern**.

13. Select cell **B5**, type Staff, and press **Enter** to display the error alert (Figure 7-15).

14. Choose **Yes** to allow the entry.

15. Choose **Manager** in cell **B6**.

16. Press **Ctrl+Home**. Click the **Save** button on the *Quick Access* toolbar to save the template with the same name.

17. Close the workbook (Figure 7-16).

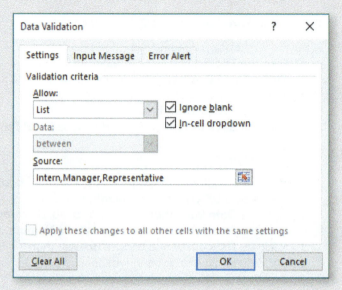

7-14 Typed validation list

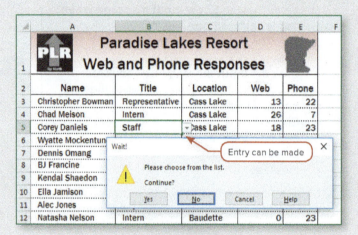

7-15 Error alert after invalid entry

| PLR | Paradise Lakes Resort | | | |
| | Web and Phone Responses | | | |
Name	Title	Location	Web	Phone
Christopher Bowman	Representative	Cass Lake	13	22
Chad Meison	Intern	Cass Lake	26	7
Corey Daniels	Staff	Cass Lake	18	23
Wyatte Mockentune	Manager	Breezy Point	25	19
Dennis Omang	Representative	Breezy Point	22	16
BJ Francine	Representative	Baudette	32	8
Kendal Shaedon	Representative	Breezy Point	5	22
Ella Jamison	Manager	Baudette	44	10
Alec Jones	Representative	Baudette	26	18
Natasha Nelson	Intern	Baudette	0	23
Nikolai Jalowiec	Manager	Walker	26	20
Tammy Christine	Representative	Walker	10	41
Josie Daddiline	Intern	Walker	1	21
Tara Miller	Intern	Breezy Point	32	17
Robert Andrew	Representative	Walker	15	10
Coryn Gomez	Representative	Baudette	35	5
Elizabeth Gabrys	Intern	Cass Lake	43	9
Rita Larson	Intern	Walker	0	36
Michael Gentile	Representative	Baudette	38	9

PLR Spa Product Inventory

Product #	Description	Department	Stock	Unit Cost	Unit Price
101	Tee shirt, blue	Apparel	12	$4.00	$9.00
102	Beach towel, tan	Apparel	12	$7.50	$16.88
103	Beach towel, green	Apparel		$7.50	$16.88
104	Beach towel, brown	Apparel	7	$7.50	$16.88
105	Stuffed animal, fish	Gifts	4	$4.75	$10.69
106	Tee shirt, green	Apparel	8	$4.00	$9.00
107	Swim shorts, small	Apparel	10	$5.50	$12.38
108	Swim shorts, medium	Apparel	12	$5.50	$12.38
109	Yoga pants, black	Apparel	5	$12.50	$28.13
110	Yoga pants, grey	Apparel	4	$12.50	$28.13
111	Sunscreen, 8 oz	Health Aids	10	$3.45	$7.76
112	Sunscreen 12 oz	Health Aids	12	$4.75	$10.69
113	Picture frame, 6"	Gifts	8	$5.50	$12.38
114	Picture frame, 12"	Gifts	6	$6.50	$14.63
115	Magnet, PLR	Gifts	15	$3.25	$7.31
116	Magnet, Minnesota	Gifts		$3.25	$7.31
117	Pen, PLR	Gifts	20	$1.24	$2.79
118	Pen, Minnesota	Gifts	24	$1.24	$2.79
119	Pen, bass boat	Gifts	12	$1.24	$2.79
120	Stuffed animal, bear	Gifts	12	$4.75	$10.69
121	Stuffed animal, raccoon	Gifts	15	$4.75	$10.69
122	Antiseptic lotion, 4 oz	Health Aids	8	$5.75	$12.94
123	Antiseptic lotion, 12 oz	Health Aids	8	$6.25	$14.06
124	Insect repellent, 8 oz	Health Aids	10	$3.50	$7.88
125	Cough syrup, 8 oz	Health Aids	6	$2.20	$4.95

7-16 Completed worksheets for PP E7-1

SLO 7.3

Using the Form button and Form Controls

Excel has commands, buttons, and tools that enable you to streamline data entry in a template so that users can quickly complete their work. Many of these tools are available from the *Developer* command tab which is not displayed on the *Ribbon* by default.

The Form Button and the Developer Tab

The *Form* button creates a screen form for data entry. The button can be displayed on the *Quick Access* toolbar or in a custom tab or group. The *Developer* tab has command groups for working with macros, controls, and add-ins, and it appears when it is toggled on in Excel *Options* (Figure 7-17).

7-17 *Form* button and *Developer* tab on the *Ribbon*

> **ANOTHER WAY**
>
> Click the arrow on the *Quick Access* toolbar and choose **More Commands** to open the *Excel Options* dialog box.

▶ HOW TO: Show the Form Button and the Developer Tab

1. Click the **Options** button [*File* tab].

2. Select **Quick Access Toolbar** in the left pane.

3. Choose **All Commands** from the drop-down list for the *Choose commands from* box.

4. Choose **Form** in the list of commands.

5. Click **Add** to add the command to the *Customize Quick Access Toolbar* list on the right (Figure 7-18).

6. Click **Customize Ribbon** in the left pane.

7. Select the **Developer** box in the *Main Tabs* group.

8. Click **OK**.

   - The *Developer* tab displays at the right end of the *Ribbon*.
   - The **Form** button is located at the right on the *Quick Access* toolbar.

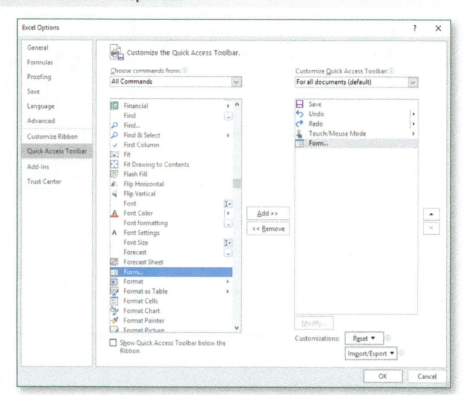

7-18 Excel *Options* dialog box to add *Form* button to *Quick Access* toolbar

Use a Data Input Form

The *Form* button creates a data input screen for list-type data. A ***data input form*** is a window or dialog box with labels and entry boxes in a vertical layout. Many users find it quicker and easier to enter data in a screen form than in a worksheet row. A data input form is a temporary view of worksheet data and is created each time you want to use it. After you complete data in one form and move to the next form, worksheet data is updated.

A data input form can display up to 32 fields or columns and shows one row (record) at a time. In the form, you can delete or add a record as well as filter the records.

▶ HOW TO: Create and Use a Data Input Form

1. Select the cell range including column headings.

2. Click the **Form** button on the *Quick Access Toolbar* (Figure 7-19).

   - A data entry form opens and displays the first record (row) in the range.
   - When there are more fields than can be displayed at one time, a scroll bar is available for viewing all fields.

3. Click **New** to open a blank form.

4. Enter data for the new record and click **New**.

   - The row is added to the list.

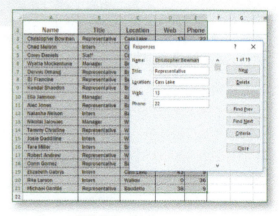

7-19 Selected range and data entry form

5. Click **Criteria** to open a blank form.

6. Click the field to be used for filtering data.

7. Type the criteria (Figure 7-20).

   - You can use wildcard characters.
   - Criteria are not case-sensitive.

8. Click *Find Next* or *Find Prev* to find a matching record.

   - The search begins at the current form.
   - The first matching record displays in the form.

9. Click **Close** to close the form.

7-20 Data entry criteria form

Form Controls

A *form control* is an object that you can use to display a choice, to run a command, or to perform an action in a worksheet. Form controls make data entry easier and can improve the appearance of your work. You use form controls when you select from a drop-down list, choose an option button, or click a check box.

Two categories, *Form Controls* and *ActiveX Controls*, are available from the **Insert Controls** button in the *Controls* group on the *Developer* tab. *ActiveX Controls* require that you write code in **VBA (Visual Basic for Applications)** a programming language for enhanced commands and features in Excel. *Form Controls* accomplish similar tasks without programming.

A selected form control has handles for sizing, a move arrow for positioning, and a context menu. The *Format Control* dialog box includes properties and settings specific to each type of control. When a form control is selected, the *Drawing Tools Format* tab is available, too.

> **MORE INFO**
>
> If a control's context menu shows *Assign Macro*, it is a *Form* control. If the context menu includes *Properties*, it is an *ActiveX* control.

Option Button Control

An *Option Button* control is a radio button that allows the user to select one choice from a set of possibilities. An option button control has a default label "Option Button N" in which "n" is a number. You edit the label to specify the option names. Option button controls are usually organized in a *Group Box* control or a rectangle shape.

▶**HOW TO:** Insert an Option Button Form Control

1. Click the **Insert Controls** button [*Developer* tab, *Controls* group].

2. Click the **Option Button (Form Control)** button in the *Form Controls* group (Figure 7-21).

   - The pointer is a thin cross or plus sign.

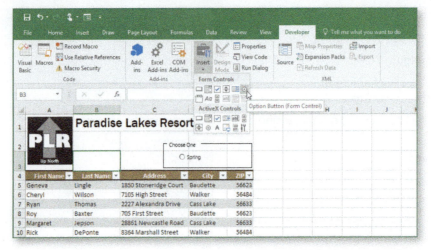

7-21 Form controls gallery

3. Click and drag the pointer to draw the control.
   - The control is selected immediately after it is created.
   - An option button control includes a default label.
   - To select a control, point to display the link select pointer and right-click.

4. Click the **Properties** button [*Developer* tab, *Controls* group].
   - The *Format Control* dialog box opens.

5. Verify that the **Control** tab is selected.

6. Select the **Unchecked** button for *Value*.
   - Options depend on the type of control.

7. Select the **3-D shading** box (Figure 7-22).

8. Click **OK**.

9. Point to the control and right-click.

10. Select **Edit Text**.
    - The insertion point displays next to the default label.

11. Delete the default label.

12. Type a new label for the option button (Figure 7-23).

13. Select a worksheet cell to deselect the control.
    - You can drag the control to the desired position on the sheet.
    - You can use *Drawing Tools* to align multiple controls.

7-22 *Format Control* dialog box

7-23 New control in worksheet

Combo Box Control

A ***Combo Box*** control creates a drop-down list from which you select one option. The options in the list are from a cell range in the workbook. You link the control to a cell which displays a value that represents the position of the choice in the range. You can display the result displayed in the combo box in a worksheet cell by using an *INDEX* command.

▶ HOW TO: Use a Combo Box Form Control with Index

1. Click the **Insert Controls** button [*Developer* tab, *Controls* group].

2. Click the **Combo Box (Form Control)** button in the *Form Controls* group.

   - The pointer is a thin cross or plus sign.

3. Click and drag the pointer to draw the control.

   - The control is selected immediately after it is created.
   - To select a control, point to display the link select pointer and right-click.

4. Right-click the control and select **Format Control**.

   - The *Format Control* dialog box opens.
   - You can also click the **Properties** button in the *Controls* group [*Developer* tab].

5. Verify that the **Control** tab is selected.

6. Click the **Input range** box and select the cells with data for the combo box drop-down list.

   - You can type a range name, but you cannot paste a range name.

7. Click the **Cell link** box.

8. Click the worksheet cell where the choice made in the combo box will display.

   - You can type a cell address.
   - The linked cell can be hidden by positioning the control over it.

9. Click the **Drop down lines** box and enter the number of lines to display in the combo box.

10. Select the **3-D shading** check box (Figure 7-24).

11. Click **OK**.

12. Select the cell for the *INDEX* function.

    - Select a cell other than the *Cell link* cell.
    - The control is deselected.

13. Start an *INDEX* function and select the **array, row_number, column_num** argument list.

14. Select the same cell range used as the input range in the combo box for the *Array* argument.

    - You can type or paste a range name.

15. Click the **Row_num** box.

16. Select the same cell used as the *Cell link* in the control.

    - You can type the cell address.

17. Click **OK** to complete the *INDEX* formula.

18. Click the combo box arrow and make a choice.

    - The number indicating the position of your choice displays in the linked cell.
    - The *INDEX* formula returns the text of the choice (Figure 7-25).

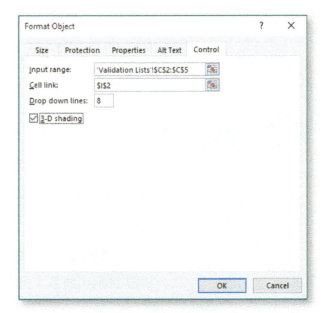

7-24 *Format Object* dialog box for a combo box

7-25 Combo box selection and *INDEX* result

Reset the Ribbon

You can hide the *Form* button or the *Developer* tab and reset the *Ribbon* to its previous settings.

> ▶ **HOW TO:** Hide the Form Button and the Developer Tab

1. Click the **File** tab and select **Options**.
2. Click **Quick Access Toolbar** in the left pane.
3. Choose **Form** in the *Customize Quick Access Toolbar* list on the right.
4. Click **Remove**.
5. Click **Customize Ribbon** in the left pane.
6. Deselect the **Developer** box in the *Main Tabs* group.
7. Click **OK**.

- The *Developer* tab is removed from the *Ribbon*.
- The *Form* button is removed from the *Quick Access* toolbar.

> **SLO 7.4**

Setting Worksheet and Workbook Protection

Worksheet protection allows you to choose which cells can be edited. When you share work with others, worksheet protection safeguards your work from accidental changes by others. You can also prohibit changes to the size and position of workbook windows as well as not permit the addition or deletion of worksheets.

Worksheet Protection

Worksheet protection is a simple way to prevent changes to your work. When the *Protect Sheet* command is enabled, you can select a cell but you cannot edit it. If you attempt to edit a cell, you see an error message box as shown in Figure 7-26. Many *Ribbon* commands are grayed out when a worksheet is protected.

7-26 Message box when cells are not editable

The *Protect Sheet* command works in conjunction with the ***Locked*** cell property which is active for all cells and objects by default. Setting worksheet protection requires you to determine which cells and objects should be unlocked for editing.

Unlock Worksheet Cells

After you have completed the template for Paradise Lakes, you do not want labels, images, product IDs, and descriptions to be changed. Data such as the number in stock and the price, however, can be edited. Cells that are editable must be unlocked before setting worksheet protection.

You can toggle the *Locked* property on and off from the *Format* button menu [*Home* tab, *Cells* group]. When a cell is locked, the icon with the *Locked* command name in the menu is outlined. The *Locked* property is also available on the *Protection* tab in the *Format Cells* dialog box.

▶ HOW TO: Unlock Cells for Editing

1. Select the cell(s) to be unlocked.
   - You can select noncontiguous cells or ranges.
2. Click the **Format** button [*Home* tab, *Cells* group].
   - The icon for *Lock Cell* is outlined to indicate that cells are locked (Figure 7-27).
   - All cells are locked by default.
3. Choose **Lock Cell**.
   - The selected cells are unlocked for editing.
4. Click the **Format** button [*Home* tab, *Cells* group].
   - The icon for *Lock Cell* is not outlined.
5. Click a cell to close the menu.

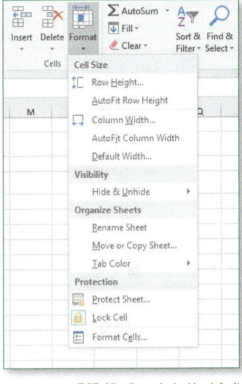

7-27 All cells are locked by default

▶ MORE INFO

The *Locked* property should be enabled for formula cells in a protected sheet so that formulas are not accidentally changed or deleted.

Protect a Worksheet

The *Locked* property setting has no effect until you add worksheet protection. The *Protect Sheet* button is in the *Changes* group on the *Review* tab. The *Protect Sheet* button becomes the *Unprotect Sheet* button when a sheet is protected. You can also protect a worksheet from the *Format* button [*Home* tab, *Cells* group] or from the *Info* command on the *File* tab.

The *Protect Sheet* dialog box has a list of editing options for locked cells, *PivotTables*, objects, hyperlinks, and more. These options include allowing cells to be selected or formatted, permitting rows and columns to be modified, and allowing *PivotTables* to be used.

As you activate worksheet protection, you can set an optional password. Worksheet protection without a password is not very secure, because you only need know how to unprotect the sheet.

▶ HOW TO: Protect a Worksheet

1. Unlock cells as needed.
2. Click the **Protect Sheet** button [*Review* tab, *Changes* group].
   - The *Protect Sheet* dialog box opens.
3. Type a password, as desired.
   - You see placeholders as you type a password.

4. Select the box for each editing capability that should be available (Figure 7-28).

5. Click **OK**.

   - The *Confirm Password* dialog box opens if you set a password.

6. Retype the password.

   - Passwords are case sensitive.

7. Click **OK**.

   - The *Protect Sheet* button displays *Unprotect Sheet*.

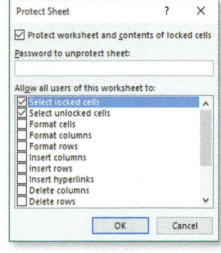

7-28 *Protect Sheet* dialog box

MORE INFO

You cannot recover a lost or forgotten password without the use of a password recovery program.

Unprotect a Worksheet

Sheet protection must be removed to edit a protected sheet. Click the **Unprotect Sheet** button [*Review* tab, *Changes* group]. If a password was used, enter the password in the *Unprotect Sheet* dialog box and click **OK**.

▶ **HOW TO:** Unprotect a Worksheet

1. Click the **Unprotect Sheet** button [*Review* tab, *Changes* group].

   - Protection is removed if no password exists.
   - The *Unprotect Sheet* dialog box opens if a password exists.

2. Type the password.

3. Click **OK**.

Protect Workbook Structure

Workbook structure includes the number and arrangement of sheet tabs. By setting this protection, you can prohibit others from deleting or inserting a sheet, from moving a tab, or from unhiding a worksheet. When workbook protection is active, unavailable commands are grayed out or cannot be selected.

You can protect workbook structure with or without a password. You can remove workbook structure protection by clicking the **Protect Workbook** button [*File* tab].

ANOTHER WAY

You can set and remove workbook protection by clicking the *Protect Workbook* button [*Review* tab, *Changes* group].

▶HOW TO: Protect Workbook Structure

1. Arrange worksheet tabs and hide sheets as desired.
2. Click the **Protect Workbook** button [*Review* tab, *Changes* group].
   - The *Protect Structure and Windows* dialog box opens.
   - The *Windows* setting is disabled by default.
3. Verify that the **Structure** box is selected (Figure 7-29).
4. Type a password in the *Password* box.
   - A password is optional.
   - If you include a password, click **OK**, and retype it in the *Confirm Password* dialog box.
5. Click **OK** in the *Protect Structure and Windows* dialog box.
   - The **Protect Workbook** button [*Review* tab, *Changes* group] is highlighted.
6. Click the **File** tab.
   - The *Info* command describes the current protection setting.
7. Click the **Protect Workbook** button.
8. Select **Protect Workbook Structure**.
   - Enter the password if needed and click **OK**.
   - The protection is removed.

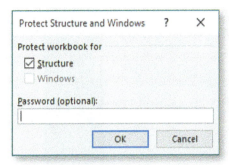

7-29 *Protect Structure and Windows* dialog box

PAUSE & PRACTICE: EXCEL 7-2

In this project, you create a workbook from a template and use a data input form. You add a combo box control, unlock cells, and set worksheet protection.

File Needed: *[your initials] PP E7-1Template.xltx*
Completed Project File Name: *[your initials] PP E7-2.xlsx*

1. Create a workbook from a template.
   a. Click the **File** tab and select **New**.
   b. Click **PERSONAL** (Figure 7-30).
   c. Select *[your initials] PP E7-1Template* completed in *Pause & Practice 7-1* to create a workbook based on the template. (If your template is not available in the *Personal* category, open it from your usual location for saving files.)
   d. Save the workbook as an Excel workbook named [your initials] PP E7-2 in your usual location.

2. Display the *Form* button and the *Developer* tab.
   a. Click the **Customize Quick Access Toolbar** arrow at the right edge of the *Quick Access* toolbar.
   b. Choose **More Commands** to open the *Excel Options* dialog box.
   c. Select **All Commands** in the *Choose commands from* list.
   d. Scroll to find **Form. . .** in the list and select it.
   e. Click **Add**.
   f. Click **Customize Ribbon** in the left pane.

7-30 User-created templates are in the *PERSONAL* category

   g. Select the **Developer** box in the *Main Tabs* group.

   h. Click **OK**.

3. Verify that the **Responses** sheet is selected.

4. Create and use a data input form.

   a. Select cells **A2:E21**.

   b. Click the **Form** button on the *Quick Access* toolbar. The form displays the first of 19 records.

   c. Click **Find Next** in the data form. The second record (row) displays in the form.

   d. Click **Criteria** in the form to open a blank form.

   e. Type tam* in the *Name* box to find the record for Tammy Christine.

   f. Click **Find Next**. The record displays in the form.

   g. Click **Delete** and select **OK**. The record is deleted from the worksheet.

   h. Click **New** in the data form to display a blank form.

   i. Type John Jones in the *Name* box and press **Tab**. (If you accidentally press **Enter**, the form is completed. Click **Criteria**, type john*, and click **Find Next** to find the incomplete form.)

   j. Type Intern in the *Title* box and press **Tab**. Data validation settings do not function in a simple data form.

   k. Type Walker in the *Location* box and press **Tab**.

   l. Type 12 in the *Web* box and press **Tab**.

   m. Type 10 in the *Phone* box and press **Enter**. A new blank form opens, and data is added as the last row (Figure 7-31).

   n. Click **Close** to close the data form and press **Ctrl+Home**.

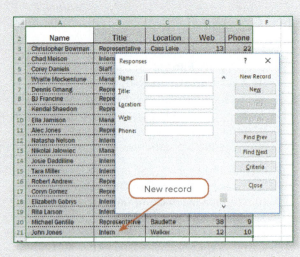

7-31 One record deleted and one added in the data form

5. Insert a combo box form control.
   a. Click the **Name** box arrow and choose **Location**. This range includes the four location names for Paradise Lakes Resort.
   b. Click the **Data Entry** worksheet tab.
   c. Click the **Insert Controls** button [*Developer* tab, *Controls* group].
   d. Click the **Combo Box (Form Control)** button.
   e. Draw a control directly over and the same width and height as cells **G2:H2** (Figure 7-32).
   f. Right-click any border of the control and choose **Format Control**. If the command is not listed, click a cell to deselect the control and right-click the control again.
   g. Type location in the *Input range* box on the *Control* tab.
   h. Click the **Cell link** box and select cell **I2**. The selection made in the combo box will display in this cell as a value to mark the relative position of the choice in the range.
   i. Select the **3-D shading** box (Figure 7-33).

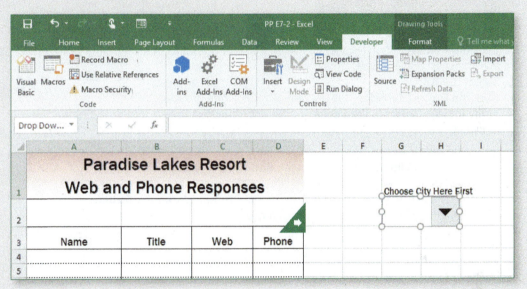

7-32 **Combo box drawn on sheet**

   j. Click **OK**. Click cell **H3** to deselect the combo box control.
   k. Click the **combo box** arrow and choose **Baudette**. The label displays in the control and **1** displays in the linked cell (I2), because Baudette is the first item in the input range.

6. Use *INDEX* to display the city name from the combo box.
   a. Select cell **A2**.
   b. Click the **Lookup & Reference** button [*Formulas* tab, *Function Library* group].
   c. Choose **Index** and choose the **array, row_num, column_num** argument group.

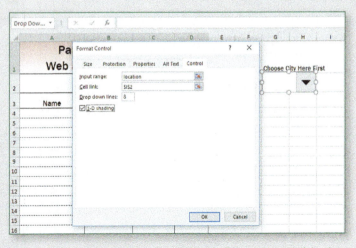

7-33 **Combo box defined in *Format Control* dialog box**

d. Press **F3** (**FN+F3**) and select **Location** for the *Array* argument.

e. Click the **Row_num** box, select cell **I2**, and click **OK**. The city name represented by the value in cell I2 displays in cell A2 and in the combo box.

f. Right-click the combo box control to display its context menu.

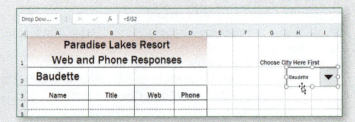

7-34 Combo box covers linked cell

g. Point to a border of the control and left-click to hide the menu.

h. With the four-pointed move arrow, drag the control to cells **H2:I2** so that it covers the linked cell (Figure 7-34).

i. Deselect the control object.

j. Click the combo box arrow and choose **Cass Lake**.

7. Unlock cells and protect a sheet.
   a. Click the **Inventory** sheet tab.
   b. Select cells **C5:D29**.
   c. Click the **Format** button [*Home* tab, *Cells* group] and select **Lock Cell**. Data in columns C and D are unlocked and editable.
   d. Select cell **A5**.
   e. Click the **Protect Sheet** button [*Review* tab, *Changes* group].
   f. Verify that the **Select locked cells** and **Select unlocked cells** boxes are selected.
   g. Click **OK**.

8. Protect workbook structure.
   a. Right-click the **Validation Lists** sheet tab and choose **Hide**.
   b. Click the **File** tab and choose **Info**.
   c. Click the **Protect Workbook** button and select **Protect Workbook Structure**.
   d. Click **OK** to protect the structure without a password.

9. Save and close the workbook (Figure 7-35).

10. Move the template from the default folder and hide the **Form** button and the *Developer* tab.
    a. Click the **File** tab and choose **Open**.
    b. Click **Browse**.

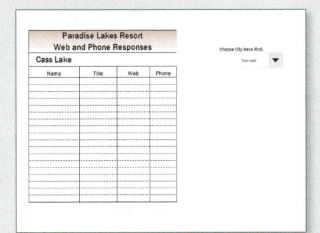

	Name	Title	Location	Web	Phone
	Christopher Bowman	Representative	Cass Lake	13	22
	Chad Melson	Intern	Cass Lake	26	7
	Corey Daniels	Staff	Cass Lake	18	23
	Wyatte Mockentune	Manager	Breezy Point	25	19
	Dennis Omang	Representative	Breezy Point	22	16
	BJ Francine	Representative	Baudette	32	8
	Kendal Shaedon	Representative	Breezy Point	5	22
	Ella Jamison	Manager	Baudette	44	10
	Alec Jones	Representative	Baudette	26	18
	Natasha Nelson	Intern	Baudette	0	23
	Nikolai Jalowiec	Manager	Walker	26	20
	Josie Daddiline	Intern	Walker	1	21
	Tara Miller	Intern	Breezy Point	32	17
	Robert Andrew	Representative	Walker	15	10
	Coryn Gomez	Representative	Baudette	35	5
	Elizabeth Gabrys	Intern	Cass Lake	43	9
	Rita Larson	Intern	Walker	0	36
	Michael Gentile	Representative	Baudette	38	9
	John Jones	Intern	Walker	12	10

Paradise Lakes Resort
Web and Phone Responses

7-35 Completed worksheets for PP E7-2

c. Expand the *Quick access* list in the left pane and select **Documents**.
d. Double-click **Custom Office Templates** in the pane on the right.
e. Right-click *[your initials] PP E7-1Template* and choose **Cut**.
f. Navigate to and open your folder for saving files.
g. Right-click an unused area of the *Open* dialog box and choose **Paste**.
h. Click **Cancel** to close the dialog box.
i. Click the **File** tab and choose **Options**.
j. Click **Customize Ribbon** in the left pane and deselect the **Developer** box in the *Main Tabs* group.
k. Click **Quick Access Toolbar** in the left pane.
l. Click **Form . . .** on the right and click **Remove**.
m. Click **OK**.

Sharing and Merging Workbooks

A *shared workbook* is one that multiple people edit, either simultaneously or at different times. When a shared workbook is maintained on a network and all users have access to it, each person can work on it as needed. In other cases, a shared workbook is copied so that each user has his or her own copy. After all members of the work group have completed their work, the copies are combined into a merged workbook.

Paradise Lakes Resort can use a shared workbook for inventory or customer management. As representatives work from various locations, they record their own data, and all copies are merged to create a final report with the latest data.

Not all commands are available in a shared workbook such as deleting sheets, merging cells, inserting or editing charts, setting conditional formatting or data validation, setting worksheet protection, and using passwords. Most of these tasks, however, can be completed before the workbook is shared.

Share a Workbook

When a workbook is shared, any user who has access permission can edit it. Most shared workbooks are stored on a network so that editing is live. When that is not possible, each person in the work group simply makes a copy of the workbook.

One person shares the workbook and is considered the "owner." When a workbook is shared, the word *[Shared]* appears after the file name in the title bar. As you edit a shared workbook, the user name of the computer identifies each change.

The *Share Workbook* dialog box has two tabs, *Editing* and *Advanced*. On the *Editing* tab, you indicate that the workbook is to be shared (Figure 7-36). The *Advanced* tab includes settings that determine how changes are tracked. You can set the number of days that edits are kept, when edits are saved, and what happens if two users make conflicting edits at

7-36 *Editing* tab in the *Share Workbook* dialog box

the same time. A shared workbook maintains a *change history*, a record of each edit. This history includes the name of the user, the date, and a brief description of the change. When multiple copies of a shared workbook are combined, the change history helps you decide which changes should be accepted for the final report.

 HOW TO: Share a Workbook

1. Click the **Share Workbook** button [*Review* tab, *Changes* group].

2. Select the **Allow changes by more than one user at the same time** box on the *Editing* tab.

   - The user name is shown as the person who has the workbook open.

3. Click the **Advanced** tab (Figure 7-37).

4. Set the number of days for keeping the change history in the *Track changes* group.

   - You can also indicate that the change history not be kept.

5. Choose how often edits are saved in the *Update changes* group.

   - You can save edits only when the file is saved.
   - If you set an automatic save at a specific time interval, you can further manage changes.

6. Choose how to handle conflicts in the *Conflicting changes between users* group.

   - You can review each conflicting edit to accept or reject it.
   - You can keep only those edits being saved by you.
   - The *Include in personal view* group enables each user to save print and filter choices for the workbook.

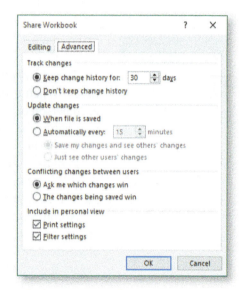

7-37 *Advanced* tab in the *Share Workbook* dialog box

7. Click **OK**.

   - The message box notes that the workbook will be saved, using the same file name.

8. Click **OK**.

   - The file name in the title bar displays **[Shared]**.
   - If a shared workbook has features that are not editable, a pop-up window may alert you to that information.

Protect a Shared Workbook

When you protect a shared workbook, no user can delete the change history. If the number of days set in the *Advanced* tab of the *Share Workbook* window has been reached and you have not added this protection, the change history is deleted and you will not be able to combine individual copies of the workbook into a final report.

The *Protect Shared Workbook* button is on the *Review* tab in the *Changes* group. It is a toggle that shows *Unprotect Shared Workbook* when protection is active.

▶HOW TO: Protect a Shared Workbook

1. Click the **Protect Shared Workbook** button [*Review* tab, *Changes* group].

   - The *Protect Shared Workbook* dialog box opens.

2. Select the **Sharing with track changes** box (Figure 7-38).

   - You can encrypt a workbook with a password before sharing it.

3. Click **OK**.

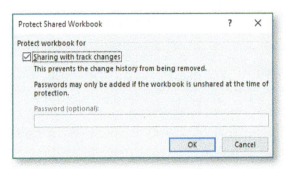

7-38 *Protect Shared Workbook* **dialog box**

Insert Comments

A ***comment*** is a pop-up text box attached to a cell (Figure 7-39). A default comment is automatically inserted in a shared workbook for each edit. You can insert your own comments, too, for clarification or discussion. Comments are useful when you or a member of your team wants to add an explanation or ask a question.

You insert comments from the *Review* tab or from a cell's context menu. After you add a comment to a cell, a small red triangle (called an ***indicator***) appears in the upper-right corner of the cell. To view the comment, hover the pointer over a cell with an indicator.

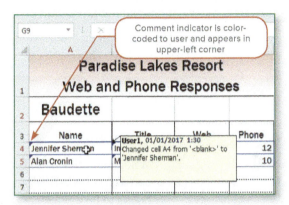

7-39 **A comment is attached for each edit in a shared workbook**

> ▶ **ANOTHER WAY**
>
> Display all comments in a sheet by clicking the *Show All Comments* button on the *Review* tab.

Open the Excel *Options* and select the **Advanced** tab. Scroll to the *Display* group and set whether comments display or if only the indicator displays in the cell. You can also display or hide comments from the *Review* tab.

> ▶ **MORE INFO**
>
> Comments do not print by default. Choose the option to print them on the *Sheet* tab in the *Page Setup* dialog box.

After a comment is created, you can edit or delete it by selecting the cell and the desired command on the *Review* tab. You can also execute comment-related commands by right-clicking the comment cell and choosing from the context menu.

▶ **HOW TO:** Insert a Comment

1. Select the cell for the comment.
2. Click the **New Comment** button [*Review* tab, *Comments* group].
   - A comment box opens and displays the user name.
   - You can delete or replace the user name.
3. Type the text of the comment (Figure 7-40).
4. Click any cell away from the comment cell.
5. Click the **Show All Comments** button [*Review* tab, *Comments* group] to toggle on/off the display of all comments in the worksheet.
   - A small red triangle displays in the upper-right corner of the cell with the comment.
6. View the comment by hovering the pointer over the cell.

7-40 Comment text for a user-defined comment

Compare and Merge Workbooks

When multiple copies of a shared workbook exist, the copies are combined using the *Compare and Merge Workbooks* command to create a final report. Here are the requirements for workbooks to be merged:

- The original shared workbook must have the change history active.
- Each copy must have been made from the original shared workbook.
- Each copy must have a different file name and cannot have a password.

Customize the *Quick Access* toolbar to add the *Compare and Merge Workbooks* button or add the button to a custom group on the *Ribbon*.

▶ **HOW TO:** Compare and Merge Workbooks

1. Click the **File** tab and choose **Options**.
2. Click **Quick Access Toolbar** in the left pane.
3. Choose **All Commands** from the *Choose commands from* list.
4. Select **Compare and Merge Workbooks** from the list.
5. Click **Add** to add the command to the *Customize Quick Access Toolbar* list.
6. Click **OK**.
   - The **Compare and Merge Workbooks** button appears on the right of the *Quick Access* toolbar (Figure 7-41).
7. Open the original shared workbook.
8. Click the **Compare and Merge Workbooks** button.
9. Click **OK** to save the workbook.
   - The *Select Files to Merge into Current Workbook* dialog box opens.

7-41 *Compare and Merge Workbooks* button on the *Quick Access* toolbar

10. Navigate to the folder with the first file to be merged and select the file name (Figure 7-42).

    • You can select multiple files from the same folder using the **Ctrl** key.

11. Click **OK**.

    • If a workbook has no changes, you see a notification message box.

12. Click the **File** tab and choose **Options**.

13. Click **Quick Access Toolbar** in the left pane.

14. Choose **Compare and Merge Workbooks** on the right.

15. Click **Remove** and then click **OK**.

7-42 *Select Files to Merge into Current Workbook* **dialog box**

Highlight Changes

After a workbook has been shared or merged, you can track changes to accept or reject edits. Each user's edits are highlighted by colored cell borders and triangles in the upper left corners. A comment box displays for each change and identifies the user name and the edit. To see the comment, click a highlighted cell.

In the *Highlight Changes* dialog box, you specify which changes should be highlighted. The *When* setting provides options that include seeing all edits or edits made since a particular date. The *Who* option can be set to show changes by everyone including you, by everyone else, or by a specific user. The *Where* setting is used to select a range of cells for review rather than the entire worksheet.

You can choose to see the changes on screen or in a printed change history sheet. The history sheet is a generated sheet that is automatically deleted when the workbook is saved.

▶ **HOW TO:** Highlight Changes in a Shared Workbook

1. Click the **Track Changes** button [*Review* tab, *Changes* group].

2. Choose **Highlight Changes** (Figure 7-43).

    • The *Highlight Changes* dialog box opens.
    • Verify that the **Track changes while editing** box is selected.

3. Verify that the **When** box is selected.

    • You can use *When*, *Who*, and *Where* or just one of these categories.

4. Click the **When** arrow and select an option.

    • *Not yet reviewed* shows all edits that you have not seen.

5. Select the **Who** box and click its arrow.

    • Choose *Everyone* to review edits by all users.
    • Choose a user name to review only those edits.

6. Select the **Where** box to limit highlighted edits to a cell range.

    • Select the range in the worksheet or type the range address.

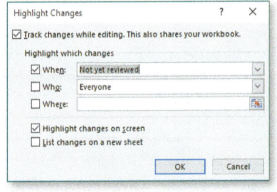

7-43 *Highlight Changes* **dialog box**

7. Verify that the **Highlight changes on screen** box is selected.

   - You can print the change history by selecting the *List changes on a new sheet* box.

8. Click **OK**.

   - If there are no edits, click **OK** to close the message box.

9. Hover at a cell with a revision triangle to see a description of the edit.

Accept or Reject Changes

The *Accept or Reject Changes* command opens a dialog box for each change, and you choose to accept or reject the edit. If you reject a change, the data is reset to the original content. When there have been multiple edits to the same cell, the *Accept or Reject Changes* dialog box lists each change so that you can select one to accept or keep the original value.

▶ **HOW TO:** Accept or Reject Changes in a Shared Workbook

1. Click the **Track Changes** button [*Review* tab, *Changes* group].

2. Choose **Accept/Reject Changes**.

   - If the workbook has not yet been saved, you must save it.
   - The *Select Changes to Accept or Reject* dialog box is similar to the *Highlight Changes* dialog box.

3. Click the **When** arrow and choose **Not yet reviewed**.

4. Click **OK**.

   - The first change is detailed in the *Accept or Reject Changes* dialog box (Figure 7-44).
   - If there are multiple edits for the cell, the changes are listed in the dialog box.

5. Click **Accept** to accept the edit and move to the next edit.

   - Click **Accept All** to accept all changes in the workbook without further review.

6. Click **Reject** to reject the edit and move to the next edit.

   - Click **Reject All** to reject all changes without further review.
   - The dialog box closes after all edits have been accepted or rejected.

7. Save the workbook.

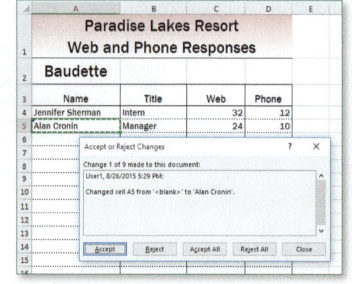

7-44 Each edit is shown in the *Accept or Reject Changes* dialog box

---

SLO 7.6 ## Checking a Workbook for Distribution Issues

Before distributing a workbook to clients or coworkers, you can ensure that the workbook does not include properties that should not be shared and that the workbook is compatible with all Excel versions. There is even a command to gauge how much of your work is accessible for persons with visual impairment.

Inspect a Workbook

The **Inspect Document** command looks for metadata and personal information in a workbook. **Metadata** are embedded file properties such as user name and date at the time of creation, the original file location, and user comments. Some metadata can be removed. For example, if you insert comments for your team members while working on a shared workbook, you can remove those comments before a customer sees the workbook. The **Document Inspector** is the dialog box that lists properties and data that can be removed.

▶ **HOW TO:** Inspect a Workbook

1. Click the **Check for Issues** button [*File* tab].
2. Choose **Inspect Document**.
3. Click **Yes** to save the workbook.
   - The *Document Inspector* lists categories of content that can be searched (Figure 7-45).
   - All categories are selected by default.
   - Deselect the box for any category that should not be searched.
4. Click **Inspect**.
   - The *Document Inspector* identifies what is included in the workbook.
   - Not all metadata can be removed.
5. Click **Remove All** for each category of content to be cleared (Figure 7-46).
   - You can close the dialog box to review content that needs further investigation.
   - You can run the *Document Inspector* again when needed.
6. Click **Close**.

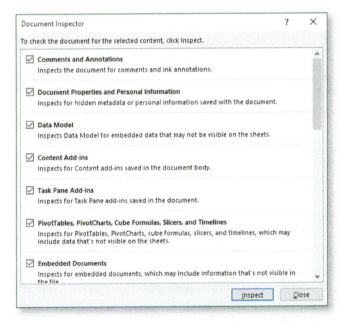

7-45 *Document Inspector* dialog box

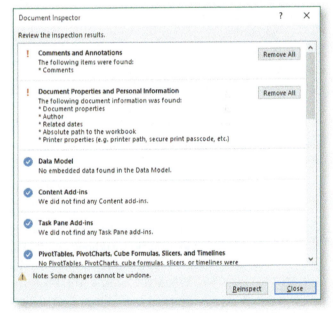

7-46 *Document Inspector* dialog box after inspection

After you run the *Document Inspector*, a workbook property is assigned to automatically remove that metadata each time you save the file. This property can interfere with commands such as sharing a workbook. You can disable the property by clicking *Allow this information to be saved in your file* in the *Check for Issues* group in *Backstage* view.

Check Compatibility

The **Check Compatibility** command opens the *Compatibility Checker* which identifies commands, features, and objects that are not supported in earlier versions of Excel. For example, early versions of Excel did not have *SmartArt* graphics. Several Excel 2016 functions do not work in earlier versions of Excel, and select formatting features are not compatible.

The *Compatibility Checker* gives you an opportunity to edit incompatible data or objects before you save the workbook in a different file format. A few issues are significant but most are minor. When you save a workbook in Excel 97-2003 format, the *Compatibility Checker* automatically runs to alert you to potential issues. You can run the command, however, for any workbook at any time.

▶ **HOW TO:** Check Compatibility

1. Click the **Check for Issues** button [*File* tab].
2. Choose **Check Compatibility**.
   - The *Compatibility Checker* describes each unsupported feature (Figure 7-47).
   - Click **Select versions to show** to choose a particular Excel version.
   - The dialog box can be sized or scrolled to view all issues.
3. Click **Copy to New Sheet** to create a sheet that details the issues.
   - A new sheet named **Compatibility Report** displays and provides documentation.
   - This command is unavailable in a shared workbook.
4. If you do not copy the issues to a new sheet, click **OK**.
   - The features are unchanged and you can save the workbook in the desired format.
   - Run the *Compatibility Checker* again when needed.

7-47 The *Compatibility Checker* locates unsupported features

Define a Trusted Location

Workbooks with data from a questionable source open in **Protected View** so that you can confirm that you trust the document and its source. Workbooks from the Web open in *Protected View* as do workbooks with macros and *ActiveX* controls.

A **Trusted Location** is a folder that is identified as one that stores workbooks that are safe. When you open a workbook from a trusted location, it does not open in *Protected View* and you can avoid the protected view message. Trusted locations are identified in the *Trust Center* in the Excel *Options* dialog box.

▶ **HOW TO:** Define a Trusted Location

1. Choose the **Options** command [*File* tab].
2. Choose **Trust Center** in the left pane.
   - The initial dialog box explains Microsoft security features.

3. Click **Trust Center Settings**.
    - The left pane lists security categories.
4. Select **Trusted Locations** in the left pane.
    - Trusted folders for your computer are listed.
5. Click **Add new location**.
6. Click **Browse** (Figure 7-48).
7. Locate the folder to be trusted, select its name, and click **OK**.
    - Type the path to the folder if you prefer.
8. Select the **Subfolders of this location are also trusted** box.
9. Click the **Description** box.
    - Type an optional description for the folder (Figure 7-49).
10. Click **OK** to add the folder to the list of trusted locations.
11. Click **OK** to close the **Trust Center**.
12. Click **OK** to close the Excel *Options* dialog box.

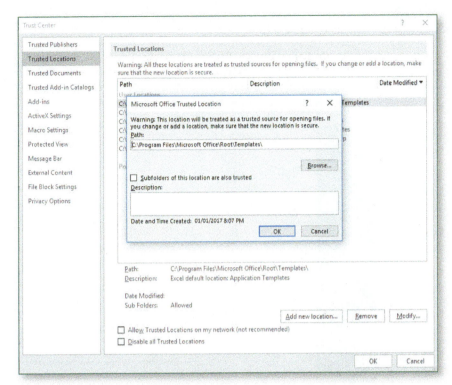

7-48 *Trust Center* options

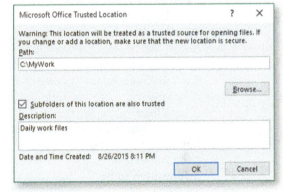

7-49 Trusted folder description

In this project, you inspect a workbook, check it for compatibility, and share it. You make edits as different users and insert comments. Finally, you merge the workbooks to accept or reject the changes.

File Needed: *[your initials] PP E7-2.xlsx*
Completed Project File Names: *[your initials] PP E7-3User1.xlsx*, *[your initials] PP E7-3User2.xlsx*, and *[your initials] PP E7-3Merged.xlsx*

1. Open the *[your initials] PP E7-2* workbook completed in *Pause & Practice 7-2* and save it as [your initials] PP E7-3User1.

2. Inspect the workbook and remove sheet and structure protection.
   a. Click the **Check for Issues** button [*File* tab, *Info* group] and choose **Inspect Document**. The message box notes that you cannot inspect a workbook that has protected sheets (Figure 7-50).
   b. Click **OK** in the message box.

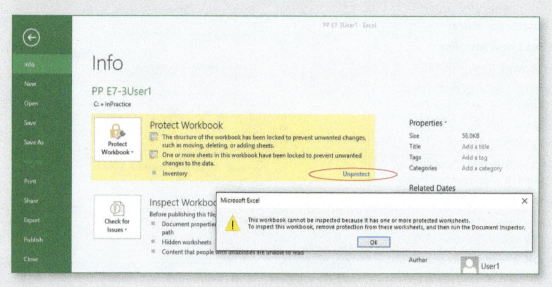

7-50 Workbook with sheet protection cannot be inspected

   c. Click **Unprotect** in the *Protect Workbook* group.
   d. Click the **Check for Issues** button and choose **Inspect Document**.
   e. Select **Yes** to save the workbook without sheet protection.
   f. Click **Inspect**. Properties and personal information that can be removed are noted.
   g. Click **Remove All** for *Document Properties and Personal Information*.
   h. Scroll the list to see the *Hidden Worksheets* tag but do not remove the sheets.
   i. Click **Close**.
   j. Click the **File** tab. Note in the *Inspect Workbook* group that personal information will be removed each time this workbook is saved (Figure 7-51).
   k. Click **Allow this information to be saved in your file**. This property must be disabled in order to share the workbook.
   l. Click the **Protect Workbook** button and select **Protect Workbook Structure**.

3. Check compatibility.
   a. Click the **Check for Issues** button [*File* tab, *Info* group] and choose **Check Compatibility**.

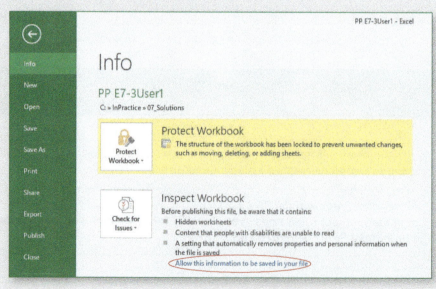

7-51 Setting changed after removing metadata

b. Review the issues in the *Compatibility Checker* dialog box.

c. Click **Copy to New Sheet**. The report displays on its own sheet (Figure 7-52).

4. Share the workbook.

   a. Select the **Data Entry** sheet tab.

   b. Click the **Share Workbook** button [*Review* tab, *Changes* category]. You cannot share a workbook that has an Excel table.

   c. Click **OK** in the message box.

   d. Click the **Guests** worksheet tab and click any cell in the table.

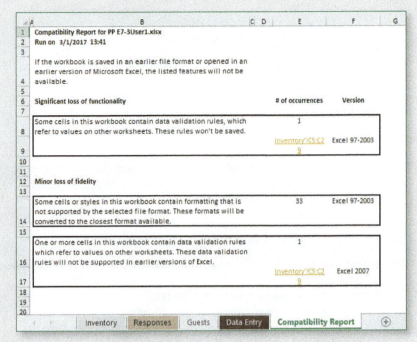

7-52 Documentation for unsupported commands and features

   e. Click the **Convert to Range** button [*Table Tools Design* tab, *Tools* group].

   f. Click **Yes** to convert the table to a range.

   g. Select the **Data Entry** tab and click the **Share Workbook** button [*Review* tab, *Changes* category].

   h. Select the **Allow changes by more than one user at the same time** box.

   i. Click the **Advanced** tab.

   j. Set the *Keep change history for* option to **25** days.

   k. Click **OK** to close the *Share Workbook* dialog box.

   l. Click **OK** to resave the shared workbook. Look for *[Shared]* at the end of the file name in the title bar.

   m. Select cell **A4**.

5. Make a copy of the shared workbook in the same folder.

   a. Click the **File** tab and choose **Save As**.

   b. Save the workbook as [your initials] PP E7-3User2 in your usual folder.

6. Click the combo box control arrow and choose **Baudette**.

7. Select cell **A4**. Enter the data shown here in row 4. Use the validation list to select the title.

   Jennifer Sherman   Intern 32   12

8. Insert a comment.

   a. Select cell **F4**.

   b. Click the **New Comment** button [*Review* tab, *Comments* group].

   c. Select the default user named, type User 2:, and press **Enter**.

   d. Type Jennifer spent two days in Baudette. (Figure 7-53).

   e. Select cell **F3**. If the comment still displays, click the **Show All Comments** button [*Review* tab, *Comments* group] to hide it. It appears when you hover over the cell.

7-53 New comments inserted for cell F4

9. Save the workbook in your usual location and close it.

10. Open **[your initials] PP E7-3User1.xlsx**.

11. Click the combo box control arrow and choose **Walker**.

12. Click cell **A5** and type the following data:

    Alan Cronin   Manager   24   10

13. Insert a comment.
    a. Select cell **F5**.
    b. Click the **New Comment** button [*Review* tab, *Comments* group].
    c. Select the default user named, type User 1:, and press **Enter**.
    d. Type Alan spent time at all locations.
    e. Select cell **F3**.

14. Save the workbook. This is the original shared workbook.

15. Add the *Compare and Merge Workbooks* command to the *Quick Access* toolbar.
    a. Select cell **A1**.
    b. Select the **Options** command [*File* tab].
    c. Click **Quick Access Toolbar** in the left pane.
    d. Choose **All Commands** from the *Choose commands from* list.
    e. Select **Compare and Merge Workbooks** and click **Add**.
    f. Click **OK**.

16. Merge copies of the shared workbook.
    a. Click the **Compare and Merge Workbooks** button on the *Quick Access* toolbar. If asked, click **OK** to save the workbook before merging.
    b. Navigate to the folder with **[your initials] PP E7-3User2** in the *Select Files to Merge Into Current Workbook* dialog box.
    c. Click the **[your initials] PP E7-3User2** file name and click **OK**. The copied workbook is merged into the workbook on screen. Cells with typed comments are indicated by a red triangle in the upper-right corner of the cell.
    d. Point to cell **F4** and then to cell **F5** to see the comments.

17. Highlight changes.
    a. Click the **Track Changes** button [*Review* tab, *Changes* group].
    b. Choose **Highlight Changes**.
    c. Choose **Not yet reviewed** for the *When* command.
    d. Click **OK**. Cells with changes display a triangle in the upper-left corner.
    e. Point to cell **D5** to see the generated comment (Figure 7-54).

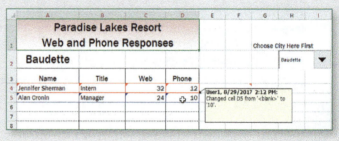

7-54 All cells with changes include a triangle

18. Accept or reject changes.
    a. Click the **Track Changes** button [*Review* tab, *Changes* group].
    b. Choose **Accept/Reject Changes**.
    c. Choose **Not yet reviewed** for the *When* box.
    d. Click **OK**. The first change was the combo box selection; the linked cell for this control is cell **I2** (Figure 7-55).

7-55 First edit is identified

e. Click **3 (Original Value)** and click **Accept**. The value in cell **A2** is reset to Cass Lake, but the control is not reset until you complete the current task. The next change is the addition of a person's name in cell **A5**.

f. Click **Accept All** to accept all edits. The dialog box closes, and the combo box control is updated.

19. Save the merged workbook as *[your initials] PP E7-3Merged* and close it (Figure 7-56).

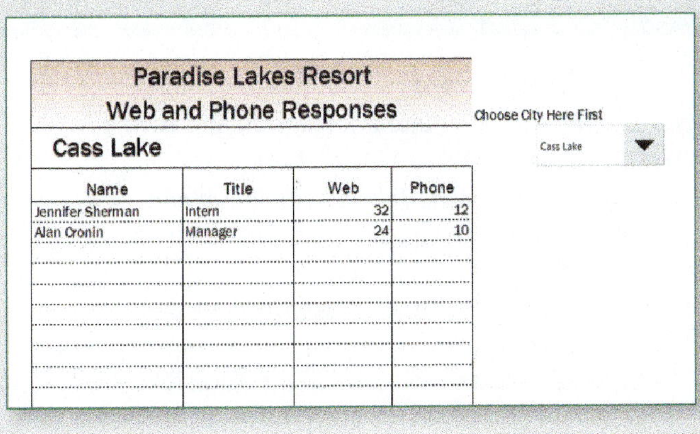

7-56 Completed worksheet for PP E7-3Merged

20. Remove the *Compare and Merge Workbooks* button from the *Quick Access* toolbar.
    a. Click the **Options** command [*File* tab].
    b. Click **Quick Access Toolbar** in the left pane.
    c. Click **Compare and Merge Workbooks** in the list on the right.
    d. Click **Remove** and click **OK**.

Chapter Summary

7.1 Use a template to create a workbook and save a workbook as a template (p. E7-435).

- A **template** is a model workbook that can include data, formulas, formatting, controls, and more.
- Templates are available from the *New* pane in *Backstage* view.
- Excel templates are saved in a default folder which can be changed in the *Save* pane, Excel *Options*.
- Templates saved in the default folder are listed in the *Personal* category in the *Backstage* view.
- Template workbooks have an .xltx file name extension.
- Templates are often saved with a thumbnail image, set in the *Save As* dialog box.
- When you create a workbook from a template, a new workbook opens as a copy of the template.

7.2 Set data validation, input messages, and error alerts (p. E7-437).

- **Data validation** is the process of matching data with specifications as the data is entered.
- **Validation settings** are rules applied to data as it is entered.
- Data validation settings can be statements with relational operators, choices made from lists, limits set on dates or times, or a formula.
- An **input message** is a comment box that appears as soon as a cell is selected, informing the user about the validation rule.
- An **error alert** is a comment box that appears when invalid data is entered in a cell, and the type of alert determines whether the entry is allowed.
- If data validation is set after data has been entered, you can use the *Circle Invalid Data* command to identify those cells.

7.3 Use the *Form* button and *Form Controls* (p. E7-443).

- The *Form* button creates a data entry form in a vertical arrangement for data.
- You can enter, delete, and filter data in a data form.
- The *Form* button must be added to the *Quick Access* toolbar or to a custom group on the *Ribbon*.

- A **form control** is an object or shape used to make a selection or to run a command in a worksheet.
- Form controls include option buttons, combo boxes, check boxes, and list boxes.
- The *Developer* tab on the *Ribbon* includes the *Controls* group.
- The *Developer* tab can be shown or hidden by opening the Excel *Options* dialog box and selecting the *Customize Ribbon* pane.

7.4 Set worksheet and workbook protection to manage editing (p. E7-448).

- The *Protect Sheet* command prohibits changes to cells unless they have been unlocked.
- The **Locked** property is enabled for all cells but has no effect unless the *Protect Sheet* command is applied.
- Cells that are editable must be unlocked before the worksheet is protected.
- **Worksheet protection** can be set with or without a password.
- The *Protect Workbook Structure* command allows a user to edit data but not move, copy, delete, insert, hide, or unhide sheets.

7.5 Share a workbook, track changes, and compare and merge workbooks (p. E7-455).

- A **shared workbook** is a workbook that is edited by multiple users, either at the same time on a network, or separately using individual copies of the workbook.
- Each copy must have been made from the original shared workbook and have a unique file name.
- When you share a workbook, you can set how long changes are tracked, when changes are saved, and how conflicts are resolved.
- The *Share Workbook* command maintains a **change history** for each user.
- When users have individual copies of the shared workbook, the copies are merged into a final workbook.
- The *Compare and Merge Workbooks* button must be displayed on the *Quick Access* toolbar or in a custom group in the *Ribbon*.
- In a shared or merged workbook, you can highlight, accept, or reject changes as you are working or after copies are combined.

- Changes can be highlighted in the worksheet or printed on a separate sheet.
- Each cell in a shared workbook that was edited has a **comment**, a pop-up text box that describes the change.
- You can insert a comment with a descriptive or explanatory message in any cell.

7.6 Inspect a workbook for metadata, check compatibility, and define a trusted location (p. E7-460).

- The **Inspect Document** command locates metadata and personal information that can be removed from the file.
- The **Check Compatibility** command identifies features, commands, and objects that might not work properly in an earlier version of Excel.
- The *Inspect Document* and *Check Compatibility* commands can be run as many times as necessary for a workbook.

- A **trusted location** is a folder that contains secure, safe workbooks that do not open in *Protected View*.
- You can define a folder as a trusted location in the *Trust Center* from the Excel *Options* dialog box.

Check for Understanding

The SIMbook for this text (within your SIMnet account) provides the following resources for concept review:

- Multiple choice questions
- Matching exercises
- Short answer questions

Guided Project 7-1

In this project, you develop a template for group instructors at Sierra Pacific Community College District (SPCCD). You create data validation with input and error messages and insert a form control. After inspecting the workbook and checking compatibility, you share the workbook.
[Student Learning Outcomes 7.1, 7.2, 7.3, 7.4, 7.5, 7.6]

File Needed: **SierraPacific-07.xlsx** (Student data files are available in the Library of your SIMnet account)
Completed Project File Names: **[your initials] Excel 7-1Template.xltx, [your initials] Excel 7-1User1.xlsx, [your initials] Excel 7-1User2.xlsx,** and **[your initials] Excel 7-1Merged.xlsx**

Skills Covered in this Project

- Set data validation with an error alert.
- Set data validation with an input message.
- Insert an option button control.
- Inspect a workbook.
- Check compatibility.
- Add worksheet and workbook protection.
- Save a workbook as a template.
- Create a workbook from a template.
- Share a workbook and track changes.

1. Open the **SierraPacific-07** workbook from your student data files.

2. Save the workbook as a template.
   a. Click the **File** tab and select **Save As**.
   b. Choose **This PC** and click the **More options** link.
   c. Type the file name [your initials] Excel 7-1Template in the *File name* box.
   d. Verify that the **Save Thumbnail** box is selected or select it.
   e. Choose **Excel Template** from the *Save as type* drop-down box. The default templates folder opens.
   f. Click **Save**.

3. Set data validation for a range.
   a. Select cells **C5:C29**.
   b. Click the **Data Validation** button [*Data* tab, *Data Tools* group] and verify that the **Settings** tab is selected.
   c. Click the **Allow** arrow and choose **Decimal**.
   d. Verify that the *Data* option displays **between**.
   e. Type .1 for the *Minimum* and 20 for the *Maximum*.
   f. Do not click **OK**.

4. Create an error message for data validation settings.
   a. Click the **Error Alert** tab.
   b. Verify that the **Show error alert after invalid data is entered** box is selected.
   c. Click the **Style** arrow and choose **Warning** to allow an invalid entry.
   d. Click the **Title** box and type Class Points.
   e. Click the **Error message** box and type Enter a value between 0.1 and 20.
   f. Click **OK**.
   g. Select cell **C5**, type 21 and press **Enter** to display the error alert (Figure 7-57).
   h. Click **Cancel** to keep the current value.

5. Set data validation with an input message.
   a. Select cells **D5:D29** and click the **Data Validation** button [*Data* tab, *Data Tools* group].
   b. Click the **Allow** arrow and choose **Decimal** on the *Settings* tab.
   c. Verify that **between** is the *Data* option.
   d. Click the **Minimum** box and type 50.
   e. Enter 100 for the *Maximum*.
   f. Click the **Input Message** tab.
   g. Verify that the **Show input message when cell is selected** box is selected.
   h. Click the **Title** box and type Project Points.
   i. Click the **Input message** box and type Enter a value between 50 and 100.
   j. Click **OK**.

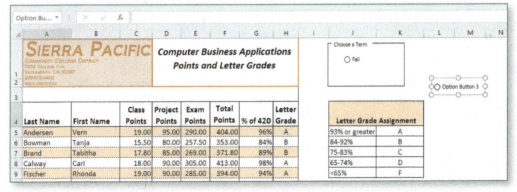

7-57 Error alert for invalid data

6. Select cells **E5:E29** and set data validation to limit the entry to any decimal number between 150 and 300. Do not use an input or error alert message.

7. Display the *Developer* tab on the *Ribbon* if it is not shown.
   a. Click the **Options** button [*File* tab] and click **Customize Ribbon** in the left pane.
   b. Select the **Developer** box in the *Main Tabs* group on the right and click **OK**.

8. Insert an option button form control.
   a. Click the **Insert Controls** button [*Developer* tab, *Controls* group] and select the **Option Button (Form Control)** button.
   b. Draw a control that covers cells **L3:M3** (Figure 7-58).

7-58 New option button form control

   c. Right-click any border of the control and choose **Edit Text**.
   d. Delete the default label and type Spring.
   e. Click cell **M1** to deselect the control.
   f. Right-click the control with the link select pointer.
   g. Point to a border of the control and click to hide the context menu.
   h. Point again to the border to display the move pointer.
   i. Drag the control to position it below the *Fall* control in the group box.
   j. Press **Ctrl** and click the *Fall* control so that both controls are selected (Figure 7-59).
   k. Click the **Align** button on the *Drawing Tools Format* tab and choose **Align Left**.

9. Insert a comment.
   a. Select cell **A4**.
   b. Click the **New Comment** button [*Review* tab, *Comments* group].
   c. Type Select and delete cells A5:E29 to begin a new grade sheet. (Figure 7-60).
   d. Select cell **F4** to hide the comment.

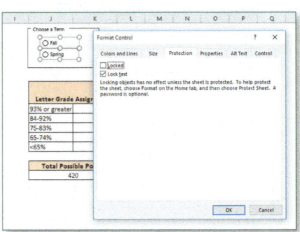

7-59 Both controls selected

10. Inspect the workbook and check compatibility.
    a. Click the **Check for Issues** button [*File* tab, *Info* group] and choose **Inspect Document**.
    b. Choose **Yes** to save the document.
    c. Click **Inspect**. Scroll the *Document Inspector* dialog box to confirm what has been found.
    d. Click **Remove All** for *Document Properties and Personal Information*. Do not remove the comment.
    e. Click **Close**.
    f. Click the **File** tab.
    g. Click **Allow this information to be saved in your file** in the *Inspect Workbook* group. This property must be disabled in order to share the workbook.
    h. Click the **Check for Issues** button [*File* tab, *Info* group] and choose **Check Compatibility**.
    i. Click **Copy to New Sheet**.

7-60 New comment in cell A4

11. Unlock cells and controls, protect the worksheet, and protect the structure.
    a. Click the **Grade Sheet** worksheet tab and select cells **A5:E29**. These are cells in which instructors enter student names and points.
    b. Right-click cell **A5** and choose **Format Cells**.
    c. Click the **Protection** tab and deselect the **Locked** box.
    d. Click **OK**.
    e. Point to the *Fall* option button control and right-click.
    f. Press **Ctrl** and right-click the *Spring* control so that both controls are selected.
    g. Right-click the *Fall* control and choose **Format Object** (Figure 7-61).
    h. Click the **Protection** tab, deselect the **Locked** box, and click **OK**.
    i. Select cell **A4**.
    j. Click the **Protect Sheet** button [*Review* tab, *Changes* group].

7-61 Format two controls at once

    k. Allow options to select locked and unlocked cells, do not use a password, and click **OK**.

    l. Click the **Protect Workbook** button [*Review* tab, *Changes* group].

    m. Do not assign a password and click **OK**.

12. Save and close template.

13. Create a workbook from a template.

    a. Click the **File** tab and select **New**.

    b. Click **PERSONAL** near the top of the gallery.

    c. Click the icon for *[your initials] Excel 7-1Template* to create a new workbook.

    d. Point to cell **A4** to read the comment.

    e. Select and delete the contents of cells **A5:E29** and select cell **A5**.

    f. Save the workbook as [your initials] Excel 7-1User1 in your usual location for saving workbooks. The *Save As* dialog box displays the most recently used folder which may be your *Custom Office Templates* folder.

14. Share the workbook.

    a. Click the **Share Workbook** button [*Review* tab, *Changes* category]. (If a message box says that privacy measures are in place, click the **File** tab, and click **Allow this information to be saved in your file** in the *Inspect Workbook* group.)

    b. Verify that the **Allow changes by more than one user at the same time** box is selected.

    c. Click the **Advanced** tab and set the *Keep change history for* option to **25** days.

    d. Click **OK** to close the *Share Workbook* dialog box.

    e. Click **OK** to resave the shared workbook.

15. Make a copy of the shared workbook in the same folder.

    a. Click the **File** tab and choose **Save As**.

    b. Save the workbook as [your initials] Excel 7-1User2 in the same folder as the original shared workbook.

    c. Type the following data in cells **A5:E5**. When the error alert message displays, click **Yes** to complete the entry.

        Goldstone   Violet   29   75   295

    d. Select the **Spring** radio button (Figure 7-62).

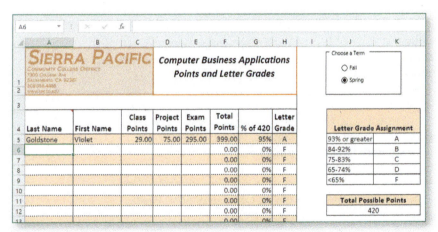

7-62 Data entry for User 2

    e. Save and close the workbook.

    f. Open the *[your initials] Excel 7-1User1* workbook.

    g. Select the **Spring** radio button.

h. Type the following data in cells **A6:E6**:

Gomez   Andre   12   95   250

i. Save the workbook and leave it open.

16. Add the **Compare and Merge Workbooks** button to the *Quick Access* toolbar.
   a. Select the **Options** command [*File* tab] and select **Quick Access Toolbar** in the left pane.
   b. Choose **All Commands** from the *Choose commands from* list.
   c. Select **Compare and Merge Workbooks** in the commands list.
   d. Click **Add** and click **OK**.

17. Merge copies of the shared workbook.
   a. Click the **Compare and Merge Workbooks** button on the *Quick Access* toolbar. (Save the workbook if prompted.)
   b. Navigate to the folder with the *[your initials] Excel 7-1User2* workbook in the *Select Files to Merge Into Current Workbook* dialog box.
   c. Click the *[your initials] Excel 7-1User2* file name and click **OK**.

18. Accept or reject changes.
   a. Click the **Track Changes** button [*Review* tab, *Changes* group] and choose **Accept/Reject Changes**.
   b. Verify that **Not yet reviewed** displays for the *When* setting.
   c. Click **OK**. The first change is identified as cell **A6**.
   d. Click **Accept**. The next change is in cell **B6**.
   e. Click **Accept All**.

19. Save the merged workbook as [your initials] Excel 7-1Merged and close it (Figure 7-63).

20. Move the template from the default folder.
   a. Click the **File** tab, select **Open**, and click **Browse**.
   b. Expand the *Quick access* list in the left pane and select **Documents**.
   c. Double-click **Custom Office Templates**.
   d. Right-click *[your initials] Excel 7-1Template* and choose **Cut**.
   e. In the left pane, navigate to and select your folder for saving files.
   f. Right-click an unused area of the dialog box and choose **Paste**.
   g. Click **Cancel** to close the dialog box.

7-63 Merged workbook for Excel 7-1

21. Remove the **Compare and Merge Workbooks** button and the *Developer* tab.
   a. Select the **Options** command [*File* tab] and click **Quick Access Toolbar**.
   b. Click **Compare and Merge Workbooks** in the list on the right.
   c. Click **Remove**.
   d. Click **Customize Ribbon** in the left pane.
   e. Deselect the **Developer** box in the *Main Tabs* group and click **OK**.

Guided Project 7-2

In this project, you complete the purchase order for Blue Lake Sports by adding a data validation list and check box form controls. You protect the sheet and the workbook, save it as a template, and share it for testing.
[Student Learning Outcomes 7.1, 7.2, 7.3, 7.4, 7.5, 7.6]

File Needed: ***BlueLakeSports-07.xlsx*** *(Student data files are available in the* Library *of your SIMnet account)*
Completed Project File Names: *[your initials]* ***Excel 7-2Template.xltx,*** *[your initials]* ***Excel 7-2User1.xlsx,***
[your initials] ***Excel 7-2User2.xlsx***, and *[your initials]* ***Excel 7-2Merged.xlsx***

Skills Covered in this Project

- Set data validation to use a list.
- Use an error alert for data validation.
- Insert a check box form control.
- Unlock worksheet cells and protect a worksheet.
- Save a workbook as a template.
- Create a new workbook from a template.
- Share a workbook and track changes.
- Accept or reject changes.

1. Open the ***BlueLakeSports-07*** workbook from your student data files.

2. Save the workbook as a template.
   a. Click the **Save As** button [*File* tab] and choose **This PC**.
   b. Click the **More Options** link.
   c. Type the file name [your initials] Excel 7-2Template in the *File name* box.
   d. Verify that the **Save Thumbnail** box is selected or select it.
   e. Choose **Excel Template** from the *Save as type* drop-down box.
   f. Click **Save**.

3. Set data validation with an error alert to use a list.
   a. Click the **Purchase Order** sheet tab, select **B17**, and click the **Data Validation** button [*Data* tab, *Data Tools* group].
   b. Click the **Allow** arrow and choose **List** on the *Settings* tab.
   c. Click the **Source** entry box.
   d. Click the **Departments** worksheet tab and select cells **A2:A14**.
   e. Click the **Error Alert** tab.
   f. Verify that the **Show error alert after invalid data is entered** box is selected.
   g. Use **Stop** for the *Style* to prohibit an invalid entry.
   h. Click the **Title** box and type Wait!.
   i. Click the **Error message** box and type Please choose from the list.
   j. Click **OK**.

4. Display the *Developer* tab and the *Compare and Merge Workbooks* button.
   a. Select the **Options** command [*File* tab] and click **Customize Ribbon** in the left pane.
   b. Select the **Developer** box in the *Main Tabs* group.
   c. Click **Quick Access Toolbar** in the left pane.
   d. Choose **All Commands** from the *Choose commands from* list.
   e. Click **Compare and Merge Workbooks** in the commands list.
   f. Click **Add** and click **OK**.

5. Insert a check box form control.
   a. Click the **View** tab and check the **Gridlines** box in the *Show* group to draw and position controls with gridlines visible.
   b. Click the **Insert Controls** button [*Developer* tab, *Controls* group] and click the **Check Box (Form Control)** button.
   c. Draw a control directly over cell **B15**.

d. Click the **Properties** button [*Developer* tab, *Controls* group].

e. Verify that the **Unchecked** radio button is selected on the *Control* tab.

f. Select the **3-D shading** box.

g. Click the **Protection** tab and deselect the **Locked** box.

h. Click **OK**.

i. Click two times near the word "Check" with the control to place an insertion point.

j. Delete **Check Box 1**, press **Spacebar**, and type Yes (Figure 7-64).

k. Click cell **E15** to deselect the control. If you accidentally placed a check mark within the control, point and click to remove it.

7-64 Edited label for check box control

6. Copy a check box form control.

a. Point to the check box control label **Yes** and right-click.

b. Choose **Copy** from the menu and then press **Ctrl+V** to paste the control.

c. Point to any border of the copied control to display a move pointer.

d. Drag the copy to cell **C15**.

e. Press **Ctrl** and right-click while pointing to the first check box control to select both controls (Figure 7-65).

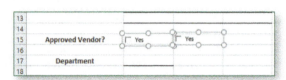

7-65 Two controls selected

f. Click the **Align** button [*Drawing Tools Format* tab, *Arrange* group] and choose **Align Middle**.

g. Select cell **E15** to deselect both controls.

h. Right-click the copied control and choose **Edit Text** to place an insertion point.

i. Delete **Yes** and type No (Figure 7-66).

j. Select cell **E15**. Remove check marks that were accidentally entered.

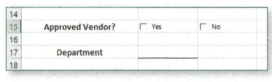

7-66 Controls are aligned

7. Protect the worksheet and the workbook structure.

a. Select **D7**.

b. Press **Ctrl** and select cell **D9**, cells **B11:D13**, cell **B17**, and cells **A20:D28**.

c. Click the **Format** button [*Home* tab, *Cells* group].

d. Select **Lock Cell** to remove the *Locked* property.

e. Click cell **D7**.

f. Click the **Protect Sheet** button [*Review* tab, *Changes* group].

g. Allow the options to select locked and unlocked cells. Do not use a password.

h. Click **OK**.

i. Click the **Protect Workbook** button [*Review* tab, *Changes* group].

j. Do not use a password and click **OK**.

8. Save and close the template.

9. Create a workbook from a template.

a. Click the **New** button [*File* tab] and click **PERSONAL** near the top of the gallery.

b. Click **[your initials] Excel 7-2Template** to create a workbook.

c. Type BLS00120 in cell **D7** and press **Tab**.

d. Type **=to** in cell **D9**, press **Tab** to select **TODAY**, and press **Enter**.

e. Type the following in cells **B11:B13**:

Outdoor Apparel, Inc
4232 South Water Street
Omaha, NE 68107

f. Select the check box control for **Yes**.

g. Select cell **B17**, click the data validation arrow, and choose **Apparel**.

h. Save the workbook as an Excel workbook named [your initials] Excel 7-2User1 in your usual location for saving files.

10. Inspect the workbook.

a. Click the **File** tab. You cannot inspect a worksheet that is protected.

b. Click **Unprotect** in the *Protect Workbook* area (Figure 7-67).

c. Click the **Check for Issues** button and choose **Inspect Document**.

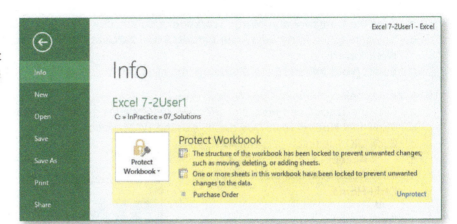

7-67 Remove protection from the *Backstage* view

d. Choose **Yes** to save the document before inspection.

e. Click **Inspect** in the *Document Inspector* dialog box.

f. Click **Remove All** to remove all personal information and document properties.

g. Click **Close**.

11. Check compatibility.

a. Click the **Protect Workbook** button [*Review* group, *Changes* group]. In order to generate a compatibility report, the *Protect Workbook* property must be disabled.

b. Click the **Check for Issues** button [*File* tab, *Info* group] and choose **Check Compatibility**.

c. Click **Copy to New Sheet**.

d. Click the **Purchase Order** sheet tab.

12. Share the workbook.

a. Click the **File** tab.

b. Click **Allow this information to be saved in your file** in the *Inspect Workbook* group. This property was activated when you removed metadata; it prohibits sharing the workbook.

c. Return to the **Purchase Order** sheet and click the **Share Workbook** button [*Review* tab, *Changes* category].

d. Select the **Allow changes by more than one user at the same time** box.

e. Click the **Advanced** tab and set the *Keep change history for* option to **15** days.

f. Click **OK** to close the *Share Workbook* dialog box.

g. Click **OK** to resave the shared workbook.

13. Make a copy of the shared workbook in the same folder.

a. Click the **File** tab and choose **Save As**.

b. Select **This PC** and click the **More Options** link.

c. Navigate to and choose your folder and save the workbook as [your initials] Excel 7-2User2.

d. Type the following in cells **A20:D20**:

Ladies Parka   LP10Blue   4   87

e. Save and close the workbook.

14. Open *[your initials] Excel 7-2User1* and select cell **A21**.
    a. In cells **A21:D21**, type the following:

    Men's Parka   MP16Black   4   98

    b. Save the workbook and leave it open.

15. Merge copies of the shared workbook.
    a. Click the **Compare and Merge Workbooks** button. (Save the file if prompted.)
    b. Navigate to the folder with *[your initials] Excel 7-2User2* in the *Select Files to Merge Into Current Workbook* dialog box.
    c. Select *[your initials] Excel 7-2User2* and click **OK**.

16. Accept or reject changes.
    a. Click the **Track Changes** button [*Review* tab, *Changes* group] and choose **Accept/Reject Changes**.
    b. Verify that **Not yet reviewed** displays as the *When* option.
    c. Click **OK**. The first edit is cell **A21**.
    d. Click **Accept** to locate the next edit.
    e. Click **Accept All** and then press **Ctrl+Home**.

17. Save the workbook as
    [your initials] Excel 7-2Merged in
    your folder and close it (Figure 7-68).

18. Move the template from the default folder.
    a. Click the **File** tab, select **Open**, and click **Browse**.
    b. Expand the *Quick access* list in the left pane and select **Documents**.
    c. Double-click **Custom Office Templates**.
    d. Right-click *[your initials] Excel 7-2Template* and choose **Cut**.
    e. In the left pane, navigate to and select the folder for saving files.
    f. Right-click an unused area of the dialog box and choose **Paste**.
    g. Click **Cancel** to close the dialog box.

19. Remove the **Compare and Merge Workbooks** button and the *Developer* tab.
    a. Select the **Options** command [*File* tab] and click **Quick Access Toolbar** in the left pane.
    b. Click **Compare and Merge Workbooks** in the list on the right.
    c. Click **Remove**.
    d. Click **Customize Ribbon** in the left pane.
    e. Deselect the **Developer** box in the *Main Tabs* group and click **OK**.

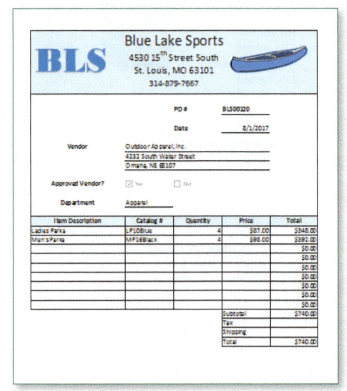

7-68 Merged workbook for Excel 7-2

Guided Project 7-3

Agents for Placer Hills Real Estate (PHRE) have built a worksheet to help clients compare monthly payments. You clear and reset data validation and insert a spin box form control for the agent's ID. The workbook is saved as a template.
[**Student Learning Outcomes 7.1, 7.2, 7.3, 7.4, 7.6**]

File Needed: **_PlacerHills-07.xlsx_** _(Student data files are available in the_ Library _of your SIMnet account)_
Completed Project File Names: **_[your initials] Excel 7-3.xlsx_** and **_[your initials] Excel 7-3Template.xltx_**

Skills Covered in this Project

- Save a workbook as a template.
- Find and clear data validation settings.
- Set data validation with an error alert.
- Insert a spin box form control.
- Protect a worksheet.
- Create a workbook from a template.

1. Open the **_PlacerHills-07_** workbook from your student data files. The #NUM error appears in three cells because data for the _PMT_ formula in cell H15 is missing.

2. Save the workbook as a template.
   a. Select **Save As** [_File_ tab] and choose **This PC**.
   b. Click the **More options** link to open the _Save As_ dialog box.
   c. Type the file name [your initials] Excel 7-3Template in the _File name_ box.
   d. Verify that the **Save Thumbnail** box is selected or select it.
   e. Choose **Excel Template** from the _Save as type_ drop-down box.
   f. Click **Save**.

3. Find and clear data validation settings.
   a. Click the **Find & Select** button [_Home_ tab, _Editing_ group] and choose **Go To Special**.
   b. Select the option button for **Data validation** (Figure 7-69).
   c. Click **OK**. Cells with data validation settings are highlighted.
   d. Click the **Data Validation** button [_Data_ tab, _Data Tools_ group].
   e. Click **Clear All** on the _Settings_ tab and leave the dialog box open.

4. Set data validation with an error alert.
   a. Verify that the following cells in the worksheet are selected: **C9:C12, H9, H11, H13:H14**, and **H16**. (If they are not, close the _Data Validation_ dialog box, select the cells, and click the **Data Validation** button [_Data_ tab, _Data Tools_ group].)
   b. Click the **Allow** arrow and choose **Decimal** on the _Settings_ tab.
   c. Click the **Data** arrow and choose **greater than or equal to**.
   d. Click the **Minimum** box and type 0.
   e. Click the **Error Alert** tab and verify that the **Show error alert after invalid data is entered** box is selected.
   f. Verify that **Stop** displays as the **Style**.
   g. Click the **Title** box and type Required.
   h. Click the **Error message** box and type Please enter a positive value. (Figure 7-70).
   i. Click **OK**.

7-69 Locate cells with data validation using _Go To Special_

7-70 Data validation error alert

5. Display the *Developer* tab on the *Ribbon* if it is not shown.
   a. Select the **Options** command [*File* tab] and click **Customize Ribbon** in the left pane.
   b. Select the **Developer** box in the *Main Tabs* group and click **OK**.

6. Insert a spin button form control.
   a. Show the gridlines on the worksheet [*View* tab].
   b. Click the **Insert Controls** button [*Developer* tab, *Controls* group].
   c. Click the **Spin Button (Form Control)** button.
   d. Draw a control directly over cells **I21:I22** (Figure 7-71).

7-71 Spin button form control

   e. Right-click the control and choose **Format Control**.
   f. Click the **Minimum value** box on the *Control* tab and type 1.
   g. Set a maximum value of **8**. These are agent identification numbers (1 through 8).
   h. Click the **Cell link** box and select cell **H22**. The choice made by the spin button will be placed in this cell (Figure 7-72).

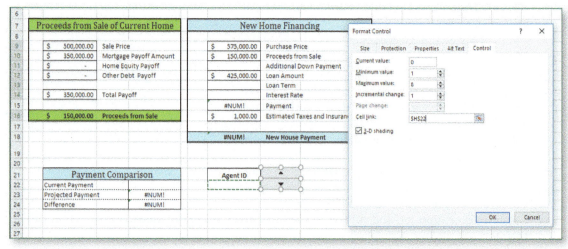

7-72 Options set for spin button control

   i. Verify that the **3D shading** box is selected and click **OK**.
   j. Click cell **D4** to deselect the control.

7. Protect the worksheet for data entry.
   a. Select cells **D4:E4**.
   b. Press **Ctrl** and select cells **C9:C12**, **H9**, **H11**, **H13:H14**, **H16**, **H22**, and **E22**.
   c. Click the **Format** button [*Home* tab, *Cells* group].
   d. Select **Lock Cell** to remove the *Locked* property.
   e. Click the **Protect Sheet** button [*Review* tab, *Changes* group].
   f. Allow the options to select locked and unlocked cells. Do not use a password.
   g. Click **OK**.

8. Delete the contents of cells **C9:C10**, **H9** and **H16**.

9. Select cell **D4** to position the insertion point on the template.

10. Save and close the template.

11. Create a workbook from a template.
    a. Click the **New** button [*File* tab] and click **PERSONAL** near the top of the gallery.
    b. Click *[your initials] Excel 7-3Template*.
    c. Save the workbook as a regular Excel workbook named [your initials] Excel 7-3 in your usual location for saving files.

12. Select cell **C9**, type 450000, and press **Enter**. The cells are formatted and formulas are calculated.

13. Type 275000 in cell **C10** and press **Enter**.

14. Select cell **H9**, type 485000, and press **Enter**.

15. Type 75000 in cell **H11**.

16. Enter data in cells **H13**, **H14**, and **H16** as shown in Figure 7-73.

17. Click the spin box control arrows to select **3** as the agent ID.

18. Select cell **E22**, type 1875, and select cell **D4**.

19. Save and close the workbook.

20. Move the template from the default folder.
    a. Click the **File** tab, choose **Open**, and click **Browse**.
    b. Expand the *Quick access* list in the left pane and select **Documents**.
    c. Double-click **Custom Office Templates**.
    d. Right-click *[your initials] Excel 7-3Template* and choose **Cut**.
    e. Navigate to and open your folder for saving files.
    f. Right-click an unused area of the dialog box and choose **Paste**.
    g. Click **Cancel** to close the dialog box.

21. Remove the *Developer* tab.
    a. Click the **Options** button [*File* tab] and click **Customize Ribbon** in the left pane.
    b. Deselect the **Developer** box in the *Main Tabs* group and click **OK**.

7-73 Completed worksheet for Excel 7-3

Independent Project 7-4

Classic Gardens and Landscapes (CGL) monitors employee hours by task and by day. The task hour worksheet has a data entry form, and the employee hours worksheet has formulas and data validation. The workbook is saved as a template for sharing.

[Student Learning Outcomes 7.1, 7.2, 7.3, 7.4, 7.5, 7.6]

File Needed: **ClassicGardens-07.xlsx** *(Student data files are available in the Library of your SIMnet account)*
Completed Project File Names: *[your initials] Excel 7-4Template.xltx, [your initials] Excel 7-4User1.xlsx, [your initials] Excel 7-4User2.xlsx,* and *[your initials] Excel 7-4Merged.xlsx*

Skills Covered in this Project

- Create a data entry form.
- Insert a comment.
- Set data validation with an error alert.
- Save a workbook as a template.
- Create a workbook from a template.
- Share a workbook.
- Compare and merge workbooks.
- Highlight, accept, and reject changes.

---

1. Open the **ClassicGardens-07** workbook from your student data files.

2. Save the workbook as a template with a thumbnail named [your initials] Excel 7-4Template in the default *Custom Office Templates* folder.

3. Display the **Compare and Merge Workbooks** and **Form** buttons on the *Quick Access* toolbar.

4. Create and use a data input form.
   a. Select cells **A9:E17** on the **Task Hours** worksheet and click the **Form** button.
   b. Press **Tab** and type 22 for Week 1 brick and stone paving. If you accidentally press **Enter** and move to the next record, click **Find Prev** in the data form to return to the unfinished form.
   c. Press **Tab** and type 18 for Week 2.
   d. Press **Tab** and type 30 for Week 3.
   e. Press **Tab**, type 8 for Week 4, and press **Enter**. The next data form opens, and the data displays in the worksheet (Figure 7-74).

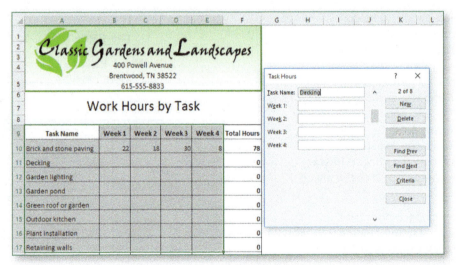

7-74 Data form to enter new records

f. Enter data for the second task, decking:

Week 1   15
Week 2   28
Week 3   0
Week 4   12

g. Close the data form and select cell **G1**.

5. Insert a comment in cell **G1**.
   a. Type Delete the sample data in cells B10:E11. in the comment box.
   b. Select cell **G3**.
   c. If the comment is not visible, click the **Show All Comments** button in the *Comments* group [*Review* tab] to display it.

6. Set data validation with an error alert.
   a. Click the **Employee Hours** worksheet tab.
   b. Select cells **B8:G13** and set data validation to use a decimal value less than **8.1**.
   c. Use an **Information** type error alert with the title Overtime.
   d. Type the error message Overtime pay starts at greater than 8 hours.

7. Enter *SUM* formulas for the totals in column **H** and row **14**.

8. Select cells **B8:G13** and remove the **Locked** property. Select cell **B8** to cancel the selection.

9. Protect the sheet without a password.

10. Save and close the template.

11. Create a new workbook based on the template and save it as [your initials] Excel 7-4User1 in your usual folder for saving files.

12. Share the workbook with default settings.

13. Make a copy of the shared workbook in the same folder and name it [your initials] Excel 7-4User2.

14. In *[your initials] Excel 7-4User2*, enter the following hours for Alvarez and accept the invalid entry.

Mon   9
Tue   8
Wed   7

15. Save and close *User2*'s workbook and open *[your initials] Excel 7-4User1*.

16. As *User1*, enter the following hours for Alvarez. Accept the invalid entry and note that the days of the week are different from those entered by *User2*.

Wed   9
Thu   8
Fri   7

17. Save *User1*'s workbook and leave it open.

18. Merge *User2*'s workbook into *User1*'s workbook.

19. Click the **Track Changes** button [*Review* tab, *Changes* group] to accept or reject changes. For the conflict in cell D8, select and accept **9** as the value. Accept all other changes.

20. Save the merged workbook as [your initials] Excel 7-4Merged and leave it open.

21. Click the **Share Workbook** button [*Review* tab, *Changes* group] and deselect the **Allow changes by more than one user at the same time** box. Click **OK** and then click **Yes** to unshare the workbook.

22. Remove sheet protection.

23. Inspect the workbook and remove all comments and personal information.

24. Open the *Properties* dialog box [*File* tab], and deselect the **Show Thumbnails for All Excel Documents** box on the *Summary* tab, and click **OK**.

25. Save and close the merged workbook (Figure 7-75).

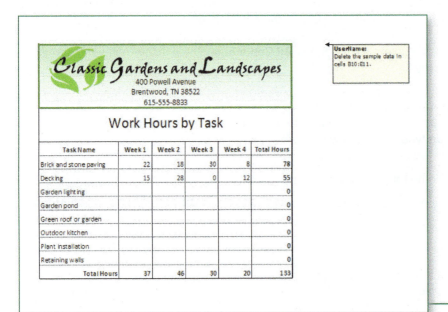

26. Remove the **Form** and **Compare and Merge Workbooks** buttons from the *Quick Access* toolbar.

27. Move the template from the *Custom Office Templates* folder to your folder.

Independent Project 7-5

In the Courtyard Medical Plaza workbook, you add items to the pharmacy inventory using a data entry form. On the Optometry worksheet, you find and correct invalid data. Finally, you inspect the workbook and check its compatibility with earlier versions of Excel.
[Student Learning Outcomes 7.2, 7.3, 7.6]

File Needed: ***CourtyardMedical-07.xlsx*** *(Student data files are available in the Library of your SIMnet account)*
Completed Project File Name: ***[your initials] Excel 7-5.xlsx***

Skills Covered in this Project

- Create and use a data entry form.
- Circle invalid data.
- Inspect a workbook.
- Check workbook compatibility.

---

1. Open the ***CourtyardMedical-07*** workbook from your student data files. It is marked as final.

2. Click **Edit Anyway** in the message bar, and save the workbook as [your initials] Excel 7-5.

3. Display the **Form** button on the *Quick Access* toolbar.

4. Create and use a data input form.
   a. Select cells **A9:D24** on the **Pharmacy** sheet.
   b. Create the data entry form.
   c. Enter data for two items shown here. The currency symbol is included in format settings so you need not type it.

Product ID	Description	Cost	Retail
CMP-016	Swim ear drops	4.59	6.89
CMP-017	Peptic relief tablets (25)	2.50	3.99

   d. Close the data form.

5. Click the **Optometry** worksheet tab and circle invalid data.

6. Review the data validation settings for any cell in column A. Correct the invalid entries based on the settings.

7. Inspect the workbook. Remove personal data and document properties and hidden worksheets.

8. Check compatibility and copy the results to a new sheet.

9. Mark the workbook as final and close it (Figure 7-76).

10. Remove the **Form** button from the *Quick Access* toolbar.

Product ID	Description	Cost	Retail
CMP-006	Acetaminophen	$2.50	$3.99
CMP-001	Tongue depressor	$0.55	$1.99
CMP-002	Cough drops	$0.85	$1.29
CMP-003	Nasal spray	$3.45	$5.99
CMP-004	Antiseptic wash	$2.75	$4.99
CMP-005	Disinfectant wipes	$1.25	$3.99
CMP-007	Bandage, 1 inch strips	$1.25	$3.99
CMP-008	Bandage, 2 inch strips	$1.25	$3.99
CMP-009	Bandage, assorted	$3.75	$4.99
CMP-010	Ibuprofen	$2.50	$3.99
CMP-011	Cough syrup	$2.25	$4.99
CMP-012	Antibiotic ointment	$2.25	$5.99
CMP-013	Moisture lotion	$1.55	$4.99
CMP-014	Dandruff shampoo	$2.75	$5.99
CMP-015	Insect bite gel	$3.55	$6.99
CMP-016	Swim ear drops	$4.59	$6.89
CMP-017	Peptic relief tablets (25)	$2.50	$3.99

7-76 Completed worksheets for Excel 7-5

Independent Project 7-6

The Hamilton Civic Center is developing a template with a calorie-tracking sheet for member exercise and a report about off-site seminars. You create the template, set data validation, complete formulas, and insert a combo box control. You create a new workbook from the template and share it with co-workers.
[Student Learning Outcomes 7.1, 7.2, 7.3, 7.4, 7.5, 7.6]

File Needed: *HamiltonCC-07.xlsx* (Student data files are available in the Library of your SIMnet account)
Completed Project File Names: *[your initials] Excel 7-6Template.xltx*, *[your initials] Excel 7-6User1.xlsx*, *[your initials] Excel 7-6User2.xlsx*, and *[your initials] Excel 7-6Merged.xlsx*

Skills Covered in this Project

- Set data validation to use a list.
- Set data validation to use a date restriction.
- Create an error alert message.
- Insert a combo box control.
- Protect a worksheet and workbook structure.
- Check compatibility.
- Save a workbook as a template.
- Share a workbook.
- Track, accept, and reject changes.

1. Open the **HamiltonCC-07** workbook from your student data files and save it with a thumbnail image as [your initials] Excel 7-6Template in the default templates folder.

2. Select cell **D2** on the **Data** sheet and review the formula. The formula divides calories by time and rounds the results to three decimal places.

3. Select cells **D2:D10** and open the *Format Cells* dialog box.

4. Select the **Custom** category on the *Number* tab. Choose **0.00** in the sample list and edit the *Type* box to show 0.000. The number of zeros indicates how many positions display after the decimal point (Figure 7-77).

5. Select cell **D2** and click the **Format Painter** button [*Home* tab, *Clipboard* group]. Click the **Calorie Tracking** tab and paint the format to cells **E3:E33**.

6. Select cell **E3** on the **Calorie Tracking** sheet. Start a *VLOOKUP* function to lookup the label in cell **C3**. For the array, use an absolute reference to cells **A2:D10** on the **Data** sheet. The *Col_index_num* is **4** for the calories per minute column. The result of the *VLOOKUP* formula is the calories per minute for the exercise (Figure 7-78).

7. Edit the formula in cell **E3** to multiply the results by the number of minutes in cell **D3**.

8. Copy the formula in cell **E3** to cells **E4:E33**. The #N/A error message displays in rows where there is no data.

9. Select cells **C3:C33** and set data validation to use the list of activity names on the **Data** sheet. Do not use an input message or an error alert.

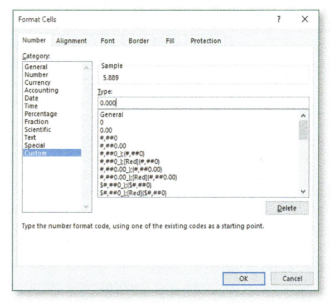

7-77 Custom format for values

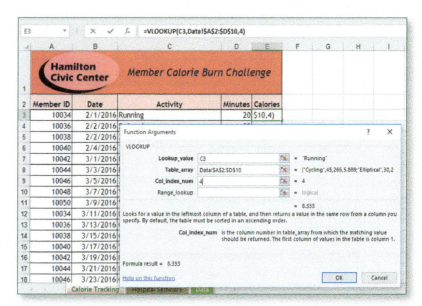

7-78 VLOOKUP formula

10. On the **Calorie Tracking** sheet, delete the data in cells **A3:D23**.

11. Select cells **B3:B33** and set data validation to use a **Date** that is less than or equal to *TODAY* (Figure 7-79). Include a *Stop* error alert with a title of Check Date and a message of Date must be today or in the past.

12. Select cells **A3:D33** and remove the **Locked** cell property. Select cell **A3** to position the insertion point.

13. Display the **Developer** tab on the *Ribbon* and click the **Data** worksheet tab.

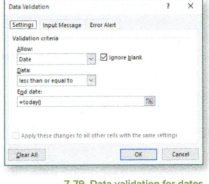

7-79 Data validation for dates

14. Draw a combo box control to cover cell **F8** and open its *Format Control* dialog box. Select cells **G8:G11** for the *Input range* and cell **F8** for the *Cell link* (Figure 7-80).

15. Deselect the control and then select **Second** from it. The linked cell is under the control and hidden from view.

16. Click the **Hospital Seminars** tab and select cell **D4**. This cell has *Center Across Selection* alignment applied.

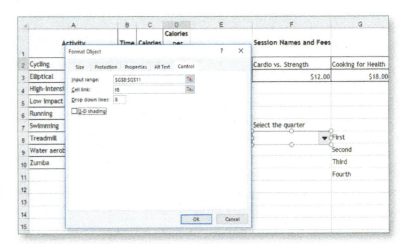

7-80 Combo box settings

17. In cell **D4**, use *CONCAT* and *INDEX* to display the result from the combo box, concatenating the *Index* results to the word "Quarter."

    a. Start a *CONCAT* function [*Text* group].
    b. Use the *INDEX* function with the first arguments list as the *Text1* argument.
    c. The *Array* argument is cells **G8:G11** on the *Data* sheet, and the *Row_num* argument is cell **F8** on the *Data* sheet. The combo box control covers cell F8, so type f8 after the sheet name (Figure 7-81).

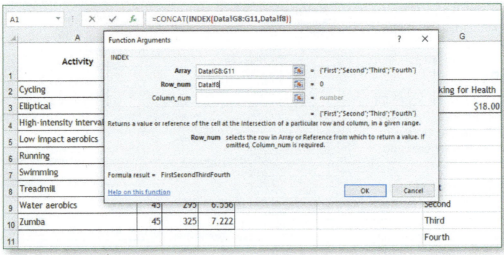

7-81 *INDEX* is nested within *CONCAT*

d. Click between the two ending parentheses in the *Formula* bar to return to the *CONCAT* arguments and type a comma , to move to the *Text2* argument. (If you accidentally clicked *OK*, click the **Insert Function** button to re-open the *Function Arguments* dialog box.)

e. Click the **Text2** box, press **Spacebar**, and type Quarter, and click **OK**. (Figure 7-82).

f. Format cell **D4** as **bold italic 16 pt**.

7-82 Space character is included with *Text2* argument

18. On the *Data* sheet, select **Third** from the combo box control, and return to the *Hospital Seminars* sheet to see the results.

19. Select cell **D4** and cells **D6:G10** on the *Hospital Seminars* sheet and remove the **Locked** property.

20. Delete the contents of cells **D6:G10** and select cell **D6**.

21. Protect the **Hospital Seminars** sheet and the **Calorie Tracking** sheet, both without passwords.

22. Save and close the template.

23. Create a workbook from the template. Save the new workbook as [your initials] Excel 7-6User1 in your usual folder for saving files.

24. Share the *[your initials] Excel 7-6User 1* workbook with the default settings.

25. Make a copy of the shared workbook named [your initials] Excel 7-6User2.

26. In *[your initials] Excel 7-6User2*, enter the data shown here on the *Calorie Tracking* sheet. Do not type the word "Yesterday" or "Two days ago," but enter date values using *mm/dd/yy* format.

Member ID	Date	Activity	Minutes
10001	Yesterday	Elliptical	45
10003	Two days ago	Water aerobics	40

27. Enter the data shown here on the *Hospital Seminars* sheet for *User2*.

	Henderson	Advocate	Mercy	Gallatin
Cardio vs. Strength	14	22	31	15
Know Your Numbers	32	21	18	21

28. Save and close the *[your initials] Excel 7-6User2* workbook.

29. Open *[your initials] Excel 7-6User1*. Starting in cell **A5** on the *Calorie Tracking* sheet, enter the following data. Enter date values and use *mm/dd/yy* format.

Member ID	Date	Activity	Minutes
10007	Today	Running	30
10003	Two days ago	High-intensity interval training	40

30. Starting in cell **D9** on the *Hospital Seminars* sheet, enter the data shown here.

	Henderson	Advocate	Mercy	Gallatin
Pamper Your Joints	10	20	15	18
Vitamins are Best	14	31	27	15

31. Save the **[your initials] Excel 7-6User1** workbook. Then merge the **[your initials] Excel 7-6User2** workbook into it.

32. Highlight the changes and accept all of them.

33. Save the merged workbook as [your initials] Excel 7-6Merged and close it (Figure 7-83).

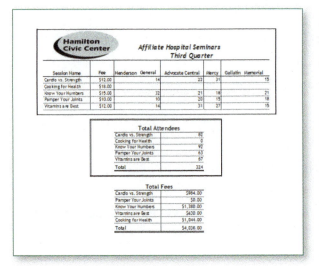

7-83 Completed worksheets for Excel 7-6

34. Hide the **Developer** tab and remove the **Compare and Merge Workbooks** button from the *Quick Access* toolbar.

35. Move the template from the *Custom Office Templates* folder to your usual work folder.

Improve It Project 7-7

Staff at Life's Animal Shelter (LAS) use an Excel template to maintain lists of animal adoptions. You open and edit the template to add data validation and a check box form control. In addition, you inspect the workbook, check its compatibility with earlier versions, and test it.
[Student Learning Outcomes 7.1, 7.2, 7.3, 7.4, 7.6]

File Needed: **LASTemplate-07.xltx** (Student data files are available in the Library of your SIMnet account)
Completed Project File Names: **[your initials] Excel 7-7.xlsx** and **[your initials] Excel 7-7Template.xltx**

Skills Covered in this Project

- Set data validation to use lists.
- Insert and format a check box control.
- Inspect a workbook and remove metadata.
- Check workbook compatibility.
- Protect a worksheet and workbook structure.
- Save a template as a different template.
- Create a workbook from a template.

1. Open the **LASTemplate-07** template from your student data files. The template has one row of sample data.

2. Press **F12** (**FN+F12**) to open the *Save As* dialog box. The *Save as type* shows *Excel Template*, but the current folder is your usual storage location.

3. Click the **Save as type** arrow and choose **Excel Workbook**.

4. Click the **Save as type** arrow again and choose **Excel Template** to reset the folder to the *Custom Office Templates* folder.

5. Type [your initials] Excel 7-7Template in the *File name* box and click **Save**.

6. Set data validation for the *Species* column to use the animal types on the **Lists** worksheet. Do not use an input or an error message.

7. Set data validation for the *City* column to use data on the **Lists** worksheet without input or error messages.

8. Build a *VLOOKUP* formula in cell **G5** to lookup the city name in cell **F5** in the array on the **Lists** worksheet and display the ZIP code. Use the sample data to verify that your formula is correct and then copy the formula (Figure 7-84).

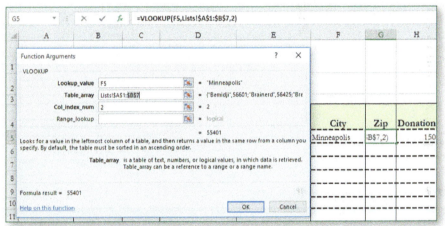

7-84 VLOOKUP to display ZIP code

9. Format the cells in the *Donation* column to display **Currency** with no decimal places.

10. Format the cells in column **A** to show the **Short Date** format.

11. Determine the custom format used for *Pet IDs* on the *Animals* worksheet and then apply the same format to the *Animal ID* data on the *Adoptions* worksheet.

12. Draw a check box form control to cover cells **G2:H2**. Format the control to be unchecked with 3-D shading. On the *Colors and Lines* tab in the *Format Control* dialog box, set a **1 pt. solid black** line for the control. On the *Protection* tab, remove the **Locked** property. Edit the text in the control to display All donations cleared. (Figure 7-85).

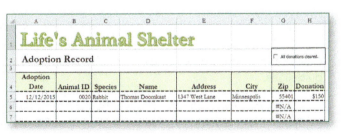

7-85 Check box control completed

13. Delete the test data in cells **A5:F5** and cell **H5**. Data validation is not deleted when you delete cell contents.

14. Inspect the workbook and remove all personal information.

15. Check compatibility and copy the results to a new sheet.

16. Remove the **Locked** property from cells **A5:H29** on the **Adoptions** sheet.

17. Select cell **A5** and protect the **Adoptions** sheet without a password.

18. Delete the **Animals** worksheet and hide the **Lists** and **Compatibility Report** worksheets.

19. Protect the workbook structure without a password.

20. Resave the template and close it.

21. Create a new workbook from the template and enter the following data:

Adoption Date	Animal ID	Species	Name	Address	City	Zip	Donation
2/5/17	10	Dog	John Doe	4567 Western Trail	Cass Lake		125

22. Save your workbook in your usual folder as [your initials] Excel 7-7 (Figure 7-86).

23. Close the workbook and hide the *Developer* tab.

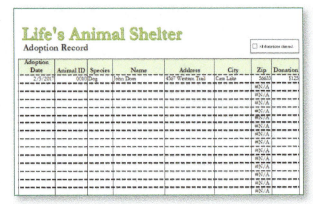

7-86 Completed worksheet for Excel 7-7

Challenge Project 7-8

In this project, you build a list of television or streaming shows and series that you regularly watch or would like to watch. You add data validation for the genre of show, inspect the workbook, and check it for compatibility.
[**Student Learning Outcomes 7.1, 7.2, 7.6**]

File Needed: None
Completed Project File Name: *[your initials] Excel 7-8.xlsx*

Create and save a workbook as [your initials] Excel 7-8. Modify your workbook according to the following guidelines:

- In cells **A3:A12**, type the names of ten network, cable, or Internet shows, series, or specials.
- Type Title in cell **A2**. Type Network/Site in cell **B2**, Day in cell **C2**, and Time in cell **D2**. Name this sheet Watch List.

- Type a main title for the data. Apply formats based on the type of data. Add borders, shading, or other attributes to enhance the look of the worksheet.
- On another worksheet in the same workbook, create a list of network call letters, web URLs, or other identifiers for providers of your shows. Sort the data in a logical order. Then use this list to set data validation for the appropriate column on the *Watch List* sheet.
- Complete your worksheet using real or fictitious data.
- Inspect the workbook and remove personal information.
- Check the workbook's compatibility and show the results on a new sheet.

Challenge Project 7-9

In this project, you select an Excel template from the *Featured* group and create a workbook. You explore features used in the template and edit the workbook to customize it.
[Student Learning Outcomes 7.1, 7.2, 7.3, 7.5, 7.6]

File Needed: None
Completed Project File Name: *[your initials] Excel 7-9.xlsx*

Explore available templates in the *Backstage* view and choose one. Create a new workbook and save it as [your initials] Excel 7-9. Modify your workbook according to the following guidelines:

- Review sample data and formulas in the workbook.
- Unhide worksheets, columns, and rows, if they exist.
- Enter data for your own work or personal circumstances.
- Use *Find & Select* and *Go To Special* to locate existing data validation, if any. If the workbook includes data validation, edit the settings to make a change that fits the worksheet. If the template has no data validation, identify a cell range and build and apply data validation.
- Insert a form control to further personalize your workbook.
- Insert a comment to explain the purpose of the workbook.
- Inspect the workbook and remove metadata that you think can be safely removed.
- Check the workbook's compatibility and copy the results to a new sheet.

Challenge Project 7-10

In this project, you create a template to keep track of your course grades. You will include a combo box control to select the semester as well as data validation to select course codes and grades.
[Student Learning Outcomes 7.1, 7.2, 7.3]

File Needed: None
Completed Project File Names: *[your initials] Excel 7-10Template.xltx* and *[your initials] Excel 7-10.xlsx*

Create and save a workbook as [your initials] Excel 7-10Template in the *Custom Office Templates* folder. Modify your workbook according to the following guidelines:

- In cells **A3:D3**, type the labels Code, Number, Name, and Grade.
- Format cells **A4:D9** with borders or shading to accommodate six courses per semester.
- Create and use list data validation in the *Code* and *Grade* columns. "Code" is the department or discipline indicator such as BUS, MIS, or COM; "Name" is the course title. You can type lists on another sheet or enter the list information in the *Source* entry box on the *Settings* tab for data validation.
- Type a main label in cell **A1** to indicate the purpose of the worksheet. Type a second label in cell **A2** to mark where a student enters his or her name on the sheet.
- To the right of the *Grade* column, insert a combo box control to choose the semester.
- Complete formatting for the sheet. Then copy cells **A1:D9** and the control to create a second grouping starting in cell **A12** for another semester.
- Save and close the template.
- Create a workbook from the template, complete data for two semesters, and save the workbook as [your initials] Excel 7-10.
- Remove the *Developer* tab and move the template from the *Custom Office Templates* folder to your work folder.

CHAPTER 8

Exploring Data Analysis and Business Intelligence

CHAPTER OVERVIEW

Excel provides self-service business intelligence (BI) with its data analysis tools so that you can use Excel to accomplish what previously required the help of an information technology department. In this chapter, you explore scenarios, *Goal Seek*, *Solver*, data tables, and more.

STUDENT LEARNING OUTCOMES (SLOs)

After completing this chapter, you will be able to:

SLO 8.1 Create and manage scenarios for worksheet data (p. E8-496).

SLO 8.2 Use *Goal Seek* to backsolve a cell value for a formula (p. E8-498).

SLO 8.3 Use *Solver* to find a solution for a formula (p. E8-500).

SLO 8.4 Build data tables with one and two variables (p. E8-508).

SLO 8.5 Create a forecast sheet for time-based data (p. E8-511).

SLO 8.6 Get and transform data in a query (p. E8-515).

SLO 8.7 Explore *PivotTable* tools (p. E8-522).

SLO 8.8 Use the *Analysis ToolPak* to calculate statistical measures (p. E8-529).

CASE STUDY

In the Pause & Practice projects in this chapter, you create scenarios for Paradise Lakes Resort (PLR) and build a Solver problem. You build data tables to assess revenue and expense levels, create a query, and work with PivotTables.

Pause & Practice 8-1: Create scenarios and use *Goal Seek* and *Solver* to find solutions.

Pause & Practice 8-2: Build one- and two-variable data tables and create a forecast sheet.

Pause & Practice 8-3: Build a query from multiple sources, insert a timeline in a *PivotTable*, and use GETPIVOTDATA.

Creating and Managing Scenarios

A *scenario* is a saved set of values in a worksheet allowing you to vary numbers and see potential results. Scenarios are simple what-if analysis tools, often used to review best and worst possibilities.

A worksheet can have up to 32 scenarios, each one named and saved. Paradise Lakes Resort, for example, can change the value for one revenue category to calculate the effect on total revenue. Each test value is an input, is saved in the scenario, and can be shown in the worksheet.

> **MORE INFO**
>
> Because each scenario input value must be typed in the *Scenario Values* dialog box, use scenarios for data with only a few sets of values.

Create a Scenario

The first scenario that you should create is a scenario for current data so that you can always return to those values. After that, you create additional scenarios using the same cells with different values. You can display any scenario when needed, but only one scenario can be displayed at a time. Although it is optional, it is helpful to name input and result cells so that summary reports are easily understood.

You create a scenario by choosing **Scenario Manager** from the *What-if Analysis* button in the *Forecast* group on the *Data* tab.

▶ **HOW TO:** Create and Show a Scenario

1. Click the **What-if Analysis** button [*Data* tab, *Forecast* group].
2. Select **Scenario Manager**.
   - The *Scenario Manager* dialog box opens.
   - Existing scenarios, if any, are listed in the dialog box.
3. Click **Add**.
   - The *Add Scenario* dialog box opens.
4. Type a name for the saved set of values in the *Scenario name* box.
   - Name the original set of values Original or a similar name.
   - Use a short, descriptive name.
   - Use capitalization and spaces as desired.
5. Click the **Changing cells** box and select the cells whose values will be changed.
   - You can select the cell range before starting the *Scenario Manager* command.
6. Click the **Comment** box to type an optional description or explanation (Figure 8-1).
   - A default comment that includes the user name and date displays for each scenario.

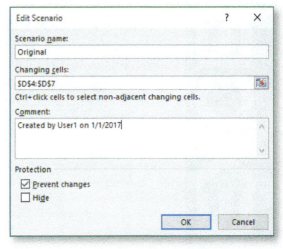

8-1 Scenario setup for original values

7. Click **OK**.

- The *Scenario Values* dialog box opens.
- The values currently displayed in the worksheet are shown for each cell address or name.
- Leave the values unchanged when creating a scenario for the original set of values.

8. Type a new value for each cell name or address (Figure 8-2).

9. Click **OK** in the *Scenario Values* dialog box.

- The *Scenario Manager* dialog box shows the scenario name.

10. Click **Show**.

- The values from the selected scenario replace the values in the worksheet.
- Select another scenario name and click **Show**.

11. Click **Close** in the *Scenario Manager* dialog box.

- The values currently displayed remain visible.

8-2 **New values entered in the *Scenarios Values* dialog box**

Edit a Scenario

When a scenario displays, you can change the values in the affected cells as a regular edit. The scenario itself is unchanged. To change the values saved in a scenario, open the *Scenario Manager*, select the scenario name, and click *Edit*. From the *Edit Scenario* dialog box, you can change a scenario name, redefine which cells are changed, and open the *Scenario Values* dialog box.

▶ **HOW TO:** Edit a Scenario

1. Click the **What-if Analysis** button [*Data* tab, *Forecast* group].

2. Select **Scenario Manager**.

3. Select the scenario name in the *Scenarios* list.

4. Click **Edit**.

- The *Edit Scenario* dialog box is the same as the *Add Scenario* dialog box.

5. Change the scenario name in the *Scenario name* box.

6. Adjust the cell range if needed in the *Changing cells* box.

- A default comment is generated each time the scenario is edited (Figure 8-3).

7. Click **OK**.

- The *Scenario Values* dialog box shows the current values for the scenario.

8. Type a new value for each cell address or range name as needed.

- You can leave some cell values as is.

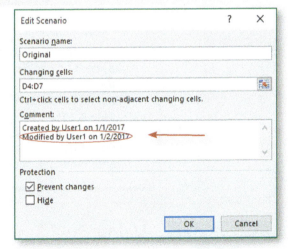

8-3 **Comments are inserted each time a scenario is edited**

9. Click **OK**.

10. Click **Show** to view the edited scenario in the worksheet.

11. Click **Close**.

Scenario Summary Reports

A *scenario summary report* is a generated worksheet that describes each scenario in a workbook. It is formatted as an Excel outline with two row outline levels and two column outline levels. In the report, you can hide or display details about the changing cells and the result cells. For a large worksheet with many scenarios, you can generate a scenario summary report as a *PivotTable*.

If you edit a scenario after creating a summary report, the report is not updated. You can, however, quickly generate another scenario summary report.

▶ HOW TO: Create a Scenario Summary Report

1. Click the **What-if Analysis** button [*Data* tab, *Forecast* group].

2. Select **Scenario Manager**.

3. Click **Summary**.
   - The *Scenario Summary* dialog box appears.

4. Choose **Scenario summary** as the *Report type*.

5. Click the **Result cells** box and select the cell or range (Figure 8-4).
   - These can be changing cells or cells that are affected by changing cells.
   - Press **Ctrl** to select nonadjacent cells or type a comma (,) to separate cell addresses.

6. Click **OK** (Figure 8-5).
   - The report is generated on a sheet named **Scenario Summary**.
   - It is formatted as an outline in a default style.
   - You can hide or display details, delete blank columns and rows, and format the sheet as desired.

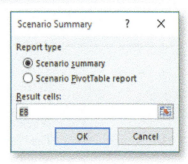

8-4 *Scenario Summary* dialog box

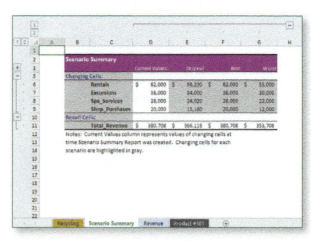

8-5 *Scenario Summary* report

SLO 8.2

Using Goal Seek

Goal Seek is a what-if analysis command that tests values in a cell to *backsolve* a formula. *Backsolving* means knowing the results and determining the value needed to reach those results. When buying a car, use *Goal Seek* to determine how much money to borrow if you can afford a $500 per month payment.

Use Goal Seek

Goal Seek solves a formula for one cell (one argument) in the formula. In the *Goal Seek* dialog box, you enter the cell reference for the formula in the *Set cell* box. You type a target or goal number in the *To value* box. In Figure 8-6, the formula in cell D4 is backsolved by adjusting the value in cell B4 so that the formula result is $50. The solution appears in the *Goal Seek Status* dialog box shown in Figure 8-7 and in the worksheet. You can accept it or keep the original value.

The *Goal Seek* command is an option for the *What-if Analysis* button [*Data* tab, *Forecast* group].

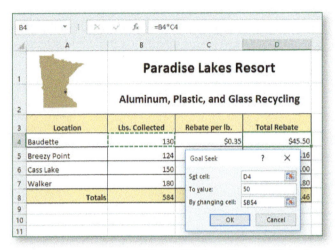

8-6 *Goal Seek* problem and dialog box

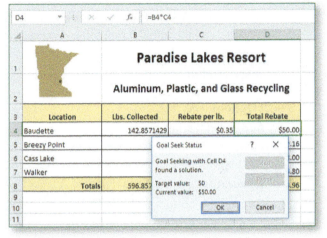

8-7 *Goal Seek Status* shows a solution

▶ **HOW TO:** Use Goal Seek

1. Click the cell with the formula.
2. Click the **What-if Analysis** button [*Data* tab, *Forecast* group].
3. Choose **Goal Seek**.
   - The *Goal Seek* dialog box opens.
   - Verify the formula address in the *Set cell* box.
4. Click the **To value** box and type the target value.
   - This is the result you want the formula to return.
5. Click the **By changing cell** box and click the cell to be adjusted (see Figure 8-6).
   - The address is entered as an absolute reference.
   - *Goal Seek* can change only one cell.
   - You can key the address instead of selecting the cell.
6. Click **OK**.
   - The *Goal Seek Status* dialog box indicates that a solution was calculated (Figure 8-7).
   - The solution displays in the cell.
7. Click **OK** to accept the solution.
   - You can also press **Enter** to accept the solution.
   - Choose **Cancel** to ignore the solution and keep the original data.

Using Solver

Solver is an analysis tool that finds the lowest, the highest, or a specific result for a formula by changing values in other cells within limitations that you set. Using *Solver* can be described as solving a problem in reverse, because you start with the desired answer and *Solver* calculates how to reach that answer. Paradise Lakes Resort, for example, might set a goal for quarterly revenue and use *Solver* to determine the best way to reach that goal by calculating a target for each revenue category.

 Solver is a sophisticated analysis tool, but it may not be able to find a solution to every problem. When it cannot do so, the *Solver Results* dialog box informs you that it could not find a solution.

Install and Run Solver

Solver is an Excel ***add-in***. An add-in is an enhanced command or feature that is not installed with the initial Excel setup. You can install add-ins from the *Add-Ins* dialog box in Excel *Options*.

▶**HOW TO: Install Solver**

1. Select **Options** [*File* tab].
2. Click **Add-Ins** in the left pane.
   - The *View and manage Microsoft Office Add-ins* dialog box opens.
   - Applications that are currently active are listed near the top of the window.
3. Click **Solver Add-in** in the list of *Inactive Application Add-Ins* (Figure 8-8).
4. Click **Go** near the bottom of the dialog box to open the *Add-ins* dialog box.
5. Select the **Solver Add-in** box (Figure 8-9).
   - You can remove *Solver* by deselecting the box.

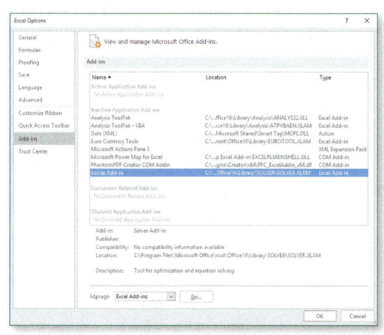

8-8 *Add-ins* dialog box in Excel *Options*

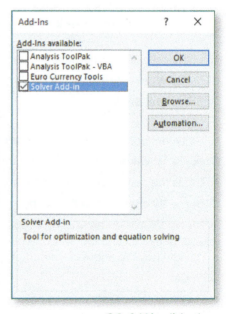

8-9 *Add-ins* dialog box

6. Click **OK**.
   - The **Solver** button is located in the *Analyze* group on the *Data* tab.

A *Solver* problem
has three components,
known as *parameters*.
A parameter is infor-
mation used by *Solver*
to find a solution. The
parameters are the
objective cell, variable
cells, and constraints.

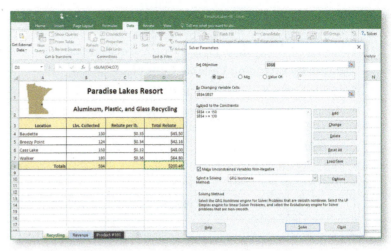

8-10 *Solver* problem for Paradise Lakes

The Objective Cell

The *objective cell* is a
cell with a formula to
be calculated to reach
a desired result. It is
sometimes referred to
as the *target cell*. You can set the objective cell to the maximum or minimum or to a value. In
Figure 8-10, Paradise Lakes wants to determine a maximum total rebate. The formula in cell
D8 is the objective cell.

Variable Cells

In order to reach the desired result in the objective cell, *Solver* changes the cells identified as
variable cells. These cells may also be called *decision cells* or *changing cells*. In Figure 8-10,
the variable cells are cells B4:B7.

Constraints

A *constraint* is a restriction or limitation. It could be a limitation on the formula, on one or
more of the variable cells, or a limitation on other cells that are directly related to the objective cell. In Figure 8-10, a constraint for cell B4, the Baudette value, is that pounds collected
cannot be fewer than 130 or greater than 150. When *Solver* cannot find a solution, it is often
due to how constraints are defined.

Solving Method

Solver uses an *algorithm*, a step-by-step procedure, to find a solution. Three solving methods
are available: GRG Nonlinear, LP Simplex, and Evolutionary. For most problems, start with
GRG Nonlinear. If *Solver* cannot find a solution, try either of the other methods. For sophisticated *Solver* problems with complicated constraints, identify the type of problem and explore
the solving methods in detail.

To run *Solver*, click the **Solver** button on the *Data* tab in the *Analyze* group and define
each parameter in the *Solver Parameters* dialog box.

▶ **HOW TO:** Run Solver

1. Click the **Solver** button [*Data* tab, *Analyze* group].
   - The *Solver Parameters* dialog box opens.
2. Click the **Set Objective** box and click the cell with the formula to be solved.
   - The objective cell must include a formula.

3. Make a selection for the **To** parameter.
   - You can solve the formula for the minimum or maximum value.
   - You can choose *Value Of* and type a specific value in the entry box.
4. Click the **By Changing Variable Cells** box.
5. Select the cells that can be changed.
   - You can paste or type a range name instead of selecting cells.
   - Press **Ctrl** to select nonadjacent cells.
6. Click **Add** to the right of the *Subject to the Constraints* box.
   - The *Add Constraint* dialog box opens.
   - You can set multiple constraints for a cell.
7. Click the **Cell Reference** box and select the first cell or range that has a limitation.
8. Click the middle drop-down arrow and choose an operator.
   - The *int* operator limits the value to a whole number.
   - The *bin* operator requires a binary value, either 0 or 1.
   - The *dif* operator is used to specify that all values in a range must be different.
9. Click the **Constraint** box and enter a value (Figure 8-11).
   - You can click a cell with a value for the constraint.
10. Click **Add** in the *Add Constraint* dialog box to add another constraint.
    - If you click **OK** but want to add another constraint, click **Add** to the right of the *Subject to the Constraints* box.
11. Click **OK** in the *Add Constraint* dialog box when all constraints are identified.
    - The constraints are listed in the *Solver Parameters* dialog box.
12. Select the **Make Unconstrained Variables Non-Negative** box.
    - If you leave this box unchecked, a variable cell without a constraint can be solved to a negative number.
13. Click the **Select a Solving Method** arrow and choose a method (Figure 8-12).
    - If *Solver* cannot find a solution, try a different method.
14. Click **Solve**.
    - The *Solver Results* dialog box includes an option to keep the solution or to return to the original values.
    - You can generate *Solver* reports.
    - You can save the results as a scenario.
15. Click **OK** to keep the solution.

8-11 *Add Constraint* dialog box

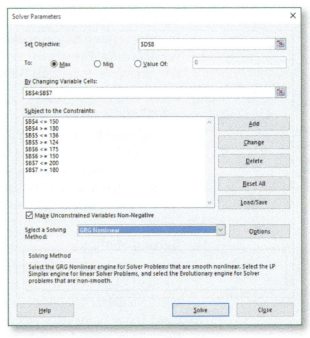

8-12 Completed *Solver* parameters with constraints

Solver Reports

Select an option in the *Solver Results* dialog box to generate statistical analysis reports about the problem and the solution. Three reports for a solved problem are listed: *Answer*, *Sensitivity*, and *Limits*. These reports are straightforward to generate, but you should have an understanding of statistical concepts and terms to understand and interpret the reports.

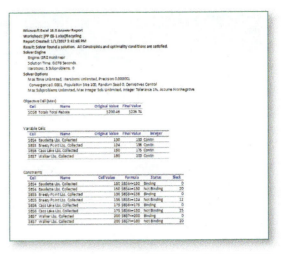

> ### MORE INFO
>
> When *Solver* cannot find a solution, print the *Feasibility* and *Feasibility-Bounds* reports to help identify constraint issues.

Answer Report

The **Answer report** identifies and lists each parameter and serves as documentation of your work. The report includes original values and values suggested by *Solver* as shown in Figure 8-13.

8-13 A *Solver Answer* report

The first *Answer* report is inserted in the workbook in a sheet named *Answer Report 1*. If you run *Solver* multiple times, you can generate an answer report each time, and the sheets are named *Answer Report 2*, and so on.

▶ **HOW TO:** Create an Answer Report

1. Complete the *Solver Parameters* dialog box as needed.
2. Click **Solve**.
3. Select **Answer** in the *Reports* section in the *Solver Results* dialog box. (Figure 8-14).
   - You can also select *Sensitivity* and *Limits* to generate all three reports.
4. Select the **Outline Reports** box if the report should be formatted as an Excel outline.
5. Click **OK**.
   - The report is generated on a new sheet.
6. Select the **Answer Report 1** sheet tab.
   - The report documents how *Solver* reached the solution.

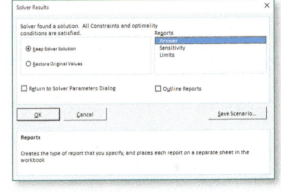

8-14 *Solver Results* window

If *Solver* returns a runtime error in a message box, uninstall the command from the *Add-Ins* dialog box in Excel *Options*, and exit Excel. Then restart Excel and install *Solver* again.

▶ **HOW TO:** Uninstall Solver

1. Select **Options** [*File* tab] and click **Add-Ins** in the left pane.
   - The *View and manage Microsoft Office Add-ins* dialog box opens.
   - Active applications are listed near the top of the window.
2. Select **Solver Add-in** in the list of *Active Application Add-Ins*.
3. Click **Go** near the bottom of the dialog box.
4. Deselect the **Solver Add-in** box and click **OK**.

In this project, you create three scenarios for March revenue at Paradise Lakes Resort. You also use *Goal Seek* and *Solver* to analyze rebate amounts for recyclables at the current rates.

File Needed: ***ParadiseLakes-08.xlsx*** *(Student data files are available in the* Library *of your SIMnet account)*
Completed Project File Name: ***[your initials] PP E8-1.xlsx***

---

1. Open the **ParadiseLakes-08** workbook from your student data files and save it as [your initials] PP E8-1.

2. Click the **Revenue** worksheet tab.

3. Create a scenario for the original data.
   a. Select cells **D4:D7**.
   b. Click the **What-if Analysis** button [*Data* tab, *Forecast* group].
   c. Select **Scenario Manager**. No scenarios exist in the workbook.
   d. Click **Add**.
   e. Type Original as the name in the *Add Scenario* dialog box. The *Changing cells* box displays the selected cells **D4:D7** and a default comment (Figure 8-15).

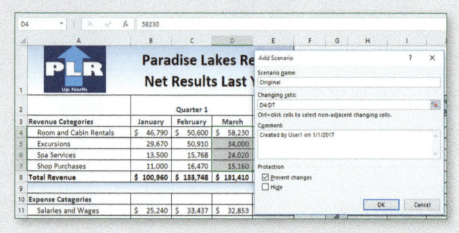

8-15 *Scenario Manager dialog box*

   f. Click **OK**. Note that the changing cells were named.
   g. Do not change any values in the *Scenario Values* dialog box and click **OK**.
   h. Click **Close**.

4. Create scenarios with new data.
   a. Click the **What-if Analysis** button [*Data* tab, *Forecast* group] and select **Scenario Manager**. The *Original* scenario name is listed.
   b. Click **Add** to add a second scenario to the workbook.
   c. Type Best as the name in the *Add Scenario* dialog box.
   d. Verify that the *Changing cells* are cells **D4:D7**.
   e. Click **OK**.
   f. Type 62000 for **Rentals** in the *Scenario Values* dialog box and press **Tab**. If you accidentally press **Enter** and return to the *Scenario Manager* dialog box, click **Edit** and **OK** to return to the *Scenario Values* dialog box.

g. Edit the values as shown here:

Excursions	36000
Spa_Services	28000
Shop_Purchases	20000

h. Click **OK** and then click **Add** to add a third scenario.
i. Type Worst as the name and click **OK**.
j. Edit the values as shown here:

Rentals	55000
Excursions	30000
Spa_Services	22000
Shop_Purchases	12000

k. Click **OK** and click **Close**. The original values are still displayed in the workbook.

5. Show a scenario.
   a. Click the **What-if Analysis** button [*Data* tab, *Forecast* group] and select **Scenario Manager**. The three scenario names are listed (Figure 8-16).
   b. Click **Best** to highlight the name.
   c. Click **Show**. The values for the *Best* scenario display in the worksheet.
   d. Click **Close**.
   e. Select cell **A2**.

6. Create a scenario summary report.
   a. Click the **What-if Analysis** button [*Data* tab, *Forecast* group] and select **Scenario Manager**.
   b. Click **Summary**.
   c. Verify that **Scenario summary** is selected as the *Report type* in the *Scenario Summary* dialog box.
   d. Select cell **E8** in the *Result cells* box.
   e. Click **OK**. The report is inserted on a new sheet named *Scenario Summary* (Figure 8-17).

7. Use *Goal Seek* to determine number of pounds of recycling.
   a. Click the **Recycling** sheet tab and select cell **D4**.
   b. Click the **What-if Analysis** button [*Data* tab, *Forecast* group] and choose **Goal Seek**.
   c. Click the **To value** box and type 50.
   d. Click the **By changing cell** box and select cell **B4** (Figure 8-18).
   e. Click **OK** to run *Goal Seek*. Recycling must increase to more than 142 pounds to reach the target.
   f. Click **OK** to accept the solution.
   g. Select cell **D5** and run *Goal Seek* to determine how many pounds are required to reach $50 for Breezy Point.
   h. Select cells **B4:B8** and click the **Decrease Decimal** button [*Home* tab, *Number* group] to display all values with two decimal places.

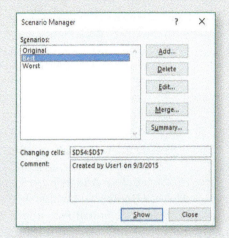

8-16 Scenario names in the dialog box

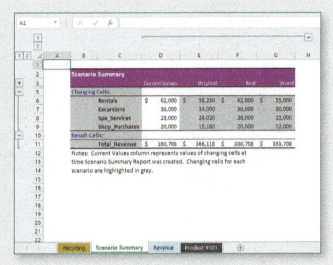

8-17 *Scenario Summary* report sheet

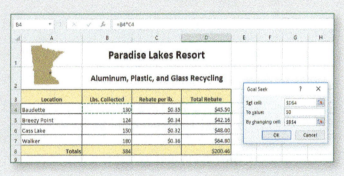

8-18 *Goal Seek* dialog box

8. Create a scenario for current data.
   a. Select cells **B4:B7** and click the **What-if Analysis** button [*Data* tab, *Forecast* group].
   b. Select **Scenario Manager** and click **Add**. Scenarios are associated with a worksheet, and this sheet currently has no scenarios.
   c. Type Current as the name in the *Add Scenario* dialog box.
   d. Click **OK**.
   e. Do not change any values and click **OK** and then click **Close**.

9. Install *Solver*. (Skip this step if *Solver* is already installed.)
   a. Select the **Options** command [*File* tab].
   b. Click **Add-Ins** in the left pane.
   c. Click **Solver Add-in** in the *Inactive Application Add-ins* list.
   d. Click **Go** near the bottom of the window.
   e. Select the **Solver Add-in** box and click **OK**.

10. Set *Solver* parameters.
    a. Select cell **D8**. This cell has a *SUM* formula.
    b. Click the **Solver** button [*Data* tab, *Analyze* group] to open the *Solver Parameters* dialog box.
    c. Verify that cell **D8** is selected in the *Set Objective* box; it is an absolute reference.
    d. Verify that the **Max** radio button is selected for the *To* parameter.
    e. Click the **By Changing Variable Cells** box and select cells **B4:B7**.

11. Add constraints to a *Solver* problem.
    a. Click **Add** to the right of the *Subject to the Constraints* box.
    b. Select cell **B4** for the *Cell Reference* box.
    c. Verify that **<=** is the operator.
    d. Click the **Constraint** box and type 150 (Figure 8-19).
    e. Click **Add** to add another constraint. If you accidentally closed the *Add Constraint* dialog box, click **Add** in the *Solver Parameters* dialog box.
    f. Select cell **B4** again for the *Cell Reference* box.
    g. Choose **>=** as the operator and type 130 as the constraint. The value in cell B4 must be equal to or less than 150 and equal to or greater than 130 (between 130 and 150).
    h. Add the following constraints:

       B5   <=   160
       B5   >=   150
       B6   <=   175
       B6   >=   150
       B7   <=   200
       B7   >=   180

8-19 *Add Constraint* dialog box

    i. Click **OK** in the *Add Constraint* dialog box when all constraints are identified (Figure 8-20).
    j. Select the **Make Unconstrained Variables Non-Negative** box if needed.
    k. Choose **GRG Nonlinear** for the *Select a Solving Method*.
    l. Click **Solve**. A possible solution to the problem is shown in the worksheet.

12. Manage *Solver* results.
    a. Click **Save Scenario** in the *Solver Results* dialog box.
    b. Type Max as the scenario name.
    c. Click **OK** to return to the *Solver Results* dialog box.

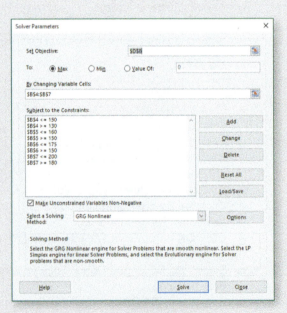

8-20 All constraints are listed

d. Select **Answer** in the *Reports* list.

e. Click **OK**. The generated report is inserted.

13. Create a scenario summary report.

a. Click the **What-if Analysis** button [*Data* tab, *Forecast* group] and select **Scenario Manager**.

b. Click **Summary**.

c. Verify that **Scenario summary** is selected as the *Report type*.

d. Click the **Result cells** box and verify or select cell **D8**.

e. Click **OK**. The report displays on a sheet named *Scenario Summary 2*.

14. Save and close the workbook (Figure 8-21).

15. Uninstall *Solver*.

a. Select **Options** [*File* tab] and click **Add-Ins** in the left pane.

b. Select **Solver Add-in** in the list of *Active Application Add-Ins*.

c. Click **Go** near the bottom of the dialog box.

d. Uncheck the **Solver Add-in** box and click **OK**.

Paradise Lakes Resort
Net Results Last Year

Revenue Categories	January	February	March	Total
		Quarter 1		
Room and Cabin Rentals	$ 46,790	$ 50,600	$ 62,000	$ 159,390
Excursions	29,670	50,910	36,000	116,580
Spa Services	13,500	15,768	28,000	57,268
Shop Purchases	11,000	16,470	20,000	47,470
Total Revenue	$ 100,960	$ 133,748	$ 146,000	$ 380,708
Expense Categories				
Salaries and Wages	$ 25,240	$ 33,487	$ 36,500	$ 95,177
Administrative	15,144	20,062	21,900	57,106
Marketing	10,096	13,375	14,600	38,071
Operations and Maintenance	28,269	37,449	40,880	106,598
Total Expenses	$ 78,749	$ 104,323	$ 113,880	$ 296,952
Net Income	$ 22,211	$ 29,425	$ 32,120	$ 83,756

Paradise Lakes Resort
Aluminum, Plastic, and Glass Recycling

Location	Lbs. Collected	Rebate per lb.	Total Rebate
Baudette	150.00	$0.35	$52.50
Breezy Point	160.00	$0.34	$54.40
Cass Lake	175.00	$0.32	$56.00
Walker	200.00	$0.36	$72.00
Totals	685.00		$234.90

Constraints

Cell	Name	Cell Value	Formula	Status	Slack
$B$4	Baudette Lbs. Collected	150.00	$B$4<=150	Binding	0
$B$4	Baudette Lbs. Collected	150.00	$B$4>=130	Not Binding	20.00
$B$5	Breezy Point Lbs. Collected	160.00	$B$5<=160	Binding	0
$B$5	Breezy Point Lbs. Collected	160.00	$B$5>=150	Not Binding	10.00
$B$6	Cass Lake Lbs. Collected	175.00	$B$6<=175	Binding	0
$B$6	Cass Lake Lbs. Collected	175.00	$B$6>=150	Not Binding	25.00
$B$7	Walker Lbs. Collected	200.00	$B$7<=200	Binding	0
$B$7	Walker Lbs. Collected	200.00	$B$7>=180	Not Binding	20.00

Microsoft Excel 16.0 Answer Report
Worksheet: [PP E8-1.xlsx]Recycling
Report Created: 1/1/2017 2:33:46 PM
Result: Solver found a solution. All Constraints and optimality conditions are satisfied.
Solver Engine
  Engine: GRG Nonlinear
  Solution Time: 0.125 Seconds.
  Iterations: 5 Subproblems: 0
Solver Options
  Max Time Unlimited, Iterations Unlimited, Precision 0.000001
  Convergence 0.0001, Population Size 100, Random Seed 0, Derivatives Central
  Max Subproblems Unlimited, Max Integer Sols Unlimited, Integer Tolerance 1%, Assume NonNegative

Objective Cell (Max)

Cell	Name	Original Value	Final Value	
$D$8	Totals Total Rebate	$212.80	$234.90	

Variable Cells

Cell	Name	Original Value	Final Value	Integer
$B$4	Baudette Lbs. Collected	142.86	150.00	Contin
$B$5	Breezy Point Lbs. Collected	147.06	160.00	Contin
$B$6	Cass Lake Lbs. Collected	150.00	175.00	Contin
$B$7	Walker Lbs. Collected	180.00	200.00	Contin

Scenario Summary

	Current Values:	Current	Max
Changing Cells:			
$B$4	150.00	142.86	150.00
$B$5	160.00	147.06	160.00
$B$6	175.00	150.00	175.00
$B$7	200.00	180.00	200.00
Result Cells:			
$D$8	$234.90	$212.80	$234.90

Notes: Current Values column represents values of changing cells at time Scenario Summary Report was created. Changing cells for each scenario are highlighted in gray.

8-21 Completed worksheets for PP E8-1

Building One- and Two-Variable Data Tables

A *data table* is a range of cells that shows calculated results for one or more formulas. The *Data Table* command is an option on the *What-If Analysis* button on the *Data* tab [*Forecast* group]. It inserts the function {=TABLE(row_input, column_input)} as an array formula, because the same formula is executed in each cell in the selected range. In *SLO 6.3: Exploring Lookup & Reference Functions*, you learned about array formulas when you used *TRANSPOSE*.

Build a One-Variable Data Table

A *one-variable data table* substitutes values for one argument in a formula and displays results for each substituted value. Figure 8-22 shows a data table in columns H:J; column G is a descriptive label. The data table has two formulas, one for January expenses (cell I3) and one for January income (cell J3). The *Data Table* command calculates results in cells I4:J14.

8-22 Data table shows expense and income numbers when total revenue amounts are varied

The *Data Table* command uses an *input value*. The input values in Figure 8-22 are the revenue numbers in column H. These values are substitute values for the formula result in cell B8. In this example, each value in column H is substituted for cell B8 in the net income formula. A one-variable data table uses one input value in the command, and the substitute numbers are either in a column or a row.

When substitute input values are in a column, the data table formulas must start in the column to the right and one row above where the values start. When the data table has multiple formulas, the formulas must be in the same row. In Figure 8-22, the first formula is in cell I3. In the example, cell I3 is a reference to cell B15 so that you need not retype the formula. The second formula is in cell J3, a reference to the net income formula in cell B17. Both of these formulas have a relationship to cell B8.

> **MORE INFO**
>
> When input values are in a row, the first formula must be one column to the left of the first value and one row below.

For the *Data Table* command, select the entire data table range including the formulas, the input values, and the result cells. In Figure 8-22, the data table range is cells H3:J14.

You can edit an input value after the data table is calculated, and the results are updated. You cannot delete the contents of an individual cell in a data table, because that would "shrink" the array. You can, however, select all result cells and delete them.

▶ HOW TO: Create a One-Variable Data Table

1. Enter input values in a single column or row.
   - You can fill a series of values or key specific numbers.

2. Enter the first formula.
   - If input values are in a column, enter the formula one row above and one column to the right of the first input value.
   - If input values are in a row, enter the formula one column to the left and one row below the first input value.
   - You can type a reference to an existing formula.
   - You can type or build the formula with sample data and sample cell references.

3. Enter additional formulas in the same row (Figure 8-23).

4. Select the data table range.
   - Select all input values, all formulas, and the cells for results.
   - The top-left cell in the range is empty.

5. Click the **What-If Analysis** button [*Data* tab, *Forecast* group].

6. Choose **Data Table**.
   - The *Data Table* dialog box opens.

7. Enter a column or a row input cell reference (Figure 8-24).
   - In a one-variable data table, enter either a row input or a column input reference.
   - You can select the cell for which the input values will be substituted.
   - You can type the cell address.

8. Click **OK**.
   - The data table cells display results for each input value.
   - You can format a data table to add number styles, fill, borders, or explanatory labels.
   - The *TABLE* function is used in an array formula and is entered in each result cell.

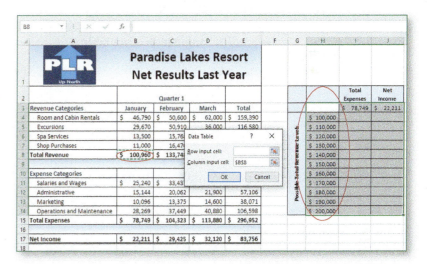

8-23 Input values are in a column; formulas are in the row above, one column to the right

8-24 Values in column H will replace the value in cell B8 in the data table to calculate expense and income amounts

Build a Two-Variable Data Table

A ***two-variable data table*** uses two sets of input values, one in a column, the other in a row, and the table has only one formula. Figure 8-25 shows a two-variable data table in which January revenue *and* expenses are varied to calculate net income. The net income formula is in cell B17 and is referenced in cell H4. Substituted revenue amounts are column input values (cells H5:H17), and substituted expense amounts are row input values (cells I4:P4).

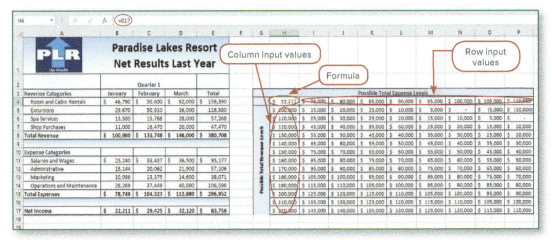

8-25 Two-variable data table

In a two-variable data table, row input values start one column to the right of the column values and one row above the first column value, cell I4 in the figure. Place the formula above the column values and to the left of the row values (cell H4 in the example).

The data table range includes the formula, the input column, the input row, and the result cells, cells H4:P17. In Figure 8-25, the column input cell for the *Data Table* command is cell B8 because revenue values are in *column* H. The row input cell is cell B15, because expense values are in *row* 4. The input values are substituted for both the revenue and expense amounts to complete the data table.

> **MORE INFO**
>
> A data table must be on the same worksheet as its formulas.

▶ HOW TO: Create a Two-Variable Data Table

1. Enter column input values in a single column.
   - Type values or fill a series.
   - You can prepare either the row or column input values first.
2. Enter row input values in a single row.
   - Start the first row value one row above and one column to the right of the first column value.
3. Enter the formula or a reference to the formula.
   - It is easier to refer to an existing formula than to re-enter the formula.
   - Place the formula reference in the cell above the column input values and to the left of the row input values.
4. Select the data table range.
   - Include the formula, column input values, row input values, and result cells.

5. Click the **What-If Analysis** button [*Data* tab, *Forecast* group].

6. Choose **Data Table**.

7. Select the row input cell.

   - You can type the cell address.

8. Select the column input cell or type the cell address (Figure 8-26).

9. Click **OK**.

   - The result cells calculate the formula results in each cell.
   - Each result cell substitutes a column and a row input value in the formula.
   - Change any column or row input value to recalculate the data table.

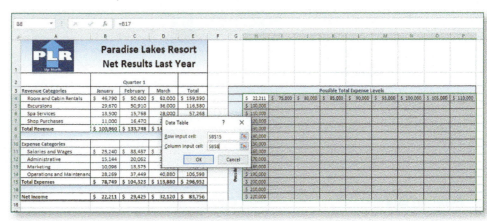

8-26 Two-variable data table setup

Creating a Forecast Sheet

A *forecast sheet* is a worksheet with an Excel table and a chart that illustrates past data and predicts future values, generated from data in the workbook. A forecast sheet can be created quickly to estimate future values for product sales, work hour requirements, or expense levels.

Create a Forecast Sheet

A forecast sheet uses two data series to build either a line or a column chart. One data series must be a date or time field, and the other series is the values used for forecasting. The date or time series must follow an interval, such as every hour, every other day, every month, and so on. The generated sheet is formatted as an Excel table and displays existing dates/times and values in adjacent columns. At the end of the table, forecast dates display with estimated values in a third column.

> **MORE INFO**
>
> A forecast sheet inserts *FORECAST* functions [*Statistical* category] in its tables. Explore these functions to learn more about them.

The *Create Forecast Sheet* dialog box has options for calculating statistics such as alpha, beta, and gamma values, and more. You can also redefine the time and value ranges if needed.

After the forecast sheet is created, format the table from the *Table Tools Design* tab. The *Chart Tools Design* and *Format* tabs are also available for limited formatting of the chart.

▶ **HOW TO:** Create a Forecast Sheet

1. Select the two data series.

   - One column must be a time or date field.
   - The columns need not be adjacent.

2. Click the **Forecast Sheet** button [*Data* tab, *Forecast* group].

   - The *Create Forecast Worksheet* window opens (Figure 8-27).

3. Select the line or column chart type.

   - The chart preview displays.

4. Click the calendar icon for **Forecast End** and set the ending date or time for estimated values.

5. Select the **Options** arrow to expand the window.

   - You can change the ranges used for the data series.
   - The default confidence interval is 95% which measures how likely a value is to occur within the range of forecasted values.

6. Select the **Include forecast statistics** box.

   - This option generates alpha, beta, gamma, and additional statistical measures.

7. Click **Create** (Figure 8-28).

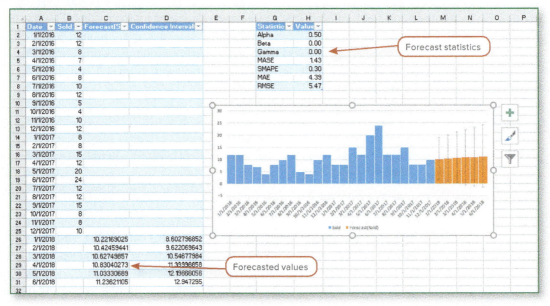

8-27 Create Forecast Worksheet window

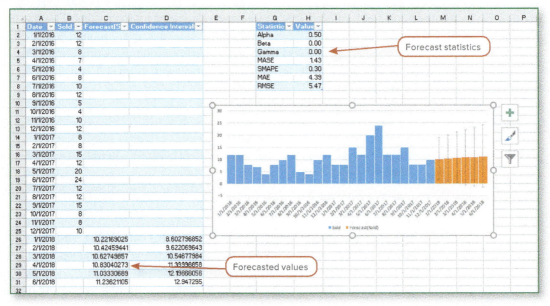

8-28 Forecast table and chart

- The forecast sheet includes the table, forecast statistics, and the chart.
- Forecasted values are at the bottom of the table.
- Forecast statistics are displayed in a separate table.

In this project, you build a one- and a two-variable data table to determine revenue, expense, and income levels for Paradise Lakes Resort. You also create a forecast sheet for a product sold at PLR spas.

File Needed: *PP E8-1.xlsx*
Completed Project File Name: *[your initials] PP E8-2.xlsx*

1. Open the *[your initials] PP E8-1* workbook completed in *Pause & Practice 8-1* and save it as [your initials] PP E8-2.

2. Select the **Revenue** worksheet tab.

3. Create a one-variable data table.
   a. Select cell **I3**. This cell is one column to the right of and one row above the first input value.
   b. Type **=**, select cell **B15**, and press **Enter** to create a reference to the total expenses formula for January.
   c. Select cell **J3** and create a reference to cell **B17** for the net income formula (Figure 8-29).
   d. Select cells **H3:J14** as the data table range.
   e. Click the **What-If Analysis** button [*Data* tab, *Forecast* group] and choose **Data Table**.
   f. Click the **Column input cell** entry box and select cell **B8**. The total revenue amount will be replaced by the input values in column H in both formulas.
   g. Click **OK** to create the data table.
   h. Select cells **I4:J14** and format them as **Accounting Number** format with **0** decimal places.
   i. *AutoFit* columns that do not display all the data (Figure 8-30).

4. Create a two-variable data table.
   a. Select cell **H17** to place the formula one row above the column input values and one column to the left of the row values.
   b. Type **=**, select cell **B17**, and press **Enter** to create a reference to the net income formula.
   c. Select cells **H17:P30** as the data table range.
   d. Click the **What-If Analysis** button [*Data* tab, *Forecast* group] and choose **Data Table**.
   e. Select cell **B15** for the *Row input cell* box. The values in row 17 will be substituted for the value in cell B15.
   f. Click the **Column input cell** box and select cell **B8**. The values in column H will be substituted for the value in cell B8 (Figure 8-31).
   g. Click **OK** to build the data table. Some results are negative, meaning a net loss.
   h. Format all cells in the data table as **Accounting Number** format with **0** decimal places.
   i. **AutoFit** columns that do not display all the data.

5. Edit input values for a table.
   a. Select cell **I17** and type 75000 as a new value.
   b. Select cell **J17** and type 80000 to start a new series.

		Total Expenses	Net Income
		$ 78,749	=B17
	$ 100,000		
	$ 110,000		
	$ 120,000		
	$ 130,000		
	$ 140,000		
	$ 150,000		
	$ 160,000		
	$ 170,000		
	$ 180,000		
	$ 190,000		
	$ 200,000		

Possible Total Revenue Levels

8-29 Formula reference in the data table

		Total Expenses	Net Income
		$ 78,749	$ 22,211
	$ 100,000	$ 78,000	$ 22,000
	$ 110,000	$ 85,800	$ 24,200
	$ 120,000	$ 93,600	$ 26,400
	$ 130,000	$ 101,400	$ 28,600
	$ 140,000	$ 109,200	$ 30,800
	$ 150,000	$ 117,000	$ 33,000
	$ 160,000	$ 124,800	$ 35,200
	$ 170,000	$ 132,600	$ 37,400
	$ 180,000	$ 140,400	$ 39,600
	$ 190,000	$ 148,200	$ 41,800
	$ 200,000	$ 156,000	$ 44,000

Possible Total Revenue Levels

8-30 One-variable data table results

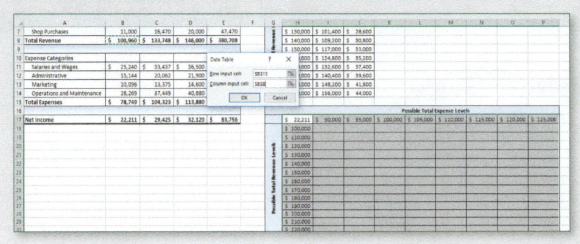

8-31 *Data Table* dialog box for a two-variable table

c. Select cells **I17:J17** and use the *Fill* handle to fill values to reach cell **P17**. The data table updates and there are fewer negative results (Figure 8-32). When revenue and expenses are equal, there is no profit, shown as a hyphen (-) in the *Accounting Number* format.

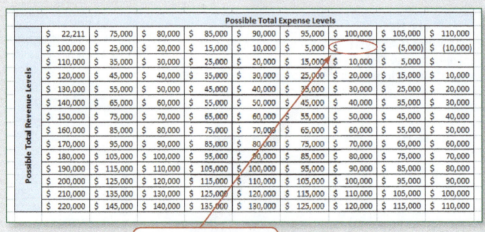

Revenue and expense are equal

8-32 Completed two-variable table

6. Create a forecast worksheet.
   a. Select the **Product #101** worksheet tab.
   b. Select cells **A4: B28** and click the **Forecast Sheet** button [*Data* tab, *Forecast* group].
   c. Click the **Create a line chart** button.
   d. Click **Create** to generate the forecast worksheet.
   e. Name the new sheet tab Forecast Sheet.

7. Format a forecast chart sheet.
   a. Move the chart to its own sheet named Forecast Chart.
   b. Format the chart with **Style 9**.
   c. Click the **Chart Elements** drop-down list [*Chart Tools Format* tab, *Current Selection* group] and select **Horizontal (Category) Axis** to select the dates along the bottom axis.
   d. Click the **Format Selection** button [*Chart Tools Format* tab, *Current Selection* group].
   e. Select the **Axis Options** button in the *Format Axis* pane.
   f. Expand the **Labels** group in the task pane and set the **Specify interval unit** at **2** to show every other month.

g. Click the **Chart Elements** button at the top right corner of the chart and insert a **Centered Overlay** chart title.

h. Edit the placeholder text to Forecasted Sales for Product #101.

i. Click the chart background to deselect the title object.

j. Point at the chart title object to display a move pointer and drag the title as shown in Figure 8-33.

8. Save and close the workbook.

	A	B	C	D	E
1	Date	Sold	Forecast(Sold)	Lower Confidence Bound(Sold)	Upper Confidence Bound(Sold)
2	1/1/2016	12			
3	2/1/2016	12			
4	3/1/2016	8			
5	4/1/2016	7			
6	5/1/2016	4			
7	6/1/2016	8			
8	7/1/2016	10			
9	8/1/2016	12			
10	9/1/2016	5			
11	10/1/2016	4			
12	11/1/2016	10			
13	12/1/2016	12			
14	1/1/2017	8			
15	2/1/2017	8			
16	3/1/2017	15			
17	4/1/2017	12			
18	5/1/2017	20			
19	6/1/2017	24			
20	7/1/2017	12			
21	8/1/2017	12			
22	9/1/2017	15			
23	10/1/2017	8			
24	11/1/2017	8			
25	12/1/2017	10	10	10.00	10.00
26	1/1/2018		10.22169025	1.62	18.82
27	2/1/2018		10.42459441	0.80	20.05
28	3/1/2018		10.62749857	0.08	21.17
29	4/1/2018		10.83040273	-0.57	22.23
30	5/1/2018		11.03330689	-1.16	23.23
31	6/1/2018		11.23621105	-1.71	24.18

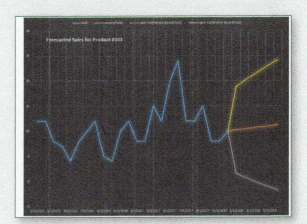

8-33 Completed forecast worksheet and chart for PP E8-2

SLO 8.6

Getting and Transforming Data in a Query

You can import data from various sources in queries and transform the data to fit your Excel needs. A **query** is a combination of instructions, filters, and formats that establishes a connection to and displays data. You define and save a query once and refresh it when necessary to extract current data. You can combine queries to build an Excel table or *PivotTable* that would otherwise be impossible or difficult to create. Queries can use corporate data, online public data, or data on your computer. As for tables and *PivotTables*, data for queries is always in list-type format.

The *Query Editor* is a window that floats on top of the worksheet as shown in Figure 8-34. It opens with its own *Ribbon* and displays the *Query Settings* pane on the right. You define and organize the data for loading into Excel in the *Query Editor*. The *New Query* button is located on the *Data* tab in the *Get & Transform Data* group.

Get and Transform an XML File

XML represents *Extensible Markup Language*, a file format for exchanging data on the Web. An XML file is a text file that can be imported into many applications; it has an .xml file name extension. To create a query, you can use an XML file on your computer, on a corporate network, or in a *OneDrive* folder.

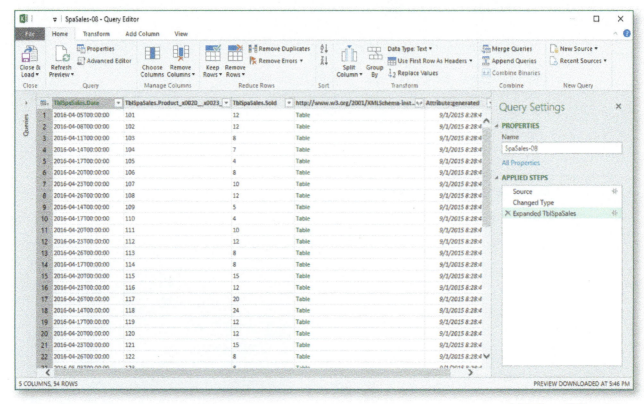

8-34 *Query Editor* window

> **MORE INFO**
>
> An XML file has a related .xsd file that provides data scheme information.

> **ANOTHER WAY**
>
> You can open an XML file in Excel and save it as a regular workbook.

▶**HOW TO:** Get an XML File for a Query

1. Click the **New Query** button [*Data* tab, *Get & Transform* group] and choose **From File**.
2. Choose **From XML**.
   • The *Import Data* dialog box opens.
3. Navigate to the folder with the XML file.
4. Select the file name, click **Import**, and then click **Edit**.
   • The *Query Editor* window opens with the *Query Settings* pane at the right.
5. Click the **Expand** button next to the file name at the top of the first column (Figure 8-35).
   • All of the fields are selected.
   • You can deselect fields as desired.

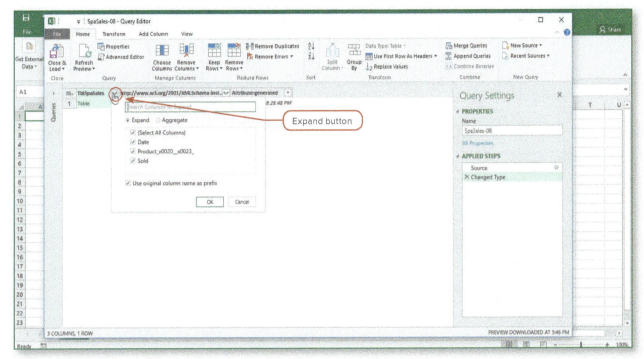

8-35 XML data is ready to be expanded

6. Click **OK**.

- Each field is expanded so that data is visible in the query sheet.
- The *Applied Steps* in the *Query Settings* pane lists each action you perform (Figure 8-36).
- You can delete steps to undo actions.

Data in a query can be "cleaned" or prepared for use in Excel. The labels, for example, can be edited to use simple, descriptive terms. You can also choose the data type for each column to match your plans for use in Excel.

Queries are named with the same name as the source file, but you can change the name in the *Query Settings* pane. Each field has a *Filter* arrow for displaying only the rows that you need for your Excel worksheet.

After you have prepared the data in the *Query Editor*, you load the results to Excel. The data is formatted as an Excel table on a new worksheet with a default name which you can edit as desired.

▶ **HOW TO: Edit and Load a Query**

1. Double-click a column name, type a new name, and press **Enter**.
   - You can also edit labels later in the Excel table or *PivotTable*.
2. Click a column name and click the **Data Type** button [*Home* tab, *Transform* group].
3. Choose the data type (see Figure 8-36).
   - If you plan to use a field in calculations, it must be a number-type field.
4. Right-click the column name for a field to be removed.
5. Select **Remove**.
   - You can also click the column name and press **Delete** on the keyboard.

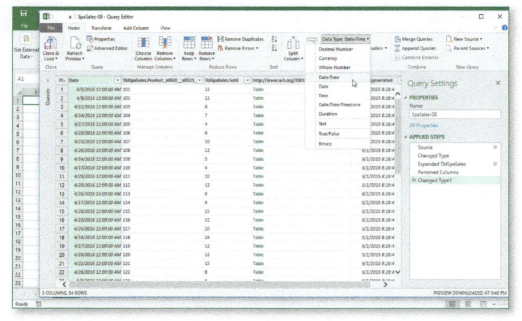

8-36 Select the appropriate data type for each field

6. Click a *Filter* arrow and build a filter for a column as desired.

   - Only filtered rows are loaded to the worksheet.

7. Click the **Close & Load** button [*Home* tab, *Close* group].

   - Query results display in an Excel table on a new sheet.
   - You can rename the sheet tab as desired.
   - The *Workbook Queries* pane is open and lists existing queries (Figure 8-37).

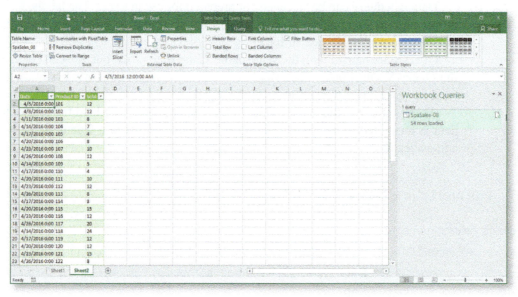

8-37 Query results and the *Workbook Queries* pane

8. Save the workbook.

Get and Transform a Database Table

Queries can be built from tables in Access or SQL databases to which you have permission. The fields are placed in the *Query Editor* with the field names used in the database, and you have the same query editing features as you have for an XML file.

▶ **HOW TO: Build a Query for a Database Table**

1. Click the **New Query** button [*Data* tab, *Get & Transform* group] and choose **From Database**.

2. Choose **From Microsoft Access Database**.
   - The *Import Data* dialog box opens.

3. Navigate to the folder with the database file.

4. Select the database name and click **Import**.
   - The *Navigator* window opens and lists the names of tables and queries in the Access database.

5. Select the name of the table or query.
   - The *Navigator* shows a preview of the data that will be imported (Figure 8-38).

6. Click **Edit** at the bottom of the window.
   - The *Query Editor* opens and displays all the fields from the selected table or query.
   - Database field names are used in the header row.

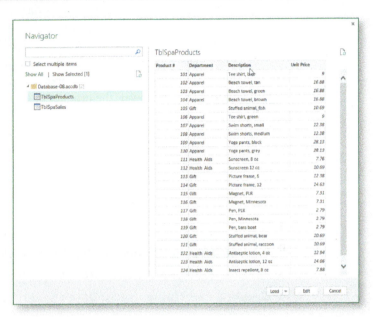

8-38 *Navigator* window for getting files from a database

7. Click a column name to select the field and click the **Data Type** button [*Home* tab, *Transform* group].

8. Choose the data type.
   - If you plan to use a field in calculations, it must be a number-type field.

9. Right-click a column name to open its menu (Figure 8-39).

10. Select **Remove**.
    - The *Applied Steps* in the *Query Settings* pane lists each action you perform.

11. Double-click a column name, type a new name, and press **Enter**.

12. Click the **Close & Load** button [*Home* tab, *Close* group].
    - Query results display in an Excel table on a new sheet.
    - You can rename the sheet tab as desired.
    - The *Workbook Queries* pane lists queries in the workbook.

13. Save the workbook.

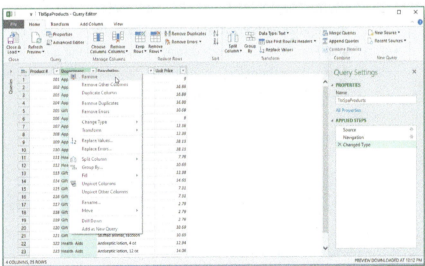

8-39 Remove unnecessary data from the query

Create a PivotTable from Multiple Queries

Queries are part of the workbook and are listed in the *Workbook Queries* pane. The pane opens immediately after you load a query, and it can be toggled off and on from the *Data* tab. When you select a cell in a query table, the *Query Tools* tab displays as well as the *Table Tools Design* tab. From the *Query Tools* tab, you can edit the query, refresh the data, delete the query, and combine queries. From the *Table Tools Design* tab, you can create a new *PivotTable*.

You can use multiple queries to create a *PivotTable* when a common field exists in each of the queries. A ***common field*** is data that is the same in each of the queries, allowing for a relationship between the queries. Many relationships are one-to-many in which there is a key field in one of the queries. The ***key field*** is a column in which each data piece appears only once. The related query uses the same field, but it can appear many times. In a product list query, each product number appears only once with the description of the item. In a product sales query, however, the product number appears each time a sale is recorded.

> **MORE INFO**
>
> Relationships in Excel queries follow the same logic as database rules for relating tables.

As you create queries, Excel automatically and invisibly builds a data model. A ***data model*** is a collection of tables in the workbook available for use in creating a *PivotTable*.

▶**HOW TO:** Create a PivotTable from a Data Model

1. Select a cell in one of the query tables.
   - The *Query Tools* and *Table Tools Design* tabs open.
2. Click the **Summarize with PivotTable** button [*Table Tools Design* tab, *Tools* group].
   - The *Create PivotTable* dialog box displays the name of the query and highlights the range in the sheet.
3. Select the **New Worksheet** radio button.
4. Select the **Add this data to the Data Model** box.
5. Click **OK**.
   - A blank *PivotTable* layout displays on a new sheet.
   - The *Workbook Queries* and the *PivotTable Fields* panes are open.
6. Select the fields from the active query to be shown in the *PivotTable*.
   - Fields are placed in areas in the *PivotTable* layout.
   - You can move fields as needed by dragging a field name from one area to another.
7. Click **All** at the top of the *PivotTable Fields* pane to see the related query name.
8. Select the name of the related query and expand it to see the fields.
   - The fields are available for placement in the *PivotTable*.
9. Select the fields to be shown in the *PivotTable*.
   - Fields display in the *PivotTable* layout but may not show accurate data (Figure 8-40).
   - A warning box in the *PivotTable Fields* pane states that *Relationships between tables may be needed*.
10. Click **AutoDetect**.
    - A message box notes that a relationship has been created.
    - If a relationship cannot be found, edit the queries to verify data types for related fields.

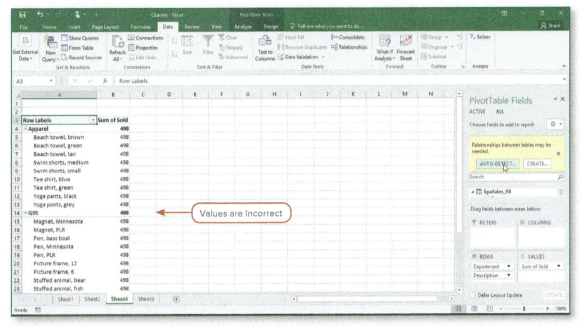

8-40 Fields in *PivotTable* are not yet matched by relationship

11. Click **Close** in the message box.

   - Data in the *PivotTable* is accurate when the relationship is valid.

12. Click the **Relationships** button [*PivotTable Tools Analyze* tab, *Calculations* group].

   - The *Manage Relationships* dialog box identifies how the queries are related (Figure 8-41).

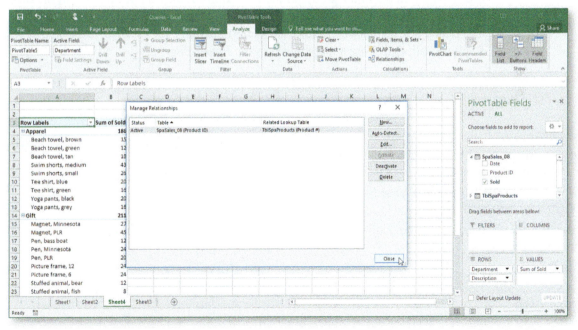

8-41 *Manage Relationships* dialog box

13. Close the dialog box.

SLO 8.7

Exploring PivotTable Tools

You learned in *SLO 4.8: Building and Formatting PivotTables*, how to create, format, and rearrange a *PivotTable*. *PivotTables* and *PivotCharts* have many features that allow you to manage and adjust the data. You can display a timeline for date fields, show values as ratios or percentages, or create a calculated field. A *PivotTable* and its *PivotChart* are linked, so changes you make in either are immediately reflected in the other.

PivotTable Slicers

The *Slicer* tool creates a visual filter for a field in a *PivotTable*, like a slicer for an Excel table. For a large *PivotTable*, a slicer allows you to display only the data you need at the moment. In the Paradise Lakes worksheet, for example, you can create a slicer that displays items sold by department as shown in Figure 8-42.

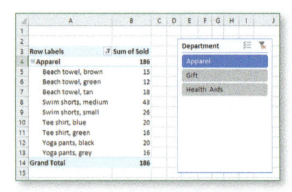

8-42 Department slicer filters data to show only apparel sales

You create a slicer by clicking the ***Insert Slicer*** button in the *Filter* group on the *PivotTable Tools Analyze* tab. From the *Insert Slicers* dialog box, you select fields to be displayed in slicers, each field in its own slicer window. The dialog box includes all fields used as the data range for the *PivotTable* so that you can use fields in a slicer that are not displayed in the *PivotTable*.

▶ **HOW TO:** Insert a Slicer in a PivotTable

1. Click a cell in the *PivotTable*.
2. Click the **Insert Slicer** button [*PivotTable Tools Analyze* tab, *Filter* group].
   - The *Insert Slicers* window lists each field in the data source for the *PivotTable*.
3. Select the box for each field to be used for filtering data (Figure 8-43).
4. Click **OK**.
   - A *Slicer* window opens for each field.
   - No filter applied.
   - When a slicer button is grayed out, there are no matching items in the *PivotTable*.
5. Click the item name to be used as criteria in the *Slicer* window (Figure 8-44).
   - The *PivotTable* is filtered to display data that matches your selection.

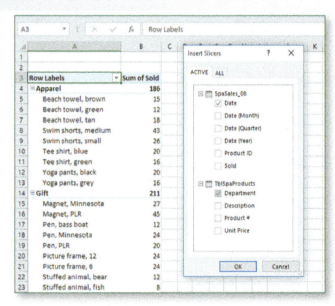

8-43 Choose one or more fields to be used in slicers

- Click the **Multi-Select** button to select more than one field, or press **Ctrl** and click each field.
- Remove a filter by clicking the **Clear Filter** button in the top-right corner of the slicer.

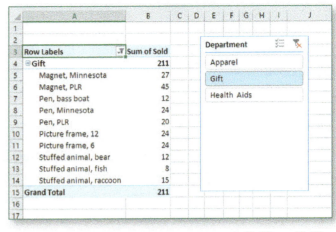

8-44 Slicer with filter

Slicer Tools Options

A slicer is an object that can be sized and moved. When a slicer window is selected, the *Slicer Tools Options* tab is available. It includes commands to format the slicer, change its caption, and to size and position the object.

▶ HOW TO: Format a PivotTable Slicer

1. Select the slicer.
2. Click the **More** button [*Slicer Tools Options* tab, *Slicer Styles* group].
3. Select a style.
4. Click the **Columns** box [*Slicer Tools Options* tab, *Buttons* group].
5. Type the number of columns to be displayed in the slicer.
   - You can set a width and height for each button in the slicer.
6. Size the slicer to display the buttons in a row (Figure 8-45).
   - You can also set a width and height for the slicer window.

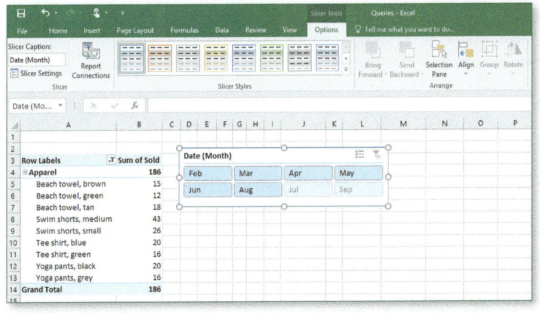

8-45 Slicer with four columns

7. Click the **Slicer Settings** button [*Slicer Tools Options* tab, *Slicer* group].
   - The *Slicer Settings* dialog box opens.

8. Click the **Caption** box and type a label for the slicer (Figure 8-46).

- You can change the default sort order in the slicer.

9. Click **OK**.

A slicer is saved with the *PivotTable*. If you no longer need the slicer, select it and press **Delete** to remove it.

Insert Timeline

A *timeline* is a visual filter for a date field in a *PivotTable*. In a timeline, you select days, months, quarters, or years for filtering. A timeline is a selectable object that can be sized, positioned, and formatted.

The *Insert Timeline* button is on the *PivotTable Tools Analyze* tab in the *Filter* group. When a timeline object is selected, it displays selection handles, and the *Timeline Tools Options* tab appears. Timeline options include light and dark styles and height and width settings.

> **MORE INFO**
>
> You can insert a timeline for dates in an Excel table.

▶ **HOW TO:** Insert and Format a Timeline in a PivotTable

1. Click a cell in the *PivotTable*.

- The *PivotTable Tools Analyze* and *Design* tabs open.

2. Click the **Insert Timeline** button [*PivotTable Tools Analyze* tab, *Filter* group].

- The *Insert Timelines* dialog box lists date fields in the *PivotTable*.

3. Select the box for the date field to be shown in the timeline.

- The date field for the timeline need not be shown in the *PivotTable*.

4. Click **OK**.

- The *Timeline* object displays.
- The *Timeline* displays months as the time level.

5. Click the **Months** arrow and choose the time level as desired.

6. Click the time group to use for filtering in the timeline.

- The *PivotTable* is filtered to show rows based on the item selected in the timeline (Figure 8-47).

7. Click the **More** button [*Timeline Tools Options* tab, *Timeline Styles* group] and choose a style.

8. Point to a border to display a move pointer and drag the timeline object to a new location.

9. Point to a corner handle to display a size arrow and resize the timeline object.

8-47 *Timeline* filter for Q2 in 2017

Custom Calculations

A **custom calculation** is a built-in percentage, ranking, or ratio in a *PivotTable*. Custom calculations are listed in the *Value Field Settings* dialog box on the *Show Values As* tab. In Figure 8-48, the *Sold* field is shown twice in the *PivotTable*, once as a value (column B) and once as a percentage of the total (column C). You can see the field listed twice in the *Values* area in the *PivotTable Fields* pane.

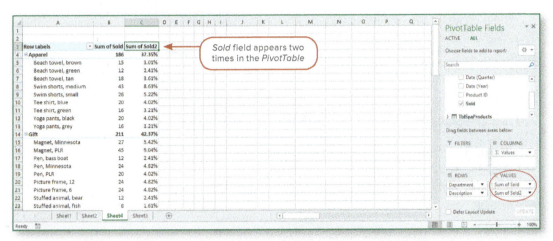

8-48 Value field displayed twice with different calculations

▶HOW TO: Use a Custom Calculation in a PivotTable

1. Right-click a value in the *PivotTable* column.
2. Select **Show Values As**.
   - Custom calculations are listed.
   - *No Calculation* is the first option.
3. Choose a calculation (Figure 8-49).
   - The column in the *PivotTable* displays the custom calculation results.

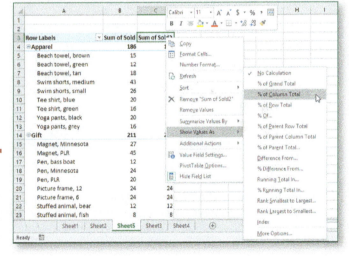

8-49 Value field set to show a custom calculation

> **ANOTHER WAY**
>
> Click a cell in the *PivotTable* column, click the **Field Settings** button [*PivotTable Tools Analyze* tab, *Active Field* group] and click the *Show Value As* tab to use a custom calculation.

Calculated Fields

A **calculated field** is a field in the *PivotTable* that is not in the source data. A calculated field uses a value field from the *PivotTable's* underlying data in a formula. When you insert a calculated field, it displays as the rightmost field in the *PivotTable*, but you can move it and edit its *Value Field Settings*, too.

A calculated field can be created in a *PivotTable* based on workbook data but not in a *PivotTable* that uses data from multiple queries or online sources.

▶ HOW TO: Insert a Calculated Field

1. Click a cell in the *PivotTable*.
2. Click the **Fields, Items, and Sets** button [*PivotTable Tools Analyze* tab, *Calculations* group].
3. Select **Calculated Field**.
4. Click the **Name** box in the *Insert Calculated Field* dialog box.
5. Type a name for the calculated field.
   * The name must be unique.
6. Click the **Formula** box and delete the zero and the space after the equals sign.
7. Enter the formula (Figure 8-50).
   * Double-click a field name in the *Fields* list to insert it in the formula.
   * Fields names display within single quotation marks.
   * You can select a field name and click **Insert Field**.
   * Type an operator or a constant value to build the formula.
8. Click **OK**.
   * The calculated field is added at the right in the *PivotTable* (Figure 8-51).

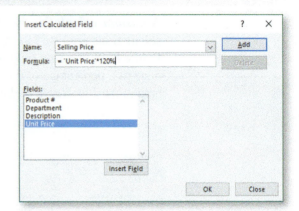

8-50 A calculated field uses a *PivotTable* field in a formula

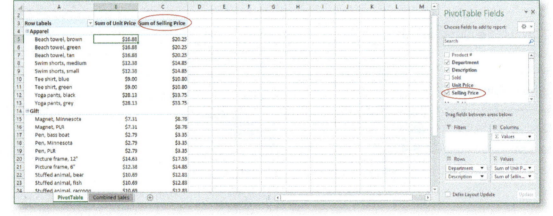

8-51 Calculated field inserted in *PivotTable*

   * The field name is included in the *PivotTable Fields* pane.
   * An associated *PivotChart* is updated to include the new field.

> ▶ **MORE INFO**
>
> Delete a calculated field by right-clicking a cell in the column and choosing *Remove "Field Name."*

PivotTable Layout

The *Layout* group on the *PivotTable Tools Design* tab allows you to alter the appearance of a *PivotTable*. You can hide or display subtotals and grand totals, insert a blank row after items, or repeat row labels. The *Options* command on the *PivotTable Tools Analyze* tab opens the *PivotTable Options* dialog box which includes settings to customize display, print, and data features.

1. Click a cell in the *PivotTable*.

2. Click the **Subtotals** button [*PivotTable Tools Design* tab, *Layout* group].

   - Subtotals can be hidden or shown.
   - Subtotals can be placed at the top or the bottom of each item.

3. Select an option for subtotals.

4. Click the **Grand Totals** button in the *Layout* group [*PivotTable Tools Design* tab].

   - You can show grand totals for both columns and rows.
   - You can turn off the display of grand totals.

5. Select an option for grand totals.

6. Click the **Report Layout** button [*PivotTable Tools Design* tab, *Layout* group].

   - A *Compact* format places row data in one column and occupies the least amount of horizontal space.
   - An *Outline* form places row data in separate columns (Figure 8-52).
   - *Tabular* form starts row data in the same row but in separate columns.
   - *Repeat Item Labels* displays the row data in each row like an Excel table.

7. Click the **Blank Rows** button [*PivotTable Tools Design* tab, *Layout* group].

   - You can display a blank row before or after each item.

8. Click the **Options** button [*PivotTable Tools Analyze* tab, *PivotTable* group] (Figure 8-53).

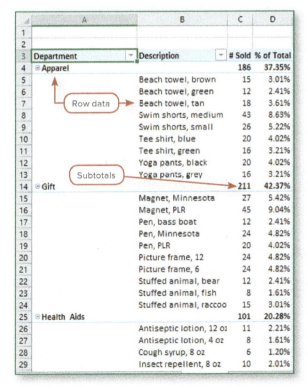

8-52 **Subtotals at the top with data in outline layout**

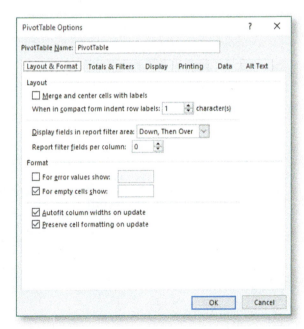

8-53 *PivotTable Options* **dialog box**

- The *PivotTable Options* dialog box has six tabs.
- Some options are also available in the *Layout* group on the *PivotTable Tools Design* tab.

9. Click **OK**.

Use GETPIVOTDATA

When you refer to a value in a *PivotTable* in another worksheet, you cannot simply click the cell because the cell content at that address may change if the *PivotTable* is rearranged. To refer to specific *PivotTable* results in another sheet, use the *GETPIVOTDATA* function from the *Lookup & Reference* category. If the *PivotTable* is pivoted to another view, your formula displays the results from the original *PivotTable* layout as long as that result is still somewhere in the *PivotTable*. GETPIVOTDATA works in *PivotTables* that are based on a range of data in the workbook, not *PivotTables* built from queries or multiple online sources.

> **MORE INFO**
>
> When the original data referenced in *GETPIVOTDATA* is no longer displayed in the *PivotTable*, the function returns the error message #REF!

Although you can insert the *GETPIVOTDATA* function from the *Formulas* tab, it is easier to enter a 3D reference to the cell in the *PivotTable*. The function is entered automatically with required arguments. The syntax for *GETPIVOTDATA* is:

=GETPIVOTDATA(Data_field,Pivot_table,Field,Item)

▶ **HOW TO: Use GETPIVOTDATA**

1. Select the cell where the *PivotTable* result should be displayed.
   - This cell is in a worksheet other than the sheet with the *PivotTable*.
2. Type **=** to start a formula.
3. Click the sheet tab that includes the *PivotTable*.
4. Select the cell with the desired result in the *PivotTable*.
5. Press **Enter** (Figure 8-54).
   - The focus returns to the worksheet.
   - The *GETPIVOTDATA* formula is inserted in the cell with a 3D reference to the *PivotTable* sheet name.
   - The result from the *PivotTable* appears in the cell.

8-54 *GETPIVOTDATA* inserted in the cell

6. Click the *PivotTable* sheet tab name.
7. Pivot the table to a different arrangement as desired.
   - The original result used in the *GETPIVOTDATA* formula must be shown somewhere in the *PivotTable*.
8. Return to the sheet with the *GETPIVOTDATA* formula.
   - *GETPIVOTDATA* returns the same result.

PowerPivot

When you build a *PivotTable* from multiple-source queries, not all *PivotTable* tools are available due to data storage and refresh procedures in queries. Calculated fields, for example, are not possible.

PowerPivot is a COM add-in, a compiled add-in designed to work with Excel. *PowerPivot* stores data from multiple sources for use in its own *PowerPivot* tables. It operates in a separate window and can analyze millions of records. In a *PowerPivot* worksheet, you can access and extract data from online public databases as well as company databases. *PowerPivot* is available for many, but not all, versions of Excel. It must be installed from the *Add-Ins* dialog box [Excel *Options*].

PowerPivot displays data in a *PowerPivot* table that resembles an Excel worksheet without row or column headings. You cannot edit data in a *PowerPivot* sheet, because the data is maintained at its source. You can build calculations and formulas, sort and filter data, and link tables for use in a *PowerPivot* report.

> **MORE INFO**
>
> *PowerPivot* ribbons, windows, dialog boxes, and commands are similar to the Excel *Query Editor* and *PivotTables*.

SLO 8.8

Using the Analysis ToolPak

The *Analysis ToolPak* is an Excel add-in with statistical and engineering functions. Each analysis tool performs its task when you provide the data and define the required components. For concepts such as covariance and regression, the *Analysis ToolPak* helps you analyze data with a minimum of steps and time.

Install the Analysis ToolPak

The *Analysis ToolPak* is installed from the *Add-Ins* dialog box in Excel *Options*. Its button appears on the *Data* tab in the *Analyze* group.

▶ **HOW TO:** Install the Analysis ToolPak

1. Select **Options** [*File* tab].
2. Click **Add-Ins** in the left pane.
   - The *View and manage Microsoft Office Add-ins* dialog box opens.
   - Active applications are listed near the top of the window.
3. Select **Analysis ToolPak** in the *Inactive Application Add-Ins* list.
4. Click **Go** near the bottom of the dialog box to open the *Add-ins* dialog box.
5. Select the **Analysis ToolPak** box.
   - You can remove the *ToolPak* by deselecting the box.
6. Click **OK**.
   - The *Data Analysis* button appears in the *Analyze* group on the *Data* tab.

Generate Descriptive Statistics

Descriptive statistics are summary measures for a data range such as the mean or average, the maximum, the minimum, and a count. Additional statistics that are generated automatically include the mode, the standard deviation, and the range. You already know how to calculate several of these measures using functions from the *Statistical* and *Math & Trig* categories.

The ***Descriptive Statistics*** command is a quick and easy way to prepare a summary report about a set of values. You simply select the range and indicate where results should display. The resulting report is a two-column layout of labels and values.

▶ HOW TO: Generate Descriptive Statistics

1. Click the **Data Analysis** button [*Data* tab, *Analyze* group].

   - The *Data Analysis* dialog box lists calculations available in the *ToolPak* (Figure 8-55).

2. Choose **Descriptive Statistics** and click **OK**.

   - The *Descriptive Statistics* dialog box opens.

3. Click the **Input Range** box and select the cell range on the sheet.

   - These are the cells with data points to be analyzed.
   - Include a column label if there is one and select the **Labels in first row** box.

4. Select the **Columns** radio button if the data is in a column.

   - Select the **Rows** button when the data is in a row.

5. Select the **Output Range** radio button.

6. Click the **Output Range** box and select an empty cell on the sheet.

   - Select a cell where there is room for a two-column report.
   - A worksheet *ply* is a new sheet tab that you can name.

7. Select the **Summary statistics** box (Figure 8-56).

   - You can include a confidence interval and *Kth* values in the report.
   - *Kth* numbers are used to order values. If you set a *Kth Largest* at 2, the result is the second largest value in the range.

8. Click **OK**.

   - The two-column report is generated (Figure 8-57).
   - The column label is the report title.
   - Format the report as desired.

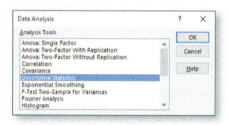

8-55 *Data Analysis* dialog box

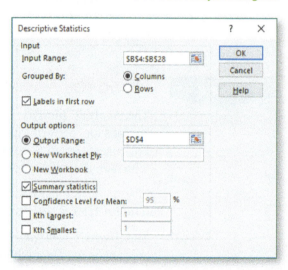

8-56 *Descriptive Statistics* dialog box

Prepare a Moving Average

A moving average calculates a series of averages for a set of values. It is sometimes called a rolling or running average. A moving average is often used to smooth out unequal measurement periods or values in the data. Paradise Lakes Resort, for example, can determine average

	A	B	C	D	E
1					
2	**PLR Product #101**				
3					
4	*Date*	*Sold*		*Sold*	
5	1/1/2016	12			
6	2/1/2016	12		Mean	10.66667
7	3/1/2016	8		Standard Error	0.945368
8	4/1/2016	7		Median	10
9	5/1/2016	4		Mode	12
10	6/1/2016	8		Standard Deviation	4.631336
11	7/1/2016	10		Sample Variance	21.44928
12	8/1/2016	12		Kurtosis	2.135365
13	9/1/2016	5		Skewness	1.157482
14	10/1/2016	4		Range	20
15	11/1/2016	10		Minimum	4
16	12/1/2016	12		Maximum	24
17	1/1/2017	8		Sum	256
18	2/1/2017	8		Count	24
19	3/1/2017	15			

8-57 Generated summary statistics report

three-month rental revenue on April 1 from January–March values. Then, on May 1, they average February–April, and so on throughout the year. At the end of a year, they can average all the averages.

The ***Moving Average*** command analyzes past results and predicts future values. It generates a column of averages and can also create a chart and a list of forecast errors.

▶HOW TO: Calculate a Moving Average

1. Click the **Data Analysis** button [*Data* tab, *Analyze* group].

   - The *Data Analysis* dialog box lists available calculations.

2. Choose **Moving Average** and click **OK**.

   - The *Moving Average* dialog box opens.

3. Click the **Input Range** box and select the cell range on the sheet.

   - These are the values to be averaged.
   - If the values are in a row with labels directly above, select the **Labels in First Row** box.

4. Click the **Interval** box and type the number of cells to be averaged in each set.

   - An interval of 3 means that an average is calculated for every 3 values in the list.
   - An interval of 3 also means that there are no results for the first two values in the input range.

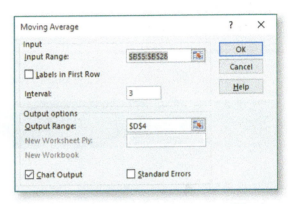

8-58 *Moving Average* dialog box

5. Click the **Output Range** box and select an empty cell on the sheet.

   - The resulting list will be at least as many rows as the input range.

6. Select the **Chart Output** box to generate a moving average chart (Figure 8-58).

7. Select the **Standard Errors** box to generate a list of deviation errors.

8. Click **OK**.

   - The list is generated (Figure 8-59).
   - You can position, size, and format the chart as desired.

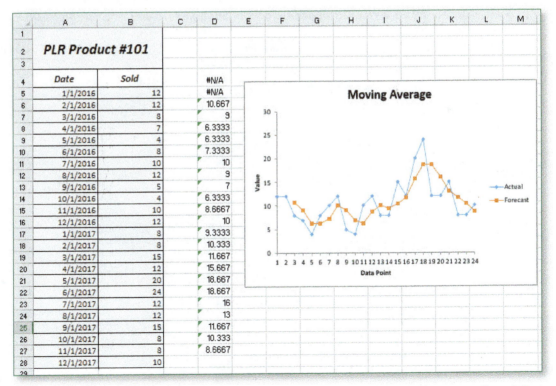

8-59 Generated moving average list and chart

The **Data Analysis** button remains in the *Data* tab until you remove the *Analysis ToolPak*. You remove the *ToolPak* from the *Add-Ins* dialog box in Excel *Options*.

> **HOW TO:** Uninstall the Analysis ToolPak

1. Select **Options** [*File* tab].
2. Click **Add-Ins** in the left pane.
   - The *View and manage Microsoft Office Add-ins* dialog box opens.
   - Active applications are listed near the top of the window.
3. Select **Analysis ToolPak** in the list of *Active Application Add-Ins*.
4. Click **Go** near the bottom of the dialog box to open the *Add-ins* dialog box.
5. Deselect the **Analysis ToolPak** box and click **OK**.

PAUSE & PRACTICE: EXCEL 8-3

In this project, you use *GETPIVOTDATA* in a *PivotTable* and work with the *Analysis ToolPak*. So that your queries use a clean data model, you build two queries as sources for a *PivotTable* with a timeline in another workbook.

Files Needed: ***PP E8-2.xlsx*, *Database-08.accdb*, *SpaSales-08.xml*,** and ***SpaSales-08.xsd*** (*Student data files are available in the* Library of your SIMnet account)
Completed Project File Names: ***[your initials] PP E8-3.xlsx*** and ***[your initials] PP E8-3a.xlsx***

1. Open the ***[your initials] PP E8-2*** workbook completed in *Pause & Practice 8-2* and save it as [your initials] PP E8-3.

2. Right-click the leftmost tab scrolling button to open the *Activate* dialog box (Figure 8-60).

3. Select **Combined Sales** and click **OK**.

4. Use *GETPIVOTDATA* to display results from a *PivotTable*.
   a. Select cell **I5**.
   b. Type = to start the formula.
   c. Click the **PivotTable** sheet tab, select cell **B4**, and press **Enter**.
   d. Select cell **I6** and use *GETPIVOTDATA* to display the total for the Gift department.
   e. Select cell **I7** and use *GETPIVOTDATA* (Figure 8-61).
   f. Click the **PivotTable** sheet tab and click a cell in the *PivotTable*.
   g. With the four-pointed arrow, drag the *Department* field name in the *Rows* area of the *PivotTable Fields* pane into the *Columns* area. The *PivotTable* is pivoted (Figure 8-62).
   h. Click the **Combined Sales** sheet tab. *GETPIVOTDATA* shows the same results even though the content at the original cell locations has changed.

8-60 *Activate* dialog box with sheet names

5. Format a *PivotTable*.
   a. Click the **PivotTable** sheet tab and click a cell in the *PivotTable*.
   b. Click the **More** button [*PivotTable Tools Design* tab, *PivotTable Styles* group].

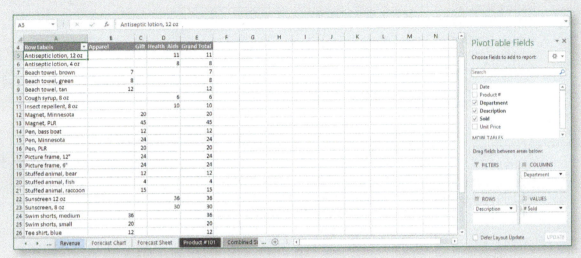

8-61 *GETPIVOTDATA* displays results from the *PivotTable*

8-62 Data in *PivotTable* is rearranged

   c. Select **Pivot Style Medium 8** in the gallery.
   d. Click the **Grand Totals** button [*PivotTable Tools Design* tab, *Layout* group].
   e. Select **On for Columns Only** to remove Column E, the grand totals column.

6. Install the *Analysis ToolPak*.
   a. Select **Options** [*File* tab] and click **Add-Ins** in the left pane.
   b. Select **Analysis ToolPak** in the *Inactive Application Add-Ins* list.
   c. Click **Go** near the bottom of the dialog box.
   d. Select the **Analysis ToolPak** box and click **OK**.

7. Calculate descriptive statistics for a data range.
   a. Select the **Product #101** worksheet tab.
   b. Click the **Data Analysis** button [*Data* tab, *Analyze* group].
   c. Choose **Descriptive Statistics** and click **OK**.
   d. Select cells **B4:B28** for the **Input Range** box.
   e. Verify that the **Columns** radio button is selected.
   f. Select the **Labels in First Row** box.
   g. Select the **Output Range** radio button.
   h. Click the **Output Range** box and select cell **E4**.
   i. Select the **Summary statistics** box.
   j. Select the **Kth Largest** box and type 3 in the entry box to calculate the third largest value in the range (Figure 8-63).

8-63 *Descriptive Statistics* dialog box

k. Click **OK**.

l. **AutoFit** column **E** (Figure 8-64).

8. Calculate a moving average for a data range.

   a. Click the **Data Analysis** button [*Data* tab, *Analyze* group].

   b. Choose **Moving Average** and click **OK**.

   c. Select cells **B5:B28** for the **Input Range** box.

   d. Click the **Interval** box and type 3 to average groups of three cells in the range.

   e. Click the **Output Range** box and select cell **E21**.

   f. Select the **Chart Output** box.

   g. Click **OK**.

   h. Select the chart object and move it so that its top-left corner is at cell **G21**.

   i. Size the chart object to reach cell **P42** (Figure 8-65).

	A	B	C	D	E	F
2	**PLR Product #101**					
4	**Date**	**Sold**			*Sold*	
5	1/1/2016	12				
6	2/1/2016	12			Mean	10.6667
7	3/1/2016	8			Standard Error	0.94537
8	4/1/2016	7			Median	10
9	5/1/2016	4			Mode	12
10	6/1/2016	8			Standard Deviation	4.63134
11	7/1/2016	10			Sample Variance	21.4493
12	8/1/2016	12			Kurtosis	2.13537
13	9/1/2016	5			Skewness	1.15748
14	10/1/2016	4			Range	20
15	11/1/2016	10			Minimum	4
16	12/1/2016	12			Maximum	24
17	1/1/2017	8			Sum	256
18	2/1/2017	8			Count	24
19	3/1/2017	15			Largest(3)	15
20	4/1/2017	12				
21	5/1/2017	20				
22	6/1/2017	24				
23	7/1/2017	12				

Forecast Chart | Forecast Sheet | Product #101 | Combined Sales

8-64 Generated statistics report

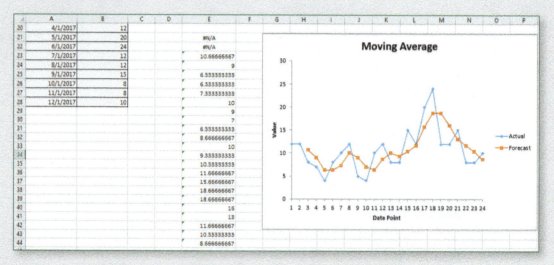

8-65 Moving Average results and chart

9. Uninstall the *Analysis ToolPak*.

   a. Select **Options** [*File* tab] and click **Add-Ins** in the left pane.

   b. Select **Analysis ToolPak** In the list of *Active Application Add-Ins*.

   c. Click **Go** near the bottom of the dialog box.

   d. Deselect the **Analysis ToolPak** box and click **OK**.

10. Save and close the workbook.

11. Open a new workbook.

12. Get and transform data from an XML file.

   a. Click the **New Query** button [*Data* tab, *Get & Transform* group], choose **From File**, and **From XML**.

   b. Navigate to the folder with the **SpaSales-08** XML file from your student data files.

c. Select the file name **SpaSales-08**, click **Import**, and then click **Edit**.

d. Click the **Expand** button next to the **TblSpaSales** label at the top of the first column in the *Query Editor*.

e. Select all field boxes and click **OK**.

f. Click the **TblSpaSales.Date** column label, click the **Data Type** button [*Home* tab, *Transform* group], and choose **Date/Time**.

g. Click the **TblSpaSales.ProductID** label, click the **Data Type** button [*Home* tab, *Transform* group], and choose **Whole Number**.

h. Select the **Whole Number** data type for the *Sold* column.

i. Click the **http://...Schema...** label.

j. Click the **Remove Columns** button [*Home* tab, *Manage Columns* group].

k. Remove the **Attribute:generated** column (Figure 8-66).

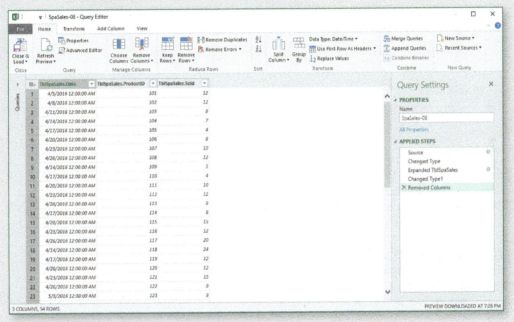

8-66 XML data in the *Query Editor*

l. Click the **Close & Load** button [*Home* tab, *Close* group].

m. Rename the query results sheet as XML Query.

13. Get and transform data from an Access database file.
    a. Click the **New Query** button [*Data* tab, *Get & Transform* group] and choose **From Database**.
    b. Choose **From Microsoft Access Database**.
    c. Navigate to the folder with the **Database-08** database file from your student data files.
    d. Select the **Database-08** name and click **Import**.
    e. Select **TblSpaProducts** in the *Navigator* window.
    f. Click **Edit** at the bottom of the window.
    g. Click the **Product #** column name and click the **Data Type** button [*Home* tab, *Transform* group] in the *Query Editor*.
    h. Choose **Whole Number**. This is the field that will establish a relationship between the query tables (Figure 8-67).
    i. Click the **Close & Load** button [*Home* tab, *Close* group].
    j. Rename the query results sheet as Database Query.

14. Create a *PivotTable* from two queries.
    a. Select cell **A2** in the table on the **Database Query** sheet.

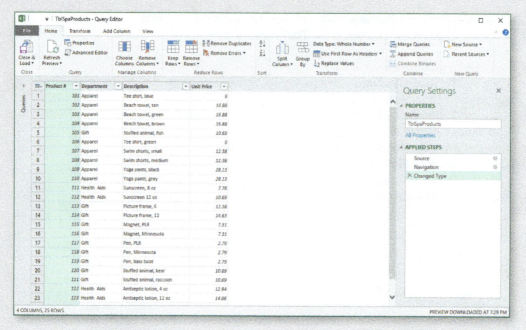

8-67 Access table in *Query Editor*

b. Click the **Summarize with PivotTable** button [*Table Tools Design* tab, *Tools* group].
c. Select the **Existing Worksheet** radio button.
d. Click the **Location** box and click cell **A3** on **Sheet1**.
e. Select the **Add this data to the Data Model** box and click **OK**.
f. Select the boxes for the **Department** and **Description** fields In the *PivotTable Fields* pane.
g. Click **All** at the top of the *PivotTable Fields* pane.
h. Select **SpaSales-08** to expand the field list from the XML query.
i. Select the **TblSpaSales.Sold** box.
j. Click **AutoDetect** in the warning box to create a relationship between the tables.
k. Click **Close** in the message box (Figure 8-68).
l. Rename the sheet as Timeline.

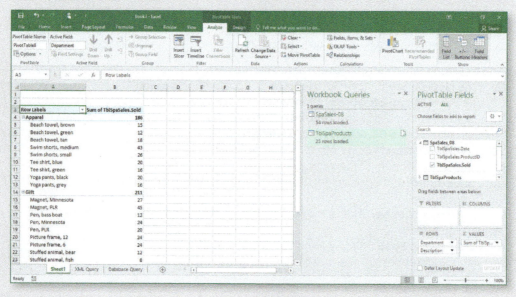

8-68 *PivotTable* created from two queries

15. Insert a timeline for a *PivotTable*.
    a. Click any cell in the *PivotTable* on the **Timeline** sheet.
    b. Click the **Insert Timeline** button [*PivotTable Tools Analyze* tab, *Filter* group].
    c. Select the **TblSpaSales.Date** box and click **OK**.
    d. Click the **Months** button in the time-line and select **Quarters**.
    e. Click **Q3** In the timeline for 2017.
    f. Click the **More** button [*Timeline Tools Options* tab, *Timeline Styles* group].
    g. Find and select **Timeline Style Dark 5** in the gallery.
    h. Position the timeline with its top-left corner in cell **C3** (Figure 8-69).

16. Click a worksheet cell.

17. Save the workbook as [your initials] PP E8-3a and close it.

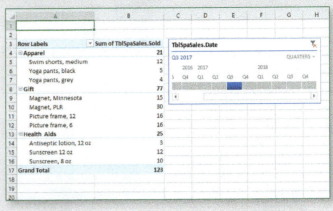

8-69 Timeline filters the data by quarter

Chapter Summary

8.1 Create and manage scenarios for worksheet data (p. E8-496).

- A **scenario** is a saved set of values in a workbook.
- A *scenario* is a what-if analysis tool because it allows you to display and compare multiple data possibilities in a worksheet.
- The **Scenario Manager** command is available from the *What-if Analysis* button in the *Forecast* group in the *Data* tab.
- In the *Add Scenario* dialog box, you name each scenario and select cells to be changed.
- In the *Scenario Values* dialog box, you accept or type new values for each scenario.
- Only one scenario can be displayed in the worksheet at a time.
- From the *Scenario Manager* dialog box, you can create a **scenario summary report** that lists details about changing cells and result cells for all scenarios in a workbook.

8.2 Use *Goal Seek* to backsolve a cell value for a formula (p. E8-498).

- **Backsolving** is a problem-solving method that starts with the result and calculates the value to reach that result.
- The **Goal Seek** command tests values for one cell in a formula.
- *Goal Seek* determines what value should be in the cell so that the formula results in a specified value.
- The *Goal Seek* command is an option on the *What-if Analysis* button in the *Forecast* group in the *Data* tab.

8.3 Use *Solver* to find a solution for a formula (p. E8-500).

- The *Solver* **add-in** is an analysis tool that solves a problem in reverse.
- **Solver** determines the highest, the lowest, or a specific result for a formula by adjusting values in cells used in the formula.
- A *Solver* problem has three components known as **parameters**, identified in the *Solver Parameters* dialog box.
- The **objective cell** is a cell with a formula that will be solved for specific results. It is also called the **target cell**.

- **Variable cells**, also known as **decision** or **changing cells**, are cells that *Solver* can adjust to reach the objective.
- **Constraints** are restrictions or limitations on variable cells, the formula, or other worksheet cells that are related to the objective cell.
- The *Solver Results* dialog box includes options to keep the solution, to return to the original values, and to save the results as a scenario.
- The *Solver Results* dialog box has a *Reports* section with analysis reports that can be generated for each solution.
- *Solver* is activated from the *Add-Ins* dialog box in the Excel *Options* dialog box.
- The *Solver* button displays in the *Analyze* group on the *Data* tab.

8.4 Build data tables with one and two variables (p. E8-508).

- A **data table** is a range of cells in a worksheet that shows multiple results for one or more formulas.
- A data table is created from the *What-If Analysis* button in the *Forecast* group on the *Data* tab.
- A **one-variable data table** substitutes values for one argument in one or more formulas.
- A **two-variable data table** substitutes values for two arguments in a single formula.
- The values that are substituted are known as **input values**.
- Input values can be in a row or a column, and the formula must be entered in a specific location based on whether the table uses one or two variables.
- In the data table range, the formula can be typed or entered as a reference to the formula in the worksheet.
- In the *Data Table* dialog box, you specify a row or column input cell for a one-variable table and both for a two-variable table.
- The row or column input is the cell address in the formula that is replaced with input values.
- A *Data Table* command inserts the *TABLE* function in an array formula in each result cell.

8.5 Create a forecast sheet for time-based data (p. E8-511).

- A **forecast sheet** is a generated worksheet that uses existing data to analyze and predict results.

- A forecast sheet includes a table and a related chart.
- Two data series are required to build a forecast sheet; one series must be a date or time field.
- The date or time field must use a recognizable time interval.
- The forecast chart can be a line or a column chart.
- The *Forecast Sheet* button is in the *Forecast* group on the *Data* tab.

8.6 Get and transform data in a query (p. E8-515).

- A **query** stores instructions for getting data from an external source for display in a worksheet.
- A query can get data from online and in-house sources including database or text files, **XML** data, and others.
- A query establishes a data connection to the source so that the data can be refreshed.
- Data is cleaned or prepared in the *Query Editor* before it is loaded into Excel.
- Query results are displayed in an Excel table.
- Queries are named and saved with the workbook.
- When a **common field** exists in two or more queries, those queries can be used to create a *PivotTable*.
- The *New Query* button is in the *Get & Transform* group on the *Data* tab.

8.7 Explore *PivotTable* tools (p. E8-522).

- A slicer is a visual filter for a *PivotTable*, a small window that floats on the sheet.
- You can insert a slicer for any field in the data source for the *PivotTable*.
- A **timeline** is a visual filter for a date field in a *PivotTable*.
- The **Insert Slicer** and **Insert Timeline** buttons are in the *Filter* group on the *PivotTable Tools Analyze* tab.
- Slicers and timelines are objects that can be positioned, sized, and formatted.
- The *Value Field Settings* for a field in a *PivotTable* determine how values are summarized.

- You can change the calculation used for value fields, show custom calculations, or insert a calculated field.
- A **custom calculation** is a built-in percentage, ranking, or ratio.
- A **calculated field** is a field that is not in the data source for a *PivotTable* and is built from a formula with one of the fields in the source data.
- Insert a calculated field from the **Fields, Items, & Sets** button [*PivotTable Tools Analyze* tab, *Calculations* group].
- *PivotTable* fields can be formatted from the *Value Field Settings* dialog box or from the *Number* group on the *Home* tab.
- Layout options for a *PivotTable* include how and where totals display and the report format.
- The *GETPIVOTDATA* function displays results from a particular cell in a *PivotTable*.
- For expanded *PivotTable* functions and commands, the *PowerPivot* add-in can access millions of records for analysis in a report.

8.8 Use the *Analysis ToolPak* to calculate statistical measures (p. E8-529).

- The *Analysis ToolPak* is an Excel add-in with built-in statistical and engineering calculations.
- After the add-in is installed, the *Data Analysis* button appears in the *Analyze* group on the *Data* tab.
- The **Descriptive Statistics** command calculates and generates a list of popular measures for a data range.
- The **Moving Average** command calculates and generates a list of running or rolling averages for a set of values with a related chart.
- Other *Analysis ToolPak* commands include covariance, regression analysis, and random number generation.

Check for Understanding

The SIMbook for this text (within your SIMnet account) provides the following resources for concept review:

- Multiple choice questions
- Matching exercises
- Short answer questions

Guided Project 8-1

Wear-Ever Shoes uses *Solver* to analyze advertising for greatest exposure. You use scenarios, a data table, and *Goal Seek* in the analysis. You also build a query for an Access table to create a *PivotTable* that relates customer satisfaction and cost.
[Student Learning Outcomes 8.1, 8.2, 8.3, 8.4, 8.5, 8.6, 8.7, 8.8]

Files Needed: **WearEverShoes-08.xlsx** and **Database-08.accdb** *(Student data files are available in the Library of your SIMnet account)*
Completed Project File Name: *[your initials] Excel 8-1.xlsx*

Skills Covered in this Project

- Create and manage scenarios.
- Use *Solver*.
- Use *Goal Seek*.
- Build a one-variable data table.
- Build a two-variable data table.

- Create and format a *PivotTable* with a *PivotChart*.
- Build a query to get data from an Access table.
- Use the data model to create a *PivotTable*.
- Generate *Descriptive Statistics* using the *Analysis ToolPak*.
- Create a forecast sheet.

1. Open the **WearEverShoes-08** workbook from your student data files and save it as [your initials] Excel 8-1.

2. Review marketing formulas.
   a. Select cell **E7** on the **Marketing Analysis** tab. The *SUMPRODUCT* formula multiplies the cost per ad (cells C7 and D7) by the number of ads (cells C13 and D13).
   b. Select cell **E10** and then cell **G4** to review the *SUMPRODUCT* formulas.

3. Create a scenario for original data.
   a. Select cells **C13:D13** and click the **What-if Analysis** button [*Data* tab, *Data Tools* group].
   b. Select **Scenario Manager**. No scenarios exist in the workbook.
   c. Click **Add**.
   d. Type Original in the *Add Scenario* dialog box.
   e. Verify that the *Changing cells* box shows cells **C13:D13**.
   f. Click **OK**.
   g. Do not edit the *Scenario Values* dialog box and click **OK**.
   h. Click **Close**.

4. Install *Solver* and the *Analysis ToolPak*.
   a. Select the **Options** command [*File* tab].
   b. Click **Add-Ins** in the left pane.
   c. Click **Go** near the bottom of the window.
   d. Select the **Solver Add-in** box.
   e. Select the **Analysis ToolPak** box.
   f. Click **OK**.

5. Set *Solver* parameters.
   a. Click the **Solver** button [*Data* tab, *Analyze* group].
   b. Click cell **G4** for the **Set Objective** box. This cell has a *SUMPRODUCT* formula.

c. Verify that the **Max** radio button is selected to find the maximum value.

d. Click the **By Changing Variable Cells** box and select cells **C13:D13**. *Solver* will test values for the number of TV and magazine ads.

6. Add constraints to a *Solver* problem.

a. Click **Add** to the right of the *Subject to the Constraints* box.

b. Select cell **C13** for the *Cell Reference* box.

c. Verify that **<=** is the operator.

d. Click the **Constraint** box and select cell **C15**. This constraint is that the number of TV ads (cell C13) be less than or equal to the value in cell C15.

e. Click **Add**. (If you accidentally closed the dialog box, click **Add** to reopen it.)

f. Select cell **E7** for the *Cell Reference* box and use **<=** as the operator.

g. Click the **Constraint** box and type 3750 as the budget amount.

h. Add another constraint that cell **E10** be greater than or equal to **12**. This means that the audience reach must be at least 12 million.

i. When all constraints are identified, click **OK** in the *Add Constraint* dialog box.

j. Choose **GRG Nonlinear** for the *Select a Solving Method* box.

k. Verify that the **Make Unconstrained Variables Non-Negative** box is selected (Figure 8-70).

8-70 *Solver* parameters

l. Click **Solve**. A solution displays in the worksheet, and the *Solver Results* dialog box is open. The maximum total exposure is 14,500. (If *Solver* did not return that value, uninstall *Solver*, exit Excel, restart Excel, and install *Solver* again. Then try Steps 5-6 again. If the error persists, go to Step 7f.)

7. Save *Solver* results as a scenario. (If *Solver* has not returned the indicated result, start at Step f.)

a. Click **Save Scenario** in the *Solver Results* dialog box.

b. Type Max Exposure as the scenario name.

c. Click **OK** to return to the *Solver Results* dialog box.

d. Select **Answer** in the *Reports* list.

e. Click **OK**. The generated report is inserted, and *Solver* results are shown in the worksheet.

f. If *Solver* has not worked as indicated, type 6 in cell **C13** and type 3 in cell **C15** and proceed to Step 7g.

g. If *Solver* has not worked as indicated, create a scenario named Max Exposure with cells **C13:D13** as the changing cells.

8. Create a scenario summary report.
   a. Click the **What-if Analysis** button [*Data* tab, *Data Tools* group] and select **Scenario Manager**.
   b. Click the **Summary** button.
   c. Verify that the **Scenario summary** button is selected.
   d. Click the **Result cells** box, select cells **C13:D13**, type a comma , and then select cell **G4** (Figure 8-71).
   e. Click **OK** in the *Scenario Summary* dialog box. The report displays in a new worksheet.

9. Show a scenario.
   a. Click the **Marketing Analysis** worksheet tab.
   b. Click the **What-if Analysis** button [*Data* tab, *Data Tools* group] and select **Scenario Manager**.
   c. Click **Original** to highlight the name.
   d. Click **Show** and click **Close**.

10. Create a one-variable data table.
    a. Select cells **B20:B21** and fill values to reach cell **B30** as column input values.
    b. Select cell **C19**, one column to the right and one row above the first input value.
    c. Type =, click cell **E7**, and press **Enter** to reference the budget formula.
    d. Select cells **B19:C30** as the data table range.
    e. Click the **What-If Analysis** button [*Data* tab, *Data Tools* group] and choose **Data Table**.
    f. Click the **Column input cell** box and select cell **C7** to indicate that the cost per TV ad will be replaced by the input values in column B.
    g. Click **OK** to create the data table (Figure 8-72).
    h. Click the **What-if Analysis** button [*Data* tab, *Data Tools* group] and select **Scenario Manager**.
    i. Click **Max Exposure** to highlight the name and click **Show**.
    j. Click **Close**. The data table is updated.

11. Use *Goal Seek* to find the number of ads.
    a. Select cell **E10**.
    b. Click the **What-if Analysis** button [*Data* tab, *Data Tools* group] and choose **Goal Seek**.
    c. Click the **To value** box and type 15 as the target.
    d. Click the **By changing cell** box and select cell **D13** to determine how many magazine ads must be run to reach 15 million people.
    e. Click **OK**. Note the result shown in cell **D13** in the worksheet.
    f. Click **Cancel** and type the result value in cell **G23**.
    g. Select cell **E10** and use *Goal Seek* to change cell **C13** to calculate how many TV ads must be run to reach 15 million people. Do not keep the results, but type the resulting value in cell **G26** (Figure 8-73).

12. Create a two-variable data table.
    a. Click the **Inventory** worksheet tab. Current costs and increase percentages are shown at the right.
    b. Select cell **K4** to place the formula one row above column input values and one column left of the row values.
    c. Type =, click cell **J7**, type *(1+, click cell **J4**, and press **Enter**. The closing right parenthesis was necessary.
    d. Click **Yes** in the message box to accept the correction with closing right parenthesis. The formula multiplies the cost times 1 plus the percentage increase. Because cells **J4** and **J7** contain labels,

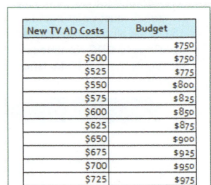

Scenario Summary	?	X

Report type

○ Scenario summary
○ Scenario PivotTable report

Result cells:

=$C$13:$D$13,$G$4

| OK | Cancel |

8-71 Nonadjacent cells used in the report

New TV AD Costs	Budget
	$750
$500	$750
$525	$775
$550	$800
$575	$825
$600	$850
$625	$875
$650	$900
$675	$925
$700	$950
$725	$975
$750	$1,000

8-72 Data table results with *Original* scenario

the result is a standard error message (Figure 8-74).

e. Select cells **K4:N10** as the data table range.

f. Click the **What-If Analysis** button [*Data* tab, *Data Tools* group] and choose **Data Table**.

g. Select cell **J4** for the *Row input cell* box because the percentage values in row 4 will replace the label in cell J4.

h. Click the **Column input cell** box and select cell **J7** so that the costs in column K replace the label in cell J7.

i. Click **OK** to build the data table.

j. Format cells **L5:N10** as **Currency** with two decimal places.

k. Format cell **K4** to use a **White, Background 1** font color.

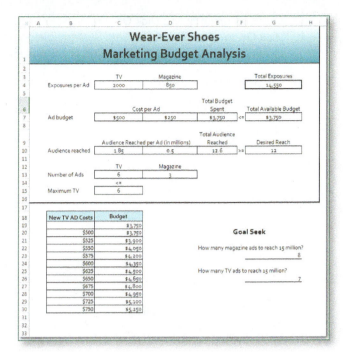

8-73 Completed Marketing Analysis sheet

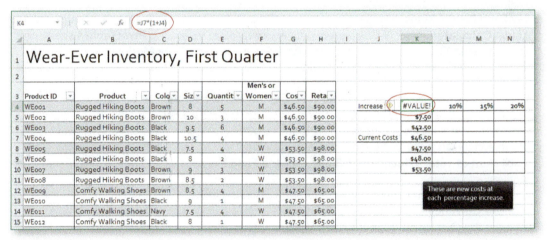

8-74 The result is an error in the placeholder formula.

13. Create a *PivotTable* for the **Inventory** data.

   a. Select cell **A3** and click the **PivotTable** button [*Insert* tab, *Tables* group].

   b. Verify that the **New Worksheet** button is selected.

   c. Deselect the **Add this data to the Data Model** box. You cannot insert a calculated field in a *PivotTable* built from the data model.

   d. Click **OK**.

   e. Name the worksheet tab PivotTable 1.

   f. Select the **Product ID, Product, Quantity**, and **Cost** field boxes in the *PivotTable Fields* pane. Label fields are added to the *Rows* area, and numeric fields are added in the *Values* area.

   g. Right-click **Sum of Cost** in cell **C3** and select **Value Field Settings**.

   h. Edit the name to display Our Cost in the *Custom Name* box.

   i. Click **Number Format** in the *Value Field Settings* dialog box.

j. Choose **Currency** and click **OK**.

k. Click **OK** to close the *Value Field Settings* dialog box.

l. Edit the name in cell **B3** to show **Current Stock** (Figure 8-75).

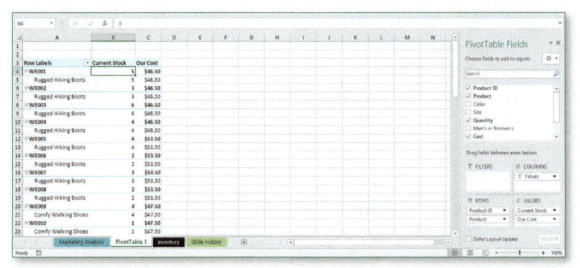

8-75 Inventory *PivotTable*

14. Insert a calculated field.

   a. Click any cell in the *PivotTable*.

   b. Click the **Fields, Items, and Sets** button [*PivotTable Tools Analyze* tab, *Calculations* group] and select **Calculated Field**. (If *Calculated Field* is unavailable, delete the **PivotTable 1** sheet, and return to step 13. Be sure to deselect the **Add this data to the Data Model** box.)

   c. Type Total Value as the name for the calculated field in the *Name* box in the *Insert Calculated Field* dialog box.

   d. Click the **Formula** box and delete the zero and the space after the equals sign.

   e. Double-click **Cost** in the *Fields* list.

   f. Type * after ='Cost' in the *Formula* box to multiply.

   g. Double-click **Quantity** in the *Fields* list and click **OK**.

   h. Click **Sum of Total Value** in cell **D3** and click the **Field Settings** button [*PivotTable Tools Analyze*, *Active Field* group].

   i. Click **Number Format** in the *Value Field Settings* dialog box.

   j. Choose **Currency** and click **OK**.

   k. Change the *Custom Name* to Inventory Value.

   l. Click **OK**.

15. Insert a slicer.

   a. Verify that any cell in the *PivotTable* is active.

   b. Click the **Insert Slicer** button [*PivotTable Tools Analyze* tab, *Filter* group].

   c. Select the **Product** box and click **OK**.

   d. With the four-pointed arrow, drag the slicer so that the top-left corner is in cell **E3**.

   e. Click **Comfy Walking Shoes** in the slicer (Figure 8-76).

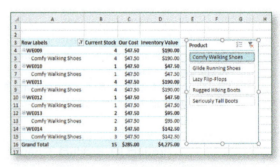

8-76 Data is filtered by the slicer

16. Create a *PivotChart*.

   a. Select a cell in the *PivotTable* and click the **PivotChart** button [*PivotTable Tools Analyze*, *Tools* group].

   b. Click **Pie** in the list, **3-D Pie** as the subtype, and click **OK**.

   c. With the four-pointed arrow, drag the *PivotChart* so that its top-left corner is in cell **I3**.

d. Point to the bottom-right sizing handle and drag it to reach cell **S24**.

e. Click **Rugged Hiking Boots** in the slicer (Figure 8-77).

f. Select cell **A1**.

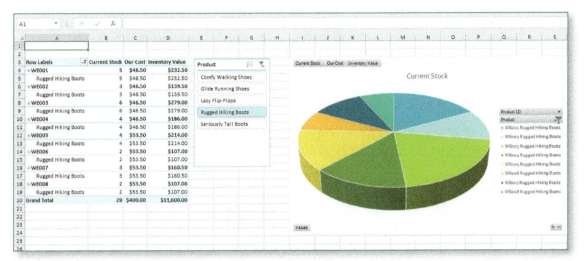

8-77 Filtered *PivotTable* and *PivotChart*

17. Get and transform data from an Access database.

   a. Click the **New Query** button [*Data* tab, *Get & Transform* group], select **From Database**, and choose **From Microsoft Access Database**.

   b. Navigate to the folder with ***Database-08*** from your student data files and click to select the file name.

   c. Click **Import** to open the *Navigator* window.

   d. Select **TblWearEver** in the list and click **Load**.

   e. Select the **D:H** columns headings and click the **Home** tab.

   f. Click the **Number Format** arrow in the *Number* group and select **Number** as the format.

   g. Click the **Decrease Decimal** button [*Home* tab, *Number* group] two times.

   h. Name the new sheet Ratings (Figure 8-78).

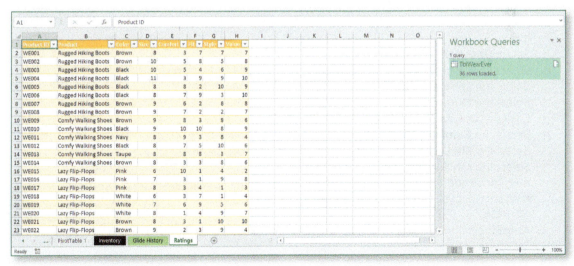

8-78 Query results are loaded without editing

18. Create a *PivotTable* from the data model.

   a. Click cell **A2** in the query results table on the **Ratings** sheet.

   b. Click the **Summarize with PivotTable** button [*Table Tools Design* tab, *Tools* group].

c. Verify that the **New Worksheet** button is selected.

d. Verify or select the **Add this data to the Data Model** box and click **OK**.

e. Expand the **TblWearEver** field list in the *PivotTable Fields* pane if the fields are not listed.

f. Select the **Product ID**, **Comfort**, **Fit**, **Style**, and **Value** boxes to place the fields in the *PivotTable* layout.

g. Click **All** at the top of the *PivotTable Fields* pane and expand the **InventoryTable** list.

h. Select the **Cost** box to add it to the *PivotTable* layout.

i. Click **Auto-Detect** to create the relationship. The *Product ID* fields from the query and the table are used to link or relate the data.

j. Click **Close** in the message box (Figure 8-79).

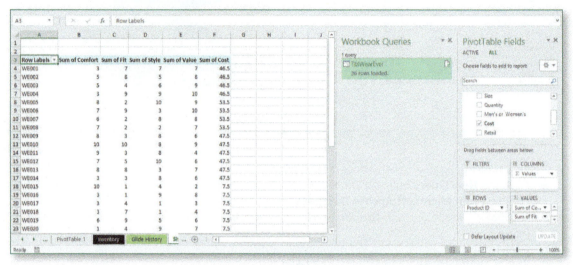

8-79 *PivotTable* from related query and table

k. Name the sheet tab PivotTable 2.

l. Close the *Workbook Queries* pane.

19. Generate *Descriptive Statistics* for a rating category.

a. Click the **Ratings** sheet tab and select cell **J1**.

b. Click the **Data Analysis** button [*Data* tab, *Analyze* group].

c. Select **Descriptive Statistics** and click **OK**.

d. Select cells **H1:H37** for the *Input Range* box.

e. Select the **Labels in First Row** box.

f. Select the **Output Range** button.

g. Click the **Output Range** box and click cell **J1**.

h. Select the **Summary statistics** box.

i. Select the **Kth Largest** box and type 3 in its entry box.

j. Select the **Kth Smallest** box and type 3 in its entry box. These settings will calculate the third largest and third smallest values in the input range (Figure 8-80).

k. Click **OK**.

l. **AutoFit** column **J**.

m. Select cell **J1** and edit the label to display Value Rating Analysis (Figure 8-81).

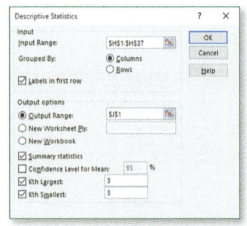

8-80 *Descriptive Statistics* dialog box with *Kth* values

20. Create a forecast sheet.

a. Click the **Glide History** sheet tab.

b. Select cells **A4:B16**. One data series is time-based, and the other represents values.

c. Click the **Forecast Sheet** button [*Data* tab, *Forecast* group].

d. Click the **Create a column chart** button at the top-right of the window.

e. Click the **Options** button to expand the window.

f. Set the forecast to end at 12/31/19 if it does not already show that date (Figure 8-82).

g. Click **Create** to build the new sheet and chart.

h. Select the chart object and position its top-left corner to start in cell **E2**.

	A	B	C	D	E	F	G	H	I	J	K
1	Product ID	Product	Color	Size	Comfort	Fit	Style	Value		Value Rating Analysis	
2	WE001	Rugged Hiking Boots	Brown	8	3	7	7	7			
3	WE002	Rugged Hiking Boots	Brown	10	5	8	5	8		Mean	6.916667
4	WE003	Rugged Hiking Boots	Black	10	5	4	6	9		Standard Error	0.433471
5	WE004	Rugged Hiking Boots	Black	11	3	9	9	10		Median	7
6	WE005	Rugged Hiking Boots	Black	8	8	2	10	9		Mode	10
7	WE006	Rugged Hiking Boots	Black	8	7	9	3	10		Standard Deviation	2.600824
8	WE007	Rugged Hiking Boots	Brown	9	6	2	8	8		Sample Variance	6.764286
9	WE008	Rugged Hiking Boots	Brown	9	7	2	2	7		Kurtosis	-0.887
10	WE009	Comfy Walking Shoes	Brown	9	8	3	8	6		Skewness	-0.52239
11	WE010	Comfy Walking Shoes	Black	9	10	10	8	9		Range	8
12	WE011	Comfy Walking Shoes	Navy	8	9	3	8	4		Minimum	2
13	WE012	Comfy Walking Shoes	Black	8	7	5	10	6		Maximum	10
14	WE013	Comfy Walking Shoes	Taupe	8	8	8	3	7		Sum	249
15	WE014	Comfy Walking Shoes	Brown	8	3	3	8	6		Count	36
16	WE015	Lazy Flip-Flops	Pink	6	10	1	4	2		Largest(3)	10
17	WE016	Lazy Flip-Flops	Pink	7	3	1	9	8		Smallest(3)	2
18	WE017	Lazy Flip-Flops	Pink	8	3	4	1	3			
19	WE018	Lazy Flip-Flops	White	6	3	7	1	4			
20	WE019	Lazy Flip-Flops	White	7	6	9	5	6			
21	WE020	Lazy Flip-Flops	White	8	1	4	9	7			
22	WE021	Lazy Flip-Flops	Brown	8	3	1	10	10			
23	WE022	Lazy Flip-Flops	Brown	9	2	3	9	4			

Glide History | PivotTable 2 | **Ratings**

8-81 Generated statistics report

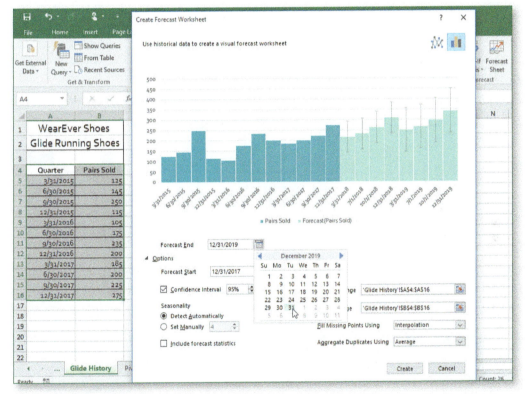

8-82 Options for a forecast sheet

i. Select a **Pairs Sold** column in the chart and change its **Shape Fill** color to **Lime, Accent 3**.

j. Select cell **A1**.

k. Name the sheet tab Glide Forecast.

21. Save and close the workbook (Figure 8-83).

22. Uninstall *Solver* and the *Analysis ToolPak*.

a. Select the **Options** command [*File* tab] and click **Add-Ins** in the left pane.

b. Select **Solver Add-In** in the list of *Active Applications Add-Ins*.

c. In the *Manage* section near the bottom of the window, click **Go**.

d. Deselect the **Solver Add-in** and **Analysis ToolPak** boxes.

e. Click **OK**.

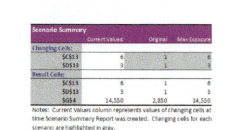

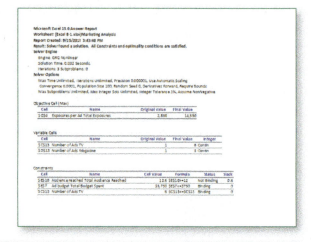

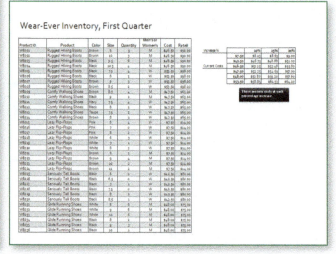

Guided Project 8-2

Sierra Pacific Community College (SPCC) has a worksheet for evaluating student loan offerings with data tables that you must build. You also determine how to reach a goal capacity for the freshmen orientation seminar and build a *PivotTable* to analyze departmental course fees.
[**Student Learning Outcomes 8.1, 8.2, 8.3, 8.4, 8.5, 8.6, 8.7, 8.8**]

Files Needed: ***SPCC-08.xlsx***, ***SPCC-08.xml***, and ***SPCC-08.xsd*** *(Student data files are available in the Library of your SIMnet account)*
Completed Project File Name: *[your initials] Excel 8-2.xlsx*

Skills Covered in this Project

- Create and manage scenarios.
- Use *Goal Seek*.
- Build data tables with one and two variables.
- Use *Solver* to determine capacity.
- Use data to create a forecast sheet.
- Calculate a moving average using the *Analysis ToolPak*.
- Get and transform XML data.
- Create a *PivotTable* from the data model.
- Use *PivotTable* tools.
- Insert and format a slicer for a *PivotTable*.

1. Open the ***SPCC-08*** workbook from your student data files and save it as [your initials] Excel 8-2.

2. Review the loan formulas on the **Loan Tables** worksheet.
   a. Select cell **C7**. The PMT function determines the monthly payment for a $10,000 loan at 4.5% for five years.
   b. Select cell **F4**. The total interest is the payment times the number of years times 12 minus the loan amount.
   c. Select cell **F6**. The total interest plus the loan amount are added.

3. Create scenarios in a worksheet.
   a. Select cell **C5** and click the **What-if Analysis** button [*Data* tab, *Data Tools* group].
   b. Select **Scenario Manager**. No scenarios exist in the workbook.
   c. Click **Add**.
   d. Type 5 Year as the name in the *Add Scenario* dialog box.
   e. Verify that the *Changing cells* box displays cell **C5** as the argument to be changed.
   f. Click **OK**.
   g. Do not edit the *Scenario Values* entry and click **OK**.
   h. Click **Add** to add another scenario.
   i. Type 7 Year as the name and keep the *Changing cells* as cell **C5**.
   j. Click **OK**.
   k. Change the value to 7 in the *Scenario Values* dialog box and click **OK**.
   l. Add another scenario for a nine-year loan and close the *Scenario Manager* dialog box.

4. Display a scenario in a worksheet.
   a. Click the **What-if Analysis** button [*Data* tab, *Data Tools* group] and select **Scenario Manager**.
   b. Select **7 Year** in the list and click **Show**.
   c. Click **Close**.

5. Use *Goal Seek* to find a target payment.
   a. Select cell **C7**.
   b. Click the **What-if Analysis** button [*Data* tab, *Data Tools* group] and choose **Goal Seek**.
   c. Click the **To value** box and type 125 as the target.
   d. Click the **By changing cell** box and select cell **C6** to determine the interest rate that results in this payment.
   e. Click **OK** (Figure 8-84).

6. Save *Goal Seek* results as a scenario.
   a. Select cell **C6** and click the **What-if Analysis** button [*Data* tab, *Data Tools* group].
   b. Select **Scenario Manager** and click **Add**.
   c. Type $125 Payment as the scenario name.
   d. Verify that the *Changing cells* box displays cell **C6**.
   e. Click **OK**.
   f. Do not change the *Scenario Values* entry, click **OK**, and click **Close**.

7. Create a scenario summary report.
   a. Click the **What-if Analysis** button [*Data* tab, *Data Tools* group] and select **Scenario Manger**.
   b. Click the **Summary** button.
   c. Verify that the **Scenario summary** is selected.
   d. Click the **Result cells** box and select cells **C5:C7**.
   e. Click **OK** in the *Scenario Summary* dialog box. The report is generated in a new worksheet (Figure 8-85).

8. Create a one-variable data table to calculate the payment and total interest charges based on different rates.
   a. Select the **Loan Tables** worksheet tab.
   b. Select cells **B15:B16** and fill percentages to reach cell **B23**. These are column input values.
   c. Select cell **C14**. The first formula must be one column to the right and one row above the first input value.
   d. Type **=**, select cell **C7**, and press **Enter** to reference the payment formula.
   e. Select cell **D14**. Additional formulas must be in the same row.
   f. Type **=**, select cell **F4**, and press **Enter** to reference the total interest formula.
   g. Select cells **B14:D23** as the data table range.
   h. Click the **What-If Analysis** button [*Data* tab, *Data Tools* group] and choose **Data Table**.
   i. Click the **Column input cell** entry box and click cell **C6**. The input values will be substituted for this cell in the data table formula (Figure 8-86).

8-84 *Goal Seek* results

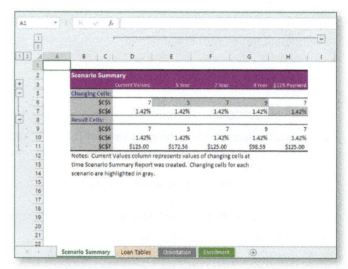

8-85 Scenario summary report results

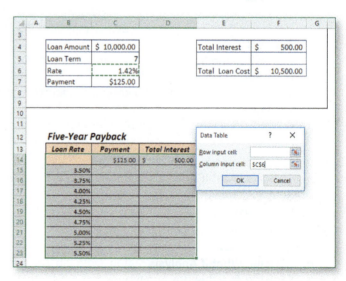

8-86 One-variable data table setup

j. Click **OK** to create the data table.

k. Format cells **C15:D23** as **Currency** with two decimal places.

9. Create a two-variable data table to calculate monthly payments at different rates and payback years.

    a. Select cell **B26** to place the formula one row above column input values and one column left of row values.

    b. Type =, click cell **C7**, and press **Enter**.

    c. Select cells **B26:F35** as the data table range.

    d. Click the **What-If Analysis** button [*Data* tab, *Data Tools* group] and choose **Data Table**.

    e. Select cell **C5** for the *Row input cell* box. The number of years are in the row of this data table.

    f. Click the **Column input cell** box and select cell **C6**. The changing interest rates are in a column.

    g. Click **OK** to build the data table. The standard error message #VALUE! appears in all the cells.

    h. Select **C27** and click its **Trace Error** button. An *Error in Value* results because the content in row 26 is recognized as text (Figure 8-87).

    i. Click cell **C26**, type 6, and press **Tab**. The first column of the data table is refreshed.

    j. Type 8 in cell **D26** and press **Tab**.

    k. Correct the row input values in cells **E26:F26**.

    l. Format cells **C27:F35** as **Currency** with two decimal places.

    m. Format cell **B26** to use **Orange, Accent 2, Lighter 60%** as the font color.

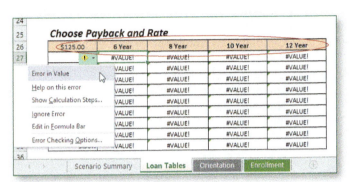

8-87 Year values were entered as text

10. Install *Solver* and the *Analysis ToolPak*.

    a. Select the **Options** command [*File* tab].

    b. Click **Add-Ins** in the left pane.

    c. Click **Go** near the bottom of the window.

    d. Select the **Solver Add-in** box.

    e. Select the **Analysis ToolPak** box.

    f. Click **OK**.

11. Use *Solver* to find a capacity goal.

    a. Select the **Orientation** sheet tab. The college wants to maximize the number of students who can be accommodated in the orientation seminar.

    b. Click the **Solver** button [*Data* tab, *Analyze* group].

    c. Select cell **E9** for the *Set Objective* box. This cell has a *SUM* formula.

    d. Verify that the **Max** radio button is selected for the *To* parameter.

    e. Click the **By Changing Variable Cells** box and select cells **D5:D8**.

12. Add constraints to a *Solver* problem.

    a. Click **Add** to the right of the *Subject to the Constraints* box.

    b. Select cell **D5** for the *Cell Reference* box.

    c. Use **<=** as the operator.

    d. Click the **Constraint** box and type 4. The Davis campus can hold four or fewer sessions.

    e. Click **Add**. (If you accidentally closed the dialog box, click **Add** to reopen it.)

    f. Select cell **D5** again for the *Cell Reference* box.

    g. Choose **>=** as the operator.

    h. Click the **Constraint** box and type 1. The Davis campus must have at least one session.

i. Click **Add**. Complete constraints for the problem as shown here:

D6   <=   3
D6   >=   1
D7   <=   1
D7   >=   1
D8   <=   4
D8   >=   1

j. When all constraints are identified, click **OK** in the *Add Constraint* dialog box.

k. Choose **GRG Nonlinear** for the *Select a Solving Method*.

l. Confirm that the **Make Unconstrained Variables Non-Negative** box is selected (Figure 8-88).

m. Click **Solve**. A solution is shown in the worksheet, and the *Solver Results* dialog box is open. The maximum number of students is 870.

n. Select the **Keep Solver Solution** button and click **OK**. (If you see a *Solver* run-time error message, type 4, 3, 1, 4 in cells **D5:D8** so that you can continue.)

13. Create a forecast sheet.

a. Click the **Enrollment** sheet tab.

b. Select cells **D7:E13**. One data series is time-based, and the other is the enrollment numbers.

c. Click the **Forecast Sheet** button [*Data* tab, *Forecast* group].

d. Click the **Create a line chart** button at the top-right of the window.

e. Click the **Options** button to expand the window.

f. Set the forecast to end at **12/31/19**.

g. Click **Create** to build the new sheet and chart. Excel supplies additional dates to smooth out the intervals.

h. Select the chart object and position its top-left corner to start in cell **A20**.

i. Drag the bottom right sizing handle so that the chart object reaches cell **E36**.

j. Select the **Total** line and change its **Shape Outline** color to **Black, Text 1**.

k. Select the **Chart Area** and set its **Shape Outline** color to **Black, Text 1** and a **½ pt Weight** (Figure 8-89).

l. Select cell **A1**.

m. Name the sheet tab **IMS Forecast**.

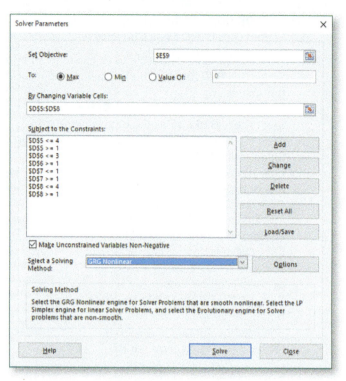

8-88 *Solver* **constraints for the capacity problem**

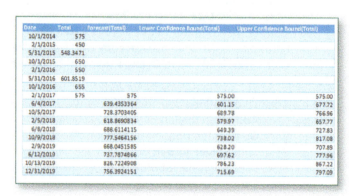

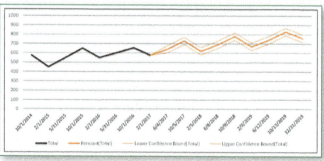

8-89 Forecast sheet and chart

14. Calculate a moving average.
    a. Click the **Enrollment** sheet tab.
    b. Click the **Data Analysis** button [*Data* tab, *Analyze* group].
    c. Choose **Moving Average** and click **OK**.
    d. Select cells **B8:B13** for the *Input Range* box.
    e. Click the **Interval** box and type 2 so that every two years are averaged.
    f. Click the **Output Range** box and select cell **B16**.
    g. Click **OK**.
    h. Click the **Data Analysis** button [*Data* tab, *Analyze* group], choose **Moving Average**, and click **OK**.
    i. Select cells **E8:E13** for the **Input Range** box.
    j. Click the **Interval** box and type 2.
    k. Click the **Output Range** box, select cell **E16**, and click **OK**.
    l. Calculate the moving average for the PHI department in column **H** (Figure 8-90).

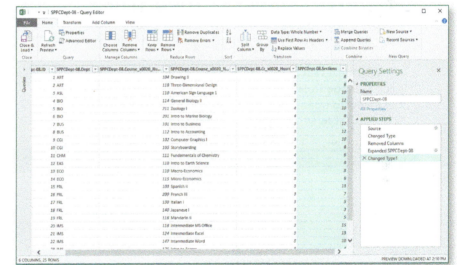

8-90 Moving average results

15. Get and transform XML data.
    a. Click the **New Query** button [*Data* tab, *Get & Transform* group] and choose **From File**.
    b. Choose **From XML**.
    c. Navigate to the folder with the **SPCCDept-08** XML file.
    d. Select the **SPCCDept-08** file name, click **Import**, and then click **Edit**.
    e. Click the **http://. . .Schema. . .** column label in the *Query Editor*.
    f. Click the **Remove Columns** button [*Home* tab, *Manage Columns* group].
    g. Remove the **Attribute:generated** column.
    h. Click the **Expand** button next to the **SPCCDept-08** label and click **OK** to display all fields.
    i. Click the **SPCCDept-08.ID** column label, click the **Data Type** button [*Home* tab, *Transform* group], and choose **Whole Number**.
    j. Click the **SPCCDept-08.Course. . .** label in the third column, click the **Data Type** button [*Home* tab, *Transform* group], and choose **Whole Number**.
    k. Select the **Whole Number** data type for the **Hours** and **Sections** columns (Figure 8-91).

8-91 XML file ready to be loaded to Excel

    l. Click the **Close & Load** button [*Home* tab, *Close* group].

    m. Rename the query results sheet as XML Dept.

16. Get and transform XML data.

    a. Click the **New Query** button [*Data* tab, *Get & Transform* group] and choose **From File** and **From XML**.

    b. Navigate to the folder with the *SPCCFees-08* XML file.

    c. Select the **SPCCFees-08** file name, click **Import**, and click **Edit**.

    d. Click the **http://. . .Schema. . .** column label and click the **Remove Columns** button [*Home* tab, *Manage Columns* group].

    e. Remove the **Attribute:generated** column.

    f. Click the **Expand** button next to the **SPCCFees-08** label and click **OK**.

    g. Click the **SPCCFees-08.ID** column label, click the **Data Type** button [*Home* tab, *Transform* group], and choose **Whole Number**.

    h. Click the **SPCCFees-08.Fee** label, click the **Data Type** button [*Home* tab, *Transform* group], and choose **Currency**.

    i. Click the **Close & Load** button [*Home* tab, *Close* group].

    j. Rename the query results sheet as XML Fees.

17. Create a *PivotTable* from the data model.

    a. Click the **XML Dept** worksheet tab and select cell **A1**.

    b. Click the **Summarize with PivotTable** button [*Table Tools Design* tab, *Tools* group].

    c. Verify that the **New Worksheet** button is selected.

    d. Select the **Add this data to the Data Model** box and click **OK**.

    e. Expand the **SPCCDept-08** query list in the *PivotTable Fields* pane if it is not expanded.

    f. Select the **Dept**, **Course. . . Name**, and **Sections** boxes to place the fields in the *PivotTable* layout. Point to a long field name to see its complete name.

    g. Click **All** at the top of the *PivotTable Fields* pane and expand the **SPCCFees-08** list.

    h. Select the **Fee** box to add it to the *PivotTable* layout.

    i. Click **Auto-Detect** to create the relationship. No relationship is detected.

    j. Click **Manage Relationships** in the message box (Figure 8-92).

    k. Click **New** to open the *Create Relationship* dialog box.

    l. Click the **Table** arrow and choose **SPCCFees-08** as the table name.

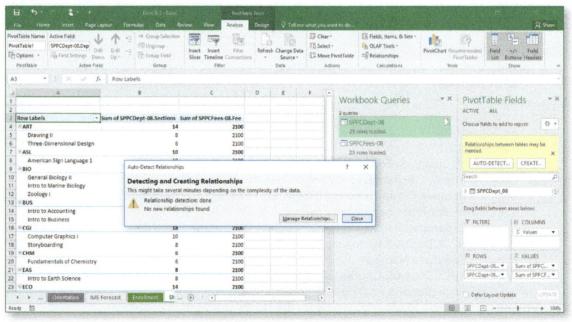

8-92 No relationship is detected

m. Click the **Column (Foreign)** arrow and choose **SPCCFees-08.ID** as the field name.

n. Click the **Related Table** arrow and choose **SPCCDept-08**.

o. Click the **Related Column (Primary)** arrow and choose **SPCCDept-08.ID** as the field name (Figure 8-93).

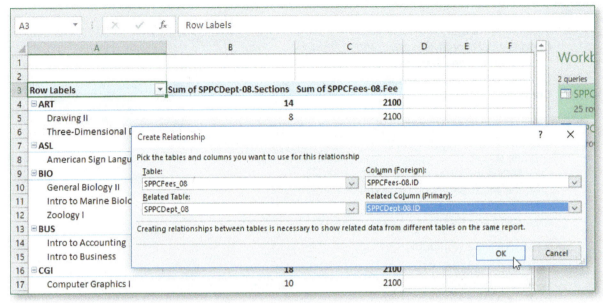

8-93 *Create Relationship* dialog box

p. Click **OK** and then click **Close**.

q. Name the sheet tab XML PivotTable.

18. Pivot and format a *PivotTable*.

a. Drag the **Fee** field on top of the **Section** field in the *Values* area in the *PivotTable Fields* pane to arrange the *Fee* field on the left of the *Sections* field in the *PivotTable*.

b. Select cell **B3** and type Course Fee as the *Custom Name*.

c. Click the **Field Settings** button [*PivotTable Tools Analyze*, *Active Field* group].

d. Click **Number Format** in the *Value Field Settings* dialog box.

e. Choose **Currency**, set zero (0) decimal places, click **OK**, and close the *Value Field Settings* dialog box.

f. Right-click cell **C3** and select **Value Field Settings**.

g. Type Number of Sections in the *Custom Name* box and click **OK**.

h. Click the **Subtotals** button [*PivotTable Tools Design* tab, *Layout* group].

i. Select **Do Not Show Subtotals**.

j. Click the **More** button [*PivotTable Tools Design* tab, *PivotTable Styles* group] and choose **Pivot Style Medium 1**.

k. Select the **Banded Columns** box [*PivotTable Tools Design* tab, *PivotTable Style Options* group] (Figure 8-94).

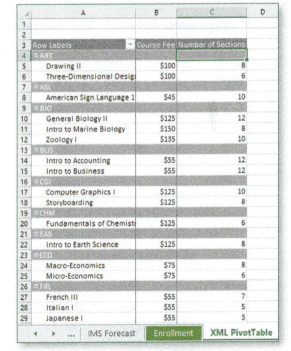

8-94 Formatted *PivotTable*

19. Insert a slicer.
    a. Click any cell in the *PivotTable*.
    b. Click the **Insert Slicer** button [*PivotTable Tools Analyze* tab, *Filter* group].
    c. Select the **SPCCDept-08.Dept** box and click **OK**.
    d. Use the four-pointed arrow to drag the slicer so that the top-left corner is in cell **E3**.

20. Format a slicer.
    a. Click the **More** button [*Slicer Tools Options* tab, *Slicer Styles* group] and choose **Slicer Style Dark 3**.
    b. Click the **Up** spin arrow for the **Columns** button [*Slicer Tools Options* tab, *Buttons* group] and to reach **4**.
    c. Size the slicer to reach column **H** and row **9**.
    d. Click **BIO** in the slicer (Figure 8-95).
    e. Click the **Multi-Select** button in the slicer.
    f. Click **CHM** and **EAS** in the slicer.

8-95 Filtered *PivotTable* and its slicer

21. Save and close the workbook.

22. Uninstall *Solver* and the *Analysis TookPak*.
    a. Select the **Options** command [*File* tab] and click **Add-Ins** in the left pane.
    b. Select **Solver Add-In** in the list of *Active Applications Add-Ins*.
    c. Click **Go** in the *Manage* section near the bottom of the window.
    d. Deselect the **Solver Add-in** and **Analysis ToolPak** boxes and click **OK**.

Guided Project 8-3

Courtyard Medical Plaza has new worksheets for weight loss workshops. You use *Solver* with sample data and add scenarios and data tables to complete a sample set. You also create *PivotTables* to analyze dental insurance data.
[**Student Learning Outcomes 8.1, 8.3, 8.4, 8.7, 8.8**]

File Needed: ***CourtyardMedical-08.xlsx*** *(Student data files are available in the* Library *of your SIMnet account)*
Completed Project File Name: *[your initials] Excel 8-3.xlsx*

Skills Covered in this Project

- Create and manage scenarios.
- Use *Solver* in a worksheet to find a solution.
- Build a one-variable data table.

- Build a two-variable data table.
- Create and customize a *PivotTable*.
- Insert a slicer in a *PivotTable*.
- Insert a *PivotChart*.
- Generate *Descriptive Statistics* for a set of data.

1. Open the ***CourtyardMedical-08*** workbook from your student data files and save it as [your initials] Excel 8-3.

2. Install *Solver* and the *Analysis ToolPak*.
    a. Select the **Options** command [*File* tab].

b. Click **Add-Ins** in the left pane.
c. Click **Go** near the bottom of the window.
d. Select the **Solver Add-in** box.
e. Select the **Analysis ToolPak** box.
f. Click **OK**.

3. Click the **Workout Plan** worksheet tab and select cell **E10**. Five activities are included in this plan to burn calories for weight loss. This cell includes a *SUM* formula.

4. Add scenarios in a worksheet.
   a. Click the **What-if Analysis** button [*Data* tab, *Data Tools* group] and select **Scenario Manager**.
   b. Click **Add**.
   c. Type Basic Plan as the name.
   d. Click the **Changing cells** box, select cells **D5:D9**, and click **OK**.
   e. Do not edit the *Scenario Values* and click **OK**.
   f. Click **Add** to add another scenario.
   g. Type Double as the name, keep the *Changing cells* as is, and click **OK**.
   h. Change the values to 2, 2, 4, 2, 2, doubling each current value, in the *Scenario Values* dialog box and click **OK** (Figure 8-96).
   i. Click **Close**.

5. Use *Solver* to find a target calorie burn.
   a. Click the **Solver** button [*Data* tab, *Analyze* group].
   b. Select cell **E10**, the cell with a *SUM* formula, for the **Set Objective** box.
   c. Click the **Value Of** radio button and type 3500 in the entry box.
   d. Click the **By Changing Variable Cells** box and select cells **D5:D7**. *Solver* finds how many times each activity should be performed to burn 3,500 calories subject to the constraints.

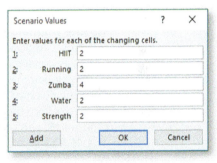

8-96 Edited scenario values

6. Add constraints to a *Solver* problem.
   a. Click **Add** to the right of the *Subject to the Constraints* box.
   b. Select cell **D5** for the *Cell Reference* box.
   c. Choose **>=** as the operator.
   d. Click the **Constraint** box and type 2. The constraint requires that the exercise be done at least twice a week.
   e. Click **Add** to add each of the five remaining constraints shown here:
      D5   <=4
      D6   <=3
      D6   >=1
      D7   <=4
      D7   >=1
   f. When all constraints are identified, click **OK** in the *Add Constraint* dialog box.
   g. Choose **GRG Nonlinear** for the *Select a Solving Method*.
   h. Confirm that the **Make Unconstrained Variables Non-Negative** box is selected (Figure 8-97).
   i. Click **Solve**. A solution displays in the worksheet, and the *Solver Results* dialog box is open.

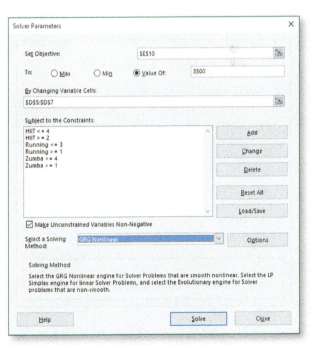

8-97 *Solver* parameters and constraints

7. Save *Solver* results as a scenario.
   a. Click **Save Scenario** in the *Solver Results* dialog box.
   b. Type 3500 Burn as the scenario name.
   c. Click **OK** to return to the *Solver Results* dialog box.
   d. Click the **Restore Original Values** button.
   e. Select **Answer** in the *Reports* list.
   f. Click **OK**. The generated report is inserted, and the original values are restored in the worksheet.

8. Create a scenario summary report.
   a. Click the **What-if Analysis** button [*Data* tab, *Data Tools* group] and select **Scenario Manager**.
   b. Click the **Summary** button.
   c. Verify that the **Scenario summary** button is selected.
   d. Click the **Result cells** box, select cells **D5:D9**, type a comma , and then select cell **E10**.
   e. Click **OK** in the *Scenario Summary* dialog box. The report is generated in a new worksheet. Since the results cells are named, the range names appear in the report (Figure 8-98).

9. Create a one-variable data table to calculate total calories if dinner calories are adjusted.
   a. Click the **Calorie Journal** worksheet tab and select cell **I5**. The *SUM* formula calculates total calories consumed per day.
   b. Select cell **E15**. The formula for the data table must be one column to the right and one row above the first input value.
   c. Type = , click cell **I5**, and press **Enter**.
   d. Select cells **D15:E23** as the data table range.
   e. Click the **What-If Analysis** button [*Data* tab, *Data Tools* group] and choose **Data Table**.
   f. Click the **Column input cell** box and select cell **G5**. The input values will be substituted for this cell in the data table formula.
   g. Click **OK** (Figure 8-99).

10. Create a two-variable data table to calculate total calories if both lunch and dinner calories are adjusted.
    a. Select cell **L15**. A two-variable table has one formula, one row above column inputs and one column left of row values.
    b. Type = , click cell **I5**, and press **Enter**.
    c. Select cells **L15:T23**.
    d. Click the **What-If Analysis** button [*Data* tab, *Data Tools* group] and choose **Data Table**.
    e. Select cell **E5** for the *Row input cell* box. Lunch calories are in the row of this data table.
    f. Click the **Column input cell** box and select cell **G5**. Dinner calories are in the column.
    g. Click **OK** to build the data table (Figure 8-100).

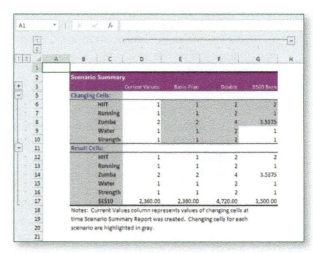

8-98 Generated scenario summary

Dinner Calories	Total Calories
	2,450
500	2,150
600	2,250
700	2,350
800	2,450
900	2,550
1,000	2,650
1,100	2,750
1,200	2,850

8-99 One-variable data table with results

Dinner Calories	Lunch Calories							
2,450	500	600	700	800	900	1000	1100	1200
500	2050	2150	2250	2350	2450	2550	2650	2750
600	2150	2250	2350	2450	2550	2650	2750	2850
700	2250	2350	2450	2550	2650	2750	2850	2950
800	2350	2450	2550	2650	2750	2850	2950	3050
900	2450	2550	2650	2750	2850	2950	3050	3150
1000	2550	2650	2750	2850	2950	3050	3150	3250
1100	2650	2750	2850	2950	3050	3150	3250	3350
1200	2750	2850	2950	3050	3150	3250	3350	3450

8-100 Two-variable data table with results

11. Select cell **J1** and insert a page break [*Page Layout* tab, *Page Setup* group].

12. Create a *PivotTable* for dental insurance data.
    a. Click the **Dental Insurance** worksheet tab and select cells **A4:E35**.
    b. Click the **Recommended PivotTables** button [*Insert* tab, *Tables* group].
    c. Choose **Sum of Billed by Service Code** and click **OK**. Label fields are in the *Rows* area, and numeric fields are in the *Values* area.
    d. Name the worksheet tab PivotTable 1.
    e. Point to **Billed** in the *Choose fields to add to report* area and drag the field name to the **Values** area to show the field twice in the *PivotTable*.

13. Edit value field settings.
    a. Click **Sum of Billed** in cell **B3** and click the **Field Settings** button [*PivotTable Tools Analyze*, *Active Field* group].
    b. Type Total Billed as the *Custom Name*.
    c. Click **Number Format**, choose **Currency**, set **0** (zero) decimal places, and click **OK** two times to close the dialog boxes.
    d. Right-click **Sum of Billed2** in cell **C3** and select **Value Field Settings**.
    e. Type Average Billed as the *Custom Name*.
    f. On the *Summarize Values By* tab, choose **Average** as the function.
    g. Click **Number Format**, choose **Currency**, set **0** (zero) decimal places, and close the dialog boxes.

14. Use *PivotTable* tools to format the report.
    a. Click any cell in the *PivotTable* and apply **Pivot Style Medium 6**.
    b. Select the **Banded Rows** and **Banded Columns** boxes [*PivotTable Tools Design* tab, *PivotTable Style Options* group].
    c. Click the **Grand Totals** button [*PivotTable Tools Design* tab, *Layout* group] and choose **Off for Rows and Columns**.

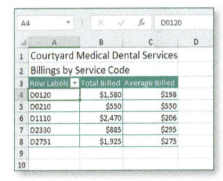

8-101 Completed *PivotTable*

15. Select cell **A1** and type Courtyard Medical Dental Services.

16. Type Billings by Service Code in cell **A2**.

17. Format both labels as **14 pt**. (Figure 8-101).

18. Create a *PivotChart*.
    a. Select a cell in the *PivotTable* and click the **PivotChart** button [*PivotTable Tools Analyze*, *Tools* group].
    b. Choose **Column** and **Clustered Column** as the subtype and click **OK**.
    c. Drag the chart object so that its top-left corner is in cell **E3**.
    d. Size the chart object to reach cell **M24**.
    e. Click one of the **Average Billed** columns and click the **Change Chart Type** button [*PivotChart Tools Design* tab, *Type* group].
    f. Click the **Chart Type** arrow for the *Average Billed* series and choose **Line with Markers** (Figure 8-102).
    g. Click **OK**.

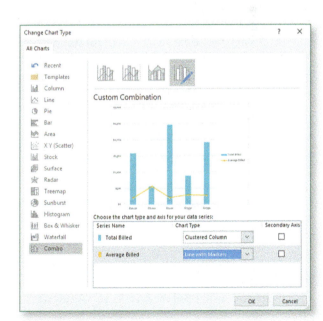

8-102 Change the chart type for one of the data series

h. Click one of the **Total Billed** columns and change its **Shape Fill** [*PivotChart Tools Format* tab, *Shape Styles* group] to **Teal, Accent 5, Darker 25%**.

19. Insert a slicer.
    a. Click any cell in the *PivotTable* and click the **Insert Slicer** button [*PivotTable Tools Analyze* tab, *Filter* group].
    b. Select the **Insurance** box and click **OK**.
    c. Position the slicer so that the top-left corner is in cell **O3**.
    d. Format the slicer with **Slicer Style Dark 5**.
    e. Click **CompDent** in the slicer to filter the *PivotTable* and *PivotChart* (Figure 8-103).
    f. Select cell **A1**.

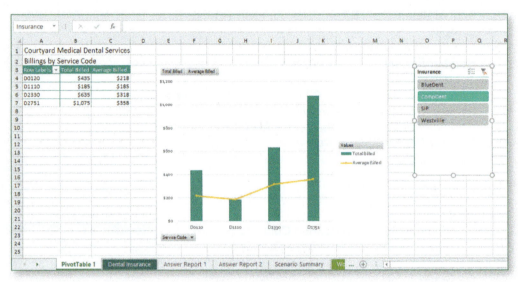

8-103 Completed *PivotTable*, *PivotChart*, and slicer

20. Generate *Descriptive Statistics* for a rating category.
    a. Click the **Dental Insurance** sheet tab.
    b. Click the **Data Analysis** button [*Data* tab, *Analyze* group].
    c. Select **Descriptive Statistics** and click **OK**.
    d. Select cells **E4:E35** for the **Input Range** box.
    e. Select the **Labels in First Row** box.
    f. Select the **Output Range** button.
    g. Click the **Output Range** box and click cell **G4**.
    h. Select the **Summary statistics** box and click **OK**.
    i. **AutoFit** column **G** (Figure 8-104).

21. Save and close the workbook.

22. Uninstall *Solver* and the *Analysis TookPak*.
    a. Select the **Options** command [*File* tab] and click **Add-Ins** in the left pane.
    b. Select **Solver Add-In** in the list of *Active Applications Add-Ins*.
    c. Click **Go** in the *Manage* section near the bottom of the window.
    d. Deselect the **Solver Add-in** and **Analysis ToolPak** boxes and click **OK**.

8-104 Summary statistics for the billed amounts

Independent Project 8-4

Central Sierra Insurance has assembled data about clients in a *PivotTable*. The data source has been updated, but the *PivotTable* has not been refreshed. You also insert a calculated field and complete formatting. You create a commission calculator with a two-variable data table and get data from an Access database file to create a second *PivotTable*.
[Student Learning Outcomes 8.4, 8.6, 8.7]

Files Needed: ***CentralSierra-08.xlsx*** and ***Database-08.accdb*** *(Student data files are available in the Library of your SIMnet account)*
Completed Project File Name: *[your initials] Excel 8-4.xlsx*

Skills Covered in this Project

- Work with *PivotTable* tools.
- Insert a calculated field in a *PivotTable*.
- Build a two-variable data table.
- Get and transform data from an Access table.
- Create a *PivotTable* from the data model.

1. Open the ***CentralSierra-08*** workbook from your student data files and save it as [your initials] Excel 8-4.

2. Click the **Client Stats** worksheet tab. Note the column labels and city and state names.

3. Click the **PivotTable1** worksheet tab. The state names on this sheet are different.

4. Click a cell in the *PivotTable*. The field name "Number of Volunteers" in the *PivotTable Field List* pane is not part of the data on the **Client Stats** sheet.

5. Click the **Refresh** button on the *PivotTable Tools Analyze* tab (Figure 8-105).

6. Edit the *PivotTable* to show # of Females and # of Males as column labels. Center align both labels.

7. Click the *Filter* arrow for cell **A5** and sort the state names in ascending order.

8. Apply **PivotStyle Light 22** and show **Banded Rows**.

9. Insert a calculated field in a *PivotTable*.
   a. Click the **Fields, Items, and Sets** button [*PivotTable Tools Analyze* tab, *Calculations* group] and choose **Calculated Field**.
   b. Type All in the *Name* box.
   c. Click the **Formula** box and delete the zero and the space after the equals sign.
   d. Double-click **Females** and type + for addition.
   e. Double-click **Males** and click **OK** (Figure 8-106).
   f. Edit the label in cell **D5** to show Total and center it.
   g. Press **Ctrl+Home**.

10. Click the **Commissions** worksheet tab and enter a formula in cell **E6** to calculate commission dollars (multiply the premium by the rate).

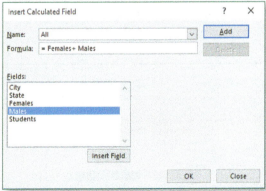

8-105 Refreshed *PivotTable*

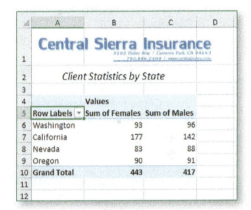

8-106 *Insert Calculated Field* dialog box

11. Build a two-variable data table to calculate commissions. Format the results as **Currency** with no decimal places (Figure 8-107).

12. Get and transform data from a Microsoft Access database.
    a. Click the **New Query** button [*Data* tab, *Get & Transform* group], choose **From Database**, and then select **From Microsoft Access Database**.
    b. Find and select *Database-08* from your student data files and click **Import**.
    c. In the *Navigator* window, select **TblCentralSierra** in the list and click **Edit**.
    d. Remove the **ID** and **State** columns in the *Query Editor*.
    e. Close the query and load it to Excel.
    f. Name the new sheet Client Stats2.

13. Create a *PivotTable* from the data model.
    a. Click cell **A2** in the table on the **Client Stats2** sheet.
    b. Click the **Summarize with PivotTable** button [*Table Tools Design* tab, *Tools* group].
    c. Add the data to the data model and place the *PivotTable* on a new worksheet.
    d. Expand the **TblCentralSierra** list in the *PivotTable Fields* pane and place all the fields in the *PivotTable* layout.
    e. Click **All** in the *PivotTable Fields* pane and expand the list for the table that includes the male, female, and student fields.
    f. Select the **Students** box to add it to the *PivotTable* layout.
    g. Click **Auto-Detect** to create the relationship. The *City* field is the common field in these two tables.
    h. Click **Close** in the message box (Figure 8-108).
    i. Name the sheet tab PivotTable2.

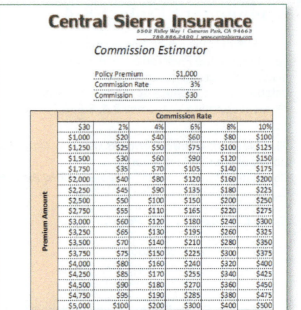

Central Sierra Insurance
5502 Ridley Way | Cameron Park, CA 94663
780.886.2400 | www.centralsierra.com

Commission Estimator

Policy Premium	$1,000
Commission Rate	3%
Commission	$30

	Commission Rate				
$30	**2%**	**4%**	**6%**	**8%**	**10%**
$1,000	$20	$40	$60	$80	$100
$1,250	$25	$50	$75	$100	$125
$1,500	$30	$60	$90	$120	$150
$1,750	$35	$70	$105	$140	$175
$2,000	$40	$80	$120	$160	$200
$2,250	$45	$90	$135	$180	$225
$2,500	$50	$100	$150	$200	$250
$2,750	$55	$110	$165	$220	$275
$3,000	$60	$120	$180	$240	$300
$3,250	$65	$130	$195	$260	$325
$3,500	$70	$140	$210	$280	$350
$3,750	$75	$150	$225	$300	$375
$4,000	$80	$160	$240	$320	$400
$4,250	$85	$170	$255	$340	$425
$4,500	$90	$180	$270	$360	$450
$4,750	$95	$190	$285	$380	$475
$5,000	$100	$200	$300	$400	$500

Premium Amount

8-107 Completed data table for commissions

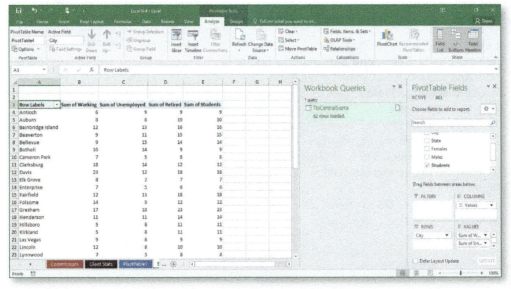

8-108 *PivotTable* from the data model

14. Edit the column labels as show here. The display label cannot be the same as the field name in the *PivotTable* list.

        B3   Employeed
        C3   Not Working
        D3   Retirees
        E3   Undergrad

15. Apply **PivotTable Style Medium 15** with **Banded Rows** and **AutoFit** each column.

16. Save and close the workbook (Figure 8-109).

Row Labels	Employeed	Not Working	Retirees	Undergrad
Antioch	6	9	9	9
Auburn	8	8	10	10
Bainbridge Island	12	13	16	16
Beaverton	9	11	15	15
Bellevue	9	15	14	14
Bothell	10	14	9	9
Cameron Park	7	5	8	8
Clarksburg	18	14	12	12
Davis	23	12	18	18
Elk Grove	8	2	7	7
Enterprise	7	5	6	6
Fairfield	12	13	18	18
Folsome	14	9	12	12
Gresham	17	18	23	23
Henderson	11	11	14	14
Hillsboro	5	8	11	11
Kirkland	5	8	11	11
Las Vegas	9	8	9	9
Lincoln	12	8	10	10
Lynnwood	7	5	8	8
Milwaukie	8	8	9	9
North Las Vegas	5	9	8	8
Oak Grove	7	5	8	8
Paradise	10	14	9	9
Parkland	8	4	2	2
Portland	10	10	14	14
Poulsbo	9	12	5	5
Redmond	8	7	5	5
Reno	9	15	14	14
Roseville	14	10	15	15
Sacramento	6	6	9	9
Spring Valley	9	5	7	7
Stockton	15	15	18	18
Tacoma	11	10	8	8
Tigard	12	13	16	16
Vancouver	10	10	15	15
Walnut Grove	12	8	13	13
Winchester	10	8	10	10
Witney	13	13	13	13
Woodland	22	20	24	24
Yakima	14	8	7	7
Yuba City	12	11	14	14
Grand Total	443	417	483	483

Central Sierra Insurance
5502 Ridley Way | Cameron Park, CA 94664
780.956.7400 | www.centralsierra.com

Client Statistics by State

Row Labels	Values # of Females	# of Males	Total
California	177	142	319
Nevada	83	88	171
Oregon	90	91	181
Washington	93	96	189
Grand Total	**443**	**417**	**860**

8-109 Completed *PivotTables* for Excel 8-4

Independent Project 8-5

At Placer Hills Real Estate, the commission and fee split between the listing and selling agents depends on price tiers (levels). You create a one-variable data table to display commissions and net earnings for various split rates. You copy the sheet and edit it to show results for another price tier. Additionally, you create scenarios for selling price and commission, generate summary statistics, and create a forecast sheet.
[Student Learning Outcomes 8.1, 8.3, 8.4, 8.5, 8.8]

File Needed: **PlacerHills-08.xlsx** (Student data files are available in the Library of your SIMnet account)
Completed Project File Name: **[your initials] Excel 8-5.xlsx**

Skills Covered in this Project

- Build a one-variable data table.
- Use *Solver*.
- Create and manage scenarios.
- Generate descriptive statistics.
- Create a forecast sheet.

1. Open the **PlacerHills-08** workbook from your student data files and save it as [your initials] Excel 8-5.

2. Review formulas.
   a. Select cell **C14** on the **Tier 2** worksheet. The total commission is calculated by multiplying the selling price by the listing rate.
   b. Select cell **C15**. The *IFS* function checks the selling price (C12) to determine the commission split percentage (column D).
   c. Select cell **C16**. The *IFS* function checks the selling price (C12) to determine the fee percentage (column E) and multiplies the commission (C15) to calculate the fee in dollars.
   d. Select cell **C17**. The net commission is calculated by subtracting fees from the PHRE amount.

3. Build one-variable data tables.
   a. Select cell **C20** and create a reference to cell **C15**.
   b. Select cell **D20** and create a reference to cell **C17**. Both formulas in the data table refer to cell **C12**, the one variable.
   c. Use cell **D8** as the column input for the data table. (You can use any percentage from column D because its value is replaced by the possible rates in the data table.) (Figure 8-110).
   d. Decrease the decimal two times for the results in the data table.
   e. Make a copy of the **Tier 2** worksheet and name the copy Tier 1.
   f. Edit the label in cell **A23** to show **Tier 1**.
   g. Edit the selling price in cell **C12** to **$1,000,000**.
   h. Recalculate the data table with cell **D7** as the column input for *Tier 1*.

4. Name cell ranges.
   a. Click the **Price Solver** worksheet tab.
   b. Click cell **C12** and name the range **Selling_Price**. You cannot use spaces in a range name.
   c. Name cell **C14** as Total_Commission and cell **C17** as PHRE_Commission.

5. Install the *Solver Add-in* and the *Analysis ToolPak*.

6. Use *Solver* to find target PHRE net commission amounts.
   a. Build a *Solver* problem with cell **C17** as the objective cell. For the first solution, set the objective to a value of **50000** by changing cell **C12**. Save the results as a scenario named $50,000.
   b. Restore the original values and run another *Solver* problem to find a selling price for a PHRE commission of 75000. Save these results as a scenario named $75,000.

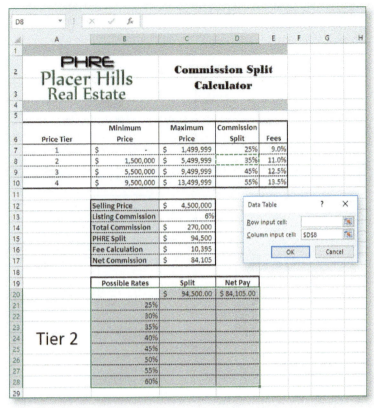

8-110 Data table setup for *Tier 2*

c. Restore the original values and run a third *Solver* problem to find a selling price for a net commission of $100,000. Save these results as a scenario.

7. Manage scenarios.
   a. Show the **$50,000** scenario in the worksheet.
   b. Create a **Scenario summary** report for cells **C12**, **C14**, and **C17**.

8. Generate *Descriptive Statistics* for recent sales.
   a. Click the **Sales Forecast** sheet tab.
   b. Generate **Descriptive Statistics** for cells **E4:E26** and note that the label is in the first row.
   c. Select the **Output Range** button, click the entry box, and select cell **G4**.
   d. Select the **Summary statistics** box and include the largest and smallest (*Kth* values) in the report.
   e. **AutoFit** column **G** (Figure 8-111).

9. Create a forecast sheet for the date and price data on the **Sales Forecast** sheet using a column chart. End the forecast three months from the last date in the table. Position the chart object with its top-left corner in cell **E1**. Size the chart object to reach cell **P20**. Name the generated sheet as Forecast.

Sale Price	
Mean	370593.2
Standard Error	19986.61
Median	365000
Mode	#N/A
Standard Deviation	93745.5
Sample Variance	8.79E+09
Kurtosis	-1.23251
Skewness	0.01939
Range	294100
Minimum	228900
Maximum	523000
Sum	8153050
Count	22
Largest(1)	523000
Smallest(1)	228900

8-111 Descriptive statistics for sales

10. Save and close the workbook (Figure 8-112).

11. Uninstall the *Solver Add-in* and the *Analysis ToolPak*.

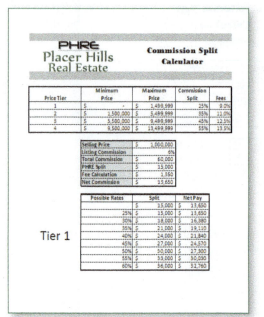

Tier 1

Tier 2

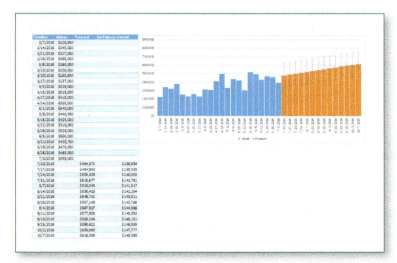

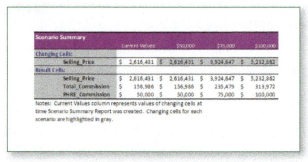

8-112 Completed worksheets for Excel 8-5

Independent Project 8-6

Wilson Home Entertainment Systems calculates selling price based on cost and profit margin. You create scenarios for the worksheet and build a two-variable data table. Other tasks include getting data from an XML file and creating a *PivotTable* and *PivotChart*.
[**Student Learning Outcomes 8.1, 8.2, 8.3, 8.4, 8.5, 8.6, 8.7, 8.8**]

Files Needed: **WilsonHome-08.xlsx**, **WilsonHome-08.xml**, and **WilsonHome-08.xsd** *(Student data files are available in the* Library *of your SIMnet account)*
Completed Project File Name: *[your initials] Excel 8-6.xlsx*

Skills Covered in this Project

- Create and manage scenarios.
- Create a scenario summary report.
- Build a two-variable data table.
- Create a forecast sheet.

- Use the *Analysis ToolPak* to generate a moving average.
- Use *Solver* to find a solution.
- Use *Goal Seek* to backsolve a problem.
- Get and transform XML data.
- Create and customize a *PivotTable*.

1. Open the **WilsonHome-08** workbook from your student data files and save it as [your initials] Excel 8-6.

2. Install *Solver* and the *Analysis ToolPak*.

3. Review pricing formulas.
   a. Select cell **F5** on the **Product Pricing** worksheet. Shipping and handling charges are calculated at 10% of the manufacturer's cost.
   b. Select cell **F6**. An insurance cost is calculated at 6% of the cost.
   c. Select cell **F7**. Total investment is the sum of the cost, shipping and handling, and insurance.
   d. Select cell **F9**. The suggested selling price is the total investment multiplied by 1 plus the margin. These results are rounded to show zero (0) decimal places.

4. Create and manage scenarios.
   a. Create a scenario named **12%** with cell **F8** as the changing cell but do not edit the value. This is the original data set.
   b. Add another scenario named **13**% and change the value.
   c. Add scenarios for **15%** and **17%** profit margins.
   d. Generate a scenario summary report for cells **F4**, **F8**, and **F9**.
   e. Edit the labels in cells **C6** and **C8:C10** in the *Results Cells* section of the summary report to display **Cost**, **Margin** (C6 and C9), and **Selling Price**. Right-align these labels.
   f. Show the **15%** scenario in the **Product Pricing** worksheet.

5. Select cell **B12** and create a reference to the selling price formula for the two-variable data table.

6. Build the data table and format results as **Currency** with zero (0) decimal places (Figure 8-113).

| | Manufacturer's Cost | Profit Margin | | | | | | |
		8%	10%	12%	14%	16%	18%	20%
	$133							
	$200	$251	$255	$260	$264	$269	$274	$278
	$225	$282	$287	$292	$298	$303	$308	$313
	$250	$313	$319	$325	$331	$336	$342	$348
	$275	$345	$351	$357	$364	$370	$376	$383
	$300	$376	$383	$390	$397	$404	$411	$418
	$325	$407	$415	$422	$430	$437	$445	$452
	$350	$438	$447	$455	$463	$471	$479	$487
	$375	$470	$479	$487	$496	$505	$513	$522
	$400	$501	$510	$520	$529	$538	$548	$557
	$425	$532	$542	$552	$562	$572	$582	$592
	$450	$564	$574	$585	$595	$606	$616	$626
	$475	$595	$606	$617	$628	$639	$650	$661
	$500	$626	$638	$650	$661	$673	$684	$696
	$525	$658	$670	$682	$694	$706	$719	$731
	$550	$689	$702	$715	$727	$740	$753	$766
	$575	$720	$734	$747	$760	$774	$787	$800
	$600	$752	$766	$780	$793	$807	$821	$835
	$625	$783	$798	$812	$827	$841	$856	$870
	$650	$814	$829	$844	$860	$875	$890	$905
	$675	$846	$861	$877	$893	$908	$924	$940
	$700	$877	$893	$909	$926	$942	$958	$974
	$725	$908	$925	$942	$959	$976	$992	$1,009
	$750	$940	$957	$974	$992	$1,009	$1,027	$1,044

8-113 Completed data table for *Product Pricing* sheet

7. Create a forecast sheet for the data on the **Soundbar Sales** sheet with a line chart. End the forecast at the end of the third month from the last date in the data. Position the chart object with its top-left corner in cell **A20**.

8. Change the outline color for the **Values** series in the chart to **Blue-Gray, Text 2**. Change the outline color for the **Forecast** series to **Orange, Accent 4**. Select the chart area and format the outline color as **Black, Text 1**.

9. Rename the sheet tab as Forecast Sheet and select cell **A1** (Figure 8-114).

10. Create a moving average list with chart for cells **B4:B16** on the **Soundbar Sales** sheet with an interval of **2**. Output the results to cell **D4**. Position the chart object to start at cell **E4** and size it to reach cell **M18**.

11. Change the outline and shape fill color for the **Forecast** series to **Gold, Accent 3**. Select cell **A3** (Figure 8-115).

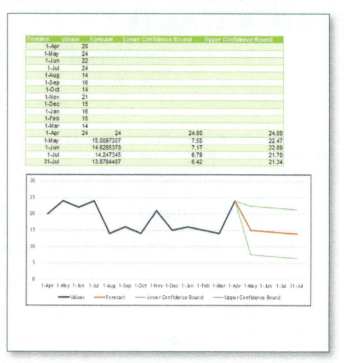

8-114 Completed forecast sheet and chart

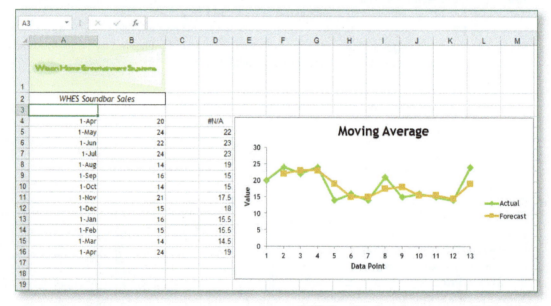

8-115 Completed moving average and related chart

12. Use *Solver* to find target total wages for one day.
    a. Click the **Man Hours** sheet tab.
    b. Select cells **C5:C8** and save the values as a scenario named **Current**.
    c. Build a *Solver* problem to find the minimum result for cell **E9** subject to the following constraints:
       C5   Between 16 and 18
       C6   Between 6 and 10

C7   Between 12 and 15
C8   Between 4 and 12

   d. Save the results ($2,085) as a scenario named Minimum and show the results in the worksheet.

13. Use *Goal Seek* to set cell **E9** to a value of **1800** by changing cell **C5**. Accept the solution and save cells **C5:C8** as a scenario named $1800.

14. Create a scenario summary report for cells **C5:C8** and cell **E9** (Figure 8-116).

15. Get and transform XML data.
   a. Create a new query for the XML file **WilsonHome-08** from your student data files.
   b. Display all fields in the *Query Editor*.
   c. Remove the two generated columns at the right of the data.
   d. Set the data type to **Date/Time** for the **WilsonHome.Date** field and to **Currency** for the **WilsonHome.Price** column.
   e. Load the query and name the query results sheet as XML Sales.
   f. Select the **WilsonHome.Date** column in the worksheet and apply the **Short Date** format.

16. Create a *PivotTable* from the data model.
   a. Select cell **A2** on the **XML Sales** sheet.
   b. Create a *PivotTable* on a new worksheet and add the data to the workbook data model.
   c. Show the **ID** and **Style** fields. Drag the **Style** field to the *Columns* area in the *PivotTable Fields* pane.
   d. Click **All** in the *PivotTable Fields* pane, expand the **TableQty** list, and add the **Quantity** field to the *PivotTable* layout.
   e. Click **Create** in the *PivotTable Fields* task pane to open the *Create Relationship* dialog box.
   f. Click the **Table** arrow and choose **TableQty** as the table and **ID** as the *Column (Foreign)* field.
   g. Click the **Related Table** arrow and select **WilsonHome_08** with **WilsonHome.ID** as the *Related Column (Primary)* field (Figure 8-117).
   h. Click **OK** and then click **Close**.
   i. Name the sheet tab XML PivotTable.
   j. Close the *Workbook Queries* pane if it is open.

17. Work with *PivotTable* tools.
   a. Click any cell in the *PivotTable* and insert a timeline for the *Date* field.
   b. Format the timeline to show quarters and then display data for the second quarter 2017.
   c. Position the timeline to start in cell **F2**.
   d. Apply **PivotTable Style Medium 4** with banded columns and rows to the *PivotTable* and **Timeline Style Light 3** to the timeline.
   e. Change the label in cell **A3** to Transaction ID.
   f. Change the label in cell **B3** to Product.
   g. Select cell **A1**.

18. Use *GETPIVOTDATA* on the **Quantities** sheet to get data for column F (Figure 8-118).

8-116 **Scenario summary report after** *Solver* **and** *Goal Seek*

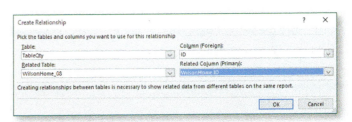

8-117 *Create Relationship* **dialog box**

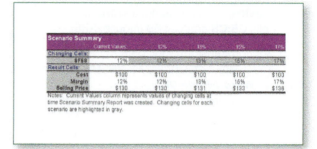

8-118 Completed worksheets for Excel 8-6

19. Save the workbook, click **Continue** in the *Compatibility Checker*, and close the workbook.

20. Uninstall *Solver* and the *Analysis ToolPak*.

Improve It Project 8-7

Pool and Spa Oasis forecasts sales for three categories of business. You create scenarios with different growth rates and build a one-variable data table. On another worksheet, you use *Solver* to find minimum total wages for a work crew.
[Student Learning Outcomes 8.1, 8.3, 8.4]

File Needed: **Pools&Spa08.xlsx** *(Student data files are available in the Library of your SIMnet account)*
Completed Project File Name: **[your initials] Excel 8-7.xlsx**

Skills Covered in this Project

- Create and manage scenarios.
- Build a one-variable data table.
- Use *Solver* with constraints.

1. Open the **Pools&Spa-08** workbook from your student data files and save it as [your initials] Excel 8-7.

2. Review formulas.
   a. Select cell **D5** on the **Forecast** worksheet. The text box explains the formula which uses 3D references to the **Factors** sheet.
   b. Select cell **B12**. This is a reference to the growth factor in cell **F3** on the **Factors** sheet.
   c. Click the **Factors** worksheet tab. The company uses a general growth rate, but each category's potential is increased or reduced by an adjustment factor.

3. Create scenarios for the growth rate.
   a. Create a scenario named .15% on the **Factors** sheet for the existing data with cell **F3** as the changing cell.
   b. Add another scenario named .5% and change the value to .005.
   c. Add scenarios for **1.25%** and **1.75%** growth rates. In the *Scenarios Values* dialog box, you must enter the decimal equivalent of the percentage.
   d. Show the **1.25%** scenario in the worksheet.
   e. Return to the **Forecast** worksheet.

4. Complete the growth rate series for the data table in cells **D20:D27**. The formula references are already entered in row 17.

5. Build the data table with column input cell **B12**. The results are incorrect, because input values and the formula reference must be on the same worksheet.

6. Edit formulas to use a reference on the same sheet.
   a. Click cell **D5**. The data table indirectly refers to this formula which uses the growth factor in cell **F3** on the **Factors** sheet.
   b. Edit the formula to show (1+$B$12) in place of the reference to cell **F3** on the **Factors** sheet. This is the input value for the data table (Figure 8-119).
   c. Copy the formula to the cells **E5:G5** and then to cells **D6:G7**. Redefine borders as needed.

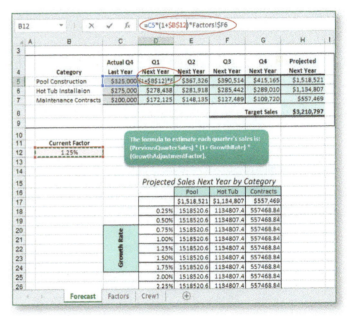

8-119 Edited formula to refer to cell on the same sheet as the data table

7. Format data table results as **Currency** with no decimal places.

8. Use *Solver* to find minimum wages.
   a. Click the **Crew1** worksheet tab.
   b. Build a *Solver* problem to find the minimum value for cell **E9** by changing cells **D5:D8**. Constraints for cell **D8** are already entered in the *Solver Parameters* dialog box.
   c. Add constraints for each of cells **D5:D7** that reflect the information in column C in the worksheet.
   d. Add a constraint that cell **D9** be less than or equal to 150 (Figure 8-120).
   e. Keep the *Solver* results.

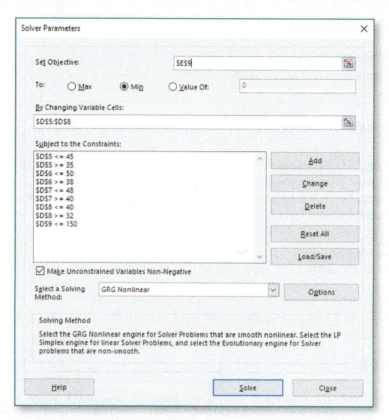

Solver Parameters

Se_t Objective: $SE$9

To: ○ _Max   ● Mi_n   ○ _V_alue Of: 0

_B_y Changing Variable Cells: $D$5:$D$8

Subject to the Constraints:

```
$D$5 <= 45
$D$5 >= 35
$D$6 <= 50
$D$6 >= 38
$D$7 <= 48
$D$7 >= 40
$D$8 <= 40
$D$8 >= 32
$D$9 <= 150
```

Add   Change   Delete   Reset All   Load/Save

☑ Ma_k_e Unconstrained Variables Non-Negative

S_e_lect a Solving Method: GRG Nonlinear   Options

Solving Method

Select the GRG Nonlinear engine for Solver Problems that are smooth nonlinear. Select the LP Simplex engine for linear Solver Problems, and select the Evolutionary engine for Solver problems that are non-smooth.

Help   Solve   Close

8-120 *Solver* constraints for work crew problem

9. Save and close the workbook (Figure 8-121).

10. Uninstall the *Solver Add-in*.

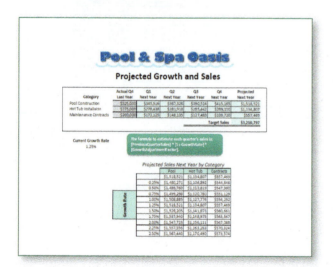

8-121 **Completed worksheets for Excel 8-7**

Challenge Project 8-8

In this project, you create a worksheet for a carpet/flooring business. You plan to build a data table that shows cost based on total square footage and cost per square foot of the flooring product.
[Student Learning Outcome 8.4]

File Needed: None
Completed Project File Name: *[your initials] Excel 8-8.xlsx*

Create and save a workbook as [your initials] Excel 8-8. Modify your workbook according to the following guidelines:

- Enter a label in row 4 for Costs per square foot. In row 5, type the label Total square footage. In row 6, type Total cost.
- In the adjacent column enter a sample cost and square footage for carpet or wood flooring in a home. Build a formula in row 6 to calculate the cost for your sample values.
- Starting in row 9, create column input values that represent cost per square foot. Use an increment of $2. Start at an average price and fill at least 20 costs in the column.
- In row 8, type an initial row input value that reflects square footage for a single room. Use an increment of 5 and fill values so that you have 9 or 10 columns.
- Build the two-variable data table for total costs for flooring.
- Determine a name for the company and enter main and secondary titles for your worksheet. Add borders, shading, or other format attributes to enhance the interpretation of the worksheet.

Challenge Project 8-9

In this project, you use a statistical measure from in the *Analysis ToolPak* and prepare an informational worksheet to describe and demonstrate one of the calculations.
[Student Learning Outcome 8.8]

File Needed: None
Completed Project File Name: *[your initials] Excel 8-9.xlsx*

Create and save a workbook as [your initials] Excel 8-9. Modify your workbook according to the following guidelines:

- In cell A3, enter the label Statistical Measure. In cell A4, type Purpose.
- In cells B3:B4, enter the name of one of the statistical measures in the *Analysis ToolPak* that you used in this chapter. In row 4, type a brief description of its use and purpose.
- Starting in row 6, develop worksheet data that will illustrate the measure you have chosen, using work, school, or personal data. Include labels and values that clearly illustrate the goal of using your statistical measure.
- Calculate the measure.
- Format the sheet and related results in a professional manner.

Challenge Project 8-10

In this project, you create a worksheet for a trip that you are planning. Some costs are fixed, but you use *Solver* to help determine how much you can spend on lodging and meals.
[Student Learning Outcome 8.1, 8.2, 8.3]

File Needed: None
Completed Project File Name: *[your initials] Excel 8-10.xlsx*

Create and save a workbook as [your initials] Excel 8-10. Modify your workbook according to the following guidelines:

- Enter labels in column A for Airfare, Hotel, Meals, Car Rental, and two other spending categories for your trip.
- In column B, enter average values for your trip. Calculate a total and format the data in an easy-to-understand style.
- Save the original values as a scenario with the changing cells as hotel and meal costs.
- Run *Solver* with a lower total cost as your objective by adjusting the hotel and meal categories. Decide if you need to set constraints for the other categories. If *Solver* cannot find a solution, redefine constraints until it can find a solution. Save the results as a scenario.
- Run *Solver* with a higher cost as your objective. Save the results as a scenario and generate a *Solver* Answer report.
- Generate a scenario summary report for the hotel and meal categories.
- Use *Goal Seek* with the total cost cell set at an optimum cost for your trip by adjusting only the hotel cost. Show these results in the worksheet.

CHAPTER 9

Recording and Editing Macros

CHAPTER OVERVIEW

Routine tasks such as entering the same label or calculating results for the same range can often be handled by macros. A **macro** is a series of instructions and keystrokes that executes a command. In this chapter, you learn how to run and record a macro, how to edit a macro in the Visual Basic Editor, and how to create a macro-enabled template.

STUDENT LEARNING OUTCOMES (SLOs)

After completing this chapter, you will be able to:

SLO 9.1   Run a macro (p. E9-576).

SLO 9.2   Record a macro (p. E9-578).

SLO 9.3   Assign a macro to a *Button* form control (p. E9-582).

SLO 9.4   Edit a macro in the Visual Basic Editor (VBE) (p. E9-584).

SLO 9.5   Record a macro with relative references (p. E9-588).

SLO 9.6   Save a macro-enabled template (p. E9-590).

SLO 9.7   Create a macros-only workbook (p. E9-590).

CASE STUDY

In the Pause & Practice projects in this chapter, you work with a macro-enabled Excel workbook for Paradise Lakes Resort (PLR). You run and record macros, assign them to buttons, and create macro-enabled templates.

Pause & Practice 9-1: Run and record a macro.

Pause & Practice 9-2: Assign a macro to a button and edit a macro.

Pause & Practice 9-3: Record a macro with relative references and save a macro-enabled template.

Running a Macro

A macro is saved in an Excel macro-enabled workbook which has an **.xlsm** file name extension. When you open a macro-enabled workbook, a security message bar informs you that macros are disabled. In order to run or edit macros, you must enable them.

Macro Security

Because macros are targets for viruses, malware, or malicious code, the default option in the Excel *Trust Center* disables all macros as a workbook is opened. You should enable macros only when you know they can be trusted.

You can check macro security settings in the *Trust Center* [*File* tab, *Options* group]. Alternatively, the *Developer* tab has a *Macro Security* button that opens the *Macro Settings* pane in the *Trust Center*.

▶ **HOW TO: Display the Developer Tab and Check Macro Settings**

1. Click the **File** tab and select **Options**.
   - The *Excel Options* dialog box opens.
2. Click **Customize Ribbon** in the left pane.
3. Select the **Developer** box in the *Main Tabs* list and click **OK**.
4. Click the **Macro Security** button [*Developer* tab, *Code* group].
   - The *Trust Center* window opens to the *Macro Settings* pane (Figure 9-1).
5. Verify or select the **Disable all macros with notification** button.
6. Click **OK** to close the *Trust Center*.
   - A workbook with macros opens with a security message bar.
   - The macros are not usable or editable.
7. Click **Enable Content** in the message bar to enable macros for each workbook.

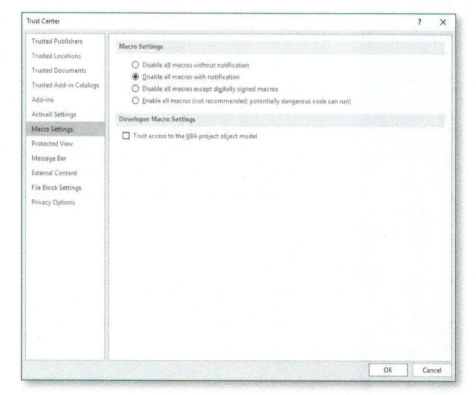

9-1 *Macro Settings* in the *Trust Center*

▶ **MORE INFO**

If you select *Enable All Macros* in the *Trust Center*, the *Security Warning* bar does not open when you open a workbook with macros.

Run a Macro

Once macros are enabled, you run a macro to execute its commands, such as inserting data or formatting cells. You run a macro by selecting the macro name in the *Macro* dialog box and clicking *Run*. Macros can also be saved and run with keyboard shortcuts.

As long as a workbook is open, its macros are available in any open workbook. You can, for example, run a macro stored in *Workbook 2* while working in *Workbook 1* as long as *Workbook 2* is open. The *Macro* dialog box lists the names of macros from all open workbooks. When a macro runs, it carries out the commands or enters data in the current workbook. After the macro is run, edit data entered by the macro as usual.

Macro-related commands are in the *Code* group on the *Developer* tab. You can also run and record a macro from the *Macros* button on the *View* tab.

> **HOW TO: Run a Macro**

1. Open the workbook.
2. Click **Enable Content** in the security bar (Figure 9-2).
   - The security bar may not display if you enabled macros in the workbook in your current work session.
3. Click the **Macros** button [*Developer* tab, *Code* group].
   - The *Macro* dialog box lists the names of available macros.
   - The list includes macros from all open workbooks.
4. Select the macro name in the list (Figure 9-3).

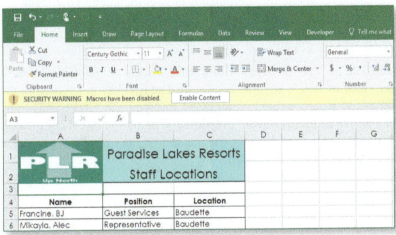

9-2 *Security Warning* **bar for a workbook with macros**

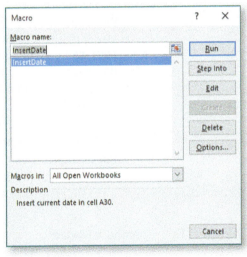

9-3 *Macro* **dialog box**

5. Click **Run**.
   - The macro executes its commands in the worksheet.
   - You can delete a macro by selecting its name and clicking **Delete** in this dialog box.

> **ANOTHER WAY**
>
> Click the **Macros** button on the *View* tab to open the *Macro* dialog box.

Recording a Macro

Macros are programs that carry out routine, repetitive tasks. If you always print two copies of completed worksheets, for example, you can record a macro that performs the steps for the print command. Then, with the click of a button or a keyboard shortcut, your print command runs.

Excel macros are recorded. You perform all the steps in a worksheet, and Excel encodes each action. The code underlying a macro uses the programming language *Visual Basic for Applications*, referred to as *VBA*. Because you "record" a macro, you don't need to know VBA to create a macro.

Macros are saved in a workbook. You can save a macro in the current workbook, in a new workbook, or in a special macros-only workbook.

Record a Macro

Almost any Excel command can be recorded in a macro. Before you begin to record, practice what you want to do so that your steps while recording are error-free. For example, if you want to record a macro to open an inventory workbook, carry out the task before you record the macro to identify folder and file names. A macro records every step and every keystroke, including incorrect or unnecessary steps.

Once you know all the steps, you can start to record. As you record, you perform the commands or type the data to be included in the macro. When you are finished, click the **Stop Recording** button. To test your macro, delete the data or undo the commands that you carried out during recording and run your macro.

By default, a macro is recorded with absolute references to the cell locations for each command or data entry task so that positioning commands are not included in the macro. If you type the company name in cell A32 while recording, the macro records that the company name is entered in cell A32. The active cell can be any worksheet cell when you run the macro.

Macros must be named. The name must begin with a letter and cannot contain spaces or special characters. A macro may include a keyboard shortcut. The first key in a macro shortcut is always **Ctrl**. Experienced macro writers recommend that you use **Ctrl+Shift+any alphabetic character** for a macro shortcut to avoid overriding Windows or Excel commands. For example, if you use **Ctrl+P** as a macro shortcut, the macro overrides the *Print* command shortcut when the workbook with that macro is open.

> **HOW TO: Record a Macro**

1. Click the **Record Macro** button [*Developer* tab, *Code* group].
   - The *Record Macro* dialog box opens.
   - A default name displays.
2. Type a name for the macro in the *Macro Name* box.
   - Begin the name with a letter.
   - Do not space between words; you can separate words with an underscore.
3. Click the **Shortcut key** box.
4. Press **Shift** and type a letter for the shortcut.
   - A shortcut is optional.
5. Click the **Store macro in** box and choose **This Workbook** from the drop-down list.

6. Press **Tab** and type an optional explanation in the *Description* box (Figure 9-4).

   - The description is included as a comment in the VBA code.

7. Click **OK**.

   - The *Record Macro* button toggles to the *Stop Recording* button.

8. Complete each task for the macro.

   - Select a cell and enter data.
   - Select cells and give a command.
   - If you make an error, correct it as usual.

9. Click the **Stop Recording** button [*Developer* tab, *Code* group].

   - The data and commands performed as you recorded the macro are part of the worksheet.

10. Delete the data or undo commands that were completed while recording the macro.

11. Run the macro to test it.

9-4 Macro name, shortcut, and description

> **ANOTHER WAY**
>
> The *Status* bar includes a *Record Macro* button next to the mode indicator. Its *ScreenTip* is *No macros are currently being recorded. Click to begin recording a new macro.* This button toggles to a button to stop recording.

> **MORE INFO**
>
> To change the shortcut for a macro, open the *Macro* dialog box and select **Options**.

Save a Macro-Enabled Workbook

You can begin the process of recording macros in a regular Excel workbook. To save macros, however, you must save the workbook as a macro-enabled workbook. The *.xlsm* format allows for the inclusion of VBA modules where macros are stored. If you try to save a workbook with macros as a regular Excel workbook, a message box, shown in Figure 9-5, reminds you that your VBA work cannot be saved in a regular workbook.

9-5 Macros can only be saved in macro-enabled workbooks

Macros cannot be removed by the *Document Inspector* as shown in the message box in Figure 9-6. You must delete macros to remove data that should not be included in a file that is shared with others.

9-6 Macros cannot be removed by the *Document Inspector*

▶HOW TO: Save a Macro-Enabled Workbook

1. Click the **File** tab and select **Save As**.

2. Navigate to the desired folder location.
   - You can save macro-enabled workbooks in any folder.

3. Type or edit the file name.

4. Click the **Save as type** arrow and choose **Excel Macro-Enabled Workbook** (Figure 9-7).

5. Click **Save**.
   - The workbook is saved and remains open.

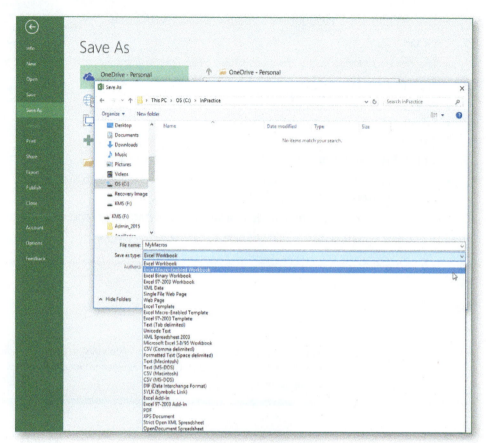

9-7 Choose the file type for a macro-enabled workbook

PAUSE & PRACTICE: EXCEL 9-1

In this project, you open a macro-enabled workbook for Paradise Lakes Resort. You enable the macros, run a macro to enter the current date, and record a new macro to enter a label in cell A32.

File Needed: ***ParadiseLakes-09.xlsm*** *(Student data files are available in the Library of your SIMnet account)*
Completed Project File Name: ***[your initials] PP E9-1.xlsm***

1. Check macro security and show the *Developer* tab.
   a. Click the **Options** command [*File* tab] and click **Trust Center** in the left pane.
   b. Select **Trust Center Settings**.
   c. Click **Macro Settings** in the left pane.
   d. Verify or select the **Disable all macros with notification** button.
   e. Click **OK**.

f. Click **Customize Ribbon** in the left pane.

g. Select the **Developer** box in the *Main Tabs* list and click **OK**.

2. Open the ***ParadiseLakes-09.xlsm*** workbook from your student data files and click **Enable Content** in the security bar.

3. Save the workbook as a macro-enabled workbook.

   a. Click the **File** tab and select **Save As**.

   b. Navigate to your folder for saving files.

   c. Edit the file name to [your initials] PP E9-1.

   d. Click the **Save as type** arrow and choose **Excel Macro-Enabled Workbook**.

   e. Click **Save**.

4. Run a macro.

   a. Click the **Macros** button [*Developer* tab, *Code* group] to open the *Macro* dialog box.

   b. Select **InsertDate** in the macros list (Figure 9-8). The description for the macro explains what it will do.

   c. Click **Run** to insert the current date in cell A30.

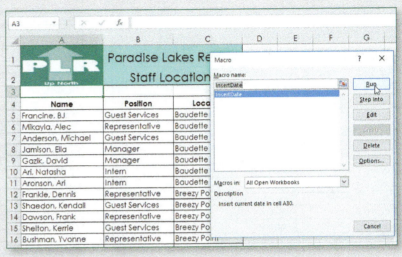

9-8 *Macro* dialog box with existing macro names

5. Record a macro.

   a. Click the **Record Macro** button [*Developer* tab, *Code* group].

   b. Type FirstQuarter in the *Macro name* box.

   c. Click the **Shortcut key** box.

   d. Press **Shift** and type q. The keyboard shortcut for the macro is **Ctrl+Shift+Q**.

   e. Verify that **This Workbook** is the choice in the *Store macro in* box.

   f. Click the **Description** box and type Display First Quarter in cell A32. (Figure 9-9).

   g. Click **OK** to begin recording.

   h. Select cell **A32**. This is the first step in the macro, to move the active cell to cell A32.

   i. Type First Quarter and press **Enter**. This action enters the label and moves to cell A33 (Figure 9-10).

   j. Click the **Stop Recording** [*Developer* tab, *Code* group].

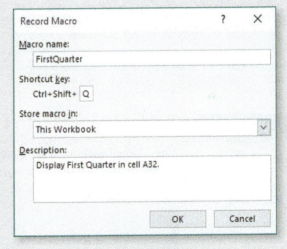

9-9 Details for the *FirstQuarter* macro

6. Run a macro with a shortcut.

   a. Delete the contents of cell **A32**. The label was entered as you recorded the macro.

   b. Press **Ctrl+Home** to move the pointer to cell A1.

   c. Press **Ctrl+Shift+Q** to run the macro. The macro inserts the quarter name in cell A32.

7. Save and close the workbook (Figure 9-11).

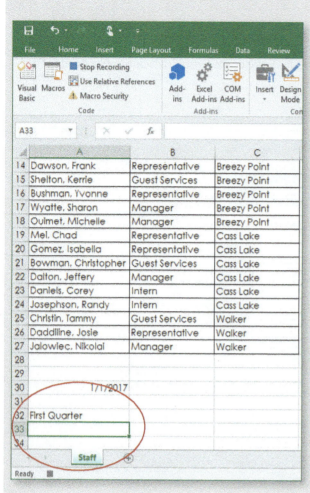

Name	Position	Location
Francine, BJ	Guest Services	Baudette
Mikayla, Alec	Representative	Baudette
Anderson, Michael	Guest Services	Baudette
Jarnison, Ella	Manager	Baudette
Gazik, David	Manager	Baudette
Ari, Natasha	Intern	Baudette
Aronson, Ari	Intern	Baudette
Frankie, Dennis	Representative	Breezy Point
Shaedon, Kendall	Guest Services	Breezy Point
Dawson, Frank	Representative	Breezy Point
Shelton, Kerrie	Guest Services	Breezy Point
Bushman, Yvonne	Representative	Breezy Point
Wyatte, Sharon	Manager	Breezy Point
Ouimet, Michelle	Manager	Breezy Point
Mei, Chad	Representative	Cass Lake
Gomez, Isabella	Representative	Cass Lake
Bowman, Christopher	Guest Services	Cass Lake
Dalton, Jeffery	Manager	Cass Lake
Daniels, Corey	Intern	Cass Lake
Josephson, Randy	Intern	Cass Lake
Christin, Tammy	Guest Services	Walker
Daddiline, Josie	Representative	Walker
Jalowiec, Nikolai	Manager	Walker

1/1/2017

First Quarter

9-10 Data is entered as macro is recorded   9-11 PP E9-1 completed

---

SLO 9.3

Assigning a Macro to a Button

You worked with form controls in Chapter 7 when you learned how to insert combo box and option button controls in a worksheet. The ***Button*** is a form control that runs a macro with a single click.

 ANOTHER WAY

In a workbook with macros, choose **Quick Access Toolbar** in Excel *Options*. Select **Macros** from the *Choose commands from* list and add your macro name to the toolbar. An icon is placed in the *Quick Access* toolbar that you can click to run the macro.

Assign a Macro to a Button

The *Button* form control is available from the *Insert Controls* button on the *Developer* tab [*Controls* group]. As soon as you draw the control, the *Assign Macro* dialog box opens so that you can select a macro to be assigned to the control.

▶ HOW TO: Assign a Macro to a Button

1. Click the **Insert Controls** button [*Developer* tab, *Controls* group].

2. Click the **Button (Form Control)** command in the *Form Controls* category (Figure 9-12).

3. Draw a button control in the worksheet.

   - The *Assign Macro* dialog box opens.
   - You can choose a macro from any open workbook.

4. Select the macro name to assign to the button (Figure 9-13).

5. Click **OK**.

   - The button displays the default name *Button N,* where *N* is a number.
   - The button control is selected and displays selection handles.

6. Click inside the button to position the I-beam pointer.

7. Delete the default text and type a label for the button.

8. Right-click the button and choose **Exit Edit Text** from the menu (Figure 9-14).

   - Resize the button by dragging a selection handle.
   - While selection handles are visible, point to a border to display a four-pointed move arrow and drag the button to another location.

9. Click a worksheet cell to deselect the *Button* control.

10. Click the *Button* form control to run the macro.

    - The pointer displays a hand with a pointing finger when it is ready to run the macro.
    - To select the *Button* control without running the macro, right-click the control, and then left-click a border.
    - To delete a *Button* control, right-click the control, left-click a border to close the menu, and then press **Delete**.

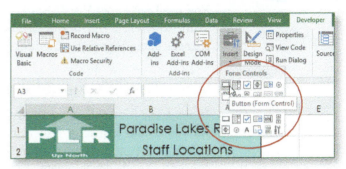

9-12 The *Button* control is in the *Controls* group on the *Developer* tab

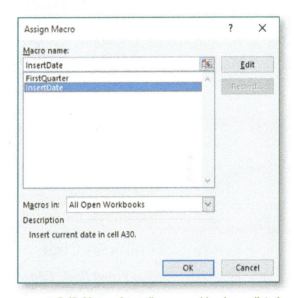

9-13 Macros from all open workbooks are listed

9-14 Type a new label for a *Button* control and exit editing

---

> ▶ **MORE INFO**
>
> Right-click the **Button** control and choose **Assign Macro** from the context menu to assign a different macro to the button.

Editing a Macro in the Visual Basic Editor (VBE)

You need not know Visual Basic for Applications (VBA) programming to record a macro. With experience and practice, you will find it relatively straightforward to make minor changes in the Visual Basic Editor (VBE).

Visual Basic for Applications (VBA)

Visual Basic for Applications (VBA) is the programming language that underlies Excel macros. As you record a macro, Excel and VBA convert your keystrokes into VBA code. *Code* describes the programming commands required for a task to run. VBA uses the following concepts in code development.

- *Objects:* An *object* is a tool or element with functions, properties, and data. Examples of objects are *workbook, sheet, cell, range,* and *button.*
- *Properties:* A *property* is a characteristic or attribute. A worksheet object has name, default font, or print area properties. A cell object has a value property.
- *Methods:* A *method* is a function, service, or action for an object. A method for a workbook object might be to open another workbook.
- *Collections:* A *collection* is a group of similar objects. Collections allow you to apply a method to multiple objects.

> **MORE INFO**
>
> VBA is an object-oriented programming language.

Edit VBA Code

The *Visual Basic Editor (VBE)* is an application that runs in a window separate from Excel. It opens when you choose the command to edit a macro from the *Macro* dialog box or when you click the *Visual Basic* button on the *Developer* tab.

> **ANOTHER WAY**
>
> You can open the *VBE* window with the keyboard shortcut **Alt+F11**.

The VBE window has three panes, the *Code* window, the *Project Explorer,* and the *Properties* window. Figure 9-15 shows a macro with these three panes visible. The panes are displayed from the *View* menu in the *Visual Basic Editor* window.

To edit macro actions, you make changes in the *Code* window. In Figure 9-15, for example, you can change the location of the date to cell A31 instead of cell A30 by editing that line in the code as well as the line that shows where the pointer ends.

Be careful about punctuation, spacing, and special characters while editing code because they are part of the programming. Some errors are identified immediately and highlighted in red with a message box as shown in Figure 9-16.

Macros follow a pattern so that you can become familiar with simple code as you analyze your own macros. Note the following similarities in macros:

- The first line displays *Sub* followed by the name of the macro and a set of parentheses. *Sub* means *subroutine* or *sub procedure.* A sub procedure macro runs from the workbook or from another macro. Sub procedure macros end with *End Sub.*

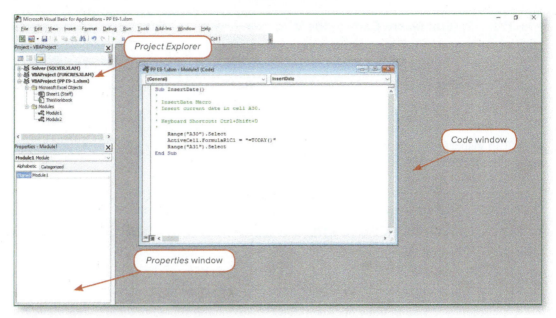

9-15 The Visual Basic Editor with *Code* window, *Project Explorer*, and *Properties* window

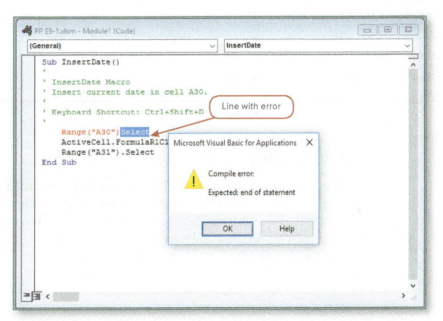

9-16 Coding error in the Visual Basic Editor

- Each line preceded by an apostrophe and shown in green is a ***comment.*** Comment lines are not part of the code. They describe the code, show the shortcut, or separate sections of the macro. Comment lines in Figures 9-15 and 9-16 were entered automatically as the macro was recorded. You can enter your own comments if you write a macro in the Visual Basic Editor.
- Lines of text shown in black between *Sub* and *End Sub* are the *code*. These are Visual Basic commands and properties that control the macro actions.

A macro is stored in a ***module.*** In VBA, a module is a container for the statements, declarations, and procedures. When macros are in the same module, they are separated by a solid border. Macros can also be in separate modules. When you select a macro in the *Macro* window to be edited, the module is automatically selected. You can also select a module from the *Project Explorer* pane.

▶ HOW TO: Edit Macro Code in the VBE

1. Click the **Macros** button [*Developer* tab, *Code* group].
   - Macro names are listed in the *Macro* dialog box.
2. Select the macro name to be edited.
3. Click **Edit**.
   - The Visual Basic Editor (VBE) opens.
   - If the *Code* window is not displayed, choose **Code** from the *Edit* menu.
   - Display or hide the *Project Explorer* or the *Properties Window* from the *View* menu.
4. Edit each line as needed (Figure 9-17).
   - Add or delete code if you know VBA programming commands.

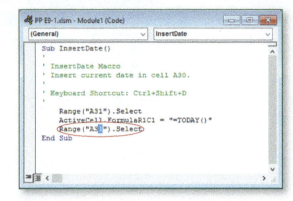

9-17 Edit code lines in the Visual Basic Editor

5. Click the **Close** button in the top right corner of the *VBE* window to return to the worksheet.
   - You can also click the **View Microsoft Excel** button at the left of the toolbar. This leaves the *VBE* window open.
   - Press **Alt+F11** to return to the workbook.
6. Run the macro to test it.
7. Save and close the workbook.
   - The revised macro is saved with the workbook.

Macro Issues

Common issues arise from running or recording a macro. Syntax errors are messages that identify code that Visual Basic does not recognize. Syntax errors can result from typographical errors in the code or from incorrectly used statements. You can usually select the problematic line in the VBE window and press **F1** to access a Help screen. The following table describes problems that prohibit a macro from running successfully.

Common Macro Issues and Solutions

Macro Issue	Solution
Macros are disabled without notification when the workbook is open.	Select **Disable all macros with notification** from the *Macro Security* button [*Developer* tab, *Code* group].
Another macro is currently running.	End the current macro before running or recording another macro.
The worksheet is in *Edit* mode.	Press **Enter** to end *Edit* mode and then run or record the macro.
The worksheet tab is being renamed.	Press **Enter** to complete renaming the worksheet and then run or record the macro.
The workbook is protected.	Unprotect the workbook and then run or record the macro.
A dialog box is open.	Close the dialog box and then run or record the macro.

In this project, you assign a macro to a button. You edit the *InsertDate* macro to change the cell location and test the edited macro using the button.

File Needed: ***[your initials] PP E9-1.xlsm***
Completed Project File Name: ***[your initials] PP E9-2.xlsm***

1. Display the *Developer* tab if it is not shown.

2. Open the *Trust Center* and set macro security to **Disable all macros with notification**.

3. Open the ***[your initials] PP E9-1.xlsm*** workbook completed in *Pause & Practice 9-1*.

4. Click **Enable Content** in the security bar. (The security bar may not open if you completed PP E9-1 during the same work session.)

5. Save the workbook as a macro-enabled workbook named [your initials] PP E9-2.

6. Assign a macro to a *Button* form control.
   a. Click the **Insert Controls** button [*Developer* tab, *Controls* group].
   b. Click the **Button (Form Control)** command in the *Form Controls* category.
   c. Draw a button control that covers cells **E2:F2**.
   d. Select **InsertDate** in the *Assign Macro* dialog box and click **OK** (Figure 9-18).
   e. Click inside the button control to display an I-beam pointer.
   f. Delete the default text and type Insert Date as the caption for the button.
   g. Click cell **C3** to deselect the control.
   h. Right-click the **Button** control and choose **Format Control** (Figure 9-19).
   i. Select **Bold Italic** as the *Font style* on the *Font* tab and click **OK**.
   j. Select cell **C3** to deselect the control.

9-18 ***Button* control object in the worksheet**

7. Edit a macro in the Visual Basic Editor.
   a. Click the **Macros** button [*Developer* tab, *Code* group].
   b. Select **InsertDate** in the list of macro names.
   c. Click **Edit** to open the Visual Basic Editor (VBE) window. (If the *Code* window is not displayed, choose **Code** from the *Edit* menu.)
   d. Click to place an insertion point after **A30** in the comment line "Insert current date in cell A30."
   e. Edit the comment line to show A31.
   f. Edit the first code line *Range("A30").Select* to show A31.
   g. Edit the last line *Range("A31").Select* to display A32 (Figure 9-20).
   h. Click the **View Microsoft Excel** button at the left side of the toolbar.

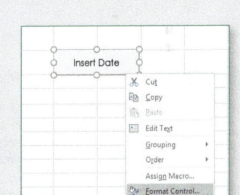

9-19 **Context menu for a *Button* control**

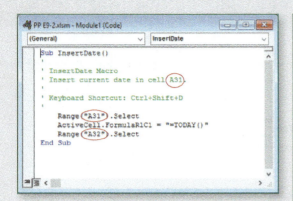

9-20 Edited code for the macro

Name	Position	Location
Francine, BJ	Guest Services	Baudette
Mikayla, Alec	Representative	Baudette
Anderson, Michael	Guest Services	Baudette
Jamison, Ella	Manager	Baudette
Gazik, David	Manager	Baudette
Ari, Natasha	Intern	Baudette
Aronson, Ari	Intern	Baudette
Frankie, Dennis	Representative	Breezy Point
Shaedon, Kendall	Guest Services	Breezy Point
Dawson, Frank	Representative	Breezy Point
Shelton, Kerrie	Guest Services	Breezy Point
Bushman, Yvonne	Representative	Breezy Point
Wyatte, Sharon	Manager	Breezy Point
Ouimet, Michelle	Manager	Breezy Point
Mei, Chad	Representative	Cass Lake
Gomez, Isabella	Representative	Cass Lake
Bowman, Christopher	Guest Services	Cass Lake
Dalton, Jeffery	Manager	Cass Lake
Daniels, Corey	Intern	Cass Lake
Josephson, Randy	Intern	Cass Lake
Christin, Tammy	Guest Services	Walker
Daddiline, Josie	Representative	Walker
Jalowiec, Nikolai	Manager	Walker

Paradise Lakes Resorts
Staff Locations

8. Run a macro from a *Button* form control.
   a. Delete the contents of cell **A30** and press **Ctrl+Home**.
   b. Click the **Insert Date** *Button* control. The date is inserted in cell A31 and the active cell is cell A32.

9. Save and close the workbook (Figure 9-21).

1/1/2017

First Quarter

9-21 PP E9-2 completed

SLO 9.5

Recording a Macro with Relative References

Recorded macros use absolute references, and the active cell can be anywhere in the worksheet when you run the macro. Cell addresses are included in the code. Alternatively, you can record a macro with relative references. In this type of macro, keyboard movement commands are recorded. In Figure 9-22, you can see positioning commands in the line *ActiveCell.Offset(2,0)*. The number 2 is the row offset and zero (0) is the column offset to move the insertion point down two times in the same column.

Before you run a macro that was recorded with relative references, you must set the active cell at the presumed starting location, because the macro executes its commands relative to that cell.

> **MORE INFO**
>
> A positive row offset number moves the insertion point down in the worksheet; a negative number moves it up. A positive column offset number moves the pointer to the right; a negative number moves it left.

9-22 Macro recorded with relative references includes positioning commands

The *Use Relative References* button is located in the *Code* group on the *Developer* tab. It is off or inactive by default.

> **HOW TO:** Record a Macro with Relative References

1. Select the cell at which the commands will begin.
2. Click the **Use Relative References** button [*Developer* tab, *Code* group].
   - The button is shaded when it is active (Figure 9-23).
   - The button remains active until you click to turn it off.

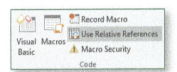

9-23 *Use Relative References* is active

3. Click the **Record Macro** button [*Developer* tab, *Code* group].
4. Type a name for the macro in the *Macro name* box.
   - Begin the name with a letter and do not use spaces between words.
5. Click the **Shortcut key** box, press **Shift**, and type a letter.
   - A shortcut is optional.
6. Verify that **This Workbook** is selected in the *Store macro in* box.
7. Type an optional explanation in the *Description* box.
   - The description appears as a comment in the Visual Basic Editor.
8. Click **OK**.
   - The *Record Macro* button toggles to the *Stop Recording* button.
   - All keyboard positioning commands are recorded.
   - Position the insertion point using keyboard arrow keys or keyboard shortcuts.
9. Complete each task for the macro.
   - Enter and format data.
   - Select cells and give commands.
   - Use the keyboard to position the pointer.
10. Click the **Stop Recording** button [*Developer* tab, *Code* group].
11. Click the **Use Relative References** button [*Developer* tab, *Code* group] to turn off the feature.
12. Delete data or undo commands that were entered as the macro was recorded.
13. Save the workbook.
    - Select the starting cell before running the macro.

SLO 9.6

Saving a Macro-Enabled Template

Templates, because they are model workbooks, often include macros. A *macro-enabled template* is an Excel template that includes macros in addition to formats and data. A macro-enabled template has an *.xltm* file name extension and is automatically saved in the default templates folder for your computer. You can save a macro-enabled template in any folder, but its name appears in the *Personal* group in the *Backstage* view for the *New* command when it is stored in the default folder.

Recording a macro in a template is no different from recording a macro in a regular workbook. When you create a workbook from a macro-enabled template, you must click **Enable Content** to use the macros.

▶ HOW TO: Save a Macro-Enabled Template

1. Enter data and formatting for the template.
2. Record and test macros.
3. Delete data and undo commands that were entered as macros were recorded.
4. Choose **Save As** from the *File* tab.
5. Navigate to any available folder.
   - The folder will update to the default macros folder when you choose the file type.
6. Type the file name for the macro-enabled template.
7. Choose **Excel Macro-Enabled Template** from the *Save as type* list (Figure 9-24).
8. Note the default folder location or choose another folder.
9. Click **Save**.

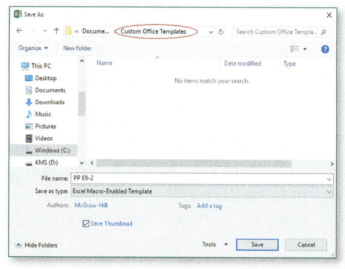

9-24 Macro-enabled templates are saved in the default templates folder

SLO 9.7

Creating a Macros-Only Workbook

A *macros-only workbook* is an Excel workbook saved in *.xlsm* format that includes only macros, no data. As long as this type of workbook is open, you can use its macros in any open workbook. A macros-only workbook enables you to build a library of your macros.

> **MORE INFO**
>
> Use Microsoft Help to learn more about the *PERSONAL.XLSB* workbook.

The *Personal Macro* workbook that is an option in the *Record Macro* dialog box is a macros-only workbook. It is saved in the *XLSTART* folder for the current user with a default name of *PERSONAL.XLSB*. After you have saved a macro in this workbook, *PERSONAL. XLSB* opens automatically as a hidden workbook each time you start Excel so that its macros are always available.

E9-590

Excel 2016 Chapter 9 Recording and Editing Macros

You can create your own macros-only workbook, save it in your usual working folder, and open it each time you start Excel. Since a macros-only workbook includes no data, it is good practice to type a list of macro names with explanations on *Sheet1* as a reminder to not use the workbook for other work.

> **HOW TO: Create a Macros-Only Workbook**

1. Create a new workbook.
2. Record and test macros.
3. Delete data and undo commands that were entered as macros were recorded.
4. Select cell **A1** and type Macros Workbook.
5. Select cell **A3** and type the name of the first macro.
6. Select cell **B3** and type a brief description of the macro.
   - You can include the keyboard shortcut, date of creation, and similar information about the macro.
   - Use as many cells as necessary to document each macro.
7. Use additional rows to document macros in the workbook (Figure 9-25).
8. Choose **Save As** from the *File* tab.
9. Navigate to your folder for saving files.
10. Type a file name for the macros-only workbook.
    - Use a name such as "MacroLibrary" or "MyMacros."
11. Click the **Save as type** arrow and choose **Excel Macro-Enabled Workbook**.
12. Click **Save** and leave the workbook open.
13. Create or open another workbook and use the macros as desired.

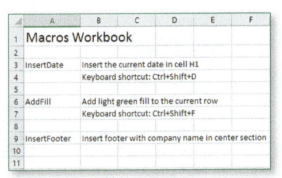

9-25 Include documentation in a macros-only workbook

In this project, you record a macro with relative references to apply shading to a row in the Paradise Lakes Resort worksheet. You save the workbook as a macro-enabled template.

File Needed: *[your initials] PP E9-2.xlsm*
Completed Project File Names: *[your initials] PP E9-3.xltm* and *[your initials] PP E9-3.xlsm*

1. Set macro security to **Disable all macros with notification** in the *Trust Center*.

2. Open the *[your initials] PP E9-2.xlsm* workbook completed in *Pause & Practice 9-2* and click **Enable Content** in the security bar if necessary.

3. Display the *Developer* tab if it is not shown.

4. Record a macro with relative references.
   a. Select cell **A5**. This is where the macro will start its commands.
   b. Click the **Use Relative References** button [*Developer* tab, *Code* group].
   c. Click the **Record Macro** button [*Developer* tab, *Code* group].
   d. Type AddFill in the *Macro name* box.
   e. Click the **Shortcut key** box, press **Shift**, and type f.
   f. Verify that **This Workbook** is selected in the *Store macro in* box.
   g. Click the **Description** box, type Add fill to row., and click **OK**. All keyboard commands will be recorded.
   h. Press **Shift+** press **right arrow** two times to select cells **A5:C5**.
   i. Click the **Fill Color** arrow [*Home* tab, *Font* group] and choose **Dark Green, Accent 3, Lighter 80%** to apply the fill color to the selected cells.
   j. Press **Home** and then press the **down arrow** two times to move the active cell to cell **A7** (Figure 9-26).
   k. Click the **Stop Recording** button [*Developer* tab, *Code* group].

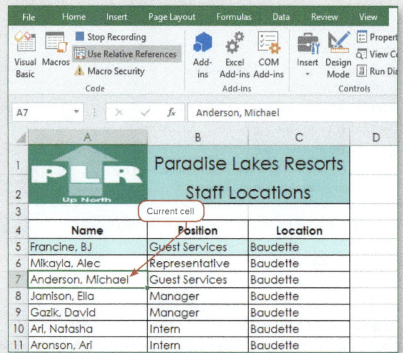

9-26 Macro records all positioning commands

5. Click the **Undo** button in the *Quick Access* toolbar to remove the fill that was applied as you recorded the macro.

6. Select cell **A5** to position the active cell for the start of the macro.

7. Press **Ctrl+Shift+F** to test the macro.

8. Press **Ctrl+Shift+F** to run the macro in row 7.

9. Press **Ctrl+Home** (Figure9-27).

10. Save the workbook as a macro-enabled template.
    a. Choose **Save As** from the *File* tab.
    b. Navigate to any available folder.

9-27 Fill is applied to two rows by the macro

c. Type [your initials] PP E9-3 as the file name for the macro-enabled template.

d. Choose **Excel Macro-Enabled Template** from the *Save as type* list (Figure 9-28).

e. Click **Save** to save the template.

11. Close the workbook.

12. Click the **Use Relative References** button [*Developer* tab, *Code* group] to turn off the command.

13. Click **New** on the *File* tab and click **Personal**.

14. Click the icon for *[your initials] PP E9-3* in the *Personal* category to create a workbook from the template.

15. Click **Enable Content** in the *Security Warning* message bar.

16. Select cell **A9** and press **Ctrl+Shift+F** to run the macro.

17. Press **Ctrl+Shift+F** to run the macro in every other row up to and including row 27 (Figure 9-29).

18. Press **Ctrl+Home**.

19. Save the workbook as a macro-enabled workbook named [your initials] PP E9-3 in your usual folder for saving workbooks.

20. Close the workbook.

21. Delete the template from the *Custom Office Templates* folder.

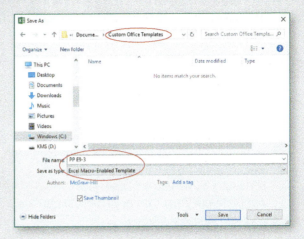

9-28 Macro-enabled template is saved in the default *Templates* folder

9-29 PP E9-3 completed

Chapter Summary

9.1 Run a macro (p. E9-576).

- A *macro* is a series of commands saved in a workbook in a **Visual Basic for Applications (VBA)** programming module.
- Macros must be saved in a macro-enabled workbook which has an *.xlsm* file name extension.
- Because macros may hide viruses and malicious code, you should choose the option in the *Trust Center* to disable macros as a workbook is opened.
- Macros must be enabled to be run.
- From the *Macros* button on the *Developer* tab, you can open the *Macro* dialog box to see the names of existing macros for all open workbooks.
- You can run a macro from the *Macro* dialog box or by pressing the macro's keyboard shortcut keys.

9.2 Record a macro (p. E9-578).

- A macro is recorded, because you perform the steps and your actions are converted to *VBA code* automatically.
- Practice the commands that you want to record as a macro so that your actual recording is error-free.
- Enter a name for the macro and an optional shortcut in the *Record Macro* dialog. You can also type a description.
- Macro names must begin with a letter and cannot include spaces or special characters.
- All macro shortcuts include **Ctrl** with an alphabetic character, but it is recommended to include **Shift** with the shortcut.
- While recording a macro, commands are carried out and data are entered in the worksheet. You can delete or undo these commands before saving the macro-enabled workbook.

9.3 Assign a macro to a *Button* form control (p. E9-582).

- The **Button** form control runs a macro when clicked.
- When you release the pointer after drawing a *Button* control, the *Assign Macro* dialog box opens.
- You can assign a macro from any open workbook.

- To edit or format a *Button* control, right-click the control and choose a command from the context menu.

9.4 Edit a macro in the Visual Basic Editor (VBE) (p. E9-584).

- Excel macros are saved in a *Visual Basic for Applications* module, a container for the statements, commands, and data from a macro.
- The **Visual Basic Editor (VBE)** is a separate application that runs in its own window.
- The Visual Basic Editor has three panes: the *Code* window, the *Project Explorer,* and the *Properties Window.*
- The *Code* window displays programming statements and properties for each command in the macro.
- The *Code* window includes **comment** lines which are preceded by an apostrophe and shown in green.
- For many simple changes, you can edit code lines in the *Code* window.
- Changes made in the Visual Basic Editor are saved when you save the workbook.

9.5 Record a macro with relative references (p. E9-588).

- By default, a macro is recorded with cell addresses (absolute references) for each command.
- The active cell can be anywhere in the worksheet when you run a macro that was recorded with absolute references.
- You can record a macro with relative references by enabling the *Use Relative References* command in the *Code* group on the *Developer* tab.
- For a macro that is recorded with relative references, you must select the appropriate cell before running the macro.
- In the Visual Basic Editor *Code* window for a macro with relative references, you can view and edit positioning commands.

9.6 Save a macro-enabled template (p. E9-590).

- A template with macros must be saved as an Excel **macro-enabled template** with an *.xltm* extension.

- Macro-enabled templates are saved, by default, in the same folder as Excel workbook templates.
- Macro-enabled templates appear in the *Personal* category for the *New* command in the *Backstage* view when saved in the default templates folder.

9.7 Create a macros-only workbook (p. E9-590).

- A ***macros-only workbook*** is saved with an **.xlsm** file name extension and includes no data.
- A macros-only workbook is a way of building a macros library for use in all workbooks.
- When a macros-only workbook is open, you can use its macros in any open workbook.

- You can save a macros-only workbook in your usual folders for saving work.
- From the *Record Macro* dialog box, you can create the ***Personal Macro workbook*** which is named *PERSONAL.XLSB* and saved in the *XLSTART* folder.

Check for Understanding

The SIMbook for this text (within your SIMnet account) provides the following resources for concept review:

- Multiple choice questions
- Matching exercises
- Short answer questions

Guided Project 9-1

Boyd Air has a macros-only workbook and a related Excel template workbook. You edit the *InsertDate* macro and record a macro to apply fill. In the template, you create a macro to delete data using a *Button* form control.
[Student Learning Outcomes 9.1, 9.2, 9.3, 9.4, 9.5, 9.6, 9.7]

Files Needed: ***BoydAir-09.xlsx*** and ***BoydAirMacros-09.xlsm*** *(Student data files are available in the* Library *of your SIMnet account)*
Completed Project File Names: *[your initials] Excel 9-1Macros.xlsm*, *[your initials] Excel 9-1.xltm*, and *[your initials] Excel 9-1 Complete.xlsm*

Skills Covered in This Project

- Set macro security options.
- Edit a macro in the Visual Basic Editor.
- Record a macro.
- Create a macros-only workbook.
- Run a macro.
- Record a macro with relative references.
- Save a macro-enabled template.
- Assign a macro to a *Button* form control.

---

1. Set macro security and display the *Developer* tab.
   a. Click the **Options** command [*File* tab] and click **Trust Center** in the left pane.
   b. Click the **Trust Center Settings** button and click **Macro Settings** in the left pane.
   c. Verify or select **Disable all macros with notification** and click **OK**.
   d. Click **Customize Ribbon** in the left pane and display the *Developer* tab.

2. Open the **BoydAirMacros-09.xlsm** workbook from your student data files, a macros-only workbook (Figure 9-30). Enable the macros if necessary.

3. Save the workbook as a macro-enabled workbook.
   a. Choose **Save As** from the *File* tab.
   b. Navigate to your folder for saving files.
   c. Type [your initials] Excel 9-1Macros as the file name.
   d. Verify or choose **Excel Macro-Enabled Workbook** in the *Save as type* list.
   e. Click **Save**.

4. Run and edit a macro to place the date in column H.
   a. Click the **Test Sheet** worksheet tab.
   b. Press **Ctrl+Shift+D** to run the *InsertDate* macro. The date is inserted in cell E1.
   c. Delete the contents of cell **E1** and press **Ctrl+Home**.
   d. Click the **Macros** button [*Developer* tab, *Code* group].
   e. Verify that the macro name **InsertDate** is selected and click **Edit** to open the Visual Basic Editor (VBE) window. (If the *Code* window is not displayed, choose **Code** from the *View* menu.)

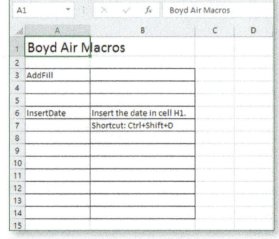

9-30 Workbook includes only macros

f. Click after the left quotation mark in **"E1"** in the code to place an insertion point.

g. Edit the code *Range("E1").Select* to show H1.

h. Edit the last line of code to show H2 instead of "E2" (Figure 9-31).

i. Click the **Close** button at the top-right corner of the VBE window.

j. Click the **Macros** button [*Developer* tab, *Code* group].

k. Verify that **InsertDate** is selected and click **Run**.

l. Delete the date in cell **H1** and press **Ctrl+Home**.

5. Record a macro with relative references to highlight a row of data.

a. Click the **Use Relative References** button [*Developer* tab, *Code* group] to enable the command.

b. Select cell **A5** and click the **Record Macro** button [*Developer* tab, *Code* group].

c. Type ApplyFill in the *Macro name* box.

d. Click the **Shortcut key** box, press **Shift**, and type a.

e. Verify or choose **This Workbook** in the *Store macro in* box.

f. Click the **Description** box, type Apply fill to current row., and click **OK**.

g. Press **F8 (FN+F8)** to start *Extend Selection* mode to use directional arrows to select cells.

h. Press the **right arrow** seven times to select cells **A5:H5**.

i. Click the **Fill Color** arrow [*Home* tab, *Font* group] and choose **Green**, **Accent 6**, **Lighter 80%**. *Extend Selection* mode is canceled.

j. Press **Home** to return the insertion point to cell **A5**.

k. Click the **Stop Recording** button [*Developer* tab, *Code* group].

l. Click the **Undo** button in the *Quick Access* toolbar.

m. Select cell **A5** and press **Ctrl+Shift+A** to test the macro.

6. Save a macros-only workbook.

a. Click the **Macro Info** worksheet tab.

b. Select cell **B3**, type Apply fill to current row., and press **Enter**.

c. Type Shortcut: Ctrl+Shift+A in cell **B4** (Figure 9-32).

d. Save the workbook and leave it open.

7. Open the **BoydAir-09.xlsx** workbook.

8. Record a macro with absolute references to delete data.

a. Click the **Use Relative References** button [*Developer* tab, *Code* group] to disable the command.

b. Click the **Record Macro** button [*Developer* tab, *Code* group].

c. Type DeleteData in the *Macro name* box.

d. Do not use a shortcut key, and store the macro in **This Workbook**.

e. Click the **Description** box, type Delete past data., and click **OK**.

f. Select cell **A5** to record the cell address in the macro.

g. Press **F8 (FN+F8)** to start *Extend Selection* mode so that you can use directional arrows to select cells and rows.

h. Press **Ctrl** and press the **right arrow** one time to highlight to the end of the data in the row.

i. Press **Ctrl** and press the **down arrow** one time to highlight to the bottom row of data.

j. Press **Delete**. *Extend Selection* mode is canceled.

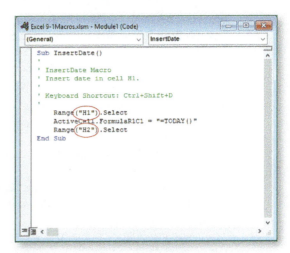

9-31 Edited code for the macro

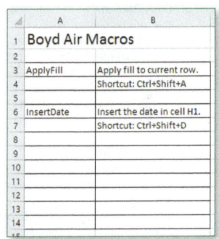

9-32 Documentation for the macros

k. Select cell **A5** to position the active cell.

l. Click the **Stop Recording** button [*Developer* tab, *Code* group].

m. Click the **Undo** button in the *Quick Access* toolbar and select cell **A5**.

9. Assign a macro to a *Button* form control.

a. Click the **Insert Controls** button [*Developer* tab, *Controls* group].

b. Click the **Button (Form Control)** command in the *Form Controls* category.

c. Draw a *Button* control that covers cells **I2:J2**.

d. Select **DeleteData** in the *Assign Macro* dialog box and click **OK** (Figure 9-33).

e. Click inside the *Button* control to place an I-beam pointer.

f. Delete the default text and type Delete Data as the label.

g. Select cell **A1** to deselect the *Button* control. Do not test the macro.

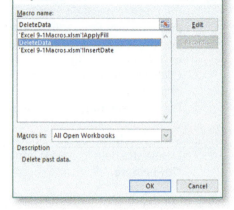

9-33 Assign the macro to the *Button* control

10. Save the workbook as a macro-enabled template.

a. Choose **Save As** from the *File* tab and navigate to your folder.

b. Type [your initials] Excel 9-1 as the file name.

c. Click the file type arrow and choose **Excel Macro-Enabled Template**. The folder updates to the *Custom Office Templates* folder for your computer.

d. Click **Save** to save the template.

e. Close the template. The macros workbook is still open.

11. Create a workbook from the template and run macros.

a. Click the **File** tab and select **New**.

b. Click **Personal** as the category and select **[your initials] Excel 9-1** to create a workbook from the template.

c. Click **Enable Content** in the security bar.

d. Press **Ctrl+Shift+D** to run the date macro. This macro is stored in the macros workbook.

e. Format the font size for cell **H1** to **11 pt**.

f. Click the *Button* control to run its macro.

g. Select cell **A5** and press **Ctrl+ Shift+A** to add fill to the row.

h. Run the *ApplyFill* macro in rows **7** and **9**.

i. Save the workbook as an **Excel Macro-Enabled Workbook** named [your initials] Excel 9-1Complete in your usual location for saving files (Figure 9-34).

j. Close the workbook.

12. Save and close **[your initials] Excel 9-1Macros.**

13. Delete the template from the *Custom Office Templates* folder.

14. Hide the *Developer* tab.

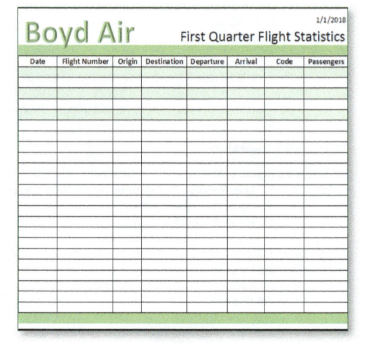

9-34 Excel 9-1 worksheet completed

Guided Project 9-2

Eller Software Services uses a template for client data. You record macros to remove fill, to filter and extract data, and to clear data.
[Student Learning Outcomes 9.1, 9.2, 9.3, 9.5, 9.6]

File Needed: **EllerSoftware-09.xlsx** *(Student data files are available in the* Library *of your SIMnet account)*
Completed Project File Names: *[your initials] Excel 9-2.xltm*, *[your initials] Excel 9-2a.xlsm*, and *[your initials] Excel 9-2b.xlsm*

Skills Covered in This Project

- Set macro security options.
- Record a macro.
- Run a macro.
- Record a macro with relative references.
- Assign a macro to a *Button* form control.
- Save a macro-enabled template.
- Print macro code.

1. Set macro security and display the *Developer* tab.
   a. Select the **Options** command [*File* tab] and click **Trust Center** in the left pane.
   b. Click the **Trust Center Settings** button.
   c. Click **Macro Settings** in the left pane.
   d. Verify or select **Disable all macros with notification** and click **OK**.
   e. Click **Customize Ribbon** in the left pane and display the *Developer* tab.

2. Open the **EllerSoftware-09.xlsx** workbook from your student data files.

3. Save the workbook as an Excel macro-enabled template.
   a. Choose **Save As** from the *File* tab.
   b. Navigate to any available folder.
   c. Type [your initials] Excel 9-2 as the *File name*.
   d. Choose **Excel Macro-Enabled Template** from the *Save as type* list. The folder updates to the *Custom Office Templates* folder for your computer.
   e. Click **Save** to save the template and leave it open.

4. Record a macro with relative references to remove fill from a row.
   a. Click the **Use Relative References** button [*Developer* tab, *Code* group] to enable the command.
   b. Select cell **A5** on the *Clients* worksheet and click the **Record Macro** button [*Developer* tab, *Code* group].
   c. Type RemoveFill in the *Macro name* box.
   d. Click the **Shortcut key** box, press **Shift**, and type r.
   e. Choose **This Workbook** for the *Store macro in* box.
   f. Click the **Description** box, type Remove fill from current row, and click **OK**.
   g. Press **Shift** and press the **right arrow** six times to select cells **A5:G5**. Positioning commands are recorded.
   h. Click the **Fill Color** arrow [*Home* tab, *Font* group] and choose **No Fill**.
   i. Press **Home** to return the insertion point to cell **A5**.
   j. Click the **Stop Recording** button [*Developer* tab, *Code* group].
   k. Select cell **A7** and press **Ctrl+Shift+R** to remove the fill.
   l. Remove the fill in odd-numbered rows up to and including row 15 (Figure 9-35).

5. Record a macro to filter clients.
   a. Click the **Use Relative References** button [*Developer* tab, *Code* group] to disable the command.
   b. Press **Ctrl+Home**.

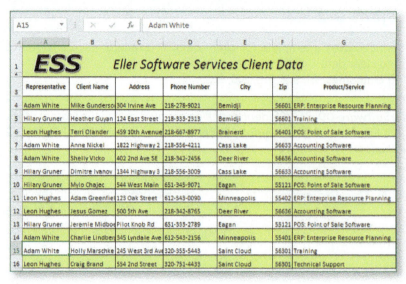

9-35 Macro removes the fill from each row in which it is run

c. Click the **Record Macro** button [*Developer* tab, *Code* group].

d. Type FilterData in the *Macro name* box.

e. Do not use a shortcut key and store the macro in **This Workbook**.

f. Click the **Description** box, type Filter for selected representative, and click **OK**. All commands and selections to build an advanced filter are recorded.

g. Click the **Advanced** button [*Data* tab, *Sort & Filter* group] and select the **Copy to another location** radio button.

h. Verify or select cells **A3:G16** for the **List range** box.

i. Click the **Criteria range** box and select cells **A1:A2** on the **Criteria** tab.

j. Click the **Copy to** box and select cells **B19:G19** on the **Clients** tab (Figure 9-36).

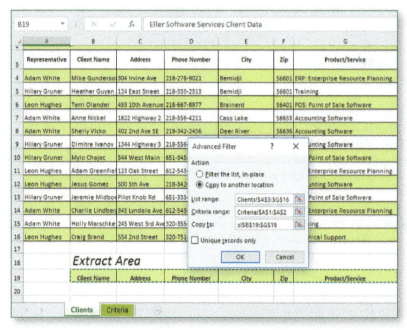

9-36 *Advanced Filter* dialog box

k. Click **OK** to run the filter.

l. Click the **Stop Recording** button [*Developer* tab, *Code* group]. Four records display in the extract area.

6. Record a macro to clear filter results.

   a. Click the **Record Macro** button [*Developer* tab, *Code* group].

   b. Type ClearResults in the *Macro name* box.

   c. Do not use a shortcut key and store the macro in **This Workbook**.

   d. Click the **Description** box, type Clear filter, and click **OK**.

   e. Select cell **B20**, the first cell that displays filter results.

   f. Press **F8 (FN+F8)** to start *Extend Selection* mode.

   g. Press the **right arrow** five times.

   h. Press **Ctrl** and then press the **down arrow** once to highlight to the end of the filter results.

   i. Click the arrow on the **Clear** button [*Home* tab, *Editing* group] and select **Clear All**.

   j. Press **Ctrl+Home**.

   k. Click the **Stop Recording** button [*Developer* tab, *Code* group].

7. Assign a macro to a *Button* form control.

   a. Click the **Insert Controls** button [*Developer* tab, *Controls* group].

   b. Click the **Button (Form Control)** command in the *Form Controls* category.

   c. Draw a *Button* control that covers cell **I17**.

   d. Select **FilterData** in the *Assign Macro* dialog box and click **OK**.

   e. Click inside the *Button* control to place an I-beam pointer.

   f. Delete the default caption and type Show Results as the label.

   g. Select cell **I16** to deselect the control.

   h. Create another *Button* form control in cell **J17** and assign the **ClearResults** macro to it. Edit the caption to display Clear Results.

8. Size and align controls.

   a. Right-click the **Show Results** button to select it.

   b. Press **Ctrl** and right-click the **Clear Results** button. Both buttons display selection handles.

   c. Click the **Height** box [*Drawing Tools Format* tab, *Size* group] and type 0.35 and press **Enter**. The controls are the same height.

   d. Click the **Align** button [*Drawing Tools Format* tab, *Arrange* group] and select **Align Top** (Figure 9-37).

   e. Select cell **A1**.

9. Save and close the template.

   a. Click the **Save** button in the *Quick Access* toolbar.

   b. Close the template.

9-37 Button controls inserted, sized, and aligned

10. Create a workbook from the template and run macros.

   a. Click the **File** tab and select **New**.

   b. Click **Personal** as the category and click **[your initials] Excel 9-2** to create a workbook from the template. Enable the macros.

c. Click the combo box control arrow and select **Adam White**. The name displays in the combo box and in cell **I20**. Cell **I20** has an *INDEX* formula that displays the choice made in the combo box, and cell **A2** on the **Criteria** sheet is a reference to cell **I20**.

d. Click the **Show Results** *Button* control to run its macro.

e. Select cell **B20** and press **Ctrl+Shift+R** to remove the fill.

f. Remove the fill from each result row in the extract area that has a fill color applied.

11. Save the workbook as a macro-enabled workbook.

a. Choose **Save As** from the *File* tab.

b. Navigate to your folder for saving files.

c. Type [your initials] Excel 9-2a as the file name.

d. Choose **Excel Macro-Enabled Workbook** from the *Save as type* list.

e. Click **Save** (Figure 9-38).

f. Click the **Clear Results** *Button* control to test its macro.

g. Close the workbook without saving.

12. Create another workbook from the template.

a. Click the **File** tab and select **New**. Select **Personal** as the category and **[your initials] Excel 9-2** as the template and enable the macros.

b. Click the combo box control arrow and select **Leon Hughes**. The name displays in the combo box and in cell **I20**.

c. Click the **Show Results** *Button* control to run its macro.

d. Select cell **B20** and press **Ctrl+Shift+R** to remove the fill.

e. Remove the fill from each result row in the extract area that has a fill color applied (Figure 9-39).

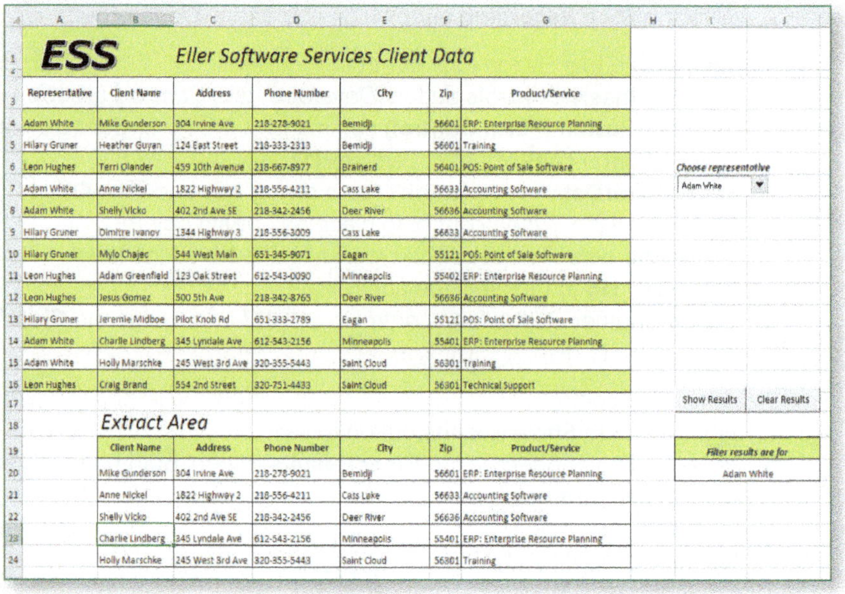

9-38 Excel 9-2a completed

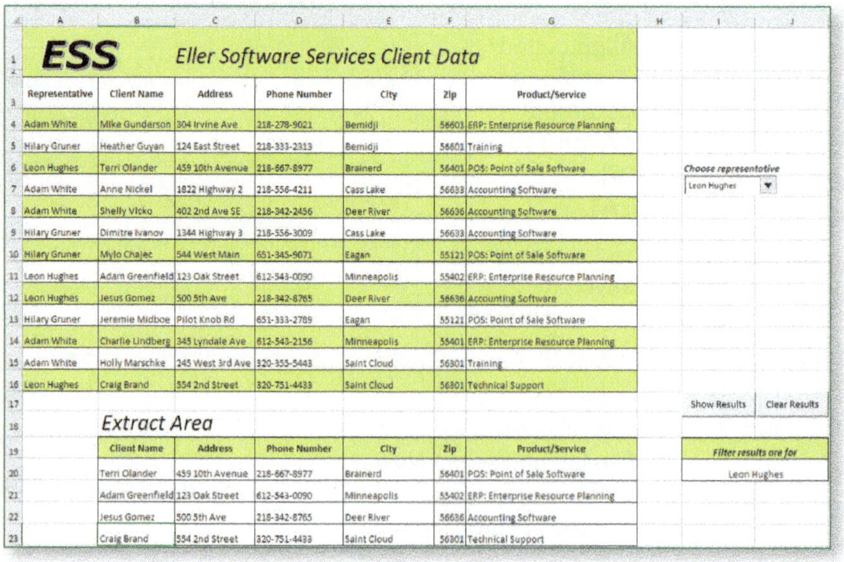

9-39 Excel 9-2b completed

f. Choose **Save As** from the *File* tab and navigate to your folder for saving files.

g. Type [your initials] Excel 9-2b as the file name.

h. Choose **Excel Macro-Enabled Workbook** from the *Save as type* list and click **Save**.

13. Print macro code in a workbook.

a. Click the **Macros** button [*Developer* tab, *Code* group] and select **Edit**.

b. Display the *Code* window if necessary [*View* menu]. Three macros are contained in Module 1. (If your macros are not all in Module 1, complete the steps to print the first group as listed here. Then expand the second module and print the remaining macro(s).)

c. Size the *Code* window to display your macros.

d. Click **File** in the menu and select **Print**.

e. Verify or select the **Current Module** radio button.

f. Verify or select the **Code** box (Figure 9-40).

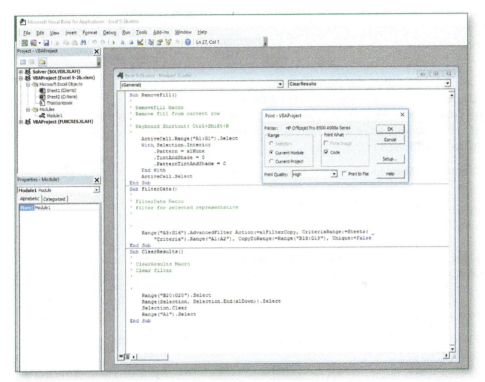

9-40 Macro code for Excel 9-2 workbooks

g. Click **OK** to send the document to the current printer.

h. Press **Alt+F11** to close the Visual Basic Editor and return to Excel.

i. Close the workbook.

14. Delete the template from the *Custom Office Templates* folder and hide the *Developer* tab.

Guided Project 9-3

Clemenson Imaging LLC uses a macros-only workbook and a macro-enabled template for procedures tracking. You edit a macro to insert a label and create a macro for weekly data. You also record a macro to print the workbook and then use these macros in a separate workbook.
[Student Learning Outcomes 9.1, 9.2, 9.3, 9.4, 9.7]

Files Needed: ***Clemenson-09.xlsx*** and ***ClemensonMacros-09.xlsm*** *(Student data files are available in the Library of your SIMnet account)*
Completed Project File Names: ***[your initials] Excel 9-3Macros.xlsm*** and ***[your initials] Excel 9-3.xlsx***

Skills Covered in This Project

- Set macro security options.
- Edit and save a macros-only workbook.
- Copy and edit a macro.
- Edit a macro in the Visual Basic Editor.
- Record a macro.
- Run a macro.
- Assign a macro to a *Button* form control.

1. Set macro security and display the *Developer* tab.
   a. Select **Options** (*File* tab) and then click **Trust Center**.
   b. Click the **Trust Center Settings** button and click **Macro Settings** in the left pane.
   c. Verify or select **Disable all macros with notification** and click **OK**.
   d. Click **Customize Ribbon** in the left pane and display the **Developer** tab.

2. Open the **ClemensonMacros-09** workbook from your student data files and click **Enable Content**.

3. Save the workbook as an Excel macro-enabled workbook.
   a. Choose **Save As** from the **File** tab.
   b. Navigate to your folder for saving files.
   c. Type [your initials] Excel 9-3Macros for the *File name*.
   d. Choose **Excel Macro-Enabled Workbook** from the *Save as type* list if necessary.
   e. Click **Save** and leave the workbook open. The workbook includes a macro that inserts a label in cell A3.

4. Click the **New sheet** worksheet tab to insert a blank worksheet.

5. Press **Ctrl+Shift+Q** to run the macro. The label "Second Quarter Procedures" displays in cell A3, and the active cell is cell A4.

6. Edit a macro in the Visual Basic Editor (VBE).
   a. Click the **Macros** button [*Developer* tab, *Code* group], and select **QtrLabel**.
   b. Click **Edit** to open the Visual Basic Editor (VBE) window. (In the *Project Explorer* window, expand the *Modules* folder if necessary, and double-click **Module 1**. Choose **Code** from the *View* menu if the *Code* window is not displayed.)
   c. Select **Second Quarter** in the code and type Quarterly as shown in Figure 9-41.

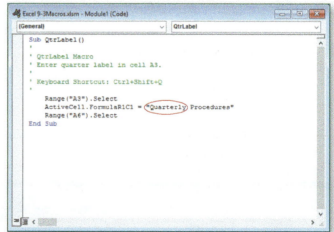

9-41 Code window for the *QtrLabel* macro

d. Edit the code *Range ("A4"). Select* to show "A6."
e. Click the **Close** button at the top-right corner of the VBE window.
f. Delete the contents of cell **A3** and press **Ctrl+Home**.
g. Press **Ctrl+Shift+Q** to run the edited macro.
h. Delete the contents of cell **A3** and press **Ctrl+Home**.

7. Copy and edit a macro.
a. Click the **Developer** tab, click the **Macros** button, and select **QtrLabel**.
b. Click **Edit** to open the Visual Basic Editor (VBE) window.
c. Drag the lower-left corner of the *Code* window to resize the window to approximately twice its current height.
d. Starting at *Sub QtrLabel()* at the top of the *Code* window, select all the code (Figure 9-42).
e. Press **Ctrl+C** to copy the code.
f. Click after **End Sub**, press **Enter** to start a new line, and press **Ctrl+V** to copy the code. A horizontal line is inserted to separate the routines.
g. Edit the copied code as shown here. Be careful about punctuation and spelling (Figure 9-43).

> **Sub WkLabel ()**
> **'**
> **'WkLabel Macro**
> **'Enter weekly label in cell A3.**
> **'**
> **'Keyboard Shortcut: Ctrl+Shift+W**
> **'**
>   **Range("A3").Select**
>   **ActiveCell.FormulaR1C1 = "Weekly Procedures"**
>   **Range("A6"). Select**
> **End Sub**

h. Click the **Close** button at the top-right corner of the VBE window.
i. Press **Ctrl+Shift+W** to test the macro; it does not run.

8. Change macro options to define the shortcut for a macro.
a. Click the **Macros** button on the *Developer* tab and select **WkLabel**.
b. Click **Options** to open the *Macro Options* dialog box (Figure 9-44).
c. Press **Shift** and type w in the *Shortcut key* box.
d. Click **OK** in the *Macro Options* dialog box.

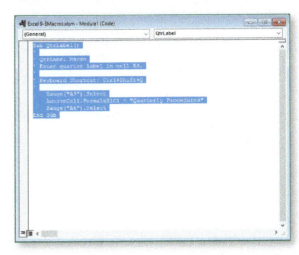

9-42 Codes lines are selected for copying

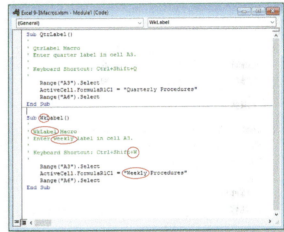

9-43 Copied code is edited to create a new macro

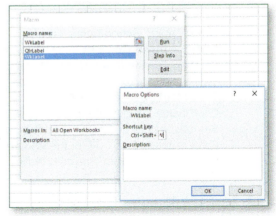

9-44 *Macro Options* dialog box

    e. Click **Cancel** to close the *Macro* dialog box.
    f. Press **Ctrl+Shift+W** to test the macro.
    g. Delete the contents of cell **A3**.

9. Record a macro to print the workbook. (Make sure the default printer is ready).
    a. Click the **Record Macro** button [*Developer* tab, *Code* group].
    b. Type PrintWB in the *Macro name* box.
    c. Do not use a shortcut key and store the macro in **This Workbook**.
    d. Type Print all worksheets. in the *Description* box and click **OK**.
    e. Click the **File** tab and choose **Print**.
    f. Choose **Print Entire Workbook** in the *Settings* group.
    g. Click **Print**. The workbook is sent to the printer.
    h. Click the **Stop Recording** button [*Developer* tab, *Code* group]. (If a printer was not ready, open the printer dialog box and cancel the print job.)

10. Complete documentation for the macros.
    a. Click the **Sheet1** worksheet tab and select cell **B6**.
    b. Type Ctrl+Shift+W and press **Enter**.
    c. Type Enter the weekly label in cell A3. in cell **B7** and press **Enter**.
    d. Select cell **A9**, type PrintWB, and press **Tab**.
    e. Type Print entire workbook. in cell **B9** and press **Enter** (Figure 9-45).
    f. Rename the sheet as **Macros** and press **Ctrl+Home**.

11. Click the **Save** button in the *Quick Access* toolbar to resave the macros-only workbook.

12. Open the **Clemenson-09.xlsx** workbook from your student data files and save it as [your initials] Excel 9-3 in your folder.

13. Assign macros to *Button* form controls.
    a. Click the **Insert Controls** button [*Developer* tab, *Controls* group].
    b. Click the **Button (Form Control)** command and draw a *Button* control that covers cells **H3**. The *Assign Macro* dialog box opens.
    c. Select **QtrLabel** and click **OK**.
    d. Click inside the button control, delete the default caption, and type Quarter.
    e. Select cell **I3** to deselect the control.
    f. Draw a button in cell **J3** for the **WkLabel** macro. Change its caption to Week.
    g. Draw a button that covers cells **I4:I5** for the **PrintWB** macro. Change its caption to Print (Figure 9-46).

14. Select cell **A1**.

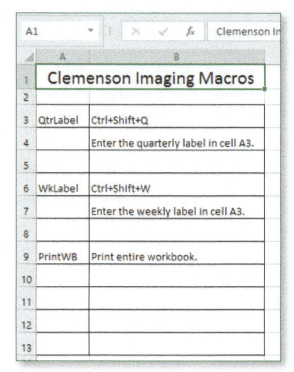

9-45 Documentation for the macros workbook

9-46 Completed button controls

15. Run macros.
   a. Click the button to run the weekly label macro and then select cell **A6**.
   b. Make sure the printer is ready.
   c. Click the button to run the print macro.

16. Save and close the *[your initials] Excel 9-3* workbook (Figure 9-47).

17. Save and close the *[your initials] Excel 9-3Macros* workbook.

9-47 Excel 9-3 completed

Independent Project 9-4

At Wear-Ever Shoes, you use a macro to identify products to be reordered. The macro is written but requires editing before being assigned to the *Button* control. You also record a macro to insert the current date.
[Student Learning Outcomes 9.1, 9.2, 9.3, 9.4]

File Needed: ***WearEver-09.xlsm*** *(Student data files are available in the* Library *of your SIMnet account)*
Completed Project File Name: *[your initials] Excel 9-4.xlsm*

Skills Covered in This Project

- Set macro security options.
- Run a macro.
- Edit a macro in the Visual Basic Editor.
- Assign a macro to a *Button* form control.
- Record a macro.

---

1. Set macro security to **Disable all macros with notification** and display the **Developer** tab.

2. Open the **WearEver-09** workbook from your student data files and click **Enable Content**.

3. Save the workbook as an **Excel Macro-Enabled Workbook** named [your initials] Excel 9-4 in your usual location for saving files. (Click **OK** in the message box about the *Document Inspector* if it opens.)

4. Run the **Reorder** macro. It applies conditional formatting to cells in the *Quantity* column with a value less than or equal to 2.

5. Click a blank cell to see the formatting.

6. Click the **Conditional Formatting** button [*Home* tab, *Styles* group] and clear the formatting from the sheet.

7. Press **Ctrl+Home**.

8. Edit a macro to add a line of code.
   a. Click the **Macros** button [*Developer* tab, *Code* group] and edit the **Reorder** macro.
   b. Click after the word *False* at the end of the code and press **Enter** to insert a blank line.
   c. Point in the left margin area next to the line that displays *Range("E4:E39"). Select* to display a white arrow pointer and click to select the line (Figure 9-48). This code indicates that a cell range is active or selected.
   d. Press **Ctrl+C** to copy the line.
   e. Click the empty line that you inserted in step b.
   f. Press **Ctrl+V** to copy the code.
   g. Edit the copied code to display *Range("A2").Select*. This returns the insertion point to cell A2 after conditional formatting is applied (Figure 9-49).
   h. Click the **Close** button in the top-right corner of the window.

9. Assign a macro to a *Button* form control.
   a. Right-click the *Button* control and choose **Assign Macro** (Figure 9-50).
   b. Select **Reorder** in the *Assign Macro* dialog box and click **OK**.
   c. Deselect the control and then click it to run the macro.
   d. Press **Ctrl+Home**.

10. Record a macro to insert the date.
    a. Disable the **Use Relative References** button [*Code* group] if it is active.
    b. Record a macro named Today with a shortcut of **Ctrl+Shift+D** in **This Workbook**.
    c. Type Insert date in cell A2 as the *Description* and click **OK**.
    d. Click cell **A2** and type =to and press **Tab**. Then press **Enter**.
    e. Stop recording and delete the contents of cell **A2**.
    f. Press **Ctrl+Home**.
    g. Press **Ctrl+Shift+D** to run the macro.

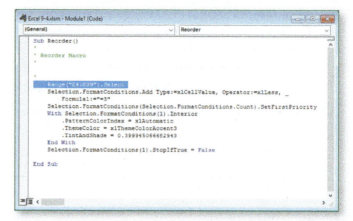

9-48 Code line selected in the VBE

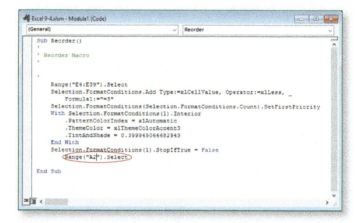

9-49 Copied and edited code line

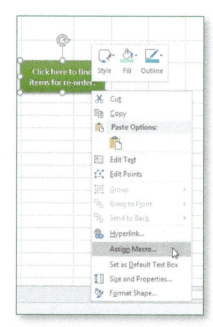

9-50 Right-click the control to assign the macro

11. Hide the *Developer* tab. Save and close the workbook (Figure 9-51).

9-51 Excel 9-4 completed

Independent Project 9-5

Courtyard Medical Plaza developed a trainer's worksheet for personalized workout plans. You record and edit macros for a macros-only workbook and run the macros in the trainer's workbook.
[Student Learning Outcomes 9.1, 9.2, 9.4, 9.5, 9.7]

File Needed: ***CourtyardMedical-09.xlsx*** *(Student data files are available in the* Library *of your SIMnet account)*
Completed Project File Names: *[your initials]* ***Excel 9-5Macros.xlsm*** and *[your initials]* ***Excel 9-5.xlsx***

Skills Covered in This Project

- Set macro security options.
- Create a macros-only workbook.
- Record a macro with relative references.
- Run a macro.
- Edit a macro in the Visual Basic Editor.

---

1. Set macro security to **Disable all macros with notification** and display the **Developer** tab.

2. Create a new workbook and save it as an *Excel Macro-Enabled Workbook* named
   [your initials] Excel9-5Macros in your usual location for saving files.

3. Activate the **Use Relative References** command and select cell **A1**.

4. Record a macro with relative references.
   a. Record a macro named Titles with a shortcut of **Ctrl+Shift+T** in **This Workbook**.
   b. Type Enter column titles for the *Description* and click **OK**.
   c. Type Activities and press the **right arrow** key.
   d. Type Calories and press the **right arrow** key.
   e. Type Times and press the **right arrow** key. Type Burned and press the **right arrow** key.
   f. Press the **left arrow** key four times to return to the "Activities" label.
   g. Select cells **A1:D1** and apply **bold** and **italic**.
   h. Stop recording.
   i. Select cell **A4** and record a macro with relative references named Activities with a shortcut of **Ctrl+Shift+A** in **This Workbook**. Type Enter activities for the *Description*.
   j. Type the labels shown here and press **Enter** after each one to move from row to row.

      Dance Fusion

      High Intensity Interval

      Pilates/Yoga

      Running

      Strength Training

      Swimming

      Water Aerobics

   k. Stop recording (Figure 9-52).

5. Select cell **F1** and type Titles Macro.

6. Remove bold and italic from cell **F1**.

7. Select cell **F2** and type Ctrl+Shift+T.

8. Select cell **F4** and type Activities Macro.

9. Type Ctrl+Shift+A in cell **F5** (Figure 9-53).

10. Edit the **Titles** macro to change the word "Activities" in the code to Activity.

11. Size the *Code* window so that you can see most of both macros. Print the code [*File* menu] (Figure 9-54).

12. Save the macros-only workbook and leave it open.

13. Open the **CourtyardMedical-09** workbook from your student data files and save it as [your initials] Excel 9-5.

14. Run the **Titles** macro in cell **A3**. Run it again in cells **F3**, **A15**, and **F15**.

15. Run the **Activities** macro in cells **A4**, **F4**, **A16**, and **F16**.

16. Save and close the workbook and hide the *Developer* tab (Figure 9-55).

17. Save and close the macros-only workbook.

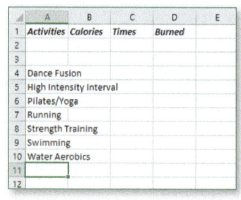

9-52 Data is entered as macros are recorded

9-53 Documentation for the macros workbook

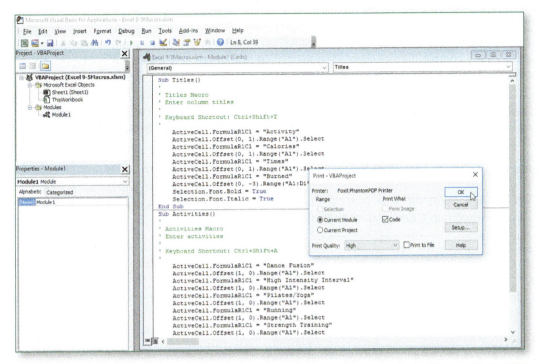

9-54 Print code from the *File* menu in the VBE

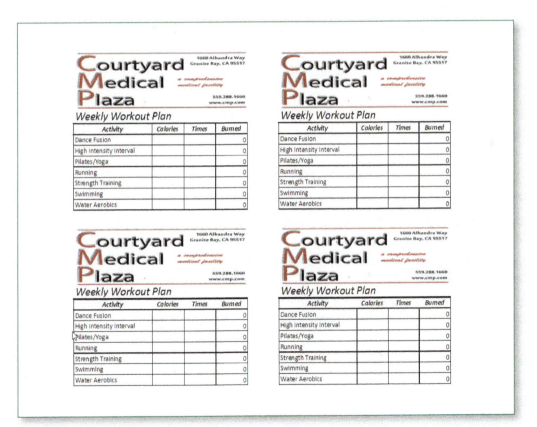

9-55 Excel 9-5 completed

Independent Project 9-6

Classic Gardens and Landscapes (CGL) tracks task hours in a macro-enabled workbook. You record a macro with a combination of absolute and relative references and a *Text* function.
[Student Learning Outcomes 9.1, 9.2, 9.3, 9.4, 9.5, 9.6]

File Needed: ***ClassicGardens-09.xlsm*** *(Student data files are available in the* Library *of your SIMnet account)*
Completed Project File Names: *[your initials] Excel 9-6.xltm* and *[your initials] Excel 9-6.xlsm*

Skills Covered in This Project

- Set macro security options.
- Assign a macro to a *Button* form control.
- Run a macro.
- Record a macro.
- Record a macro with relative references.
- Edit a macro in the Visual Basic Editor.
- Save a macro-enabled template.

1. Set macro security to **Disable all macros with notification** and display the *Developer* tab.

2. Open the **ClassicGardens-09** macro-enabled workbook from your student data files and enable the macros.

3. Save the workbook as a macro-enabled template.
   a. Choose **Save As** from the *File* tab and navigate to any available folder.
   b. Type [your initials] Excel 9-6 as the *File name*.
   c. Choose **Excel Macro-Enabled Template** from the *Save as type* list and click **Save**.
   d. Leave the template open.

4. Insert a *Button* form control to cover cell **H2** and assign the **CurrentDate** macro. Edit the caption to show "Today."

5. Deselect the *Button* control and run the macro from it. **AutoFit** column **F** if necessary to see the date in cell F20.

6. Select cell **H5** and enable the **Use Relative References** command.

7. Record a macro named **InsertLabel** with a shortcut of **Ctrl+Shift+L**. The description is Row 7 label. Click **OK** to begin recording.

8. Type Week of and press **Ctrl+Enter** to keep the insertion point cell **H5**.

9. Right-align the label and press the **right arrow** one time (Figure 9-56).

10. Disable the **Use Relative References** command. You are still recording the macro.

11. Start a **Text** function [*Formulas* tab, *Function Library* group, *Text* button].

12. Click cell **F20** for the *Value* argument and make the reference absolute. Type mmm dd for the *Format_text* argument and click **OK** (Figure 9-57).

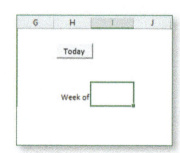

9-56 Macro includes data and positioning commands

13. Stop recording.

14. Delete the contents of cells **H5:I5**.

15. Select cell **H7** and press **Ctrl+Shift+L** to test the macro. Delete the contents of cells **H7:I7**.

16. Edit the macro.
    a. Click the **Macros** button [*Developer* tab, *Code* group] and edit the **InsertLabel** macro.
    b. Find the code with the *Text* function.
    c. Edit the format codes to show "*mmmm dd*" so that the month is spelled out (Figure 9-58).
    d. Close the VBE and test the macro in cell **H7**.
    e. Delete the contents of cells **H7:I7**.
    f. Delete the contents of cell **F20** and press **Ctrl+Home**.

17. Save the macro-enabled template with the same name and close it.

18. Create a workbook from the template.
    a. Create a new workbook from the **[your initials] Excel 9-6** template and enable the macros.
    b. Click the **Button** form control to run the date macro.
    c. Select cell **B7** and press **Ctrl+Shift+L**.

19. Save the workbook as an **Excel Macro-Enabled Workbook** named [your initials] Excel 9-6 in your usual location for saving files (Figure 9-59).

20. Close the workbook.

21. Delete the template from the *Custom Office Templates* folder and hide the *Developer* tab.

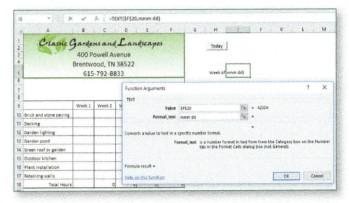

9-57 *Function Arguments* dialog box for the *Text* function

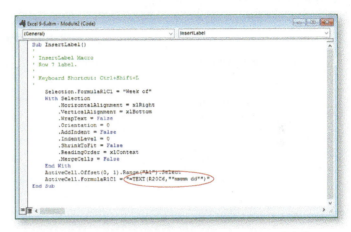

9-58 Edited code for the *InsertLabel* macro

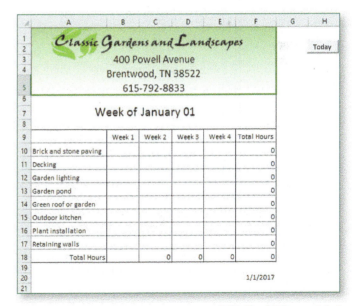

9-59 Excel 9-6 completed

Improve It Project 9-7

In the Blue Lake Sports invoice form worksheet, you record a macro to copy the active sheet. In addition, you edit the macro to delete data. You save your work as a macro-enabled template.
[Student Learning Outcomes 9.1, 9.2, 9.4, 9.6]

File Needed: ***BlueLakeSports-09.xlsm*** *(Student data files are available in the* Library *of your SIMnet account)*
Completed Project File Names: *[your initials]* ***Excel 9-7.xltm*** and *[your initials]* ***Excel 9-7.xlsm***

Skills Covered in This Project

- Set macro security options.
- Edit a macro in the Visual Basic Editor.

- Record a macro.
- Run a macro.
- Save a macro-enabled template.

1. Set macro security to **Disable all macros with notification** and display the **Developer** tab.

2. Open the **BlueLakeSports-09** macro-enabled workbook from your student data files and enable the macros.

3. Review the **DeleteData** macro in the Visual Basic Editor. It was recorded to delete the contents of cells so that a new invoice can be created. Note its keyboard shortcut.

4. Return to the worksheet and note the addresses of cells that should be cleared to enter data for a new order. Formulas should not be deleted.

5. Edit the macro code so that it will delete the contents of cells **A14:E29** (Figure 9-60).

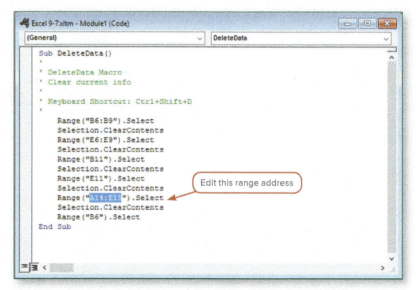

9-60 Code for *DeleteData* macro

6. Record a new macro named **CopySheet** with a shortcut of **Ctrl+Shift+C**. Record commands to copy the current worksheet and move it to the end. Record commands to copy the current worksheet and move it to the end. Stop recording when the sheet is copied.

7. Run the **DeleteData** macro on the copied worksheet.

8. Delete the copied sheet.

9. Save the workbook as a macro-enabled template named [your initials] Excel 9-7 in the *Custom Office Templates* folder. Close the template.

10. Create a new workbook from the template. Run the **CopySheet** macro and then run the **DeleteData** macro.

11. Save the workbook as a macro-enabled workbook named [your initials] Excel 9-7 in your usual folder (Figure 9-61).

12. Delete the template from the *Custom Office Templates* folder and hide the *Developer* tab.

9-61 Excel 9-7 completed

Challenge Project 9-8

In this project, you create a macros-only workbook for an automobile dealership. You record one macro to enter main labels, another to enter model names, and a third to enter column labels. In a separate workbook, you run these macros to build a worksheet.
[Student Learning Outcomes 9.1, 9.2, 9.4, 9.5, 9.7]

File Needed: None
Completed Project File Names: *[your initials] Excel 9-8Macros.xlsm* and *[your initials] Excel 9-8.xlsx*

Create and save a macro-enabled workbook named [your initials] Excel 9-8Macros. Modify your workbook according to the following guidelines:

- Record a macro with absolute references and a keyboard shortcut to display the name of the dealership, address lines, telephone and fax numbers, and a web site address in cells **A1:A5**. Format each label with a font size and bold or italic and stop recording.

- In cell **F1**, enter the name of the macro used to display the main labels. In cell **G1**, type the keyboard shortcut.
- Select cell **A7**. Record a macro with relative references and a keyboard shortcut that enters Week 1, Week 2, Week 3, and Week 4 in a single row, using the *Fill* handle or the **right arrow** key to move from column to column.
- In cell **F7**, type the name of the macro. In cell **G7**, type the keyboard shortcut.
- Select cell **A9** and record a macro with relative references and a keyboard shortcut that enters the names of eight automobile makes/models sold at the dealership in a single column. Press the **down arrow** key or **Enter** to move from row to row.
- In cell **F9**, type the name of the macro. In cell **G9**, type the keyboard shortcut.
- Insert a blank sheet and test your macros. Make edits if you can, or delete a macro and re-record it.
- Save the macros-only workbook and leave it open.
- Create a new workbook and run the labels macro.
- Select cell **B7** and run the week macro.
- Select cell **A8** and run the makes/models macro.
- Format the worksheet using font styles, alignment, fill, and borders.
- Save the workbook as [your initials] Excel 9-8. It is not macro-enabled; you simply ran macros in it.

Challenge Project 9-9

In this project, you create a quarterly results worksheet for a management consulting firm. You record a macro to copy the sheet and assign it to a *Button* control. You record another macro to delete data on the copied sheet. Finally, you print your macro code.
[**Student Learning Outcomes 9.1, 9.2, 9.3, 9.4**]

File Needed: None
Completed Project File Name: *[your initials] Excel 9-9.xlsm*

Create and save a macro-enabled workbook named [your initials] Excel 9-9. Modify your workbook according to the following guidelines:

- In cell **A1**, type the name of a management consulting firm. In cell **A2**, type Quarterly Results, and in cell **A3**, type the name of a city followed by Office (e.g., New York Office).
- In cells **B4:D4**, enter three month names for any quarter, spelled out.
- In cells **A5:A9**, type the names of five tasks typically billed by a consulting firm.
- Prepare formulas to show totals in column **E** and in row **10**.
- Name the sheet tab Quarter Results. Format the worksheet with fonts, styles, alignment, fill, borders, or other attributes.
- Enter values in cells **B5:D9** that indicate number of tasks or dollars billed. Format these cells based on the type of value you chose.
- Write a macro to copy the worksheet and place it at the end.
- Draw a *Button* form control on the **Quarter Results** sheet and assign the macro that copies the worksheet to the control.

- On the copied sheet, write a macro to delete the contents of cells **B5:D9** and the cells with month names. Use a keyboard shortcut for this macro.
- Delete the copied sheet and test both macros.
- Open the Visual Basic Editor and the *Code* window for *Module 1*. From the *File* menu, print the code for the macro. If your macros are in separate modules, open *Module 2* and print the code.

Challenge Project 9-10

In this project, you explore how to use the *Personal.xlsb* workbook, an option in the *Store Macro In* list in the *Record Macro* dialog box. *Personal.xlsb* is a hidden workbook that is created and named automatically when you choose it as the location for a recorded macro. The workbook opens each time you start Excel, and its macros are available in any open workbook.
[Student Learning Outcomes 9.1, 9.2, 9.4, 9.5, 9.7]

File needed: None
Completed project file name: *[your initials] Excel 9-10.xlsx* and *Personal.xlsb*

Open a new Excel workbook and modify your workbook according to the following guidelines:

- In the blank workbook in cell **A1**, record a macro with relative references named MyName. Use a shortcut of **Ctrl+Shift+N**. In the *Record Macro* dialog box, select **Personal Macro Workbook** to store the macro.
- Type your name, your street address, your city, state, and ZIP code in three rows, typical address style, and stop recording.
- Close the blank workbook used for recording the macro without saving it. The *PERSONAL* macro workbook now includes your macro.
- Open another new workbook. Press **Ctrl+Shift+N** to run the macro. The *Personal.xlsb* workbook is hidden, but its macros are available.
- Click the **View** tab and note that the **Unhide** button is available.
- Click the **Macros** button [*View* tab] and choose **View Macros**. The available macros list identifies the *PERSONAL.XLSB!* workbook. Select the **MyName** macro and choose **Edit**. You cannot edit a macro in a hidden workbook. Click **OK** in the message box and close the *Macro* dialog box.
- From the *View* tab, choose **Unhide** and show the **PERSONAL** workbook. It opens but has no visible data, only your macro. (If you are using a shared computer, the *PERSONAL* workbook may include macros and documentation from another user.)
- Click the **Macros** button [*View* tab] and choose **View Macros**. Select the **MyName** macro and choose **Edit**. The Visual Basic Editor opens.
- In the VBE, edit your address. Add a personal title or your middle initial, a street direction, or spell out the state name. Be careful when editing code to not alter punctuation or commands unless you are familiar with Visual Basic for Applications programming. Close the VBE and return to the Excel window.
- From the *View* tab, choose **Hide** to hide the *PERSONAL* workbook. It is important that this workbook be hidden so that you don't accidentally enter data or unwanted commands.

- Delete any data in the open workbook (or open a new workbook) and press **Ctrl+Shift+N** to run the edited macro. Save the workbook as [your initials] Excel 9-10. Close the workbook.
- The *Personal Macro Workbook* remains available until you delete it. It is usually stored in *Users\UserName\AppData\Roaming\Microsoft\Excel\XLSTART,* which may be a hidden folder. In order to find and delete the *Personal Macro Workbook,* you must exit Excel. The file name does not appear in any Explorer window until you do that.
- Exit Excel and select **Save** in the message box to save changes to the *Personal Macro Workbook.* Do not restart Excel yet.
- You must use a File Explorer window so that you can unhide the **XLSTART** folder if it is hidden. Click the **File Explorer** button on the Windows taskbar or choose **File Explorer** from the **Start** menu.
- Navigate to *C:\Users\UserName. UserName* is the name for the computer at which you are currently working.
- If you do not see the *AppData* folder, click the **View** tab and select the **Hidden items** box. This command displays folders that are hidden.
- Continue navigating to find *C:\Users\UserName\AppData\Roaming\Microsoft\Excel\XLSTART.* You should see *PERSONAL.XLSB* in this folder; file name extensions may be hidden on your computer. (Do not delete *PERSONAL* workbook if you are using a shared computer on which users store macros.)
- Select and delete the file. You cannot delete it if Excel is running because the file is open whenever Excel is running.
- Navigate once more to *C:\Users\UserName.*
- Click the **View** tab, deselect the **Hidden items** box, and close the File Explorer window.

CHAPTER 10

Customizing Excel and Using OneDrive and Office Online

CHAPTER OVERVIEW

You can personalize your Excel working environment and use related online services and tools. Excel 2016 integrates "cloud" technology so that you can store workbooks on local media, in *OneDrive*, and with *Office Online*. Cloud services allow you to access your work from anywhere on any computer with Internet access.

STUDENT LEARNING OUTCOMES (SLOs)

After completing this chapter, you will be able to:

SLO 10.1 Customize Excel 2016 options, the *Ribbon*, and the *Quick Access* toolbar to personalize your working environment (p. E10-620).

SLO 10.2 View and modify Office account settings and install an Office add-in (p. E10-628).

SLO 10.3 Create a folder, add a file, and move and copy a file in *OneDrive* (p. E10-636).

SLO 10.4 Share *OneDrive* files and folders (p. E10-642).

SLO 10.5 Open, create, and edit an Excel workbook in *Office Online* (p. E10-646).

SLO 10.6 Explore *Office Online* applications and productivity tools (p. E10-655).

CASE STUDY

In the Pause & Practice projects in this chapter, you customize Excel settings and use cloud services to save, edit, and share workbooks for Paradise Lakes Resort (PLR).

Pause & Practice 10-1: Customize Excel and Office account settings and install an add-in.

Pause & Practice 10-2: Use *OneDrive* and *Excel Online* to save and share a workbook.

Pause & Practice 10-3: Create and share an *Excel Survey*.

Customizing Excel 2016

You have learned ways to customize an individual workbook such as changing the tab color or choosing a zoom size. The *Excel Options* dialog box includes customization choices that globally alter Excel settings and apply to all workbooks you create.

Excel Options

In the *Excel Options* dialog box, settings and commands are grouped into categories. The following list shows the names of the panes or categories in the *Excel Options* dialog box. Each category is discussed in the sections that follow.

- *General*
- *Formulas*
- *Proofing*
- *Save*
- *Language*
- *Advanced*
- *Customize Ribbon*
- *Quick Access Toolbar*
- *Add-ins*
- *Trust Center*

▶ HOW TO: Customize Excel Options

1. Click the **File** tab to open the *Backstage* view.
2. Choose **Options** to open the *Excel Options* dialog box (Figure 10-1).
3. Click the category or pane name at the left to display options at the right.
4. Make selections using check boxes, text boxes, drop-down lists, or buttons.
   - When you click a button, a dialog box with related settings opens.
5. Click **OK** to close the *Excel Options* dialog box and apply the settings.

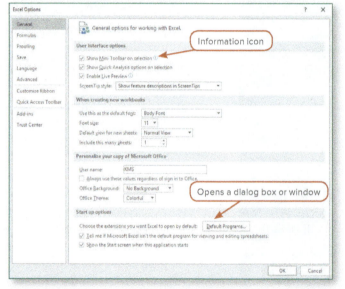

10-1 *Excel Options* dialog box, *General* pane

General

The *General* category includes four groups of settings: *User Interface options*, *When creating new workbooks*, *Personalize your copy of Microsoft Office*, and *Start up options* (see Figure 10-1).

In the *User Interface options* group, you can choose whether the mini toolbar displays for selected data and if the *Quick Analysis* button appears for selected cells. You can enable or disable *Live Preview* and customize the *ScreenTip* style.

The *When creating new workbooks* area has options to select the default font and the default view. You can also choose the number of sheets in a new workbook. Changes that you make do not affect workbooks already saved, only new workbooks created after you customize these options.

In the *Personalize your copy of Microsoft Office* area, you can change your user name, enforce your Excel settings for all users on the computer, and choose the Office background and theme.

The *Start up options* group allows you to select compatible file name extensions for Excel, so that Excel starts when you double-click the file name in a *File Explorer* window. From this group, you can also choose whether or not the *Start* screen displays when Excel opens.

Formulas

The *Formulas* pane includes settings for calculation and for formula and error handling (Figure 10-2). In the *Calculation options* area, choose automatic or manual calculation. Manual calculation can speed editing for exceptionally large worksheets, but you must calculate formulas by clicking the *Calculate Now* button [*Formulas* tab, *Calculation* group] or by pressing **F9** (**FN+F9**). Iterative calculations are used in *Goal Seek* and *Solver* problems to find a solution and also affect calculation speed for a workbook.

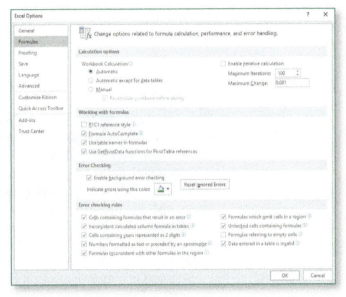

10-2 *Formulas* options in the *Excel Options* dialog box

Select the cell reference style in the *Working with formulas* group. The default setting is the column letter and row number convention with cell addresses such as A1, B15, and D25. The *R1C1* option identifies rows and columns by numbers with cell addresses such as R2C4 for row 2, column 4. Some macro commands use the *R1C1* style in the code.

From the *Formulas* pane, disable *Formula AutoComplete* if you prefer to not see a list of function and range names when you type an entry in a formula. Table names and structured references are supplied when you refer to a cell in a table unless you deselect the *Use table names in formulas* box. Finally, you can prohibit the use of the *GETPIVOTDATA* function when you refer to a cell in a *PivotTable*.

Two groups in the *Formulas* pane affect how formula errors are handled. In the *Error Checking* options area, you can disable background error checking and determine the color for the error triangle in the cell. The rules that Excel uses for background checking are shown in the *Error checking rules* list. Note that the default setting does not identify formulas that refer to empty cells.

▶ HOW TO: Customize the Cell Reference Style

1. Create a new blank workbook.
2. Click the **File** tab and choose **Options** to open the *Excel Options* dialog box.
3. Click **Formulas**.
4. Select the **R1C1 reference style** box in the *Working with formulas* group.
   - Point to the *Information* icon to see details about the option.
   - Deselect the box to use the standard A1 reference style.
5. Click **OK** to close the *Excel Options* dialog box.
   - The row and column headings are numbered (Figure 10-3).

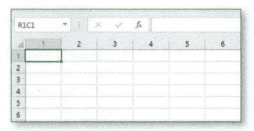

10-3 Workbook in R1C1 reference style

Proofing

The *Proofing* category in the *Excel Options* dialog box has settings for text entries in a workbook (Figure 10-4). When you click the *AutoCorrect Options* button, the *AutoCorrect* dialog box opens and has tabs for *AutoCorrect*, *AutoFormat As You Type*, *Actions*, and *Math AutoCorrect*. The *Math AutoCorrect* list is a Word feature that converts text into math symbols; it does not apply to Excel.

The *When correcting spelling in Microsoft Office programs* group lists settings for all Office programs, so that a choice you make in Excel applies to a Word document. Excel does not highlight spelling errors as you enter data, but it does correct two initial uppercase letters in a word in a cell.

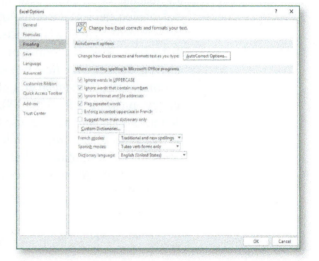

10-4 *Proofing* pane in the *Excel Options* dialog box

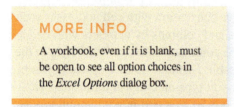

> **MORE INFO**
>
> A workbook, even if it is blank, must be open to see all option choices in the *Excel Options* dialog box.

Save

In the *Save* pane, you control how and where workbooks are saved (Figure 10-5). You can select the default file format in the *Save workbooks* group. The *AutoRecover* feature saves open

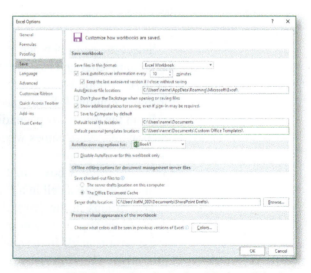

10-5 *Save* options in the *Excel Options* dialog box

workbooks, and you can determine where and how often recovery files are stored. The *AutoRecover exceptions for* area allows you to disable *AutoRecover* for an individual workbook.

The *Backstage* view displays when you press **Ctrl+O** or **Ctrl+S** to open or save a workbook unless you deselect the *Don't show the Backstage view when opening or saving files* box. From the *Save* pane, you can also set the default save location for files and templates.

The *Offline editing options for document management server files* group pertains to documents shared in Microsoft SharePoint. *Preserve visual appearance of the workbook* controls how colors display when a workbook is opened in earlier versions of Excel.

Language

The *Language* pane is used to set the language preference in all Office programs (Figure 10-6). The selected language affects spelling, grammar, dictionaries, and sorting. You can add a new language, set a language as the default, or remove a language. In the *Choose Display and Help Languages* group, you choose the language for tabs, buttons, and *Help* screens.

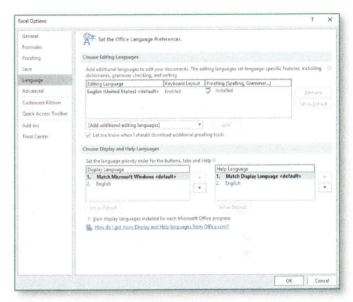

10-6 *Language* options in the *Excel Options* dialog box

> **MORE INFO**
>
> Language settings in Office are determined by the selected language when you install Windows.

Advanced

The *Advanced* pane has 14 categories of settings. Figure 10-7 shows the first category, *Editing options*. This group includes options that display the *Fill Handle*, allow for editing in the cell, and permit typing the percent sign (%) with a value, all features you have used in this book. The following list shows the names of the categories in the *Advanced* pane. Scroll through these areas to familiarize yourself with the choices.

- *Editing options*
- *Cut, copy, and paste*

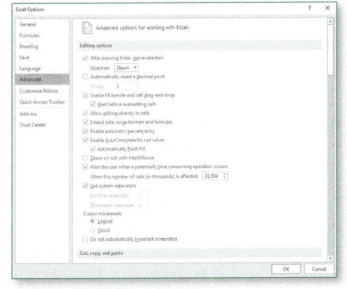

10-7 *Advanced* pane in the *Excel Options* dialog box

- *Pen*
- *Image size and quality*
- *Print*
- *Chart*
- *Display*
- *Display options for this workbook*
- *Display options for this worksheet*
- *Formulas*
- *When calculating this workbook*
- *General*
- *Data*
- *Lotus compatibility*
- *Lotus compatibility Settings for*

> **MORE INFO**
>
> The *Customize Ribbon* and *Quick Access Toolbar* panes are covered later in this section.

Add-ins

The add-in commands or programs that are available on your computer depend on your Office product and installation (Figure 10-8).

Active add-ins are listed in the top half of the *Add-ins* pane. When the *Manage* box displays *Excel Add-ins*, click **Go** to open the *Add-ins* dialog box and install an inactive feature or remove an active one. In the *Manage* list, you can choose *COM Add-ins* to see a list of compiled programs that are available for installation on your computer. Many of these programs must be downloaded separately from Excel.

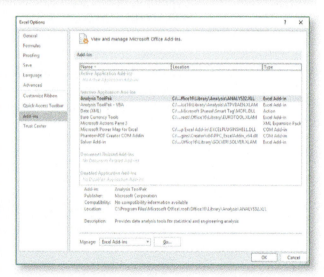

10-8 *Add-ins* pane in the *Excel Options* dialog box

Trust Center

You used the *Trust Center* in *SLO 9.1: Running a Macro* to set macro security and in *SLO 7.6: Checking a Workbook for Distribution Issues* to define a trusted location. Additional settings in the *Trust Center* include the use of *Protected View*, the appearance of the message bar, and handling of external data (Figure 10-9). It is generally recommended that you use the default settings in the *Trust Center* to keep your files and computer safe.

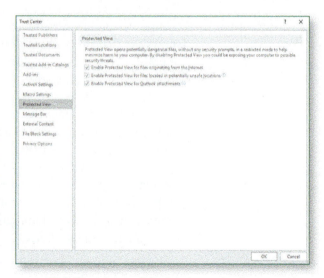

10-9 *Trust Center* dialog box for setting *Protected View*

Customize the Ribbon

You can customize the *Ribbon* to display your own tabs and groups. New groups may be added to standard command tabs or your custom tabs. Command buttons can be added only to a custom group.

▶ HOW TO: Add a Tab, a Group, and a Command to the Ribbon

1. Right-click the **Ribbon** and select **Customize the Ribbon** from the context menu.

   - The *Excel Options* dialog box opens to the *Customize Ribbon* pane.
   - The leftmost list shows available commands; the rightmost list displays *Ribbon* tab and group names.

2. On the right, click the tab name after which you want to insert a new tab.

3. Click the **New Tab** button.

   - A new custom tab and custom group are inserted.

4. Click **New Tab (Custom)** and then click **Rename**.

   - The *Rename* dialog box opens.

5. Type the name of the new tab and click **OK** (Figure 10-10).

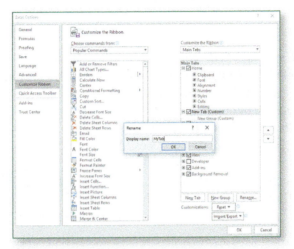

10-10 Rename a custom *Ribbon* tab

6. Select **New Group (Custom)** and click **Rename**.

7. Type the name of the new group in the *Display name* box and click **OK**.

   - Symbols are optional; they appear only when the Excel window is scaled so small that *Ribbon* and group names are not visible.
   - You will not see a custom group name in the *Ribbon* until you add a button to the group.

8. Select the custom group name to which you want to add a command.

9. Click the **Choose commands from** drop-down list and select **All Commands**.

10. Select the command name and click **Add** to place the command in the group (Figure 10-11).

11. Click **OK** to close the *Excel Options* dialog box.

    - The custom tab and group display on the *Ribbon* (Figure 10-12)

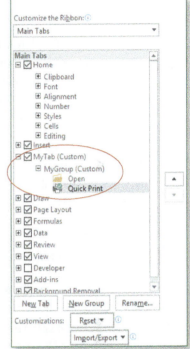

10-11 Commands added to a custom group on a custom tab

10-12 Custom tab and group in the *Ribbon*

In addition to adding tabs, groups, and commands to the *Ribbon*, you can rearrange the order of tabs or groups by dragging and dropping the tab or group names in the *Excel Options* dialog box. You can also rearrange names by clicking the *Move Up* or *Move Down* button in the *Excel Options* dialog box.

▶ HOW TO: Move Tabs, Groups, and Commands on the Ribbon

1. Right-click the **Ribbon** and select **Customize the Ribbon** from the context menu.
   - The *Excel Options* dialog box opens to the *Customize Ribbon* pane.
2. Select the command, group, or tab to be moved.
3. Click the *Move Up* or *Move Down* button to rearrange the selected item (Figure 10-13).
   - You can also drag and drop the tab or group name to a new position.
4. Click **OK** to close the *Excel Options* dialog box.
   - The tabs, groups, and commands appear in the new arrangement.

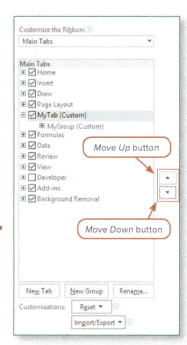

10-13 Move item names up or down to rearrange the *Ribbon*

Customize the Quick Access Toolbar

The *Save*, *Undo*, and *Redo* commands display on the *Quick Access* toolbar by default. If you have a computer with a touch screen, you also see the *Touch/Mouse Mode* button. You can add commands to the toolbar by using the *Customize Quick Access Toolbar* drop-down list or the *Quick Access Toolbar* pane in the *Excel Options* dialog box. From the *Excel Options* dialog box, you can choose to show changes in the *Quick Access* toolbar globally or for only the current workbook.

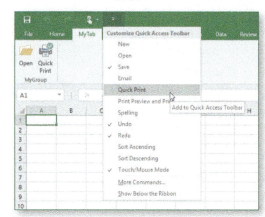

10-14 Commonly-used commands are available from the drop-down list

▶ HOW TO: Customize the Quick Access Toolbar

1. Click the **Customize Quick Access Toolbar** drop-down list on the right edge of the *Quick Access* toolbar (Figure 10-14).
   - Commands that display on the *Customize Quick Access* toolbar include a check mark.
2. Select a command to display it on the *Quick Access* toolbar.
   - A default button for the command appears on the *Quick Access* toolbar.
3. Click the **Customize Quick Access Toolbar** drop-down list and select **More Commands**.
   - The *Excel Options* dialog box opens to the *Quick Access Toolbar* pane.
4. Select a command in the list and click **Add** (Figure 10-15).
   - The command name displays in the list on the right.
   - The list on the left is filtered to show **Popular Commands**. You can display all commands by selecting **All Commands** from the **Choose commands from** drop-down list.
   - You can select **For WorkbookName.xlsx** from the *Customize Quick Access Toolbar* drop-down list (above the rightmost list) to limit the changes to the current workbook.
5. Click **OK** to close the *Excel Options* dialog box.

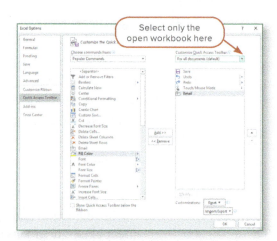

10-15 *Customize Quick Access Toolbar* pane

Remove Commands from the Ribbon and the Quick Access Toolbar

You can remove commands from the *Quick Access* toolbar and remove commands, groups, or tabs from the *Ribbon*.

▶ **HOW TO:** Remove Items from the Quick Access Toolbar and the Ribbon

1. Right-click the button to be removed in the *Quick Access* toolbar.
   - The context menu opens (Figure 10-16).
2. Select **Remove from Quick Access Toolbar**.
   - The button is removed from the toolbar.
   - Click the **Customize Quick Access Toolbar** drop-down list and deselect the command name to remove the button.
3. Right-click the **Ribbon** and select **Customize the Ribbon** from the context menu.
   - The *Excel Options* dialog box opens to the *Customize Ribbon* pane.
4. In the list on the right, select the command, group, or tab name to be removed.
   - Expand or collapse the tab or group as needed.
5. Click **Remove**.
6. Click **OK** to close the *Excel Options* dialog box.
   - The *Ribbon* displays modified groups and tabs.

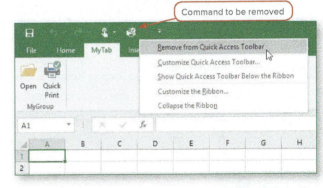

10-16 Remove a command from the *Quick Access* toolbar using the context menu

Reset the Ribbon and the Quick Access Toolbar

Reset both the *Ribbon* and the *Quick Access* toolbar to their original settings from their panes in the *Excel Options* dialog box. When resetting the *Ribbon*, you can limit the reset to a selected tab.

▶ HOW TO: Reset the Ribbon and the Quick Access Toolbar

1. Click the **File** tab and choose **Options**.

2. Select *Customize Ribbon* or *Customize Quick Access Toolbar.*

   - To reset a specific *Ribbon* tab, select the tab name in the list on the right.

3. Click **Reset** and choose a command (Figures 10-17 and 10-18).

   - The *Reset only selected Ribbon tab* option is grayed out when no custom groups exist.
   - The *Reset only Quick Access Toolbar* option is grayed out if only the default buttons display in the toolbar.

4. Select **Reset all customizations**.

   - A message box asks you to confirm that all customizations will be removed.

5. Click **Yes** (Figure 10-19).

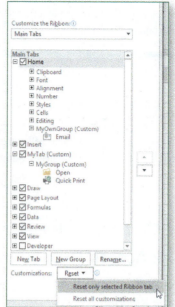

10-17 Reset the *Ribbon*

10-18 Reset the *Quick Access toolbar*

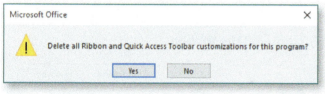

10-19 Message box to confirm resetting of the *Ribbon* and the toolbar

6. Click **OK** to close the *Excel Options* dialog box.

   - The *Ribbon* and the *Quick Access* toolbar reset to their default displays.

SLO 10.2

Customizing Office Account Settings

When you install Office 2016 or 365, you use your Microsoft account information to set up and log in to Windows and Office. You can view and customize your Office account settings in the *Backstage* view, add connected services such as LinkedIn or Twitter, and install *Office Add-ins* for extra commands and features in all your programs.

> **MORE INFO**
>
> If you don't have a Microsoft account, you can create a free account at https://signup.live.com.

Microsoft Account Information

Office 2016 and 365 provide portability of your account settings. When you sign in to Windows 10, you log in with your Microsoft account user name and password and Microsoft Office uses this information to apply your Office settings to whatever computer you are using.

You see your name in the upper right corner of the Excel window, and the context menu enables you to open the *Account* pane in the *Backstage* view (Figure 10-20).

10-20 Microsoft account information

> **HOW TO: View Account Settings in Excel**

1. Click your name in the upper right corner of the Excel window (see Figure 10-20).
   - If your name is not displayed, you are not signed in to Office. Find and click the **Sign in** link and sign-in to your Microsoft account.
2. Select **Account settings** to open the *Account* area on the *Backstage* view (Figure 10-21).
   - Your account information displays.
   - You can also click the **File** tab and select **Account**.

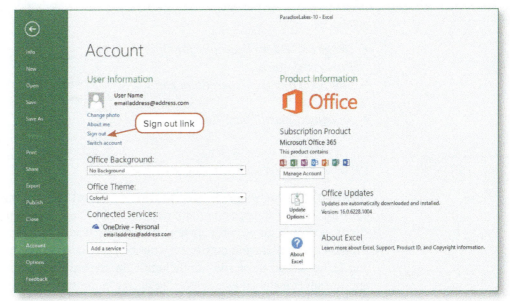

10-21 Office user information and settings

Office Background and Theme

You can change the **Office Background** and **Office Theme** in the *Account* area in the *Backstage* view (see Figure 10-21). The background choice displays a graphic pattern in the upper right corner of the Excel window. The theme controls colors in the *Ribbon*, the *Backstage* view, and dialog boxes. Your background and theme selections apply to all Office applications. The default *Office Theme* for Office 2016 is *Colorful*.

Connected Services

Office 2016 allows you to connect to online services as part of your account settings (Figure 10-22). When you add a service, you are usually prompted to enter your user name and password for the service. You can also remove a service from **Connected Services**.

The following services are currently available:

- **Images & Video**: *Facebook for Office*, *Flickr*, and *YouTube*
- **Storage**: *Office365 SharePoint* and *OneDrive*
- **Sharing**: *LinkedIn* and *Twitter*

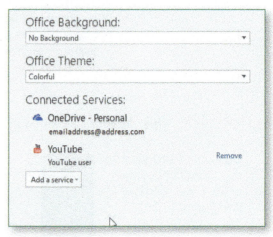

10-22 Add an online service to your Office account

Office Add-ins

Office add-ins are programs that provide enhanced features and commands to your Office software, similar to apps on your smartphone. In Excel, for example, you can add specialized charts, a People graph, or a currency converter. These programs may be from Microsoft or from other suppliers and may or may not be free. Each program has its own set of commands and features, and most add-ins include help screens, instructions, or a tutorial. The add-in application is installed as a selectable object in the worksheet or in a pane at the right of the Excel window.

▶ **HOW TO:** Install an Office Add-in

1. Open the workbook in which the add-in will be used.
2. Click the **Store** button [*Insert* tab, *Add-ins* group].
   - The *Office Add-ins* dialog box opens and displays the names of popular or featured add-ins for Excel (Figure 10-23).
   - Add-ins are regularly updated and featured.
   - Click the **My Add-ins** link to display add-ins currently installed for your account.
3. Select a category name to filter the list.
   - You can type a keyword in the search box to locate specific types of add-in programs.
4. Select the name of an add-in.
   - A dialog box opens that contains details about the program.

10-23 *Office Add-ins* **dialog box from the** *Store*

5. Click **Trust It** to install the add-in.

- The *Add-in* window for the selected application opens (Figure 10-24).
- The add-in appears as a floating selectable object or in a pane at the right of the window.
- When the add-in is a selectable object, you can select, size, and position the object.
- For some add-ins, a web site may open for installation of the program.

6. Use the add-in features and commands as desired in the workbook.

7. Select the add-in object and press **Delete**, or close the add-in pane.

- The add-in window is closed.
- The add-in is available in your account for use when needed.

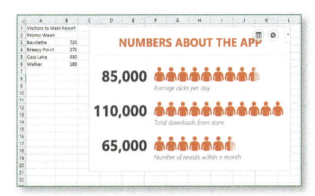

10-24 *Add-in* displayed in a selectable object or window

Manage Office Add-ins

You can manage add-ins by clicking the *My Add-ins* button [*Insert* tab, *Add-ins* group]. Review details about installed add-ins, rate or review an installed program, or remove an add-in from the *Office Add-ins* dialog box. When you remove an add-in, it is deactivated and not shown as part of your Office account in the *Office Add-ins* dialog box. You can reactivate an add-in at any time. Microsoft add-ins may place a button in the *Add-ins* group [*Insert* tab] so that you can reactivate the add-in from the button.

> **MORE INFO**
>
> The add-ins in *Excel Options* [*Add-ins* pane] are not the same as those available in the *Office Store*.

> **HOW TO:** Manage Office Add-ins

1. Open a workbook.

2. Click the **My Add-ins** button [*Insert* tab, *Add-ins* group] (Figure 10-25).

- The *Office Add-ins* dialog box opens.
- Installed add-in names and icons display.
- You can click the **My Add-ins** drop-down list and choose **Manage Other Add-ins** to open the *Add-ins* pane in the *Excel Options* dialog box.

3. Select an add-in and click **Insert**.

- The add-in opens in a separate window or pane in the workbook (see Figure 10-24).
- If the add-in placed a button in the *Add-ins* group [*Insert* tab], you can click the button to start the add-in program.

4. Complete work in the worksheet.

5. Delete the add-in object or close its pane when finished.

10-25 *Office Add-ins* dialog box lists currently available programs

6. To deactivate an add-in, click the **My Add-ins** button [*Insert* tab, *Add-ins* group].

   - The *Office Add-ins* dialog box opens.

7. Right-click an add-in name or click the ellipses (**...**) in the upper right corner.

8. Select **Remove** to remove an add-in.

   - A message box informs you that the add-in will be removed from your Microsoft account (Figure 10-26).
   - You can also view add-in details or rate and review the add-in from the context menu.

9. Click **Remove** in the message box.

   - The add-in is deactivated and not listed in the *Office Add-ins* dialog box.
   - Some Microsoft add-in buttons remain in the *Ribbon*.

10. Close the *Office Add-ins* dialog box.

10-26 Remove an add-in from your Office account

> **ANOTHER WAY**
>
> Click the **Manage My Add-ins** link in the *Office Add-ins* dialog box to open your Office *Store* account. From this window, *Hide* an add-in to remove it from your account or *Retrieve* the add-in.

PAUSE & PRACTICE: EXCEL 10-1

For this project, you customize Excel options, add items to the *Ribbon* and the *Quick Access* toolbar, customize your Office account settings, and add and remove an Office add-in.

Note: You need a Microsoft account (https://signup.live.com) to complete this project.

File Needed: ***ParadiseLakes-10.xlsx*** *(Student data files are available in the Library of your SIMnet account)*
Completed Project File Name: ***[your initials] PP E10-1.xlsx***

1. Open Excel and verify that you are signed in to your Microsoft account.

2. Open the ***Paradise Lakes-10*** workbook from your student data files.

3. Customize Excel options.
   a. Click the **File** tab and select **Options** to open the *Excel Options* dialog box.
   b. Select **Formulas** at the left to open the *Formulas* pane.
   c. Select the **Manual** radio button in the *Calculation options* group.
   d. Select the **R1C1 reference style** box in the *Working with formulas* group.
   e. Click **OK** to close the *Excel Options* dialog box and apply the changes.

4. Select cell **R7C2** on the **Revenue** sheet and delete the contents. The formulas do not recalculate.

5. Click the **Formulas** tab and click the **Calculate Now** button [*Calculation* group].

6. Add a tab, a group, and commands to the *Ribbon*.
   a. Right-click the **Ribbon** and select **Customize the Ribbon**.
   b. Click **Home** in the *Main Tabs* list on the right.
   c. Click the **New Tab** button at the bottom of the list.
   d. Select **New Tab (Custom)** below the *Home* tab and click **Rename**.
   e. Type your first name for the *Display name* and click **OK**.
   f. Select **New Group (Custom)** and click **Rename**.
   g. Type My Commands as the **Display name** and click **OK**.
   h. Select the **My Commands** group name.
   i. Select **Open** in the *Popular Commands* list on the left and click **Add**.
   j. Select **Print Preview and Print** in the list and click **Add**.
   k. Add the **Save As** command to the *My Commands* group (Figure 10-27).
   l. Click **OK** to close the *Excel Options* dialog box.

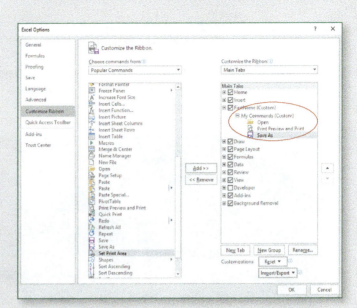

10-27 **Custom tab and group with commands added in the *Excel Options* dialog box**

7. Click the **[your first name]** tab in the *Ribbon*.

8. Click the **Save As** button in the **My Commands** group and save the workbook as [your initials] PP E10-1 in your folder for saving files.

9. Add commands to the *Quick Access* toolbar.
   a. Click the **Customize Quick Access Toolbar** drop-down list and select **New** to add the button to create a new workbook to the toolbar.
   b. Click the **Customize Quick Access Toolbar** drop-down list and select **More Commands**.
   c. Click the **Choose commands from** drop-down list and select **All Commands**.
   d. Select **Insert Comment** and click **Add**.
   e. Click **OK** to close the *Excel Options* dialog box (Figure 10-28).

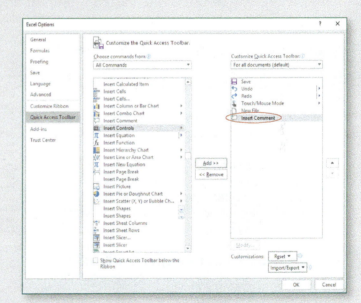

10-28 ***New* and *Insert Comment* buttons added to the *Quick Access* toolbar**

10. Select cell **R7C2** and click the **Insert a Comment** button in the *Quick Access* toolbar.

11. Type Re-enter values ASAP. in the comment box and click cell **R7C1**.

12. Click the **Review** tab and click the **Show All Comments** button [*Comments* group] to hide comments if they are shown.

13. Customize your Office account settings.
    a. Click the **File** tab and select **Account**.
    b. Click the **Office Background** drop-down list and choose **Circles and Stripes**.
    c. Click the **Office Theme** drop-down list and select **Dark Gray**.
    d. Click the **Add a service** drop-down list, select **Images & Videos**, and then click **YouTube** (Figure 10-29).
    e. Return to the workbook.

10-29 Office Account settings affect all Office applications

14. Add an Office add-in. (You must be logged in to your Microsoft account and have permission to install an add-in. If you are unable to install an add-in, go to Step 16.)

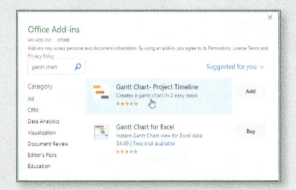

10-30 *Office Add-ins* search results

    a. Click the **Gantt Chart** worksheet tab.
    b. Click the **Store** button [*Insert* tab, *Add-ins* group].
    c. Click the **Search** box and type gantt chart. A Gantt chart is a bar chart that plots start and end dates for tasks or stages in a project.
    d. Press **Enter** to find related add-ins. Current add-ins may be different from what is shown in Figure 10-30. Choose an add-in that is free.
    e. Select **Gantt Chart – Project Timeline** (or similar free application). A dialog box opens with information about the add-in.
    f. Click **Add** to install the add-in. The add-in opens in a separate selectable object.

15. Use an Office add-in in a workbook. (If your add-in is different from the add-in shown here, follow the prompts or guidelines to build the chart.)
    a. Select cell **R10C1** in the worksheet.
    b. Click the **Next** button in the add-in object (right-pointing arrow in an ellipse) to display a table layout for the data (Figure 10-31).
    c. Select cells **R2C1:R5C5** in the worksheet and click the **Copy** button [*Home* tab, *Clipboard* group].
    d. Select cell **R11C1** and click the **Paste** button [*Home* tab, *Clipboard* group].

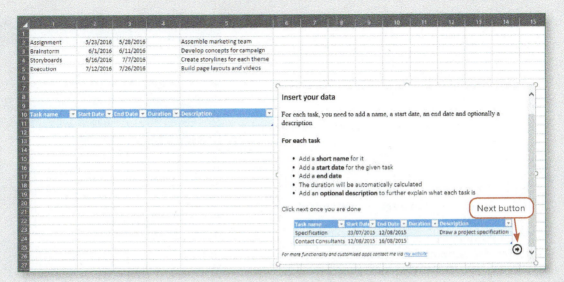

10-31 Table layout for the add-in

e. Click the **Next** button in the add-in object to create the chart.

f. Select cell **R14C5** and press **Tab** to add data to the table.

g. Type Evaluation in cell **R15C1** and press **Tab**.

h. In cell **R15C2**, use *mm/dd/yy* format, type the date that is four days after the date displayed in cell **R14C3**, and press **Tab**.

i. In cell **R15C3**, use *mm/dd/yy* format, type the date that is the same date three months from the date in cell **R15C2**, and press **Tab**.

j. Leave cell **R15C4** blank.

k. Select cell **R15C5** and type Review and assessment.

l. Locate and click the refresh or reload button in the add-in object (Figure 10-32).

m. Select cell **R16C1** to deselect the object.

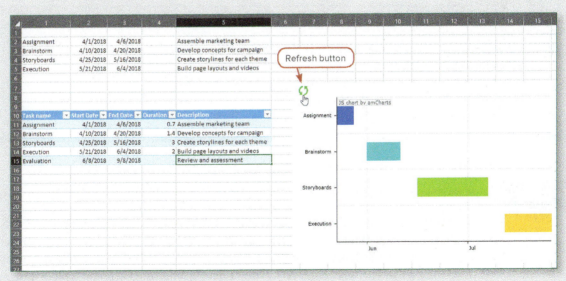

10-32 Each add-in has specific commands and options

16. Save and close the workbook (Figure 10-33).

17. Reset your Office account settings.
    a. Open a new blank workbook.
    b. Click the **File** tab and select **Account**.
    c. Click the **Office Background** drop-down list and choose **No Background**.
    d. Click the **Office Theme** drop-down list and select **Colorful**.
    e. Click **Remove** for the **YouTube** service in the *Connected Services* area and select **Yes**.
    f. Select **Options** and **Customize Ribbon**.
    g. Click **Reset**, choose **Reset all customizations**, and then click **Yes**.
    h. Click **Formulas** on the left.
    i. Select the **Automatic** radio button.
    j. Deselect the **R1C1 reference style** box.
    k. Click **OK** to close the *Excel Options* dialog box.

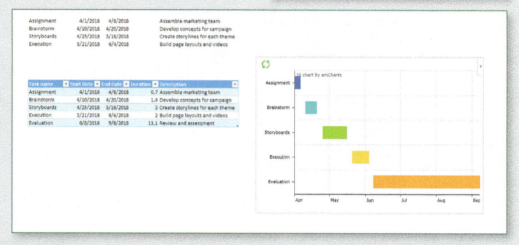

10-33 PP E10-1 completed

18. Deactivate the add-in. (Skip this step if you did not install the add-in.)
    a. Click the **My Add-ins** button [*Insert* tab, *Add-ins* group].
    b. Right-click the name of your **Gantt Chart** add-in and select **Remove**.
    c. Click **Remove** in the message box.
    d. Close the *Office Add-ins* dialog box.

SLO 10.3

Using OneDrive

OneDrive is "cloud" storage where you store files in an online location for access from any computer. Cloud storage means that you are not limited to a single computer and that you do not need to transport files on portable media. When you have a Microsoft account, you also have a *OneDrive* account. If you don't have a Microsoft account, create a free account at https://signup.live.com/.

You can save, open, and edit documents from your *OneDrive* account as well as create folders and rename, move, or delete files. *OneDrive* is listed in the *Open*, *Save*, and *Save As* commands in the *Backstage* view. When you open the *Save As* or *Open* dialog box, *OneDrive* is one of the listed folders. In *Excel Options*, you can set *OneDrive* as your default save location.

Use OneDrive in a File Explorer Window

In a Windows 10 *File Explorer* window, *OneDrive* is a storage location, similar to your *Documents* or *Pictures* folders (Figure 10-34). The difference between your *OneDrive* folder and other Windows folders is the physical location. When you save a workbook in the *Documents* folder on *This PC*, the file is stored on your computer. You have access to the file only from your computer. When you save a document in your *OneDrive* folder, the workbook is stored in the cloud, and you have access to the file from any computer with Internet access.

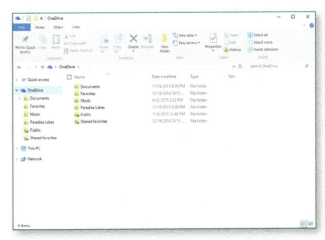

10-34 *OneDrive* folder displayed in a *File Explorer* window

Use OneDrive Online

You can sign-in directly to the *OneDrive* site with your Microsoft account. Your *OneDrive* account lists category names to the left of the window: *Files, Recent, Photos, Shared* and *Recycle bin*. The *Files* group includes default folders named *Documents, Favorites, Music, Public*, and *Shared favorites*.

HOW TO: Use OneDrive Online

1. Open an Internet browser window and navigate to the *OneDrive* web site (www.onedrive.com).
   - You can use any browser (e.g., Microsoft Edge, Google Chrome, or Mozilla Firefox).
2. Click the **Sign in** button.
   - If you are signed in to Windows with your Microsoft account and use Microsoft Edge as your browser, you may be automatically signed in to your *OneDrive* account.

3. Type your Microsoft account email address if necessary and click **Next**.

   - If you are signed in to Windows and Office, your email address may already be displayed.

4. Type your Microsoft account password and click **Sign in**.

   - Category names are listed at the left (Figure 10-35).
   - If you have multiple Windows or Office installations associated with your Microsoft account, you will see a *PCs* category that displays your installation names when expanded.

5. Select **Files** to display folder and file names.

   - Default folder names are *Documents*, *Favorites*, *Music*, *Public*, and *Shared favorites*.

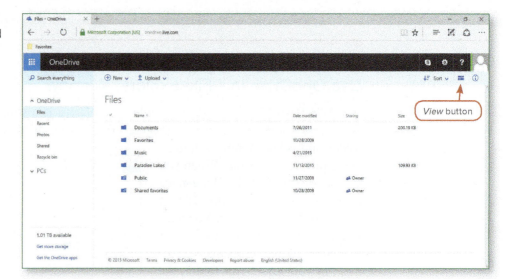

10-35 *OneDrive* window in *List* view

6. Click the **Sort** drop-down list to select a sort option.

   - You can arrange the folder or file names by name, date modified, or size.

7. Click the **View** button to toggle between *List* and *Tiles* views.

   - In *Tiles* view, a folder that holds files shows a pages icon and the number of documents in the folder.

8. Click a folder name to open it (Figure 10-36).

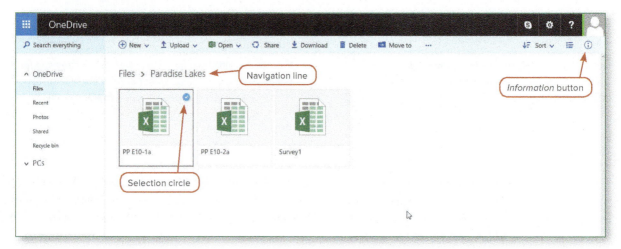

10-36 **Folder contents displayed in** *OneDrive* **in** *Tiles* **view**

   - File names are displayed.

9. Point to the folder or file icon and click the selection circle.

   - You can click the **Information** button on the right to display details about a selected folder or file.

10. Click a workbook name to launch *Excel Online*.

   - The workbook opens in its own window (Figure 10-37).
   - If the workbook has data connections, they are disabled; close the related security bar.

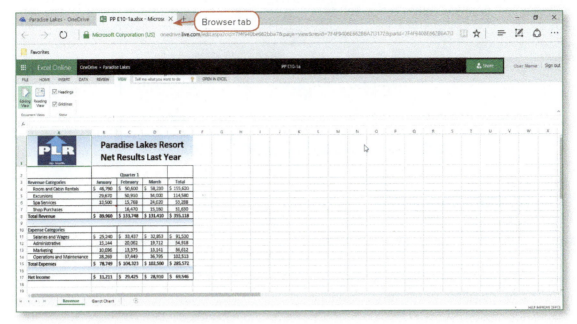

10-37 Workbook from *OneDrive* opened in *Excel Online*

11. Close the workbook by closing its browser tab.
   - Do not click the **Close** button at the top right corner of the window; this will close *OneDrive*.
   - Edits are saved automatically to the *OneDrive* folder.

12. Click **Files** to return to the *OneDrive* folder list.
   - You can click **Files** in the category list on the left or in the navigation line in the center pane (see Figure 10-36).

13. Click your name or picture in the upper right corner of the window and select **Sign out**.

> **MORE INFO**
>
> Do not check the *Keep me signed in* box when you use a public computer so that your *OneDrive* files are not available to the next person who uses the computer.

Create a Folder

You can upload workbooks to the default folders in *OneDrive*, or you can create folders to organize your work. After you create a folder in *OneDrive*, you will see its name in the *Backstage* view or in the dialog boxes for the *Open* and *Save* commands as well as in a *File Explorer* window.

▶ **HOW TO: Create OneDrive Folders**

1. Click **Files** on the left in *OneDrive*.
   - Default folder and file names stored in the *Files* folder are displayed.

2. Click the **New** button and select **Folder** (Figure 10-38).
   - The *Folder* dialog box opens.

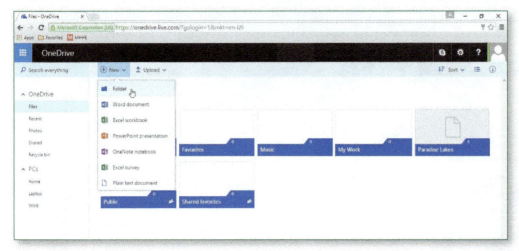

10-38 Create a new *OneDrive* folder

3. Type the name of the new folder and click **Create**.

   - You can invite others to share a folder as you create it.

4. Click a folder name to open the folder.

   - You can create a new folder inside an existing folder.
   - Right-click a folder name and select **Delete** to delete the folder from *OneDrive*.

5. Click **Files** to return to the *OneDrive* list.

   - Click **Files** in the list on the left or in the navigation line above folder names.

Upload a File or Folder

You can upload files to *OneDrive* from the hard drive or portable media for your computer. When you upload files to *OneDrive*, the files are copied to *OneDrive* and maintained in the original location.

> **MORE INFO**
>
> You can upload a folder with some browsers. Experiment and investigate to learn if you can upload a folder with your browser.

▶ **HOW TO:** Upload Files to OneDrive

1. Click **Files** on the left to display file and folder names in *OneDrive*.

   - If you are uploading a file to a specific folder, click the folder name to open it.

2. Click the **Upload** button (Figure 10-39).

3. Select **Files** or **Folder**.

   - If you choose *Files*, the *Open* dialog box displays.
   - If you select *Folder*, the *Select Folder* (Microsoft Edge) or the *Browse For Folder* (Google Chrome) dialog box opens (Figure 10-40).

4. Select the file or folder name to upload.

   - Press **Ctrl** or **Shift** to select multiple file names.
   - You can select only one folder name.

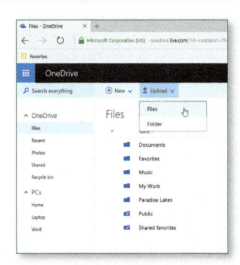

10-39 Upload a file to *OneDrive*

5. Click **Open**, **Select Folder**, or **OK**.
   - The name on the button to start the upload depends on the browser and whether you are uploading files or a folder.
   - An uploading status message appears in the upper right corner.
   - The uploaded file or folder names appear in *OneDrive*.

Move, Copy, or Delete a File or Folder

You can move or copy files and folders in *OneDrive* among your own folders. You can also delete files or folders for which you are the owner.

10-40 *Select Folder* dialog box

▶ **HOW TO:** Move, Copy, or Delete OneDrive Files

1. Click the selection **circle** for the file or folder to be moved or copied.
   - In *Tiles* view, the selection circle is in the top right corner of the folder or file icon.
   - In *List* view, the selection circle is to the left of the folder or file name.
   - You can select multiple items to be moved or copied to the same destination.

2. Click the *Move to* or the *Copy to* button.
   - The task pane opens.
   - If you don't see the *Copy to* button, click the ellipsis to open the menu of additional commands.

3. Select the name of the destination folder (Figure 10-41).

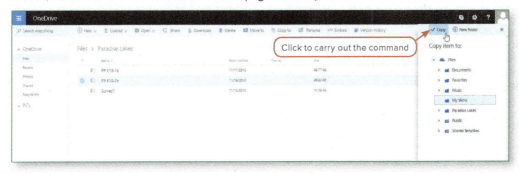

10-41 Select the destination folder

   - You can also click **New folder** to create a folder for moved or copied items.

4. Click the **Move** or **Copy** button at the top of the pane.
   - A message appears in the task pane while the files are copied or moved.
   - You can click the **Close** button in the task pane to cancel the move or copy action.

5. Click the selection **circle** for a file or folder to delete.

6. Click the **Delete** button.
   - The file or folder is deleted.
   - A message box opens with an **Undo** button to restore the item(s).

Download a File or Folder

You can download a file or folder from your *OneDrive* folder to your computer. When you download items from *OneDrive*, the items are copied to the destination and the originals remain in the *OneDrive* folder. After you edit the file, you must upload it to *OneDrive* if you want the revised work available on *OneDrive*.

1. Click the selection **circle** for the file or folder to be downloaded.

   - In *Tiles* view, the selection circle is in the top right corner of the icon.
   - In *List* view, the selection circle is to the left of the name.
   - If you select multiple files or folders, a compressed (zipped) folder downloads with the selected files/folders.

2. Click the **Download** button.

   - Results depend on the Internet browser.
   - The file or the zipped folder is downloaded to the *Downloads* folder on your computer, and a message box appears on the *Status* bar (Figure 10-42).

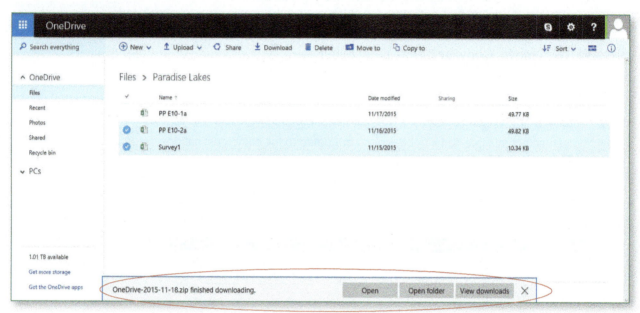

10-42 Download process and message depends on the browser

3. Open the file in the application program.

 MORE INFO

When you store and work directly with files on *OneDrive*, all of your work is "in sync."

SLO 10.4

Sharing OneDrive Files and Folders

In addition to retrieving your *OneDrive* files from any computer or mobile device, you can share files and folders so that you can collaborate on work with other people. When you share a file or a folder, you determine how others can use your work, because you assign permission to view or to edit files.

Share an Excel Workbook

Save any workbook to your *OneDrive* folder by selecting that location in the *Save* or *Save As* dialog box in Excel. A workbook must be saved to your *OneDrive* account before you can share it. When you share the workbook, you enter email addresses and specify a permission level. You can also type a brief message that is included in the notification email.

▶ HOW TO: Share a Workbook in Excel

1. Save the workbook to your *OneDrive* folder.
   - You can choose any folder in your *OneDrive* account.
   - Leave the workbook open.
2. Click the **Share** button in the upper right corner.
   - The *Share* pane opens.
3. Type or select email addresses for those with whom you are sharing the workbook.
   - If Outlook is your email program, click the **Address Book** button to the right of the *Invite people* box, select recipient names, and click **OK**.
   - Separate multiple email addresses with semicolons (**;**).
4. Select *Can edit* or *Can view* from the drop-down list.
5. Type an optional message in the *Message* area (Figure 10-43).
6. Click the **Share** button.
   - An email is sent to each recipient with a link to your file on *OneDrive*.
   - The *Share* pane lists recipient names.
   - You can right-click a recipient name to remove the name from the list or to change the permission.
7. Close the *Share* pane.

10-43 Share a workbook

▶ **ANOTHER WAY**

You can open the *Share* pane from the *Backstage* view. Click the **File** button, select **Share**, and then click the **Share with People** button.

Create a Sharing Link

A ***sharing link*** is a text hyperlink that you copy and email to others. You can generate an *Edit link* or a *View-only link*.

▶ HOW TO: Create a Sharing Link

1. Open the workbook to be shared.
   - The workbook must be saved in your *OneDrive* account.
2. Click the **Share** button next to your user name.
   - The *Share* pane opens.
3. Click **Get a sharing link** at the bottom of the *Share* pane (see Figure 10-43).
   - The *Share* pane updates to the second pane or page (Figure 10-44).
4. Click *Create an edit link* or *Create a view-only link*.
   - A link is created and displayed in the text box.
5. Click the **Copy** button (Figure 10-45).
   - You can paste the copied link in an email or in an online location.

10-44 Create a sharing link

10-45 Copy a sharing link for pasting in an email or in an online location

6. Click the **Back** arrow to the left of *Get a sharing link*.
   - The *Share* pane displays the first pane (page).
7. Close the *Share* pane.

Change the Sharing Permission

After you have shared a file, you can change the sharing permission or remove permission to edit the file. If you created a sharing link, you can disable the link.

10-46 Remove a user or change the permission

1. Open the shared workbook.
2. Click the **Share** button near your user name.
   - The *Share* pane opens.
3. Right-click the name of a recipient with whom you have shared the document.
4. Select *Remove User* or *Change permission to: Can view* (or *Can edit*) (Figure 10-46).
5. Right-click **Anyone with a sharing link**.
6. Select **Disable Link**.
   - Click **Copy Link** to copy and share the link with additional recipients.
7. Close the *Share* pane.

Email Options in Excel

The *Share* command [*File* tab] includes an *Email* group with commands to attach an Excel workbook to an email message or send a PDF version of the file. Both commands open a new message in Outlook with the file attached. You simply enter recipient addresses and send the message. You must have Outlook installed on your computer.

You can also send an XPS file, a document that can be viewed but not easily edited, if Outlook is installed. This format is similar to a PDF file. Finally, you can send a workbook as an Internet fax if you have a fax service provider.

Share a File or Folder in OneDrive

Share a file or folder directly from your *OneDrive* account without opening the workbook in Excel. You can send an email with a link to the shared workbook or get a link for pasting in an email or other online location.

> ▶ **MORE INFO**
>
> Microsoft regularly updates *OneDrive* online. Figures and steps in this chapter may be slightly different from *OneDrive* in your Internet browser. Figures and steps in this chapter display *OneDrive* using the Google Chrome web browser.

▶ HOW TO: Get a Link in OneDrive

1. Sign in to your *OneDrive* account.
2. Check the selection **circle** for the file or folder to be shared.
   - You can select multiple items.
   - When you share a folder, users have access to all files in the folder.
3. Click the **Share** button.
   - The *Share* window opens.
4. Click **Anyone with this link can edit this item**.
   - Deselect the **Allow editing** check box to create a view-only link.
   - Make this choice before you get the link.
   - Click **Manage Permissions** to open the *Information* pane.
5. Click **Get a link**.
   - Click the button or the text.
   - The link displays (Figure 10-47).
6. Click **Copy**.
   - The link is copied to the Windows *Clipboard*.
   - Click the **More** link to paste the link on Facebook, Twitter, or LinkedIn.
7. Close the dialog box.
   - Paste the link in an email or post it in an online location.

10-47 *Share* window in *OneDrive*

From your *OneDrive* account, you can send an email with a link. You enter email addresses and a brief message and send the email from the *OneDrive* folder.

▶ HOW TO: Share a OneDrive File or Folder in an Email

1. Sign in to your *OneDrive* account.
2. Check the selection circle for the file or folder to be shared.
   - You can select multiple items.
   - When you share a folder, users have access to all files in the folder.
3. Click the **Share** button.
   - The *Share* window opens.
4. Click **Email**.
   - The dialog box displays an address box and a message box.
5. Type email address(es) in the first text box.
   - Press **Tab** after typing an email address to add another recipient.
6. Click the **Can edit** arrow and select **Can view** to change the sharing permission.
7. Click the message text box and type a brief note to the recipient(s).
8. Click the **Share** button to send the email (Figure 10-48).
   - Recipients receive an email from you with a subject line indicating that you have shared a file.
   - The link and your message appear in the body of the email.

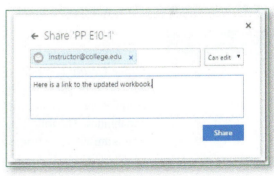

10-48 Send a sharing email in *OneDrive*

Change Sharing Permission in OneDrive

You can change the sharing permission or remove sharing for a file or folder from your *OneDrive* account. The *Information* pane displays properties of the selected file or folder.

▶ HOW TO: Change or Remove OneDrive Sharing

1. Sign in to your *OneDrive* account.
2. Check the selection **circle** for the shared file.
   - You can remove sharing permissions for one file or folder at a time.
3. Click the **Information** button.
   - The *Sharing* area in the *Information* pane displays email addresses and links (Figure 10-49).
   - Expand the *Sharing* area if it is collapsed.
4. Click the **Can edit** arrow below an email address and make a selection (Figure 10-50).
   - You can reset the permission to *Change to view only*.
   - Choose *Stop Sharing* to remove sharing permission.
5. Click the **Disable link** button to remove a sharing link.
   - The *Remove Link* dialog box opens.
6. Click **Remove link**.
7. Click the **Information** button to close the *Information* pane.

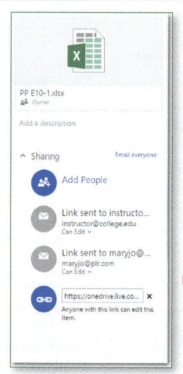

10-49 *Information* pane for shared file

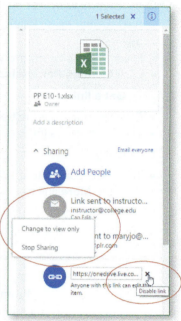

10-50 Change sharing permission or stop sharing

SLO 10.5

Using Office Online

Office Online is a free scaled-down version of popular Office 2016 applications, available from Microsoft or your *OneDrive* account page. Each online application looks and performs like the complete program but with fewer features and capabilities. The following *Office Online* programs are available from any Internet browser:

- **Word Online**: word processing
- **Excel Online**: electronic worksheet and charting
- **PowerPoint Online**: slide presentations
- **OneNote Online**: note-taking and organization

You can see all available applications by clicking *the List of Microsoft Services* button in the upper left corner of the *OneDrive* window (Figure 10-51). You will see the

10-51 List of Microsoft services

same button in each of the online applications, too. You need not have a purchased version of Office to use any of these applications.

> **MORE INFO**
>
> Microsoft Access is currently not available in *Office Online*.

Edit a Workbook in Excel Online

You can create, edit, and save *OneDrive* workbooks using *Excel Online*. You can build basic formulas, use functions, create charts, and format worksheets. *Excel Online* does not have all the features and commands as Excel 2016, but you can start a workbook in *Excel Online* and complete it in Excel 2016 if necessary. When Excel 2016 is installed on the computer, *Excel Online* includes an option to open the workbook in Excel 2016.

Excel Online has a *Ribbon* and command tabs, and you insert functions from the *Insert* tab.

> **HOW TO:** Edit a Workbook in Excel Online

1. Log in to your *OneDrive* account.
2. Click the name of an Excel workbook in a *OneDrive* folder.
   - The workbook opens in *Excel Online*.
   - The workbook opens in its own browser tab, and *OneDrive* is open in the previous tab.
   - You can also right-click the file name and select **Open in Excel Online**.
   - If the workbook has links, they are disabled. Close the message bar to continue working (Figure 10-52).

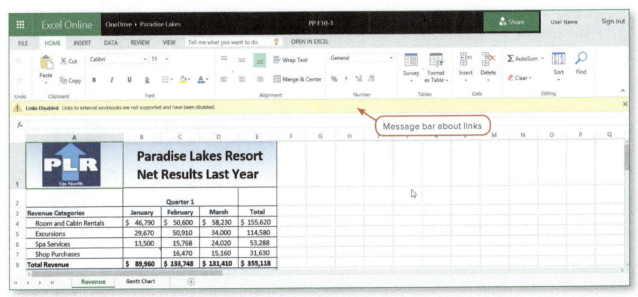

10-52 Workbook opened in *Excel Online*

3. Edit the workbook.
4. Close the browser tab to close the *Excel Online* workbook.
   - *Excel Online* automatically saves the workbook in your *OneDrive* folder.
   - The *OneDrive* tab displays.

Create and Print an Excel Online Workbook

A new workbook created in *Excel Online* has a default name, such as *Book1* or *Book2*, and is saved automatically when you close the browser tab. To use a more descriptive file name, click the default name in the *Title* bar and type a new name, or you can click the *File* tab and choose *Save As*. Workbooks are saved to your *OneDrive* account, and the *Save As* command includes an option to download a copy of the workbook to your computer.

The *Print* command is listed in the *Backstage* view and first displays a printer-friendly view. The *Print Options* dialog box asks you to print the selection or the entire sheet. After you make a choice, the workbook opens in a separate window and uses your default Windows printer.

▶ **HOW TO:** Create and Print an Excel Online Workbook

1. Log in to your *OneDrive* account.
2. Click the folder name for the folder where you want to store the workbook.
3. Click the **New** button and select **Excel workbook** (Figure 10-53).
   - *Excel Online* starts and a blank workbook is open.
4. Enter data for the worksheet.
5. Click the default *Book1* name in the *Title* bar.
6. Type the new file name and press **Enter** (Figure 10-54).
   - The workbook is saved in the folder you selected in *OneDrive*.
   - Click the **File** tab, select **Save As**, and then click the **Save As** button to choose a folder and name the workbook.

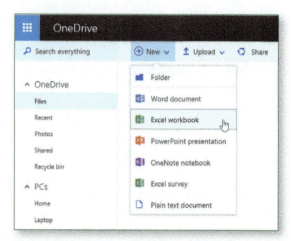

10-53 Create a new workbook in *Excel Online*

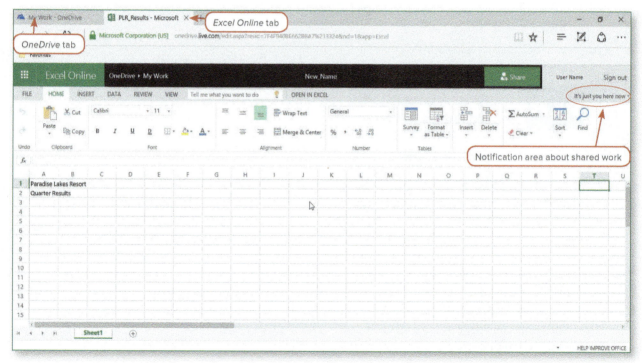

10-54 Rename the workbook in the *Title* bar

7. Click the **File** tab and choose **Print**.

8. Click the *Print* button.

   - The *Print Options* dialog box opens (Figure 10-55).
   - You can print selected cells or the entire sheet.

9. Make a selection and click **Print**.

   - A browser print window opens.

10. Click **Print** in the browser window.

    - The dialog box for your default printer opens.

11. Click **Print**.

12. Close the browser tab to close the workbook.

    - You can leave the workbook open and click the *OneDrive* tab to return to your *OneDrive* folders and files.

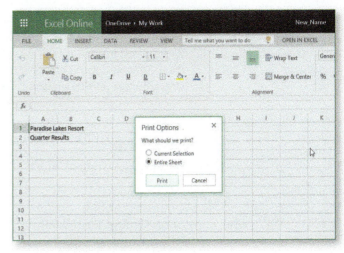

10-55 *Print Options* dialog box for an *Excel Online* workbook

Create a Chart in Excel Online

You can create a chart object in *Excel Online*. Basic chart types are available including column, bar, and pie charts. After a chart is created and selected, the *Chart Tools* tab is available in the *Ribbon* with a limited number of options for chart layout.

> **HOW TO:** Create a Chart in an Excel Online Workbook

1. Open the workbook in *Excel Online*.

2. Select the data for the chart.

   - The selected cells must be contiguous.

3. Click the **Insert** tab and click the desired chart button [*Charts* group].

4. Choose the chart subtype.

   - The chart object displays in the worksheet.
   - The *Chart Tools* tab is available.

5. Size and position the chart object as desired.

   - You cannot select individual chart elements.

6. Click the **Chart Title** button [*Chart Tools* tab, *Labels* group].

7. Choose a position for the chart title.

   - The *Edit Title* dialog box opens.

8. Type the title for the chart and click **OK** (Figure 10-56).

9. Use commands in the *Labels* group [*Chart Tools* tab] to add or remove chart elements.

10. Close the browser tab to save the workbook.

    - You can download a copy of the workbook to your computer to enhance the chart.

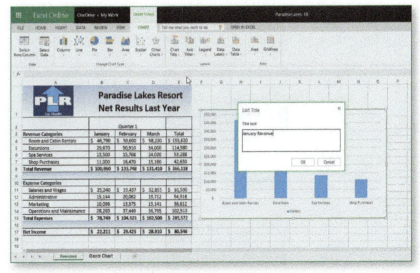

10-56 Create a chart in *Excel Online*

Share an Excel Online Workbook

You can share a workbook in *Excel Online*. The steps are similar to sharing a file or folder in *OneDrive*.

HOW TO: Share an Excel Online Workbook

1. Open a workbook in *Excel Online*.
2. Click the **Share** button in the *Title* bar.
   - The *Share* window opens.
   - You can *Invite people* (send an email) or *Get a link*.
3. Type or select email addresses.
   - Press **Tab** to separate multiple email addresses.
   - If *Outlook Mail* is your email program and you have completed contact information, click the **Address Book** button to the right of the *Invite people* box, select names, and click **OK**.

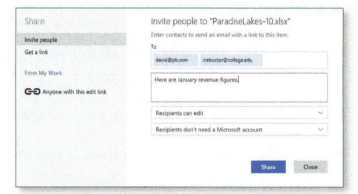

10-57 Share an *Excel Online* workbook

4. Click the **Recipients can edit** link.
   - You can select **Recipients can only view**.
   - You can also require recipients to sign in to their Microsoft account by selecting **Recipients need to sign in with a Microsoft account** from the drop-down list.
5. Type an optional message in the *Add a quick note* box (Figure 10-57).
6. Click the **Share** button.
   - An email is sent to each recipient with a link to your file on *OneDrive*.
   - The *Share* window lists recipient email addresses.
   - Select an email address and click the drop-down list to remove or change sharing.

> **ANOTHER WAY**
>
> You can get a link in the *Share* dialog box to share an *Excel Online* workbook using the same steps as when getting a link for a *OneDrive* file.

Use Comments in Excel Online

In *Excel Online*, you can add a comment in a worksheet, review and reply to comments from other users, or delete a comment. Comments in *Excel Online* are slightly different from comments in Excel 2016. When online, comments appear in a pane to the right of the window and are identified in the worksheet by a red triangle. When you select a cell with a red triangle, a comment balloon appears which opens the *Comments* pane when you click the balloon.

► **HOW TO: Add a Comment in Excel Online**

1. Open the workbook in *Excel Online*.
2. Right-click the cell in which you want to add a comment.
3. Choose **Insert Comment** from the context menu.
   - The *Comments* pane opens on the right.
   - The selected cell and your user name are indicated in the comment box.
   - You can also click the **Insert** tab and click the **Comment** button [*Comments* group] to open the pane.
   - Comments inserted in Excel 2016 appear in the pane and in the worksheet.
4. Type the text of the comment in the comment box (Figure 10-58).

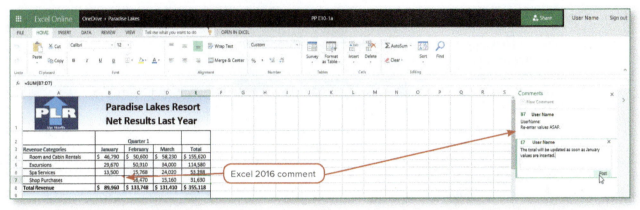

10-58 Insert a comment in *Excel Online*

5. Click **Post** in the *Comments* pane.
   - The comment is attached to the cell and posted to the workbook.
6. Close the *Comments* pane.

Collaborate in Excel Online

Excel Online allows you to work with others on a workbook simultaneously or at different times; the workbook must be shared with the other users. If two or more of you work at the same time in *Excel Online*, everyone's sign-in information is visible in the *Excel Online* window (see Figure 10-54), and you are notified when an edit is made. Changes are automatically saved and marked with the name of the person who made the edit.

PAUSE & PRACTICE: EXCEL 10-2

For this project, you create a folder in *OneDrive*, save a file to *OneDrive*, upload a file to *OneDrive*, edit a workbook in *Excel Online*, and share a *OneDrive* folder.

Note: You need a Microsoft account (https://signup.live.com) to complete this project.

File Needed: *[your initials] PP E10-1.xlsx*
Completed Project File Names: *[your initials] PP E10-2.xlsx*, *[your initials] PP E10-2a.xlsx*, and *[your initials] PP E10-1a.xlsx*

1. Open the *[your initials] PP 10-1.xlsx* workbook completed in *Pause & Practice 10-1*.

2. Save the workbook as [your initials] PP E10-2 in your usual location for saving files on your computer.

3. Log in to your *OneDrive* account.
   a. Open an Internet browser window and go to the *OneDrive* web site (www.onedrive.live.com).
   b. Click the **Sign in** button. (You may be signed in to *OneDrive* if you use Microsoft Edge as your browser; go to step 4).
   c. Type your Microsoft account email address and click **Next** (or similar command).
   d. Type your Microsoft account password and click **Sign in**.

4. Create a *OneDrive* folder.
   a. Click **Files** on the left to display the contents of your *OneDrive* folder.
   b. Click the **View** button to use a *List* view if the *Tiles* view is current.
   c. Click the **New** button and select **Folder** from the drop-down list.
   d. Type PLR as the name for the new folder (Figure 10-59).
   e. Click **Create**.

5. Save a workbook to a *OneDrive* folder.
   a. Click the Excel icon on the Windows task bar to return to *[your initials] PP E10-2*.
   b. Click the **File** tab and choose **Save As**.
   c. Select **OneDrive – Personal** in the locations list.
   d. Click **OneDrive – Personal** above the file name box to open the *Save As* dialog box.
   e. Double-click the **PLR** folder name to open it.
   f. Edit the file name to [your initials] PP E10-2a (Figure 10-60).
   g. Click **Save**.
   h. Close the workbook and leave Excel open.
   i. Click the browser icon on the Windows task bar to return to your *OneDrive* folder.
   j. Click the **Refresh** button or the **Reload this page** button. (The name of the button depends on your browser; your page may have refreshed automatically.)

6. Upload a workbook to a *OneDrive* folder.
   a. Click the **PLR** folder name to open the folder if it is not the current folder.
   b. Click the **Upload** button and choose **Files**.

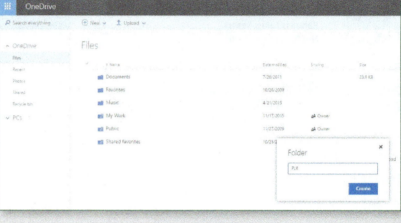

10-59 Create a folder in *List* view

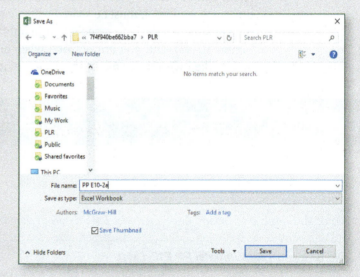

10-60 *Save As* dialog box for a *OneDrive* folder

E10-652

c. Navigate to and select the *[your initials] PP E10-1* workbook on your computer.
   d. Click **Open** to upload the workbook to the *PLR* folder.
   e. Right-click the *[your initials] PP E10-1* file name in the *PLR* folder and select **Rename**.
   f. Edit the file name to [your initials] PP E10-1a in the *Rename* dialog box (Figure 10-61).
   g. Click **Save**.

7. Edit a workbook in *Excel Online*.
   a. Click the *[your initials] PP E10-2a* file name to launch *Excel Online*.
   b. Close the security message bar about links if it opens. The Gantt chart does not display when the add-in is inactive.
   c. Click the **Revenue** sheet tab, select cell **B7**, type 15400, and press **Enter**.

10-61 Rename a *OneDrive* file

   d. Click the **Data** tab and click the **Calculate Workbook** button [*Calculation* group] if the formulas did not recalculate.
   e. Click cell **B7** again and click the comment balloon.
   f. Click the **Delete** button in the *Comments* pane (Figure 10-62).

10-62 Delete a comment in *Excel Online*

8. Add a comment to the workbook.
   a. Select cell **A2**.
   b. Click the **Insert** tab and click the **Comment** button [*Comments* group].
   c. Type I completed all values in Excel Online.
   d. Click **Post** in the *Comments* pane (Figure 10-63).

10-63 Insert a comment in *Excel Online*

e. Close the *Comments* pane.

f. Close the *Excel Online* browser tab to save and close the **[your initials] PP E10-2a** workbook and display the *OneDrive* tab.

9. Get a sharing link for the **PLR** folder.

a. Select **Files** at the left to display your *OneDrive* folders.

b. Check the circle to the left of the **PLR** folder name (Figure 10-64).

c. Click **Share** to open the *Share* window.

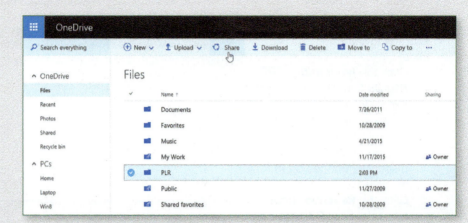

10-64 *PLR folder in OneDrive*

d. Click the **Anyone with this link can edit this item** drop-down list.

e. Click the **Allow Editing** box to deselect it (Figure 10-65).

f. Select **Get a link**.

g. Click **Copy**.

h. Close the *Share* window.

10. Sign out of your *OneDrive* account.

a. Click **[your name]** or picture in the top right corner of the window.

b. Choose **Sign out** from the *Account* drop-down list.

c. Close the *OneDrive* browser tab.

10-65 Copy the link

11. Email the sharing link to your instructor.

a. Open the email account that you use for your course.

b. Create a new message with your instructor's email address in the *To* area.

c. Type Your Name, Course Code, PLR as the subject line.

d. Type Here is a link to my PLR folder. in the body of the message and press **Enter**.

e. Press **Ctrl+V** to paste the link and press **Enter**. Your link will be different from the link shown in Figure 10-66.

f. Send the email.

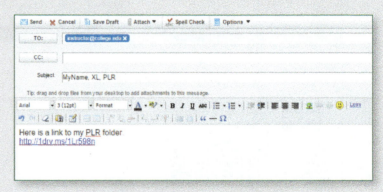

10-66 Pasted link in the email message

Exploring Office Online Applications

With your Microsoft account, you have access to applications in addition to *OneDrive*, *Excel Online*, and the other Office programs. These include *Outlook.com* for email, *People* to store your contact list, *Calendar* to organize your schedule, and more.

Excel Survey

An **Excel Survey** is an electronic survey that gathers responses in a worksheet and is shared by a link in an email or in an online environment. Respondents complete the survey online and submit their responses. Each response is added to the *OneDrive* workbook and can be tabulated using *Excel Online* commands. You can also download the workbook to a computer with Excel 2016 for analysis.

Build a survey from your *OneDrive* account or from within *Excel Online*. You type labels and questions in a wizard-like window and save the survey as an *Excel Online* workbook in one of your *OneDrive* folders. In an *Excel Survey*, you can select the following response types for your questions: *Text*, *Paragraph Text*, *Number*, *Date*, *Time*, *Yes/No*, and *Choice*. You can also specify if a response is required.

▶ **HOW TO:** Create an Excel Survey

1. Log in to your *OneDrive* account.
2. Select the *OneDrive* folder in which you want to store the survey.
3. Click the **New** button and select **Excel survey**.
   - The *Edit Survey* window opens in a new *Excel Online* workbook.
   - From a blank *Excel Online* workbook, click the *Insert* tab and then click the **Survey** button [*Tables* group].
4. Click **Enter a title for your survey here** and type a title.
5. Click **Enter a description for your survey here** and type an optional description.
   - The optional description appears below the main label in the survey.
6. Click **Enter your first question here**.
   - The *Edit Question* dialog box opens.
7. Click the **Question** box and type the first question.
   - You can include an optional subtitle for each question as desired.
8. Click the **Response Type** drop-down list and select the type of answer.
   - The type of response affects options in the *Edit Question* dialog box (Figure 10-67).
9. Select the **Required** box if each respondent must answer the question.
10. Click the **Default Answer** box and type an optional automatic response.
    - A default answer can save respondent time if you know that most of them will respond with the same answer.

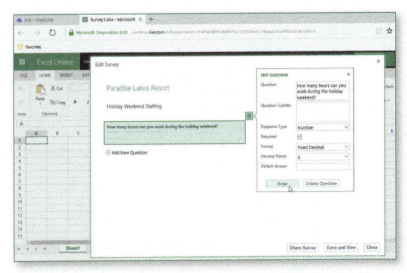

10-67 Build an *Excel Survey*

11. Click **Done** to add the question to the survey.

12. Click **Add New Question** to add another question.

    - Click the **Edit Question** button to edit an existing question.
    - Edit the question or click the **Delete Question** button to remove a question from the survey.

13. Drag a question box up or down in the *Edit Survey* window to reorder the questions.

14. Click **Save and View** to save and preview your survey (Figure 10-68).

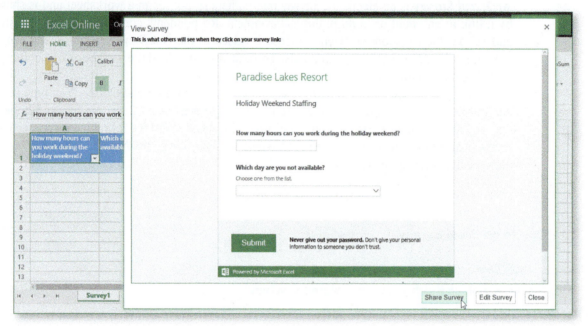

10-68 Preview the survey before sharing

15. Click **Share Survey** to get a link for the online survey.

16. Click **Create Link** (Figure 10-69).

17. Select the link, press **Ctrl+C** to copy the link, and click **Done**.

18. Click the default file name in the *Title* bar, type a descriptive file name, and press **Enter**.

19. Close the *Excel Online* browser tab.

20. Prepare the email for recipients, paste the link, and send the email.

    - You can also copy the link in an online location for your recipients.

10-69 Get a link for the *Excel Survey*

> ### MORE INFO
>
> When it is important to identify recipient responses to an *Excel Survey*, one of your questions should request a name or other identifier.

After the survey is distributed, view results in *Excel Online* by opening the workbook. The results are formatted as a table with *AutoFilters* for each column. You can filter data in *Excel Online*, add formulas, or apply formats. From the *Tables* group on the *Home* tab, click the *Survey* button to view, edit, delete, or share the survey.

Sway

Sway is a digital storytelling application. A *Sway* is an interactive presentation in which you can place text, images, videos, charts, tweets, and links. Your *Sways* and their associated data are stored in the cloud in central data centers. They are always available through your Microsoft account. You can share a *Sway* the same way you share a *OneDrive* file or an *Excel Survey*.

The *Sway* application includes sample *Sways* that you can view to learn how to build your own presentations, newsletters, or stories. *Sways* can be displayed on a PC, a tablet, or a mobile device.

> ### MORE INFO
> The working area for a *Sway* is the ***storyline*** and each element or part is a ***card***. Cards can be grouped.

▶ **HOW TO:** View a Sway

1. Log in to your *OneDrive* account.
2. Click the **List of Microsoft Services** button and select **Sway**.
   - *Sway* launches.
3. Click **Get started**.
   - You may need to enter your email address and click **Next**.
   - Sample sways are listed.
   - If you select **Create New**, a new blank *Sway* opens (Figure 10-70).

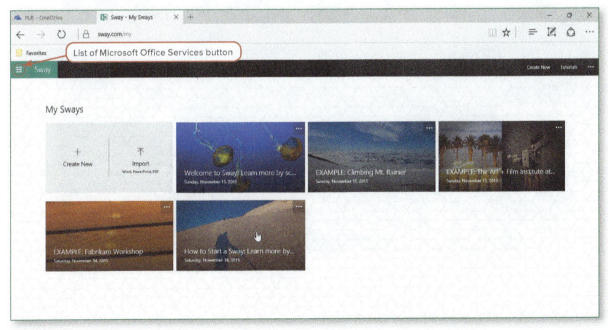

10-70 Sample sways are available for review

4. Choose one of the sample sways.

- The *All Cards* pane is on the left, the *Storyline* pane is in the center, and the *Preview* pane is on the right (Figure 10-71).

10-71 Three panes for a *Sway*

5. Scroll the *Storyline* pane to see the cards.

- The content on a card appears in a white rectangular background.
- Cards can be organized into a group.
- A group of cards displays an expand/collapse arrow in the top left corner of the rectangle.

6. Click the *Preview* pane to start the *Sway*.

- The *Storyline* pane moves to the left.

7. Click **Play** in the top right corner of the window (Figure 10-72).

10-72 Preview a *Sway* to watch how it runs

8. Scroll right or down to watch the *Sway*.

- The design and layout of the Sway determines whether you scroll left and right or up and down.

9. Click **Storyline** on the left to open the *Storyline* pane.
   - If the *Storyline* pane is not accessible, click the **Edit** button in the *Preview* pane.
   - If the *All Cards* pane is not displayed, click **Cards** in the *Title* bar to open the pane.
10. Close the browser tab to close the *Sway*.
    - *Sways* are saved automatically and are identified visually by the first card.

You can view tutorials from within the *Sway* application to explore features in depth. *Sway* is also available as a free application for Windows 10 from the Windows Store.

Outlook Mail

The **Mail** application launches *Outlook Mail*, the email program that is part of *Office Online*. Send an email message from this program, and the recipient sees your usual email address. To receive emails in *Outlook Mail*, however, you must add a second email address to your Microsoft account which has the address *[your identifier]@outlook.com* and is known as an **alias**. You can sign in to your Microsoft account with the alias or with your primary address.

People

People is a service to store names and information about your contacts for use with *Outlook Mail*. Connect to social media sites to sync those contacts, or import your contact list from most email services.

Calendar

Calendar is an appointments and events schedule. Your *Calendar* can be shared so that others see your availability. You can view your calendar in several layouts including by month, by week, or by day (Figure 10-73). From the *Agenda* view, you can see a list of upcoming appointments or events. From the *Calendar* application, you can also enter tasks to build a to-do list.

OneNote Online

OneNote Online is a productivity tool for taking notes and recording audio. Your notes are searchable, stored in the cloud, and immediately accessible with *OneNote Online* and your Microsoft account.

10-73 *Calendar* displayed in *Month* view

You type your notes on a *page* which can be part of a *section*. Sections and pages are stored in a *notebook* (Figure 10-74). Your first notebook is named with your Microsoft user name, but you can create multiple workbooks for keeping separate note groupings. *OneNote Online* has an abbreviated *Ribbon* with commands and format options similar to Excel and Word. *OneNote* is also a desktop and mobile application. Your *OneNote* data syncs across all devices when you log in with your Microsoft account.

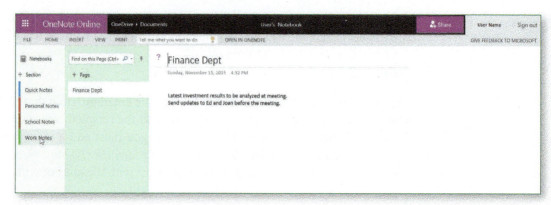

10-74 *OneNote Online* notebook

PAUSE & PRACTICE: EXCEL 10-3

For this project, you create an *Excel Survey*, share it, and analyze results in the worksheet. You need email addresses for your instructor and two classmates or friends who are available to complete the survey. You also download a copy of the survey results to your computer.

*Note: You need a Microsoft account (*https://signup.live.com*) to complete this project.*

File Needed: None
Completed Project File Name: **[your initials] PP E10-3.xlsx**

1. Log in to your *OneDrive* account.
   a. Open an Internet browser window and go to the *OneDrive* web site (www.onedrive.live.com). (You may be signed in to *OneDrive* if you use Microsoft Edge as your browser; go to step 2).
   b. Click the **Sign in** button, type your Microsoft account email address, and click **Next**.
   c. Enter your password and click **Sign in**.

2. Open a *OneDrive* folder.
   a. Click **Files** to display the contents of your *OneDrive* folder.
   b. Click **PLR** to open the Paradise Lakes folder that you created in *Pause & Practice 10-2*.

3. Create an *Excel Survey*.
   a. Click the **New** button and select **Excel survey**.
   b. Click **Enter a title for your survey here** in the *Edit Survey* window.
   c. Type Paradise Lakes Resort in the title box to replace the placeholder text.
   d. Click **Enter a description for your survey here**.
   e. Type Holiday Weekend Schedule in the description box.

4. Add a *Text* question to an *Excel Survey*.
   a. Click **Enter your first question here**.
   b. Click the **Question** box and type Your Name.
   c. Click the **Question Subtitle** box and type Type your first and last name.
   d. Click the **Response Type** drop-down list and select **Text**.
   e. Check the **Required** box.
   f. Click **Done** (Figure 10-75).

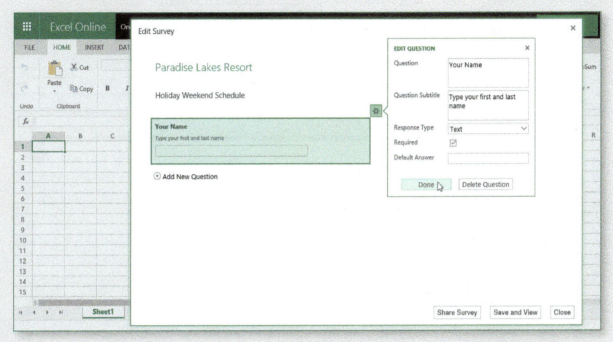

5. Add a question with a *Number* response.
   a. Click **Add New Question**.
   b. Click the **Question** box and type How many hours can you work during the holiday weekend?.
   c. Leave the *Question Subtitle* box blank.
   d. Click the **Response Type** drop-down list and select **Number**.
   e. Click the **Format** drop-down list and select **Fixed Decimal**.
   f. Click the **Decimal Places** drop-down list and select **0**.
   g. Check the **Required** box and click **Done**.

6. Add a question with a *Choice* response.
   a. Click **Add New Question**.
   b. Click the **Question** box and type Which day are you not available?
   c. Click the **Question Subtitle** box and type Select one of the three days listed.
   d. Click the **Response Type** drop-down list and select **Choice**.
   e. Triple-click the **Choices** box and type the following three day names. Press **Enter** after each day except *Sunday*.

   Friday
   Saturday
   Sunday
   f. Check the **Required** box and click **Done** (Figure 10-76).

7. Save, view, and rename the survey.
   a. Click **Save and View** to preview the survey (Figure 10-77).
   b. Click **Close** to close the *View Survey* window.
   c. Click the **Survey1** name in the *Title* bar, type [your initials] PP E10-3, and press **Enter**.

8. Share the survey.
   a. Click the **Survey** button [*Home* tab, *Tables* group] and select **Share Survey**.
   b. Click **Create Link**.

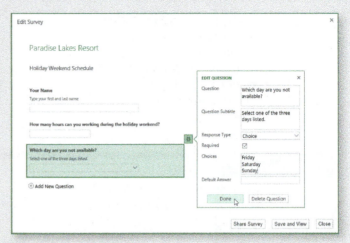

10-76 Required *Choice* question in an *Excel Survey*

10-77 Preview the *Excel Survey*

   c. Click the link to select it and press **Ctrl+C** to copy it.
   d. Click **Done**.
   e. Close the *Excel Online* browser tab for **[your initials] PP E10-3**.

9. Email the *Excel Survey* link.
   a. Open your email program and create a new message.
   b. Type your instructor's, your two other recipients', and your email addresses in the *To* area for a list of four names. Separate the names by pressing **Tab** or by typing a semicolon (;).
   c. Type [your name] Excel Survey as the subject.
   d. In the message area, type Please complete the survey and submit your answers., and press **Enter**.
   e. Press **Ctrl+V** to paste the link and press **Enter**.
   f. Send the email.

10. Review survey results after recipients have replied.
    a. Log in to your *OneDrive* account.
    b. Open the **PLR** folder.

c. Click the **[your initials] PP E10-3**
   file name to open the workbook in
   Excel Online. Responses in your
   workbook will not match those in
   Figure 10-78.
d. Select all cells with data and apply
   All Borders (Figure 10-78).

11. Download a copy of the survey
    workbook.
    a. Click the **File** tab and select **Save As**.
    b. Click the **Download a Copy Button**
       to download a copy to your default
       folder for downloads.

12. Close the browser tab for **[your initials]**
    PP E10-3.

13. Sign out of *OneDrive* and close the browser.

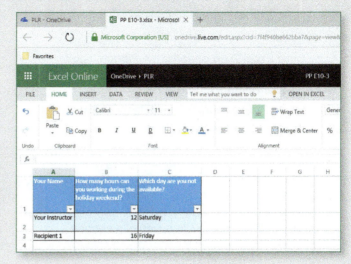

10-78 *Excel Survey* with two responses

Chapter Summary

10.1 Customize Excel 2016 options, the *Ribbon*, and the *Quick Access* toolbar to personalize your working environment (p. E10-620).

- The *Excel Options* dialog box allows you to choose global settings for new workbooks.
- The *Excel Options* dialog box has the following command and feature categories: *General*, *Formulas*, *Proofing*, *Save*, *Language*, *Advanced*, *Customize Ribbon*, *Quick Access Toolbar*, *Add-ins*, and *Trust Center*.
- From the *General* category, you can choose whether the *Quick Analysis* button displays and select a default font.
- The *Formulas* pane has an option to use manual calculation and the *R1C1* cell reference style.
- Changes made in the *Proofing* pane affect the *AutoCorrect* command group in all Office programs (Access, Excel, PowerPoint, and Word).
- The *Advanced* pane has categories and settings for display of the *Fill Handle*, *AutoComplete*, *Flash Fill*, and more.
- You can customize the *Ribbon* to create a new tab or group, add commands to custom groups, rearrange and rename tabs and groups, and similar tasks.
- When you customize the *Quick Access* toolbar, you can choose a command from the *Customize Quick Access Toolbar* drop-down list or use the *Excel Options* dialog box to add any command.
- Both the *Ribbon* and the *Quick Access* toolbar can be reset to their original settings from the *Excel Options* dialog box.

10.2 View and modify Office account settings and install an Office add-in (p. E10-628).

- The *Account* area in the *Backstage* view displays user and product information for your Microsoft Office account.
- Your account information and settings are applied when and where you log in to your Microsoft account.
- **Office Background** displays a graphic pattern in the upper right corner of the application window.
- **Office Theme** determines *Ribbon* and other screen colors.

- You can use **Connected Services** to add services such as YouTube or Facebook to your account.
- An **Office add-in** provides additional features and commands to Excel and other Office programs.
- Add-ins are available in the *Office Store*; many are free.

10.3 Create a folder, add a file, and move and copy a file in OneDrive (p. E10-636).

- **OneDrive** is "cloud" or online storage for your files, available with your Microsoft account.
- You can access documents stored in your *OneDrive* account from any computer that has Internet access.
- *OneDrive* is listed as a storage location in a *File Explorer* window in Windows 10.
- *OneDrive* has default folders and you can create and name new folders.
- When you upload a saved workbook to *OneDrive*, it is copied to the cloud and remains in its original location on the computer.
- When you download a file from a *OneDrive* folder, it is copied to your computer.

10.4 Share *OneDrive* files and folders (p. E10-642).

- You can share a *OneDrive* file or folder.
- The *Share* command sends an email with a link to a shared workbook.
- You can get a **sharing link** to be copied into a different email program or to an online location.
- After a file has been shared, you can change the sharing permission or remove it from recipients.
- A workbook can be shared from within Excel 2016 but it must first be saved to your *OneDrive* account.

10.5 Open, create, and edit an Excel workbook in *Office Online* (p. E10-646).

- **Office Online** is free online software available with your Microsoft account.
- *Office Online* includes condensed versions of Word, PowerPoint, Excel, and OneNote.
- **Excel Online** has features and commands similar to Excel 2016 including a *Ribbon*.
- You can edit an Excel 2016 workbook in *Excel Online* or create a new workbook.

10.6 Explore *Office Online* applications and productivity tools (p. E10-655).

- Your Microsoft account gives you access to productivity tools for use with *Office Online* software.
- **Excel Survey** is used to build an online survey that is sent, by link, to recipients.
- Recipient responses to an *Excel Survey* are gathered in a table in an *Excel Online* workbook.
- **Sway** is a digital storytelling application that can include text, images, videos, and links.
- **Outlook.com** is an email feature that uses your primary Microsoft account information and a second email address for receipt of messages.

- The **People** application is a contact manager for creating an online address book.
- You can use the **Calendar** application to maintain a schedule of events, appointments, and tasks.
- **OneNote Online** is a notetaking application for text and audio.

Check for Understanding

The SIMbook for this text (within your SIMnet account) provides the following resources for concept review:

- Multiple choice questions
- Matching exercises
- Short answer questions

Guided Project 10-1

Courtyard Medical Plaza (CMP) has assembled data about dental patient insurance. You change Excel options, use an add-in, and upload the file to *OneDrive*. After you edit the workbook in *Excel Online*, you share it. Finally, you build an Excel *Survey*.
[Student Learning Outcomes 10.1, 10.2, 10.3, 10.4, 10.5, 10.6]

Note to Instructor and Students:

For this project, you use your Microsoft and OneDrive account. You can create a free Microsoft account at https://signup.live.com.

File Needed: ***CourtyardMedical-10.xlsx*** *(Student data files are available in the* Library *of your SIMnet account)*
Completed Project File Names: *[your initials] **Excel 10-1.xlsx**, [your initials] **Excel 10-1a.xlsx**, and [your initials] **Excel 10-1b.xlsx***

Skills Covered in This Project

- Customize *Excel Options* to use manual calculation.
- Customize *Excel Options* to use the *R1C1* cell reference style.
- Install and use an Office add-in.
- Create a *OneDrive* folder.
- Upload a workbook to a *OneDrive* folder.
- Edit a workbook in *Excel Online*.
- Share a *OneDrive* workbook.
- Create an *Excel Survey*.

1. Open the **CourtyardMedical-10** workbook from your student data files.

2. Save the workbook as [your initials] Excel 10-1 in your usual location for saving files on your computer.

3. Customize Excel options to use manual calculation and the *R1C1* reference style.
   a. Click the **File** tab and select **Options** to open the *Excel Options* dialog box.
   b. Select **Formulas** on the left.
   c. Select the **Manual** radio button in the **Calculation options** group.
   d. Select the **R1C1 reference style** box in the **Working with formulas** group.
   e. Click **OK** to close the *Excel Options* dialog box.

4. Select cell **R5C5**, type 145 and press **Enter**.

5. Type 195 in cell **R6C5** and press **Enter**.

6. Click the **Formulas** tab and click the **Calculate Now** button [*Calculation* group].

7. Install an Office add-in. (If you are unable to install an add-in, go to Step 8e.)
   a. Log-in to your Microsoft account if you have not already done so.
   b. Click the **Store** button [*Insert* tab, *Add-ins* group].
   c. Select **Visualization** in the *Category* list.
   d. Find and click **Bubbles**, a free add-in.
   e. Click **Add** to install the add-in.

8. Use an Office add-in in a workbook.
   a. Select the add-in object and drag it to position the top left selection handle at cell **R2C12**.
   b. Click the **Select Table** bubble in the add-in.
   c. Select cells **R4C9:R8C10** in the worksheet and click **OK** (Figure 10-79).

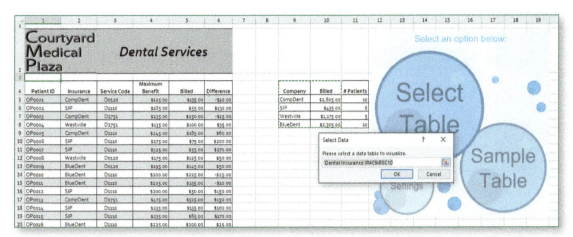

   d. Select cell **R3C1** to deselect the object (Figure 10-80). Bubbles may move as you scroll the worksheet.

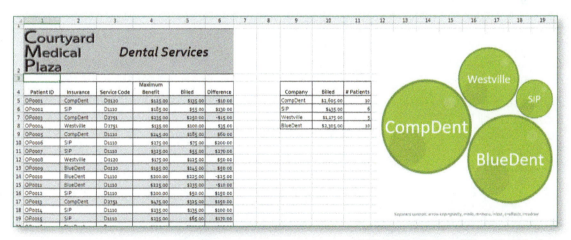

   e. Save the workbook with the same file name in the same folder on your computer.

9. Create a *OneDrive* folder.
   a. Log in to your *OneDrive* account.
   b. Click **Files** to display the contents of your *OneDrive* folder.
   c. Click the **View** button and choose a **List** view.
   d. Click the **New** button and select **Folder**.
   e. Type Courtyard Med and click **Create**.

10. Save a workbook to a *OneDrive* folder.
   a. Click the Excel icon on the Windows task bar to return to *[your initials] Excel 10-1*.
   b. Click the **File** tab and choose **Save As**.
   c. Click **OneDrive - Personal** in the locations list.
   d. Select **OneDrive** in the navigation list at the left.

e. Click the **Courtyard Med** folder name.

f. Edit the file name to [your initials] Excel 10-1a (Figure 10-81).

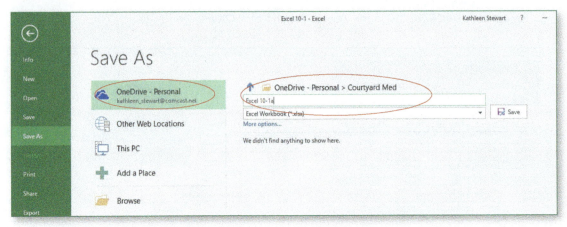

10-81 Workbook is renamed and saved on *OneDrive*

g. Click **Save**. The *OneDrive* workbook is open in Excel 2016.

h. Close the workbook.

11. Edit a workbook in *Excel Online*.

a. Return to your *OneDrive* account.

b. Click the **Courtyard Med** folder name to open it.

c. Click the **[your initials] Excel 10-1a** file name to launch *Excel Online*. The add-in object reloads in Step 11e.

d. Select cell **E5**, type 525, and press **Enter**.

e. Click the **Data** tab and click the **Calculate Workbook** button [*Calculation* group]. The add-in object refreshes.

12. Add a comment to the workbook.

a. Select cell **E4**.

b. Click the **Insert** tab and click the **Comment** button [*Comments* group].

c. Type Billed amounts are still being adjusted.

d. Click **Post** in the *Comments* pane (Figure 10-82).

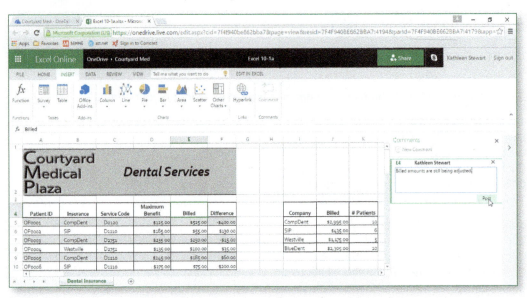

10-82 A comment in *Excel Online*

e. Close the *Comments* pane.

f. Close the *Excel Online* browser tab to save and close the **[your initials] Excel 10-1a** workbook and return to your *OneDrive* account.

13. Share a *OneDrive* workbook.

a. Verify or open the **Courtyard Med** folder.

b. Click the selection circle for the **[your initials] Excel 10-1a** file name.

c. Click the **Share** button.

d. Click **Email** and type your instructor's email address in the first entry box.

e. Click the message box and type Here is the insurance workbook.

f. Click **Share** to send the sharing email (Figure 10-83).

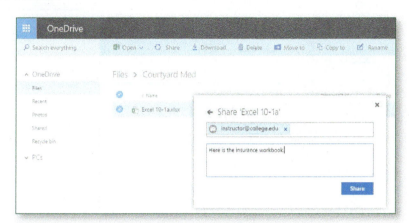

10-83 Share a *OneDrive* workbook

14. Create an *Excel Survey*.

a. Click **Files** to display the contents of your *OneDrive* folder.

b. Click **Courtyard Med** to open the folder.

c. Click the **New** button and select **Excel survey**.

d. Click **Enter a title for your survey here** in the *Edit Survey* window.

e. Type Courtyard Medical Plaza to replace the placeholder text.

f. Click **Enter a description for your survey here**.

g. Type Your Visits to CMP in the description box.

15. Add a *Number* question to an *Excel Survey*.

a. Click **Enter your first question here**.

b. Click the **Question** box and type Number of Visits.

c. Click the **Question Subtitle** box and type How many times per week do you work with your therapist?

d. Click the **Response Type** drop-down list and select **Number**.

e. Click the **Format** drop-down list and select **Fixed Decimal**.

f. Click the **Decimal Places** drop-down list and select **0**.

g. Check the **Required** box and click **Done**.

16. Add a question with a *Yes/No* response.

a. Click **Add New Question**.

b. Click the **Question** box and type Have you made progress with your therapist?

c. Click the **Response Type** drop-down list and select **Yes/No**.

d. Check the **Required** box and click **Done** (Figure 10-84).

17. Save, view, and rename the survey.

a. Click **Save and View** to preview the survey.

b. Click **Close** to close the *View Survey* window.

c. Click the workbook name in the *Title* bar, type [your initials] Excel 10-1b, and press **Enter** (Figure 10-85).

18. Download a copy of the survey workbook.

a. Click the **File** tab and select **Save As**.

b. Click the **Download a Copy Button** to download a copy to your default folder for downloads.

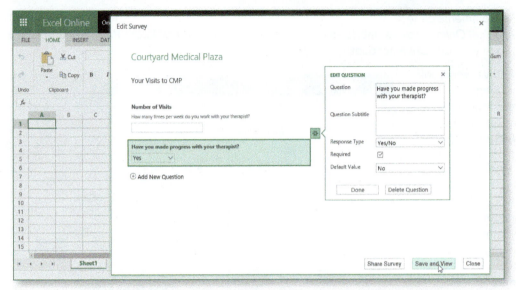

10-84 *Yes/No survey question*

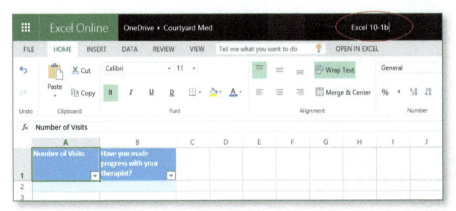

10-85 Rename the *Excel Survey*

19. Close the *Excel* Online browser tab for *[your initials] Excel 10-1b*.

20. Sign out of *OneDrive* and close the browser.

21. Reset *Excel Options*.
     a. Return to Excel 2016 and open a new blank workbook.
     b. Click the **File** tab and select **Options**.
     c. Click **Formulas** on the left.
     d. Select the **Automatic** radio button.
     e. Deselect the **R1C1 reference style** box.
     f. Click **OK** to close the dialog box.

22. Deactivate the add-in. (Skip this step if you did not install the add-in.)
     a. Click the **My Add-ins** button [*Insert* tab, *Add-ins* group].
     b. Right-click the **Bubbles** add-in and select **Remove**.
     c. Click **Remove** in the message box.
     d. Close the *Office Add-ins* dialog box.

Guided Project 10-2

In the workbook for Blue Lake Sports, you customize the *Ribbon* to display your own command tab and group. You change Office settings, save the workbook to your *OneDrive* account, edit it online, and share the workbook.
[Student Learning Outcomes 10.1, 10.2, 10.3, 10.4, 10.5]

Note to Instructor and Students:

For this project, you use your Microsoft and OneDrive account. You can create a free Microsoft account at https://signup.live.com.

File Needed: ***BlueLakeSports-10.xlsx*** *(Student data files are available in the* Library *of your SIMnet account)*
Completed Project File Names: *[your initials] Excel 10-2.xlsx*, *[your initials] Excel 10-2a.xlsx*, and *[your initials] Excel 10-2b.xlsx*

Skills Covered in This Project

- Modify Office account settings to choose a theme.
- Add a custom command tab and group to the *Ribbon*.
- Add command buttons to a custom group in the *Ribbon*.
- Save a workbook to a *OneDrive* folder.
- Edit a workbook in *Excel Online*.
- Share a *OneDrive* workbook.

1. Open the **BlueLakeSports-10** workbook from your st nt data files.

2. Save the workbook as [your initials] Excel 10-2 in your usual location for saving files on your computer.

3. Customize the *Ribbon* to add a tab and a group.
   a. Right-click the **Ribbon** and select **Customize the Ribbon**.
   b. Select **Insert** in the *Main Tabs* list on the right.
   c. Click **New Tab** to insert a custom tab and group.
   d. Click **New Tab (Custom)** and click **Rename**.
   e. Type [your initials] Tab and click **OK**.
   f. Select **New Group (Custom)** and click **Rename**.
   g. Type [your initials] Group and click **OK**.

4. Add command buttons to a custom group.
   a. Select **[your initials] Group**.
   b. Select **Save As** in the *Popular Commands* list on the left.
   c. Click **Add** to place the button in the custom group.
   d. Click the **Choose commands from** drop-down list and select **All Commands**.
   e. Select **Screenshot** in the list and click **Add** (Figure 10-86).
   f. Click **OK**.

5. Select an Office theme.
   a. Click the **File** tab and select **Account**.
   b. Click the **Office Theme** drop-down list and select **Dark Gray**.
   c. Return to the workbook.

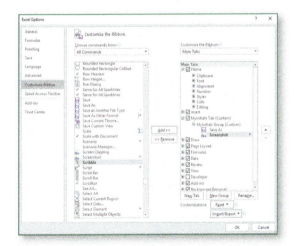

10-86 Custom tab, group, and buttons

6. Use a custom group to take a screenshot.
   a. Press **Ctrl+N** to open a new blank workbook.
   b. Press **Ctrl+F6** to return to **[your initials] Excel 10-2**.
   c. Click the **[your initials] Tab** command tab in the *Ribbon*.
   d. Click the **Screenshot** button and choose **Screen Clipping**.
   e. With the crosshair pointer, select from the top left corner of the blank workbook window to cell **P20**.
   f. Click the **Height** box on the *Picture Tools Format* tab in the *Size* group.
   g. Type 4 as the new height and press **Enter**. The width is proportional.
   h. Select the picture object and position its top left selection handle at cell **H1**.
   i. Select cell **G6** (Figure 10-87).

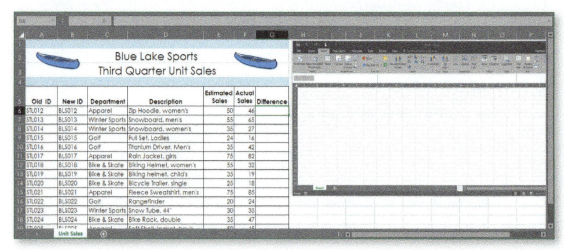

10-87 Sized and positioned screenshot

7. Save a workbook to a *OneDrive* folder.
   a. Click the **File** tab and choose **Save As**.
   b. Select **OneDrive - Personal** in the locations list.
   c. Click the **Documents** folder name.
   d. Edit the file name to [your initials] Excel 10-2a.
   e. Click **Save**. The *OneDrive* workbook is open in Excel 2016.
   f. Close the workbook.

8. Edit a workbook in *Excel Online*.
   a. Open your browser and sign in to your *OneDrive* account.
   b. Click the **Documents** folder name to open it.
   c. Click the **[your initials] Excel 10-2a** file name to launch *Excel Online*.
   d. Select cell **G6** and type a formula to subtract actual sales from estimated sales.
   e. Copy the formula to cells G7:G20 (Figure 10-88).
   f. Close the *Excel Online* browser tab to save and close the **[your initials] Excel 10-2a** workbook and return to your *OneDrive* account.

9. Share a *OneDrive* workbook.
   a. Verify or check the selection circle for the **[your initials] Excel 10-2a** file name.
   b. Click the **Share** button and select **Email**.
   c. Type your instructor's email address in the entry box and type a semicolon (;).
   d. Type your email address after your instructor's address.
   e. Click the message box and type Excel 10-2a with screenshot.
   f. Click **Share** to send the sharing email.

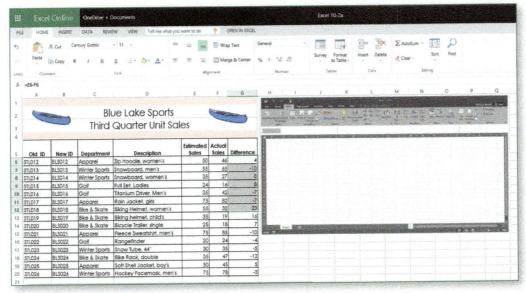

10-88 *Excel Online* workbook with screenshot

10. Sign out of *OneDrive* and close the browser.

11. Reset the *Ribbon*.
    a. Return to Excel 2016 and the blank workbook.
    b. Click the **File** tab and select **Options**.
    c. Select **Customize Ribbon** on the left.
    d. Click **Reset** and choose **Reset all customizations**.
    e. Click **Yes** in the message box.
    f. Click **OK** to close the dialog box.

12. Reset the Office theme.
    a. Click the **File** tab and select **Account**.
    b. Click the **Office Theme** drop-down list and select **Colorful**.
    c. Return to the blank workbook.

Guided Project 10-3

The aging detail worksheet for Livingood Accounting Services has an error that you correct using *Excel Online*. You use *Outlook Mail* to send a sharing link in an email message and upload a CSV file (comma-separated values) to the *People* application.
[**Student Learning Outcomes 10.3, 10.4, 10.5, 10.6**]

Note to Instructor and Students:

For this project, you use your Microsoft and OneDrive account. You can create a free Microsoft account at https://signup.live.com.

Files Needed: ***Livingood-10.xlsx*** and ***Livingood-10.csv*** *(Student data files are available in the Library of your SIMnet account)*
Completed Project File Names: *[your initials]* ***Excel 10-3.xlsx*** *and* *[your initials]* ***Excel 10-3a.xlsx***

Skills Covered in This Project

- Save a workbook to a *OneDrive* folder.
- Insert the *TODAY* function in a workbook in *Excel Online*.
- Get a sharing link for a *OneDrive* workbook.
- Send a sharing link in an *Outlook Mail* message.
- Import contacts into the *People* application.

---

1. Open the **Livingood-10** workbook from your student data files. (You can point to a file name to see a *ScreenTip* to distinguish the Excel workbook from the CSV file with the same name.)

2. Save the workbook as [your initials] Excel 10-3 in your usual location for saving files on your computer.

3. Save a workbook to a *OneDrive* folder. (You must be signed in to your Microsoft account.)
   a. Click the **File** tab and choose **Save As**.
   b. Click **OneDrive - Personal** in the locations list.
   c. Select **Documents** to open the folder.
   d. Edit the file name to [your initials] Excel 10-3a.
   e. Click **Save**.
   f. Close the **[your initials] Excel 10-3a** workbook in Excel 2016.

4. Edit a workbook in *Excel Online* to insert the TODAY function.
   a. Open your browser and go to your *OneDrive* account.
   b. Click the **Documents** folder name.
   c. Click the **[your initials] Excel 10-3a** file name to launch *Excel Online*.
   d. Select cell **G1** and type =to to display the *Formula AutoComplete* list.
   e. Press **Tab** to select the function (Figure 10-89).
   f. Press **Enter** to complete the function. The formulas in column **E** are calculated.
   g. Close the *Excel Online* browser tab to save and close the **[your initials] Excel 10-3a** workbook and return to your *OneDrive* account.

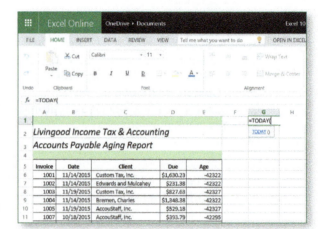

10-89 Enter the *TODAY* function in *Excel Online*

5. Get a sharing link for a *OneDrive* workbook.
   a. Verify or check the selection circle for the **[your initials] Excel 10-3a** file name.
   b. Click the **Share** button.
   c. Click **Anyone with this link can edit this item**.
   d. Deselect the **Allow editing** box to create a view-only link.
   e. Click **Get a link**.
   f. Click **Copy** to copy the link to the Windows *Clipboard* (Figure 10-90).
   g. Close the *Share* window.

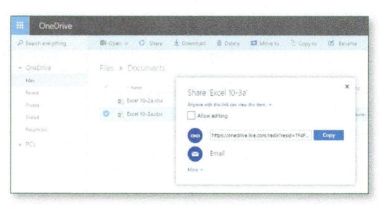

10-90 Get a sharing link for a workbook in *OneDrive*

6. Paste the link in an *Outlook Mail* email message.
   a. Click the **List of Microsoft Services** button and choose **Mail**.
   b. Close any welcome or introductory screens and click the **New** button. Your Microsoft email account name appears as the sender.
   c. Type your instructor's email address in the *To* box.
   d. Click **Add a subject** and type Updated File.
   e. Click **Add a message or drag a file here** in the body area.
   f. Press **Ctrl+V** to paste the link.
   g. Press **End** to position the pointer and press **Enter**.
   h. Type Click this link for the corrected file. and press **Enter** (Figure 10-91). (Your link will be different from the link displayed in the figure.)
   i. Click **Send**.
   j. Close the *Outlook Mail* browser tab to return to the *OneDrive* tab.

10-91 Send a link in an *Outlook Mail* message

7. Import a CSV file into the *People* application.
   a. Click the **List of Microsoft Services** button and select **People**.

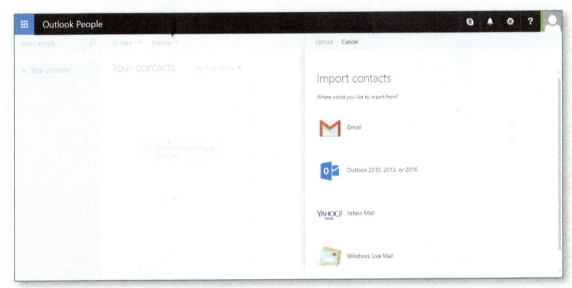

10-92 *People* application

   b. Click the **Manage** button and select **Import contacts** (Figure 10-92).
   c. Click **Gmail**. This choice enables you to locate and import a CSV file; it does not need to be a *Gmail* email list.
   d. Click **Browse**.
   e. Navigate to your student data files folder and select **Livingood-10.csv**. (Figure 10-93). (You can point to a file name to see a *ScreenTip* to distinguish the CSV file from the Excel file with the same name.)
   f. Click **Upload**. The contact names and data are imported.

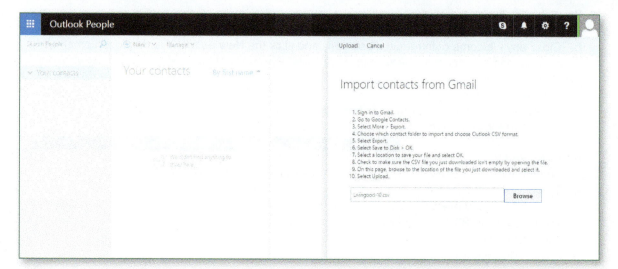

10-93 Use Gmail to import a *csv* file

g. Click **Cancel** in the *Import successful* window (Figure 10-94).

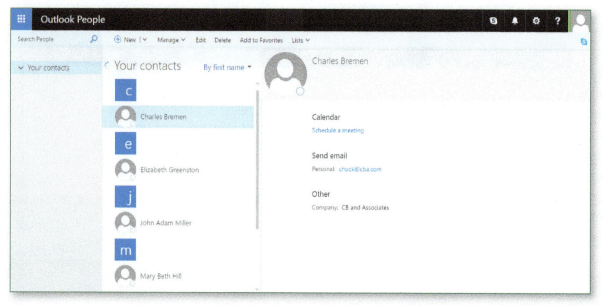

10-94 Imported contacts are added

8. Close the *People* browser tab.

9. Sign out of *OneDrive* and close the browser.

Independent Project 10-4

For the Hamilton Civic Center, you use an Excel add-in to illustrate the number of seminar attendees in relation to their goal number. You upload the workbook and a related Word document to *OneDrive* for sharing. [Student Learning Outcomes 10.2, 10.3, 10.4]

Note to Instructor and Students:

For this project, you use your Microsoft and OneDrive account. You can create a free Microsoft account at https://signup.live.com.

Files Needed: *HamiltonCC-10.xlsx* and *HamiltonCC-10.docx* (Student data files are available in the Library of your SIMnet account)
Completed Project File Names: *[your initials] Excel 10-4.xlsx* and *[your initials] Excel 10-4Word.docx*

Skills Covered in This Project

- Install an Excel add-in.
- Use an Excel add-in to illustrate data.
- Create a *OneDrive* folder.
- Upload files to *OneDrive*.
- Share a *OneDrive* folder.

1. Copy the **HamiltonCC-10.docx** Word document from your student data files to your usual location for saving files on your computer.

2. In a *File Explorer* window, rename the copied Word file as [your initials] Excel 10-4Word.

3. Open the **HamiltonCC-10** Excel workbook from your student data files.

4. Save the workbook as [your initials] Excel 10-4 in your usual location for saving files on your computer.

5. Click the **Store** button [*Insert* tab, *Add-ins* group] and select the **Visualization** category. Find and install the free **Gauge** add-in.

6. Click **Insert Gauges** in the add-in object, select cell **E20** on the **Hospital Seminars** worksheet, and click **OK** (Figure 10-95).

7. Click the **Settings** button in the add-in object, to the left of the *Help* question mark. Set the maximum value at **350** (Figure 10-96).

8. Scroll in the add-in object and select the **digital** theme.

9. Click the **Back** button next to *Settings* in the add-in object.

10. Drag the gauge object so that it aligns at row 13 to the right of the *Total Attendees* information (Figure 10-97).

11. Select cell **E23** and save and close the workbook.

12. Open your browser and go to your *OneDrive* account.

10-95 *Gauge* add-in for Excel

10-96 Add-in settings

13. Create a folder named Hamilton CC in the *Files* category and open the folder.

14. Click the **Upload** button and find and select *[your initials] Excel 10-4.xlsx* and *[your initials] Excel 10-4Word.docx* in your folder for saving files. Upload both files to the *Hamilton CC* folder on *OneDrive*.

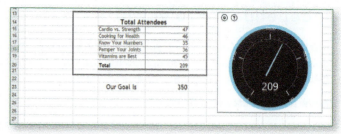

10-97 Completed gauge add-in

15. Display the *Files* category and select the *Hamilton CC* folder.

16. Share the folder in an email with your instructor.

17. Sign out of your *OneDrive* account and close the browser.

18. Open a blank workbook in Excel. Click the **My Add-ins** button [*Insert* tab, *Add-ins* group] and remove the **Gauge** add-in from your account.

Independent Project 10-5

You add two buttons to the *Quick Access* toolbar so that you can complete a workbook for Sierra Pacific Community College District (SPCC) and upload the workbook to *OneDrive*. You enter labels for a new workbook using *Excel Online* and save it to the SPCC folder.
[Student Learning Outcomes 10.1, 10.3, 10.4, 10.5]

Note to Instructor and Students:

For this project, you use your Microsoft and OneDrive account. You can create a free Microsoft account at https://signup.live.com.

File Needed: **SPCC-10.xlsx** *(Student data files are available in the* Library *of your SIMnet account)*
Completed Project File Names: *[your initials] Excel 10-5.xlsx and [your initials] Excel 10-5a.xlsx*

Skills Covered in This Project

- Customize the *Quick Access* toolbar.
- Create a *OneDrive* folder.
- Upload a workbook to *OneDrive*.
- Create a new workbook in *Excel Online*.
- Share a *OneDrive* folder.

1. Open the **SPCC-10** workbook from your student data files.

2. Save the workbook as [your initials] Excel 10-5 in your usual location for saving files on your computer.

3. Click the **Customize Quick Access Toolbar** drop-down list and select **More Commands**.

4. Click the **Choose commands from** drop-down list and select **All Commands**

5. Select **Rename Sheet** in the list and click **Add**.

6. Add the **Thick Bottom Border** button to the toolbar and close the *Excel Options* dialog box (Figure 10-98).

7. Click the **Rename Sheet** button in the *Quick Access* toolbar and type Capacity as the new sheet name.

8. Select cells **B2:E2** and click the **Thick Bottom Border** button in the *Quick Access* toolbar.

9. Select cell **F1**. Save and close the workbook.

10. Leave Excel 2016 running. If a blank workbook is not open, press **Ctrl+N**.

11. Open your browser and go to your *OneDrive* account.

12. Create a folder named SPCC in the *Files* category and upload a copy of *[your initials] Excel 10-5* to the folder.

13. From the **SPCC** folder window, create a new *Excel Online* workbook. Click the default file name in the *Title* bar and name the workbook as [your initials] Excel 10-5a.

14. Enter the data shown in Figure 10-99.

15. Close the browser tab for *[your initials] Excel 10-5a*.

16. Share the **SPCC** folder in an email to your instructor.

17. Sign out of your *OneDrive* account and close the browser.

18. Return to Excel 2016 and reset the *Quick Access* toolbar.

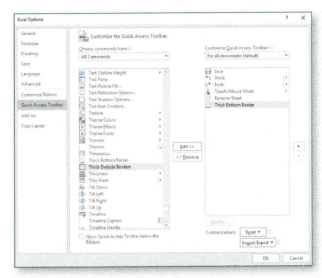

10-98 Command buttons for the *Quick Access* toolbar

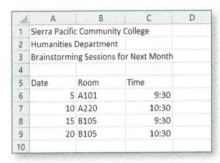

10-99 Data for new *Excel Online* workbook

Independent Project 10-6

You plan to take notes using *OneNote Online* for the planning meeting at Mary's Rentals. You will share your notes and attach a copy of the related workbook so that the rental manager can complete the workbook using your notes.
[Student Learning Outcomes 10.4, 10.6]

Note to Instructor and Students:

For this project, you use your Microsoft and OneDrive account. You can create a free Microsoft account at https://signup.live.com.

File Needed: ***MarysRentals-10.xlsx*** *(Student data files are available in the* Library *of your SIMnet account)*
Completed Project File Name: *[your initials]* ***Excel 10-6.xlsx***

Skills Covered in This Project

- Upload a workbook to *OneDrive*.
- Use *OneNote Online*.
- Share a *OneNote* notebook.

1. Open the **MarysRentals-10** workbook from your student data files.

2. Save the workbook as [your initials] Excel 10-6 in your usual location for saving files on your computer.

3. Edit the workbook properties to show your first and last name as *Author*. Type New Maintenance Costs as the *Title*.

4. Save and close the workbook.

5. Open your browser and go to your *OneDrive* account.

6. Upload a copy of *[your initials] Excel 10-6* to the *Documents* folder in the *Files* category.

7. Click the **List of Microsoft Services** button and select **OneNote**. Enter your Microsoft account information and password if prompted. The default notebook is named **[Your User Name's] Notebook**.

8. If the section is empty, press **Enter** or click where indicated to create a new page.

9. Type Mary's Rental Planning Meeting as the title for the page and press **Enter** (Figure 10-100).

10-100 New notebook and page in *OneNote Online*.

10. Type the data shown in Figure 10-100. To create a table, enter the first ID number and press **Tab**. Then press **Enter** or **Tab** to move to the next item in the table. After the last item in the table, press **Enter** or **Tab** and then press **Backspace** to exit the table format.

11. Press **Enter** and type the sentence shown below the table in Figure 10-100.

12. Click **Insert** in the *Ribbon* and click the **File Attachment** button [*Files* group]. Click **Choose File**, navigate to *OneDrive* in the locations lists at the left of the *Open* dialog box. Open the *Documents* folder in your *OneDrive* account, select *[your initials] Excel 10-6*, and click **Open**. Then click **Insert** to attach the workbook to the notebook.

13. Click **Share** in the *Title* bar and share the notebook with your instructor. Type Here are notes from the meeting as a quick note (Figure 10-101).

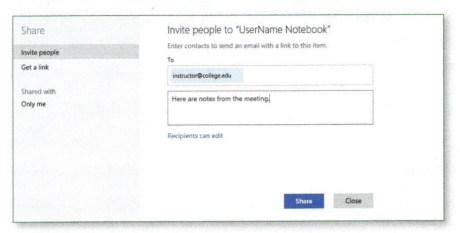

10-101 Share the *OneNote Online* notebook item

14. Close the *OneNote* browser tab. (To delete a note page, start the *OneNote* application, right-click the page title in the pane, select **Delete** and click **Yes**. To delete a notebook, go to your *OneDrive* account and display the *Documents* folder. Select the selection circle for the notebook name and click **Delete** in the *Title* bar.)

15. Sign out of your *OneDrive* account and close the browser.

Improve It Project 10-7

The Pool & Spa Oasis wants to use the *Calendar* application to schedule work crews. You have volunteered to enter the current schedule in *Calendar* and share your work. Microsoft regularly updates its online applications, but you should be able to use the steps here as a guideline in building a calendar. [Student Learning Outcomes 10.4, 10.6]

Note to Instructor and Students:

For this project, you use your Microsoft and OneDrive account. You can create a free Microsoft account at https://signup.live.com.

File Needed: ***Pool&Spa-10.xlsx*** *(Student data files are available in the* Library *of your SIMnet account)*
Completed Project File Name: ***[your initials] Excel 10-7.xlsx***

Skills Covered in This Project

- Upload a workbook to *OneDrive*.
- Use the *Calendar* application.
- Share a calendar.

1. Open the **Pool&Spa-10** workbook from your student data files.

2. Save the workbook as [your initials] Excel 10-7 in your usual location for saving files on your computer.

3. Enter the *TODAY* function in cell **A12**.

4. Type 1000 Street Address in cell **B12**.

5. Type ro in cell **C12** and press **Tab** to accept the *AutoComplete* suggestion.

6. Type the start time at 1 PM and end time of 2 PM.

7. Resave the workbook.

8. Open your browser and go to your *OneDrive* account.

9. Size and position the Excel window and the *OneDrive* window so that you can see both windows side-by-side, or print a copy of the worksheet for reference as your work in the *Calendar* application.

10. Click the **List of Microsoft Services** button and select **Calendar**. The current month displays with today highlighted. (If the calendar is not displayed in monthly view, click **Month** from the view choices at the right of the window).

11. Click **Add calendar** and select **Secondary calendar**.

12. Type Pool&Spa in the entry box in the *My calendars* list and press **Enter**.

13. Click **Pool&Spa** in the *My calendars* list. Your default calendar and the *Pool&Spa* calendars are open.

14. Point to the Calendar name and click the **X** to close it (Figure 10-102).

15. Click the **New** button to create an event for today.

16. Type Routine maintenance in the *Add a title for the event* box.

17. Select the *Add a location box*, type 1000 Street Address, and ignore suggested locations.

18. Select **1:00 PM** as the *Start* time and **2:00 PM** for the *End* time box.

19. Click **Save** (Figure 10-103).

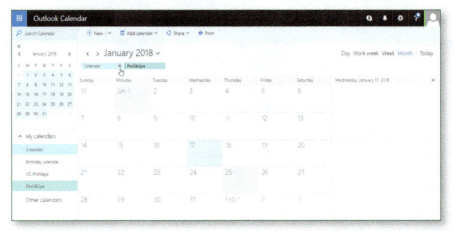

10-102 Close a calendar

20. Refer to your workbook to complete data for the remaining four dates. If your dates reach into next month, click the **Next** button to the left of the current month name.

21. Click **Share** when all dates are entered and select the **Pool&Spa** calendar for sharing.

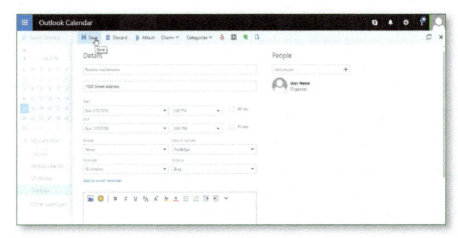

10-103 Enter and save data for an event

22. Type your instructor's email address in the entry box and verify that the *Can view all details* option is selected. Then click **Share**.

23. Close the *Calendar* browser tab. (To delete a calendar, right-click the calendar name in the *My Calendars* list and select **Delete**).

24. Open the **Documents** folder in the *Files* category in *OneDrive* and upload a copy of **[your initials] Excel 10-7** to the folder.

25. Sign out of your *OneDrive* account and close the browser.

26. Save and close the workbook.

Challenge Project 10-8

In this project, you add a custom tab to the *Ribbon* with two groups of commands. You insert a screen-shot of the customized *Ribbon* in a new workbook and share that workbook with your instructor.
[**Student Learning Outcomes 10.1, 10.2, 10.3, 10.4**]

Note to Instructor and Students:

For this project, you use your Microsoft and OneDrive account. You can create a free Microsoft account at https://signup.live.com.

File Needed: None
Completed Project File Name: **[your initials] Excel 10-8.xlsx**

Create and save a workbook as [your initials] Excel 10-8. Modify your workbook according to the following guidelines:

- Modify the *Office Theme* to *Dark Gray* and choose an *Office Background* other than *No Background*.
- Customize the *Ribbon* to add a new tab after the *View* tab. Name the new tab [your last name] Tab. Name the new custom group as Group 1.
- Add a new group to the **[your last name]** tab and name it as Group 2.
- Add three commands to the **Group 1** group.
- Add three commands to the **Group 2** group, different from the three you added to the *Group 1* group.
- Open a second blank workbook and click the **[your last name]** command tab. Return to the **[your initials Excel 10-8]** workbook and take a screenshot of the blank workbook (not a screen clipping).
- In **[your initials] Excel 10-8**, format the height of the picture image to **5** inches.
- Save and close **[your initials] Excel 10-8**.
- Go to your *OneDrive* account and upload a copy of **[your initials] Excel 10-8** to the *Documents* folder.
- Share the **[your initials] Excel 10-8** file in the *Documents* folder with your instructor in an email.
- Sign out of your *OneDrive* account and close the browser.
- Modify the *Office Theme* to **Colorful** and choose **No Background** for your Office account settings.
- Reset all customizations for the *Ribbon*.

Challenge Project 10-9

In this project, you create a workbook that lists tasks with start and end dates for stages of a project. You search for and install an *Add-in* from the Office *Store* to create a Gantt chart.
[Student Learning Outcome 10.6]

Note to Instructor and Students:

For this project, you use your Microsoft and OneDrive account. You can create a free Microsoft account at https://signup.live.com.

File Needed: None
Completed Project File Name: ***[your initials] Excel 10-9.xlsx***

Create and save a workbook as [your initials] Excel 10-9. Modify your workbook according to the following guidelines:

- In cell **A1**, type Task 1. Type Task 2 in cell **A2**. Fill the labels to "Task 5" in cell **A5**.
- In cell **B1**, type today's date. In cells **B2:B5**, enter a date for each task that is after today but within six months of today. These dates are starting dates for each task.
- In cell **C1**, type the date for one week from today. This is the end date for Task 1.
- In cells **C2:C5**, type ending dates for each task so that there is some overlap of dates for two of the tasks. For example, Task 3 can start before Task 2 is complete.
- Search the Office *Store* in the *Project Management* category for a free add-in to create a Gantt chart. Install the add-in.
- Review guidelines in the add-in and click an empty cell if that is indicated. Copy your data where it is needed for the add-in to work.
- After the Gantt chart is created, edit the task labels to display the names of tasks in an actual project. Develop tasks for a project such as remodeling your kitchen, deciding whether to buy or lease a new automobile, writing an historical novel, etc.
- Reload or refresh the data for the Gantt chart if necessary.
- Save and close ***[your initials] Excel 10-9***.
- Remove the add-in from your Office account.

Challenge Project 10-10

In this project, you create and distribute an *Excel Survey* to gather information about school or work activities. After recipients have responded, you download a copy of the Excel workbook to your computer.
[Student Learning Outcomes 10.4, 10.5, 10.6]

Note to Instructor and Students:

For this project, you use your Microsoft and OneDrive account. You can create a free Microsoft account at https://signup.live.com.

File Needed: None
Completed Project File Name: ***[your initials] Excel 10-10.xlsx***

Assemble the email addresses of four classmates or colleagues who agree to respond to your survey within 24 hours of receiving it. You plan to ask them questions about arrival time at campus or work, time commuting, how they commute, and so on.

- Log in to your *OneDrive* account.
- Open the *Documents* folder and create a new *Excel Survey*.
- Determine and enter a title and a description for your survey.
- For the first question, ask what time the individual arrives for work or for class and use a *Time* response type.
- For the next three questions, ask recipients how long they spend getting to work or campus, if they drive, bike, or take public transportation, or similar questions.
- For the last question, ask what time they leave work or campus.
- Rename the survey as [your last name] Excel 10-10.
- Share the survey with your classmates or colleagues and your instructor.
- After all responses are received, download a copy of the survey to your computer.
- Open *[your last name] Excel 10-10* in Excel 2016 on your computer.
- Format the table with a different style and make other format choices to enhance the appearance of the survey results.
- Save and close *[your initials] Excel 10-10*.

appendices

- **APPENDIX A:** Office 2016 Shortcuts
- **APPENDIX B:** Business Document Formats (online resource)

Office 2016 Shortcuts

Using Function Keys on a Laptop

When using a laptop computer, function keys perform specific Windows actions on your laptop, such as increase or decrease speaker volume, open Windows *Settings*, or adjust the screen brightness. So when using a numbered function key in an Office application, such as **F12** as a shortcut to open the *Save As* dialog box, you may need to press the **function key** (**Fn** or **fn**) on your keyboard in conjunction with a numbered function key to activate the Office command (Figure Appendix A-1). The *function key* is typically located near the bottom left of your laptop keyboard next to the *Ctrl* key.

**Appendix A-1
Function key**

Common Office 2016 Keyboard Shortcuts

Action	Keyboard Shortcut
Save	**Ctrl+S**
Copy	**Ctrl+C**
Cut	**Ctrl+X**
Paste	**Ctrl+V**
Select All	**Ctrl+A**
Bold	**Ctrl+B**
Italic	**Ctrl+I**
Underline	**Ctrl+U**
Close *Start* page or *Backstage* view	**Esc**
Open *Help* dialog box	**F1**
Activate *Tell Me* feature	**Alt+Q**
Switch windows	**Alt+Tab**

Excel 2016 Keyboard Shortcuts

Action	Keyboard Shortcut
File Management	
Open a new blank workbook	**Ctrl+N**
Open an existing workbook from the *Backstage* view	**Ctrl+O**
Open an existing workbook from the *Open* dialog box	**Ctrl+F12**
Close	**Ctrl+W**
Save	**Ctrl+S**

(continued)

Action	Keyboard Shortcut
Move to cell A1	**Ctrl+Home**
Next worksheet	**Ctrl+Page Down**
Previous worksheet	**Ctrl+Page Up**
Editing	
Cut	**Ctrl+X**
Copy	**Ctrl+C**
Paste	**Ctrl+V**
Undo	**Ctrl+Z**
Repeat/redo	**Ctrl+Y**
Underline	**Ctrl+U**
Bold	**Ctrl+B**
Italics	**Ctrl+I**
Open *Format Cells* dialog box	**Ctrl+1**
Edit mode (insertion point appears within the cell)	**F2**
Manual line break in a cell	**Ctrl+Enter**
Toggle between formula view and results view	**Ctrl+~**
Customizing Sheets	
Hide row	**Ctrl+9**
Hide column	**Ctrl+0**
Unhide row	**Ctrl+Shift+(**
Insert dialog box (cell, row, or column)	**Ctrl+plus sign (+)**
Insert worksheet	**Shift+F11**
Insert chart object	**Alt+F1**
Formula Creation	
Open *Insert Function* dialog box	**Shift+F3**
Insert a plus sign	**Shift+=**
Insert a multiplication sign	**Shift+8**
Insert an exponent sign	**Shift+6**
Insert an open parenthesis	**Shift+9**
Insert a closed parenthesis	**Shift+0**
Insert the *SUM* function	**Alt+=**
Absolute symbol toggle	**F4**
Open *Paste Name* dialog box (insert range name)	**F3**

glossary

3D cell reference A cell address in another worksheet in the same workbook.

A

absolute cell reference A cell address with dollar signs such as $B$2.

active cell A cell that is ready for editing, surrounded with a solid border.

add-in Enhanced command or feature available for Excel.

Advanced Filter Filter process that uses a criteria range and an optional output range.

algorithm A step-by-step procedure used by *Solver* to reach a solution.

alignment Vertical and horizontal position of data in a cell.

Analysis Toolpak Add-in for Excel with built-in statistical and engineering calculations.

annuity A series of equal payments.

argument A cell reference, value, or other element required for a function.

array A range of cells in a row or a column.

array formula A formula that calculates and displays results across a range of cells.

Array1 Argument in a *SUMPRODUCT* function that identifies the first range of cells to be multiplied.

Array2 Argument in a *SUMPRODUCT* function that identifies the second range of cells to be multiplied.

ascending order Alphabetically from A to Z or from smallest to largest value.

attribute Setting or property for a cell.

Auto Outline Summary that inserts groups based on formula location.

AutoCalculate *Status* bar area that displays calculations for selected cells.

AutoComplete Feature that suggests an entry for a cell based on data already in the column.

AutoFilter Arrow in a header row used for sorting or filtering data.

AutoFit Feature that fits column or row to accommodate largest entry.

axis Horizontal or vertical boundary of plotted data in a chart.

axis title Title for categories or values in a chart.

B

backsolve Problem-solving method in which the result is known and a value necessary to reach that result is determined.

border Outline for a cell or range.

business intelligence (BI) Tools, applications, and processes used to analyze data.

Button Form control that runs a macro with a single click.

C

calculated field Field in a *PivotTable* that is built from a formula with an existing *PivotTable* field.

Calendar Free time and appointment scheduling application available with a Microsoft account.

cash flow Future payment or receipt.

category axis Describes data shown in a chart; the horizontal axis in a column chart and the vertical axis in a bar chart.

category label Text label that described a data series in a chart.

cell Intersection of a column and a row in a worksheet.

cell address Column letter and row number that identifies location of cell or range; also called cell reference.

cell style Set of formatting elements for data in a cell.

change history Record of edits made in a shared workbook.

changing cells Variable cells in a *Solver* problem.

chart A visual representation of numeric worksheet data.

chart area Background rectangle area for a chart.

chart element Separate, selectable, editable object or part in a chart.

chart floor Base or bottom for a 3D chart.

chart layout Set of charts elements and their locations.

chart object Selectable chart with clickable elements.

chart sheet Chart displayed in its own tab or sheet in a workbook.

chart style Combination of colors and effects for a chart and its elements.

chart title Name or main label for a chart.

chart wall Vertical background for a 3D chart.

circular reference Formula error in which the formula refers to the cell in which it is located.

code Programming statements and commands in a Visual Basic for Applications module.

col_index_number Argument in a *VLOOKUP* functions for the column with data to be displayed in the result.

collections (vba) Group of similar objects.

Combo Box Form control that displays as a drop-down list used to make a choice.

comment Pop-up text box attached to a cell. Also a line preceded by an apostrophe in the Visual Basic Editor, that is not part of the code.

common field Data field that is the same data type and displays the same data in a query.

Compatibility Checker Dialog box that identifies command and features that are not supported in earlier versions of Excel.

concatenate To link or join data.

conditional formatting Format settings that are applied based on rules, rankings, or other criteria.

confidence interval Range of values that includes an estimated or forecasted number, expressed as a percentage.

connection Identifier and a link to external data in a workbook.

consolidated worksheet Worksheet that gathers and summarizes values from more than one worksheet.

constant A value used in a formula.

constraints Solver parameter that sets a restriction or limitation.

criteria Function argument which sets a restriction or condition.

criteria range Two or more rows of data used to specify advanced filter conditions.

Cse formula An array formula, executed by pressing **Ctrl + Shift + Enter**.

custom autofilter Criteria set in a dialog box from an Auto-Filter arrow.

custom calculation Built-in percentage, ranking, or ratio for a value field in a *PivotTable*.

D

data input form Dialog box that displays data from a row in a vertical layout for data entry.

data label Object that displays value for each data marker in a chart.

data marker Bar, column, slice, or other object used to graph a value in a chart.

data model Collection of tables or queries in a workbook, available for building PivotTables.

data point A value in a chart represented by a cell; a single value graphed in a chart.

data series A group of values or data points shown in a chart as columns, bars, slices, or other objects.

data table Columnar display of values for each data series in a chart located below the chart; also a range of cells with calculated results for one or more formulas.

data validation Process of setting rules for data entry.

Data visualization Formatting that uses colored bars, color variations, or icons based on rules or rankings.

database Software applications that use related tables, queries, forms, and reports; also a cell range in a worksheet with label and data rows.

database function A function that performs a mathematical or statistical calculation only for data that meet its criteria.

decision cells Changing cells in a *Solver* problem.

delimited File that separates data into column with a special character.

delimiter Character used to separate columns.

dependent Cell that is affected by the active cell.

dependent workbook Workbook that has a linking or external reference formula.

descending order Alphabetically from Z to A or from largest to smallest value.

Descriptive Statistics Group of popular statistical measures for a data range.

destination cell Cell location for pasted data.

Developer tab Ribbon command tab with tools for working with form controls, macros, and XML data.

deviation A forecast error.

dimension Number of row and columns in an array.

discount rate The cost of financing or a competing rate of return.

Document Inspector Dialog box that lists metadata in a workbook.

document panel Horizontal window below the *Ribbon* that lists editable document properties.

document property Information about a workbook such as file name, creation and edit dates, size, etc.

duplicate row Record in a table with the same content as another record in one or more columns.

dynamic consolidation Consolidation command that inserts a formula that updates when changes are made to the source data.

E

ellipse Oval shape.

error alert Message box that appears when invalid data is entered in a cell with data validation settings.

Excel Start page Opening screen when Excel is started.

Excel Survey Free electronic survey application available with a Microsoft account.

exporting Saving or copying data for use in another program or application.

external data Data that originated in another program or format.

external reference A formula or cell address that refers to cells in another workbook.

extract range One row of labels for results of an advanced filter.

F

field One column of data, a column in a database.

field name Label in a header row.

fill Color or pattern used a background for a cell or range.

fill handle Small black square at lower right corner of a cell or range used to complete a series or copy data.

filter Requirement or condition that identifies data to be shown or hidden.

fixed width Specific number of characters assigned to a field or column.

Flash Fill Excel feature that completes column data based on first entry.

font Named design of type for characters, punctuation, and symbols.

font style Thickness or angle of characters.

footer Data that prints at the bottom of each page.

forecast error The difference between actual and predicted values.

forecast sheet Generated worksheet with a table and chart built from two data series, one of which is a time or date field.

form control Object used to display a choice, run a command, or perform a task.

Format Painter Tool that copies format from one cell to others.

formula A calculation in a cell that displays a result.

formula auditing Process of reviewing formulas for accuracy.

Formula Autocomplete Feature that displays a list of function and range names after a character is typed.

Formula bar Bar below the *Ribbon* that displays active cell contents.

function A built-in formula.

Fv Argument in *Financial* functions for the future value.

G

Goal Seek What-if analysis command that finds a value that will provide a specified formula result.

gradient Blend of two or more colors used as fill.

gridline Horizontal or vertical line across the plot area in a chart.

gridlines Vertical and horizontal lines on screen that form columns and rows in a worksheet.

group Set of rows with the same entry in at least one column.

H

header Data that prints at the top of each page.

header row First row of a table with labels.

Hidden Worksheet Worksheet whose tab is not visible.

hierarchy Division of data into groups and related subgroups.

hyperlink Clickable jump text or object in a worksheet.

I

identifier Character used in a cell address that labels a component of the address.

importing Process of getting data from an outside source.

indent Command that moves data away from the left edge of a cell.

indicator Triangle in the upper-right corner of a cell to identify a comment.

input message Comment box that appears at data entry as part of a cell's data validation settings.

input value Number of value in a column or row that is substituted for a value in a formula in a data table.

invalid data Cell data that does not conform to data validation settings.

K

key field Data field that is a common field but each data piece is used only once in a query.

L

label Text data in a worksheet that is not used in calculations.

legend Chart element that describes colors, symbols, or textures used in a chart.

linebreak Start of a new line in a cell made by pressing **Alt+Enter**.

link A live data connection to another workbook.

linking Process of referring to data in another workbook.

Logical_test Argument in *Logical* functions for the statement to be evaluated.

Looup_value Argument in *Lookup* functions for the cell or data to be found.

M

macro Series of commands and keystrokes that executes a command.

macro-enabled template Excel template that includes macros.

macros-only workbook Macro-enabled workbook that include only macros.

Mark as Final Workbook property that sets the file as read-only.

marker Data point in a sparkline.

math hierarchy Sequence of arithmetic calculations in a formula.

mathematical order of operations Sequence of arithmetic operations in a formula.

mean Value determined by adding all values in a range and dividing by the number of values.

mean absolute deviation (MAD) Popular measure of how spread out values are from the average.

metadata Properties and settings that are embedded in a workbook and stored with the file.

methods (VBA) Function, action, or service for an object.

Microsoft Access Relational database management system available with the Office suite.

mixed cell reference A cell address with one dollar sign such as $B2 or B$2.

module Container or folder for Visual Basic for Applications statements and procedures.

Moving Average A series of averages for a set of values.

N

Name box Area in *Formula* bar that displays cell address of the active cell.

nested function A function within another function; a function used as an argument in another function.

Normal view Worksheet view used to create and modify a worksheet.

nper Argument in financial functions for the term of a loan or investment that specifies the number of periods.

O

objective cell Cell with a formula used as a *Solver* parameter.

Objects (VBA) Tools or elements with properties, functions, or data.

Office add-in Application programs for enhanced features and commands in Excel and other Office software.

Office Background Graphic pattern displayed in the top right corner of the application window.

Office Clipboard Storage location for cut or copied data shared by all Office applications.

Office Online Free, abbreviated versions of Office 2016 applications.

Office Theme Ribbon, tab, and dialog box colors for Office applications.

OneDrive Online or cloud storage available with a Microsoft account.

OneNote Online Free note-taking and audio recording application available with a Microsoft account.

one-variable data table Range of cells that calculates results by substituting values for one argument in one or more formulas.

Option Button Form control that displays as a radio button used to make one choice in a group.

Order of precedence Sequence of arithmetic calculations in a formula.

Outline Summary that groups records with collapse/expand buttons.

Outlook.com Free email application available with a Microsoft account.

P

Page break Printer code to start a new page.

Page Break preview Worksheet view that shows printed pages with dashed or dotted lines to mark where new pages start.

Page Layout view Worksheet view that opens header and footer areas, indicates margin areas, and shows rulers.

parameter Information used in a Solver problem.

Paste Options Gallery of choices for how data is copied.

Pattern Crosshatches, dots, or stripes used as fill.

People Free contact management application available with a Microsoft account.

Personal Macro workbook Hidden macros-only workbook named PERSONAL.XLSB, saved in the XLSTART folder, that is automatically opened each time Excel is started.

PivotChart Summary chart built from a PivotTable or a range of data.

PivotTable Summary report for a range of data with interactive field and filter buttons.

Pixel One screen dot used as measurement.

Plot area Chart element bounded by the horizontal and vertical axes.

Point Font measurement of 1/72 of an inch.

population All data available for analysis.

PowerPivot Add-in for Excel that accesses and extracts data from large databases for use in PowerPivot reports.

precedent Cell that contributes to a formula's result.

Print area Defined data that prints.

print title Row or column that prints on each page.

product Result of a multiplication formula.

Protected View Status of a workbook opened or copied from an Internet source.

Pv Argument in *Financial* functions for the present or current value.

Q

query Set of instructions, filters, and formats that connects to and gets data for use in Excel.

Quick Analysis Tool that displays for a selected cell range with suggested command groups.

R

range Rectangular group of cells such as A1:B3.

Range Finder Feature that highlights and color-codes a formula cell range in Edit mode.

range name Label assigned to a single or a group of cells.

Range_lookup Optional argument in *Lookup* functions to specify exact or close matches for the results.

rate Argument in many Financial functions that specifies an interest rate for the time period.

record One row of data, a row in a database.

relative cell reference A cell address such as B2.

Row_index_number Argument in a HLOOKUP functions for the row with data to be displayed in the result.

S

sample A subset of a population.

scenario Set of values saved with the worksheet.

scenario summary report Generated worksheet outline that describes scenarios for the sheet.

scope A worksheet set as the location for a range name.

screenshot Picture of an application window or any part of the window.

selection handle Small shape on each corner and middle edge of an object or element.

serial number Value assigned to a date.

series List of labels or values that follow a pattern.

shape effects Design elements such as shadows, bevels, or soft edges for a chart element or object.

shape fill Background color for a chart element or object.

shape outline Border color and thickness for a chart element or object.

shape style Set of fill colors, borders, and effects for a chart element or object.

shared workbook Workbook that is edited by more than one user, simultaneously or separately, but prepared as a final report.

SharePoint server Web platform designed for collaboration via the Internet.

sharing link Text hyperlink that can be copied into an email to share a file.

sheet Individual page or tab in a workbook.

SmartArt Text-based line illustration available for use in a worksheet.

Solver What-if analysis command that finds lowest, highest, or specific result for a formula.

sorting Process of arranging rows of data in an identified order.

source Text, database, or other file from which data is imported.

source cell Cell data that is copied or cut.

source data Cell range with values and labels graphed in a chart.

source workbook Workbook that provided data to another workbook in a consolidation command or an external reference formula.

source worksheet Worksheet that provides data to a consolidation command or to an external reference formula.

sparklines Miniature charts embedded in a worksheet cell.

splitter bar Horizontal or vertical gray bar that divides a worksheet into panes.

spreadsheet Individual page or sheet in a workbook.

standard deviation Popular measure of how broadly values vary from the average.

static consolidation Consolidation command that inserts a value result that does not update when changes are made to the source data.

structured reference Name assigned to specific parts of an Excel table.

subtotal Summary row for grouped data.

SUM *Math & Trig* function that adds cell values.

Sunburst chart Hierarchy chart similar to a pie chart with concentric rings for each level in the hierarchy.

Sway Free storytelling application available with a Microsoft account.

syntax Required elements and the order of those elements for a function.

T

tab Identifier at the bottom left of a worksheet that displays the name of sheet.

tab scrolling buttons Buttons to the left of tab names used to move through all worksheet tabs.

table Excel data formatted with a header row followed by data rows.

table style Predesigned set of format settings.

table_array Argument in *Lookup* functions for the cell range with data to be displayed in the result.

target cell Objective cell in a *Solver* problem.

template Model workbook with any combination of data, formulas, formatting, charts, images, controls, and more.

text file File format that includes data with no formatting.

Text Import Wizard Step-by-step guide for importing a text file.

theme Collection of fonts, colors, and special effects for a workbook.

thumbnail Small image of a worksheet in a dialog box.

tick mark Small line on a chart axis to guide in reading values.

timeline Visual filter for a date field, displayed as a floating dialog box.

trendline Chart element that averages and forecasts chart data.

Trusted Location Folder, network, or cloud location that is considered a safe source for a workbook.

two-variable data table Range of cells that calculates results by substituting values for two arguments in one formula.

type Argument in *Financial* functions for the timing of a payment.

V

validation settings Rules or requirements applied to data as it is entered.

value Numerical data in a worksheet that can be used in calculations.

value axis Shows the numbers in a chart; the vertical axis in a column chart and the horizontal axis in a bar chart.

Value_if_false Argument in *Logical* functions for the result when the *logical_test* statement is false.

Value_if_true Argument in *Logical* functions for the result when the *logical_test* statement is true.

variable cells Cells that can be changed in a Solver problem.

Visual Basic Editor (VBE) Application with three panes that displays programming for a macro.

Visual Basic for Applications (VBA) Underlying programming language used in Excel macros and ActiveX controls in a workbook.

Volatile Description for function results that depend on the date and time set in the computer.

W

Watch Window Floating dialog box that displays selected cell references.

waterfall chart A chart that depicts a running total based on negative and positive values.

WordArt Text box with font style, color, fill and effects.

workbook Saved Excel document file that contains worksheets.

worksheet Individual page or sheet in a workbook.

worksheet protection Property that sets which cells can be edited.

X

.xlsm File name extension for an Excel macro-enabled workbook.

.xltm File name extension for an Excel macro-enabled template.

.xltx File name extension for an Excel template.

.xlxs Excel file format for workbooks.

.xml Text file format that uses Extensible Markup Language.

index

Symbols

A

B

C